D0745680

American Masculinities

Bret E. Carroll is an associate professor of history at California State University, Stanislaus. He received his Ph.D. from Cornell University in 1991. He is author of *The Routledge Historical Atlas of Religion in America* (1997), *Spiritualism in Antebellum America* (1997), and several articles on nineteenth-century masculinity.

American Masculinities

A Historical Encyclopedia

Bret E. Carroll Editor

California State University – Stanislaus

SAGE Publications

International Educational and Professional Publisher

Thousand Oaks ■ London ■ New Delhi

339 Fifth Avenue, New York, New York 10016
www.mosgroup.com

SAGE REFERENCE
Publisher: Rolf Janke

THE MOSCHOVITIS GROUP
Publisher: Valerie Tomaselli
Executive Editor: Hilary W. Poole
Senior Editor: Stephanie Schreiber
Associate Editor: Sonja Matanovic
Editorial Coordinator: Nicole Cohen Solomon
Design and Layout: Annemarie Redmond
Production Coordinator: K. Nura Abdul-Karim
Editorial Intern: Jessica Rosin
Copyediting: Peter Jaskowiak
Proofreading: Sharae Johnson
Index: Barber Indexing

For information:
Sage Publications, Inc.
2455 Teller Road
Thousand Oaks, California 91320
Email: order@sagepub.com

Sage Publications Ltd.
6 Bonhill Street
London EC2A 4PU
United Kingdom

Sage Publications India Pvt. Ltd.
M-32 Market
Greater Kailash I
New Delhi 110 048 India

Printed in the United States of America

Library of Congress Cataloging-in-Publication Data
American masculinities : a historical encyclopedia / Bret E. Carroll, editor.
p. cm. — (Sage reference publication)
Includes bibliographical references and index.
ISBN 0-7619-2540-6 (Cloth)
1. Men—United States—Encyclopedias. 2. Masculinity—United States—Encyclopedias. I. Carroll, Bret E., 1961- II. Series.
HQ1090.3.A453 2004
305.31_03—dc22

2003017571

Contents

List of Entries
vii

Reader's Guide
ix

Foreword
xiii

Introduction
1

American Masculinities: A Historical Encyclopedia
5–514

Bibliography
515

Contributors
533

Index
537

List of Entries

Abolitionism
Adolescence
Adventures of Huckleberry Finn
Advertising
Advice Literature
African-American Manhood
Agrarianism
Alcohol
Alger, Horatio, Jr.
American Dream
American Revolution
Antiwar Movement
Apprenticeship
Art
Arthur, Timothy Shay
Artisan
Asian-American Manhood
Atlas, Charles
Automobile

Bachelorhood
Baseball
Beat Movement
Beecher, Henry Ward
Birth of a Nation
Bisexuality
Black Panther Party
Body
Bodybuilding
Bogart, Humphrey
Boone, Daniel
Boxing
Boyhood
Boy Scouts of America
Brando, Marlon
Breadwinner Role
Buddy Films
Bureaucratization
Business/Corporate America

California Gold Rush
Capitalism
Catcher in the Rye, The
Character
Chivalry
Citizenship
Civil Rights Movement
Civil War
Class
Cold War
Common Sense Book of Baby and Child Care, The
Confidence Man
Conscientious Objection
Consumerism
Contrast, The
Cooper, Gary
Cop Action Films
Counterculture
Cowboys
Crèvecoeur, J. Hector St. John
Crisis of Masculinity
Crockett, Davy
Cult of Domesticity

Darwinism
Dean, James
Death of a Salesman
Deliverance
Democratic Manhood
Detectives
Divorce
Douglass, Frederick
Dueling

Eastwood, Clint
Easy Rider
Education
Emancipation
Emerson, Ralph Waldo
Emotion
Ethnicity
Eugenics
Evangelicalism and Revivalism

Fashion
Fatherhood
Father Knows Best
Father's Day
Fathers' Rights
Feminism
Fishing
Fitzgerald, F. Scott
Football
Franklin, Benjamin
Fraternal Organizations
Fraternities
Freudian Psychoanalytic Theory

Gambling
Gangs
Gangsters
Gays in the Military
Gilded Age
Graham, Sylvester
Grant, Cary
Grapes of Wrath, The
Great Depression
Gulick, Luther Halsey
Guns

Hall, Granville Stanley
Health
Hemingway, Ernest
Heroism
Heterosexuality
Higginson, Thomas Wentworth
Hoboes
Hollywood
Home Improvement
Homosexuality
Hudson, Rock
Hunting

Immigration
Imperialism
Individualism
Industrialization
Insanity
Invisible Man
Irish-American Manhood
Iron John: A Book About Men
Italian-American Manhood

Jackson, Andrew
James, William
Jesus, Images of
Jewish Manhood
Jungle, The
Juvenile Delinquency

Kellogg, John Harvey
Kerouac, Jack
King, Martin Luther, Jr.
Kramer vs. Kramer

Labor Movement and Unions
Latino Manhood
Lawrence, D. H.
Leatherstocking Tales
Leave It to Beaver
Leisure
Lincoln, Abraham
London, Jack
Lone Ranger, The

Malcolm X
Male Friendship
Manifest Destiny
Market Revolution
Marlboro Man
Marriage
Martial Arts Films
Masculine Domesticity
Masturbation
Medicine
Men and Religion Forward Movement

Men's Clubs
Men's Movements
Men's Studies
Middle-Class Manhood
Militarism
Military
Ministry
Minstrelsy
Moby Dick
Momism
Mother–Son Relationships
Mr. Mom
Muscular Christianity
Music

Nationalism
Nation of Islam
Native American Manhood
Nativism
New Deal
Noyes, John Humphrey
Nuclear Family

Odd Couple, The
Old Age
Organization Man, The
Outdoorsmen

Passionate Manhood
Patriarchy
Patriotism
Playboy Magazine
Politics
Populism
Pornography
Postmodernism
Professionalism
Progressive Era
Promise Keepers
Property
Prostitution

Race
Rambo
Reagan, Ronald
Rebel Without a Cause
Reform Movements
Religion and Spirituality
Reproduction
Republicanism
Reverse Sexism
Romanticism
Roosevelt, Theodore

Sandow, Eugen
Sawyer, Tom
Schwarzenegger, Arnold
Seduction Tales
Self-Control
Self-Made Man
Sensitive Male
Sentimentalism
Sexual Harassment
Sexual Revolution
Shaft
Slave Narratives
Slavery
Social Gospel
Sons of Liberty
Southern Manhood
Spanish-American War
Sports
Springsteen, Bruce
Strenuous Life
Suburbia
Success Manuals
Suffragism
Sunday, Billy
Superman

Tarzan
Technology
Television
Temperance
Thoreau, Henry David
Transsexuality
Transvestism
Travel
Travel Narratives
Twain, Mark

Uncle Sam
Urbanization

Victorian Era
Vietnam War
Violence

War
Washington, George
Wayne, John
Western Frontier
Westerns
Whiteness
White Supremacism
Whitman, Walt
Work
Working-Class Manhood
World War I
World War II
Wright, Richard

Young Men's Christian Association
Youth

Reader's Guide

This list is provided to assist readers in finding articles on related entries. It classifies articles into fourteen general thematic categories: Art and Literature; Body and Health; Class, Ethnic, and Racial Identities; Concepts and Theories; Family and Fatherhood; Historical Events and Processes; Icons and Symbols; Leisure and Work; Media and Popular Culture; Movements and Organizations; People; Political and Social Issues; Religion and Spirituality; Sexual Identities and Sexuality. Some article titles appear in more than one category.

Art and Literature

Adventures of Huckleberry Finn
Alger, Horatio, Jr.
Art
Arthur, Timothy Shay
Beat Movement
Catcher in the Rye, The
Common Sense Book of Baby and Child Care, The
Contrast, The
Crèvecoeur, J. Hector St. John
Death of a Salesman
Emerson, Ralph Waldo
Fitzgerald, F. Scott
Grapes of Wrath, The
Hemingway, Ernest
Invisible Man
Iron John: A Book About Men
Jesus, Images of
Jungle, The
Kerouac, Jack
Lawrence, D. H.
Leatherstocking Tales
London, Jack
Moby Dick
Organization Man, The
Romanticism
Sawyer, Tom
Seduction Tales
Slave Narratives
Thoreau, Henry David
Travel Narratives
Twain, Mark
Whitman, Walt
Wright, Richard

Body and Health

Atlas, Charles
Body
Bodybuilding
Darwinism
Eugenics
Fashion
Freudian Psychoanalytic Theory
Graham, Sylvester
Gulick, Luther Halsey
Hall, Granville Stanley
Health
Higginson, Thomas Wentworth
Insanity
James, William
Kellogg, John Harvey
Lawrence, D. H.
Masturbation
Medicine
Muscular Christianity
Old Age
Reproduction
Roosevelt, Theodore
Sandow, Eugen
Schwarzenegger, Arnold
Self-Control
Strenuous Life
Temperance

Class, Ethnic, and Racial Identities

Abolitionism
African-American Manhood
Apprenticeship
Artisan
Asian-American Manhood
Beecher, Henry Ward
Black Panther Party
Breadwinner Role
Business/Corporate America
Civil Rights Movement
Class
Douglass, Frederick
Ethnicity
Graham, Sylvester
Grapes of Wrath, The
Hall, Granville Stanley
Immigration
Invisible Man
Irish-American Manhood
Italian-American Manhood
Jewish Manhood
King, Martin Luther, Jr.
Labor Movement and Unions
Latino Manhood
Malcolm X
Middle-Class Manhood
Minstrelsy
Nation of Islam
Native American Manhood
Nativism
Populism
Race
Shaft
Slavery
Southern Manhood
Springsteen, Bruce
Sunday, Billy
Whiteness
White Supremacism
Work
Working-Class Manhood
Wright, Richard

Concepts and Theories

Agrarianism
American Dream
Breadwinner Role
Capitalism
Character
Chivalry
Citizenship
Class
Conscientious Objection
Consumerism
Cult of Domesticity
Darwinism
Democratic Manhood
Emotion
Ethnicity
Eugenics
Evangelicalism and Revivalism
Fathers' Rights
Feminism
Freudian Psychoanalytic Theory
Heroism
Imperialism
Individualism
Manifest Destiny
Market Revolution
Masculine Domesticity
Men's Studies
Militarism
Momism
Muscular Christianity
Nationalism

Nativism
Passionate Manhood
Patriarchy
Patriotism
Populism
Postmodernism
Professionalism
Property
Race
Republicanism
Romanticism
Self-Control
Sentimentalism
Strenuous Life
White Supremacism

Family and Fatherhood

Adolescence
Bachelorhood
Boyhood
Breadwinner Role
Common Sense Book of Baby and Child Care, The
Cult of Domesticity
Divorce
Fatherhood
Father Knows Best
Father's Day
Fathers' Rights
Freudian Psychoanalytic Theory
Hall, Granville Stanley
Home Improvement
Leave It to Beaver
Marriage
Masculine Domesticity
Momism
Mother–Son Relationships
Mr. Mom
Noyes, John Humphrey
Nuclear Family
Old Age
Patriarchy
Promise Keepers
Property
Reproduction
Suburbia
Youth

Historical Events and Processes

Abolitionism
American Revolution
Antiwar Movement
California Gold Rush
Civil Rights Movement
Civil War
Cold War
Emancipation
Gilded Age
Great Depression
Immigration
Imperialism
Industrialization
Manifest Destiny
Market Revolution
New Deal
Politics
Populism
Progressive Era
Reform Movements
Sexual Revolution
Spanish-American War
Suffragism
Urbanization
Victorian Era
Vietnam War
War
Western Frontier
World War I
World War II

Icons and Symbols

Alger, Horatio, Jr.
American Dream
Atlas, Charles
Automobile
Bogart, Humphrey
Boone, Daniel
Brando, Marlon
Confidence Man
Cooper, Gary
Cowboys
Crockett, Davy
Dean, James
Detectives
Eastwood, Clint
Franklin, Benjamin
Gangsters
Grant, Cary
Hoboes
Hollywood
Hudson, Rock
Jesus, Images of
Kerouac, Jack
Lincoln, Abraham
Lone Ranger, The
Malcolm X
Marlboro Man
Outdoorsmen
Rambo
Reagan, Ronald
Sawyer, Tom
Self-Made Man
Sensitive Male
Springsteen, Bruce
Suburbia
Superman
Tarzan
Uncle Sam
Washington, George
Wayne, John

Leisure and Work

Agrarianism
Alcohol
Apprenticeship
Artisan
Automobile
Baseball
Boxing
Breadwinner Role
Bureaucratization
Business/Corporate America
Consumerism
Dueling
Fashion
Fishing
Football
Fraternal Organizations
Fraternities
Gambling
Hunting
Industrialization
Labor Movement and Unions
Leisure
Male Friendship
Medicine
Men's Clubs
Ministry
Music
Outdoorsmen
Professionalism
Self-Made Man
Slavery
Sports
Suburbia
Success Manuals
Technology
Travel
Work
Working-Class Manhood
Young Men's Christian Association

Media and Popular Culture

Advertising
Advice Literature
Automobile
Birth of a Nation
Bogart, Humphrey
Brando, Marlon
Buddy Films
Cooper, Gary
Cop Action Films
Cowboys
Crockett, Davy
Dean, James
Deliverance
Detectives
Eastwood, Clint
Easy Rider
Fashion
Father Knows Best
Gangsters
Grant, Cary
Hollywood

Home Improvement
Hudson, Rock
Kramer vs. Kramer
Leave It to Beaver
Lone Ranger, The
Marlboro Man
Martial Arts Films
Minstrelsy
Mr. Mom
Music
Odd Couple, The
Playboy Magazine
Rambo
Reagan, Ronald
Rebel Without a Cause
Schwarzenegger, Arnold
Seduction Tales
Shaft
Springsteen, Bruce
Success Manuals
Superman
Tarzan
Television
Wayne, John
Westerns

Movements and Organizations

Abolitionism
Antiwar Movement
Beat Movement
Black Panther Party
Boy Scouts of America
Civil Rights Movement
Counterculture
Eugenics
Feminism
Fraternal Organizations
Fraternities
Iron John: A Book About Men
Kerouac, Jack
King, Martin Luther, Jr.
Labor Movement and Unions
Malcolm X
Men and Religion Forward Movement
Men's Clubs
Men's Movements
Military
Muscular Christianity
Nationalism
Nation of Islam
Nativism
Populism
Promise Keepers
Reform Movements
Sexual Revolution
Social Gospel
Sons of Liberty
Suffragism
Temperance
White Supremacism
Young Men's Christian Association

People

Alger, Horatio, Jr.
Arthur, Timothy Shay
Atlas, Charles
Beecher, Henry Ward
Bogart, Humphrey
Boone, Daniel
Brando, Marlon
Cooper, Gary
Crèvecoeur, J. Hector St. John
Crockett, Davy
Dean, James
Douglass, Frederick
Eastwood, Clint
Emerson, Ralph Waldo
Fitzgerald, F. Scott
Franklin, Benjamin
Graham, Sylvester
Grant, Cary
Gulick, Luther Halsey
Hall, Granville Stanley
Hemingway, Ernest
Higginson, Thomas Wentworth
Hudson, Rock
Jackson, Andrew
James, William
Kellogg, John Harvey
Kerouac, Jack
King, Martin Luther, Jr.
Lawrence, D. H.
Lincoln, Abraham
London, Jack
Malcolm X
Noyes, John Humphrey
Reagan, Ronald
Roosevelt, Theodore
Sandow, Eugen
Schwarzenegger, Arnold
Springsteen, Bruce
Sunday, Billy
Thoreau, Henry David
Twain, Mark
Washington, George
Wayne, John
Whitman, Walt
Wright, Richard

Political and Social Issues

Abolitionism
Adolescence
Antiwar Movement
Citizenship
Civil Rights Movement
Class
Conscientious Objection
Crisis of Masculinity
Darwinism
Divorce
Education
Emotion
Ethnicity
Eugenics
Fathers' Rights
Feminism
Gangs
Gays in the Military
Guns
Health
Immigration
Imperialism
Insanity
Juvenile Delinquency
Medicine
Momism
Nativism
Old Age
Pornography
Promise Keepers
Race
Reform Movements
Reverse Sexism
Self-Control
Sexual Harassment
Social Gospel
Temperance
Violence
War
White Supremacism

Religion and Spirituality

Beecher, Henry Ward
Conscientious Objection
Emerson, Ralph Waldo
Evangelicalism and Revivalism
Gulick, Luther Halsey
Higginson, Thomas Wentworth
Iron John: A Book About Men
Jesus, Images of
Kerouac, Jack
King, Martin Luther, Jr.
Malcolm X
Men and Religion Forward Movement
Ministry
Muscular Christianity
Nation of Islam
Noyes, John Humphrey
Promise Keepers
Religion and Spirituality
Social Gospel
Sunday, Billy
Young Men's Christian Association

Sexual Identities and Sexuality

Bachelorhood
Bisexuality

Deliverance
Freudian Psychoanalytic Theory
Heterosexuality
Homosexuality
Hudson, Rock
Marriage
Masturbation
Noyes, John Humphrey
Playboy Magazine
Pornography
Prostitution
Reproduction
Seduction Tales
Sexual Harassment
Sexual Revolution
Transsexuality
Transvestism
Whitman, Walt

Foreword

"Scholarship is a product of the specialization." This maxim is a cornerstone of the modern research university. Professors advise doctoral students to lay claim to a small piece of turf, the smaller the better. A scholarly monograph, senior scholars inform their charges, is a narrow one. Such folk often dismiss encyclopedias, which embrace the contrary principles of brevity and breadth, as of little importance.

They are wrong. A well-crafted encyclopedia is an important tool for advancing knowledge. This point was hammered home two and a half centuries ago when Denis Diderot and his bookish friends in France began work on the first great encyclopedia. Having witnessed a flowering of new ideas in science, mathematics, geography, literature, music, architecture, and many other fields, they perceived a need to transform these independent discoveries into the knowledge revolution. New ideas in one branch of knowledge field had implications for all of the others. Diderot conceived of the encyclopedia form as a means of synthesizing specialized knowledge and presenting it in a form readily accessible to diverse readers.

American Masculinities: A Historical Encyclopedia encompasses another revolution in knowledge. Masculinity studies scarcely existed in the 1970s; it could be discerned, if at all, as a faint echo to the explosion of work on women. But since then, hundreds of scholars in scores of disciplines have been drawn to various specialized aspects of the topic. Issues of masculinity are highlighted at scholarly conferences, and the term pops up in countless book titles and scholarly papers and articles.

This encyclopedia marks an important step in the evolution of masculinity as a field of historical study. It not only tracks recent scholarship in masculinity studies but also, like all encyclopedias, suggests through its organization new ways of looking at the relation among essays. Diderot observed that the alphabetical arrangement of his encyclopedia produced "burlesque contrasts" by, for example, juxtaposing an article on art with another on artisans. Modern scholars might say instead that the inherent randomness of an encyclopedia format provides a means of "deconstructing" customary topics, thereby facilitating a creative rearrangement of the ideas.

So, too, the present volume. Consider the early pages. The article on "Adolescence" features Granville Stanley Hall's 1904 book of that title, which contended that the teenage years, for boys especially, were tumultuous. The next entry is "*Adventures of Huckleberry Finn*," a tale of adolescent boys who chafe at social constraints. The essay on "Alcohol" discusses the enduring centrality of drinking rituals among young males, ranging from the colonial tavern to contemporary frat parties. The article on "Alger, Horatio, Jr.," details how that hack writer's books encouraged generations of boys to transform their adolescent restlessness into a climb from "rags to riches."

These essays, connected through their alphabetical proximity, outline a familiar rendering of boyhood and give it an interesting depth of detail. The essay on Alger also goes beyond the familiar account to show that this apostle of conventional boyhood was himself what we would now describe as gay. Other essays within the same cluster of pages further complicate the conventional picture of American masculinity. The essay on "Abolitionism" shows that many leaders of the movement embraced a masculine ethos of Christian love, as did the author of antebellum advice books, Timothy Shay Arthur (as described in the article about the writer). An essay on the "American Dream" similarly shows the broad range of gender-linked yearnings. Every reader of this volume will approach it from a different perspective, gleaning a host of interesting facts, but also assembling new insights from the wealth of synthesis.

Encyclopedias do not exist to freeze knowledge within the bound pages of a book, like a bug in amber, but to advance knowledge and push it in new directions. "An Encyclopedia should be begun, carried through, and finished within a certain interval," Diderot insisted. "Our moment passes and hardly will a great [reference] enterprise be completed before our generation exists no longer." Bret E. Carroll's encyclopedia synthesizes one generation's rendering of a new body of knowledge. Because of his labors, what will come afterwards will be all the better.

—Mark C. Carnes
Ann Whitney Olin Professor of History
Barnard College, Columbia University

Introduction

This is an encyclopedia about American masculinities. Its purpose is to provide a reference guide and an introduction to the many ways in which men have defined, imagined, and experienced male identity in the social, cultural, and political contexts of the United States.

A work such as this would have been virtually unimaginable in 1980, when men's studies was only beginning to emerge as a field of scholarly inquiry. It would still have been unfeasible as recently as the early 1990s, when the first book-length history of American masculinity—E. Anthony Rotundo's *American Manhood* (1993)—appeared in the nation's libraries and bookstores. But the study of masculinity, both in and outside the United States, has blossomed and flourished since then, and it has been incorporated increasingly into academic curricula. The publication of *American Masculinities: A Historical Encyclopedia,* intended to serve professional scholars and students alike, is one sign that the field has reached maturity. This work serves as a marker of how the field has developed in the decade since Rotundo's seminal book used the analytical concept of masculinity to open new vistas for exploration and research into American history, society, and culture.

Masculinity Studies and the Encyclopedia: Assumptions and Scope

Scholars in several disciplines—including history, literary studies, anthropology, sociology, religion, and media studies—have cultivated this new field. This encyclopedia has been developed to reflect these diverse foundations, with articles examining men's family lives, work, sexuality, bodies, and behaviors; images of masculinity in literature, film, art, music, television shows, and cultural iconography; social and political ideologies and power structures; controversial issues; the relation between notions of masculinity and historical events, processes, and periods; and group identities in which gender has intersected with race, class, ethnicity, age, religion, and region. The encyclopedia's categories, as listed in the Reader's Guide, are intended to represent the range of exploration in the field as well as to guide users toward those dimensions of American masculinity that most interest them.

The contributors to this volume share the assumption that men's lives have been grounded fundamentally in gender; that is, in their awareness of themselves as males. Their concern is with men not merely as politicians, scientists, intellectuals, professionals, leaders of social movements, or military officers—the stuff of traditional scholarship—but as *men.* They owe this approach to the women's studies scholars of the 1970s and 1980s, who revealed the importance of gender as a category of social, cultural, and historical analysis. Some view masculinity studies as a threat to women's studies, fearing that it might be a means by which men can remain at the center of scholarly inquiry, and that the study of masculinity will blur, if not eclipse, the study of women. But because constructions of manhood and womanhood are, and have always been, relational—each necessarily being defined with reference to the other—the two fields are very much interrelated and mutually dependent.

The contributors also understand that masculinity is not monolithic and not simply dependent on biological sex. Rather, it is historically, socially, and culturally rooted. It is variable across time, and it is conceptualized and lived in ways that shape and are shaped by men's differing self-perceptions, needs, and aspirations. Nowhere is its variability clearer than in the dynamic and multiform culture of the United States. Nor is understanding masculinity simply a matter of examining the images and masculine types conveyed by popular culture and the media. Such images are certainly influential in U.S. society, which is highly dependent on the media, and they are by no means neglected in this book, but these representations often tell us more about what men are *supposed to be* than about what they actually *are.* This encyclopedia is informed by a sensitivity to the similarities and differences—and to the complex interrelations—between image and reality, prescription and practice.

Although, or perhaps because, this encyclopedia aims to convey the state of the art in gender studies, there is much that it *cannot* do. Since the field of American masculinity studies is continually developing and redeveloping, the encyclopedia necessarily omits topics that have not yet received much scholarly attention. The encyclopedia may also appear to privilege some periods over others, with entries on the Victorian and Progressive eras specifically, but not one on the colonial era. This reflects scholars' conviction that some periods have clearly defining cultural characteristics. Of course, they continue to search for synthetic understandings of other periods or groups whose defining cultural characteristics (if there are any) remain unclear. Finally, limitations of space required selectivity in choosing entry topics. This encyclopedia is not intended to be exhaustive, but rather to convey a sense of the scope of the field.

The encyclopedia, then, is offered to its users as a tool. Each entry offers suggestions for further reading, including academic books and scholarly journal articles, and each directs the user to related entries in the encyclopedia. At the end of the encyclopedia, a comprehensive bibliography provides readers with a list of sources—organized according to important thematic categories in the field—that will provide additional directions for further study. An extensive index offers users an additional means of locating topics of interest. By encapsulating the current state of scholarly interpretation, *American Masculinities: A Historical Encyclopedia* is intended to help students and scholars advance their studies, develop new questions for research, and stimulate new ways of exploring the history of American life.

Masculinity and U.S. History

Perhaps the primary lesson of masculinity studies as applied to U.S. history is that because American history (like all history) has been fundamentally about relations of power (e.g., political, economic, social, cultural), it has also been fundamentally about the social and cultural constructions of gender and masculinity used to support or seek power. In particular, white males of the middle and upper classes virtually monopolized power and public life until well into the twentieth century, and they have continued to dominate them into the early twenty-first. Thus, concepts and experiences of masculinity, infused with related concepts and experiences of race and class, have been at the heart of American life. They are the proverbial elephant in the closet, figuring prominently, but sometimes so obviously as to be overlooked.

White men in power have deployed race- and class-based ideologies and rhetorics of manhood in an attempt to justify their hold on power, to maintain their power, and to address challenges to their power. Since the initial establishment of the United States, this group of men associated American citizenship, patriotism, and even national identity itself with white masculinity, using implicitly and explicitly gendered metaphors to describe these associations. At the same time, in a democratic and increasingly multiracial and multicultural society in which existing power arrangements have continually been contested and reconfigured, masculinity has also been contested and reconfigured. Women and nonwhites have challenged or attempted to claim constructions of (white) masculinity in their efforts to attain power, and white males have responded through defensive reactions couched in terms of perceived threats to their manhood. In short, one may view the sweep of U.S. history as, in large part, the establishment and ongoing erosion of the power of white men and white masculinity as an initially preindustrial and agrarian American society became modern and industrial, and then postmodern and postindustrial. Viewing U.S. history through the lens of gender and masculinity—while recognizing and examining the elephant in the closet—has yielded new insights into American culture, called our attention to previously overlooked facets of the American experience, and revealed new dimensions of familiar events, movements, and institutions.

The lens of gender and masculinity studies has revealed that the founders of the United States were heirs to a European worldview grounded in an agrarian, preindustrial economy and in patriarchal social arrangements that assigned males the responsibilities and privileges of public and domestic power and consigned women to subordination. Viewing this system as an expression of a divinely ordained natural order, the earliest European colonizers sought to re-establish it in colonial America—and, with only a few exceptions, they largely succeeded. Their notions of masculinity shaped not only gender hierarchies but also racial hierarchies. They concluded from the very different gender arrangements of Amerindian and African peoples that the men of these groups were aberrantly masculine, and thus fit for subjugation. Yet colonizing a new environment forced them to adapt European patriarchy to new patterns and perceptions of land availability, and to the relative absence of European institutional infrastructures. Europeans also brought with them developing political, economic, and religious notions, such as the Protestant emphasis on individual experience, the political ideology of republicanism, and the developing economic system of market capitalism, that eventually transformed the patriarchal social and political order.

The founding of the United States was led by a generation of white male patriot leaders who were both inspired by and fearful of democracy's subversive potential. This dual outlook shaped their conceptions of the new nation's political and social structure, as well as the definitions of manhood upon which they grounded it. Determined to legitimate their own seizure of power and maintain the patriarchal system they deemed essential to order, they confined the exercise of political power to white property-owning males and developed a conception of republican citizenship that privileged the qualities they associated with manhood and whiteness. It is no coincidence that the most well known of the Revolutionary-era patriot organizations called itself the Sons of Liberty, that George Washington quickly became known as the "father of his country," that later generations of Americans would refer to those who established the nation as "founding fathers," or that the most prominent personification of the United States became, and remains, the decidedly white male figure of Uncle Sam. At the same time, the American Revolution inspired other men—namely those who did not own property and belonged to what were sometimes called the "lower orders"—to incorporate into their lives different understandings of republicanism and manliness, which helped them press their own claims to power during the political and social upheaval of the Revolutionary period.

Because the American political system developed amid an exaltation of republican manhood and assumed its modern features as the right to vote was being expanded to include all adult white males, it is hardly surprising that ideologies and rhetorics of masculinity became central to American political culture. The presidential election of 1828 set a key pattern of American electioneering. Andrew Jackson was presented to voters as a frontier-dwelling, Indian-fighting, heroic military general with a decided penchant for physical confrontation and defending his wife's honor. In the elections that followed, every campaign sought to emphasize a candidate's manliness. Similarly, American political leaders seeking to justify domestic and international applications of their power have historically used the rhetoric of manliness to underscore the presumed moral righteousness, and ostensibly protective purposes, of their policies. Beginning in the late eighteenth and early nineteenth centuries, and continuing into the twenty-first century, the U.S. government has cast itself in its domestic and foreign policies as a paternal and chivalric protector (often of emasculated dependents) while labeling perceived internal and external enemies as either demasculinized conspirators or as hypermasculine brutes.

In the late eighteenth and early nineteenth centuries, another important pattern emerged: Americans conceptualized in masculine terms the capitalist economic system that was becoming virtually synonymous with national life. This development was hardly surprising, since the national market economy was, like the democratic political system, confined largely to white men. In defining white men alone as possessed of the qualities of self-control, rationality, competitiveness, and ambition necessary to succeed, and thus naturally suited to the amoral roughness of the marketplace, Americans effectively defined the public world of economic exchange as a masculine sphere of activity, and financial success was thus seen as a masculine achievement. In the South, slave-owning southern men grounded their particular brand of capitalist production in an ideology of gender and racial hierarchy that cast white male slave-owners as paternalistic patriarchs presiding over their profitable plantations and enslaved laborers. Even in the twentieth century, as women and nonwhites increasingly enjoyed access to economic opportunity, many Americans continued to gender the nation's economic system male—and to color it white. Most Americans remained less likely to think that the rough-and-tumble world of economic competition had become feminized than to think that successful women had become masculinized. Similarly, economically successful nonwhite men have often been assumed to lose their racial or ethnic identities—to become "white." Like American national identity itself, the so-called American Dream began, and remains, ideologically linked to white masculinity.

The social and cultural use of gender to underwrite male power during the nineteenth century was by no means confined to those areas of life called "public." In domestic life, too, men assumed and usually sought to monopolize family leadership, typically by appealing to the same ideologies of masculinity that they used to justify their public political and economic power. While the market and industrial revolutions of the nineteenth century undermined the household economy on which patriarchy had rested in the preindustrial United States, these transformations also generated new ideologies of the family that preserved, and even enhanced, male domestic power in the "private" sphere of the home. Older patriarchal practices survived among those groups, such as yeoman farmers and the industrial working class, who resisted or were dislocated by the wrenching social and economic changes of the period. But during the early decades of the nineteenth century an emerging middle class produced a "cult of domesticity," as well as new and more modern ideals of masculinity (the "breadwinner" and the "family man"), which located the father at the apex of the nuclear family. These ideals eventually spread well beyond the white middle class, and they have retained enormous influence into the twenty-first century.

Although the advent of an urban-industrial society in the nineteenth century benefited white middle-class men, it became clear by midcentury that these men were also troubled by the transformation. They feared that the transition from nature's rhythms and vigorous physical labor to corporate work environments and urban and suburban living alienated them from important foundations of masculine identity. In response, they developed new ideals intended to accommodate the new order. One of them, which found scientific support in Darwinian biology and in contemporary psychological theories of human development, was an emphasis on strenuous exercise, outdoor activity, martial spirit, and the romantic ruggedness of nature (particularly in the West). The growing identification of manliness with physical strength, virility, and prowess was evident throughout American culture by the late nineteenth century, and it remained strong throughout the twentieth. Indeed, the cultural premium on masculine toughness found new sustenance during the twentieth century in the growth of leisure time and a consumer economy, and it acquitted new impetus and urgency as a result of the nation's rise to global power, the two world wars, the Cold War, and growing threats from domestic and global terrorism.

Other new ideals were intended to empower men for success in the emerging corporate and bureaucratic world. If earlier men had required an inwardly wrought individual "character," men of the late nineteenth and twentieth centuries were increasingly advised to cultivate "personality" and external appearance and to practice teamwork in order to achieve success amid increasingly large organizations and bureaucratic chains of command. Manliness in the twentieth century increasingly meant being a "team player," a successful businessman, or an effective salesman. It required men to cultivate a winning manner and to "dress for success" by wearing "power" clothes.

White men in power asserted these new concepts of masculinity with particular urgency, for their power was being increasingly challenged. Waves of immigration—which started in the mid–nineteenth century, accelerated in the late nineteenth and early twentieth centuries, and resumed after 1965—began to deprive whites of northern and western European descent of their numerical dominance as the nation became more multiracial and multiethnic. Nativist groups appeared in response, casting racial and ethnic "others" as un-American intruders in a white masculine America, and labeling them as either hypersexualized beasts (as in the case of southern Europeans, Jews, or Latinos) or effeminate (as in the case of Asians and, again, Jews). Even those who did not join nativist organizations often accepted these stereotyped images. During the late nineteenth century, in particular, whites of self-proclaimed Anglo-Saxon ancestry, drawing on theories of social Darwinism, anxiously perceived themselves as losing a competitive struggle for survival among the races. These men placed their hopes in the ideals of manly vigor and strenuous living—and in reproduction by racially responsible white couples. Physicians, psychologists, and other cultural authorities agreed that "normal" male sexuality was oriented toward procreation, and any other form was viewed as deviant.

The most direct challenges to the power of white males during the late nineteenth and twentieth centuries came from organized groups of women and nonwhite men who—with particular intensity and success during the late twentieth century—were seeking power of their own. Women's rights activists and feminists sought to end the identification of citizenship and economic and professional opportunity with masculinity; civil rights activists and ethnic and racial militants sought to end their identification with *white* masculinity; and gay rights activists sought to end their identification with *heterosexual* masculinity. These groups were supported by white men of the counterculture and political left who were increasingly critical of American political, economic, and social institutions, and thus sought new ways to distribute power in American society. All of these groups sought to redefine the relation between manliness and American life by offering their own visions of manhood.

By the end of the twentieth century, these movements had made considerable headway in creating an American nation that was not for white men only, and not so thoroughly grounded in concepts of masculinity and whiteness. Furthermore, traditional male power was increasingly undermined during the late twentieth century by growing divorce rates, economic circumstances that prompted a growing incidence of dual-income families, and postmodern questioning not only of white male power, but of whether masculinity and whiteness had any objective existence or meaning at all. In response, a growing number of white men defensively asserted in film, television, and talk-show radio what they considered to be traditional American values—that is, those ideas that supported the power of white masculinity—and they turned to conservative political and religious groups, and sometimes to right-wing militia and patriot organizations, in an effort to express and defend these values.

At the dawn of the twenty-first century, then, the meaning of American masculinity—or masculinit*ies*—is hotly contested. The masculinity-whiteness-heterosexuality-Americanism complex has eroded, generating a search for new ways to conceptualize the relation between manhood and American life. That search pervades the nation's political and religious life, has infused its popular culture, is powerfully evident in academia, and is at the heart of this encyclopedia.

—Bret E. Carroll

Abolitionism

Although opposition to the institution of slavery in North America dates back into the eighteenth century, the 1831 publication of William Lloyd Garrison's newspaper, the *Liberator*, is often cited as the inaugural event of the abolition movement in America. In the decades prior to the Civil War, abolitionists built a social movement and a political campaign aimed at ending slavery in the United States—a goal that was accomplished with the ratification of the Thirteenth Amendment in 1865. The definitions of manhood used by abolitionists varied in detail, but they generally included economic, political, and spiritual independence. Slavery had to be abolished, at least in part, because it threatened these cherished ideals.

Historians are increasingly emphasizing the significant contributions of different African-American communities to the movement, particularly in its early years; nonetheless, the majority of both the abolitionist leadership and the rank-and-file of the movement came from the white, northern middle class. Not surprisingly, in many respects abolitionist conceptions of manhood resembled those common in the North. Influenced by the ideals of political equality, spiritual empowerment, and economic independence associated with the American Revolution, the religious revivals of the Second Great Awakening, and the market revolution, antebellum northerners articulated a vision of manhood defined by the liberty and power of the individual male citizen. Abolitionists shared the northern middle-class's conception of an ideal society in which a "man" owned his own labor, and thus possessed both the means and the opportunity to acquire property, which would, in turn, ensure his political rights and his family's economic security. However, unlike the rest of the northern middle class, abolitionists desired to include African Americans in the American community and to extend to them, in varying degrees, the rights and opportunities associated with republicanism, evangelicalism, and liberalism. This did not mean that most abolitionists thought of African Americans as the equals of whites, or that they believed African-American men could ever embody "manhood." But many did consider slavery and racial prejudice fundamental contradictions of their most highly valued economic and political ideals, including their notions of manhood.

While all abolitionists shared the common goal of ending slavery in the United States, the internal politics of the movement were often contentious and always complex, with differing constructions of masculinity represented. Radical abolitionists, such as William Lloyd Garrison and Angelina and Sarah Grimké, considered spiritual equality and the ultimate authority of the conscience to be divine truths, and they regarded contemporary gender roles relegating men and women to distinct and separate spheres of activity as a sinful violation of both of these principles. They believed that women had both the right and the spiritual duty to enter the "male" world of abolitionist politics, and that men were in turn obligated to embody "female" virtues of love and sympathy in their concern for slaves. Many radical male abolitionists sought to embody their notions of gender in their personal lives, laboring to create fairly egalitarian relationships with

This image of a male slave pleading for help, which accompanied the 1837 broadside publication of John Greenleaf Whittier's antislavery poem "Our Countrymen in Chains," suggests both abolitionists' association of manhood with independence and their belief that male slaves were not fully masculine. (From the collections of the Library of Congress)

women (particularly with their wives) and unusually affectionate, supportive, and loving friendships with other men.

More conservative abolitionists, such as Arthur and Lewis Tappan, neither accepted the radicals' critique of gender conventions nor supported their feminist agenda. Instead, they insisted that American gender conventions reflected divinely ordained biological and spiritual differences between men and women—with men more naturally suited to political and economic activity in the public realm. From this perspective, gender reform distracted the movement from its abolitionist goals.

Radical and conservative abolitionists also had differing views about the most "manly" way to eradicate slavery. Defining manliness as the following of conscience and moral principle, radical abolitionists emphasized the use of "moral suasion" (appealing to people's moral sense to convince them of slavery's sinful nature) and regarded cooperation with the political system and the use of violence as corruptions of manly conscience and moral purity. But partly because this strategy emulated the middle-class conception of "feminine" influence, which held that women's power came from the virtuous, informal influence they wielded within the family, conservative abolitionists eventually rejected moral suasion and its advocates as too "feminine," and therefore ineffective. Conservatives turned instead during the 1840s to active engagement in electoral politics—a right exclusive to white men and a key identifier of antebellum manhood—and during the 1850s they increasingly advocated the use of violence.

In 1840, conservative abolitionists led by the Tappan brothers withdrew from Garrison's American Anti-Slavery Society, which had just elected the female abolitionist Abby Kelly to its business committee, and formed the American and Foreign Anti-Slavery Society. This rejection of the "feminine," and of the feminist politics of the radical wing of the movement, initiated a masculinization of abolitionist politics that continued throughout the Civil War. This process accelerated during the 1840s and 1850s, spurred by the eruption of national debate over the status of slavery in new western territories acquired by the United States during the Mexican War and by the Fugitive Slave Law passed in 1850. These events moved the issue of slavery to the center of the nation's politics, and they moved abolitionists away from the strategy of moral suasion and toward a policy of "masculine" political measures and "manly" violence.

In 1848 the new Free-Soil Party was formed to preserve land and republican independence for white men by preventing the expansion of the slave labor system into territory just won in the Mexican War. This "free soil" ideology became central to the platform of the Republican Party, which emerged in 1854. Many northerners praised the manliness and righteous violence of John Brown, who was executed after failing in his attempt to incite a slave rebellion in the South in 1859. The abolitionist strategy of focusing upon the power of the male citizen, especially in terms of voting rights, culminated in 1870 with the ratification of the Fifteenth Amendment, which granted the vote to former male slaves, but, despite the objections of some prominent feminist abolitionists, did not extend the vote to women.

Abolitionists contributed to changing understandings of manhood in antebellum America in complex and contradictory ways. While their belief in individual independence had the potential to radically challenge antebellum notions of masculinity and femininity, it also legitimated an emerging system of market capitalism and a related liberal middle-class conception of manhood that emphasized men's role as autonomous, self-interested actors in the economic marketplace. The abolitionists' emphasis in the 1830s on Christian love and political sympathy across racial and gender lines had contributed to a critique of the market model of manhood that celebrated competition in the public sphere. Yet in the 1840s and 1850s male abolitionists increasingly identified themselves with the exclusively male roles of voter and soldier, figures who struggled politically and violently to determine the fate of American polity.

Bibliography

Dixon, Chris. *Perfecting the Family: Antislavery Marriages in Nineteenth-Century America.* Amherst: University of Massachusetts Press, 1997.

Dorsey, Bruce. *Reforming Men and Women: Gender in the Antebellum City.* Ithaca, N.Y.: Cornell University Press, 2002.

Kraditor, Aileen S. *Means and Ends in American Abolitionism: Garrison and His Critics on Strategy and Tactics, 1834–1850.* New York: Pantheon, 1969.

Stauffer, John. *The Black Hearts of Men: Radical Abolitionists and the Transformation of Race.* Cambridge, Mass.: Harvard University Press, 2002.

Yacovone, Donald. "Abolitionists and the 'Language of Fraternal Love.'" In *Meanings for Manhood: Constructions of Masculinity in Victorian America,* edited by Mark C. Carnes and Clyde Griffen. Chicago: University of Chicago Press, 1990.

Further Reading

Abzug, Robert H. *Cosmos Crumbling: American Reform and the Religious Imagination.* New York: Oxford University Press, 1994.

Ginzberg, Lori D. *Women and the Work of Benevolence: Morality, Politics, and Class in the Nineteenth-Century United States.* New Haven, Conn.: Yale University Press, 1990.

Hoganson, Kristin. "Garrisonian Abolitionists and the Rhetoric of Gender, 1850–1860." *American Quarterly,* 45 December 1993, 558–595.

Stewart, James Brewer. *Holy Warriors: The Abolitionists and American Slavery.* Rev. ed. New York: Hill and Wang, 1997.

RELATED ENTRIES

African-American Manhood; Civil War; Douglass, Frederick; Evangelicalism and Revivalism; Feminism; Male Friendship; Middle-Class Manhood; Politics; Property; Race; Reform Movements; Religion and Spirituality; Sentimentalism; Slavery; Victorian Era; Violence

—*Robert K. Nelson*

ADOLESCENCE

Throughout American history, parents, journalists, educators, politicians, and young people have debated the meaning of the transitional period between childhood and adulthood. Views of adolescence have had powerful but varied gender implications, shifting between the extremes of applauding youthful male vitality and condemning youthful male rebellion. Debates about adolescence often showed the concerns of adults who hoped to train young men to use their energies to assume their proper place in public life, but also feared that those energies could lead to various crises.

During colonial times, both the ideas about the roles of young males and their actual experiences differed significantly by region. In New England, boys were sent away to learn a trade, a practice intended by parents to undercut their sons' rebellious tendencies, teach them Puritan values, and lead them to their calling, all of which were considered essential to the achievement of manhood. But young men's dependence on the patriarchal family often lasted until their late twenties, when marriage marked their postponed entry into the adult world.

In the South, where church and family were less central aspects of society, many young, unmarried males labored as indentured servants, thus lacking independence for an extended time. Even in later decades, when native-born men grew up in family settings, adolescence in the colonial South remained a stage of life associated with great insecurity. Only in the early to mid-1700s did large numbers of elite southern parents begin to train their sons to assume roles of power and mastery.

The situation was considerably different for young African Americans. Growing up in slavery, most of them felt the brutal reality of bondage early in life. Slave communities usually discouraged youthful male rebellion and established norms that emphasized family stability. Though evidence on slave courtship is rare, some sources point to young male slaves gaining self-esteem through competition for the attention of young women.

After the American Revolution, parents wanted their sons to aspire to the values of a republican citizenry, and young men themselves endorsed this spirit of national strength, liberty, and virtue. But in the long run, republicanism encouraged young white men to challenge parental authority. In the early nineteenth century, college students confronted traditional rules at their institutions, and many young men moved to urban centers and created a youth subculture with clubs and fraternal organizations. Many conservatives attributed this subculture to a decreasing influence of traditional institutions, such as church and family, and viewed this "urban youth crisis" as a symbol of national decline.

Mid-nineteenth-century attempts to socialize and control young men were inextricably intertwined with the anxieties of an emerging middle class. As industrialization and growing immigration swelled the ranks of the working class, middle-class reformers, who viewed young working-class men as a social danger, established houses of refuge and reform schools to teach middle-class values and morals to working-class youth. With regard to their own sons, middle-class parents began to stress prolonged education and insisted on their sons living at home until their early twenties. This practice promoted a stronger relationship between mother and son, with the intention of fostering morality, self-restraint, and sexual fidelity. The ideal of Victorian manhood thus emphasized a devotion to mother and family as a counter to youthful male impulses, and as a prerequisite to fulfilling manly independence in the public sphere of business and politics.

During the late nineteenth and early twentieth centuries, dramatic changes in American society prompted the identification of adolescence as a distinct stage of life. An emerging cadre of white middle-class professionals concerned with maintaining stability in an urbanizing, industrializing society understood adolescence as a universally valid concept, but they tied it closely to their ideas about class, race, and gender. In 1904 the psychologist Granville Stanley Hall's study *Adolescence* offered the first systematic analysis of youth behavior. Hall argued that the development of each individual recapitulated the evolution of the human race, and that adolescence paralleled a prehistoric time of restless nomadic migration, upheaval, and uprooting. This natural adolescent restlessness, he said, was exacerbated—especially in boys—by modern, artificial, and sexually stimulating urban-industrial environments. To prevent destructive male adolescent behavior, he counseled the channeling of young men's energy into play. Yet his writings signified his belief that adolescent masculinity required repressive control and regimentation.

Hall's work strongly influenced early twentieth-century educators, social workers, and others engaged in socializing adolescents. It was especially popular with "boy-workers," who founded homosocial clubs and organizations for white middle- and upper-class boys that offered structured physical activities and directed adolescent male energy into the development of morality and self-discipline. Believing that adult men were best able to achieve this result, these educators put boys under explicitly male authority and sought to minimize the "feminine influences" that they thought were dominating schools, churches, and other organizations of the time.

During the twentieth century, several waves of lively debates assessed how to tame the "young rebel." During the 1920s, amid an increasing challenge to Victorian middle-class moral standards, many middle-class parents feared that their sons and daughters might emulate the behavior of working-class adolescents, stimulating a debate among parents about youthful morality. During the Great Depression of the 1930s, fears of adolescent male disorder were intensified by rising unemployment and a growing number of hoboes.

During the 1950s and 1960s, amid liberalizing sexual attitudes, fears of internal and external subversion, and a growing youth population, public debates about the American teenager became even more pronounced. The Cold War, with its simultaneous celebration of American freedom and demands for conformity, shaped 1950s debates and generated a new type of rebel that combined these contradictions. Fiercely independent and self-reliant, but also volatile, sexually charged, and potentially delinquent, seeking both autonomy and attachment, these figures—such as James Dean in *Rebel Without a Cause* (1955) and Marlon Brando in *The Wild One* (1953)—were considered both dangerous and glamorous at the same time. In the turbulent 1960s, adolescent males attracted public attention by joining student protests and the anti–Vietnam War movement, defying authority and conventional middle-class manhood, wearing long hair, and refusing military service. To the older generation, such behavior was strongly associated with femininity, disloyalty, and subversiveness.

For African-American men and members of other minority groups, the issue of race further complicated the problem of adolescent rebellion. Trying to enhance their families' opportunities for upward mobility, or to stabilize upward mobility already achieved, parents of the African-American underclass and middle class tended to observe their sons' rebellious behavior as counterproductive. Whites who feared for the disruption of social stability and harbored racist assumptions likewise made those young black men who "acted out" into objects of anger. Yet these young men themselves, and even many of their parents, also defended their behavior as expressions of a necessary struggle for social justice—and of racial pride.

By the close of the twentieth century, new issues once again made male adolescents the topic of anxious debate. Concerns about the destructive potential of adolescent male energy have been evident in controversies over rap musicians who appear to condone and encourage misogyny and gang violence; cybersurfers who seem withdrawn, antisocial, lacking adult guidance, and possibly inclined toward illegal computer hacking; teenage males who turn anger into school violence; and "slackers" who demonstrate an apparent lack of ambition. Discussions of all of these problems suggest the continuing perception that control of adolescent masculinity is necessary to maintain social order.

BIBLIOGRAPHY

Alexander, Ruth M. "Adolescence." In *Encyclopedia of American Social History*, Vol. III, edited by Mary Kupiec Cayton, Elliott J. Gorn, and Peter W. Williams. New York: Scribners, 1993.

Fass, Paula. *The Damned and the Beautiful. American Youth in the 1920's.* New York: Oxford University Press, 1977.

Kett, Joseph. *Rites of Passage: Adolescence in America, 1790 to the Present.* New York: Basic Books, 1977.

Macleod, David I. *Building Character in the American Boy: The Boy Scouts, YMCA, and their Forerunners, 1870–1920.* Madison: University of Wisconsin Press, 1983.

Novak, Steven J. *The Rights of Youth: American Colleges and Student Revolt.* Cambridge, Mass.: Harvard University Press, 1977.

Thompson, Roger. "Adolescent Culture in Colonial Massachusetts." *Journal of Family History* 9, no. 2 (1984): 127–144.

Wallach, Glenn. *Obedient Sons: The Discourse of Youth and Generations in American Culture, 1630–1860.* Amherst: University of Massachusetts Press, 1997.

FURTHER READING

Graebner, William. *Coming of Age in Buffalo: Youth and Authority in the Postwar Era.* Philadelphia: Temple University Press, 1990.

Hall, G. Stanley. *Adolescence: Its Psychology and Its Relations to Psychology, Anthropology, Sociology, Sex, Crime, Religion and Education.* 2 Vols. New York: Appleton, 1905.

King, Wilma. *Stolen Childhood: Slave Youth in Nineteenth-Century America.* Bloomington: Indiana University Press, 1995.

Modell, John. *Into One's Own: From Youth to Adulthood in the United States, 1920–1975.* Berkeley: University of California Press, 1989.

RELATED ENTRIES

African-American Manhood; American Revolution; Apprenticeship; Boy Scouts of America; Brando, Marlon; Character; Citizenship; Class; Consumerism; Counterculture; Dean, James; Education; Gangs; Hall, Granville Stanley; Hoboes; Juvenile Delinquency; Leisure; Marriage; Masculine Domesticity; Mother–Son Relationships; Nuclear Family; *Rebel Without a Cause*; Victorian Era; Young Men's Christian Association; Youth

—*Olaf Stieglitz*

ADVENTURES OF HUCKLEBERRY FINN

In his novel *Adventures of Huckleberry Finn* (1884), Mark Twain used nineteenth-century conventions of American writing about boyhood, but he created a literary classic in the ways he overturned those conventions. The book's main character, Huckleberry Finn, is an American male icon, both in the challenges he faces moving from boyhood to manhood and in the definitions of manhood he witnesses and rejects.

Huck feels constrained by a domestic life that many men in Victorian America perceived as excessively feminized. He wants freedom from the proper and maternal Miss Watson, who expects the poor and unkempt Huck to clean up, go to school and church, and become a respectable boy. But while Huck defies the rules and self-control of Victorian manners, he also challenges the extravagant playfulness he associates with his friend Tom Sawyer, who attempts to turn children's play into affairs of great drama. Huck considers both Tom's games and Miss Watson's Sunday school to be foolish wastes of time.

To escape the restraints of Victorian conventions that he associates with women, Huck considers two options. First, his father Pap offers him a yeoman life of leisure outside any norms of time and community. Huck describes living with Pap as "kind of lazy and jolly, laying off comfortable all day, smoking and fishing, and no books nor study" (30). But the negative side of yeoman life is the absolute power of the father; so, after enduring some beatings, Huck chooses his second option: running away.

As Huck Finn journeys along the Mississippi River, Mark Twain dramatizes the flaws and failures of several definitions of American manhood. Traditional expressions of honor, associated in particular with southern manhood, fail. The Grangerford and Shepherdson families kill each other in a feud whose origin no one can remember. A minor character named Sherburne, claiming to be protecting his own honor, kills a drunk who insulted him and then faces down a potential lynch mob that comes looking for vengeance. Town residents respond to the antics of con men by tarring and feathering them. Manly violence abounds, none of it for good reason.

Huck ultimately chooses two meanings of mature masculinity as preferable to both Victorian respectability and aggressive manhood. Rejecting the notion that masculinity

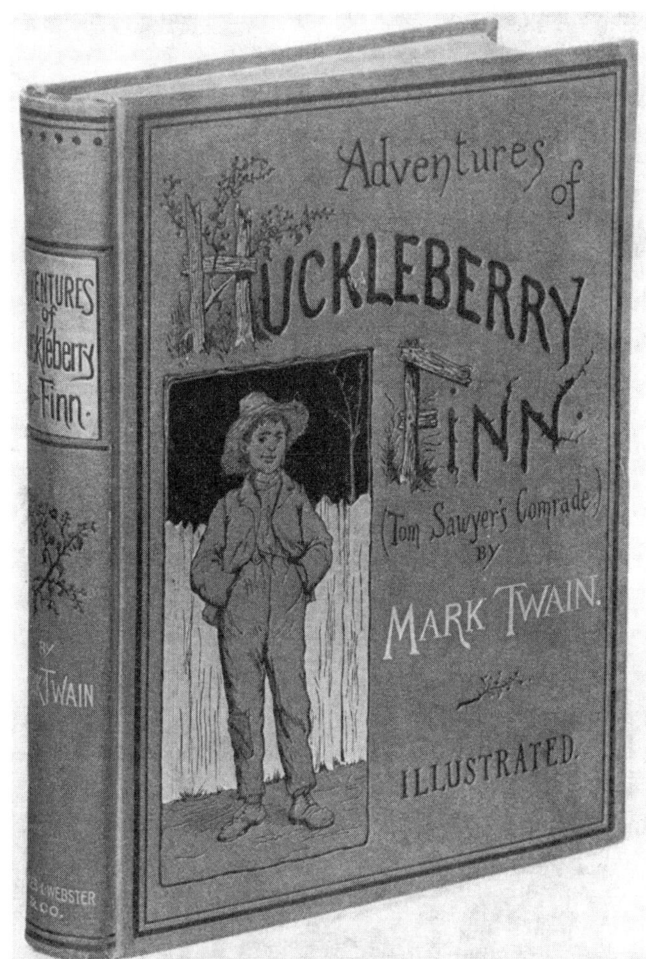

This image of the fictional Huckleberry Finn, from the cover of the first American edition of Mark Twain's novel Adventures of Huckleberry Finn *(1884), suggests Huck's rejection of Victorian gentility and embrace of the frontier in his transition from boyhood to manhood. (© Bettmann/Corbis)*

means whiteness and domination—a meaning that his impoverished father shares with other white men in the book—Huck humbles himself and apologizes after playing a trick on Jim, a runaway slave who becomes his travel companion. Later, Huck overcomes his own inherited beliefs about slavery when he protects Jim from being discovered. The only way Huck can envision living without either dominating other people or fitting into flawed moral codes is to keep moving. So, in the end, Huck decides to "light out for the Territory," embracing a definition of manhood grounded in personal autonomy and freedom from social convention.

Adventures of Huckleberry Finn undermines a conventional dichotomy in representations of boyhood. One strand of that literature, represented by the writers Horatio Alger, Jr., and Oliver Optic, depicts the boy as a moral innocent who redeems society through his innate goodness—and usually reaps the benefits. The other portrays the boy as a prankster—as a Tom Sawyer or Bart Simpson—whose high-spirited subversiveness shows the foolishness of social conventions. Huck rejects social conventions through his moral observations and actions. Rather than improving society, however, he chooses to escape it, like the frontiersmen and raftsmen Huck admires, and like contemporary figures such as Jack Kerouac and Bruce Springsteen.

Bibliography

Griswold, Jerry. *Audacious Kids: Coming of Age in America's Classic Children's Books.* New York: Oxford University Press, 1992.

Jacobson, Marcia. *Being a Boy Again: Autobiography and the American Boy Book.* Tuscaloosa: University of Alabama Press, 1994.

Rodgers, Daniel T. "Socializing Middle-Class Children: Institutions, Fables, and Work Values in Nineteenth-Century America." In *Growing Up in America,* edited by N. Ray Hiner and Joseph M. Hawes. Urbana: University of Illinois Press, 1985.

Twain, Mark. *Adventures of Huckleberry Finn.* 1884. Reprint, edited by Walter Blair and Victor Fischer. Berkeley: University of California Press, published in cooperation with the University of Iowa, 1985.

West, Mark I. *Children, Culture, and Controversy.* Princeton, N.J.: Princeton University Press, 2001.

Wieck, Carl F. *Refiguring Huckleberry Finn.* Athens: University of Georgia Press, 2000.

Further Reading

Calvert, Karin. *Children in the Home: The Material Culture of Early Childhood, 1600–1900.* Boston: Northeastern University Press, 1992.

Fishkin, Shelley Fisher. *Was Huck Black? Mark Twain and African-American Voices.* New York: Oxford University Press, 1993.

Marten, James. *The Children's Civil War.* Chapel Hill: University of North Carolina Press, 1998.

Sattelmeyer, Robert, and J. Donald Crowley, eds. *One Hundred Years of Huckleberry Finn: The Boy, His Book, and American Culture.* Columbia: University of Missouri Press, 1985.

West, Elliott, and Paula Petrik, eds. *Small Worlds: Children and Adolescents in America, 1850–1950.* Lawrence: University Press of Kansas, 1992.

Related Entries

Alger, Horatio, Jr.; Boyhood; Kerouac, Jack; Sawyer, Tom; Southern Manhood; Springsteen, Bruce; Travel; Travel Narratives; Twain, Mark; Whiteness; Youth

—Ted Ownby

Advertising

Advertising typically associates products with lifestyle choices and seeks to influence individual and social-group behavior through appeals to mass audiences. In doing so, advertising also shapes gender identities by conforming to, and producing expectations about, male and female behavior. Through simplified and idealized images of masculinity—often presented as realistic through the use of photography, testimonials, and other techniques—advertising aimed at men has defined manhood and confirmed traditional male authority and dominance by associating consumer products with success and power. In particular, advertisements have identified men with public authority and women with the home, family, and emotions. They have represented the male as expert in the worlds of business, technology, and science; presented white businessmen and professionals as typical representatives of masculinity; and associated masculine success with the acquisition of money and the exercise of power over women. Although advertising began in the 1980s and 1990s to broaden its depictions of men by including minorities and gay men, it continued to legitimate the cultural dominance of men who fit within a narrow range of masculine identities.

Masculinity and the Rise of Modern Advertising

Advertising emerged as an important cultural phenomenon near the end of the nineteenth century. Before that time, ads were often mistrusted, since they were used to hock unnecessary products of questionable repute. Advertisements also began to look different, relying on words, which were considered more informative than visual images. By the early twentieth century, massive economic and social changes, including the centralization of production and the development of national markets, generated a consumer economy in which producers sought national publicity through advertising. This consumer-based economy spawned the modern advertising industry as structural changes in the nature of work, including shorter working hours, increased leisure time, and higher wages, gave men spending money and time to spend it on the new products rolling off assembly lines. Advertising now served an important social function: inform people about, and stimulating their desire for, these products. With new print technologies and rural free delivery enabling them to expand their readership, newspapers and periodicals increasingly included advertising as a significant source of revenue, selling their audience markets to advertisers.

During the 1920s, advertising agencies sought to reach men by appealing to their aspirations for upward mobility and by drawing heavily on psychology and dominant constructions of middle-class masculinity. Ads used emotional, and often irrational, appeals to men's sexuality, hunger, and safety. They tapped men's insecurity about employment, success, and their bodies and featured images of well-to-do businessmen and professionals in order to encourage personal dissatisfaction (the belief that one was insufficiently masculine) and suggest that consumer products could foster self-improvement. A soap ad, for example, featured a pile of men grasping to reach the top, while Gillette promoted its shaving products by suggesting that men who shaved daily were satisfied and successful. Such ads introduced new and enduring standards of male physical appearance, encouraging men to view themselves as marketable commodities at a time when manliness and success in business were increasingly associated with the cultivation of personality and a winning external appearance—an approach that was replacing the nineteenth century values of community service and inner strength as signs of success.

Masculinity and Advertising: 1930s–1950s

During the Great Depression, advertisers attempted to reach men by addressing male anxieties generated by economic uncertainty, which had the effect of both soothing and increasing their fears. Although the authority of men as family breadwinners was threatened by unemployment, ads confirmed male domestic authority. Home-product advertisements depicting husbands lurking behind their wives, for example, suggested that women belonged in the home and that their husbands retained final power over domestic purchasing. Ads also assumed a new inspirational tone, assuring men left uncertain of their manhood that continued hard work would produce success and a return to traditional breadwinning responsibilities. Using new visual techniques of persuasion, such as close-up photography to emphasize extreme emotions, they played on feelings of guilt and fear, and made the national economic crisis into a personal challenge by encouraging men to keep trying. Conversely, at a time when unemployment was straining many marriages and driving some men to abandon their families, ads were depicting angry or bored husbands confronting their wives over perceived threats to the father's provider role and the family's financial security. In an ad for Lux detergent, for example, a husband fearful that a run in his wife's stocking could cost him his job chides her, "You would get a run at the boss's party!" while a photograph shot from an unusual angle below emphasizes the run and dramatizes the threatening nature of the situation.

With the return of economic prosperity and the continuing expansion of consumerism following World War II, advertising began to target, and to define, a new masculine figure, the suburban dad, through the powerful new medium of television. Enormously expanding the reach of advertising's gendered imagery, television ads (like the shows they sponsored) presented the white, middle-class, breadwinner father as the ideal man, his success indicated and measured by his ability to provide consumer products for his children and his homemaker wife. Advertisers also sought to reach the new and potentially huge postwar market of "baby boomer" boys by using the images of masculinity (e.g., heroic, tough, individualistic, patriotic) being emphasized in an anxious Cold War culture.

Expanding consumerism also tapped another emerging model of American masculinity: the freewheeling bachelor. As cultural commentators criticized what they considered a repressive suburban middle-class lifestyle, *Playboy* magazine (established in 1953) and its advertisements proposed an alternative mode of manliness grounded in open sexuality, personal freedom, and consumption of luxury goods. Speaking to an exclusively male audience, advertisers in *Playboy* celebrated the self-made bachelor-consumer by associating their brand names and products (e.g., liquor, automobiles, cigarettes, domestic luxuries) with masculine freedom and fulfillment.

New Male Audiences and Images: The Late Twentieth Century

In response to the counterculture and movements for civil rights, women's rights, and gay rights during the 1960s and early 1970s, advertisers began targeting newly empowered groups of men and, to a limited degree, withdrawing from traditional identifications of masculinity with whiteness, breadwinning, and heterosexuality. Ads appealing to rebellious young men who questioned conventional values addressed their audiences in a new, informal vernacular that linked their products (Volkswagen vehicles, for example) with such countercultural values as sexual liberation, anti-consumerism, and a rejection of office work. At the same time, with more married women entering the workforce, advertisers constructed a superwoman image—though taking care to preserve conventional gender roles to a significant degree. Thus, a commercial for Enjoli perfume featured a professional woman claiming that she could "bring home the bacon, fry it up in a pan," but would also satisfy her husband sexually. Similarly, a Folger's coffee commercial introduced a "new man" who assumed domestic responsibilities, while also, by suggesting his inability to function effectively in the kitchen, continuing to depict domestic work as belonging properly to women.

The civil rights movement brought increased recognition of the spending power of minority groups, leading advertisers to target black and Latino men in ways that both challenged and reinforced traditional racial stereotypes. In television and magazine advertisements aimed at these groups, images of upper-class, and often light-skinned, minority men represented a change from earlier racist advertising (exemplified by the figure of Uncle Ben) that had presented African-American men as servile. Some welcomed the new representations while others argued that such limited portrayals flattened the diversity of their communities. Another advertising tactic featured images of sports celebrities such as Michael Jordan and associated minority men with financial success, while also suggesting that such success was achieved through physical rather than intellectual pursuits. Nonwhite men also figured disproportionately in advertisements for alcoholic beverages, cigarettes, and fast food that were strategically placed in urban environments on billboards and other prominent locations.

The gay rights movement, meanwhile, brought greater acceptance and awareness of gay male sexuality to advertising, while a new cultural focus on the self and the body generated greater use of the partially unclothed male body and a growing tendency toward androgynous depictions of men. Beginning in the 1980s, men's fashion advertising, addressing both gay and straight male markets and exemplified by ads for Calvin Klein jeans and underwear, featured handsome, scantily-clad male models. Adopting a more fluid notion of gender, which alongside the rise of health clubs and exercise culture focused on the body as a site of transformation, advertisers offered men a new range of personal hygiene and grooming products such as hair sprays and scented shampoos—while guaranteeing that their use did not compromise one's masculinity. A body spray called "Axe," for example used its name and advertising to reaffirm a phallic association with violence rather than any liberation from mainstream social values.

As a reaction to these enormous structural changes, and in reflection of the militaristic foreign policy of the Ronald Reagan administration, an aggressively hypermasculine American male protagonist emerged in 1980s ads. Superhuman action figures resembling film characters Rambo and the Terminator, and whose bodies could become weapons, appeared in advertising for children's toys and video games. Cartoon advertising mascots like Joe Camel or the Budweiser frogs presented to young men—and even to boys—a less aggressive, humorous version of this angry male consumer. Marketing tie-ins in films and television programs, such as those promoting new James Bond films, expanded the reach of this new masculinity. In these ads, the classy but violent and faintly misogynistic hero Bond drives the car and wears the watch and clothing that male viewers are intended to desire. The widespread concentration of media ownership in the 1990s expanded such images of Western machismo and individualism internationally as well, as American advertising reached the former Soviet republics as well as China.

Evaluating Advertising's Impact

The advertising industry is a major American export representing American values as well as products. As such, scholars are concerned with its impact on global politics. Studies of advertising and masculinity are also beginning, in the wake of the school murders at Columbine High School, to evaluate the impact of advertising on social behavior, particularly on young boys. Some scholars argue that understanding the effect of advertising on men requires an analysis of social, economic, and cultural forces, including its relationship to other media, while others take a behavioral approach that links advertising directly with violent, impulsive, and antisocial behavior.

BIBLIOGRAPHY

Berger, John. *Ways of Seeing.* New York: Penguin, 1972.

Bordo, Susan. *The Male Body: A New Look at Men in Public and in Private.* New York: Farrar, Straus and Giroux, 1999.

Clarke, Eric, and Matthew Henson. "Hot Damme! Reflections on Gay Publicity." In *Boys: Masculinities in Contemporary Culture,* edited by Paul Smith. Boulder, Colo.: Westview Press, 1996.

Ewen, Stuart. *Captains of Consciousness: Advertising and the Social Roots of the Consumer Culture.* New York: McGraw-Hill, 1976.

Goffman, Erving. *Gender Advertisements.* New York: Harper & Row, 1979.

Katz, Jackson. "Advertising and the Construction of a Violent White Masculinity." In *Gender, Race and Class in Media: A Text Reader,* edited by Gail Dines and Jean M. Humez. Thousand Oaks, Calif.: Sage, 1995.

Marchand, Roland. *Advertising the American Dream: Making Way for Modernity, 1920-1940.* Berkeley: University of California Press, 1985.

Pendergrast, Tom. *Creating the Modern Man: American Magazines and Consumer Culture, 1900–1950.* Columbia: University of Missouri Press, 2000.

Rotundo, E. Anthony. *American Manhood: Transformations in Masculinity from the Revolution to the Modern Era.* New York: Basic Books, 1993.

Further Reading

Dávila, Arlene M. *Latinos, Inc.: The Marketing and Making of a People.* Berkeley: University of California Press, 2001.

Frank, Thomas. *The Conquest of Cool: Business Culture, Counterculture, and the Rise of Hip Consumerism.* Chicago: University of Chicago Press, 1997.

Jhally, Sut. *The Codes of Advertising: Fetishism and the Political Economy of Meaning in the Consumer Society.* New York: St. Martin's, 1987.

Nixon, Sean. *Hard Looks: Masculinities, Spectatorship and Contemporary Consumption.* New York: St. Martin's, 1996.

Strate, Lance. "Beer Commercials: A Manual on Masculinity." In *Men, Masculinity, and the Media,* edited by Steve Craig. Newbury Park, Calif.: Sage, 1992.

Twitchell, James B. *ADCULT USA: The Triumph of Advertising in American Culture.* New York: Columbia University Press, 1996.

Wallace, Michelle. "Masculinity in Black Popular Culture." In *Constructing Masculinity,* edited by Maurice Berger, Brian Wallis, and Simon Watson. New York: Routledge, 1995.

Related Entries

Adolescence; Alcohol; American Dream; Breadwinner Role; Business/Corporate America; Civil Rights Movement; Consumerism; Cowboys; Fashion; Freudian Psychoanalytic Theory; Great Depression; Marlboro Man; *Playboy* Magazine; Television; Urbanization

—Danielle K. Schwartz

Advice Literature

Commercially printed advice literature began appearing in America in the eighteenth century, with the intent being to instruct boys (and men) on how to "act like a man." Although not exclusive to the United States, advice literature is characteristically American in its faith that individuals can improve themselves through knowledge and effort. Advice literature has historically conveyed social constructions of ideal masculinity, often in response to perceived crises in masculinity.

Advice literature has addressed several different dimensions of male identity and behavior. Child-rearing advice literature aimed at parents reveals cultural expectations about how to rear the proper boy. Advice literature written for boys and adolescents reflects societal images of appropriate masculine behavior and values. Other literature addressed styles of fathering, helped husbands understand their social responsibilities, and helped men perform in such extrafamilial social roles as youth leader, athletic coach, teacher, boss, employee, and business colleague. It is not known whether readers of this literature actually followed the advice they were given, so it is dangerous to make generalizations from these texts about actual behavior, but the literature itself serves as important evidence of prevailing historically and socially conditioned expectations regarding appropriate masculine conduct.

Eighteenth- and Nineteenth-Century Advice

Religious leaders and physicians authored the earliest advice books for parents and young men, which stressed the moral responsibility of the man in the family. Colonial advice literature viewed the family as a microcosm of society, making little distinction between the public and private roles of fathers and, by example, of their sons.

During the early to mid-nineteenth century—amid rising nationalism, urbanization, the transition to a market economy, and the erosion of traditional preindustrial village restraints on male behavior—advice-manual writers such as Sylvester Graham, William Alcott, and O. S. Fowler continued to infuse advice literature with strong religious overtones. But there was a new emphasis on self-control and self-discipline of the body. Often considered an essential component of good "character," self-control provided new mechanisms of moral and social order and reinforced the traits men were thought to need to contribute to economic growth. Advice manuals urged young men to avoid sexual indulgence (especially masturbation), and the language used in the manuals suggests that the writers saw the young (white) man's body as a powerful metaphor for the strength and purity of the nation.

Family life was a major concern in these early advice manuals. Men were urged both to be effective providers by seeking economic success and to cultivate domestic ties as a counteractive force to the amorality of capitalist competition. There was a growing sense that the family was a safe haven from an increasingly stressful public world, and that the husband/father was the crucial link between the public world and the increasingly private domestic sphere.

The role of emotions raised troubling questions about the performance of masculinity. Women were thought to be much more emotional than men. Early Victorian-era Americans saw male anger as a dangerous loss of self-control, and advice literature for parents of boys and for husbands recommended its suppression. Following the Civil War, however, advice writers increasingly saw anger as a natural emotion in men, one that should be constructively channeled.

The Late Nineteenth and Early Twentieth Centuries

The rise of scientific psychology in the 1880s challenged religion's authority in matters of child rearing and moral education, and the emergence of what historians have called a "therapeutic society" transformed religious questions into psychological ones. A key inventor of the scientific idea of adolescence, the psychologist Granville Stanley Hall, addressed the implications of evolutionary science for understanding the psychology and sociology of male adolescents. He advised parents, educators, and youth workers on how to fashion socialization experiences that would use, rather than resist, the powerful biological forces of male adolescence. Like other nineteenth-century proponents of "muscular Christianity," Hall firmly advised physical activity for boys as a necessary foundation for their mental and moral education. Hall also combined Romantic and Darwinian views, seeing adolescence as a special period for the development of young men's religious and moral sensibilities. He believed that young men were naturally inclined toward selflessness and altruism, and he advised parents, teachers, and leaders of such youth movements the Young Men's Christian Association and the Boy Scouts of America to nourish these proclivities.

Just as anxiety about the fate of the new nation colored advice to young men in the early national period, so anxiety about several economic, social, and ideological forces that were converging in the 1890s, particularly the emergence of urban-industrial living, made adults worry about the development of boys, and also made white middle-class men worry that they were less manly than their fathers had been. Books such as William B. Forbush's *The Boy Problem* (1902), relying upon the same evolutionary psychology that Hall had used, recommended that boys' physicality be channeled into positive activities. Boy gangs was seen as "natural" from this perspective, but Forbush and others encouraged socially useful alternatives to the gang, from the athletic team to the Boy Scout patrol.

The Mid- to Late Twentieth Century

By the 1950s, advice literature for parents, especially for the parents of boys, was increasingly geared toward rearing children to be comfortable with an emotionally neutral conformity suited to middle-class life. But the postwar period also witnessed the rise of new sorts of advice literature aimed at men, much of which suggested a dissatisfaction with the breadwinner ethic. Men's magazines such as *Playboy* (established in 1953) emphasized the pursuit of self-fulfillment through leisure activities and consumption.

By the 1970s, amid rising divorce rates, the emergence of second-wave feminism, and a corresponding awareness of men's issues, books and magazines offered advice on "men's liberation" and "men's rights," especially the rights of divorced fathers with regard to their children. Some of this advice literature of the 1970s and the 1980s—such as Warren Farrell's *The Liberated Man* (1975)—displayed profeminist sentiments, but some of it reflected the male backlash against the women's liberation movement. From the 1970s to the 1990s, advice literature addressed health, physical and emotional fitness, romantic relationships and sexual practices (both heterosexual and homosexual), workplace relationships, and fathering or stepfathering. The growth of literature related to fitness and health during this period demonstrates that the male body continued to stand as a powerful social symbol.

By the 1990s, economic developments (such as corporate downsizing), affirmative action programs, conflicting claims of "rights," and a backlash against feminism contributed to a new sense of crisis in white, middle-class, heterosexual masculinity. A broad range of men's movements, including the mythopoetic men's movement led by the poet Robert Bly, responded to the crisis, generating literature advising men on how to be better husbands, fathers, and sons.

The advice literature of the 1990s reflected societal anxiety about boys and about fatherhood. After considerable concern about the socialization and schooling of girls in the 1980s, public attention in the 1990s turned to worrying about boys, spurred by incidents such as school shootings, gang rapes, and other violent acts. A flood of books, led by William

Pollack's best-seller *Real Boys* (1998), offered parents, teachers, and youth workers advice (usually based on therapeutic work with troubled boys) on how to combat restrictive definitions of masculinity—definitions that unfairly and unreasonably expect boys to be stoic, independent, competitive, and aggressive. The authors of these advice books recommended instead an "emotional" socialization of boys that could extend their emotional repertoire beyond anger.

High divorce rates and ideological battles over the relative benefits of "traditional" and "nontraditional" (especially fatherless) families at the beginning of the twenty-first century intensified public debate about fatherhood in America. Advice literature for fathers has kept pace with these concerns, generally extolling the importance of fathers and encouraging men to take a greater role in the rearing of their children, especially their sons.

The expansion of the Internet has meant an increase in the volume of advice literature for men and boys. Electronic advice literature, such as Go Ask Alice, a health information website maintained by Columbia University, addresses a wide range of topics, including health, sexuality, dating, and drugs, that young men might not feel comfortable discussing with parents or peers. This is an especially important development, as there are many more advice-based print magazines for girls (e.g., *Seventeen*) than for boys. At the same time, the easy accessibility and absence of systematic controls of Internet literature has raised concerns about its quality and reliability, and there are many adults who want to restrict children's access to information about sexuality. Still, young men will likely continue to rely increasingly on Internet sites more than on books and magazines for advice. Similarly, adult men will supplement the printed advice literature they read with information from the Internet.

Conclusion

As a number of social and economic factors have made boys and men increasingly anxious about what sorts of masculinity society expects them to demonstrate, males have turned to advice literature for guidance. Whereas earlier advice typically promoted socially sanctioned conduct, by the late twentieth century some advice literature tried to be an agent of social change, moving men away from traditional definitions of masculinity toward new and more varied understandings of manhood. Boys and men have available to them, both in print and electronically, advice about every possible anxiety and problem, and the trend seems to be toward greater diversity and flexibility in the literature's understanding of what it means to "be a man."

Bibliography

Ehrenreich, Barbara. *The Hearts of Men: American Dreams and the Flight from Commitment.* New York: Anchor Press, 1983.

Pollack, William. *Real Boys: Rescuing Our Sons from the Myths of Boyhood.* New York: Random House, 1998.

Smith-Rosenberg, Carroll. *Disorderly Conduct: Visions of Gender in Victorian America.* New York: Knopf, 1985.

Stearns, Carol Zisowitz, and Peter N. Stearns. *Anger: The Struggle for Emotional Control in America's History.* Chicago: University of Chicago Press, 1986.

Further Reading

Grant, Julia. *Raising Baby by the Book: The Education of American Mothers.* New Haven, Conn.: Yale University Press, 1998.

Lasch, Christopher. *Haven in a Heartless World: The Family Besieged.* New York: Basic Books, 1977.

Mechling, Jay. "Advice to Historians on Advice to Mothers." *Journal of Social History* 9 (1975): 44–63.

Parke, Ross D., and Peter N. Stearns. "Fathers and Child Rearing." In *Children in Time and Place: Developmental and Historical Insights,* edited by Glen H. Elder, Jr., John Modell, and Ross D. Parke. Cambridge, England: Cambridge University Press, 1993.

Stearns, Peter N. *Jealousy: The Evolution of an Emotion in American History.* New York: New York University Press, 1989.

Related Entries

Adolescence; Boyhood; Character; *Common Sense Book of Baby and Child Care, The*; Crisis of Masculinity; Divorce; Emotion; Fatherhood; Hall, Granville Stanley; Health; Heterosexuality; Homosexuality; Marriage; Masturbation; Medicine; Men's Movements; Men's Studies; Middle-Class Manhood; *Playboy* Magazine; Success Manuals; Violence; Work; Youth

—*Jay Mechling*

African-American Manhood

Constructions of, and challenges to, black manhood have been central to American and African-American history. African-American men have typically understood their historic movements for liberation as struggles to realize or reclaim black manhood, and they have often viewed white racism and dominance as emasculating obstructions of their ability to act effectively as providers, husbands, and fathers. White Americans, meanwhile, have justified slavery and racism, and developed their approaches to race relations, through the images of black masculinity they have created. A struggle to define black masculinity is evident throughout African-American history and discourse.

Black Manhood Under Slavery

Manhood under slavery was highly problematic, for enslavement denied African-American men a range of experiences that they and white Americans associated with manhood, including earning a living, providing for a family, enjoying personal independence, and defending one's freedom. It also impaired their ability to protect their wives and daughters from sexually aggressive masters and denied them the right to resist slavery and its brutality, for acts of rebellion and carrying weapons were punishable by death. At the same time, however, many slave owners promoted family life as a counter to rebellion and desertion, and male slaves were therefore able to develop masculine identities around marriage and fatherhood.

White defenders of slavery, associating manhood with freedom and independence, defined black men as feminine and lacking the qualities of true masculinity. Black men, they said, were naturally dependent and needed to be subservient to paternalistic white masters because they were incapable of taking care of themselves. Nineteenth-century proslavery advocate George Fitzhugh explicitly feminized male slaves when he compared the relation between master and slave to that between husband and wife. Even white abolitionists associated black men with femininity. The abolitionist Theodore Tilton, for instance, called blacks a "feminine people" possessing a "strange moral, instinctive insight that bellows more to women than to men" (Tilton, 11–12).

Black abolitionists, on the other hand, asserted black manhood, linking its fulfillment to liberation from slavery and protection of family. Advocating armed insurrection, if necessary, Frederick Douglass and David Walker believed that acceptance of servitude signified weakness and femininity, while redemptive violence, grounded in courage, intelligence, and self-reliance, demonstrated an authentic black masculinity. Henry Highland Garnett complained in his 1843 *Address to Slaves* that male slaves "tamely submit, while your lords tear your wives from your embraces," and he asked "are you men?"

Emancipation and African-American Manhood

While African-American men associated masculinity with freedom, it became clear to them after emancipation that black manhood also required what many white Americans, influenced by agrarianism and republicanism, considered fundamental to manliness: land ownership, labor contracts, and the vote (guaranteed by the Fifteenth Amendment but often denied in practice by property requirements, poll taxes, literacy tests, among other restrictions). But continuing racism and discrimination limited their ability to fulfill these roles and responsibilities and achieve the status they associated with manhood. In the North, 80 percent of jobs available to blacks were in menial and unskilled labor (generally defined by whites as unmanly), and 75 percent of blacks in the South were sharecroppers. White middle-class society associated manliness with status as a land owner or sole family breadwinner, but black men were unlikely to secure work that allowed them this status. Their desire to acquire the economic, legal, social, and political underpinnings of American manhood shaped much of African-American activism for civil rights and racial justice during the late nineteenth and twentieth centuries.

Defining African-American Manhood in the Post-Emancipation Era

The post-emancipation reality of racism kept concerns about the realization and the meaning of African-American manhood at the top of blacks' social and intellectual agenda, but black leaders offered differing definitions of masculinity and varying prescriptions for achieving it. For Booker T. Washington, author of *Up From Slavery* (1901) and founder of the Tuskegee Institute (1881), black manhood involved self-employment and ownership of land and small businesses. He advised black men to seek this status not through agitation for legal rights, but through hard work, which would disprove white stereotypes and ultimately prompt whites to accept them as equals and as men.

The Harvard sociologist W. E. B. Du Bois, meanwhile, argued instead that black masculinity must be demonstrated and achieved through ceaseless agitation against American racism. In his 1903 *The Souls of Black Folk*, he wrote that education and voting were "necessary to modern manhood," while Washington's accommodationist position compromised masculinity by slighting black men's "manhood rights" and leaving them "unmanned" (Du Bois, 36, 38–39). Du Bois sought to move blacks to the center of American national life through the leadership of a "talented tenth"—an elitist vision that associated manliness with expertise in the fashion of contemporary white progressive reformers. His hope for the future of black masculinity in white America underlay his founding of the National Association for the Advancement of Colored People (NAACP) in 1909.

A third vision of black manhood was offered by Marcus Garvey, founder of the Universal Negro Improvement Association (UNIA). Like Washington, he sought to realize black masculinity through internal changes in African-American men themselves, rather than in social agitation. Yet he differed from both Washington and Du Bois in suggesting that black manhood be sought apart from white society. Urging African Americans to establish and patronize their own businesses and embrace the physical features of blackness (his newspaper, Negro World, refused to advertise hair straighteners and skin-lightening makeup), Garvey believed that black masculinity required complete independence. He therefore questioned the integrationist goals of Washington and Du Bois and advocated repatriation to Africa. Resisting the psychological legacy of slavery, Garvey concluded, in Third Stage of "Contact with the White Man," that "all the manhood within the race must throw off all the conditions that affected us" (Gayfield, 5). The tensions represented by Washington, Du Bois, and Garvey—between accommodation and militancy, integrationism and separatism—continued to shape conceptions of African-American masculinity through the twentieth century.

Defining African-American manhood was a central concern of the Harlem Renaissance, a black literary and cultural movement of the 1920s and 1930s. Although its writers and artists differed in artistic style and political ideology, they agreed that black masculinity was grounded in racial identity and required the creation of an independent artistic voice. Alain Locke announced this new approach to black manhood by rejecting the label "colored" and declaring the birth of the "new Negro." James Weldon Johnson, in *Autobiography of an Ex-Colored Man* (1912) explores the difficulties facing its biracial protagonist, who, in passing as white, denies his blackness and thus his manhood. Claude McKay likewise linked the struggle for masculine identity with the struggle for racial identity; he commented in his autobiography, *A Long Way from Home* (1937), that his "white education" had robbed him of the "primitive vitality," "pure stamina," and "unwaggering strength" that he associated with black masculinity (McKay, 229). In "The Negro Artist and the Racial Mountain" (1926), Langston Hughes wrote that black artists could "express themselves freely" and convey black masculinity through their art only by refusing to be beholden to the white patrons on whom they had traditionally depended. The dilemma of black manhood defined by Harlem Renaissance writers—the difficulty of achieving it in a white America and the resulting alienation—continued to inform the works of such subsequent writers as Richard Wright, Ralph Ellison, and James Baldwin.

Visions of Black Manhood in the Civil Rights Era

African-American men sought to demonstrate their manhood, and thus improve their status in American society in the Civil War, World War I, and World War II. But after World War II, during which the United States fought against a white racist enemy in the name of freedom and democracy, black men (and women) increased their resistance to American racism and segregation in the South, producing during the 1950s and 1960s a highly effective movement for racial justice—and a corresponding burst of new visions and styles of African-American manhood. The Baptist minister Martin Luther King, Jr., promoted a model of masculinity and social agitation grounded in nonviolent struggle and the inner cultivation of Christian love and spiritual freedom.

The Nation of Islam and its national spokesman Malcolm X, meanwhile, criticized King's moderate approach. The NOI shared King's emphasis on an internally wrought black manhood grounded in racial pride, leadership, morality, spirituality, and patriarchal gender roles. But it associated Christianity and nonviolence with a long history of black subservience and emasculation in America, advocating instead militancy and violent self-defense as the bases of African-American manhood. This approach grew increasingly influential during the mid- to late 1960s, when boxing champion Cassius Clay adopted Islam and the name Muhammad Ali and represented himself as a model of black manhood. The Student Nonviolent Coordinating Committee chair Stokely Carmichael renounced nonviolence, expelled white members, and stated that the only position for women in the movement was "prone." (Coming to doubt that black manhood was achievable in the United States, Carmichael later assumed the name Kwame Ture and moved to Guinea.)

The Black Panther Party, established in 1966, offered another style of African-American masculinity. It developed a model of black manhood grounded in physical prowess, the embrace of violence, community action, aesthetic presence, and social and economic independence from whites. Calling for the establishment of a separate black nation, they brandished weapons, wore black leather jackets and berets, used brash rhetoric, and espoused Marxism as a means of black economic empowerment.

Black Manhood in a Post–Civil Rights Era

With the passage of the Civil Rights Act in 1964, racism lost its legal basis. However, poverty and alienation in black communities persisted, eliciting considerable public comment during the latter decades of the twentieth century, much of it addressing perceived failings of African-American manhood.

The failure of black men to provide emotionally, spiritually, financially, and politically was continuously cited as the basis of contemporary black problems. A seminal statement of this view was white sociologist Daniel Patrick Moynihan's 1965 report *The Negro Family: The Case for National Action,* in which he blamed irresponsible fathers and fatherless families for the social problems facing the black community and urged the re-establishment of patriarchal family structure to stabilize the black family.

Many black commentators agreed. Nathan and Julia Hare argued in *The Endangered Black Family* (1984) that Western culture had caused a "corrosion of black masculinity" and left blacks alienated from their "natural origins" (Hare and Hare, 64). The Hares were particularly concerned about what they considered Western culture's introduction of homosexuality to the black community. Unable to reproduce normalized conceptions of manhood and femininity within its families, they said, African-American culture had generated numerous social problems by leaving black men without an understanding of the responsibilities of a man, such as breadwinning, heading the household, and caring for dependents. The conviction that revitalizing African-American life required revitalizing African-American manhood underlay the Million Man March of October 16, 1995. Offering a traditional vision of manhood and liberation, Louis Farrakhan, its chief organizer, called upon black men to return to their communities and assume their rightful position as patriarchal leaders of their families, organizations, and communities.

The New Black Aesthetic: Black Masculinity and Popular Culture

Since at least the nineteenth century, African-American manhood in the United States has shaped, and been shaped by, popular-culture images. Until well into the twentieth century, these images—from minstrel shows to the film *Birth of a Nation* (1915) to the radio and television series Amos 'n Andy (1928–53)—were created largely by whites and conveyed a strongly stereotyped vision of black masculinity characterized

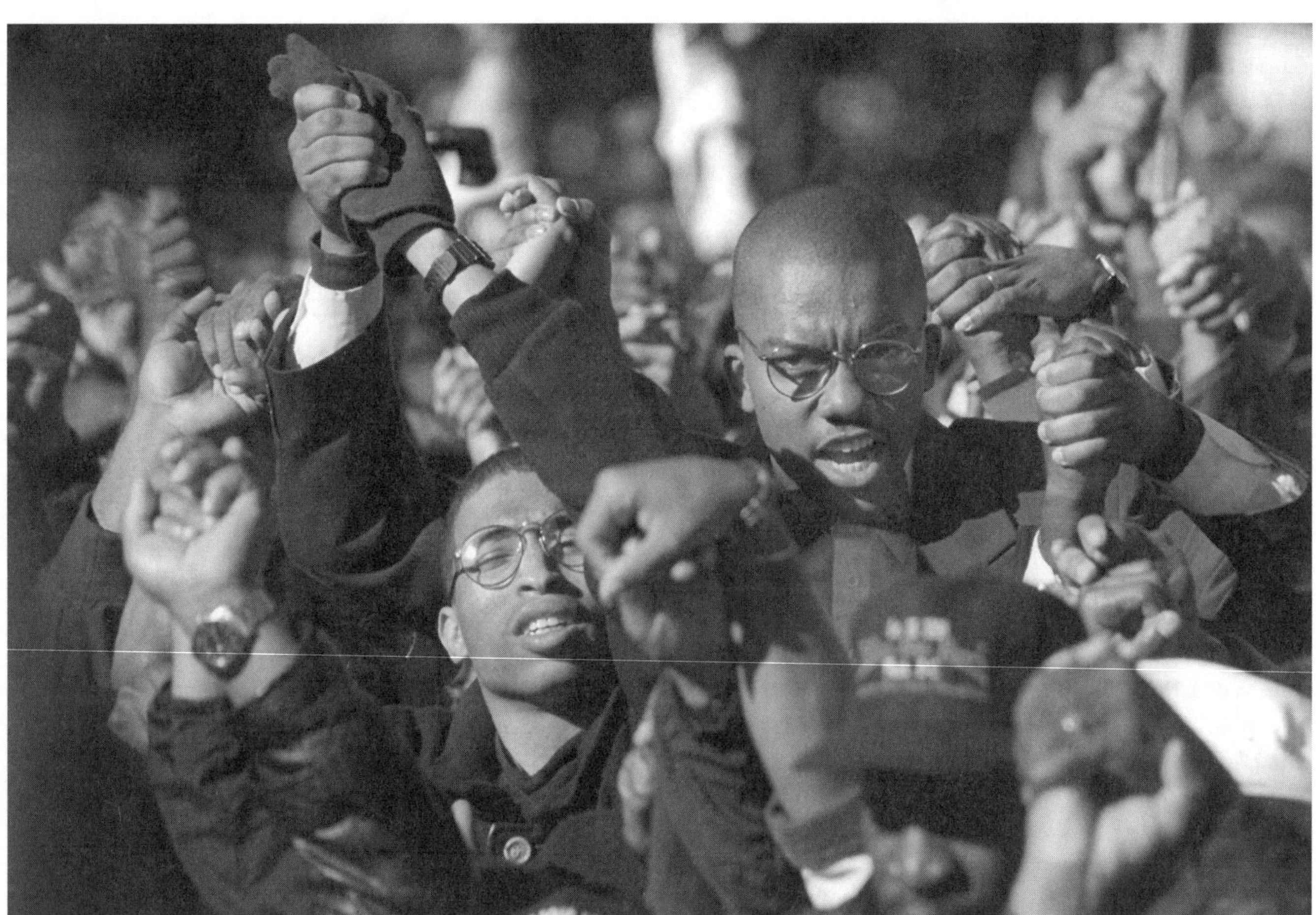

African-American men participating in the Million Man March, organized by Nation of Islam leader Louis Farrakhan and held on the Mall in Washington, D.C., in 1995. The event promoted a vision of African-American manhood that emphasized pride, empowerment, liberation, and patriarchal family leadership. (AP/Wide World Photos)

by stupidity, laziness, satisfaction with subservience, brute physicality, and hypersexuality. During the 1970s, however, the civil rights movement made an impact on American culture and African-American men began to create their own images, and more realistic and subtle representations began to emerge.

Media images of African-American men multiplied during the early 1970s with the release of the films *Shaft* (1971) and *Superfly* (1972); the premier of such television series as *Sanford and Son* (1972–77), *Good Times* (1974–79), and *The Jeffersons* (1975–85); and the airing of the television miniseries *Roots* (1977). Some of these cast black men in strong and heroic roles as crime fighters or hard-working fathers. Yet critics claimed that these images—as well as later ones in such films as *Boyz 'n the Hood* (1991) and *Menace II Society* (1993)—perpetuated negative stereotypes by representing black manhood as urban, ghetto-bound, violent, sexual, and dangerous. *The Jeffersons* title character, George Jefferson, represented a model of successful middle-class black manhood, though his verbal abusiveness (particularly of the show's female characters) was criticized as a hypermasculine caricature and his self-consciousness of his class status underscored the awkwardness of his relationship to middle-class life.

By the 1980s, new, less controversial, and more complex images appeared. *The Cosby Show* (1984–92), in which the physician Cliff Huxtable displays fatherly wisdom and is married to a lawyer, offered an image of middle-class African-American masculinity relatively free of stereotype. Meanwhile, the film *Do the Right Thing* (1989), directed by the African-American filmmaker Spike Lee, questioned simple approaches to black masculinity by attempting to reconcile competing models. The moderate main character, Mookie, works for white pizzeria owners; the muscular Radio Raheem represents an aggressive militancy; and the mentally disabled Smiley symbolizes the search for a new black manhood by selling copies of a photograph of Martin Luther King, Jr., and Malcolm X together.

While some African-American men sought to distance black manhood from images of urban violence during the 1990s, a growing number of publicly visible figures in professional sports and the music industry embraced and promoted the image of urban, muscular, violent, aggressive, (hetero) sexual, and brash black manhood as the basis of their masculine aesthetic and as a vehicle of economic success. In particular, hip-hop musicians such as Puff Daddy and Jay-Z and boxers such as Mike Tyson, successfully represented themselves as authentic representations of African-American masculinity. These commodified black male images represented an essential definition of black masculinity into the twenty-first century.

BIBLIOGRAPHY

Boyd, Todd. *Am I Black Enough For You? Popular Culture From the 'Hood and Beyond.* Bloomington: University of Indiana Press, 1987.

Carby, Hazel. *Race Men.* Cambridge, Mass.: Harvard University Press, 1998.

Du Bois, W. E. B. *The Souls of Black Folk.* 1903. Reprint, New York: Bantam Classic Books, 1989.

Fredrickson, George. *The Black Image in the White Mind: The Debate on Afro-American Character and Destiny, 1817–1914.* New York: Harper & Row, 1971.

Gayfield, Donnie. "On the Periphery of Manhood: The African American Community's Marginalization of Black Male Homosexuality." *The 2000 Berkeley McNair Research Journal* (Winter 2000). <http://www-mcnair.berkeley.edu/2000journal/Gayfield/Gayfield.html> (April 9, 2003).

Hare, Nathan, and Julia Hare. *The Endangered Black Family: Coping With the Unisexualization and Coming Extinction of the Black Race.* San Francisco, Calif.: Black Think Tank, 1984.

Harper, Phillip Brian. *Are We Not Men? Masculine Anxiety and the Problem of African American Identity.* New York: Oxford University Press, 1996.

Hill, Robert A., and Carol A. Rudisell, eds. *The Marcus Garvey and Universal Negro Improvement Association Papers.* Berkeley: University of California Press, 1983.

Horton, James Oliver. "The Manhood of the Race: Gender and the Language of Black Protest in the Antebellum North." <http://www.law.yale.edu/outside/pdf/centers/sc/Horton-Manhood.pdf> (February 19, 2003).

Hughes, Langston. "The Negro Artist and the Racial Mountain." *The Nation* (1926). <http://www.english.uiuc.edu/maps/poets/g_l/hughes/mountain.htm> (February 19, 2003).

Johnson, James Weldon. *Autobiography of an Ex-Colored Man.* 1912. Reprint, New York: Penguin Classics, 1990.

McKay, Claude. *A Long Way from Home.* 1937. Reprint, New York: Arno Press, 1969.

Moynihan, Daniel Patrick. *The Negro Family: The Case for National Action.* 1965. <http://www.dol.gov/asp/programs/history/webid-meynihan.htm> (February 19, 2003).

Thomas, Kendall. "'Ain't Nothing Like the Real Thing': Black Masculinity, Gay Sexuality, and the Jargon of Authenticity." In *The House That Race Built: Black Americans, U.S. Terrain,* edited by Wahneema Lubiano. New York: Vintage Books, 1998.

Tilton, Theodore. *The Negro: A Speech at Cooper Institute.* New York, May 12, 1863.

Washington, Booker T. *Up From Slavery.* 1901. Reprint, New York: Oxford University Press, 2000.

FURTHER READING

Boyd, Herb, and Robert Allen, eds. *Brotherman: The Odyssey of Black Men in America.* New York: One World, 1996.

Carbado, Devon. *Black Men on Race, Gender and Sexuality: A Critical Reader.* New York: New York University Press, 1999.

Golden, Thelma. *Black Male: Representations of Masculinity in Contemporary American Art.* New York: Whitney Museum of American Art, 1994.

Hare, Nathan, and Julia Hare. *Bringing the Black Boy to Manhood: The Passage.* San Francisco, Calif.: Black Think Tank, 1985.

Hine, Darlene Clark, Earnestine Jenkins, and Bill Strickland. *A Question of Manhood: A Reader in U.S. Black Men's History.* Bloomington: University of Indiana Press, 1999.

Hutchinson, Earl Ofari. *The Assassination of the Black Male Image.* New York: Simon & Schuster, 1996.

Majors, Richard, and Janet Mancini Billson. *Cool Pose: The Dilemmas of Black Manhood in America.* New York: Simon & Schuster, 1993.

Stecopoulos, Harry, and Michael Uebel. *Race and the Subject of Masculinities.* Durham, N.C.: Duke University Press, 1997.

RELATED ENTRIES

Black Panther Party; Civil Rights Movement; Douglass, Frederick; Emancipation; Hollywood; *Invisible Man*; King, Martin Luther, Jr.; Malcolm X; Nationalism; Nation of Islam; Patriarchy; Race; Religion and Spirituality; *Shaft*; Slavery; Television; Violence; White Supremacism; Wright, Richard

—*David J. Leonard*

AGRARIANISM

Agrarianism, a complex set of ideas that celebrates the moral, spiritual, and political superiority of men who cultivate the soil, was a central cultural theme of early American society, and it has heavily influenced American understandings of manhood. For agrarian thinkers, farming provided a basis for manly virtue and egalitarian ideals of republicanism and democratic citizenship. The agrarian ideal was personified in the image of the male yeoman-citizen, a land-owning farmer who embodied the republican ideal of economic independence and public-minded democratic participation.

Imported to early America from Great Britain and France, agrarian ideas were evident as early as the eighteenth century. Benjamin Franklin, for example, believed that rural people—particularly male farmers—embodied the values of thrift, hard work, and self-reliance. Similarly, J. Hector St. John Crèvecoeur, who came to America from France and took up farming in New York, wrote in *Letters from an American Farmer* (1782), a popular and widely read work upon its publication, that the nation's farmers were the happiest, most virtuous, and most independent citizens, and that they would be the strength of the new republic.

Agrarian ideals were not only expressed in rhetoric, but were to a considerable degree embodied in American social and political reality. Because cheap land was abundant and social relations relatively fluid in the early republic, farming did provide the large majority of white American men of the lower and middling classes the opportunity to own property, enjoy social status and economic security, and exercise the privileges of political citizenship. Thus, agrarianism became a key component in constructing white masculine definitions of citizenship and republicanism.

The agrarian belief in a close relation among land ownership, economic self-sufficiency, political independence, and manhood became foundational to the political and economic philosophy of the young nation. Agrarians articulated a belief in a close relationship between economic independence and political independence. Thomas Jefferson most eloquently expressed the political philosophy of agrarianism in *Notes on the State of Virginia* (1782), where he wrote that "Those who labour in the earth are the chosen people of God, if ever he had a chosen people, whose breasts he has made his peculiar deposit for substantial and genuine virtue"(Koch and Peden, 280). Leaders such as Jefferson and John Adams believed that the agrarian bases of republican manhood would be corrupted and destroyed by industrial and urban development, since men employed in manufacturing would become dependent upon wages. This dependency would render them subservient, and thus unfit for political citizenship. Jefferson and other agrarian thinkers also contrasted the idealized virtuous yeoman with corrupt and unmanly urban bankers, merchants, and industry owners, whose commercial interests were perceived as anathema to the tenets of republicanism. Thus, by the early nineteenth century, agrarianism reflected a perceived dualism between the independent white masculinity of the rural yeomanry and the degraded or immoral manhood of their urban counterparts.

Throughout the nineteenth century, Jefferson's agrarian vision of manly land ownership and independence fueled a national expansion, with people migrating westward in search of more land and greater economic opportunity. During the Jacksonian era, as the northeastern region of the country grew more industrialized, agrarianism became more closely associated with the western and southern regions of the expanding nation. As the American frontier expanded westward, agrarianism became increasingly tied to cultural assumptions about pioneer masculinity, rugged self-reliance, and the celebration of the self-made man. By the mid–nineteenth century, agrarianism had become inextricably linked with the populist sentiment of Jacksonian democracy. As the ranks of clerks swelled in urban centers, proponents of agrarianism came to associate city occupations with emasculating weakness and dependence, while a closeness to the land and to nature was associated with such masculine qualities as courage, virility, and independence.

Agrarian ideology emerged forcefully as an overt political expression of white masculine identity with the formation in 1848 of the Free-Soil Party. The Free-Soilers drew much of their support from small farmers, and they argued that excluding slavery from western expansion was critical to keeping western land open to white settlement, and thus to the preservation of manly republican independence. Although the Free-Soil Party had initially been founded by political abolitionists, the party's goals had shifted quickly from ending slavery to promoting the settlement of free white men in the West. Still, its vision of a republic of free white landowner-citizens powerfully influenced the ideology of the Republican Party that emerged in 1854, as well as that of the Union cause in the Civil War.

Agrarian notions of manhood inspired major unrest in the decades after the Civil War. As farmers became increasingly dependent upon credit and in danger of losing their land, they felt that their manly dignity, economic independence, and political liberty were being assaulted by rapacious capitalists and industrialists. The most significant of the agrarian movements was the Farmers' Alliance, which emerged in Texas during the late 1870s as a cooperative agricultural movement and became prominent in the 1880s and 1890s. The Alliance represented the interests of both large and small farmers, but it was built primarily around farmers defending a manhood defined in terms of land ownership and whiteness. Most southern Alliance members opposed the membership of black farmers, whose own association of manhood with land ownership and economic independence led them to organize the Colored Farmers' National Alliance in 1886. Both Alliances spread rapidly through the 1880s. At their height, they claimed over one million members and effectively organized farmers into collective associations throughout the country. Agrarian unrest similarly informed the political ideology of the People's Party (or Populists), which emerged as a major national party in 1892 and held that the nation was "one united brotherhood of freedom."

The agrarian critique of industrial capitalism's emasculating effects on traditional American manhood ceased to be a major political force after the election of 1896, but agrarian sensibilities have continued to inform American constructions of masculinity. For example, when dust storms ravaged the American heartland during the Great Depression of the 1930s, agrarian sentiment resurfaced in American popular culture. Works such as John Steinbeck's *The Grapes of Wrath* (1939) portrayed displaced farmers as independent, hard-working men swindled by eastern bankers. Cut adrift from the land, the "Okies" became symbols of a once virile yeomanry reduced to an emasculated pauperism by the greed of urban capitalists.

Agrarianism has also re-emerged in the contemporary men's movement. Some members of the movement draw upon a modern agrarian sentiment that offers "the farmer's regenerative masculinity" as a superior alternative to the "potentially toxic masculinity of the warrior" (Bliss). Agrarian concepts of masculinity have also been recently influenced and reshaped by the rural philosophy of sustainable agriculture. Sustainable agriculture, unlike industrial agriculture, offers farm men a male identity that incorporates a sense of interdependency with family and community, which contrasts sharply with the more traditional agrarian rhetoric of independence and self-sufficiency.

Bibliography

Argersinger, Peter H. *The Limits of Agrarian Radicalism: Western Populism and American Politics.* Lawrence: University Press of Kansas, 1995.

Bliss, Shepherd. "Beyond the Warrior: Coming Home to the Land." MenWeb, April 1995. <http://www.menweb.org/blisbeyo.htm> (March 10, 2003).

Goodwyn, Lawrence. *Democratic Promise: The Populist Moment in America: A Short History of the Agrarian Revolt in America.* New York: Oxford University Press, 1978.

Inge, M. Thomas. *Agrarianism in American Literature.* New York: Odyssey Press, 1969.

Koch, Adrienne, and William Peden, eds. *The Life and Selected Writings of Thomas Jefferson.* New York: Random House, 1972.

Peter, Gregory, Michael Mayerfield Bell, Susan Jarnagin, and Donna Bauer. "Coming Back Across the Fence: Masculinity and the Transition to Sustainable Agriculture." *Rural Sociology* 65, no. 2 (2000): 215–233.

Wirzaba, Norman. "Caring and Working: An Agrarian Perspective." *Christian Century*, 22–29 (September 1999): 598.

Further Reading

Crèvecoeur, J. Hector St. John. *Letters from an American Farmer and Sketches of 18th-Century Life.* 1782. Reprint, New York: Penguin, 1981.

Fink, Deborah. *Agrarian Women: Wives and Mothers in Rural Nebraska, 1880-1940.* Chapel Hill: University of North Carolina Press, 1992.

Murphy, Paul V. *The Rebuke of History: The Southern Agrarians and American Conservative Thought.* Chapel Hill: University of North Carolina Press, 2001.

Palmer, Bruce. *"Man over Money": The Southern Populist Critique of American Capitalism.* Chapel Hill: University of North Carolina Press, 1980.

Rogers, William Warren. *The One-Gallused Rebellion: Agrarianism in Alabama, 1865–1896.* Tuscaloosa: University of Alabama Press, 2001.

Steinbeck, John. *The Grapes of Wrath.* New York: The Viking Press, 1939.

RELATED ENTRIES

Abolitionism; Capitalism; Citizenship; Civil War; *Contrast, The*; Crèvecoeur, J. Hector St. John; Democratic Manhood; Franklin, Benjamin; Gilded Age; *Grapes of Wrath, The*; Industrialization; Jackson, Andrew; Men's Movements; Politics; Populism; Property; Republicanism; Self-Made Man; Southern Manhood; Western Frontier; Whiteness; Work; Working-Class Manhood

—*Rebecca Hartman*

ALCOHOL

Throughout American history, alcohol consumption has been an important element in defining male identity and establishing standards of male public behavior. Since colonial times, the pressure to drink could be so strong in some all-male spaces that liquor consumption came to be considered a badge of honor. Paradoxically, while male culture has typically required drinking to establish one's social standing, excess consumption has generally been viewed as a sign of weakness.

From the outset, public consumption of alcohol in America was a male prerogative. This practice originated in Europe, where the alehouse served as a place for males to share camaraderie over drinks, and the early settlers brought these traditions with them. Authorities in Puritan New England sought to regulate alcohol consumption by limiting both the number of taverns and their hours of operation, but the Puritans themselves practiced temperance or moderation rather than abstinence, and the growing population and increasing diversity frustrated attempts at regulation. Taverns became important throughout colonial America as gathering places for men to transmit news concerning politics and, during the 1760s and 1770s, deteriorating relations with Great Britain. They also functioned as meeting sites where political activists organized resistance to crown policies and articulated republican concepts of manhood.

The importance of alcohol in relation to manliness also affected relations between white colonists and Native Americans. White frontiersmen, who often drank regularly, undoubtedly influenced Native American's drinking habits by presenting alcohol consumption as an accepted behavior. Whites also encouraged Indians to drink to create demand for liquor as a trade good. Ironically, white advocates of western expansion ultimately pointed to the apparent inability of Native Americans to handle liquor consumption as a sign of weakness, and thus as a justification for conquest. As a result, Native American men increasingly viewed alcohol as a threat to their manhood and their ability to resist white encroachment.

In the household economy of the eighteenth and early nineteenth centuries, liquor consumption bonded master craftsmen with their employees in artisan workshops controlled by the master. The easy mixing of work and leisure softened the conflicts inherent in master–apprentice relations. During the nineteenth century, as industrialization and urbanization spread and transformed men's work patterns, the relationship of alcohol consumption to male identity shifted among white Americans. With the rise of the factory system, drinking became a focus of class tensions. Many factory owners sought to control their employees and improve productivity by defining a standard of manhood that emphasized sobriety, self-control, and the man's role as a family provider. As alcohol disappeared from the workplace, its centrality to working-class leisure and working-class manhood increased. Symbolizing artisan independence and resistance to emerging bourgeois standards of manhood, social drinking fostered class consciousness, as well as solidarity among factory workers and immigrants (such as the Irish) who poured into the cities of the Northeast and Midwest beginning in the mid–nineteenth century. The homosocial setting of the urban neighborhood saloon was a hub for machine politics, labor-union activity, and immigrant bonding.

Even in the supportive environment of the saloon, however, there was an element of risk to male public drinking. The very qualities that made the saloon a male place—the conviviality and comradeship of the regulars—could also threaten manhood. Male saloon patrons knew that excessive alcohol consumption or a failure to meet challenges to their virility, physical strength, or athletic prowess were perceived as signs of weakness. Any threat to one's manhood could result in a fistfight or worse, particularly if the protagonists were drunk. During the Victorian era, as excessive drinking became associated with irresponsibility and loss of self-control, many men had trouble maintaining accepted standards of male behavior while consuming alcohol. Advice literature repeatedly emphasized that alcohol dependency could impair a man's capacity as a breadwinner by crippling his work performance, threatening his job security, destroying his health, diverting his earnings from household expenses to the saloon, and possibly causing him to abuse his wife and children.

During the nineteenth and early twentieth centuries, drinking became a divisive gender issue as middle-class women came to perceive drinking as a threat to the home and family. Facing destitution and abuse by alcoholic husbands at a time when divorce and property laws still favored men, growing numbers of women joined temperance, prohibition, and antisaloon organizations such as the Women's Christian Temperance Union. Anti-alcohol sentiment helped fuel the drive for female suffrage as women sought a political voice to attain their goals. In addition, the contradiction between drinking to establish one's masculinity and the dangers that excessive drinking posed to the male provider role created an ambivalence among many men than undermined their resistance to temperance advocates and suffragists.

Prohibition and woman suffrage, enacted with the Eighteenth and Nineteenth Constitutional Amendments (in 1919 and 1920 respectively), did not end men's alcohol consumption, but it did erode the predominance of male public drinking. Ironically, by forcing drinking underground into speakeasies, Prohibition created spaces that were at once private and public, in that they were unregulated places where all drinkers were welcome, regardless of gender. Women, benefiting from political empowerment and a growing economic autonomy, could drink respectably. By the time of Prohibition's repeal in 1933, women were an entrenched presence in the previously male-dominated drinking environment. The reappearance of legally sanctioned public drinking did not, therefore, entail the retreat of women to the home. Nevertheless, unescorted females were frowned upon in many public taverns and entirely unwelcome in others. Those places that remained all-male bastions, such as fraternal organizations, continued to serve as sites for all-male drinking and bonding. Yet the barriers to public female alcohol consumption had crumbled; alcohol consumption disappeared as a gender-based political issue; and, in gender-integrated drinking environments, demonstrations of manliness became increasingly sexually charged—intended to impress women as much as men.

World War II further eroded the male prerogative on public consumption of alcohol. Women increasingly entered the workforce and became a permanent part of the culture that sanctioned socializing with coworkers in taverns and other public sites. These previously all-male spaces remained open to women in the postwar years, while some private men's organizations remained closed to women until the 1970s. The transformation of public drinking from a space of male exclusivity and homosociality to one of gender equality has resulted from factors both external and internal to men themselves, particularly the impact of economic and social change on U.S. gender dynamics and male uncertainty about the relation between drinking and masculinity.

Bibliography

Conroy, David W. *In Public Houses: Drink and the Revolution of Authority in Colonial Massachusetts.* Chapel Hill: University of North Carolina Press, 1995.

Duis, Perry. *The Saloon: Public Drinking in Chicago and Boston, 1880–1920.* Urbana: University of Illinois Press, 1983.

Frank, John W., et. al. "Historical and Cultural Roots of Drinking Problems among American Indians." *American Journal of Public Health* 90, no. 3 (2000): 344–351.

Johnson, Paul E. *A Shopkeeper's Millennium: Society and Revivals in Rochester, New York, 1815–1837.* New York: Hill and Wang, 1978.

Murdock, Catherine Gilbert. *Domesticating Drink: Women, Men, and Alcohol, 1870–1940.* Baltimore: Johns Hopkins University Press, 1998.

Parsons, Elaine Franz. "Risky Business: The Uncertain Boundaries of Manhood in the Midwestern Saloon." *Journal of Social History* 34, no. 2 (2000): 283–307.

Powers, Madelon. *Faces Along the Bar: Lore and Order in the Workingman's Saloon, 1870–1920.* Chicago: University of Chicago Press, 1998.

Rotundo, E. Anthony. *American Manhood: Transformations of Masculinity from the Revolution to the Modern Era.* New York: Basic Books, 1993.

Further Reading

Barr, Andrew. *Drink: A Social History of America.* New York: Carroll & Graf, 1999.

Burnham, John C. *Bad Habits: Drinking, Smoking, Taking Drugs, Gambling, Sexual Misbehavior, and Swearing in American History.* New York: New York University Press, 1993.

Mendelson, Jack H., and Nancy K. Mello. *Alcohol, Use and Abuse in America.* Boston: Little, Brown, 1985.

Powers, Madelon. "Women and Public Drinking, 1890-1920." *History Today* 45, no. 2 (1995): 46–52.

Rorabaugh, W. J. *The Alcoholic Republic: An American Tradition.* New York: Oxford University Press, 1979.

RELATED ENTRIES

Advice Literature; Artisan; Fraternal Organizations; Immigration; Industrialization; Leisure; Male Friendship; Men's Clubs; Middle-Class Manhood; Republicanism; Self-Control; Sports; Suffragism; Temperance; Urbanization; Work; Working-Class Manhood

—*Walter F. Bell*

ALGER, HORATIO, JR.

1832–1899
Author

The author of over one hundred novels, Horatio Alger, Jr., has come to be associated with a rags-to-riches narrative that combines moral uplift with social mobility. In the majority of his novels, a young, destitute street boy is discovered by an older, wealthy man who enlists the boy's services, offers assistance and guidance, and enables him to ascend the social ladder. Alger's novels address the consequences of urbanization and economic transformation for changing notions of manhood in Gilded Age America.

Alger's emphasis on paternalistic relations as a means of uplift may have a biographical background: In 1866, Alger had to leave his post as minister of a Unitarian church in Brewster, Massachusetts, over charges of having sexually abused young boys. Upon arriving in New York, Alger befriended several of the street urchins that served as inspiration for his novels. Later in his life, Alger appears to have assumed the role of wealthy patron of street boys, entertaining and helping hundreds of these boys.

Alger's stories present a concept of republican manhood that predates the emergence of market capitalism. As such, they emphasize homosocial, paternalistic nurture, rather than celebrating the ideals of self-made manhood and entrepreneurial masculinity encouraged by the laissez-faire capitalist marketplace of the late nineteenth century. Lacking in formal education, Alger's protagonists have a strong moral sense and work ethic, and they tend to disrespect any social hierarchy not based on merit. Frequently defying an arrogant superior, Alger's protagonists willingly and eagerly respond to the offer of guidance and assistance from nurturing wealthy men, usually business owners.

On the other hand, Alger, his stories, and the model of manhood he represents are implicated in the late-nineteenth-century capitalist marketplace. As an author of popular fiction, Alger's own livelihood was uncertain, and he had to cater to mass-marketing structures and an emerging commodity culture in order to succeed. While his stories often celebrate the small producer values of a bygone past, the sentimental relation between the wealthy patron and the plucky boy in Alger's stories, which have a decidedly homoerotic tone, can be read as a support of capitalist class and market structures. By providing guidance and counsel and opening a path toward economic opportunity, the businessmen in Alger's stories almost always uplift and assimilate the "gentle boys" (who are also potential future members of "the dangerous classes") into the ranks of the petit bourgeoisie. As their reward, the protagonists achieve a modest degree of social mobility offered by an emerging corporate, capitalist order, but never gain great wealth, for which they do not express a desire. Excluding women from the plots, Alger's stories affirm capitalism as a male enterprise and the marketplace as a male domain. The masculine bond between patron and street boy follows capitalist structures of exchange, while protecting both from the marketplace's exploitative aspects.

Alger's tales reflect the close relationship between economic change and shifting articulations of masculinity in Gilded Age America. Torn between a celebration of pre-market small-producer values (and paternalistic nurture) and an acceptance of capitalist market structures, Alger's narratives exhibit an ambivalent relation to capitalism and its mechanisms of exchange.

BIBLIOGRAPHY

Moon, Michael. "'The Gentle Boy from the Dangerous Classes': Pederasty, Domesticity, and Capitalism in Horatio Alger." *Representations* 19 (Summer 1987): 87–110.

Nackenoff, Carol. *The Fictional Republic: Horatio Alger and American Political Discourse.* New York: Oxford University Press, 1994.

Scharnhorst, Gary, with Jack Bales. *The Lost Life of Horatio Alger, Jr.* Bloomington: Indiana University Press, 1985.

Zuckerman, Michael. "The Nursery Tales of Horatio Alger." *American Quarterly* 24, no. 2 (May 1972): 191–209.

FURTHER READING

Banta, Martha. *Failure and Success in America: A Literary Debate.* Princeton, N.J.: Princeton University Press, 1978.

Hilkey, Judy A. *Character Is Capital: Success Manuals and Manhood in Gilded Age America.* Chapel Hill: University of North Carolina Press, 1997.

Weiss, Richard. *The American Myth of Success: From Horatio Alger to Norman Vincent Peale.* Urbana: University of Illinois Press, 1969.

SELECTED WRITINGS

Alger, Horatio, Jr. *Fame and Fortune.* Philadelphia: Porter & Coates, 1868.
———. *Ragged Dick, Or, Street Life in New York with the Boot Blacks.* Boston: Loring, 1868.
———. *Ben, the Luggage Boy, or, Among the Wharves.* Philadelphia: Porter & Coates, 1870.
———. *Rufus and Rose, or, The Fortunes of Rough and Ready.* Philadelphia: Porter & Coates, 1870.
———. *Rough and Ready, or, Life among the New York Newsboys.* Philadelphia: J. C. Winston, 1897.

RELATED ENTRIES

Advice Literature; American Dream; Boyhood; Capitalism; Gilded Age; Homosexuality; Individualism; Male Friendship; Middle-Class Manhood; Republicanism; Self-Made Man; Urbanization; Victorian Era

—*Thomas Winter*

AMERICAN DREAM

The phrase "American Dream" refers to a set of promises and ambitions closely identified with national identity, particularly economic opportunity and prosperity, wealth and land ownership, and equal access to the "good life." This concept has also been closely associated with American ideals of masculinity, and the notion of America as a land of opportunity has nurtured an enduring cultural ideal in which success—not only as an American, but also as a man—has been measured in predominantly economic terms. Furthermore, it has reinforced a race- and class-based ideal of manhood, for white men, through their domination of the nation's power structures, have been most able to define, pursue, and fulfill the terms of the American Dream.

The interdependent relationship between masculinity, American identity, and material success can be traced back to what the German sociologist Max Weber identified as the Puritan origins of American capitalism. Although the doctrines of the first Puritan colonies—and the vision of America as a religious utopia—were short-lived, the practical tenets of the Puritan lifestyle left an indelible stamp on conceptions of the American Dream. In *The Protestant Ethic and the Spirit of Capitalism* (1905), Weber argued that, removed from their religious context, Puritan values of diligence and thrift contributed to a rationalized lifestyle that made capitalist development possible. Although women could enact these values within the private sphere, men involved in the public arenas of politics and the market gained material success through their demonstration of these qualities.

The Colonial Period

The explicit formulation of the American Dream began in the eighteenth century. Benjamin Franklin's Autobiography (written between 1771 and 1789), which has established him as the colonial era's archetypal self-made man, led Weber to identify him as the personification of the capitalist work ethic. Through his own example, Franklin promoted an organized and virtuous lifestyle as the best means to secure wealth in an expanding commercial economy. J. Hector St. John de Crèvecoeur offered an agrarian counterpart: Touting the promise of American agrarian life, he suggested in *Letters from an American Farmer* (1782) that the availability of land in America promised the individual who worked hard the opportunity to become a "new man." Configured as a product of character and self-determination, the American Dream of wealth and success thus became a defining aspiration for white American men.

The Nineteenth Century

If Franklin and Crèvecoeur embodied formulas by which economic success could be achieved, the market revolution, urbanization, and industrialization, provided many Americans in the nineteenth century with the conditions necessary for its fulfillment and prompted the emergence of a middle class that associated manliness with character and the achievement of success. The United States' rapidly expanding cities offered business and industry as paths to the American Dream, and Horatio Alger's stories of impoverished urban male characters rising to positions of affluence encouraged a belief in economic mobility, the myth of the self-made man, and the notion that hard work would assure business success. Meanwhile, western expansion reinforced the association between manhood, agrarianism, and the American Dream by bolstering American men's aspirations to land ownership. By 1893, the historian Frederick Jackson Turner could affirm that the interrelation between land availability, economic opportunity, and manhood was the defining feature of American history and the basis of American national identity. In Turner's view, the availability of land in the West provided men with a chance to succeed, while the practical experience of western life reinforced qualities of individualism, self-reliance, and perseverance, all considered essential to both success and manliness.

Yet the American Dream served to exclude nonwhite men from prevailing constructions of manhood, since racial discrimination prevented most of them from achieving, or even hoping to achieve, economic success. Indeed, the economic prosperity enjoyed by white men often came directly at the expense of minorities: Western settlement necessitated the usurpation of Native American inhabitants, whom whites defined as uncivilized, while agricultural success in the South often depended upon the labor of African-American slaves, whom whites characterized as childlike. Even among white men, real wealth was achieved by only a small segment of the population.

While industrialization and market capitalism created a prosperous middle class, white men left behind by these developments questioned the availability of the American Dream. At the same time, they measured their own masculinity and formed their agendas for social change according to the ideals associated with the American Dream. Beginning in the 1830s, working-class Americans, who were losing hope that their work would result in self-employment or land ownership, formed labor organizations in an effort to secure the higher wages and shorter hours that they considered necessary to a comfortable lifestyle. During the late nineteenth century, they were joined in their anxiety by movements of southern and western farmers who were fearful that industrialization and corporate capitalism would undermine the manly economic independence that they associated with agriculture.

Even middle-class men were forced to rethink the relation between masculinity and the American Dream during the late nineteenth and early twentieth centuries, as the growth of bureaucratic, hierarchical corporations made their work more routinized and less likely to result in independent entrepreneurship or land ownership. While owners of large corporations—called "captains of industry" by their admirers—viewed their success as a vindication of the American Dream and as proof of their manliness, their critics charged that they undermined the American Dream and its associated notions of manhood by exemplifying greed and threatening the business aspirations of others through their monopolistic practices. Growing numbers of middle-class men responded to the new economic conditions by developing new ideals of manly success. They grounded their masculine identities more in leisure activities than in work, sought promotion within the corporation rather than through independent business ownership, and increasingly cultivated an externally directed "personality" rather than an internally rooted "character" as the key to success.

The Twentieth Century

Continuing economic growth during the early twentieth century reinforced the association between masculinity and the American Dream. In 1928, Herbert Hoover would win the presidency with assurances that American business culture fostered and rewarded "rugged individualism." The Great Depression of the 1930s tested the belief that ambition, hard work, and competence contributed to economic success, as widespread unemployment and poverty appeared to discredit the American Dream and its ideal of American masculinity. Yet the fact that most men attributed their economic adversity to their own shortcomings revealed the continuing power of those values.

During the post–World War II era, the viability of economic prosperity as a stable basis for masculine identity was strengthened. The passage of the G.I. Bill in 1941 suggested that the federal government was obliged to provide veterans with the opportunity to attain the American Dream. This legislation funded unprecedented access to job skills, college degrees, and home ownership, while also supplanting the traditional emphasis on unaided effort with a new sense of entitlement. In the postwar era, the American Dream would be fulfilled on the new suburban frontier, as America's newly expanded middle-class established a vision of the "good life" of material consumption and abundant leisure—the provision of which became a dominant model of male success.

Yet this revitalized link between manliness and the American Dream was questioned in some circles. Some critics argued that the means by which the American Dream was now to be achieved—through standardized corporate employment, consumerism, and status seeking—threatened masculine individualism. In the 1950s, C. Wright Mills, David Riesman, William Whyte, Vance Packard, and others decried what they saw as an exchange of manly individual freedom and opportunity for the conformity and security of the American Dream. They saw the American Dream, configured as an entitlement or expectation, as the achievable goal of an unheroic middle-class male motivated by a desire to belong rather than to excel. Another group of critics—those of the Beat Generation—offered an alternative model of the American Dream grounded in personal spiritual liberation from perceived middle-class materialism and conformity. Youth of the 1960s counterculture embraced similar alternatives as growing numbers of young men rejected their fathers' standards of success.

The latter half of the twentieth century witnessed powerful challenges to the assumption that white men alone were entitled to pursue the American Dream—and that white masculinity, therefore, could be defined through this sense of entitlement. Revolutionary protest in the 1960s and 1970s, such as Martin Luther King, Jr.'s, dream of a multiracial society and the women's movement's exposure of gender oppression, challenged the longstanding association between the American Dream and white middle-class manhood. Political reforms, including the Civil Rights Act (1964), the Equal Rights Amendment (reintroduced 1967; defeated 1982) and affirmative action programs (initiated in 1964), attempted to broaden opportunity and secure economic, political, and educational equality, thereby creating a more inclusive American Dream.

As the exclusive interrelationship between white masculinity and the American Dream eroded, some white men reacted adversely to their loss of entitlement, in many cases attempting to preserve that exclusivity. Others celebrated the change on the basis that the American Dream, by definition, should not be tied exclusively to either whiteness or manhood. Although more elusive, unstable, and problematic, the American Dream, through the weight of its history and its enduring mythic appeal, continues to exert a powerful influence on what it means to be an American man.

BIBLIOGRAPHY

Adams, James Truslow. *The Epic of America.* London: Routledge, 1943.

Crèvecoeur, J. Hector St. John. *Letters from an American Farmer and Sketches of 18th-Century Life.* 1782. Reprint, New York: Penguin, 1981.

Trilling, Lionel. *The Liberal Imagination: Essays on Literature and Society.* Garden City, N.Y.: Doubleday, 1950.

Turner, Frederick Jackson. *The Frontier in American History.* 1920. Reprint, Tucson: University of Arizona Press, 1986.

Weber, Max. *The Protestant Ethic and the Spirit of Capitalism.* 1905. Reprint, translated by Talcott Parsons. New York: Routledge, 1992.

FURTHER READING

Franklin, Benjamin. *Benjamin Franklin's Autobiography: An Authoritative Text, Backgrounds, Criticism.* Edited by J. A. Leo Lemay and P. M. Zall. New York: Norton, 1986.

Gitlin, Todd. *Twilight of Common Dreams: Why America is Wracked by Culture Wars.* New York: Metropolitan Books, 1995.

Packard, Vance. *The Status Seekers: An Exploration of Class Behavior in America.* New York: Pocket Books, 1961.

Riesman, David, in collaboration with Reuel Denney and Nathan Glazer. *The Lonely Crowd: A Study of the Changing American Character.* New Haven, Conn.: Yale University Press, 1970.

RELATED ENTRIES

Advice Literature; Agrarianism; Alger, Horatio, Jr.; Beat Movement; Capitalism; Character; Class; Counterculture; Crèvecoeur, J. Hector St. John; Franklin, Benjamin; *Grapes of Wrath, The*; Labor Movement and Unions; Middle-Class Manhood; *Organization Man, The*; Populism; Property; Self-Made Man; Suburbia; Success Manuals; Western Frontier; Whiteness; Work; Working-Class Manhood

—*Erica Arthur*

AMERICAN REVOLUTION

The American Revolution (1775–83) was a crucial moment in the history of American masculinity. It not only severed the political relationship between the American colonies and Great Britain, but it also grounded the new nation in a set of principles that became fundamental to American understandings of manhood. Yet the Revolution's impact on constructions of masculinity was complex, both reinforcing and challenging the patriarchal social and political relations that had arrived with the earliest European colonists.

The notions of manhood that informed the Revolution were grounded primarily in a social and political ideology called republicanism and had long historic roots. The ancient Greeks and Romans, to whom American patriots looked for inspiration, had defined political participation and the rights of democratic citizenship as the purview of free men. The expansion of the early Roman republic into the Roman Empire, the American revolutionaries believed, had undermined its citizens' manliness as its republican government decayed under the influence of imperial luxury and corruption.

Revolutionary republicanism also drew on the thinking of the Whigs, political activists in eighteenth-century England. Living in an expanding British Empire, the Whigs argued that the growth of monarchical power, at the expense of the elected representatives of the House of Commons, endangered both their rights as property-owning men and their ability to act manfully and virtuously in the political realm—meaning independently of corrupting outside influence, and on the basis of moral principle rather than narrow self-interest. Whigs portrayed their concerns in sharply gendered terms: theirs was a heroic and manly defense of liberty (envisioned as a virtuous white female) against a tyrannical hypermasculine power and a seductively female corruption.

American political leaders increasingly interpreted their own position in the empire in terms of this ideology, particularly after a newly expanded British Empire began to tax the colonies for revenue after its 1763 victory over France in the Seven Years' War. Having previously been taxed only by their own elected assemblies, which defended their rights in the absence of representation in the House of Commons, many colonists opposed British taxation measures as efforts to reduce them to "slavery"—the opposite of independent manhood. The 1765 Stamp Act sparked a resistance movement led by groups whose names, such as the Sons of Liberty, suggested their perception of their activities as acts of manly heroism. They dramatized and put into action their movement and its attendant notion of manhood in the kinds of public spaces and activities—particularly taverns and street demonstrations—that were associated primarily with men.

Such events as the Boston Massacre (1770); the British government's response to the Boston Tea Party (1773); and the outbreak of hostilities (1775) prompted growing charges that King George III was a tyrannical patriarch whose unchecked authority and corrupt government had to be cast off. In Common Sense (1776), Thomas Paine called the king the "pretended . . . FATHER OF HIS PEOPLE," and, in the first of his "Crisis" papers (1776), denounced him as "a sottish, stupid, stubborn, worthless, brutish man" (Fast, 25, 52). Many colonists further questioned the manhood of George III by noting his relative youth and inexperience—having assumed the crown in 1760 at age twenty, he was charged with lacking the maturity to govern effectively and being easily swayed by his advisers. Thomas Jefferson made George III the primary target of American grievances in the Declaration of Independence, and he praised colonial assemblies for "opposing, with manly firmness, his invasions on the rights of the people" (Koch and Peden, 23).

The rhetoric of patriot leaders suggested that they understood the Revolution as largely a man's war; men did the bulk of the fighting, wrote the political rationale for separation from Great Britain, devised new state and national governments, and assumed political offices, while women supported boycotts of British tea and cloth and served primarily as nurses, cooks, and laundresses. (Patriot men also boycotted tea, calling tea drinking an effete luxury more suitable to the British Empire than to sturdy republican farmers and craftsmen in the colonies.) The political philosophy of the resulting republic—grounded in a longstanding European belief in a natural social and political hierarchical order—similarly identified equality and the rights of citizenship with manhood, whiteness, and property ownership. It defined white men of property alone as capable of independent self-governance, while women, African Americans, Native Americans, and those without property were defined as unmanly and dependent. When Abigail Adams wrote her husband John, asking him to "remember the ladies" as the new nation defined its political system, he spoke for most patriot leaders in responding that extending political rights beyond white men of property opened the door to chaos. The Revolution thus affirmed the fundamentally patriarchal relations characteristic of contemporary Western society.

The close association of virtuous republican citizenship with white property-owning American manhood was also visible in the artistic and cultural productions of the Revolutionary period. John Trumbull's 1792 painting General George Washington at the Battle of Trenton, for instance, depicted Washington—now president and widely perceived as an iconic embodiment of American manhood—in a pose of heroic generalship. Royall Tyler's play *The Contrast* (1787) juxtaposed the virtuous and heroic American republican, named Colonel Manly, with his servant Jonathan and the foppish British rake Billy Dimple.

Yet the Revolution also had a radical potential to undermine Revolutionary leaders' patriarchal elitism and their restrictions on manly citizenship. Men without property who had participated in the Revolution sought and received suffrage rights in many of the new states on the grounds that they had proven their manhood by fighting in the war. Women's wartime activities, meanwhile—including participation in anti-British economic boycotts, running of family farms and businesses in men's absence, and camp services—made them increasingly aware of their identities as citizens and blurred the contemporary line between male and female roles. The Revolutionary rejection of tyrannical governance—called by scholar Jay Fliegelman an "American Revolution against patriarchal authority"—prompted a new model of domestic relations that emphasized greater egalitarianism and affection and led to a rise in the divorce rate, as women increasingly sought liberation from unhappy marriages. The Revolutionary rhetoric of independence and equality stigmatized all forms of dependence and "slavery," and, in the decades that followed, stimulated a growing democratization of citizenship and economic opportunity. By the 1830s, men of an emerging industrial working class began to resist "wage slavery" and to assert a "democratic manhood" that challenged older notions of social and political hierarchy. Beginning later in the nineteenth century, women, African Americans, and members of other groups in American society drew on the ideology of the Revolution to resist oppression and assert their rights, challenging the traditional association of citizenship with whiteness and manhood. Despite these challenges, the Revolution's association of manhood with personal independence, self-governance, and resistance to authority has remained integral to American constructions of masculinity.

Bibliography

Bailyn, Bernard. *The Ideological Origins of the American Revolution.* Cambridge, Mass.: Belknap Press, 1967.

Fast, Howard. *The Selected Work of Tom Paine and Citizen Tom Paine.* New York: Random House, 1945.

Fliegelman, Jay. *Prodigals and Pilgrims: The American Revolution Against Patriarchal Authority, 1750–1800.* Cambridge, England: Cambridge University Press, 1982.

Koch, Adrienne, and William Peden, eds. *The Life and Selected Writings of Thomas Jefferson.* New York: Random House, 1972.

Norton, Mary Beth. *Founding Mothers and Fathers: Gendered Power and the Forming of American Society.* New York: Knopf, 1996.

Further Reading

Bloch, Ruth H. "The Gendered Meanings of Virtue in Revolutionary America." *Signs: Journal of Women in Culture and Society* 13, no. 1 (1987): 37–58.

Kann, Mark E. *The Gendering of American Politics: Founding Mothers, Founding Fathers, and Political Patriarchy.* Westport, Conn.: Praeger, 1999.

Related Entries

Art; Citizenship; Democratic Manhood; Divorce; Marriage; Patriarchy; Politics; Property; Republicanism; Seduction Tales; Sons of Liberty; Suffragism; War; Washington, George; Whiteness

—*Bret E. Carroll*

Antiwar Movement

Although every American war has had opponents within the country, the opposition has not usually implied a critique of the dominant definition of manhood. However, opposition to the Vietnam War during the 1960s and early 1970s frequently involved more than criticism of the nation's foreign policy. Occurring during a time of pervasive cultural turmoil, this antiwar movement both promoted and reflected a widespread redefinition of masculinity.

American society's stance on the Vietnam War varied. Some older men opposed the war, many younger ones supported it, and there were women on both sides of the issue. However, the domestic debate over the war may be seen in part as a dispute over the meaning of manhood between two generations of American males. On one side were the baby boomers (those born after World War II). Members of this generation were disillusioned by the actions of a country that their upbringing during the 1950s had taught them was above reproach. On the other side were the fathers of the baby boomers, who were often veterans of the less controversial World War II and Korean War.

Many young American men not only opposed the Vietnam War, but, as part of the "counterculture," they also questioned the American ethic of material achievement, competition, and other values that their fathers treasured. Many in the older generation viewed American military action during World War II and the Korean War positively, as an unqualified good, and—like most Americans of the Cold War era—associated military toughness with aggressive manliness. They identified their material success and the period's rigid division of gender roles with an American way of life that they believed they and their government had successfully defended during times of economic depression and war. This generation often viewed their sons' dissent as outright ingratitude against themselves and the country—and as an indication that growing up in affluence had made their sons soft. Wearing short military haircuts, they criticized the long hair frequently worn by antiwar activists, associating it with femininity, and they portrayed antiwar protesters as effeminate cowards.

Many antiwar protesters, on the other hand, rejected the older generation's definition of masculinity. Confronting a public image that depicted them as cowardly, they portrayed resistance as a courageous and manly act and embraced a model of manhood emphasizing pacifism, commitment to social justice, and, in many cases, a more androgynous appearance. They also projected an image of sexual virility; among the most popular slogans of the draft resistance movement, for example, was "Girls Say Yes to Guys Who Say No!"

Not all antiwar protesters embraced the model of manhood constructed by white, college-educated opponents of the war. Draft deferments for college students left disproportionate numbers of working-class males, especially poor black men, among the ranks of infantrymen in Vietnam, providing ample reason for African-American men to question the war. But for black antiwar protesters, many of whom were simultaneously involved in the civil rights movement, the attempt to overcome racism made the educated white protesters' model of pacifism and androgyny less appealing than militant assertiveness. Additionally, many antiwar activists were veterans of the Vietnam War, and these individuals were often more focused on helping to end the war than on challenging definitions of manhood.

The generational argument over Vietnam was particularly concentrated in the homes of the elite and the middle class, where it often severely strained father–son relationships. Lieutenant General Joseph Carroll, director of the Defense Intelligence Agency, watched the growing alienation of his son James, a young Catholic priest, due to their contrasting opinions on the war. President Lyndon Johnson's defense secretary, Robert S. McNamara, was a fervent and active participant in waging the Vietnam War; the secretary's own son Craig, however, was a passionate opponent of his father's efforts. When Tom Hayden (who was instrumental as a Michigan undergraduate in founding the dissident Students for a Democratic Society [SDS] in 1962) became nationally known for his antiwar protests in the late 1960s, his father, an Eisenhower Republican, severed all contact with his son for a decade.

Despite such intergenerational tensions, in several respects participants in the antiwar movement supported traditional gender roles. The protesters' sense of their own importance and moral superiority, as well as the common belief that they had the world's attention and held the world's fate in their hands, reflected a distinctly American conceit fundamental to notions of manliness that spanned from the time of the Puritan leader John Winthrop (1588–1649), through reform activists of the nineteenth and twentieth centuries, to the very leaders planning the Vietnam War. The antiwar movement was also rigidly conventional in the extent to which males dominated leadership positions. According to movement leader Todd Gitlin in his 1993 book *The Sixties: Years of Hope, Days of Rage*, "the SDS Old Guard was essentially a young boys network" (367). Young women gained organizational experience that subsequently served them well in the women's movement, but many resented being relegated to such traditional female roles as running mimeograph machines and serving coffee. Tom Hayden's wife, Sandra Cason (Casey) Hayden, left her husband and wrote an important critique of women's inferior status in both the antiwar and civil rights movements. David Harris, a celebrated antiwar protestor who went to prison for his activities, would later demonstrate his own conventional maleness in a memoir resentful of the strength of his ex-wife, the activist folk singer Joan Baez, and defensively disdainful of the homosexuality of his former movement mentor, Allard Lowenstein.

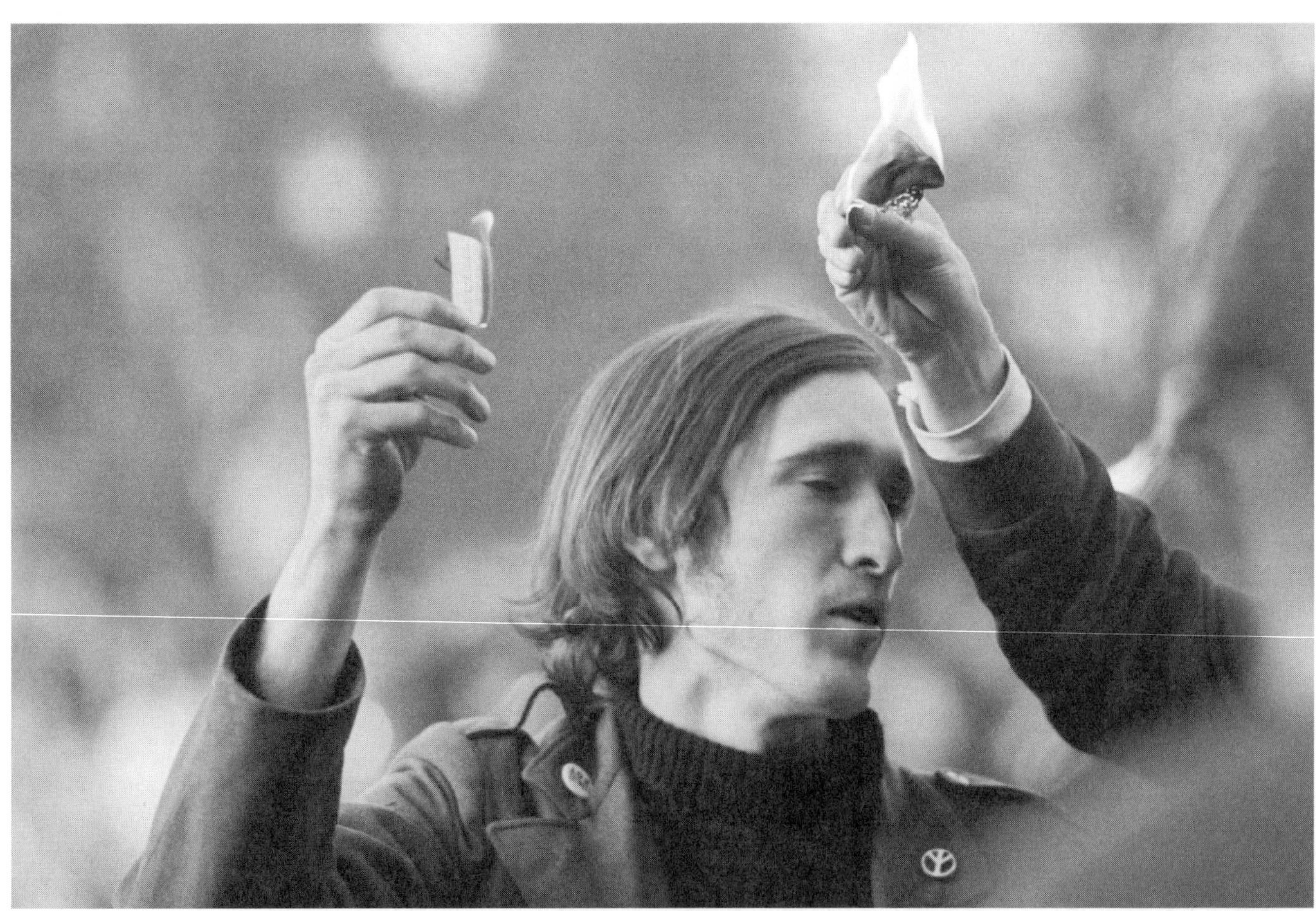

A young man burns his draft card in 1967 during an anti-Vietnam War demonstration. This image illustrates protestors' association of manhood with pacifism, defiance of established authority, and commitment to justice. (© Bettmann/Corbis)

A distinctly unconventional sort of male, however, might also be drawn to the antiwar protest. Allard Lowenstein was only one of a disproportionately large number of gay men in the antiwar and civil rights movements. Although the time was not yet right for openness about their sexuality, participation in causes that often challenged traditional notions of American manhood may well have had special meaning for these men. As also happened when they joined the military, involvement in the antiwar movement undoubtedly made many gay men aware for the first time that their numbers were much larger than the conventional wisdom would have had them believe.

Generational differences over the Vietnam War, and the conflicting constructions of masculinity that accompanied the conflict, remain important in American life, particularly since some antiwar protestors have now assumed positions of power and authority. Bill Clinton, once a young opponent of the war, later proved himself to be a distressingly conventional man in certain ways, but he is nonetheless a profoundly different sort of American male than the elder George Bush, his predecessor in the presidency and a World War II veteran. Clinton's contemporary and successor, on the other hand, the younger George Bush, a man who as an undergraduate was more interested in fraternity pranks than either protests or class work, is a reminder that neither the antiwar movement nor other reform efforts of the period prompted as much immediate change as some at the time feared (and others hoped) would be the case. Yet the movement left a definite legacy, weakening conventional notions of masculinity and helping open the way for alternative notions of American life in areas ranging from foreign policy to private lives.

BIBLIOGRAPHY

Carroll, James. *An American Requiem: God, My Father, and the War that Came Between Us.* Boston: Houghton Mifflin, 1996.

Chalmers, David Mark. *And the Crooked Places Made Straight: The Struggle for Social Change in the 1960s.* 2nd ed. Baltimore: Johns Hopkins University Press, 1996.

Echols, Alice. *Daring to Be Bad: Radical Feminism in America, 1967–1975.* Minneapolis: University of Minnesota Press, 1989.

Gitlin, Todd. *The Sixties: Years of Hope, Days of Rage.* Rev. ed. New York: Bantam, 1993.

Harris, David. *Dreams Die Hard: Three Men's Journey Through the Sixties.* San Francisco: Mercury House, 1993.

Hayden, Tom. *Reunion: A Memoir.* New York: Random House, 1988.

Isserman, Maurice, and Michael Kazin. *America Divided: The Civil War of the 1960s.* New York: Oxford University Press, 2000.

FURTHER READING

Baritz, Loren. *Backfire: A History of How American Culture Led Us into Vietnam and Made Us Fight the Way We Did.* Baltimore: Johns Hopkins University Press, 1998.

Burner, David. *Making Peace with the 60s.* Princeton, N.J.: Princeton University Press, 1996.

RELATED ENTRIES

American Dream; Breadwinner Role; Civil Rights Movement; Cold War; Conscientious Objection; Counterculture; Feminism; Imperialism; Militarism; Military; Reform Movements; Vietnam War; Violence; Youth

—*John Ibson*

APPRENTICESHIP

During the colonial period and the early nineteenth century, many young men indentured themselves as apprentices to master craftsmen for a period of approximately seven years before moving on to the status of journeyman (a skilled craftsman who had finished his apprenticeship but had not yet opened his own shop). Apprenticeship served as an important social institution, providing young men with practical and moral training, while also serving as a vehicle for social control and citizenship training. Apprenticeship also upheld the hierarchical structure of society. Young men at this stage of their lives learned codes of masculine prerogative grounded in the ideals of manly republican citizenship and the independent producer.

Apprenticeship was embedded in late-eighteenth-century and early-nineteenth-century republicanism, in which manliness and citizenship were understood to be based on property ownership and the resulting political and economic independence. Republican political theory contended that the economic independence enjoyed by master craftsmen ensured their political independence by rendering them impervious to corrupting influence and inclining them toward political virtue (the ability to act toward the common good, as opposed to narrow self-interest). Apprentices and other dependents, conversely, were considered unready for the privileges of republican citizenship. Living in and sustained by the households of master craftsmen, apprentices were to learn the workings of a hierarchical republican social order and prepare themselves to assume the status of master craftsman, household head, independent citizen, and property owner.

Apprenticeship was also an essential component of traditional artisanal craft culture, a male institution that, like republicanism, reinforced patriarchal social hierarchies. By requiring an extended period of training in a craft and requiring that the apprentice achieve mastery before opening shop as an independent producer, it insured quality of production, provided a role model for the apprentice, and encouraged the apprentice to develop the sense of manly pride that was to become a foundation of his own artisanal manhood. Apprenticeship also served as an instrument of social control by providing moral guidance for young men within a system of paternal relationships. The apprentice was to emerge from this system fully prepared both for economic independence and republican citizenship.

Apprenticeship began at about the age of fourteen, when a boy would indenture himself to a master craftsman, pledging obedience and dependence in exchange for training and room and board. Living with masters, apprentices worked alongside journeymen while they learned their trades. At the end of their indentures, they were given a suit of clothes and their wages as journeymen, thus passing into manhood.

Apprenticeship continued to function as a socializing institution in young men's lives as long as traditional artisanal culture remained a viable method of production and employment. However, social and economic changes during the Revolutionary period and the early nineteenth century had a profound impact on the role of apprenticeship in young men's lives.

The American Revolution altered the hierarchical relationship of master and apprentice in several ways. First, it provided expanded opportunities for young men. Boycotts of British goods created an increased demand for colonial production of finished goods, which increased the demand for skilled journeymen and apprentices in master craft workshops. This new demand for labor changed the power dynamic in the artisanal workshop by enhancing the bargaining power of journeymen and apprentices. In addition, the army lured many young men out of workshops with promises of higher wages and patriotic adventure. Although state laws varied regarding private property and masters' rights to the labor of their apprentices, they generally allowed apprentices to enlist (often with half of their pay going to their masters). Masters were also often allowed to send apprentices in their place as substitutes for military service. Such practices disrupted the traditional artisanal culture and hierarchy.

The Revolution also altered master–apprentice relations by generating new concepts of independence and liberty (and thus of American manhood) that undermined traditional notions of paternal hierarchy, thereby creating new sources of tension and conflict within craft workshops. Young men who had fought for their country's independence believed they had demonstrated their republican manhood and fitness for citizenship, and they were therefore reluctant to return to apprenticeships and positions of dependence. Other men who had fought were given the status of citizenship without rising through the system of apprenticeship to property ownership. Additionally, many artisans, including apprentices, had been active in patriotic organizations such as the Sons of Liberty, which gave them increased political access and consciousness and loosened the bonds of craft hierarchy.

The breakdown in craft hierarchy eroded the practice of apprenticeship, as well as the social system and the ideals of manhood that had sustained it. Journeymen began to assert their rights based on their identity as independent citizens rather than within craft traditions. During the 1790s, furthermore, as relative prosperity increased the desire for goods and, therefore, the number of apprentices, journeymen's wages decreased, leading journeymen to form associations that demanded restrictions on the number of apprenticeships indentured in particular trades. This development marked the beginning of labor organizing and a new kind of male consciousness among workers based on their class status, rather than on their perception of belonging to a family of tradesmen within a craft workshop.

The Industrial Revolution further eroded the apprenticeship system by changing methods of production and relations between men in workshops and factories. Machines speeded production and reduced the skills required to produce goods, thus reducing the need for prolonged periods of training. Young men, observing that the mastery of a trade no longer insured future success or the achievement of the independent producer ideal, became reluctant to enter into apprenticeships. Further, mechanization allowed master workshops to expand into factories with more workers. It was no longer feasible to house journeymen and apprentices within master households, so masters introduced wages to all employees, with which they were to find their own housing. Without the household training or paternal bonds of traditional artisan culture, apprenticeship no longer served as a formative stage in the lives of young men.

The decline of apprenticeship as a socializing institution for young men occurred alongside stark changes in the lives of American men in general. As the United States underwent the process of industrialization, changes in the workplace devalued skilled labor, reducing manly pride of craft and encouraging the formation of class-based, rather than craft-based, definitions of manhood among workers. Apprentices had willingly submitted to obedience in order to learn mastery of a craft and achieve independent republican manhood. Ironically, however, expanded notions of republican manhood and independence helped dismantle the artisanal system of apprenticeship, for it ennobled young men refused to submit to such hierarchical patriarchal relationships.

BIBLIOGRAPHY

Baron, Ava. "Acquiring Manly Competence: The Demise of Apprenticeship and the Remasculinization of Printers' Work." In *Meanings for Manhood: Constructions of Masculinity in Victorian America,* edited by Mark Carnes and Clyde Griffen. Chicago: University of Chicago Press, 1990.

Rorabaugh, W. J. *The Craft Apprentice from Franklin to the Machine Age in America.* New York: Oxford University Press, 1986.

Wilentz, Sean. *Chants Democratic: New York City and the Rise of the American Working Class, 1788–1850.* New York: Oxford University Press, 1984.

FURTHER READING

Rotundo, E. Anthony. *American Manhood: Transformations in Masculinity from the Revolution to the Modern Era.* New York: Basic Books, 1993.

Stokes, Melvyn, and Stephen Conway. *The Market Revolution in America: Social, Political, and Religious Expressions, 1800–1880.* Charlottesville: University Press of Virginia, 1996.

RELATED ENTRIES

American Revolution; Boyhood; Character; Citizenship; Class; Crisis of Masculinity; Labor Movement and Unions; Market Revolution; Patriarchy; Republicanism; Sons of Liberty; Working-Class Manhood; Youth

—*Jeffrey Trask*

ART

American art, although a substantially younger tradition than its international counterparts, represents humankind's desire to represent itself—sometimes realistically, but also abstractly or in an idealized form. The many schools of American art, as well as vernacular forms of male imagery such as advertising, graphic novels, comic books, living art exhibitions, and graffiti, reveal complex combinations of American social ideals and complex definitions of masculinity.

One powerful link between popular and classical art forms is the regular reliance on the male body by male artists. Up until the early twentieth century, American art was almost exclusively a male endeavor, and American art continues to reveal deeply ingrained ideologies of American masculinity (in form, content, and theme). Within the numerous variations of masculinity in American art, two themes reoccur with enough frequency to be termed major archetypes: the hero and anti-hero. Although not limited to American art, these archetypes reflect particular ideologies of masculinity and the deep complexity of the images that maintain them.

The Hero

The hero is arguably the most recognizable masculine archetype in American art. Characterized by either the use of a single male or groups of men as subject, the hero projects strength, virility, control, power, and dominance. In Eastern and European art, the hero symbolically represents exaggerated and hyper-idealized masculinity. In American art, however, the male form tends to be less idealized than it is standardized; that is, it has historically been used to create social and cultural norms of manhood, defined by characteristics of race (white), class (wealthy), and physical stature (grand). All of these traits exist in art as ideals of the form to which men of all backgrounds should aspire.

Early colonial and Jacksonian art focused largely upon the portrait, which was used to convey complex meanings of manhood, such as republican ideals of citizenship, individuality, and controlled mastery of the dual worlds of nature and science. For example, John Trumbull's painting *General George Washington at the Battle of Trenton* (1792) depicts Washington in immaculate dress (despite the circumstances of war) with his gaze cast slightly upward and to the left, one arm outstretched, presumably toward battle, and the other arm resting nobly upon the hilt of his sword. Romanticized and reminiscent of ancient Greek form, Trumbull's painting nonetheless succeeds in conveying the potency of powerful leadership embodied in one individual, Washington.

Equally telling of man's role as conqueror is a later work, *The Gross Clinic* (1875), by Thomas Eakins. Within the setting of an operating amphitheater, a group of learned, stoic, white men hover over the exposed tendons and bright red blood of the patient, while the patient's mother, pictured in the background, hides her face in horror. Thus, not only was science explicitly the arena of men, but the taxing responsibility for forging new frontiers implicitly resided solely within the spectrum of male ability.

Masculinity, then, in early American art, was defined largely by man's involvement within the world and his control over it. This theme also pervades works in which nature served as the subject, such as those of the Hudson River

School of painting that emerged in the mid- to late nineteenth century. Asher B. Durand's *Kindred Spirits* (1849) epitomizes the grandeur of the rugged and raw American frontier, though the presence in the painting of two well-dressed men standing upon a bluff offers a reminder that American men have properly tamed the wild forces of nature for the benefit of civilization.

In early American art, the hero is often readily visible, often taking the form of the military commander, the scientist, or the politician. Notably, after the Civil War a shift occurred in which the common man also emerged as hero. Still reflecting the basic republican ideals of early America, the average male as a subject was still invested with the ethos of American individuality. The best examples of this come from the many two- and three-dimensional images of the New Deal era, in which blue-collar, industrial, and farm workers are often the main subjects. The photographic work of Lewis Hine, such as *Steelworker* (1931), captures the essence of masculinity in the machine age. In these types of works, man once again battles for supremacy, but rather than fighting against nature or science, man struggles against the very limits of both within the larger context of a civilized world. Hine's photographs seem to ask how far, how fast, and how high man can go.

Throughout the many periods of American art and the developments of various mediums for artistic expression, the core theme of American masculinity usually depicts man overcoming a great challenge, sometimes in the struggle of upholding the very definition of manhood. In all cases, the power dynamic conveyed through the subject matter is that of male prerogative and dominance—in sharp contrast to much more passive conceptions of femininity (or less-romanticized types of masculinity).

The Antihero

The hero and the antihero share many similar traits, especially power. Unlike the hero, however, the antihero has often represented masculinities outside of the standardized republican ideal. Although the antihero often carries negative connotations, in reality it is a contrasting interpretation of masculinity, one that provides alternative definitions outside of white, mainstream contexts. Much of the hero art exists with the counterpart of antihero, not unlike a negative image of a positive photograph.

One of the first antiheroes to emerge in American art was the Native American. Although most typical in this genre are the noble profile portraits of Native American males, more pejorative images, such as John Vanderlyn's *The Death of Jane McCrea* (1804) contrast masculine ("civilized") white men with caricatures of Native Americans as brutal savages, usually depicted partially nude and in a state of rage. Both exist as types of masculinity, but the images imply that only the civilized manhood of white men is distinctly American, and thus acceptable.

Other points of sharp departure from the early stoic republican ideal are the satirical images of nineteenth-century artists John Quidor and David Gilmour Blythe, whose depiction of poverty and male rowdiness earned them little acclaim in an otherwise optimistic and hero-oriented art world. Quidor's Antony van Corlear Brought into the *Presence of Peter Stuyvesant* (1839) shows mostly overweight white men smoking, in generally disheveled and slovenly positions, while one African-American man is grossly exaggerated in physical appearance and stance. All of the figures represented in the painting lack any sense of a standardized masculinity, and thus true manliness as defined by other early art.

Race figures heavily into the American antihero, especially in post–Civil War images of African Americans. The famous bronze sculpture *Emancipation* (1874), by Thomas Ball, serves as one example. Ball's outdoor monument depicts Abraham Lincoln standing stoically erect holding in one hand the Emancipation Proclamation that freed black slaves, while the other hand beckons an African-American man who is kneeling at his feet to stand. Lincoln, the immaculately dressed epitome of white manliness, serves as a contrast to the African American, who is chained at the wrists and wearing only a loin cloth. Again, two opposing ideologies of masculinity dominate the piece: civilized whiteness and uncivilized blackness. Other images that rely on caricatures or exaggerations of racial difference to denigrate or demonize the subjects' antiheroic masculinities span the history of American art, ranging from images of immigrants to government propaganda used during both world wars. Despite the differing subject matters, all these depictions share the reinforcing power of socially acceptable masculinity defined along the terms of the hero, rather than the antihero.

The broad cultural space that often divides the two competing types of masculinity, hero and antihero, has been substantially narrowed in some ways, while remaining unaltered in others. For instance, in the art of the New Deal era, the qualifier of wealth diminishes, whereas race and the explicit emphasis on whiteness remain almost unchanged. The most notable and powerful images of the period include the unemployed transient and the noble American worker. Raphael Soyer's photograph *Transients* (1936) shows a group of white men stunned by the events that led to their lowly state, but also resigned to their fate. The men in the photograph lack any sense of individuality, or any ability to overcome the boundaries of nature or science. Instead, they are placed in the context of a struggle for survival, and their manhood diminished as a result. The hero archetype suffered more direct attacks as well, as is the case with Jack Levine's painting *Welcome Home* (1946), which depicts older, wealthy, white men gorging themselves on a dinner feast, oblivious to any interest other than their own. Like their transient counterparts, they are no longer individuals but part of a different group—moneyed employers who bear no similarities to the average blue-collar working man, their masculinity diminished through overcivilization.

Within postmodern American art, androgyny and homosexuality have added to the complexity of the antihero. In the 1950s and early 1960s, Andy Warhol's blatant gender-bending (blurring sexual barriers between what defines male and female) and exaggerations of pop icons subverted virtually all of the standardized republican masculinity traits. Likewise, Robert Mapplethorpe's overtly homosexual and erotic photography deeply challenges the idealized hero—his male subjects typically exhibit heroic traits such as fitness, strength, virility, but the themes involved defy white heterosexuality. Other examples, such as Diane Arbus's photograph *A Young Man in Curlers at Home on West Twentieth Street* (1966), defy the borders of sexuality, at least as they exist within American art, presenting the viewer with the image of a male possessing definitively female characteristics. The hero, in essence, became the antihero, and vice versa.

The substantial artistic tradition of masculinity in American art reaches far beyond the obvious theme of single or multiple male subjects. Male artists, themselves invested with ideologies of masculinity, have helped engender and maintain cultural and social hierarchies of meaning for men along racial, economic, and physical lines. Within the competition between the "normal" and "abnormal" images of American masculinity rests the audience—groups of men (and women) who have been informed by the images, and who have absorbed their meanings to varying degrees. That the two dominant archetypes, hero and antihero, continue to express parallel ideals of masculinity in the modern era attests to their durability and power, even as new images seek to challenge them.

Bibliography

Bordo, Susan. *The Male Body: A New Look at Men in Public and in Private.* New York: Farrar, Straus and Giroux, 1999.

Craven, Wayne. *American Art: History and Culture.* New York: Abrams, 1994.

Foxhall, Lin, and John Salmon, eds. *Thinking Men: Masculinity and its Self-Representation in the Classical Tradition.* London: Routledge, 1998.

Hirsch, Robert. *Seizing the Light: A History of Photography.* Boston: McGraw-Hill, 2000.

Lash, John. *The Hero: Manhood and Power.* New York: Thames and Hudson, 1995.

Melosh, Barabara. *Engendering Culture: Manhood and Womanhood in New Deal Public Art and Theater.* Washington, D.C.: Smithsonian Institution Press, 1991.

Solomon-Godeau, Abigail. *Male Trouble: A Crisis in Representation.* New York: Thames and Hudson, 1997.

Further Reading

Bjelajac, David. *American Art: A Cultural History.* New York: Abrams, 2001.

Hyde, Sarah. *Exhibiting Gender.* Manchester, England: Manchester University Press, 1997.

Righe, Mary Ann, and Elizabeth Ewing Lang. *Art America.* New York: McGraw-Hill, 1977.

Smith, Terry, ed. *In Visible Touch: Modernism and Masculinity.* Chicago: University of Chicago Press, 1997.

Related Entries

Advertising; African-American Manhood; Body; Citizenship; Emancipation; Fashion; Great Depression; Heroism; Heterosexuality; Hoboes; Hollywood; Homosexuality; Individualism; Jesus, Images of; Marlboro Man; Native American Manhood; New Deal; Outdoorsmen; Pornography; Postmodernism; Race; Republicanism; Television; Transsexuality; Whiteness; Working-Class Manhood

—Elizabeth Myers

Arthur, Timothy Shay

1809–1885
Writer and Editor

Timothy Shay Arthur, perhaps the most prolific and popular writer of the nineteenth-century United States, published uncounted short pieces in magazines and more than two hundred novels and collections of short pieces. Remembered primarily for his temperance writings, including *Ten Nights in a Bar-Room and What I Saw There* (1854), Arthur also contributed to nineteenth-century ideas about business success and middle-class manhood.

Arthur, born in New York's Hudson Valley, lived most of his life in Baltimore and Philadelphia. A learning disability may have limited his formal education. He completed an apprenticeship as either a tailor or watchmaker (historians are not sure which), but problems with his eyes kept him from practicing a trade. Instead, he taught himself bookkeeping and spent about three years as a financial clerk. He then turned to writing and editing, making these his lifelong professions.

Arthur's writing explored many topics, including mesmerism (an early form of hypnotism), women's rights, and the philosophy of the scientist and theologian Emanuel Swedenborg, but he focused primarily on the emerging urban middle-class world of commercial business and the self-made man. He addressed ideals of middle-class manhood directly and systematically in *Advice to Young Men* (1848), one of many such manuals published in the nineteenth century. It was very popular and was reprinted by different publishers for at least twenty years. In *Advice*, as in his fiction, Arthur encouraged men to adopt a specific ideology of manhood as a strategy for success in business and in life. Arthur advised them to be ambitious but to proceed cautiously; to work hard, but always morally; to aspire toward independent business ownership, but not go into debt; to learn to dance, but to refrain from alcohol and tobacco; and to form friendships, but avoid men who encouraged bad habits. He decried dueling and supported respect for parents and elders. Arthur stressed purposeful activity—he wrote in the story "Retiring from Business" (1843) that "no man can be unoccupied and happy" (Arthur 1843, 286)—and thus promoted a model of manliness suitable to an expanding commercial capitalism. But he also hearkened back to traditional republican models of manhood by reminding his readers that wealth and success should be pursued for the good of society as a whole, rather than for its own sake or out of mere self-interest.

In *Advice* and in his fiction, Arthur put forth—in conformity with prevailing middle-class Victorian gender constructs bolstered by his Swedenborgian beliefs—the idea that men are "in the province of the understanding" and women "in the province of the affections" (Arthur 1848, 112). He suggested that young men spend as much time as possible with their sisters and marry early, so that their understanding and reason could be leavened by the emotional truths and understandings he associated with femininity.

Arthur's popularity helped him spread his temperance beliefs, but he was less able to use his popularity to influence the emerging entrepreneurial model of middle-class manhood His exhortations and homilies undoubtedly affected individual young men, but in the larger society his vision of honorable merchants who eschewed debt and alcohol and contented themselves with an orderly and simple life in an unostentatious home remained an ideal that competed with—and ultimately lost to—a model of success that was ruthless, ambitious, and focused on material gains.

Bibliography

Arthur, T. S. "Retiring from Business." *Godey's* 26 (June 1843).

———. *Advice to Young Men on their Duties and Conduct in Life.* Boston: Elias Howe, 1848.

French, Warren G. "Timothy Shay Arthur: Pioneer Business Novelist." *American Quarterly* 10, no. 1 (1958): 55–65.

Hemphill, C. Dallett. *Bowing to Necessities: A History of Manners in America, 1620-1860.* New York: Oxford University Press, 1999.

Johnson, Claudia Durst. "Timothy Shay Arthur." In *American National Biography*. New York: Oxford University Press, 1998.

Ruppel, Tim. "Gender Training: Male Ambition, Domestic Duties, and Failure in the Magazine Fiction of T. S. Arthur." *Prospects* 24 (1999): 311–337.

Further Reading

French, Warren. "Timothy Shay Arthur's Divorce Fiction." *The University of Texas Studies in English* 33 (1954): 90–96.

Lauricella, Jr., Francis. "The Devil in Drink: Swedenborgianism in T.S. Arthur's Ten Nights in a Bar-Room (1854)." *Perspectives in American History* 12 (1979): 353–385.

Selected Writings

Arthur, T. S. *Ten Nights in a Bar-Room and What I Saw There.* 1854. Reprint, Bedford, Mass.: Applewood Press, 2000.

———. "How to Manage a Husband." Edinborough Press. 2002. <http://www.edinborough.com/Life/SocialLife/Husband.htm>. (August 9, 2002).

Related Entries

Advice Literature; Alger, Horatio, Jr.; Business/Corporate America; Capitalism; Middle-Class Manhood; Self-Made Man; Temperance; Urbanization; Work

—*JoAnn E. Castagna*

Artisan

In the years following the American Revolution, independent artisans embodied the ideal of virtuous, republican manhood. By the nineteenth century, however, the market revolution and industrialization made it increasingly unlikely that a craftsman could become a property-owning artisan. Although artisanal manhood remained a prominent ideal in American culture throughout the nineteenth century, it faded during the twentieth century as manhood ceased to be defined by the combination of skilled labor, control of production, and property ownership.

In the eighteenth and early nineteenth centuries, artisanal manhood was embodied in the daily process of work itself, which reinforced the association between craftsmanship, property ownership, production, manual labor, and self-control. As property owners, artisans labored with their own tools in their own shops, which were usually located on the ground floor of their homes. They employed a small number of apprentices (young men training in the craft) and journeymen (men who had completed their training) who aspired to become masters themselves. Artisans also controlled their own labor time. Artisans and their employees were task-oriented, working to complete a particular job rather than laboring for a set number of hours. Often, recreational activities such as games, drinking, and breaks for cakes and sweets occurred throughout the workday. The fluid mix of work and recreation tied masters and journeymen together as men and craftsmen, since both participated in the work and leisure activities of the all-male shops. This combination of labor and play also continually reasserted artisans' control of themselves and their labor, reinforcing their positions as the "yeomen of the cities."

Popular images of artisans from the early nineteenth century depict them as the physical embodiment of republican manhood: self-sufficient, sturdy, hard working, and personally independent. Illustrations typically show artisans as tall, muscular men, standing erect with firmly planted feet. Their sleeves usually are rolled up to reveal sinewy forearms. At their sides rest the tools of their trade, material symbols of their ownership of property both in real estate (such as shops) and in skill and knowledge. Their position as property owners assured their economic, and consequently political, independence, which Thomas Jefferson and other supporters of republican manhood considered necessary for a virtuous and effective citizenry.

Artisanal manhood rested not only on property ownership but also on the ideology of producerism, which contended that artisans' wealth and independence stemmed from their role as creators of commodities. The skill, time, and knowledge put into making each commodity determined its value; consequently, commodity value was a reflection of an artisan's skill and work. Producerism suggested that work created wealth, which revealed a continuing belief in work as a means to self-advancement. Artisans defined themselves in opposition to groups they deemed nonproductive and therefore unmanly—particularly male and female wage earners; women in the home; slaves who did not control their own work; and speculators, stockbrokers, and lawyers, whose wealth resulted from the manipulation of the products of other men's labor. Like women and slaves, wage earners were dependent on another man for economic sustenance, and, as dependents, male wage earners risked forfeiting their positions as independent citizens.

An 1889 image of an "Arm and Hammer" engraving representing the laboring class. A popular symbol of working-class manhood from the late eighteenth through the late nineteenth century, it suggests many American workers' identification of manliness with manual labor and whiteness. (© Bettmann/Corbis)

Wage earning was particularly troubling to artisans in the early nineteenth century, for industrialized production, the expansion of market capitalism, the transportation revolution, and cyclic economic panics increasingly forced artisans into the ranks of wage laborers. Artisans understood this prospect as a threat to their masculinity, for they believed that wage earners had only a tenuous claim to manly independence. Many spoke of "wage slavery" and interwove whiteness into their constructions of artisanal manhood to distinguish their identities as laborers from those of black slaves.

The change from artisan to wageworker did not happen instantaneously, nor did it occur at the same pace in each trade. Before the Civil War, many men could reasonably hope to achieve the status of independent artisan. Until 1860, as many as 90 percent of white men owned their land or shop, and half of the 10 percent who were wage earners worked in shops with ten or fewer employees, where the traditional mixture of work and play, task-oriented work, and close master–journeyman relationships survived.

But the small, familial shops of the artisans began to disappear in northeastern urban centers as early as the 1810s. Increasingly, some artisanal masters hired more journeymen, while others struggled to compete with larger shops—facing the possibility of becoming dependent employees themselves if their shops failed. Most wage labor was now time-oriented rather than task-oriented. Masters no longer labored alongside journeymen, work discipline limited or eliminated recreation, and journeymen lost hope of becoming masters themselves. Faced with the prospect of dependence on another man for wages, craftsmen adhered more closely than ever to the traditional ideal of artisanal manhood.

After the Civil War, wage work, rather than independent artisanal production, increasingly became the norm. With the emergence of both a large proletariat and ever-larger corporations, the notion of a manly citizen based on production and self-employment became both increasingly problematic and increasingly romanticized. The figure of the artisan remained vivid in the public imagination, but it increasingly represented an elusive and fading ideal. Likewise, the artisan remained prominent in labor rhetoric, becoming for labor organizations such as the Knights of Labor a symbolic image invoked in resistance to wage work and male dependency.

Artisanal manhood largely disappeared from American culture in the twentieth century. Although images of the artisan remain on products such as Arm & Hammer baking soda, the specific connection between the muscular arm grasping a large hammer and the property-owning craftsman has been lost. During the twentieth century, working-class manhood came to be defined more in terms of recreational activities, such as sports, hobbies, and outdoor activities, than in terms of control of labor time or property ownership. However, the traditional ideals of the artisan endure in popular images of the small-business owner and the family farmer.

Bibliography

Johnson, Paul E. *A Shopkeepers Millennium: Society and Revivals in Rochester, New York, 1815-1837.* New York: Hill and Wang, 1978.

Kimmel, Michael. *Manhood in America: A Cultural History.* New York: Free Press, 1996.

Laurie, Bruce. *Artisans into Workers: Labor in Nineteenth-Century America.* New York: Hill and Wang, 1989.

Rogers, Daniel T. *The Work Ethic in Industrial America, 1850–1920.* Chicago: University of Chicago Press, 1978.

Further Reading

Blewett, Mary. *Men, Women, and Work: Class, Gender, and Protest in the New England Shoe Industry.* Urbana: University of Illinois Press, 1988.

Dawley, Alan. *Class and Community: The Industrial Revolution in Lynn.* Cambridge, Mass.: Harvard University Press, 1976.

Fink, Leon. *Workingmen's Democracy: The Knights of Labor and American Politics.* Urbana: University of Illinois Press, 1983.

Licht, Walter. *Industrializing America: The Nineteenth Century.* Baltimore: Johns Hopkins University Press, 1995.

Roediger, David R. *The Wages of Whiteness: Race and the Making of the American Working Class.* New York: Verso, 1999.

Schultz, Ronald. *The Republic of Labor: Philadelphia Artisans and the Politics of Class, 1720–1830.* New York: Oxford University Press, 1993.

Wilentz, Sean. *Chants Democratic: New York City and the Rise of the American Working Class.* New York: Oxford University Press, 1984.

Related Entries

Agrarianism; Alcohol; Apprenticeship; Breadwinner Role; Citizenship; Industrialization; Labor Movement and Unions; Market Revolution; Property; Race; Republicanism; Whiteness; Work; Working-Class Manhood

—*Rosanne Currarino*

Asian-American Manhood

Despite their roots in strongly patriarchal Asian cultures, American men of Asian extraction have continually struggled against the idea that they are somehow less masculine than men from other cultures. For nearly a century after Asian immigration to the United States began, this idea was more than simply a cultural stereotype, it was also embodied in the U.S. legal code. Until 1870 only white males had enjoyed the full benefits of U.S. citizenship, but that year these benefits were extended to men of African descent by the Nationality

Act. According to this act, however, Asian Americans were designated as "aliens ineligible to citizenship." The enfranchisement of women by the Nineteenth Amendment in 1919 further eroded the legal standing of Asian-American men and reinforced the idea that Asian men were naturally inferior to other men. Although the Immigration and Nationality Act of 1952 finally enfranchised Asian Americans by removing nationality and race from consideration in determining eligibility for immigration or naturalization, the emasculation of the Asian-American man would remain an ongoing problem for Asian-Americans into the twenty-first century.

Early Asian Immigrants in the Nineteenth Century

Asian immigration to the United States began in the mid-nineteenth century as an almost exclusively male phenomenon. In 1849, 325 Chinese men arrived in California to take part in the California gold rush, followed by 450 more the following year. Beginning in 1851, the number of Chinese men emigrating to California began to rise dramatically, with more than 2,500 arriving that year and more than 20,000 arriving in 1852, bringing the total number of Chinese immigrants to about 25,000.

These Chinese emigrants called themselves *gam saan haak* (travelers to the Gold Mountain) and they thought of themselves, at least initially, as sojourners (*dekaseginin*) who would earn enough money working in the United States to return home rich within a few years. Largely from the province of Canton, these immigrants came from a patriarchal, Confucian culture that regarded men as naturally superior to women, who were taught to be obedient to their fathers, husbands, and (in the case of widows) sons. Women were left behind because the expense of paying their passage to the United States would have decreased the profitability of the trip, and most women from the better classes were unfit for difficult journeys because their feet had been disformed by the practice of foot binding. Chinese immigrants worked initially as miners, and in the 1860s more than ten thousand Chinese were working on the construction of the western portions of the Central Pacific Railroad. By the 1880s, male Chinese in the United States outnumbered female Chinese by almost twenty to one.

Throughout the 1850s, California's popular press presented favorable portraits of Chinese immigrants, who were welcomed as visitors who could assist in fostering California's economic growth. However, because the Chinese lived in highly concentrated enclaves such as San Francisco's Chinatown, were largely non-Christian, and were willing to accept low-paying jobs that were shunned by whites, many white Americans soon began to regard the Chinese and other Asian immigrants to the United States as a "yellow peril" that posed a threat to American democracy. Chinese men came to be regarded as less masculine than men of other races, in part because Chinese culture seemed to be the antithesis of American individualism, and in part because male Chinese dress and hairstyles differed from those of Euro-American men. Putting self-interest aside, the Chinese banded together and managed to undercut white labor by working harder and for lower wages. In both political documents and yellow-peril fictions such as P. W. Dooner's *Last Days of the Republic* (1880), the Chinese were depicted as insectlike automata who were inhuman in their ability to subsist on starvation wages. Popular stereotypes also portrayed "chinamen" as naturally suited only to feminized, service-oriented jobs such as washing laundry and waiting on tables, despite the early association of Chinese men with mining and work on the railroads. With the suspension of the Burlingame Treaty with China in 1881 and the passage of the first Chinese Exclusion Act in 1882, the Chinese became the only ethnic group that could not immigrate freely to the United States. A series of subsequent acts ensured that the Chinese would remain ineligible to emigrate to the United States until 1943, when the Chinese exclusion laws were finally repealed by Congress.

Emigration from Japan began in the late 1860s, when small groups arrived in both Hawaii and California. Japanese emigration also began as a predominantly male phenomenon, with most of the immigrants working as agricultural laborers. Japan's relative domestic prosperity, its openness to Western technology, and its military victories over China gave it international prestige and meant that relatively few of its citizens were seeking to emigrate to the United States. Because the U.S. government held Japan in higher esteem than it did China, the Japanese at first suffered less from anti-Asian sentiment than did the Chinese. In the early 1890s, Japanese immigrants began to arrive in California in significant numbers, but like the Chinese before them, these first-generation immigrants, known as Issei, regarded themselves as sojourners whose goal was to make money and return to Japan. By the turn of the century, Issei attitudes toward the United States had changed, and a significant number settled down in California to become farmers.

The United States and Japan established the so-called Gentleman's Agreement of 1907–8, through which Japan voluntarily limited the emigration of Japanese laborers to the United States. The agreement did, however, allow laborers already present in the United States to send for their wives and families back in Japan, and therefore by the 1920s the Japanese-American population did not have the gender imbalance that marked the Chinese-American population. Because Asians were prohibited by U.S. anti-miscegenation laws from marrying whites, Chinese men were unable to marry and start families at the same rate as the Japanese. The Chinese thus constituted a bachelor population, in which old men far outnumbered young men (although many of these "bachelors" were actually married men whose wives remained in China).

What Chinese and Japanese men had in common, however, was their continued pursuit of traditionally Asian models of masculinity. Issei wives, for example, were expected both to contribute to the farm work and to keep house, and many felt that their husbands were more imperious and less helpful than white husbands. Meanwhile, as the century progressed, whites began to make fewer distinctions between Chinese and Japanese, disparaging the masculine qualities of men from these groups equally. By the mid-1920s, the anti-Chinese exclusion laws were extended to Japanese and other Asians, who were all treated as aliens ineligible for citizenship and denied the rights held by men and women from other racial and ethnic backgrounds.

From Yellow Peril to Model Minority

The experience of Chinese-American men looms large in any history of Asian-American manhood because the Chinese dominated the early years of Asian immigration to the United States, when the abiding stereotypical attitudes toward Asian cultures were formed. Even after the passage of the Immigration Act of 1965, which opened up Asian immigration on a quota basis, immigrants from other nations in Asia tended to suffer from the same set of stereotypes. The Chinese-American playwright, novelist, and critic Frank Chin has argued that throughout the period leading up to World War II, the stereotype of the emasculated Asian male "came out of the laws, out of the schools, out of the white literary lights of the time, out of the science, out of the comics, movies, and radio night and day" (Chin, 12). As a result, not only white Americans, but also many Asian Americans came to internalize it. The force of the stereotype remained undiminished even after World War II, when considerable publicity was given to the many heroic acts performed by *Nisei* (second-generation Japanese-American) soldiers in the service of the United States, including a presidential reception for the highly decorated 442nd Regimental Combat Team, composed of Nisei from Hawaii and from internment camps in California.

After World War II, however, the idea of the less-than-masculine Asian man was given a new stereotypical basis. Asian Americans were no longer considered unassimilable aliens; instead, they were stereotyped as the "model minority," in contradiction to those minorities—particularly African Americans and Chicanos—who were growing increasingly militant in their calls for social equality. The years after the Immigration Act of 1965 saw a rapid increase in immigrants not only from China and Japan, but also from the Philippines, Korea, Vietnam, and South Asia. These groups have adopted different approaches to the problem of assimilation into U.S. society: Far more than Filipinos, Japanese, or South Asians, Asian Americans with roots in China, Korea, and Vietnam have tended to emphasize the maintenance of ethnic communities into which economic resources can be invested. All, however, have found themselves affected by the stereotype of the model minority, according to which Asians have been portrayed by the white mainstream (in the words of the literary scholar Elaine Kim) as "restrained, humble, and well-mannered, a people who respect law, love education, work hard, and have close-knit, well-disciplined families" (Kim, 177). Asian-American men, consequently, have often been depicted by the U.S. mainstream as domesticated and meek.

Thus, while the myth of the model minority does promote respect for Asians as intelligent and diligent, it also associates them with conformity rather than individuality, setting them at odds with the values most promoted by U.S. cultural mythology. This association, combined with the fact that at the close of the twentieth century Asian men still tended to be employed in service-oriented, secondary-sector jobs (e.g., janitors, waiters, machinists, clerks), perpetuated stereotyped perceptions of Asian-American men as less than fully masculine. Even when they managed to penetrate the primary sector, companies pursuing them for technical jobs often shunned them for managerial jobs, in part due to the stereotype that they are too passive to be effective managers and administrators.

At the same time, the late twentieth century saw the emergence of an alternative stereotype, as the popularity of martial arts films promoted an image of Asian hypermasculinity. Indeed, because the better known of the Asian martial arts has roots in Zen Buddhist practice, it is possible to find in these arts a model of individuality that arises from a communally oriented masculine ethos and that might offer an alternative to the rugged individualism that looms so large in U.S. popular culture. Perhaps, as the proportion of Asian Americans grows in relation to the rest of the U.S. population, this model of masculinity may increasingly pose a challenge to the models that traditionally dominate in the United States. However, it is more likely that white audiences view the Asian kung-fu fighter as an escapist fantasy, rather than a threat, precisely because Asian-American manhood is assumed to be safely feminized or domesticated. At the start of the twenty-first century, many Asian-American writers have set themselves the task of both combating the stereotypical portrayals of Asian-American manhood and leading both white Americans and Asian Americans to recognize the diversity of Asian—and Asian-American—cultures.

Bibliography

Chin, Frank. "Come All Ye Asian American Writers of the Real and the Fake." In *The Big Aiiieeeee! An Anthology of Chinese American and Japanese American Literature,* edited by Jeffrey Paul Chan, et al. New York: Penguin, 1991.

Daniels, Roger. *Coming to America: A History of Immigration and Ethnicity in American Life.* New York: HarperCollins, 1990.

Eng, David L. *Racial Castration: Managing Masculinity in Asian America.* Durham, N.C.: Duke University Press, 2001.

Kim, Elaine. *Asian American Literature: An Introduction to the Writings and Their Social Context.* Philadelphia: Temple University Press, 1982.

Takaki, Ronald. *Strangers from a Different Shore: A History of Asian Americans.* Boston: Little, Brown, 1989.

Wu, Cheng Tsu, ed. *"Chink!": A Documentary History of Anti-Chinese Prejudice in America.* New York: World Publishing, 1972.

Further Reading

Cheung, King Kok, ed. *An Interethnic Companion to Asian American Literature.* Cambridge, England: Cambridge University Press, 1997.

Lowe, Lisa. *Immigrant Acts: On Asian American Cultural Politics.* Durham, N.C.: Duke University Press, 1996.

Tchen, John Kuo Wei. *New York Before Chinatown: Orientalism and the Shaping of American Culture, 1776–1882.* Baltimore: Johns Hopkins University Press, 1999.

Related Entries

California Gold Rush; Citizenship; Crisis of Masculinity; Immigration; Martial Arts Films; Patriarchy; Race; Work; World War II

—*Cyrus R. K. Patell*

Atlas, Charles

1894–1972
Bodybuilder

As early-twentieth-century industrialization brought more women into areas that were traditionally male, men began to depend on physical development to maintain a sense of power and manliness. Mechanized production, decreases in the need for skilled labor, and the mass influx of immigrants all challenged traditional notions of masculinity. During this period, the bodybuilder Charles Atlas preached that the road to economic and social success began with physical improvement. Atlas's popular fitness and health program offered a way for millions of young men in factory and office jobs to achieve this new masculinity through exercise.

Born Angelo Siciliano in Acri, Italy, Atlas immigrated to the United States in 1904 with his mother after his parents separated. A physically weak young boy, Angelo worked in a women's pocketbook factory and was prone to sickness. After enduring taunts and regular beatings by Brooklyn neighborhood bullies, he decided to transform his physique and developed an idea for isometric exercises that he would later trademark as Dynamic Tension. Through a regular workout routine he was able to sculpt his body into the award-winning shape that became his ticket to achieving the American dream.

Atlas adopted his new name after spotting a poster of the Greek god Atlas holding the world, and he went on to win the World's Most Beautiful Man contest in 1921. He then won a national muscle building contest the next two years in a row, earning him the title of World's Most Perfectly Developed Man. At 5′ 10″, 180 pounds, with a 47-inch chest, his physical measurements were judged by experts to be masculine perfection. Atlas modeled for artists, and parts of his body have been reproduced for more than seventy-five statues around the world.

In 1927, Atlas published his total fitness and health program and created a correspondence course that promised to help other "weaklings" transform their bodies. Ads were placed in boy's magazines and comic books with headlines such as "Are You a Red-blooded Man?" and "Yes! I turn Weaklings into He-Men, " suggesting that young boys could become self-dependent, powerful, and attractive to women just like their favorite superheroes.

It was also in 1927 that Atlas built his first gymnasium, in New York, and in 1929 he teamed up with marketing whiz Charles Roman to form Charles Atlas, Ltd. Together they attracted thousands of customers by suggesting that physical stamina would help men compete successfully in the harsh and strenuous conditions of industrial society. Program materials, which were translated into seven languages and Braille, used effective advertising techniques, including cartoons, to promote the company. Atlas also performed amazing public feats: he pulled a 731.5-ton railroad car and towed six linked automobiles for a mile. By the 1950s, his company had recruited nearly a million pupils all over the world, including Gandhi, Joe DiMaggio, Rocky Marciano, and Robert Ripley.

By promoting self-discipline and a health-conscious routine, Atlas symbolized the ideal masculine physique and inspired other men to achieve the same results. He preached that physical transformation alone, without intellectual or emotional development, was enough to achieve success as a man, presenting himself as living proof that through hard work and self-discipline the average man could become superior if he developed his body's potential.

Bibliography

Butler, George, and Charles Gaines. *Yours in Perfect Manhood, Charles Atlas: The Most Effective Fitness Program Ever Devised.* New York: Simon & Schuster, 1982.

Gaines, Charles. "The Return of Hercules." In *Dream Streets: The Big Book of Italian American Culture,* edited by Lawrence DiStasi. New York: Harper & Row, 1989.

Kimmel, Michael. *Manhood in America: A Cultural History.* New York: Free Press, 1996.

Further Reading

Bushyeager, Peter. "The World of Atlas." *Men's Health* 6 (September/October 1991): 56–61.

Gaines, Charles. "Hulk Triumphant." *Esquire* 105 (June 1986): 117–118.

Gustaitis, Joseph. "Charles Atlas: 'The World's Most Perfectly Developed Man." *American History Illustrated* 21 (Sept. 1986): 16–17.

Toon, Elizabeth, and Janet Golden. "Rethinking Charles Atlas." *Rethinking History* 4, no. 1 (2000): 80–84.

Related Entries

Advertising; Body; Bodybuilding; Health; Heterosexuality; Immigration; Industrialization; Passionate Manhood; Self-Made Man

—*Fred Gardaphe*

Automobiles

For over a century, men have used the activities of making, purchasing, driving, racing, and working on cars to assert and reinforce American perceptions of masculine work, consumption, skill, and technological prowess. At the same time, women and minority males have faced limits and challenges to their access to and authority over automotive technology.

Automobiles debuted in the United States at the turn of the twentieth century, a time when the ongoing processes of industrialization, bureaucratization of white-collar work, and feminization of office spaces were undermining older work-based sources of masculinity. The automobile industry played a significant part in accelerating these changes, particularly after Henry Ford introduced the moving assembly line in 1913. Autoworkers, like other male industrial workers during the twentieth century, responded by asserting their masculinity through a shop-floor culture that sought control over the work process and fostered increased homosocial leisure activities such as drinking, gambling, and hunting.

As a commodity, the automobile offered early-twentieth-century American males a new form of consumption to salve the psychic wounds of modern industrialized manhood: a unique consumption of comfort, convenience, and often luxury that was also an unquestionably masculine activity conducted in an all-male retail setting. Once purchased, automobiles offered multiple avenues for exercising and expressing manly independence, freedom, and control. Automobile drivers were in complete control of their destiny, free of the limits of horse-drawn or rail transportation. Even when the machine broke down or became mired in the mud, it provided men the opportunity to display masculine traits of technical knowledge and mechanical skill as they tinkered with and, they hoped, asserted mastery over an expensive industrial product that they owned, operated, and (ideally) understood mechanically.

Women and minority men also sensed the freedom and power of automobiles, and they exploited opportunities to master the new machines. Before World War I, women drove, raced, and worked on cars in defiance of strong social pressures against such behavior. In the face of widespread racism and segregation, African-American men established their own networks of automobile clubs and auto-related businesses to facilitate black motoring. However, automakers inundated the popular print media with images that both exploited and perpetuated ideals of white men as controllers of automotive technology and women as passengers, spectators, or trophies of motorized male sexual conquest. The advent of federally funded vocational education in public schools during the 1920s established an enduring system of gender-segregated technical training that made automotive technological knowledge a rigidly masculine, and often racially segregated, terrain.

Following World War II, as suburbanization, automatic transmissions, and fatherhood domesticated automobile consumption, the now rigidly male culture of automotive technology found renewed expression in a plethora of regional and national motor-sports activities, such as drag racing, stock-car racing, and the annual Indianapolis 500 automobile race. Racecar drivers such as Don Garlits, Richard Petty, and A. J. Foyt provided young males with icons of masculine bravado and achievement. During the 1960s, U.S. automakers tapped into suburban male anxieties by offering a new line of muscle cars, sparking a "horsepower war" that rhetorically equated powerful piston engines with strength and virility—a design and marketing strategy that has continued into the twenty-first century.

Women and minorities are still vastly underrepresented in almost all automotive activities except driving and consumption, and the automobile remains a vehicle for sexual and racial discrimination. African-American motorists continue to face increased police surveillance in some areas, and women continue to encounter patronizing male behavior on car lots and in repair shops. As contemporary constructions of American masculinity evolve in response to a postindustrial economy, automobiles are likely to remain strongly associated with American manhood and masculinity for quite some time.

Bibliography

McShane, Clay. *Down the Asphalt Path: The Automobile and the American City.* New York: Columbia University Press, 1994.

Meyer, Stephen. "Work, Play, and Power: Masculine Culture on the Automotive Shop Floor, 1930-1960." In *Boys and Their Toys?: Masculinity, Technology, and Class in America,* edited by Roger Horowitz. New York: Routledge, 2001.

Scharff, Virginia. *Taking the Wheel: Women and the Coming of the Motor Age.* Albuquerque: University of New Mexico Press, 1992.

Shackleford, Ben A. "Masculinity, the Auto Racing Fraternity, and the Technological Sublime." In *Boys and Their Toys?: Masculinity, Technology, and Class in America,* edited by Roger Horowitz. New York: Routledge, 2001.

Stearns, Peter N. *BE A MAN!: Males in Modern Society.* 2nd ed. New York: Holmes & Meier, 1990.

Further Reading

Daniel, Pete. *Lost Revolutions: The South in the 1950s.* Chapel Hill: University of North Carolina Press, 2000.

Gilroy, Paul. "Driving While Black." In *Car Cultures,* edited by Daniel Miller. Oxford: Berg, 2001.

Lawson, Helen M. *Ladies on the Lot: Women, Car Sales, and the Pursuit of the American Dream.* Lanham, Md.: Rowman & Littlefield, 2000.

Marusza, Julia. "Skill School Boys: Masculine Identity Formation Among White Boys in an Urban High School Vocational Autoshop Program." *Urban Review* 29, no. 3 (1997): 175–187.

Oldenziel, Ruth. *Making Technology Masculine: Men, Women, and Modern Machines in America, 1870–1945.* Amsterdam: Amsterdam University Press, 1999.

Wachs, Martin, and Margaret Crawford, eds. *The Car and the City: The Automobile, the Built Environment, and Daily Urban Life.* Ann Arbor: University of Michigan Press, 1992.

Related Entries

Advertising; Business/Corporate America; Consumerism; Education; Gambling; Hunting; Industrialization; Kerouac, Jack; Labor Movement and Unions; Leisure; Masculine Domesticity; Middle-Class Manhood; Southern Manhood; Sports; Suburbia; Technology; Travel; Work

—*Kevin L. Borg*

Bachelorhood

Bachelorhood has long provoked contradictory responses among Americans: Men and women alike have found single men's freedom from the strictures of family deeply compelling, but Americans have also perceived bachelorhood as a grave danger to social order. Shirking traditional marital obligations and lacking both the domesticating influence and legitimate sexual outlet of a wife, bachelors have threatened to destabilize the complex relationships governing social and political life in the United States. Bachelorhood, then, has represented both a masculine ideal—the self-invented man unconstrained by obligations—and its opposite—the rootless hedonist ungoverned by propriety.

The Troubling and Troubled Man Alone: Bachelorhood before the Civil War

In colonial America, concerns about the dangers of bachelorhood outweighed envy of single men's freedom. Fearful that unmarried men would become lustful degenerates, many New England colonies assessed a special tax on single men who lived independently, and several forbade entirely their living outside "family rule." Bachelors also presented a political challenge. For example, seventeenth-century political theorists such as Robert Filmer closely linked the origins and aims of family governance and state governance. Although Filmer's analogy between the state and the family had declined by the late seventeenth century, when it was eclipsed by the philosopher John Locke's conception of citizenship as a contract between the individual and the state, marriage continued to serve as a central unifying ritual in the early republic. A common rite of passage, marriage not only distinguished men from boys, it also linked males across class and ethnic lines.

By the mid–nineteenth century, despite the centrality of marriage in defining adult masculinity, perceptions of bachelorhood had begun to change in two important ways. Most importantly, along with the emergence of a recognizable American middle class came a redefinition of bachelors as single men of means. No longer simply unmarried males of any economic status, bachelors came to be understood as those with the income or prospects to support a family in acceptable style. Given the social and economic discrimination against African Americans, this definition effectively excluded black men. Secondly, middle-class single manhood was increasingly interpreted in deeply sentimental terms in literature. If earlier depictions had represented unmarried men as suspicious or contemptible, new literature was much more forgiving. Frequently attributing mature bachelorhood to youthful tragedy, especially the loss of an early love, narratives invited pity rather than reproach for men who did not wed. Indeed, sentimental narratives often depicted bachelors as uniquely situated observers of society, suggesting that bachelors could feel as deeply as women yet remain unperturbed by an emotional sensibility culturally associated with femininity.

The rhetoric of bachelor sentimentality, with its reassurance about the virtue of unmarried men, contrasted with the far more complicated reality of bachelors' lives from the mid–nineteenth century onward. While rural bachelors remained largely under the control of both their families and local communities, young single men who moved to the cities to seek jobs as white-collar workers could enjoy urban pleasures with relative impunity. Heedless of guidebooks that warned against urban temptations, many youthful bachelors

This undated image of two bachelors conveys the model of masculinity associated with bachelorhood in American culture. Many such bachelors enjoyed a close friendship with other men and a comfortable lifestyle characterized by urbane leisure activity and freedom from marital and paternal obligations. (Wisconsin Historical Society, WHi-6639)

participated in such morally questionable activities as drinking binges, attendance at bare-knuckle prize fights, and liaisons with prostitutes.

The Pleasures of the City: Bachelorhood in the Late Nineteenth Century

The quantity and availability of indulgent pleasures increased after the Civil War, when immigration from both the countryside and abroad dramatically increased the number of unmarried men in urban areas. Between 1890 and 1920, about 40 percent of the population in major cities were single adult males. Many of these men did not enjoy the middle-class status traditionally associated with bachelorhood, but they helped to foster and support a commercial infrastructure that made it possible to live comfortably independent of the family. Amenities such as restaurants, laundry facilities, lodging houses, and bathhouses multiplied, offering for a fee what men previously had relied on wives to provide. The number of commercial leisure institutions catering to single men—including saloons, billiard halls, gymnasiums, and cheap theaters—multiplied as well.

Critics chided bachelors for selfishly avoiding marriage and continued to accuse unwed men of immorality. In the late nineteenth century, however, these criticisms proved relatively unpersuasive. For one thing, observers who were not themselves bachelors frequently coveted rather than condemned the opportunities available to single men. Many single women in the late nineteenth century, for example, began calling themselves "bachelor girls" as a way of claiming the privileges single men enjoyed. Additionally, the increased material expectations of middle-class life allowed men to argue that they did not marry because they could not afford a wife, and that profligate women, rather than single men, were responsible for bachelors' refusal to marry.

Women's entry into the paid workforce at the end of the nineteenth century, and their growing patronage of the new sites of urban leisure, dramatically changed social relations. Middle-class husbands (who evinced a growing orientation toward domesticity in the late nineteenth century) previously had spent much of their labor and leisure time with male friends in sites largely closed to women. However, as men and women spent more time together, a new model of heterosocial companionability, or friendships with the opposite sex, began to replace the older model of same-sex friendships. Although this process occurred gradually, by the 1920s it was expected that unmarried middle-class men would spend most of their leisure time in the company of women, seeking an emotionally and physically rewarding relationship that would culminate in marriage.

The Stigmatized Single: Bachelorhood after 1920

The late-nineteenth-century emergence of heterosocial companionship exposed bachelorhood to a whole new set of suspicions—especially homosexuality. Whereas previously bachelors had been accused of transgressions involving the exploitation of women, few critics associated bachelorhood per se with a sexual interest in other males (despite the presence of urban gay subcultures), and the emphasis on intimate homosocial friendship had exonerated bachelorhood from suspicions of "perversion." By the 1920s, however, bachelorhood beyond the average age of marriage was increasingly and explicitly associated with homosexuality—as well as with such psychological and physical dysfunctions as mental illness, increased criminality, and susceptibility to early mortality.

Changing social mores and new ideas about deviance had important implications for bachelorhood. First, age began to replace class status as the most salient characteristic of bachelorhood. Young or not-yet-married men, even those financially able to support a wife, were referred to much less frequently as bachelors. By contrast, older never-married men were labeled bachelors almost irrespective of their incomes. In addition, young single men enjoyed many new privileges denied to older bachelors. As doctors and social critics condemned older or 'confirmed' bachelors as a threat to society, young single men enjoyed novel opportunities for premarital physical intimacy with women who were prospective mates.

Ambiguous Legacies: Bachelorhood after World War II

Despite the growing stigma associated with bachelorhood in the early twentieth century, the term never fully lost its earlier association with prosperity, privilege, and freedom. Bachelorhood was thus ripe for rehabilitation following World War II. As men returned from wartime service, married, and started families, the responsible husband and father triumphed as the dominant model of adult masculinity in the 1950s to such an extent that many Americans associated singleness beyond a certain age with both homosexuality and political subversion. Yet economic prosperity, expanding consumerism, and new and more relaxed attitudes toward male sexuality fostered the ideal of the footloose and fancy-free bachelor as an alternative identity. Figured most prominently in *Playboy*, the men's magazine begun by Hugh Hefner in 1953, bachelorhood in the 1950s and 1960s celebrated both sexual access to women and the world of material goods. Even as contemporary bachelorhood defied some conventional gender expectations (many early *Playboy* articles were devoted to advice about bachelor domesticity, for example) it reinforced older ideas of the bachelor as hedonist. Indeed, the new bachelor was depicted as even more committed to luxury and leisure than his forebears, as well as to the changing social mores that sanctioned casual sexual relationships between consenting adults.

The term bachelor has become somewhat antiquated since the 1960s, in part because of the concept's enigmatic heritage. Its intimations of male privilege and an ambiguous preference for same-sex companionship seem unsuited to an age of sexual egalitarianism, open heterosocial intimacy, and proud gay identity. Yet the term continues to resonate in the American imagination. For example, one of the most popular television shows of 2002 was *The Bachelor.* The "plot" of this reality show, in which several women vied for a marriage proposal from a handsome, affluent, single white man in his mid-thirties, captures some of the term's persistent associations. The man at the show's center qualified as a bachelor in part because of his class and age, and in part because he enjoyed privileged social and sexual opportunities with several attractive women. Yet the point of the show was to find the bachelor a mate and thereby contain the identity that animated the show in the first place.

Despite the centrality of bachelorhood to masculine identity, its history is only starting to be written. Most inquiries have focused either on institutional sites such as saloons that catered to urban single men or on the ways that literary texts construct the bachelor. More work needs to be done on how bachelors have interpreted their own experience; on how they have mediated the tensions between independence and dependence, and between roughness and respectability; and on the nature and significance of regional, racial, and ethnic variations in bachelor life.

Bibliography

Chauncey, George. *Gay New York: Gender, Urban Culture, and the Making of the Gay Male World, 1890–1940.* New York: Basic Books, 1994.

Chudacoff, Howard. *The Age of the Bachelor: Creating an American Subculture.* Princeton, N.J.: Princeton University Press, 1999.

Fass, Paula. *The Damned and the Beautiful: American Youth in the 1920's.* New York: Oxford University Press, 1977.

Kann, Mark. *On the Man Question: Gender and Civic Virtue in America.* Philadelphia: Temple University Press, 1992.

Laipson, Peter. "I Have No Genius for Marriage: Bachelorhood in Urban America, 1870–1930," Ph.D. diss., University of Michigan, 2000.

Norton, Mary Beth. *Founding Mothers and Fathers: Gendered Power and the Forming of American Society.* New York: Knopf, 1996.

Osgerby, Bill. *Playboys in Paradise: Masculinity, Youth and Leisure-Style in Modern America.* Oxford: Berg, 2001.

Ryan, Mary. *Cradle of the Middle Class: The Family in Oneida County, New York, 1790–1865.* Cambridge, England: Cambridge University Press, 1981.

Snyder, Katherine. *Bachelors, Manhood, and the Novel, 1850–1925.* New York: Cambridge University Press, 1999.

Further Reading

Bailey, Beth L. *From Front Porch to Back Seat: Courtship in Twentieth-Century America.* Baltimore: Johns Hopkins University Press, 1985.

Boyer, Paul S. *Urban Masses and Moral Order in America, 1820–1920.* Cambridge, Mass.: Harvard University Press, 1978.

Carnes, Mark C. *Secret Ritual and Manhood in Victorian America.* New Haven, Conn.: Yale University Press, 1989.

Courtwright, David. *Violent Land: Single Men and Social Disorder from the Frontier to the Inner City.* Cambridge, Mass.: Harvard University Press, 1996.

Ehrenreich, Barbara. *The Hearts of Men: American Dreams and the Flight from Commitment.* Garden City, N.Y.: Anchor Press, 1983.

Gorn, Elliot J. *The Manly Art: Bare-Knuckle Prize Fighting in America.* Ithaca, N.Y.: Cornell University Press, 1986.

Mintz, Steven, and Susan Kellogg. *Domestic Revolutions: A Social History of American Family Life.* New York: Free Press, 1988.

Modell, John. *Into One's Own: From Youth to Adulthood in the United States, 1920–1975.* Berkeley, Calif.: University of California Press, 1989.

Nasaw, David. *Going Out: The Rise and Fall of Public Amusements.* New York: Basic Books, 1993.

Rotundo, E. Anthony. *American Manhood: Transformations in Masculinity from the Revolution to the Modern Era.* New York: Basic Books, 1993.

Related Entries

Class; Consumerism; Fraternal Organizations; Gilded Age; Heterosexuality; Homosexuality; Leisure; Male Friendship; Marriage; Masculine Domesticity; Middle-Class Manhood; *Odd Couple, The; Playboy* Magazine; Sentimentalism; Urbanization

—*Peter Laipson*

Baseball

Baseball has long been intertwined with constructions of masculinity in the United States. In popular American mythology, it has been understood as a rite of passage between fathers and sons, as well as a nostalgic commemoration of a manliness achieved away from urban complications and corruptions. In reality, however, baseball has played important roles in indoctrinating working-class men into industrial society and, by excluding women and people of color for many decades, reaffirming the dominance of white middle-class men. Even after racial barriers fell, baseball remained a contested site in which minority players continued to have to prove their worth and their manhood by complying with white standards.

Baseball's origins can be traced back to the mid–nineteenth century. It evolved from the British game of cricket, which was played by upper-class gentlemen at exclusive country clubs. By 1868 baseball was both rivaling cricket in popularity in the United States and challenging accepted class-based views of masculinity. It became representative of working-class manhood, whereas cricket, defined as a manly sport earlier in the nineteenth century, was dismissed by century's end as an effete game for dandies. Albert Spalding, the leading manufacturer of baseball equipment in the United States, claimed that men who played cricket saw it as an opportunity to "drink afternoon tea, flirt, gossip, smoke, [and] take a whisky and soda at the customary hour," while he praised baseball for instilling "American Courage, Confidence, Combativeness; American Dash, Discipline, Determination; American Energy, Eagerness, Enthusiasm; American Pluck, Persistence, Performance; American Spirit, Sagacity, Success; American Vim, Vigor, Virility" (Kimmel, 55).

Baseball engendered a nationalist spirit among enthusiasts, while it also became a way for boys to be socialized into prescribed gender roles and prove their manhood. Baseball became popular at a moment in U.S. history when white middle-class men felt that their manhood was being threatened. Industrialization and urbanization had forced many men into blue- and white-collar professions that alienated them from the ideals of artisanship, ownership, and self-sufficiency that had defined masculinity in previous generations.

The Jeffersonian agrarian tradition that strongly associated manhood with the physical labor, closeness to nature, and economic autonomy characteristic of farming (as well as with whiteness) seemed endangered among the new generation of men growing up in urban metropolises and working in factories and offices. By 1910, less than one-third of American men were economically autonomous, and the social and cultural dominance of white middle-class manhood appeared to be besieged by increased immigration from Europe, the emancipation of black slaves and their migration to northern cities, and the rise of the woman's movement.

On the surface, baseball provided a solution to white, middle-class, masculine angst. As a sport, it became an important outlet for aggression and a site to prove one's physical prowess. The organization of the game, in which each player receives his turn at bat and stands alone facing the opposing pitcher, accentuates the autonomy of the individual and provides ample opportunity for personal achievement. The symmetry of the game, divided as it is into nine innings with a minimum of three players batting in each inning, also gives the sport an allure of egalitarianism among white men (while obscuring the omission of women and, until 1948, African Americans from baseball's most esteemed leagues).

At the same time, baseball's rigid structure, team-first philosophy, and the myriad of rules also reinforced middle-class values of obedience, self-sacrifice, and discipline in working-class male enthusiasts, which in turn assured the continued success of industrial capitalism and legitimated middle-class mores and understandings of manhood. Although the masculinity expressed on the baseball field suggested individual competition and achievement, its containment of such male expression within a space carefully supervised and controlled by white male elites promoted an obedience that served the interests of an emergent industrial capitalism.

Over the years, baseball has become a central arena for men of differing ethnic origins to prove their place amid "real" (i.e., white) men. Black ballplayers in the Negro Leagues had long desired to test their skills against the perceived "best of the best," seeing competition with and, later, participation in the Major Leagues as a means of asserting black manhood by proving its right to be fairly compared with dominant definitions of masculinity. This motive is still invoked today by Asian and Hispanic players, though often it is used to mask the financial advantages that also accompany service in the Major Leagues. Even after the "gentlemen's agreement" among Major League owners to bar blacks from playing at the Major League level was lifted, misconceptions of white male superiority remained. African-American and Hispanic ballplayers were often lauded for their "natural" athletic gifts, but in a thinking man's sport where the development of skills and the deployment of strategies were the ultimate signs of mastery, African Americans, Latinos, and other minorities deemed intellectually inferior by whites would be denied equal respect and excluded from managerial positions until the late 1970s.

During the 1970s, three interrelated developments—the arrival of free agency, the gradual escalation of salaries that followed, and the growing cultural emphasis on personal fulfillment and expression—led baseball players to prove their manhood less through teamwork than through the attainment of individual records. While earlier star personas, such as Babe Ruth, Mickey Mantle, and Reggie Jackson, were celebrated both for personal glory and the success they brought to their ball clubs, media coverage of baseball during the 1990s increasingly focused on the achievements of individual players such as Mark McGwire, Sammy Sosa, and Barry Bonds, regardless of their team efforts.

At the same time, the media attention focused on stars and the increased corporatization and commercialization of sports made the individual player's goal of proving his manhood—of overcoming the trappings of a society that seeks to hold him down—increasingly problematic. Fan's charges of disloyalty, greed, and selfishness, and the importance placed on media endorsements, suggested a growing commodification and decreasing moral wholesomeness of the game and its players, whose primary motivation increasingly appeared to be economic. Media attention also focused on the personal lives of ballplayers, highlighting the fact that success on the field did not necessarily indicate either acceptable manly behavior off the field or happiness and fulfillment at home.

Meanwhile, individual records, long considered unquestionable evidence of an athlete's masculine success and achievement, also met with anxious incredulity among baseball enthusiasts, who seemed to yearn for a mythical past in which baseball was a game rather than a career. There was speculation about whether performance-enhancing drugs nullified the value of the new records. Author Tara Rodgers' observations on Mark McGwire's star status neatly summarize the problematic contemporary relationship between manhood and baseball. According to Rodgers, McGwire is "a home run king who participates in psychotherapy to cope with the trauma of his divorce, and whose androstenedione-enhanced body is frequently problematized . . . for being as much a product of medical science as old-fashioned hard work." Rodgers' emphasis on McGwire's troubled psyche and artificially pumped-up physique suggests that baseball has become less a validating arena of (white, middle-class) male strength of body or fortitude of character than a contradictory space representative of masculinity's continuing redefinition.

Bibliography

Kimmel, Michael. "Baseball and the Reconstitution of American Masculinity, 1880–1920". In *Baseball History from Outside the Lines,* edited by John E. Dreifort. Lincoln: University of Nebraska Press, 2001.

Rodgers, Tara. "Take Me 'Out' to the Ballgame: Interventions Into the Transformation of the Village People's 'YMCA' from Disco Anthem to Ballpark Fun." pinknoises.com, October 2000. <http://www.pinknoises.com/ymca.shtml> (March 10, 2003).

Further Reading

Altimore, Michael. "Gentleman Athlete: Joe DiMaggio and the Celebration and Submergence of Ethnicity." *International Review for the Sociology of Sport* 34, no. 4 (1999): 359–367.

Bloom, John. *A House of Cards: Baseball Card Collecting and Popular Culture.* Minneapolis: University of Minnesota Press, 1997.

Messner, Michael A. *Power at Play: Sports and the Problem of Masculinity.* Boston: Beacon Press, 1992.

Miller, Toby. *Sportsex.* Philadelphia: Temple University Press, 2001.

Trujillo, N. "Hegemonic Masculinity on the Mound: Media Representations of Nolan Ryan and American Sports Culture." *Critical Studies in Mass Communication* 8 (1991): 290–308.

Related Entries

African-American Manhood; Agrarianism; Business/Corporate America; Character; Ethnicity; Football; Individualism; Industrialization; Latino Manhood; Middle-Class Manhood; Race; Self-Made Man; Sports; Urbanization; Whiteness; Work; Working-Class Manhood

—*Avi Santo*

Beat Movement

The Beat movement, which spanned from the late 1940s to the early 1960s, emerged from the stylistic example of a small group of unconventional writers known collectively as the Beat Generation or, more simply, the Beats. The meaning of beat for these writers combined a sense of being socially marginalized, oppressed, and cast-off with the saintly, spiritual connotations of beatific. Critics debate who rightly belongs in the Beat category, but most agree on the importance of three young white men who formed a kind of literary community in New York City in the 1940s: Jack Kerouac, Allen Ginsberg, and William S. Burroughs. In their major works—*On the Road* (1957), *Howl* (1956), and *Naked Lunch* (1959), respectively—they adopted innovative styles marked by spontaneity, improvisation, and self-expression to convey both their deep alienation from consumer society and their rejection of a postwar masculine ideal that stressed hard work, family responsibility, and strict heterosexuality.

Unlike the explosion of political activism in the early 1960s, the Beats stood more for a kind of personal spiritual liberation than for social revolution. Beat writers were the heirs to the legacy of nineteenth-century American Romanticism, drawing especially on the ideas of the transcendentalist philosopher Ralph Waldo Emerson and the poetry of Walt Whitman in formulating their social critiques and personal explorations. Just as Emerson and Whitman responded to an emergent market capitalism by fashioning a concept of manhood grounded in spirituality, spontaneity, and a belief in a transcendent reality, so the Beats constructed their version of a spiritually liberated masculinity in opposition to the perceived oppressiveness of consumer capitalism in the mid–twentieth century. Moreover, Walt Whitman's homosexuality and the erotic energy in his poetry also likely appealed to the sexually unconventional Beats. More contemporary influences on Beat style included the improvisational techniques of African-American jazz musicians, whose marginal status and lifestyles suggested to the Beats a bohemianism and a natural, sensual, "primitive" masculine style that stood in direct contrast to the artificiality and repression of white middle-class gender conventions.

The Beats openly challenged what they considered the oppressive conformist mentality of white middle-class America, from suburban family life to corporate employment to the availability of mass-produced consumer goods. They rejected the suburban ideal that millions of Americans embraced after World War II, perceiving the nuclear family, the rise of materialist values, and the responsibility associated with a steady job and support of a wife and children as threats to the individual male spirit. Rejecting the middle-class ideal of monogamous family life, the Beats were generally interested in women only as sexually objectified "chicks" or as poor non-Anglo "Earth mother" types—in both cases, women who were young, attractive, available, compliant, and silent. In that sense, they reflected more conventional notions of male sexual dominance and gender hierarchy.

As an alternative to widely accepted middle-class ideals of manhood, the Beats nurtured a defiant masculine subculture founded on male comradeship and dedicated to a kind of personal freedom defined by sexual license, casual drug and alcohol use, and literary experimentation. The perceived importance of male friendships to the quest for freedom and to the realization of one's artistic potential is evident in Beat writings and, often, in the explicit dedication of their work to one another. Male bonding for the Beats also extended to various degrees of homosexual behavior. Allen Ginsberg was openly gay, for example, and William S. Burroughs cultivated a homosexual identity that was defiant, rebellious, and masculine—a misogynistic rejection of women and what he saw as their threat to male freedom. Overall, the Beats cultivated their brand of masculinity as a critique of postwar American society and culture. Interpreting middle-class life as a kind of prison for men, they responded by fashioning themselves as maverick adventurers seeking physical and spiritual fulfillment and liberation in the company of other men on the margins of respectable society.

Popular awareness of the Beats as a cultural movement grew out of the media attention initially devoted to two key 1957 events: the San Francisco obscenity trial of the poet Lawrence Ferlinghetti for publishing Ginsberg's poem *Howl*, and the publication of Kerouac's *On the Road*. Reviewers and interviewers quickly moved beyond discussions of literary technique and content to focus instead on issues of lifestyle and masculinity; they celebrated the Beats' supposed personal and sexual freedom as representative of longstanding American ideals of manhood, while also denigrating as unmanly their perceived laziness and detachment. Men's magazines such as *Esquire* and *Playboy*, themselves promoting a new model of masculinity based on sexual indulgence, tended to ignore the harsher and more transgressive aspects of Beat behavior, playing up instead their easy, uncomplicated sexual relationships with beautiful "chicks."

What turned the Beats' alternative style into a movement was the transformation of their critique into a simplistic male rebelliousness that appealed to adolescents and alarmed parents. In this form, the Beat movement became a national phenomenon, a focal point for parental anxieties and youthful alienation. Adults in the late 1950s associated the Beats with their fears of juvenile delinquency and gang violence, while their children flocked to movie theaters to watch Marlon Brando in *The Wild One* (1953), James Dean in *Rebel Without a Cause* (1955), and other young male stars who projected the cool, hip style of the "bad boy." The Beats became an important precursor to other strands of adolescent defiance in the 1960s and beyond, helping to establish the rebellious, free-spirited, and sexually charged male persona as a popular model of masculinity for young American men.

BIBLIOGRAPHY

Foster, Edward Halsey. *Understanding the Beats.* Columbia: University of South Carolina Press, 1992.

Lee, A. Robert, ed. *The Beat Generation Writers.* London: Pluto Press, 1996.

Sterritt, David. *Mad to Be Saved: The Beats, the '50s, and Film.* Carbondale: Southern Illinois University Press, 1998.

Van Minnen, Cornelis A., et. al., eds. *Beat Culture: The 1950s and Beyond.* Amsterdam: VU University Press, 1999.

FURTHER READING

Charters, Ann, ed. *The Portable Beat Reader.* New York: Penguin, 1992.

Ehrenreich, Barbara. *The Hearts of Men: American Dreams and the Flight from Commitment.* Garden City, N.Y.: Anchor Press, 1984.

Tytell, John. *Naked Angels: The Lives and Literature of the Beat Generation.* New York: McGraw-Hill, 1976.

Watson, Steven. *The Birth of the Beat Generation: Visionaries, Rebels, and Hipsters, 1944–1960.* New York: Pantheon Books, 1998.

RELATED ENTRIES

Emerson, Ralph Waldo; Juvenile Delinquency; Kerouac, Jack; Male Friendship; Middle-Class Manhood; Religion and Spirituality; Romanticism; Whitman, Walt; Working-Class Manhood; Youth

—*Eric Combest*

BEECHER, HENRY WARD

1813–1887
Minister, Lecturer, Writer, and Social Reformer

The scion of a famed family of ministers and reformers, Henry Ward Beecher was a chief spokesman of the nineteenth-century middle class. Although charges of adultery ultimately undermined his influence, he promoted an ethos of middle-class Protestant masculinity that addressed the challenges posed by the market economy and industrial capitalism of the nineteenth century.

Beecher was ordained in 1837, and he became the pastor of the Plymouth Congregational Church in Brooklyn, New York, ten years later. He attracted a large following among the urban middle class in Brooklyn—more than 3,000 people attended his sermons every Sunday. His early preaching articulated a style of Victorian manhood at once entrepreneurial and religious, calling upon men to exercise moral and sexual restraint and to reject the temptations of immoral business dealings, gambling, and prostitution that were by-products of the new market economy. He encouraged young men to channel their masculine energies into their own salvation and the salvation of the world by taking up the causes of abolitionism, temperance, and even woman suffrage.

Beecher's *Lectures to Young Men* (1844), part of a growing body of advice literature for urban men, brought his ideas on masculinity to a national audience. He urged the upwardly mobile young men streaming into America's growing cities—a group that reformers considered particularly prone to immorality—to avoid excessive secularism as they sought economic success. Beecher encouraged these men to embrace Christianity and practice the virtues of self-made manhood: self-discipline, industry, sobriety, and piety. He maintained that these virtues, which blended capitalism and Christianity into a coherent model of American masculinity, could bring purpose and success to the lives of young men.

In 1874, Beecher became embroiled in a sex scandal that severely tarnished his public image. His friend, Theodore Tilton, filed suit against Beecher, alleging that Beecher had committed adultery with Tilton's wife, Elizabeth. The controversy raised questions about the relationship between male ministers like Beecher, who possessed authority, influence, and charisma, and the women who constituted a majority of most congregations. It also suggested disparities between public Victorian-era pronouncements about male sexuality and the actual sexual identities and practices of men. A months-long trial ended in acquittal, but rumors of his alleged affair would continue even after Beecher's death.

In the years following the trial, Beecher increasingly became an apologist for established, Victorian male authority. An advocate of social Darwinism, he sanctioned economic and social competition among men as natural and identified success as a mark of manliness. Beecher viewed the labor radicalism of the late-nineteenth century as an inappropriate challenge by inferior and unreasonable men to the social order. In marked contrast to his earlier warnings, he increasingly encouraged middle-class men to enjoy their hard-earned affluence. He also began advocating "muscular Christianity," calling for increased male membership in the church, emphasizing the connection between physical fitness and spiritual strength, and he was one of the first to advocate the building of gymnasiums within the facilities of the Young Men's Christian Association (YMCA).

Although often remembered as a hypocrite, a man whose success brought about the betrayal of his earlier ideals, Beecher's significance should not be underestimated. In the early decades of the nineteenth century, he was among the most prominent advocates of self-made Christian manhood and, later in his career, he became one of the most well-known defenders of the middle-class hegemony made possible by that ideology.

BIBLIOGRAPHY

Clark, Clifford E. *Henry Ward Beecher: Spokesman for a Middle-Class America.* Urbana: University of Illinois Press, 1978.

Fox, Richard Wightman. *Trials of Intimacy: Love and Loss in the Beecher–Tilton Scandal.* Chicago: University of Chicago Press, 1999.

McLoughlin, William G. *The Meaning of Henry Ward Beecher: An Essay on the Shifting Values of Mid-Victorian America, 1840–1870.* New York: Knopf, 1970.

Putney, Clifford. *Muscular Christianity: Manhood and Sports in Protestant America, 1880–1920.* Cambridge, Mass.: Harvard University Press, 2001.

Waller, Altina L. *Reverend Beecher and Mrs. Tilton: Sex and Class in Victorian America.* Amherst: University of Massachusetts Press, 1982.

FURTHER READING

Caskey, Marie. *Chariot of Fire: Religion and the Beecher Family.* New Haven, Conn.: Yale University Press, 1978.

Halttunen, Karen. *Confidence Men and Painted Women: A Study of Middle-Class Culture in America, 1830–1870.* New Haven, Conn.: Yale University Press, 1982.

Rotundo, E. Anthony. *American Manhood: Transformations in Masculinity from the Revolution to the Modern Era.* New York: Basic Books, 1993.

Rugoff, Milton. *The Beechers: An American Family in the Nineteenth Century.* New York: Harper & Row, 1981.

SELECTED WRITINGS

Beecher, Henry Ward. *Lectures to Young Men, on Various Important Subjects.* 1844. Reprint, New York: J. B. Alden, 1889.

———. *Life Thoughts, Gathered From the Extemporaneous Discourses of Henry Ward Beecher.* Edited by Edna Dean Procter and A. Moore. 1858. Reprint, Glasgow: Collins, 1871.

RELATED ENTRIES

Abolitionism; Advice Literature; Crisis of Masculinity; Gilded Age; Immigration; Industrialization; Jesus, Images of; Market Revolution; Middle-Class Manhood; Ministry; Muscular Christianity; Reform Movements; Religion and Spirituality; Seduction Tales; Self-Control; Self-Made Man; Sentimentalism; Suffragism; Temperance; Urbanization; Victorian Era; Young Men's Christian Association

—*Scott Miltenberger*

BIRTH OF A NATION

The film *Birth of a Nation* (1915), directed by D. W. Griffith, depicts the founding of the Ku Klux Klan and an idealized Southern way of life. A commercial and artistic milestone in American cinema, the film impressed its stereotyped portrayals of black men on the national consciousness through its sophisticated cinematic style, serious moral tone, epic length, and historical content.

Birth of a Nation portrays the Ku Klux Klan as heroic defenders of white manhood against the perceived threat of Northern politicians and African-American freedmen during the Reconstruction period. The film attempted to unify white society by juxtaposing the image of manly Ku Klux Klan "knights" against a demonized image of black male sexuality and political power. A key sequence in the film shows African-American senators in the South Carolina legislature passing pro-miscegenation laws, which would allow individuals of different races to marry or cohabitate.

While many of the stereotypes of African-American men featured in the film had a long history in popular culture, the film includes the first cinematic representation of the "buck"—the young black male who is brutally aggressive, highly sexed, and thus threatening to the dominance of the white male protagonist. This threat is visually represented by the physical bodies of the actors playing each role: Gus, played by Walter Long (a white actor in blackface), is a large, muscular man, while the film's protagonist, Ben Cameron (played by Henry Walthall) has a slight build and is called "the little colonel." One of Griffith's influential techniques was to balance the personal with the epic, and the sexualized threat posed by the young black males in the film has a range of victims: one of Cameron's sisters is attacked by Gus, another sister is threatened by a gang of black men, and Cameron's fiancée is at the mercy of a mulatto protegé of Northern politicians. During the climax of the film, with his "last-minute rescue" technique, Griffith cuts between scenes in which white men, women, and children are being menaced by black men. The Klan arrives just in time to save them all, thus dramatizing the triumph of white manhood.

Birth of a Nation's influence on popular attitudes toward African Americans was compounded by the millions of people who saw it. Membership in the Ku Klux Klan, which was reconstituted the same year the film was released, reached new highs as a direct result of the film's popularity, and the number of lynchings in 1915 increased significantly over previous years. At the same time, the National Association for the Advancement of Colored People (NAACP) achieved national recognition through its protests against the film's negative portrayals of African-American manhood. Birth of a Nation established a lasting pattern—persisting into the late twentieth century—of stereotyping black men in film, and thereby marginalizing them in American popular culture.

The film's most problematic legacy may be its status as a cinematic masterpiece. Despite deploring its racism and its potential to perpetuate negative stereotypes of African-American masculinity, film scholars argue that *Birth of a Nation* must continue to be shown because of its importance to American cinema history. The film remains notorious: the

Library of Congress's nomination of the film for inclusion in its National Film Registry in 1993 caused an outcry from the NAACP, and in 1994 the British Board of Film Classification ruled against the video release of the film. Such incidents suggest that the film—and its depictions of African-American masculinity—remain controversial.

Bibliography

Allen, Michael. *Family Secrets: The Feature Films of D. W. Griffith.* London: BFI, 1999.

Bogle, Donald. *Toms, Coons, Mulattoes, Mammies, and Bucks: An Interpretive History of Blacks in American Films.* 3rd ed. New York: Continuum, 1994.

Guerrero, Ed. *Framing Blackness: The African American Image in Film.* Philadelphia: Temple University Press, 1993.

Lang, Robert, ed. *The Birth of a Nation: D. W. Griffith, Director.* New Brunswick, N.J.: Rutgers University Press, 1994.

Wiegman, Robyn. "Race, Ethnicity, and Film." In *The Oxford Guide to Film Studies,* edited by John Hill and Pamela Church Gibson. Oxford: Oxford University Press, 1998.

Further Reading

Bogle, Donald. *Blacks in American Films and Television: An Encyclopedia.* New York: Garland, 1988.

Geduld, Harry M., ed. *Focus on D. W. Griffith.* Englewood Cliffs, N.J.: Prentice Hall, 1971.

MacLean, Nancy. *Behind the Mask of Chivalry: The Making of the Second Ku Klux Klan.* New York: Oxford University Press, 1994.

Simmon, Scott. *The Films of D. W. Griffith.* Cambridge, England: Cambridge University Press, 1993.

Smith, Valerie, ed. *Representing Blackness: Issues in Film and Video.* New Brunswick, N.J.: Rutgers University Press, 1997.

Related Entries

African-American Manhood; Emancipation; Hollywood; Slavery; Southern Manhood; Whiteness; White Supremacism

—*Sandy Camargo*

Bisexuality

Bisexuality, the sexual attraction to both men and women, has long been considered incompatible with masculinity. While a few early experts on sexuality, such as Havelock Ellis and Alfred Kinsey, acknowledged bisexuality as an important facet of human sexuality, most distinguished male bisexuality from a secure heterosexual masculine identity. Most writers also identified bisexuality as a form of homosexuality, which they likewise defined as being in opposition to normative heterosexual masculinity. When bisexuals began to organize in the 1970s, they challenged the conventional binaries of masculine-feminine and heterosexual-homosexual that had long been used to define dominant American concepts of manhood.

In the late nineteenth and early twentieth centuries, as industrialization, urbanization, bureaucratization, and immigration generated among many American men a sense that masculinity, and therefore the social order itself, was in crisis, psychologists and other social scientists interested in sexuality and its relation to society created the category of bisexuality. Most experts, using emerging evolutionary theories of human society, interpreted bisexuality (like homosexuality) as a form of psychological and social deviance—or as a stage preceding the formation of mature heterosexual identity. The bisexual male was thus stigmatized as an incomplete man and a potential threat to social order. This attitude prevailed through the mid-twentieth century, as two world wars and an extended economic depression in the 1930s reinforced beliefs linking heterosexual manhood to national strength.

American perceptions of bisexuality and its relation to masculinity began to change in 1948, when the publication of Alfred Kinsey's *Sexual Behavior in the Human Male* prompted scholars to acknowledge and discuss bisexuality as a common phenomenon among adult men, and to rethink the notion of normative heterosexual manhood. Yet most of the literature on male sexuality continued to categorize bisexuality as a variety of homosexuality, thus retaining the heterosexual-homosexual dyad that structures U.S. understandings of sexual identity, and also leaving bisexual men without a clear theoretical basis for conceptualizing bisexual maleness.

Attempts by bisexual men to develop bisexual male identities received a new impetus and visibility with the emergence of the modern gay rights and liberation movement in the late 1960s. Many bisexuals were active in New York's early Gay Liberation Front (GLF), founded in 1969 to "free the homosexual in everyone." Like contemporary womanist and feminist organizations, the GLF challenged traditional gender concepts, a stance that allowed for the inclusion of bisexual men. But as gay activism turned to rights-based strategies during the early 1970s and embraced the dominant culture's heterosexual-homosexual binary, bisexual activists founded their own organizations, including the National Bisexual Liberation Group, founded in 1972. That same year the Quaker Committee of Friends on Bisexuality issued its "Ithaca Statement on Bisexuality," which distinguished bisexual from homosexual identity (the statement was published in the *Advocate*, a national gay news magazine). Other bisexual organizations followed, including the Bisexual Center, founded in San Francisco in 1976, and BiWays, established in Chicago in 1978. Except for the Bisexual Center, most of these early organizations were dominated by men and heavily concerned with challenging prevailing paradigms of male sexuality and masculine gender roles. Early activism by homosexual and bisexual men helped produce some major successes, including the decision by the American Psychiatric Association (APA) to remove homosexuality as an illness from its diagnostic manual in 1973.

Despite such efforts, discrimination against bisexuals and misunderstandings of bisexuality persisted. During the late twentieth and early twenty-first centuries, evangelical Christian groups and other conservative organizations seeking to defend conventional gender categories and models of masculinity continued to conflate homosexuality with bisexuality—or to group them together as the same social evil. Similarly, as acquired immunodeficiency syndrome (AIDS) emerged as a major public concern during the 1980s, popular magazines such as *McCall's* and *Ladies' Home Journal* portrayed bisexual men as threats to heterosexual women and as conduits by which the virus passed from gay communities to the nuclear family. Such organizations and publications reinforced the longstanding fear and stigmatization of bisexual men.

Bisexual organizations and political action groups continued to proliferate, helping bisexuality to become less stigmatized during the 1980s and 1990s. New educational and political organizations continued to emerge, included BiPOL, a national organization established in 1983 in San Francisco; Boston's BiCEP, established in 1988; and BiNet USA, a national Bisexual network established in 1990. BiNet activists, in particular, worked with gay organizations to increase awareness of distinctive bisexual identities and to alleviate tensions between bisexuals and gays. The publication of Thomas Geller's *Bisexuality: A Reader and Sourcebook* (1990) and the inclusion of the word bisexual in the 1993 March on Washington for gay rights further heightened the public profile of bisexuality and aided bisexuals' attempts to articulate new approaches to gender and masculine identity. The 1990s also witnessed an intensifying discussion of gender and masculinities within bisexual organizations, particularly as transgender activists such as Dallas Denny called attention to the connections between a fear of people who reject rigid categories of sexual orientation and a fear of people who reject conventional gender roles. The activities of these figures suggest that dominant American constructions of gender and sexuality, which remain structured through dyadic rather than fluid models, continue to view bisexuality as incompatible with masculinity.

BIBLIOGRAPHY

Beemyn, Brett, and Erich Steinman, eds. *Bisexual Men in Culture and Society.* New York: Haworth Press, 2002.

Boswell, John. *Christianity, Social Tolerance, and Homosexuality: Gay People in Western Europe from the Beginning of the Christian Era to the Fourteenth Century.* Chicago: University of Chicago Press, 1980.

Bristow, Joseph, and Angelina R. Wilson. *Activating Theory: Lesbian, Gay, Bisexual Politics.* London: Lawrence and Wishart, 1993.

Firestein, Beth. *Bisexuality: The Psychology and Politics of an Invisible Minority.* Thousand Oaks, Calif.: Sage, 1996.

Hutchins, Loraine, and Lani Ka'ahumanu, eds. *Bi Any other Name: Bisexual People Speak Out.* Boston: Alyson Publications, 1991.

Klein, Fred. *The Bisexual Option.* New York: Haworth Press, 1993.

FURTHER READING

Fast, Julius, and Hal Wells. *Bisexual Living.* New York: M. Evans, 1975.

Geller, Thomas. *Bisexuality: A Reader and Sourcebook.* Ojai, Calif.: Times Change Press, 1990.

Hall, Donald E., and Maria Pramaggiore. *RePresenting BiSexualities: Subjects and Cultures of Fluid Desire.* New York: New York University Press, 1996.

Tucker, Naomi, ed. *Bisexual Politics: Theories, Queries, and Visions.* New York: Hawthorn, 1995.

Weinberg, Martin S., Colin J. Williams, and Douglas W. Pryor. *Dual Attraction: Understanding Bisexuality.* New York: Oxford University Press, 1994.

Williams, Mark. *Sexual Pathways: Adapting to Dual Sexual Attraction.* Westport, Conn.: Praeger. 1999.

RELATED ENTRIES

Freudian Psychoanalytic Theory; Heterosexuality; Homosexuality; Transsexuality

—Linda Heidenreich

BLACK PANTHER PARTY

In response to the civil rights movement's failure to address the challenges of postindustrial capitalism, urban blight, and social dislocations, the Black Panther Party (BPP) articulated a construction of black masculinity based on violent self-defense and the promotion of self-determination. For the BPP, living as black men meant meeting violence with violence, resisting threats from the (white) police, and providing for a black community that was starving physically, emotionally, politically, and spiritually.

Huey Newton and Bobby Seale founded the Black Panther Party in Oakland, California, in 1966. Originally intended to

A poster from around 1970 depicting members of the Black Panther Party holding machine guns. Black Panthers proposed—and expressed through their attire—an ideal of African-American masculinity grounded in brash aggressiveness and defiant social protest. (From the collections of the Library of Congress)

protect the black community from police brutality, the organization evolved into a revolutionary nationalist group that responded to African Americans' educational, social, and economic needs. Its agenda—"land, bread, housing, education, clothing, justice, peace and people's community control of modern technology"—reflected a vision of black manhood that was grounded in men's traditional roles as breadwinners, protectors, and leaders.

The Panthers identified several inner-city institutions—particularly law enforcement, the school system, and social welfare—as white-run attempts to emasculate black men by limiting their ability to govern, teach, and protect their communities. They established street patrols and community service programs designed to offer political hope and social assistance. These alternative institutions provided social spaces in which Panther men enacted their vision of black masculinity.

Although the Panthers used masculine imagery in their rhetoric—one statement called the group "the cream of Black manhood"—their public postures did more to attract followers than did their political statements or ideology. Seeking to create a new aesthetic of black masculinity, they cultivated an image of brash aggressiveness and coolness. Thus, they wore black leather coats, black berets, and dark glasses, and they brandished weapons and ammunition at their public appearances. A portrait of Huey Newton, dressed in a black leather jacket and beret, holding a spear in one hand and a shotgun in the other, suggests that their aesthetic looked as much to traditional African cultural models as to contemporary American urban life.

Although the BPP's vision of black manhood was in some ways traditional, they also challenged conventional notions of femininity that called for black women to "support their men" through domestic or secretarial work. Within the party, women and men alike engaged in community patrols and shoot-outs, while its male members often did work that other black men might have associated with women, including teaching in their community schools, working in the free breakfast programs, and helping to develop community service programs. Despite these challenges to traditional definitions of masculinity and femininity, conventional gender constructs persisted within the organization: community service programs were defined as feminine and police patrols as masculine. The BPP privileged masculine activities in its rhetoric, viewing patrols as sites of revolutionary resistance to white supremacist emasculation in which participants, whether male or female, were acting as "men."

The Panthers' model of black masculinity, grounded in militancy and an unwillingness to take any "shit" from "da man," continues to impact those discourses—ranging from the Shaft films to the performances and lyrics of rap and hip-hop music—that address the oppression of urban blacks and that surround definitions of black masculinity within urban popular culture.

BIBLIOGRAPHY

Cleaver, Kathleen. "Women, Power, and Revolution." In *Liberation, Imagination, and the Black Panther Party: A New Look at the Panthers and their Legacy,* edited by Kathleen Cleaver and George Katsiaficas. New York: Routledge, 2001.

Le-Blanc-Ernest, Angela. "'The Most Qualified Person to Handle the Job': Black Panther Party Women, 1966–1982." In *The Black*

Panther Party Reconsidered, edited by Charles E. Jones. Baltimore: Black Classic Press, 1998.

Matthews, Tracye. "'No One Ever Asks, What a Man's Role in the Revolution is': Gender and the Politics of The Black Panther Party, 1966–1971." In *The Black Panther Party Reconsidered,* edited by Charles E. Jones. Baltimore: Black Classic Press, 1998.

Reid-Pharr, Robert. "Once You Go Black: Performance, Seduction, and the (Un)Making of Black American Innocence." George Mason University, Fall 2001. <http://culturalstudies.gmu.edu/cultural_matters/index.html> (March 10, 2003).

FURTHER READING

Brown, Elaine. *A Taste of Power: A Black Woman's Story.* New York: Anchor Books, 1994.

Cleaver, Eldridge. *Soul on Ice.* 1967. Reprint, New York: Delta Trade Paperbacks, 1999.

Harper, Phillip Brian. *Are We Not Men? Masculine Anxiety and the Problem of African American Identity.* New York: Oxford University Press, 1996.

Hilliard, David, and Donald Weise, eds. *The Huey P. Newton Reader.* New York: Seven Stories Press, 2002.

Hilliard, David, and Lewis Cole. *The Autobiography of David Hilliard and the Story of The Black Panther Party.* Boston: Little, Brown, 1993.

Wallace, Michelle. *Black Macho and the Myth of Superwoman.* New York: Dial Press, 1979.

RELATED ENTRIES

African-American Manhood; Civil Rights Movement; Class; Emancipation; Ethnicity; Feminism; Guns; Heterosexuality; Malcolm X; Militarism; Nationalism; Nation of Islam; Patriarchy; Race; *Shaft*; Slavery; Urbanization; Violence; White Supremacism; Working-Class Manhood

—*David J. Leonard*

BODY

The male body has been an object of widespread interest, admiration, and social contemplation at least since the time of the ancient Greeks. Contemporary American society has in some ways returned to the classical tradition of idealizing the male form, but with a number of troubling consequences that would have seemed unimaginable as recently as the mid–twentieth century. During the nineteenth and twentieth centuries, American culture increased its scrutiny of the male body and viewed it as both a symbol of an idealized masculinity (often a symbol laden with moral values) and an aesthetic object in itself.

The Nineteenth Century

Charismatic health experts and dietary reformers such as Sylvester Graham and John Harvey Kellogg contributed greatly to nineteenth-century American constructions of masculinity and of the idealized male body. Both men exemplified an inward-looking approach to the male body and constructions of masculinity; that is, they defined the manly body in terms of health and moral purity rather than aesthetics and physical appearance. Graham, one of the most influential antebellum commentators on masculinity, believed that manliness required adherence to nutritional restrictions and to moral and, even among married men, sexual restraint. Graham's vision of ideal manhood remained influential through the late nineteenth century, in part because of Kellogg, who similarly associated manliness with healthful eating and moral and sexual purity.

The Early Twentieth Century

By the early twentieth century, modernization—particularly the growing incidence of sedentary office work among middle-class men—prompted concerns about male vigor and an accompanying shift from inward to aesthetic approaches to the idealized male body that emphasized strength and outward appearance as physical indicators of moral purity. This new focus on the visible features of the male body paralleled a cultural shift from a focus on inner "character" to outward "personality" as markers of manliness, as well as the rise of a "muscular Christianity" that identified physical strength with moral strength. Seeking idealized masculine forms that demonstrated individualism and physical prowess in an increasingly corporatized and bureaucratized society, Americans admired such figures as the vaudeville performer and bodybuilder Eugen Sandow, whose muscular physique was considered a representation of purity and the ideal male body; the fictional hero Tarzan, whose physical skills and strength suggested a natural male body uncorrupted by urban-industrial civilization; the escape artist Harry Houdini, whose abilities suggested that the male body aspired to freedom and resisted physical constraints; and (somewhat later, amid the loosening sexual standards of the 1920s), the bodybuilder Charles Atlas, who frankly linked male sexual appeal to physical brawn by stigmatizing the "ninety-seven-pound weakling." Such popular heroes reflected Americans' anxious turn to the male body amid the perceived emasculating tendencies of modern life.

The Mid–Twentieth Century

Cultural concerns with the male body persisted during the mid–twentieth century, but it assumed forms quite different from those of earlier decades and, in some ways, resembled the inward approach of the nineteenth century. World War II and the Cold War that followed generated among many Americans an anxiety about national strength. During the 1950s, in particular, fears of Soviet communism and of internal threats to the nation prompted concern that capitalist prosperity, suburban living, and white-collar work had made American men overweight, and thus soft and flabby compared to the men of the regimented Soviet Union. Cold War–era fitness enthusiasts such as Jack LaLanne typically framed their promotion of exercise in terms of health and moral fitness, which they considered the key to a stronger America. LaLanne downplayed the aesthetic or erotic aspects of the body, since—amid fears of homosexuality as a form of deviance akin to juvenile delinquency and communism—much of the American public looked with suspicion upon bodybuilding. LaLanne's signature jumpsuits exemplified this de-emphasis on the unclad male form, as did many of the other idealized males of this era. For instance, the appeal of movie stars such as Humphrey Bogart significantly depended on facial good looks and appropriate masculine conduct, rather than on an ideal of overall physical perfection.

The Late Twentieth Century

During the 1960s and 1970s, the counterculture (a revolution in sexual standards and practices) and the growing appeal of self-realization movements encouraged a tendency among men to identify bodily with spiritual well-being and view their bodies as the most important expression of masculinity. American men demonstrated their new and often sexualized body consciousness in several ways: they participated in new exercise fads, such as jogging; adopted new fashions, like small bathing suits and open-chest shirts; and embraced the revival of bodybuilding.

A resurgence of bodybuilding followed the popular success of Arnold Schwarzenegger, a new masculine force on the cultural radar screen who capitalized on the changing social and cultural climate of the 1970s. A charismatic and highly successful professional bodybuilder who was then making an unprecedented transition from bodybuilding success to movie stardom, Schwarzenegger promoted bodybuilding as a suitable activity for middle-class American men, though more for the sake of health and fitness than for the aesthetic goals central to competitive bodybuilding. Wearing bikini-style trunks and explicitly associating bodybuilding with heterosexuality and appeal to women, Schwarzenegger ushered in an era in which explicit attention to the unclad male body became widely accepted and the body became more important than ever as a way that American men measured and defined their manhood.

In the 1980s and 1990s, widespread acceptance of the muscular and hairless body as a masculine ideal—reinforced by the emphasis on military toughness prevalent during the presidency of Ronald Reagan—became increasingly visible throughout American culture. This new emphasis was most obviously visible in advertising and media images like those in such popular men's magazines as *Men's Health* and *Men's Fitness*. In films like those in the *Rambo* and *Terminator* series, Sylvester Stallone and Schwarzenegger, respectively, portrayed characters whose muscularity and physical strength were expressed through violence and associated with Americanism and heroic resistance to evil. Television wrestling, which was especially popular among adolescent males, featured ever more muscular bodies engaged in increasingly violent competition. Television advertisements featuring similar figures hawked "body-sculpting" equipment for the home, promising male audiences that they could achieve the muscular ideal. The idealized muscular body also began to influence mannequins (the most common type of American statuary) and children's action figures, and the resulting effect on consumers, and particularly on boys, added to and perpetuated the cultural power of this ideal.

Gay advocate and journalist Michelangelo Signorile has persuasively argued that this new American male-body aesthetic has another (and more surprising) source than the revival of bodybuilding and the action films and figures of the 1980s. Signorile's *Life Outside: The Signorile Report on Gay Men* (1997) traces the rise of the current hairless and muscular body aesthetic directly to American gay communities, and specifically to gay pornography. His report claims that this ideal assumed a new visibility in the wake of the Sexual Revolution and gay rights movement of the late 1960s and 1970s.

Male Body-Image Anxiety in the Late Twentieth Century

The new pervasiveness of the muscular body aroused considerable concern among cultural commentators. Lynne Luciano, for example, argued in *Looking Good* (2001) that the internalization of the new bodily ideal led American men to consider their bodies the most important marker of their masculinity, and therefore generated an explosion of male self-image anxieties and body-image disorders. Luciano and others were concerned that, while surveys conducted in the early 1970s indicated that American men were generally content with their bodies, the proliferation of advertising and media images of extremely muscular male bodies beginning in the mid-1980s diminished that sense of satisfaction. In 2000, Harrison Pope, Katharine Phillips, and Roberto

Olivardia offered persuasive arguments and statistical evidence of a "crisis of male body obsession," which they called the "adonis complex," and they linked this crisis to a host of male body-image disorders.

One such disorder—previously virtually unheard of outside of bodybuilding gyms—is muscle dysmorphia. Generally known around American gyms by the informal names "biggerexia" or "reverse anorexia," it is a condition in which men who may in fact be quite large and muscular, nevertheless feel that they are not nearly large or muscular enough. Through various methods, including the use of steroids to enhance muscle mass, these men continually try to make their bodies even bigger and stronger. Beginning around 1980, sociologists and psychologists began to document increases in this pattern of thinking, not just among hard-core bodybuilders, but also among American males in general. The origin of this disorder is difficult to pinpoint, in part because bodybuilders regarded it as typical of gym life long before cultural critics began to study it and publicize it in the early 1990s. A closely related male body disorder, fueled by the stigmatization of excess body fat, is male anorexia. Long considered almost exclusive to women, anorexia began to manifest itself among American men with increasing frequency in the early 1990s.

Concerns about body hair became another manifestation of male body anxiety during the late twentieth century, particularly its presence in desirable places and absence in others. Like extreme muscularity, the absence of chest hair moved, under the impact of advertising campaigns featuring hairless male torsos, from an object of suspicion to a sought-after ideal during the last two decades of the twentieth century. The growing stigmatization of baldness, meanwhile, prompted the marketing of an array of antibaldness drugs such as Rogaine.

In another indication that bodily strength and vigor became highly important measures of manhood in the late twentieth century, the sports sections of most major metropolitan newspapers increasingly included advertisements for penis-enlargement surgery. Like many other plastic or cosmetic surgeries, these procedures were marketed to men less because of legitimate medical need than because of a widespread male anxiety about the size and shape of body parts. Similarly, this period witnessed the growing appeal of sexual enhancement drugs like Viagra, as men increasingly measured their masculinity by their sexual performance. These procedures and drugs suggested that male body anxiety had extended to include the most private of physical attributes. That Viagra became at once both very popular and widely mocked was an indicator both of the importance of sexual potency to American constructions of masculinity and of American men's fear that seriously discussing the issue would raise suspicion that they were failing to meet body-centered expectations of manhood.

All of these disorders and anxieties became included in late-twentieth-century discussions of a "crisis" of masculinity. As American men sought to define manhood in a postmodern culture, critics argued, they were being presented with an unattainable hypermasculine physical ideal while being told that they might achieve it through weight-training equipment, surgery, and pharmaceutical products. The result was the spread of distorted ideas of how to be a man. While the potential effects of this trend on the psyches and body images of adult American males troubled critics, the question of how the trend might affect future generations was even more worrisome.

The long-term effects of twentieth-century changes in American male body images are impossible to predict with any accuracy. It seems reasonable, however, to conclude that the disparity between the idealized male body and the actual bodies of typical American males will continue to grow in an increasingly sedentary society. In this regard, American males will likely come to be more susceptible to the sorts of body-image anxieties, dissatisfactions, and disorders that were until recently considered exclusively women's concerns.

Bibliography

Griswold, Robert L. "The 'Flabby American,' the Body, and the Cold War." In *A Shared Experience: Men, Women, and the History of Gender,* edited by Laura McCall and Donald Yacovone. New York: New York University Press, 1998.

Kasson, John. *Houdini, Tarzan, and the Perfect Man: The White Male Body and the Challenge of Modernity in America.* New York: Hill and Wang, 2001.

Kimmel, Michael. "Consuming Manhood: The Feminization of American Culture and the Recreation of the Male Body, 1832–1920." *Michigan Quarterly Review* 33 (1994): 7–36.

Luciano, Lynne. *Looking Good: Male Body Image in Modern America.* New York: Hill and Wang, 2001.

Pope, Harrison G., Katharine A. Phillips, and Roberto Olivardia. *The Adonis Complex: The Secret Crisis of Male Body Obsession.* New York: Free Press, 2000.

Signorile, Michelangelo. *Life Outside: The Signorile Report on Gay Men: Sex, Drugs, Muscles, and the Passages of Life.* New York: HarperCollins, 1997.

Further Reading

Anderson, Arnold, Leigh Cohn, and Thomas Holbrook. *Making Weight: Men's Conflicts with Food, Weight, Shape, and Appearance.* Carlsbad, Calif.: Gürze Books, 2000.

Kimmel, Michael, and Michael A. Messner. *Men's Lives.* New York: Allyn & Bacon, 2001.

Lehman, Peter. *Masculinity: Bodies, Movies, Culture.* New York: Routledge, 2001.

Paris, Bob. *Gorilla Suit: My Adventures in Bodybuilding.* New York: St. Martin's, 1997.

RELATED ENTRIES

Advertising; Atlas, Charles; Bodybuilding; Crisis of Masculinity; Graham, Sylvester; Health; Heterosexuality; Homosexuality; Kellogg, John Harvey; Men's Movements; Muscular Christianity; Rambo; Sandow, Eugen; Schwarzenegger, Arnold; Sports; Tarzan

—*Sean Heuston*

BODYBUILDING

From Theodore Roosevelt to Charles Atlas to Arnold Schwarzenegger, the story is a familiar one: A weak or sickly boy, riddled with self-doubt and powerlessness, develops into a strong, confident, and magnetic man through a disciplined bodybuilding regimen. Bodybuilding had its origins in the United States in the late nineteenth century, and it has grown in popularity, both as a fitness practice and a competitive sport, into the twenty-first century. Throughout its history, bodybuilding has been fundamentally concerned with the transformation of the self. This metamorphosis through muscle building represents a fundamentally modern ideal of masculinity that emerged at a time of vast social and cultural change.

As constructions of masculinity in the United States became increasingly grounded in the biological and medical aspects of the male body during the late nineteenth century, America witnessed a craze in physical-culture regimens aimed at developing the physique and promoting health. Theodore Roosevelt was the best-known example of this new ethic of "strenuous manhood," but the push toward a muscular virility extended outside of elite circles to a wider American populace. The Prussian-born bodybuilder Eugen Sandow became an instant celebrity when he toured the United States in the 1890s, performing feats of strength and displaying his (near-naked) muscular physique. Bernarr Macfadden, a health reformer and canny businessman, was inspired to develop his own body after seeing Sandow perform, and he attracted more than 100,000 readers to his monthly magazine *Physical Culture* (founded in 1898) through a combination of sensational images and health advice.

This new focus on strength and fitness reflected widespread anxieties about the status of white middle-class manhood in turn-of-the-century industrial America. Fitness promoters capitalized on fears that white middle-class men were becoming weak and "overcivilized" in corporate America, and that their influence was being eroded by the threats posed by labor unrest, immigration, and the emerging women's movement. In contrast, the developed body combined classical Greek ideals of beauty with aggressiveness and sexuality, thereby co-opting the strength and vitality associated with races perceived as more primitive, while still preserving a mantle of civilization for white men. Celebrity strongmen such as Sandow and Macfadden became part of a new society of spectacle and mass consumption, displaying their erotically charged bodies in front of mixed-gender audiences and through mass-produced photographs and widely circulated magazines.

Following the initial enthusiasm for strength training around 1900, muscle building continued to be promoted over the next several decades by popular figures such as Charles Atlas (the 97-pound weakling) and Bob Hoffman, the owner of York Barbell and *Strength and Health* magazine. Whereas the turn-of-the-century physical culture movement had emphasized the revitalization of white Anglo-Saxon men, most of the weightlifters who congregated in Bob Hoffman's "muscletown" of York, Pennsylvania, during the mid-twentieth century were first- or second-generation immigrants who sought success and acceptance in America through a rigorous regimen of weight training. Hoffman even identified the hard work and discipline of his immigrant corps as the true sources of American power, arguing that a physically fit, democratic America could overcome the threats posed by world dictators and communism.

In contrast to the feats of strength demonstrated in weightlifting, bodybuilding focused on the development of a particular physique. In the mid-twentieth century, weightlifting enthusiasts distinguished themselves from the more narcissistic, and therefore less manly, practice of building muscles for the sake of appearance rather than function. By the 1970s, however, bodybuilding had gained a cultural notoriety that weightlifting lacked, while became increasingly regarded as compatible with masculinity. The 1974 documentary film *Pumping Iron* and the emerging celebrity status of Arnold Schwarzenegger introduced the arena of professional bodybuilding to many Americans. By the late 1970s, bodybuilding started to attract a small minority of female competitors as well, though many Americans deemed such women unfeminine.

At the same time that competitive bodybuilding was reaching a mainstream audience, a health and fitness movement began to emerge. The beauty ideals of the late twentieth century reflected this focus on "hard" bodies, which signify control, discipline, and sexual power. To an unprecedented degree, Americans are encouraged in the mass media to shape and manipulate their bodies into a desired form that defies aging and denies the vulnerability of the flesh. Competitive bodybuilding has a complex relationship to these more widespread exercise practices and standards of beauty, and its relation to cultural constructions of masculinity remains ambivalent. Some critics argue that professional bodybuilding takes the muscular ideal to such a hypermasculine extreme that it verges on farce or caricature. Others note the traditionally feminine activities involved in competitive bodybuilding, such as posing in front of a mirror, dieting, and shaving and oiling one's body. Still other observers suggest that professional bodybuilding, especially the use of performance-enhancing drugs, carries health risks. Since its origins in the late nineteenth century, bodybuilding has occupied a middle space between fitness and performance, and between health and erotic display. Bodybuilders have transformed their bodies into very particular cultural products that have reflected both the anxieties of their historical moment and the potential they see for individual achievement and mastery over the self.

BIBLIOGRAPHY

Bederman, Gail. *Manliness and Civilization: A Cultural History of Gender and Race in the United States, 1880–1917.* Chicago: University of Chicago Press, 1996.

Bordo, Susan. *The Male Body: A New Look at Men in Public and in Private.* New York: Farrar, Straus and Giroux, 1999.

Dutton, Kenneth R. *The Perfectible Body: The Western Ideal of Male Physical Development.* New York: Continuum, 1995.

Fair, John D. *Muscletown USA: Bob Hoffman and the Manly Culture of York Barbell.* University Park: Pennsylvania State University Press, 1999.

Green, Harvey. *Fit for America: Health, Fitness, Sport and American Society.* New York: Pantheon, 1986.

Kasson, John F. *Houdini, Tarzan, and the Perfect Man: The White Male Body and the Challenge of Modernity in America.* New York: Hill and Wang, 2001.

Klein, Alan M. *Little Big Men: Bodybuilding Subculture and Gender Construction.* Albany: State University of New York Press, 1993.

Moore, Pamela L., ed. *Building Bodies.* New Brunswick, N.J.: Rutgers University Press, 1997.

FURTHER READING

Balsamo, Anne. *Technologies of the Gendered Body: Reading Cyborg Women.* Durham, N.C.: Duke University Press, 1996.

Chapman, David L. *Sandow the Magnificent: Eugen Sandow and the Beginnings of Bodybuilding.* Urbana: University of Illinois Press, 1994.

Fussell, Samuel Wilson. *Muscle: Confessions of an Unlikely Bodybuilder.* New York: Poseidon Press, 1991.

Heywood, Leslie. *Bodymakers: A Cultural Anatomy of Women's Body Building.* New Brunswick, N.J.: Rutgers University Press, 1998.

Ian, Marcia. "How Do You Wear Your Body? Bodybuilding and the Sublimity of Drag." In *Negotiating Lesbian and Gay Subjects,* edited by Monica Dorenkamp and Richard Henke. New York: Routledge, 1995.

Long, Ron. "The Fitness of the Gym." *Harvard Gay and Lesbian Review* 4 (Summer 1997): 20–22.

Schwarzenegger, Arnold. *The New Encyclopedia of Modern Bodybuilding.* New York: Simon & Schuster, 1998.

RELATED ENTRIES

Atlas, Charles; Body; Health; Roosevelt, Theodore; Schwarzenegger, Arnold; Sports; Strenuous Life

—*Karen P. Flood*

BOGART, HUMPHREY

1899–1957
Actor

Humphrey Bogart is remembered as one of Hollywood's biggest stars, and he remains an icon of masculinity in American culture. After years of setbacks, false starts, and failed marriages, Bogart spent fifteen years at the height of his profession. In the 1940s he was ranked among the top money-making stars; by 1947 he was the highest paid actor in the world; and in 1948 he established his own film company. "Bogie," as he came to be known, personified both toughness and elegance as the quintessential romantic antihero.

Bogart was born in 1899 to a noted Manhattan surgeon and his wife, who was a successful magazine illustrator. He had a minor career in New York theater in the 1920s and a few failed attempts at film acting in the 1930s before becoming one of Hollywood's most distinctive leading men in the 1940s and 1950s. He began his career playing juveniles—young, handsome romantic leads—on Broadway, but as the tolerance of American audiences for the carefree juvenile diminished with the Great Depression, Bogart found himself playing the role of the tough guy. With this shift to playing heavies and gangsters, Bogart achieved success and fame in Hollywood. His breakthrough role was playing escaped convict Duke Mantee in Robert Sherwood's play *The Petrified Forest* on Broadway in 1935, a role he reprised in the 1936 Warner Brothers film.

In the 1940s, Bogart shifted roles again, and began playing film noir antiheroes. In these roles he echoed the mood of post-World War II American masculinity, reflecting the disillusionment and masculine crisis of returning veterans who found themselves displaced, unemployed, alienated, and often disabled. At the same time, he embodied the personal integrity, individualism, and sentimentalism that lay behind this disillusionment. As the antihero in such films as *High Sierra* (1941), *The Maltese Falcon* (1941), *Casablanca* (1942), and *Key Largo* (1948), Bogart achieved enormous critical success and popularity, and won a best-actor Oscar for his role in *The African Queen* (1951).

Despite his tough-guy persona, Bogart was dependent on the women in his life. He married four times, concluding one marriage with the embarkation on another. He married Helen Menken in 1926, Mary Philips in 1928, Mayo Methot in 1938, and Lauren Bacall in 1945. Bogart and Bacall had two children and remained happily married until Bogart's death in 1957. They were seen as one of Hollywood's most loved celebrity couples, and their relationship forms part of the Bogie myth: a tough guy whose heart could be won by a beautiful woman who was as tough as he was.

For contemporary audiences, Bogart encapsulates the antihero: tough, smooth-talking, with his collar turned up, his gun in his pocket, and a cigarette dangling from his lip. As the tough guy, Bogart did not so much mirror the reality of American masculinity as offer a model to which it could aspire. Even today, Bogart remains an ideal of American masculinity, embodying an individualism, integrity, and heroism that seem absent in today's culture. He remains a true Hollywood legend.

BIBLIOGRAPHY

Coe, Jonathan. *Humphrey Bogart: Take it and Like it.* New York: Grove Weidenfeld, 1991.

Fuchs, Woolfgang. *Humphrey Bogart: Cult-Star—A Documentation.* Berlin: Taco, 1987.

Pascall, Jeremy. *Hollywood and the Great Stars: The Stars, the Sex Symbols, the Legend, the Movies and How It All Began.* New York: Crescent Books, 1976.

Shipman, David. *The Great Movie Stars.* Vol. 1, *The Golden Years.* Rev. ed. New York: Hill and Wang, 1979.

Sklar, Robert. *City Boys: Cagney, Bogart, Garfield.* Princeton, N.J.: Princeton University Press, 1992.

Spoto, Donald. *Camerado: Hollywood and the American Man.* New York: New American Library, 1978.

FURTHER READING

Bogart, Stephen. *Bogart: In Search of My Father.* New York: Dutton, 1995.

Eyles, Allen. *Humphrey Bogart.* London: Sphere, 1990.

Hyams, Joe. *Bogart and Bacall: A Love Story.* New York: D. McKay, 1975.

Meyer, Jeffrey. *Bogart: A Life in Hollywood.* Boston: Houghton Mifflin, 1997.

Pettigrew, Terence. *The Bogart File.* London: Golden Eagle Press, 1977.

Sperber, A. M., and Eric Lax. *Bogart.* New York: William Morrow, 1997.

RELATED ENTRIES

Crisis of Masculinity; Detectives; Gangsters; Great Depression; Heroism; Hollywood; Individualism; World War II

—*Philippa Gates*

BOONE, DANIEL

1734–1820
American Frontiersman

Pictured as a buckskin-clad, rifle-toting, backwoods hunter, Daniel Boone has represented in American culture the settlement of the West and an archetypal American masculinity. During the late eighteenth century and the nineteenth century, Boone was transformed into a legendary embodiment of the masculine ideals of a new nation experiencing westward expansion, the market revolution, and urbanization.

Born in Pennsylvania, Boone received a rudimentary education and spent his youth on the North Carolina frontier. He married Rebecca Bryan in 1756 but rejected a settled life of farming to take up hunting and exploring in the Appalachian Mountains of Kentucky. Interested in opening the West to settlement, he helped construct a road across the Cumberland Gap in 1775 and established the Kentucky settlement of Boonesborough. He became involved in several unsuccessful land dealings, losing land in Kentucky for failure to meet preemption requirements and land in Missouri for failure to cultivate it. He fought in the American Revolution as a local militia captain, though primarily to defend his community against Native Americans. The aging Boone, already famed as a frontiersman, reacquired a portion of his land holdings from Congress six years before his death.

Despite Boone's missteps, biographers made him a symbol of heroic American manhood, embodying and reconciling several contradictory masculine ideals in post-Revolutionary and antebellum American culture. On one level, he exemplified republican manhood in choosing a life of simple virtue over what one nineteenth-century biographer called the "luxury and effeminacy" of an increasingly commercialized America (Herman, 436). At the same time, however, he became a model of urban, entrepreneurial, and individualistic middle-class manhood, resembling the ideal conveyed by contemporary writers of advice and success manuals for young men. Hunting in an unrestrained natural setting that symbolized the aggressively competitive urban marketplace, Boone mastered his environment and achieved self-made success, while also maintaining the internalized moral self-control that Americans called "character."

Although the Boone ideal included a "wild" masculinity associated with Native American men and the American natural environment (particularly athleticism and hunting prowess), it also reflected most nineteenth-century Americans' association of manhood with whiteness. Called a "Romulus of Saxon blood" by one antebellum biographer (Herman, 450), the mythic Boone was an agent of Manifest Destiny (the idea that the expansion of the United States and its Euro-American institutions was divinely ordained), bringing commerce, cities, and white "civilization" to the frontier. Far from producing the savagery that white Americans perceived in Native Americans, hunting instilled in the idealized Boone the mental discipline, enterprise, aggression, and perseverance characteristic of middle-class manhood. Indeed, the fictional Boone was a gentle man influenced by the domestic affection and romantic love of the ideal Victorian husband.

The mythic Boone embodied the sporting aspirations of many middle-class men in the urbanizing, industrializing society of the nineteenth century. Concerned that nonmanual labor feminized men, many middle-class Americans saw in Boone an exemplar of the outdoor activities they deemed essential to male reinvigoration. Furthermore, Boone's idealized exploits in a violent world unsuitable for his wife reassured middle-class men that their competitive struggle in the commercial marketplace was a masculinizing rather than feminizing endeavor. During the late nineteenth century, these dimensions of the Boone ideal became increasingly important as the frontier disappeared and growing numbers of white middle-class American men embraced the "strenuous life."

The Boone masculine ideal inspired many other iconic American figures, including Congressman Davy Crockett, Buffalo Bill, Kit Carson, and the fictional Natty Bumppo. As the television adventure program *Daniel Boone* (1964–70) suggests, the Boone image continued to appeal to the American imagination—and to enjoy considerable commercial success—in the increasingly technological and suburbanized society of the twentieth century.

BIBLIOGRAPHY

Faragher, John Mack. *Daniel Boone: The Life and Legend of an American Pioneer.* New York: Henry Holt, 1992.

Herman, Daniel J. "The Other Daniel Boone: The Nascence of a Middle-Class Hunter Hero, 1784-1860." *Journal of the Early Republic* 18, no. 3 (1998): 429–457.

Slotkin, Richard. *Regeneration through Violence: The Mythology of the American Frontier, 1600–1860.* Norman: University of Oklahoma Press, 2000.

FURTHER READING

Aron, Stephen. *How the West Was Lost: The Transformation of Kentucky from Daniel Boone to Henry Clay.* Baltimore: Johns Hopkins University Press, 1996.

Kimmel, Michael. *Manhood in America: A Cultural History.* New York: Free Press, 1996.

Sweeney, J. Gray. *The Columbus of the Woods: Daniel Boone and the Typology of Manifest Destiny.* St. Louis, Mo.: Washington University Gallery of Art, 1992.

RELATED ENTRIES

Advice Literature; Character; Crockett, Davy; Heroism; Hunting; Individualism; Leatherstocking Tales; Manifest Destiny; Market Revolution; Middle-Class Manhood; Outdoorsmen; Republicanism; Self-Made Man; Strenuous Life; Success Manuals; Western Frontier; Whiteness

—Bret E. Carroll

BOXING

Boxing matches in the United States have historically carried important symbolic meanings. They have highlighted ethnic differences, reflected racial divides, and served as high-profile expressions of national chauvinism. Above all, attitudes toward boxing have been keen indicators of popular ideas about American manhood.

Bare-knuckle boxing and other blood sports thrived in the sporting culture of the colonial South. Living in a violent and competitive world, men gathered in taverns to wager on and participate in bare-knuckle fights to settle differences and demonstrate such traits of southern manliness as physical strength and honor. Puritans and evangelical Protestants, however, condemned boxing as an unwholesome corruption of the human body and antithetical to the patriarchal values of hard work and familial responsibility.

During the second half of the nineteenth century, boxing began to become more widely accepted as an indicator of manliness. New England intellectuals, concerned that urbanization and industrialization threatened men's physical vigor, preached a "muscular Christianity" and cautiously embraced

Male spectators watch a boxing match between Irish-American heavyweight champion John L. Sullivan and Jake Kilrain in 1889. Boxing matches created homosocial environments in which spectators associated manhood with physical brawn, strenuous exertion, competitive sport, and, in many cases, ethnic identity. (From the collections of the Library of Congress)

sparring as a healthy tonic. Boxing and other athletic activities were incorporated into the Young Men's Christian Associations being established in northern cities. Still, middle-class Victorians continued to view prizefighting—literally, fighting for a prize—as antithetical to such traits of manliness as self-restraint and steady achievement.

The emerging working class, however, was defining its own ideals of masculinity and more fully embraced boxing. With the dissolution of the craftsman system and workplace autonomy, bourgeois calls for sobriety and self-discipline rang increasingly anachronistic to working-class sensibilities. Working-class men turned to an elemental form of masculine expression that rejected austerity and the regimented control over one's body, and instead celebrated the aggressive use of that body. The brawny prizefighter, hailed as a virile and valiant figure, was held up as the apogee of this new masculine ethos. Fight clubs began appearing in urban working-class neighborhoods nationwide.

The boxing arena itself was a masculine public space, but attendance at fights held different meanings for different men, depending on class and marital status. For the wealthy, a prizefight dramatized the ethos of individual competition and validated their own status as winners. For the laboring class, boxing matches were a celebration of brawn and skill and promised that toughness and dedication would be rewarded with heroic status. Married men attended the fights to reconnect with the bachelor subculture, while bachelors went to cultivate friendships and quasi-familial bonds grounded in the shared experience of sports spectatorship. For all men, the fights were a space where one could celebrate the autonomous man and enjoy membership in an all-male community. When, at the end of the nineteenth century, American boxing adopted the Marquess of Queensbury Rules, which mandated timed rounds and gloved fists, the sport seemed less brutal and more rational and began appealing to lower and upper classes equally.

While boxing forged a sporting family, nineteenth-century prizefights also served as physical allegories of ethnoreligious difference. In urban areas where white Protestant Americans resented competition from African American and

Irish-born men, prizefights between members of these rival groups were symbolic battles for group supremacy. At the pinnacle of these conflicts stood John L. Sullivan, the son of Irish immigrants, who seized the heavyweight title in 1882. Sullivan was a brawny figure whose prodigious feats appealed most especially to Irish-American men, but also to turn-of-the-century American men enamored with the notions of rugged individualism and the "strenuous life" promoted by Theodore Roosevelt.

When Jack Johnson became the first African-American heavyweight champion in 1908, black America rejoiced, while white America scurried to find a "Great White Hope" to defeat him. In an era when the heavyweight champion was held up as the pinnacle of American manhood, African Americans celebrated Johnson as a figure of masculine achievement who laid waste the doctrine of white supremacy. When Johnson defeated Jim Jeffries in a 1910 bout billed as a battle for racial supremacy, white mobs lynched black men, the press demanded that films of the fight be censored, and Progressive Era politicians sought to banish the sport.

Prizefighting underwent a renaissance in the 1920s, as the aftermath of World War I left many Americans longing for a more honorific era when men settled differences with their fists. The mass media soon transformed the sport into a commercial spectacle. Boxing's new cultural resonance resided in such iconic champions as "Manassa Mauler" Jack Dempsey, an itinerant brawler who personified the virility and impulsiveness of the Roaring Twenties and appealed to men mired in an emerging world of sedentary, white-collar work. Equally influential was black champion Joe Louis, whose 1936 knockout of the German boxer Max Schmeling was a high-profile battering of Nazi ideology. This symbolic victory of democracy and American manhood in the years immediately preceding World War II transformed the "Brown Bomber" from race hero to national treasure.

The postwar rise of television ushered in a brief golden age for boxing, as watching Friday night fights sponsored by beer and shaving-cream companies became a ritual linking viewers to a male-specific consumer culture. But the infatuation with televised boxing prompted the decline of the neighborhood fight club, and a deterioration of the quality of televised bouts due to a paucity of skilled fighters undercut boxing's hold on popular male consciousness. Equally damaging to the sport was a Congressional investigation revealing that boxers were forced to fix fights in order to get title shots.

Boxing and the racially-charged issues of masculinity associated with it were catapulted back into the public eye during the 1960s after the dynamic heavyweight Cassius Clay won the title in 1964. Soon after his victory over Sonny Liston, Clay embraced Islam and changed his name to Muhammad Ali. Against the backdrop of a civil rights movement in which black male activists adopted the slogan "I am a Man," Ali used the heavyweight title as a pulpit for a politicized masculine expression, presenting himself as the proud black athlete in militant revolt. His assertion of individual pride ("I am the greatest," he boasted), his outspokenness against racial injustice, and his refusal to serve in the Vietnam War emboldened liberal-minded individuals of all races. Ali's heavily hyped 1971 fight against Joe Frazier became a referendum on black masculinity itself, with Ali personifying the confrontational "Black Power" stance and Frazier representing quiet patriotism and duty. During the decades that followed, Latino men became a growing presence in professional boxing, and they likewise found in it a vehicle for asserting and forging definitions of manhood.

Questions about the relation between boxing and masculinity re-emerged in the late twentieth century when the controversial boxer Mike Tyson invoked contested ideas about the relationship between race, masculinity, and rage. Many Americans responded to Tyson's annihilation of the heavyweight division, his 1992 rape conviction, and his biting of an opponent by charging that the black male boxer represented a predatory and hypermasculine animalism. But others, particularly African-American men living in the context of urban deindustrialization, lionized "Iron Mike" as the embodiment of black working-class resiliency and authenticity.

The boxing ring has been contested cultural terrain, a masculine space in which claims of individual prowess and group honor are forcefully articulated and demeaning stereotypes are challenged. Boxing continues to resonate in tough, urban environments, where blacks, Latinos, and other young men disconnected from paths of social mobility hope to punch their way to the American Dream. For aspiring pugilists and the sport's many fans, boxing is a physical event in which violence is celebrated as art, fighters are considered the manifestation of American individualism, and champions are extolled as the most manly of men.

Bibliography

Gorn, Elliott J. *The Manly Art: Bare-Knuckle Prize Fighting in America.* Ithaca, N.Y.: Cornell University Press, 1986.

Hietala, Thomas R. *The Fight of the Century: Jack Johnson, Joe Louis, and the Struggle for Racial Equality.* Armonk, N.Y.: M. E. Sharpe, 2002.

Sammons, Jeffrey T. *Beyond the Ring: The Role of Boxing in American Society.* Urbana: University of Illinois Press, 1988.

Further Reading

Gorn, Elliot J. "The Manassa Mauler and the Fighting Marine: An Interpretation of the Dempsey-Tunney Fights." *Journal of American Studies* 19 (1985): 1, 27-47.

Levine, Peter. "'Oy Such a Fighter!': Boxing and the American Jewish Experience." In *The New American Sport History: Recent Approaches and Perspectives,* edited by S. W. Pope. Urbana: University of Illinois Press, 1997.

Marqusse, Mike. *Redemption Song: Muhammad Ali and the Spirit of the Sixties.* London: Verso, 1999.

Oates, Joyce Carol. *On Boxing.* Hopewell, N.J.: Ecco Press, 1995.

Roberts, Randy. *Papa Jack: Jack Johnson and the Era of White Hopes.* New York: The Free Press, 1983.

Related Entries

African-American Manhood; Bachelorhood; Body; Civil Rights Movement; Crisis of Masculinity; Democratic Manhood; Ethnicity: Heroism; Individualism; Irish-American Manhood; Leisure; Middle-Class Manhood; Muscular Christianity; Nationalism; Nativism; Passionate Manhood; Progressive Era; Race; Roosevelt, Theodore; Self-Made Man; Sports: Victorian Era; Violence; Working-Class Manhood

—*Matthew Andrews*

Boyhood

Throughout U.S. history, the meaning of boyhood—a life stage that begins when a male child becomes socialized to behaviors defined as masculine—has shifted along with changing definitions of manhood, varied along lines of class and region, and been transformed by changing social and economic circumstances. In the premodern patriarchal society of early America, boyhood typically ended in one's late teens with the achievement of economic independence. The onset of modernization in the nineteenth century, however, including industrialization and the development of a concept of adolescence, altered ideas about when boyhood ended. More constant have been the settings in which boyhood masculinity has been experienced (family, peer groups, school, work, and leisure) and a cultural ambivalence about whether boys' boisterous energies should be encouraged as essential to healthy masculine development or controlled for the sake of social order.

The Colonial Period

Native American boys lived in culturally diverse tribes, but their lives invariably involved preparation for manhood in societies whose reality was defined by cosmos, landscape, economy, and culture. Through ritual, oral stories, shaming, and the example of older men, they learned to hunt large game (a male task in most hunting tribes) and seek the required relationship with animal spirits. Typically, boyhood culminated in the vision quest, in which the boy separated from the group and sought contact with the animal spirits that would guide him through manhood. The use of ridicule and shaming to correct unsanctioned behavior remains central to the raising of boys in Native American cultures.

Euro-Americans, meanwhile, considered social stability to be dependent on social hierarchy and deferential respect for authority. They therefore believed boyhood should be devoted to learning proper obedience. Likewise, they believed that boyhood was to be spent acquiring the skills one would need to assume the responsibilities of manhood—defined as becoming established in a trade and achieving status as a head of household. Thus, boys typically worked from their early youth in their parents' household, contributing to their fathers' artisanal labor or doing agricultural work on the family farm—or else as servants or apprentices in other people's households.

Boyhood experience varied by region. For New England Puritans, it was shaped by the doctrine of infant depravity. Because Puritans considered boys naturally prone to sin, they severely punished rebelliousness so that boys might avoid damnation. They encouraged young males to seek the conversion and salvation they deemed necessary to full spiritual manhood. Most boys in the colonial and antebellum South, meanwhile, were raised in preparation for a manhood grounded in agrarianism and racial hierarchy. On plantations, white boyhood involved learning about honor, paternalistic care for slaves, plantation business, and such gentlemanly leisure activities as hunting and horse racing. For slaves, boyhood served as an introduction to the problematic nature of masculine identity as a slave: performing difficult and involuntary agricultural labor, living under the domination of whites, learning lessons in survival, and facing the possibility of separation from one's family.

Americans' understandings of child rearing—and thus of boyhood—began to change in the eighteenth century. With the growing influence of Enlightenment ideas and republican political philosophy, commentators on child rearing increasingly regarded boyhood as a stage of life in which the growing man developed the faculties of reason and judgment, as well as an understanding of the responsibilities of political citizenship, which was considered fundamental to manhood. Later, in the early nineteenth century, Romantic ideas of natural childhood purity and a growing challenge to the Calvinist doctrine of human depravity reinforced this more positive view of boyhood and encouraged the indulgence of natural boyhood playfulness as important to healthy manhood.

The Nineteenth Century

During the nineteenth century, industrialization and the growth of commercial capitalism had an impact on boyhood that, while always powerful, varied with social class. Among the middle class, particularly in the urbanizing Northeast and upper Midwest, child labor became less necessary to the domestic economy and family size decreased as economic production and the earning of income moved outside the home. As a result, boyhood became less devoted to preparing for a trade and more devoted to moral nurture and education in preparation for the entrepreneurial or professional activities now associated with manhood.

Concerned that competitive capitalism and the increasing impersonality of an urbanizing, commercializing society encouraged amorality and threatened social cohesion, middle-class Victorian Americans came to believe that the proper masculine development of boys required substantial domestic influence. Mothers, in particular, defined as models of moral purity and piety, would teach boys moral restraint and self-control. At the same time, boys were encouraged to develop a separate boy culture grounded in adventure and demonstrations of courage outside the home and in the company of other boys. Reflected in such literary works as *Adventures of Tom Sawyer* (1876) and *Adventures of Huckleberry Finn* (1884), this boy culture was considered essential to the development of the individualism and competitiveness that boys would need to become economically successful men. This culture survived through the twentieth century.

For boys outside the urban middle class, boyhood was very different. In rural areas, boys continued to experience more traditional styles of boyhood: they helped with farm chores, hunted small game, and fished. For working-class and immigrant boys in the nation's growing industrial cities, whose labor was still necessary to their families' economic survival, masculine identity was forged through labor and games played on the streets—and sometimes through acts of vandalism and delinquency. For immigrant boys, boyhood in the American city meant acculturation into value systems often radically different from those of their fathers, and the resulting strains in familial relationships often intensified as boys grew older.

The Late Nineteenth and Early Twentieth Centuries

During the late nineteenth and early twentieth centuries, modernization continued to transform the meaning and experience of boyhood, and boyhood became a focus of increasingly anxious concern. One source of concern was the belief that maternal influence and urban-industrial "overcivilization" had sissified white middle-class American boys by minimizing their physical labor, outdoor activity, and fatherly influence. Such anxieties generated the growth of organized sport for boys, the establishment of the Boy Scouts of America (1910) and similar organizations, and a growing movement to encourage fathers to increase their involvement in their sons' lives—all of which were intended to use disciplined activity to raise boys into healthy men characterized by physical and mental toughness rather than excessive emotionalism and sentimentalism.

Psychologists reached similar conclusions about boys' development. Granville Stanley Hall suggested that male development from boyhood to adulthood recapitulated the evolution of human society from a primitive to an increasingly civilized state. He therefore encouraged the channeled release of aggressive and competitive boyhood impulses as necessary to the achievement of well-adjusted manhood and the curtailment of juvenile destructiveness. Influenced by such thinking, Progressive reformers seeking to alleviate crime and delinquency among working-class and immigrant boys grounded their efforts in the belief that the nation's cities needed to provide "safe" outlets for boyhood playfulness. Too many urban boys, they argued, were exposed to dangerous notions of masculine behavior on the streets or in theaters.

The belief that the transition from boyhood to manhood required discipline and the suppression of behaviors defined as "feminine" remained powerful through the early decades of the twentieth century. In his influential *Psychological Care of Infant and Child* (1928), the psychologist John B. Watson urged parents to treat boys as young adults who had to follow specific rules and regulations, and to respond to disobedience with severe punishment. Boys, he said, should be taught to be tough, control their feelings, avoid playing with dolls, and resist asking for sympathy or expressing fear. This model of boyhood, according to Watson, would prepare boys to inherit the patriarchal system of power.

For African-American boys, meanwhile, boyhood was shaped by experiences of racism, segregation, and the denial of equal educational opportunity. Although schools and colleges for blacks began to appear during Reconstruction and school attendance increased greatly during the early twentieth century, inferior schooling and a focus on vocational training for blue-collar jobs produced many learning deficiencies and low expectations. The African-American novelist Richard Wright's autobiographical *Black Boy* (1945) suggests that African-American boyhood in this period involved choosing between resistance and submission to racism, as well as the growing frustration and alienation that came with realizing that the achievement of full manhood was difficult, if not impossible, in white America. School desegregation in the wake of the Supreme Court case *Brown v. Board of Education of Topeka* (1954), combined with the impact of the 1964 Civil Rights Act and Operation Head Start, a federal program aimed at educating poor urban youth, began to alter the nature of African-American boyhood by improving education and increasing opportunity. But even into the early twenty-first century, the appeal of gang activity and drugs (also a problem for other groups of boys) suggested that alienation remained a concern for many African-American boys.

For both white and black boys, growing public school attendance during the early to mid-twentieth century—reaching 74.8 percent of five- to nineteen-year-olds by 1940 and 88.6 percent by 1960—effectively increased the influence of peer groups on their behavior and their ideas of desirable male conduct. For the sons of immigrants, who were exposed to and encouraged in "American" patterns of thought and behavior, such social interactions increased the cultural distance between them and their parents. Likewise, all boys learned generationally specific behaviors that they believed distinguished them from their fathers.

Boyhood in Postwar America

During and after World War II, as American leaders sought to bolster and demonstrate American toughness in the face of fascist militarism and Soviet communism, Watson's concept of masculinity grew more prevalent. Both popular culture and politicians encouraged patriotism and a martial spirit among the nation's boys. During the Cold War, in particular, as fears of internal and external threats to American society mounted, boys were taught to conform to social mores, obey social and political authority, and avoid such "deviant" behaviors as juvenile delinquency, homosexuality, and communism. In an increasingly corporatized economy and society, experts advised social acceptance as necessary to success. Fathers were deemed especially important to the effort to raise a nation of strong, well-adjusted boys.

Postwar economic expansion also allowed consumerism to play an ever larger role in shaping ideals of masculinity, and American boys, often in the company of their peers, consumed ideas about appropriate manliness in a variety of forms. They viewed models of rugged masculine individualism in movie theaters, to which they flocked to see Westerns and war films; on television, where they saw the adventures of western frontiersman Davy Crockett; and in such consumer goods as coonskin caps and G.I. Joe toy soldiers. They also watched television programs such as *The Adventures of Ozzie and Harriet* (1952–66) and *Leave It to Beaver* (1957–63), which portrayed idealized families and interactions between boys and their fathers intended to convey lessons about appropriate masculine behavior. As men became increasingly inclined to define their manhood through their leisure activities and domestic lives, and as they sought to minimize effeminacy and deviance in their sons, boys spent more time with their fathers in such activities as camping, fishing, and other forms of sport, and organizations devoted to encouraging activities between boys and their fathers multiplied.

At the same time, however, some experts sought to inspire a different type of masculinity among American boys. In *The Common Sense Book of Baby and Child Care* (1946), one of the most influential books ever written on American childhood, Dr. Benjamin Spock rejected the militaristic approach to child rearing in favor of an affectionate, nurturing style of parenting. Spock argued that boys should express love toward family and friends, be unrestricted in their emotions, accept crying as an entirely normal behavior, and temper aggression with sensitivity to others.

This challenge to conventional notions of boyhood emotional suppression gained momentum during the 1960s and 1970s, when a growing youth counterculture, an increasingly powerful feminist movement, and an emerging men's movement all questioned traditional models of masculinity. As members of these movements urged men to devote more time to household responsibility, to avoid identifying their manhood too closely with their work, and to become aware of their emotions, they argued that boyhood experience should foster a more nurturing, more sensitive, and less competitive model of manhood. By the end of the twentieth century, such calls took on added urgency amid growing fears that conventional models generated school violence, gang membership, lawlessness, and other destructive patterns of behavior. These fears were reinforced by growing divorce rates, parental abdication in dual-income families, the influence of peer groups, and violence in such consumer products as movies, television programs, rap music, and video games. This new anxiety about American boyhood was exemplified by the popularity of William Pollack's best-selling *Real Boys: Rescuing Our Sons from the Myths of Boyhood* (1998), which examined the primary causes of male behavior problems and offered advice on contemporary child-rearing techniques. At the beginning of the twenty-first century, then, the meaning of boyhood, like that of masculinity itself, was at a crossroads.

BIBLIOGRAPHY

Beales, Ross W., Jr. "In Search of the Historical Child: Miniature Adulthood and Youth in Colonial New England." *American Quarterly* 27, no. 4 (1975): 379–398.

Fass, Paul S., and Mary Ann Mason, eds. *Childhood in America.* New York: New York University Press, 2000.

Garbarino, James. *Lost Boys: Why Our Sons Turn Violent and How We Can Save Them.* New York: Free Press, 1999.

Hiner, N. Ray, and Joseph M. Hawes. *Growing Up in America.* Chicago: University of Illinois Press, 1985.

Hoff Sommers, Christina. *The War against Boys: How Misguided Feminism is Harming Our Young Men.* New York: Simon & Schuster, 2000.

Kindlon, Daniel J., and Michael Thompson, with Teresa Barker. *Raising Cain: Protecting the Emotional Life of Boys.* New York: Ballantine Books, 1999.

Maccoby, Eleanor. *The Two Sexes: Growing Up Apart, Coming Together.* Cambridge, Mass.: Belknap Press, 1998.

Pollack, William. *Real Boys: Rescuing Our Sons from the Myths of Boyhood.* New York: Random House, 1998.

Rotundo, E. Anthony. *American Manhood: Transformation in Masculinity from the Revolution to the Modern Era.* New York: Basic Books, 1993.

West, Elliott. *Growing Up in Twentieth Century America: A History and Reference Guide.* Westport, Conn.: Greenwood Press, 1996.

Wright, Richard. B*lack Boy: A Record of Childhood and Youth.* New York: World Publishing, 1945.

FURTHER READING

Bremner, Robert H, ed. *Children and Youth in America: A Documentary History.* Cambridge, Mass.: Harvard University Press, 1974.

Cable, Mary. *The Little Darlings: A History of Child Rearing in America.* New York: Scribners, 1975.

Graff, Harvey J. *Conflicting Paths: Growing Up in America.* Cambridge, Mass.: Harvard University Press, 1995.

Graff, Harvey J., ed. *Growing Up in America: Historical Experiences.* Detroit: Wayne State University Press, 1987.

King, Wilma. *Stolen Childhood: Slave Youth in Nineteenth-Century America.* Bloomington: Indiana University Press, 1995.

Macleod, David I. "Act Your Age: Boyhood, Adolescence, and the Rise of the Boy Scouts of America." *Journal of Social History* 16, no. 2 (1982): 3–20.

———. *The Age of the Child: Children in America, 1890-1920.* New York: Twayne, 1998.

Rotundo, E. Anthony. "Boy Culture: Middle-Class Boyhood in Nineteenth-Century America." In *Meanings for Manhood: Constructions of Masculinity in Victorian America,* edited by Mark C. Carnes and Clyde Griffen. Chicago: University of Chicago Press, 1990.

West, Elliott. *Growing Up in Twentieth-Century America: A History and Reference Guide.* Westport, Conn.: Greenwood, 1996.

RELATED ENTRIES

Adolescence; *Adventures of Huckleberry Finn*; Baseball; Boone, Daniel; Boy Scouts of America; *Common Sense Book of Baby and Child Care, The*; Crockett, Davy; Fatherhood; *Father Knows Best;* Fishing; Gangs; Hall, Granville Stanley; *Home Improvement;* Juvenile Delinquency; *Leave It to Beaver*; Mother–Son Relationships; Progressive Era; Romanticism; Sawyer, Tom; Sports; Television; Wright, Richard; Young Men's Christian Association; Youth

—Bret E. Carroll and Annette Richardson

BOY SCOUTS OF AMERICA

The Boy Scouts of America (BSA) was founded in 1910 as an organized youth movement meant to revitalize American manhood. Based on a philosophy of "muscular Christianity," the group created a practical program of activities meant to develop the young man's physical, mental, and moral fitness.

At the beginning of the twentieth century, devastating economic cycles, immigration, and urbanization generated anxiety among white middle-class men about the future of American manhood. Just as the military hero Lord Robert S. S. Baden-Powell created the Boy Scouts in England in 1908 to toughen young British men in physical fitness and moral character, so the men who founded the BSA worried that an increasingly urban, industrial civilization was distancing men from the positive effects of the more primitive wilderness. They also feared that the increasing influence of women in the domestic sphere and in more public roles, such as teaching, was leading to a feminization of American boyhood.

In 1910 several men gathered to create the BSA, including Ernest Thompson Seton, the founder of the Woodcraft Indians, a youth movement and organization based on Native American cultures; Daniel Carter Beard, who had founded the Sons of Daniel Boone, an organization for boys based on pioneer life; and three men with extensive experience in the Young Men's Christian Association (YMCA)—Edgar M. Robinson, John L. Alexander, and James E. West. Borrowing heavily from Baden-Powell's ideas, the BSA also Americanized the movement in its first Handbook (1911) and in the design of its uniform, ranks, badges, and programs.

The BSA bases its programs on the idea of the "patrol," which typically consists of eight boys who form the basic friendship group in a larger "troop" of patrols. Adult men serve as scoutmasters of troops (usually sponsored by schools, religious organizations, and fraternal organizations), and boys ages eleven through seventeen fill the leadership positions in the troop and in patrols. Boys learn to lead other boys and to teach each other a range of skills, including first aid, camping, lifesaving, and other skills for living. The program also stresses character training, including service to others.

Through most of its history, the BSA has enjoyed great public support and admiration for its work. The Eagle Scout, the organization's highest earned rank, is widely recognized as a mark of fine manhood. The organization became very popular in the 1950s, especially for white middle-class boys, and the BSA's fusing of citizenship, patriotism, masculinity, and America's "public religion" (a generalized Judeo-Christian, largely Protestant, ethic) suited the culture of the Cold War. The antimilitary and antiestablishment culture of the Vietnam War era, however, began to make the BSA a more controversial organization, and by the 1980s the BSA was defending itself against a series of lawsuits. Atheists sued the BSA when they were denied membership, and girls and women sued to be admitted to the organization. The most visible controversy in the 1990s was the battle over the BSA policy of excluding openly gay men and boys from membership. In June 2000, a five-to-four split decision by the U.S. Supreme Court affirmed the BSA's position that they are a private organization with the right to exclude members whose beliefs and practices differ significantly from the official philosophy and goals of the organization. The court's decision did not settle the controversy, however, and social and political organizations, such as Scouting for All, still work to get the BSA to change its policies on admitting gays and atheists. Various local governments and charitable organizations have struggled with conflicts between their own antidiscrimination rules and the special status they have accorded BSA troops.

Although the BSA has tried to respond to social changes and move beyond its white, middle-class base, the BSA stands on the side of traditional values in the so-called culture wars. Its 1990s advertising slogan, "Character Counts," and its stress on male honor reflect the nineteenth-century values of its origins. As in the 1890s, the middle class in the United States in the 1990s felt grave concern about white, middle-class, heterosexual masculinity, and a number of popular books and magazine articles addressed the worries of parents, teachers,

A boy scout at the U.S. Capitol delivering U.N. posters in support of the war effort in 1941. This image illustrates the masculine ideal of citizenship, patriotism, and physical and moral fitness that the Boy Scouts of America sought to cultivate in boys. (From the collections of the Library of Congress)

coaches, and youth workers over American society's impact on the development of boys. The BSA, an organization that has registered over 100 million members since its founding, had over four million American members in 2002, and it continues to find itself at the center of the public debate over the meaning of American boyhood and manhood.

Bibliography

Macleod, David I. *Building Character in the American Boy: The Boy Scouts, YMCA, and Their Forerunners, 1870–1920.* Madison: University of Wisconsin Press, 1983.

Mechling, Jay. *On My Honor: Boy Scouts and the Making of American Youth.* Chicago: University of Chicago Press, 2001.

Further Reading

Hunter, James Davison. *Culture Wars: The Struggle to Define America.* New York: Basic Books, 1991.

———. *Death of Character: Moral Education in an Age Without Good or Evil.* New York: Basic Books, 2000.

Related Entries

Boyhood; Citizenship; Cold War; Crisis of Masculinity; Heterosexuality; Homosexuality; Industrialization; Leisure; Muscular Christianity; Patriotism; Religion and Spirituality; Urbanization; Young Men's Christian Association; Youth

—*Jay Mechling*

Brando, Marlon

1924–
American Movie Star

A major Hollywood star during the second half of the twentieth century, Marlon Brando has offered American audiences complex models of masculinity that reflect various transformations in American society. His characters have suggested the impact of postwar alienation and changing conceptions of sexuality in America.

Brando's portrayals resonated with broader contemporary cultural messages and debates about masculinity during the 1950s. On the one hand, McCarthyism and Cold War rhetoric demanded adherence to traditional concepts of familial and nationalist virility. But at the same time, new cultural currents generated different understandings of masculine behavior. The Kinsey Report's research on male sexuality (1948) located sexuality at the center of masculine identity; *Playboy* magazine, first published in 1953, made the distribution of sexually suggestive material more popular and socially acceptable; and the Beat Generation challenged mainstream values by identifying nonconformity, unrestrained sexuality, and homosexuality as acceptable male behaviors. Brando's characters embodied these conflicting understandings of American manliness.

Brando's first role reveals the fragility and vulnerability of postwar masculinity. In the significantly titled *The Men* (1950), Brando plays a paraplegic war veteran who learns bitter lessons about male identity while readjusting to American society. The lead character's broken body exposes the dependency (on women) lying beneath the contemporary veneer of macho posturing. Similarly, as Stanley Kowalski in *A Streetcar Named Desire* (1951), Brando's swaggering, loud-mouthed, working-class antihero displays an aggressive masculinity that masks his insecurities. Kowalski's rape of his sister-in-law Blanche represents not so much the triumph of the brute male as an effort to destroy the feminine he fears within himself.

Throughout the late 1950s and 1960s, Brando's roles continued to reflect the insecurities and fears of Cold War society. His characters offered a tough, autonomous, and sometimes (as in 1953's *The Wild One*) rebellious exterior, while at the same time challenging images of American men as securely patriarchal. They also questioned body-centered ideals of manly toughness through severe beatings—as in *On the Waterfront* (1954), Brando's self-directed *One-Eyed Jacks* (1961), and *The Chase* (1966).

The combination of a macho facade and personal vulnerability appears in his portrayal of the homosexual Major Pendleton in *Reflections in a Golden Eye* (1967). Brando's ambivalence about the relationship between masculinity and homosexuality is suggested by the officer's closeted and obsessive fascination with an army private, as well as his character's misogyny. Despite the film's release date, the depiction owes more to 1950s repressiveness than to the influence of the counterculture of the 1960s.

While Brando's troubled characters confronted the disintegration of "official" masculinity during the 1950s and the further fragmentation of male identity during the Sexual Revolution of the 1960s, his major movies of the 1970s closely associated him with patriarchy and aggressiveness. Most notable in this respect are his Oscar-winning portrayal of Don Vito Corleone in Francis Ford Coppola's *The Godfather* (1972), and his fiercely independent military commander Colonel Kurtz in the same director's *Apocalypse Now* (1979). Yet the self-loathing and sexual disgust memorably encapsulated on screen in *Last Tango in Paris* (1972) suggest Brando's continuing challenge to self-assured manhood. The spectacular declension of Brando's physique during and after the 1970s—the subject of considerable public notice and comment—may be read as a potent symbol of Brando's persistent ambivalence about the meaning of American masculinity.

Bibliography

Anderson, Lindsay. "The Last Sequence of On the Waterfront." In *Coming to Terms with Hollywood,* edited by Jim Cook and Alan Lovell. London: British Film Institute, 1981.

Downing, David. *Marlon Brando.* New York: Stein and Day, 1984.

Klinger, Barbara. *Melodrama and Meaning: History, Culture, and the Films of Douglas Sirk.* Bloomington: Indiana University Press, 1994.

MacKinnon, Kenneth. *Love, Tears, and the Male Spectator.* Madison, N.J.: Fairleigh Dickinson University Press, 2002.

Naremore, James. "Marlon Brando in On the Waterfront." In *Film and Theory: An Anthology,* edited by Robert Stam and Toby Miller. Malden, Mass.: Blackwell, 2000.

Further Reading

Biskind, Peter. *Seeing is Believing: How Hollywood Taught Us to Stop Worrying and Love the Fifties.* New York: Henry Holt, 2000.

Hanks, Pamela Anne. "The Viewer's Role in Filmed Versions of A Streetcar Named Desire." *Journal of Popular Film and Television* 14 (1986): 114-122.

MacKinnon, Kenneth. *Uneasy Pleasures: The Male as Erotic Object.* London: Cygnus Arts, 1997.

McCann, Graham. *Rebel Males: Clift, Brando, and Dean.* New Brunswick, N.J.: Rutgers University Press, 1993.

Reeves, Saskia. "Caged Birds." *Sight and Sound* 6 (1996): 61.

Related Entries

Beat Movement; Cold War; Dean, James; Hollywood; Homosexuality; *Playboy* Magazine; Sensitive Male; Violence; Working-Class Manhood

—*Kenneth MacKinnon*

Breadwinner Role

Since the nineteenth century, the ideal of the breadwinner role designated men as solely responsible for supporting their wives and children. Failure to meet this ideal (and subsequent reliance on the incomes of wife and children) publicly demonstrated a husband's failure as a provider—and as a man. Although the increasing number of women in the workforce since the 1960s has effectively challenged the male's role as the sole breadwinner, providing for a family remains integral to an understanding of masculinity in America.

The Colonial Period and the Nineteenth Century

In colonial America, the family was the dominant unit of production. Although male heads of household were theoretically responsible for the economic and material well-being of their families, economic sustenance was assured through the labor of the entire family. In most cases, fathers and husbands were the sole property owners and controlled their wives' wages or money (if they had any). It was not until the nineteenth century, however, that men became exclusively accountable for the economic comfort of their families, and that women become excluded (in theory at least) from productive labor.

The ideal of the male breadwinner as the primary economic provider and reliable family man emerged during the market revolution of the early to mid-nineteenth century, as economic production ceased to occur within the home and increasingly became a male activity taking place in the public realm. Men, particularly those of the emerging middle class, now traveled to work, leaving their wives and children within the confines of the home. The division between male public realms and female private realms—what historians have called the "cult of domesticity"—mirrored divisions of responsibility between husbands and wives. Men were now responsible for earning enough money for the entire family, while wives oversaw household duties, child rearing, and consumption. Both publicly and privately—through success in the world of business and in providing for one's family—the role of primary breadwinner became a key marker of middle-class manhood. It also became a potential source of anxiety and self-doubt for men, for failing at business in the precarious boom-and-bust economy of antebellum America meant failing as a breadwinner, and thus as a man.

Many middle-class men and highly skilled workers adhered to (or attempted to adhere to) the ideal of the male breadwinner, but for most semiskilled and unskilled workers the ideal remained unattainable. Throughout the nineteenth century, most working-class families required the incomes of children and wives for at least part of the year in order to maintain even a low level of subsistence. Until after World War I, depressions, unemployment, and consistent job insecurity threatened skilled working men's positions as economic providers and household heads, and made semiskilled and unskilled men's adherence to the breadwinner norm seem increasingly untenable. But the ideal remained central to the aspirations of working-class men, strongly influencing the agendas of the emerging labor unions. At the turn of the twentieth century, for example, United Mine Workers president John Mitchell argued that job insecurity and low wages not only undermined workers' independence, but also infantilized and emasculated male workers by forcing "full-grown men [to] stay home minding babies or mending stockings" while their wives and older children worked for the family wage (Mitchell, 26). Similarly, American Federation of Labor president Samuel Gompers insisted that men earn sufficient incomes to provide their families with comfort as well as sustenance, pointing out in an 1890 issue of the *Louisville Courier Journal* that a working man "wants to have . . . a pretty picture on the wall, or perhaps a piano or organ in his parlor," as well as a well-dressed wife (Kaufman, 311).

At the turn of the twentieth century, large numbers of working women began to challenge the image of the male breadwinner, insisting that they be able to earn and manage their own wages. These women linked consumption with economic independence, something middle-class social reformers often found quite troubling. Fearing that boisterous young women would not become suitable wives for breadwinners, reformers often sought to redirect working women's recreational activities toward more domestic pursuits. Belief in the social and economic primacy of the male breadwinner among both the working class and the middle class effectively marginalized the importance of female wage work. Some reformers insisted that women not work at all, while others, assuming that women's labor was either temporary or secondary to a male breadwinner's, felt that women did not need to be paid as much as men. The adherence of craft unions to the ideal of breadwinner masculinity meant that they were often ambivalent about supporting female workers' demands for higher or equal wages. Instead, they joined with middle-class reformers to push for legislation protecting women workers from long hours or especially harsh working conditions.

The Twentieth Century

The rise of skilled workers' incomes in the first decades of the twentieth century, as well as the increase in stable, long-term, white-collar jobs for middle-class men, reinforced the ideal of the male breadwinner. For middle-class men, in particular, the emergence of professional career paths and consistent, well-paid employment strengthened the connection between breadwinning, consumerism, and middle-class masculinity. The correlation of manhood and breadwinner was so strong through most of the twentieth century that many men felt their masculinity to be seriously threatened by unemployment during the Great Depression (as they had by the depressions of the nineteenth century). Many Americans, including employers, social reformers, and union members, sought to bolster the vulnerable male-breadwinner role by removing women from the workforce. They even accused working women of taking jobs away from men and subverting the "proper" social order. Unemployed men, feeling their manliness weakened by their failure to live up to the breadwinner norm (a feeling sometimes reinforced by critical wives measuring them by that standard) were often emotionally traumatized. A contemporary psychiatrist explained that "[t]he women punished the men. . . . [These men] felt despised, they were ashamed of themselves" (Kimmel, 200).

The increase in jobs during and after World War II removed the specter of unemployment for many American men. To ensure that men could return to their "proper" place as breadwinners after the war, the majority of women who had entered the workforce during the 1940s were quickly laid off. Movies like *Tender Comrade* (1943), in which Ginger Rogers plays a defense-plant worker pining for her husband to return so that everything can go back to normal, further emphasized the supposed naturalness of men's reclaiming jobs from women by showing wives happily exchanging work pants and tools for dresses and domestic duties.

The Postwar Period

During the 1950s, economic prosperity and the growth of suburbia continued to bolster the ability of middle- and working-class men to conform to the breadwinner ideal, while also increasing pressure on breadwinning fathers to supply their families with consumer goods. Faced with threats of global war and nuclear holocaust during the Cold War, Americans found reassurance in the perceived stability of the patriarchal, nuclear family as depicted in the new medium of television, which attempted to reinforce male breadwinning as both natural and the normative American experience. Television series such as *Life with Father* (1953) depicted the prototypical suburban family: upper-middle-class working father, cheerful homemaker mother, and three happy children. The father, Jim Anderson, exemplified the masculinity of the new middle-class breadwinner. He demonstrated his masculinity not through an exciting or daring job (he worked as an advertising executive) but through acceptance of his responsibility to earn a living for his family. Some men no doubt chafed at the dull routine of their lives, but in the 1950s, according to sociologist Talcott Parsons, "virtually the only way to be a real man in our society [was] to have an adequate job and earn a living" (Kimmel, 245).

Despite popular images of male breadwinners and unemployed wives, the social realities of the 1950s directly challenged the male breadwinner's primacy in the home and workplace. In the mid-1950s, married women joined the workforce in increasing numbers, and 30 percent of married women were working for a salary by 1960. Employment rates increased the most among middle-class women during this period.

Nonetheless, Americans continued to believe in the norm of the male breadwinner. The welfare state reinforced this belief, consistently assuming that male heads of households were the main economic provider for the family. Consequently, the federal government favored workman's compensation and unemployment insurance (both designed to protect a man's family in hard economic times) over aid to mothers (especially mothers' pensions) and children. Daniel Patrick Moynihan, in his 1965 report *The Negro Family: A Case for National Action*, charged that African-American poverty was the result of too few fathers, and reformers have continually upheld the male breadwinner norm and blamed African-American poverty on "irresponsible" men. Moynihan used African-American men and families as foils through which to associate non-normative masculinity (absence of breadwinner identity) with non-normative family life, implicitly bolstering the seemingly endangered ideal of breadwinner masculinity.

Conclusion

The male breadwinner has gradually disappeared from American life, although the ideal retains a powerful hold on the popular imagination. In 1960, 70 percent of American families corresponded to the ideal of the male breadwinner and the unemployed wife. By the end of the twentieth century, however, only about 15 percent of families conformed to this ideal, with approximately 60 percent of white married women in the workforce.

A 2001 study conducted by Pennsylvania State University concluded that men whose wives earned more than they did suffered a "decline in well-being." Some psychiatrists have labeled this psychological distress breadwinner anxiety, a condition that includes ailments such as panic attacks, excessive worry, sleep problems, and fear of sexual inadequacy. Such anxieties suggest that, despite the large number of two-income families, the male breadwinner role remains an integral part of American men's sense of their masculinity.

BIBLIOGRAPHY

Hartman, Susan M. "Women's Employment and the Domestic Ideal in the Early Cold War Years." In *Not June Cleaver: Women and Gender in Postwar America, 1945–1960,* edited by Joanne Meyerowitz. Philadelphia: Temple University Press, 1994.

Kaufman, Stuart B., et al, eds. *The Samuel Gompers Papers.* Vol. 2. Urbana: University of Illinois Press, 1987.

Kimmel, Michael. *Manhood in America: A Cultural History.* New York: Free Press, 1996.

May, Elaine Tyler. *Homeward Bound: American Families in the Cold War Era.* New York: Basic Books, 1999.

Mintz, Steven. "Mothers and Fathers in America: Looking Backward, Looking Forward." Gilder Lehrman Institute of American History. <http://www.gliah.uh.edu/historyonline/mothersfathers.cfm> (January 6, 2003).

Mitchell, John. *Organized Labor: Its Problems, Purposes and Ideals and The Present and Future of American Wage Earners.* Philadelphia: American Book and Bible House, 1903.

Peiss, Kathy. *Cheap Amusements: Working Women and Leisure in Turn-of-the-Century New York.* Philadelphia: Temple University Press, 1986.

Rogers, Daniel T. *The Work Ethic in Industrial America, 1850–1920.* Chicago: University of Chicago Press, 1978.

Rogers, S. J., and D. D. DeBoer. "Changes in Wives' Income: Effects on Marital Happiness, Psychological Well-Being, and the Risk of Divorce." *Journal of Marriage and the Family* 63, no. 2 (2001): 458–472.

FURTHER READING

Blumin, Stuart M. *The Emergence of the Middle Class: Social Experience in the American City, 1760–1900.* New York: Cambridge University Press, 1989.

Enstad, Nan. *Ladies of Labor, Girls of Adventure: Working Women, Popular Culture, and Labor Politics at the Turn of the Twentieth Century.* New York: Columbia University Press, 1999.

Ginzberg, Lori D. *Women and the Work of Benevolence: Morality, Politics, and Class in the Nineteenth-Century United States.* New Haven, Conn.: Yale University Press, 1990.

Griswold, Robert L. *Fatherhood in America: A History.* New York: Basic Books, 1993.

Kessler-Harris, Alice. *Out to Work: A History of Wage-Earning Women in the United States.* New York: Oxford University Press, 1982.

Laurie, Bruce. *Artisans into Workers: Labor in Nineteenth-Century America.* Urbana: University of Illinois Press, 1997.

Milkman, Ruth. *Gender at Work: The Dynamics of Job Segregation by Sex during World War II.* Urbana: University of Illinois Press, 1987.

Montgomery, David. *Citizen Worker: The Experience of Workers in the United States with Democracy and the Free Market during the Nineteenth Century.* Cambridge, England: Cambridge University Press, 1993.

Rotundo, E. Anthony. *American Manhood: Transformations in Masculinity from the Revolution to the Modern Era.* New York: Basic Books, 1993.

Skocpol, Theda. *Protecting Soldiers and Mothers: The Political Origins of Social Policy in the United States.* Cambridge, Mass.: Belknap Press, 1992.

RELATED ENTRIES

Artisan; Consumerism; Cult of Domesticity; Fatherhood; Great Depression; Industrialization; Labor Movement and Unions; *Leave It to Beaver*; Market Revolution; Marriage; Middle-Class Manhood; New Deal; Patriarchy; Property; Suburbia; Television; Work; Working-Class Manhood

—*Rosanne Currarino*

BUDDY FILMS

Whether categorized as road movies, Westerns, comedies, or cop action films, all buddy films embrace the same premise: two men of differing personalities and/or backgrounds are thrown together, and their initial lack of understanding of one another is eventually transformed into friendship and mutual respect. Buddy films negotiate crises of masculinity centered on questions of class, race, and gender, and they tend to conclude with a narrative resolution of these questions through the buddies' acceptance of each other's differences. They offer male movie-going audiences an opportunity to indulge in a form of male bonding and behavior usually discouraged by social constraints.

For the most part, the desire for male bonding is a feature particular to American society; the popular culture of other Western nations tend not to share this preoccupation with the intimacy of the male bond, focusing instead on the male–female romantic relationship or the heroism of the individual male. American popular culture is replete with texts concerned with the potency of the male bond in the face of danger and the empowerment each man experiences as part of the male duo. In buddy films, the male–female romantic couple is replaced with the male–male couple, setting up a contemplation of intimacy relatively free from social convention and entirely without need for a sexual/marital union at the end of the film. The genre has followed a general development, featuring mainly comedy duos until the 1960s, outlaws in the late 1960s, biracial cop action heroes in the 1980s, sensitive males in the early 1990s, and male–female detectives in the late 1990s.

Until the 1960s, comedic male couples dominated the buddy film genre. These include Laurel and Hardy and Abbott and Costello in the 1930s, Bing Crosby and Bob Hope in the 1940s, Dean Martin and Jerry Lewis in the 1950s, and Walter Matthau and Jack Lemmon in the 1960s in *The Odd Couple* (1969). The 1960s and 1970s witnessed two overlapping shifts in the buddy film. First, feminist gains and an incipient men's movement prompted more serious dramatic, and sometimes tragic, explorations of male friendship. Second, a widespread questioning of social institutions, a celebration of youthful and rebellious individualism, and Hollywood's attempt to attract young audiences spawned films focusing on outlaws whose adventures reflected a desire for freedom from the domestic restraints imposed by women and society. Both shifts were evident in such films as *Butch Cassidy and the Sundance Kid* (1969), *Easy Rider* (1969), *Midnight Cowboy* (1969), *Thunderbolt and Lightfoot* (1974), and *Dog Day Afternoon* (1975).

During the 1980s, in the midst of President Ronald Reagan's right-wing politics and intensified Cold War concerns, buddies became law-enforcing action heroes, often with pumped-up bodies and violent tendencies. These action heroes blended masculinity, heroism, and patriotism into an idealized image, and their bodies became sites for articulating national concerns through repeated physical injuries. In a reflection of the advancement of African Americans in the decade following the civil rights movement, these action-hero buddies tended to consist of a biracial couple, most notably Eddie Murphy and Nick Nolte in the *48 Hours* films and Mel Gibson and Danny Glover in the *Lethal Weapon* films. In this subgenre, pioneered by the television series *I Spy* in the 1960s, the African-American character is typically the sidekick to the white hero and isolated from the African-American community. He thus offers his skills and bravery for the preservation of mainstream (white) cultural values. The sidekick is presented in stereotypical terms, either as a representative of black subculture through his behavior and taste in music and clothes (e.g., Eddie Murphy in *48 Hours* [1982]), or as a domesticated, professional, devoted father and husband (e.g., Danny Glover in *Lethal Weapon* [1987]).

Biracial buddy films explore issues of masculinity by moving women to the periphery and exploring the differing personalities and racial backgrounds of the two male heroes. Each man comes to realize the value of the other because of his difference, and both experience personal growth and empowerment through the male bond they forge while fighting their common enemy. Despite the exploration of racial differences, however, the emphasis on shared masculinity and the heroes' eventual acceptance of each other suppress, rather than expose, issues of race.

In the 1990s, the violent and retributive hero of the 1980s was replaced by the sensitive male, and masculinity in film became less idealized and more realistic. Some buddy films—such as *The Fisher King* (1991) and *The Shawshank Redemption* (1994)—contemplated a masculinity that required sensitive relations between men. But the on-screen preoccupation with male bonding seemed to lessen in the 1990s, and the buddy film developed new permutations, including the female–female couple (as in *Thelma and Louise* [1991]) and the male–female platonic couple (as in *The Pelican Brief* [1993]). The male–male biracial couple was transformed as well, most notably in the *Rush Hour* films that teamed the Hong Kong action star Jackie Chan and the African-American comedian Chris Tucker. These shifts reflect both Hollywood's desire to attract broader audiences and the advances made by women and ethnic minorities toward greater representation and equality in American society. In particular, the shift away from physically imposing white male heroes reflects the empowerment of minority masculinities and the valuation of vulnerability over violence.

Buddy films have changed to reflect shifting social and cultural concerns involving race, class, and gender. Yet despite these differences of personality and background, the heroes' shared masculine identity overrides other identifiers, including race, in the face of threats to masculinity—typically represented by women in the comedy buddy film, the law in the outlaw buddy film, or criminals in the cop-action buddy film. Buddy films express a perennial theme in American culture: the escapist male fantasy of rejecting heterosexual coupling, domesticity, and prescribed social roles in order to find freedom and adventure through male bonding.

Bibliography

Ames, Christopher. "Restoring the Black Man's Lethal Weapon: Race and Sexuality in Contemporary Cop Films." *Journal of Popular Film and Television* 20, no. 3 (1992): 52–60.

Fuchs, Cynthia. "The Buddy Politic." In *Screening the Male: Exploring Masculinities in Hollywood Cinema*, edited by Steven Cohan and Ina Rae Hark. London: Routledge, 1993.

Goldstein, Patrick. "The Big Picture: It's Still a Guy Thing: The Evolution of Buddy Movie." *Los Angeles Times*, 9 October 2001, Calendar section.

Guerrero, Ed. "The Black Image in Protective Custody: Hollywood's Biracial Buddy Films of the Eighties." In *Black American Cinema*, edited by Manthia Diawara. New York: Routledge, 1993.

Holmlund, Chris. "Masculinity as Multiple Masquerade: The 'Mature' Stallone and the Stallone Clone." In *Screening the Male: Exploring Masculinities in Hollywood Cinema*, edited by Steven Cohan and Ina Rae Hark. London: Routledge, 1993.

Further Reading

Cohan, Steven, and Ina Rae Hark, eds. *The Road Movie Book*. New York: Routledge, 1997.

Jeffords, Susan. *Hard Bodies: Hollywood Masculinity in the Reagan Era*. New Brunswick, N.J.: Rutgers University Press, 1994.

King, Neal. *Heroes in Hard Times: Cop Action Movies in the U.S.* Philadelphia: Temple University Press, 1999.

Null, Gary. *Black Hollywood: From 1970 to Today*. Secaucus, N.J.: Carol Publishing, 1993.

Tasker, Yvonne. *Spectacular Bodies: Gender, Genre, and the Action Cinema*. London: Routledge, 1993.

Related Entries

African-American Manhood; Asian-American Manhood; Civil Rights Movement; Class; Cop Action Films; Detectives; *Easy Rider*; Ethnicity; Heroism; Hollywood; Male Friendship; *Odd Couple, The*; Race; Sensitive Male; Westerns

—*Philippa Gates*

Bureaucratization

Bureaucracy, or bureaucratization, refers to routinized, depersonalized, and dispersed processes devoted to the execution of a variety of administrative tasks, and to the regulation and assessment of these tasks. Within a bureaucratic system of governance, authority is dispersed and disconnected from ownership or physical production. Notions of a "bureaucratic manhood," or a "bureaucratic team player," slowly began to appear in U.S. society as bureaucratic systems of governance and administration emerged after 1830. This development enabled men to articulate masculine power and authority outside the contexts of craft skills (which were slowly displaced by industrialization after 1830) and ownership and entrepreneurial control (which were transformed by corporatization after 1880). In addition, a mode of bureaucratic manhood gained ground after 1880 that linked masculinity to the exercise of social, economic, and political power and authority in an increasingly capitalistic society.

Bureaucracy in the United States

A federal bureaucracy remained largely undeveloped until the presidency of Andrew Jackson (1829–37), when an informal process of institutional regulation was replaced by a formalized administrative system. The emergence and expansion of a federal bureaucracy was a consequence of the implementation of universal white-male suffrage. In an age characterized by political majority rule by white men, power had to be abstracted, divided, recombined, and allocated —a process that required a formalization of administrative hierarchies, a specialization of administrative procedures, a division of responsibilities, and an explicit definition of jurisdiction and powers. This bureaucratization of government was instrumental in shaping a democratic and national system of political organization.

In the aftermath of the Civil War, antebellum moral reformers who had gained positions of power adopted an ideal of a masculine "scientific morality," which combined moral imperatives with abstract standards of bureaucratic efficiency and rational performance. This ideal significantly informed the policies of the Freedmen's Bureau, created in 1865, and of the Civil Service Commission, created by the 1883 Pendleton Act, which set out to regularize the process of selecting and appointing federal office holders. With the rise of the corporation in the late nineteenth century, processes of bureaucratic governance quickly spread into the private sector as well.

The idea that government should be in the hands of trained administrators instead of partisan legislators received a boost during the Progressive Era and the "managerial revolution" of the New Deal, both of which saw a host of new bureaucratic agencies emerge, including the Federal Reserve Board (1913) and the Social Security Administration (1935). In the 1930s and 1940s, private businesses, nongovernmental organizations, and labor unions (which all began to interact and cooperate more closely with the emerging corporate state) increasingly adopted bureaucratic forms of governance. By 1945, bureaucratization had transformed much of the public and private sectors in the United States.

Bureaucratization received a new boost in the 1960s, when the federal government added 400,000 new positions and state and local governments added another 4 million new jobs. The decade also witnessed a dispersion of administrative functions from the federal to the local level, and a subsequently closer intertwining of federal, state, and local governments. As part of President Lyndon B. Johnson's Great Society program, as well as his War on Poverty, the federal government funded over 150 Community Action Agencies under the Community Action Program. Built on an idea of "maximum feasible participation," these programs localized bureaucracy and accountability. Johnson's Creative Federalism and Richard Nixon's New Federalism appeared to work against centralization of power, but actually promoted a dissemination of bureaucracy. Despite attempts to stem bureaucratization through deregulation in the 1980s and the new populism that emerged in the 1990s, attempts to control bureaucracies have usually led to the creation of new bureaucracies.

Bureaucratization in the late nineteenth and twentieth centuries generated depersonalized definitions of masculine authority and power based less on physical labor than on intellectual work and efficiency within large-scale institutional structures. (From the collections of the Library of Congress)

Bureaucratization and Masculinity

Definitions of manhood have historically stood in an ambiguous relation to bureaucracy and bureaucratization. Some scholars have emphasized that men's desire for individualistic self-assertion and affirmation are fundamentally at odds with both the need for men to surrender to a larger collective and the depersonalized patterns of authority that exist within a bureaucratic culture. Others have emphasized that service and the ability (and even eagerness) to submit to larger collectives, such as an institution, the nation, or other social groupings, constitute a spirit of teamwork that is inherent in cultural constructions of masculinity. Becoming part of a bureaucracy, then, poses the potentially complex problem for men of how to be assertive and in control as individuals, while also surrendering self-interest and accepting the individual subordination inherent in bureaucratic authority and control.

For men, the fragmentation and dispersal of control, authority, and individuality within a larger administrative process complicated notions of manhood, especially when bureaucracies became more prevalent in the late nineteenth century. However, the ability to be part of these dispersed patterns of power, and to act on behalf of a larger authority, has provided some compensation for these difficulties. In other words, while bureaucratization has restricted male individualism, it has also empowered men in other ways.

The need to conform to systemized behavior and professional routines, and to the depersonalized exercise of authority within an administrative, bureaucratic apparatus, has placed greater emphasis on interpersonal skills among men, generating a "bureaucratic manhood." For instance, advice books such as Dale Carnegie's *How to Win Friends and Influence People* (1936) emphasize the need to cultivate interpersonal skills in order to interact with others and achieve one's goals in bureaucratic settings. After World War II, bureaucratic manhood, and the ideal of man as a bureaucratic team player, gained increasing acceptance. In 1956, William H. Whyte published *The Organization Man*, a sociological study detailing the impact of corporate, bureaucratized mass society on social patterns and notions of middle-class masculinity. While critical of the developments he observed, Whyte discovered that, by the mid-1950s, masculine individualism had found its expression within and through an integration into routinized bureaucratic structures in both the public and private sectors.

Yet while bureaucratization and bureaucratic forms of governance have provided institutional sites for the articulation of masculinity, they have also, according to sociobiological arguments, challenged conventional constructions of masculinity and undermined men's claim of exclusive control over large areas of social and political life. Bureaucratization and technological change have disconnected large areas of work from the physical power traditionally associated with men. Furthermore, while bureaucratic or corporate white-collar jobs require the mental work and rational thought that men have traditionally claimed as their domain, many of these positions also require social skills traditionally associated with femininity, such as the ability to negotiate social distance and social intimacy and to handle emotional encounters with colleagues or clients. In the end, the bureaucratization of society may have contributed to the undermining of traditional gender roles.

Bureaucratic Manhood and its Critics

Finding an accommodation between traditional ideals of manliness and the bureaucratic demands of service, teamwork, and surrender to authority has often been an uneasy process. Whereas the futuristic vision of a corporatist society that Edward Bellamy unfolds in his book *Looking Backward, 2000–1887* (1888) implicitly praises bureaucratic efficiency as a means to address human needs, critics have challenged this perspective in both popular culture and academic circles. Ayn Rand's books—particularly her novel *The Fountainhead* (1949)—celebrate an individualism unfettered by restraints in an increasingly bureaucratized society. David Riesman's *The Lonely Crowd* (1950), C. Wright Mills' *White Collar* (1951), and Norman Mailer's "The White Negro" (1957) all bemoan the impact that bureaucratization and mass society have had on masculinity and the role and value of the individual. Critical works such as Herbert Marcuse's *The One-Dimensional Man* (1956) have held bureaucratized, corporatized mass society directly responsible for a host of social and personal ills. More recently, Sam Keen's *Fire in the Belly* (1991), Robert Bly's *Iron John* (1990), and Robert Moore and Douglas Gillette's *King, Warrior, Magician, Lover* (1990) have encouraged men to foster behavioral and emotional qualities that may compensate for a perceived loss of individuality in a bureaucratized society. But such advice appears difficult to reconcile with the behavioral and performance imperatives of a bureaucratic apparatus, and thus with the success so often associated with manliness.

Conclusion

In both the public and private sectors, bureaucracy and bureaucratization have been accused of assuming power at the expense of transparent decision making and the larger democratic process, and of paying insufficient attention to individual needs. Yet modern needs of governance and administration appear to require ever-growing bureaucracies to execute the many administrative tasks that have become part and parcel of modern life. In modern society, power has become depersonalized in systems that subject all citizens to sets of rules and record-gathering activities. The modern corporate society has steadily replaced a process of male individuation and gender identity formation mediated solely through participation in the marketplace with a process of individuation that also requires compliance with bureaucratic rules and regulations.

Bibliography

Clawson, Dan. *Bureaucracy and the Labor Process: The Transformation of U.S. Industry, 1860–1920.* New York: Monthly Review Press, 1980.

Crenson, Matthew A. *The Federal Machine: Beginnings of Bureaucracy in Jacksonian America.* Baltimore: Johns Hopkins University Press, 1975.

Dandeker, Christopher. *Surveillance, Power, and Modernity: Bureaucracy and Discipline from 1700 to the Present Day.* New York: St. Martin's Press, 1990.

Galambos, Louis, ed. *The New American State: Bureaucracies and Policies Since World War II.* Baltimore: Johns Hopkins University Press, 1987.

Hochschild, Arlie Russell. *The Managed Heart: The Commercialization of Feeling.* Berkeley: University of California Press, 1983.

Morone, James A. *The Democratic Wish: Popular Participation and the Limits of American Government.* Rev. ed. New Haven, Conn.: Yale University Press, 1998.

Nelson, William E. *The Roots of American Bureaucracy, 1830–1900.* Cambridge, Mass.: Harvard University Press, 1982.

Stearns, Peter N. *Be A Man! Males in Modern Society.* 2nd ed. New York: Holmes & Meier, 1990.

Woll, Peter. *American Bureaucracy.* 2nd ed. New York: Norton, 1977.

Further Reading

Bellamy, Edward. *Looking Backward, 2000–1887.* Boston: Ticknor & Company, 1888.

Foucault, Michel. *Discipline and Punish: The Birth of the Prison.* Translated by Alan Sheridan. 2nd ed. New York: Vintage, 1995.

Giddens, Anthony. *The Class Structure of the Advanced Societies.* 2nd ed. London: Hutchinson, 1981.

———. *The Consequences of Modernity.* Stanford, Calif.: Stanford University Press, 1990.

———. *Modernity and Self-Identity: Self and Society in the Late Modern Age.* Stanford, Calif.: Stanford University Press, 1991.

Karl, Barry D. *The Uneasy State: The United States from 1915 to 1945.* Chicago: University of Chicago Press, 1983.
Mills, C. Wright. *White Collar: The American Middle Classes.* New York: Oxford University Press, 1951.
Stillman, Richard J. *The American Bureaucracy.* Chicago: Nelson-Hall, 1987.
Whyte, William H. *The Organization Man.* New York: Simon & Schuster, 1972.

RELATED ENTRIES

Breadwinner Role; Business/Corporate America; Citizenship; Individualism; Industrialization; Middle-Class Manhood; Nationalism; *Organization Man, The*; Postmodernism; Professionalism; Self-Made Man; Work

—*Thomas Winter*

BUSINESS/CORPORATE AMERICA

In 1925, Calvin Coolidge uttered the oft-repeated remark: "The business of America is business." Over the course of the twentieth century, the United States underwent a profound transformation in its industrial practices, as small factories and local crafts gave way to large national and multinational corporations. In the process, the ways that Americans work changed dramatically, for this change has had an enormous impact on the places, products, and psyches of American male workers. It increased the desire to own a business, left management–worker relations more impersonal and bureaucratic, and distanced owners from managers and workers in salary and prestige. In the midst of these trends, traditional definitions of manhood gave way to newer definitions grounded in the social reality of corporate hierarchies.

The Rise of Corporate Work

Prior to the rise of corporations in the late nineteenth century, the majority of American men worked as small farmers or local craftsmen under a system where task completion, rather than time schedules, determined the rhythm of the day. A finished job was determined not by eight or ten hours spent on a particular task but by the completion of a finished product. This preindustrial system of production demanded hard labor, particularly at times of high demand or harvest, but also afforded considerable self control over one's workplace. By the late nineteenth century, the lifestyle that this work environment created and the economic independence it afforded had come to be seen as essential to manhood.

By the 1880s, this preindustrial workplace was rapidly being replaced by a new system based on large-scale factories and complex corporations, both of which altered previous definitions of masculine work. New factories, represented by Henry Ford's River Rouge plant outside of Detroit, employed thousands of men in the production of uniform products. By the 1910s, Ford's assembly-line production system, which would become the model for American factories, had dramatically changed the way work was done. Although workers were still male, they no longer worked individually to craft finished products. Instead they worked collectively, each person performing one brief, routine task as the product moved from worker to worker until it was completed. This change resulted in employee dissatisfaction and a high turnover rate until Ford instituted the five-dollar day (a doubling of the previous minimum wage) in 1914 and deliberately crafted a masculine atmosphere in the factory through company publications like Ford Man and the continued exclusion of women employees.

Emerging corporations found that selling masculinity to white-collar workers required similar efforts, for new positions in urban offices offered young men a workplace dramatically different from that experienced by their fathers. This new environment was largely incompatible with traditional notions of masculine labor and individualism. Photographs of the period taken for large corporations like Metropolitan Life Insurance in New York reveal large rooms with hundreds of similarly dressed white male clerks sitting at identical desks and shuffling identical papers,. Such work was typically done in high-rise structures, with each floor specializing in a particular area of corporate work. Thus, the building functioned as an organism, with each employee providing a component part of the whole. Employees frequently performed an entire day's labor without traveling beyond the papers and phones at their desks. Documentation was of the utmost importance in a system where thousands of employees worked simultaneously, and employees were frequently required to submit productivity reports monitoring their daily performance and progress.

The corporate environment fostered new ideals of masculine identity and achievement grounded in mental work, entrepreneurship, competitiveness, pursuit of economic success, and breadwinning. Whereas distinctions between owner and worker had frequently been minimized in a small business where everyone labored, corporate systems developed elaborate hierarchies and "ladder" systems to chart employees' positions and progress, using frequent promotions and raises in a conscious effort to retain workers. Few men were eager to give up their vision of nineteenth-century workplace independence; however, ranking systems and frequent promotions made men feel that hard work resulted in constant progress toward the top and a share in the wealth and status of corporate leaders.

Creating masculine spaces within the new world of business required excluding women and defining the bulk of the work as masculine. As late as the 1940s, Ford's River Rouge complex employed 70,000 men and no women. In corporations like Metropolitan Life, where women were frequently employed as a source of congenial and inexpensive labor, they were kept far from masculine spaces. Women entered and exited the building from different entrances, used separate staircases, worked in distinct units (typically phone operating and stenography) that did not involve expert knowledge or advanced technology, and rarely climbed the ladder to positions of rank and authority. Minorities were similarly excluded, particularly in ethnically mixed regions like Los Angeles, where business elites openly discriminated. In spite of these efforts, corporate workplaces still had to contend with complaints that they had been feminized. Their desire to create clean, presentable, and modern workspaces meant the prohibition of chewing tobacco, spittoons, and unrestricted smoking—all bastions of nineteenth-century workplace masculinity.

Men's attitudes toward the corporate workplace varied in the early twentieth century. Some, particularly salesmen, took pride in bringing new products from a modern company to small-town America. For these men, corporate culture offered the chance to be an entrepreneur with the security of a corporate salary. For others, like Edgar Rice Burroughs, the author of the popular *Tarzan* book series (1912–47), corporate life meant suffocation. Burroughs revealed the ambivalence many men felt upon entering the corporate world. After early ventures in independent business failed, Burroughs found himself working for *System*, a business magazine that dispensed "expert" advice for a fifty-dollar fee. Possessing no expertise himself, Burroughs' employment convinced him of the fallacies of American business, and he turned to fiction for relief. The popularity of his character, Tarzan, a child of gentility who grows strong and agile while being raised in the wild, reflects his dissatisfaction with white-collar masculinity.

By the 1950s, sociologists, psychologists, and other commentators emerged to quantify and evaluate—often critically—the new phenomenon of the white-collar American male. William Whyte's *The Organization Man* (1956), David Riesman's *The Lonely Crowd* (1950), and C. Wright Mills' *White Collar* (1951) lamented the decline in American ingenuity, the rise of other-directedness (excessive reliance on others when forming one's own opinions) and the devaluation of production caused by corporate work habits. Arthur Miller's play *Death of a Salesman* (1948) dramatizes the decline of the independent entrepreneur, depicting Biff Loman railing against his father's life of corporate passivity, staleness, and repetition. Much of the disillusionment of the 1950s Beat movement, and of the 1960s counterculture movement, can be traced to this spirit of corporate condemnation. At its heart, this was a critique of the corporatization of masculinity. With the decline of male entrepreneurship and craftsmanship, few men maintained control over their work hours, work product, and work relationships. Blending into the system, a requisite for corporate success, seemed to require abandoning the self-direction that had long defined masculine work.

At the same time, white-collar work remained closely associated with white middle-class manhood. Many female and nonwhite workers found only entry-level corporate work open to them, while others found that those industries that would offer them an opportunity for advancement, such as the service and retail industries, tended to offer low pay and little job security.

Modern Corporate Masculinity

After a period of economic stagflation in the 1970s, Ronald Reagan's corporate-friendly policies, termed Reaganomics, revitalized the relationship between masculinity and business in the 1980s. His administration's elimination of federal regulations and reduction of corporate taxes, combined with his own Hollywood leading-man star appeal, created a popular image of the masculine entrepreneur as patriot. The economic boom of the 1990s, and its accompanying hi-tech frenzy, facilitated and revealed changes in this masculine corporate image. Publicized reports of stocked mini bars and pick-up ball games helped a generation of young people envision corporations as dynamic, creative spaces where the entrepreneurial spirit is very much alive. To attract the best and brightest talent, many companies eschewed hierarchies for teamwork, breaking up the traditional divisions between owner, manager, and employee that had separated labor from craft. In embracing creativity and synergy and moving away from traditionally masculine styles of work and labor organization, these companies made gender less of a determinant in corporate success.

In spite of these innovations, much of American corporate culture remains highly masculine. In an era when corporate CEOs are increasingly female and men and women are recruited equally for top corporate positions, many women continue to see themselves as outsiders in a men's club. As late as the 1970s, business students, when asked to describe their ideal managers, used masculine pronouns in their replies. More recent research reveals that men and women continue to have a gendered vision of corporate leadership, associating "masculine" rationality more closely with success than "female" egalitarianism. Additionally, studies on corporate paternity leave have found that men frequently refuse to take advantage of company leave policies for fear of reprisals. Corporate culture as a whole continues to base its identity on exclusion, whether by distancing entry-level workers from managers and managers from CEOs, by devaluing female leadership traits, or by equating success with the distance an employee maintains from the home.

Bibliography

Davis, Clark. "The Corporate Reconstruction of Middle-Class Manhood." In *The Middling Sorts: Explorations in the History of the American Middle Class*, edited by Burton Bledstein and Robert Johnson. New York: Routledge, 2001.

Hacker, Helen Mayer. "The New Burdens of Masculinity," *Marriage and Family Living* 19, no. 3 (1957): 227–233.

Hill, Anita F. "Insider Women With Outsider Value." *The New York Times*, 6 June 2002.

Kasson, John F. *Houdini, Tarzan, and the Perfect Man: The White Male Body and the Challenge of Modernity in America.* New York: Hill and Wang, 2001.

Lewchuk, Wayne A. "Men and Monotony: Fraternalism as a Managerial Strategy at the Ford Motor Company," *Journal of Economic History* 5, no. 4 (1993): 824–856.

Linstedt, Sharon. "Do Real Men Go On Paternity Leave?" *The Buffalo News*, 11 September 2000.

Milkman, Ruth. *Gender at Work: The Dynamics of Job Segregation by Sex During World War II.* Urbana: University of Illinois Press, 1987.

Whyte, William H. *The Organization Man.* 1956. Reprint, New York: Simon & Schuster, 1972.

Zunz, Oliver. *Making America Corporate, 1870–1920.* Chicago: University of Chicago Press, 1990.

Further Reading

Davis, Clark. *Company Men: White-Collar Life and Corporate Cultures in Los Angeles, 1892–1941.* Baltimore: Johns Hopkins University Press, 2000.

Kwolek-Folland, Angel. *Engendering Business: Men and Women in the Corporate Office, 1870–1930.* Baltimore: Johns Hopkins University Press, 1994.

Maier, Mark. "Gender Equity, Organizational Transformation & Challenger." *Journal of Business Ethics* 16 (1997): 943–962.

Marchand, Roland. *Advertising the American Dream: Making Way for Modernity, 1920–1940.* Berkeley: University of California Press, 1985.

———. *Creating the Corporate Soul: The Rise of Public Relations and Corporate Imagery in American Big Business.* Berkeley: University of California Press, 1998.

Mills, C. Wright. *White Collar: The American Middle Classes.* New York: Oxford University Press, 1951.

Powell, Gary N., and D. Anthony Butterfield. "The 'Good Manager': Masculine or Androgynous?" *The Academy of Management Journal* 22, no. 20 (1979): 395–403.

Reisman, David. *The Lonely Crowd: A Study of the Changing American Character.* 1950. Reprint, New Haven, Conn.: Yale Nota Bene, 2001.

Related Entries

Bureaucratization; *Death of A Salesman*; Individualism; Masculine Domesticity; Middle-Class Manhood; *Organization Man, The;* Professionalism; Reagan, Ronald; Tarzan; Work; Working-Class Manhood

—Carolyn Thomas de la Peña

California Gold Rush

The California gold rush of 1849 through 1851 was the largest and most significant of American mineral rushes. Thousands of young men made their way to California after the discovery of gold in 1848 in the foothills of the Sierra Nevada Mountains. Most hoped to strike it rich and return home wealthy within a few months, a hope that usually failed to materialize. But the gold rush experience of these men, and especially their immersion in the virtually all-male world of the mining camp, illuminates the tenuous quality of constructions of manliness in this period.

The news of the discovery of gold in California spread east slowly, but by late 1848 interest in the strike, spurred by newspaper publicity, had grown into a mania, and men all over the country prepared to go west. It was a difficult and dangerous journey, whether on the Overland Trail or by sea through Panama or around Cape Horn, but thousands attempted it, including men from Mexico, Europe, Australia, China, and Chile. It is almost impossible to know how many people passed through California between 1848 and 1852, when the rush began to wane, but there were certainly hundreds of thousands.

The great majority of the new arrivals in California were young men. In the 1850 census women made up only 8 percent of California's non-Indian population of 92,597, while 72 percent (66,230) were males between the ages of twenty and forty. Three-quarters of the total population were native-born white Americans, while 962 were black. In the mining regions women were even more rare: Calaveras County in 1850 had 16,537 men and 265 women. The California gold rush was thus very different from the situation in Oregon and other western states that were settled by families and had a large female population from the beginning. California in the 1850s was masculine space, and the few women who did come shared with Eliza W. Farnham, the wife of a Santa Cruz farmer, "a universal feeling of being sadly out of place" (Farnham, 155).

The main appeal of California was not just the gold, but the gold-rush experience: adventure, sightseeing, and the latitude of the masculine California world. As young men left their homes and set out across the prairie or sailed from New York harbor into the Atlantic, they left behind the familiar world (and responsibilities) of family and relations, of farm, shop, and factory. After they arrived in San Francisco, they headed up into the mountains and found mining settlements with names like Hangtown, Whiskey Creek, and Rough and Ready, where they came into contact with men from all over the globe.

Strict new standards of propriety had been adopted by most American men earlier in the nineteenth century as a result of the religious revivals of the Second Great Awakening and the temperance movement. Women, whose moral virtue was deemed superior to that of men, were central to both crusades, and their scarcity in California seemed, in the minds of many men, to release them from the strictures of Protestant respectability. As troubled eastern moralists had foreseen, all too many men living on their own without women or churches proved incapable of refined behavior, and a construction of manliness that predated the period of moral reforms reappeared in gold-rush California. Heavy consumption of alcohol had once been common throughout the United States, but the temperance movement caused it to decline sharply in the 1840s. In California, however, men resumed the drinking habits of earlier generations, and with drinking came brawling and gambling. Men also went unshaven and dressed to suit only themselves. Religion withered. For many miners, the heaviest drinker, fiercest fighter, and best gambler was the most respected man. "All the *restrictive influence* of fair women is lost," explained twenty-four-year-old miner Edward Ely, "and the ungoverned tempers of men run wild" (Ely, 57).

The masculine, profane lifestyle of gold-rush California, combined with the necessity of working together at the hard, dirty job of extracting gold, erased any social distinctions between miners and created a strong sense of fraternity. Benevolence and openhandedness toward fellow white "forty-niners," as the miners were called, were a routine part of daily life. The camaraderie was so potent, in part, because it was so selective—there were sharply delineated groups of outsiders to mark the boundary of the community. Examples of extraordinary generosity among white miners can be juxtaposed with examples of incredible brutality and violence toward Hispanics, Chinese, and Native Americans, all of whom the white men viewed as racially incapable of true manhood.

Ultimately, most California gold miners expressed not so much an outright rejection of bourgeois manliness as an ambivalence toward it. Not every man succumbed to the lifestyle that some distressed clerics labeled "the California pox," and even those who did slip into the heavy-drinking, hard-playing habits of earlier generations felt free to reject the tenets of bourgeois conventionality not only because of the absence of women, but also because their California sojourn was a temporary spree. Most of the men involved knew that the day would come when the binge would be over and they would return east. Those men who decided to settle permanently in California usually improved their deportment and adopted norms of Victorian manhood. For those who eventually returned east, indulging their unruly impulses during their gold-rush experience may have helped accommodate them to their more sedate later lives in the field, workshop, or office and thus facilitated their embrace of the values they had temporarily abandoned. For a smaller number of men, however, the experience exposed the fragility of eastern standards of respectability by whetting their appetite for disorderly comportment—an appetite that prompted a boom in prizefighting and gambling in eastern cities in the years after the gold rush.

BIBLIOGRAPHY

Bancroft, Hubert Howe. *California Inter Pocula.* 1888. Reprint, New York: Arno Press, 1967.

Beiber, Ralph P. "California Gold Mania," *Mississippi Valley Historical Review* 35 (June 1948): 3–28.

Borthwick, John David. *Three Years in California.* Edited by Joseph A. Foster. Edinburgh: W. Blackwood and Sons, 1857.

Clappe, Louise A. K. S. *The Shirley Letters from the California Mines, 1851–1852.* 1922. Reprint, Berkeley, Calif.: Heyday Books, 1998.

Ely, Edward. *The Wanderings of Edward Ely: A Mid-Nineteenth Century Seafarer's Dairy.* Edited by Anthony and Allison Sirna. New York: Hastings House, 1954.

Farnham, Eliza Woodson Burhans. *California, In-doors and Out; or, How We Farm, Mine, and Live Generally in the Golden State.* New York: Dix, Edwards, 1856.

Johnson, Susan Lee. *Roaring Camp: The Social World of the California Gold Rush.* New York: Norton, 2000.

Maffly-Kipp, Laurie F. *Religion and Society in Frontier California.* New Haven, Conn.: Yale University Press, 1994.

Roberts, Brian. *American Alchemy: The California Gold Rush and Middle-Class Culture.* Chapel Hill: University of North Carolina Press, 2000.

FURTHER READING

Holliday, J. S. *Rush for Riches: Gold Fever and the Making of California.* Berkeley: University of California Press, 1999.

Marks, Paula Mitchell. *Precious Dust: The American Gold Rush Era, 1848–1900.* New York: William Morrow, 1994.

Orsi, Richard J., and Kevin Starr, eds. *Rooted in Barbarous Soil: People, Culture, and Community in Gold Rush California.* Berkeley: University of California Press, 2000.

Rohrbough, Malcolm J. *Days of Gold: The California Gold Rush and the American Nation.* Berkeley: University of California Press, 1997.

RELATED ENTRIES

Alcohol; Bachelorhood; Cult of Domesticity; Gambling; Male Friendship; Middle-Class Manhood; Religion and Spirituality; Self-Control; Temperance; Travel; Travel Narratives; Western Frontier; Whiteness

—*Richard Stott*

CAPITALISM

Capitalism is an economic system grounded in the concept of free enterprise, and, in American culture, it is generally considered fundamental to national identity and prosperity. It is based upon the theory that economies should be market driven, with private owners or suppliers providing products and services at whatever cost consumer demand makes feasible. Motivated by the potential for profits, private owners and investors will presumably produce whatever commodities are required or desired by a population willing to pay enough to make the investment worthwhile. This economic system assumes that the investment of capital and the employment of labor will keep the national economy strong with little or no government intervention.

In theory, capitalism should be genderless, rewarding the incentive and inventiveness of any individual. In practice, it has usually benefited men, whose capital and position as heads of households have given them a clear advantage in dealing with market issues, and it has been crucial in defining manhood for economically successful males. In addition, by placing work and earning as central male virtues, capitalism has often treated consumption as a female activity, perhaps even a female weakness.

In 1776, the Scottish moral philosopher and economist Adam Smith published *The Wealth of Nations,* the pioneering text on capitalism. This treatise on free trade and market economics challenged the restrictive system of mercantilism, insisting that the principles of free competition and choice were the keys to economic development. These ideas were widely embraced in England, Europe, and the United States during the Industrial Revolution in the eighteenth and nineteenth centuries. As a new bourgeoisie developed, with bankers, merchants, factory owners, and professionals displacing the aristocracy as the most economically and, hence, politically and socially powerful community, the advantages of capitalism seemed evident. The laws of supply and demand would create an opportunity for all men to become prosperous, regardless of their station at birth—a prospect that became closely tied to American notions of an ideal democratic political economy. These men would then be able to demonstrate their manhood by achieving economic success and fulfilling their roles as financial providers for the nuclear family. Furthermore, Smith's perception of capitalism as a system driven by rational decision making, combined with the tendency of Enlightenment thought to associate rationality and public economic activity with manhood, reinforced the association of capitalism with male endeavor in European and American thought.

The move away from hereditary wealth toward entrepreneurship and professionalism had the potential to expand opportunities for common people and women (who had most often been ineligible to own property). However, for moneyed men, who had access to the franchise (the right to vote) and professional training, the possibilities seemed boundless. The idealized capitalist was an entrepreneurial man who formed alliances with others like himself, developed profitable business plans, and cemented deals in social settings inaccessible to women and other outsiders. The wealth that he created allowed his wife to remain in the home tending to domestic responsibilities and facilitated the education of his children, who might develop professional skills and become prosperous bourgeois capitalists themselves. While the aristocracy lost favor, the supremacy of wealthy men was reaffirmed, with those who earned their wealth growing in prestige. The successful capitalist was, after all, presumed to be responsible for the economic growth of the entire nation. Not surprisingly, the most capable businessmen soon took positions of political as well as economic leadership. Leading American capitalists of the late nineteenth century justified their leadership (and grounded their sense of manliness) in the ideas of Adam Smith and of social Darwinism, which defined human society in terms of competitive struggle and economic success as a mark of fitness.

Opponents of capitalism have criticized capitalists, capitalism, and the profit motive for encouraging ruthless and amoral male behavior. They accuse the system of promoting an unfair distribution of wealth; encouraging crime, greed, and such egregious moral wrongs as child and slave labor; and exploiting and quelling dissent among the working classes, whose working conditions have often been abysmal. According to opponents of capitalism, the drive for profit cannot assure the social and moral welfare of a society (the proper goal of society's male leadership), since it encourages valuing human beings for their wealth or regarding them as marketable commodities rather than respecting their inherent worth.

Critiques of capitalism have been infused with considerations of gender and masculinity. Some nineteenth- and twentieth-century Americans articulated their moral concerns by developing such male symbols as the slick "confidence man" and cigar-chomping "robber baron." Other critics charged that a capitalist system dominated by white men undermined meritocracy by excluding women and minorities from the social milieu that supports successful capitalists. Still others argued that the identification of masculinity with proficiency as a capitalist effectively undervalued, or even emasculated, men who offered other skills or failed to produce economic profit.

The nineteenth-century German philosopher Karl Marx launched the most infamous critique against capitalism—one thoroughly informed by nineteenth-century gender constructs—in *The Communist Manifesto* (1848) and *Das Kapital* (1867) both written in collaboration with Friedrich Engels. Marx insisted that human history could be described as a class struggle between those who own (or have access to) the means of production and those who do not. The subordinate class of laborers (understood by Marx as men) has always been in the majority and produced the wealth of society, but has been oppressed by a minority (also men) who hold a disproportionate share of the wealth. By the mid–eighteenth century, this historic battle among men was no longer between serfs and lords or plebeians and patricians, but between workers (proletariat) and capitalist owners (bourgeoisie).

To address this problem, Marx promoted communism, a political, economic, and social system that, at least theoretically, supports a more equal distribution of wealth and power. Interestingly, even within this model, Marx assumed that women should be limited to the household, responsible only for child rearing and other reproductive labor. In so doing, he affirmed the patriarchal family structure and excluded women from the public exchange of resources. Marx's ideas became increasingly influential in the United States during the late nineteenth century and the twentieth century, particularly among social critics and social scientists.

Still, *The Communist Manifesto* enjoyed only limited appeal in the United States. American capitalists railed against it through the late nineteenth and twentieth centuries—particularly in the context of the Cold War struggle against the communist Soviet Union, when many Americans embraced capitalism and breadwinning masculinity as the foundations of American life. By the end of the twentieth century, many pointed to the failure of communist governments and the embrace of private enterprise in the former Soviet Union and Eastern Europe as proof of capitalism's superiority. For those who defended the superiority of capitalism over communism, considerations of gender figured prominently. Critics of communism charged that a system that requires both males and females to perform labor for the state undermines women's responsibility to focus primarily upon domestic duties and men's right to choose the most lucrative career paths and demand good wages.

Yet capitalism also continued to draw gender-related criticism in late-twentieth-century America. Critics faulted the system for devaluing and undercompensating the work that women traditionally perform. In this view, the focus on capital is particularly detrimental for women because they shoulder a disproportionate burden of unpaid reproductive labor. Many contend that a capitalist system marginalizes poor women (especially single mothers) and disabled and elderly men because they cannot compete as profit-making adults. In order to address some of these issues, men and women have pressed for universal health care, government-sponsored child care, and other forms of regulation that would focus on human need above market demands.

Whatever the political and social vagrancies or advantages, to its proponents the system of capitalism essentially affirms that the pursuit of personal profit and the right to own property are the best economic stimuli. A free market economy, they argue, is morally defensible and legitimate as a means to create wealth while simultaneously ensuring a social order that supports traditional gender roles.

Bibliography

Gibson-Graham, J. K. *The End of Capitalism (As We Know It): A Feminist Critique of Political Economy.* Cambridge: Blackwell, 1996.

Marx, Karl. *Capital: The Communist Manifesto and Other Writings.* Edited with an introduction by Max Eastman. 1848. Reprint, New York: Modern Library, 1932.

———. *Capital.* Edited by Friedrich Engels. 1867. Reprint, Chicago: Encyclopedia Britannica, 1952.

Schumpeter, Joseph. *Capitalism, Socialism, and Democracy.* 5th ed. London: Allen & Unwin, 1976.

Smith, Adam. *An Inquiry into the Nature and Causes of the Wealth of Nations.* Edited by Edwin Cannan, introduction by Max Lerner. 1776. Reprint, New York: Modern Library, 1937.

Stigler, George. *The Citizen and the State: Essays on Regulation.* Chicago: University of Chicago Press, 1975.

Further Reading

Adam Smith Institute. <www.adamsmith.org> (December 1, 2002).

Burns, Emile. *A Handbook of Marxism: Being a Collection of Extracts from the Writings of Marx, Engels, and the Greatest of their Followers.* New York: Haskell House, 1970.

Eisner, Robert. *The Misunderstood Economy: What Counts and How to Count It.* Boston: Harvard Business School Press, 1994.

Engels, Friedrich. *Socialism: Utopian and Scientific.* Translated by Edward Aveling. Westport, Conn.: Greenwood Press, 1977.

Inozemtsev, N. N. *Contemporary Capitalism: New Developments and Contradictions.* Moscow: Progress Publishers, 1974.

Rothschild, Emma. *Economic Sentiments: Adam Smith, Condorcet, and the Age of Enlightenment.* Cambridge, Mass.: Harvard University Press, 2001.

Sweezy, Paul Marlor. *The Transition from Feudalism to Capitalism.* Atlantic Highlands, N.J.: Humanities Press, 1976.

Wilson, Carter. *Racism: From Slavery to Advanced Capitalism.* Thousand Oaks, Calif.: Sage, 1996.

Young, Jeffrey T. *Economics as a Moral Science: the Political Economy of Adam Smith.* Cheltenham, England: Edward Elgar, 1997.

Related Entries

Business/Corporate America; Class; Cold War; Consumerism; Industrialization; Market Revolution; Patriarchy; Work; Working-Class Manhood

—Calinda N. Lee

The Catcher in the Rye

Since its publication in 1951, critics have regarded J. D. Salinger's *The Catcher in the Rye* as the definitive literary personification of mid-twentieth-century American angst. The novel, which examines the main character Holden Caufield's adventures during the three days immediately following his expulsion from an exclusive all-male preparatory school, effectively captures the zeitgeist of the 1950s and addresses the instability of gender roles and expectations in postwar America.

Although post-World War II Americans were reinforcing traditional gender roles amid a booming postwar economy and a rising national birthrate, concerns about the state of

American masculinity were gripping the nation. Many women had assumed the traditional male role of family breadwinner during the war, and they were reluctant to relinquish this new independence, causing a generation of men to question their understanding of masculine identity.

The Catcher in the Rye highlights some symptoms of this problem. Caufield's virginity and pacific tendencies are great sources of anxiety for him, and he repeatedly reminds the reader that he has never "gave a girl the time" and that he is "partly yellow" (Salinger, 89, 92). Caufield's decidedly non-masculine demeanor is particularly interesting in light of contemporary world events and cultural currents: He desires to be a peacekeeper at precisely the time that the United States was emerging as a world super power, and he fears women at a time when many Americans identified homosexuality as deviant and unpatriotic. This paradox indicates the uncertainties surrounding gender roles during this time period.

The novel's most profound statement about masculinity is suggested in its title: Caufield's ambition to be the "catcher in the rye." The phrase is derived from Robert Burns's "Coming Thro the Rye," a song that questions the moral implications of an adulterous rendezvous. As a catcher, Caufield hopes to save youth from the perils of adulthood, a life stage that he perceives to be fraught with phoniness and perverse sexuality. His ambition reflects cultural expectations of men as the primary defenders of innocence, justice, and freedom. Caufield aspires to this mythic image of manhood, despite the treachery that he perceives to be around him. However, he ultimately dismisses this desire as impractical, an admission that suggests the impotency of masculinity during the second half of the twentieth century.

The passage of time since its publication has not dampened the relevancy of Salinger's first, and only, published novel. As a character, Holden Caufield has come to represent the struggles and conflicting expectations inherent to American manhood; his story addresses several issues considered incompatible with his gender: homosexuality, cowardice, martyrdom. Perhaps it is because of these themes—and their inherent challenge to traditional American masculinity—that *The Catcher in the Rye* has been consistently banned from the curriculum of countless American schools. However, the novel remains widely referenced in American popular culture, most likely because the anxiety it addresses has persisted into the early twenty-first century.

BIBLIOGRAPHY

Pinsker, Stanford. *The Catcher in the Rye: Innocence Under Pressure.* New York: Twayne, 1993.

Rowe, Joyce. "Holden Caulfield and American Protest." In *New Essays on The Catcher in the Rye*, edited by Jack Salzman. Cambridge, England: Cambridge University Press, 1991.

Salinger, J. D. *The Catcher in the Rye.* 1951. Reprint, Boston: Little, Brown, 2001.

Steinle, Pamela. "'If a Body Catch a Body': The Catcher in the Rye Censorship Debate as Statement of Nuclear Culture." In *Popular Culture and Political Change in Modern America,* edited by Ronald Edsforth and Larry Bennett. Albany: State University of New York Press, 1991.

FURTHER READING

Laser, Marvin. *Studies in J. D. Salinger: Reviews, Essays, and Critiques of The Catcher in the Rye, and Other Fiction.* Edited by Marvin Laser and Norman Fruman. New York: Odyssey Press, 1963.

Steinle, Pamela Hunt. *In Cold Fear: The Catcher in the Rye Censorship Controversies and Postwar American Character.* Columbus: Ohio State University Press, 2000.

RELATED ENTRIES

Adolescence; Capitalism; Cold War; Consumerism; Heterosexuality; Homosexuality; Patriotism; Youth

—*Kristen M. Kidder*

CHARACTER

The concept of character has been an important one in the lives of American men and in American constructions of masculinity. It can be defined as an internalized commitment to moral or ethical principles, such as honesty, industry, frugality, sobriety, punctuality, and diligence. Men were first encouraged to cultivate character in the eighteenth century, but its prime period of importance was during the late nineteenth and early twentieth centuries, when it became an essential tool for middle-class economic advancement. Character's relative importance to manhood declined during the twentieth century, but it remained an important foundation for a man's success.

In colonial America, men were not concerned explicitly with character. The term did not even appear in relation to masculinity until the eighteenth century, for within the structure of the colonial family and community the prime tenets of what would later be understood as character were so embedded in the definition of masculinity that there was little reason to stress their conscious development.

During the eighteenth and nineteenth centuries, however, as American men became increasingly involved in transatlantic commerce and a burgeoning domestic market economy, traditional family and community structures gradually lost their power to ensure a masculine sense of societal duty. As a result, calls for an internally grounded masculine character became more pronounced. *Benjamin Franklin's Autobiography*, written between 1771 and 1789, reveals an early concern with male character. Franklin advised young men to cultivate and display sincerity and moral integrity in order to succeed in an emerging world of capitalist enterprise. In so doing he articulated the foundation for the nineteenth-century concept of character.

During the first half of the nineteenth century, character became fundamental to middle-class constructions of manhood and recipes for success. At first, discussions of character were heavily steeped in religion. For example, Timothy Dwight, a Congregational minister and the president of Yale College from 1795 to 1817, advised Yale's male student body that their salvation, and the salvation of the society that they would someday lead, required acting responsibly and correctly of one's own accord, rather than relying upon externally imposed rules of behavior.

Gradually, concepts of character and character-based manhood became tied to economic ends and class definition. During the late nineteenth century, advice manuals emphasized character as an important asset for lower-class men who sought wealth, favor, white-collar positions, and middle-class status. Male readers learned that possessing the traits associated with character was akin to possessing capital and fortune. By setting those who possessed it apart from greedy capitalists and the immigrant underclass, character became an important way for men to define themselves as members of an emerging middle class. This new ideology of middle-class manhood, in turn, adapted American ideals of manhood to a growing national market economy by defining those ideals in terms of capitalist exchange.

Many nineteenth-century institutions were geared toward building male character. Proponents of character emphasized, first and foremost, the role of the family. Three major developments enhanced the importance of the nineteenth-century middle-class home in the formation of male character. First, the household declined in importance as a site of economic production during the early nineteenth century, enhancing the importance of its socialization functions. Second, whereas young men in colonial America had frequently been "bound out" to neighboring families to learn productive skills, the new market economy of the nineteenth century encouraged young men to stay at home, often into their twenties. Third, the ideology of "separate spheres," according to which men were responsible for work in the public realm and women for work in the private realm, defined the home as a haven of morality where men were to receive the nurture necessary to achieve success in the commercial marketplace. Advice writers such as Horace Bushnell and Catharine Beecher, who defined women as naturally more virtuous than men, urged upon mothers in particular the importance of instilling morality in their sons (though many writers also advised fathers to help build their sons' character).

Character was formally taught outside the home through an institutional matrix consisting of advice manuals, schools, and young men's organizations. From grammar school primers to high school moral philosophy texts, nineteenth-century schoolbooks were increasingly concerned with character education. These were augmented with advice books, such as Daniel Eddy's *Young Man's Friend* (1855) and Dale John's *The Way to Win* (1891), which instructed: "Your character is your best capital and fortune" (Hilkey, 125). Finally, young men, particularly those who had left home to pursue urban ventures, found character encouraged by debating clubs, literary societies, fraternal organizations, and groups such as the Young Men's Christian Association (YMCA).

During the twentieth century, changes in American business life generated new ideals of middle-class manliness. The nineteenth-century economy of restraint and scarcity was replaced by an economy of exuberance and abundance, and increasing corporatization and bureaucratization meant that social and economic relations became increasingly impersonal. Within this new culture, virtues such as loyalty, honesty, diligence, and determination were no longer deemed sufficient to guarantee success. Instead, a new generation of success manuals increasingly encouraged men to cultivate a magnetic personality that could command people's attention. Perhaps the most influential representatives of this new "cult of personality" were Dale Carnegie's *How to Win Friends and Influence People* (1936) and racy, physique-focused magazines like Bernarr Macfadden's *Physical Culture*. In this environment, character remained a core virtue, but the new premium on masculine personality required a shiny exterior coating of vibrance and charisma.

Character remained important to late-twentieth-century definitions of manhood, but the impact of the cult of personality has rendered its precise place in such definitions problematic. The 1996 and 2000 presidential campaigns, in which the candidates' characters were frequently discussed, provide a case in point. In 1996, for instance, Americans who were asked to identify the qualities of a good leader detailed several traits, such as honesty, intelligence, dedication to hard work, and self-made success, that would have been recognizable to nineteenth-century character advocates. Yet the same Americans who valued a candidate's character also valued a potential leader's charisma, attractiveness, speaking skills, and ability to influence others. At the beginning of the twenty-first century, more than in earlier periods, ideal manhood requires a precise blending of character and personality. The difficulty in achieving the right mix of these traits can be seen in the political misfortunes of Bill Clinton, whom Americans perceived as lacking character, and Al Gore, whom they perceived as lacking charisma.

At the same time, character has become less closely tied to masculinity, and its defining standards have been applied increasingly across gender lines. As women have acquired equal footing in the workplace and political arena—and sought success in a public world until recently defined largely by men—they too have learned the necessity of negotiating the uneasy relation between character and personality.

BIBLIOGRAPHY

Clark, Clifford Edward. *The American Family Home, 1800–1960.* Chapel Hill: University of North Carolina Press, 1986.

Franklin, Benjamin. *Benjamin Franklin's Autobiography: An Authoritative Text, Backgrounds, Criticism.* Edited by J. A. Leo Lemay and P.M. Zall. New York: Norton, 1986.

Hilkey, Judy. *Character is Capital: Success Manuals and Manhood in Gilded Age America.* Chapel Hill: University of North Carolina Press, 1997.

Marsh, Margaret. "Suburban Men and Masculine Domesticity, 1870–1915." In *Meanings for Manhood: Constructions of Masculinity in Victorian America,* edited by Mark C. Carnes and Clyde Griffen. Chicago: University of Chicago Press, 1990.

Rotundo, E. Anthony. *American Manhood: Transformations in Masculinity from the Revolution to the Modern Era.* New York: Basic Books, 1993.

Susman, Warren. *Culture as History: Transformations of American Society in the Twentieth Century.* New York: Pantheon, 1984.

"Teens Tell What They Expect in Character of a President." *The Plain Dealer,* 30 September 1996, 4(E).

FURTHER READING

Bennett, William J., ed. *The Book of Virtues: A Treasury of Great Moral Stories.* Parsippany, N.J.: Silver Burdett Press, 1996.

Boyer, Paul. *Urban Masses and Moral Order in America, 1820–1920.* Cambridge, Mass.: Harvard University Press, 1978.

Carnes, Mark, and Clyde Griffen, eds. *Meanings for Manhood: Constructions of Masculinity in Victorian America.* Chicago: University of Chicago Press, 1990.

Cott, Nancy F. *The Bonds of Womanhood: "Woman's Sphere" in New England, 1780–1835.* New Haven, Conn.: Yale University Press, 1997.

Gelber, Steven M. "Do-it-Yourself: Constructing, Repairing, and Maintaining Domestic Masculinity." *American Quarterly* 49, no. 1 (March, 1997): 66–113.

Greene, Theodore P. *America's Heroes: The Changing Models of Success in American Magazines.* New York: Oxford University Press, 1970.

Haller, John S., and Robin M. Haller. *The Physician and Sexuality in Victorian America.* Carbondale: Southern Illinois University Press, 1995.

Kasson, John F. *Houdini, Tarzan, and the Perfect Man: The White Male Body and the Challenge of Modernity in America.* New York: Hill and Wang, 2001.

RELATED ENTRIES

Advice Literature; Business/Corporate America; Capitalism; Confidence Man; Cult of Domesticity; Franklin, Benjamin; Market Revolution; Middle-Class Manhood; Success Manuals; Young Men's Christian Association

—Carolyn Thomas de la Peña

CHIVALRY

The concept of chivalry developed in France and Spain during the eleventh and twelfth centuries. Derived from the French word chevalier, meaning "horseman," chivalry refers to the code of ethics that governed the behavior of mounted soldiers (knights) in feudal states. Motivated by a profound sense of duty, the ideal knight was to demonstrate grace, courtesy, gallantry, piety, chastity, valor, and loyalty at all times, and especially in relations with women. In American culture, the idea of a gallant man who rules and protects his home and lover authoritatively, though benevolently, has shaped constructions of masculinity from colonial times into the modern era.

In colonial America, ideals of chivalry were most clearly evident among the southern gentry, who by the early eighteenth century began aspiring to the lifestyle of England's landed aristocracy. Their notions of chivalric guardianship were grounded in their property (land and slaves) and in the racial and gender hierarchies that defined the southern social structure. The ideal southern gentleman and his sons were to protect the honor of their family; the virtue of their mothers, wives, and daughters; and the welfare of their slaves. Sometimes this required the ritualized violent confrontation of the duel.

Yet chivalric notions of manliness were by no means an entirely southern phenomenon. Throughout the colonies, this ideal underlay the rhetoric of Revolutionary protest against British imperial policy. Many patriots, gendering liberty and republican virtue as female, identified themselves as heroic "sons" and protectors of liberty against the encroaching and corrupt "male" power of King George III. This cultural association among chivalry, manhood, militarism, and patriotism has persisted into the twenty-first century.

As the nation expanded westward during the nineteenth century, writers such as James Fenimore Cooper—influenced by the popular romantic fiction of Sir Walter Scott—infused their archetypal western heroes with chivalric traits of gallantry and principled dedication to the protection of women. Similarly, chivalry informed the ideologies and assumptions underlying the Monroe Doctrine, Manifest Destiny, and U.S. imperialism. In all of these, white Americans justified national expansion, global interventionism, and resistance to European colonization in the Western hemisphere as being part of their perceived obligation to protect republican liberty among (or bring it to) the nonwhite and "feminized" peoples of the Americas and the world.

In the nineteenth century, chivalry remained a marker not only of masculinity and whiteness, but also of class status. The Victorian middle- and upper-class idea that men were to represent their families in the public sphere (called the "cult of domesticity" by historians) was solidified by social mores that dictated that upper-class women remain in the home, guarded from the toil and ugliness of public life by their male patrons. Such imperatives were, however, not extended to lower-class and African-American women, whose partners and families relied upon their income to ensure family survival. Unable to approach the chivalric ideal of womanhood, these women could be used by a gentleman for labor and sex without endangering his respectability.

In the South, Victorian domesticity accentuated aristocratic notions of gallant masculinity, though chivalric manhood took on increasingly political overtones amid the growing sectional crisis that preceded and then sparked the Civil War. During the 1840s and 1850s, defenders of slavery criticized the northern free-labor system on the grounds that male industrialists had immorally abandoned their traditional obligation to protect the weak. The rhetoric leading to secession and war—and the ideology and violent practices of such Reconstruction-era white supremacist organizations as the Ku Klux Klan—relied heavily upon the notion that southern men must heroically guard the virtue of white women against northern carpetbaggers and the threat of sexual predation by black men. The wide currency of this image of chivalric, white, southern manhood in the early twentieth century was evident in the popularity of the film *Birth of a Nation* (1915), which features scenes of heroic white Klansmen on horseback.

By the late nineteenth century, fears among many white, middle-class, American men that urban-industrial "overcivilization" threatened their physical vigor generated among them an ideal of "passionate manhood" that encouraged emotionally charged displays of prowess and loyalty. In American literature, authors such as Mark Twain and, in the twentieth century, Ernest Hemingway focused their classic prose on the fraternal bonds that tie both boys and men. They glorified the physical challenges that tested men's allegiances in battle, hunting, and sport. In American social life, lodges and mutual aid societies required chivalrous oaths of fidelity and even secret rituals, and labor unions relied upon the supremacy of brotherhood and honor to compel members' loyalty. In American foreign policy, Theodore Roosevelt and the "Rough Riders" assumed the image of horse-riding chivalric protectors during the 1898 Spanish-American War.

In the twentieth century, white Americans continued to associate chivalric manhood with their whiteness, but the black nationalist movements of the 1910s, 1920s, and 1960s also embraced chivalrous ideals as they argued that the black man was responsible for racial uplift and should be the ultimate authority in the home and community. Groups like the Black Panther Party, founded in 1966, operated largely as fraternal organizations and offered the chivalric elements of group life.

Chivalry came under increasing attack as feminists of the late twentieth century formulated a systematic critique of male patriarchal power and the models of masculinity that informed it. Noting that, in feudal times, women had few rights and were regarded, essentially, as the property of their male patrons, these critics claimed that the focus upon male chivalry and courtly love further objectified women, affirming their status as prizes to be won or lost in male-centered battles. The supposed attributes of chivalry, they charged, actually presume women's weakness, inferiority, and a need to rely upon men. Although chivalry's viability in contemporary society has become controversial, the continuing appeal of popular films in which male heroes rescue damsels in distress, as well as the publicity given in 2001 to oppressed women being liberated from the Taliban regime in Afghanistan by U.S. military forces, testifies to its continuing influence in American life.

BIBLIOGRAPHY

Brod, Harry, and Michael Kaufman, eds. *Theorizing Masculinities.* Thousand Oaks, Calif.: Sage, 1994.

Broughton, Bradford B. *Dictionary of Medieval Knighthood and Chivalry: Concepts and Terms.* New York: Greenwood Press, 1986.

Chickering, Howell, and Thomas H. Seiler, eds. *The Study of Chivalry: Resources and Approaches.* Kalamazoo: Consortium for the Teaching of the Middle Ages, Western Michigan University, 1988.
Fraser, John. *America and the Patterns of Chivalry.* Cambridge, England: Cambridge University Press, 1982.
Friedan, Betty. *The Second Stage.* New York: Summit, 1981.
Hall, Jacquelyn Dowd. *Revolt against Chivalry: Jessie Daniel Ames and the Women's Campaign against Lynching.* New York: Columbia University Press, 1993.
Hoganson, Kristin L. *Fighting for American Manhood: How Gender Politics Provoked the Spanish-American War.* New Haven, Conn.: Yale University Press, 1998.
Kerber, Linda K. *No Constitutional Right to Be Ladies: Women and the Obligations of Citizenship.* New York: Hill and Wang, 1998.
Moeller, C. H. "Chivalry." In *The Catholic Encyclopedia.* Vol. III. <http://www.newadvent.org/cathen/03691a.htm> (May 22, 2003).
Van DeBurg, William L. *New Day in Babylon: The Black Power Movement and American Culture, 1965–1975.* Chicago: University of Chicago Press, 1992.
Wyatt-Brown, Bertram. *Southern Honor: Ethics and Behavior in the Old South.* New York: Oxford University Press, 1982.

FURTHER READING
Creel, George. *Chivalry versus Justice: Why the Women of the Nation Demand the Right to Vote.* New York: National Woman Suffrage Publishing, 1915.
Nicholson, Helen. *Love, War, and the Grail: Templars, Hospitallers, and Teutonic Knights in Medieval Epic and Romance, 1150–1500.* Leiden, the Netherlands: Brill, 2001.
Velde, Francois. History of Orders of Chivalry: A Survey. <http://www.heraldica.org/topics/orders/ordhist.htm> (May 22, 2003).
Wood, Charles T. *The Age of Chivalry: Manners and Morals, 1000–1450.* London: Weidenfeld & Nicolson, 1920.

RELATED ENTRIES
African-American Manhood; *Birth of a Nation*; Cult of Domesticity; Dueling; Hemingway, Ernest; Heroism; Imperialism; Leatherstocking Tales; Manifest Destiny; Militarism; Nationalism; Patriotism; Sons of Liberty; Southern Manhood; Western Frontier; Whiteness

—*Bret E. Carroll and Calinda N. Lee*

CITIZENSHIP

Throughout most of U.S. history, citizenship has been largely the right of white men. It has, therefore, been integral to the definition of masculinity for white men. Participatory citizenship has, of course, expanded since the early nineteenth century to include African Americans, Native Americans, women, and other groups, but this expansion has occurred in conjunction with attempts (often successful) to exclude non-whites and women.

The Colonial and Revolutionary Eras

In colonial America (as in England), citizenship and voting rights were grounded in property ownership and whiteness, which were inextricably intertwined with constructions of masculinity. Citizenship, voting rights, and (in most cases) property holding were confined to white men and were considered the foundations of manly independence. They were also thought to ensure disinterested political action, by men, in the best interest of society's propertyless dependents—such as women and African-American slaves. Many more men could vote in the American colonies than in England—in both the North and the South, approximately 50 percent of white men met the property requirement. But citizenship and voting remained the privilege of white male property owners—a minority of the population in every colony. As much as 80 percent of the total population—women, slaves, servants, children, and propertyless white men—were excluded from the rights of citizenship.

The republican ideology that informed the American Revolution reaffirmed, at least initially, the interrelationships among citizenship, manhood, whiteness, independence, and property ownership. For Thomas Jefferson, the ideal citizen was a yeoman farmer whose small landholdings assured that he was not politically or economically dependent upon any other individual. After the Revolution, citizenship and the franchise (the right to vote) remained confined to property-owning white men. While the ability to vote was a public sign of prosperity and manly competence, it also entailed recognizing the manly virtue of others. Men were expected to vote for a candidate based on their knowledge of his character. Male virtue, demonstrated through property ownership and the acknowledgment of voting peers, provided the main qualifications, in theory at least, for political office. Republicanism and deferential politics, then, assumed a hierarchy of manliness: Officeholders presumably possessed superior and more virtuous manliness than other men. In practice, this meant that local elites dominated politics, influencing votes through intimidation, or by supplying alcohol and entertainment on Election Day. Alcohol consumption and other forms of Election Day recreation reasserted the homosocial nature of both political participation and access to the public sphere of civil society.

The Era of the Common Man

Historians have labeled the early nineteenth century the Era of the Common Man in the United States because, although most Americans remained excluded from the political process, the period from 1800 to 1860 did witness an extension of the franchise to include propertyless white men, with a general increase in these men's social and political power. By the 1830s, most states had abolished property-based suffrage (voting) requirements for white men over twenty-one years of age. This extension of voting rights was part of a larger move from strict social hierarchy and deference to a democratized understanding of citizenship.

Universal white-male suffrage brought large numbers of white men—including landless "squatter" farmers, urban working men, and Irish laborers—into active political participation. This meant that whiteness and masculinity, rather than property ownership, became the primary markers of citizenship, and political parties courted their new and broadened audience by appealing to this new ideological complex. Andrew Jackson and the Democratic Party successfully claimed to represent the "common man," meaning a man who was white, plainspoken, an urban worker or a frontiersman, and rough in manners but devoted to individual freedom, popular democracy, and participatory citizenship. Political gatherings emphasized "democratic manhood"—the individual liberty and equal citizenship status of most white men—and successfully combined the homosocial election rituals with a populist conception of political participation. The Whig Party quickly followed suit. William Henry Harrison's 1840 presidential campaign, for example, used images of hard cider and Harrison's imagined beginnings in a log cabin to garner support from the male electorate.

Urban workers who supported Jackson, not needing property to vote (and increasingly unlikely to become property owners) enthusiastically contributed and responded to this understanding of citizenship, at times asserting it through mob violence against those they considered outside the community of citizens, including African Americans and some white immigrants. Many native-born Americans, particularly in eastern cities, saw Irish and other Catholic immigrants as a political threat, for they viewed the Catholic Church hierarchy, with its leadership in Rome, as antidemocratic. Anti-immigrant sentiment, or nativism, found expression throughout the period from 1830 to 1860 in political parties and secret societies, most notably the American Party (known as the Know-Nothing Party because members would reply "I know nothing" when asked about the party) of the 1850s.

African-American Men and Citizenship During Reconstruction

The exclusive association of citizenship with manhood and whiteness was challenged by women's-rights activists as early as the 1840s, but understandings of citizenship as the province of white men began to break down only with the end of slavery, when African Americans began asserting their rights as American citizens. With emancipation and the passage of the Fourteenth Amendment (1868) and the Fifteenth Amendment (1870) to the Constitution (the former granting African Americans the rights of U.S. citizenship; the latter excluding race as a basis for denying voting rights), the grounding of citizenship in whiteness formally ended. However, citizenship remained firmly linked to masculinity. Attempts by women to secure the vote through the Fifteenth Amendment failed, and only African-American men were admitted to the political process. These men entered politics forcefully: In the fall of 1867, between 70 and 90 percent of eligible black men voted in all southern states, and 265 African-American men were elected to state offices. For African-American men, citizenship meant not merely voting, but the right to move about freely, to own land, to set the terms of their labor, to build independent churches, and to seek an education.

But the ability of blacks to claim full citizenship proved short-lived in many places. By 1868 the Ku Klux Klan was effectively terrorizing African-American men and women who sought to buy land, protested over low wages, or sought to exercise voting and officeholding rights. Racist propaganda that asserted whiteness and masculinity as the most desirable bases of citizenship attacked African Americans' manliness, portraying black voters and politicians as imbeciles, children, or animals. The Supreme Court also counteracted the extension of citizenship rights beyond white men through its narrow interpretations of the rights granted by the Fourteenth Amendment, confining them to interstate travel and use of the nation's waterways. The Supreme Court also left voting requirements up to the individual states, allowing southern states to impose poll taxes or literacy requirements that effectively excluded black voters.

The Progressive Era

The Progressive Era (1890–1915) witnessed concerted efforts to preserve the equation of citizenship with both whiteness and masculinity in the face of increasing immigration by people deemed nonwhite and un-American—particularly those from Asia and eastern and southern Europe. Not only did southern states embrace literacy requirements in order to prevent African-American men from voting, but other states, such as Connecticut (1856), Wyoming (1890), Maine (1894), California (1896), and New York (1922), imposed literacy requirements, making some knowledge of English a requirement to vote. In addition, a stated intention of naturalization no longer allowed a man to vote. U.S. citizenship became a prerequisite for voting, reflecting the rising tide of anti-immigrant feeling in the United States and a growing conviction among white native-born men that Anglo-Saxon manhood was in danger of disappearing. The anti-Chinese (and later anti-Japanese) laws of the late nineteenth and early twentieth centuries, such as the Naturalization Act of 1870 (which specifically prohibited Asians from becoming citizens), the Chinese Exclusion Act of 1882, and the Immigration Act of 1924, represented the most extreme version of such beliefs, preventing Asians from becoming naturalized citizens and voting. Anti-Asian legislation was often justified by portraying Chinese and Japanese men as suspiciously feminine (illustrations emphasized Asian clothing and Chinese men who wore their hair in a queue, or long braid) or inhuman.

Even as the Progressive Era witnessed the reaffirmation of a notion of citizenship based on white masculinity, it also saw the successful culmination of the decades-old challenge by women of citizenship's association with manhood. Proponents of woman suffrage, incensed by the exclusion of women from Fifteenth Amendment voting rights, became increasingly outspoken and organized in defense of women's suitability for full participatory citizenship. Their campaign resulted in the passage of the Nineteenth Amendment (1920), which guaranteed women the right to vote and broke the male monopoly on political participation.

The Social Citizen: The Twentieth Century

The relation between citizenship, masculinity, and whiteness was further eroded by the rise of the welfare state in the twentieth century. Americans increasingly embraced a new ideal of "social citizenship" in which citizens could demand both economic security and social equality. On the one hand, this new ideal encouraged social and political movements (such as the civil rights movement) that defined the vigorous pursuit of education, jobs, and salaries as a manly endeavor. Within these movements, however, men defended their agendas as necessary to secure self-reliance, and they often excluded women from leadership roles. On the other hand, social citizenship also encouraged these same activists—as well as advocates for women's and other groups' rights—to critique and challenge white men's longstanding monopoly on full citizenship privileges. Indeed, gay rights groups have exposed heterosexuality to be just as equally important as whiteness and masculinity in determining access to the rights of citizenship.

Furthermore, the welfare state (especially the programs of the New Deal in the 1930s and the Great Society in the mid-1960s), which sought to guarantee all Americans equal economic opportunity and a small amount of economic security, altered the longstanding relation between citizenship, masculinity, independence, property ownership, and whiteness by making all citizens dependent (or potentially dependent) on the government for economic protection. Perceived as threats to manly citizenship and self-reliance, such programs are popularly associated with women and nonwhites (groups long associated with dependence) and were resisted by conservatives, especially those of the 1980s and 1990s, in the name of "traditional" manhood.

Conclusion

The number of Americans who claim the rights of citizenship has expanded tremendously since the founding of the country. Whereas only propertied white men could participate in public life in the early republic, all Americans, regardless of race or gender, now have the theoretical right to claim the entitlements of full citizenship. But when Americans do make claims for social and economic equality, they are often portrayed as dependent women or people of color (regardless of their sex or race) taking advantage of the hard work of real (male) citizens. Thus, Ronald Reagan's references to "Cadillac-driving welfare queens" were interpreted by Americans as denunciations of African-American women whose dependence on government welfare exploited the hard work of nonblack, nonfemale taxpayers. The virtuous and independent citizen, the "real" citizen who is not dependent on "handouts" from the federal government, tends to be associated with men in American culture.

BIBLIOGRAPHY

Baker, Paula. "Domestication of Politics: Women and American Political Society, 1780–1920." *American Historical Review* 89, no. 3 (June 1984): 620–647.

Foner, Eric. *Reconstruction: America's Unfinished Revolution, 1863–1877.* New York: Harper & Row, 1988.

Ignatieff, Michael. "The Myth of Citizenship." In *Theorizing Citizenship*, edited by Ronald Beiner. Albany: State University of New York Press, 1995.

Kimmel, Michael. *Manhood in America: A Cultural History.* New York: Free Press, 1996.

Marshall, T. H. *Class, Citizenship, and Social Development: Essays.* Chicago: University of Chicago Press, 1977.

Roediger, David R. *The Wages of Whiteness: Race and the Making of the American Working Class.* London: Verso, 1999.

Schudson, Michael. *The Good Citizen: A History of American Civic Life.* New York: Martin Kessler, 1998.

Shklar, Judith N. *American Citizenship: The Quest for Inclusion.* Cambridge, Mass.: Harvard University Press, 1991.

FURTHER READING

Dawley, Alan. *Struggles for Justice: Social Responsibility and the Liberal State.* Cambridge, Mass.: Belknap Press, 1991.

Dimock, Wai Chee. *Residues of Justice: Literature, Law, and Philosophy.* Berkeley: University of California Press, 1996.

Fraser, Nancy, and Linda Gordon. "Civil Citizenship against Social Citizenship?" In *The Condition of Citizenship*, edited by Bart van Steenbergen. London: Sage, 1994.

Isenberg, Nancy. *Sex and Citizenship in Antebellum America.* Chapel Hill: University of North Carolina Press, 1998.

Jacobson, Matthew Frye. *Whiteness of a Different Color: European Immigrants and the Alchemy of Race.* Cambridge, Mass.: Harvard University Press, 1998.

Macpherson, C. B. *The Political Theory of Possessive Individualism: Hobbes to Locke.* Oxford: Oxford University Press, 1990.

Pocock, J. G. A. "The Ideal of Citizenship Since Classical Times." In *Theorizing Citizenship,* edited by Ronald Beiner. Albany: State University of New York Press, 1995.

Rogin, Michael Paul. *Fathers and Children: Andrew Jackson and the Subjugation of the American Indian.* New Brunswick, N.J.: Transaction Publishers, 1991.

Smith, Rogers M. *Civic Ideals: Conflicting Visions of Citizenship in U.S. History.* New Haven, Conn.: Yale University Press, 1997.

Tilly, Louise A. "Scholarly Controversy: Women, Work, and Citizenship." *International Labor and Working Class History Journal* 52 (Fall 1997): 1–41.

Twine, Fred. *Citizenship and Social Rights: The Interdependence of Self and Society.* London: Sage, 1994.

Watson, Harry L. *Liberty and Power: The Politics of Jacksonian America.* New York: Hill and Wang, 1990.

RELATED ENTRIES

African-American Manhood; Agrarianism; Asian-American Manhood; Breadwinner Role; Civil Rights Movement; Democratic Manhood; Emancipation; Feminism; Immigration; Industrialization; Irish-American Manhood; Jackson, Andrew; Labor Movement and Unions; Market Revolution; Nativism; New Deal; Politics; Property; Republicanism; Suffragism; Whiteness; Work; Working-Class Manhood

—*Rosanne Currarino*

CIVIL RIGHTS MOVEMENT

The civil rights movement of the 1950s and 1960s sought social and political equality for racial minorities in the United States. In challenging racial discrimination, civil rights activists also raised questions about traditional American gender identities, paving the way for the modern feminist movement and creating new possibilities for minority men to define their own masculine identities. With voting rights, increased educational opportunities, and access to better jobs, minority men became better able to fulfill traditional male roles as fathers, husbands, and community leaders. They also challenged racist stereotypes about who they were and what types of men they could be, constructing models of manhood grounded in racial identity and the struggle for racial justice.

The U.S. Supreme Court's 1954 *Brown* v. *Board of Education* decision outlawing racial segregation in public schools is often seen as the beginning of the civil rights movement. Yet African-American activism for equal rights reached back at least as far as the Revolutionary era, and was long intertwined with models of African-American manhood that emphasized black identity. A more immediate precursor to the civil rights movement was minority men's participation in the U.S. Armed Forces during World War II and the Korean War. Serving in the military was not the only way to "become a man," but it was a traditional rite of passage for young men and an obligation of American (especially male) citizenship. When minority men risked their lives to defend democracy in Europe and Asia, they gained a new sense of themselves as men and saw clearly the hypocrisy of disfranchisement (denial of the right to vote) and segregation in the United States. The activism of returning black veterans and the Brown decision inspired protests against racial discrimination in education, public transportation, and electoral politics from the mid-1950s through the 1960s.

Southern white men responded to black activism and challenges to white male supremacy by calling for "massive resistance" to the civil rights movement. The Citizens' Council, a segregationist group founded by middle-class southern white men in Mississippi in 1954, called on white husbands and fathers to fulfill a longstanding duty of white southern manhood: to "defend" white women and children from racial integration. This rhetoric inspired vigilante violence—often considered an expression of traditional white southern manhood and honor—such as the 1955 lynching of fourteen-year-old Emmett Till for supposedly whistling at a white woman in rural Mississippi and the 1957 castration of a black man in a Ku Klux Klan initiation ritual in Birmingham, Alabama.

Southern political leaders did little to stop such atrocities. In fact, governors Ross Barnett (Mississippi), George Wallace (Alabama), and Orval Faubus (Arkansas) based their political careers on opposition to integration. Like the Citizens' Council and the Klan, southern elected officials tapped into a fear that miscegenation (interracial sexual relations) would result from social integration. These southern white men demonized black men as hypersexual beasts in an effort to galvanize opposition to civil rights, just as their political forefathers had done in the 1890s to justify disfranchisement, segregation, and lynching.

Civil rights activists fought such racist stereotyping and discrimination with a variety of strategies. On the one hand, there were advocates of nonviolent direct action protests in the Congress of Racial Equality (CORE), the Student Nonviolent Coordinating Committee (SNCC), and the Southern Christian Leadership Conference (SCLC). SCLC's founder and long-time president, Martin Luther King, Jr., was one of the most eloquent advocates of the nonviolent philosophy, not only in the pursuit of civil rights, but also in protesting American involvement in the Vietnam War. King and other advocates of nonviolence sought to put into practice a conception of American manhood based not on physical power and domination, but on brotherly love, moral principle, spiritual strength, interracial cooperation, and—for African Americans—group empowerment and pride in blackness. The nonviolent protests of the civil rights movement caricatured, and were intended to expose, the unchristian violence on which white male supremacy stood. The movement's successes served to stigmatize and stereotype traditional white southern manhood in the minds of many Americans.

Civil rights activists also called on the federal government to fulfill the nation's egalitarian ideals. After much prodding, Washington lawmakers, responding positively to nonviolent protest and the model of manhood that informed it, guaranteed social equality with the Civil Rights Act of 1964 and political equality with the Voting Rights Act of 1965. Federal officials were less successful in guaranteeing economic equality, though they tried with President Lyndon Johnson's War on Poverty programs. One ill-fated federal initiative, outlined by Johnson's assistant secretary of labor Daniel Moynihan in *The Negro Family: A Case for National Action* (1965), suggested that a "culture of poverty" and family breakdown in minority communities could be addressed by bolstering minority male employment. Movement leaders applauded Moynihan's focus on minority employment, but his patriarchal policy proposals and critique of "matriarchal" black families proved controversial.

Nonviolence generated new conceptions of American manhood and effectively won federal support for civil rights initiatives, but it could not defend minority communities from vigilante violence in the absence of media coverage and federal protection. Thus, some civil rights activists dismissed King's model as insufficient and proposed alternatives. Robert Williams, former leader of the National Association for the Advancement of Colored People (NAACP) in North Carolina, and the Nation of Islam minister Malcolm X felt that African Americans must defend themselves, in Malcolm's words, "by any means necessary." These men argued that it was their duty as men, husbands, and fathers to protect themselves and their loved ones from white violence. Williams and Malcolm inspired younger activists to form groups like the Black Panther Party in the late 1960s and early 1970s. These groups advocated armed self-defense and fashioned a bold new identity for minority men based on militancy, brash self-assertion, and moral superiority to whites. Discomfiting to the white liberals who dominated American politics during the mid-1960s, this model of African-American manliness did not produce the legislative successes that the nonviolent model had.

When movement activists carried signs bearing the slogan "I Am a Man" in the 1968 Memphis sanitation workers' strike, they demanded both recognition of their rights and respect as men. As this slogan revealed, questions about gender were intertwined with concerns for racial justice. Civil rights activism allowed minority men an equal voice in determining their own political destinies and masculine identities, diversifying the concept of manhood in America. The struggle for civil rights also inspired the re-emergence of the feminist movement, which challenged male monopolization of political, economic, and social power in America; launched a full-scale assault on patriarchy; and proposed new models of manhood separated from traditional notions of sexual difference. Although the defeat of the Equal Rights Amendment in the 1980s and the organization of the Million Man March in the 1990s suggest that these struggles continue, there is little doubt that the civil rights movement profoundly redirected American understandings of masculinity in the late twentieth century.

Bibliography

Cleaver, Eldridge. *Soul On Ice.* New York: Dell, 1968.

Evans, Sara. *Personal Politics: The Roots of Women's Liberation in the Civil Rights Movement and the New Left.* New York: Vintage, 1979.

King, Martin Luther, Jr. *Where Do We Go From Here: Chaos or Community?* New York: Harper & Row, 1967.

Tyson, Tim. *Radio Free Dixie: Robert F. Williams and the Roots of Black Power.* Chapel Hill: University of North Carolina Press, 1999.

X, Malcolm, with Alex Haley. *The Autobiography of Malcolm X.* New York: Grove, 1965.

Further Reading

Branch, Taylor. *Parting the Waters: America in the King Years 1954–1963.* New York: Simon & Schuster, 1988.

Ling, Peter J., and Sharon Monteith, eds. *Gender in the Civil Rights Movement.* New York: Garland, 1999.

Matthews, Tracye. "'No One Ever Asks, What a Man's Place in the Revolution Is': Gender and the Politics of the Black Panther Party, 1966–1971." In *The Black Panther Party (Reconsidered),* edited by Charles E. Jones. Baltimore: Black Classic Press, 1998.

Wallace, Michele. *Black Macho and the Myth of the Superwoman.* London: Verso, 1999.

Related Entries

African-American Manhood; Black Panther Party; Feminism; King, Martin Luther, Jr.; Malcolm X; Military; Politics; Southern Manhood; World War II

—*Steve Estes*

Civil War

The American Civil War (1861–65) between the North (the Union) and the South (the Confederacy) was a conflict over issues of national identity, economic development, western expansion, and slavery. With roughly 2 million soldiers fighting for the Union and about 800,000 for the Confederacy, the war wrought transformations in the lives of both black and white men and altered ideas about manhood in both the North and the South. It served as a juncture between two regional sets of ideals of manhood and highlighted the race, gender, and class hierarchies on which they were contingent.

For men on both sides, the Civil War accelerated processes of maturation and of male gender-identity formation. Loyalty to, and sacrifice for, community, region, and cause played a significant role. Most troops (94 percent of Union soldiers and 82 percent of Confederate soldiers) were volunteers, and in many cases entire communities of men formed into military companies. Losses of 20 percent in a single artillery charge were not uncommon.

The war was an especially formative experience for the 40 percent of the soldiers that were 21 years old or younger. The army imposed institutional discipline on soldiers, while at the same time promoting male bonding and competition and giving freer reign to the social impulses, such as sexuality and violence, that were a part of antebellum America. Sexuality was part of a military culture that consisted largely of single men, whereas violence was encouraged, and at times considered necessary, in conflicts between soldiers.

In the North, the war's demand for discipline, courage, and physical strength changed men's lives and notions of manliness. For middle-class men in particular, an emphasis on a "strenuous life" of struggle in overcoming obstacles replaced the idealism and transcendental intellectualism of antebellum reform causes. Wartime industrialization also affected constructions of middle-class and working-class manhood by emphasizing a class-based differentiation of manhood that had begun before the war. For middle-class men, wartime industrialization advanced an ideal of entrepreneurial self-made manhood based on marketplace competition, acquisition of property through work, and power over other men in the workplace. For working-class men industrialization further eroded a traditional ideal of artisanal manliness grounded in craftsmanship, autonomy, and workplace solidarity. The Republican Party slogan of the 1850s—"free soil, free labor, free men"—appealed to traditional republican conceptions of manhood grounded in Jeffersonian ideals of landownership and craftsmanship, but the wartime industrialization promoted by a Republican administration made such ideals increasingly difficult to realize.

For Southern white men, the Civil War represented a conflict between the ideal of the chivalrous Southern patriarch and the Yankee self-made man. Since the 1830s, Southern intellectuals and politicians had upheld ideals of patriarchy, honor, paternalism, morality, and community, while criticizing Northern ideas of liberty, entrepreneurial individualism, and self-made manhood. Although articulated by Southern elites, these ideals influenced Southern white men at all social levels, for in a society founded on slave labor, white men viewed unchallenged domestic patriarchy and personal independence as their right—and as the basis of their equality with other white men.

The defeat of the South also entailed a defeat of Southern ideals of manly honor and paternalism. Northern media now represented Southern planters as failed, effete dandies and as members of a quasi-feudal aristocracy out of step with Northern entrepreneurship and ideals of the strenuous life. For example, Northern newspapers generated the legend that Jefferson Davis, the president of the defeated Confederate

States of America, was disguised in women's clothes when he was captured in Richmond, Virginia.

Southern white men also felt emasculated by the emancipation of slaves. Their resulting hostility toward black men resulted in approximately 150 lynchings per year between 1889 and 1898 alone. Lynchings were typically justified with claims that the black victim had sexually offended a white woman. Such explanations reflected the participants' sense of lost patriarchal control over their households (and over the South as an independent political entity), as well as their perception of free black men as a threat to traditional definitions of Southern white manhood. Similar feelings underlay the activities of fraternal organizations such as the Ku Klux Klan, established in 1866 in Tennessee to resist the power of blacks and Republicans in the South. In the absence of new constructions of Southern white manhood appropriate to a changing South, the traditional ideal based on patriarchy, racial superiority, and the protection of white Southern womanhood persisted into the twentieth century, finding cinematic expression in such films as D. W. Griffith's *Birth of a Nation* (1915).

African American men—200,000 of whom served in the war—hoped the Civil War would end slavery and enhance their manhood by allowing them to achieve equality, independence, and mastery over their own households, free from white surveillance and control. From the beginning, black men realized the significance of a Union victory for their aspirations and sought to volunteer. The Union army at first refused to enlist black men, but the Emancipation Proclamation of 1863 changed Union policies on black enlistment and dispelled the notion that the Civil War was a white man's war. African-American men joined the fight in large numbers—although they represented only 1 percent of the Northern population, they made up 10 percent of the Union army. Black recruiters relied on a racially universalizing language of manhood in their appeals for enlistment. In 1863, the politician and abolitionist Frederick Douglass confidently proclaimed that once black men would be allowed to join the Union army, they would be paragons of upright manliness and worthy of the rights of citizenship. The performance of the 54th Massachusetts Infantry—though a disaster in military terms—helped to reinforce African-American men's claim to equal citizenship and dispelled contemporary associations of black men with cowardice. Many African-American men, such as the African Methodist Episcopal church minister and Civil War army chaplain Henry McNeal Turner, continued to insist long after the Civil War that the war had liberated African men by proving their manhood.

One unifying factor of the Civil War, which affected many men regardless of region or race, was serious injury leading to disfigurement or amputation. During the Civil War, doctors performed approximately 60,000 amputations—more than during any other U.S. war—and 35,000 survived the procedure. Soldiers who lost limbs displayed visible evidence of heroic self-sacrifice, but at the same time they felt that their manhood had been compromised, for they had been left physically disempowered, dependent on others, and visibly altered at a time when American men were increasingly defining manhood in terms of body image.

The Civil War instilled among generations of American men the notion that war can build or regenerate manhood, by creating a notion of the strenuous life. By the 1880s, many young white men born too late to participate in the war articulated a new passionate manhood that emphasized courage, promoted physical exercise, and motivated men to support or participate in the Spanish-American War (1898).

The war's legacy differs for white and black men. Civil War re-enacters, mostly white, continue to represent men as heroic warriors and depict war as a masculine rite of passage and a way to reinvigorate manhood. For black men (and women), the Civil War remains primarily associated with the emancipation and the rights of citizenship, particularly as lingering Confederate sympathies continue to represent a challenge to black pride.

Bibliography

Clinton, Catherine, and Nina Silber, eds. *Divided Houses: Gender and the Civil War.* New York: Oxford University Press, 1992.

Fredrickson, George M. *The Inner Civil War: Northern Intellectuals and the Crisis of the Union.* New York: Harper & Row, 1965.

Kimmel, Michael. *Manhood in America: A Cultural History.* New York: Free Press, 1996.

O'Leary, Cecilia Elizabeth. *To Die For: The Paradox of American Patriotism.* Princeton, N.J.: Princeton University Press, 1999.

Rose, Anne C. *Victorian America and the Civil War.* New York: Cambridge University Press, 1992.

Further Reading

Cimbala, Paul A., and Randall M. Miller, eds. *Union Soldiers and the Northern Home Front: Wartime Experiences, Postwar Adjustments.* New York: Fordham University Press, 2002.

Edwards, Laura F. *Gendered Strife and Confusion: The Political Culture of Reconstruction.* Urbana: University of Illinois Press, 1997.

Linderman, Gerald. *Embattled Courage: The Experience of Combat in the American Civil War.* New York: Free Press, 1987.

Whites, LeeAnn. *The Civil War as a Crisis in Gender: Augusta, Georgia, 1860–1890.* Athens: University of Georgia Press, 1995.

Wyatt-Brown, Bertram. *Southern Honor: Ethics and Behavior in the Old South.* New York: Oxford University Press, 1982.

Related Entries

Abolitionism; Adolescence; African-American Manhood; *Birth of a Nation*; Citizenship; Douglass, Frederick; Emancipation; Gilded Age; Lincoln, Abraham; Middle-Class Manhood; Militarism; Military; Nationalism; Passionate Manhood; Slavery; Southern Manhood; Strenuous Life; Victorian Era; War; Whiteness; White Supremacism; Youth

—*Thomas Winter*

Class

The economic and social transformations engendered by industrialization, urbanization, and the emergence of a market economy in the nineteenth century led to processes of class formation, class difference, and class identity that have profoundly shaped definitions of manliness in the United States. A man's position in the process of production, the type of work he performs, and the amount of managerial and entrepreneurial control he exercises are determinants of class status and are intricately connected to notions of masculinity and gender. As an expression of a man's economic status, and of the cultural attitudes and perceptions that it engenders, class and class difference are connected to articulations of gender and manliness in U.S. society.

Manhood and Social Hierarchy in Preindustrial Society

The notion of class divisions did not exist in preindustrial America, but emerged with the separation of labor from managerial control and ownership of the means of production that were part of the Industrial Revolution. Yet preindustrial society recognized social hierarchies and status distinctions that were closely intertwined with definitions of manhood. Status distinctions were reflected in three different paradigms of manliness that prefigured subsequent class-based definitions of masculinity: patrician, artisan, and yeoman. The patrician, who inherited European aristocratic ideals of manhood based on honor, cultural refinement in taste and conduct, and substantial property ownership, saw himself as one of the trustworthy few who fulfilled his duties and obligations and served the republic by providing leadership to society. In turn, the patrician expected and received the deference of those below him in social standing. The artisan and the yeoman both emphasized economic self-sufficiency and independence as the basis of citizenship and manliness, but they had different economic foundations. The artisanal ideal of manliness, rooted in craft-based production, emphasized workplace autonomy and craft-based solidarity, whereas the yeoman emphasized access to and ownership of land as the marks of autonomy and manliness.

Industrialization and the Market Revolution

In the early nineteenth century, industrialization and the market revolution fundamentally reshaped processes of economic production, manufacturing, and distribution, as well as the social experiences of work and business. These economic transformations created new forms of social stratification and new notions of manliness based on class difference.

Class-based constructions of masculinity were grounded in experiences of work, income-generating activity, and economic transactions. The control over one's labor power and the ability to participate in an expanding marketplace—called "transactional manhood" by the historian Scott Sandage—increasingly set the standards by which men defined themselves as men and as members of particular social classes. Industrialization and the market revolution slowly replaced an ideal of manliness grounded in propertied independence with an ideal rooted in acquisitive individualism and the ability to engage in economic transactions.

Merchants, lawyers, and those artisans who were able to expand their operations formed the core of an emerging middle class and conformed most closely to a notion of transactional manhood. For these men, entrepreneurial control over one's business operations, and one's workforce became fundamental both to class status and to class-based definitions of manliness. Middle-class manhood meant, above all, espousing an individualistic ethos, being continually "on the make," and embracing those behaviors deemed necessary for economic success—particularly self-control, industry, sobriety, rationality, and competitiveness.

For upper-class men, ideas of manhood remained grounded in property, power, wealth, quasi-aristocratic status, and social leadership (not unlike the eighteenth-century patrician). They aspired through their wealth, social position, and political clout to conduct themselves as civic stewards, offering guidance and giving shape to an urbanizing and industrializing society by holding political office, performing charitable work, and serving in informal advisory functions. With the market revolution and the shift of economic transactions from barter and local exchange to cash and credit in domestic and trans-Atlantic markets, control over the circulation of money through credit or speculatory activity became a critical aspect of upper-class manliness.

Not all men could achieve this ideal of transactional manhood. Artisans and journeymen, who aspired to become master artisans and to realize an artisanal masculine ideal based on skill, entrepreneurial control, and craft autonomy, found themselves increasingly pressed into the ranks of an emerging working class. Industrialization and the market revolution curtailed their ability to transact. Nor could older ideals of propertied independence ground their notions of manliness, since the ownership of land or a house became increasingly unattainable for them. The ability to establish their sons in jobs and careers of their own became more important to their sense of manhood—but this rested on uncertain foundations, since its success depended largely on the occupation, labor demand, and skill level required. Instead, working-class men grounded their manliness in their ability to earn a family wage. Many skilled craftsmen were able to retain traditional notions of craft control and workplace autonomy in their definitions of working-class manliness. For factory operatives and skilled craft-workers alike, awareness of their shared class status, and solidarity with other men of the same class background, became a significant aspect of their manliness.

Corporate Capitalism in the Late Nineteenth and Early Twentieth Centuries

The second wave of industrialization in the late nineteenth century, and the subsequent rise of corporations, further reshaped class-based social structures and class-based definitions of manliness. Mechanization and the so-called deskilling of many work processes, the continuing significance of craft-based control and craft autonomy, the increasing significance of bureaucratic and corporate structures, and the further spatial expansion of cities (and the spatial distribution of social functions within them) all contributed to the reshaping of class-based social structures and class-based definitions of manliness.

Mechanization and the deskilling of an increasing number of work processes increased the entrepreneurial power and control of industrialists. For a small group of upper-class businessmen, the power and ability to direct the flow of production, cash, and credit—to function as "captains of industry"—became a crucial aspect of their definitions of manliness. Their control over large labor forces and national distribution networks, as well as social Darwinist ideas linking success with power and strength, figured into their perceptions of their manliness.

By the turn of the twentieth century, the United States witnessed the formation of a whole new substratum of middle managers for whom the administration and supervision of others was a critical aspect of their manliness. These new middle-class men belonged to an emerging corporate class of employers, entrepreneurs, professionals, managers, advertisers, ministers, academics, and others who were united by their profound agreement as to the benefits of a corporate capitalist society—and who shared in its administration, control, and ideological justification. Men of this corporate class defined manliness through corporate, bureaucratic, and professional codes that emphasized productivity, efficiency, teamwork, and public status.

Class-based constructions of manhood among industrial workers continued to vary, depending on one's level of skill. In some areas, such as glove-making, glass-blowing, printing, and steel manufacturing, craft skills retained significance and craft autonomy continued to play a significant aspect of the definition and experience of working-class masculinity. But for the increasing ranks of semiskilled and unskilled operatives and workers, craft autonomy became unattainable.

For a growing segment of the male working class, the paycheck, or the ability to provide for one's family, became the yardstick of manliness and social worth. With the introduction of the continuous-motion assembly line, older artisanal ideals emphasizing skill content and physical power withered, and some manufacturers replaced men with women. Men in many industrial work settings compensated for this development by defining certain jobs as suitable for men only. The affirmation of masculinity through such gender-typing became an important part of the cultural wage that working-class men derived from their work. Working-class men also looked increasingly to labor unions (such as the Knights of Labor, founded in 1869, and the American Federation of Labor, founded in 1886) to define and collectively affirm class-based definitions of manliness. While men across class lines tended to share a belief in the importance of individual effort for economic success and well-being, working-class men increasingly realized that mutual loyalty among men of the same class background allowed them to protect their economic interests and their claims to manhood in a transactional society.

The Great Depression intensified class-based definitions of manliness. Those who struggled to survive were reaffirmed in linking manhood to economic status and the ability to provide, while wealthier Americans who weathered the storm were confirmed in their belief in their own strength. Among working-class men, class solidarity and unionization became an even more salient dimension of working-class manhood, as was evidenced by the large number of strikes, in particular in 1934 and 1937, and the rise of the Congress of Industrial Organizations (CIO), which organized previously unorganized workers. Yet militant assertions of working-class masculinity, critical of and potentially in opposition to capitalism, was reined in by the New Deal. By supporting unionization through the Wagner Act (1935), the federal government generated new loyalties between the federal government and the working class, thus bringing working-class men and their definitions of manhood into a closer alliance with the corporate class and a closer conformity with transactional standards of manliness.

Manhood and Class in Postwar America

The long cycle of global economic expansion that followed World War II and that lasted until the late 1960s had a tremendous impact on class-based definitions of manliness in U.S. society. This economic upswing stabilized the lives and careers of middle-class men and enabled many working-class men to aspire to, and even achieve, middle-class status. Suburban living, including the ownership of a home, household appliances, and an automobile, became an important expression of a man's success as breadwinner and a pervasive symbol of a man's class status. Yet some cultural critics suggested that the security, comforts, and social status associated with suburban manhood undermined rather than bolstered masculine identity. Others, such as Sloan Wilson, the author of *The Man in the Grey Flannel Suit* (1955), and William Whyte, the author of *The Organization Man* (1956), feared that the new middle-class male lacked autonomy.

Manhood and Class in a Postindustrial Economy

Between the mid-1950s and the 1980s, a series of structural changes in the U.S. economy altered the class structure of American society and challenged older class-based definitions of manliness. According to the sociologist Daniel Bell, the United States economy was, by the mid-1950s, entering a new "postindustrial" phase based less on production and manufacturing than on theoretical knowledge and professional expertise. By the late 1960s a long stretch of post–World War II economic expansion had given way to stagnation and inflation. During the 1970s and 1980s, U.S. companies began adjusting to changing global realties by means of a restructuring—often called "de-industrialization." The increasing significance of white-collar and service occupations, the end of continuous economic growth, and the decline of heavy industry (which meant a loss of jobs in previously male preserves) made the class distinctions and class-based notions of manhood generated by industrialization less meaningful. Michael Moore's documentary film *Roger and Me* (1988), a study of the decline of Flint, Michigan, as a result of GM plant closures, suggested that workingmen felt powerless, alienated, and unable to adjust to new realities by articulating new and meaningful definitions of manliness and class.

The corporate restructuring of the U.S. economy affected not only working-class men but also, by the mid-1980s, middle-class men as well. After an initial expansion of the corporate sector in the early 1980s, corporations began to "downsize," resulting in the loss of white-collar management positions. Men began to lose their sense of security in their jobs and their work-based masculine identities.

As old frameworks of class-based notions of manhood emphasizing entrepreneurial control lost significance, new class divisions and class-based definitions of manliness emerged. Class distinctions grounded in the social relations of production in an industrial economy did not vanish. But the most meaningful postindustrial class divisions—sometimes overlapping with, and sometimes replacing, corporate industrial class distinctions—became those between men (and increasingly women as well) who possessed and administered scientific knowledge and expertise and those who were subjected to such knowledge and expertise without exercising any control over it. Class-based definitions of manliness increasingly became defined through participation in corporate networks of codification, application, and distribution of knowledge. The development of these new postindustrial definitions of manhood suggests that class remains a powerful shaper of masculinity in American society.

BIBLIOGRAPHY

Aron, Cindy Sondik. *Ladies and Gentlemen of the Civil Service: Middle-Class Workers in Victorian America.* New York: Oxford University Press, 1987.

Bell, Daniel. *The Coming of Post-Industrial Society: A Venture in Social Forecasting.* New York: Basic Books, 1973.

Blumin, Stuart M. *The Emergence of the Middle-Class: Social Experience in the American City, 1760–1900.* Cambridge, England: Cambridge University Press, 1989.

Davis, Clark. *Company Men: White-Collar Life and Corporate Cultures in Los Angeles, 1892–1941.* Baltimore: Johns Hopkins University Press, 2000.

DeVault, Illeen A. *Sons and Daughters of Labor: Class and Clerical Work in Turn-of-the-Century Pittsburgh.* Ithaca, N.Y.: Cornell University Press, 1990.

Giddens, Anthony. *The Class Structure of the Advanced Societies.* New York: Harper & Row, 1975.

Kimmel, Michael. *Manhood in America: A Cultural History.* New York: Free Press, 1996.

Montgomery, David. "Worker's Control of Machine Production in the Nineteenth Century." *Labor History* 17 (Fall 1976): 486–509.

Sandage, Scott A. "Gender and the Economics of the Sentimental Market in Nineteenth-Century America." *Social Politics* 6, no. 2 (1999): 105–130.

Sklar, Martin J. *The Corporate Reconstruction of American Capitalism, 1890-1916: The Market, The Law, and Politics.* Cambridge, England: Cambridge University Press, 1988.

Thompson, E. P. *The Making of the English Working Class.* 1964. Reprint, London: Penguin, 1980.

Trachtenberg, Alan. *The Incorporation of America: Culture and Society in the Gilded Age.* New York: Hill and Wang, 1982.

Further Reading

Baron, Ava, ed. *Work Engendered: Toward a New History of American Labor.* Ithaca, N.Y.: Cornell University Press, 1991.

Bendix, Reinhard. *Work and Authority in Industry: Ideologies of Management in the Course of Industrialization.* Berkeley: University of California Press, 1974.

Clawson, Mary Ann. *Constructing Brotherhood: Class, Gender, and Fraternalism.* Princeton, N.J.: Princeton University Press, 1989.

DeMott, Benjamin. *The Imperial Middle: Why Americans Can't Think Straight about Class.* New York: Morrow, 1990.

Gorn, Elliott Jacob. *The Manly Art: Bare-Knuckled Prize Fighting and the Rise of American Sports.* Ithaca, N.Y.: Cornell University Press, 1986.

McNall, Scott G., Rhonda F. Levine, and Rick Fantasia, eds. *Bringing Class Back In: Contemporary and Historical Perspectives.* Boulder, Colo.: Westview Press, 1991.

Winter, Thomas. *Making Men, Making Class: The YMCA and Workingmen, 1877–1920.* Chicago: University of Chicago Press, 2002.

Related Entries

Agrarianism; Artisan; Automobile; Boxing; Business/Corporate America; Capitalism; Darwinism; Great Depression; Individualism; Industrialization; Labor Movement and Unions; Leisure; Market Revolution; Middle-Class Manhood; New Deal; *Organization Man, The*; Professionalism; Property; Self-Made Man; Suburbia; Urbanization; Work; Working-Class Manhood

—*Thomas Winter*

Cold War

The Cold War, which began after World War II and lasted through the 1980s, was a geopolitical rivalry between the United States and the Soviet Union grounded in an ideological rivalry between capitalism and communism. The Cold War raised concerns about both external and internal threats to American strength, social stability, and security, and particularly to material abundance, middle-class lifestyles, and cultural norms about masculinity. Motivated by fears of emasculation, effeminization, and homosexuality, Americans anxiously defined their nation and their way of life in terms culturally associated with masculinity, including power, diplomatic and military assertiveness, economic success, sexual and physical prowess, moral righteousness, and patriotism.

Postwar Anxieties

A major basis of Cold War anxiety was the fear that the defining features of American life weakened both American men and the nation, thus rendering both unable to confront the perceived threat of Soviet communism abroad and at home. In an often contradictory fashion, American commentators of the 1940s and 1950s identified the sources of this weakness as postwar material abundance, conformity (as well as nonconformity), overprotective mothers, negligent parents, governmental and corporate paternalism, and rampant homosexuality (which Alfred Kinsey's *Sexual Behavior in the Human Male* (1948) had shown to be far more widespread in U.S. society than most had believed). Corporate capitalism, in particular, caused anxious concerns. Bureaucratic and regimented workplaces, critics argued, seemed to have undermined the manhood of American men. Suggesting that American men had become alienated and emasculated by corporate work and suburban life, C. Wright Mills's *White Collar* (1951) and William H. Whyte's *The Organization Man* (1956) maintained that manliness could be affirmed through independence, self-determination, and the exercise of power.

Masculinity and 1950s Domesticity

Cold War anxieties regarding American manhood often equated communism with voracious femininity or seductive female sexuality. In the novels of Mickey Spillane, such as *One Lonely Night* (1951) and *Kiss Me Deadly* (1952), women who work for communists take advantage of weak men who are unable to resist their seductive wiles. In these tales, only the protoganist/hero Mike Hammer—whose name suggests the association many Americans perceived between masculinity, physical toughness, and Americanism—possesses the fortitude necessary for triumph over these figures. In an even more frightening image, the 1962 film *The Manchurian Candidate* showed a brainwashed U.S. soldier accepting orders from a female enemy agent. Such popular-culture images suggested that any effective containment of communism would require the containment of femininity and an assertion of the traditional gender hierarchy. The Cold War thus provided a powerful impetus for a pronounced cultural emphasis on conventional domesticity as a pillar of American life.

The importance of traditional ideals of domesticity and femininity to American Cold War posturing was apparent in 1959, when Vice President Richard M. Nixon traveled to Moscow to open and attend an American exhibit that consisted mostly of an average American suburban home with all the modern conveniences. This exhibit became the site of the famous "kitchen debate" between Nixon and Soviet premier Nikita Khrushchev. In the debate, Nixon praised the material abundance of American life as a sign of the superiority of the American capitalist system. His argument that U.S. superiority and freedom ultimately depended less on weaponry than on material abundance and a middle-class suburban lifestyle implied that it also rested on full-time female homemakers and male providers. The containment of communism abroad, Nixon suggested, required the containment of female sexuality through motherhood—and the activity of American men in the public world of capitalist exchange.

This connection between containing communism abroad and female sexuality at home was satirized in Stanley Kubrick's 1963 film *Dr. Strangelove, Or, How I Stopped Worrying and Learned to Love the Bomb.* Rife with exaggerated images of male sexual prowess, the film tells the story of a preventive nuclear assault on the Soviet Union, launched to fend off a Soviet threat to American masculine sexual potency. In the film, the Soviet Union retaliates by exploding a nuclear device that will destroy all life on Earth within a year. At that point, the president's scientific advisor, Dr. Strangelove, unveils a plan for survival that suggests sexually charged domestic containment: A select sample of the U.S. population with a gender ratio of ten women to every man will be sent underground into bunkers built in abandoned mine shafts, thus guaranteeing the survival of the U.S. nation and way of life.

Masculinity and Cold War Politics

In American politics, the postwar competition between the Soviet Union and the United States was often represented in terms of masculinity. Whereas the U.S. victory in World War II and President Harry Truman's confrontation of communist threats in Greece and Turkey in 1947 appeared to confirm the masculine vigor of U.S. society, the Communist victory in China in 1949 and the subsequent invasion of South Korea in 1950 seemed to suggest that U.S. politics lacked manly stamina. Losing hold over a region geopolitically important to the United States and populated by a people traditionally depicted as effeminate and decadent caused political enemies of Truman and the Democratic Party to suggest that they had become "soft" on communism.

The Republican Party, which gained control of the White House when Dwight D. Eisenhower won the presidential election in 1952, infused the vocabulary of U.S. diplomacy and military policy with a distinctly masculine vocabulary intended to signal stamina and aggressiveness, introducing such concepts as brinkmanship (taking the power struggle to the brink of nuclear war), massive retaliation (responding to an isolated incident, or conflict, with an all-out attack), and rollback (a commitment to push back Soviet influence wherever it had gained a foothold). This unencumbered expression of masculine strength and boldness reassured Americans worried about national toughness.

Amid this concern with American male toughness, Republican Senator Joseph R. McCarthy of Wisconsin and his anticommunist campaign emerged and gained widespread acceptance between 1950 and 1954. McCarthy purposefully used a flamboyantly aggressive and masculine posturing. Charging that his opponents were either communist, homosexual, or both, McCarthy equated support for him and his party with heterosexual, patriotic American manliness. Although his accusations about communists in government quickly turned out to be as unsubstantiated as his claims about his wartime exploits as "Tailgunner Joe" were false, his political persona may have held a certain appeal for at least some American men. It certainly reflected broader cultural anxieties and powerfully influenced subsequent politics—particularly the policies of Democrats, who felt compelled to demonstrate their toughness.

The Cold War premium on asserting American masculinity was especially evident in the presidency of Democrat John F. Kennedy (1961–63). His campaign presented him as a youthful, vigorous, and sexually appealing contrast to the aging incumbent, Dwight D. Eisenhower. His promise of a "New Frontier" appealed to longstanding mythologies of American manhood, and his call to "ask not what your country can do for you" but "what you can do for your country" assured American men that there would be opportunities to demonstrate their masculine vigor. On December 26, 1960, President-elect John F. Kennedy launched his campaign to reinvigorate American men and the nation with a *Sports Illustrated* article titled "The Soft American." He wrote that prosperity, suburban life, television, movies, and everyday conveniences had enervated Americans, leaving them and the nation unable to compete with communists. Closing the "muscle gap," he said, would allow the nation to close the "missile gap" and compete successfully in the space race with the Soviet Union, which had launched the first satellite, *Sputnik*, in 1957. Presenting space as the ultimate frontier of masculine endeavor and space technology as symbolic of American power and prowess, Kennedy made the space program a top priority.

Kennedy's foreign policy suggested similar concerns. His persistent confrontations with Cuban Communist leader Fidel Castro—who himself viewed his relation with the United States as a contest of masculine strength—was driven by a conscious need to assert his and America's might, as was his brinkmanshiplike confrontation with the Soviet Union during the Cuban Missile Crisis in 1961. More portentous was his determination to resist communism in Vietnam and avoid the loss of another Asian nation. This commitment led his vice president and successor, Lyndon B. Johnson, who was equally anxious to assert his, his party's, and his nation's masculine power, into a full-scale war. Men who opposed such policies, particularly the U.S. military involvement in Vietnam, found their masculinity questioned and were depicted as effeminate or homosexual.

In 1980 the Cold War ideological complex of containment and masculinity received a new boost with the election of Ronald Reagan, a Republican, as president. During the presidencies of Reagan and his successor, George H. W. Bush, a compulsive masculinity again informed American foreign policy, often casting minor states, such as Grenada or Panama, in the role of global enemies. Reagan's proposal to install a missile defense system in orbit indicated that space had once again become an arena for proving American masculinity. Political supporters and sympathetic historians credit Reagan's rhetoric of masculine toughness with contributing decisively to the end of the Cold War in the late 1980s.

Conclusion

The Cold War tapped currents of masculinity that had been activated during the second half of the nineteenth century, particularly the notion that warfare validates and invigorates manliness, the idea that national survival requires masculine toughness, an equation of masculinity with bodily strength and vigor, and a concern with the dangers of unbridled female sexuality. It both reinvigorated and reinforced these pre-existing currents, thus contributing to the persistence of masculine rhetoric and militarism in American foreign policy after the Cold War itself ended.

Bibliography

Cuordileone, Kyle A. "'Politics in an Age of Anxiety': Cold War Political Culture and the Crisis in American Masculinity, 1949–1960." *Journal of American History* 87 (September 2000): 515–545.

Faludi, Susan. *Stiffed: The Betrayal of Modern Man*. New York: William Morrow, 1999.

Griswold, Robert. "The 'Flabby American,' the Body, and the Cold War." In *A Shared Experience: Men, Women, and the History of Gender*, edited by Laura McCall and Donald Yacovone. New York: New York University Press, 1998.

Kimmel, Michael. *Manhood in America: A Cultural History*. New York: Free Press, 1996.

May, Elaine Tyler. *Homeward Bound: American Families in the Cold War Era*. New York: Basic Books, 1988.

Savran, David. *Taking It Like A Man: White Masculinity, Masochism, and Contemporary American Culture*. Princeton, N.J.: Princeton University Press, 1998.

Further Reading

Boyer, Paul S. *By The Bomb's Early Light: American Thought and Culture at the Dawn of the Atomic Age*. Chapel Hill: University of North Carolina Press, 1994.

Dean, Robert D. *Imperial Brotherhood: Gender and the Making of Cold War Foreign Policy*. Amherst: University of Massachusetts Press, 2001.

Ehrenreich, Barbara. *The Hearts of Men: American Dreams and the Flight from Commitment*. New York: Anchor Press/Doubleday, 1984.

Epstein, Barbara. "Anti-Communism, Homophobia, and the Construction of Masculinity in the Postwar U.S." *Critical Sociology* 20 (1994): 21–44.

Mills, C. Wright. *White Collar: The American Middle Classes*. New York: Oxford University Press, 1951.

Smith, Geoffrey. "National Security and Personal Isolation: Sex, Gender, and Disease in the Cold-War United States." *International History Review* 14 (May 1992): 307–337.

Whyte, William H. *The Organization Man*. New York: Simon & Schuster, 1956.

Winkler, Allan M. *Life Under A Cloud: American Anxiety About The Atom*. New York: Oxford University Press, 1993.

Related Entries

Body; Bureaucratization; Business/Corporate America; Capitalism; Crisis of Masculinity; Heroism; Imperialism; Militarism; Military; *Organization Man, The*; Patriarchy; Patriotism; Politics; Reagan, Ronald; Technology; Vietnam War; War

—*Thomas Winter*

Common Sense Book of Baby and Child Care, The

With more than fifty million copies in print, *The Common Sense Book of Baby and Child Care* is the best-selling nonfiction book after the Bible. First published in 1946 by the pediatrician Dr. Benjamin Spock, this guide played a vital role in shaping millions of fathers and sons of the baby boom generation.

Although Spock's philosophy evolved over time, initially his vision was in harmony with the emphasis on conformity and strict gender roles of Cold War America. He advocated raising boys to work and compete in the public realm and raising girls to be homemakers. He also reinforced the idea that child rearing was largely a mother's responsibility (although fathers might "occasionally" assist). But Spock departed from conventional beliefs by rejecting predominant child-rearing philosophies that advocated harsh discipline. Instead, he argued that parents should nurture, rather than dominate, children, and that fathers should show affection to their children. His idea that children should be encouraged, and even pampered, reflected the idealism of a nation wishing to raise a postwar generation of healthy, competitive citizens.

Drawing from the psychoanalytic theories of Sigmund Freud, Spock's guide provided insights into issues such as jealousy, anxiety, puberty, and identity. It explained all stages of a child's development, making clear distinctions between boy and girls. From age three to five, for example, boys will model themselves after their "admired fathers" while developing a "strong romantic attachment" to their mothers. Next, boys will attempt to assert their independence through dress, manners, and interests. Although Spock recognized that this stage of male development presented the dangerous possibility of producing juvenile delinquency—an intense fear among Cold War Americans who associated conformity with social and political stability—he viewed even the most disturbing behavior as "natural" and counseled parents to maintain an even-tempered, loving approach in responding to it. He cautioned that either excessive or insufficient discipline might lead to "neuroses" that could hinder a boy's healthy progression to manhood, marriage, and productive citizenship.

Spock's vision of the ideal father combined the qualities of firmness and attentiveness reflected in numerous popular portrayals of fathers in the postwar era, such as in the television show *Father Knows Best* (1954–63). In countering earlier notions of fatherhood, Spock instructed fathers to abandon the role of distant authoritarian—a posture associated by Cold War Americans with communist threats to American democracy—and assured them that they could be simultaneously affectionate and masculine. Further, because boys must "pattern" themselves on a role model to develop into men, Spock encouraged fathers to limit teasing and "roughhousing." Arguing that girls also need their fathers' approval, Spock suggested that fathers compliment their daughters on, for example, their cooking or clothes.

In the 1960s, as Spock began to speak out against the Vietnam War, critics from the political right attacked his politics, blaming his "permissive" child-rearing philosophy for the rise of an antiauthoritarian counterculture and a perceived softness and effeminacy among young men. Meanwhile, feminists labeled his philosophy as fundamentally sexist and promotive of an antiquated masculine ideal. Spock later revised his guide in an effort to rid it of sexism (ceasing, for example, to use only "he" to refer to a child), and updating it with sections on homosexuality, working mothers, and divorce. He also advocated a more expansive view of boyhood and fatherhood by loosening the strict boundaries between gender roles and advocating shared responsibilities of both parents.

Bibliography

Maier, Thomas. *Dr. Spock: An American Life.* New York: Harcourt Brace, 1998.

Spock, Benjamin. *The Common Sense Book of Baby and Child Care.* New York: Duell, Sloan, and Pearce, 1946.

Spock, Benjamin, with Michael Rothenberg. *Baby and Child Care.* 6th ed. New York: Dutton, 1992.

Further Reading

Coontz, Stephanie. *The Way We Never Were: American Families and the Nostalgia Trap.* New York: Basic Books, 2000.

May, Elaine Tyler. *Homeward Bound: American Families in the Cold War Era.* New York: Basic Books, 1999.

Spock, Benjamin. *A Better World for Our Children: Rebuilding American Family Values.* Bethesda, Md.: National Press Books, 1994.

Spock, Benjamin, and Mary Morgan. *Spock on Spock: A Memoir of Growing Up in the Twentieth Century.* New York: Pantheon Books, 1989.

Spock, Benjamin, with Mitchell Zimmerman. *Dr. Spock on Vietnam.* New York: Dell, 1968.

Related Entries

Adolescence; Advice Literature; Antiwar Movement; Boyhood; Cold War; Counterculture; Fatherhood; Feminism; Freudian Psychoanalytic Theory; Juvenile Delinquency; Suburbia; Vietnam War

—*Jenny Thompson*

CONFIDENCE MAN

The confidence man—a man who takes advantage of people by gaining their confidence, convincing them to trust him with their possessions, and then stealing those possessions—was a male archetype of Victorian middle-class culture. He symbolized middle-class Americans' anxieties about the potential for predatory male behavior in the increasingly anonymous, impersonal, and competitive social world being created by urbanization and the market revolution.

The term confidence man first appeared in 1849 in a *New York Herald* story about the arrest of Samuel (William) Thompson, who had robbed about one hundred people. Approaching strangers in the streets like an old acquaintance, Thompson asked his unsuspecting victims, after a short conversation, "have you confidence in me to trust me with your watch until to-morrow?" The *Herald*'s term would quickly achieve wide currency.

The figure of the confidence man acquired literary fame in Herman Melville's novel *The Confidence-Man: His Masquerade* (1857). Set on a steamboat, the story revolves around a group of passengers whose refined appearances and conduct conceal their corruption and greed. Neither the real-life confidence man Thompson nor Melville's characters were isolated phenomena. An 1860 survey of New York police officers estimated that one out of ten criminals in New York was a confidence man.

The confidence man was a product of growing urbanization in antebellum America. In 1830, 9 percent of Americans lived in cities with twenty-five hundred or more inhabitants—a figure that rose to 20 percent by 1860. Antebellum cities were characterized by high mobility and population turnover rates, a lack of pronounced spatial boundaries between residential and commercial areas, and only limited residential segregation along lines of class, ethnicity, or race. The resulting social fluidity and anonymity enabled the confidence man to thrive.

The confidence man also served as a threat in his ability to corrupt transient young men. In his guises as seducer and gambler, the confidence man was ready to entice young men into an emerging urban subculture of theaters, brothels, and gambling dens. Another type of confidence man, generated by the emergence of modern political parties and campaigns, was the party man, a demagogue who sought personal power by using the rhetoric of republican civic-mindedness to solicit political support. American society had just begun to accept political parties and partisan politics, and the party man was often seen as a socially divisive force and a source of moral corruption. At a time when such traditional small-town mechanisms of moral order as family and the church were losing force, suspicion of the confidence man reflected republican fears of corruption, conspiracy, and social and political instability.

The confidence man was implicated in the changing ideals of middle-class manhood in antebellum America. The market revolution generated the ideal of the self-made man, who, unfettered by communal bonds, was enterprising, thrifty, and ready to take advantage of opportunities. Another model of manhood that emerged at this time was the Yankee, who became a national symbol by 1850, around the time the confidence man first appeared. A man of great ingenuity, the Yankee was hardworking and willing to take advantage of others for his own gain. The confidence man was also a man-on-the-make who acted on the opportunities offered by an expanding market economy, but his behavior highlighted the potential social and ethical dangers of an amoral public world.

The confidence man embodied an identity problem among middle-class men in antebellum America. The problem was how to pursue self-interest and success in an anonymous market-driven society without resorting to manipulation of appearance or dishonest conduct. The confidence man represented a violation of the morally stable and sincere character that Americans thought was essential to true manhood and necessary to maintain personal trustworthiness amid the increasing impersonality of market relations and urban life. The confidence man, able to instill confidence in others while remaining unrestrained by the requirements of character, represented a profound threat to the social and moral order.

By the 1870s, the skills of the confidence man were being transformed into a more benign model for men who wished to get ahead in an emerging urban consumer society. Advice books and success manuals of the time encouraged men to gain the confidence of others by cultivating the ability to impress them. This new success ideology peaked with books such as Dale Carnegie's *How to Win Friends and Influence People* (1936). The development of modern American business culture in the twentieth century put a premium on the skills of the confidence man, making them mainstream masculine ideals.

BIBLIOGRAPHY

Bergmann, Johannes Dietrich. "The Original Confidence-Man." *American Quarterly* 21 (1969): 560–577.

Haltunen, Karen. *Confidence Men and Painted Women: A Study of Middle-Class Culture in America, 1830–1870.* New Haven, Conn.: Yale University Press, 1982.

Kasson, John F. *Rudeness & Civility: Manners in Nineteenth-Century Urban America.* New York: Hill and Wang, 1990.

Meyer, Donald. *The Positive Thinkers: Religion as Pop Psychology, from Mary Baker Eddy to Oral Roberts.* New York: Pantheon, 1980.

Robertson-Lorant, Laurie. *Melville: A Biography.* Amherst: University of Massachusetts Press, 1998.

FURTHER READING

Harvey, David. *Consciousness and the Urban Experience.* Baltimore: Johns Hopkins University Press, 1985.

Hilkey, Judy. *Character Is Capital: Success Manuals And Manhood In Gilded Age America.* Chapel Hill: University of North Carolina Press, 1997.

Lasch, Christopher. *The Culture of Narcissism: American Life in an Age of Diminishing Expectations.* New York: Norton, 1991.

Melville, Herman. *The Confidence-Man: His Masquerade.* 1857. Reprint, Oxford: Oxford University Press, 1999.

Rogin, Michael Paul. *Subversive Genealogy: The Politics and Art of Herman Melville.* Berkeley: University of California Press, 1985.

Rose, Anne C. *Voices of the Marketplace: American Thought and Culture, 1830-1860.* New York: Twayne, 1995.

Wadlington, Warwick. *The Confidence Game in American Literature.* Princeton, N.J.: Princeton University Press, 1975.

RELATED ENTRIES

Advice Literature; Capitalism; Character; Democratic Manhood; Market Revolution; Middle-Class Manhood; Republicanism; Self-Made Man; Sentimentalism; Success Manuals; Urbanization; Victorian Era

—*Thomas Winter*

CONSCIENTIOUS OBJECTION

Male identity and war making are often related in American life, but American culture has also encouraged conscientious objection—a refusal to participate in warfare on religious or political grounds—as a masculine standard. Because individual and societal determinations about manliness help dictate how power is distributed, consideration of how men have resisted and avoided conscription reveals important ties between gender norms and cultural values. Physical courage has historically been a key element of Western masculinity, and many Americans connect violence and aggression to their ideas of manliness. Furthermore, American male patriotism often equates commitment to country with a willingness to sacrifice one's life in war. These models of manliness dictate military service as a masculine duty and imply that refusal is unmanly. But at the same time, the individualism and freedom often associated with masculinity in America has justified resistance to military service.

The earliest conscientious objectors came from pacifist Christian sects, whose male adherents looked for their model of manliness to their interpretation of Jesus as an advocate of nonviolence, peace, and love. Their notion of masculinity was viewed with ambivalence by most colonists, whose definitions of manhood involved defense of community as well as adherence to Christian precepts. But whereas pacifist Christians prioritized religious doctrine, most colonists emphasized pragmatic need. Thus Maryland and North Carolina fined Quakers for refusing to fight against Native Americans, while several other colonies recognized conscientious objection as a right and excused from service those who paid a special tax.

During the era of the American Revolution, the tenets of republicanism and republican manhood—which focused on the belief that individual rights and religious freedom should be protected from perceived government tyranny—helped to build respect for conscientious objection into American political culture. George Washington exempted from his Revolutionary War draft order those with "conscientious scruples against war," and the framers of the U.S. Constitution considered including a military exemption for conscientious objectors in the Second Amendment.

Still, conscientious objection continued to arouse ambivalent responses through much of the nineteenth century. The Mexican War of 1846–47 provoked transcendentalist writer Henry David Thoreau to refuse to pay taxes, suffer imprisonment, and codify a philosophy of civil disobedience, though his was a minority position. During the Civil War, Amish and Mennonite conscientious objectors challenged conscription with varying success, in some cases purchasing an exemption, hiring a substitute, or caring for soldiers wounded in battle. The nation's growth into a global military power during the twentieth century intensified Americans' tendency to identify masculinity and patriotism with militarism—and the view of conscientious objectors as unmanly also intensified. During World War II, thousands of Jehovah's Witnesses were sentenced to federal prison for refusing military service.

Disagreement over the meaning of masculinity in wartime has been dramatically visible in the treatment of conscientious objectors. The belief that refusing military service violates normative manhood has led government authorities to impose severe penalties, while conscientious objectors, motivated by religious or moral principle, have often viewed these punishments as a form of martyrdom or self-sacrifice, and therefore as an important signifier of their manhood. They have therefore accepted even the most severe sentences—in many cases long prison terms, and in some cases death. Of the 450 conscientious objectors found guilty at military hearings during World War I, for example, 17 were sentenced to death, 142 received life sentences, and 73 received twenty-year prison terms. Only 15 were sentenced to three years or less. Many imprisoned conscientious objectors endured abuse, torture, and mistreatment. During World War I, conscientious objectors at Fort Leavenworth in Kansas were placed in solitary confinement, manacled to their cell walls for nine hours every day, fed a bread-and-water diet, and beaten by guards. During World War II, pacifists were either jailed or sent to labor camps.

For African-American conscientious objectors, resistance to military service has been an expression of both spiritually grounded and racially grounded ideas of masculinity. While many African-American men have contributed to U.S. war efforts in an attempt to demonstrate their manliness and stake a claim to the rights of citizenship, others have concluded from their identification of manhood with citizenship that they should refuse to represent a country that segregated the armed forces and denied them their rights. The Nation of Islam leader Elijah Muhammad served four years in prison during World War II for his intransigence. Also rejecting military service during World War II was the pacifistic Fellowship of Reconciliation, a nondenominational religious organization led by Bayard Rustin, who later helped found the Congress of Racial Equality (CORE). Rustin, like Martin Luther King, Jr., and other twentieth-century conscientious objectors, saw in the examples of Thoreau, charismatic Hindu leader Mahatma Gandhi, and radical reformer A. J. Muste a model of nonviolent manhood useful for pursuing racial justice in America.

During the 1960s, many African-American civil rights activists again opposed the war and sought conscientious-objector status. They were joined by large numbers of young whites who, influenced by the New Left and countercultural youth movements, questioned conventional associations of masculinity with militarism, defended individual freedom against what they perceived as political and corporate threats, and objected to the Vietnam War on moral and spiritual grounds. Members of all of these movements expressed their ideals of manliness through nonviolent demonstrations. Perhaps the most famous draft resistor during the Vietnam War—proof to many that conscientious objection and masculine toughness were compatible—was the heavyweight boxing champion Muhammad Ali, who was sentenced to five years in prison for draft evasion when a federal court refused his claim for exemption as a minister of Islam.

Substantial public opposition to the Vietnam War, combined with the Supreme Court's broadening of eligibility for conscientious-objector status to include secular, moral, and ethical systems in the *United States* v. *Seeger* (1965) and *Welsh* v. *United States* (1970) cases, led to a dramatic increase in the willingness of American authorities to grant conscientious-objector status. Whereas there were only 0.14 conscientious objector grants per 100 inductees during World War I and 0.15 during World War II, there were 42.62 in 1971 and 130.72 in 1972—marking the first time in American history when conscientious objectors outnumbered draftees.

While the increasing instance of conscientious objection prior to the elimination of the military draft in 1973 appears to imply that militarism and war service have become less important signifiers of masculinity, the premium on American military toughness since 1980 suggests that notions of violence, aggression, and dominance remain central to U.S. constructions of patriotism and manhood. While the growing acceptance of conscientious objection represents a triumph for those who wish to challenge the longstanding ideal that real men make war, it is perceived as an affront by those who feel that military service is a vital component of American male patriotism.

BIBLIOGRAPHY

Chambers, John Whiteclay, II. "Conscientious Objection." In *The Oxford Companion to American Military History*, edited by John Whiteclay Chambers II. New York: Oxford University Press, 1999.

Kohn, Stephen M. *Jailed for Peace: The History of American Draft Law Violators, 1658–1985.* Westport, Conn.: Greenwood Press, 1986.

Schlissel, Lillian. *Conscience in America: A Documentary History of Conscientious Objection in America, 1757–1967.* New York: Dutton, 1968.

FURTHER READING

Flynn, George Q. *The Draft, 1940–1973.* Lawrence: University Press of Kansas, 1993.

Frazer, Heather T., and John O'Sullivan. *"We Have Just Begun to Not Fight": An Oral History of Conscientious Objectors in Civilian Public Service during World War II.* New York: Twayne, 1996.

Gara, Larry, and Lenna Mae Gara, eds. *A Few Small Candles: War Resisters of World War II Tell Their Stories.* Kent, Ohio: Kent State University Press, 1999.

Goossen, Rachel Waltner. *Women Against the Good War: Conscientious Objection and Gender on the American Home Front, 1941–1947.* Chapel Hill: University of North Carolina Press, 1997.

May, Larry. *Masculinity and Morality.* Ithaca, N.Y.: Cornell University Press, 1998.

Sprunger, Mary. *Sourcebook: Oral History Interviews with World War One Conscientious Objectors.* Akron, Pa.: Mennonite Central Committee, 1986.

Stearns, Peter N. *Be A Man! Males in Modern Society.* 2nd ed. New York: Holmes & Meier, 1990.

Wright, Edward Needles. *Conscientious Objectors in the Civil War.* Philadelphia: University of Pennsylvania Press, 1931.

Related Entries

American Revolution; Antiwar Movement; Character; Citizenship; Civil Rights Movement; Civil War; Emancipation; Individualism; Militarism; Military; Nationalism; Nation of Islam; Patriotism; Religion and Spirituality; Republicanism; Vietnam War; Violence; War; World War I; World War II

—*Michael Ezra*

Consumerism

Consumerism has often been at odds with American conceptions of masculinity. Historically, commodity consumption has been considered principally a feminine realm, for women's social roles have been centered on the home and family, while men's roles have been focused on work. Nevertheless, men have not been entirely excluded from consumer practices and desires. The family responsibilities that have accompanied the father's traditional provider role, for example, provide an inherent incentive toward consumerism. During the twentieth century, America has also seen the steady growth of masculine cultures predicated on hedonistic forms of personal consumption.

The Eighteenth and Nineteenth Centuries

During the eighteenth and early nineteenth centuries, dominant codes of masculinity rejected the pleasures of personal consumption. Among the white middle class, productiveness and respectability were core values, and men were expected to be the family's breadwinner, a term that denoted an ideal of mature and hard-working masculinity. This ethos of masculine productivity and self-sacrifice was augmented during the nineteenth century as the self-made man, embodied in the novels of Horatio Alger, Jr., emerged as an influential cultural icon.

Masculine ideals oriented around work and the fulfillment of family needs also pertained to working-class culture. By the end of the century, however, many urban workingmen—both white and African American—were also embracing models of masculinity that privileged personal recreation and stylish display. Making a virtue of flamboyant consumption, these "mashers" and Bowery B'hoys were highly visible figures in urban centers of commercial leisure. More widely, however, consumption related to personal pleasure remained an uncertain territory for men. During the late nineteenth century markedly feminine associations still surrounded consumerism, exemplified by the prominence of the "dandy," or "dude," as a stock character in popular humor. Distinguished by his dapper clothes and self-conscious urbanity, he was ridiculed in popular culture as an effete "pussyfoot." Bachelors—men not bound by provider responsibilities—also were viewed with suspicion and deemed unmanly by middle-class culture.

Nevertheless, by the turn of the century, growing urbanization and the rise of a modern consumer economy were drawing greater numbers of men into cultures founded on consumption. Alongside the working-class mashers, many middle-class men also embraced a culture based on personal consumption, and a network of businesses developed specifically geared to men's consumer interests. At the seamier end of the scale were brothels, blood sports, and other illicit pleasures, but a host of restaurants, barbershops, tobacconists, tailors, bars, and theaters also thrived on the patronage of affluent "men-about-town." Traditional notions of heterosexual masculinity, however, were still pervasive and dictated that men carefully distance themselves from the feminine connotations of shopping. Therefore, commodities purchased by women were called consumer goods, whereas men's purchases were accorded the more manly label of expenditure.

The 1920s and 1930s

Amid the prosperity of the 1920s, men's involvement in consumerism became more pronounced. The expanding consumer industries brought higher earnings to many workers, a trend heralded in 1914 by the "five-dollar day" introduced at Henry Ford's automobile factories. Combined with the easier availability of consumer credit, this growth in spending power brought a deluge of new consumer goods—including better clothes and new forms of entertainment such as the cinema—within working men's reach. White-collar workers, too, enjoyed higher standards of living, and middle-class suburbs became important markets for cars, household appliances, and other commodities that grew to be symbols of middle-class respectability. For many, this transformation brought a more comfortable way of life, but it also increased the pressures of the breadwinner role and caused many men to overextend themselves financially. Moreover, economic inequality and entrenched racism effectively excluded many men from the consumer boom. During the 1920s the consumer society's benefits were, for example, less accessible to African Americans, Mexican Americans, and men from other minority ethnic groups, a disparity that continued throughout the twentieth century.

In addition to the growth of family-oriented purchases, the 1920s also saw men's increasing participation in personal consumption. The glamorous celebrities and movie stars of the age—such as Douglas Fairbanks, Rudolph Valentino, and John Gilbert, showcased the possibilities for masculine self-realization in the new consumer society. In popular novels and films, the lavish lifestyle of the gangster (denoted by his expensive suits and jewelry) also came to embody both the promise and the pitfalls surrounding the new paths to individual fulfillment offered by consumerism. For instance, in F. Scott Fitzgerald's *The Great Gatsby* (1925), Jay Gatsby's palatial home, fabulous parties, and expensive clothes epitomize the growth of a masculine style defined by hedonistic materialism. Gatsby's gleaming car represents the emergence of the automobile as an archetypal symbol of the new union of consumerism with masculine independence, power, and status. These figures, both real and fictional, helped break down longstanding perceptions that manhood and consumerism were incompatible, and they offered models of male deportment that a growing number of American men sought to emulate.

The onset of the economic depression following the stock market crash of 1929 was a blow to the American economy. For men whose identity depended upon their role as breadwinner, unemployment was a crushing and even emasculating experience, robbing them of the ability to provide for their families. The growth of consumerism, however, was not halted. Indeed, during the Great Depression, masculine identities based upon the pleasures of individual consumption not only survived, but in some respects thrived. In 1933, for example, the launch of *Esquire* magazine testified to the endurance of a culture of fashionable leisure among many men who had escaped the economic blight. During the late nineteenth century magazines such as *McClure's* and *Vanity Fair* had already targeted men as a market for particular goods and services, but *Esquire*'s consumerist agenda was more forthright. The magazine encouraged its readers to think of themselves as autonomous individuals who expressed their identities through the purchase of distinctive goods. With its circulation soaring to 728,000 by 1938, *Esquire* combined color illustrations of men's fashions with features on foreign travel, cuisine, and interior décor—a formula that underlined the magazine's appeal to a readership of affluent and style-conscious male consumers.

The Swinging Bachelor and the Counterculture

After World War II, American economic growth was phenomenal. Between 1945 and 1960 the gross national product soared by 250 percent, and the economy was pushed forward by a steady growth in earnings. Much of the postwar explosion in consumption was concentrated in the growing suburbs and centered on family life—prosperity unveiled new vistas of household appliances, home furnishings, toys, and holidays. This growth of family-oriented spending underscored men's breadwinning role across the social scale, but the pressure to provide was felt especially by middle-class men, whose status often depended on their ability to furnish their family with all the accoutrements of "the good life."

Additionally, in the 1950s and 1960s, masculine identities based around personal consumption became both more visible and more socially acceptable. The icon of the "swinging bachelor" came into vogue as a personification of a form of masculinity oriented around sexual and material gratification. The success of *Playboy* magazine, launched in 1953, testified to the ascendance of this masculine archetype; the magazine's combination of soft-core pornography and a celebration of stylish leisure prompted many imitators. *Gentlemen's Quarterly*, originally published in 1928 as a menswear trade journal, also enjoyed success after it was revamped in 1957 as a high-class fashion magazine for the 1950s man of style. Throughout popular culture, style-conscious consumption was increasingly celebrated as a desirable masculine ideal. In the entertainment industry, for example, movie stars such as Rock Hudson and Tony Curtis established a niche in roles as jet-set playboys, while a boisterous clique known as the Rat Pack—comprising Frank Sinatra, Sammy Davis, Jr., Dean Martin, and their associates—carved out a reputation for high-living and licentious horseplay.

The counterculture of the 1960s was often critical of the consumer society's political and economic structures, but it also generated a code of optimism, excitement, and stylishness that was in many respects commensurate with modern consumer lifestyles. Laying an emphasis on self-expression and personal fulfillment, many of the aesthetic expressions of the counterculture found an affinity with the tastes and attitudes of fashionable consumers. The role of the counterculture in affirming and extending a hedonistic consumer ethos was especially evident in men's fashion. In what was dubbed the Peacock Revolution, conservative lounge suits gave way to flared trousers, colorful shirts, and gold medallions—a shift that marked a boom for American menswear, with sales climbing steeply throughout the late 1960s. In this context, the consumerist male was given full legitimation as, more than ever before, American men immersed themselves in the pleasures of personal consumption.

The Late Twentieth Century

In the 1980s, the economic ethos of free market competition that prevailed during Ronald Reagan's presidency found its cultural counterpart in a renewed emphasis on personal gratification. Business shifts from manufacturing and distribution to financial and information services laid the way for a new generation of young, urban professionals—derisively labeled Yuppies in popular culture—whose self-obsession and elitist materialism took male consumerism to dizzying heights. During the 1990s, however, the neurotic pursuit of status became unfashionable and was eclipsed by modes of masculinity more subtle in their hedonism. The success of magazines such as *Men's Health* (launched in 1988), for example, signaled the rise of a masculine identity oriented around personal physical transformation, while magazines such as *Maxim* (originally a British title, launched in America in 1997) and *FHM* (another British magazine, launched in the United States in 2000) celebrated sexual license and ironic humor. In both configurations of masculinity, however, practices of individual and acquisitive consumerism remained pronounced.

Overall, the rise of commodity consumption has had a mixed impact on American men. On one hand, it has enabled men to fulfil the American promise of self-realization and material well-being, thus offering visible evidence of manly success. On the other hand, poor men, who have been denied the benefits of consumerism by social inequality, and middle-class men, who have felt pressured to satisfy the demands and expectations generated by consumerism, have sometimes questioned or doubted their ability to meet American standards of manhood.

BIBLIOGRAPHY

Breazeale, Keanon. "In Spite of Women: Esquire Magazine and the Construction of the Male Consumer." *Signs* 20, no. 1 (1994): 1–22.

Chudacoff, Howard. *The Age of the Bachelor: Creating an American Subculture.* Princeton, N.J.: Princeton University Press, 1999.

Ehrenreich, Barbara. *The Hearts of Men: American Dreams and the Flight From Commitment.* New York: Doubleday, 1984.

Rotundo, E. Anthony. *American Manhood: Transformations in Masculinity from the Revolution to the Modern Era.* New York: Basic Books, 1993.

Swiencicki, Mark A. "Consuming Brotherhood: Men's Culture, Style and Recreation as Consumer Culture, 1880–1930." *Social History* 31, no. 4 (1998): 207–240.

FURTHER READING

Beynon, John. *Masculinities and Culture.* Buckingham, England: Open University Press, 2002.

Chapman, Rowena, and Jonathan Rutherford, eds. *Male Order: Unwrapping Masculinity.* London: Lawrence & Wishart, 1988.

Osgerby, Bill. *Playboys in Paradise: Masculinity, Youth, and Leisure-Style in Modern America.* Oxford, England: Berg, 2001.

Pendergast, Tom. *Creating the Modern Man: American Magazines and Consumer Culture, 1900–1950.* Columbia: University of Missouri Press, 2000.

RELATED ENTRIES

Advertising; Alger, Horatio, Jr.; American Dream; Automobile; Bachelorhood; Breadwinner Role; Capitalism; Class; Counterculture; Fashion; Fatherhood; Fitzgerald, F. Scott; Gangsters; Great Depression; Heterosexuality; Hollywood; Hudson, Rock; Industrialization; Leisure; *Playboy* Magazine; Pornography; Reagan, Ronald; Self-Made Man; Sexual Revolution; Suburbia; Urbanization; Victorian Era; Work

—*Bill Osgerby*

THE CONTRAST

Royall Tyler's *The Contrast* (1787)—the first comedy written by a native-born American to be produced professionally, and the first professional play that addresses specifically American issues—portrays romantic interactions between several couples in New York City just after the Revolutionary War. The play dramatizes the difference between emerging American mores and older European behavioral ideals by contrasting republican masculinity with a cultured but effete European masculinity.

The plot focuses on a struggle between Colonel Henry Manly and Billy Dimple for the affections of Maria. The aptly named Manly represents the republican ideal of masculinity: subordination of personal interest to duty, an abstracted sense of virtue, and the ability to master one's material and sexual desires. Manly's masculinity was a desirable yet flawed ideal: Americans deemed it essential to the health of the republic, but it also made Manly (like his hero George Washington) stiff and dull. Manly ultimately wins Maria's love, for his republican masculinity fits perfectly with the expectations of ideal manhood she has formed through reading sentimental novels. But he must contend with Dimple, to whom Maria's father had engaged her, and whose mannered falseness represents an essentially antirepublican model of manhood.

In the play's final act, Dimple tries to rape Manly's sister Charlotte, and he loses Maria when Maria's father learns of Dimple's gambling debts. Both the attempted rape and the debts dramatize Dimple's failure to meet the standards of republican self-mastery. Through gambling he surrenders his economic independence to chance, and his debt compromises his ability to determine his own destiny. By contrast, Manly had set his love for Maria aside after learning she was betrothed, dramatizing his republican virtue. Manly's ultimate betrothal to Maria represents republican superiority over cosmopolitan influences.

Dimple's servant Jessamy and Manly's servant Jonathan provide another contrasting pair of masculinities. Jessamy is a parody of his master; he cannot be trusted and he continually seeks to take advantage of others. Jessamy is a comic precursor of the nineteenth-century confidence man, who corrupted virtuous newcomers to the city. Meanwhile, Jonathan, who represents the comic Yankee or country bumpkin, is on his first trip to the city and symbolizes, in exaggerated form, the vulnerability of republican virtue. Jessamy tutors Jonathan in wooing city women, attending the theater, and creating deceitful emotional responses. Jonathan's mangling of his newly learned vocabulary, and his inability to distinguish staged performance from real life, generates the play's humor. His innate virtue, however, allows him to escape his troubles. An avatar of an emerging democratic masculinity, the youthful Jonathan rejects European sophistication in a sweeping fashion that implies a rejection of all intellectual and cultural aspirations and prefigures the association in American culture of masculinity with anti-intellectualism.

The Contrast portrays the vulnerabilities inherent in American ideals of masculinity. Manly's own sister mocks his lack of fashion sense, dramatizing the emerging threat to republican masculinity posed by consumer capitalism. Both Manly and Jonathan, moreover, exhibit a simplicity and naiveté that makes them vulnerable to their more sophisticated European counterparts. Manly is susceptible to Dimple's superficial expressions of patriotism, and Jonathan proves to be insufficiently educated. Tyler thus expresses the anxieties of a new nation before resolving them with patriotic reassurances. *The Contrast* remains important because the dichotomies between intellectual and working-class sensibilities, between republican virtue and cultural pursuits, and between rural and urban lifestyles have continued to shape American understandings of masculinity.

Bibliography

Carson, Ada Lou, and Herbert L. Carson. *Royall Tyler.* Boston: Twayne, 1979.

Moses, Montrose J., ed. *Representative Plays by American Dramatists.* 1918. Reprint, New York: B. Blom, 1964.

Tanselle, G. Thomas. *Royall Tyler.* Cambridge, Mass.: Harvard University Press, 1967.

Vaughn, Jack A. *Early American Dramatists: From the Beginnings to 1900.* New York: Frederick Ungar, 1981.

Further Reading

Appleby, Joyce. *Capitalism and a New Social Order: The Republican Vision of the 1790s.* New York: New York University Press, 1984.

Carson, Cary, Ronald Hoffman, and Peter J. Albert, eds. *Of Consuming Interests: The Style of Life in the Eighteenth Century.* Charlottesville: University of Virginia Press, 1994.

Fliegalman, Jay. *Prodigals and Pilgrims: The American Revolution Against Patriarchal Authority, 1750–1800.* Cambridge: Cambridge University Press, 1982.

Halttunen, Karen. *Confidence Men and Painted Women: A Study of Middle-Class Culture in America, 1830–1870.* New Haven, Conn.: Yale University Press, 1982.

Hofstadter, Richard. *Anti-Intellectualism in American Life.* New York: Vintage, 1966.

Pocock, J. G. A. *Virtue, Commerce, and History: Essays on Political Thought and History, Chiefly in the Eighteenth Century.* Cambridge: Cambridge University Press, 1985.

Related Entries

American Revolution; Character; Confidence Man; Democratic Manhood; Republicanism; Sentimentalism

—*Greg Beatty*

Cooper, Gary

1901–1961
American Actor

Alongside John Wayne, Humphrey Bogart, and Jimmy Stewart, the actor Gary Cooper has become one of the foremost masculine archetypes in classic American film. In his most memorable roles, Cooper manifested a quiet, self-effacing, and long-suffering strength that earned him the epithet, "The Last American Hero." Best known for his Oscar-winning performances in *Sergeant York* (1941) and *High Noon* (1952), as well as for his portrayal of Lou Gehrig in *The Pride of the Yankees* (1942), Cooper became an ideal of American masculinity for moviegoers from the 1930s through the early 1950s.

Born Frank Cooper, Gary Cooper began his film career as a stunt rider in early Westerns. As his fame grew, Cooper became acutely conscious of cultural expectations, explaining at one point that "[t]o get folks to like you . . . I figured you had to be sort of their ideal. I don't mean a handsome knight riding a white horse, but a fella who answered the description of a right guy" (Lanche). Throughout the course of his career, both on- and offscreen, Cooper constructed such an image so effectively that, by the 1950s, his universal appeal seemed unimpeachable. He was the quiet, capable, principled man, his vulnerability offset by a commitment to his unerring moral compass.

Cooper's image evokes the simple confidence of an America flush with the patriotic triumph of the post–World War II era, as well as the moral certainty that typically characterized the United States through much of the conservative 1950s. During the Cold War era, despite his involvement in Senator Joseph McCarthy's efforts to root out suspected communists in Hollywood, the politically conservative Cooper managed to placate both sides. Appearing as a friendly witness at McCarthy's hearings, but not naming names, he maintained both patriotism and integrity. As the author Ernest Hemingway, a close friend of Cooper's, once observed, "If you made up a character like Coop, nobody would believe it. He's just too good to be true" (Meyers, 175).

Cooper made his greatest cultural impact as Will Kane in Fred Zinnemann's 1952 Western *High Noon*. Portraying a heroic marshall abandoned by the town he protects, Cooper became ingrained in the American imagination as the lone hero who refused to desert the community that betrayed him, embodying simultaneously the masculine virtues of self-sufficiency and dutiful protection. Although interpretations of the film's ultimate message differ widely, Cooper's image as the vulnerable but unyielding marshall has become his most enduring legacy.

Cooper's portrayals of humble, beleaguered, but legendary heroes made him an indelible part of the American cultural imagination. In many contemporary discussions of masculinity, the masculine ideal that Cooper exemplifies has come under scrutiny and attack by gender theorists: he epitomized the strong, silent type, suffering adversity with stoicism and perseverence, but rarely communicating emotion. His significance as a national icon has become similarly dated, though perhaps more nostalgically remembered, evoking a system of belief and a means of dealing with adversity that seem untenable in an increasingly complex world.

Throughout his career, Cooper's embodiment of both wise, paternalistic authority and frontier self-sufficiency represented a mid-twentieth-century masculine ideal. His screen persona embodied the American optimism—the faith in the ultimate triumph of simple and self-evident justice—that prevailed until the turmoil of the 1960s saw that confidence undermined. Since his death, he has come to signify the loss of American innocence.

Bibliography

Girgus, Sam B. *Hollywood Renaissance : The Cinema of Democracy in the Era of Ford, Capra, and Kazan.* New York: Cambridge University Press, 1998.

Lanche, Jerry. The Gary Cooper Homepage. 1997. <http:www.geocities.com/Athens/5376/coopquot.htm.> (April 15, 2003).

Meyers, Jeffrey. *Gary Cooper: American Hero.* New York: Cooper Square Press, 1998.

Mitchell, Lee Clark. *Westerns: Making the Man in Fiction and Film.* Chicago: University of Chicago Press, 1996.

Further Reading

Arce, Hector. *Gary Cooper: An Intimate Biography.* New York: William Morrow, 1979.

Swindell, Larry. *The Last Hero: A Biography of Gary Cooper.* Garden City, N.Y.: Doubleday, 1980.

Whitfield, Stephen J. *The Culture of the Cold War.* Baltimore: Johns Hopkins University Press, 1991.

Related Entries

Bogart, Humphrey; Cold War; Emotion; Hemingway, Ernest; Heroism; Hollywood; Wayne, John; Westerns; World War II

—*Anthony Wilson*

Cop Action Films

The cop action film, as a genre, first appeared in the 1970s, though police officers and detectives had emerged as heroes in the detective films of the 1940s and 1950s. This era was preceded by primarily negative portrayals of law enforcement in Depression-era films that celebrated the outlaw. In films, the cop went from being an average figure in the 1940s to a vengeful loner in the 1970s and a wisecracking action hero in the

1980s. The cop remains the most common hero in the detective genre, offering an opportunity to evaluate issues of class, gender, and race in American culture, as well as the idealization of law enforcement and masculine heroism,.

In the midst of the professionalization of crime detection in the 1940s and Cold War concerns for national security, the cop emerged as the hero of the detective genre. The police *procedural* (a term that refers to the official set of actions performed by police officers often highlighted in both crime literature and films) presented an idealized image of masculinity as domesticated, organized, methodical, scientific, stable, and willing to put professional duty above personal concerns. The genre thus denied the disillusionment and Cold War paranoia that plagued American society following World War II, and instead offered a hero that reflected effectiveness in the face of America's enemies. The procedural, in its pure form, continued after the 1950s only in specific instances—most notably television's Columbo—but the cop hero became firmly established in the nation's popular culture.

The procedural and its conservative representation of masculinity and law enforcement gave way to the vigilante cop film in the late 1960s and 1970s as the abolition of film censorship allowed for more violent and controversial narratives and characters. *Bullitt* (1968), *Coogan's Bluff* (1968), *The French Connection* (1971), and *Dirty Harry* (1971) established the tone for the vigilante cop film with a violent lone hero who possesses integrity and a commitment to law enforcement to the extent of employing unethical tactics to preserve American values and society. A reflection both of President Richard M. Nixon's aggressive approach to crime and U.S. society's loss of confidence in law-enforcement agencies, these films offered an independent cop who could deal with crime effectively through toughness and violence.

In the 1980s many of the privileges that men had taken for granted in American society were viewed as unearned advantages. The dominance of white, middle-class, middle-age masculinity, which had been called into question in the 1970s following the civil rights movement and second-wave feminism, was challenged on many fronts, and hegemonic masculinity began to lose ground. The cop action film became a dominant genre in the 1980s and 1990s as a result of this concern. In response to the growing opportunities for African Americans and the apparent loss of white dominance, the biracial buddy/cop film negated the threat of this empowerment by placing an African American in the role of the hero's sidekick.

The emerging equality of women, and the resulting perceived threat to male power, also generated a definition of manliness that emphasized the body, and the hero of the cop action film now typically possessed a muscular physique that symbolized sexual difference and physical power. Similarly, the dominance of middle-class, middle-age masculinity was challenged by the action hero who embodied a working-class heroism dependent on strength and bravery, though this type of hero was most often reintegrated into socially prescribed roles according to middle-class models of work and family. These two trends were evident in the 1980s, when cop films saw an emphasis on action, including fistfights, kickboxing, car chases, and gunplay, with the male body pumped up and ready for action. Exemplified by John McClane (played by Bruce Willis) in the *Die Hard* films and Martin Riggs (played by Mel Gibson) in the *Lethal Weapon* films, the cop action hero continued the tradition of the vigilante cop. He represented an idealized image of American heroism and working-class masculinity—violent, independent, white, muscular, and victorious. A personal crisis was expressed not through emotion, but through direct talk and action. The hero's body, therefore, became a site where masculine crisis was inscribed, and the spectacle of his body in action (or injured) became paramount.

Cop action films of the 1980s saw a frequent crossover into buddy films, with an increased focus on the relationship between the hero and his sidekick. As buddy narratives, these cop action films pushed women to the periphery of the narrative to allow a focus on masculinity, including issues of race and class. These films pitted opposing types of masculinity—whether from different classes, as in *Tango and Cash* (1989); different races, as in *48 Hours* (1982); or both, as in *Beverly Hills Cop* (1984). This dynamic stressed the development of a male bond that would enable the defeat of a common criminal enemy of American society. The concerns of race and class that are explored through the initial clash of the heroes are resolved through their eventual bonding, thus suppressing, rather than exposing, these issues as social problems.

The 1990s saw a shift in social conceptions of masculinity, as the valuation of brawn and violence gave way to an appreciation of brains and vulnerability. The sensitive male supplanted the retributive masculinity of the action hero as the masculine ideal. Cop action films reflected this change with a shift from toughness to intelligence as the key to solving a case—and from the working-class gun-slinging cop to a middle-class forensic detective. In a reflection of this shift, actors who played action heroes in the 1980s found themselves playing new roles in the 1990s. Bruce Willis, for example, hung up his gun to play an emotionally vulnerable detective in *Mercury Rising* (1998), and Arnold

Schwarzenegger parodied his previous action roles by playing comic and nonaction hero characters in *Kindergarten Cop* (1990) and *Junior* (1994).

Whether empowering male movie-going audiences with his physical strength, wisecracking defiance, intellectual prowess, or emotional depth, the cop action hero is a community protector and an everyman figure—an average guy who embodies male heroism simply by doing his job. Such portrayals of cop heroes perhaps reflect less of real-life policing than of Hollywood's ideals of masculinity, but they have provided important cultural tools by which American men have negotiated the turbulent cultural and political currents of the late twentieth century.

Bibliography

Cameron, Ian. *A Pictorial History of Crime Films.* New York: Hamlyn, 1975.

Fuchs, Cynthia. "The Buddy Politic." *Screening the Male: Exploring Masculinities in Hollywood Cinema,* edited by Steven Cohan and Ina Rae Hark. London: Routledge, 1993.

Inciardi, James A., and Juliet L. Dee. "From Keystone Cops to Miami Vice: Images of Policing in American Popular Culture." *Journal of Popular Culture* 21, no. 2 (1987): 84–102.

King, Neal. *Heroes in Hard Times: Cop Action Movies in the U.S.* Philadelphia: Temple University Press, 1999.

Reiner, Robert. "Keystone to Kojak: The Hollywood Cop." In *Cinema, Politics, and Society in America,* edited by Philip Davies and Brian Neve. 2nd ed. Manchester, England: Manchester University Press, 1985.

———. *The Politics of the Police.* Brighton, England: Wheatsheaf, 1985.

Further Reading

Hardy, Phil, ed. *The BFI Companion to Crime.* London: Cassell, 1997.

Jeffords, Susan. *Hard Bodies: Hollywood Masculinity in the Reagan Era.* New Brunswick, N.J.: Rutgers University Press, 1994.

Pfeil, Fred. *White Guys: Studies in Postmodern Domination and Difference.* London: Verso, 1995.

Rafter, Nicole. *Shots in the Mirror: Crime Films and Society.* New York: Oxford University Press, 2000.

Tasker, Yvonne. *Spectacular Bodies: Gender, Genre, and the Action Cinema.* London: Routledge, 1993.

Related Entries

African-American Manhood; American Dream; Body; Buddy Films; Class; Cold War; Crisis of Masculinity; Detectives; Eastwood, Clint; Emotion; Heroism; Hollywood; Male Friendship; Middle-Class Manhood; Race; Rambo; Schwarzenegger, Arnold; Sensitive Male; Vietnam War; Violence; Working-Class Manhood; World War II

—*Philippa Gates*

Counterculture

Mention of the term counterculture often invokes an image of youthful men and women in colorful tie-dyed shirts, sandals, beads, flowers, and jeans; smoking marijuana or taking LSD; and either dancing to rock music in a city park or living in a rural commune. Because the men in this image, with their long, flowing hair, so clearly departed from the male stereotype of the 1950s, it is often assumed that they were less committed to notions of masculinity than their fathers. However, the revitalization of masculinity formed an important dimension of countercultural practice.

As a result of the post–World War II "crisis of masculinity" debate, many men sought to adapt manhood to the companionate marriages and corporate employment patterns of postwar society. Counterculturalists, however, questioned the very legitimacy of such institutions, identifying them as the source of masculine malaise. Hippies (as members of the 1960s counterculture came to be called) sought to reclaim an "authentic" and "natural" masculinity by escaping the constraining, repressive consciousness they perceived as integral to industrial society. Their efforts generated a diverse range of nonconformist masculinities that still exert significant influence on American culture.

Overwhelmingly white and middle class in composition, the counterculture emphasized human consciousness as the key to self-determination. Whereas contemporary New Leftists stressed the material basis of power and organized mass movements of protest, the counterculture prioritized "mind-expansion" to recover what they considered to be the liberating psychic possibilities discarded along the road to civilization. Despite that common objective, hippies never reached consensus on the ways and means by which to achieve their goals. Hippie men's approaches to the revitalization of masculinity mirrored their commitment to one of the two principal approaches to cultural radicalism: anarchism and mysticism.

Anarchist hippies regarded the main social institutions of "straight" (conformist) society as alienating. They contended that schools, churches, and mass media (among others) programmed men to submit to the demands of breadwinning, a hypocritical double standard of sexual conduct, a spiritually barren religious life that demanded belief in the absence of ecstatic experience, and an emotionally constricted life in isolated nuclear families. Workplace relations rewarded unmanly deference to arbitrary authority and the projection of false facades to gain favor. With money as the defining value of society and thus of human consciousness, the true necessities of life seemed scarce despite American abundance, blinding men to the brotherly, communal sharing of "tribal" societies as an alternative. To hippie anarchists, it seemed absurd that a man's income could be considered a measure of his manliness when economically privileged men relied on the police, rather than themselves, to defend their unjust accumulations of property.

The Diggers, a loose collective formed in the Haight-Ashbury district of San Francisco in 1966, brought this hippie-anarchist analysis to its first full development. Through their provocative street theater, they sought to demonstrate egalitarian options to straight society. They distributed free food, opened "free stores" in which one could experience the moneyless exchange of goods, and designed street pageants to encourage direct, popular, and spontaneous participation in the creation of a new culture. Like their bohemian predecessors, the Beats, the Diggers romanticized the propertyless men of the urban streets and ghettoes as those who preserved the spirit of anarchy amid a bourgeois culture. The Diggers therefore cultivated an outlaw masculine ideal that valorized brotherly generosity, visionary artistry, candor, indifference to authority and social conventions, and trust in the legitimacy of one's own impulses. The Diggers drew significant inspiration from the manly swagger of the Black Panther Party, and for a time maintained relations with the San Francisco chapter of the Hell's Angels motorcycle gang.

Much more numerous than the anarchists were mystical hippies, who argued that straight society repressed awareness of humankind's metaphysical oneness with God and the universe. They employed eclectic means to restore that awareness, sometimes drawing heavily from the LSD experience or preindustrial religious and philosophical systems, including Zen Buddhism, Sufism, or Native American spiritual traditions. Whereas many hippie anarchists rejected pacifism, advocating the manly defense of individual liberty through force, numerous hippie mystics turned the other cheek to harassment by the police or other forces of society. Countercultural anarchists rejected all forms of hierarchical authority on principle, but hippie mystics often regarded a man's spiritual attainments as conferring leadership authority. Although it is difficult to generalize about the diverse strains of masculinity evident among mystical hippies, most embraced the proposition that gender constituted a fundamental organizing principle of the cosmos, as in the opposition of *yin* and *yang* in Chinese metaphysics.

The residents of a commune known as The Farm number among the many experiments in hippie mysticism. The spiritual teacher Stephen Gaskin, and more than 200 of his most dedicated students, left Haight-Ashbury in 1971 and founded The Farm in Summertown, Tennessee. Reaching a peak population of perhaps 1,500 in 1980, The Farm became the largest of the hippie-era communes. Gaskin taught that modern society had overemphasized manly assertiveness, failing to balance it with appreciation for feminine nurture and fertility. To recover that lost state of metaphysical balance, Gaskin exhorted men to aspire to lifetime monogamous commitment in spiritual marriages. He rejected the bombast of Digger outlaw manhood and denounced the Sexual Revolution as self-indulgent egoism. The ideal "Farmie" husband was to cultivate "knightly" comportment in his relations with "ladies." The commune's social structure evolved around the promotion, protection, and veneration of childbirth and motherhood, with men's labors dedicated to providing the material support for that sacred fertility.

Along with the New Left, the counterculture served as a precondition for the emergence of radical feminism in the late 1960s. Some women of the counterculture, including a few of those who lived at the anarchist Black Bear Ranch commune in northern California, mounted an increasingly comprehensive critique of the oppression of hippie women in the early 1970s. Responding in varying degrees to this criticism, hippie men adapted their gender identity and practice throughout the 1970s. Some responded with defensiveness and complaints that feminism ran contrary to the countercultural spirit of love and co-operation. Yet, others learned to modify their speech patterns (for example, dropping offensive references to women, such as "chick" and "old lady"). These men took on a greater share of household tasks and child care and included women in tasks once deemed "men's work," such as wood-cutting on rural communes. A few men, dedicated to the countercultural ideal of liberation through the transformation of consciousness, incorporated radical-feminist criticism of hippie gender consciousness into the ideology of the early gay liberation movement.

Thus, a wide range of nonconformist masculinities arose from the counterculture's responses to prevailing postwar models of manhood. Men in straight society have appropriated many hippie male practices, such as long hair, sensitive affect, and sexual nonconformism, reducing what once had been consciousness-transforming practices to lifestyle options. Others, such as the gay liberation movement's shortlived but significant rejection of sex roles as repressive cultural artifice, have fallen into disrepute as products of a naively optimistic era of reform. Today, the counterculture continues to leaven American manhood, even as some of its most audacious experiments lie abandoned.

BIBLIOGRAPHY

Cavallo, Dominick. *A Fiction of the Past: The Sixties in American History.* New York: St. Martin's, 1999.

January Thaw: People at Blue Mountain Ranch Write about Living Together in the Mountains. New York: Times Change Press, 1974.

Jay, Karla, and Allen Young, eds. *Out of the Closets: Voices of Gay Liberation.* 2nd ed. New York: New York University Press, 1992.

Kimmel, Michael. *Manhood in America: A Cultural History.* New York: Free Press, 1996.

Miller, Timothy. *The Hippies and American Values.* Knoxville: University of Tennessee Press, 1991.

———. *The 60s Communes: Hippies and Beyond.* Syracuse, N.Y.: Syracuse University Press, 1999.

Veysey, Laurence. *The Communal Experience: Anarchist and Mystical Counter-Cultures in America.* New York: Harper & Row, 1973.

FURTHER READING

Cain, Chelsea, ed. *Wild Child: Girlhoods in the Counterculture.* Seattle: Seal Press, 1999.

Coyote, Peter. *Sleeping Where I Fall: A Chronicle.* Washington, D.C.: Counterpoint, 1998.

Digger Archives. "A People's History of the Sixties." <www.diggers.org> (February 3, 2003).

Fike, Rupert, ed. *Voices from The Farm: Adventures in Community Living.* Summertown, Tenn.: Book Publishing, 1998.

Gaskin, Ina May. *Spiritual Midwifery.* Rev. ed. Summertown, Tenn.: Book Publishing, 1978.

Monkerud, Don, Malcolm Terence, and Susan Keese, eds. *Free Land, Free Love: Tales of a Wilderness Commune.* Aptos, Calif.: Black Bear, 2000.

Perry, Charles. *The Haight-Ashbury: A History.* New York: Vintage, 1985.

RELATED ENTRIES

Antiwar Movement; Beat Movement; Black Panther Party; Breadwinner Role; Brotherhood; Business/Corporate America; Conscientious Objection; Crisis of Masculinity; Feminism; Heterosexuality; Homosexuality; Individualism; Sensitive Male; Sexual Revolution; Vietnam War; Youth

—*Tim Hodgdon*

COWBOYS

Few figures have had as powerful and persistent an impact on representations of American masculinity as the cowboy. Popularized and romanticized during the late nineteenth century in dime novels, frontier melodramas, and Wild West shows, the cowboy became an enduring icon in the twentieth century through the influence of fiction, film, television, and advertising. In such figures as the title character of Owen Wister's best-selling 1902 novel *The Virginian,* the silent film star William S. Hart, the actor John Wayne, and the Marlboro Man, the cowboy has embodied the image of a rugged and authentic "all-American" masculinity. Throughout its history, the cowboy icon has reflected concerns over the social and economic status of Anglo-American men and the emasculating effects of urbanization, industrialization, and bureaucratization.

In contrast to his longevity as a cultural icon, the cowboy's appearance on the historical stage was fleeting. Actual cowboys rode the trail for less than a generation following the Civil War—from 1865 until the late 1880s. They were the product of the open-range cattle industry, which required the services of hired hands to round up and drive Texas cattle to

A sketch by nineteenth-century artist Frederic Remington. Amid the urbanization and industrialization of the late nineteenth and twentieth centuries, the cowboy became symbolic of a vision of masculinity that emphasized autonomy, mobility, adventure, and strenuous living in rugged, natural, outdoor environments. (© Bettmann/Corbis)

northern railheads for transport to markets in the East. Early accounts, influenced by middle-class Victorian associations of manhood with propriety and gentility, presented cowboys as antisocial and often criminal figures prone to drunken assaults on defenseless communities on the western frontier. But Wister and his friends, including the artist Frederic Remington and the future U.S. president Theodore Roosevelt, worried that overcivilization and growing immigration threatened manly vigor and Anglo-Saxon cultural and physical dominance. As a result, they recast the cowboy as an exemplar of the natural integrity and racial superiority of the Anglo-American male.

Despite the cowboy's historical status as a poorly paid laborer within a massive business enterprise, the image of the cowboy astride his horse represented the fantasy of masculine autonomy and mobility—a life free from urban-industrial concerns, domestic constraints, emotional attachments, and the feminizing influences of civilization. Roosevelt, in particular, celebrated the cowboy's reinvigorating primitive pursuits as a model of the "strenuous life"—a life of outdoor physical adventure that would cure men of the softness and nervous exhaustion brought on by modern commercial society.

The cowboy has always been a paradoxical figure, at once modern and archaic. He has embodied concerns over the fate of a traditional producer-based model of masculinity in a modern consumer society, while at the same time the cowboy image itself was created as a mass commodity and has endured due to its success as marketable entertainment. In the twentieth century, alongside such icons of rugged authenticity as Hart and Wayne, such cowboy stars of film, radio, and television as Tom Mix, the Lone Ranger, and Hopalong Cassidy have—like their nineteenth-century Wild West show brethren—eschewed manly reserve in favor of flashy costumes, daredevil stunts, and commercial product endorsements. By the latter half of the twentieth century, parodies and critiques of the image of the cowboy as a tough, laconic loner became more frequent, particularly as authoritative white masculinity came under pressure from the civil rights and liberation movements of the 1960s and 1970s. Nonetheless, the cowboy image endures, in music, fashion, and, not least of all, in political rhetoric, where politicians from Henry Kissinger to Ronald Reagan to George W. Bush have invoked the cowboy image to legitimize the moral authority of violent action in the name of the American nation.

BIBLIOGRAPHY

Savage, William W. *The Cowboy Hero: His Image in American History and Culture.* Norman: University of Oklahoma Press, 1979.

Taylor, Lonn, and Ingrid Maar. *The American Cowboy.* New York: Harper & Row, 1983.

White, G. Edward. *The Eastern Establishment and the Western Experience: The West of Frederic Remington, Theodore Roosevelt, and Owen Wister.* New Haven, Conn.: Yale University Press, 1968.

Wister, Owen. "The Evolution of the Cow-Puncher." In *Owen Wister's West: Selected Articles,* edited by Robert Murray Davis. Albuquerque: University of New Mexico Press, 1987.

FURTHER READING

Allmendinger, Blake. *The Cowboy: Representations of Labor in an American Work Culture.* New York: Oxford University Press, 1992.

Bold, Christine. *Selling the Wild West: Popular Western Fiction, 1860 to 1960.* Bloomington: Indiana University Press, 1987.

Davis, Robert Murray. *Playing Cowboys: Low Culture and High Art in the Western.* Norman: University of Oklahoma Press, 1992.

McDonald, Archie P., ed. *Shooting Stars: Heroes and Heroines of Western Film.* Bloomington: Indiana University Press, 1987.

Roosevelt, Theodore. *Ranch Life and the Hunting Trail.* New York: The Century Co., 1896.

Wister, Owen. *The Virginian: A Horseman of the Plains.* New York: Macmillan, 1902.

RELATED ENTRIES

Advertising; Cooper, Gary; Emotion; Guns; Heroism; Hollywood; Immigration; Industrialization; *Lone Ranger, The*; Marlboro Man; Roosevelt, Theodore; Urbanization; Victorian Era; Wayne, John; Western Frontier; Westerns; Whiteness

—Jonna Eagle

CRÈVECOEUR, J. HECTOR ST. JOHN

1735–1813
Colonial Franco-American Writer and Diplomat

In 1924, the writer D. H. Lawrence famously identified J. Hector St. John Crèvecoeur as the "emotional . . . prototype of the American" (Lawrence, 29). A writer known for the optimistic depiction of early America's exceptional promise in his best known work, *Letters from an American Farmer* (1782), Crèvecoeur illustrated several aspects of ideal masculinity in the pre-Revolutionary period. The qualities described in the first half of the book—including benevolence, self-reliance, exemplary fatherhood, domestic husbandry, sincerity, virtue, and sentimentality—provide a portrait of American masculinity quite different from those that would later dominate American manhood.

Born into an aristocratic Normandy family in 1735, Michel-Guillaume Jean de Crèvecoeur was educated by Jesuits before moving to England in 1754; he moved to French Canada a year later. After resigning a military commission in 1759, he anglicized his first name to J. Hector St. John and moved to upstate New York, where he married and worked a farm. In 1778, he fled to British-occupied Manhattan, and then to London, England, where he published *Letters from an American Farmer* in 1782. Abandoning his family, departing his adopted country, and espousing pro-British loyalist sentiments in Revolutionary America, he was suspected by patriots of being a loyalist spy, and by loyalists of spying for the patriots. Even without the pessimistic critique of Revolutionary America in "Distresses of a Frontier Man," the twelfth epistle of the text, one can observe that Crèvecoeur sacrificed the accepted masculine roles of family protector and public citizen.

In *Letters from an American Farmer,* Crèvecoeur stages a dialogue between his author/persona, Farmer James, his never-named wife, and their local parish in order to describe the agrarian culture and livelihood of the American farmer. In the dialogue, James suggests that an integral male identity rests on a number of public roles or symbols: the display of economic abundance signaled by "fat and well clad negroes" (43); the reputation of sober, physical industry; and the embrace of virtuous qualities. In two succeeding letters, Crèvecoeur describes the joys of the farmer's "breadwinning role" in the sketch of the successful yeoman farmer. James is happiest either at the fireside, watching his wife knit, or on the plow, carrying his son with him in his labors. Crèvecoeur sketches masculine domesticity and agricultural paternalism with a thrilling sentimentalism, claiming that his heart overflows "in involuntary tears" (47) as he recalls such happy domestic scenes.

Assuming the role of father, husband, and citizen, the Farmer James of these early letters serves as an ideal of male self-creation in the British colonies. As an author, Crèvecoeur is imagining the nation—just as, in his role of father, he is raising his children to assume his place. In other words, the America represented in the text of *Letters* is the America Crèvecoeur hopes will be his paternal legacy. As such, he describes the lineage of a lasting paternalistic settlement: "I am now doing for [my son] what my father formerly did for me" (49). The fatherly bequeath of the farm in this letter re-emerges in the letter that follows, which addresses immigration and supplies an example of one man's successful "Americanization." In this story of a Scot immigrant, Farmer James sketches the immigrant's transformation from a poor, hard-working, honest man into a rich American farmer. This third letter, included in nearly all American literature anthologies, offered an answer to the question "What is an American?" It also helped establish the ideology of the self-made man, a key element of American national and masculine identity.

Crèvecoeur's early letters celebrate this ideology and, by attaching it to an immigrant replacing a life of European servitude with one of American self-reliance, locate its possibility in the British colonies rather than in Europe. However, his later letters present a distinctly soured portrait of Revolutionary America. Harassed by patriots and the thunders of war, Farmer James imagines himself and his family fleeing into the wilderness and living with Native Americans. Life on the frontier becomes the text's new ideal, since it is closer to unspoiled nature and immune to the factious divisions of democratic politics. By associating America's potential with its wilderness rather than its Revolution for independence, Crèvecoeur turns out to be an ambivalent chronicler of the new nation. However, his fantasy of a wilderness escape initiated a new myth of American masculinity, one that later writers would develop further.

BIBLIOGRAPHY

Lawrence, D. H. *Studies in Classic American Literature.* London: M. Secker, 1924.

FURTHER READING

Carew-Miller, Anna. "The Language of Domesticity in Crèvecoeur's Letters from an American Farmer." *Early American Literature* 28 (1993): 242–254.

Kunkle, Julia Post Mitchell. *St. Jean de Crèvecoeur.* New York: Columbia University Press, 1916.

Larson, David M. "Sentimental Aesthetics and the American Revolution: Crèvecoeur's War Sketches." *Eighteenth-Century Life,* 5, no. 2 (1978): 1–12.

Philbrick, Thomas. *St. Jean de Crèvecoeur.* Boston: Twayne, 1970.

Rotundo, E. Anthony. *American Manhood: Transformations in Masculinity from the Revolution to the Modern Era.* New York: Basic Books, 1993.

Ruttenburg, Nancy. *Democratic Personality: Popular Voice and the Trials of American Authorship.* Stanford: Stanford University Press, 1998.

SELECTED WRITINGS

Crèvecoeur, J. Hector St. John. *Letters from an American Farmer and Sketches of 18th-Century Life.* 1782. Reprint, New York: Penguin, 1981.

———. *More Letters from the American Farmer: An Edition of the Essays in English Left Unpublished by Crèvecoeur.* Athens: University of Georgia Press, 1995.

Related Entries

Agrarianism; American Dream; American Revolution; Breadwinner Role; Citizenship; Fatherhood; Immigration; Masculine Domesticity; Patriotism; Property; Republicanism; Self-Made Man; Sentimentalism; Work

—*Bryce Traister*

Crisis of Masculinity

It was during the late 1960s that historians first developed the notion of a "crisis of masculinity" to describe the nervous concerns that middle-class men had regarding masculinity and the male body during the late nineteenth and early twentieth centuries. This idea not only brought scholarly attention to important changes in constructions of manhood in the twentieth century, but also raised questions about the timing of changes in cultural constructions of masculinity, the extent of uniformity and variation in men's experiences of social change, and about men's attitudes toward feminism.

During the nineteenth century, expansion in the West, Manifest Destiny, the market revolution, and, later in the century, an emphasis on the "strenuous life" all suggested the possibility of a secure, uncontestable concept of masculinity grounded in market capitalism and ideals of activity and usefulness. Toward the end of the century, however, social and economic changes, including urbanization, the transition from entrepreneurial to corporate capitalism, the rise of bureaucratic structures, and changing career paths for middle-class men, challenged this sense of security by reducing many men's sense of economic independence and achievement. Whereas mid-nineteenth-century men could at least contemplate moving to the West to restore their economic independence and male autonomy, the closing of the frontier in 1890 according to that year's U.S. Census Bureau report removed an outlet that had enabled men to compensate for the presumed loss of manliness and opportunity. Finally, by the late nineteenth century, an intensifying women's rights movement challenged men's sole control over the public sphere.

These developments led many men, sensing a threat to traditional notions of masculinity to generate new articulations of masculinity. Middle-class men hoped that embracing ideals of toughness and physical strength outside the workplace would counteract any perceived effeminization and emasculation and restore a secure and uncontestable definition of masculinity.

The phenomenon of the crisis of masculinity was first suggested in studies by George M. Fredrickson (1965), James R. McGovern (1966), John Higham (1970), and Gerald Franklin Roberts (1970). Without referring specifically to gender (which had barely emerged as an important scholarly concept) Fredrickson revealed that the social ideal of the strenuous life developed after the Civil War. McGovern discovered an obsession with virile manliness in the life and work of the muckraking journalist David Graham Phillips, while Higham found widespread interest in a "muscular Christianity," the male body, and physical exercise in late-nineteenth-century American culture. In an unpublished dissertation, Roberts indicated that a "cult of manliness" had unfolded by the time of the Progressive Era. The feminist scholar Ann Douglas also contributed to the development of this new theory, suggesting in 1977 that manhood in that period had been besieged by a process of feminization. By the late 1970s and the early 1980s, the idea of a nineteenth-century crisis of masculinity had become fully accepted in studies by Joe Dubbert (1974, 1979) and David Pugh (1983).

During the late 1980s and the 1990s, however, many scholars began to challenge this thesis. The first and perhaps most important critique was that it was based on an outdated understanding of gender that considers *male* and *female* as separate constructs, rather than in relation to one another. Second, critics charged that it reduced the range of male experience, privileging some aspects while ignoring others. They charged, for example, that the thesis overlooks the ideal of a corporate teamplayer, which incorporated changing career paths and economic opportunities into a new ideal of manhood. Third, the idea that a crisis of masculinity developed in response to feminist advances implies that all men resisted women's social and political advances during the late nineteenth and early twentieth centuries, thus ignoring such pro-feminist men as the journalist Max Eastman, the educator John Dewey, the medical expert William Sanger (husband of birth control advocate Margaret Sanger), the socialist and author Upton Sinclair, the historian Charles A. Beard (whose wife Mary Beard is often regarded as a founder of U.S. women's history), and a number of presidents of women's colleges, including Henry Durant of Wellesley and Henry Noble McCracken of Vassar (as well as Vassar's founder, Matthew Vassar).

Although the crisis of masculinity thesis is of limited value in explaining the late nineteenth and early twentieth centuries, its emergence in the 1960s and 1970s illuminates postwar changes in U.S. society that challenged the notion of a stable and unchanging (white) maleness. During the Cold War era, many Americans demanded male toughness, celebrated capitalism and the male breadwinner ideal, and associated Communism with homosexuality. At the same time, however, a growing number of American men, confronted with new opportunities for leisure, became more critical of breadwinner responsibilities. They received support from cardiologists and developmental psychologists, who provided medical and scientific rationales for greater relaxation and self-indulgence. The late 1960s saw a period of stagflation (economic stagnation with inflation), followed by recession and corporate downsizing beginning in the mid-1980s, all of which further eroded the breadwinner ideal. At the same time, the 1960s counterculture and the feminist, civil rights, and gay rights movements of the 1960s and 1970s all critiqued conventional notions of masculinity and proposed a range of alternative masculinities. Such challenges sparked the emergence of various men's movements in the 1970s and 1980s that sensed uncertainty (some scholars and commentators even called it a "crisis") in the meaning of American manhood and sought new bases for male identity. Some male activists and writers began to speak of a "masculine mystique," and Robert Bly urged a recovery of the "deep masculine" in his 1990 book *Iron John.*

By the 1990s the notion of a crisis of masculinity in contemporary life had begun to make news headlines. Concerns were raised about "deadbeat dads" and the emergence of the "angry white man" as a voter type. Groups like the Promise Keepers (a predominantly white men's organization) and the African-American Million Man March demonstrated an attempt to develop a masculine identity among men. It was against this background that a growing number of scholars began to suspect that their predecessors of the 1960s and 1970s had projected contemporary concerns about masculinity in U.S. society backward in time, thereby distorting history.

In fact, both the codifiers and critics of the thesis are correct. American men and masculinities did indeed experience a crisis that began in the 1880s. The persistent thread through this period was an underlying desire by many men for an uncontestable definition of manhood, as well as their discomfort with a proliferation of the gender roles available to both men and women—a proliferation that expanded in the twentieth and twenty-first centuries amid postmodern ideas about gender and gendered identities. The crisis of masculinity thesis and its fate in scholarly circles serve as a reminder that men's studies and men's history are better served by attempts to incorporate men's voices and issues to a multicultural canon of scholarly and cultural criticism, rather than trying to restore men to the center of academic inquiry.

Bibliography

Douglas, Ann. *The Feminization of American Culture.* New York: Noonday Press, 1998.

Dubbert, Joe. "Progressivism and the Masculinity Crisis," *The Psychoanalytic Review* 61 (Fall 1974): 433–455.

Ehrenreich, Barbara. *The Hearts of Men: American Dreams and the Flight from Commitment.* New York: Anchor Press, 1984.

Faludi, Susan. *Stiffed: The Betrayal of the American Man.* New York: William Morrow, 1999.

Fredrickson, George M. *The Inner Civil War: Northern Intellectuals and the Crisis of the Union.* Urbana: University of Illinois Press, 1993.

Griffen, Clyde. "Reconstructing Masculinity from the Evangelical Revival to the Waning of Progressivism: A Speculative Synthesis." In *Meanings for Manhood: Constructions of Masculinity in Victorian America,* edited by Mark C. Carnes and Clyde Griffen. Chicago: University of Chicago Press, 1990.

Higham, John. "The Reorientation of American Culture in the 1890s." In *Writing American History; Essays on Modern Scholarship,* edited by John Higham. Bloomington: Indiana University Press, 1970.

Kimmel, Michael. "The Contemporary 'Crisis' of Masculinity in Historical Perspective." In *The Making of Masculinities: The New Men's Studies,* edited by Harry Brod. Boston: Allen & Unwin, 1987.

Kimmel, Michael, and Thomas E. Mosmiller, eds. *Against the Tide: Pro-Feminist Men in the United States, 1776–1990. A Documentary History.* Boston: Beacon Press, 1992.

McGovern, James R. "David Graham Phillips and the Virility Impulse of Progressivism." *New England Quarterly* 39 (1966): 334–355.

Roberts, Gerald Franklin. "The Strenuous Life: The Cult of Manliness in the Era of Theodore Roosevelt." Ph.D. diss., Michigan State University, 1970.

Traister, Bryce. "Academic Viagra: The Rise of American Masculinity Studies." *American Quarterly* 52 (2000): 274–304.

Further Reading

Bly, Robert. *Iron John: A Book About Men.* Reading, Mass.: Addison-Wesley, 1990.

Dubbert, Joe L. *A Man's Place: Masculinity in Transition.* Englewood Cliffs, N.J.: Prentice Hall, 1979.

Filene, Peter Gabriel. *Him/Her/Self: Sex Roles in Modern America.* New York: Harcourt Brace Jovanovich, 1986.

Kimmel, Michael. *Manhood in America: A Cultural History.* New York: Free Press, 1996.

Pleck, Joseph H. *The Myth of Masculinity.* Cambridge, Mass.: MIT Press, 1981.

Savran, David. *Taking It Like A Man: White Masculinity, Masochism, and Contemporary American Culture.* Princeton, N.J.: Princeton University Press, 1998.

Stearns, Peter N. *Be A Man! Males in Modern Society.* 2nd ed. New York: Holmes & Meier, 1990.

RELATED ENTRIES

Breadwinner Role; Cold War; Gilded Age; *Iron John: A Book About Men*; Market Revolution; Masculine Domesticity; Men's Movements; Men's Studies; Middle-Class Manhood; Muscular Christianity; Passionate Manhood; Patriarchy; Postmodernism; Progressive Era; Promise Keepers; Sexual Revolution; Strenuous Life; World War II

—*Thomas Winter*

CROCKETT, DAVY

1786–1836
Frontiersman, Congressman, and Folk Hero

Although David Crockett was only a minor political and military figure, Davy Crockett became an important cultural icon. While the more refined Daniel Boone established western settlement for families, Crockett developed an appeal closer to that of the frontiersmen "Wild Bill" Hickok and Kit Carson and the outlaw Jesse James. By pursuing daring exploits beyond civilized borders, he represented a competing model of frontier masculinity that resisted the conforming forces of party politics and moral reformers.

Crockett left home at age twelve, working various jobs in rural Virginia before returning to his family in Tennessee. In 1813, he joined the Tennessee Volunteer Militia to fight in the Creek War; he was later elected to the rank of colonel. Failing as a farmer and entrepreneur, he supported his family through his hunting prowess. During his successful campaign for the state legislature in 1821, he derided his opponent as an unmanly "aristocrat" and highlighted his backwoods origin as a sign of his true manhood. After being defeated in a bid for U.S. Congress in 1825, he returned to hunting with amazing success, killing 105 bears in one year, including seventeen in just one week. In 1827, he was elected to the U.S. Congress, where he advocated for homesteaders and opposed Indian removal.

Politically, Crockett opposed President Andrew Jackson, a Democrat and fellow Tennessean who favored education, the rights of large land holders, and a strengthening of the federal government's executive branch. The Whig Party recognized in Crockett a true "man of the people" whose masculine image could compete with Jackson's, and—anticipating a possible presidential run—the party sponsored a Crockett speaking tour that augmented his reputation for frank speech and his talent as a frontier storyteller. In 1834, Crockett published *A Narrative of the Life of David Crockett*—possibly the first campaign autobiography. Defeated for reelection to Congress later that year, Crockett abandoned his presidential ambitions and set out for Texas, where he joined the anti-Jackson faction of the Texas government. He died on March 6, 1836, at the battle of the Alamo.

Unauthorized autobiographies, popular plays, and the eastern-produced series *The Crockett Almanacks* (1835–56) transformed Crockett into a cultural icon and folk hero by offering humorously exaggerated versions of his exploits; one such tale claimed that he rode his pet alligator up Niagara Falls. The *Almanacks* promoted an untamed, almost boyish manliness, which stood as an alternative to the middle-class ideal of the disciplined and refined gentleman. Although the first series (1835–38) of the *Almanacks* included stories of noble Indians, later editions, reflecting nineteenth-century working-class constructions of manhood, identified manhood with whiteness by depicting violent behavior toward Indians, Negroes, and Mexicans. The popular stage melodramas based on Davy Crockett promoted a less fantastic, more heroic version of Crockett, while preserving his image as a man of plain speech.

The success of Disney's film series *Davy Crockett, King of the Wild Frontier,* with the accompanying "Ballad of Davy Crockett," demonstrated Crockett's continuing resonance in the twentieth century, especially among boys. Crockett's exploits and rhetoric have made him an enduring symbol of the noble man of the wilderness, an image of a pure American masculinity that is grounded in nature and resists refinement.

BIBLIOGRAPHY

Burke, John Wakefield. *David Crockett.* Austin, Tex.: Eakin Press, 1984.

Faludi, Susan. *Stiffed: The Betrayal of the American Man.* New York: William Morrow, 1999.

Lofaro, Michael A. "David Crockett." The Handbook of Texas Online. <http://www.tsha.utexas.edu/handbook/online> (February 3, 2003).

Meine, Franklin J., ed. *Crockett Almanacks: Nashville Series, 1835–38.* Chicago: Caxton Club, 1955.

Rotundo, E. Anthony. *American Manhood: Transformations in Masculinity from the Revolution to the Modern Era.* New York: Basic Books, 1993.

Smith-Rosenberg, Caroll. *Disorderly Conduct: Visions of Gender in Victorian America.* New York: Knopf, 1985.

FURTHER READING

David, William C. *Three Roads to the Alamo: The Lives and Fortunes of David Crockett, James Bowie, and William Barrett Davis.* New York: HarperCollins, 1998.

Derr, Mark. *The Frontiersman: The Real Life and Many Legends of Davy Crockett.* New York: William Morrow, 1993.

Lofaro, Michael A., ed. *Davy Crockett: The Man, the Legend, the Legacy, 1786–1986.* Knoxville: University of Tennessee Press, 1985.

SELECTED WRITINGS

Crockett, Davy. *A Narrative of the Life of David Crockett of the State of Tennessee, with Thomas Chilton.* Philadelphia: Carey and Hart, 1834. Reprinted as *Davy Crockett's Own Story.* Bedford, Mass.: Applewood, 1993.

———. *Col. Crockett's Exploits and Adventures in Texas,* Written by Himself (Attributed to Richard Penn Smith). New York: Graham, 1848.

———. *Life and Adventures of Colonel David Crockett of West Tennessee* (Attributed to Matthew St. Clair Clarke). New York: G. Munro, 1882. Reprinted as *Sketches and Eccentricities of Colonel David Crockett of West Tennessee.* North Stratford, N.H.: Ayer, 1975.

RELATED ENTRIES

Boone, Daniel; Boyhood; Hunting; Individualism; Jackson, Andrew; Leatherstocking Tales; Politics; Property; Western Frontier

—*Elizabeth Abele*

CULT OF DOMESTICITY

The "cult of domesticity" was first explored as a historical phenomenon in antebellum U.S. society by Barbara Welter, who wrote in 1966 of a "cult of true womanhood," though the phrase itself was coined by the historian Aileen Kraditor in 1968. Part of a broader nineteenth-century northern middle-class ideology of "separate spheres," the cult of domesticity identified womanhood with the private or domestic sphere of the home and manhood with the public sphere of economic competition and politics. While the cult of domesticity primarily concerned a definition of femininity, defining the home as a space governed by women's sentimental, moral and spiritual influence, this ideology also contributed to definitions of manliness and sought to control male passions at a time when the market revolution, urbanization, westward migration, and partisan politics removed traditional communal restraints on male behavior. Through the nineteenth and early twentieth centuries, the cult of domesticity provided a powerful conceptual rationale for organizing (and reorganizing) social relations.

The Cult of Domesticity and Middle-Class Manhood in the Nineteenth Century

Between the 1780s and the 1840s, the United States developed from a preindustrial society comprised of small communities to a more urban and industrialized society. This transformation created a middle class that occupied a distinct social and cultural stratum in U.S. society, and new models of masculinity helped to define this new class. To respond to the competitive pressures and opportunities of an expanding domestic market, middle-class men relocated their businesses from their households into separate offices away from the home. This functional separation of work and production from the home environment prompted middle-class men and women to redefine the domestic sphere as a counterpoint to a competitive, and often vicarious, marketplace, making the home a private refuge from the hustle and bustle of public life. This separation also prompted the construction of new definitions of manhood and womanhood suitable to the emerging social and economic order.

The ideology of domesticity defined men as naturally competitive and aggressive providers—traits appropriate to a public world of expanding commercial capitalism and to their responsibilities as breadwinners—while it defined women as naturally suited to home life through their inclination to compassion and piety. According to the cult of domesticity, males would be morally strengthened by women in the private sphere of the home, where they would be influenced by Christian piety, moral resolve, and such sentimental values as sincerity, candor, and faithfulness. While social change encouraged men to be more assertive and pursue their individual self-interest, Victorian Americans, concerned that such characteristics threatened social cohesion, envisioned the ideal man as a Christian gentleman who abstained from excess in all walks of life while fulfilling his obligations as a breadwinner and a citizen.

The cult of domesticity expressed middle-class Americans' discomfort with the kinds of social relations fostered by market capitalism. The insistence on the separation of the private, or domestic, sphere from the public sphere was intended to prevent the intrusion of market forces into the home and the commodification of personal relations. Yet by assigning men exclusive purview of the public realm and defining them as naturally inclined to competition and aggression, it legitimated an amoral and acquisitive male individualism. The cult of domesticity thus used diametrically opposed definitions of masculinity and femininity to create a coherent middle-class value system that embraced the apparently conflicting forces of competitive capitalism and moral behavior.

While middle-class men found in the cult of domesticity a basis for a marketplace model of manhood and their monopolization of economic and political power, many of them also used it to construct a model of middle-class manhood that emphasized domestic attachment and the pleasures of private life. Such men tended to resent, rather than celebrate, the separation between their public and private lives. For example, the southern lawyer and U.S. attorney general William Wirt and his wife Elizabeth were separated by his position for most of their marriage. Wirt enjoyed his public career, but lamented his separation from his family and from the joys and duties of domestic life.

Men like Wirt perceived domestic life and its affectionate, sentimental relations as central to male life and identity. Similarly, several male authors between 1820 and 1860 cherished men's capacity for domestic life. In novels such as Nathaniel Beverly Tucker's *George Balcombe* (1836) or James Fenimore Cooper's *Wyandotte* (1837), the domestic sphere figured as a source of happiness and true fulfillment for both women and men. In these and many other works of fiction, male characters actively desired marital bliss, domestic life, and the morally and spiritually elevating influence of a wife as indispensable to male wholeness.

In the second half of the nineteenth century, middle-class men became more ambivalent toward domesticity. On the one hand, they developed an ideal of "masculine domesticity"; that is, they sought to cultivate the domestic components of masculine identity and to masculinize a domestic sphere that had become increasingly mother-centered after the market revolution began removing male labor from the home. On the other hand, middle-class men, increasingly concerned that female domestic influence left them overcivilized, excessively genteel, or even effeminate, often rejected domesticity in favor of ideals of "passionate manhood" and a "strenuous life" that emphasized duty, obligation, military valor, physical vigor and exercise, struggle against obstacles, competition in sports and business, and an attempt to recover a primitive masculine self. Proponents believed that these ideals would enable men to defy the effeminizing effects of women's domesticity and restore men to their role as patriarchs of their homes.

Domesticity and Class in the Nineteenth Century

The cult of domesticity defined an emergent middle-class manhood by contrasting middle-class men not only with middle-class women, but also with working-class men. Like middle-class men, working-class men increasingly had to seek work outside their homes. However, because working-class men were often unable to earn sufficient income to allow them to be their families' sole breadwinners, their households remained sites of income-generating work as their wives and children labored to supplement working-class men's earnings, especially during times of unemployment. The notion of the home as a moral counterpoint to the amoral public sphere, as a feminine arena where masculinity was spiritually fortified, was therefore a signifier of middle-class status unavailable to many working-class men.

At the same time, however, many working-class men used the idea of domesticity as a gauge against which to measure their own manhood and to define their class-based agendas. Regarding the domestic sphere as integral to their manliness, they argued that the higher wages and shorter hours they sought would allow them to become breadwinners responsible for nonworking spouses and children, and thus achieve greater domestic involvement.

The Twentieth Century: Domesticity Challenged and Affirmed

Through the nineteenth century and into the early twentieth century, the cult of domesticity and the ideology of separate spheres provided an influential matrix for ordering social life, defining gender roles, and conceptualizing middle-class manhood. However, with the increasing presence of women in public life, politics, and the workplace during the twentieth century, these ideologies began to appear antiquated, losing their former cultural power in ordering U.S. gender relations. Yet many Americans continued to retain nostalgic attachment to notions of domesticity and its conceptualization of manhood, particularly in response to perceived threats to the American way of life.

For example, the Great Depression of the 1930s prompted calls to give men priority in hiring as a way to stabilize domestic life amid the crisis. Similarly, Cold War anxieties of the 1950s sparked a defense of traditional patriarchal domesticity as the foundation of American society—a defense evident in such television programs as *Father Knows Best* (1954–63) and *Leave It to Beaver* (1957–63). The social and cultural upheavals of the 1960s and 1970s, including a resurgent feminist movement, rising divorce rates, and the growing incidence of dual-income households, led political conservatives and evangelical

Christians to present traditional domesticity and patriarchy as an antidote to cultural chaos—a position they continued to defend in the early twenty-first century.

These same upheavals led many other Americans, however, to once again question traditional notions of domesticity. Late-twentieth-century mass culture and television entertainment reflected this new criticism by displaying a decided ambivalence towards domesticity. For example, shows such as *The Simpsons* (premiered in 1989) and *Roseanne* (1988–97) tapped an ongoing interest in domesticity, while also exposing the unrealistic aspects of domesticity and the difficulties of achieving and maintaining it. In *The Simpsons*, housewife Marge Simpson's civilizing efforts fail to make her dysfunctional husband Homer conform to her ideal of the perfect husband and father. *Roseanne*—a show that located the majority of its plots in the family's living room—ended with the divorce of the main characters because domesticity, as nineteenth-century Americans had envisioned it, was unachievable for dual-income, lower-middle-class families in the late twentieth century. In the twenty-first century, the ideal of domesticity—often romanticized, yet frequently unattainable and regarded with increasing skepticism—continues to inform public discourse on gender and family life.

BIBLIOGRAPHY

Coontz, Stephanie. *The Social Origins of Private Life: A History of American Families, 1600-1900.* London: Verso, 1988.

Cott, Nancy F. *The Bonds of Womanhood: "Woman's Sphere" in New England, 1780-1835.* New Haven, Conn.: Yale University Press, 1977.

Frank, Stephen M. *Life with Father: Parenthood and Masculinity in the Nineteenth-Century American North.* Baltimore: Johns Hopkins University Press, 1998.

Kraditor, Aileen S., ed. *Up from the Pedestal: Selected Writings in the History of American Feminism.* Chicago: Quadrangle Books, 1968.

Lystra, Karen. *Searching the Heart: Women, Men, and Romantic Love in Nineteenth-Century America.* New York: Oxford University Press, 1989.

Marsh, Margaret. "Suburban Men and Masculine Domesticity, 1870–1915." In *Meanings for Manhood: Constructions of Masculinity in Victorian America,* edited by Mark C. Carnes and Clyde Griffen. Chicago: University of Chicago Press, 1990.

McCall, Laura. "'Not So Wild A Dream': The Domestic Fantasies of Literary Men and Women, 1820-1860." In *A Shared Experience: Men, Women, and The History of Gender,* edited by Laura McCall and Donald Yacovone. New York: New York University Press, 1998.

Rotundo, E. Anthony. *American Manhood: Transformations in Masculinity from the Revolution to the Modern Era.* New York: Basic Books, 1993.

Welter, Barbara. "The Cult of True Womanhood, 1820–1860." *American Quarterly* 18 (Summer 1966): 151–74.

Winter, Thomas. *Making Men, Making Class: The YMCA and Workingmen, 1877–1920.* Chicago: University of Chicago Press, 2002.

FURTHER READING

Epstein, Barbara Leslie. *The Politics of Domesticity: Women, Evangelism, and Temperance in Nineteenth Century America.* Middletown, Conn.: Wesleyan University Press, 1981.

Kasson, John F. *Rudeness and Civility: Manners in Nineteenth-Century Urban America.* New York: Hill and Wang, 1990.

Kerber, Linda K. "Separate Spheres, Female Worlds, Woman's Place: The Rhetoric of Women's History." *Journal of American History* 75 (June 1988): 9–39.

Kimmel, Michael. *Manhood in America: A Cultural History.* New York: Free Press, 1996.

RELATED ENTRIES

Advice Literature; Breadwinner Role; Business/Corporate America; Fatherhood; *Father Knows Best*; Labor Movement and Unions; *Leave It to Beaver*; Market Revolution; Masculine Domesticity; Middle-Class Manhood; Passionate Manhood; Patriarchy; Self-Control; Sentimentalism; Strenuous Life; Victorian Era; Working-Class Manhood

—Thomas Winter

Darwinism

The term Darwinism refers most generally to the principles of organic evolution presented by the British biologist Charles Darwin in *On the Origin of Species* (1859) and *The Descent of Man* (1871), and more specifically to the popularization of Darwin's concepts and the application of his ideas to theories of social Darwinism in the late nineteenth and early twentieth centuries. Darwinism directly challenged theological arguments for a distinct act of creation of humans—locating them, like other organisms, within the natural world. It also provided new justifications for gender and racial inequalities—suggesting that late-Victorian white masculinity was the most advanced product of evolution—and was used to define normative American manhood as economically competitive and (hetero)sexually active.

Darwin argued that species were not divinely created, static forms, but instead changed over time through the process of natural selection, in which random genetic traits that benefit an organism are passed on to offspring. Darwin's account of organic evolution by natural selection challenged prevalent religious and philosophical conceptions of humanity and masculinity, suggesting that human bodies arose from the same processes as other animals, that humans were originally less complex, and that women are neither derived from nor closer to nature than men. This contradicted Biblical accounts of the creation of Eve from Adam and of the Fall from Eden, as well as views of humans as stewards of the natural world.

Despite the paradigm shift of these perspectives, some advocates used Darwinism to legitimate the unequal race and gender relations of the late nineteenth and early twentieth centuries, attempting to ground white male dominance in natural law. Darwinism suggested to some the possibility that different racial groups represented different evolutionary stages or branches, and was thus used to assert that whites were more evolved and more intelligent, while blacks and other races were more animalistic. In the United States during the late nineteenth and early twentieth centuries, these assertions were used to justify measures such as racial segregation, antimiscegenation laws targeting African Americans, and anti-immigration legislation excluding immigrants from Asia and eastern and southern Europe. Some Darwinists also contended that men were more advanced intellectually than women and that men and women had evolved for different roles—men for competition and work outside the home, women for child care and homemaking. Such arguments were used to support the "cult of domesticity" for women, limiting women's rights outside the home and justifying men's sexual needs and pleasures as more vigorous and natural. (In response, female Darwinian theorists tended to emphasize complementarity between the sexes and the possibility of equivalence with difference.) With definitions of Victorian manhood linked to sexual reproduction, Darwinism was also used to argue that homosexuality was unnatural because it did not produce offspring.

Social Darwinism, in particular, influenced views of men as competitive, aggressive individuals and provided arguments for a natural basis for growing class inequalities. Social Darwinism represented the world as inherently competitive (epitomized by British social theorist Herbert Spencer's phrase "survival of the fittest"), suggesting that normative masculinity should embody competition to eliminate the less socially and economically fit. This focus on economic competition between individuals helped rationalize the spread of capitalism and imperialism during the Gilded Age—a position taken by Benjamin Kidd in *The Control of the Tropics* (1898). However, recent historical work suggests that Social Darwinism may explain little of American entrepreneurialism, which instead was rooted in Christian and Enlightenment ideals of self-improvement through work and accumulation. Eugenics in the United States, which received increasing support amid growing immigration in the late nineteenth and early twentieth centuries, drew on Darwinian concepts of evolutionary progress to argue against racial intermixing and for the limitation of reproduction by groups deemed biologically and morally degenerate.

Darwinism also informed the early-twentieth-century Progressive Era debate over the impact of urbanization on American masculinity. Social pathologists feared that modern cities were unnatural environments that threatened the evolutionary advancement of American manhood by permitting the survival of the unfit—and that the failure of evolution to work correctly in the urban setting was responsible for such threats to virile reproductive masculinity as homosexuality, alcoholism, and sexually transmitted diseases. Such fears led to the advocation of competitive sport, physical activity in natural settings, and the encouragement of primitive behaviors in growing boys as ways to reinvigorate masculinity. Reform-minded Darwinists were more optimistic, arguing that appropriate urban planning might allow, and even promote, the continuing evolutionary improvement of American men in urban environments.

Reactions to Darwinism in the United States generally differed along religious and regional lines, with resistance most powerful among fundamentalist Protestants and in the South, where Creationist interpretations of the Bible were strongest. The 1920 Scopes Monkey Trial, in which high school teacher John Thomas Scopes was prosecuted in Tennessee for violating state law by teaching evolution, marked a surge in antievolutionism in the South, even as it was a watershed for acceptance of Darwinian principles in the United States. Intellectual discussion centered on whether human bodies were divinely created or had organically evolved; however, debates over Darwinism implicitly included arguments over different meanings of masculinity. Many conservative Protestants upheld constructions of manhood and male sexuality grounded in the ideas of original sin and redemption, finding support for domesticity and female subordination in Biblical accounts of Eve's derivation from Adam.

Southern white masculinity likewise depended on Biblical explanations of racial differences (e.g., the mark of Cain, Noah's sons) to sustain arguments for the intellectual and moral superiority of white men. Darwinism challenged these constructions of masculinity and Biblical bases of social order by claiming that male physical, mental, social, and sexual characteristics had their origins in less complex organisms, and that relations between races and sexes were neither divinely ordained nor immutable. Darwinists held instead that masculinity, changed over time, would adapt to the conditions of modern urban society, and could be improved through progressive social change rather than individual Christian salvation.

Literary and philosophical works have reflected the impact of Darwinism on intellectual and cultural constructions of masculinity, including the anxiety about men's place in the world that it provoked and the explanations for competition that it engendered. Rather than exhibiting scientific control of nature, men, in various texts, simultaneously embrace and resist their own animalistic tendencies. In Robert Louis Stevenson's *Dr. Jekyll and Mr. Hyde* (1886), a scientist unleashes the beast he perceives within human males, leading to tragic results. Jack London, influenced by Darwinian thought, writes of a masculinity requiring struggle with and within nature rather than escape from it (e.g., *White Fang* [1906]) and he envisages competition between races, with superior whites eventually prevailing (e.g., *A Daughter of the Snows* [1902]). Edgar Rice Burroughs's *Tarzan* series (first introduced in 1912) depicts a man raised by apes whose masculinity, stunted by urban-industrial civilization, becomes fully realized only through his jungle upbringing. Sigmund Freud suggests in *Civilization and Its Discontents* (1929) that many Victorian psychological problems are the result of men's imprisonment by civilization and alienation from nature. More recently, John Updike's *Rabbit* series (1960–1990s) evokes the importance of Darwinian competition between individuals in the construction of the businessman in corporate America.

Darwinism most directly shaped constructions of masculinity in the United States by grounding humans in the natural world, identifying heterosexual and reproductive behaviors with natural explanations of normative masculinity, and justifying race, gender, and economic inequalities that privileged white middle- and upper-class men. Darwinism provided a revolutionary explanation for human origins, but at the same time reified many beliefs about the nature of white masculinity.

BIBLIOGRAPHY

Bannister, Robert C. *Social Darwinism: Science and Myth in Anglo-American Social Thought.* Philadelphia: Temple University Press, 1979.

Bowler, Peter J. *The Eclipse of Darwinism: Anti-Darwinian Evolution Theories in the Decades around 1900.* Baltimore: Johns Hopkins University Press, 1983.

Hawkins, Mike. *Social Darwinism in European and American Thought, 1860–1945: Nature as Model and Nature as Threat.* Cambridge, England: Cambridge University Press, 1997.

Hendershot, Cyndy. *The Animal Within: Masculinity and the Gothic.* Ann Arbor: University of Michigan Press, 1998.

Numbers, Ronald L. *Darwinism Comes to America.* Cambridge, Mass.: Harvard University Press, 1998.

Numbers, Ronald L., and John Stenhouse. *Disseminating Darwinism: The Role of Place, Race, Religion, and Gender.* Cambridge, England: Cambridge University Press, 1999.

Roberts, Jon H. *Darwinism and the Divine in America: Protestant Intellectuals and Organic Evolution, 1859–1900.* Madison: University of Wisconsin Press, 1988.

FURTHER READING

Conkin, Paul Keith. *When All the Gods Trembled: Darwinism, Scopes, and American Intellectuals.* Lanham, Md.: Rowman & Littlefield, 1998.

Haraway, Donna J. *Simians, Cyborgs, and Women: The Reinvention of Nature.* New York: Routledge, 1991.

Hofstadter, Richard. *Social Darwinism in American Thought, 1860–1915.* Philadephia: University of Pennsylvania Press, 1945.

Horner, Carl S. *The Boy inside the American Businessman: Corporate Darwinism in Twentieth-Century American Literature.* Lanham, Md.: University Press of America, 1992.

Kaye, Howard L. *The Social Meaning of Modern Biology: From Social Darwinism to Sociobiology.* 2nd ed. New Brunswick, N.J.: Transaction, 1997.

Young, Robert M. "The Historiographic and Ideological Contexts of the Nineteenth-Century Debate on Man's Place in Nature." In *Changing Perspectives in the History of Science,* edited by M. Teich and Robert M. Young. London: Heinemann, 1973.

RELATED ENTRIES

Capitalism; Eugenics; Freudian Psychoanalytic Theory; Heterosexuality; Homosexuality; Individualism; Race; Religion and Spirituality; Reproduction; Southern Manhood; Tarzan; Urbanization; Victorian Era; Whiteness; White Supremacism

—*Matthew R. Dudgeon*

DEAN, JAMES

1931–1955
American Actor

After a brief television and stage career, James Dean made only three movies before his death at age twenty-four in 1955. He nonetheless became one of the twentieth century's prime symbols of restless young manhood. Transcending nationality, time, and sexual orientation, Dean has remained a popular icon, and for some a cult figure. Before two of his films had even premiered, Dean died when his speeding Porsche crashed on a California highway, making his death as open to conflicting interpretations as was much of his life: What some might see as romantic recklessness others could characterize as self-destructive compulsion. Combining vulnerability, simmering rage, and sexual allure, Dean—particularly through his film characters and early death—represented a new model of American masculinity.

Like Allen Ginsberg in poetry and Elvis Presley in music, Dean seemed the antithesis of 1950s conformity. In contrast to the stiflingly conformist "man in the gray flannel suit," a phrase made famous by Sloan Wilson's 1955 novel with that title, Dean is commonly remembered wearing boots, jeans, a white t-shirt, and a black leather jacket. In *East of Eden* (1955) as Cal Trask and in *Rebel Without a Cause* (1955) as Jim Stark, Dean played vulnerable young men hungry for love. He portrayed both resentment and tenderness, an unusual combination for an American leading man in the 1950s. His characters' search for masculine identity was particularly apparent in Jim Stark's attack on his apron-clad father (Jim Backus) in *Rebel Without a Cause.* His last role, as Jett Rink in *Giant,* also released in 1955, was that of a melancholy man to whom even sudden wealth brings little satisfaction. In all of these roles, Dean played the rebellious loner, embodying the individualism, independence, and detachment long associated with masculinity in American film and literature. Dean died before he could play a part he had already signed for, the outlaw Billy the Kid.

There had not been a male role model quite like him before. "He is not a muscle-flexing hunk of beefcake" (DeAngelis, 95), wrote one columnist, while the novelist John Dos Passos wrote of all the American boys who stood "before the mirrors in the restroom/to look at themselves/and

James Dean, seen here in Rebel Without a Cause *(1955), represented a model of masculinity emphasizing rebelliousness, detachment, and sexuality that was embraced by many young American men during and after the 1950s. This image also suggests the homoeroticism and androgyny that some commentators have seen in Dean. (© Hulton/Archive)*

see/James Dean" (Dalton, 328). More prosaically, a psychiatrist remarked in 1956 that Dean was "a remarkably vivid and compelling symbol of the confusion and tumults experienced in adolescence and early maturity" (Dalton, 327). Biographies and new movies about him (and even a U.S. postage stamp with Dean's image) continued to appear decades after his death.

Cultural critics and other observers have pointed to a certain sexual ambiguity and androgynous demeanor in Dean to help explain his wide appeal. Thanks to some biographers' accounts of his love affairs with men—and Jim Stark's friendship with the homosexual Plato in *Rebel Without a Cause*—many gay males have embraced him as one of their own. In his love of race cars, his adoption of Western garb and lingo while making *Giant*, and his adolescent fondness for sports, others have seen something more conventional. Similarly, his continuing appeal has both reflected and, to some extent, shaped the shifting and sometimes contradictory definitions of American manhood.

Bibliography

Alexander, Paul. *Boulevard of Broken Dreams: The Life, Times, and Legend of James Dean.* New York: Viking, 1994.

American Legends. "James Dean." <http://www.americanlegends.com> (January 12, 2003).

Dalton, David. *James Dean, the Mutant King: A Biography.* Chicago: A Cappella, 2001.

DeAngelis, Michael. *Gay Fandom and Crossover Stardom: James Dean, Mel Gibson, and Keanu Reeves.* Durham, N.C.: Duke University Press, 2001.

JamesDean.com. "About James Dean." <http://www.jamesdean.com/> (January 12, 2003).

Further Reading

Gilmore, John. *Live Fast, Die Young: Remembering the Short Life of James Dean.* New York: Thunder's Mouth Press, 1997.

Kimmel, Michael. *Manhood in America: A Cultural History.* New York: Free Press, 1996.

Related Entries

Adolescence; Hollywood; Homosexuality; *Rebel Without a Cause*

—*John Ibson*

Death of a Salesman

Arthur Miller's play *Death of a Salesman* (1949) follows the downward spiral of Willy Loman, a traveling salesman who suffers several setbacks in his life, culminating in his dismissal from his job and eventual suicide. Loman's problems at work parallel his troubles at home, where he faces mounting debt and family tensions. The play's themes reflected anxieties about the meaning of middle-class masculinity in postwar America, and it enjoyed both critical acclaim and popular success.

In its exploration of masculinity and failure, *Death of a Salesman* addressed important concerns prompted by changing ideals of white middle-class masculinity. While the ability to provide for one's family remained an essential element of masculinity—and became even more important amid economic prosperity and the availability of new domestic products—many Americans no longer considered it sufficient. The postwar baby boom and the growth of suburbia promoted a model of family togetherness in which mature and responsible manhood required men to be engaged and emotionally accessible fathers as well as breadwinners. White middle-class men also faced transitions at the workplace as white-collar employment became increasingly bureaucratic and impersonal. These changes at home and work encouraged men to be "other-directed," striving to fit in and conform to those around them.

By these new standards of masculinity, Willy Loman considers himself a failure. He had embraced the idea of the American dream, whereby hard work would earn men a good income, recognition at the job, family harmony, and comfortable surroundings at home. Instead, he became faceless and expendable to a new boss who found his declining sales more important than his many years of loyal service. At home, Loman's attempts to provide his family with such domestic commodities as a house, car, refrigerator, and vacuum cleaner have left him drowning in debt. The ideal of family togetherness also eludes Loman as distance and disappointment mark his relationships with his two adult sons. He had tried to instill in them the idea that popularity and personality, rather than skill and character, were central to masculinity and success. His sons, however, come to regard Loman as a pathetic figure and believe that his advice contributed to their own bouts with failure.

Loman increasingly retreats into the past, revisiting and second-guessing many of his choices. As he confronts his shortcomings as a man, he idealizes his older brother Ben, who had searched successfully for adventure and entrepreneurship on the frontier of Alaska. In this way, Ben represents an alternative to postwar masculinity, one that evoked nineteenth-century ideals of manhood based on risk-taking and independence in an expanding West. Back in the present, however, Loman continues to encounter embarrassment and failure. He commits suicide, confident that his life insurance money will enable his family to succeed. Only in death can Willy Loman find success as a breadwinner and family man.

Questioning the model of masculinity generated by American business culture, Arthur Miller's *Death of a Salesman* found a receptive audience in postwar America. It resonated with American men who felt dissatisfied and suffocated by middle-class ideals of family life and white-collar work. The play also illustrated the concerns of a growing number of critics of postwar life, such as C. Wright Mills and William Whyte, who feared that postwar society was undermining the foundations of American masculinity, creating men who were feminized and weak.

BIBLIOGRAPHY

Corber, Robert J. *Homosexuality in Cold War America: Resistance and the Crisis of Masculinity*. Durham, N.C.: Duke University Press, 1997.

Ehrenreich, Barbara. *The Hearts of Men: American Dreams and the Flight from Commitment*. Garden City, N.Y.: Anchor Books, 1983.

Griswold L. Robert. *Fatherhood in America: A History*. New York: Basic Books, 1993.

Kimmel, Michael. *Manhood in America: A Cultural History*. New York: Free Press, 1996.

Murphy, Brenda. *Miller: Death of a Salesman*. Cambridge, England: Cambridge University Press, 1995.

FURTHER READING

August, Eugene R. "*Death of a Salesman:* A Men's Studies Approach." *Western Ohio Journal* 7 (Spring 1986): 53–71.

Callow, Heather Cook. "Masculine and Feminine in *Death of a Salesman*." In *"The Salesman Has a Birthday": Essays Celebrating the Fiftieth Anniversary of Arthur Miller's* Death of a Salesman, edited by Stephen A. Marino. Lanham, Md.: University Press of America, 2000.

Savran, David. *Communists, Cowboys, and Queers: The Politics of Masculinity in the Work of Arthur Miller and Tennessee Williams*. Minneapolis: University of Minnesota Press, 1992.

RELATED ENTRIES

American Dream; Breadwinner Role; Bureaucratization; Business/Corporate America; Capitalism; Cold War; Consumerism; Crisis of Masculinity; Fatherhood; Middle-Class Manhood; Nuclear Family; Western Frontier; Work

—*Elisa Miller*

DELIVERANCE

Adapted by James Dickey from his 1970 best-selling novel and directed by John Boorman, *Deliverance* (1972) follows the ordeal of four middle-aged men who must fight for their survival against a series of assaults by a group of mountain dwellers during a weekend canoeing trip. Testing the men both physically and psychologically, the adventure epitomizes the male bonding central to the emerging buddy film genre. Paralleling concerns about dominant masculinity expressed by the women's and gay liberation movements, the film examines the troubled state of traditional white, heterosexual masculinity in the United States.

Alienated by urban stress and demoralized by emasculating managerial jobs, the men are experiencing a crisis in masculine identity at the beginning of the movie. As white southerners, the loss of power engendered by the recent civil rights movement further exacerbates their uncertainty about the traditional male role. In this context, the decision to return to nature can be interpreted as an attempt to recuperate a lost masculinity.

The four principal characters in *Deliverance* represent different aspects of the late-twentieth-century male psyche. Lewis (Burt Reynolds), a man of action, relies on his muscular physique and innate athletic abilities to control others. His macho bravado ultimately masks insecurities about his traditional masculine role. Bobby (Ned Beatty), an overweight insurance salesman, appears ill-at-ease in outdoor surroundings. Sexually assaulted by a savage mountain man, Bobby responds to this affront on his manhood by disavowing the rape and persuading his friends to do the same. Drew (Ronny Cox), a sensitive musician, serves as the group's moral conscience. His desire to abide by the law places him at odds with his fellow travelers. Finally, Ed (Jon Voight), a mild-mannered businessman, taps an untested well of strength and discovers the innate instincts of a killer.

Among this group of men, two opposing models of masculinity eventually emerge. Bobby, Drew, and Ed represent various elements of a civil masculinity defined by obedience and self-restraint, alignment with the laws of society, and repression of primal urges. Lewis, an expert hunter, symbolizes a more primitive masculinity aligned with the laws of nature and expressed in domination and acts of violence. Valorizing neither model, *Deliverance* exposes the traumas these conflicting definitions of manhood create, for although primitive masculinity may inflict corporeal wounds, the self-restraint of civil masculinity pains men emotionally.

Unleashing male sexual energies deemed taboo by society, Bobby's assault arouses feelings of male eroticism and attraction. Similarly, Ed's killing of a mountain man exposes his own potential for violence. For all four men, the journey through the river's rapids and the encounter with the mountain men become metaphors for the dangers of allowing male sexual energies and violent impulses to rage out of control. Denied an outlet for displaying affection toward other men, sexual and emotional feelings between men must be repressed. By the film's end Drew drowns, and two mountain men have been murdered, their bodies buried beneath the river. In a final dream sequence, Ed sees a gun clutched by an outstretched arm resurface from its watery grave. Symbolizing the return of the repressed, his nightmare suggests that men's attempts to sublimate primitive male desire are ultimately problematic.

Notable for its morally ambiguous and flawed characters, *Deliverance* departs from the genre conventions associated with the buddy film. By leaving the film without a powerful, male hero, *Deliverance* perfectly reflects the early 1970s call to re-examine traditional gender roles.

BIBLIOGRAPHY

Farber, Stephen. "Deliverance—How It Delivers." *New York Times,* 20 August 1972. Reprinted in *New York Times Film Review Annual 1972,* 299–300.

Griffith, James. "Damned If You Do, and Damned If You Don't: James Dickey's Deliverance." *Post Script* 5, no. 3 (1986): 47–59.

Lehman, Peter, ed. *Masculinity: Bodies, Movies, Culture.* New York: Routledge, 2001.

Mellen, Joan. *Big Bad Wolves: Masculinity in the American Film.* New York: Pantheon, 1977.

Robinson, Sally. *Marked Men: White Masculinity in Crisis.* New York: Columbia University Press, 2000.

FURTHER READING

Beaton, James. "Dickey Down the River." In *The Modern American Novel and the Movies,* edited by Gerald Peary and Roger Shatzkin. New York: Ungar, 1978.

David, Deborah S., and Robert Brannon. "The Male Sex Role: Our Culture's Blueprint of Manhood, and What It's Done for Us Lately." In *The Forty-Nine Percent Majority: The Male Sex Role,* edited by Deborah S. David and Robert Brannon. Reading, Mass.: Addison-Wesley, 1976.

Dickey, James. *Deliverance.* New York: Dell, 1994.

Russo, Vito. *The Celluloid Closet: Homosexuality In The Movies.* Rev. ed. New York: HarperCollins, 1987.

RELATED ENTRIES

Body; Buddy Films; Crisis of Masculinity; Freudian Psychoanalytic Theory; Guns; Hollywood; Homosexuality; Hunting; Male Friendship; Outdoorsmen; Self-Control; Violence

—*Michael R. Meadows*

DEMOCRATIC MANHOOD

Between 1815 and the 1840s, a concept of democratic manhood emerged in the United States, marking a conscious rejection of European (especially British) notions of ascribed social status. Strongly associated with Democratic president Andrew Jackson, democratic manhood was defined as political equality and broadened political participation among white men—and by the exclusion of women and nonwhites from the privileges of citizenship. It emphasized physical prowess and boisterous patriotism, expressed by the popularity of such frontiersmen as Daniel Boone and Davy Crockett. Furthermore, the concept informed a developing urban counterculture that resisted the aristocratic pretensions and bourgeois morality of an emerging middle class.

Several developments of the early to mid–nineteenth century contributed to the emergence of democratic manhood. First, urbanization and industrialization drew increasing numbers of transient young men into the nation's expanding cities, eroding communal restraints on behavior and limiting the control that patriarchal families could exercise over their sons. Second, early industrialization challenged the manly ideal of the "heroic artisan," which was grounded in ideas about independence and producer values, by making it increasingly difficult for apprentices and journeymen to advance to the position of master craftsman and forcing them into wage labor. These men had to articulate a new concept of manhood, suitable to their social reality. Third, by 1824 all states except Virginia, Florida, and Louisiana enacted universal adult, white-male suffrage, eliminating previous tax- and property-based restrictions on voting rights and grounding citizenship in gender and racial identity.

The 1820s saw the emergence of a flourishing urban subculture of "dandies," or "sporting men," many of whom were apprentices, journeymen, or clerks, who embraced an antipatriarchal, antiaristocratic ideal of democratic manhood. Freed from the familial control and social constraints of small communities, the growing urban male population challenged paternalistic authority, looked to boardinghouses and male peers for their frame of reference, and abandoned values such as virtue and self-restraint in favor of qualities such as hedonism. The masculine libido, not yet appropriated by capitalist production, market mechanisms, and the political party system, gained free reign in these urban subcultures. Sporting men, flamboyant in dress and conduct, yet egalitarian and antiaristocratic in their values, sought to demonstrate their manliness in the urban marketplace of labor, in volunteer militia and fire companies, in street gangs such as New York's

This 1840 woodcut features presidential candidate William Henry Harrison welcoming a wounded soldier to his log cabin and offering him hard cider. With the enactment of universal white-male suffrage, political candidates increasingly conveyed an image of democratic manhood emphasizing heroic patriotism, humble origins, and frontier folksiness. (From the collections of the Library of Congress)

infamous Bowery B'hoys, and in a culture of erotic entertainments and burlesque shows. Surging immigration to the nation's cities in the 1830s and 1840s further abetted the development of this urban subculture.

The participants in this urban male subculture proved and defended their manhood through the ritualized violence of boxing and blood sports. The boxing ring was in many ways ideally suited for acting out democratic manhood, for it was an egalitarian space that defied notions of ascribed status. In this arena, victory or defeat depended solely on the masculine prowess and fighting skills of the combatants. Even though it generated social hierarchies based on merit and achievement, status in these hierarchies remained open and fluid: Since fighters and their supporters could meet for rematches, one's manhood could continually be proved.

Democratic manhood played a role in the riots that became a part of the political culture of Jacksonian America. These riots often involved issues of race, class struggle, and industrial development, and they reflected a longstanding tradition of "crowd actions" by which urban underclasses sought to enforce their political will. In 1849, for example, William Charles Macready, a British actor widely perceived as aristocratic, was performing in New York City's Astor Place Theater. Followers of Edwin Forrest, a rival American actor who was a popular symbol of patriotism among the city's sporting men, stormed the theater, prematurely ending Macready's performance. Several hundred others started a riot outside the theater that left twenty-three dead and over one hundred wounded.

Democratic manhood also affected the nation's politics, on both local and national levels. On the local level, the New York City Bowery B'hoys formed the basis of Tammany Hall, the Democratic political machine that would later control city politics during the late nineteenth century. On the national level, the presidency of Democrat Andrew Jackson (1829–37)—who was presented to the electorate as a heroic Indian fighter, general, and frontiersman with a penchant for violence—became a rallying point for political involvement among an expanded white male electorate. Jackson promised that his Native American removal policy, which would open up land between the Appalachian Mountains and the Mississippi River for settlement, would promote independence and autonomy for white men. His destruction of the Second Bank of the United States (called "Mother Bank" by its opponents) on the grounds that it allegedly suffocated white men's independence and promoted the development of a "moneyed aristocracy" carried reminders of Revolutionary-Era Republican concerns over British parental usurpation. However, although Jackson presented himself as the defender of white men's independence by opposing this key element of a capitalist market economy, he also cleared the path for further economic development. As a white, egalitarian ideal of democratic manhood became dependent upon exclusionary policies toward nonwhites, it left the very beneficiaries of these policies defenseless against capitalist development that would eventually undermine the independence of white men.

Jackson's political success prompted the opposition Whig Party, which was generally more supportive of the developing market economy, to appropriate the language of democratic manhood. In 1834, the Whigs sponsored a speaking tour featuring the Tennessean frontiersman Davy Crockett, who was running for reelection to Congress. In 1840, the party ran a victorious "Log Cabin and Hard Cider" campaign that portrayed its presidential candidate, William Henry Harrison, as a simple man of democratic values, while labeling the Democratic candidate, Martin Van Buren, as an effeminate aristocrat.

Since the nineteenth century, the notion of a democratic manhood has emerged as a significant part of cultural currents of masculinity in U.S. society. After 1815, the ideal of a democratic manhood, and the urban male subculture it sanctioned, fueled the hostility and frustration of a growing transient white male population. Antipaternalistic in nature, and a product of the social pressures of early industrialization and urbanization, this manifestation of democratic manhood represented an attempt by urban men to shape society in their own egalitarian image. Aspects of this subculture remained a part of single urban men's culture. Many of its elements would later be absorbed into a notion of the "strenuous life," understood as a combination of an active citizenship in combination with a virile and assertive masculinity, which was policed by the state and channeled into a variety of political outlets or appropriated by capitalist processes and an emerging consumer culture.

The extension of suffrage to African-American men after the Civil War and to women after World War I challenged the association of democratic values and citizenship with whiteness and manhood, while also broadening the reach of political egalitarianism inherent in the ideal of a democratic manhood. At the end of the twentieth century, the masculine appeal and association of democratic rhetoric with manhood persisted in U.S. politics and presidential campaign strategies, typified by television commercials featuring Ronald Reagan chopping wood, emphasizing Bill Clinton's humble origins, or showing Patrick Buchanan sporting a beaver hat.

BIBLIOGRAPHY

Chudacoff, Howard. *The Age of the Bachelor: Creating an American Subculture.* Princeton, N.J.: Princeton University Press, 1999.

Gorn, Elliott J. *The Manly Art: Bare-Knuckle Prize Fighting in America.* Ithaca, N.Y.: Cornell University Press, 1986.

Kasson, John F. *Rudeness & Civility: Manners in Nineteenth-Century Urban America.* New York: Hill & Wang, 1990.

Kimmel, Michael. *Manhood in America: A Cultural History.* New York: Free Press, 1996.

Rogin, Michael Paul. *Fathers and Children: Andrew Jackson and the Subjugation of the American Indian.* New Brunswick, N.J.: Transaction Publishers, 1991.

Wilentz, Sean. *Chants Democratic: New York City & The Rise of the American Working Class, 1788–1850.* New York: Oxford University Press, 1984.

FURTHER READING

Davis, Susan G. *Parades and Power: Street Theater in Nineteenth-Century Philadelphia.* Berkeley: University of California Press, 1988.

Gilfoyle, Timothy J. *City of Eros: New York City, Prostitution, and the Commercialization of Sex, 1790–1920.* New York: Norton, 1992.

Halttunen, Karen. *Confidence Men and Painted Women: A Study of Middle-Class Culture in America, 1830–1870.* New Haven, Conn.: Yale University Press, 1982.

Rose, Anne C. *Voices of the Marketplace: American Thought and Culture, 1830–1860.* New York: Twayne, 1995.

Sellers, Charles. *The Market Revolution: Jacksonian America, 1815–1846.* New York: Oxford University Press, 1991.

Smith-Rosenberg, Carroll. *Disorderly Conduct: Visions of Gender in Victorian America.* New York: Knopf, 1985.

RELATED ENTRIES

Bachelorhood; Consumerism; Crockett, Davy; Cult of Domesticity; Gilded Age; Jackson, Andrew; Leatherstocking Tales; Market Revolution; Nationalism; Patriotism; Race; Republicanism; Strenuous Life; Victorian Era; Violence; Western Frontier; Whiteness; Working-Class Manhood

—*Thomas Winter*

DETECTIVES

The detective is an icon of American masculinity that articulates the myth of the lone hero. The detective narrative is concerned, above all, with the investigation of the hero's masculinity, which must be tested and proved by solving the case. Detective heroes, who offer models of ideal manhood, have also embodied changing social attitudes toward masculinity.

Edgar Allan Poe's character C. Auguste Dupin is the literary father of all fictional detectives, including Arthur Conan Doyle's famous British sleuth Sherlock Holmes. The sleuth is characterized by the superior skills of deduction and observation associated with manhood in Victorian culture. By the 1920s and 1930s, an increasing emphasis on aggressiveness, sexuality, and the body in American constructions of male identity generated new kinds of detective figures. The hard-boiled private eye, popularized by writers such as Raymond

Chandler and Dashiell Hammett, represented a shift to a tough and street-smart hero, while film detective series followed the adventures of suave gentlemen detectives such as the Falcon and the Thin Man.

The hard-boiled detective was brought to the screen during the 1940s and 1950s, as American men struggled with the displacements of World War II and returning veterans faced a changed society, unemployment, shifting gender roles, alienation, and often disablement. During this period, *film noir* movies such as *The Maltese Falcon* (1941) and *Touch of Evil* (1958) offered audiences tough but traumatized heroes who expressed and worked through this postwar disillusionment.

Cold War concerns for security and fears of organized crime in the late 1940s and 1950s resulted in the emergence of the "cop" in films such as *The Naked City* (1948) and television's *Dragnet.* The cop put his duty first and kept his emotions and desires in check. However, the domestic turbulence of the late 1960s and 1970s, President Richard M. Nixon's hard-line politics regarding crime, America's emasculation caused by the Vietnam War, and a loss of confidence in the police culminated in the popularization of the vigilante cop. Exemplified by Harry Callahan (played by Clint Eastwood) who first appeared in 1971 in *Dirty Harry,* this detective/hero used violence, autonomy, and defiance of established legal authority to rid society of crime.

By the 1980s, the impact of second-wave feminism had thrown social conceptions of masculinity into flux and created conflicting images in the media. In this environment, the "new man" appeared. Exemplified by Thomas Magnum (played by Tom Selleck) of television's *Magnum P.I.,* the new man possessed a feminized masculinity that was sensitive and fashionable. In a backlash to these new qualities the "retributive man," appeared. The character John McClane (played by Bruce Willis) in the movie *Die Hard* (1988), exhibits the hypermasculinity characteristic of this type.

During the 1990s, society witnessed a new appreciation of masculinity that was both intellectually astute and physically and emotionally vulnerable. This shift prompted a return to a thinking detective—the criminalist. Personified by Dr. Sloan (Dick van Dyke) of television's *Diagnosis Murder,* the criminalist employs observation, forensic science, and profiling to solve a case. With this emphasis on intelligence and sensitivity, rather than muscularity, new kinds of detective heroes have emerged, including female, older, and African-American detectives. Thus, in conjunction with social changes, the icon of the detective continues to evolve beyond the traditional white male hero, offering audiences an expression of American society's shifting images of masculinity.

Bibliography

Everson, William K. *The Detective in Film.* 3rd ed. Secaucus, N.J.: Citadel, 1972.

Jeffords, Susan. *Hard Bodies: Hollywood Masculinity in the Reagan Era.* New Brunswick, N.J.: Rutgers University Press, 1994.

Krutnik, Frank. *In a Lonely Street: Film Noir, Genre, Masculinity.* London: Routledge, 1991.

Mandel, Ernest. *Delightful Murder: A Social History of the Crime Story.* London: Pluto Press, 1984.

Mellen, Joan. *Big Bad Wolves: Masculinity in the American Film.* New York: Pantheon Books, 1977.

Reiner, Robert. *The Politics of the Police.* Brighton: Wheatsheaf Books, 1985.

Further Reading

Delamater, Jerome, and Ruth Prigozy, eds. *The Detective in American Fiction, Film, and Television.* Westport, Conn.: Greenwood Press, 1988.

King, Neal. *Heroes in Hard Times: Cop Action Movies in the U.S.* Philadelphia: Temple University Press, 1999.

Lehman, David. *The Perfect Murder: A Study in Detection.* Ann Arbor: University of Michigan Press, 1999.

Naremore, James. *More than Night: Film Noir in its Contexts.* Berkeley: University of California Press, 1998.

Parish, James Robert, and Michael R. Pitts. *The Great Detective Pictures.* Metuchen, N.J.: Scarecrow Press, 1990.

Rader, Barbara A., and Howard G. Zettler, eds. *The Sleuth and the Scholar: Origins, Evolution, and Current Trends in Detective Fiction.* New York: Greenwood Press, 1988.

Related Entries

Body; Bogart, Humphrey; Buddy Films; Cold War; Cop Action Films; Eastwood, Clint; Emotion; Heroism; Hollywood; Sensitive Male; Victorian Era; Vietnam War; World War II

—*Philippa Gates*

Divorce

Throughout U.S. history, perceptions and practices regarding divorce have been closely intertwined with definitions of manhood. There have been two broad historical patterns. First, generally strict divorce laws prior to the twentieth century bolstered male domestic authority—an important element of masculine identity—by permitting men substantial leeway in domestic affairs. Beginning as early as the late eighteenth century, however, divorce laws changed (and the grounds for divorce expanded) in ways that reflected an ongoing redefinition and erosion of that authority. Second, divorce suggested until well into the twentieth century that a husband had violated prevailing standards of manhood. During the twentieth century, however, changing perceptions of marriage, the advent of "no-fault" divorce, and the growth of a new masculine ideal grounded in freedom from marital responsibility altered this longstanding association of divorce with masculine failure.

The Colonial and Revolutionary Eras

Divorce in colonial America was framed by a patriarchal social system in which the male-headed household was considered the basis of social order and the foundation of male identity. Manliness meant contributing to social stability by regulating one's household, producing offpsring, and arranging the intergenerational transfer of property. Divorce was rare, in part because it was a source of shame for colonial men. The grounds on which colonial authorities granted divorce—adultery, physical abuse, desertion, and infertility—signified that a man had failed to master the household and preserve order.

Divorce proceedings involving infertility, abandonment, and adultery were particularly revealing of colonial notions of masculinity. A man suspecting infertility in his wife might receive an annulment so that he could remarry and father heirs to his property. Similarly, abandoned women were granted divorces so that they might remarry and become wives in new patriarchal households, while male deserters were stigmatized because they rejected normative patriarchal roles. In cases of adultery, unfaithful husbands were penalized far less often than were unfaithful wives because of colonial associations of manhood with spiritual strength (aberrant male behavior emanated primarily from forgivable bodily weakness) and womanhood with innate and punishable spiritual depravity.

Understandings of manhood and divorce shifted during the era of the American Revolution. Enlightenment thought and republican political theory grounded male domestic authority in reason and voluntary consent, encouraging marital affection and consensus and delegitimizing tyrannical assertions of patriarchal power. As a result, cruelty and other oppressive male marital behaviors became widely adopted as grounds for divorce, thus weakening some traditional patriarchal prerogatives. Nonetheless, traditional views about patriarchy and permissible male behavior persisted. For example, new state laws allowing divorce in instances of physical endangerment or persistent cruelty allowed non-life-threatening and isolated acts of physical abuse to occur. Still, new ideals of rational manhood generated widening definitions of cruelty, a declining respect for authoritarian paternal styles, broadened legal justifications for divorce, and a rising divorce rate.

The Victorian Era

During the nineteenth century, the rise of a national market economy, the influence of new philosophies valuing emotional expression, and the development of a "cult of domesticity" resulted in a new Victorian masculine ideal based on breadwinning, genteel respectability, an idealization of women, and a growing emphasis on marital romance and affection, particularly among the northern middle class. By raising wives' expectations of emotional and material fulfillment, these new standards of marital manliness created greater potential for disillusionment and divorce. In addition, by defining women as weak and in need of paternal protection, emerging gender constructs encouraged divorce courts to enforce the new code of Victorian masculinity by ending the marriages of men that failed to meet it.

With the new ideal of manhood came new and broader definitions of male cruelty and failure, and an accompanying expansion of the permissible grounds for divorce. Several states began granting divorces because of drunkenness, imprisonment, and insanity, and the legal definition of marital cruelty expanded to include excessive emotional distance, failure as a breadwinner, verbal abusiveness, and inordinate sexual demands. Although fathers often retained their traditional claims to custody of minor children, new Victorian gender definitions caused courts to become increasingly sensitive to the claims of mothers seeking divorce and custody. Divorce continued to signify unmanliness, but it became an increasingly common occurrence (except in the largely agrarian South, where divorce remained relatively rare and grounded in patriarchal social structures and customs), which suggested that it was losing its traditional function as an instrument of patriarchal prerogative. The national divorce rate rose from approximately one in a thousand marriages in 1860 to almost one in twenty by 1880 and one in ten by 1910.

Modern America

Twentieth-century developments eroded traditional associations of divorce with personal failure as a man and reinforced the upward trend in divorce rates. Particularly important in framing new attitudes toward divorce and its perceived relation to masculinity was the growth of a consumer culture that emphasized personal enjoyment and the dispensability of goods, which offered Americans an increasingly wide range of leisure activities outside the home. To many in this consumer society, marriage seemed an arrangement to be judged—and either accepted or rejected—according to its consistency with personal happiness. This attitude intensified during the 1920s in the aftermath of World War I, which sparked a loss of faith in notions of honor and duty, and thus made men (and women) less likely to view the severing of marital bonds as a violation of moral principle. At the same time, conceptions of marital hierarchy based in traditional patriarchy continued to yield to a more egalitarian view of marriage as Victorian gender definitions were loosened. Under these cultural impulses, the divorce rate rose to approximately one in six by 1940.

After World War II, divorce rates temporarily decreased as many Americans, seeking order after an economic depression, a world war, and the onset of the Cold War, identified security with traditional patriarchy, marriage, and notions of manhood. But at the same time, the appearance of *Playboy* magazine in 1953 heralded a new and alternative vision—that of the sexually liberated bachelor. This new masculine ideal was reinforced by a growing inclination among Americans of the 1960s, especially younger Americans, to question and reject such traditional institutions as marriage. At the same time, an increasing presence of married women in the workforce and the growing incidence of two-income marriages contributed to an erosion of the masculine breadwinner ideal. This emboldened more women to seek divorce, and also lessened the perception of divorce as a failure of the male provider. As a result, the divorce rate again began to rise.

During the 1970s, the emergence of "no-fault" divorce dramatically altered the relation between masculinity and divorce and prompted a further hike in the incidence of divorce—including in the South—by lessening the stigma attached to divorce and solidifying a new postdivorce manhood ideal grounded in freedom of movement, conspicuous consumption, and a relative lack of responsibility. It removed blame from either party (further separating divorce from notions of failed manhood) and substantially reduced alimony and property awards to wives, allowing divorced men to continue enjoying their former standard of living. Meanwhile, a burst of self-realization and self-fulfillment movements led many men to begin viewing divorce as a liberating path to their "true selves." Divorce could thus serve as a reinforcement of, rather than a threat to, a man's masculinity. Divorce remained to some degree an indicator of masculine failure, for in many cases it still suggested that a husband had been guilty of adultery, abuse, or neglect, but it no longer did so to the degree that it once had, as was suggested by the rise in the national divorce rate to 50 percent by the 1980s (and its continued rise into the early twenty-first century).

While the experience of divorce sometimes encouraged the growth of an ideal of masculinity grounded in unmarried living, it also reinforced many divorced fathers' belief that fatherhood was essential to their masculine identities. As the incidence of divorced fatherhood grew, and as the impact of the feminist movement led divorce courts to increasingly grant custody of children to their mothers, divorced fathers began developing and supporting a fathers' rights movement that asserted their custodial rights. The figure of the divorced father—and concerns about the impact of divorce on fathers' masculinity—achieved considerable visibility in American popular culture during the late twentieth century through such films as *Kramer vs. Kramer* (1979) and *Mrs. Doubtfire* (1993).

Divorce law and divorce cases have provided a barometer of changing ideals of domestic manhood throughout U.S. history, as well as of the control that men exerted in defining that ideal. It is evident that the relation between divorce and masculinity persisted—though in attenuated form—into the early twenty-first century.

BIBLIOGRAPHY

Basch, Norma. *Framing American Divorce: From the Revolutionary Generation to the Victorians.* Berkeley: University of California Press, 1999.

Griswold, Robert L. *Family and Divorce in California, 1850–1890: Victorian Illusions and Everyday Realities.* Albany: State University of New York Press, 1982.

———. "Divorce and the Legal Redefinition of Victorian Manhood." In *Meanings for Manhood: Constructions of Masculinity in Victorian America*, edited by Mark C. Carnes and Clyde Griffen. Chicago: University of Chicago Press, 1990.

Jacob, Herbert. *Silent Revolution: The Transformation of Divorce Law in the United States.* Chicago: University of Chicago Press, 1988.

May, Elaine Tyler. *Homeward Bound: American Families in the Cold War Era.* New York: Basic Books, 1988.

Ownby, Ted. "'Hurtin' Words': Divorce and the Meaning of Cruelty in the Twentieth-Century South." In *Gender and Women in the Twentieth-Century South*, edited by Grace Elizabeth Hale, et. al., (forthcoming, 2004).

Riley, Glenda. *Divorce: An American Tradition.* New York: Oxford University Press, 1991.

Smith, Merril D. *Breaking the Bonds: Marital Discord in Pennsylvania, 1730-1830.* New York: New York University Press, 1991.

Further Reading

Cott, Nancy F. "Divorce and the Changing Status of Women in Eighteenth-Century Massachusetts." In *The American Family in Social-Historical Perspective.* 3rd ed., edited by Michael Gordon. New York: St. Martin's, 1983.

Fliegelman, Jay. *Prodigals and Pilgrims: The American Revolution Against Patriarchal Authority, 1750–1800.* Cambridge, England: Cambridge University Press, 1982.

Lystra, Karen. *Searching the Heart: Men, Women, and Romantic Love in Nineteenth-Century America.* New York: Oxford University Press, 1989.

O'Neill, William L. "Divorce in the Progressive Era." In *The American Family in Social-Historical Perspective.* 3rd ed., edited by Michael Gordon. New York: St. Martin's, 1983.

Watt, Jeffrey R. *The Making of Modern Marriage: Matrimonial Control and the Rise of Sentiment in Neuchatel, 1550–1800.* Ithaca, N.Y.: Cornell University Press, 1992.

Related Entries

American Revolution; Bachelorhood; Breadwinner Role; Cold War; Cult of Domesticity; Emotion; Fatherhood; *Father Knows Best*; Fathers' Rights; Feminism; Great Depression; *Kramer vs. Kramer*; Marriage; Middle-Class Manhood; *Odd Couple, The*; Patriarchy; *Playboy* Magazine; Property; Republicanism; Reverse Sexism; Southern Manhood; Victorian Era; Violence

—*Bret E. Carroll*

Douglass, Frederick

c. 1817–1895
Abolitionist, Author, and Politician

Frederick Douglass was a nineteenth-century abolitionist, author, and politician. Through his autobiographies, Douglass fashions himself as a representative, mid-nineteenth-century black male, though his definition of black manhood often seems to lack a specific African-American dimension. Woven into his critique of slavery and racism is an ideal of manhood shared by white middle-class men and grounded in notions of individualism, self-reliance, and entrepreneurial capitalism.

Born a slave on a Maryland plantation, Douglass became an abolitionist and supporter of women's rights after his 1838 escape. His autobiographies share similarities with other texts that celebrate the emancipation of the autonomous self, such as *Benjamin Franklin's Autobiography* (written between 1771 and 1789), Ralph Waldo Emerson's "Self-Reliance," and Walt Whitman's "Song of Myself." His work may have also inspired Henry David Thoreau's *Walden* (1854).

The central image in the early part of Douglass's *Narrative of the Life of Frederick Douglass* (1845) is that of his aunt Esther, who was punished and sexually abused by the slave owner Aaron Anthony (who was probably Douglass's biological father). Witnessing the degradation of his aunt at the hand of his biological father complicates Douglass's articulation of his own identity as a black male, for blackness is connected to oppression and femininity, whereas masculinity, associated with whiteness, independence, and power, seems unattainable for him. Grappling with this problem in his autobiographies, Douglass articulates a male identity firmly grounded in capitalist market structures and emerging northern, white middle-class definitions of manhood.

Douglass experienced his first exposure to the meanings of freedom and prosperity in 1827 while living in Baltimore as the slave of his master's relatives. Upon returning to the plantation, his owner assigned Douglass to a slave breaker, Mr. Covey. A fight with Covey, in which Douglass prevailed, proved critical to Douglass's construction of male identity. In early versions of his autobiography, this symbolic reversal of

Frederick Douglass, the former slave who became a leading abolitionist and, in his autobiography, presented a model of African-American manhood. Douglass's expression captures the self-assertion and determination that he considered fundamental to African-American manliness, while his dress suggests that he, like white abolitionists, associated manhood with middle-class status. (From the collections of the Library of Congress)

the master–slave relation gives him the independence and self-sufficiency characteristic of the traditional artisan; in subsequent revisions, it represents his achievement of an entrepreneurial manhood based on mastery over other men in the workplace. In either case, manhood for Douglass meant individualism, self-reliance, and hard work.

Douglas seems to have avoided close relationships with women, who remain at the margins throughout the numerous revisions of his autobiography. His interpretation of middle-class manhood apparently required the repression of qualities considered to be feminine, including intimacy. An ardent feminist and supporter of women's rights at the 1848 Seneca Falls women's rights convention, Douglass may have been primarily attracted to antebellum feminism because he could identify with women's demands for autonomy and independence, and with the overall middle-class nature of the movement.

Douglass's definition of manhood reflects the cultural currents and constraints of his time. His autobiographies convey a Victorian middle-class commitment to the notion of separate spheres and identify manhood in relation to economic individualism furthered by an emerging capitalist market economy—represented by the concept of the self-made man. But Douglass's writings also reflect the obstacles black men confronted in articulating an ideal of manhood in a society dominated by white middle-class values. Douglass's embrace of a white ideal of manhood may strike a modern observer as an insufficiently race-conscious solution to the predicament. However, by successfully appropriating norms of white middle-class manhood, Douglass helped to chip away at racial barriers and paved a way for others.

BIBLIOGRAPHY

Leverenz, David. *Manhood and the American Renaissance.* Ithaca, N.Y.: Cornell University Press, 1989.

Martin, Waldo E., Jr. *The Mind of Frederick Douglass.* Chapel Hill: University of North Carolina Press, 1984.

McFeely, William. *Frederick Douglass.* New York: Norton, 1991.

Sundquist, Eric J., ed. *Frederick Douglass: New Literary and Historical Essays.* New York: Cambridge University Press, 1990.

FURTHER READING

Clark Hine, Darleen, and Earnestine Jenkins, eds. *A Question of Manhood: A Reader in U.S. Black Men's History and Masculinity.* 2 vols. Bloomington: Indiana University Press, 1999–2001.

Franklin, Benjamin. *Benjamin Franklin's Autobiography: An Authoritative Text, Backgrounds, Criticism.* Edited by J. A. Leo Lemay and P. M. Zall. New York: Norton, 1986.

Gates, Henry Louis, Jr. *Figures in Black: Words, Signs, and the Racial Self.* New York: Oxford University Press, 1987.

Quarles, Benjamin. *Black Abolitionists.* New York: Oxford University Press, 1970.

Wyllie, Irvin G. *The Self-Made Man in America; The Myth of Rags to Riches.* 3rd ed. New York: Free Press, 1954.

SELECTED WRITINGS

Douglass, Frederick. *Narrative of the Life of Frederick Douglass, an American Slave.* 1845. Reprint, New Haven, Conn.: Yale University Press, 2001.

———. *Autobiographies.* New York: The Library of America, 1994.

RELATED ENTRIES

Abolitionism; African-American Manhood; Artisan; Capitalism; Cult of Domesticity; Emancipation; Emerson, Ralph Waldo; Franklin, Benjamin; Individualism; Market Revolution; Middle-Class Manhood; Race; Self-Made Man; Slave Narratives; Slavery; Thoreau, Henry David; Violence; Whiteness

—*Thomas Winter*

DUELING

Dueling in America lasted from the eighteenth century through the late nineteenth century, serving as a way for self-styled gentlemen to settle conflicts about apparent insults through a series of elaborate steps, leading ultimately to violence. The practice was especially important in dramatizing relationships between rituals and expressions of masculinity and social class.

The duel was far more common in the South than in the rest of the United States. Political figures, military leaders, lawyers, newspaper editors, and other men in public positions of authority ran the risk of being publicly insulted, and, when insulted, often turned to the duel, as many southern men put it, "to demand satisfaction." Some politicians claimed that participating in a duel was necessary to preserve their reputations as honorable men worthy of being leaders, especially as it showed they valued their principles more than their lives.

The process that might lead to a duel began when one man heard or read that another had insulted him, either by suggesting that the man was not the other's equal or by questioning his character—a concept rooted in understandings of both manhood and upper-class status. He might hear, for example, that someone questioned his courage, his honesty, or the good name of family members. Two instances involving the future president Andrew Jackson dramatize typical

Dueling represented for many elite men of the eighteenth and early nineteenth centuries, mostly in the South, a ritual defense of what they considered two central elements of manhood: honor and public reputation. This print depicts the 1804 duel between Aaron Burr and Alexander Hamilton. (From the collections of the Library of Congress)

reasons for dueling: One concerned the slow and uncertain way a man was trying, perhaps dishonestly, to pay Jackson a gambling debt. The other involved insults about the dubious divorce of Rachel Robards Jackson, who became Andrew Jackson's wife. Name-calling—coward, poltroon, and liar were among the favorites—often compelled men to protect their honor by dueling.

Honor, which was fundamental to elite southern constructions of manhood, required that a man follow a clear, formalized series of steps when insulted. If he was unsure about the process, he could check a guide to the practice, such as John Lyde Wilson's *The Code of Honor or Rules for the Government of Principles and Seconds in Duelling*, published in Charleston in 1838. First, the insulted male pondered whether what he had read or heard was really an insult. If convinced he had indeed been insulted, he took the next step and wrote the offending person, or one of his friends or relatives, asking for an explanation. The issue frequently concentrated on a central tenet of an honor-based society: that men of the same class status respect each other as equals.

At this point, networks of male friends were crucial in pushing a dispute toward either a duel or a more peaceful resolution; in either case the men were guided by a code of honor. The man who felt insulted had a close friend, his "second," contact a friend of the opposing party, either to ask for more clarification or to set a time and place for a duel. Sometimes seconds were able to discover language necessary for one man to explain his words to the other's satisfaction. If not, the seconds were responsible for making sure the weapons the duelists chose would be fair to both participants, and also for enforcing the rules at the duel itself.

Throughout the entire process, all parties were supposed to control their emotions—part of being an honorable man of elite status involved knowing how to settle disputes without becoming angry. By contrast, common folk, strangers, and slaves—people with no rank in the community—were not entitled to the formalities of the duel.

Seconds who refereed the duel had the job of judging if anyone had cheated. Most weapons were pistols, although duelists occasionally chose rifles or even swords. It is unclear how many duels led to injuries and deaths, in part because many duels went unreported. Probably no more than 15 percent of duels involved death or serious injury. Often simply going to the dueling ground gave both parties the satisfaction they desired; some participants would fire into the air instead of at their opponent to show their mastery over their emotions.

Not all duels took place in the South. The Aaron Burr–Alexander Hamilton duel took place in New Jersey in 1804, settling several years of insults and political disputes with Hamilton's death. Significantly, Hamilton had also lost a son to a duel. But the practice was so clearly identified with the South that when Congressman Jonathan Cilley of Maine dueled with Kentuckian William Graves in 1838, friends looked for something "southern" in Cilley's background.

Northern colonial governments passed antidueling laws in the eighteenth century, and southern governments followed with similar, if less aggressive, laws, most of which attempted to bar duelists and their seconds from holding office. Several other developments led to the decline of the duel. Early opponents of dueling argued that the duel did not actually resolve issues of character or settle disputes. Evangelical religion, with its call for humility, also worked against dueling. Even in the antebellum period, wealthy but religious southern men could decline challenges because of their religious beliefs. The South's economic problems and political contentiousness during and after the Civil War contributed to the decline of dueling by undercutting the wealth and status that had sustained the illusion of a fixed hierarchy in which dueling men competed to show they deserved their power and respect.

Probably the greatest reason for the decline of the duel, however, was the rise of market capitalism. In a society based increasingly on individual achievement within a faceless marketplace, men felt bound not by honor but by contract. Instead of living in local communities where men judged their reputations, they participated in complex societies that judged them, if at all, according to their place in a market society. In such a society, personal slights seemed less momentous, settling disputes through violence seemed disorderly, and the duel seemed archaic.

Bibliography

Greenberg, Kenneth S. *Masters and Statesmen: The Political Culture of American Slavery.* Baltimore: Johns Hopkins University Press, 1985.

———. *Honor and Slavery: Lies, Duels, Noses, Masks, Dressing as a Woman, Gifts, Strangers, Humanitarianism, Death, Slave Rebellions, The Proslavery Argument, Baseball, Hunting, and Gambling in the Old South.* Princeton, N.J.: Princeton University Press, 1996.

Stowe, Steven M. *Intimacy and Power in the Old South: Ritual in the Lives of the Planters.* Baltimore: Johns Hopkins University Press, 1987.

Wells, C. A. Harwell. "The End of the Affair? Anti-Dueling Laws and Social Norms in Antebellum America." *Vanderbilt Law Review* 54 (May 2001): 1805–1847.

Wyatt-Brown, Bertram. *Southern Honor: Ethics and Behavior in the Old South.* New York: Oxford University Press, 1982.

———. *The Shaping of Southern Culture: Honor, Grace, and War, 1760s–1880s.* Chapel Hill: University of North Carolina Press, 2001.

Further Reading

Ayers, Edward L. *Vengeance and Justice: Crime and Punishment in the 19th-Century American South.* New York: Oxford University Press, 1984.

Bellesiles, Michael, ed. *Lethal Imagination: Violence and Brutality in American History.* New York: New York University Press, 1999.

Bruce, Dickson. *Violence and Culture in the Antebellum South.* Austin: University of Texas Press, 1979.

Franklin, John Hope. *The Militant South, 1800–1861.* Cambridge, Mass.: Belknap Press, 1956.

Freeman, Joanne B. "Dueling as Politics: Reinterpreting the Burr–Hamilton Duel." *William and Mary Quarterly* 53 (1996): 289–318.

Moore, James T., "The Death of the Duel: The Code Duello in Readjuster Virginia, 1879–1883." *Virginia Magazine of History and Biography* 83 (1975): 259–276.

Waldrep, Christopher. *Roots of Disorder: Race and Criminal Justice in the Antebellum South, 1817–80.* Urbana: University of Illinois Press, 1998.

Wilson, Jack K. *Dueling in the Old South.* College Station: Texas A&M University Press, 1980.

Related Entries

Emotion; Guns; Jackson, Andrew; Southern Manhood; Violence

—*Ted Ownby*

Eastwood, Clint

1930–
American Actor and Director

Called icon and iconoclast, auteur and cultural product, the actor and filmmaker Clint Eastwood has profoundly influenced late-twentieth-century American ideas of masculinity. As an actor, Eastwood bridged the gap between the Western masculine archetype of the 1950s and 1960s and the action hero of the 1970s and 1980s, creating one of the most instantly recognizable onscreen presences in film history. As a director, Eastwood has reexamined and revised the genres and gender conventions of his earlier films.

Eastwood's career began in earnest in the Italian director Sergio Leone's trilogy of "spaghetti Westerns," which included *A Fistful of Dollars* (1964), *For a Few Dollars More* (1965), and *The Good, the Bad, and the Ugly* (1967). In these films Eastwood transformed the archetype of the strong, silent male hero, imbuing him with moral ambiguity as the certainties of the 1950s were called into question. His "Man with No Name" was an isolated outlaw, unmarked by the nationalistic, self-evident heroism that characterized most Western heroes of the less complicated 1950s. Unmoored from nation and community and driven by inscrutable, sometimes nihilistic, agendas, he became a fitting antihero for the anti-authoritarian climate of the late 1960s, as conceptions of what constituted heroic masculinity shifted from lawful patriotism to rebellious individualism.

This disaffection was replaced with righteous rage in the 1970s as disillusionment with government and rising concerns about violent crime replaced the more idealistic rebellion of the late 1960s. Vigilante policeman "Dirty" Harry Callahan became the role largely responsible for Eastwood's fame. Callahan's unquestioning moral certitude translated into direct and violent action—a trait, Eastwood said, meant to appeal to young American males increasingly uncertain of their futures. Although critics read the character as a fascist reactionary, Eastwood called the character's antiestablishment motivations and commitment to individual justice "the opposite of fascism." In any event, his impact on American culture is undeniable: Dirty Harry's catch-phrase from *Sudden Impact* (1983)—"Go ahead, make my day"—entered popular parlance as an expression of manly toughness and became so influential that Ronald Reagan co-opted it to respond to the possibility that Congress might raise taxes in March 1983.

As a director, Eastwood has reassessed and revised the images of masculinity raised in his early films. In *The Outlaw Josey Wales* (1976), Eastwood's lone hero becomes part of a multicultural community and family, defying persistent expectations of male isolation and emotional detachment. In his revisionist Western *Unforgiven* (1992), Eastwood examines questions of violence and legend, stripping away the layers of mythology surrounding an aging, retired killer only to reapply them in a violent climax. His directing has garnered a great deal of acclaim: Eastwood won a best-director Oscar in 1992 for *Unforgiven*, and he received the Irving Thalberg Award for lifetime achievement in 1994.

Throughout his career, Eastwood has displayed an acute consciousness of his status as an icon of individualistic, often violent, masculinity. Whether he ultimately undermines or endorses his legacy, he continues to interrogate it through his films. As both an actor and director, Clint Eastwood has left an indelible, if mercurial, impression on the American cultural imagination.

Bibliography

Schickel, Richard. *Clint Eastwood: A Biography.* New York: Knopf, 1996.

Smith, Paul. *Clint Eastwood: A Cultural Production.* Minneapolis: University of Minnesota Press, 1993.

Further Reading

Knapp, Laurence F. *Directed by Clint Eastwood.* Jefferson, N.C.: McFarland & Co., 1996.

Mitchell, Lee Clark. *Westerns: Making the Man in Fiction and Film.* Chicago: University of Chicago Press, 1996.

Related Entries

Cop Action Films; Cowboys; Emotion; Heroism; Hollywood; Individualism; Reagan, Ronald; Violence; Westerns

—*Anthony Wilson*

EASY RIDER

Released in 1969, *Easy Rider* is a movie about two motorcyclists, Wyatt (Peter Fonda) and Billy (Dennis Hopper), who travel from Los Angeles to New Orleans. Increasingly mistreated as they journey eastward, the two are killed at the movie's end. *Easy Rider* has become an iconic document of the 1960s—a signifier of the attack on American values launched by the nation's youth. As such, the film revises more traditional models of masculinity. It criticizes post–World War II constructions of manhood, and it examines the masculine ideals perpetuated by two foundational American narratives: the Western and the travel narrative.

Billy's and Wyatt's long hair, motorcycles, and use of drugs align them with counterculture models of masculinity, and the film's rock-music soundtrack further cements their identification with the era's youth movements. Billy and Wyatt stand in opposition to the ideals of their parent's generation. They reject the postwar "organization man," the suburbia-dwelling conformist who embraces traditional domestic life and subsumes his integrity and his creativity to fit in. Instead, they embrace manly individuality and self-reliance. They are men without roots or responsibilities who, in the words of George (played by Jack Nicholson), cannot "be bought and sold in the marketplace." They eschew the trappings of marriage, relegating women to the role of sexual partners.

Additionally, *Easy Rider* revises traditional ideals of masculine independence and heroism as articulated in the Western and the travel narrative. Fonda, who produced and co-wrote the film, intended to make a movie in the spirit of the 1956 film *The Searchers*—a journey narrative that focuses on the relationship between its male protagonists. *Easy Rider* places the biker in the same heroic line as the frontiersman. The main characters' costuming speaks to this aim—Wyatt is dressed in leather pants and jacket, Billy in buckskin—as does their resistance to domestication. However, Billy and Wyatt are not protectors of the community, as are Western heroes, but its victims. In the world depicted in *Easy Rider,* as in many American travel narratives, society is morally debased and intolerant, with the symbols of civilization corrupting its inhabitants. Unlike heroes in Westerns who pave the way for progress, and like the protagonists of the travel narratives, the heroes in *Easy Rider* escape society on the road. Finally, unlike the men in most travel narratives, Billy and Wyatt move from west to east along a road that leads ultimately to destruction rather than freedom.

Easy Rider addresses the perceived violence and destructiveness of American culture in the 1960s, a state the film links to conformity and intolerance, as well as to an anachronistic ideal of manhood that defines itself by the exertion of power and earning potential. Billy and Wyatt cannot survive in the nation's contemporary culture. Their murderers, similarly, are outcasts from society—southern "redneck hicks," in the words of the film, whose disempowerment in the aftermath of the civil rights movement leads them to violence.

However, the challenge to society and its prevailing models of manhood that Billy and Wyatt embody is insufficient, a position underlined by Wyatt in one of the closing scenes when he says that they "blew it." Rejecting older definitions of masculinity as dangerous and destructive, *Easy Rider* ultimately offers no viable alternative. Its pessimism mirrors other 1960s outlaw films, such as *Bonnie and Clyde* (1967) and *Alice's Restaurant* (1969), while it symbolizes the period in both its rejection of the old and its critique of the new.

BIBLIOGRAPHY

Biskind, Peter. *Easy Riders, Raging Bulls: How the Sex-Drugs-and-Rock-'n'-Roll Generation Saved Hollywood.* New York: Simon & Schuster, 1998.

Cagin, Seth, and Philip Dray. *Born to Be Wild: Hollywood and the Sixties.* 2nd ed. Boca Raton, Fla.: Coyote Books, 1994.

Fonda, Peter. *Don't Tell Dad: A Memoir.* New York: Hyperion, 1998.

Palladino, Grace. *Teenagers: An American History.* New York: Basic Books, 1996.

Slotkin, Richard. *Gunfighter Nation: The Myth of the Frontier in Twentieth-Century America.* Norman: University of Oklahoma Press, 1998.

Wright, Will. *Six Guns and Society: A Structural Study of the Western.* Berkeley: University of California Press, 1975.

FURTHER READING

Gitlin, Todd. *The Sixties: Years of Hope, Days of Rage.* New York: Bantam Books, 1993.

Klinger, Barbara. "The Road to Dystopia: Landscaping the Nation in *Easy Rider.*" In *The Road Movie Book,* edited by Steven Cohan and Ina Rae Hark. New York: Routledge, 1997.

Laderman, David. "What a Trip: The Road Film and American Culture." *Journal of Film and Video* 48, no. 1-2 (Spring-Summer 1996): 41–57.

Mordden, Ethan. *Medium Cool: The Movies of the 1960s.* New York: Knopf, 1990.

Yates, Brock. *Outlaw Machine: Harley-Davidson and the Search for the American Soul.* Boston: Little, Brown, 1999.

RELATED ENTRIES
Buddy Films; Counterculture; Cowboys; Hollywood; Kerouac, Jack; *Organization Man, The*; Suburbia; Travel Narratives; Vietnam War; Violence; Westerns; Youth

—*Allison Perlman*

EDUCATION

The formation of "manliness," or the shaping of boys into men, was until recently a central aim of American education. The system of free public educational institutions that emerged in the nineteenth century supplanted the more limited educational opportunities for boys that had existed since the colonial period, providing clearer stages of schooling that marked the progress of boys toward manhood. By the late nineteenth century, concerned with what seemed to be a threat to male dominance and the danger of effeminization posed by coeducation, public schools provided different curricula for men and women, while private institutions steadfastly adhered to their all-male status until well into the twentieth century. Yet throughout American history, education has varied from one group of men to another. Whether in coeducational or all-male settings, it has helped define differing modes of manhood deemed appropriate to a man's place in a society stratified by class and race.

Education and Manhood in Colonial America

In colonial America a basic education in literacy was widely available to boys, with the exception of slaves. This meant that education was a marker of white manhood in particular. But from the colonial era into the early nineteenth century, formal schooling ended early even for most white males, and the vast majority of boys prepared for agrarian or artisanal types of male work through individual apprenticeships and other direct training. Only the wealthiest went on to secondary schooling in grammar or Latin schools and then to private colleges—such as Harvard, the College of New Jersey (later Princeton), and William and Mary—to prepare for those careers marked in elite circles as manly (such as theology, law, and government).

Republican Manhood and Military Education

The early years of the republic saw the establishment of all-male service academies and military schools designed to instill such principles of republican manhood as citizenship, service, and sacrifice. Institutions such as the West Point Military Academy (established in 1802) in New York and the Virginia Military Institute (established in 1839) were designed to inculcate military models of American manliness that would oppose the "soft" commercial life of the nation. Yet the republican mistrust of standing armies and resistance to the formation of a dominating warrior class meant that an education in military manhood at West Point and schools modeled on it took on a distinctly American inflection. At West Point, cadets were selected from throughout the country, taught to obey civilian authority, and trained in civil engineering so they could help build the new nation.

Public Education and Coeducation in the Nineteenth Century

Beginning in the 1850s, a system of compulsory education in free public elementary schools, as well as secondary schools and universities, emerged alongside the older institutions. As formal schooling became more widely available, and as an emerging market economy produced a middle class that defined manhood in terms of upward mobility and economic and professional success, a boy was presented with clearly marked educational steps from elementary through secondary school, college, and professional training that signaled his progress from boyhood to manhood. The rite of passage to adult masculinity became (and remained through the early twenty-first century) the completion of set stages of formal education.

The emerging system of public education was marked by a decidedly male-dominated gender hierarchy: men held "manly" administrative and postsecondary-level teaching positions, while women performed the "feminine" work of teaching younger children at the elementary and secondary levels. Yet during the late nineteenth century, as the closing of the western frontier and the growth of office work for men raised fears that urban-industrial "overcivilization" threatened male physical stamina, the predominance of women in lower-level teaching positions and a trend toward coeducation in public schools prompted increasing concern that men were becoming feminized and weakened by their education.

To counter this danger, all-male private schools touted their homosocial educational environments as well-suited to raising vigorous men, while public schools from the elementary level to the university set in place a gendered curriculum with courses for men and women suited to the position of each in a patriarchal society. The requirement that boys take "shop" to acquire manly skills like woodworking and girls take "home economics" to learn such skills as cooking, sewing, and child development lasted well into the twentieth century—and was reinforced during the post–World War II era by the rise of suburbia and a growing association of manliness with home repair. Young men gravitated, or were pushed, into higher intellectual pursuits marked as manly, such as mathematics and science, while women were discouraged from these fields.

In the late nineteenth century, anxiety that manliness could not survive coeducation generated an intense opposition to opening existing all-male institutions to women. This resistance was generally successful at private elite colleges, though it failed to bar women from state universities. But whether in large state universities or private colleges, male students lived in a separate social sphere that often self-consciously fostered male bonding, muscular manliness, and competitiveness. Fear of male degeneration led male educators to encourage sports, especially football and other sports involving physical contact and teamwork. Other all-male collegiate institutions, including fraternities, literary societies, debating clubs, and student government, were valued for their ability to prepare boys for their responsibilities as men. Such homosocial worlds encouraged young men to form their identities through their relationships with their male peers, producing an emphasis on emotional stoicism and an inability to form nonsexual relations with women.

Education and Class Formation in the Nineteenth Century

With the onset of the Industrial Revolution, the individualized training characteristic of preindustrial education waned, and new educational practices emerged to reflect the appearance of new class lines and class-based models of manhood. The skills required for a working-class masculinity were increasingly obtained through vocational education, which was provided by large industrial and commercial concerns during the late nineteenth century and taken over by public schools by the beginning of the twentieth.

Meanwhile, the attainment of middle-class masculinity, defined through economic advancement and breadwinning, demanded specific educational requirements (such as a secondary school degree) to demonstrate the possession of marketable skills and such characteristics of bourgeois manhood as steadiness and application. Entry into higher-status professional manhood, such as that of the lawyer or physician, once possible through apprenticeship and private study, now required certification through an education provided by public and private schools of law, medicine, theology, and engineering.

The patriarchal elite and the newly rich aspiring to this status continued to favor elite educational institutions through the nineteenth century, sending their sons to such small private boarding schools as Andover Academy (established in 1778) in Massachusetts and Phillips Exeter (established in 1781) in New Hampshire. Here, within a world that remained all male until the mid-1970s, young men formed personal bonds that offered access in later life to positions of power in finance and government. From these schools young men moved to elite all-male universities such as Harvard, Yale, and Princeton that provided the cultural capital of upper-class manliness through a liberal arts curriculum.

Emancipation, Education, and African-American Manhood

After the Civil War, the emancipation of the slaves, who had been denied an education since colonial times, raised debates about the appropriate form of manhood for black men and about how education might contribute to it. Hampton Normal and Agricultural Institute (now Hampton University) in Virginia, founded in 1868 for blacks as well as Native Americans, sought to shape its students based on dominant American ideals of manliness such as self-reliance, hard work, and personal integrity. Tuskegee Normal and Industrial Institute in Alabama (now Tuskegee University), established by Booker T. Washington in 1881 on the model of Hampton Institute, applied the military concept of drill and moral discipline to instruct African Americans on self-control, which Washington deemed fundamental to American manhood.

Yet in training their students for work in crafts, farming, and teaching, these influential institutions relegated blacks to a position of inferior manhood. Objecting that such vocational training perpetuated inequality, other African Americans, such as the Harvard-educated W. E. B. Du Bois, advocated the entry of black men into traditional higher-education and white-only universities so that a vanguard of black professionals could forge new models of African-American manhood suitable for full integration into white society.

The Impact of Civil Rights and Feminism: The Late Twentieth Century

By the late twentieth century, the civil rights and feminist movements had effectively shattered the longstanding association of education with white masculinity. Through the civil rights movement of the 1950s and 1960s, African Americans ended the white monopolization of educational opportunities by gaining admission to public and private institutions. Yet leaders at such historically black educational institutions as Tuskegee questioned the goal of absorbing black men into what they considered hegemonic white ideals of manliness. They looked instead to foster a uniquely black masculinity suitable to leadership in the African-American community. Others, such as Henry Louis Gates, sought to promote African-American manhood among black males at integrated universities by demanding and establishing black studies programs.

The late twentieth century also saw a growing move toward gender equality that discredited the idea that a crucial function of formal education is to encourage manliness in men. The all-male educational institutions that had once been the training grounds of patriarchal power—elite private boarding schools and colleges, professional schools, and even military academies—became coeducational despite resistance by defenders of traditional homosocial education. Thus West Point admitted women in 1976, and the Virginia Military Institute followed in 1996, though only after being forced to do so by the Supreme Court. Meanwhile, there was a growing challenge to the tendency in education to discourage women from pursuing such traditionally male subjects as mathematics and science. Still, certain values marked culturally as masculine, such as competitiveness, rationality, emotional detachment, and the drive for power, continue to heavily inform American educational strategies. Education as masculinization continues in America, with the process now influencing women as well as men.

Bibliography

Gordon, Lynn D. *Gender and Higher Education in the Progressive Era.* New Haven, Conn.: Yale University Press, 1990.

Kimmel, Michael. *Manhood in America: A Cultural History.* New York: Free Press, 1996.

Lesko, Nancy, ed. *Masculinities at School.* Thousand Oaks, Calif.: Sage, 2000.

Rotundo, E. Anthony. *American Manhood: Transformations in Masculinity from the Revolution to the Modern Era.* New York: Basic Books, 1993.

Townsend, Kim. *Manhood at Harvard: William James and Others.* New York: Norton, 1996.

Wallace, Maurice O. *Constructing the Black Masculine: Identity and Ideality in African American Men's Literature and Culture, 1775–1995.* Durham, N.C.: Duke University Press, 2002.

Further Reading

Connell, R. W. *The Men and the Boys.* Cambridge: Polity, 2000.

Crackel, Theodore J. *West Point: A Bicentennial History.* Lawrence: University Press of Kansas, 2002.

Ferguson, Ann Arnett. *Bad Boys: Public Schools in the Making of Black Masculinity.* Ann Arbor: University of Michigan Press, 2001.

Related Entries

Adolescence; African-American Manhood; Apprenticeship; Boyhood; Breadwinner Role; Feminism; Football; Fraternities; Middle-Class Manhood; Military; Muscular Christianity; Sports; Working-Class Manhood

—*Herbert Sussman*

Emancipation

The 1863 Emancipation Proclamation freed four million slaves, about 90 percent of the black population of the United States at the time. Slave emancipation made it legal for Southern black men to challenge their white counterparts for control over the military, political, economic, and social spheres that constituted patriarchal dominance and masculine tradition in the United States. Because freedom from slavery did not alone insure equal rights for blacks, African-American men pursued representation within these arenas in order to gain the power necessary to assert their manhood and to demand and create first-class black citizenship.

For most freedmen, participation in areas that traditionally brought power to white males often defined their notion of freedom and informed their sense of manhood. The connections between violence and slavery produced the context for some bondsmen's (slaves') correlation of freedom and masculinity with combat. Because potential slave revolts scared white planters and inspired black slaves, African-American males sometimes physically challenged white dominance. In his classic autobiography, *Narrative of the Life of Frederick Douglass, An American Slave* (1845), Frederick Douglass associated manliness with corporeal resistance to slavery. Douglass referred to a fistfight with the brutal overseer Edward Covey as "the turning-point in [his] career as a slave. It rekindled the few expiring embers of freedom, and revived with [him] a sense of [his] own manhood (Douglass, 113)." Although the avenues for black men to pursue freedom expanded with emancipation, combat remained primary in the struggle for power.

Following emancipation, many freedmen joined the Union army, and by the end of the Civil War about 180,000 African Americans had fought against the Confederacy. Accepting the republican association of manhood with citizenship, education, and independent land ownership, black soldiers moving through the South encouraged and protected the rights of newly freed slaves to organize themselves politically and purchase land, and they helped build new schools, churches, and orphanages. African-American veterans formed political clubs and conventions, led civil rights campaigns, and, backed by the authority of the federal government, promoted black freedom through both the force of arms and the ballot. By fighting capably and bravely for the Union, freedmen destroyed the myths of black male savagery, laziness, buffoonery, and drunkenness that whites had promoted in order to maintain economic and political power.

Congress's First Reconstruction Act (1867) protected black political power, while the Fourteenth Amendment (1868) to the U. S. Constitution granted citizenship to former slaves and the Fifteenth Amendment (1870) established black men's right to vote. The Second, Third, and Fourth Reconstruction Acts, passed in 1867 and 1868, addressed voter registration, the remaking of state constitutions, and the administration of loyalty oaths to former Confederates. Throughout the South, blacks participated in state constitutional conventions. Since many Southern white leaders were barred from voting until their state's constitutions were ratified, this legislation guaranteed that black men would have a voice in postwar Southern politics.

Thomas Waterman Wood's His First Vote *(1868), depicting a freedman voting for the first time. Many African-American men liberated from slavery after the Civil War believed that realizing full manhood required the citizenship, voting rights, and political power formerly confined to white men. (Collection of Cheekwood Museum of Art, Nashville)*

Black politicians actively promoted positive images of black manhood, directly refuting stereotypes about childlike, silly, and easily manipulated black men that had been used by whites who argued for black disfranchisement. Once freedmen gained the ballot during the late 1860s, they challenged white domination in Southern politics wherever the federal government protected their right to vote. Black men played important roles in some state and local governments, while they were functionally excluded from others. Because white intimidation of black voters and politicians was pervasive, the male-dominated arenas of violence, military force, and political representation became intertwined in postwar Southern life. Although black women could not vote, they played important roles in black political movements following the Civil War, sometimes forming their own organizations, most commonly Union Leagues, when men tried to exclude them from decision-making processes.

Since colonial times, land ownership had served as perhaps the most important element in determining white men's access to political and economic power, making it a fundamental element of manhood. Following emancipation, the acquisition of land became legally possible for Southern blacks, although successful ex-slaves faced resistance from whites. Black men were determined to enjoy this newfound privilege, while whites were committed to preventing this, since land ownership would separate farmers from tenants and help determine the distribution of wealth and labor. Land ownership promised freedmen a degree of control over their time and labor. But most black men, denied the opportunity to own land, had to seek autonomy in other ways. Some achieved it through tenant farming, which gave household heads great responsibility over the process of work. However, the development of the sharecropping system during the 1870s, which eventually encompassed most African-American farmers in the South, weakened their masculine earning power by leaving them economically dependent on white landowners.

Other economic changes during the decades following emancipation likewise threatened male economic hegemony, since black women could easily find paid employment as servants, cooks, washerwomen, and "mammies" while men struggled as tenant farmers and sharecroppers. Although some black women withdrew from the labor force following the Civil War, many tailored their work schedules to accommodate both their family responsibilities and their desire to earn money.

For many emancipated men, marriage and domesticity became important mechanisms of expressing black manhood. Freedmen and their wives made their prewar matrimonial ties legal and used marriage to claim political and economic rights. Marriage also challenged stereotypes of black promiscuity and character weakness that whites had used to justify slavery. Some former slaves pursued traditional Victorian gender roles that defined men as breadwinners and excluded women from the public sphere, but recent scholarship has found that most free African-American families were neither matriarchal nor patriarchal, and that public and private matters were often inseparable during the postemancipation era.

The federal government's retreat from Reconstruction in the late 1870s threatened to undermine the newly established or newly strengthened political, legal, economic, and social foundations of black manhood. Jim Crow laws (which legalized segregation), the Ku Klux Klan, and black disfranchisement contributed to a climate of terror throughout the postbellum South. As former Confederates regained control of state governments and began to force blacks out of power through violence and legislation, blacks responded in several ways. Some, like Booker T. Washington, urged blacks to stay in the South, capitulate to white separatism, and retreat from political participation in exchange for protection of black economic endeavors by which black men might build new bases for asserting their manliness. Others called for a militant struggle for racial justice. Many other Southern blacks migrated north to start new lives. A relatively small number gave up on the prospect of achieving freedom in the United States and supported back-to-Africa movements.

Emancipation's legacy for black Americans was mixed. Although it forever ended slavery in the United States, it also brought into focus the challenges that accompanied freedom. While African-American men gained new opportunities to control their own futures, by the end of Reconstruction they faced severe limitations on their ability to pursue legal rights, political involvement and economic self-determination, all of which were seen as determinants of manhood. For all African Americans, the pursuit of political, economic, legal, social, and cultural agendas would continue through and beyond the civil rights movement of the 1950s and 1960s.

BIBLIOGRAPHY

Booker, Christopher B. *"I Will Wear No Chain!": A Social History of African American Males.* Westport, Conn.: Praeger, 2000.

Douglass, Frederick. *Narrative of the Life of Frederick Douglass: An American Slave.* 1845. Reprint, edited by William L. Andrews and William S. McFeely. New York: Norton, 1996.

Edwards, Laura F. "The Politics of Marriage and Households in North Carolina During Reconstruction." In *Jumpin' Jim Crow: Southern Politics from Civil War to Civil Rights,* edited by Jane Dailey, Glenda Elizabeth Gilmore, and Bryant Simon. Princeton, N.J.: Princeton University Press, 2000.

Foner, Eric. *Nothing But Freedom: Emancipation and Its Legacy.* Baton Rouge: Louisiana State University Press, 1983.

Frankel, Noralee. *Freedom's Women: Black Women and Families in Civil War Era Mississippi.* Bloomington: Indiana University Press, 1999.

Saville, Julie. *The Work of Reconstruction: From Slave to Wage Laborer in South Carolina, 1860–1870.* Cambridge, England: Cambridge University Press, 1994.

FURTHER READING

Bercaw, Nancy. "The Politics of Household: Domestic Battlegrounds in the Transition from Slavery to Freedom in the Yazoo-Mississippi Delta, 1850–1860," Ph.D. diss., University of Pennsylvania, 1996.

Black, Daniel P. *Dismantling Black Manhood: An Historical and Literary Analysis of the Legacy of Slavery.* New York: Garland, 1997.

Blassingame, John W. *The Slave Community: Plantation Life in the Antebellum South.* Rev. ed. New York: Oxford University Press, 1979.

Blight, David W. *Frederick Douglass' Civil War: Keeping Faith in Jubilee.* Baton Rouge: Louisiana State University, 1991.

Bolden, Tonya. *Strong Men Keep Coming: The Book of African American Men.* New York: John Wiley, 1999.

Cullen, Jim. "'I's A Man Now': Gender and African American Men." In *A Question of Manhood: A Reader in U.S. Black Men's History and Masculinity,* edited by Darlene Clark Hine and Earnestine Jenkins. Bloomington: Indiana University Press, 1999.

Genovese, Eugene D. *Roll, Jordan, Roll: The World the Slaves Made.* New York: Vintage Books, 1976.

McPherson, James M. *The Struggle for Equality: Abolitionists and the Negro in the Civil War and Reconstruction.* Princeton, N.J.: Princeton University Press, 1964.

Voelz, Peter M. *Slave and Soldier: The Military Impact of Blacks in the Colonial Americas.* New York: Garland Publishing, 1993.

RELATED ENTRIES

Abolitionism; African-American Manhood; Boxing; Breadwinner Role; Citizenship; Civil Rights Movement; Civil War; Douglass, Frederick; Lincoln, Abraham; Militarism; Property; Race; Republicanism; Slave Narratives; Southern Manhood; Violence; War; Whiteness; White Supremacism; Work

—*Michael Ezra*

Emerson, Ralph Waldo

1803–1882
Philosopher and Author

Ralph Waldo Emerson was the founder of a distinct American intellectual tradition and a key figure in the antebellum (pre–Civil War) transcendentalist movement. He espoused an ideal of manliness rooted in scholarly activity, self-knowledge, intellectual dissent, and individual autonomy, a concept that grew out of early-nineteenth-century ideas about manhood. However, although Emerson's celebration of individual autonomy suited the surging individualism engendered by the antebellum market revolution and the egalitarian spirit of Jacksonian democracy, he initially eschewed the emerging entrepreneurial model of manhood promoted by proponents of capitalist development.

In making his career choice, Emerson shunned more traditional pursuits that would have been fitting outlets for his eloquence, such as the pulpit, the press, or politics. In 1832 he abandoned a secure position as Unitarian minister at Boston's Second Church and, intent on a holistic pursuit of truth, chose the vocation of a scholar. In his lectures and essays, Emerson advocated self-knowledge and self-reliance (trusting one's own mind and seeking spiritual self-sovereignty) as quintessential manly virtues.

Emerson and the transcendentalists regarded intuition and self-knowledge as higher sources of truth than the intellect. They believed that emotion, intuition, and spirituality could guide the mind beyond the limits of pure intellect toward a transcendent form of reason. Emerson's notion of transcendental consciousness offered a new public male identity that sought to counteract the allegedly emasculating effects of the antebellum market revolution.

Seeking to redefine manliness, Emerson initially charged that the marketplace debased male self-sufficiency, and he embraced agrarian values as an alternative. He developed this theme in his essay *Nature* (1836), emphasizing it more strongly after the financial panic of 1837 and throughout the 1840s. In his famous essay "Self-Reliance" (1841), Emerson continued to advocate dissent, nonconformity, introspection, and self-knowledge as elements of the path toward truth and self-realization. This model of manhood greatly influenced Henry David Thoreau's experimental retreat to *Walden Pond* in 1845.

Ultimately, however, Emerson's insistence on self-reliant struggle as the means to build manhood generated a definition of male identity grounded in liberal marketplace economics, largely unfettered by government regulation. In his book, *The Conduct of Life* (1860), Emerson developed his earlier notion of innate individual potential into a celebration of an unfettered individualism that would be advantageous in a liberal marketplace. After 1860, Emerson emerged as an apologist for the concept of the "self-made man." This transition in Emerson's thinking about manhood anticipated new concepts of manhood that appeared after the Civil War—concepts that rejected reformist ideals of finding self-fulfillment through the moral and ethical betterment of society, and instead embraced self-discipline, professional pragmatism, and an active life.

Emerson's ideal of manhood was part of a liberal tradition in the United States that emerged in the aftermath of the American Revolution. This liberal tradition often obscured social and class conflict and used an inclusive rhetoric of manly republican virtue and independence that shrouded its elitist motives and intentions. Emerson's ideas about manhood reflected the ambivalence of middle-class men toward the spiritual and economic effects of capitalist development.

Bibliography

Cayton, Mary Kupiec. *Emerson's Emergence: Self and Society in the Transformation of New England, 1800-1845.* Chapel Hill: University of North Carolina Press, 1989.

Fredrickson, George M. *The Inner Civil War: Northern Intellectuals and the Crisis of the Union.* New York: Harper & Row, 1965.

Gilmore, Michael T. *American Romanticism and the Marketplace.* Chicago: University of Chicago Press, 1985.

Leverenz, David. *Manhood and the American Renaissance.* Ithaca, N.Y.: Cornell University Press, 1989.

Richardson, Robert D., Jr. *Emerson: The Mind on Fire.* Berkeley: University of California Press, 1995.

Further Reading

Cavell, Stanley. *Conditions Handsome and Unhandsome: The Constitution of Emersonian Perfectionism.* Chicago: University of Chicago Press, 1990.

Cheyfitz, Eric. *Trans-Parent: Sexual Politics in the Language of Emerson.* Baltimore: Johns Hopkins University Press, 1981.

Porte, Joel. *Representative Man: Ralph Waldo Emerson in His Time.* New York: Oxford University Press, 1979.

Robinson, David M. *Emerson and the Conduct of Life: Pragmatism and Ethical Purpose in the Later Work.* Cambridge: Cambridge University Press, 1993.

Steele, Jeffrey. *The Representation of the Self in the American Renaissance.* Chapel Hill: University of North Carolina Press, 1987.

Selected Writings

Porte, Joel, ed. *Ralph Waldo Emerson: Essays and Lectures.* New York: Library of America, 1983.

RELATED ENTRIES

Agrarianism; American Revolution; Capitalism; Civil War; Market Revolution; Middle-Class Manhood; Reform Movements; Religion and Spirituality; Republicanism; Self-Control; Self-Made Man; Thoreau, Henry David

—*Thomas Winter*

EMOTION

Although men are capable of the same emotional range as women, emotional expression has been distinctly gendered in Western society, particularly in the United States. In Western concepts of masculinity, emotional control has been considered central to manhood and necessary to social order, while emotion has been framed as an explosive "natural" force that can be rendered uncontrollable by feminine influences. Therefore, attempts to determine allowable expressions of emotion have characterized debates on manhood since the times of the Greek philosopher Aristotle. Although firm control of one's emotion has usually been considered essential to manliness, occasional violent outbursts have been tolerated as expected and forgivable releases from the emotional restraints imposed on men.

European Roots and Colonial America

American attitudes toward emotion have followed the ideals of European masculinity, though those ideals became modified somewhat through the influences of a conquest mentality and an American Protestant ethic. American settlement was driven by an ideology of triumphant masculinity, grounded in reason, exclusion, and extermination. Those excluded—particularly women, Catholics, and Native Americans—were often associated with a "feminine" emotionalism.

The roots of the European masculine ideal can be traced to Greek philosophical debates over the relation between emotion and masculinity. Stoic philosophers devalued emotion, while Aristotle argued that such emotions as pity and empathetic recognition among men could create the cooperation necessary to political citizenship. Some of Shakespeare's plays suggest that a similar debate occurred in early modern England. Hamlet, for example, denounces the man who is "passion's slave," yet he envies the Player who can weep for Hecuba. In *Macbeth*, when Malcolm urges Macduff to put aside his feelings, Macduff exclaims that he "must feel it as a man." These works reflect the tension between the masculine duty to control emotions and a suspicion toward men incapable of honest feelings.

The sixteenth-century Protestant Reformation and the eighteenth-century Age of Reason further codified the gendering of emotional expression as feminine and emotional control as masculine. Early Protestants viewed human beings as innately evil, and emotions were seen as dangerous forces contrary to divine order. Viewing women as weaker than men, and thus less able than men to control these forces, they held men responsible for maintaining strict emotional control. Influential eighteenth-century philosophers such as Jean-Jacques Rousseau, Immanuel Kant, and John Stuart Mill also disdained women and emotionally expressive men. They considered masculine self-control and self-discipline the only social safeguards against the forces of nature.

Other currents, meanwhile, encouraged a different relation between manhood and emotion. Early European settlers brought to colonial America not only a strict Protestant code and a mistrust of emotion, but also family practices that generated among men an emotional domestic involvement. Stern patriarchal control and emotional reserve were required for the effective religious and secular education of children; however, with survival based on the interdependent working of family members, patriarchal control was tempered by warmer connections. Eighteenth-century Enlightenment thought further promoted open expressions of male tenderness by emphasizing not only reason but also a "cult of sensibility" that criticized anger and tyranny and encouraged affection.

Nineteenth-Century America

Nineteenth-century developments again tended to associate emotion largely with women. Market capitalism and industrialization encouraged many Americans—especially middle-class Americans—to define men as rational, calculating, amoral, and aggressively competitive beings well suited to activity in a public sphere in which emotional expression was superfluous if not counterproductive. Women, on the other hand, were defined as emotional and nurturing beings ideally suited to child rearing and other activities of the domestic sphere. Phrenology, a system that sought to explain behavioral characteristics in terms of skull shape, assumed cultural prominence during this period and attempted to provide a scientific basis for this perceived difference between masculinity and femininity.

Popular notions of child rearing likewise stressed that fathers should display male emotional reserve and encourage appropriate emotional development in their sons. Fathers tended to express approval and disapproval rather than affection and anger, believing that emotional restraint was essential to teach discipline. Fathers trained their sons to develop the qualities of restraint, self-control, industry, economy, and temperance, which were seen as essential to advancing in life and achieving ideal manhood.

American literature of the mid–nineteenth century likewise encouraged a separation between manhood and emotion. Calling for a distinctly American vision, Ralph Waldo Emerson sought to eliminate the excesses of the European cult of sensibility and American sentimental writing. Emerson's self-reliant man was someone who would create a more virile art completely outside the domestic sphere of emotional experience. Novelists like Nathaniel Hawthorne and Herman Melville, as well as producers of dime novels, promoted a self-reliant masculine hero unconstrained by the domestic sphere and emotional entanglements. This masculine ideal promoted a type of independent manhood that many Americans considered essential to developing the West and the American capitalist economy.

Later in the nineteenth century, advancing urbanization and industrialization, the growth of white-collar office work, and a perception of excessive female domestic influence generated fears among many men that they had been enervated by "overcivilization." At the same time, the Darwinian view of the natural world as a place of ruthless struggle generated a desire for a more virile masculinity and an ideology of "passionate manhood" that valued primitive male emotions such as lust, greed, selfishness, ambition, and physical assertiveness. Men compared themselves readily to savage people, promoting animal behavior as an antidote to "American nervousness," and experts in the emerging field of psychology lent scientific support to this new emphasis on masculine passion. Arguing that the development of the individual male recapitulated the evolution of human society from primitive to more advanced states, Granville Stanley Hall counseled that encouraging aggressiveness in boys and adolescents would promote a healthy masculine identity.

Yet while these ideologies of masculinity emphasized the control of softer emotions, competing ideals of sentimentalism, romantic love, and domestic affection encouraged men toward more affectionate displays in their private behavior and emotional honesty in their public interactions. Sentimental literature of the Victorian period typically associated manhood with emotionally charged domestic attachments, and bachelors were frequently portrayed as longing for the love and comforts of family. Men's diaries and correspondence from the period show that men were emotionally connected to their families and friends, and that they considered these relationships to be essential to their masculine identities.

Twentieth-Century America

Around the turn of the twentieth century, the growth of American imperialism and a corporate business culture encouraged a new emphasis on masculine toughness, obedience, loyalty, reliability, and self-sacrifice. Men seeking a competitive edge in their pursuit of professional advancement were trained to hide their feelings in order to withhold information that might give others power. Outside the workplace, men's clubs reinforced this approach to emotion by fostering nonemotional and business-oriented social connections. Meanwhile, child-rearing techniques for boys were intended to mediate their mothers' softening influence and discourage crying and other forms of emotional expression. Such boys' organizations as the Boy Scouts of America, established in 1910, were designed to create reliable workers and build competition and endurance through obedience and the control of emotion. In 1923, in his *Studies in Classic American Literature,* D. H. Lawrence described the "essential American soul" as "hard, isolate, stoic and a killer" (Lawrence, 73). In 1951, the social critic Marshall McLuhan commented in *The Mechanical Bride* that such masculine icons as the cowboy and the "hard-driving executive" are "emotionally hardened" figures who "can act, but . . . cannot feel" (McLuhan, 157).

However, this model of masculinity was increasingly challenged during the twentieth century, particularly amid the economic expansion, the boom in suburban development, and the advancing corporatization of the post–World War II period. Dr. Benjamin Spock, author of *The Common Sense Book of Baby and Child Care* (1946), discouraged harsh discipline in the raising of boys and advised parents that crying was a natural emotional expression for boys and should not be discouraged. In *Eros and Civilization* (1955), and later in *One-Dimensional Man* (1964), the sociologist Herbert Marcuse warned against the damaging effects of sublimating male emotional and erotic energy in capitalist production and urged the liberation of the male psyche as necessary for the reinvigoration of American civilization. Similarly, William H. Whyte argued in *The Organization Man* (1956) that the pursuit of corporate success left American men emotionally empty and alienated from themselves and their families.

Several developments later in the twentieth century further encouraged such critiques of conventional masculinity. During the late 1960s and 1970s, second-wave feminism and emerging men's movements called for a rethinking of traditional concepts of masculinity, and for a new model of manhood grounded in a full range of emotions and greater domestic engagement. The 1970s also witnessed a new emphasis on personal self-realization and self-exploration.

Psychologists influenced by these new currents—including Joseph Pleck, Warren Farrell, and Herb Goldberg—explored men's emotional health and concluded that male inexpressiveness damaged both the male psyche and body by producing ulcers and high blood pressure. Thus, these social trends not only caused alienation and dissatisfaction, but also increased the risk of a heart attack and other ailments. By the 1990s, new and highly visible men's movements sought to promote emotional release. The Promise Keepers, an evangelical Christian movement, encouraged a more affectionate and engaged style of fathering that would solidify male domestic leadership. The mythopoetic movement, inspired by the poet Robert Bly's book *Iron John* (1990), promoted a masculine mode of emotional expression that included male mentoring, ritual, and a primitivism similar to nineteenth-century passionate manhood.

During the 1990s a growing incidence of school violence heightened concerns about the destructive effects of conventional approaches to masculinity. Alarmed commentators such as William Pollack, author of *Real Boys* (1998), argued that the longstanding acceptance of anger and violence as natural to males had fostered harmful behavior in adolescent males.

Concurrent with the rise of the men's movement was the more prominent figure of the "sensitive man," an emotionally aware masculine figure that values permanent relationships. Yet this model of manhood has proven problematic: Some men have suspected that it leaves them vulnerable, while some women suspect that men may use an emotionally superficial version of the sensitive man for manipulation. Despite the challenges in developing a new model of the emotional man, modern men remain convinced that emotional expression is essential to a more satisfactory life.

Bibliography

Chapman, Mary, and Glenn Hendler, eds. *Sentimental Men: Masculinity and Politics of Affect in American Culture.* Berkeley: University of California Press, 1999.

Frank, Stephen. *Life with Father: Parenthood and Masculinity in the Nineteenth-Century American North.* Baltimore: Johns Hopkins University Press, 1998.

Kimmel, Michael. *Manhood in America: A Cultural History.* New York: Free Press, 1996.

Lawrence, D. H. *Studies in Classic American Literature.* 1923. Reprint, Garden City, N.Y.: Doubleday, 1953.

Lystra, Karen. *Searching the Heart: Women, Men, and Romantic Love in Nineteenth-Century America.* New York: Oxford University Press, 1989.

McLuhan, Marshall. *The Mechanical Bride: Folklore of the Industrial Man.* New York: Vanguard, 1951.

Pollack, William. *Real Boys: Rescuing Our Sons from the Myths of Boyhood.* New York: Random House, 1998.

Robinson, Sally. *Marked Men: White Masculinity in Crisis.* New York: Columbia University Press, 2000.

Rotundo, E. Anthony. *American Manhood: Transformation in Masculinity from the Revolution to the Modern Era.* New York: Basic Books, 1993.

Seidler, Victor. "Masculinity, Violence and Emotional Life." In *Emotions in Social Life: Critical Themes and Contemporary Issues,* edited by Gillian Bendelow and Simon J. Williams. New York: Routledge, 1998.

Stearns, Peter. "Girls, Boys, and Emotions: Redefinitions and Historical Change." *Journal of American History* 80 (June 1993): 36–74.

Wilson, Lisa. Ye *Heart of a Man: The Domestic Life of Men in Colonial New England.* New Haven, Conn.: Yale University Press, 1999.

Further Reading

Balswick, Jack. *The Inexpressive Male.* Lexington, Mass.: Lexington Books, 1988.

Bendelow, Gillian, and Simon J. Williams, eds. *Emotions in Social Life: Critical Themes and Contemporary Issues.* New York: Routledge, 1998.

Bly, Robert. *Iron John: A Book About Men.* Reading, Mass.: Addison-Wesley, 1990.

French, Marilyn. *Beyond Power: On Women, Men, and Morals.* London: Cardinal, 1991.

Kindlon, Daniel J., and Michael Thompson, with Teresa Barker. *Raising Cain: Protecting the Emotional Life of Boys.* New York: Ballantine, 1999.

Marcuse, Herbert. *Eros and Civilization: A Philosophical Inquiry into Freud.* 1955. Reprint, Boston: Beacon, 1974.

———. *One-Dimensional Man: Studies in the Ideology of Advanced Industrial Society.* 1964. Reprint, Boston: Beacon, 1991.

Middleton, Peter. *The Inward Gaze: Masculinity and Subjectivity in Modern Culture.* London: Routledge, 1992.

Shamir, Milette, and Jennifer Travis, eds. *Boys Don't Cry?: Rethinking Narratives of Masculinity and Emotion in the U.S.* New York: Columbia University Press, 2002.

Spock, Benjamin. *The Common Sense Book of Baby and Child Care.* New York: Duell, Sloan and Pearce, 1946.

Whyte, William H. *The Organization Man.* New York: Simon & Schuster, 1956.

Related Entries

Adolescence; *Common Sense Book of Baby and Child Care, The*; Crisis of Masculinity; Cult of Domesticity; Emerson, Ralph Waldo;

Fatherhood; Hall, Granville Stanley; *Iron John: A Book About Men*; Marriage; Men's Clubs; Men's Movements; Military; *Mr. Mom*; *Organization Man, The*; Passionate Manhood; Patriarchy; Promise Keepers; Romanticism; Self-Control; Sensitive Male; Sentimentalism; Violence

—*Elizabeth Abele*

ETHNICITY

Ethnicity is an element of identity that intersects with and influences American masculinity, marking the traces of history, class, and culture that cling to groups and individuals based on their (real or imagined) shared origin. Ethnic differences within a society lead both to direct competition between men and to competing standards of masculinity. Ethnic masculinities, therefore, contribute to and challenge a society's construction of masculinity, while continuing to exist as alternative forms of masculinity. The constant reciprocal influences between "standard" masculinity and an ethnic masculinity make it a complicated task to produce a fixed definition of either.

In addition to national origin, ethnicity also encompasses differences in religion, history, and race that further characterize masculinity. Although "race" is the most extreme of ethnic definitions, most racial definitions are actually based on a rather limited number of biological characteristics. A group is often designated as racially, rather than ethnically, distinct, based on a societal need to rationalize different (and sometimes unjust) treatment. As an example of the arbitrary constructions of race, in the United Kingdom, immigrant groups of Caribbean, Indian, and Pakistani origin are all considered "black"; in the United States, however, these groups would likely be designated as "African American," "Hispanic," or "Asian"—lumped, in effect, with other ethnic groups with which they are thought to have something in common. The intersection of ethnicity and masculinity is therefore complex, and it is often complicated or obscured by both societal categorizations and personal choices. By better identifying ethnic origins, it is possible to approach a clearer understanding of how masculine ideologies and definitions have evolved.

Negotiating Ethnicity and Masculinity

Competing ethnic masculinities generally occur in cultures where immigrant groups are present. The United States is a particular example because of its lack of a single original culture. Ethnic conflicts also occur when ethnically diverse (and previously autonomous) groups are brought together under the control of a dominating group, as occurred in the former Soviet Union and the former Yugoslavia.

A major concern of masculinity is the notion of dominance, with ethnic masculinity frequently operating as the effort to maintain or achieve power. Ethnic prejudices often develop as different ethnic groups perceive the ethnic masculinities of others as actual or potential threats to their control. The construction of a hegemonic masculinity creates differences that legitimize the masculine privileges and power of a socially dominant group over marginalized groups. This illusion of a superior masculinity possessed by the group in power may work to deny, confine, and erase alternate ethnic masculinities. Dominance becomes a continual negotiation of identities, a process of constructing "the other" (a primitive, unknowable, alien masculinity that through its alleged difference and cultural inferiority defines and justifies the position of the dominant group) in an oppositional, hierarchical relation. Ironically, though this desire for dominance may divide men, unions are most likely to occur between ethnically diverse masculine groups when they perceive a shared threat, whether it be from hostile nations, women, "lesser" men, or challenges to physical or economic survival. In these alliances, a few differences will come to be perceived as assets that can benefit all the allied groups, and the valued attributes of one masculine group might even be emulated by the others, while some differences may be replaced, de-emphasized, or eliminated.

Men of differing ethnic groups judge each other on such qualities as their chivalry, comradery, expressiveness, compassion, work ethic, intelligence, physical strength, and cleanliness. Based on the performances of its members in relation to these standards of manhood, an ethnic group's men may be labeled too effeminate or too primitive—or possibly both at the same time. These judgments are, in reality, merely a projection of the judging group's fears and desires as it attempts to hide its own inability to live up to its own masculine standards, as well as a more hidden desire to escape these social expectations.

The Dynamics of Ethnic Masculinities in U.S. History

Ethnic differences have been a part of the United States since the European settlement of the North American continent. Although the American colonies that became the United States are generally viewed as founded by the English, this perspective overlooks the scattered yet consistent presence of indigenous peoples, as well as the influence of Dutch,

Spanish, French, and Mexican territories and the subsequent absorption of their settlers into the new nation. U.S. history was also characterized through the early nineteenth century by the importation of Africans as slaves, and by continual streams of immigrant populations. White Americans labeled African-American men as savages incapable of civilization, and thus suited to the slavery and powerlessness to which they had been consigned. Similarly, whites justified their ongoing dislocations of Native American groups by portraying them as uncivilizable and—with a mixture of condemnation and admiration—perceiving in them a wild masculinity and a feminized union with nature.

The first wave of immigration in the mid–nineteenth century, including the German and Irish, began the erosion of America's identity as a Protestant nation and brought tensions and controversies involving rival ethnic masculinities to the surface of American life. As different ethnic groups became part of American society, immigrant men came under attack as threats to America's progress toward Christian civilization. For instance, Irish immigrants, the first ethnic group targeted for widespread hostility, were associated with problematic masculinity and viewed as uncivilized and incapable of ever being honorable American citizens. After the Civil War, ethnic diversity exploded with the rise in immigration and the movement of freed slaves from the South to northern cities. African-American men, and such immigrant men as Italians, Jews, and Asians, were seen as simultaneously effeminate and brutish. They were suspected of being more sexually voracious and potent, tending toward violence and drunkenness, yet needing external discipline like children. Their masculinity might be dismissed as degenerate, savage, vicious, idol-worshiping, or superstitious. Northern European immigrants, on the other hand, tended to be valued for their manly strength and work ethic, yet they were suspected of lacking in intelligence and emotion.

Responding anxiously to the growing diversity of ethnic masculinities in the United States, and seeking to preserve their cultural dominance, men of Anglo-Saxon descent saw themselves as peculiarly masculine, as living proof of social Darwinism (which suggested that ethnically superior men would naturally thrive and hold positions of power), and therefore particularly suited to guide ethnically inferior men. Many Progressive Era reformers addressed urban immigration by pushing programs of "Americanization" that sought to preserve a hegemonic white Protestant masculinity, and they presented this model as the key to upward mobility and successful integration into national life.

Defining Ethnic Masculinity in the United States: Contemporary Issues

As ethnic groups have assimilated, the definition of the dominant masculinity has expanded from Anglo-Saxon Protestant to white non-Hispanic (of any faith), and it continues to evolve further. For example, judgments that were once made against Irish or Asian immigrants might now be made *by* Irish Americans or Asian Americans toward newer ethnic groups, such as Central Americans. Ethnic groups often move in their own ways through distinct phases of assimilation: first, living in immigrant communities and retaining old-country measures of manhood; second, shame and rejection of one's culture and repudiation of its norms of masculinity as impediments to success; and third, an aggressive reclamation that usually seeks to combine traditional and adopted ways of being male. At the point of full assimilation and movement into the upper middle class, an ethnic man will typically experience neither shame nor aggressiveness, and is often puzzled at why less established ethnic groups appear to adhere so awkwardly or militantly to what he considers outmoded masculinities. Acculturation in notions of masculinity has consistently been hastened when ethnically diverse men have labored together, whether in factories, in sports, or in political causes. This pattern has been especially pronounced among American military servicemen abroad. Even for those not in combat, foreign wars tend to unite American masculinities against a supposedly corrupt foreign masculinity.

Significant research supports both the "melting pot" (assimilation) and the "mixed salad" (cultural pluralism) as coexistent models of ethnic acculturation and ethnic masculinity formation operating in American culture. According to the 1990 census, of a population of 250 million, only 13 percent claimed English descent, while the remaining 87 percent identified with one or more of 200 other ancestral groups. With its lack of one originating ethnicity, the United States functions as the prototype of a country built through immigration and assimilation. However, assimilation has not prevented a number of immigrant groups from continuing to identify with their ethnic cultures. Under the "mixed salad" model, ethnic groups add flavor to the whole without losing their distinct identities, and each ethnic masculinity has remained a distinct option even while becoming part of a growing pool of American masculinities that is available for co-optation by American men of all other ethnic groups.

Ethnic masculinities should be viewed not just as static entities, but also as dynamic products of complex and continually evolving labeling and identification processes. An individual man's ethnic masculinity is a combination of his actual ancestral roots, his believed-to-be roots, his self-identification, and ethnic labels applied to him by others. Some groups, like Irish Americans and Italian Americans, have outspokenly embraced and celebrated what they proclaim to be their distinct styles of manhood. However, their definitions of these masculinities may be the product more of ethnogenesis (the development of new forms of ethnicity in America) than of Old World cultures. On the other hand, other groups, such as German Americans, may deny adhering to any ethnically distinct model of manhood, while their masculine ideals of diligence, thrift, and modesty are quietly passed from generation to generation and absorbed into American masculine ideals. Complications of ethnic masculinity are particularly common in people with mixed heritage; many contemporary Americans choosing to identity as multi-ethnic seek to combine, in varying ways, elements from their several ethnic masculinity options, while other multi-ethnic Americans may prefer to identify with only a single ethnicity and a single masculine style.

The blurring and admixing of distinct ethnic masculine identifications has been hastened through intermarriage, which has become more common as prejudicial barriers against specific ethnic groups have weakened. Through intermarriage, ethnic divisions gradually dissolve: Half of U.S.-born Asian Americans will marry white Americans; a third of Hispanic Americans marry white Americans; and intermarriages between whites and African Americans are steadily increasing. These mixed couples promote mixed values, including mixed concepts of masculine behaviors and roles.

The Influence of Ethnicity on American Masculinities

Identifying the effects and gauging the influence of ethnic masculinities on American masculinity are problematic tasks for several reasons. For one, many of those ethnic masculinities that are the most difficult to identify are also those of some of the nation's largest ancestral groups. Canadian-, Scottish-, Scotch-Irish-, German-, Polish-, Austrian-, and Slavic-American men have been less deliberate than others in preserving their ethnic heritage, in organizing around their ethnic identity, or in identifying their characteristics as significantly different than those considered "American." Some of these groups, furthermore, have also been challenged by changing national boundaries since their ancestors' immigration, and so have chosen to identify by the less complicated label—perhaps identifying themselves as German, rather than Swiss, Austro-Hungarian, or Bavarian. Thus, many of the ethnic masculinities whose influence might be suspected of being the most profound or fundamental have become all but invisible.

Ethnic masculine influences are also not evenly spread across American culture. Different skills and social networks have led to different ethnic men being concentrated in different professions. Immigrant populations have also concentrated in various regions, so that midwestern masculinity has been more influenced by German and Scandinavian masculinities; Scotch-Irish masculinity has been a larger influence in the Appalachian region; the West Coast has been more affected by Asian and Latino influences; and urban masculinities have been more directly influenced by African-American and Italian-American masculinities. As Americans have become more mobile, they take with them regional constructions of masculinity that are ethnic-inflected, even if the individual himself is not of that ethnicity.

The potential of ethnic masculinities to revitalize the dominant masculinity has been a major theme of American literature and popular culture. The interracial (or interethnic) male bonding narrative obsessively presents the mythic male union as a counter to the fragmentation of masculinity that occurs under shifting social pressures. The assumption of ethnic qualities as a way to create a more potent masculinity can be witnessed in popular culture figures such as Elvis Presley, John Travolta, and the rapper Eminem. Similarly, every American "acts" Irish on St. Patrick's Day and Mexican on Cinco de Mayo—although it is questionable how recognizable these holidays, or the accompanying masculine behaviors, would be in Ireland or Mexico. American fascination with southern Italian masculinity has led to *The Godfather*'s Michael Corleone becoming an important role model for contemporary American men, as well as to the tremendous popularity of Tony Soprano and his "soldiers." On the other hand, an illustration of the perceived difference between original and transplanted ethnic masculinities can be seen in Hollywood's casting of ethnically Chinese actors: Chinese nationals like Chow Yun Fat and Jackie Chan can play decidedly masculine heroes and villains, but Chinese-American men are not considered manly enough to be threatening. Although American men can enhance their masculinity by studying Asian martial arts, this masculine potency is not extended to Asian Americans. Because of the influences of an array of ethnic masculinities, American masculinity does not exist as a simple transplant of Anglo-Protestant masculinity, but is an ever-evolving mixture negotiated through the American ideals of tolerance, equal representation, and cultural exchange.

BIBLIOGRAPHY

Alba, Richard D. *Ethnicity and Race in the USA*. London: Routledge, 1985.

Fiedler, Leslie. *Love and Death in the American Novel*. New York: Anchor Books, 1992.

Kimmel, Michael. *Manhood in America: A Cultural History*. New York: Free Press, 1996.

Perlmutter, Philip. *The Dynamics of American Ethnic, Religious, and Racial Group Life: An Interdisciplinary Overview*. Westport, Conn.: Praeger, 1996.

Stecopoulos, Harry, and Michael Uebel, eds. *Race and the Subject of Masculinities*. Durham, N.C.: Duke University Press, 1997.

Thernstrom, Abigail, and Stephan Thernstrom, eds. *Beyond the Color Line: New Perspectives on Race and Ethnicity in America*. Stanford, Calif.: Hoover Institution Press, 2002.

Tillner, George. "Masculinity and Xenophobia: The Identity of Dominance." Paper presented at UNESCO conference Masculinity and Male Roles in the Perspective of a Culture of Peace, September 1997. <http://mailbox.univie.ac.at/~tillneg8/xenomale/OSLO.html> (March 28, 2003).

FURTHER READING

Awkward, Michael. *Negotiating Difference: Race, Gender and the Politics of Positionality*. Chicago: University of Chicago Press, 1995.

Bederman, Gail. *Manliness and Civilization: A Cultural History of Race and Gender in the United States, 1880–1917*. Chicago: University of Chicago Press, 1995.

Chapman, Rowena, and Jonathan Rutherford, eds. *Male Order: Unwrapping Masculinity*. London: Lawrence and Wishart, 1988.

Healey, Joseph F. *Race, Ethnicity, and Gender in the United States: Inequality, Group Conflict, and Power*. Thousand Oaks, Calif.: Pine Forge Press, 1997.

Holloway, Karla F. C. *Codes of Conduct: Race, Ethics and The Color of Our Character*. New Brunswick, N.J.: Rutgers University Press, 1995.

Kimmel, Michael, and Michael A. Messner. *Men's Lives*. 5th ed. Boston: Allyn & Bacon, 2001.

Levinson, David, and Melvin Ember, eds. *American Immigrant Cultures: Builders of a Nation*. New York: Macmillan Reference USA, 1997.

Tai, Robert H., and Mary L. Kenyatta, eds. *Critical Ethnicity: Countering the Waves of Identity Politics*. Lanham, Md.: Rowman & Littlefield, 1999.

RELATED ENTRIES

African-American Manhood; Asian-American Manhood; Irish-American Manhood; Italian-American Manhood; Jewish Manhood; Latino Manhood; Native American Manhood; Whiteness; Working-Class Manhood

—*Elizabeth Abele*

EUGENICS

Eugenics involves efforts to improve either the human race or a specific national, racial, or ethnic group through genetic or biological manipulation. Eugenic ideas have been associated with a wide range of social and political agendas, the most infamous being the racist and patriarchal discourses of Nazism in the first half of the twentieth century. In the United States, where the popularity and influence of eugenics peaked between the early 1910s and the late 1930s, it led to immigration restrictions and the sterilization and institutionalization of a range of persons who, for various reasons, were classed as "unfit." Although such policies were partly inspired by a Progressive Era faith in the power of science to improve society, many eugenicists in the United States used arguments about enhancing the hereditary "fitness" of the national population. These arguments supported a conservative and elitist view of power relations that privileged the white, Anglo-Saxon males of the middle and professional classes.

The importance of eugenics to social planning achieved greatest prominence following Charles Darwin's work on evolutionary biology and contributed to the application of his ideas to theories of social Darwinism, which sought to explain economic, racial, and gender inequities in U.S. society. By the 1890s, rising budgets for institutional care and correction in the United States, mass immigration from eastern and southern Europe, and perceptions of a declining fertility rate among the middle classes led to widespread fears about the degeneration of the American population. The fear of being demographically "swamped" by the fecundity of racial and class "others" was particularly troubling to Anglo-Saxon middle-class men, who believed that their authority rested on their position at the acme of evolutionary development. These men worried that they might lose their grip on power in a nation and world they understood as a perpetual struggle among races and nations for supremacy. Eugenics seemed to offer these men a utopian schema for the "perfection" of the American race and for the invigoration of white American middle-class masculinity.

Methods for redressing this perceived national genetic degeneration have been broadly classified as either "positive" or "negative" eugenics. Positive eugenics encouraged voluntary decisions about reproduction, including eugenic marriages between fit individuals and large families for the professional and middle classes. Negative eugenics—the version that most influenced American social policy in the early twentieth century—proposed state intervention to prevent the reproduction of "undesirable" persons. By 1917, sixteen states had enacted sterilization laws, most allowing for the sterilization of repeat-offender criminals, epileptics, the "feebleminded," and the mentally ill—all of whom were perceived as a threat to the genetic integrity of American manhood. After years of legal challenges, the Supreme Court ruled involuntary sterilization constitutional in 1926. In 1937, a survey found that 66 percent of the American population supported involuntary sterilization of "mental defectives," and 63 percent supported similar measures for criminals. Over 60,000 people were sterilized in these programs by 1958, 20,000 of them in California.

This popular acceptance of eugenic principles was also evident in the immigration restriction bills of 1921 and 1924, which ended the Open Door era of U.S. immigration policy and were based in part on data compiled by the Eugenic Record Office. Support for the racist assumptions of the bills was garnered from the recently-developed IQ test administered to America's draftees for World War I. Although the cultural bias of this test is obvious to the present-day reader, the data suggested that African-American men and recent immigrants, especially from southern and eastern Europe, were mentally inferior to "Nordic" American men. Partly as a result of this test, each nation was assigned a quota for immigration to the United States based on the population of people from that nation living in the United States at the time of the 1890 census, a move that sharply reduced immigration from southern and eastern Europe and almost entirely stopped immigration from the "Asiatic Barred Zone," which comprised China, Japan, Indochina, Afghanistan, Arabia, and the East Indies. The high (and rarely filled) immigration quotas for northern European countries indicated political leaders' belief that "true" American manhood was associated with this ethnic descent. Elsewhere in American life, eugenic societies sponsored publicity drives such as "fit family" contests at state fairs, while eugenicist articles regularly appeared in such popular publications as the *Saturday Evening Post.* In 1928, eugenics was endorsed by 90 percent of the biology texts used in American high schools.

Eugenics often provided a discourse of scientific support for the Anglo-Saxon supremacism and the antifeminism that was so prevalent in early-twentieth-century middle-class constructions of masculinity in the United States. It naturalized hierarchies of power that privileged Anglo-Saxon middle-class men, and it argued for the evolutionary inferiority of women and other ethnicities. Eugenics often suggested that women's primary civic responsibility was to have "fit" children, thus limiting their social role to the domestic sphere and revealing its advocates' fear that the female reproductive body had threatening potential. In its more extreme forms, eugenics was enthusiastically quoted by leaders of the Ku Klux Klan, whose growing membership—peaking at five million in the mid-1920s—suggested widespread concern about the impact of the nation's increasing ethnic diversity.

Public awareness of the implications of the Nazi eugenics program, as well as increasing scientific evidence against the efficacy of sterilization in controlling hereditary illnesses, led to the curtailment of the eugenics movement in America after World War II, although involuntary sterilizations continued until the 1970s. In addition, the feminism of the 1960s and 1970s stressed a woman's right to choose whether or not to have children, making state intervention in this decision even more controversial. Yet with the widespread availability and incidence of prenatal screening and in vitro fertilization, the advances in genetic engineering, and the strength of the anti-abortion movement, the right of the state to intervene in the reproductive choices of its citizens—a right at the heart of the eugenicist agenda—is still a very contentious issue. Thus, the proposal of eugenics that men could be "perfectible" through state regulation of reproduction, although now rarely evident in its crudely nativist and racist forms, persists.

Bibliography

Dowbiggin, Ian Robert. *Keeping America Sane: Psychiatry and Eugenics in the United States and Canada, 1880-1940.* Ithaca, N.Y.: Cornell University Press, 1997.

Greer, Germaine. *Sex and Destiny: The Politics of Human Fertility.* New York: Harper & Row, 1984.

Hasian, Marouf Arif, Jr. *The Rhetoric of Eugenics in Anglo-American Thought.* Athens, Ga.: University of Georgia Press, 1996.

Hawkins, Mike. *Social Darwinism in European and American Thought, 1860–1945.* Cambridge, England: Cambridge University Press, 1997.

Kevles, Daniel J. *In the Name of Eugenics: Genetics and the Uses of Human Heredity.* New York: Knopf, 1985.

Kimmel, Michael. *Manhood in America: A Cultural History.* New York: Free Press, 1996.

Paul, Diane B. *Controlling Human Heredity: 1865 to the Present.* Atlantic Highlands, N.J.: Humanities Press, 1995.

Further Reading

Bederman, Gail. *Manliness and Civilization: A Cultural History of Gender and Race in the United States, 1880–1917.* Chicago: University of Chicago Press, 1995.

Gould, Stephen Jay. *The Mismeasure of Man.* New York: Norton, 1996.

Haller, Mark H. *Eugenics: Hereditarian Attitudes in American Thought.* New Brunswick, N.J.: Rutgers University Press, 1984.

Higham, John. *Strangers in the Land: Patterns of American Nativism, 1860–1925.* Rev. ed. New Brunswick, N.J.: Rutgers University Press, 1988.

Larson, Edward J. *Sex, Race, and Science: Eugenics in the Deep South.* Baltimore: Johns Hopkins University Press, 1995.

Peel, Robert A, ed. *Essays in the History of Eugenics.* London: Galton Institute, 1998.

Smith, David. *The Eugenic Assault on America: Scenes in Red, White, and Black.* Lanham, Md.: George Mason University Press, 1993.

RELATED ENTRIES

Body; Class; Crisis of Masculinity; Darwinism; Ethnicity; Feminism; Immigration; Marriage; Medicine; Middle-Class Manhood; Nativism; Patriarchy; Progressive Era; Race; Reproduction; Whiteness; White Supremacism; Working-Class Manhood

—Mark Whalan

EVANGELICALISM AND REVIVALISM

Evangelical Protestantism first came to prominence in the English-speaking world in the eighteenth century, and it soon became a major strain in American religious and cultural life. As such, it has had an important influence on constructions of manhood in America, particularly in its emphasis on emotional display, self-abasement, and submission to God.

Evangelicalism first reached colonial America during the revivals of the eighteenth-century Great Awakening. In these revivals, Anglo-American evangelicals like Jonathan Edwards, George Whitefield, and John Wesley developed the emphases that became central to evangelical Christian constructions of manhood: (1) an emphasis on faith-based personal experience rather than ritualized forms of worship; (2) an antiestablishment posture privileging the individual's heartfelt relationship to God rather than adherence to church doctrine; (3) a premium on conversion, requiring that believers be "born again" in their Christian belief as adults; (4) a doctrine of submission, in which believers surrender themselves to the sovereignty of God; and (5) the primacy of emotion, or the "religious affections," in the pursuit of salvation. Public emotional display and the demand for personal abasement in religious matters, while central to evangelical understandings of manhood, differed significantly from the Enlightenment-informed model of rationalism, self-control, and moderation associated with the reigning ideologies of eighteenth-century masculinity.

Anglo-American evangelicals often compare the believer's relation to Christ with the wife's relation to her husband. Derived from the Old Testament's Song of Songs and Christ's parable of the ten virgins (Matthew 25: 1–12), the idea of Christ as a bridegroom and his believers as submissively loving spouses has a long tradition in New Testament theology. Theologically, this notion has implied an inversion of gender roles by requiring that the male believer assume a posture of wifely submissiveness and dependence, but in reality, particularly in the eighteenth century, it has reinforced normative gender roles by deeming it "natural" that husbands enjoy the "trust, submission and resignation" of wives full of "humility, modesty, purity, [and] chastity" (Greven, 128).

In the first half of the nineteenth century, for a number of reasons, evangelical Protestant identity became widely associated with femininity. During this period, republican notions of manhood began to identify masculinity with independence and self-determination rather than submissiveness, and the market revolution generated a definition of manhood grounded in aggressive competitiveness and self-made economic success. Further, evangelical males were marginalized from positions of cultural authority, and evangelical theologians of the Second Great Awakening downplayed a stern Calvinist God in favor of a loving Jesus associated with traditionally "feminine" qualities. This development was evident in the minister Horace Bushnell's suggestion that parents should strive to instill a "domesticity of character" in their male children. Other pre–Civil War evangelicals, in resistance to the feminization of Christianity, attempted to masculinize evangelical Protestantism by adopting a less emotional pulpit style and emphasizing the elements of retributive justice found in Calvinistic theology.

Mid-century evangelical Christianity also emerged as a political force, mobilizing a variety of pre–Civil War social protest movements, including abolitionism, temperance, prison reform, and (ironically enough given evangelicalism's contemporary social conservatism) women's rights. That the majority of reformers involved in these social protest movements were women further contributed to the feminization of evangelical Protestant culture, and to American literary and popular culture in general. Male evangelicals, whether ministers preaching to largely female congregations or to lecture-hall audiences, became both culturally and economically dependent on women to spread their messages.

A nineteenth-century evangelist preaches to an open-air revival meeting. Revivalists grounded their manly identities in their strenuous pulpit style, their claims to represent divine authority, and their ability to make converts. This image suggests the artist's belief that they exercised particular emotional power over women. (© The New Bedford Whaling Museum)

By the late nineteenth century, male evangelicals had intensified their efforts to counteract public perceptions of evangelicalism's feminine character. Part of this effort involved using athletic and military metaphors in an attempt to restore an essential manliness to pietistic Christianity. The Young Men's Christian Association (YMCA), which emerged in the United States in 1851, the Men and Religion Forward Movement (1911–12), and such individual preachers as "baseball evangelist" Billy Sunday attempted to foster evangelical piety among young men in urban centers by portraying Christian commitment as manly and associating spiritual strength with physical vigor. Sunday, for example, told a crowd that "the manliest man is the man who will acknowledge Jesus Christ" (Bruns, 138). Lay Christian groups like the Salvation Army modeled themselves on military units, while athletic and militaristic terms like prayer teams and Christian soldiers were used to describe the pietistic labors of evangelical males. This "muscular Christianity" intersected with contemporaneous secular appeals to rugged manhood that were popularly associated with Theodore Roosevelt and the bodybuilder Charles Atlas.

Competing with liberalized and neo-orthodox Protestantism, and publicly embarrassed by the Scopes Trial of 1925, which pitted Darwinism against creationism, evangelical Christianity faded from public prominence during the middle decades of the twentieth century. It re-emerged as a powerful cultural and political force beginning in the 1970s, coming to the aid of what many perceived as an embattled masculinity. Believing themselves undermined by feminism, civil rights, and moral liberalism, thousands of men have turned to nondenominational, experience-based, and emotionally expressive evangelical Christianity to help restore their fractured cultural authority and domestic patriarchy; while others have sought this end through the political action groups of the Christian Right and the Republican Party. Televangelist ministries like those of Jimmy Swaggart have provided the spectacles of moral revivalism and patriarchal authority desired by evangelical males. Against the perceived excesses of secular liberalism, such ministries have used the postures and ideas of traditional evangelical manhood—including moral high-mindedness, patriarchal family leadership, and public emotional display—as the basis for their conservative claims to moral authority. The continuing cultural appeal of this model of manhood in the United States became clear when Swaggart made a successful, televised, weeping plea for forgiveness after public revelations of an extramarital affair—a sharp contrast to the behavior of Jim Bakker, a minister who denied a similar charge of sexual infidelity only to lose control of his televangelical empire.

Eventually, this reactionary retrenchment produced the phenomenon of the Promise Keepers, a group of evangelical men who in the 1990s responded to feminism and recent men's movements in the United States by declaring their commitment to affectionate family leadership and embracing the morally absolutist social conservatism that has long been a part of the literalist biblical tradition of American evangelicalism. Famous for holding male-only prayer meetings and revivals in football stadiums, the Promise Keepers exploit the hypermasculine connotations of athleticism, perhaps in unconscious response to concerns about the hugging, wailing, and other emotional behaviors they display in their large gatherings. Thus, in the late twentieth century, evangelical masculinity returned to its eighteenth-century origins of emotional self-display, demonstrating to a disbelieving, secular world that conservative evangelical masculinity remains a potent cultural force.

BIBLIOGRAPHY

Balmer, Randall. *Blessed Assurance: A History of Evangelicalism in America.* Boston: Beacon Press, 1999.

Bilharz, Terry D. "Sex and the Second Great Awakening: The Feminization of American Religion Reconsidered." In *Belief and Behavior: Essays in the New Religious History,* edited by Philip R. VanderMeer and Robert P. Swierenga. New Brunswick, N.J.: Rutgers University Press, 1991.

Bruns, Roger. Preacher: *Billy Sunday and Big-Time American Evangelism.* New York: Norton, 1992.

Douglas, Ann. *The Feminization of American Culture.* New York: Noonday Press, 1998.

Douglas, Frank. *Less Than Conquerors: How Evangelicals Entered the Twentieth Century.* Grand Rapids, Mich.: W. B. Eerdmans, 1986.

Greven, Philip. *The Protestant Temperament: Patterns of Child-Rearing, Religious Experience, and the Self in Early America.* Chicago: University of Chicago Press, 1977.

FURTHER READING

Balmer, Randall. *Mine Eyes Have Seen the Glory: A Journey into the Evangelical Subculture in America.* 3rd ed. New York: Oxford University Press, 2000.

Hardesty, Nancy. *Women Called to Witness: Evangelical Feminism in the Nineteenth Century.* Knoxville: University of Tennessee Press, 1999.

Hatch, Nathan O. *The Democratization of American Christianity.* New Haven, Conn.: Yale University Press, 1989.

Lears, T. J. Jackson. *No Place of Grace: Antimodernism and the Transformation of American Culture, 1880–1920.* Chicago: University of Chicago Press, 1994.

Noll, Mark. *Evangelical Christianity: An Introduction.* Oxford: Blackwell, 2001.

SELECTED WRITINGS

Bushnell, Horace. *Views of Christian Nurture, and of Subjects Adjacent thereto.* 1847. Reprint, Delmar, N.Y.: Scholars' Fascimiles and Reprints, 1975.

Edwards, Jonathan. *The "Miscellanies."* New Haven, Conn.: Yale University Press, 1957.

———. *Treatise on the Religious Affections.* New Haven, Conn.: Yale University Press, 1957.

Whitefield, George. "Letter to Mrs. Ann D." In *The Works of the Reverend George Whitefield.* London: Edward and Charles Dilley, 1771.

RELATED ENTRIES

Atlas, Charles; Jesus, Images of; Men and Religion Forward Movement; Muscular Christianity; Promise Keepers; Religion and Spirituality; Roosevelt, Theodore; Sensitive Male; Sunday, Billy; Temperance; Young Men's Christian Association

—*Bryce Traister*

Fashion

Developments in fashion (the production, consumption, and display of dress for social purposes, typically among people with disposable wealth) have been closely related to changing constructions of masculinity in the United States. In all human societies, dress is one of the most important indicators of gender identity and difference in daily social interaction. In American society as in many others, clothing has been used to accentuate gender distinctions, uphold gender hierarchies, and convey male social and economic power.

In the patriarchal society of colonial America, as in Europe, where male authority was firmly entrenched, fashion was less attentive to gender distinctions. Elite men and women alike wore lace, rich velvets, elaborate wigs, fancy hats, powders, and rouges. But with the onset of economic and political modernization in the late eighteenth and early nineteenth centuries, particularly industrialization, democratization, and the growth of national markets, men of the emerging middle class sought to express their male authority through fashion. Anxious to accentuate gender distinctions in their dress, men came to view the adornments worn by their predecessors as feminine, and they no longer wore them.

As the adult, white, middle-class male became increasingly defined as a breadwinner, an expanding consumer economy provided him with a somber uniform—a plain, dark, three-piece suit—that represented hard work, thrift, sobriety, and economic advancement. During the 1840s the business suit became institutionalized, reflecting the new masculine ideal of "solid integrity and economic reliability" (Langner, 191). According to nineteenth-century gender dictates, men's dress served practical rather than decorative purposes, and fashion-conscious men appeared to undermine accepted notions of men as workers and providers by entering the "feminine" realm of sensuality, adornment, and consumption. Yet men evidently remained interested in stylistic flourishes. The author Harriet Beecher Stowe noted in 1865 that men's clothes, like women's apparel, "have as many fine, invisible points of fashion, and their fashions change quite as often; and they have as many knick-knacks with their studs and their sleeve-buttons and waistcoat buttons, their scarves and scarf-pins, their watch-chains and seals and sealrings" (Stowe, 174).

By the late nineteenth century, many middle-class men feared that industrialization, urbanization, and the growth of white-collar office work produced overcivilization and feminization. In response, they increasingly looked to the business suit to assert an image of masculine strength and power. Most men adopted the outfit, and those that did not risked being seen as unattractive, unmanly, or effeminate. Despite variations over subsequent decades, the suit remained a staple in defining middle-class men's economic roles and identities through the twentieth century and into the twenty-first century. Meanwhile, many working-class men considered the suit to be a symbol of genteel effeminacy, and they rejected it as not being compatible with their identities as laborers.

During the twentieth century, male fashion and its relation to masculinity were increasingly shaped by three important developments: (1) the expansion of leisure activity, particularly sports, in male experience and identity; (2) the growing importance of body-centered ideals of manliness; and (3) the ongoing expansion of a consumer culture. Manufacturers began producing clothing intended for leisure pursuits and used the emerging advertising industry to create markets for new fashions in such publications as *Gentlemen's Quarterly* (established in 1928) and *Esquire* (established in 1933).

Although the business suit (increasingly accompanied by a hat during the early twentieth century) persisted as a central component of male fashion, it came under growing attack during the decades after World War II, as cultural critics questioned American corporate life. Many of these critics—such as C. Wright Mills, author of *White Collar* (1951) and Sloan Wilson, author of *The Man in the Grey Flannel Suit* (1955)—considered the uniform of corporate work to be a symbol of excessive conformity and compromised manhood. At the same time, new, less conservative ideals of male fashion emerged. Some men embraced the new ideal of bachelor consumerism and luxurious living represented by *Playboy* magazine (established in 1953) and wore open collars. Others, particularly teenage males of the postwar "baby boom" generation, participated in the Beat movement's rejection of middle-class conformity and fashion consciousness. Still others, imitating the new "cool" style represented by actor James Dean, wore blue jeans and a leather jacket.

Male fashion developed in several new directions during the 1960s and 1970s, often being used to make personal and political statements. As a youth counterculture called many conventional American values and practices into question, various group-identity movements emerged, and many Americans turned to personal growth and fulfillment. Growing numbers of young white men (and clothing manufacturers such as Levi Strauss, eager to tap this vast market of consumers) made blue jeans, T-shirts, work shirts, and other forms of leisure dress standard elements of male attire. At the same time, African-American men used fashion—including traditional African dress; the berets, black leather jackets, and sunglasses of the Black Panthers; and the black turtleneck and leather trenchcoat of film detective Shaft—to express new, assertive, and racially grounded masculine identities. Meanwhile, men of the gay liberation movement challenged standard notions of masculinity by introducing cross-dressing into mainstream culture. While typical business attire continued to mark social class hierarchies and gender differences, new leisure clothing defied easy categorization and often (in many cases intentionally) blurred gender and class distinctions.

Still, the slipping economy of the 1970s and the growing feminist challenge to male public dominance encouraged a return to more conservative business apparel. In his book *Dress for Success* (1975), the self-styled corporate clothing consultant John Molloy (who called himself "America's first wardrobe engineer") stressed the importance of the suit, which he considered "the central power garment" (Molloy, 21). During the 1980s, as President Ronald Reagan promoted probusiness policies, "power dressing" became a distinctly masculine practice tied to a man's economic performance and authority in the workplace.

In the 1980s the growing emphasis on exercise and personal fitness generated yet another new development in male leisure dress: the emergence of athletic sportswear as a fashionable expression of masculine vigor and success. The simultaneous embrace of bodybuilding, previously regarded as a vain practice inconsistent with manliness, suggests that body-centered fashions and the popularity of male fashion magazines marked a decline in the level of unease over the possibility of "effeminate" vanity.

By the early twenty-first century, American life produced twin ideals of male fashion. Notions of masculine dress continued to draw on ideas of power and status, but the proliferation of countercultural styles (e.g., Goth, New Romantic, Psychobilly, Ragamuffin, Rastafarian, New Age Traveler, Grunge, Techno and Cyber Punk, and Leather Queen) indicated that American males had fully embraced the pleasures of fashion consumption.

Bibliography

Arnold, Rebecca. *Fashion, Desire, and Anxiety: Image and Morality in the 20th Century.* New Brunswick, N.J.: Rutgers University Press, 2001.

Craik, Jennifer. *The Face of Fashion: Cultural Studies in Fashion.* London: Routledge, 1994.

Dubbert, Joe. *A Man's Place: Masculinity in Transition.* Englewood Cliffs, N.J.: Prentice Hall, 1979.

Edwards, Tim. *Men in the Mirror: Men's Fashion, Masculinity, and Consumer Society.* London: Cassell, 1997.

Entwistle, Joanne. *The Fashioned Body: Fashion, Dress, and Modern Social Theory.* Malden, Mass.: Polity Press, 2000.

Flugel, J. C. *The Psychology of Clothes.* London: Hogarth Press, 1930.

Langner, Lawrence. *The Importance of Wearing Clothes.* New York: Hastings House, 1959.

Laver, James. *Modesty in Dress: An Inquiry into the Fundamentals of Fashion.* Boston: Houghton Mifflin, 1969.

Molloy, John T. *Dress for Success.* New York: P. H. Wyden, 1975.

Paoletti, Jo B. "Ridicule and Role Models as Factors in American Men's Fashion Change, 1880–1910." *Costume* 19 (1985): 121–134.

Rosaldo, M. Z. "Woman, Culture and Society: A Theoretical Overview." In *Woman, Culture, and Society,* edited by M. Z. Rosaldo and L. Lamphere. Stanford, Calif.: Stanford University Press, 1974.

Shapiro, Judith. "Transsexualism: Reflections on the Persistence of Gender and the Mutability of Sex." In *Body Guards: The Cultural Politics of Gender Ambiguity,* edited by Julia Epstein and Kristine Straub. New York: Routledge, 1991.

Stowe, Harriet Beecher. *House and Home Papers.* Boston: Ticknor and Fields, 1865.

Further Reading

Ash, J., and E. Wilson. *Chic Thrills: A Fashion Reader.* London: Pandora, 1992.

Chapman, R., and J. Rutherford. *Male Order: Unwrapping Masculinity.* London: Lawrence & Wishart, 1988.

Davis, Fred. *Fashion, Culture, and Identity.* Chicago: University of Chicago Press, 1992.

Johnson, Kim K. P., and Sharron J. Lennon. *Appearance and Power.* New York: Berg Publishers, 1999.

Kimmel, Michael. *Manhood in America: A Cultural History.* New York: Free Press, 1996.

Mosse, George L. *The Image of Man: The Creation of Modern Masculinity.* New York: Oxford University Press, 1996.

Related Entries

African-American Manhood; Black Panther Party; Body; Business/Corporate America; Consumerism; Counterculture; Dean, James; Leisure; Middle-Class Manhood; *Playboy* Magazine; *Shaft*; Transvestism

—*Bret E. Carroll*

Fatherhood

Fatherhood has been an all but universal experience for American men and is fundamental to understanding American masculinity. Through their experiences and conceptualizations of fatherhood, men have made sense of their lives, obligations, and responsibilities—as well as of notions attached to masculine identity, such as maturity, respectability, commitment, and breadwinning. Fatherhood has also been the foundation of male power within American society: While not all men have shared equally in such power—fatherhood is, after all, shaped by the interplay of class, race, and ethnicity—men as a sex have gained power thanks to the prerogatives and privileges that have accompanied fatherhood. The linkage between fatherhood and breadwinning, for example, has served to legitimate men's monopoly of the most desirable jobs, while consigning women to domestic obligations. The meaning of fatherhood, and its impact on masculine identity, has shifted throughout American history. While the archetypes of the Puritan patriarch, the Victorian breadwinner, and the suburban "dad" of the 1950s all connected their male identities to fatherhood, their experiences of fatherhood and masculinity differed greatly. Over time, economic, social, demographic, and cultural change have reshaped fatherhood, changed its meaning, and altered the definition of masculinity itself.

Patriarchal Fatherhood in Colonial America

For the first 150 years of European settlement in America, patriarchal power and an agrarian economy defined the experience and meaning of both fatherhood and manhood. Men were the self-anointed leaders of society, the titular and legal heads of families, and the primary locus of economic support for women and children. They represented their families' legal and political interests before the state and oversaw their children's religious upbringing. Religious and civic leaders, therefore, directed child-rearing prescriptions toward fathers. Although the stereotype of the uncaring, emotionally distant colonial father still endures, recent research suggests that men watched their children's development closely, played a critical role in their educations, and actively worked to shape their moral character. As children approached adulthood, colonial fathers helped to guide their children's courtships and their sons' selection of a vocation.

Furthermore, small homes and, for most Americans, rural living meant that fathers lived and worked in close proximity to their children. In rural areas, men helped organize the work of the household and introduced sons to the ways and rhythms of farm life; in towns and cities, fathers often labored in the home, or close to it, and introduced their sons to work at an early age. Whether in rural or more settled areas, religious and political leaders expected fathers to maintain good order within the household. A well-regulated society presupposed well-regulated families, and well-regulated families presupposed fatherly authority and engagement. In its many forms, ranging from will-crushing harshness to genteel indulgence, this regime of patriarchal fatherhood endured until the middle of the eighteenth century.

American Fatherhood in Transition: The Nineteenth Century

Sometime after the mid–eighteenth century, a variety of forces reshaped fatherhood in ways that endured for the next two centuries. The Enlightenment emphasis on religious, political, and economic individualism helped initiate this transformation. The paternal dominance and religious authority that infused Calvinist visions of manhood and family life in the seventeenth century eroded in the eighteenth century, and they were slowly replaced by an emphasis on models of manhood and fatherhood grounded in reason. Among the middling classes—though not necessarily among slaves and destitute nonslaves—family relations began to become more companionate. Romance, mutuality, companionship, and personal happiness became increasingly important barometers of spousal relationships, while male breadwinning and motherly nurture increasingly defined parental obligations.

Such trends were evident in some households even before the American Revolution, but they were decisively reinforced in the early to mid–nineteenth century as a corporate household economy gave way to a commercial–industrial world in which men began to work outside the home and women found themselves entrusted with increased child-rearing responsibilities. Masculine identity became increasingly focused on breadwinning, a development that inflated the significance and power of work outside the home, but made ties with children more difficult to sustain. Even men's abilities to shape their sons' careers became less pronounced since the dynamism of the nineteenth-century economy rendered obsolete the kinds of craft skills that fathers had traditionally passed on to their sons. For their part, middle-class fathers readied their sons for entry into the middle class through character development and access to education, a far cry from the tangible assets of land or the tools of one's craft that earlier generations of fathers could pass to their sons. Meanwhile, moralists now directed child-rearing literature to mothers, who took primary responsibility for rearing both sons and daughters. Men tried to pass on the lessons of manhood to their sons and exemplify manliness to their daughters, but their growing absence from home made this task increasingly difficult. Thus, they faced a problem that became basic to paternal masculinity in modern America: trying to ground their identities simultaneously in breadwinning and fathering.

Such generalizations, of course, must be made with caution. Rural, black, working-class, Native American, Hispanic, Jewish, and Italian fathers all had experiences that diverged from this pattern due to differing economic realities and cultural inheritances. Nevertheless, by the closing decades of the nineteenth century the general trend was that breadwinning increasingly defined American fatherhood and masculinity. This development contributed to the public power of men and undercut the emotional connections between fathers and children.

The "New Fatherhood" in Twentieth-Century America

The importance of breadwinning to American fatherhood was evidenced by the appearance of cultural lamentations about the alienation between fathers and their children in the early twentieth century. In the opening decades of the century, social scientists, psychologists, and family-life educators urged fathers to establish closer bonds with their children, arguing that involved fatherhood would replace outmoded concepts of masculinity and patriarchal power with ones attuned to the increasingly complex psychological needs of all family members. Such calls were part of a wider concern that certain aspects of modern life, such as materialism, individualism, urbanization, an emerging youth culture, and changing sexual norms, were destroying family bonds and undermining traditional masculinity. The anonymity of the city, the growing intrusiveness of government agencies in family life, and the changing nature of work itself had, experts believed, undercut male authority and identity and attenuated their former roles as religious guides, counselors, and authority figures. The antidote, they believed, was an increase in paternal companionship. This advice was reinforced by the increasing leisure time that accompanied the growth of professional, managerial, and

This 1870 Currier & Ives print depicts the idealized father as a family leader both emotionally engaged with his children and—as the industrious scene outside the window suggests—attentive to the responsibilities of work and breadwinning. (From the collections of the Library of Congress)

bureaucratic "white-collar" work during the late nineteenth and early twentieth centuries, and by the growing inclination of many middle-class men to define their identities in terms of their leisure activities.

As this "new fatherhood" took shape over the remainder of the century, a new mode of paternal masculinity began to emerge. Experts called on fathers to play a critical role in shaping their children's personality development and individual adjustment, tasks best accomplished not by stern patriarchs but by tolerant, nonauthoritarian, and flexible fathers sensitive to the emotional fulfillment and proper sex-role development of sons and daughters. By the 1930s, child experts had elaborated a psychological theory of sex-role identity that highlighted the father's crucial role as a model of masculinity for their sons to emulate and their daughters to seek in a mate.

By the middle decades of the century, men looking to define ideal fatherhood and male role modeling could look to experts of every stripe. Books, workshops, advice columns, and parent-education groups all supplied information on how and where to play with children, what to do when they misbehaved or failed in school, and how to deal with a "sissy," a bully, or a bed wetter. Such concerns, and the need for such information, suggest that fathers were indeed seeking greater involvement in their children's lives, but the existence of such advice also suggests that the new fatherhood and the new masculine vision it invoked came at a cost, for it meant a transference of child-rearing authority from fathers themselves to extrafamilial experts with specialized knowledge and their own cultural agendas. Rather than trust their own judgment and sense of paternal responsibilities and obligations, men became dependent on expert assistance for their fatherly identities, and they often lost confidence in their own paternal competency. In embracing this relocation of authority, the new fatherhood transformed the notion of the "good man" from an ideal of self-sufficiency to one of dependency grounded in good intentions and backed by knowledgeable professionals.

While this new ideal involved a surrender of authority, it also offered fathers new bases on which to ground their masculine identities. Men listening to and applying the advice of experts could take manly pride in being good fathers and good men who were sensitive to the needs of children, conversant with theories about child development, and in step with new ideals of fathering. If fathering enhanced the personality development of children, it also helped men become more nurturing and sensitive, and less slavishly devoted to the working world. Therapeutic impulses thus lurk at the center of the new fatherhood taking shape in the opening decades of the twentieth century. American men increasingly began to understand fatherhood as a "growth experience," a cultivation of one's masculinity.

But the new fatherhood was difficult to attain in a culture that measured manhood by successful breadwinning and workplace achievement. The experience of the Great Depression highlighted the enormous obstacles to close father–child bonding posed by unemployment and the resulting psychological devastation. Fathers and children often became more emotionally distant as men blamed themselves, and children blamed their fathers, for their families' suffering and economic decline. The lesson seemed clear to fathers: being a "buddy" was important, but being a breadwinner was crucial. On the other hand, prosperity also involved perils by intensifying the problem of balancing companionate fatherhood with family support. Middle-class affluence and a burgeoning youth culture elevated families' standards of housing, health, comfort, education, travel, and leisure, and thus augmented the pressure on fathers to earn money. Many middle-class fathers found it hard to be both companions and providers (more time at work meant less time with one's children) and found it easier to put their energies into jobs and careers that could bring them status and some measure of power.

This tension between breadwinning and companionship was fundamentally transformed in the second half of the twentieth century by two developments. The first, which continued through the late twentieth century, was a reorganization of the household economy. Most significantly, movement of mothers into the workforce that gained momentum in the 1950s altered the debate about male parenting. The new fatherhood first enunciated at the beginning of the twentieth century did not presuppose a fundamental change in a gender-based division of labor that defined men as breadwinners and women as mothers. But as mothers steadily increased their labor-force participation in the years after World War II, men lost the traditional basis for claiming the privileges that came with sole breadwinning, and they were increasingly required to become more fully involved in day-to-day parenting. The second important change was the re-emergence of feminism during the 1960s, which challenged the gender-based division of labor, questioned whether women were innately more suited to nurturing children, and demanded that men contribute to daily child-rearing responsibilities. Feminism asked that fathers become involved with children as more than "buddies." They were expected to be part of a restructured conception of manhood, gender roles, and family relations that struck at the core of patriarchal assumptions. This feminist vision of fatherhood invoked new forms of masculine identity far removed from traditional patriarchy.

All of these changes undermined the cultural coherence of fatherhood. During the late twentieth century, self-help enthusiasts wedded fatherhood to a wider culture of therapy, conservatives and evangelicals called for a reinvigoration of traditional fatherhood, and feminists continued their challenge that men become partners with women in the rearing of children. Meanwhile, homosexual fathers, increasingly visible after the gay rights and liberation movements of the 1960s and early 1970s, struggled to develop concepts of gay fatherhood in the face of prejudicial assumptions that they cannot be real "dads" to their children. "Deadbeat dads," who were increasingly visible amid rising divorce rates, began attracting attention for their alleged selfishness and manifest failure as breadwinners. Still other men redefined masculinity by embracing notions of self-realization and personal growth that celebrated unmarried cohabitation and a life free from the responsibilities of fatherhood. More pessimistically, many commentators worried that an epidemic of "fatherlessness" threatened the foundations of social order. Such concerns were the result of long developing changes in the lives of men that have made fatherhood increasingly politicized, unstable, fragmented, and controversial.

Bibliography

Frank, Stephen M. *Life with Father: Parenthood and Masculinity in the Nineteenth-Century American North.* Baltimore: Johns Hopkins University Press, 1998.

Griswold, Robert L. *Fatherhood in America: A History.* New York: Basic Books, 1993.

Johansen, Shawn. *Family Men: Middle-Class Fatherhood in Early Industrializing America.* New York: Routledge, 2001.

LaRossa, Ralph. *The Modernization of Fatherhood: A Social and Political History.* Chicago: University of Chicago Press, 1997.

Wilson, Lisa. *Ye Heart of a Man: The Domestic Life of Men in Colonial New England.* New Haven, Conn.: Yale University Press, 1999.

Further Reading

Ehrenreich, Barbara. *The Hearts of Men: American Dreams and the Flight from Commitment.* Garden City, N.Y.: Anchor Press/Doubleday, 1984.

Lasch, Christopher. *Haven in a Heartless World: The Family Besieged.* New York: Norton, 1995.

Related Entries

Breadwinner Role; *Common Sense Book of Baby and Child Care, The*; Cult of Domesticity; Divorce; Fathers' Rights; Leisure; Marriage; Masculine Domesticity; Middle-Class Manhood; Momism; *Mr. Mom*; Nuclear Family; Patriarchy; Suburbia

—*Robert L. Griswold*

Father Knows Best

Father Knows Best was a domestic situation comedy (1954–63) set in a typical midwestern community called Springfield. The show revolved around the trials and tribulations of the Anderson family: father and insurance agent Jim (Robert Young), mother and homemaker Margaret (Jane Wyatt), and their three children, seventeen-year-old Betty (Elinor Donahue), fourteen-year-old Jim, Jr., (Billy Gray), and nine-year-old Kathy (Lauren Chapin). The male characters in *Father Knows Best* represent influential media images of a masculine ideal (white, middle-class, Anglo-Saxon, and Protestant) shaped by emergent post–World War II and Cold War emphases on patriarchal domestic authority, family togetherness, suburban living, and conservatism.

The authoritative, self-assured masculinity of Jim Anderson (who "knew best") was intended to provide assurance for Americans who, having moved from an economic depression to a world war to the Cold War, sought social stability and moral certainty in American institutions. The bases of Jim's male identity, including moral principle, a middle-class suburban lifestyle, and conventional definitions of gender and sexuality, also represent the foundations of an idealized America. Jim's occupation as an insurance agent not only provides financial stability, but also symbolizes "insurance" against the angst of postwar America. His wisdom and domestic involvement likewise protect his family against perceived threats to the social, moral, and domestic order (particularly a disrespectful wife, a homosexual son, and assertive, career-seeking daughters).

The female characters are crucial to the preservation of this model of manhood. Margaret Anderson reinforces Jim's patriarchal domestic authority and conventional gender definitions through self-effacement. She attends to her domestic duties efficiently yet modestly, defers praise to Jim, and minimizes her own contributions to the family. When Margaret does rebel against these domestic codes, as in episodes such as "Mother Goes to School" (1957) and "It's a Small World" (1959), she suffers embarrassment, humiliation, shame, and regret. Betty, Jim's oldest daughter, is likewise punished when she attempts to assume "masculine" roles. Episodes such as "Betty, Girl Engineer" (1956), "Betty, the Pioneer Woman" (1958), and "Betty's Career Problem" (1960) suggest that girls must learn to channel athletic and career pursuits into romantic ones.

Jim, Jr., embodies postwar American ideals concerning boyhood, adolescence, and emerging manhood. Nicknamed "Bud," he is an adult male-in-training—a "budding" replica of

This promotional portrait for the television series Father Knows Best *conveys the Cold War social ideology emphasizing domestic patriarchy and the grounding of ideal middle-class male identity in family life. Clockwise from lower left: Billy Gray, Elinor Donahue, Robert Young, Jane Wyatt, and Lauren Chapin. (© Hulton/Archive)*

his father. Like the boys in *Leave It to Beaver* (1957–63), Bud learns lessons in traits and values associated by postwar Americans with ideal manhood, including positive relationships with girls, hard work, thriftiness, responsibility, selflessness, and middle-class status. For example, episodes such as "Carnival" (1957) teach Bud about ideal fatherhood; "Big Shot Bud" (1959) and "Bud Lives It Up" (1960) examine middle-class lifestyle; "Bud and the Debutante" (1959) confirms Bud's dedication to middle-class status; "Bud, the Willing Worker" (1959) offers lessons about work, determination, and reward; and "Bud Takes Up the Dance" (1954) focuses on Bud's awkward relationship with girls.

Father Knows Best offered a vision of American life that featured—and privileged—white males who were fully capable of controlling their families. This postwar ideology of family and gender made the series a comedy of reassurance and established a powerfully influential formula for subsequent sitcoms.

Bibliography

Brooks, Tim, and Earle Marsh. *The Complete Directory to Prime Time Network and Cable TV Shows, 1946–Present.* 6th ed. New York: Ballantine Books, 1995.

Frazer, June M., and Timothy C. Frazer. "'Father Knows Best' and 'The Cosby Show': Nostalgia and the Sitcom Tradition." *Journal of Popular Culture* 27, no. 3 (1993): 163–172.

Jones, Gerard. *Honey, I'm Home!: Sitcoms, Selling the American Dream.* New York: St. Martin's, 1982.

Leibman, Nina C. *Living Room Lectures: The Fifties Family in Film and Television.* Austin: University of Texas Press, 1995.

Marc, David. *Comic Visions: Television Comedy and American Culture.* 2nd ed. Malden, Mass.: Blackwell, 1997.

Further Reading

Chambers, Deborah. *Representing the Family.* London: Sage, 2001.

Eisner, Joel, and David Krinsky. *Television Comedy Series: An Episode Guide to 153 TV Sitcoms in Syndication.* Jefferson, N.C.: McFarland, 1984.

Hamamoto, Darrell Y. *Nervous Laughter: Television Situation Comedy and Liberal Democratic Ideology.* New York: Praeger, 1989.

Himmelstein, Hal. *Television Myth and the American Mind.* New York: Praeger, 1984.

Miller, Mark Crispin. "Prime Time: Deride and Conquer." In *Watching Television*, edited by Todd Gitlin. New York: Pantheon, 1986.

Related Entries

American Dream; Breadwinner Role; Class; Cold War; Consumerism; Family; Fatherhood; Heterosexuality; *Leave It to Beaver;* Marriage; Masculine Domesticity; Middle-Class Manhood; Nuclear Family; Patriarchy; Race; Suburbia; Television; Whiteness; World War II

—*Angela M. S. Nelson*

Father's Day

In 1972, fifty-eight years after Mother's Day was established as an official American holiday, Father's Day was officially proclaimed by the federal government as an observance to be held annually on the third Sunday of June. This lag suggests the cultural ambivalence about Father's Day, from its first appearance in 1910 as a religious call to "honor thy father" to its current status today as a successful commercial enterprise that celebrates the contributions of fathers to family life.

The inspiration for the holiday is traditionally traced to Sonora Smart Dodd of Spokane, Washington, who, during a Mother's Day sermon in 1909, reflected on her father's assumption of child rearing after the death of her mother. Since the mid–nineteenth century, rising expectations for male breadwinning in an industrializing society had relegated fathers to a secondary role in the home. Dodd sought to remind fathers of the religious importance of their domestic duties as well. The mayor of Spokane and the governor of Washington proclaimed the first Father's Day on July 19, 1910.

Father's Day received active support in its early years by Harry C. Meek, President of the Lions Club of Chicago. President Woodrow Wilson recognized Spokane's celebration in

1916 by pressing a button in Washington, D.C., that telegraphically unfurled a flag in the state of Washington, and in 1924 President Calvin Coolidge urged its observance at the state level. But Father's Day was not accorded full federal recognition because of broader popular disdain for its establishment. Many men scoffed at the holiday's sentimental attempts to domesticate manliness with flowers and gift-giving, or they derided the proliferation of such holidays as a commercial gimmick to sell more products—often paid for by the father himself. Still, support for fathers was expressed in the 1920s and 1930s during Mother's Day counter-rallies held in New York City's Central Park aimed at renaming it Parents' Day.

During the Depression, Father's Day was seized upon by the New York business community as a means of promoting sales by creating a "second Christmas" halfway through the year. Separate campaigns in the tobacco, neckware, and shirt industries ("Give Dad Something to Wear") were coordinated when businessmen founded the Father's Day Council in 1935. The advocacy of its first leader, advertiser Alvan Austin, combined with honors bestowed upon fathers defending the "home" during World War II, contributed to the holiday's increasing popularity.

Increasing pressures on fathers to assume more responsibility for homemaking in the 1950s did not extend to the formal recognition of Father's Day. It was only after the Sexual Revolution and the establishment of no-fault divorce in the 1960s challenged the prominence and permanence of the father's role in the home that Congress officially authorized a permanent observance in 1972. By that time the Father's Day Council estimated associated retail sales to be worth more than one billion dollars each year. Father's Day is now the fifth most popular occasion for sending greeting cards, representative gifts associated with the holiday—from ties to garden tools—symbolize the continuing tensions between labor and leisure in men's lives.

Since its official recognition, Father's Day has become a focal point for contested understandings of fathers' rights and changing familial responsibilities, especially concerning issues of custody and visitation of children. Responding to the complex composition of contemporary American families, President Bill Clinton's establishment of Parents' Day in 1994 honored multigenerational and gender-neutral contributions to child rearing, while his Father's Day proclamations in 1998 emphasized the inclusion of foster fathers, adoptive fathers, and stepfathers.

Bibliography

Krythe, Maymie R. *All About American Holidays.* New York: Harper, 1962.

LaRossa, Ralph. *The Modernization of Fatherhood: A Social and Political History.* Chicago: University of Chicago Press, 1997.

Myers, Robert J. *Celebrations: The Complete Book of American Holidays.* Garden City, N.Y.: Doubleday, 1972.

Schmidt, Leigh Eric. *Consumer Rites: The Buying and Selling of American Holidays.* Princeton, N.J.: Princeton University Press, 1995.

Further Reading

Griswold, Robert L. *Fatherhood in America: A History.* New York: Basic Books, 1993.

Related Entries

Advertising; Breadwinner Role; Consumerism; Fatherhood; Fathers' Rights; Leisure; Masculine Domesticity

—*Timothy Marr*

Fathers' Rights

Proponents of fathers' rights, which became a central issue of the late-twentieth-century men's movement, contend that changes initiated by the contemporary feminist movement have privileged women in divorce and child custody cases, to the detriment of both fathers and children. They argue that fatherhood is central to masculine identity, and men must therefore play a greater role in defining it. Focusing in particular on custody and visitation rights, child support, and abortion issues, fathers' rights groups seek to educate men and lobby for legislation that supports their agenda. The fathers' rights lobby may well represent the most active faction of the men's movement.

At the height of the feminist movement in the 1960s, some men came to share feminists' conviction that the traditional gender roles of American society needed to be transformed. Most especially, these men felt that social conventions that assigned to women the role of primary caregiver robbed men of both masculine fulfillment and crucial input into the lives of their children. Their concerns were heightened by rising divorce rates and the realization that a growing number of children were being raised by single, divorced mothers. In response, they formed male-bonding groups and shared techniques for more participatory forms of fathering, particularly after divorce. Most of these early organizations accepted the feminist premise that women had been victimized by patriarchy, but they also believed that the system of male dominance hindered the development of men who wished to explore nontraditional models of masculinity. Adherents to this philosophy sought to be more emotionally connected to their partners and children, to fulfill traditionally female-identified domestic responsibilities, and to censure men who invoked patriarchal privileges.

Many men in these early groups agitated for laws to be changed to make greater concessions for mothers, not for fathers. This was specifically in response to a court system that tended to regard children as the property of their fathers and to penalize women seeking a divorce, especially those who initiated divorce proceedings. But when no-fault divorce laws instituted in the 1970s resulted in changes that often privileged maternal child rearing, a new, decidedly nonfeminist faction of "masculinists" began to gain power. The masculinist position was first clearly articulated by Charles V. Metz, who founded the first formal fathers' rights organization, Divorce Racket Busters (later renamed United States Divorce Reform), in 1960. In his seminal book, *Divorce and Custody for Men* (1968), Metz argued that sexual discrimination was primarily perpetrated against men. Masculinists explicitly rejected the notion that women were oppressed. Instead, they believed that fathers were victimized and villainized by the new divorce laws. They felt particularly affronted when, during the 1970s, individual chapters of the National Organization for Women (NOW) began to voice opposition to joint-custody arrangements. (Their concern later intensified when, in 1996, NOW and its sympathizers officially advanced an Action Alert on Fathers' Rights in opposition to the Fathers' Count Act, which NOW claimed would weaken mothers' custodial rights).

Other masculinist groups continued to emerge in the 1970s and 1980s. In 1971, Richard Doyle established the Coalition of American Divorce Reform Elements (CADRE) in an attempt to form a united multi-organizational group that would expand divorced men's agendas beyond family arbitration (the focus of Metz's organization) to include child abuse, biological gender issues, affirmative action, paternity court, and welfare for unwed mothers. Unable to develop a singular focus and strained by competing constituencies and agendas, CADRE disbanded in 1973. Doyle then helped to create the Men's Rights Association (MRA), whose program concentrated on lobbying efforts, national legislation, and providing attorney referral and other advocacy services for fathers. The MRA thus created the template for subsequent fathers' rights organizations. Such organizations multiplied during the late 1970s and early 1980s, addressing custody and child-support matters and arguing that affirmative-action policies discriminated against men and should be illegal. The MRA reported that by 1977 there were 79 fathers' rights groups in twenty-five states and the District of Columbia; by 1981 there were 195 such groups.

Attempts to form a single umbrella association succeeded in 1982 with the establishment of the National Congress of Men (NCM), which on Father's Day of that year orchestrated a series of rallies across the nation to promote equal custodial rights for men. Later renamed the National Congress for Fathers and Children, this organization continued to grow into the twenty-first century. In 1985, amid increasing cultural conservatism and calls for the reaffirmation of traditional patriarchal domestic leadership, it was joined by the Children's Rights Council, which represented twenty-three different regional groups nationally and hosted national conferences to discuss fathers' rights issues.

In response to rhetoric during the 1990s that advocated a return to traditional family values, men's groups embracing this ideology proliferated. In 1990 the American Fathers' Coalition was created by Stuart Miller, one of the movement's most successful lobbyists. That same year evangelical Christians founded the Promise Keepers, a widely publicized organization that sought to provide guidance and support for Christian men seeking to become better fathers and family leaders.

The fathers' rights movement met with a mixed response among the general public. On the one hand, its message influenced American popular culture through such popular films as *Kramer vs. Kramer* (1979) and *Mrs. Doubtfire* (1993). On the other, it became the target of considerable criticism. While its advocates generally stressed the importance of fathers to healthy childhood development, and of fatherhood to masculine identity, some emphasized such issues as child support, the status of marital rape as a crime, and the amount of evidence required to support domestic abuse and rape cases—thus raising suspicions that the movement serves as a façade for men who are abusers or who are simply trying to avoid child-support payments. Furthermore, the harsh language used by some of the more extreme groups have fueled allegations that the movement's purpose is to affirm male dominance and erode the gains made by the women's movement.

Technological developments of the late twentieth and early twenty-first centuries have greatly affected the scope of the fathers' rights movement. The growing use of the Internet has made the diverse aims of fathers' rights groups more widely publicized, gave voice to small constituencies with relatively marginal interests, and facilitated mass conferences and demonstrations among groups that have yet to consolidate their interests in a single organization. DNA mapping has enhanced birth fathers' ability to assert their claims in adoption and abortion decisions. It seems likely that the fathers' rights movement will grow even more and raise new issues as biological and communications technologies continue to develop and multicultural constructions of fatherhood expand.

Bibliography

August, Eugene. *The New Men's Studies: a Selected and Annotated Interdisciplinary Bibliography.* 2nd ed. Englewood, Colo.: Libraries Unlimited, 1994.

Baumli, Francis, ed. *Men Freeing Men: Exploding the Myth of the Traditional Male.* Jersey City, N.J.: New Atlantis Press, 1985.

Baumli, Francis, and Tom Williamson. "The History of the Men's Movement." *Feminist Utopia,* 1992. <www.amazoncastle.com/feminism/menhist.shtml> (March 10, 2003).

Brod, Harry, and Michael Kaufman, eds. *Theorizing Masculinities.* Thousand Oaks, Calif.: Sage, 1994.

Messner, Michael A. *Politics of Masculinities: Men in Movements.* Thousand Oaks, Calif.: Sage, 1997.

Schwalbe, Michael L. *Unlocking the Iron Cage: the Men's Movement and Gender Politics and American Culture.* New York: Oxford University Press, 1996.

Further Reading

Abraham, Ken. *Who Are the Promise Keepers?: Understanding the Christian Men's Movement.* New York: Doubleday, 1997.

Doyle, Richard. "The Men's Manifesto: a Commonsense Approach to Gender Issues." Mens Defense Organization. <www.mensdefense.org/men's_manifesto.htm> (March 10, 2003).

Farrell, Warren. *The Myth of the Male: Why Men are the Disposable Sex.* New York: Simon & Schuster, 1993.

Griswold, Robert L. *Fatherhood in America: A History.* New York: Basic Books, 1993.

Harding, Christopher, ed. *Wingspan: Inside the Men's Movement.* New York: St. Martin's, 1992.

Leving, Jeffrey. *Fathers' Rights: Hard-Hitting and Fair Advice for Every Father Involved in a Custody Dispute.* New York: Basic Books, 1997.

Lingard, Bob, and Peter Douglas. *Men Engaging Feminism: Pro-Feminism, Backlashes, and Schooling.* Buckingham, England: Open University Press, 1999.

Metz, Charles V. *Divorce and Custody for Men: A Guide and Primer Designed Exclusively to Help Men Win Just Settlements.* Garden City, N.Y.: Doubleday, 1968.

Shanley, Mary Lyndon. *Making Babies, Making Families: What Matters Most in an Age of Reproductive Technologies, Surrogacy, Adoption, and Same-Sex and Unwed Parents.* Boston: Beacon Press, 2001.

Related Entries

Divorce; Fatherhood; Father's Day; Feminism; *Kramer vs. Kramer*; Men's Movements; Promise Keepers; Sensitive Male; Technology

—*Calinda N. Lee*

Feminism

Feminism in the United States is both an ideology and a political agenda, and it is grounded in the belief that women deserve rights and opportunities equal to those of men. Central to feminist thought and activity have been a critique of male-dominated power structures and, often, critiques of the models of maleness used to support that power. Feminism has therefore had a strong influence on definitions of masculinity throughout U.S. history. Frequently, it has encouraged the articulation of "profeminist" modes of manhood and other models that challenge culturally dominant ideals, provoking in response "masculinist" backlashes resisting perceived feminist threats to male authority.

Early American Feminism

Early feminist thought emerged in western Europe and America at about the time of the American Revolution. Inspired by Enlightenment philosophy and the republican ideology of equal natural rights, it appeared as part of a broader challenge to traditional Western patriarchal structures that confined political and economic power to small groups of propertied males. As American men organized an independent republic, many women, such as Judith Sargent Murray and Abigail Adams, carried republicanism to feminist conclusions that defined men and women in terms of Revolutionary American ideals.

The same ideas that inspired the earliest American expressions of feminism also produced demands for new masculine behaviors. In particular, Americans increasingly applied the Revolutionary rejection of tyrannical monarchy to domestic life, expecting husbands to temper their paternal authority with affection and a more egalitarian, less authoritarian approach to family dynamics. Women could—and in growing numbers, did—enforce this new and softer model of masculine authority by rejecting husbands that failed to adhere to it through the more liberalized divorce laws enacted in the new nation and expanded during the nineteenth century.

Feminism and the alternative models of masculinity it inspired were articulated with increasing assertiveness during the nineteenth and early twentieth centuries. During the early nineteenth century, abolitionists and other radical reformers (both women and men) began to articulate a systematic feminist ideology grounded in both the political ideology of republican democracy and a religious ideology of fundamental spiritual equality. Those who embraced this ideology expected men to embrace gender equality and reject the power structures and authoritarian behaviors that accompanied the traditional gender hierarchy. Abolitionist men were particularly inclined to encourage egalitarianism in their marital relationships and to use romantically effusive language in declaring their love for male friends. Other radical reform causes promoted by feminists, such as communitarianism, temperance, free love, and marriage reform, implied a masculine ideal that rejected drinking, competitiveness, and claims to sexual ownership of, and dominance over, women.

The Seneca Falls convention of 1848, organized as the nation's first women's rights convention by abolitionist activists Elizabeth Cady Stanton and Lucretia Mott, issued a declaration (modeled on the Declaration of Independence) stating their agenda that, by implication, offered guidelines for a feminist masculine ideal. Criticizing men for "repeated injuries and usurpations on the part of man toward woman, having in direct object the establishment of an absolute tyranny over her," the feminists at Seneca Falls—including such male abolitionists as William Lloyd Garrison and Frederick Douglass—argued that masculine identity should be separated from all claims to power over women. They also urged men to no longer "destroy [women's] confidence in [their] own powers, to lessen [their] self-respect [nor] to make [them] willing to lead a dependent and abject life"(Kerber and DeHart, 207–208). Men were to be sensitive to and encouraging of women's needs and aspirations, and less intent on preserving male-dominated power structures. This ideal of manhood continued to characterize feminist thinking through the early twenty-first century.

The Late Nineteenth and Early Twentieth Centuries

The movement for equal women's rights (first termed feminism around 1910) intensified during the late nineteenth century as female political and social activists, disappointed that the Fifteenth Amendment (1870) had not extended voting rights to women, participated in a growing suffrage campaign. Many also joined Progressive Era movements to reform politics, arguing that male-dominated governments and male politicians were inefficient, corrupt, and callous in matters of social justice. Hoping to construct a different model of political behavior, female and male Progressive reformers suggested a "maternalist" state in which political power would be shared by socially compassionate men and women and engineered for humanitarian purposes. Feminists also sought greater access to economic power and professional careers, again criticizing what they considered a male tendency toward callousness and inefficiency. Their attempt to mitigate the problems of an overmasculine political system achieved its most notable success in the 1920 ratification of the Nineteenth Amendment, which extended suffrage rights to women.

The gradually increasing influence of feminism prompted many American men to fear that female advances in America were undermining national strength and creating a state of overcivilization that threatened manly vigor and physical dominance. They responded by developing masculinist reactionary movements and ideals (including the "strenuous life," "passionate manhood," the Men and Religion Forward Movement, and "muscular Christianity") that asserted male power and authority.

The Impact of Second-Wave Feminism

Feminist activism subsided for a time during the twentieth century, as anxieties over the economic conditions of the Great Depression and national security concerns during the Cold War prompted growing calls for the reassertion of conventional gender roles and male authority. But during the latter decades of the twentieth century, feminist thought and its masculine ideal—while retaining the basic components articulated during the nineteenth century—developed in new directions and grew in influence. In the aftermath of the successes of the civil rights movement of the 1950s and 1960s, feminism and its recommended reforms of conventional masculinity also achieved new and unprecedented levels of power in American life.

Related economic and social developments of the 1960s and 1970s added new power to feminist models of manhood. Growing economic opportunity for women allowed them greater possibilities for independence and made it easier for them to divorce, which helped enforce standards of egalitarianism and sensitivity within marriage. At the same time, growing economic uncertainty, beginning in the 1970s, forced increasing numbers of middle-class families to rely on dual incomes to maintain their living standards. As a result, growing numbers of men became both more domestically engaged—in conformity with feminists' call for them to abandon the absorption in work that accompanied the breadwinner ideal of the nineteenth and twentieth centuries—and encouraging of their wives' career aspirations.

The feminism of the late twentieth century expanded both its agenda and its masculine ideal. Feminists raised public awareness of such issues as sexuality and rape, urging American men to renounce prostitution, pornography, and violence. Some feminists also linked their theories and political agenda to environmental causes, encouraging Americans to adopt a more respectful approach to "Mother Nature" by embracing the attitudes that feminist Mary Daly labeled "gyn-ecology" and ceasing the environmental "rape" being advocated by male-dominated corporations and political officials.

At the same time, female and male feminists in academia developed new fields of inquiry—such as feminist studies, women's studies, and men's studies—that questioned the "master narratives" of American life that assumed the leadership of white males as normative, and thereby legitimated patriarchal power structures. These scholars called for new approaches to the study of American life that would recognize gender as an important analytical category and treat constructions of masculinity as culturally constructed (rather than natural or essential to the self), as well as fluid, multiform, and changeable. Rejecting notions of a single model of masculinity, such scholars as Michael Kimmel discovered in U.S. history and culture profeminist men who had previously been overlooked by historical scholarship.

The models of manhood urged by feminist women and men gained a new cultural currency during the late twentieth century, as growing numbers of men sought to discover and cultivate their "feminine" sides. The term sensitive male—used to describe the man attuned to women's needs, supportive of feminist goals, and willing to express emotion—entered popular parlance, and the behaviors associated with it were explored in such popular films as *Tootsie* (1982) and *Mr. Mom* (1983) and the hit television series *Home Improvement* (1991–99).

Many men rejected these new profeminist masculine ideals, while others reacted with ambivalence, seeking to incorporate feminist critiques while preserving male authority. Religious conservatives often adopted the former approach, seeing in profeminist masculinity an undesirable surrender of domestic authority, encouraging American men to reassert their family leadership, and viewing women's work outside the home as a threat to children's well-being. Meanwhile, the Promise Keepers, a movement of evangelical Christian men established in 1991, sought to bolster male social and domestic leadership by embracing some elements of the feminist ideal, such as close domestic engagement and an embrace of emotion. The mythopoetic men's movement, inspired by Robert Bly's *Iron John* (1990), sought to reassert and cultivate an inner "essential" masculinity through all-male gatherings and rituals—an approach to masculinity that many profeminist men criticized as a reactionary denial of masculinity's adaptability to changing social reality.

The increasing visibility of both profeminist masculinity and its challengers suggests that, even if its goals for reforming male behavior remain elusive, feminism has succeeded in triggering a vigorous and highly public national debate about the meaning of American masculinity.

Bibliography

Daly, Mary. *Gyn/Ecology: The Metaethics of Radical Feminism.* Boston: Beacon Press, 1978.

Digby, Tom, ed. *Men Doing Feminism.* New York: Routledge, 1998.

Dixon, Chris. *Perfecting the Family: Antislavery Marriages in Nineteenth-Century America.* Amherst: University of Massachusetts Press, 1997.

Faludi, Susan. *Backlash: The Undeclared War Against American Women.* New York: Anchor, 1992.

Fliegelman, Jay. *Prodigals and Pilgrims: The American Revolution against Patriarchal Authority, 1750–1800.* Cambridge, England: Cambridge University Press, 1982.

Griswold, Robert L. "Divorce and the Legal Redefinition of Victorian Manhood." In *Meanings for Manhood: Cultural Constructions of Masculinity in Victorian America,* edited by Mark C. Carnes and Clyde Griffen. Chicago: University of Chicago Press, 1990.

Kerber, Linda, and Jane Sherron DeHart, eds. *Women's America: Refocusing the Past.* New York: Oxford University Press, 2000.

Kimmel, Michael. *The Politics of Manhood: Profeminist Men Respond to the Mythopoetic Men's Movement (and the Mythopoetic Leaders Answer).* Philadelphia: Temple University Press, 1995.

———. *Manhood in America: A Cultural History.* New York: Free Press, 1996.

Kimmel, Michael, and Thomas E. Mosmiller, eds. *Against the Tide: Pro-Feminist Men in the United States, 1776–1990, A Documentary History.* Boston: Beacon Press, 1992.

Rotundo, E. Anthony. *American Manhood: Transformations in Masculinity from the Revolution to the Modern Era.* New York: Basic Books, 1993.

Yacovone, Donald. "Abolitionists and the 'Language of Fraternal Love.'" In *Meanings for Manhood: Cultural Constructions of Masculinity in Victorian America,* edited by Mark C. Carnes and Clyde Griffen. Chicago: University of Chicago Press, 1990.

Further Reading

Andermahr, Sonya, et. al. *A Glossary of Feminist Theory.* London: Arnold, Andermahr, Sonya, 1997.

Bly, Robert. *Iron John: A Book About Men.* Reading, Mass.: Addison-Wesley, 1990.

Butler, Judith. *Gender Trouble.* New York: Routledge, 1999.

Echols, Alice. *Daring to Be Bad: Radical Feminism in America, 1967–1975.* Minneapolis: University of Minnesota Press, 1989.

Enloe, Cynthia. *The Morning After: Sexual Politics at the End of the Cold War.* Berkeley: University of California Press, 1993.

Faludi, Susan. *Stiffed: The Betrayal of Modern Man.* New York: Vintage, 1999.

Firestone, Shulamith. *The Dialectic of Sex.* London: Women's Press, 1979.

Friedan, Betty. *The Feminine Mystique.* New York: Norton, 1963.

Kimmel, Michael. *Men Confront Pornography.* New York: Meridian, 1991.

Lerner, Gerda. *The Creation of Patriarchy.* New York: Oxford University Press, 1986.

Millett, Kate. *Sexual Politics.* Garden City, N.Y.: Doubleday, 1970.

Pollack, William. *Real Boys: Rescuing Our Sons from the Myths of Boyhood.* New York: Random House, 1998.

Stoltenberg, John. *Refusing to Be a Man: Essays on Sex and Justice.* New York: UCL Press, 2000.

Tong, Rosemarie Putnam. *Feminist Thought: A More Comprehensive Introduction.* Boulder, Colo.: Westview Press, 1998.

Walby, Sylvia. *Theorizing Patriarchy.* Oxford: Basil Blackwell, 1990.

RELATED ENTRIES

Abolitionism; American Revolution; Divorce; *Home Improvement; Iron John: A Book About Men*; Marriage; Men's Movements; Men's Studies; *Mr. Mom*; Patriarchy; Pornography; Postmodernism; Progressive Era; Promise Keepers; Prostitution; Republicanism; Sensitive Male; Sexual Revolution

—*Bret E. Carroll*

FISHING

As a livelihood, pastime, industry, and literary theme, fishing has been perceived and portrayed as singularly masculine, and, as such, it has played a distinct role in constructions of American manhood. Both recreational and commercial fishing have long represented a haven where men can escape from society and engage in contact with the natural world. With most recreational fishing, this interaction is regarded as contemplative and sublime; with commercial fishing, it is viewed as courageous and potentially tragic.

Predating capitalism, fishing represents an atavistic masculine pursuit that recreates a primal connection to nature. The nineteenth-century naturalist and philosopher Henry David Thoreau associated fishing with "the lower orders of nature," as opposed to man's "instinct toward a higher . . . spiritual life" (Thoreau, 140, 143). But many men have regarded fishing as primal, spiritual, and transcendently philosophical. In 1653, Izaak Walton's *The Compleat Angler, or the Contemplative Man's Recreation* characterized fishing as a thinking man's practice and an artful mastery of the natural world using both human technology and one's own skills. Walton (and many who have followed him) regarded fishing as a balance of contemplation and positive action that leads to spiritual communion with a nonterrestrial, and otherwise unknowable, aquatic world. These ideas about fishing were most recently reinvigorated in American popular culture with the 1993 film adaptation of Norman Maclean's novel *A River Runs Through It* (1973), which depicts fly-fishing as a rugged yet sensitive and spiritual practice that draws a father and his two sons together, making them better men.

Recreational fishing, like hunting, has long provided a temporary escape from work and family responsibilities. The fictional character Rip Van Winkle, created by the nineteenth-century writer Washington Irving, escaped his wife and "profitable labor" by fishing "all day without a murmur" (Irving, 35). In the late nineteenth century, and throughout the twentieth century, fishing's popularity expanded as part of a general growth in leisure activities offering men an antidote to the alienating influences of industrialized and bureaucratic work experiences. Men who have "gone fishing" (as the clichéd sign left behind announces) do something that can be simultaneously passive and masculine, the opposite of work but also removed from domesticity and women's influence. Fishing retains one familial association, however, as a leisure activity that fathers can share with their sons. As a masculine activity, fishing allows fathers to fulfill a paternal role by teaching their sons to be men through close contact with nature.

Recreational fishing has also served as a therapeutic masculine ritual. The author Ernest Hemingway, for example, portrayed fishing as a means of coping with physical and

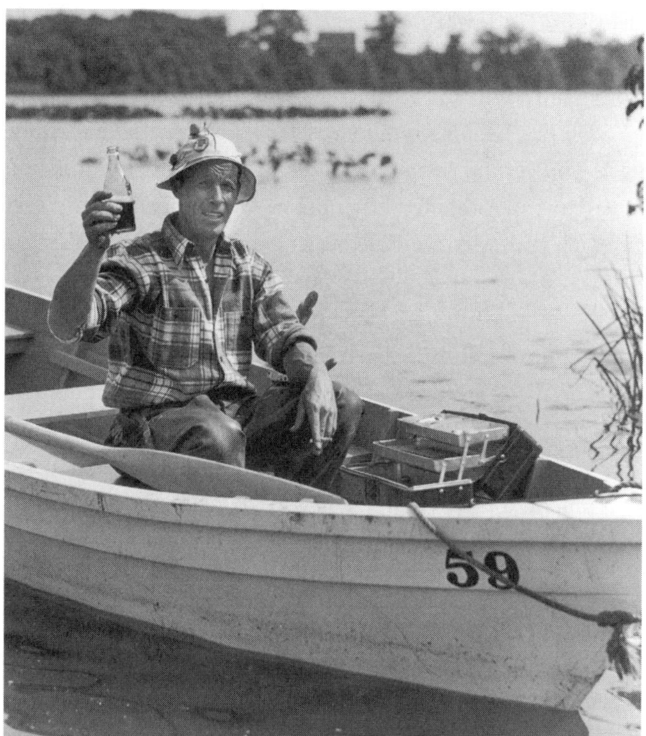

Since the late nineteenth century, American men have considered recreational fishing a leisure activity that allows escape from domestic responsibility and from industrial and bureaucratic work and promotes contemplative communion with nature. In this photo, a man fishes while enjoying a beer and a cigarette. (© Hulton/Archive)

psychological wounds inflicted by modern warfare and twentieth-century social change. In "Big Two-Hearted River" (1925), Hemingway's Nick Adams fishes to recapture "all the old feeling" and to "choke" painful memories of war, and in *The Sun Also Rises* (1926) Jake Barnes retreats to a mountain trout stream to restore a masculine identity threatened by a sexually debilitating war wound and promiscuous modern womanhood.

A different tradition portrays fishing, particularly the dangerous work of commercial fishing, as a test of manhood that can contribute to a man's alienation from society, and that can end in tragedy. Literary works ranging from Herman Melville's *Moby Dick* (1851) to Sebastian Junger's *The Perfect Storm* (1997) have portrayed maritime fishing as an exceptionally masculine pursuit that removes men from terrestrial society; exposes them to extreme risks, hardships, and natural hazards; and leads to their ultimate demise. Hemingway's *Old Man and the Sea* (1952) tells a similarly iconic story of a lone fisherman's efforts fishing for marlin in the face of adverse natural and social forces. As a dangerous and physically demanding endeavor on the one hand, and a commercial capitalist pursuit on the other, maritime fishing maintains competing masculine associations. Although some commercial fishermen are also capitalist businessmen, the masculine identities of hired crewmembers are based on their manual labor. Thus, while commercial fishing ventures create male bonding among boat crews, they also enforce hierarchies of power and command to which notions of masculinity are basic.

Despite fishing's symbolic status as an essential masculine endeavor beyond social influences, in actual practice it is not. Currently, an estimated fifty million Americans fish for pleasure each year, yet only three out of four are men or boys, making it a predominantly, but not exclusively, male pastime. Furthermore, different men fish in different ways and with varying motivations dictated in large part by their social status. Fly-fishermen, for example, are typically middle- and upper-class white men who see it as a rarefied art form, while bait- and spin-cast fishermen typically use less-expensive equipment and make up a far more demographically diverse population. The latter's version of fishing is a more widely inclusive and popular cultural practice. Although it has long been associated with a withdrawal from society to an unadulterated natural world, and as an intrinsic state of masculinity, fishing's status as an essentially manly endeavor has been, and continues to be, shaped by technologies, economics, environmental interventions, and racial and class dynamics.

BIBLIOGRAPHY

Hemingway, Ernest. *The Sun Also Rises.* New York: Scribner's, 1926.

———. *The Old Man and the Sea.* New York: Scribner's, 1952.

———. *The Complete Short Stories of Ernest Hemingway:* The Finca Vigía Edition. New York: Simon & Schuster, 1998.

Irving, Washington. *The Sketch-book of Geoffrey Crayon, Gent.* Edited by Susan Manning. Oxford: Oxford University Press, 1998.

Junger, Sebastian. *The Perfect Storm: A True Story of Men Against the Sea.* New York: Norton, 1997.

Maclean, Norman. *A River Runs Through It and Other Stories.* Chicago: University of Chicago Press, 2001.

Melville, Herman. *Moby Dick, or, The Whale,* edited by Harrison Hayford, Hershel Parker, and G. Thomas Tanselle. Evanston, Ill.: Northwestern University Press, 2001.

Thoreau, Henry David. *Walden and Resistance to Civil Government: Authoritative Texts, Thoreau's Journal, Reviews and Essays in Criticism.* Edited by William Rossi. 2nd ed. New York: Norton, 1992.

Walton, Izaak. *The Compleat Angler, or the Contemplative Man's Recreation.* 1653. Reprint, with an introduction by Thomas McGuane. New York: Harper, 1997.

FURTHER READING

Reiger, John F. *American Sportsmen and the Origins of Conservation.* 3rd ed. Corvallis: Oregon State University Press, 2001.

RELATED ENTRIES

Hemingway, Ernest; Hunting; Individualism; Leisure; Male Friendship; *Moby Dick*, Outdoorsmen; Religion and Spirituality; Work

—*Timothy Barnard*

FITZGERALD, F. SCOTT

1896–1940
American Novelist and Short-Story Writer

F. Scott Fitzgerald (Francis Scott Key Fitzgerald in full) is America's best-known chronicler of the Jazz Age, a reputation that sometimes overshadows the great merit of his work, especially *This Side of Paradise* (1920) and *The Great Gatsby* (1925). In his writings from the 1920s, Fitzgerald explored the tensions besetting the ideal of self-made American manhood. This was an era that seemed to offer incredible possibility, especially for the young, but that also made manifest the growing difficulty of achieving self-made success in modern society.

For Fitzgerald, manhood meant financial success and carefree heterosexual romance. Like some of his characters, the writer found, and then lost, both. Married to Zelda Sayre, whom he met while stationed in Alabama during World War I, Fitzgerald was a celebrity by the age of twenty-four. In the mid-1920s the Fitzgeralds joined the tiny but influential American expatriate community in Paris. Unlike the characters featured in Ernest Hemingway's work of the same period, such as soldiers and outdoorsmen exhibiting grace under pressure, Fitzgerald's male characters typically lack opportunities for vigorous, decisive action. According to Hemingway, Fitzgerald was insecure about his manhood, even at the height of his success.

Fitzgerald dreamed of acceptance as a gentleman of taste and refinement by high society. His early fiction, particularly *This Side of Paradise*, is semiautobiographical. Through the character Amory Blaine, the reader sees Fitzgerald's own anxieties as a young man from the provinces seeking definition and membership in the elite at Princeton, where the writer spent three years. His characterization of the university as "lazy and goodlooking and aristocratic" exemplifies the young Fitzgerald's sense of a gentleman. This first novel was followed by *The Beautiful and Damned* (1922), which explored a young couple's disintegration, as well as two collections of short stories, *Flappers and Philosophers* (1920) and *Tales of the Jazz Age* (1922). Fitzgerald's early work portrays young men of promise and sufficient wealth chasing or enjoying romance and fulfillment, and it suggests that these markers of manhood are most easily achieved without the distractions of family or work.

Fitzgerald's most notable work is *The Great Gatsby*, a technically brilliant novel that explores the connection between will, reputation, and success for Americans, particularly American men. As a young man, the mysterious Jay Gatsby followed a Benjamin Franklin–like path of self-improvement (even studying electricity) as he sought to make himself an image of masculinity, but he later becomes obsessed with acquiring wealth and gaining social acceptance from his rich neighbors. In chasing the beautiful but flawed Daisy Buchanan, Gatsby finds himself caught between an idealistic pursuit of the good life and a materialistic attachment to the high life. By the end of the novel, the character and his dream of success are destroyed. The title of the book, suggesting that Gatsby was a sort of magician, informs readers that Gatsby's manhood is illusory and that the novel is a cautionary fable for believers in self-made manhood.

Fitzgerald's later life brought disappointment, as he battled financial troubles stemming from extravagant living, alcoholism, and the mental deterioration of his wife. In the 1930s, as his popularity and energies waned, he nonetheless produced insightful stories and novels. In *Tender is the Night* (1934), Fitzgerald traces the career of a psychiatrist destroyed by his wealthy wife and dissipation. Fitzgerald was driven by dreams of success, and he was always haunted by a suspicion that he was somehow still an outsider who, despite his apparent accomplishments, never quite achieved the American Dream. By the time he suffered a fatal heart attack in 1940, he had lost Zelda, most of his money, and much of the fame that seemed part of his earlier success. Fitzgerald and his characters dramatize the consequences of defining masculine identity in terms of economic status.

Bibliography

Bruccoli, Matthew J. *Some Sort of Epic Grandeur: The Life of F. Scott Fitzgerald.* Rev. ed. New York: Carroll & Graf, 1991.

Chambers, John B. *The Novels of F. Scott Fitzgerald.* New York: St Martin's, 1989.

Meyers, Jeffrey. *Hemingway: A Biography.* New York: Harper & Row, 1985.

Further Reading

Berman, Ronald. *The Great Gatsby and Modern Times.* Urbana: University of Illinois Press, 1996.

Bloom, Harold, ed. *F. Scott Fitzgerald.* Broomall, Pa.: Chelsea House, 2000.

Bruccoli, Matthew J. *Fitzgerald and Hemingway: A Dangerous Friendship.* New York: Carroll & Graf, 1994.

Selected Writings

Fitzgerald, F. Scott. *Flappers and Philosophers.* 1920. Reprint, edited by James L. W. West III. New York: Cambridge University Press, 2000.

———. *This Side of Paradise.* 1920. Reprint, introduction by Susan Orlean. New York: Modern Library, 2001.

———. *The Beautiful and Damned.* 1922. Reprint, New York: Modern Library, 2002.

———. *Tales of the Jazz Age.* 1922. Reprint, edited by James L. W. West III. New York: Cambridge University Press, 2002.

———. *The Great Gatsby.* 1925. Reprint, edited with an introduction and notes by Ruth Prigozy. New York: Oxford University Press, 1998.

———. *Tender is the Night.* 1934. Reprint, New York: Scribner, 1996.

———. *The Letters of F. Scott Fitzgerald.* Edited by Andrew Turnbull. New York: Scribners, 1964.

Related Entries

American Dream; Franklin, Benjamin; Hemingway, Ernest; Self-Made Man; World War I; Youth

—*Trent Watts*

Football

Football, or American football, as it is called outside the United States, was initially a combination of European football (soccer) and rugby. It emerged as an intercollegiate sport in the 1870s in northeastern Ivy League schools. Yale University's Walter Camp, who came to be known as "the father of American football," was instrumental in developing and publicizing the sport during the 1880s and 1890s. Despite serious injuries and some deaths during its formative years, football prospered, in part because prominent men such as Camp supported it. Football also owed its initial appeal and success to what the historian Michael Oriard has called its "necessary roughness" (Oriard, 207). Football became popular in the late nineteenth century precisely because it was a rough outdoor sport that young middle- and upper-class (mostly white) men could play. In short, it became popular because it was a "manly sport."

The promotion of football during the 1880s and 1890s as a manly sport was part of the larger cult of masculinity that emerged in the United States in the late nineteenth century. Ideas about masculinity were transformed in the nineteenth century as industrialization, urbanization, and immigration altered fundamental social, economic, and political relations. With industrialization, the development of white-collar office occupations, the closing of the western frontier, and increased migration to cities, American men felt cut off from many of the outdoor activities that once defined American manliness. Social critics complained that an expanding corporate economy that valued intellectual prowess and subordination within hierarchical structures of authority over individual physical strength and endurance had "feminized" much of American culture. American males, especially middle- and upper-class white men, felt as though their power, authority, and independence, both at home and in the workplace, were in serious jeopardy. Prominent Americans such as Theodore Roosevelt issued a call to beleaguered men everywhere to reclaim their masculinity through the "strenuous life," including the new sport of football. Faced with conflicting societal demands for both aggression and self-restraint, some middle- and upper-class men turned to football as a way of defining their manliness in a rapidly changing society.

Football appealed to American men because it wed older definitions of manliness that rested upon notions of physical strength, exertion, and endurance with new ideas concerning masculinity that were being fostered by the corporate economy. This new masculinity focused on mental acuity, leadership skills, and teamwork—a combination that many men found difficult to achieve in modern America. Football required strategy and cooperative effort as well as physical strength. It provided participants with an opportunity to reclaim their physical manliness through aggression, without becoming uncivilized.

In its formative years, football was organized and played by elite white men at America's best schools. For college-age men who played the game, it represented a rite of passage from youth into adulthood. The training and education endured by younger players at the hands of their older teammates was a way of initiating boys into an adult culture characterized by a corporate hierarchy. Proponents of the new sport asserted that it developed a manly character and created assertive, charismatic leaders who went on to play important roles in industry and government. Theodore Roosevelt considered football central to a young man's training for life, and in 1890 he linked it with not only the development of character, but also with vigor and courage in the face of physical danger. He and other proponents of football argued that it developed traits in men that were necessary for the survival of both the individual male and American society.

In an effort to eliminate the extreme brutality and modernize the game, football's advocates made several modifications during the twentieth century. The implementation of the forward pass, countless rule changes, and technological improvements in the equipment that players wore made the game considerably safer, as well as more appealing to a mass consumer audience. College football quickly expanded beyond the Ivy League, becoming one of America's most popular sports and stimulating the creation of youth football, high school football, and professional football nationwide. Parents, coaches, and cultural leaders continue to claim that football teaches men essential life lessons.

Yet, football remains a violent and predominantly masculine sport. Efforts to bring women into the game have provoked substantial public skepticism. Modern television equipment and sophisticated microphones on the playing field allow spectators to see and hear all of the sights and sounds of the "battle in the trenches." Players continue to be rewarded by parents, coaches, and the media for especially violent play. One such reward, membership on the "All Madden Team," is given out annually by football commentator and former National Football League coach John Madden to the "iron men" whom he thinks best represent the game, usually the men with the most cuts and bruises; that is, the hardest hitters. Although the times and the sport have changed, football remains in many ways the rough manly sport that it was at the end of the nineteenth century.

Bibliography

Oriard, Michael. *Reading Football: How the Popular Press Created an American Spectacle.* Chapel Hill: University of North Carolina Press, 1993.

Watterson, John Sayle. *College Football: History, Spectacle, Controversy.* Baltimore: Johns Hopkins University Press, 2000.

Further Reading

Gruver, Ed. *The American Football League: A Year-by-Year History, 1960–1969.* Jefferson, N.C.: McFarland, 1997.

Nelson, David M. *The Anatomy of a Game: Football, the Rules, and the Men Who Made the Game.* Cranbury, N.J.: Associated University Presses, 1994.

Rader, Benjamin G. *American Sports: From the Age of Folk Games to the Age of Televised Sports.* Upper Saddle River, N.J.: Prentice Hall, 1999.

Staudohar, Paul D., and J. A. Mangan, eds. *The Business of Professional Sports.* Urbana: University of Illinois Press, 1991.

RELATED ENTRIES

Body; Character; Class; Crisis of Masculinity; Health; Industrialization; Leisure; Male Friendship; Men's Clubs; Middle-Class Manhood; Outdoorsmen; Sports; Strenuous Life; Urbanization; Violence; Western Frontier

—*Michael A. Rembis*

FRANKLIN, BENJAMIN

1706–1790
Statesman, Inventor, and Founding Father

In a career spanning the eighteenth century, Benjamin Franklin succeeded at nearly everything he did, leaving an indelible mark on American history, politics, and intellectual life. In his *Autobiography*, written between 1771 and 1789, one of the most widely studied texts of the American eighteenth century, Franklin portrayed himself as a consummate stylist of the eighteenth-century masculine self. Born the son of a soap-maker and regarded as a founding father of the nation upon his death, he helped created the idea of the self-made American man through his activities as a printer, entrepreneur, inventor, moralist, revolutionary, and writer.

Franklin began his career as an apprentice to his brother, James, the printer of the *New England Courant.* During this apprenticeship, Franklin took up the common eighteenth-century practice of writing under pseudonyms—including, most famously, Mrs. Silence Dogood. Anonymity allowed Franklin to pass judgment on moral and social matters (including those traditionally considered to be a woman's domain) and gave him the freedom to express his opinions in a culture prone to censure opinionists. It also bolstered the authority of his opinions by preventing his enemies from discrediting him. At a time when self-interest was thought to conflict with public-mindedness, Franklin furthered his personal agenda by representing himself, as he puts it in the *Autobiography*, as a "publick-spirited Gentleman" motivated by a desire to improve civic life. Both genuine and simulated, Franklin's civic spirit was a form of masculine virtue grounded in contemporary republican social and political theory, which defined true virtue as the subordination of self-interest to the needs of the public sphere.

Franklin associated masculinity with business activity (motivated by virtue rather than by profit), public renown, and the improvement of society. He parlayed his civic spirit into business opportunities by proposing the creation of a circulating library and the University of Pennsylvania, as well as by securing the publication rights to the laws and business of the Pennsylvania Legislature. Through such internationally celebrated inventions as the Franklin stove and his scientific studies of electricity, Franklin contributed to a mythology of American male inventiveness.

For Franklin, masculinity was achieved and expressed through self-control. The *Autobiography* recounts Franklin's plan to discipline himself by adhering to thirteen virtues (temperance, silence, order, resolution, frugality, industry, sincerity, justice, moderation, cleanliness, tranquility, chastity, and humility) that he believed would lead to ideal manhood and moral perfection. Such moral self-regulation reflected an Enlightenment understanding of manliness and a well-ordered life in which the male controlled his baser instincts for the betterment of himself and, by extension, society. While some historians have suggested that the private Franklin valued sexual prowess and a luxurious lifestyle, his public persona emphasized self-control as the basis of manliness.

Franklin has long been a celebrated figure in America's Revolutionary history and mythology. A signer of the Declaration of Independence, he has become in historical memory one of the most prominent of the founding fathers, based in part on his importance to the nation's efforts to render its revolution legitimate by investing its Revolutionary leaders with manly heroism and patriarchal authority. Given Franklin's lifelong struggle against what he perceived as tyrannical patriarchy—a struggle central to American Revolutionary ideology—it is somewhat ironic that he has been elevated to father figure status by a nation in search of authoritative masculine icons.

BIBLIOGRAPHY

Anderson, Douglas. *The Radical Enlightenments of Benjamin Franklin.* Baltimore: Johns Hopkins University Press, 1997.

Breitwieser, Mitchell Robert. *Cotton Mather and Benjamin Franklin: The Price of Representative Personality.* Cambridge: Cambridge University Press, 1984.

Warner, Michael. *The Letters of the Republic: Publication and Public Sphere in Eighteenth-Century America.* Cambridge, Mass.: Harvard University Press, 1990.

FURTHER READING

Buxbaum, Melvin H., ed. *Critical Essays on Benjamin Franklin.* Boston: G. K. Hall, 1987.

Lemay, J. A. Leo, ed. *The Oldest Revolutionary: Essays on Benjamin Franklin.* Philadelphia: University of Pennsylvania Press, 1976.

SELECTED WRITINGS

Franklin, Benjamin. *Poor Richard: An Almanack.* New York: D. McKay Co., 1976.

———. *Benjamin Franklin's Autobiography: An Authoritative Text, Backgrounds, Criticism.* Edited by J. A. Leo Lemay and P. M. Zall. New York: Norton, 1986.

RELATED ENTRIES

American Dream; American Revolution; Patriarchy; Republicanism; Self-Control; Self-Made Man

—*Bryce Traister*

FRATERNAL ORGANIZATIONS

Fraternal organizations have been a part of American life since before the American Revolution, but they achieved their greatest popularity during the second half of the nineteenth century. While groups such as the Freemasons, Elks, Odd Fellows, and Knights of Pythias are the most well known, thousands of distinct organizations have formed and disbanded during the nation's history. Fraternal organizations have played a significant role in constructions of American masculinity by creating exclusive social realms where men have been able to segregate themselves not only from women, but also from men of different races, classes, or ethnicities. They have also enabled men to enact rituals that create metaphorical brotherhoods and solidify the values of loyalty, charity, hard work, and discipline.

The Rise of American Fraternalism: The Nineteenth Century

Prior to the nineteenth century, fraternal orders were relatively few in number in the United States. The first to appear was the Masonic Order, which established its first American lodge in 1733. The Independent Order of Odd Fellows (IOOF) followed in the early nineteenth century. Membership in these early male organizations was generally confined to white urban elites in the East, and these members could foster and reinforce their public power by cultivating friendships and acquaintanceships in the worlds of business and politics.

The popularity of fraternal organizations grew rapidly during the second half of the nineteenth century, especially among the middle class. Many new orders emerged in the United States: The Knights of Pythias (KOP; 1864), the Benevolent and Protective Order of Elks (BPOE; 1867), the Fraternal Order of Eagles (FOE; 1898), the Knights of Columbus (K of C; 1882), the Modern Woodmen of America (MWA; 1883), and the Order of Patrons of Husbandry (POH; 1867), also known as "The Grange."

There were several reasons for the sudden popularity of fraternal organizations. First, a perceived "feminization" of the nation's Protestant churches, where women typically made up two-thirds of the membership, led many men to seek a homosocial spiritual community through the ritual and discipline of fraternal lodge life. Similarly, the growing mother-centered nature of the middle-class Victorian home left men seeking all-male social spaces outside it. Middle-class men also experienced a changing status in the modernizing workplace due to the growing mechanization of work and an influx of immigrants into working-class professions, fostering among them a desire for places of security, stasis, and refuge.

Lodge activities were essential to fostering particular notions of masculinity. The fact that lodges were both strictly homosocial and class- and race-based suggests that members defined their masculine identities in opposition to men of different races and classes. Lodges and their rituals, which took form in the nineteenth century and remained largely unchanged thereafter, provided a way to separate members from the outside world, establishing a secular religion free from the influence of women and the bustle of the competitive economic marketplace. Sworn to secret oaths to maintain the separation between lodge and home, and distanced from domestic life by changing work patterns, members constructed their lodges as a fictive second home and family in which they imagined themselves as brothers and where they could socialize and indulge themselves in drink, conversation, and revelry free from the prying eyes of their wives and families. By recreating the home, but simultaneously emptying it of femininity, men could remasculinize this traditionally feminine sphere without disrupting actual domestic life. Additionally, since the white middle-class "cult of domesticity" had situated morality within the sphere of women, lodge life gave men a place to create and exercise their own moral code based upon allegiance to fellow members, loyalty, trust, and self-discipline. They did this by maintaining lodge secrets and seeking advancement through the various membership levels.

Not all facets of lodge life promoted ideologies of masculinity grounded in elaborate initiation rituals, promises of exclusivity, and separation from the home and the larger society. There were more practical reasons for the lodges' appeal as well. Many lodges grew, for example, by providing death benefits for their members, anticipating the modern insurance industry. Thus, men could use lodge membership in order to fulfill their roles as family providers.

The aftermath of the Civil War furthered men's attraction to fraternal orders. The war, which had pitted "brother against brother," wreaked havoc on the nation and its sense of itself as a confraternity (united group) of citizen subjects. As a result, many men viewed the organizations' elaborate initiation rituals as a means for metaphorically reconstituting national and familial ties. Furthermore, the death and widow's benefits offered by many organizations became increasingly important following the Civil War.

By the late nineteenth century, women began lobbying their husbands for information about lodge life, and they sometimes petitioned for membership. This development aroused considerable anxiety among members, who sensed a threat to the male homosociality they deemed fundamental to fraternalism. Lodge men responded by creating associated women's clubs—such as the Elks' Emblem Club, the Masons' Order of the Eastern Star, and the Knights of Columbus's Daughters of Isabella—while maintaining male-only membership policies and a strict gender hierarchy. Men's and women's activities and meetings remained separate, and the women's orders were usually under the direct control of the men's organizations. These strategies perpetuated male-only realms distinct from the home and preserved perceived differences between masculine and feminine realms.

Race and Fraternalism

The close association white lodge members drew between homosociality, lodge membership, whiteness, and masculine identity was especially apparent in their practice of excluding social elements they deemed "other" (inferior) to white masculine identity. White fraternal lodges refused to admit African-American men and resisted attempts to integrate their organizations. White Masons, for example, regard Prince Hall (Black) Freemasonry as illegitimate despite a charter from the Grand Lodge of England and a history dating to 1775. Similarly, while the Independent Order of Good Samaritans and Daughters of Samaria accepted black members alongside whites when it was founded in 1874, white members fled the organization when the membership elected a black National Grand Sire at the 1877 convention.

Perhaps the most emphatic attempt by a fraternal organization to associate masculinity with whiteness was that of the Ku Klux Klan, founded in 1866 in the South during Reconstruction. Modeling its rituals on those of Freemasonry, it was historically dedicated to asserting an aggressive yet defensive pride in white manhood, and to keeping African Americans from exercising their constitutional rights. The Klan, in both its late-nineteenth-century and early-twentieth-century guises, promoted chivalric southern white manhood while portraying African-American men as unmanly sexual predators.

African Americans responded to their exclusion from white fraternal orders by establishing their own organizations, such as the Improved Benevolent and Protective Order of Elks of the World (1897), Grand United Order of Odd Fellows in America (1843), and Knights of Pythias of North America, Europe, Asia, and Africa (1869). As with white fraternal orders, black organizations constructed racially specific male identities among members. While most black orders embraced the same middle-class values of temperance, fidelity, and discipline as did the white orders, they also asserted the authenticity and uniqueness of their orders, fostered pride in African-American identity, and emphasized the revolutionary potential of black men fraternally bound to each other.

The Twentieth Century

Membership in fraternal organizations grew during the early twentieth century and peaked during the 1920s and 1930s. But they began to decline thereafter. Some of the reasons for this development—the 1929 onset of economic depression, the advent of the private insurance industry, the rise of men's service clubs (such as Lions, Kiwanis, and Rotary), and the growing availability of such alternative entertainments as radio, movies, and television—had little to do with issues of masculinity per se. But men did increasingly turn to other settings in which to define their manhood. New emphases on paternal involvement in domestic life led many men to spend more of their leisure time with their families. Furthermore, the experiences of fraternal interdependence and discipline that had attracted men to fraternal organizations were increasingly available in gender-segregated workplaces and in professional and recreational sports leagues. These new social spaces for fostering manhood made fraternal ritual seem increasingly archaic. Similarly, military service during the two world wars provided men with a powerful source of fraternal camaraderie, ritual, and discipline—beside which the outlandish rituals of fraternal organizations paled.

In response to declining interest, fraternal organizations sought greater interaction with the outside world during the latter half of the twentieth century, becoming involved in various charities and supporting children's causes, medical research, and scholarships. Thus, lodge membership effectively moved away from exclusive and secretive forms of masculinity to embrace styles of manhood grounded in benevolence and public service.

Conclusion

In the twenty-first century, fraternal organizations find themselves short of active members, unable to recruit new ones, and increasingly unable to maintain their once-elaborate lodges, saddled as they are with reputations for fostering outmoded notions of masculinity based on exclusivity and secrecy. Yet historically they have been pivotal in the lives of countless American men. Fraternal organizations offered men refuge during times when social roles for men were being revised due to rising industrialization, the burgeoning women's movement, and the influx of immigrants into the nation's cities. In the twenty-first century, many Americans find it difficult to take seriously the names of these groups, their elaborate costumes, and their arcane rituals, but fraternal organizations have been important to the social and cultural history of American masculinity.

BIBLIOGRAPHY

Carnes, Mark C. *Secret Ritual and Manhood in Victorian America.* New Haven, Conn.: Yale University Press, 1989.

Clawson, Mary Ann. *Constructing Brotherhood: Class, Gender, and Fraternalism.* Princeton, N.J.: Princeton University Press, 1989.

Dumenil, Lynn. *Freemasonry and American Culture, 1880–1930.* Princeton, N.J.: Princeton University Press, 1984.

Gist, Noel P. "Secret Societies: A Cultural Study of Fraternalism in the United States." *The University of Missouri Studies: A Quarterly of Research* 15, no. 4 (October 1, 1940): 9–176.

Harwood, W. S. "Secret Societies in America." *North American Review* 68 (May 1897): 617–624.

Palmer, Edward Nelson. "Negro Secret Societies." *Social Forces* 23 (December 1944): 207–212.

Stevens, Albert C. *The Cyclopædia of Fraternities.* 1896. Reprint, New York: E. B. Treat, 1907.

FURTHER READING

Ferguson, Charles W. *Fifty Million Brothers: A Panorama of American Lodges and Clubs.* New York: Farrar & Rinehart, 1937.

Muraskin, William A. *Middle-Class Blacks in a White Society: Prince Hall Freemasonry in America.* Berkeley: University of California Press, 1975.

Schmidt, Alvin J. *Fraternal Organizations.* Vol. 3 of *The Greenwood Encyclopedia of American Institutions.* Westport, Conn.: Greenwood Press, 1980.

Whalen, William J. *Handbook of Secret Organizations.* Milwaukee, Wis.: Bruce Publishing, 1966.

Williams, Loretta J. *Black Freemasonry and Middle-Class Realities.* Columbia: University of Missouri Press, 1980.

RELATED ENTRIES

Cult of Domesticity; Fraternities; Male Friendship; Men's Clubs; Men's Movements; Middle-Class Manhood; Reform Movements; Religion and Spirituality; Whiteness; White Supremacism

—*Matthew R. Davis*

FRATERNITIES

Social fraternities, quasi-secret organizations often found on college and university campuses, provide social, personal, and service opportunities for young men. Fraternities, according to the principles espoused by members, allow men to forge friendships and struggle into manhood under the guiding principles of moral integrity, honesty, and loyalty to the bonds of brotherhood. Over the years, however, they have often faced criticism for encouraging undesirable masculine behaviors, including elitism toward nonmembers, hazing (often dangerous initiation rituals) of new members, and a fun-loving social life that has sometimes bordered on decadence.

Phi Beta Kappa, organized in December 1776 at The College of William and Mary in Virginia, was the nation's first Greek-letter fraternity. Although Phi Beta Kappa ultimately became America's most renowned academic honor society for undergraduates, it established a model soon adopted by other purely social fraternal organizations. By the 1820s and 1830s, college men covertly developed regionally isolated fraternities—often meeting in members' dormitory rooms—to forge male friendships and encourage homosocial activities outside of, and in conscious opposition to, the administrative regulation of student life and the humdrum of academic recitation. The Civil War crippled fraternity life as students, especially in the South, exited classrooms for the battlefield. The prolonged and financially disruptive war undermined the practice of fraternity rituals and led to the demise of several Greek-letter organizations.

Fraternities expanded dramatically from the 1890s to the 1920s. College students were not alone in this rush to fraternalism, as hundreds of thousands of American men, anxious about the perceived female influence in American culture and experiencing what some historians have termed a "crisis of masculinity," joined all types of societies. Although fraternities maintained secret rituals, they constructed residential lodges for members, often in very prominent spaces. The fraternity house provided a visible symbol of prestige, allowed for greater independence, and encouraged the development of government and administrative skills. The fraternity man increasingly mirrored the businessman of America's growing corporate world—an aggressive and purposeful fellow who viewed membership as a possible pathway to success. Fraternities also sought to encourage manliness in members through all-male drinking and sports.

The rise of racial segregation, the growth of immigration, and the escalating number of women in college contributed to the complexity and proliferation of fraternities in the late nineteenth and early twentieth centuries. For white males, fraternity membership increasingly became a way to identify American manhood with whiteness and Protestantism, and many fraternities utilized racial and religious discrimination to restrict membership to Anglo-Saxon Protestants. Racial and religious minorities, prevented from joining old-line fraternities, soon formed their own, through which they expressed and articulated racially and ethnically grounded masculine identities. As college enrollment grew more diverse, fraternities, ever protective of their membership, became more exclusive. However, all fraternities used their prestige and popularity to increase heterosocial mingling on campus during the Jazz Age of the 1920s.

Greater fraternity exclusivity tended to exacerbate class division on campus. Fraternities attracted participants with the monetary resources for membership fees and social outings, distinguishing them from financially less fortunate peers. In the 1890s, fraternities initiated and controlled numerous campus activities, such as dances, proms, intramural athletics, and sponsorship of yearbooks and literary magazines. Fraternity men identified themselves as "Greeks," associating their manliness with a cultured and civilized historical past and berating their nonfraternity classmates as less manly "barbarians." In politics, Populist leaders attacked the elitism of many state colleges and their fraternities, culminating in the abolition of the fraternity system in South Carolina in 1893, in Arkansas in 1901, and in Mississippi in 1912.

Rushing, pledging, and joining fraternities epitomized the ultimate rite of passage for thousands of American men. Rituals of initiation often reflected the recapitulation theories of late-nineteenth-century psychologist and educational reformer Granville Stanley Hall. While most observers viewed initiation rituals as silly hijinks, critics denounced them as excessively violent and hypermasculine. Hazing, widespread among students throughout the late nineteenth and early twentieth centuries, faced greater scrutiny in the early 1930s amid rising concerns over the social embarrassment and needless deaths it produced. Despite calls for reform, however, many fraternity members and alumni defended hazing as a means to prove one's manhood. Hazing not only offered the potential fulfillment of manhood while enduring potentially dangerous physical tests, but also carried the possible exposure of sexual inadequacy and weakness. Although illegal in many states and banned by many fraternity policies, hazing continued into the early twenty-first century to lure young men into dangerous acts of bravado to prove their toughness. Many fraternity organizations responded by attempting to reframe public perception; they stressed their encouragement of civic-minded manhood through volunteer and philanthropic activities, symbolically refashioning "Hell Week" into "Help Week."

Fraternity membership slowed from the Depression through World War II, but exploded after the war as the G.I. Bill prompted thousands of men to head to college. The gritty experience of veterans, coupled with their older age, led them to question fraternity traditions and rituals. In the late 1940s, veterans helped integrate fraternities at several northeastern colleges by removing racial and religious discriminatory clauses. In 1948, Thomas Gibbs, an African-American student at Amherst College in Massachusetts, successfully pledged Phi Kappa Psi fraternity against the wishes of the national fraternity leadership, opening the door for greater flexibility in membership choice.

Clean-cut fraternity men of the 1950s presented an image of conformity, but fraternities participated in the growing currents of rebellion characteristic of the period. Many fraternity men adopted Hugh Hefner's hedonistic pursuit of a playboy culture, defining manliness in terms of freewheeling sexuality rather than traditional domesticity. African-American fraternity members, meanwhile, asserted a racially-based notion of manhood through support for civil rights advances and participation in demonstrations. Racial and religious discrimination officially continued in numerous fraternities until passage of the 1964 Civil Rights Act. That same year, the U.S. education commissioner, Francis Keppel, demanded that universities end discrimination in all of their functions in order for the college to receive federal funding. Colleges and universities responded by requiring official statements of nondiscrimination from all campus organizations, including fraternities. Despite the end of de jure segregation, de facto segregation continued unabated, and fraternities continued to foster racially and ethnically specific models of masculinity.

In the late 1960s, the Vietnam War, the Sexual Revolution, and the growth of feminism, aided in part by the abandonment of *in loco parentis* (in which the institution acts in the

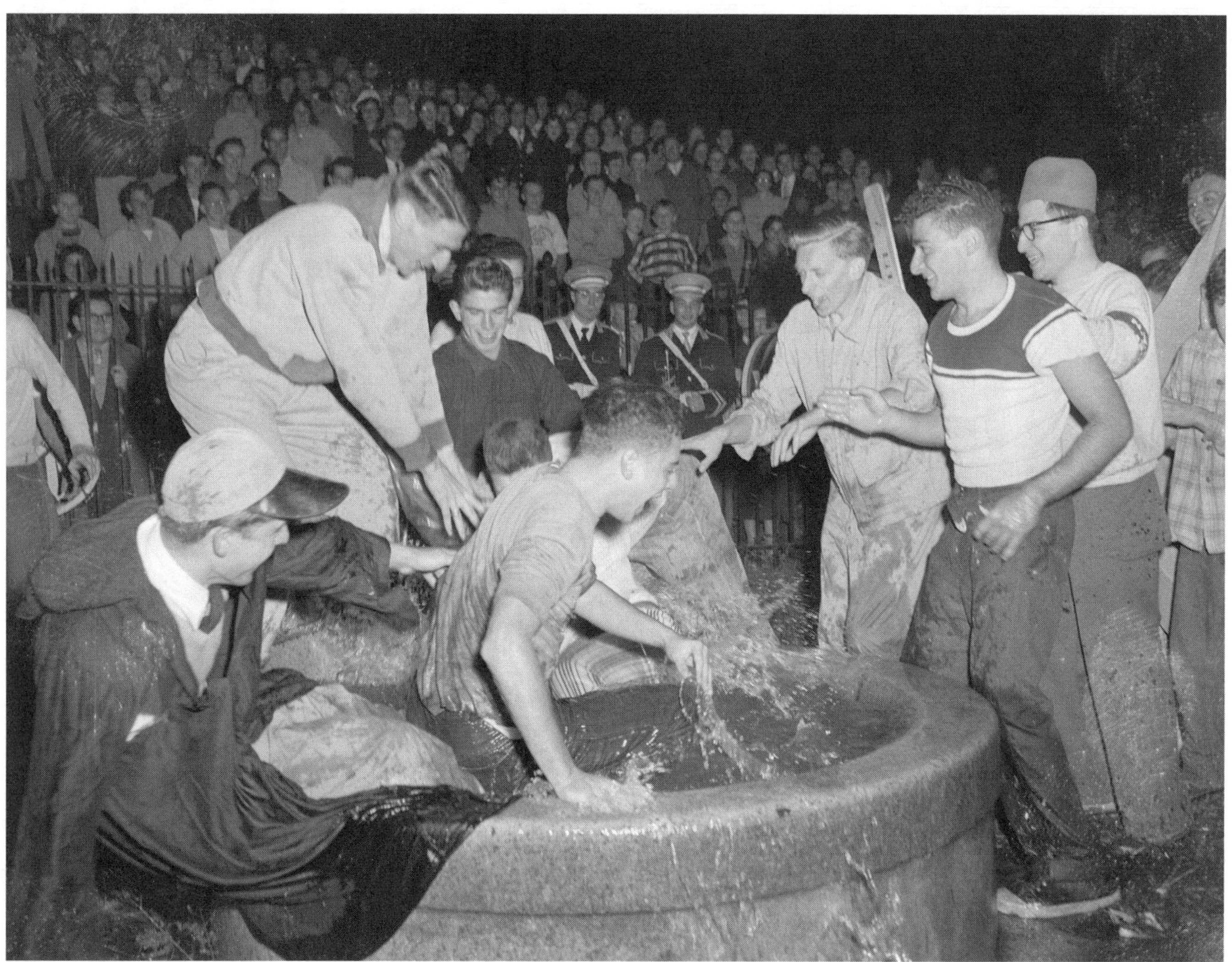

Through fraternity membership, which expanded along with university education in the late nineteenth and early twentieth centuries, young men have developed the administrative skills necessary for success in a corporate society and, as shown in this 1951 photograph, forged bonds of friendship through homosocial revelry. (© Bettmann/Corbis)

place of students' parents), eroded fraternity dominance in campus social affairs. Some critics reiterated charges identifying fraternity life with an antisocial hypermasculinity while others looked at the intimate brotherhood promoted by fraternities as a potential harbinger of homosexuality. Most fraternities responded to the latter threat by remaining unflinchingly traditional with regards to expectations for manly, heterosexual behavior—an image solidified by National Lampoon's 1978 film, *Animal House*. Yet such practices perpetuated charges of racism, sexism, and misogyny that continue to emerge with regularity. During the late twentieth and early twenty-first centuries, many fraternities sought to correct this unfavorable image by promoting racial, religious, and sexual tolerance. Despite negative publicity, fraternities continue to offer men the security of same-sex friendship, leadership development, and social engagement.

BIBLIOGRAPHY

Anson, Jack L., and Robert F. Marchesani, Jr., eds. *Baird's Manual of American College Fraternities*. 20th ed. Indianapolis, Ind.: Baird's Manual Foundation, 1991.

Fass, Paula. *The Damned and the Beautiful: American Youth in the 1920s*. New York: Oxford University Press, 1977.

Johnson, Clyde Sanfred. *Fraternities In Our Colleges*. New York: National Interfraternity Foundation, 1972.

Nuwer, Hank. *Wrongs of Passage: Fraternities, Sororities, Hazing, and Binge Drinking*. Bloomington: Indiana University Press, 1999.

Ross, Lawrence C., Jr. *The Divine Nine: The History of African American Fraternities and Sororities*. New York: Kensington Books, 2000.

FURTHER READING

Carnes, Mark C. *Secret Ritual and Manhood in Victorian America*. New Haven, Conn.: Yale University Press, 1989.

Horowitz, Helen Lefkowitz. *Campus Life: Undergraduate Cultures from the End of the Eighteenth Century to the Present.* Chicago: University of Chicago Press, 1988.

Lee, Alfred McClung. *Fraternities without Brotherhood: A Study of Prejudice on the American Campus.* Boston: Beacon Press, 1955.

Windmeyer, Shane L., and Pamela W. Freeman, eds. *Out on Fraternity Row: Personal Accounts of Being Gay in a College Fraternity.* Los Angeles: Alyson Books, 1998.

Related Entries

Adolescence; African-American Manhood; Alcohol; Brotherhood; Education; Fraternal Organizations; Hall, Granville Stanley; Male Friendship; Men's Clubs; Nativism; *Playboy* Magazine; Sports; White Supremacism; Youth

—*Anthony W. James*

Freudian Psychoanalytic Theory

Ever since the American psychologist Granville Stanley Hall invited the Austrian neurologist Sigmund Freud to deliver a series of lectures at Clark University in 1909, Freudian psychoanalytic theory has had an enormous impact on American understandings of gender and sexuality. Freudian theory has influenced conceptions of masculinity in the United States by emphasizing male heterosexual identity as a social construction maintained through the control of repressed impulses and homosexual desires. In early works such as *The Interpretation of Dreams* (1900), Freud posited the crucial role played by the unconscious mind and repression in the formation of subjectivity. In *Three Essays on the Theory of Sexuality* (1905), he made the groundbreaking claim that gender—far from an innate or inevitable consequence of biological sex—was the precarious product of a complex psychic and social process, fraught with anxiety and contradiction. While Freud viewed such a process as an essential attribute of civilization, he nonetheless emphasized the unstable, conflicted, and provisional nature of the sexual identity resulting from it. Many of Freud's assertions were considered scandalous in the United States at the time, offending Victorian propriety in their insistence upon the role of infantile sexuality and their rejection of the Victorian emphasis on the strict regulation of sexual impulses as essential to mental health.

Freud's theory of male sexual identity revolves around: (1) the Oedipus complex, and (2) the castration complex to which the Oedipus complex gives rise, and through which it is ultimately resolved. According to the theory of the Oedipus complex, the child's first love object is its mother, who through acts of feeding and caretaking provides the child with its earliest bodily pleasures and satisfactions. In the case of a boy, this early desire for the mother—whom he recognizes as "belonging to" the father in some sense—is threatened by fears of castration at the hands of the father, his rival. These fears are instigated by the boy's apprehension of anatomical sexual difference and his assumption that women—lacking the penis that he values so highly—have been castrated. Anxieties over real or imagined threats of castration lead the boy to relinquish his desire for the mother and to content himself instead with a future substitute for her. The boy's rivalry with the father, who represents the cultural authority of patriarchy, is subsumed by an intensified identification with him. This turn toward an identification with the father and the repression of the early desire for the mother pave the way for the boy's heterosexual identity. The paternal identification, and the prohibition against incest on which it is founded, provides the basis for the formation of the boy's superego—the psychical agency that censors and judges, and to which Freud attributed men's supposedly superior ethical sense.

Although Freud postulated the theoretical possibility of a "positive" resolution of the Oedipus complex along heterosexual lines—in which the boy comes to identify with members of his own sex and desire members of the opposite sex—he asserted that a complete positive resolution of the complex rarely, if ever, occurs. According to Freud, masculine and feminine traits, active and passive inclinations, and homosexual and heterosexual object choices are universal and ongoing elements of psychic life and do not correspond in any predetermined way to biological males or females. As outlined in Freud's "Analysis of a Phobia in a Five-Year-Old Boy" (1909), children are originally endowed with a fluid bisexuality comprised of active and passive aims and oriented toward both male and female objects. Heterosexual masculinity itself is founded upon the repression of an early homosexual desire for the father and the repudiation of an identification with the mother, and is maintained through the ongoing repression of homosexual attachments and passive or feminine identifications.

From the beginning, Freud's theories inspired both radical and socially conservative views in the United States, appealing to those who rejected dominant conventions of gender and sexuality, as well as those espousing the necessity of social conformity. Although Freud's theories initially attracted American intellectuals and artists interested in rebelling against restrictive Victorian sexual mores, as Freudian theory was gradually instituted within American psychiatry its more radical implications were increasingly ignored. Socially conservative applications of

Freudian theory to conceptions of masculinity were particularly prevalent after World War II, a period that saw the peak of popular Freudian revisionism in the United States. The war itself helped to bring psychoanalytic theory further into mainstream American culture, as psychoanalysts were enlisted to aid in the military's psychological screening of young recruits. This process was intended to forestall an outbreak of mass male hysteria similar to the "shell shock" epidemic of World War I by weeding out young men deemed psychologically unfit for military service.

During World War II and the Cold War, clinicians, scholars, popular commentators, and Hollywood films employed Freudian concepts and terminology to emphasize the necessity of traditional gender roles, to pathologize homosexuality as the result of psychosexual immaturity, and to diagnose a general "crisis" of American masculinity. Although Freud himself focused primarily on the significance of the role of the father, popular Freudianism in the United States became obsessed with the issue of motherhood. Particularly influential was the concept of "momism" forwarded by Philip Wylie in his best-selling *Generation of Vipers* (1942) and echoed in such influential texts as psychiatrist Edward Strecker's *Their Mothers' Sons* (1946). These men warned against the pernicious effects of domineering or over-protective mothers on their sons, and they held mothers responsible for such diverse social phenomena as male juvenile delinquency, alcoholism, and homosexuality, all of which were held to be direct threats to American national identity and security.

Alongside its role in the maintenance of dominant gender ideology, Freudian psychoanalytic theory has played a part in a wide range of radical intellectual movements of the twentieth century, and also given rise to many influential theoretical offspring (such as object-relations, Jungian, and Lacanian theories). Those insights of Freudian theory that American clinical practitioners, social commentators, and popular culture have tended to overlook have inspired feminist and queer theorists, who have been attracted to Freud's denaturalization of gender identity as a biologically determined essence. These theorists have been interested in analyzing the relationship between social institutions and individual psychosexual development, and they have also been inclined to challenge conventional definitions of masculinity. Freudian theory has been criticized for its focus on male subjectivity, lack of attention to different historical and cultural contexts, and tendency to re-assert traditional gender identities, even as it throws them into question. Nonetheless, even as critical thinkers continue to struggle with it and argue over it, Freudian psychoanalytic theory continues to provide a valuable set of analytical tools for the investigation of masculinity and male sexuality as socially constructed, rather than biologically determined, categories of identity.

Bibliography

Brenkman, John. *Straight Male Modern: A Cultural Critique of Psychoanalysis.* New York: Routledge, 1993.

Connell, R. W. "Psychoanalysis on Masculinity." In *Theorizing Masculinities,* edited by Harry Brod and Michael Kaufman. Thousand Oaks, Calif.: Sage, 1994.

Freud, Sigmund. *Three Essays on the Theory of Sexuality.* 1905. Reprint, New York: Basic Books, 1962.

———. *Three Case Histories.* New York: Macmillan, 1963.

Hale, Nathan G., Jr. *Freud and the Americans: The Beginnings of Psychoanalysis in the United States, 1876–1917.* New York: Oxford University Press, 1971.

———. *The Rise and Crisis of Psychoanalysis in the United States: Freud and the Americans, 1917–1985.* New York: Oxford University Press, 1995.

Laplanche, J., and J. B. Pontalis. *The Language of Psycho-Analysis.* Translated by Donald Nicholson-Smith. New York: Norton, 1973.

Segal, Lynne. *Slow Motion: Changing Masculinities, Changing Men.* New Brunswick, N.J.: Rutgers University Press, 1990.

Further Reading

Buhle, Mari Jo. *Feminism and Its Discontents: A Century of Struggle With Psychoanalysis.* Cambridge, Mass.: Harvard University Press, 1998.

Freud, Sigmund. *The Interpretation of Dreams.* 1900. Reprint, translated by Joyce Crick. New York: Oxford University Press, 1999.

Frosh, Stephen. *Sexual Difference: Masculinity and Psychoanalysis.* London: Routledge, 1994.

———. *For and Against Psychoanalysis.* London: Routledge, 1997.

———. *The Politics of Psychoanalysis: An Introduction to Freudian and Post-Freudian Theory.* New York: New York University Press, 1999.

Minsky, Rosalind. *Psychoanalysis and Gender: An Introductory Reader.* London: Routledge, 1996.

———. *Psychoanalysis and Culture: Contemporary States of Mind.* New Brunswick, N.J.: Rutgers University Press, 1998.

Mitchell, Juliet. *Psychoanalysis and Feminism.* New York: Pantheon Books, 1974.

Related Entries

Bisexuality; Cold War; Crisis of Masculinity; Hall, Granville Stanley; Heterosexuality; Homosexuality; Momism; Mother–Son Relationships; Nuclear Family; Patriarchy; Victorian Era; World War II

—*Jonna Eagle*

Gambling

Gambling has always been a part of American life, and attitudes about gambling have reflected long-standing disagreements over the meaning of manhood in American society. While some have stressed a sober version of manhood and condemned betting as antithetical to the values of hard work, steady achievement, and familial and religious responsibility; others have linked masculinity with risk-taking and all-male camaraderie and celebrated any man willing to wager a small fortune in the face of long odds.

Puritan leaders in colonial New England condemned gambling as contradictory to their socially prescribed work ethic and the Sabbatarian principles of piety and self-sacrifice that they associated with manhood. In the livelier Anglican South, however, the raucous and competitive flavor of the predominately male region provided a fertile environment for wagering on cockfights, bare-knuckle boxing, and horse racing. Through high-stakes betting, southern gentlemen asserted a definition of manliness that distinguished them from poor whites and black slaves. Since only the gentry had the time and money to risk outrageous amounts on a quarter-horse race, gambling was a public articulation of their financial independence, fierce competitiveness, and personal honor.

These opposing perspectives on gambling and manhood were reinforced and infused with an even stronger class dimension during the nineteenth-century market revolution. Members of the growing middle class viewed gambling as morally problematic in a capitalist society that valued the slow, steady, and rational accumulation of capital. Many middle-class Americans considered gambling evil because it produced nothing but easy earnings and addiction, and they viewed the gambler as an unmanly character who pursued profit but rejected hard work. Furthermore, because republican ideology linked manhood with a civic-minded willingness to sacrifice personal interests in the name of the common good, many Americans condemned the massive fortunes of commodities traders and land dealers as the dishonest gains of men who embodied antirepublican selfishness. Capitalist speculators responded by touting themselves as virtuous, business-minded Americans whose bold monetary risks bespoke strength of character and furthered industrial progress. Millionaires like the steel magnate Andrew Carnegie blurred the distinctions between hard work and speculative gain and came to be seen as the personification of the cherished masculine archetype, the self-made man.

For working-class men, who had little autonomy in the nineteenth-century industrial workplace, gambling served as a declaration of financial independence and mocked the middle-class standard of manhood based on thrift and sobriety. Equally important, gambling was one of the primary leisure activities around which all-male sociability coalesced. Men found daily confirmation of their masculinity in saloons, billiard parlors, and other environments that excluded women and allowed bachelors and married men alike to revel in shared drinks and friendly wagers. Gambling's most fertile ground was the western frontier. Removed from the emotional comforts of home, frontiersmen forged bonds in a common culture that celebrated risk-taking as the quintessential masculine activity. Gold-seeking "forty-niners" in California bet on everything from bull-and-bear fights to jumping frogs. Capitalists searching for silver in Comstock, Nevada, wagered personal fortunes in pursuit of the mother lode, and men toiling in mines and building the railroads risked life and limb by day, and their earnings in games of chance at night.

In the twentieth century, as the relationship between hard work and financial success became increasingly uncertain and older capitalist constructions of manhood seemed problematic, gambling remained a tonic for men seeking alternative ways to confirm their manliness. For example, as African Americans migrated from southern towns to northern cities in the century's early decades, informal urban lotteries known as policy or numbers provided young black men with a means to escape emasculating dependency on low-wage employment and earn both capital and prestige. For the street-smart hustler, it was the ability to make money while skillfully avoiding physical labor that was the mark of a real man.

Yet men ceased to hold exclusive claims on gambling by midcentury. Today, Americans of both sexes flock to Las Vegas, a post–World War II entertainment boomtown where the dream of easy money has become a product consumed by men and women alike. Underground gambling activities like dog fighting, however, remain mostly male affairs and serve as highly competitive arenas in which a bettor's masculinity is reflected in both his willingness to wager and the "gameness" of the dog he favors. Although many condemn these blood sports as a social problem, participants see the dog pit as one of the few remaining social arenas fostering male solidarity, and as an environment where the masculine traits of aggressiveness and competitiveness are still valued.

Not merely a recreational pastime, gambling has reflected significant differences in opinion about what it means to be a "real man" in American society. Whether gambling denotes an unmanly lack of self-control, or signals a cool, manly attachment to the proverb "nothing ventured, nothing gained," it has provided an accessible mix of capitalist and communal values. In either case, throughout American history, courting "Lady Luck" has been primarily a male endeavor.

Bibliography

Breen, Timothy H. "Horses and Gentlemen: The Cultural Significance of Gambling Among the Gentry in Virginia." *William and Mary Quarterly* 34 (April 1977): 329–47.

Chudacoff, Howard. *The Age of the Bachelor: Creating an American Subculture.* Princeton, N.J.: Princeton University Press, 1999.

Fabian, Ann. *Card Sharps and Bucket Shops: Gambling in Nineteenth-Century America.* New York: Routledge, 1999.

Halttunen, Karen. *Confidence Men and Painted Women: A Study of Middle-Class Culture in America, 1830–1870.* New Haven, Conn.: Yale University Press, 1982.

Powers, Madelon. *Faces Along the Bar: Lore and Order in the Workingman's Saloon, 1870–1920.* Chicago: University of Chicago Press, 1998.

Valentine, Bettylou. *Hustling and Other Hard Work: Life Styles in the Ghetto.* New York: Free Press, 1978.

Further Reading

Asbury, Herbert. *Sucker's Progress: An Informal History of Gambling in America from the Colonies to Canfield.* New York: Dodd, Mead, 1938.

Davies, Richard O., and Richard G. Abram. *Betting the Line: Sports Wagering in American Life.* Columbus: Ohio State University Press, 2001.

Findlay, John M. *People of Chance: Gambling in American Society from Jamestown to Las Vegas.* New York: Oxford University Press, 1986.

Related Entries

African-American Manhood; Alcohol; Bachelorhood; Boxing; Breadwinner Role; California Gold Rush; Capitalism; Character; Class; Individualism; Leisure; Market Revolution; Middle-Class Manhood; Religion and Spirituality; Self-Control; Self-Made Man; Sports; Victorian Era; Western Frontier; Working-Class Manhood

—*Matthew Andrews*

Gangs

As one of the fundamental social units of the American male, gangs have comprised everything from a loose-knit group of friends gathered at a street corner to a collection of individuals banded together in a hierarchical, closed unit seeking mutual protection and monetary gain. Although the term gang has often been used to denote a social problem associated with deviance and violence, throughout American history gang membership has provided young men excluded from meaningful labor, social mobility, and other traditional expressions of male achievement with the opportunity to win respect and present a tough, honor-based, masculine identity.

White youth gangs, which existed in seaboard cities at the inception of the American republic, increased in numbers and influence during the early-nineteenth-century market revolution. During this period the old craftwork system based on apprenticeship and intergenerational fellowship faded. Gang camaraderie became a surrogate for workplace fraternity and gave young men an organizational affiliation and a collective masculine identity crafted not on the job, but in saloons, commercial amusements, and the streets.

Gangs flourished in immigrant and working-class urban areas like New York's Bowery and Five Points districts, and gang identity could coalesce around ethnic affiliation (the Irish Dead Rabbits), territory (the Bowery B'hoys), or political passions such as nativism (the True Blue Americans). Tough urban spaces fostered what the historian Sean Wilentz called "republicanism of the streets" (Wilentz, 263)—an aggressive public culture marked by honor-based competitiveness and strident antiauthoritarianism. By defiantly resisting the police and combating rival gangs in battles over public space, gang members demonstrated individual prowess and strengthened group bonds.

The competitive street culture of the nineteenth-century urban gang was founded not only on masculinity, but on whiteness as well. In a world of truculent racism, gangs of European immigrants, most notably the Irish, used violence against free blacks as a means of cultural assimilation and as a public declaration of racial belonging. This violence took its most lethal expression in the New York Draft Riots of 1863. Gang membership also connected young men to the all-male world of urban politics. Youth gangs served as foot soldiers for the ward boss, and politicians provided the rent for a gang's headquarters in exchange for stuffed ballot boxes and election-day voter intimidation.

Even though the delinquent ways of street gangs were anathema to the Victorian-era middle-class creed of sober and industrious manhood, turn-of-the-century concerns that urban-industrial overcivilization threatened to feminize American youth prompted many social commentators to hail the youth gang as a masculinizing tonic. Educators like Granville Stanley Hall bemoaned a generation of young boys under the influence of female sentimentality, and J. Adam Puffer, in his book *The Boy and His Gang* (1912), suggested that gang membership was a healthy alternative for boys badly in need of male camaraderie and masculine role models.

While youth street gangs served as a basic social unit for boys transitioning from adolescence to manhood, adult gangs mirrored contemporary corporate structures, organizing along hierarchical lines and promising economic aggrandizement and social status to men who pledged their loyalty. During the Prohibition era, organized crime provided adult gangsters with avenues of rapid social mobility and access to nice homes, fancy cars, and other symbols of bourgeois respectability. When the Great Depression severely undermined the ability of many working men to earn a decent wage, the gangster's participation in the recession-proof illicit economy allowed him to continue in the masculine role of family breadwinner. Organized gangs of European ethnics, such as the Italian-American *Mafia*, and monumental crime figures like Chicago mob boss Al Capone were community benefactors and successful businessmen who embodied an underworld version of the heroic self-made man.

The number of youth street gangs surged in the years following World War II as cities like New York were radically transformed by the in-migration of large numbers of African Americans and Puerto Ricans. With rising competition for jobs on the docks and in the construction trade, many young men of color found themselves disinherited from the masculinized shop-floor culture that had nurtured the identities of previous generations of city men. For adolescent males growing up in segregated ethnic enclaves and facing a future of emasculating work in the service sector, gang violence and the defense of neighborhood turf became their primary public assertions of masculine prowess, and of racial and ethnic identity.

Modern usage of the term *gang* conjures up visions of the crime-filled and violent inner city. While the exclusion of African Americans from the urban political system and the racism of all-white police forces inhibited the widespread rise of organized crime by black adults, the rapidly growing African-American urban population during World War II led to a surge in the number of black youth gangs, many of which formed as a defensive response to white violence in the schools and city streets. Political organizations like the Black Panther Party (BPP) recruited heavily from black youth gangs that shared the Panthers' emphasis on racial pride and community autonomy, and current Los Angeles street gangs like the Crips and Bloods rose from the ruins of the BPP in the 1970s and inherited the Panthers' black masculine philosophy of abject fearlessness and group unity.

Many social commentators have condemned gang members as the pathological result of weakened community structures. Taking their cue from government reports like Daniel Moynihan's *The Negro Family: The Case for National Action* (1965), some politicians and community activists hypothesize that the deleterious effects of racism and the dearth of responsible, masculine role models have prompted young African-American males to adopt an exaggerated sense of masculinity that is articulated through intransigence, callousness, and violence against women. Less critical are those who view the inner-city gang as the street-smart articulation of group cohesiveness and economic autonomy.

In the context of strident racial segregation and urban deindustrialization, street violence is one of the most effective ways for gang members to secure neighborhood-sized economic markets. A gang member is able to express his status as a hard man or "gangsta"—a nihilistic masculine figure who defiantly welcomes violent confrontation in an environment devoid of hopeful futures. Films like John Singleton's *Boyz N the Hood* (1991) and "gangsta rap" albums like Ice Cube's *Death Certificate* (1991) document the paucity of meaningful labor available to young black and Latino men eager to fulfill the masculine role of family provider. For many gang members growing up in Watts or the *barrio* of East Los Angeles, participation in the underground drug economy has been the most promising economic opportunity.

It should be noted that gangs have not been solely an inner-city phenomenon. Outlaw groups of motorcycle gangs, such as the infamous Hell's Angels, are the legacy of the wandering gangs of the nineteenth-century Western frontier—men who displayed the masculine virtues of individualism and self-sufficiency. Biker gangs proliferated in the post–World War II decades as many men flatly rejected the staid, suburban, American dream and opted for the persona of the rebellious wanderer. Anarchic insurrection of any kind is the chief masculine expression of the motorcycle gang. In the film *The Wild One* (1953), when gang leader Marlon Brando is asked what he is rebelling against, he tellingly replies, "whaddya got?"

Another nonurban type of gang, that formed by white middle-class suburban adolescents, achieved growing public notice and notoriety during the final decade of the twentieth century. Similarly spawned by dissatisfaction with suburban life, such groups depend on suburban affluence for their existence (through the consumption of gangsta rap and drugs, for example) and rebel against schools and other institutions that represent standards of middle-class suburban propriety.

For young men passing into adulthood, gang life rooted in working-class standards of honor and toughness has offered an organizational structure in which to act out the celebrated masculine role of the "tough guy" or "hard man." Whether on the Bowery of antebellum New York or in the streets of late-twentieth-century Los Angeles, gangs have provided young men alienated from masculinized labor and the social mainstream with a space of their own in which to publicly assert a defiant masculine identity forged in individual confrontation and group camaraderie.

Bibliography

Adamson, Christopher. "Defensive Localism in White and Black: A Comparative History of European-American and African-American Youth Gangs." *Ethnic and Racial Studies* 23 (March 2000): 272–298.

Kelley, Robin D. G. "Kickin' Reality, Kickin' Ballistics: 'Gangsta Rap' and Postindustrial Los Angeles." In *Race Rebels: Culture, Politics, and the Black Working Class*, edited by Robin Kelly. New York: Free Press, 1994.

Schneider, Eric C. *Vampires, Dragons, and Egyptian Kings: Youth Gangs in Postwar New York.* Princeton, N.J.: Princeton University Press, 1999.

White, Richard. "Outlaw Gangs of the Middle Border: American Social Bandits." *Western Historical Quarterly* 12 (October 1981): 387–408.

Wilentz, Sean. *Chants Democratic: New York City and the Rise of the American Working Class, 1788–1850.* New York: Oxford University Press, 1986.

Further Reading

Asbury, Herbert. *The Gangs of New York: An Informal History of the Underworld.* 1927. Reprint, New York: Thunder's Mouth Press, 2001.

Jankowski, Martín Sánchez. *Islands in the Street: Gangs and American Urban Society.* Berkeley: University of California Press, 1991.

Puffer, Joseph Adams. *The Boy and His Gang.* Boston and New York: Houghton Mifflin Company, 1912.

Ruth, David E. *Inventing the Public Enemy: The Gangster in American Culture, 1918–1934.* Chicago: University of Chicago Press, 1996.

Shakur, Sanyika. *Monster: The Autobiography of an L.A. Gang Member.* London: Pan, 1994.

Thompson, Hunter S. *Hell's Angels: A Strange and Terrible Saga.* New York: Modern Library, 1999.

Related Entries

Adolescence; African-American Manhood; American Dream; Black Panther Party; Boyhood; Brando, Marlon; Brotherhood; Class; Ethnicity; Great Depression; Immigration; Individualism; Industrialization; Irish-American Manhood; Italian-American Manhood; Juvenile Delinquency; Latino Manhood; Market Revolution; Race; Self-Made Man; Urbanization; Western Frontier; Whiteness; Work; Working-Class Manhood; Youth

—Matthew Andrews

Gangsters

The figure of the gangster first appeared in news reports of the 1920s, and has since grown to heroic proportions, spurred in large part by a major presence in films and literature. Through powerful mass media exposure, the gangster image has provided guidelines on manhood and served as a cultural icon that has reflected the changing notions of masculinity in the United States.

The gangster, typically represented by a male figure, emerged in response to the evolution of corporate capitalism in the early twentieth century. Although criminal gangs had long occupied American cities, the Eighteenth Amendment (1919), which outlawed the manufacture, sale, or transportation of alcohol, and desperate poverty brought on by the Great Depression provided opportunities for individual crime leaders to emerge and thrive.

During the late 1920s and early 1930s, the exploits of gangsters such as Al Capone, John Dillinger, "Baby Face" Nelson, and "Pretty Boy" Floyd became national news, fueling fictional accounts and capturing the popular imagination. As corporate capitalism promoted consumerism and widened the gap between rich and poor, Americans became infatuated with the gangster, whose stylish dress and fancy cars demonstrated a victory over humble origins and defied the boundaries separating social classes, thus confirming the notion of the self-made man. Similarly, gangsters continued to appeal to the American public and attained folk-hero status by challenging the capitalist system through their autonomy and attainment of wealth outside of established channels. The gangster also counteracted the weakening of Victorian gender constructs by upholding traditional patriarchal authority over women through physical violence.

Representations of gangsters began to appear in American films during the late 1920s and early 1930s. Early films often portrayed gangsters as degenerate and overly feminized men, but later films recast them as men who wielded power through

Gangsters such as Al Capone became folk heroes during the Great Depression by forging an enduring American masculine style that emphasized self-made success, businesslike demeanor, lavish consumerism, fierce independence, violent pursuit of self-interest, and an unabashed flouting of the nation's social, economic, and legal systems. (© Bettmann/Corbis)

sexuality and guns. Historians have suggested that the gangster figure helped replace traditional qualities of ideal masculinity, such as honor, with traits such as violence, independence, and the ability to exploit the social system. This aspect of the gangster has captured the public imagination, especially male youths, from the 1930s into the twenty-first century.

Films such as *Little Caesar* (1930) and *Scarface* (1932) established a lasting association in popular culture between the gangster and particular ethnic groups, including Jewish, Irish, African, Asian, and—especially—Italian Americans. The cinematic images of masculinity associated with these ethnicities served to stereotype and marginalize these groups. This marginalization was amplified in the 1960s and 1970s when, amid growing feminist criticism of conventional understandings of manhood, the ethnic gangster embodied the masculine qualities under attack.

Through books such as Gay Talese's *Honor Thy Father* (1971) and William Kennedy's *Legs* (1975), and especially with the films of Francis Ford Coppola, Martin Scorsese, and Brian DePalma, the American ethnic gangster became more rounded, more thoughtful, and less inclined to act violently. These depictions represent the efforts of ethnic groups to take control of their own story, and they also reflect advances in cultural analysis made by feminist critiques of masculinity.

As African Americans began breaking down the social and economic barriers of earlier times, filmmakers began to exploit the black man in gangster films such as *Shaft* (1971) and *Black Caesar* (1973). The black gangster became a reflection of a more revolutionary figure as African Americans began making their own films and music. Rap groups like Public Enemy, NWA (Niggas with Attitude), and Capone-n-Noreaga adopted the powerful gangster pose to depict ghetto life in the 1980s and 1990s. Their "gangsta rap" was featured in gangster films such as *Colors* (1988), *New Jack City* (1991), *Boyz N the Hood* (1991) and *Menace II Society* (1993).

The gangster figure, whether a distilled version of the Italian stereotype, some imitative performer of gangsta rap, or the newly sensitized man (e.g., Tony Soprano), continues to reflect cultural perceptions of true manhood.

Bibliography

Munby, Jonathan. *Public Enemies, Public Heroes: Screening the Gangster from* Little Caesar *to* Touch of Evil. Chicago: University of Chicago Press, 1999.

Ruth, David. *Inventing the Public Enemy: The Gangster in American Culture, 1918-1934.* Chicago: University of Chicago Press, 1996.

Warshow, Robert. "The Gangsters as Tragic Hero." In *The Immediate Experience: Movies, Comics, Theater and Other Aspects of Popular Culture.* Garden City, N.Y.: Doubleday, 1962.

Yaquinto, Marilyn. *Pump 'Em Full of Lead: A Look at Gangsters on Film.* New York: Twayne, 1998.

Further Reading

Lippman, Walter. "The Underworld: A Stultified Conscience." *Forum* 85 (February 1931): 66.

Shadoin, Jack. *Dreams and Dead Ends: The American Gangster/Crime Film.* Cambridge, Mass.: Massachusetts Institute of Technology Press, 1977.

Tee Bee, S. "With the Gangsters." *Saturday Evening Post,* 26 June 1926, 54.

Related Entries

African-American Manhood; Asian-American Manhood; Consumerism; Ethnicity; Gangs; Great Depression; Heroism; Individualism; Irish-American Manhood; Italian-American Manhood; Jewish Manhood; Self-Made Man; Violence; Youth

—*Fred Gardaphe*

GAYS IN THE MILITARY

The military is a primary site for the social construction of ideas about gender and sexuality in the United States. The presence of gays in the military became a highly controversial issue in the late twentieth century, sparking a national public debate about the meaning of manhood because it represents a direct challenge to the traditional notion of the military as a strictly heterosexual institution designed to train young men in hegemonic masculinity. Supporters of the ban on gays in the military fear that their presence will contribute to a breakdown in morale and authority, which would lead to inefficient military performance.

During the late twentieth century, in the aftermath of the Sexual Revolution and the gay rights and liberation movements, American society increasingly recognized a variety of ways of being masculine. But the military assumed a discriminatory stance toward gays, defending a more traditional understanding of manhood and assuming homosexual men (and all women) to be incapable of physical toughness and martial discipline. It also assumed that the presence of women and gay men would threaten the intense homosocial bonding and heterosexual desire considered essential to military effectiveness. Because of such concerns, military culture forced gay military men to live closeted lives through much of U.S. history.

Gays have, in fact, served in the U.S. military throughout history, but not openly. In 1778 the U.S. military recruited a gay European military prodigy by the name of Baron Von Steuben to train American troops during the Revolutionary War. Benjamin Franklin believed that Steuben, despite the rumors of homosexuality, was a master of military strategy. Steuben lived up to his reputation and was instrumental in America's victory against Britain. Ironically, sixteen days after Steuben arrived, the army dismissed its first solider for homosexuality.

The nineteenth century brought other accounts of gays in the military. For example, the poet Walt Whitman recorded chronicles of his affairs with male soldiers during the Civil War. In addition, the Confederate Army had a famous gay general, Major General Patrick Ronayne Cleburne, who fell in love with his assistant, Captain Irving Ashby Buck. Despite repeated reports of homosexual relationships during the Civil War and various wars against Indian nations in the nineteenth century, the U.S. military did not aggressively pursue the rumors of gays in the military.

As homosexuality became increasingly stigmatized in American culture during the late nineteenth century, official military policy toward homosexuals began to change. While the U.S. military did not directly address homosexuality prior to World War I, the Articles of War of 1916 became the first official article of military regulation addressing homosexuality and sodomy as a felony. At the end of the war (in which many gay men served) Congress passed the Articles of War of 1920, which named any type of sodomy, consensual or otherwise, as an offense.

During World War II, as American officials became increasingly concerned about national toughness vis-à-vis Nazi Germany, the military treated homosexuality as a disease, employing military psychiatrists to identify and treat any homosexuals in the ranks. By 1943, formalized regulations banned homosexuals from all branches of the military. However, these regulations were malleable when periods of concern over national security required the retention of all military manpower. A research investigation conducted by the Department of Defense in 1957 led to the Crittenden Report, which concluded that gays were fit to serve in the military. The navy kept the report secret until 1976, however, when naval lawyers discovered it in Pentagon files.

During the early 1960s, the military and Federal Bureau of Investigation, led by its director J. Edgar Hoover, conducted homosexuality investigations. By October 1960, the army had initiated Project 220 and Project 440, which gathered the names of military men in San Francisco suspected of homosexual activity and investigated everyone from Central Intelligence Agency operatives to sailors and civilian employees. By 1962, Hoover was no longer able to justify these homosexuality investigations as crucial to countering national security threats and they gradually ended. The transition from a medical treatment model that encouraged integration to a policy of exclusion continued until the 1970s. In 1973 the American Psychological Association publicly declared that homosexuality was not a mental disease.

The 1970s was a pivotal period for gays in the military, for the decade witnessed two famous legal cases that challenged the ban on homosexuality in the Air Force and Navy. Although both plaintiffs, Sergeant Leonard Matlovich and Ensign Vernon Berg III, received favorable decisions in their legal battle, they eventually dropped their cases, left the military, and accepted cash settlements. During Jimmy Carter's presidency, Deputy Secretary of Defense Graham Claytor wrote a memo to the Joint Chiefs of Staff and the secretaries of the Army, Navy, and Air Force stating that "homosexuality is incompatible with military service" (Scott, xviii). Under this Department of Defense directive, anyone who engaged in homosexual behavior or made remarks suggesting that they were gay was investigated and usually discharged. Between 1980 and 1990 the U.S. military discharged an average of 1,500 service members per year under the category of "homosexuality."

Growing public acceptance of homosexuality became apparent during the 1992 presidential campaign, when Democratic candidate Bill Clinton pledged to remove the ban on gays in the military. Many gay rights advocates supported him in the hope that he would use his executive power to abolish the ban. Clinton's position aroused public opposition from such figures as Colin Powell, who was the Chairman of the Joint Chiefs of Staff at the time, and Republican senators Bob Dole and Strom Thurmond. Intense public debate over the issue led the Clinton administration to adopt the compromise measure popularly known as the "Don't Ask, Don't Tell" policy, which was drafted by Secretary of Defense Les Aspin in July 1993 and signed into law by President Clinton in November of that year. This policy prevented the military from questioning people about their sexuality, thus extending the rights of gay men to serve in the military without harassment, while instructing military personnel not to discuss their homosexuality with their employer, thus perpetuating their forced secretiveness.

Activity on the issue of gays in the military decreased in the late 1990s, and the "Don't Ask, Don't Tell" policy remained in effect into the early twenty-first century. Despite a high-profile court victory by Colonel Greta Cammermeyer, the highest-ranking U.S. military officer to challenge the policy, the military's stance on gays in the military remains a hostile one. Between March 1995 and February 1996, the Servicemembers Legal Defense Network documented 363 violations of the policy in which military personnel openly admitted that they were gay. This demonstrated that military leaders were resistant to implementing it by discharging these individuals. During periods of military conflict, the military has feigned ignorance about gays in uniform in order to keep as many soldiers available as possible. Although the military, by lifting the outright ban on gays, hinted at its ability to initiate a re-examination of gender expectations and be a chief social agent of change in contemporary society, it has remained bound by traditional definitions of masculinity in the United States.

BIBLIOGRAPHY

Anderson, Clinton W., and H. Ron Smith. "Stigma and Honor: Gay, Lesbian, and Bisexual People in the U.S. Military." In *Homosexual Issues in the Workplace,* edited by Louis Diamant. Washington, D.C.: Taylor & Francis, 1993.

Cohn, Carol. "Gays in the Military: Texts and Subtexts." In *The "Man" Question in International Relations,* edited by Marysia Zalewski and Jane Parpart. Boulder, Colo.: Westview Press, 1998.

Osburn, C. Dixon, and Michelle M. Benecke. "Conduct Unbecoming: Second Annual Report on 'Don't Ask, Don't Tell, Don't Pursue'" In *Wives and Warriors: Women and the Military in the United States and Canada,* edited by Laurie Weinstein and Christie C. White. Westport, Conn.: Bergin & Garvey, 1997.

Scott, Wilbur J., and Sandra Carson Stanley, eds. *Gays and Lesbians in the Military: Issues, Concerns, and Contrasts.* New York: Aldine De Gruyter, 1994.

Shilts, Randy. *Conduct Unbecoming: Lesbians and Gays in the U.S. Military: Vietnam To the Persian Gulf.* New York: St. Martin's, 1993.

Zeeland, Steven. *Barrack Buddies and Soldier Lovers: Dialogues with Gay Young Men in the U.S. Military.* New York: Haworth Press, 1993.

FURTHER READING

Bostdorff, Denise M. "Clinton's Characteristic Issue Management Style: Caution, Conciliation, and Conflict Avoidance in the Case of Gays in the Military." In *The Clinton Presidency: Images, Issues, and Communication Strategies,* edited by Robert E. Denton, Jr., and Rachel L. Holloway. Westport, Conn.: Praeger, 1996.

Diamond, Diane, Michael Kimmel, and Kirby Schroeder. "'What's This About a Few Good Men': Negotiating Gender in Military Education." In *Masculinities at School,* edited by Nancy Lesko. Thousand Oaks, Calif.: Sage, 2000.

Hall, Edmund. *We Can't Even March Straight: Homosexuality in the British Armed Forces.* London: Vintage, 1995.

Halley, Janet E. *Don't: A Reader's Guide to the Military's Anti-Gay Policy.* Durham, N.C.: Duke University Press, 1999.

Humphrey, Mary Ann. *My Country, My Right to Serve: Experiences of Gay Men and Women in the Military, World War II to the Present.* New York: HarperCollins, 1988.

Shawver, Lois. *And the Flag Was Still There: Straight People, Gay People, and Sexuality in the U.S. Military.* New York: Haworth Press, 1995.

Wells-Petry, Melissa. *Exclusion: Homosexuals and the Right to Serve.* Washington D.C.: Regnery Gateway, 1993.

RELATED ENTRIES

American Revolution; Civil War; Heroism; Homosexuality; Male Friendship; Militarism; Military; Patriotism; Rambo; Sexual Harassment; Vietnam War; Violence; War; Whitman, Walt; World War I; World War II

—*Michelle L. Robertson*

GILDED AGE

The Gilded Age (1873–1900) takes its name from the title of an 1873 novel by Mark Twain and Charles Dudley Warner. The social transformations that prompted Twain and Warner to characterize this period as materialistic, shallow, and corrupt also affected definitions of manliness. Amid the increasing pace and growing scale of urban industrial life, the Gilded Age witnessed the emergence of corporate and bureaucratic structures, new technologies, new forms of work, and changing career paths for men. Those who considered work, productive effort, and artisanal or entrepreneurial autonomy critical to their definitions of manliness found themselves in a social setting that no longer seemed to furnish men of different class backgrounds with a sense of achievement. The social transformations of the late nineteenth century put further pressures on men to articulate new definitions of manliness suitable to a rapidly changing social environment. Since the 1830s, the processes of urbanization, industrialization, class formation, and economic development had forced men across a range of social backgrounds to rethink concepts of male gender identity. In the late nineteenth century, these developments entered a new stage and inaugurated new articulations of manliness that would shape ideas of manhood, leisure, work, and consumption throughout the twentieth century.

Urban-Industrial Life, Neurasthenia, and Middle-Class Manliness

With the emergence of corporations and the concomitant rise of white-collar career paths, the ideal of the "self-made man" became more and more difficult to realize in the realms of work, economic achievement, and the marketplace. Instead, growing numbers of middle-class men felt strained while fulfilling their societal obligations amid the increasing velocity, pace, and scale of urban-industrial society. According to doctors, this resulted in large numbers of middle-class men suffering from a form of overwork or fatigue known as neurasthenia. Defined by Dr. George M. Beard in 1869, neurasthenia afflicted men and women in mentally demanding occupations, such as artists, authors, scholars, and businessmen. Neurasthenia consisted of a wide range of psychological and physical symptoms, including headaches, nosebleeds, lack of concentration, and a general state of weakness. By far the most common psychiatric diagnosis of the time, neurasthenia affected 69 percent of all men between the ages of twenty-five and forty-five at some point in their lives. As a marker of hard work, neurasthenia served as a badge of middle-class manliness. The prescription for this condition was a period of rest followed by a return to an active life.

Leisure and the "Strenuous Life"

As an antidote to the pace and scale of urban-industrial society, many middle-class men embraced an active life away from work. They discovered athletics, the great outdoors, a primitive inner self, and a new ideal of the "strenuous life" (a notion popularized by Theodore Roosevelt in a speech before an all-male audience at Chicago's Hamilton Club on April 10, 1899) as sources of a revitalized masculinity. By choosing this path, men expected to achieve a new balance between civilized manly conduct and an assertive masculinity that would enable them to compensate for the constraints of society. Men felt and acted more passionately about their masculinity, the foundation of which began to shift away from work and toward leisure and consumer behavior.

Articulated largely by white Anglo-Saxon middle-class men concerned with revitalizing their manhood, and drawing on the increasingly influential concept of Darwinian struggle, the strenuous life carried connotations of racial and sexual survival of the fittest. By focusing on racial and sexual difference and defining white manhood as being apart from nonwhite and nonmale "others," it provided another means by which Gilded Age men could assure themselves of the possibility of a stable masculine identity amid powerful social change. By the 1880s, definitions of (white) manliness became increasingly contingent on notions of difference along lines of race, gender, and sexuality.

Difference, Masculinity, and Empire

White men became increasingly inclined to define themselves explicitly along lines of race and gender as women and nonwhite immigrants entered the workforce in growing numbers during the late nineteenth century. Gender distinctions were increasingly apparent in men's tendency to define professions in law, politics, medicine, and science as male enclaves, and to exclude women from these areas of work.

Another crucial marker of difference was sexuality. Cities such as New York and Chicago witnessed the emergence of thriving same-sex subcultures. Whereas Victorian men had accepted, and even celebrated, close-knit male-male friendships (which frequently had physical dimensions such as the sharing of beds), same-sex relations became increasingly suspect by the late nineteenth century. By the end of the century, medical practitioners had "discovered" homosexuality and defined it as a deviant form of sexuality. Categorizing men who acted effeminate and desired male partners as homosexuals also served as an affirmation of a presumably stable, unified heterosexual manliness.

Further, at a time when large numbers of southern and southeastern Europeans and Asians emigrated to the United States, white men linked definitions of masculinity to a notion of Anglo-Saxonism. Influenced by the Darwinian idea of evolution, and by new scientific inquiries into racial descent, white Euro-Americans depicted Anglo-Saxons as a superior race. Amid economic upheavals, labor radicalism, and rising levels of immigration, this ideological construct postulated the exceptionality and greatness of Anglo-Saxon nations, emphasizing a love of freedom and a capacity for self-government as supreme Anglo-Saxon virtues.

An emphasis on racial difference as a marker of manliness played a significant role in late-nineteenth-century western expansion and imperialism. Both of these endeavors afforded Anglo-Saxon men opportunities to prove their masculinity in a Darwinian struggle for survival against allegedly primitive races and lesser men, both at home and abroad. Defeating Native Americans in the wars on the Great Plains in the late nineteenth century and confining them to reservations secured for white Euro-American men not only control of vast natural resources, but also the belief that they were of a racially superior and more virile stock. The Spanish-American War (1898), the Philippine-American War (1900–02), and subsequent U.S. expansion abroad likewise reflected this aggressive masculinity.

The Defense of Artisanal Manhood

Both middle- and working-class men sought to restore what they perceived as a loss of male identity grounded in work and economic independence. Working-class men resisted the quickening pace of production and their employers' workplace authority, seeing in both an intrusion on their traditional craft-based prerogatives. A nationwide series of strikes in 1877 and 1886, the 1892 steelworkers' strike at the Carnegie plant in Homestead, Pennsylvania, and the American Railway Union strike against the Pullman Car Company in Chicago in 1894 exemplified workingmen's defense of traditional notions of manhood. Yet, with the founding of the American Federation of Labor in 1886, the American labor movement de-emphasized notions of workplace authority and emphasized pay and benefits instead, shifting the foundations of working-class manliness toward breadwinning and an ability to participate in expanding consumer markets.

Similarly, some middle-class men chose to compensate for changing work settings and shifting career paths by turning to craftsmanship as a model of manliness. At a time when forces of industrialization and mechanization severely retrenched the control that skilled craft workers exercised on the shop floor, middle-class culture rediscovered the artisan and the craftsman (seen as embodying skill, autonomy, control, and simplicity) as a metaphor of manliness. This metaphor appeared in a variety of settings. The Social Gospel and muscular Christianity movements, which emerged in the Protestant churches in the Gilded Age, replaced the mid-nineteenth-century image of a sentimental, androgynous, and nurturing Jesus with the image of a vigorous, manly carpenter and noble craftsmen. The prizefighter John L. Sullivan likewise owed his popularity, at least in part, to the image of the "heroic artisan" that he projected to his all-male audiences through his physique and Irish working-class background. After the cattle drives across the Great Plains ended in the 1880s, the figure of the cowboy, yet another heroic artisan and strenuous craftsman, gained popularity in popular culture through pulp fiction and novels such as Owen Wister's *The Virginian* (1902). The artisan metaphor was also at the foundation of the many fraternal orders that were established in the late nineteenth century and modeled on medieval craft guilds. Finally, the late-nineteenth-century arts and crafts movement, inspired by the British craftsmen and intellectuals John Ruskin and William Morris, encouraged men to adorn their homes with furniture made in the simple, presumably masculine, craftsman style.

Despite the fact that the image of the artisan as a metaphor for a revitalized manliness was grounded in work and skill, it also firmly tied articulations of masculinity to leisure and the growing consumer culture of the Gilded Age. Craftsman-style furniture, cowboy novels, or fraternal regalia had to be purchased before they could be used, and masculinity became increasingly tied to consumption.

Conclusion

In the Gilded Age, definitions of masculinity shifted away from their traditional moorings in work and economic achievement and became slowly bound up with the leisure and consumerism of a commercializing society. Men would find ways to reintegrate ideas about work with ideas of manliness through notions of the corporate or bureaucratic team player, the breadwinner, or the worker-as-consumer. Yet the Gilded Age witnessed a fragmenting of paths to masculinity. Men came to embrace the notion that manhood was not a stable core that one possessed, but that it could be created through performance and outward representation.

BIBLIOGRAPHY

Bederman, Gail. *Manliness and Civilization: A Cultural History of Gender and Race in the United States, 1880–1917.* Chicago: University of Chicago Press, 1995.

Carnes, Mark C. *Secret Ritual and Manhood in Victorian America.* New Haven, Conn.: Yale University Press, 1989.

Haller, John S., and Robin M. Haller. *The Physician and Sexuality in Victorian America.* New York: Norton, 1974.

Kimmel, Michael. *Manhood in America: A Cultural History.* New York: Free Press, 1996.

Kwolek-Folland, Angel. *Engendering Business: Men and Women in the Corporate Office, 1870–1930.* Baltimore: Johns Hopkins University Press, 1994.

Lears, T. J. Jackson. *No Place of Grace: Antimodernism and the Transformation of American Culture, 1880–1920.* New York: Pantheon, 1981.

Further Reading

Budd, Michael Anton. *The Sculpture Machine: Physical Culture and Body Politics in the Age of Empire.* New York: New York University Press, 1997.

Hilkey, Judy. *Character Is Capital: Success Manuals and Manhood in Gilded Age America.* Chapel Hill: University of North Carolina Press, 1997.

Hoganson, Kristin. *Fighting for American Manhood: How Gender Politics Provoked the Spanish-American War.* New Haven, Conn.: Yale University Press, 1998.

Kasson, John F. *Houdini, Tarzan, and the Perfect Man: The White Male Body and the Challenge of Modernity in America.* New York: Hill and Wang, 2001.

Putney, Clifford. *Muscular Christianity: Manhood and Sports in Protestant America, 1880–1920.* Cambridge, Mass.: Harvard University Press, 2001.

Rodgers, Daniel. *The Work Ethic in Industrial America, 1850–1920.* Chicago: University of Chicago Press, 1978.

Rotundo, E. Anthony. *American Manhood: Transformations in Masculinity from the Revolution to the Modern Era.* New York: Basic Books, 1993.

Related Entries

Artisan; Body; Bureaucratization; Capitalism; Class; Consumerism; Cowboys; Crisis of Masculinity; Darwinism; Fraternal Organizations; Heterosexuality; Homosexuality; Imperialism; Individualism; Jesus, Images of; Labor Movement and Unions; Middle-Class Manhood; Muscular Christianity; Passionate Manhood; Professionalism; Progressive Era; Race; Self-Made Man; Social Gospel; Strenuous Life; Urbanization; Victorian Era; Western Frontier; Whiteness; White Supremacism; Work; Working-Class Manhood

—*Thomas Winter*

Graham, Sylvester

1794–1851
Health Reformer and Minister

Sylvester Graham, a Presbyterian minister and antebellum health reformer, addressed medical, dietary, and sexual aspects of manhood. Graham's emphasis on restraint in these areas meshed well with Victorian concerns about physical purity and bodily discipline in all aspects of life. While Victorian Americans valued self-control and bodily discipline in general, they were particularly inclined to identify these with ideal manhood.

Ordained in 1830, Graham began lecturing that same year for a temperance organization, the Pennsylvania Society for Discouraging the Use of Ardent Spirits. Graham was suddenly propelled into a position of cultural influence in 1832, when, amid fears of a cholera outbreak, he advised Americans of the preventive value of proper eating habits and food preparation. The physical self-restraint that Graham preached represented for him the essential quality of middle-class Victorian manhood. Graham began to consider the subject of sexuality in his 1834 *A Lecture to Young Men.* Graham advised his audiences, consisting largely of Northeastern white middle-class men, against any form of sexual indulgence, especially masturbation.

Graham feared that a loss of male self-control threatened Victorian society, and he therefore urged men to avoid any form of excitement. To cleanse the body and prevent debilitating overstimulation of the nervous system, he encouraged physical exercise, sleeping on a hard bed, avoidance of meat and spicy foods, and consumption of water and a coarse bread made of unsifted flour. (His original bread recipe eventually found a more appealing successor in the Graham Cracker.) Most importantly, Graham urged the utmost sexual restraint, even in marriage.

Influenced by the perfectionist impulse of the Second Great Awakening, which emphasized the possibility and duty of achieving total freedom from sin, Graham cast sin in a physical framework by defining it in terms of bodily appetite and desire. He urged men to embrace an antierotic, antilibidinal definition of manhood, identifying bodily self-restraint as the way to salvation. Graham's male ethos reflects the contradictions of an age that witnessed the first wave of industrialization and the emergence of a national market economy. On the one hand, his resistance to sensual indulgence can be interpreted as a critique of the materialism he feared would result from the nascent industrialization and market capitalism of the 1830s. On the other hand, his condemnation of self-indulgent behavior reflected a quintessentially capitalist ethos of delayed gratification.

A highly sought-after speaker in the Northeast, Graham was very influential. In 1837, his followers formed the American Physiological Society, with William Alcott, the author of *The Young Man's Guide* (1846), as its first president. The society published the *Graham Journal of Health and Longevity,* which ceased publication in 1839. While the society used his name and ideas, which became widely shared among contemporary reformers, Graham himself played no leading role in it.

Although Graham's best known legacy might be the Graham Cracker, his ideas also anticipated and shaped later shifts in cultural constructions of masculinity in the United States. His emphasis on bodily self-restraint and suppression of libidinal impulses helped to lay the foundation for the body-centered understanding of manhood that emerged later in the nineteenth century.

Bibliography

Nissenbaum, Stephen. *Sex, Diet, and Debility in Jacksonian America: Sylvester Graham and Health Reform.* Westport, Conn.: Greenwood Press, 1980.

Sellers, Charles. *The Market Revolution: Jacksonian America, 1815–1846.* New York: Oxford University Press, 1991.

Sokolow, Jayme. *Eros and Modernization: Sylvester Graham, Health Reform, and the Origins of Victorian Sexuality in America.* Rutherford, N.J.: Fairleigh Dickinson University Press, 1983.

Walters, Ronald G. *American Reformers, 1815–1860.* New York: Hill and Wang, 1978.

Further Reading

Barker-Benfield, G. J. *The Horrors of the Half-Known Life: Male Attitudes toward Women and Sexuality in Nineteenth-Century America.* New York: Routledge, 2000.

Haller, John S., and Robin M. Haller. *The Physician and Sexuality in Victorian America.* New York: W. W. Norton, 1974.

Walters, Ronald G., ed. *Primers for Prudery: Sexual Advice to Victorian America.* Updated ed. Baltimore: Johns Hopkins University Press, 2000.

Selected Writings

Graham, Sylvester. *A Lecture to Young Men, on Chastity.* 1834. Reprinted in *Primers for Prudery: Sexual Advice to Victorian America,* edited by Ronald G. Walters. Baltimore: Johns Hopkins University Press, 2000.

———. *Treatise on Bread and Bread-Making.* 1837. Reprinted in *Primers for Prudery: Sexual Advice to Victorian America,* edited by Ronald G. Walters. Baltimore: Johns Hopkins University Press, 2000.

———. *Lectures on Science and Human Life.* 1839. Reprinted in *Primers for Prudery: Sexual Advice to Victorian America,* edited by Ronald G. Walters. Baltimore: Johns Hopkins University Press, 2000.

Related Entries

Body; Capitalism; Health; Heterosexuality; Industrialization; Market Revolution; Marriage; Masturbation; Middle-Class Manhood; Reform Movements; Religion and Spirituality; Self-Control; Temperance; Victorian Era

—*Thomas Winter*

Grant, Cary

1904–1986
Actor

During the 1940s and 1950s, Cary Grant became the model of urbane, heterosexual masculinity for a generation of American filmgoers. Standing over six feet tall, Grant was strikingly handsome, and he was often cast as an upper-class character—such as C. K. Dexter Haven in *The Philadelphia Story* (1940)—whose charms made him irresistible to women. A popular romantic leading man from the 1930s through the 1960s, Grant's image of on-screen manhood evolved from that of a screwball comedian, featuring physical gags and self-deprecating wit, to that of a tanned, suave, self-contained hero.

Born in Bristol, England, as Archibald Alexander Leach, Grant grew up in modest circumstances. Coming to the United States in 1920, he found work on Broadway in New York City. By the 1930s he had moved to California and begun to appear in films—and changed his name at his studio's request.

Grant appeared in more than eighty films from 1932 to 1966. His early roles tended toward light comedy. The actress Mae West famously invited Grant to "come up and see me" in *She Done Him Wrong* (1933). The early Grant's screen image differed significantly from his later roles. In *Sylvia Scarlett* (1935), for instance, Grant plays a Cockney con man: sympathetic, funny, but hardly elegant. By the 1940s, however, Grant appeared as the romantic lead opposite his generation's best actresses. His characters from this period conveyed the idealized masculine type for which Grant is best remembered: handsome, graceful, elegant, stylish, and witty.

Grant's personal life was more complicated than his savoir-faire screen image would suggest, and he found it difficult to attain the ease and assurance that his film roles and publicity conveyed. "Everybody wants to be Cary Grant," the actor once said, "even I want to be Cary Grant" (McCann, xi). For years he was reticent in speaking about private matters. Yet even as he became an icon of American manhood, his sexuality became the object of fascination and speculation. He shared a house for a time with the actor Randolph Scott, and gossip linked the two romantically. Grant's career was dependent on the overt heterosexuality of his characters, however, and he refused to address such rumors. In his early roles, Grant did play his masculinity broadly and with humor, particularly in screwball comedies such as *Bringing Up Baby* (1938), in which Grant, attired in a woman's dressing gown, famously claimed, "I just went gay all of a sudden!"

In the 1950s, Grant starred in a series of critical and popular successes, including *To Catch a Thief* (1955), *An Affair to Remember* (1957), *Indiscreet* (1958), and *North By Northwest* (1959). His calm, capable, and assured characters, whether retired cat burglars or playboys, relied on wit and intelligence rather than coarse physicality. In a post–World War II America that imagined itself as mature and worldly, Grant's image of grace under pressure represented American manhood as most American men (and women) imagined it could be.

BIBLIOGRAPHY

Deschner, Donald. *The Films of Cary Grant.* Secaucus, N.J.: Citadel, 1973.

Higham, Charles, and Roy Moseley. *Cary Grant: The Lonely Heart.* San Diego, Calif.: Harcourt, Brace, Jovanovich, 1989.

McCann, Graham. *Cary Grant: A Class Apart.* New York: Columbia University Press, 1996.

FURTHER READING

Butters, Ronald R. "Cary Grant and the Emergence of Gay 'Homosexual'." *Dictionaries: Journal of the Dictionary Society of North America* 19 (1998): 188–204.

Nelson, Nancy. *Evenings with Cary Grant: Recollections in His Own Words and by Those Who Knew Him Best.* New York: William Morrow, 1991.

Wansell, Geoffrey. *Haunted Idol: The Story of the Real Cary Grant.* New York: William Morrow, 1984.

RELATED ENTRIES

Cold War; Heterosexuality; Hollywood; Homosexuality; Self-Control

—*Trent Watts*

GRAPES OF WRATH, THE

Published in 1939, John Steinbeck's novel *The Grapes of Wrath* tells the story of the Joads, a farming family that migrates to California in search of work after being dispossessed of their Oklahoma farm amid the horrific drought that struck the Midwest during the 1930s (causing the region to be called the Dust Bowl). Centering on Tom Joad, the young adult son of Ma and Pa, the story may be read as his attempt to retain and rethink his manhood amid the emasculating circumstances of the Great Depression.

The Grapes of Wrath reflects the agrarian definition of manhood that had characterized American culture since the colonial period and had become codified in the republican thought of Thomas Jefferson. According to this definition, economic, political, and spiritual manhood were fully realized through agricultural work, land ownership, providing for one's family, and the self-sufficiency and personal independence that property ownership provided. By the late nineteenth century, small farmers in the South and West became increasingly alienated by rapid industrialization in the Northeast. With their growing dependence on credit and the increased risk of foreclosure, they came to view government policies as favoring bankers, industrialists, and wealthy landowners.

Steinbeck's novel suggests that these longstanding agrarian concerns were aggravated by the economic uncertainties of the Depression. The story opens as government agents remove the Joads from their farm. The family packs a jalopy and—in keeping with many other American travel narratives that associate westward travel with a search for freedom and manhood—heads for California to find agricultural work and retrieve their economic independence. Grandpa, deprived of the foundation of his manly identity and spirituality, dies at the outset of the trip, while Pa's diminished manhood causes him to lose decision-making authority to Ma.

In California, the Joads become migrant farm laborers, dependent on large landowners for their livelihood. Yet the resulting feeling of emasculation draws Tom Joad and other migrant workers together, fostering a new ideal of manhood grounded partly in their shared commitment to traditional agrarianism, but also in their emerging class consciousness, their concern for social justice, and their brewing resistance to the power of large landowners and government officials. Tom and other male workers find a model of this new kind of manhood in Jim Casy, a preacher whose call for class struggle eventually leads to his death at the hands of landowners' agents during a violent outbreak at one of the camps. Casy becomes a martyr to the cause, as his religiously charged initials imply. The novel closes as Tom, identified by the authorities as a troublemaker, leaves his family to heroically take up Jim's larger cause.

The Grapes of Wrath reflects the Great Depression's impact in disrupting older concepts of masculinity based on individualism and self-sufficiency and fostering more socially and politically radical notions grounded in collective class identity. The novel has assumed the status of a twentieth-century classic and remains widely read, and Tom Joad has been used as a symbol of the heroic male worker in songs written by Woody Guthrie in the 1940s and Bruce Springsteen in the late twentieth century. Steinbeck's vision of an essentially

American agrarian manhood—radicalized and endangered but proud—therefore remains a powerful presence in American culture.

BIBLIOGRAPHY

Martin, Stoddard. *California Writers: Jack London, John Steinbeck, the Tough Guys.* New York: St. Martin's, 1983.

Pells, Richard H. *Radical Visions and American Dreams: Culture and Social Thought in the Depression Years.* New York: Harper & Row, 1973.

Simon, Bryant, and William Deverell. "Come Back Tom Joad: Thoughts on a California Dreamer." *California History* 79, no. 4 (2000): 180–191.

FURTHER READING

Dunbar-Ortiz, Roxanne. "One or Two Things I Know About Us: 'Okies' in American Culture." *Radical History Review* 59 (1994): 4–34.

Inge, M. Thomas, ed. *Agrarianism in American Literature.* New York: Odyssey Press, 1969.

Steinbeck, John. *The Grapes of Wrath.* New York: The Viking Press, 1939.

RELATED ENTRIES

Agrarianism; American Dream; Crévecoeur, J. Hector St. John; Great Depression; Heroism; Industrialization; Populism; Property; Religion and Spirituality; Republicanism; Springsteen, Bruce; Travel Narratives; Western Frontier

—*Bret E. Carroll*

GREAT DEPRESSION

The worst economic disaster in American history, the Great Depression of the 1930s affected almost all aspects of life in the United States, including American notions of masculinity. Social scientists of the time and historians interested in American manhood have highlighted men's inability to live up to the breadwinner ideal and provide for their families during this period, thus underscoring the important concepts of work and family in relation to male identity. Yet the Great Depression's effects on American men and masculinity were more complex, varying sharply by class and other forms of social identity.

Within a climate of general economic insecurity, induced by the stock market crash of October 1929, wages declined considerably and unemployment rates rose dramatically. This perilous situation motivated Mirra Komarovsky, Winona Morgan, and other sociologists of the time to research the interrelations between the economy and male authority—particularly changing roles and shifting power relations in families due to the economic crisis. While limited in scope, these studies had a lasting effect on notions about the depression's impact on American masculinity. They described men who felt humiliated and ashamed by unemployment, which was previously thought to be a working-class problem but was now increasingly experienced by the middle class. The dominant middle-class ethos of breadwinning and self-reliance weighed heavily on these men, with varying consequences: marriage rates declined steadily until the mid-1930s, marital relations often deteriorated, reports of domestic violence increased, and some husbands and fathers deserted their families. Feeling emasculated, many men blamed themselves for their difficulties. But many also blamed the growing number of women in the labor force and insisted that they be replaced by unemployed men. Early New Deal relief programs appeared to respond to this call for a reassertion of traditional male breadwinning, for they clearly favored male employment over female work.

On one level, then, the Great Depression stressed the ideology of work as a core element of male identity and reconfirmed the existing American gender system of male providers and female housewives. In fact, sociologists Robert S. and Helen M. Lynd found evidence that many Americans of the period denied any change in the gender system. In *Middletown in Transition* (1937), perhaps the most well-known and influential of the sociological studies undertaken during the 1930s, the Lynds argued that American men and their families relied heavily on tradition to ease the burdens of economic hardship.

But such studies reveal only part of a much more complex reality. Examining trends of the mid-1930s and the experiences of nonwhite, working-class, and homosexual men expose variations in the consequences of the Great Depression on constructions of masculinity. After the first shock of hard times eased and New Deal programs restored a sense of confidence, American men increasingly reconsidered their notion of masculinity in light of the now more limited prospects for success. In particular, they turned to a "modern" masculine ideal that emphasized personality over character and flexibility over determination and pride. This ideal had developed during the 1920s, but it lost much of its persuasive power with the stock market crash. Dale Carnegie's bestselling book *How to Win Friends and Influence People* (1936) set this new tone. Carnegie argued that if male success is no longer preordained but precarious, then modern men had to advertise themselves in order to gain status and income.

An unemployed man sells apples on the street in the nation's capitol amid the Great Depression of the 1930s. During the depression, many men struggled to maintain their identities as family breadwinners and, increasingly, looked to the federal government's New Deal programs for assistance. (From the collections of the Library of Congress)

Although success at the workplace and stability at home remained touchstones of male identity, this new concept of masculinity also encouraged equal partnership in marriage and an expanded role for fathers by stressing both teamwork and leadership as highly important personality traits. So while the Great Depression in some ways reinforced traditional constructions of masculinity, in others, at least as indicated in the advice literature of the period, it served to advance the ongoing modernization of American masculinity.

For many blue-collar workers, a large number of whom were immigrants, the experience of uneven and unpredictable incomes before 1929 allowed them to cope with the Great Depression and preserve their sense of male identity more easily than middle-class men did. Since most working-class families had traditionally relied on working wives and children for income, a perceived failure to live up to the sole breadwinner ideal did not challenge working-class men's sense of manhood as much as it did middle-class men's. Many men from immigrant backgrounds, moreover, could continue to rely on the ethnic social networks in which their sense of masculinity had traditionally been grounded.

Furthermore, the intense industrial conflicts of the 1930s and the New Deal's strengthening of unionism gave participants a sense of manhood that was grounded in values of working-class solidarity rather than middle-class male individualism. Although we still know too little about men's interests and intentions on picket lines or at hobo camps, the hard times certainly fostered ideas about cooperation. This becomes evident both in the arts—in *The Grapes of Wrath* (1939) and other writings of John Steinbeck, for example—and in politics, where the language of collectivity contributed to the appeal of the New Deal and enhanced the appeal of the Communist Party.

For homosexual men, much as for middle-class men, the effects of the Great Depression were decidedly negative, though for different reasons. Gay men, marginalized by the dominant heterosexual culture, had created a lively subculture in major American cities during the 1920s. After the crash, however, economic insecurity, its perceived threat to traditional constructions of male identity, and a resulting intensification of public anxieties about homosexuality and effeminacy sparked antihomosexual campaigns in the tabloid press and eroded these subcultures quickly and decisively.

A conclusive assessment of the Great Depression's importance for American masculinity is not easy. This is in part because it simultaneously retarded and promoted change in the nation's ever-shifting gender dynamic, thus making simple conclusions impossible. Furthermore, more is currently known about the depression's impact on white middle-class men than on other groups, such as African-American men. Given what is known, however, it appears likely that new research will reaffirm the complex nature of its impact on varying American constructions of masculinity.

Bibliography

Chauncey, George. *Gay New York: Gender, Urban Culture and the Makings of the Gay Male World, 1890–1940.* New York: Basic Books, 1994.

Filene, Peter G. *Him/Her/Self: Sex Roles in Modern America.* Rev. ed. Baltimore: Johns Hopkins University Press, 1986.

Green, Harvey. *The Uncertainty of Everyday Life, 1915–1945.* New York: HarperCollins, 1992.

Kimmel, Michael. *Manhood in America: a Cultural History.* New York: Free Press, 1996.

McElvaine, Robert S. *The Great Depression: America, 1929–1941.* New York: Times Books, 1984.

Pendergast, Tom. *Creating the Modern Man. American Magazines and Consumer Culture, 1900–1950.* Columbia: University of Missouri Press, 2000.

Further Reading

Cohen, Lizabeth. *Making a New Deal: Industrial Workers in Chicago, 1919–1939.* Cambridge, England: Cambridge University Press, 1990.

Cross, Gary. *Time and Money: The Making of Consumer Culture.* London: Routledge, 1993.

Komarovsky, Mirra. *The Unemployed Man and His Family—the Effect of Unemployment Upon the Status of Man in Fifty-Nine Families.* New York: Dryden Press, 1940.

Lynd, Robert S., and Helen M. Lynd. *Middletown in Transition. A Study in Cultural Conflicts.* New York: Harcourt, Brace, 1937.

McElvaine, Robert S., ed. *Down and Out in the Great Depression. Letters from the "Forgotten Man."* Chapel Hill: University of North Carolina Press, 1983.

Morgan, Winona L. *The Family Meets the Depression. A Study of a Group of Highly Selected Families.* Westport, Conn.: Greenwood Press, 1939.

Related Entries

Advertising; American Dream; Breadwinner Role; Capitalism; Class; Consumerism; Cult of Domesticity; *Grapes of Wrath, The*; Hoboes; Labor Movement and Unions; Marriage; Middle-Class Manhood; New Deal; Work; Working-Class Manhood

—*Olaf Stieglitz*

Gulick, Luther Halsey

1865–1918
Physical Educator and Author

Luther Halsey Gulick contributed to the field of physical education and helped redefine middle-class manhood during the Progressive Era (1890–1915). Born into a family of Congregational ministers, Gulick devoted his life to promoting and intertwining physical education and male spirituality.

Gulick held several influential positions in the field of physical education. He headed the gymnasium department at the Young Men's Christian Association (YMCA) Training School in Springfield, Massachusetts (1887–1900); served as director of physical education in the public schools of New York City (1903–08); held the presidencies of the American Physical Education Association (1903–06) and the Public School Physical Training Society (1905–08); and cofounded the Playground Association of America with educator Joseph Lee in 1906 (and served as its first president).

Central to Gulick's thinking on masculinity and physical education were the concept of organic memory and the so-called recapitulation theory of play. According to the concept of organic memory, each individual inherits the history of his or her own race. Gulick asserted that only white men have the ability to fully establish control of mind over body. According to recapitulation theory, as a child grows to maturity it relives past stages of evolution, moving from primitive forms of behavior to civilized forms of social organization by learning to take control of the atavistic layers of its personality.

Central to the concepts of white manhood in the early twentieth century was the ability to shape this civilized self-possession during a child's adolescent years. Proponents of recapitulation theory argued that manhood could be shaped through physical exercise. Gulick believed that training the body's motor reflexes and subjecting them to conscious control of the mind would build the necessary moral reflexes of an individual.

Gulick shared the definition of manhood and the concerns with the male physique espoused by advocates of the "strenuous life," but he rejected an exclusive emphasis on the body as a symbol of self-confident manliness. Achieving manhood, Gulick believed, required not simply muscle building, but a symmetrical development of body, mind, and spirit—as represented by the inverted red triangle that he persuaded the YMCA to adopt as its symbol in 1891. Gulick favored team sports such as basketball and volleyball because they promoted the moral principles of loyalty, self-control, self-sacrifice, and teamwork, which he considered to be the foundations of Christianity and an altruistic Christian manhood.

Although Gulick advocated a "muscular Christianity" that emphasized a greater balance between body and spirit, his emphasis on making the male physique an expression of Christian manhood ultimately led him to place sexuality and sexual difference at the center of male gender identity. In *The Dynamic of Manhood* (1918), Gulick followed a path charted earlier by his friend Granville Stanley Hall and urged men to channel their sexual impulses and reproductive energies into emotional expressions as a part of their outwardly directed, embodied selves. Gulick's prescription for establishing manliness by externalizing physical desires and functions contributed to the cultural separation of sexuality from reproduction.

Gulick made lasting contributions to ideas about masculinity and physical exercise. His ideas about manhood contributed to a body-centered definition of male gender identity.

He also helped to pioneer calisthenics, an early form of aerobics, and each year the American Alliance for Health, Physical Education, Recreation and Dance awards a medal in his name to an individual who has made outstanding contributions to the field of physical education.

BIBLIOGRAPHY

Dorgan, Ethel Josephine. *Luther Halsey Gulick, 1865–1918.* New York: Bureau of Publications, Teacher's College, Columbia University, 1934.

Gustav-Wrathall, John D. *Take The Young Stranger By The Hand: Same-Sex Relations and the YMCA.* Chicago: University of Chicago Press, 1998.

Hopkins, C. Howard. *History of the Y.M.C.A. in North America.* New York: Association Press, 1951.

Rader, Benjamin G. "The Recapitulation Theory of Play: Motor Behaviour, Moral Reflexes, and Manly Attitudes in Urban America, 1880–1920." In *Manliness and Morality: Middle-Class Masculinity in Britain and America, 1800–1940,* edited by J. A. Mangan and James Walvin. New York: St. Martin's, 1987.

FURTHER READING

Putney, Clifford Wallace. *Muscular Christianity: Manhood and Sports in Protestant America, 1880–1920.* Cambridge: Harvard University Press, 2001.

Tomko, Linda J. "Fete Accompli: Gender, 'Folk Dance,' and Progressive Era Political Ideals in New York City." In *Corporealities: Dancing, Knowledge, Culture and Power,* edited by Susan Leigh Foster. New York: Routledge, 1996.

Wallach, Stephanie. "Luther Halsey Gulick and the Salvation of the American Adolescent." Ph.D. Diss., Columbia University, New York, 1989.

Winter, Thomas. "'The Healthful Art of Dancing': Luther Halsey Gulick, Gender, the Body, and the Performativity of National Identity." *Journal of American Culture* 22 (Summer 1999): 33–38.

SELECTED WRITINGS

Gulick, Luther Halsey. *The Efficient Life.* New York: Doubleday, Page, 1907.

———. *Mind and Work.* New York: Doubleday, Page, 1909.

———. *The Dynamic of Manhood.* New York: Association Press, 1918.

———. *A Philosophy of Play.* New York: Scribners, 1920.

RELATED ENTRIES

Body; Bodybuilding; Boy Scouts of America; Darwinism; Hall, Granville Stanley; Health; Heterosexuality; Middle-Class Manhood; Muscular Christianity; Progressive Era; Race; Religion and Spirituality; Sports; Victorian Era; Whiteness; Young Men's Christian Association; Youth

—*Thomas Winter*

GUNS

Guns were considered a necessity in settling the American frontier during the colonial era, for they provided personal and familial protection and enabled colonists to kill game for survival. In the twenty-first century, guns remain central to popular images of the self-sufficient pioneer and mythic gunfighter, and they are an essential tool of film and television heroes. American men, in particular, are associated with guns, which they have used to assert their power and dominate people in warfare, law enforcement, and personal conflicts.

Although there is some controversy regarding the development of America's gun culture, it is generally believed that guns were essential to notions of republican manhood and an emerging national identity in Revolutionary America. The Second Amendment of the U.S. Constitution granted citizens "the right . . . to keep and bear arms." The association of guns with a manly defense of liberty was apparent in Ralph Waldo Emerson's poetic celebration, in his "Concord Hymn," of the embattled farmers who began the American Revolution with "the shot heard round the world." This association between guns, Americanism, and manliness was reinforced by subsequent wars.

Guns became particularly important to southern ideals of manhood. After the French and Indian War (1754–63), colonists, especially in the South, adopted from French and British aristocrats the tradition of dueling, which was part of a code of manly honor that demanded ritualized combat between two equals when one had questioned the integrity of the other. At the same time, southern white men were particularly troubled by the possibility that black men might use guns to challenge a social system grounded in white patriarchy, racial hierarchy, and paternalism. As early as 1640, laws were passed making it illegal for African Americans to carry weapons. After the Civil War, Southern states passed the "Black Codes," which included provisions denying former slaves the right to own weapons.

During the antebellum period, burgeoning firearms manufacturers like Samuel Colt helped bolster the nation's gun culture by making guns affordable, accurate, and durable. Inspired by Unionist shooting enthusiasts, rifle shooting became such a popular sport after the Civil War that the members of the National Guard formed the National Rifle Association (NRA) in 1871 to advance the sport. Membership in the NRA boomed after World War I as hunters in rural areas joined the organization.

During the twentieth century, American gun culture continued to facilitate the formation of masculine identity. Gun ownership became a rite of passage, particularly in rural areas where boys were given a progressive assortment of firearms upon reaching a certain age. Hunting became a vital part of many young males' initiation into manhood. After the late-nineteenth-century disappearance of the western frontier left many American men anxious about the future of American manhood, shooting and marksmanship became popular sports, and such organizations as the Boy Scouts of America (established in 1910) awarded boys badges for demonstrating these skills. Marksmanship competitions, historical re-enactments, firearms collecting, and gun shows provided a range of activities that appealed to various social classes and subcultures as ways of fashioning masculine identity.

The relation between gun ownership and masculinity became a powerful political issue during the late twentieth century. Research indicated that many African-American males viewed guns as a way to express power and masculinity, that they were the most common homicide perpetrators and victims, and that since 1969 homicide had been the leading cause of death for black males ages fifteen to nineteen. Meanwhile, a series of school shootings by suburban white adolescents during the 1990s indicated disturbing new trends in gun violence. In this setting, the NRA and its self-consciously masculine president Charlton Heston assumed growing visibility amid an intensifying public debate over whether gun ownership encouraged hypermasculine violence or was necessary to the protection of one's family.

At the start of the twenty-first century gun advocates assert that ownership is a freedom epitomizing American individualism and the intent of the founding fathers. Gun control advocates, meanwhile, argue that gun ownership reinforces an obsolete and potentially dangerous male fantasy of returning to an idealized past of hunters and cowboys. Both sides underscore the continuing association of guns with masculinity.

Bibliography

Bailey, Beth. "Manners and Etiquette." In the *Encyclopedia of American Social History*, edited by Mary Kupiec Cayton, Elliott J. Gorn, and Peter W. Williams. New York: Scribner, 1993.

Doss, Erika. "Imaging the Panthers: Representing Black Power and Masculinity, 1960s–1990s." *Prospects 23: An Annual of American Studies* (1998): 470–493.

Hawley, Fred. "Guns." In the *Encyclopedia of Southern Culture*, edited by Charles R. Wilson and William Ferris. Chapel Hill: University of North Carolina Press, 1989.

Karlson, Trudy Ann, and Stephen W. Hargarten. *Reducing Firearm Injury and Death: A Public Health Sourcebook On Guns*. New Brunswick, N.J.: Rutgers University Press, 1997.

Spraggins, Johnnie David, Jr. "African American Masculinity: Power and Expression." *Journal of African American Men* 4 (Winter 1999): 45–72.

Further Reading

Bellesiles, Michael A. *Arming America: The Origins of a National Gun Culture*. New York: Knopf, 2000.

Diaz, Tom. *Making a Killing: The Business of Guns in America*. New York: New Press, 1999.

Dizard, Jan E., Robert M. Munth, and Stephen P. Andrews. *Guns in America: A Reader*. New York: New York University Press, 1999.

Rosa, Joseph G. *Age of the Gunfighter: Men and Weapons on the Frontier, 1840–1900*. Norman: University of Oklahoma Press, 1995.

Related Entries

African-American Manhood; American Revolution; Boy Scouts of America; Cowboys; Dueling; Hunting; Republicanism; Southern Manhood; Violence; War; Western Frontier

—*Rebecca Tolley-Stokes*

Hall, Granville Stanley

1844–1924
Psychologist and Pedagogue

The founder and first president of Clark University, Granville Stanley Hall formulated theories on child development, psychology, play, and race that greatly influenced theories about white manhood and male sexuality around the turn of the twentieth century.

Hall's chief concern was neurasthenia, a medical condition of mental and physical exhaustion first diagnosed by the physician George M. Beard in 1869. Neurasthenia tended to affect white middle-class men who feared that industrialization and urbanization undermined their ability to meet contemporary expectations of manhood. While men such as Theodore Roosevelt advocated the "strenuous life" as an antidote, Hall supported a preventive approach that targeted adolescent boys.

The concept of organic memory, which states that each individual inherits the history of his or her own race, informed Hall's thinking on child development, race, and the formation of the self. Hall advocated organized play as means through which boys could counteract the allegedly debilitating and effeminizing effects of urban-industrial "overcivilization" and achieve a reinvigorated white masculinity by tapping the primitive energy embedded in their genetic make-up. Under proper guidance, Hall believed, the primitive impulses in boys could be directed into a forceful adult masculinity able to withstand the pressures of urban, industrial life.

This prescription for the reinvigoration of white, middle-class masculinity influenced Hall's understanding of sexuality. Influenced by his New England Protestant background, and by middle-class Victorian attitudes generally, Hall initially regarded sexuality as a morally and physiologically enervating force that needed to be contained and restricted. But his insistence on tapping and directing atavistic impulses through organized play for the purpose of creating a forceful, reinvigorated masculinity eventually led Hall to suggest that the sexual energy of boys and young men could serve as a substitute for depleted nervous energy. This new link between sexuality and the development of adult masculinity became one of the main themes in Hall's two-volume study on pedagogy and child psychology, *Adolescence* (1904).

Changing scientific theories of genetic inheritance helped to stimulate this change in Hall's views on sexuality. As he began his work on *Adolescence* in the early 1890s, scientists had begun to abandon the postulate developed by the French naturalist Jean-Baptiste-Pierre-Antoine de Monet Chevalier de Lamarck, which maintained that genetic inheritance was shaped by parental behavior, and instead began to recognize the role and function of chromosomes. This shift in scientific knowledge about genetic inheritance prompted Hall to alter his earlier repressive views on manhood and male sexuality as he completed *Adolescence*.

While Hall did not advocate free sexual expressiveness, his acceptance of sexuality as a positive force in a man's life nonetheless represented a profound departure from a Victorian emphasis on restraint and suppression. In *Adolescence*, Hall argued that sex was not immoral, but sacred because it was part of God's purpose of evolution through procreation. This new appreciation of sexuality and the body led Hall to embrace the concept of "muscular Christianity" as an ideal of male spirituality.

Hall's writings helped to redefine men's approach to their sexuality and played a critical role in shifting understandings of manliness from the self-restrained manhood characteristic of middle-class Victorian culture to the more assertive, and at times aggressive, masculinity that developed at the turn of the twentieth century.

Bibliography

Bederman, Gail. *Manliness and Civilization: A Cultural History of Race and Gender in the United States, 1880–1917.* Chicago: University of Chicago Press, 1995.

Ross, Dorothy. *G. Stanley Hall: The Psychologist as Prophet.* Chicago: University of Chicago Press, 1972.

Further Reading

Cavallo, Dominick. *Muscles and Morals: Organized Playgrounds and Urban Reform, 1880–1920.* Philadelphia: University of Pennsylvania Press, 1981.

Gosling, F. G. *Before Freud: Neurasthenia and the American Medical Community, 1870–1910.* Urbana: University of Illinois Press, 1987.

Lutz, Tom. *American Nervousness, 1903: An Anecdotal History.* Ithaca, N.Y.: Cornell University Press, 1991.

Russett, Cynthia Eagle. *Sexual Science: The Victorian Construction of Womanhood.* Cambridge, Mass.: Harvard University Press, 1989.

Selected Writings

Hall, Granville Stanley. *Adolescence: Its Psychology and Its Relations to Physiology, Anthropology, Sociology, Sex, Crime, Religion and Education.* 2 vols. New York: Appleton, 1904.

———. *Life and Confessions of a Psychologist.* New York: Appleton, 1923.

Related Entries

Adolescence; Body; Boyhood; Freudian Psychoanalytic Theory; Health; Gulick, Luther Halsey; Medicine; Middle-Class Manhood; Muscular Christianity; Progressive Era; Roosevelt, Theodore; Victorian Era; Whiteness

—*Thomas Winter*

Health

Throughout American history, issues of health, ranging from hygiene to disease prevention to diet, have been fundamental to cultural constructions of masculinity. In the late eighteenth century a series of transformations in American life, especially the American Revolution and such modernizing developments as urbanization and industrialization, raised questions and concerns about the meaning of American manhood and the nature of American life. In this environment, the strength and vigor of the male body began to be linked to the well-being of the nation. Since then, the cultural link between health and masculinity has been reinforced by the fact that the chief spokespersons regarding matters of health have overwhelmingly been men. Further, in the late nineteenth century a growing tendency to define masculinity in physical and biological terms emerged.

The Revolutionary Era

The first strong cultural link between health and masculinity in American life accompanied the founding of the nation in the late eighteenth century. As American patriots sought to define American nationhood by proposing a distinction between virtuous republican American men and the corrupt and effete British government and aristocracy, the Philadelphia physician Benjamin Rush formulated a version of republican manhood grounded in bodily health. Rush counseled American men that a strict vegetarian diet would improve strength and virility, while meats, spicy foods, and alcohol would produce disease by overstimulating the body. He associated a plain diet with the simple and virtuous living characteristic of the ideal republican man, and rich foods, by contrast, with the luxurious living of foppish British aristocrats. For Rush and the many American men who took his advice, good health became a manifestation of manly citizenship and the basis of a stable republic.

The Nineteenth Century

The association between health and manhood was reinforced during the early to mid–nineteenth century as industrialization, urbanization, and the rise of a national market economy raised new and interrelated concerns about male behavior and the direction of national development. By the 1830s, these concerns had produced a spate of reform movements—many of them influenced by the Protestant revivalism of the Second Great Awakening—intended to shape American male behavior and the emerging urban-industrial capitalist system. Many of these movements were grounded in the assumption that American men, loosed from traditional moral restraints of church and community, required self-control and spiritual grounding (called "character" by nineteenth-century Americans) to ensure social stability, moral order, and economic productivity.

Among these movements was a push for health and dietary reform, led by Sylvester Graham. Although Graham addressed both men and women, his advice primarily targeted young men, on whose shoulders he rested the future of the nation. Believing that consumption of meat, alcohol, tea, coffee, and tobacco would lead to disease, Graham urged American men to adopt a strict diet of vegetables, grains, and water, as well as a regimen of moderate exercise. The resulting physical and spiritual health, he counseled, would direct the energies of the body away from wasteful and debilitating sensual indulgence and toward the self-discipline and the competitive economic success that he and his contemporaries deemed fundamental to manliness and national strength. Joining many Americans in associating masculinity with public economic activity and the threat of overindulgence (and women with moral purity, motherhood, and domesticity), Graham suggested that men's health began at home, in dietary practices and foods regulated and prepared by their wives and mothers. He thus rooted his notions of healthy manhood firmly in the emerging Victorian gender dichotomy that historians call the "cult of domesticity." Indeed, many Victorian Americans underscored their association of health with masculinity by suggesting that women were naturally weak and prone to unhealthfulness.

The link between masculinity and health, and concerns about the vigor of American men, grew stronger still during the late nineteenth century. Advancing urbanization and industrialization, combined with the growing number of men in corporate and bureaucratic positions, prompted anxiety that a state of "overcivilization" was weakening the health of American men and sapping national strength by overtaxing men's intellectual capacity and removing them from vigorous physical labor. According to male physicians and psychologists, the results were evident in a rising incidence of what the psychologist George Beard, in 1869, labeled neurasthenia, a condition characterized by such "feminine" physical and behavioral traits as nervousness, fatigue, and a withdrawal from the competitive world of business.

Experts agreed that the physical and mental reinvigoration of American manhood lay in sufficient exercise and outdoor activity. Thus an emerging "muscular Christianity" movement encouraged men to cultivate physical health as a necessary counterpart to their spiritual health. In addition, a "muscular vegetarianism" movement, led by John Harvey Kellogg, urged men to increase their physical strength and energy by consuming vegetables rather than meat. At the same time, the Young Men's Christian Association, first established in the United States in 1851, increasingly emphasized athletic activities in its programs and the ideal of a "strenuous life" became a highly popular masculine ideal. By the early twentieth century, Progressive Era reformers applied this thinking to their attempts to reduce delinquency and crime and increase the psychological wellness of urban boys. Perhaps the most visible advocate of this new masculine imperative was Theodore Roosevelt, who touted his personal transformation from asthmatic youth to vigorous soldier, outdoorsman, and president. Roosevelt declared his readiness for his 1912 Progressive Party presidential campaign by pronouncing himself "fit as a bull moose."

The Twentieth Century

The turn of the twentieth century witnessed another, related development in the relation between American masculinity and health. As a developing corporate business culture generated as growing emphasis on external "personality" over internal "character" as the key to manliness and success, so notions of male health began to focus on the appearance or physique of the male body. This trend was evident during the late nineteenth century, when bodybuilding advocates Bernarr McFadden and Eugen Sandow gained national attention as representatives of a new ideal of male muscularity. But the cultural emphasis on bodybuilding as a signifier of health became particularly powerful with the growing prominence of Charles Atlas in the 1920s. Creator of the Dynamic Tension exercise system, Atlas added to Victorian ideals of self-control and mental vigor with new emphases on the healthful power of milk and the sexual appeal of the sculpted and muscular masculine body. New and more liberal attitudes about sexuality, the emergence of the emancipated "New Woman," and the proliferation of entertainment venues encouraging the commingling of the sexes combined to make Atlas's ideal of outwardly manifest physical health (and his denigration of the unmanly "ninety-seven pound weakling") compellingly attractive to men in the 1920s and, indeed, through the remainder of the twentieth century.

The bodybuilding impulse waned around the mid–twentieth century as post–World War II economic prosperity and the expansion of suburbia encouraged Americans strained by the recent experiences of the Great Depression and world war to enjoy the fruits of material abundance. Yet the sedentary nature of middle-class existence, combined with Cold War anxieties that American life fostered flabbiness rather than toughness in its men and the nation, kept issues of health and masculinity—and the attempt to define the one in terms of the other—culturally prominent. Cultural critics argued that consumerism (long considered "feminine" in American cultural discourse) was making American men weak and overweight, and that capitalist competition and the pressures of breadwinning were leaving them vulnerable to heart attack, impotence, and other serious health problems. In response to such concerns, campaign managers for the 1960 presidential candidate John F. Kennedy emphasized his manly youthfulness and vigor, carefully distracting public attention from his serious health problems. The 1960s witnessed a renewed flurry of exercise advice offered by such highly visible fitness advocates as Jack LaLanne.

National attention to health issues grew enormously during the 1970s along several fronts. Feminists increasingly challenged and loosened the traditional cultural association between health and masculinity by pushing a medical profession long dominated by male practitioners to pay greater attention to women's health. At the same time, the growth of self-realization and self-fulfillment movements reinforced among American men the belief that both physical and psychological healthfulness was fundamental to their manhood. The men's movements that emerged during this decade likewise encouraged men to define themselves in terms of aspects of their lives other than their work, and to pay closer attention to their physical and emotional health and reduce stressful activities that might undermine their well-being. Thus, the decade witnessed a renewed bodybuilding impulse, led by such figures as Arnold Schwarzenegger; a jogging fad promoted by Jim Fixx, the author of the best-selling *Complete Book of Running* (1977); and a growing popularity of the martial arts. Although women became increasingly involved in these and other kinds of exercise, the prominence of male spokespersons tended to reinforce the belief that manliness, in particular, required healthfulness. Careful attention to matters of diet and exercise among both men and women remained salient features of American cultural life into the twenty-first century, but the popularity of such drugs as Viagra suggested that Americans continued to associate healthfulness with masculinity.

BIBLIOGRAPHY

Berrett, Jesse. "Feeding the Organization Man: Diet and Masculinity in Postwar America." *Journal of Social History* 30, no. 4 (1997): 805–826.

Cassedy, James H. *Medicine in America: A Short History.* Baltimore: Johns Hopkins University, 1991.

Money, John. *The Destroying Angel: Sex, Fitness, and Food in the Legacy of Degeneracy Theory: Graham Crackers, Kellogg's Corn Flakes, and American Health History.* Buffalo, N.Y.: Prometheus, 1985.

Toon, Elizabeth, and Janet Golden. "'Live Clean, Think Clean, and Don't Go to Burlesque Shows': Charles Atlas as Health Advisor." *Journal of the History of Medicine* 57 (January 2002): 39–60.

White, Kevin. *The First Sexual Revolution: the Emergence of Male Heterosexuality in Modern America.* New York: New York University Press, 1993.

FURTHER READING

Haller, John, and Robin Haller. *The Physician and Sexuality in Victorian America.* Carbondale: Southern Illinois University Press, 1995.

Kimmel, Michael. *Manhood in America.* New York: Free Press, 1996.

Nissenbaum, Stephen. *Sex, Diet, and Debility in Jacksonian America: Sylvester Graham and Health Reform.* Westport, Conn.: Greenwood Press, 1980.

Pugh, David G. *Sons of Liberty: The Masculine Mind in Nineteenth-Century America.* Westport, Conn.: Greenwood Press, 1983.

Rotundo, E. Anthony. *American Manhood.* New York: Basic Books, 1993.

RELATED ENTRIES

Atlas, Charles; Body; Bodybuilding; Character; Graham, Sylvester; Kellogg, John Harvey; Medicine; Muscular Christianity; Republicanism; Roosevelt, Theodore; Sandow, Eugen; Schwarzenegger, Arnold; Self-Control; Sports; Strenuous Life

—*Bret E. Carroll and Catherine Maybrey*

HEMINGWAY, ERNEST

1899–1961
American Novelist and Short Story Writer

Ernest Hemingway was one of the most popular writers of the twentieth century. His rich personal life, critically praised fiction, and declarative and unsentimental prose style all exerted a profound influence on twentieth-century American literature and shaped twentieth-century notions of manhood and masculinity.

Rather than rely simply on pure imagination for creative material, Hemingway lived a life that was in many ways influenced by the early twentieth-century ideal of the "strenuous life." He sought out traditionally masculine adventures (often risking death in war, bullfighting, and hunting), and these dangerous experiences shaped and defined him and his works. Neither an armchair writer nor bookish intellectual, Hemingway was a man of action—he was an avid outdoor sportsman, big-game hunter, heavy drinker, bar brawler, boxer, bullfight enthusiast, and, over his lifetime, either a volunteer or correspondent in five wars.

War, in particular, defines Hemingway's literary legacy, serving as the backdrop for three of his best known and most popular novels: *The Sun Also Rises* (1926), *A Farewell to Arms* (1929), and *For Whom the Bell Tolls* (1940). In these early novels, Hemingway delineates a particular model of twentieth-century masculine literary hero: the man of action, a lone individualist with primitive emotions who struggles bravely against personal or cosmic circumstances. Jake Barnes, the protagonist of *The Sun Also Rises,* loses both sexual potency and psychological balance because of his experiences in World War I. Jake seeks both to consummate his love for Brett Ashley and to find existential meaning in the postwar world, telling himself, "I did not care what it [the world] was all about. All I wanted to know was how to live in it" (Hemingway 1996, 137). He achieves neither goal, yet survives both failures. Although Jake is unsuccessful in the end, Hemingway instills in him the unshakeable and unsentimental quality of grace under physical and psychological pressure.

Such qualities are readily evident in Hemingway's other young protagonists as well. Robert Jordan in *For Whom the Bell Tolls* and Frederic Henry in *A Farewell to Arms* are both American war volunteers (also in World War I) who suffer internal and external injuries and loss only to find disillusionment and death. For Hemingway, man is always at war with himself—the internal struggle is always paired with external warfare. His model of male heroism is grounded more in the fight itself than in the final outcome.

In Hemingway's works, this struggle continues to play out at all stages of a man's life. In the highly regarded *The Old Man and the Sea* (1952), the elderly protagonist Santiago's four-day struggle to catch, kill, and bring home a huge marlin serves as an extended metaphor for male perseverance in the face of powerful natural forces. Having gone eighty-four days without a catch, Santiago is nearly killed by his fight with the fish, and later by the sharks, despite all his skill, experience, and tenacity. A humble Santiago returns home with the skeleton of the marlin lashed to his boat, and with renewed faith that "a man is not made for defeat. . . . A man can be destroyed but not defeated" (Hemingway 1996, 114).

Hemingway's life and writings stand as examples of an archetypal manhood in which a man makes his way in the world alone, and an activist artistry in which the creation of masculinity and literature are the same process. Although biographical truths and literary fiction are often conflated, Hemingway is revered as a "man's man" and a "man's writer" who has influenced subsequent generations of war correspondents, journalists, and writers.

Bibliography

Baker, Carlos. *Ernest Hemingway: A Life Story.* New York: Bantam, 1970.

Hemingway, Ernest. *The Sun Also Rises.* 1926. Reprint, New York: Scribner, 1996.

———. *The Old Man and the Sea.* 1952. Reprint, New York: Scribner, 1996.

Mellow, James R. *Hemingway: A Life without Consequences.* Boston: Houghton Mifflin, 1992.

Oliver, Charles M. *Ernest Hemingway A to Z: The Essential Reference to the Life and Work.* New York: Facts On File, 1999.

Reynolds, Michael. *Hemingway: The Paris Years.* New York: Norton, 1999.

Further Reading

Fitch, Noel Riley. *Sylvia Beach and the Lost Generation: A History of Literary Paris in the Twenties and Thirties.* New York: Norton, 1983.

Trogdon, Robert W., ed. *Ernest Hemingway: A Literary Reference.* New York: Carroll & Graf, 2002.

Wagner, Linda W., ed. *Ernest Hemingway: Six Decades of Criticism.* East Lansing: Michigan State University Press, 1987.

Selected Writings

Hemingway, Ernest. *Men Without Women.* 1927. Reprint, New York: Scribner, 1997.

———. *A Farewell to Arms.* 1929. Reprint, New York: Scribner, 1997.

———. *The Green Hills of Africa.* 1935. Reprint, New York: Touchstone, 1996.

———. *For Whom the Bell Tolls.* 1940. Reprint, New York: Scribner, 1996.

Related Entries

Fishing; Hunting; Individualism; Outdoorsmen; Sports; Strenuous Life; War; World War I

—*Carlos Rodríguez*

Heroism

American ideals of heroism have been historically inseparable from ideals of masculinity. While heroism has been tied to such masculine ideals as gallantry, chivalry, nobility, and courage, the basis of American notions of both heroism and manliness has been a tension between virtuous devotion to a higher cause and the quest for personal achievement. Various heroic types have emerged and captivated the American imagination.

The earliest model of heroic masculinity in American culture was the patriotic citizen-soldier. Emerging at the time of the American Revolution, this figure embodied ideals of republican citizenship, particularly fraternalism, public virtue, and self-sacrifice on behalf of a national cause. But in a society already beginning to embrace a liberal-democratic commitment to individual liberty, the public spiritedness of the youthful soldier-patriot set the stage for self-interested pursuits later in life. By valorizing the youthful soldier and juxtaposing him to the mature, freedom-loving, civic individual, American culture resolved the tension between civic virtue and personal liberty in generational terms.

This model of heroism—emphasizing both the citizen-soldier's civic kinship with other Americans and the sacrifices that set him apart—has persisted through all subsequent American wars and been immortalized in countless novels and films. After being challenged during the 1960s by young Americans uncertain of the rightness of American involvement in the Vietnam War, it was strongly revived during the 1980s. This return to heroic masculinity can be seen in President Ronald Reagan's efforts to restore American military might, and in the popularity of the films of such actors as Arnold Schwarzenegger and Sylvester Stallone.

During the early nineteenth century, another model of American heroic masculinity emerged: the frontier hero. Like the citizen-soldier, the frontier hero embodied the tension between public spiritedness and personal achievement. Early frontier heroes such as Daniel Boone and the fictional Natty Bumppo were both civic-minded agents of civilization and freedom-loving fugitives from civilization. Invariably white, they achieved their status through mastery of the hunting and survival skills characteristic of romanticized Native American manhood—and through the application of these skills to the conquest of the frontier and the westward expansion of Euro-American institutions. They thus tied heroic manhood specifically to whiteness. These contradictory characteristics re-emerged in such nineteenth- and twentieth-century figures as the frontiersman Kit Carson, the buffalo hunter William Cody (popularly known as Buffalo Bill), and the actor John Wayne. However, these were commercialized, mass-mediated versions intended to entertain audiences by appealing to the nostalgia that accompanied and followed the disappearance of the western frontier.

Amid the market revolution of the early to mid–nineteenth century, the "self-made man," representing personal achievement and economic success, became a new type of heroic American man. Represented early in the century by Benjamin Franklin, and later in the century by immigrant industrialist Andrew Carnegie and Horatio Alger, Jr.'s, upwardly mobile street urchins, the self-made man became a hero by helping to justify the individualistic pursuit of self-interest. But his heroism also lay in his moral virtue and his application of his wealth to philanthropic ends.

As the growing corporatization and bureaucratization of American life challenged the possibility of achieving self-made success, the self-made man became even more heroic. The continued vitality of this heroic ideal—and its expansion to embrace nonwhites—was evident in the twentieth-century works of writers Abraham Cahan (a Jewish immigrant) and Richard Rodriguez (a Mexican American), and in the success stories of twentieth-century sports heroes such as African Americans Jackie Robinson and Michael Jordan.

The manly worker, or "heroic artisan," emerged as an important cultural icon in the late nineteenth century, when the mechanization of production was undermining older ideals of artisan labor. Featured in Gilded Age dime novels—and celebrated anew in the proletarian art and fiction of the Great Depression of the 1930s, the Depression-era songs of Woody Guthrie, and the music of late-twentieth-century rock musician Bruce Springsteen—this figure embodied moral virtue and rose above other men through determination and personal fortitude. Yet at the same time he remained satisfied with modest material success and turned his heroic energies toward the betterment of the working-class community.

During the late nineteenth and twentieth centuries, movements for racial justice and rights for nonwhites made race leaders into exemplars of heroic masculinity. Figures like Frederick Douglass, Booker T. Washington, W. E. B. Du Bois, Martin Luther King, Jr., and Malcolm X—the last two of whom were assassinated by people disinclined to view them as heroes—became heroic advocates for racial equality. Similarly, labor organizer César Chavez sought justice for Mexican-American farm workers during the middle decades of the twentieth century. Part of what made these figures heroic was their ability to rise above humble origins to achieve personal success, but even more important was their public devotion to their racially defined communities.

While notions of heroic masculinity have varied by race, ethnicity, and class, and while they have been subjected to multiple interpretations and specific historical conditions, all of them have helped to define ideals of manliness by which ordinary American men judge themselves. In doing so, they have provided utopian resolutions to the tension between public spiritedness and individualism that has long been at the foundation of American life.

Bibliography

Browne, Ray B., Marshall Fishwick, and Michael T. Marsden, eds. *Heroes of Popular Culture.* Bowling Green, Ohio: Bowling Green University Popular Press, 1972.

Denning, Michael. *Mechanic Accents: Dime Novels and Working-Class Culture in America.* New York: Verso, 1987.

Greene, Theodore P. *America's Heroes: The Changing Model of Success in American Magazines.* New York: Oxford University Press, 1970.

Kann, Mark. *On the Man Question: Gender and Civic Virtue in America.* Philadelphia: Temple University Press, 1991.

Kimmell, Michael. *Manhood in America: A Cultural History.* New York: Free Press, 1996.

Lewis, R. W. B. *The American Adam: Innocence, Tragedy, and Tradition in the Nineteenth Century.* Chicago: University of Chicago Press, 1955.

Rotundo, E. Anthony. *American Manhood: Transformations in Masculinity from the Revolution to the Modern Era.* New York: Basic Books, 1990.

Westbrook, Robert. "'I Want a Girl, Just Like the Girl That Married Harry James': American Women and the Problem of Political Obligation in World War II." *American Quarterly* 42, no. 4 (1990): 587–614.

Further Reading

Dalton, Kathleen. *Theodore Roosevelt: A Strenuous Life.* New York: Knopf, 2002.

Faragher, John Mack. *Daniel Boone: The Life and Legend of an American Pioneer.* New York: Henry Holt, 1992.

Gaines, Kevin K. *Uplifting the Race: Black Leadership, Politics, and Culture in the Twentieth Century.* Chapel Hill: University of North Carolina Press, 1996.

Jeffords, Susan. *The Remasculinization of America: Gender and the Vietnam War.* Bloomington: Indiana University Press, 1989.
Mitchell, Lee Clark. *Westerns: Making the Man in Fiction and Film.* Chicago: University of Chicago Press, 1996.
Susman, Warren. "Culture Heroes: Ford, Barton, and Ruth." In *Culture As History: The Transformation of American Society in the Twentieth Century.* New York: Pantheon, 1984.

Related Entries

Alger, Horatio, Jr.; Boone, Daniel; Chivalry; Individualism; Leatherstocking Tales; Patriotism; Rambo; Reagan, Ronald; Republicanism; Schwarzenegger, Arnold; Self-Made Man; Springsteen, Bruce; Western Frontier; Westerns

—*Holly Allen*

Heterosexuality

Heterosexuals are people who desire and engage in sexual activity exclusively with the opposite sex. Contemporary Americans generally define heterosexuality as the opposite of homosexuality, and consider the two mutually exclusive. The rise of this duality is important for its insistence on the difference between men and women. This emphasis on difference has played a large role in definitions of masculinity and femininity in the twentieth century.

History of Heterosexuality as a Medical Term

Heterosexuality is a modern concept that made its way into English as a medical term late in the nineteenth century and gained popular usage in the first half of the twentieth century. It emerged at the same time as the term *homosexuality*, and the emergence of these concepts together marked a change in the ideology of sexuality. Nineteenth-century norms, especially among the middle class, posited that humans naturally wanted to procreate, and that a desire for sex for any other reason was abnormal. Beginning in the 1890s, the German sexologist Richard von Krafft-Ebing and others argued that desire for sex itself was normal and natural, as long as that desire was for the other sex and included the desire to reproduce. The 1893 translation of Krafft-Ebing's *Psychopathia Sexualis* was the first work to use the term *heterosexual* to refer to a person attracted to the opposite sex. Krafft-Ebing set up an oppositional relationship between heterosexual and homosexual, and he defined heterosexuals as being normal, and homosexuals as being deviant.

Sigmund Freud built on Krafft-Ebing's concept of heterosexuality and gave it much of its current meaning. Freud argued that all humans were driven in large part by sexual desire, and that the inappropriate development or channeling of that drive made one mentally unhealthy. Freud saw this desire as having little, if any, basis in the desire to reproduce, instead attributing sexual desire entirely to the desire for pleasure. He considered a lack of heterosexual desire to be a sign of mental illness. Freud is also important for locating the formation of heterosexuality or homosexuality not in the nature of the individual, but rather in one's childhood experiences. His theories of psychological growth posited heterosexuality as the end result of successful sexual development. A truly mature (and masculine) male, he argued, would invariably desire women. Of course, these writings did not immediately change Americans' perceptions. Freud would become most influential in U.S. popular culture after World War II.

Heterosexuality and Changing Ideas of Masculinity

The term *heterosexuality* came into popular usage in the late nineteenth century at about the same time that *masculinity* was becoming a widespread term. Victorian (especially middle- and upper-class) ideals of manhood had prized self-control, civilized behavior, and same-sex platonic love. Middle-class Victorians considered love by a man (whomever the object) to be ideal—as long as that love was without sexual expression. They considered sexual activity for any other reason than reproduction to be a wasteful drain of bodily energy.

In the late 1800s, however, ideals of manhood and of love began to change. Growing numbers of middle-class men, fearful that urban-industrial life had threatened masculine vigor by severing their contact with nature, embraced a new model of masculinity that idealized men who could not entirely control their physical passions. Physical aggression and the inability to rein in sexual desire were two of the most important aspects of this new masculinity. The concept of heterosexuality became intertwined with this new idea, since it assumed the appropriateness of physical sexual desire itself. The developing association between masculinity and heterosexuality was also encouraged by the Darwinian ideas of natural and sexual selection, which were gaining popularity at this time. These ideas suggested that the "fittest" men were those who had physical strength with which to defend themselves and instinctually desired to have sex (and therefore reproduce) with as many women as possible. Instead of being signs of moral weakness, such manifestations of overt heterosexuality as adultery and premarital sexual experience increasingly came to be viewed as signs of masculine virility.

Other social and cultural currents of the late nineteenth century reinforced the increasingly close connection between manliness and heterosexuality. As child labor became less important to the family economy, reproduction became less central to sexual practice than it had been, and birth rates dropped. Birth-control methods became increasingly legal and respectable after the turn of the twentieth century, and sex within marriage purely for pleasure became, for many, a central element of a successful marriage. The medical community began to see heterosexual activity as healthy, especially for men, rather than as a drain on their mental powers. This new emphasis on sex in marriage for pleasure was part of a larger nineteenth-century shift to a marital ideal emphasizing companionship between husband and wife. Heterosexual romance became, in the minds of many Americans, the single most important part of a marriage. Just as marital love came to be associated with sexual desire, love between members of the same sex—once viewed as an expression of platonic feelings—also became associated with sexual desire and was therefore perceived as taboo. These changes likely had an effect on the sexual behaviors of many men.

By the 1950s these sexual beliefs became predominant throughout American culture, and prevailing American notions of masculinity became dependent on heterosexual identity and exclusively heterosexual activity. Heterosexuality in men, especially around the mid–twentieth century, became associated with marriage, children, and the role of the breadwinner, and men married at younger ages after World War II than they had before. Yet dominant norms of heterosexual masculinity also permitted a significant degree of sexual experimentation. Because the distinction between homosexuality and heterosexuality emphasized the importance of gender, rather than focusing on behavior, it therefore allowed heterosexual men to engage in behaviors that might earlier have been considered perverse and unhealthy, such as oral sex, as long as they were performed with a woman. Furthermore, teenage dating without adult supervision became increasingly possible with the proliferation of cars, movie theaters, and restaurants. Premarital heterosexual experience for men, through "petting" and even intercourse, became a regular part of teenage experience and was often practiced with teenage girls from the same social background.

In the 1950s, Americans increasingly understood heterosexual sex that occurred before, and even outside of, marriage as normal behavior for men. This model of heterosexual masculinity was most explicitly articulated in Hugh Hefner's *Playboy* magazine, which lauded the mature, heterosexual bachelor as a man to be envied. His ability to have multiple sexual partners made him seem even more masculine and heterosexual than the supposedly monogamous married man. This new idealization of nonmarital sexuality, along with the increasing availability and reliability of contraceptives (especially with the introduction of the birth control pill in 1960), separated sexual behavior from reproduction and broadened the range of culturally acceptable manifestations of male heterosexuality.

The counterculture of the 1960s and 1970s further increased the separation of heterosexuality from traditional notions of masculinity, as heterosexual men grew their hair long and idealized androgynous behavior, while still believing in the normality and naturalness of heterosexuality. Throughout these periods, the average age of marriage for men rose, and their prolonged bachelorhood allowed heterosexual men more time for premarital sex.

Some disagreement about the category of heterosexuality still existed, however, even in the 1950s. Alfred Kinsey, for example, famous for his studies of sexuality in the 1940s and 1950s, argued that there was no natural division of people into homosexuals and heterosexuals. Overall, however, the concept of heterosexuality would remain mostly unquestioned until the rise of feminism and gay rights activism in the 1970s.

Heterosexual Masculinity Challenged

Beginning in the 1970s, feminists and gay rights activists challenged the dualistic categories of homosexuality and heterosexuality, and especially the idea that heterosexuality is more natural, healthy, and masculine than homosexuality. Such challenges were used to examine prevailing ideas about masculinity and femininity, which were already under attack from the androgynous counterculture. For example, Kate Millett's *Sexual Politics* (1970) called for the overthrow of heterosexual supremacy in society, arguing that men's "heterosexual posturing" in order to meet the demands of masculine standards involved the dangerous potential for violence against women. Feminists also argued that compulsory heterosexuality serves as a support for male privilege. Many feminists rejected marriage, and even heterosexuality, in their attempts to overcome oppression.

Similarly, gay and lesbian activists questioned the desirability of heterosexual and masculine identification, viewing the close association between them as part of an oppressive system. They questioned the link between heterosexuality and masculinity, especially the idea that homosexuality and masculinity were mutually exclusive. Feminists and queer theorists also problematized the validity of the categories *heterosexual* and *homosexual*, as well as *masculine* and *feminine*, arguing that these concepts were cultural constructs that failed to accurately describe anyone's sexual desire or behavior.

Heterosexual men reacted to these challenges in different ways. Some men, especially in the late 1970s, actively tried to change ideals of manhood to allow heterosexual men to support feminism. Other men, predominantly white middle-class heterosexuals, read Robert Bly's *Iron John* in the early 1990s and embraced his reinforcement of gender difference and the innate power of manhood. Similarly, cultural conservatives continued to argue for heterosexuality as the only natural and moral behavior for men. Debates on whether people can be neatly divided into homosexuality and heterosexuality are sure to continue in the future, as are questions over the links between heterosexuality and masculinity.

Bibliography

Bederman, Gail. *Manliness and Civilization: A Cultural History of Gender and Race in the United States, 1880–1917.* Chicago: University of Chicago Press, 1995.

Brod, Harry, and Michael Kaufman, eds. *Theorizing Masculinities.* London: Sage, 1994.

Katz, Jonathan Ned. *The Invention of Heterosexuality.* New York: Dutton, 1995.

Krafft-Ebing, Richard von. *Psychopathia Sexualis, With Especial Reference to Contrary Sexual Instinct: A Clinical-Foresnic Study.* Translated by F.J. Rebman. New York: Medical Arts Agency, 1906.

Millett, Kate. *Sexual Politics.* 1970. Reprint, Chicago: University of Chicago Press, 2000.

Rich, Adrienne. "Compulsory Heterosexuality and Lesbian Existence." In *Powers of Desire: The Politics of Sexuality*, edited by A. Snitow, C. Stansell, and S. Thompson. New York: Monthly Review, 1983.

Further Reading

D'Emilio, John, and Estelle Freedman. *Intimate Matters: A History of Sexuality in America.* 2nd ed. Chicago: University of Chicago Press, 1997.

Foucault, Michel. *History of Sexuality.* Vol. 1. New York: Vintage, 1990.

Richardson, Diane, ed. *Theorising Heterosexuality: Telling It Straight.* Buckingham, England: Open University Press, 1996.

Segal, Lynne. *Straight Sex: Rethinking the Politics of Pleasure.* Berkeley: University of California Press, 1994.

Related Entries

Bachelorhood; Bisexuality; Darwinism; Emotion; Feminism; Freudian Psychoanalytic Theory; Homosexuality; *Iron John: A Book About Men*; Marriage; Men's Movements; Patriarchy; Reproduction; Violence

—*Christy Erin Regenhardt*

Higginson, Thomas Wentworth

1823–1911
Health Reformer and Minister

The Unitarian minister Thomas Wentworth Higginson was among a growing number of nineteenth-century reformers concerned with the health and physical fitness of middle-class American men. As one of the earliest proponents of "muscular Christianity," Higginson formulated what became a highly influential ideal of middle-class manhood.

Born in Cambridge, Massachusetts, Higginson graduated from Harvard Divinity School in 1847 and became involved in several antebellum-era reforms, especially abolitionism and women's rights. Like many Unitarian ministers of the period, he emphasized the close relation between nature and human spirituality—an idea closely associated with Romanticism—and like many reformers he promoted the cultivation of moral perfection in both individuals and American society.

By the late 1850s, Higginson was increasingly focused on health reform. He drew inspiration from the English novelists Charles Kingsley and Thomas Hughes, who were harbingers of the muscular Christianity movement and whose works emphasized the importance of physical exercise and competitive sport in building Christian character among young men. He became convinced that urbanization, industrialization, and poor dietary habits were undermining the health and vigor of middle-class men. He also criticized the nation's Protestant churches for teaching "that physical vigor and sanctity were incompatible" and filling the ministry with clergy who lacked a "manly life" (Putney, 21). Convinced that both personal and national spiritual strength required a healthy diet, outdoor activity, and physical education, he published his views in a series of *Atlantic Monthly* essays during the late 1850s and early 1860s, including "Saints, and their Bodies," "A Letter to a Dyspeptic," "Physical Courage," "Gymnastics," and "My Outdoor Study."

Although Higginson addressed women's health as well—one of his essays focused on "The Health of Our Girls"—his primary concern was the necessity of physical fitness in preparing middle-class boys and men for the roles, responsibilities, and imperatives of Victorian middle-class manhood. He considered good health "a necessary condition of all permanent success" (Borish, 146) and believed that the moral discipline fostered by exercise and sport would make men more effective in business, politics, the ministry, and the conquest and settlement of the western frontier. He therefore actively promoted organized camping (so that men might learn from nature's "magnificent strength" [Lucas, 32]), boating ("without a boat, one is so much less a man"), and football ("to those whose animal life is sufficiently vigorous to enjoy it") (Borish, 148, 149).

Higginson's ideal of middle-class manhood was decidedly white, genteel, and heterosexual. Although he led a regiment of freed slaves in South Carolina during the Civil War and was fascinated by what he considered the "splendid muscular development" (Nelson and Price, 504) of black men's bodies, he thought that "neither their physical nor moral temperament gave them that toughness, that obstinate purpose of living, which sustains the . . . Anglo-Saxon" (Borish, 148). He harshly distinguished his own model of American manliness from what he called the "unmanly manhood" of poet Walt Whitman, who celebrated rough working-class masculinity, open sexual expression, and homosexual love, and who chose nursing over field duty during the Civil War.

Higginson's ideas at first remained confined largely to eastern elites and theologically liberal ministers, but by the closing decades of the nineteenth century they achieved much wider popularity. Higginson remained actively involved with muscular Christianity in his later life, becoming a patriarch to the movement he had helped to establish.

Bibliography

Borish, Linda J. "The Robust Woman and the Muscular Christian: Catharine Beecher, Thomas Higginson, and Their Vision of American Society, Health, and Physical Activities." *International Journal of the History of Sport* 4 (1987): 139–154.

Lucas, John A. "Thomas Wentworth Higginson: Early Apostle of Health and Fitness." *Journal of Health, Physical Education, and Recreation* 42 (February 1971): 30–33.

Nelson, Robert K., and Kenneth M. Price. "Debating Manliness: Thomas Wentworth Higginson, William Sloane Kennedy, and the Question of Whitman." *American Literature* 73 (2001): 497–524.

Putney, Clifford. *Muscular Christianity: Manhood and Sports in Protestant America, 1880–1920.* Cambridge, Mass.: Harvard University Press, 2001.

Tuttleton, James W. *Thomas Wentworth Higginson.* Boston: Twayne, 1978.

Further Reading

Edelstein, Tilden G. *Strange Enthusiasm: A Life of Thomas Wentworth Higginson.* New Haven, Conn: Yale University Press, 1968.

Looby, Christopher. "'As Thoroughly Black as the Most Faithful Philanthropist Could Desire': Erotics of Race in Higginson's Army Life in a Black Regiment." In *Race and the Subject of Masculinities,* edited by Harry Stecopoulos and Michael Uebel. Durham, N.C.: Duke University Press, 1997.

Selected Writings

Higginson, Thomas Wentworth. "Saints, and Their Bodies." *Atlantic Monthly* 1 (1858): 582–595.

———. "Physical Courage." *Atlantic Monthly* 2 (1858): 728–737.

———. "A Letter to a Dyspeptic." *Atlantic Monthly* 3 (1859): 465–474.

———. "Gymnastics." *Atlantic Monthly* 7 (1861): 283–302.

———. "My Outdoor Study." *Atlantic Monthly* 8 (1861): 302–309.

———. "The Health of Our Girls." *Atlantic Monthly* 9 (1862): 722–731.

———. *Army Life in a Black Regiment.* 1869. Reprint, New York: Crowell-Collier, 1962.

______. "Unmanly Manhood." *Woman's Journal,* April 13, 1882.

Related Entries

Abolitionism; Beecher, Henry Ward; Body; Boyhood; Character; Civil War; Football; Graham, Sylvester; Health; Heterosexuality; Homosexuality; Industrialization; Middle-Class Manhood; Ministry; Muscular Christianity; Reform Movements; Religion and Spirituality; Romanticism; Sports; Strenuous Life; Urbanization; Victorian Era; Western Frontier; Whiteness; Whitman, Walt

—Bret E. Carroll

Hoboes

Hoboes, or tramps, were unskilled workers that traveled across America in large numbers between 1870 and 1940 seeking employment. Almost exclusively white, fluent English speakers, and overwhelmingly male, they often rode illegally on freight trains between cities and rural areas, where they found jobs in construction, on the railroads, or on farms. Sacrificing the respectability of settled male gender roles in exchange for freedom from social responsibility, hoboes were either demonized as hypermasculine predators who threatened the family or romanticized as freedom-loving wanderers. Yet their labor was critical to the expansion and consolidation of America's industrial economy during the late nineteenth and early twentieth centuries.

For the few middle-class men that experienced hoboing, train riding and manual labor served as a rite of passage into a muscular and adventurous masculine world—an initiation into a "strenuous life" that rejected the genteel and artificial overcivilization often criticized in the Progressive Era. Most hoboes, however, were young working-class men, and hoboing was integral to traditions and practices of young working-class manhood. Although working-class hoboes performed unskilled labor, their mobility continued an earlier pattern of artisan life in which journeymen in the skilled crafts of printing and railroading traveled between apprenticeship and craft employment. Hoboing also preserved settled jobs for working-class fathers and husbands, who were often threatened by industrial layoffs, and provided some unattached men an opportunity to accumulate capital or escape family conflict or claims of paternity.

Many aspects of hobo life challenged masculine gender conventions. Urban "hobohemias" fostered a nondomestic bachelor subculture of single residence hotels and flop houses, saloons and cheap restaurants, second-hand clothing stores, burlesque shows, and prostitution. Public perception usually associated hoboes, who lived in urban "jungles" or in rural camps, with tasks commonly considered feminine: laundering shirts to kill lice and cooking mulligan stew (made from whatever was handy) in tomato cans. While many hoboes remained single for economic reasons, some found in hoboing a space for engaging in homosexual relations. Some hoboes created a group identity outside of the economic and cultural mainstream, including publishing a monthly newspaper, *The Hobo News/Review.*

Public fear of hoboes resulted in the passage of Tramp Acts (vagrancy statutes) in the 1870s. Directly derived from the southern Black Codes used to control the freedmen's movement and re-establish white supremacy in the aftermath of the Civil War, these laws disciplined the male labor force into a large and impersonal work culture; undermined workers' self-conceptions as independent artisans; and demonized those who refused to adapt. Tramp laws also helped reinforce the relegation of middle-class women to the domestic sphere by implying that they needed to be protected from these unattached men.

Because their lifestyle defied acceptable male behavior in multiple ways, hoboes stood on the margins of society. Their freedom from the new American industrial social order appeared either as effeminate or disreputable and threatening. By the 1920s, however, their challenge to social conventions had been recast by the actor Charlie Chaplin and others into a romanticized or comic image. The iconography of the hobo thereafter became established in American popular films, cartoons, and literature as representative of a long American tradition, stretching from Huckleberry Finn to Dean Moriarty (in Jack Kerouac's *On the Road*), fantasizing a masculine escape from domestic and corporate fetters. In this idealized form the hobo powerfully contributed to popular constructions of masculinity.

Bibliography

Adrian, Lynne M. "'The World We Shall Win for Labor': Early Twentieth-Century Hobo Self-Publication." In *Print Culture in a Diverse America,* edited by James P. Danky and Wayne A. Wiegand. Urbana: University of Illinois Press, 1998.

Anderson, Nels. *On Hobos and Homelessness,* edited and with an introduction by Rafaele Rauty. Chicago: University of Chicago Press, 1998.

Bruns, Roger. *Knights of the Road: A Hobo History.* New York: Methuen, 1980.

Cresswell, Tim. *The Tramp in America.* London: Reaktion Books, 2001.

Fox, Charlie. *Tales of an American Hobo.* Introduction by Lynne M. Adrian. Iowa City: University of Iowa Press, 1989.

Kusmer, Kenneth L. *Down and Out, On the Road: The Homeless in American History.* New York: Oxford University Press, 2002.

Monkkonen, Eric H. *Walking to Work: Tramps in America, 1790–1935.* Lincoln: University of Nebraska Press, 1984.

Further Reading

Feied, Frederick. *No Pie in the Sky: The Hobo as American Cultural Hero in the Works of Jack London, John Dos Passos, and Jack Kerouac.* New York: Citadel Press, 1964.

Guthrie, Woody. *Bound for Glory.* 1943. Reprint, New York: New American Library, 1983.

London, Jack. *The Road.* New York: Macmillan, 1907. Reprinted in *Novels and Social Writings.* New York: Literary Classics of the United States, 1982.

———. *Jack London on the Road: The Tramp Diary and Other Hobo Writings,* edited by Richard W. Etulain. Logan: Utah State University Press, 1979.

Minehan, Thomas. *Boy and Girl Tramps of America.* 1934. Reprint, Seattle: University of Washington Press, 1976.

Willard, Josiah Flynt. *Tramping with Tramps: Studies and Sketches of Vagabond Life.* New York: Century Company, 1899.

Related Entries

Adventures of Huckleberry Finn; Agrarianism; Alcohol; Artisan; Bachelorhood; Beat Movement; *Grapes of Wrath, The*; Great Depression; Industrialization; *Jungle, The*; Kerouac, Jack; London, Jack; Masculine Domesticity; Middle-Class Manhood; Progressive Era; Travel; Working-Class Manhood

—Lynne M. Adrian

HOLLYWOOD

Since the 1910s, Hollywood, in Los Angeles, California, has been home to the American film industry, which has produced iconic representations of masculinity that have reflected and helped define notions of manhood in the United States. Its role in doing so, however, has always been complex and fundamentally contradictory. Filmed, processed, edited, and then projected on-screen, Hollywood's film images of men have achieved cultural power by being compellingly realistic, natural, and embodied, yet also by being imaginary, constructed, and disembodied. Hollywood films have supported heterosexual male dominance by constructing film narratives that objectify women and assume a heterosexual male perspective, while at the same time they have also objectified manhood by presenting images of men performing masculine roles for popular consumption.

A large and highly profitable industry, "Hollywood" (the term is virtually synonymous with the California film industry) has culturally and economically empowered male actors, directors, producers, screenwriters, and technicians, allowing them to exemplify a particular kind of successful modern manhood. The men who make films, and the male viewers who consume them, have had their masculine identities and ideas about manhood shaped by Hollywood's products and by-products, making Hollywood a powerful cultural industry fundamental to formulations of twentieth-century masculinity.

Movie Manhood in the Silent Era

Hollywood's complex relationship to masculinity dates back to the silent film era at the beginning of the twentieth century. D. W. Griffith's Civil War epic *Birth of a Nation* (1915) juxtaposed images of heroic white southern gentlemen with corrupt and handicapped northern men, as well as with stereotyped representations of African-American men, portrayed (by white actors in blackface) as comic fools, political usurpers, and menacing sexual predators. By dramatizing white masculine fears and fantasies of both empowerment and disempowerment, and by circulating racialized constructions of masculinity among mass audiences, Griffith became the first of a lasting off-screen masculine type in Hollywood: the powerful directorial auteur capable of cinematic artistry and overseeing big budgets, complex technologies, and numerous personnel.

On-screen, Hollywood reflected and contributed to body-centered definitions of masculinity of the period. Men's performances were emphatically physical, portraying physical prowess, malleability, vulnerability, and resilience—ranging from the athleticism of Douglas Fairbanks to the overt sexuality of Rudolph Valentino to the physical humor of Charlie Chaplin and Buster Keaton. Through exaggerated physical movements that created dramatic and comic narratives, these male stars offered viewers compelling, albeit fictional, versions of masculinity. By and large, film images of masculinity depicted standard archetypes, including the morally upright male hero and the hypermasculine villain.

Masculinity in Hollywood's Golden Age

The advent of sound film in 1927 heralded Hollywood's "Golden Age" of the 1930s and 1940s. As the film industry gained increasing cultural power, its efforts to avoid government regulation led to a self-imposed production code in 1930 that ensured its conformity to conservative social conventions and traditional notions of manhood. However, far more ambivalent and contested versions of masculinity were embedded in many film narratives and production processes.

During the 1930s, the experiences of economic depression and world war shaped two of Hollywood's most distinctively masculine genres—Westerns and war films—which showed nostalgic and escapist images of iconic men maintaining self-control in antagonistic environments. While Westerns depicted stoic heroes and antiheroes deliberately and decisively meting out violence in a bygone era, war films depicted men bravely facing the violence and chaos of modern warfare. Gangster and detective films of the noir genre combined elements of Westerns and war films, depicting modern gunslingers attempting to control a hostile and morally ambiguous urban world. Meanwhile, Hollywood's romantic comedies and melodramas portrayed men moving from the masculine independence of bachelorhood to the domesticated manhood of marriage. Such iconic masculine actors as John Wayne, Gary Cooper, Humphrey Bogart, James Cagney, James Stewart, and Cary Grant became stars in these genres, while the directors Howard Hawks, John Ford, and John Huston established their masculine filmmaking reputations through their Westerns and war films. Other directors, such as Orson Welles, Frank Capra, and George Cukor, represented an alternative model of male prowess: the sensitive, creative intellectual maverick.

Contrasting models of masculinity often informed the film industry's volatile gender politics. During the production of *Gone With The Wind* (1939), for example, the male lead, Clark Gable, considered a virile and brutish star, denounced director George Cukor for his homosexuality; accused him of offering more scenes to the female lead, Vivian Leigh; and refused to work with him. Producer David O. Selznick replaced Cukor with director Victor Fleming, a friend of Gable's with a reputation as a "man's man." Cukor, meanwhile, developed a reputation as a successful "woman's director" for his ability to elicit strong performances from female stars. Cukor's situation also demonstrated Hollywood's ambivalence about homosexual masculinity: On-screen, homosexuals were portrayed as weak, ineffectual, deviant, and psychologically unstable. Off-screen, however, homosexuality was not necessarily a barrier to success, even though discrimination existed in the industry. Cukor, director James Whale, and actors Cary Grant, Gene Kelly, Rock Hudson, Montgomery Clift, and Anthony Perkins are all men whose fame as masculine Hollywood icons has since been linked to either acknowledged homosexuality or ambiguous homoeroticism in their films.

This poster for the 1942 film Casablanca *suggests Hollywood's importance in purveying images of masculinity for popular consumption, lionizing and objectifying the heterosexual male. American filmgoers of the World War II era idealized Humphrey Bogart as a morally principled, emotionally detached fighter of evil. (Warner Brothers/The Kobal Collection)*

Hollywood's rationalized studio system during the Golden Age also gave rise to an oligarchy of powerful, predominantly Jewish, male studio heads—such as Adolph Zukor, Carl Laemmle, Samuel Goldwyn, William Fox, Harry and Jack Warner, and Louis B. Mayer—who reigned over actors and directors. Following filmmaking pioneers Thomas Edison and Griffith, who established the early technology and techniques of filmmaking, these men created another kind of Hollywood masculinity by transforming the business into a cultural and economic empire and establishing themselves as captains of a new American industry. While fostering the careers of these and other European immigrants, Hollywood reinforced broader cultural associations of masculinity with whiteness. In this process, it relegated Asian- and African-American men to off-screen manual labor or to minor film roles as attendants, bandits, musicians, dancers, and racial caricatures of entertaining, inferior, or menacing masculinity.

Hollywood Masculinity in Postwar America

In postwar America, the Golden Age of filmmaking came to an end when a 1948 Supreme Court ruling broke up the studio system for violating antitrust laws. Meanwhile, television became a new form of popular entertainment in the 1950s, further lessening Hollywood's power. However, Hollywood's influence on American masculinities persisted. Big-budget technicolor musicals continued to reinforce masculine ideals through male performers like Fred Astaire, Gene Kelly, and Frank Sinatra, whose star personas rested on their physical or musical grace. But Hollywood also began exploring more frankly the tensions, ambiguities, and uncertainties underlying masculine identity. *The Best Years of Our Lives* (1946) swept the Oscars by dramatizing World War II veterans struggling to reassimilate as physically and psychologically damaged misfits. The 1950s also saw a new type of male star, characterized by vulnerability, inner turmoil, and rebelliousness. These young actors, including Montgomery Clift, Paul Newman, Marlon Brando, and James Dean, found success using the new introspective "method" acting, in which an actor uses his emotions to identify with his character.

Models of masculine toughness and vulnerability were further revised in the 1960s and 1970s amid a rise in youthful rebellion and the growth of feminism. Clint Eastwood's "man-with-no-name" Westerns of the 1960s established him as a masculine icon and moved the genre toward new extremes of violence and stoicism. In the 1970s Eastwood's influence as a hip yet conservative man expanded with his directorial debut *Play Misty for Me* (1971), a film about a man stalked by an ex-lover that reflected a backlash against the era's feminist critique of masculinity. His roles in the "Dirty Harry" detective series depicted a vigilante, "might-makes-right" version of manhood that supported the conservative ideologies of the Cold War. In contrast stood the vulnerable and sensitive, yet strongly iconoclastic, masculine rebels portrayed in *The Graduate* (1967) and *Easy Rider* (1969)—youth films that launched Dustin Hoffman and Jack Nicholson as influential actors.

During the 1960s and 1970s, Hollywood's centrality to American filmmaking and its leadership in manufacturing film images of American masculinity waned as a variety of new film production locations, styles, and strategies arose—most influentially in New York City—in conjunction with a proliferation of new versions of movie manhood. The maverick actor-director Woody Allen, for example, positioned himself against Hollywood in autobiographical films portraying a neurotic New York Jew as a comic antihero. In the mid-1960s, groundbreaking performances by Sidney Poitier marked more progressive depictions of African-American men imbued with strength, intelligence, and dignity, while "blaxploitation" films oriented to black audiences—beginning with *Shaft* (1971)—invoked numerous racialized masculine stereotypes by portraying pimps, avengers, and a virile detective as urban black antiheroes. Meanwhile, the Italian-American directors Francis Ford Coppola and Martin Scorsese, working with actors Al Pacino and Robert De Niro, forged a New York filmmaking dynasty depicting the urban plight of Italian-American criminals, cops, and boxers. In the early 1970s, the actor Bruce Lee established the martial arts genre as a vehicle for depicting Asian masculine physical prowess, self-discipline, and ancient wisdom.

New Hollywood Masculinities in the Late Twentieth Century

During the 1980s and 1990s, Hollywood images of masculinity moved in two major directions. On the one hand, Hollywood produced new physical and violent film versions of manhood that reflected a more conservative political climate. In 1981 the former actor Ronald Reagan had become president and launched an aggressive foreign policy seeking to reassert American military strength after the defeat in Vietnam and the Iran hostage crisis. In films of this period, Sylvester Stallone and Arnold Schwarzenegger transformed Hollywood masculinity into an excessive "musculinity" in grotesque caricatures of physical prowess. On the other hand, the impact of feminism was evident in film portrayals that destabilized gender stereotypes, challenged conventional masculine norms, and proposed new models of manliness. Such gender-bending films as *Tootsie* (1982), *Mr. Mom* (1983), *Three Men and a Baby* (1987), and *Mrs. Doubtfire* (1993) encouraged audiences to consider men as sensitive and nurturing partners and fathers, rather than as unemotional, work-obsessed breadwinners or hypermasculine bullies. Similarly, in feminist filmmaker Jane Campion's *The Piano* (1993), Harvey Keitel portrayed an emotionally stifled physical brute who becomes transformed into a caring, sexually desirable man.

Hollywood's varied masculinities also changed off-screen. Beginning in the 1970s, George Lucas and Steven Spielberg emerged as new and powerful types in the film industry: creative visionaries who were also businessmen capable of making lucrative blockbusters on an unprecedented scale. Using sensational special effects technologies, these director-moguls recycled elements from old genres in self-consciously escapist depictions of swashbuckling masculine prowess. They also capitalized on new marketing techniques and merchandising tie-ins. Through their films and their magnate personas, they reflected the postmodern tendency to recycle the old in new ways.

Meanwhile, the director Spike Lee established himself as a pioneer of mainstream African-American filmmaking by directing films that achieved interracial appeal by offering frank explorations of contemporary sexuality and race relations from a distinctly African-American perspective. Although Poitier and comedians like Richard Pryor and Eddie Murphy had achieved on-screen stardom before him, Lee's success heralded the rise of many more African Americans in Hollywood, including the directors Mario Van Peebles and John Singleton, and numerous dramatic actors, including Denzel Washington, Samuel L. Jackson, Laurence Fishburne, Morgan Freeman, and Danny Glover, whose star performances portray intelligent, tenaciously principled black men with power and self-possession.

Although Asian-American men continued to lack substantial presence in Hollywood, the 1990s martial arts and action films of actor Jackie Chan and director John Woo were highly successful and represented a formidable new Asian Hollywood manhood both on and off-screen. Chan's persona as a personable Asian superman draws from his status as both actor and virtuoso stuntman who blends physical prowess with disarming self-deprecation. Like Chan, Woo moved from Hong Kong martial arts filmmaking and achieved crossover fame as a gifted Hollywood stylist making ultraviolent mainstream films.

Hollywood's status as a leader in creating film masculinities remained ambiguous. After Hollywood actor/director Robert Redford's 1991 inauguration of the Sundance Film

Festival in Utah, which promotes independent filmmaking outside of Hollywood, many hybridized independent/Hollywood figures arose as actors, directors, and producers. The careers of men like Billy Bob Thorton, Matt Damon, and Ben Affleck suggest that filmmakers and actors are likely to serve as models of manhood outside of Hollywood, while also working from within the system. Still, director James Cameron's triumphant quip that "size matters!"(referring to the unprecedented financial success of his over-budgeted special-effects 1997 behemoth *Titanic*) illustrates the continuing link between the big-budget productions of Hollywood and a man's claim to masculine prowess.

Conclusion: The Elusiveness of Hollywood Manhood

The basis of the film industry's relationship to masculinity remains fundamentally complex in its simultaneous support for and threat to what it means to be a man in America. The wide distribution and aggressive marketing of Hollywood films and stars powerfully reinforces cultural associations of manhood with power, self-control, and triumph over circumstance, giving actors and filmmakers a seemingly superhuman cultural omnipotence. At the same time, Hollywood actors maintain only limited control over the larger phenomenon of their celebrity as they get transformed into objectified, fictional representations of manhood.

A similar dilemma also confronts the male moviegoer, whose masculinity is made problematic by its comparative passivity. Viewing a shadow image of a sensational and usually idealized version of manhood, the male moviegoer regularly encounters versions of manliness at odds with his own experience. For all participants in the Hollywood film industry, masculinity remains an elusive ideal.

Bibliography

Cohan, Steven, and Ina Rae Hark, eds. *Screening the Male: Exploring Masculinities in Hollywood Cinema.* New York: Routledge, 1993.

———. *Masked Men: Masculinity and the Movies in the Fifties.* Bloomington: Indiana University Press, 1997.

Ehrenstein, David. *Open Secret: Gay Hollywood, 1928–1998.* New York: William Morrow, 1998.

Lehman, Peter. *Running Scared: Masculinity and the Representation of the Male Body.* Philadelphia: Temple University Press, 1993.

Lehman, Peter, ed. *Masculinity: Bodies, Movies, Culture.* New York: Routledge, 2001.

Silverman, Kaja. *Male Subjectivity at the Margins.* New York: Routledge, 1992.

Studlar, Gaylyn. *This Mad Masquerade: Stardom and Masculinity in the Jazz Age.* New York: Columbia University Press, 1996.

Trice, Ashton D., and Samuel A. Holland, eds. *Heroes, Antiheroes, and Dolts: Portrayals of Masculinity in American Popular Films, 1921–1999.* Jefferson, N.C.: McFarland, 2001.

Further Reading

Bingham, Dennis. *Acting Male: Masculinities in the Films of James Stewart, Jack Nicholson, and Clint Eastwood.* New Brunswick, N.J.: Rutgers University Press, 1994.

Cohan, Steven. *Masked Men: Masculinity and the Movies in the Fifties.* Bloomington: Indiana University Press, 1997.

Davies, Jude, and Carol R. Smith. *Gender, Ethnicity and Sexuality in Contemporary American Film.* Chicago: Fitzroy Dearborn, 2000.

Jeffords, Susan. *Hard Bodies: Hollywood Masculinity in the Reagan Era.* New Brunswick, N.J.: Rutgers University Press, 1994.

Kirkham, Pat, and Janet Thumim, eds. *You Tarzan: Masculinity, Movies, and Men.* New York: St. Martin's, 1993.

———. *Me Jane: Masculinity, Movies, and Women.* New York: St. Martin's, 1995.

Mellen, Joan. *Big Bad Wolves: Masculinity in the American Film.* New York: Pantheon, 1977.

Sklar, Robert. *City Boys: Cagney, Bogart, Garfield.* Princeton, N.J.: Princeton University Press, 1992.

Tasker, Yvonne. *Spectacular Bodies: Gender, Genre and the Action Cinema.* New York: Routledge, 1993.

Related Entries

Birth of a Nation; Bogart, Humphrey; Brando, Marlon; Buddy Films; Cooper, Gary; Cop Action Films; Cowboys; Dean, James; *Deliverance*; Detectives; Eastwood, Clint; *Easy Rider*; Feminism; Gangsters; Grant, Cary; Homosexuality; Hudson, Rock; *Kramer vs. Kramer*; Martial Arts Films; Men's Movements; Men's Studies; *Mr. Mom*; *Odd Couple, The*; Rambo; Reagan, Ronald; *Rebel Without a Cause*; Schwarzenegger, Arnold; Sensitive Male; *Shaft*; Technology; Television; Wayne, John; Westerns

—*Timothy Barnard*

HOME IMPROVEMENT

In 1991 (the year after Robert Bly's *Iron John* was published) *Home Improvement*, starring comedian Tim Allen as Tim "The Toolman" Taylor, brought the complicated state of contemporary masculinity to prime-time television. While many TV families of the late 1980s and early 1990s featured single fathers (e.g., *Who's the Boss, Empty Nest, Full House*) and workplace settings (e.g., *Cheers, Murphy Brown, Designing Women*),

Home Improvement thrust the middle-class WASP family back into the spotlight, challenging popular notions of ideal fatherhood and masculinity within the nuclear family. Whereas family shows of the 1950s, such as *Father Knows Best,* featured a flawless breadwinner and family man, *Home Improvement* introduced a father struggling to understand himself and his family; and whereas mastery of home improvement had typified the ideal suburban father, Tim Taylor is comically danger-prone. Until the program ended in 1999, Allen's trademark combination of hypermasculinity, testosterone, and power tools parlayed into a top-rated sitcom.

Living in Michigan with his outspoken wife Jill (Patricia Richardson) and three sons, Tim embodies characteristics often associated with crude masculinity: vulgarity, desire for unyielding power, and egocentrism. During each episode, however, his masquerade of manliness crumbles as his attempts to interact with his wife and children, or simply to accomplish tasks around the house turn disastrous through family squabbles or exploding appliances.

When Tim cannot recognize his own inadequacies, he seeks the wisdom of his Zen-like neighbor, Mr. Wilson (Earl Hindman), who advises Tim while enacting tribal or spiritual customs in his backyard. (Many reviewers have identified Wilson's actions with Robert Bly's emphasis on recapturing masculinity through a communal return to the primitive, but his uncontested inner peace and constant depiction as a loner distance him from the communal weekend warriors associated with Bly's faction of the men's movement.) Like Jill, Wilson attempts to make the egocentric Tim more aware of others' needs—to educate him in the "sensitive male" model of manhood—but Tim exhibits the weekly amnesia of most situation-comedy characters, repeatedly forgetting lessons that have already been learned.

Tim's style of masculinity is also scrutinized through juxtaposition with a "sensitive male" during his public performances on his do-it-yourself television show *Tool Time.* Playing a foil to Tim's tactless rube, his co-host and much-tortured sidekick Al Borland (Richard Karn) sports a stereotypically masculine flannel shirt and beard, but he personifies a softer model of manhood: emotional, aware of his feminine side, and respectful to women (especially his mother). As Tim's show objectifies women with sexy *Tool Time* Girls Lisa and Heidi (Pamela Anderson and Debbe Dunning) and promotes male power, his own bumbles and Al's higher level of competence and more "sensible" masculinity repeatedly undermine Tim's position.

Home Improvement offered a friendly critique of the men's movement while also providing variable representations of acceptable masculinity. Tim's constant struggle for a peaceful equilibrium between a preconceived notion of "real" masculine behavior and that encouraged by the feminist movement appealed to viewers, landing the show as high as number two in ratings during its eight-year run. While many shows of the 1990s sought to diverge from the nuclear family, *Home Improvement* reappropriated the white middle-class male for critique, destabilizing the notion of traditional manhood in favor of more conflicted masculinities.

Bibliography

Brooks, Tim, and Earle Marsh, eds. *The Complete Directory to Prime Time Network and Cable TV Shows, 1946–Present.* 7th rev. ed. New York: Ballantine Books, 1999.

Gabriel, Trip. "In Touch with the Tool-Belt Chromosome." *New York Times,* 22 September 1991.

Schindehette, Susan. "Real Men Laugh Last." *People,* 6 July 1992, 105–108.

Waters, Harry F. "That Old Familiar Feeling." *Newsweek,* 9 September 1991, 50.

Zoglin, Richard. "Home Improvement." *Time,* 3 May 1993, 72–75.

Further Reading

Allen, Tim. *Don't Stand Too Close to a Naked Man.* New York: Hyperion, 1994.

Cotter, Bill. *The Wonderful World of Disney Television: A Complete History.* New York: Hyperion, 1997.

Craig, Steve. "More (Male) Power: Humor and Gender in 'Home Improvement.'" *The Mid-Atlantic Almanack* 5 (1996): 61–84.

Hirshey, Gerri. "Dressed to Drill." *Gentleman's Quarterly,* March 1994.

McEachern, Charmaine. "Bringing the Wildman Back Home: Television and the Politics of Masculinity." *Continuum: The Australian Journal of Media & Culture* 7, no. 2 (1994): 1–15.

Vernon, Scott. "Patricia Richardson: 'If I Were Married to Tim, I'd Have Done Away with Him Long Ago.'" *Good Housekeeping,* June 1994, 62.

Related Entries

Fatherhood; *Father Knows Best*; Feminism; *Iron John: A Book About Men*; Marriage; Masculine Domesticity; Men's Movements; Middle-Class Manhood; Sensitive Male; Television

—*Kelly Kessler*

Homosexuality

Homosexuality, defined variously as same-sex love, desire, and/or sexual activity, has been, in one form or another, a universal phenomenon. In the United States, male homosexuality, like all same-sex attraction and behavior, has often challenged entrenched gender systems that define and maintain masculinity. Although the term *homosexual* referred to both sexes when it was coined in the nineteenth century, male homosexuality has been a more prominent concern in American society. This is due to the larger public role that men have played, and to the resulting concern with definitions of, and conformity to, a masculine ideal. For these reasons—in addition to moral opposition to sexual acts between same-sex partners—homosexuality has been among the most controversial and divisive issues in the United States.

Homosexuality has been classified as a sin, a crime, and an illness, with changes in the dominant view reflecting both the general secularization of life in the United States and the power of legal and medical institutions in the twentieth century. The history of homosexuality in the United States might be divided into two broad eras: Before about 1900, when there was a wide range of categories for sexual behavior and identity (with a gradual narrowing of options over time); and the period after 1900, which has been dominated by the homosexual/heterosexual duality and the mid-twentieth-century emergence of political movements and organizations asserting a gay identity.

Before 1900

In most indigenous American cultures, some individuals dressed and acted as the opposite sex or engaged in same-sex acts and relationships. But the Europeans who colonized North America arrived with sexual codes. Having already made the Judeo-Christian sin of sodomy a capital crime in the New World, they considered the indigenous peoples that they encountered inferior (and Native American men wanting in masculinity) in part because of the more fluid gender roles and sexual behaviors that existed among native peoples. Some sodomy laws were liberalized in the eighteenth century, but antisodomy laws still remained in force in many U.S. states at the beginning of the twenty-first century.

As the United States took shape in the nineteenth century, the emerging middle class developed separate public and private spheres—with public roles for males and private roles for females. In practice this division contributed to homosocial behavior and created an environment conducive to and supportive of intense same-sex friendships, with varying degrees of sexual activity in these "romantic friendships" (such as those associated with poet Walt Whitman). Scholars debate whether such relationships, as well as same-sex acts in single-sex communities (such as those on the nineteenth-century frontier) should be viewed in terms of later concepts of sexuality, since the idea of homosexuals and heterosexuals as types of people was not yet common.

The Twentieth Century

Recent scholarship suggests that the modern concepts of heterosexuality and homosexuality were "invented" in Western society in the late nineteenth century. Each was conceived in relation to the other, and both, as identities, were considered products of specific historical conditions rather than biologically or physically constant. The emerging sciences of psychology and sexology created the sexual "invert" (also called "variant," "deviant," and "Uranian"), meaning one whose biological sex did not correspond to his or her gender behavior and, possibly, to a person sexually attracted to the same sex. At best, the invert represented immature development, and at worst a threat to society and a need for therapy or more drastic treatment (e.g., institutionalization, castration and, later, shock therapy). Thus, the types of romantic friendships that had often been freely expressed during the previous century, were now stigmatized as abnormal, and many who were involved in such friendships felt the need to appear and live according to heterosexual norms.

Several late-nineteenth-century developments contributed to this new environment for sexual and gender nonconformists. Intensifying industrial capitalism and nationalism encouraged a fixed gender system in which a virile masculinity was seen as both the cause and effect of U.S. economic and political ascendancy. In addition, a new focus on "companionate marriage" idealized the romantic heterosexual couple. The link that was made between masculine traits and national strength—(reflected in the "muscular Christianity" movement and the new emphasis on the "strenuous life") coupled with intensified concerns for social order, rendered traits and behaviors considered feminine less tolerable in men. Violation of prevailing gender codes became an offense against Americanism itself and led to the persecution of gender inverts and homosexuals from that time forward.

The defining and stigmatizing of homosexuality made homosexual subcultures more visible, especially in the 1920s and 1930s in Bohemian enclaves in New York, such as Greenwich Village and Harlem, as well as in other large cities. These subcultures embraced a variety of definitions and behaviors, falling along racial and class lines (for example, "normal" men could have sex with men as long as they took only the "active" role), but most visible were effeminate, or gender-inverted, males, often referred to as "fairies" or "pansies." It was also at this time that drag balls, bars, and bath houses provided sites for the expression of multiple masculinities and same-sex expression and community. Drag queens, in particular, challenged conventional notions of maleness. The onset and deepening crisis of the Great Depression, however, combined with new liquor licensing laws, revitalized rigid gender roles and the desire to remove sexual and gender outlaws from public spaces.

World War II and Postwar America

The climate of Cold War America—in which "deviant" homosexuality was identified with national weakness and communism and "normal" heterosexuality with national strength and Americanness—further encouraged public fear of homosexuality. The virulent anticommunism of the 1950s merged with notions of gender normalcy to exaggerate fears of effete men in government and military service, resulting in the firing of thousands of known or suspected homosexuals. Rooted in limited notions of masculinity, the conceptual link between political and sexual "subversion" has contributed to homophobia in the United States.

Still, the massive mobilization of troops and industries after the United States entered World War II provided new opportunities for realizing and expressing homosexual identity and community by throwing together previously isolated individuals who had always felt "different." Significantly, homosexuals at this time began using same-sex sexuality, rather than the medically imposed conflation of homosexuality with gender inversion (e.g., "effeminacy" in men) as the basis for their identity. After the war, homosexuals increasingly politicized their identity, resulting in the emergence of a self-described homophile movement, represented by the Mattachine Society, which was founded in Los Angeles by 1951. Organization around the concept of homosexual rights, which had first been attempted in 1924 in Chicago by Henry Gerber's Society for Human Rights, slowly gained adherents, becoming the conceptual basis of subsequent gay rights movements.

During the 1960s, the growth of movements asserting civil rights and expressing pride in racial and gender identities enhanced the momentum of what became known (as homosexuals sought new names in an attempt to jettison older medical and legal stigmas) as the gay rights and gay liberation movements. During the 1960s and 1970s, gay people achieved an unprecedented public presence in the United States and developed a flourishing culture that included books and magazines; bars and baths; political, religious, and social organizations; symbols and fashion representing gay pride; and marches and celebrations. Highly visible communities emerged in New York, San Francisco, and other large cities. After New York's 1969 Stonewall riot—which erupted when police raided a gay bar—"gay pride" became a rallying cry. Gay rights activists achieved a major victory in 1973 when the American Psychiatric Association removed homosexuality from its list of mental disorders.

Eventually, however, the gay rights movement divided over goals and strategy. Those who conformed more to prescribed gender images, and were hence less visible, often sided with more accommodationist principles and emphasized sexual-object choice as the only salient difference between heterosexuals and homosexuals. On the other hand, advocates of gay liberation, like radical feminists, offered a more thorough critique of prevailing codes of gender and heterosexuality and sought to articulate a variety of gay, straight, and bisexual masculinities. Dissention also occurred around the relationship of gay rights activism to other movements and groups, and around the appearance of sexism and male domination within the movement's organizations. The association of a gay identity with maleness led to the addition of the term *lesbian* to the movement and prompted some homosexual women to develop a lesbian-separatist theory and practice.

By the 1970s, gay masculinities had become highly varied, ranging from the "macho men" (as exemplified by the pop group The Village People) who incorporated, in exaggerated form, traditionally masculine characteristics to the drag queens who continued to seek male identities that included characteristics traditionally considered feminine.

AIDS and Beyond

Gay liberation and gay pride were forced in different directions with the 1981 discovery of Acquired Immune Deficiency Syndrome (AIDS) and its initial link to the sexual activities and multiple partners of many gay men (AIDS was called a "gay plague" in early 1980s media accounts). New organizations—notably the Gay Men's Health Crisis (founded in 1982), and AIDS Coalition to Unleash Power (ACT-UP, founded in 1987)—emerged to address and debate responses to the epidemic.

Public reactions to AIDS were informed by a climate of backlash: Conservatives resisted or overturned the gains of most gay rights movements and touted conventional heterosexuality as "traditional family values." Yet events of the 1980s and 1990s also prompted productive dialogue and analysis within gay culture and politics. Concepts of sexuality and masculinity as fluid—varying from one individual to another and across time, place, and culture—began to replace the essentialist notion that homosexual/heterosexual and masculine/feminine are fixed dualities. Scholars, including postmodernists and queer theorists, began reexamining intersections among gender, sexuality, race, and class in American society, both past and present. In the popular mass media, too, a variety of gay and male identities were explored in the 1990s with increasing frequency and acceptance—examples include the feature films *Philadelphia* (1993) and *In and Out* (1997) and the television series *Will and Grace* (premiered 1998) and *Queer as Folk* (premiered 1999). Political controversies erupted over ongoing discrimination against gay men (and lesbians) in the military and in the workplace, while the newer visibility, activism, and variety of gay youth began adding a new dimension to debates over gender and sexuality. At the beginning of the twenty-first century, however, the legal rights of same-sex couples to marry and raise children had yet to be gained, and same-sex organizations (such as the Boy Scouts) continued to rely on stereotypes of masculinity to deny openly gay males equal participation.

Bibliography

Chauncey, George. *Gay New York: Gender, Urban Culture, and the Making of the Gay Male World, 1890–1940.* New York: Basic Books, 1994.

D'Emilio, John. *Sexual Politics, Sexual Communities: The Making of a Homosexual Minority in the United States, 1940–1970.* 2nd ed. Chicago: University of Chicago Press, 1998.

Katz, Jonathan Ned. *Gay American History: Lesbians and Gay Men in the U. S. A.* Rev. ed. New York: Meridian, 1992.

Rupp, Leila J. *A Desired Past: A Short History of Same-Sex Love in America.* Chicago: University of Chicago Press, 1999.

Further Reading

Bérubé, Allan. *Coming Out Under Fire: The History of Gay Men and Women in World War Two.* New York: Plume, 1991.

Greenberg, David F. *The Construction of Homosexuality.* Chicago: University of Chicago Press, 1990.

Hawkeswood, William G. *One of the Children: Gay Black Men in Harlem.* Edited by Alex W. Costley. Berkeley: University of California Press, 1996.

Katz, Jonathan Ned. *The Invention of Heterosexuality.* New York: Dutton, 1995.

———. *Love Stories: Sex Between Men Before Homosexuality.* Chicago: University of Chicago Press, 2001.

Plummer, David. *One of the Boys: Masculinity, Homophobia, and Modern Manhood.* New York: Harrington Park Press, 1999.

Related Entries

Bachelorhood; Bisexuality; Civil Rights Movement; Cold War; Cult of Domesticity; Freudian Psychoanalytic Theory; Gays in the Military; Heterosexuality; Male Friendship; Middle-Class Manhood; Nationalism; Postmodernism; Transsexuality; Transvestism; Whitman, Walt

—*Vicki L. Eaklor*

Hudson, Rock

1925–1985
American Film and Television Actor

A popular movie and television star from the 1950s into the 1980s, Rock Hudson seemed, in his power and charm, to epitomize mainstream masculinity. That status changed in 1985, however, when he became the first major celebrity known to have died of AIDS, and when his long-hidden homosexuality was thereupon disclosed. The poignant and public wasting away of a body that was once a prime symbol of American virility altered the public discourse about AIDS and contributed to the redefining of American masculinity late in the twentieth century.

In a studio-inspired refashioning, Roy Fitzgerald was renamed Rock Hudson, just as other male actors of the postwar period were given the supposedly alluring names of Tab, Gig, and Troy. More than a name change was thought advisable for Hudson, though. In a decade when homosexuality was often as feared as (and was often linked to) communism, a public affirmation of heterosexuality could seem mandatory. In spite of his numerous (though certainly not public) sexual involvements with other men, Hudson married his agent's secretary in 1955, the union lasting but three years.

It is as an object of a woman's sexual desire and as a representative of various male archetypes that Hudson is most vividly remembered. In more than sixty movies from 1948 to 1986 he would play, among other roles, a boxer, an Indian, a surgeon, a Texas oil baron, a banker, and a high school counselor who murdered pretty female students. But he is perhaps most remembered for his parts opposite Doris Day in *Pillow Talk* (1959) and *Lover Come Back* (1961), films full of the innocent sexual innuendo distinctive to the period. A later generation knew Hudson as a San Francisco police commissioner in the popular 1970s television series whose very name, *McMillan and Wife,* stressed the star's heterosexual identity.

Hudson's handsome face and physique epitomized the body-based masculine ideals of the twentieth century and were essential elements of his stardom. "I became the beefcake king" (Hudson and Davidson, 62), he recalled of the days when fan magazines would so often show him shirtless, supposedly engaged in such masculine activities as washing his car or painting his house. In 1954, *Life* magazine wondered whether his attraction "lies primarily in his basic honesty or his bare chest" (Hudson and Davidson, 73). Other magazines began to wonder why Hudson had no wife, but his marriage, though brief, seemed to quiet those questions for years. Much later in Hudson's career, as American society experienced a newly assertive movement for gay rights, public allusions to Hudson's possible homosexuality resurfaced.

Rock Hudson played a much more significant role in the cultural reassessment of homosexuality and masculinity when his affliction with AIDS was made public. At a time when President Ronald Reagan, ironically a friend of Hudson's, had not even spoken publicly of the disease, Hudson's highly publicized final days made AIDS much more difficult to ignore. The revelation that a man who had so looked the part of the ideal American male was gay challenged widespread stereotypes of homosexual men as effeminate weaklings.

BIBLIOGRAPHY

Hudson, Rock, and Sara Davidson. *Rock Hudson: His Story*. New York: William Morrow, 1986.

Oppenheimer, Jerry, and Jack Vitek. *Idol: Rock Hudson: The True Story of an American Film Hero*. New York: Villard, 1986.

Shilts, Randy. *And the Band Played On: Politics, People, and the AIDS Epidemic*. New York: St. Martin's, 2000.

FURTHER READING

Clark, Tom. *Rock Hudson, Friend of Mine*. New York: Pharos Books, 1990.

Gates, Phyllis, and Bob Thomas. *My Husband, Rock Hudson: The Real Story of Rock Hudson's Marriage to Phyllis Gates*. New York: Doubleday, 1987.

Gross, Larry. *Up from Invisibility: Lesbians, Gay Men, and the Media in America*. New York: Columbia University Press, 2001.

RELATED ENTRIES

Body; Cold War; Health; Heterosexuality; Hollywood; Homosexuality

—*John Ibson*

HUNTING

Hunting wild animals has been a primary male undertaking and a source of masculine identity throughout human history. It has provided food, clothing, bone tools, fuel, ritual paraphernalia, folk medicine, and trade goods such as skins, fur, and feathers. But its chief cultural significance, whether done for subsistence or sport, has been its function as a primal drama for the initiation of boys into manhood and for the ritual bonding of the male hunters.

The earliest European settlers in North America—especially the Protestant settlers arriving in the seventeenth century—associated hunting not with manliness, but with disorder, danger, and primitive savagery. Nor were manhood and hunting widely associated in eighteenth-century and early-nineteenth-century America. Republican values defined American manhood in terms of agrarianism rather than hunting—it was the yeoman farmer, not the backwoods hunter, on whom Thomas Jefferson and others rested their faith for the future of the republic. Nonetheless, a culture of hunting thrived in some regions of the colonies and the early United States, especially in the South, where the planter class embraced hunting as a class tradition, seeing the hunt as an important activity for demonstrating white masculine supremacy.

It was during the early nineteenth century that white settlement of game-rich western frontier land, romanticization of Native American male hunters, and a decidedly masculine nationalism encouraged the association of hunting with manliness and American identity. Such figures as Meriwether Lewis, Daniel Boone, Davy Crockett, and Andrew Jackson, for example, came to stand for a potent masculinity representative of a powerful nation. At the same time, an emerging northeastern urban middle class that cultivated genteel styles of manhood associated the West with rowdiness and disorder, and continued to link hunting with savagery. This association remained alive after the Civil War as the advent of industrialized food production, the spread of urban and suburban living, and a growing influx of immigrants from European societies and social classes without hunting traditions prompted a decline in subsistence hunting.

During the late nineteenth and early twentieth centuries, however, other social and cultural changes made hunting for sport a perceived imperative of American manhood and an important activity of middle- and upper-class men. Concerned that urbanization, industrialization, and domestication had enervated American men by removing them from nature, advocates of the "strenuous life," such as Theodore Roosevelt, urged men to seek reinvigoration through hunting and other outdoor activities. Several outdoor sports magazines began appearing during the 1870s, and in 1887 Roosevelt and George Bird Grinnell, the editor of *Forest and Stream*, founded the Boone and Crockett Club. This club, and many others modeled on it, served as exclusively male spheres where middle-class men could escape what they perceived as the increasing feminization of society. The dramatic loss of game animals for sport hunting in the closing decades of the nineteenth century helped spur the conservation movement of the Progressive Era, as hunting clubs and similar organizations pressed for the establishment of game preserves and other protected wilderness areas where men might continue to demonstrate their manhood through hunting.

A similar perception of a "crisis" in white, middle-class, heterosexual masculinity—and a similar belief that masculinity is revitalized through contact with nature—prompted the men's movements of the 1990s to practice what the scholar Stephen Kellert calls "nature hunting," in which hunters engage in the activity for its spiritual dimensions. The mythopoetic men's movement, in particular, promoted a link between hunting and the actualization of masculinity, and some hunting organizations and clubs have made explicit connections with these men's movements. Some defenders of hunting recommend the activity as therapeutic for men's modern fears and troubles—and as an important socialization experience for boys raised in urban environments, especially boys raised by single mothers.

Although there have always been women hunters, and although there are signs that an increasing proportion of licensed hunters in the United States are women, hunting continues to be—and is perceived to be—an overwhelmingly male activity. In a society with few formal initiation rituals for its young men, the boy's first hunting trip with his father and male family members and friends has served that function in parts of the nation. In fact, novels, personal accounts, and ethnographic accounts of the folk cultures of hunters suggest that it is the ritual closeness of the male friendship group in the hunting party, rather than the actual shooting of the animals, that holds the greatest meaning for participants. Even when women join the hunting party, they find themselves in a decidedly masculine world.

A long tradition in American fiction uses hunting as the primary vehicle for a young man's journey or initiation meant to prove his manhood. William Faulkner's short story, "The Bear," which appears in *Go Down, Moses* (1942), epitomizes the hunt as a male rite of passage. Ernest Hemingway's own love of hunting and his views of the hunt as a test of manhood pervade many of his stories and novels, while Norman Mailer used a hunting trip to Alaska by two young men and their fathers as the central, telling metaphor in his novel, *Why are We in Vietnam?* (1967).

In film, perhaps the major genre for American mythological narratives in the twentieth and twenty-first centuries, hunting often appears, both literally and metaphorically, as a test of manhood. In John Boorman's *Deliverance* (1972; based on the 1972 James Dickey novel), a band of men travel into the woods to test their manhood, with the hunt as a central metaphor. Michael Cimino used the hunting metaphor in his highly acclaimed Vietnam War buddy film, *The Deer Hunter* (1978); and Stephen Hopkins's *The Ghost and the Darkness* (1996) uses a lion hunt in Africa to explore white middle-class masculinity.

This hunting world is shrinking. As measured by the number of hunting licenses issued, fewer Americans hunt each year. By the end of the twentieth century, the portrait of the typical hunter was fairly clear: male; white; with some schooling beyond high school; working in a services, managerial, or manual-labor job; and earning a household annual income under $50,000. The increasing expense of hunting means that wealthy hunters will continue participating in the sport, using private clubs and guided hunting trips to distant places, while people with more modest incomes will curtail their hunting or abandon the activity altogether. Antihunting activities by animal rights groups highlight the social class struggle in this debate, as middle-class and upper-middle-class animal activists (mainly women) seek to disrupt the activities of the working- and middle-class hunters (mainly men). As actual hunting declines in the United States, its power as a symbolic activity in the proving of manhood remains strong.

BIBLIOGRAPHY

Dizard, Jan E. *Going Wild: Hunting, Animal Rights, and the Contested Meanings of Nature.* Amherst: University of Massachusetts Press, 1999.

Herman, Daniel Justin. *Hunting and the American Imagination.* Washington, D.C.: Smithsonian Institution Press, 2001.

Hufford, Mary. *Chaseworld: Foxhunting and Storytelling in New Jersey's Pine Barrens.* Philadelphia: University of Pennsylvania Press, 1992.

Swan, James A. *In Defense of Hunting.* San Francisco: HarperCollins, 1995.

Warren, Louis S. *The Hunter's Game: Poachers and Conservationists in Twentieth-Century America.* New Haven: Yale University Press, 1997.

FURTHER READING

Ives, Edward D. *George Magoon and the Down East Game War: History, Folklore, and the Law.* Urbana: University of Illinois Press, 1988.

Proctor, Nicolas W. *Bathed in Blood: Hunting and Mastery in the Old South.* Charlottesville: University Press of Virginia, 2002.

Reiger, John F. *American Sportsmen and the Origins of Conservation.* 3rd ed. Corvallis: Oregon State University Press, 2001.

Stange, Mary Zeiss. *Woman the Hunter.* Boston: Beacon Press, 1997.

RELATED ENTRIES

Agrarianism; Boone, Daniel; Crockett, Davy; *Deliverance*; Fishing; Guns; Hemingway, Ernest; Leatherstocking Tales; London, Jack; Men's Movements; Native American Manhood; Outdoorsmen; Republicanism; Roosevelt, Theodore; Southern Manhood; Strenuous Life

—*Jay Mechling*

Immigration

Processes of immigration have interacted with concepts and experiences of masculinity throughout U.S. history. As male immigrants moved from their countries and cultures of origin to the United States, both their notions of manliness and the dominant American culture's masculine ideals were sometimes challenged, and sometimes affirmed, by the encounter. Leaving one's country of origin and relocating over vast distances for economic betterment or to escape political or cultural persecution corresponded to traditional ideas about manliness, which portrayed a man as a successful provider, family caretaker, and guardian. This ideal was accepted by the immigrants themselves and by the larger American society. But while most immigrant men arrived in the United States prepared to embrace American definitions of manhood grounded in economic independence, productive effort and endeavor, and work, they also had to recast, renegotiate, and sometimes abandon some of their inherited definitions of manliness as they sought to mediate between their culture of origin and their newly adopted culture. Immigration, therefore, has created opportunities to articulate new understandings of manliness as it has forced immigrants to mediate between bonds of ethnicity, family, and kin networks on the one hand and the individualizing forces of city, market, and industry on the other.

Colonial America

As the American colonies became settlement societies, the British government and the joint stock companies that ran most of the early colonies appealed to men's desire for economic opportunity and to religious dissenters' desire for greater freedom of religious expression. Immigration, then, and the ideals of manhood that shaped it, were grounded in notions of economic opportunity and greater liberty.

The dynamics and demographics of immigration shaped the transfer of English ideals of patriarchal manhood to colonial America. In New England, the immigration of whole families allowed for a relatively stable transmission of social structures and relations, including patriarchal forms of family and political governance. In the Chesapeake region, however, a mostly male immigration and a low life expectancy due to disease produced clear departures from strict patriarchal household governance and economic power. In this setting, family structures were destabilized and women were allowed greater opportunities to own property. But as natural population growth gradually supplanted immigration, life expectancy increased, and the gender ratio became more balanced, patriarchal social patterns became more firmly entrenched.

The development of the American colonies into settlement societies encouraged more immigration, with significant consequences for notions of manliness. Coming from Germany, Sweden, and Switzerland, as well as Great Britain, colonial-era immigrants organized their ideas about manliness less around loyalty to British colonial forces and notions specific to British culture than around more abstract notions of political liberty, equality, religious freedom, and independent property ownership. The French aristocrat J. Hector St. John Crèvecoeur, for example, felt that coming to colonial America had made him into a new type of man, one who defined his manliness and self-worth around landownership and productive endeavor rather than aristocratic status. Such notions of manliness played a significant part in the development of proindependence sentiment during the 1770s.

Early National and Antebellum America

Immigration was disrupted by the American Revolution, and by European wars during the decades that followed, but it began to surge after the end of the Napoleonic wars in 1815. It was further stimulated and facilitated by new developments in transportation and communication, such as canals, railroads, steamships, and the telegraph, as well as by such social and political crises in Europe as the revolutions of 1830 and 1848 and the Irish potato famine of the late 1840s. Between the 1830s and 1850s, German and Irish immigrants—by far the most numerous groups—relocated to the United States for differing reasons and developed different ideals of manhood.

Averaging twenty to twenty-five years in age, most of these immigrants were in early adulthood. Many of them became wage laborers and developed their mature masculine identities as industrial workers in an expanding urban population. Manhood for them was typically grounded in class awareness and in a world of taverns, theaters, and other urban amusements. Affected by urbanization and industrialization in greater proportions than native-born men, immigrant men were the first to reconcile their expectations with a rapidly changing social reality, and also the first to articulate new notions of manhood suitable to an urbanizing and industrializing society. In this way immigration helped catalyze emerging models of urban and industrial masculinity in antebellum America.

The Irish in particular, who came to the United States in increasing numbers in the 1840s, were likely to be poor and unskilled, to join the ranks of an emerging urban proletariat, and to embrace working-class definitions of manliness. Male conviviality based on alcohol consumption formed an important part of these definitions. Yet their understanding of manhood was shaped by other aspects of the immigrant experience as well. Confronted by strong anti-Catholic, anti-immigrant, and nativist sentiments, they sought to demonstrate their Americannness and seek power through participation in urban politics. In Boston, New York, and other cities, they became a powerful force in city politics, joined urban police forces in substantial numbers, and developed a pragmatic ideal of manhood grounded in a clear understanding of the realities of urban life.

Along with the Irish, German immigrants pursued forms of leisure that emphasized alcohol, and male sociability in beer gardens characterized urban culture in cities such as Milwaukee, St. Louis, and Cincinnati until prohibition in 1919. Yet in other ways the experiences of German men differed from those of Irish men. Drawn by the desire for economic opportunity and to escape political persecution, Germans coming to the United States after 1830 (and especially after 1848) brought with them notions of manliness that were grounded in strong traditions of political and religious dissent, and these meshed well with U.S. notions of republican and democratic manhood. Those Germans who brought sufficient financial resources to purchase land embraced the ideals of agrarian manliness promoted by Thomas Jefferson.

The "New" Immigration: 1880–1924

Between the 1880s and the early twentieth century, the social and economic impact of the commercialization of agriculture, industrialization, and urbanization in southern, eastern, and southeastern Europe stimulated growing Italian, Jewish, and Slavic immigration to the United States. This "new" immigration differed significantly from earlier currents of immigration. The majority of these immigrants were of Catholic, Eastern Orthodox, or Jewish background, and their religions and strongly patriarchal Old World cultures significantly shaped their notions of manliness. Notions of patriarchal family leadership also shaped the demographic patterns of immigration. Whereas earlier immigrants had tended to come unmarried or in nuclear family units, new immigrants often came as extended stem families, consisting of the conjugal (married) units of brothers. Furthermore, two-thirds of the immigrants relocating to the United States between 1880 and 1914 were men.

Culturally, as well as demographically, manliness played a very significant role in the immigration stream that arrived in the United States between the late nineteenth and early twentieth centuries. The complex impact of immigration on masculinity was particularly apparent in immigrants' family lives. Immigrant men understood their relocation to America as an expression of their patriarchal leadership, and they expected their authority to be preserved—even enhanced—by it. But the immigration process often weakened social hierarchies based on patriarchy. Since men usually came first, their wives and children learned to support themselves before following their husbands and fathers to the United States. Furthermore, sons caught between old traditions and a new social setting—often finding themselves subject to new behavioral demands—tended to reject their fathers' patriarchal ways and adopt new standards of masculinity, bringing them into conflict with their fathers. These sons, and their sons in turn, often combined traditional ethnic masculine styles with newer ones to create new hybrid models of manhood. Their fathers, meanwhile, either vigorously asserted their traditional patriarchal prerogatives or felt their manhood challenged and undermined (or both).

The cultural interaction between the experiences of "new" immigrants and their masculine identities also occurred in labor and work-related settings, where traditional social bonds and notions of manliness grounded in kinship and ethnicity helped to shape newly emerging ideas about working-class manliness. Whereas many earlier immigrants found that their skills transferred well to the United States, "new" immigrants more typically found it necessary to acquire new skills, and they viewed their ability to do so as a significant measure of their social worth and masculinity. One outlet for new work-related articulations of manliness was contract labor systems, such as the Italian *padrone* system, in which established Italian immigrants functioned as mediators between newly arrived Italian men and U.S. society. In this system, however, newer immigrants were also exploited as cheap labor. Grounded in Old World traditions of patriarchy, social reciprocity, and shared kin identity, the padrone system, and other contract labor systems like it, were highly exploitative, yet those immigrants who managed and gained from these systems were able to articulate a definition of manliness that joined shared ethnicity and individualistic entrepreneurial impulses.

Old World loyalties of kin, ethnicity, and stem family also shaped industrial work settings and unionization. Slavs, for example, were known in many industries as assertive and aggressive unionizers, and they viewed their activities as expressions of manliness. The development of ethnically based, work-related masculinities was facilitated by the fact that, within certain communities, immigrants gravitated towards specific industries. In Newark, New Jersey, for example, the Irish dominated leather making, and in Buffalo, New York, Italians dominated construction. These occupations and the skills they required constituted important arenas in which immigrants assimilated and developed new definitions of manliness.

The Twentieth Century: 1924–Present

During the twentieth century, the social context for the interaction between immigration and notions of manliness changed considerably, as did the demographic profile of the immigration stream. The 1924 Johnson-Reed Act (also called the National Origins Act) supplemented and extended previous laws that had excluded Asian immigration, and it virtually cut off immigration from southern, eastern, and southeastern Europe. In so doing, the act helped to facilitate the assimilation of those immigrants who had already arrived, and thus heightened their aspirations to realize mainstream ideals of manliness. Furthermore, the rise of extremely racist fascist regimes in Europe, and their discrediting and defeat in World War II, made many native-born Americans less inclined to view immigrants from southern, eastern, and southeastern European backgrounds as racially different. Finally, the concentration of many immigrant men in the industrial working-class gave labor unions a significant role in integrating immigrant men into the wider culture, helping them to attain the financial resources necessary to effective breadwinning. The Congress of Industrial Organizations (CIO), formed in 1937, appealed to unskilled and semiskilled workers in industries with largely first- and second-generation immigrant workforces, and thus played a key role in this process.

The Cold War climate, including a U.S. desire to project an international image of promoting freedom and economic opportunity, prompted a greater openness to immigration, which culminated in the Immigration and Nationality Act amendments of 1965. This act overturned the 1924 National Origins Act and reopened the United States to immigration. The immigrants arriving under the new legislation were to a large extent nonwhite, including many African, Asian, and Hispanic (Mexican and Cuban in particular) immigrants. Their social profile, again, differed fundamentally from earlier generations of immigrants.

Immigrants arriving after 1965 were not only predominantly nonwhite, but they also possessed, on average, more skills and a higher education than those who came between 1830 and 1924. While often discriminated against based on their race or skin color, these immigrants brought with them skills and resources that enabled them to aspire to definitions of manliness organized around breadwinning, economic independence, and entrepreneurial drive that white men had long embraced.

While there are considerable differences between immigrants according to their national background, Asians tend to have fewer children, to experience lower unemployment and poverty rates, and to obtain higher levels of education. These immigrants differ substantially from those of earlier generations, who expected to start at the bottom and possibly work their way up. Immigrants from the Far East and from South Asia, in particular, tend to be graduates of professional and graduate schools. Education, professional work, and sustaining middle-class lifestyles have been significant components of masculinity among these groups. Many other Asian immigrants, as well as many from Latin America, joined the ranks of a segment of petty entrepreneurs, owning restaurants and grocery stores, in many American cities. These men embraced traditional American notions of manliness based on property, business ownership, and economic independence.

Late-twentieth-century immigrants not only embraced pre-existing American models of manhood, but they began to change the cultural landscape of American masculinity as well. They tended to be in their family-forming and child-bearing years, they included many different ethnicities, and they have contributed to a demographic shift in the U.S. population that is generating the formation of multiple overlapping and layered identities of race, ethnicity, and manliness in U.S. society. Furthermore, as members of these groups intermarry with members of other groups, their offspring will define their cultural and gender identities in new and different ways. As such, immigration will continue to transform cultural constructions of masculinity and to serve as an important catalyst in changing definitions of manliness in U.S. society.

BIBLIOGRAPHY

Archdeacon, Thomas. *Becoming American: An Ethnic History.* New York: Free Press, 1983.

Bodnar, John. *The Transplanted: A History of Immigrants in Urban America.* Bloomington: Indiana University Press, 1985.

Daniels, Roger. *Coming to America: A History of Immigration and Ethnicity in American Life.* New York: HarperCollins, 1990.

Jacobson, Matthew Frye. *Whiteness of a Different Color: European Immigrants and the Alchemy of Race.* Cambridge, Mass.: Harvard University Press, 2000.

Ueda, Reed. *Postwar Immigrant America: A Social History.* Boston: Bedford Books, 1994.

FURTHER READING

Brodkin, Karen. *How Jews Became White Folks and What That Says About Race in America.* New Brunswick, N.J.: Rutgers University Press, 1998.

Handlin, Oscar. *The Uprooted.* 1951. Reprint, Philadelphia: University of Pennsylvania Press, 2002.

Higham, John. *Send These to Me: Immigrants in Urban America.* New York: Atheneum, 1975.

Ignatiev, Noel. *How the Irish Became White.* New York: Routledge, 1995.

Thernstrom, Stephen, ed. *Harvard Encyclopedia of American Ethnic Groups.* Cambridge, Mass.: Belknap Press, 1980.

RELATED ENTRIES

American Dream; Asian-American Manhood; Breadwinner Role; Citizenship; Crèvecoeur, J. Hector St. John; Ethnicity; Gilded Age; Individualism; Industrialization; Irish-American Manhood; Jewish Manhood; Latino Manhood; Nationalism; Nativism; Patriarchy; Postmodernism; Race; Urbanization; Whiteness; White Supremacism; Work

—*Thomas Winter*

IMPERIALISM

U.S. imperialism developed and peaked during the late nineteenth and early twentieth centuries, when the nation attempted to expand overseas and control the political and economic systems of lesser developed nations in the Pacific and the Caribbean. American activities in the Philippines, which came into the possession of the United States after the Spanish-American War of 1898, embodied the assumptions underlying this expansion. Among the factors driving American imperialism was a new gender dynamic that surfaced in the years after the Civil War. Overseas expansion and the acquisition of colonial territories provided opportunities for young men to prove their masculinity and affirm the male virtues of bravery, loyalty, and endurance. At the same time, expansionists believed that the new possessions in Asia, the Pacific, and the Caribbean created chances for men to fulfill their role as warrior/protectors and as paternal tutors of "inferior" peoples, to establish their manhood in American society in response to women's political activism, and to assert their supremacy in new colonial gender systems.

Challenges to American Masculinity in the Late Nineteenth Century

The notions of masculinity that influenced American imperialism drew on several cultural currents of the late nineteenth century. The first was the closing of the frontier and the end of western expansion. The image of the North American frontier as a cradle of American democracy and as a proving ground for generations of young American men to prove their masculinity (a thesis espoused by the historian Frederick Jackson Turner in 1893) sparked concern among white men at the end of the nineteenth century that an important source of American manhood had disappeared. For this new generation and its leaders, the disappearance of the strenuous labor of frontier life, and of the male icons associated with that labor (e.g., the yeoman farmer, the independent artisan, the frontiersman, the hunter, the Indian fighter), left them with few models of manhood and few chances to prove themselves either as provider or protector.

The romantic mystique that enshrouded the collective memory of the Civil War, including the national reverence felt toward both Union and Confederate veterans, further heightened American men's concerns about their masculinity. Veterans' sons and grandsons, feeling inadequate by comparison, sought new ways to conceptualize and demonstrate their manhood. From Darwinism, which suggested that the struggle for survival strengthened species, and social Darwinism, which held that nations gained strength through commercial, political, and military competition, American men concluded that war could be a means of personal, social, and national regeneration. Similarly, the notion of the "strenuous life" among the Victorian middle class promised that men turned soft by the domestication and materialism of an urban-industrial "overcivilization" could reinvigorate American masculinity through hunting, outdoor activity, athletic competition, and male camaraderie. All these concerns caused the intellectual and political leaders of the post–Civil War generation (such as the rising politicians Theodore Roosevelt and Henry Cabot Lodge and the naval historian Alfred Thayer Mahan, whose 1890 book *The Influence of Sea Power Upon History* triggered a wave of navalism in the United States and Europe) to look overseas for new worlds to conquer.

Expansionist rhetoric—like that of Manifest Destiny, which was used in the 1840s to justify the acquisition of territory in the American West and white dominance over African Americans, Mexicans, and Native Americans—cast white American men as heroic republicans. The nonwhite peoples of the Caribbean, Latin America, and the Pacific, on the other hand, were described in feminine terms as undisciplined and indulgent savages who were incapable of self-defense or self-government and needed the benevolent supervision that only a paternalistic, white, and democratic society could bring them. White American men saw a close connection between the maintenance of white male supremacy; the masculine virtues of strength, bravery, resourcefulness, and loyalty; and a healthy democracy in which strong men elected government leaders and maintained political and social stability. Attempts by minorities to assert their independence would undermine the natural social order, threaten families, and undermine white male identity and self-esteem. According to many white male Americans, the strength of the United States and the stability of the international order ultimately rested on white male dominance.

The Gendered Rhetoric of Overseas Expansion

Advocacy for the acquisition of territory outside the continental United States first surfaced shortly after the Civil War, but it gained little support until the last two decades of the nineteenth century. The controversies surrounding the 1889 establishment of an American presence in Samoa in the western Pacific Ocean and the initial rejection of the annexation of Hawaii by the Grover Cleveland administration in 1895 sparked some expansionist activity, but it was the Cuban crisis of 1898, followed by the Spanish-American War and the annexation of the Philippines and Hawaii, that propelled the imperialists to the forefront of American politics. Their gender-based discourse became part of the cultural mainstream. Supporters of the wars against Spanish forces in Cuba and the Filipino insurgents, who rebelled against the American presence on their islands between 1899 and 1902, successfully cast both conflicts as tests of American manhood. The liberation of Cuba was portrayed in gender terms: heroic white civilized American soldiers were rescuing the helpless, downtrodden, feminized Cuban people from the predatory, hypermasculine Spanish oppressor. Imperialists used similar rhetoric to justify the Philippine war.

Advocates of overseas expansion faced formidable opposition from a large anti-imperialist movement. In response to this resistance among some Americans, supporters of retaining the Philippines as an American possession following the Spanish-American War used gender symbols to reinforce their case. They believed that for the United States to yield to the "savage" Filipino rebels would undermine the collective manhood of American society and leave thousands of Spanish residents and "decent" upper-class Filipinos (particularly the women, whom they saw in Victorian terms as symbols of feminine purity and virtue but incapable of defending themselves) to the mercy of backward, brutish, and hypermasculine rebel peasant soldiers. Imperialists argued that failure to hold the islands would indicate that the present generation of young men lacked the strength of previous generations, and thus would be a confession of impotence. Theodore Roosevelt, for example, wrote that when men fear war, "they tremble on the brink of doom" (Hoganson 1998, 53).

Imperialism stirred national political debates that were, in effect, debates about the meaning of American manhood. Imperialists exploited anxieties about the effects of industrialization and materialism by portraying their anti-imperialist opponents as soft and cowardly products of a feminized culture. They sought to undercut the "anti's" political authority by questioning their manhood, circulating political cartoons that portrayed male anti-imperialist politicians in women's clothing, and suggesting that they lacked the manly character needed for political authority. The fact that the anti-imperialist opposition consisted of a large number of activist women's groups reinforced their arguments. Supporters of imperialism linked their perception that only men willing to pursue imperial goals were fit to govern to arguments against woman suffrage and gender equality at home. Anti-imperialist men also sought to defend their position through gendered appeals. Sharing imperialist assumptions that nonwhite peoples needed the protection of white men, they cast themselves as heroic defenders of both national honor and the rights of nonwhite peoples. At the same time, they portrayed advocates of imperialism as arrogant hypermasculine aggressors.

Gender Relations in U.S. Colonial Societies

The colonial societies that evolved in the new U.S. possessions (particularly the Philippines) reflected the same assumptions about masculinity and race that had driven the Spanish-American War. In fact, such assumptions also drove other Western imperialist powers, such as Great Britain, France, and the Netherlands. The United States and the European powers promoted systems of imperial governance that viewed white men, whether administrators or soldiers, as the embodiment of the masculine virtues of strength, courage, and resourcefulness needed to govern the overseas possessions. Under this system, the task of colonial administration involved the tutelary bonding between the white American father/teacher and the native child/apprentice. Strict codes of conduct separated the white rulers from their subjects, and rigid sexual and social hierarchies assured white male control in the areas of commerce, government, and household conduct. The U.S. colonial government in the Philippines barred Filipino men from senior positions and minimized their social contacts with white males and females. The restriction of the privileges of manhood to white men also applied to social clubs such as the Army and Navy Club in Manila, which provided facilities for activities defined in American culture as masculine—such as athletics and gambling—and limited membership to a white elite consisting of senior male American military officers and civilian administrators.

This system of governance sprang from a culture of fear that sought to affirm white masculinity through the subordination of native peoples to a position of inferiority. It was believed that any display of weakness would undermine the established system and send the Philippine archipelago into chaos, possibly leading to wholesale massacres of white men, women, and children. The tutelary measures of the U.S. imperial government created limited reforms aimed less at assuring self-government and genuine improvements in the quality of life of the people than at co-opting the male native elites into collaboration with American rule.

The patriarchal assumptions that drove American imperialism resulted in a sexual colonialism—a system of gender hierarchy in which ruling white men sought to control the bodies and sexuality of both white and native women. This system relegated women to a position of childlike inferiority. White women were a subordinate class that served to reinforce white male dominance and natives' second-class status—as well as to rationalize the preservation of these race and gender systems. White American women in the Philippines might be employed as schoolteachers or nurses, but they were excluded from administrative positions requiring policy decisions. The wives of American administrators and military officers were obliged to provide a respectable domestic environment and models of idealized womanhood, including exemplifying sexual purity and maintaining a respectable domestic environment, so that native women might achieve "white" womanhood themselves through imitation.

Native Filipino men were also defined as feminine and subordinate in day-to-day relations. As cooks and houseboys, they served white women and offered whites the leisure that defined their privileged class status. At the same time, the presence of native domestic servants in the homes of white imperialists raised fears that young native males might achieve intimacy with white women. These native men were thus emasculated through their service to whites while also serving as a potential sexual threat that could undermine the superiority of white men. This paradox generated anxieties toward native male workers that pervaded all of the European and American possessions in Asia and the Pacific.

In the 1920s and 1930s, post–World War I disillusionment with global political and military activism led the United States to limit its overseas obligations. Beginning with its entrance into World War II, however, the nation entered a period of globalism that still persists. The masculine rhetoric of imperialism remained part of American cultural and political discourse—and of U.S. foreign policy decisions regarding Africa, Asia, the Pacific, and the Middle East—for most of the twentieth century. However, a significant shift occurred: The defeat of Nazi Germany, the nation's drive to forge alliances with nonwhite countries during the Cold War, and a wave of anticolonial independence movements during the 1960s and 1970s prompted the disappearance of the earlier emphasis on whiteness. Yet American policymakers continued to portray U.S. activities in gendered terms. For instance, the notion of the American male warrior/protector shielding weak, dependent "family" members against treacherous "savages" who violated American concepts of civilized manhood would be applied in conflicts in Korea, Vietnam, the Persian Gulf, and Afghanistan. Debates about American globalism continue to be couched in masculine terms, and the image of a generous, paternalistic America protecting and tutoring its children still holds a powerful appeal in its affirmation of masculine values and nationalist sentiment. For critics of American imperialism in the early years of the twentieth century and, later, for critics of American globalist policies, such paternalistic attitudes reflect a dangerous arrogance.

BIBLIOGRAPHY

Bederman, Gail. *Manliness and Civilization: A Cultural History of Gender and Race in the United States, 1880–1917.* Chicago: University of Chicago Press, 1995.

Hoganson, Kristin L. *Fighting for American Manhood: How Gender Politics Provoked the Spanish-American and Philippine-American Wars.* New Haven, Conn.: Yale University Press, 1998.

———. "As Badly Off As the Filipinos': U.S. Women's Suffragists and the Imperial Issue at the Turn of the Twentieth Century." *Journal of Women's History* 13, no. 2 (2001): 9–33.

Kaplan, Amy, and Donald E. Pease, eds. *Cultures of United States Imperialism.* Durham, N.C.: Duke University Press, 1993.

LaFeber, Walter. *The New Empire: An Interpretation of American Expansion, 1860–1898.* Ithaca, N.Y.: Cornell University Press, 1963.

Linn, Brian McAllister. *Guardians of Empire: The U.S. Army and the Pacific, 1902–1940.* Chapel Hill: University of North Carolina Press, 1997.

Miller, Stuart Creighton. *"Benevolent Assimilation": The American Conquest of the Philippines, 1899–1903.* New Haven, Conn.: Yale University Press, 1982.

Slotkin, Richard. *Gunfighter Nation: The Myth of the Frontier in Twentieth-Century America.* New York: Macmillan, 1992.

Stoler, Ann Laura, et. al. "Empires and Intimacies: Lessons from (Post) Colonial Studies: A Round Table." *Journal of American History* 88, no. 3 (2001): 829–897.

FURTHER READING

Anderson, Warwick. "The Trespass Speaks: White Masculinity and Colonial Breakdown." *American Historical Review* 102, no. 5 (1997): 1343–1370.

Horsman, Reginald. *Race and Manifest Destiny: The Origins of American Racial Anglo-Saxonism.* Cambridge, Mass.: Harvard University Press, 1981.

Hugill, Peter J. "Imperialism and Manliness in Edwardian Boys Novels." *Ecumene* 6, no. 3 (1999): 310–340.

Janiewski, Dolores E. "Engendering the Invisible Empire: Imperialism, Feminism, and U.S. Women's History." *Australian Feminist Studies* 16, no. 36 (2001): 279–293.

Welch, Richard E. *Response to Imperialism: The United States and the Philippine-American War, 1899–1902.* Chapel Hill: University of North Carolina Press, 1979.

Wexler, Laura. *Tender Violence: Domestic Visions in an Age of U.S. Imperialism.* Chapel Hill: University of North Carolina Press, 2000.

RELATED ENTRIES

Civil War; Cold War; Crisis of Masculinity; Gilded Age; Heroism; Industrialization; Militarism; Nationalism; Patriotism; Progressive Era; Roosevelt, Theodore; Spanish-American War; Urbanization; Vietnam War; War; Western Frontier; White Supremacism; World War I; World War II

—*Walter F. Bell*

INDIVIDUALISM

Individualism has been a key component of American culture and identity, and in the shaping of American masculinity. Individualism in the United States has taken various forms. Politically, it has emphasized personal freedom and liberty in the face of social constraints—as well as the narrow self-interest and overzealous egotism that may prevent others from enjoying their freedom and liberty. Religiously, it has emphasized the primacy of individual faith and conscience over external authorities. Economically, it has connoted the competitive pursuit of self-interest in the laissez-faire market. Changing notions of the individual's relationship to society over time have affected Americans' perceptions of the relation between individualism and masculinity, and differences of race and class have further complicated this relationship. In all cases, however, Americans have defined manhood in terms of a proper balance between individualism and social obligation.

The Colonial and Revolutionary Periods

Socially, colonial Americans understood individualism to be incompatible with virtuous manhood, which they defined in terms of selfless service to family and community. Social restraints and communal sanctions tempered individual greed and avarice. Spiritually, meanwhile, individualism was an important value. The Calvinist and other Protestant theologies to which most colonial Americans subscribed emphasized the primacy of the individual's relationship with God and encouraged regular introspective self-assessment, self-discipline, and struggle against sin as equally necessary to a man's spirituality.

The American Revolution strengthened the link between individualism and masculinity by making a republican model of manhood (emphasizing self-government, freedom from tyranny, and independence) fundamental to American political life. At the same time, however, republicanism reinforced the belief that true manhood involved an awareness of one's social and civic obligation and a willingness to sacrifice selfish interests for the public good. Republican individualism was associated with white men in particular; women and African Americans were excluded from suffrage and citizenship.

The Nineteenth Century

Republican and religious concepts of individualism, the latter reinforced by the growth of evangelical Christianity in the 1810s and 1820s, remained fundamental to American constructions of manhood through the nineteenth and twentieth centuries. Yet the market revolution and westward expansion of the early nineteenth century placed a new emphasis on economic individualism. In place of the colonial notion of manhood, in which communal sanctions disciplined greed, came a new premium on both the legitimate pursuit of self-interest in a competitive society and the necessity of individual moral self-discipline. As young men began seeking economic opportunities in the nation's cities or on the frontier, they increasingly measured manhood in terms of "self-made" success in the marketplace rather than self-sacrifice to family and community. Amid the search for new markets in the unsettled West, frontier individualism, in particular, offered American men the possibility of testing their ability to make it on their own in a hostile environment.

Yet despite changes in the relation between individualism and masculinity, important continuities remained. First, economic individualism, like older forms of manly individualism, was identified with white men in particular. As with public political activity, market activity was largely denied to women and nonwhite men. Second, American notions of ideal manhood continued to imply the necessity of balancing individualism with social awareness. Indeed, fears of unfettered individualism were typically articulated through the symbolic use of hypermasculine figures. During the 1830s and 1840s, popular depictions of Davy Crockett in editions of the *Crockett Almanac* represented a masculinity run amok on an uncivilized frontier, and Americans began to fear the urban "confidence man" who, unrestrained by morality or social obligation, used unethical business practices to conquer the competitive marketplace.

While individualism for white men meant the pursuit of economic success and self-sufficiency, its primary meaning for most antebellum African Americans involved resistance to and escape from slavery. Yet many African-American men combined this racially specific definition of manly individualism with the political, religious, and economic definitions characteristic of the larger American culture. The abolitionist Frederick Douglass, for example, equated blackness with oppression and effeminacy and white manhood with independence and power. Likewise, because Douglass overpowered his overseer, gained his freedom, and later achieved literary success, he equated manhood with economic individualism.

The Twentieth Century

Economic, social, and political changes in the first half of the twentieth century challenged the competitive individualism that had been the measure of manhood in the previous century, prompting both a defense of these older models of masculine individualism and the development of new models. The declaration in 1890 that the western frontier was "closed"—according to that year's U.S. Census Bureau report—led many American men, anxious that a longstanding arena of manly individualism had disappeared, to challenge themselves and assert their personal mastery over physically challenging natural environments. Darwinian theory—according to which individuals in nature compete for survival—reinforced this concept of masculine individualism.

At the same time, the apparent threat to economic competition, and thus to manhood, posed by the rise of monopolistic businesses in the late nineteenth and early twentieth centuries generated heated national debate. Business leaders claimed that their activities and power underscored the link between manliness and economic individualism, a point that led their admirers to dub them "captains of industry." Critics, however, claimed that their excessive greed had made them insensitive to social obligation and to workers' and small-business owners' hopes for economic self-sufficiency. Progressive reformers of the early twentieth century supported antitrust measures to preserve men's economic and political individualism against corporate power and corruption, while managers and others working for large corporations asserted their individualism by competing for career advancement. By the 1920s an environment of economic prosperity led many Americans to agree with Republican presidential candidate Herbert Hoover's 1928 declaration that the American business world was a system of "rugged individualism" that government interference would only stifle.

The association between masculinity and economic individualism persisted even amid the upheavals of the Great Depression in the 1930s. Many men tended to blame financial setbacks on their own individual failings and to view government handouts as humiliating. Similarly, critics of the New Deal (government relief and social programs introduced by President Franklin D. Roosevelt) charged that it undermined individual initiative. To be sure, the Great Depression also gave a decisive impetus to unionization among workers, many of whom supplemented their ideals of individualism with newer notions of manhood emphasizing social solidarity. This new emphasis on collectivist notions of masculinity contributed to the relatively wide appeal of socialism and communism in the 1930s, and in the 1932 presidential election the Socialist Party candidate, Norman Thomas, won over 800,000 votes, while the Communist Party candidate, William Z. Foster, received over 100,000 votes. Yet the fact that these large numbers constituted only a small percentage of the electorate suggests that individualistic definitions of manhood enjoyed far greater appeal.

The continuing growth of a corporate economy after World War II raised new concerns that masculine individualism was endangered. William H. Whyte's *The Organization Man* (1956) gloomily portrayed powerless white-collar men adrift in a world controlled by anonymous corporations that required conformity and obliterated individual initiative, while the rebellious youth of the Beat movement sought personal spiritual liberation through a rejection of such middle-class conformity. In 1962, male leaders of the activist student organization Students for a Democratic Society declared in their Port Huron Statement that corporate society had reduced men' s potential for self-cultivation, independence, and creativity. They called for individual fulfillment through democracy, while also urging a manly commitment to social justice and cautioning against equating independence with egotism.

Similarly, though with less emphasis on social activism, participants in the 1960s counterculture sought personal liberation from mainstream institutions in an effort to recover what they considered an authentic, natural masculinity.

Masculinity and individualism remained closely associated during the 1970s. As a turn away from the social activism of the 1960s and a growing cultural emphasis on self-examination and self-realization led the writer Tom Wolfe to dub this period the "me decade," American men sought to assert their masculinity through attention to personal health and physical fitness. Bodybuilding, once deemed narcissistic, enjoyed a new popularity among men seeking extreme physical forms of self-realization.

Ronald Reagan's presidency suggested that rugged individualism once again became a primary element of American manliness in the 1980s. Reagan sought to project an image of virile masculinity, an image he consistently associated with personal responsibility, individual initiative, and self-assurance. His probusiness and antiwelfare policies, which appealed particularly to male business leaders and other white men, likewise signaled a return to traditional individualism. That Reagan and his conservative political supporters simultaneously ended feminists' hope for passage of the Equal Rights Amendment to the U.S. Constitution in 1982 suggests that his was a particularly male brand of individualism.

Yet the twentieth century also witnessed a gradual erosion of the traditional association between individualism and (white) masculinity. The growing success of movements advocating the rights of women and nonwhite men meant that white males ceased to maintain their domination of the political and economic worlds, and that others besides white males participated in established American patterns of individualism.

By the late 1980s and 1990s, the traditionally close relation between masculinity and individualism was further challenged by new intellectual trends. Influenced by postmodernism, scholars in gender studies emphasized that gender definitions are socially constructed rather than innately connected to biological sex, and that masculinity thus varies across human societies. In addition, the unified notion of selfhood that had informed the traditional concept of individualism in American culture gave way to a fragmented sense of self that included multiple, and sometimes conflicting, self-identities. With the concepts of both masculinity and individualism called into question, the nature of the relation between them—or whether there was any meaningful relation at all—became unclear. The sense of a fixed, hegemonic model of individualism associated with white men continues to be eroded by a dynamic, diverse model that recognizes differing individual experiences of masculinity along racial, ethnic, class, and sexual-preference lines.

BIBLIOGRAPHY

Hayden, Tom. *Port Huron Statement: The Founding Manifesto of Students for a Democratic Society.* Chicago: Charles H. Kerr, 1990.

Kimmel, Michael. *Manhood in America: A Cultural History.* New York: Free Press, 1996.

Rotundo, E. Anthony. *American Manhood: Transformations in Masculinity from the Revolution to the Modern Era.* New York: Basic Books, 1993.

Whyte, William H. *The Organization Man.* New York: Simon & Schuster, 1956.

Wills, Gary. *Reagan' s America: Innocents at Home.* New York: Doubleday, 1987.

FURTHER READING

Bellah, Robert, et al. *Habits of the Heart: Individualism and Commitment in American Life.* Berkeley: University of California Press, 1985.

Clark, Keith. *Black Manhood in James Baldwin, Ernest J. Gaines, and August Wilson.* Urbana: University of Illinois Press, 2002.

Connell, R. W. *Masculinities.* Berkeley: University of California Press, 1995.

RELATED ENTRIES

Abolitionism; African-American Manhood; American Revolution; Bodybuilding; Business/Corporate America; Capitalism; Confidence Man; Counterculture; Crockett, Davy; Darwinism; Douglass, Frederick; Great Depression; Market Revolution; Men's Movements; Men's Studies; *Organization Man, The*; Postmodernism; Reagan, Ronald; Reform Movements; Republicanism; Self-Made Man; Slave Narratives

—*Erika Kuhlman*

INDUSTRIALIZATION

The process of industrialization, which began in the United States during the early nineteenth century, had an enormous impact on American constructions of masculinity. It complicated preindustrial notions of manhood based on male patriarchal control over family and household, while also generating new and often class-based definitions of gender. For some segments of the male population, industrialization eroded two critical foundations of preindustrial male patriarchy: It reduced the importance of property ownership and moved productive, income-generating labor out of the home. In doing so, it opened up opportunities for social and cultural experimentation with definitions of manhood both in and outside the workplace. Men were able to shape these new articulations of masculinity to some extent, but the impact of industrialization on their work and on the economic foundations of their lives also set the parameters for their redefinition of themselves as men.

Household Production, Proto-Industrialization, and Patriarchy

Through the late eighteenth century, most American households were sites of preindustrial production grounded firmly in patriarchal authority, which in turn was a fundamental component of masculine identity. Between 1790 and 1815, however, the nature of both household production and household patriarchy began to shift. Commodity production in the countryside and in urban households intensified as merchants increased investment in domestic markets and the development of manufactures. This early commodity production, or proto-industrialization, actually relied on the patriarchal family unit and its social relations to organize, mobilize, and discipline a spatially dispersed workforce and produce goods for expanding markets. In and around Lynn, Massachusetts, for instance, merchants and artisans began in the 1780s to create a thriving shoe industry based on a "putting out" system in which entrepreneurs supplied raw materials to widely dispersed farm families working out of their own homes. Such forms of household-based commodity production actually reinforced domestic patriarchy, since the father/husband mediated the relation between the income-generating family members and the artisan or merchant who supplied the raw material.

Eventually, however, the success and profitability of this form of household production enabled master artisans, merchants, and shopkeepers to relocate and concentrate work processes into workshops, thus undermining traditional household patriarchy. This process was uneven in its application. In the 1790s, Samuel Slater hired whole family units for his textile mills in Massachusetts and Rhode Island, and even purchased land for heads of households to support a combination of industrial labor and subsistence agriculture. He then sought to incorporate household patriarchy and the family as a productive unit, and to channel the social discipline these relations helped to generate into industrial manufacturing. But while the Slater Mills relied on the patriarchal family unit to maintain industrial discipline among its workers, the textile mills at Waltham and Lowell, Massachusetts, which were built later, involved no similar effort to preserve preindustrial patriarchal relations.

The Breadwinner Ideal

Across class lines, men counteracted the limitations that industrialization imposed on patriarchy by monopolizing income-generating productive labor. Accompanying and justifying this development was a new definition of manhood, that of primary family breadwinner. This concept was grounded in an increasing emphasis on gender difference, and on the notion of men's unique suitability for the new forms of work generated by industrialization. The breadwinner ideal had a mixed effect on male domestic authority and masculine identity. On the one hand, it made men, their manliness, and their ability to provide economic security for their families dependent on market forces beyond their control. By disrupting the link between men's work and their households, moreover, it reduced the time that most fathers spent at home, which limited their control over their wives and children. It also rendered them less able to validate themselves by transmitting their skills to a son or apprentice or by steering their sons into their own career paths. Yet at the same time, the male breadwinner actually held a greater share of domestic economic power than had the preindustrial patriarch, and breadwinning reinforced men's ability to provide for their wives and children.

Masculinity and Class

Industrialization created a new social division between those who owned or managed business establishments (the emergent middle class) and those who worked under these owners and managers as working-class wage earners. Male experiences, and the definitions of masculinity that these generated, varied across this class line. In general, working-class men found that the craft-based skills in which they had traditionally grounded their ideas of manly labor were undermined and increasingly replaced by new technologies. Middle-class men, meanwhile, were able to form new definitions of masculinity around their work, particularly the appropriation and administration of entrepreneurial and organizational prerogatives formerly under the purview of artisans and small-scale producers. Both groups of men formed and expressed new class-based ideals of manhood inside and outside the workplace.

For working-class men, a heightened emphasis on male physical ability enabled them to reassure themselves of their manliness and respond to the pressures of industrialization. Although industrialization would ultimately result in the mechanization and de-skilling of many work tasks, early industrialization, with its demand for productivity and its comparatively primitive machinery, actually increased the demand for physical strength in such industries as metallurgy, mining, and textiles. In many trades, working-class men expressed their class-based masculinity by asserting their independence, craft skills, and control over the shop floor, thus challenging managerial prerogatives and control of work processes. In trades such as steel, glass blowing, or printing, craft skills remained significant in many aspects of the production process, and craftworkers continued to define their identities as workers and as men around their craft-based autonomy on the shop floor.

Resistance at work represented another such outlet available to working-class men. Labor and crowd action, bread riots, and price riots did not represent a new phenomenon, but in the eighteenth century such social uprisings were community-based rather than work- or class-based, and they also included both men and women. While women workers in such industries as textiles and needlework went on strike just as men did, the nineteenth century witnessed a masculinization of such forms of protest, which were increasingly organized through labor and trade unions that grew out of men's homosocial workplace bonds.

Working-class men also defined and asserted their masculinity off the job. The industrializing city offered a range of boisterous amusements that became key settings for public demonstrations of manliness. Drinking alcohol—a traditional element of artisanal labor, but increasingly stigmatized by middle-class men as incompatible with productive efficiency—became for the new industrial labor force both an important badge of one's physical stamina and a rejection of middle-class morality. Theaters in working-class neighborhoods, where middle-class male patrons were often unwelcome and risked forced removal, served a similar function.

By the late nineteenth century, as advancing mechanization increasingly de-skilled more and more tasks and work processes and undermined craft-based prerogatives at work, working-class men's responses to industrialization began to change. More traditional segments of the working class, inspired by a craft-based ideal of manhood, sought to resurrect artisanal production and a community of producers by organizing the relatively short-lived Knights of Labor organization, which did not survive a series of strikes in 1886. A more accommodationist wing of the labor movement, represented by the American Federation of Labor, accepted the loss of workplace prerogatives and sought better financial compensation of its members to attain the newer breadwinner ideal. This mostly male labor organization paved the way for the notion of the working man as a consumer that emerged in the twentieth century.

Whereas industrialization imposed more rigid forms of workplace discipline and control over working-class men, it generated outlets for masculine self-expression at work for middle-class men. With the onset of new technologies, administrative and scientific functions (such as engineering, accounting, and chemistry) gained significance in industry around the mid–nineteenth century. As new machinery replaced craft and physical skills, it generated demands for administrative skills and produced an inclination among middle-class men to distinguish between their intellectual labor and what they considered the inferior, and even animalistic, physical labor of working-class men. Middle-class men increasingly defined their masculinity in terms of those qualities that characterized business in industrializing America: rationality, competitiveness, efficiency, and frugality. With the growing bureaucratization of American business that accompanied advancing industrialization later in the nineteenth century, definitions of middle-class manhood expanded to include teamwork, loyalty, and professionalism. Off the job, middle-class men of the nineteenth century cultivated a genteel model of manly deportment that—in conscious distinction from working-class behavioral patterns—embraced temperance, social etiquette, and refinement.

Industrialization also generated new patterns of fathering in the middle class. Whereas working-class fathers had to worry about how they might prepare their sons for the new industrial workplace, middle-class fathers had to provide their offspring with more formal education to enable sons to choose their own career paths. Middle-class men, in particular, measured their manhood through their ability to ensure their sons' upward social mobility, and thereby preserve their families' often tenuous middle-class status. For these men, the role of the breadwinner included the expectation to provide their children with increasing numbers of years of schooling. Their sons, meanwhile, enjoyed greater autonomy than had their preindustrial counterparts in choosing their own careers, and they viewed their freedom in determining their professional life as an expression of their own achievement of manhood.

Gender Hierarchy in the Industrial Workplace

Industrialization posed a potential threat to the traditional gender hierarchy of preindustrial patriarchy by creating opportunities for women to enter the labor force and achieve economic independence. But in such industries as textiles and needlework, which relied heavily on female workforces, men held supervisory positions, in effect restoring some measure of patriarchal control. Furthermore, in those industries that tended to rely on women as a cheap labor supply, male workers and middle-class reformers demanded a reduction in working hours for women on the grounds that women either lacked men's physical strength and stamina or were required in their homes as mothers. Working men who supported such laws most probably had the well-being of their daughters and wives in mind, yet their aspiration to the domestic power of the sole breadwinner was probably also a factor. Middle-class men, on the other hand, justified the gender division of labor and their dominance of emerging entrepreneurial, professional, and bureaucratic work not on technological or physical necessity, but on what they considered to be women's lack of capacity for rational thought and self-control. New codes of manliness that emphasized expertise, knowledge, and mental power supported this belief.

Masculinity and Sexuality in Industrializing America

Industrialization and the accompanying process of urbanization provided one final arena for defining and demonstrating masculinity: sexuality. During the nineteenth century, sex became an increasingly important signifier of manliness (particularly among working-class men) and the age at which men tended to become sexually active dropped from twenty-five to eighteen. No longer able to rely on property as a means of patriarchal control and with work often no longer an integral part of household activities, sex became a last resort for the exercise of patriarchal power among men. As industrialization made the achievement of manhood through work dependent on the shifts in labor markets, and as the acquisition of property became uncertain, men could validate themselves through sexual domination of women. Indeed, antebellum New York City witnessed an increase in rapes and sexual assaults on women. Industrialization made sex available as a compensatory outlet for men in more direct ways as well: Female needle workers, working out of their own homes in New York under abysmal conditions in the 1830s and 1840s, frequently had to resort to casual prostitution to make ends meet.

For middle-class men, meanwhile, sexuality became a new territory for asserting the self-control so crucial to middle-class definitions of manhood. Advice writers such as William Alcott, Sylvester Graham, Augustus Kingsley Gardiner, and John Todd counseled self-restraint in all bodily matters, and especially in all sexual matters. Masturbation, while never encouraged in preindustrial society, was now condemned as wasteful of potentially productive male energy. Sexual activity, contemporary observers advised, was best restricted to procreation only. Middle-class men, then, were admonished to synchronize their bodies and their bodily conduct with an emerging capitalist regime of accumulation and delayed gratification. As middle-class men emphasized self-restraint and self-control to the point of repressing their libidos, they also linked definitions of manliness to class difference, as working-class men did not follow the same mandates.

Conclusion

Industrialization affected definitions and cultural constructions of manliness by undermining patriarchal control over the household, cutting the spatial link between work and home, and prompting the formation of new class-based masculinities. Men redefined manliness through the role of the breadwinner, by generating new codes of manliness on the job, and through sexuality. While the separation of masculinity from property ownership and household patriarchy cut across class lines, industrialization also affected men and masculinity in class-specific ways. Middle-class men had more cultural and economic resources at their command to actively generate new articulations of manliness than did working-class men. As a social and cultural construct, American masculinity took new forms as industrialization generated the social and cultural dynamics of a modern society.

BIBLIOGRAPHY

Barker-Benfield, Graham J. *The Horrors of the Half-Known Life: Male Attitudes toward Women and Sexuality in Nineteenth-Century America.* New York: Harper & Row, 1976.

Blumin, Stuart. *The Emergence of the Middle Class: Social Experience in the American City, 1760–1900.* Cambridge, England: Cambridge University Press, 1989.

Coontz, Stephanie. *The Social Origins of Private Life: American Families, 1600–1900.* New York: Verso, 1988.

Gorn, Elliot J. *The Manly Art: Bare-Knuckle Prize Fighting in America.* Ithaca, N.Y.: Cornell University Press, 1986.

Kimmel, Michael. *Manhood in America: A Cultural History.* New York: Free Press, 1996.

Licht, Walter. *Industrializing America: The Nineteenth Century.* Baltimore: Johns Hopkins University Press, 1995.

McGaw, Judith A. *Most Wonderful Machine: Mechanization and Social Change in Berkshire Paper Making, 1801–1885.* Princeton, N.J.: Princeton University Press, 1987.

Stearns, Peter N. *Be a Man! Males in Modern Society.* 2nd ed. New York: Holmes & Meier, 1990.

FURTHER READING

Baron, Ava, ed. *Work Engendered: Toward a New History of American* Labor. Ithaca, N.Y.: Cornell University Press, 1991.

Bensman, David. *The Practice of Solidarity: American Hat Finishers in the Nineteenth Century.* Urbana: University of Illinois Press, 1985.
Clawson, Mary Ann. *Constructing Brotherhood: Class, Gender, and Fraternalism.* Princeton, N.J.: Princeton University Press, 1989.
Cooper, Patricia A. *Once A Cigar Maker: Men, Women, and Work Culture in American Cigar Factories, 1900–1919.* Urbana: University of Illinois Press, 1987.
Montgomery, David. *The Fall of the House of Labor: The Workplace, The State, and American Labor Activism, 1865–1925.* Cambridge, England: Cambridge University Press, 1987.

RELATED ENTRIES

Artisan; Breadwinner Role; Bureaucratization; Business/Corporate America; Capitalism; Class; Fatherhood; Heterosexuality; Labor Movement and Unions; Leisure; Market Revolution; Middle-Class Manhood; Patriarchy; Professionalism; Property; Self-Control; Self-Made Man; Technology; Urbanization; Work; Working-Class Manhood

—*Thomas Winter*

INSANITY

Throughout the history of the Western world, and of the United States, insanity has been recognized as a mental illness that prevents its victims from conforming to societal definitions of rational behavior and judgment. Physicians and psychiatrists have studied insanity since the eighteenth century. Its association with weakness and childlike behavior has been understood to undermine masculine identity, thus contributing to the shame experienced by its male sufferers.

Insanity in the Early Republic

Insanity became an important public concern at the time of the nation's founding. After the American colonies declared their independence by separating from England, a new nation was established based on Enlightenment concepts of science and reason and republican ideals grounded in a patriarchal government and a citizenship of rational, independent white males. But mental illness seemed to pose a challenge to a society founded upon these principles. Political leaders feared that male insanity weakened the new nation by reducing male citizens to the mental level of their supposed intellectual inferiors; namely women, children, and slaves.

The association that early American leaders drew between manhood, rationality, and republicanism resulted in the construction of numerous mental asylums in the early republic. The Pennsylvania Hospital, directed by the physician Benjamin Rush from 1783 to 1813, treated patients as dependent children (the opposite of independent manhood), with physicians and attendants acting as parents. The paternalistic environment that pervaded asylums in the early nineteenth century encouraged physicians to focus on the behavior of the patient, on observable symptoms, rather than on the disease itself. Rather than attempting to find the cause of emotional outbursts or childlike behavior, physicians attempted to retrain men to act within the confines of an accepted masculine ethos. Once male patients consistently avoided their so-called errant behavior, physicians released them into society with their abilities to reason and rights as citizens fully restored. In this context, Rush's method of treatment fully embraced republican concepts of manhood, supporting the paternal hierarchy and male intellectual supremacy.

The Nineteenth Century: Masturbatory Insanity and Neurasthenia

The American belief that insanity was inconsistent with manhood and republican citizenship remained consistent throughout the nineteenth century. However, the onset of the market revolution and rapid urbanization prompted physicians to identify "new" mental illnesses that, while affecting both genders, were particularly troubling in men, since men were primarily responsible for economic production and other public endeavors.

One newly identified form of insanity was masturbatory insanity, which began to appear in record numbers beginning in the 1830s. Concerned that masturbation threatened the emerging masculine imperatives of the market society (i.e., the self-control, economic productivity, and reproduction necessary to national strength), physicians increasingly linked it to insanity. Physicians generally agreed that masturbatory insanity was caused by excessive stimulation, but they disagreed over what kinds of stimulation were most dangerous. Some believed that the proliferating leisure activities available in growing urban centers, such as going to saloons, attending theaters, and reading newspapers, corrupted men's minds with sexual images that encouraged masturbation, which led to insanity. Others argued that the pressures of market competition drove men to masturbate in an effort to relieve their tension. Both of these theories linked insanity to men's failure to conform to cultural expectations of masculinity; that is, to operate effectively in a market society and to exercise self-control.

Another newly identified form of mental illness was called *neurasthenia*. The physician George Beard introduced this term in 1869 to label a range of mental and physical symptoms—such as nervousness, weakness, exhaustion, and an inability to work—that were commonly associated with women in Victorian America. Assuming that men of different social classes embodied very different kinds of manhood, Beard and other neurologists distinguished two varieties of neurasthenia. Professional middle- and upper-class men, considered "brain workers," contracted cerebral neurasthenia due to the overexertion of their intellectual capacities and the pressures of trying to achieve self-made success in an urbanizing, industrializing economy. Meanwhile, working-class men, defined as less capable of manly self-control, developed spinal neurasthenia as a result of sexual overindulgence and frustration at being barred from self-made manhood by the physicality of their labor. By defining neurasthenia along class lines, physicians identified upper- and middle-class men with normative manhood, but effectively emasculated working-class men by grouping them with women.

The Twentieth Century

The advent of modern psychiatry in the late nineteenth and early twentieth centuries brought new theories about insanity and masculine identity. The Viennese psychologist Sigmund Freud argued that masculine identity was grounded in sexuality and shaped by early childhood experience. To Freud, insanity in men was linked to the incomplete or imperfect formation of mature masculinity, and women could never achieve full maturity due to their "inferior" genitalia. Freudian psychology thus reinforced, even as it recast, the opposition between manhood and insanity, while also reinforcing the rationale for male power. It remained powerfully influential through the twentieth century, shaping most subsequent approaches to the examination of insanity and masculinity.

The advent of modern warfare and America's growing global power produced new mental stresses on men and new ideas about male insanity in its relation to national strength. During World War I, psychiatrists encountered the first cases of shell shock and faced new questions about the meaning of manhood. While patients attempted to repress their memories of the horrors of war, their reluctance to return to battle conflicted with prevailing concepts of masculinity and national toughness. Psychiatrists suggested an ambivalent relation between shell shock and masculinity—they noted that victims exhibited the same signs as women diagnosed with hysteria, but they gave the condition a different name in order to reinforce its association with male activity.

Similar questions about men's mental health arose during and after the Vietnam War, as psychiatrists observed and examined the symptoms of a condition they termed *post-traumatic stress disorder*. As military strength became more important to national identity, American society became increasingly inclined to question the mental health of men who deviated from such masculine imperatives as bravery, duty, and toughness.

During the late twentieth century, psychiatrists were increasingly able to treat mental illnesses with drugs, and conditions such as depression became less stigmatized. Furthermore, as feminists challenged conventional notions of masculinity that emphasized emotional reserve and toughness, society urged men to acknowledge their vulnerabilities. But because the cultural connection between masculinity and strength remained unshaken, insanity continued to be a gendered phenomenon and to retain feminine connotations. Schizophrenia, multiple personality disorder, depression, and other disorders maintain their cultural association with female instability, thereby distancing men from the stigma associated with mental illness.

Bibliography

Engelhardt, H. Tristram. "The Disease of Masturbation: Values and Concepts of Disease." In *Sickness and Health in America.* Madison: University of Wisconsin Press, 1978.

Haller, John, and Robin Haller. *The Physician and Sexuality in Victorian America.* Urbana: University of Illinois Press, 1974.

Lunbeck, Elizabeth. *The Psychiatric Persuasion: Knowledge, Gender, and Power in Modern America.* Princeton, N.J.: Princeton University Press, 1994.

Nissenbaum, Stephen. *Sex, Diet, and Debility in Jacksonian America: Sylvester Graham and Health Reform.* Westport, Conn.: Greenwood Press, 1980.

Further Reading

Barker-Benfield, G. J. *The Horrors of the Half-Known Life.* New York: Harper & Row, 1976.

Bullough, Vern. *Sexual Attitudes: Myths and Realities.* Amherst, N.Y.: Prometheus, 1995.

Gamwell, Lynn, and Nancy Thomas. *Madness in America: Cultural and Medical Perceptions of Mental Illness before 1914.* Ithaca, N.Y.: Cornell University Press, 1995.

Kimmel, Michael. *Manhood in America.* New York: Free Press, 1996.

Stengers, Jean. *Masturbation: The History of a Great Terror.* New York: St. Martin's, 2001.

Related Entries

Body; Freudian Psychoanalytic Theory; Health; Masturbation; Middle-Class Manhood; Republicanism; Self-Control; Work; Working-Class Manhood

—*Catherine Maybrey*

INVISIBLE MAN

Ralph Ellison's *Invisible Man* (1952) traces the life of its African-American male protagonist—significantly left unnamed—as he moves from college in the South to New York City. The experiences of the protagonist captures the ways in which African Americans were deemed "invisible" by whites in order to dehumanize and marginalize them in American life. Although Ellison addresses African-American leadership and cultural relations in the black community, his primary concern is to inspect and critique whites' use of a pejorative construction of African-American masculinity, particularly the stereotyping of black males as brutish and libidinous, to dominate the social and political power dynamic of post–World War II America.

Several scenes in the novel symbolically depict white America's stereotyping of African-American masculinity and marginalizing of black men. At one point, the protagonist is forced to participate in a boxing match before a white male audience in order to receive a briefcase and a scholarship to a black college. Before the match, the protagonist and nine other young African-American men are forced to watch what the white men believe to be black men's ultimate object of desire: a nude, white, female dancer. Forced to sexual arousal, the youths are objectified by the all-white male audience, who proceed to live out their own racist fantasies of the "black buck" and the "black brute" as they scream racial obscenities to spur the teenagers into battle. The protagonist, by performing as a brutish black body, conforms to the white audience's expectations and blinds them to his intellectual potential.

The scenes with the dancer and the boxing match include a strongly homoerotic element—and an accompanying critique of white male sexuality and power. Since homosexuality was stigmatized by mainstream American culture, having the white men gaze upon virile males in boxing gear not only grounds the whites' power in the objectification of black men, but also calls that power into question by grounding it in homoerotic desire. This message becomes more explicit later in the text, when the young Emerson, a covert white homosexual, offers the protagonist a job as his manservant when previous attempts to sexually lure the black youth fail.

The dominant theme of African-American male disempowerment is further illustrated when the protagonist is demoted from a leadership role in the Marxist Brotherhood, a white-led communist group, because he resists their ideological practice of conflating the racial and economic oppression of African Americans. In the process, he is again reduced from a position of intellectual empowerment to the status of a sexual object, subjected to the sexual advances of several white women attempting to fulfill their fantasies of being overtaken by a libidinous black "buck." The protagonist reflects on a tradition of African-American manhood sexually subjugated to white women (and thereby emasculated) through performance as servants, chauffeurs, and Pullman porters.

Invisible Man examines the way in which African-American males are often objectified and eroticized by the dominant white culture in terms of physicality and sexuality, while at the same time denied power and autonomy—the definitive measures of manhood mandated by the white patriarchal system. Ellison's central message was that African-American men would achieve this manhood only when they achieved true visibility and equality. His message foreshadowed the declaration, "I AM A MAN" proclaimed by black men during the civil rights movement as they demanded full representation and equal rights for all African Americans.

BIBLIOGRAPHY

Benston, Kimberly W., ed. *Speaking for You: The Vision of Ralph Ellison.* Washington, D.C.: Howard University Press, 1987.

Ellison, Ralph. *Invisible Man.* New York: Random House, 1952.

Nadel, Alan. *Invisible Criticism: Ralph Ellison and the American Canon.* Iowa City: University of Iowa Press, 1988.

O'Meally, Robert G. *The Craft of Ralph Ellison.* Cambridge, Mass.: Harvard University Press, 1980.

FURTHER READING

Butler, Robert J., ed. *The Critical Response to Ralph Ellison.* Westport, Conn.: Greenwood Press, 2000.

Schor, Edith. *Visible Ellison: A Study of Ralph Ellison's Fiction.* Westport, Conn.: Greenwood Press, 1993.

Sundquist, Eric J., ed. *Cultural Contexts for Ralph Ellison's Invisible Man.* Boston: Bedford Books, 1995.

Watts, Jerry Gafio. *Heroism and the Black Intellectual: Ralph Ellison, Politics, and Afro-American Intellectual Life.* Chapel Hill: University of North Carolina Press, 1994.

RELATED ENTRIES

African-American Manhood; Body; Boxing; Civil Rights Movement; Homosexuality; Race; Violence; Whiteness

—*Angelo Rich Robinson*

IRISH-AMERICAN MANHOOD

Irish immigration into the United States became substantial early in the nineteenth century, and Irish-American men have since achieved positions throughout the American social structure. Although these men form a diverse group, subtle scrutiny reveals common notions and experiences of manhood among them.

While recognizing the cultural complications brought about by extensive marriage across ethnic lines by Irish Americans, two broad generalizations can still be made about the history of Irish-American manhood. First, Irish-American men have constructed their notions of masculinity through cultural accretion or substitution, rather than simply either rejecting or retaining traits from the "old country." They have thus supplemented and recast beliefs and behaviors previously promoted in their homeland. Second, Irish-American men moved from widespread poverty in the nineteenth century to a largely middle-class status by the end of the twentieth century, and they have usually adopted at least the appearance of the restraint commonly associated with middle-class males in the United States.

Manhood in Ireland

Most of the Irish males who came to the United States at the end of the nineteenth century had experienced materially sparse lives in Ireland. The typical male immigrant had farmed a small plot of rented land on which he grew potatoes and perhaps kept a few pigs, chickens, and cattle. Irish manhood prized verbal and physical aggression rather than acquisitiveness. Learning to appreciate the material priorities of American life and the tenets of American entrepreneurial manhood would therefore be difficult for many Irish males and their descendants. The Irish faced harsh treatment by Protestant landlords in Ireland, which accentuated their sense of distinctiveness as Catholics and caused many peasants to dislike rural life. This alienation from the land was intensified by the failure of the potato, the Irish peasant's primary food, during the several famines of the nineteenth century, the most devastating of which occurred during the late 1840s. Excessive drinking among men—often of poteen, a powerful homemade concoction—was extremely common in rural Ireland. In the United States, this distinctively intense affection for alcohol would continue to characterize Irish-American males, though it would often become a source of tension and embarrassment among those who aspired to blend into American society.

Geographical and Economic Mobility during the Nineteenth Century

Although Irish emigration to North America began early in the nineteenth century (and has continued to the present), intertwined factors of famine, eviction from the land, and political turmoil in Ireland made the middle and later years of the nineteenth century the time of heaviest Irish movement into the United States. About 1.5 million Irish entered the United States from 1847 to 1860, and about another 1.5 million followed from 1870 to 1900. Most arrived in poverty. While many nineteenth-century immigrants came from societies around the world in which men and women were often segregated from each other in everyday life, rural Ireland in the nineteenth century seems to have been a place of unusually pervasive separation, and even outright hostility, between the sexes. The journey to the United States often reflected this sexual segregation, with Irish women and men emigrating individually or with members of their own sex rather than in family units.

For the Irish, as for many other immigrant groups, American life accentuated some features of Old World manhood, while also prompting changes in others, and many Irish-American men sought to prove both their manhood and their American identity. Factors of social class and geographical region, in particular, shaped Irish-American manhood, with those Irish Americans who remained in the working class and the urban Northeast remaining the most distinctively Irish in their behaviors and beliefs. Those who moved either up the economic ladder or to other parts of the country sometimes embraced the emphasis on emotional restraint and material acquisitiveness characteristic of middle-class American notions of manhood. Yet social and geographical mobility did not completely erase cultural distinctiveness among Irish-American men.

In the nineteenth century, dire poverty and a sense of betrayal by the land tended to keep many Irish males in or near the American cities in which they had initially landed, though some enterprising or lucky men found ways to reach more promising areas. While countless Scandinavians and Germans (and a few Irish) headed west to farm, many Irish males instead went to the western frontier to lay track for the transcontinental railroad. The descendants of these men help account for the substantial Irish-American communities today in cities like Butte, Montana.

Constructing Irish-American Manhood in the Nineteenth and Twentieth Centuries

Characterized by many native-born Americans as inferior, unmanly, and as racially "other"—and as inclined to laziness, irresponsibility, and a lack of self-control—Irish-American men sought to demonstrate their manhood in a variety of ways. One important mechanism, particularly pronounced among those in the nation's cities, was to assert their whiteness. Seeking to differentiate themselves from slaves or from the free black laborers with whom they competed for jobs, and to counteract the hostility of native-born Americans, they sought to forge a psychologically (if not materially) advantageous racial identity, including an excessive racism against African Americans. In the United States, according to the historian Noel Ignatiev, the Irish "became white."

Another mechanism, perhaps reflecting a survival skill and an outlet for aggression derived from the Irish experience of severe English authority, was a style of pretense and fanciful loquacity that Queen Elizabeth I derisively christened "blarney" in the sixteenth century. Irish-American men displayed a particular fondness for talk, and especially exaggeration—an inclination well suited to their new American imperative of asserting manliness. Such affection for pretense may help explain why many men in Ireland and the United States showed great interest and skill in the acting profession. On stage and screen, from nineteenth-century playwrights and actors Dion Boucicault and Edward Harrigan to twentieth-century film stars James Cagney, Pat O'Brien, Spencer Tracy, Martin Sheen, and Sean Penn, Irish-American men have been revealingly conspicuous in the ranks of gifted actors in the United States.

The need to assert their manhood in the United States also led Irish-American men to gain a new appreciation for wielding power and influence, as well as for material success. A keen sense of the importance of holding political power made local politics a frequent focus of male attention and activity, particularly in the taverns around which much of Irish-American male social life centered. East Boston's Patrick Kennedy, the grandfather of President John F. Kennedy, was one of many Irish Americans who used his tavern as a political meeting place. The aggressive pursuit of political influence led some Irish-American men to participate in the emergence of powerful new urban male types in both the late nineteenth century and the twentieth century. New York City's Tammany Hall, Kansas City's Pendergast machine, and Chicago's Daley machine, all primarily run by (and sometimes named after) Irish-American males, became prototypical urban political organizations. Irish-American men—from Knights of Labor leader Terence Powderly in the nineteenth century to American Federation of Labor head George Meany in the twentieth—also occupied instrumental leadership positions in the formative years of the labor movement.

Religion, too, became an important arena in which Irish Americans asserted and defined manhood and sought power and influence. The sometimes defensive identification with Catholicism that had flourished in Ireland persisted in an America dominated by Protestantism. Irish-American males typically took their Catholicism seriously and practiced it strictly, making Catholic identity and practice an integral part of Irish-American masculinity itself. Accustomed to, and sometime preferring, all-male groups, and savoring authoritative roles, Irish-American men were particularly attracted to the priesthood and regarded it as a manly calling. For instance, Cardinal James Francis McIntyre of Los Angeles, a powerful mid-twentieth-century prelate, left a promising career on Wall Street for the priesthood, perhaps finding the one occupation as manly as the other. The Irish would dominate the American Catholic hierarchy (and the priesthood) beginning in the late nineteenth century and through much of the twentieth.

American culture also perpetuated the tendency toward pugnacity already present in Irish manhood. An aggressive and sometimes violent defense of honor, long elemental to urban working-class manhood in the United States, became especially important to Irish-American men because of the discrimination they faced in America. Likewise, the emphasis on sport and physicality in the rapidly modernizing society of the late-nineteenth-century United States was embraced by Irish-American men, who were particularly inclined to emphasize vigorously competitive athletics in an effort to overcome the stereotype of the Irish male as an aimless drinker. Thus, bare-knuckle prizefighter John L. Sullivan, the son of Irish immigrants, became a hero to Irish-American men in the late nineteenth century. Both Irish Americans and other Americans have closely associated Irish-American manhood with determination and aggressiveness—an association well symbolized by the University of Notre Dame's nickname, "The Fighting Irish."

At the same time, Irish-American men sought to turn their reputed aggressiveness into a basis for acceptance by other Americans through soldiering and patriotism, both longstanding badges of maleness in the United States. After their arrival in the United States, Irish-American men had been viewed with mistrust by Protestant Americans, who associated them with hypermasculine drinking and violence and suspected them of disloyalty because of their religious allegiance to the Roman Pope. Such suspicions were reinforced by Irish-American leadership of mobs during the New York Draft Riots of 1863, and again a half century later by Irish Americans' opposition to U.S. support of England during World War I. By the time of World War II, therefore, and continuing into the postwar period, Irish-American men tended to display an unusually aggressive patriotism, represented well by the bombastic 1950s anticommunism of "Tail Gunner Joe" McCarthy, the often excessively patriotic performances of George M. Cohan, and James Cagney's famous portrayal of Cohan in the World War II-era film *Yankee Doodle Dandy* (1942). Indeed, the popularity of 1940s film actor Pat O'Brien, often cast as a soldier, and the fame of the five Sullivan brothers in actual (and ultimately deadly) combat during World War II generated in American culture a pronounced connection between Irish-American masculinity and military service, and many war stories thereafter included a character with an Irish name. Characters such as Father Mulcahy in *M*A*S*H*, a popular film (1970) and television series (1972–83), and CIA operative Jack Ryan in Tom Clancy's popular novels of the late twentieth and early twenty-first centuries exemplify the persistence of this tradition.

Competing Models of Irish-American Manhood

As Irish immigrants and their descendants sought to adapt to American culture, the meaning of manhood became a contested issue within the Irish-American community. On the one hand, characteristics associated with boyishness—such as irresponsibility, drinking, a fondness for fancy and fantasy, reluctance to marry, and living with one's parents into middle age—were often accepted components of male behavior in both Irish and Irish-American culture. Yet such elements of masculinity did raise concerns among Irish Americans, particularly in the face of anti-Irish discrimination and the cultural power of middle-class values in the United States. High rates of domestic violence and desertion of family have been especially troubling issues throughout much of the Irish-American experience, persisting until well into the twentieth century. In many fictional works, such as Betty Smith's *A Tree Grows in Brooklyn* (1947), an Irish-American mother represented the group's adaptation to a sternly sober, materialistic American culture, while a carefree father symbolized a less acculturated Irish masculinity. Protestant American advice writers of the late nineteenth century urged greater domestic engagement among fathers. Yet the contemporaneous reform effort in the Irish-American community to integrate the father into the home was even more fervent, a drive that sought no less than a redefinition of Irish-American manhood itself.

Furthermore, many Irish-American men of the late nineteenth and twentieth centuries challenged traditional boyishness by enacting an opposing model of Irish-American masculinity reflective of American middle-class ideals of manliness and grounded in sobriety, practicality, and hard-headedness. This notion of masculinity was apparent in the development of an Irish-American political and religious leadership during the late nineteenth century, and it continued to develop thereafter. During the 1960s, for example, men such as Chicago's dour mayor Richard J. Daley and Los Angeles's shrewd Cardinal James Francis McIntyre challenged the stereotype of the Irish-American male, sarcastically described by novelist John Gregory Dunne as a "harp twinkler" (Dunne, 136). This awareness of the realities and stereotypes stemming from the traditional inclination to drink may have stimulated a powerful emphasis on temperance among many Irish-American men, sometimes to the point of total abstinence solemnized by an oath.

Manhood and Melancholia in the Irish-American Experience

Irish-American manhood has been shaped by another important element; namely the singular pain of the encounter between Irishness and modernity, a pain perhaps felt with particular intensity by those Irish males who emigrated to the rapidly modernizing United States of the nineteenth century and among their descendants in subsequent generations. Some historians and psychologists, noting this tendency toward melancholia, have connected it with what they allege is an unusually high rate of schizophrenia among twentieth-century Irish males and American men of Irish ancestry. Less dramatic (and more widely recognized, especially by scholars, novelists, and playwrights) has been an ongoing fascination with death in the cultures of both Ireland and Irish America. Such phenomena suggest that Irish-American manhood has been grounded to a significant degree in a profound unease with American life.

Bibliography

Dezell, Maureen. *Irish America: Coming into Clover.* New York: Doubleday, 2001.

Dunne, John Gregory. *True Confessions.* New York: Pocket Books, 1978.

Fallows, Marjorie R. *Irish Americans: Identity and Assimilation.* Englewood Cliffs, N.J.: Prentice Hall, 1979.

Ibson, John Duffy. *Will the World Break Your Heart? Dimensions and Consequences of Irish-American Assimilation.* New York: Garland, 1990.

Ignatiev, Noel. *How the Irish Became White.* New York: Routledge, 1995.

McCaffrey, Lawrence J. *Textures of Irish America.* Syracuse, N.Y.: Syracuse University Press, 1992.

Miller, Kerby A. *Emigrants and Exiles: Ireland and the Irish Exodus to North America.* New York: Oxford University Press, 1985.

Further Reading

Casey, Daniel J., and Robert E. Rhodes, eds. *Modern Irish-American Fiction: A Reader.* Syracuse, N.Y.: Syracuse University Press, 1989.

Fanning, Charles, ed. *The Exiles of Erin: Nineteenth-Century Irish-American Fiction.* Notre Dame, Ind.: University of Notre Dame Press, 1987.

———. *New Perspectives on the Irish Diaspora.* Carbondale: Southern Illinois University Press, 2000.

Hayden, Tom. *Irish on the Inside: In Search of the Soul of Irish America.* New York: Verso, 2001.

Meagher, Timothy J. *Inventing Irish America: Generation, Class, and Ethnic Identity in a New England City, 1880–1928.* Notre Dame, Ind.: University of Notre Dame Press, 2001.

Related Entries

African-American Manhood; Alcohol; American Dream; Class; Ethnicity; Fitzgerald, F. Scott; Gangs; Immigration; Insanity; Mother–Son Relationships; Nativism; Patriotism; Politics; Race; Religion and Spirituality; Temperance; Whiteness

—*John Ibson*

Iron John: A Book About Men

Iron John: A Book About Men (1990), the American poet Robert Bly's interpretation of the German fairy tale "Der Eisenhans," became a foundational text for the mythopoetic men's movement of the 1990s. Concerned that modern American men had become alienated from the source of their masculinity, he proposed the recovery of that identity through a regimen of healing ritual.

In the book, Bly measures late-twentieth-century American manhood against a romanticized preindustrial past in which males lived in close contact with nature, received ritual instruction in their passage through adolescence, and learned healthy male behavior by working alongside their fathers. According to Bly, the Industrial Revolution separated fathers from sons and robbed men of their connection with nature and each other, leaving men unable to feel or express compassion properly or form healthy relationships with other men. Furthermore, the elevation of women's authority in the American home had feminized men by giving mothers too great a hold on their sons' affections and encouraging maternal smothering of young boys. The Vietnam War reinforced these developments by undermining young men's faith in the paternal authority of the government and alienating them from their fathers. Because modern American men lack strong mentoring models of strength, passion, and decisiveness they have become spiritually damaged and are fearful of expressing their natural appetites and desires.

For Bly, the key to recovering lost masculine identity lay in the figure of the strong man, the Iron John figure, that was prominent in most cultures' myths and fairy tales. This archetype represents an essential manliness that must be kindled within a boy and nurtured throughout his lifetime. Traditional ritual initiation of boys by men into a broad range of male roles and experiences would allow boys to define themselves in relation to powerful male figures and apart from their mothers. By initiating, or "wounding," the boy, the older man facilitates the boy's escape from his mother and allows the boy to carry through life the healthy, passionate spirit of the natural inner warrior. According to Bly, a boy nurtured and mentored by men will grow into a man respectful and tolerant of both men and women, and he will be able to constructively manage disappointment and anger. *Iron John* counsels men to identify a cause or a quest and to chase it with singleness of purpose. Bly's emphasis on healing and fellowship, rather than grass-roots, public policy–oriented action, distinguished the mythopetic men's movement from the male liberationist and fathers' rights advocates of the 1970s and 1980s, as well as their Christian contemporaries, the Promise Keepers.

Bly's conceptualization of a new masculine ideal draws from a variety of sources, particularly the psychologist Carl Jung and the mythologist Joseph Campbell. *Iron John*, however, is frankly poetic and literary rather than historical or sociological. The text features Bly's retellings of myths of masculinity, his readings of those myths, and selections of poetry, including his own. Although Bly is careful not to blame feminism for the woes of contemporary men, *Iron John* stands in the tradition of other twentieth-century lamentations about the baleful effects of too much maternal love, as well as fears that urban, industrialized men have lost their vitality.

Bibliography

Bly, Robert. *Iron John: A Book About Men.* Reading, Mass.: Addison-Wesley, 1990.

Kriegel, Leonard. "Gender and Its Discontents." *Partisan Review* 60 (Summer 1993): 453–458.

Zipes, Jack. "Spreading Myths about Fairy Tales: A Critical Commentary on Robert Bly's Iron John." *New German Critique* 55 (Winter 1992): 3–19.

Further Reading

Harding, Christopher, ed. *Wingspan: Inside the Men's Movement.* New York: St. Martin's, 1992.

Kimmel, Michael, ed. *The Politics of Manhood: Profeminist Men Respond to the Mythopoetic Men's Movement (And the Mythopoetic Leaders Answer).* Philadelphia, Penn.: Temple University Press, 1995.

Schwalbe, Michael L. *Unlocking the Iron Cage: The Men's Movement, Gender Politics, and American Culture.* New York: Oxford University Press, 1996.

Related Entries

Adolescence; Boyhood; Crisis of Masculinity; Emotion; Fathers' Rights; Male Friendship; Men's Movements; Men's Studies; Momism; Mother–Son Relationships; Passionate Manhood; Promise Keepers; Sensitive Male; Youth

—*Trent Watts*

Italian-American Manhood

Modern conceptions of the "Italian-American man" are the result of centuries of Italianate masculinities coming into contact with the variety of masculinities present in America. The results of this encounter are more varied and complex than the stereotypical representations of the Latin lover, the brutish bully, and the flashy gangster that have dominated American popular culture since the early 1920s. Rather, qualities of Italian-American manhood are based primarily on the family order and the expectations of men to procreate, provide, and protect the family.

Italianate Masculinities

Descriptions of Italian masculinity go back as far as ancient Roman times (roughly the fifth century B.C.E.). The writings of Cicero and Tacitus reveal that men in this period were expected to protect the honor of the family and preserve their public reputation by monitoring the behavior of their wives and daughters. Any incident involving a woman's *injuria* (dishonor) required that the offended man take responsive (and often violent) action, against both the woman (whether it be a daughter, wife, or sister) and the man who had led her into dishonor. Such action was not only expected but, until recently, also sanctioned by Italian law.

After the fall of the Roman Empire in the fifth century C.E., Italian manhood became an ever changing synthesis of the many cultures, such as Germanic, Arab, and Spanish, that invaded and occupied the Italian peninsula over the ensuing centuries. Codes of Italian manhood, as they had developed by the sixteenth century, were outlined in Baldassare Castiglione's *The Book of the Courtier* (1528) and Niccolò Machiavelli's *The Prince* (1513), both of which were originally designed for the nobility, though they eventually became influential at all levels of Italian society. According to these works, a man was expected to handle his problems with coolness and detachment and to control his public behavior. This concept of one's *figura* (public figure) stemmed from the perennial need to protect oneself from one's enemies. Self-control had to be achieved in such a way as to appear effortless—a quality called *sprezzatura.* Another imperative of Italian manhood was *omertà* (silence) a term said to be derived from *ombredad*, the Spanish word for "manhood." Italian men were expected to express their manhood through actions rather than through words, as suggested by an Italian saying, "*Le parole sono femmine, I fatti sono maschi*" (words are feminine, actions are masculine). This approach to public behavior formed a distinctive Italian masculinity that required public demonstration of actions befitting males.

After the fall of the Roman Empire, Italy was constantly invaded and ruled by foreign powers. Under such conditions, Italians found social stability through *l'ordine della famiglia* (the order of the family), in which the father was patriarch and the rest of the family deferred to his authority. The mother, however, ruled within the home, setting up a relationship with her male children that was quite different from those in other cultures. The model for this relationship was that between Jesus and his mother, Mary, as she prepared him for public life—as it was depicted in Italian religious and secular art. Responsible for socializing the children, the Italian mother used her sons as buffers between home and the outside world: sons would represent their mothers in the public arena and serve as their emissaries. Through devoted attention extending into adulthood, she exacted unconditional and unwavering loyalty, resulting in the son's perception of having incurred an unpayable debt requiring constant attention to the family's (and her) needs. Mass emigration during the late nineteenth and early twentieth centuries would threaten this longstanding order of the family and bring Italian notions of masculinity into contact with those of the United States.

The Americanization of Italian Manhood

Between 1831 and 1908, nearly three million Italians immigrated to the United States, and over 60 percent of these immigrants were men. Most Italian male immigrants came to the United States to make money, with plans of eventually returning to Italy. Many of these men lived with fellow Italian workers or boarded with Italian families, typically in urban areas such as New York, Boston, Philadelphia, and Chicago. Many Italian men took jobs as laborers, wielding picks and shovels to help build railroads, subway systems, skyscrapers, and other structures. Time away from work was usually spent in the company of other Italians in local bars and cafes. Many of these workers were veterans of Italian labor movements, and they became instrumental in the development and advancement of the American labor movement.

Public displays of homosocial physical affection among men—including greetings with hugs and kisses on the cheeks (and sometimes on the mouth)—were common in Italy, and continued among Italian immigrants in the United States. Considered entirely compatible with heterosexual masculinity in both Italian and Italian-American culture, such gestures further fueled suspicions of Italian-American manhood among non-Italians in the United States, especially in the context of rising concerns over homosexuality in the late nineteenth and early twentieth centuries. This public behavior was displayed often during religious festivals, such as those devoted to the Madonna and patron saints, during which the men—who shared the burden of carrying statues—would hug, kiss, and cry in each other's arms at the culmination of rituals. In Italian-American culture, such public displays of affection established and intensified friendships among those who had publicly endured pain and suffering during the rituals (suffering that was viewed as symbolic of Christ's suffering).

In spite of public displays of affection between men, a great deal of homophobia existed, and still exists, within Italian-American male culture, though not to the same extent as found in other ethnic American cultures. Homosexuality, while more accepted in the Greco-Roman culture of Italy than in the United States, represented a threat to the family order because it did not contribute to the strengthening of the family through procreation. Still, many Italian-American homosexuals have gained acceptance by their families.

The radicalism and distinctive customs of nineteenth-century Italian workers made them seem more "foreign" than other ethnic groups, and they were therefore viewed as more of a threat by most Americans, who became concerned about the influence of Italian immigrant men in the United States. Italian immigrant men were frequently associated with urban crime and disorder, and they were often depicted as dark, dirty, and dangerous strangers. In the late nineteenth century, the writer Henry James depicted Italian workers in Boston as intimidating in terms of their physical qualities. The films of the 1920s and 1930s reinforced these negative stereotypes—examples include the exotic, oversexed sensuality of Rudolph Valentino and the criminality of Rico Bandello (as portrayed by Edward G. Robinson) in *Little Caesar* (1931). Newspapers of the 1920s offered sensationalized accounts of presumed anarchists Nicola Sacco and Bartolomeo Vanzetti, while accounts of the dapper lifestyles and defiant behavior of such gangsters as Al Capone, Lucky Luciano, and Frank Costello reinforced notions that Italian men had explosive tempers and were predisposed to violence. Through such accounts, the American media suggested that the Italian-American man symbolized hypersexuality, crime, and other breaches of civility.

During and after World War II, Americanization increasingly transformed traditional Italian manhood and drew Italian-American men away from the margins of American life toward positions of middle-class respectability and public fame. During World War II, nearly 500,000 Italian Americans—a higher proportion than any other ethnic group—served in the U.S. armed forces. As a result, Italian-American men became more directly exposed to models of masculinity beyond their own culture. On the home front, traditional male–female divisions of domain and labor began to break down as women took jobs traditionally held by men and experienced an independence that had previously been denied to them. At the same time, public images of Italian-American manhood, based on the examples of men who succeeded economically and in popular culture, became more positive. The baseball player Joe DiMaggio and the singer Frank Sinatra, for example, brought the Italian *bella figura* (good image) into the national spotlight for emulation by American men. In the postwar United States, increasing numbers of Italian-American men joined the exodus from ethnic urban neighborhoods to suburbia, where they worked outside the neighborhood and away from the home. Without the traditional male presence, Italian family dynamics changed dramatically and the foundations of the old-world patriarchy began to weaken.

Contemporary Italian-American Masculinities

More recent developments in Italian-American manhood have occurred as proponents of feminism, gay liberation, and the men's movement have increasingly challenged male dominance. For instance, the feminist movement of the 1960s and the men's movements developed in the 1970s by such figures as the poet Robert Bly encouraged men to become active participants in the domestic sphere, urged them to be more emotionally expressive and sensitive, and challenged traditional notions of heterosexuality and the breadwinning role. Many Italian Americans have adjusted to these changing American models of manhood, while continuing to evidence traditional European patriarchy. For instance, the idea of using violence to establish and maintain honor persists, even as the efficacy of patriarchy is disappearing.

Representations of Italian-American masculinity in popular culture continue to reflect stereotypes, and the absence of recent scholarly studies of Italian-American men makes them the most useful existing windows on Italian-American manhood in contemporary American culture. Fictional figures in the movies of the 1970s, such as Don Vito Corleone (*The Godfather,* 1972), Rocky Balboa (*Rocky,* 1976), and Tony Manero (*Saturday Night Fever,* 1977), all exhibit physical power and aggressiveness, criminality, and overt sexuality. Such characters can be seen as attempts by Hollywood filmmakers to marginalize troublesome characteristics of traditional patriarchy by associating them with ethnic cultures from the Old World.

In the early twenty-first century, however, fictional gangsters such as Tony Soprano of the television series *The Sopranos* (premiered in 1999) represent a more complex rendering of Italian-American manhood, as well as an examination of the challenges facing contemporary Italian-American men as they struggle to adjust to changing American conceptions of masculinity. Focused on the life of a contemporary gangster, the show explores Soprano's psychological responses to a changing world. He eventually realizes that he is not as tough as his gangster father, and that his son, while not afraid to defy him, is too soft and sensitive to ever be a gangster. As he questions the traditional family order that created his roles as son, husband, father, and gangster, Soprano signals the end of the line of the traditional model of Italian manhood. Furthermore, his interactions with women, such as his therapist, represent a recovery of the original mother–son paradigm so crucial in the formation of Italian men. This trend may lead to more in-depth and diverse representations of what it means to be an American man of Italian descent.

Bibliography

Belmonte, Thomas. "The Contradictions of Italian American Identity: An Anthropologist's Personal View." In *The Italian American Heritage: A Companion to Literature and Arts,* edited by Pellegrino D'Acierno. New York: Garland Publishing, 1999.

Gambino, Richard. *Blood of My Blood: The Dilemma of the Italian-Americans.* Toronto: Guernica Editions, 1996.

Kertzer, David I., and Richard P. Saller, eds. *The Family in Italy from Antiquity to the Present.* New Haven, Conn.: Yale University Press, 1991.

La Cecla, Franco. "Rough Manners: How Men are Made." In *Material Man: Masculinity, Sexuality, Style,* edited by Giannino Malossi. New York: Harry N. Abrams, 2000.

Orsi, Robert. *The Madonna of 115th Street: Faith and Community in Italian Harlem, 1880–1950.* New Haven, Conn.: Yale University Press, 1985.

Posen, Sheldon, and Joseph Sciorra."Brooklyn's Dancing Tower." *Natural History* 92, no. 6 (June 1983): 30–37, 77.

Further Reading

La Sorte, Michael. *La Merica: Images of Italian Greenhorn Experience.* Philadelphia, Penn.: Temple University Press, 1985.

Mangione, Jerre, and Ben Morreale. *La Storia: Five Centuries of the Italian American Experience.* New York: Harper Collins, 1992.

Mecca, Tommi Avicolli, Denise Nico Leto, and Giovanna Capone. *Hey Paesan!: Writing by Lesbians and Gay Men of Italian Descent.* Oakland, Calif.: Three Guineas Press, 1999.

Signorile, Michelangelo. *Queer in America: Sex, the Media, and the Closets of Power.* New York: Random House, 1993.

Tamburri, Anthony Julian, ed. *Fuori: Essays by Italian/American Lesbians and Gays.* West Lafayette, Ind.: Bordighera, 1996.

Related Entries

Advertising; Body; Breadwinner Role; Crisis of Masculinity; Ethnicity; Fatherhood; Gangs; Gangsters; Heterosexuality; Homosexuality; Immigration; Individualism; Industrialization; Mother–Son Relationships; Nuclear Family; Patriarchy; Race; Religion and Spirituality; Self-Made Man; Television; Violence; War; Youth

—Fred Gardaphe

Jackson, Andrew

1767–1845
American General and President

Andrew Jackson served as a role model for many nineteenth-century working men and small farmers by presenting a hypermasculine image of action, decisiveness, and determination. Rising from humble beginnings to become the hero of the War of 1812 and president of the United States (1829–37), Jackson became the first leader to exploit class-based resentment. His aggressive, sometimes violent style and his emphasis on independence appealed to the common man of the late 1820s and the 1830s.

Born on the western North Carolina frontier, Jackson endured a poverty-stricken childhood before studying law. Quick to anger, he reacted violently to anyone who threatened his masculinity, and he fought his first duel in 1788 against a rival attorney who had embarrassed him in court. He fought additional duels to preserve his standing in southern society, killing one man who had insulted his wife in 1806. Jackson's willingness, even eagerness, to resolve disputes through bloodshed would later make him a hero among working men who associated manhood with violent defense of personal honor.

Jackson moved to Tennessee in 1788 and soon sought military office to boost his status. He was appointed a major general in 1801. His 1814 victory against the Creek Indians at Horseshoe Bend, Alabama, brought him national fame, the rank of brigadier general in the U.S. Army, and command of the entire Gulf of Mexico region. He hoped that service in the War of 1812 would rescue his reputation from its harmful association with Aaron Burr, who had been tried for treason after he tried to establish a new republic in the southwest. His defeat of the British at the Battle of New Orleans in 1815 made Jackson a national hero and helped to propel him into the White House.

In 1828, Jackson defeated John Quincy Adams (who had defeated him in the 1824 presidential election) in a presidential campaign that his supporters promoted as pitting the masculine working man against the effete intellectual. As president, Jackson asserted his manhood by patronizing others. His paternalism and taste for vengeful, punitive maneuvering informed his treatment of Native Americans—his Indian policy aimed to replace the autonomy of what he considered the primitive, childlike Creek, Choctaw, and Cherokee with the fostering care of the federal government. Calling himself "your father the President" in communications with Native Americans, Jackson insisted that they evacuate their ancestral lands to avoid violence at the hands of whites, whose aspirations for independent land ownership—in accordance with Jeffersonian ideals of republican and agrarian manhood—he supported.

Issues and constructions of masculinity also shaped Jackson's approach to the other major controversy of his administration: the destruction of the Second Bank of the United States. Jackson and his supporters claimed to be liberating the nation (particularly white men seeking independent property ownership) from dependence on an all-powerful motherlike bank and what he labeled the "effete aristocracy" who used the bank to undermine manly republican independence. His action was supported by working men and small farmers, who associated manhood with independence.

Fiercely independent, quick to violence, and domineering, Jackson became a model of mid-nineteenth-century southern and frontier manhood. His struggles against Native Americans' "primitive" manhood and his political opponents' effete, overcivilized manhood reflected the impulsively democratic beliefs of that era's working men. More importantly, he inspired male politicians to use images of masculinity for political purposes. Jackson's health failed soon after he left office in 1837 and he died at his home in Tennessee in 1845.

Bibliography

Curtis, James C. *Andrew Jackson and the Search for Vindication.* Boston: Little, Brown, 1976.

Kimmel, Michael. *Manhood in America: A Cultural History.* New York: Free Press, 1996.

Rogin, Michael Paul. *Fathers and Children: Andrew Jackson and the Subjugation of the American Indian.* New Brunswick, N.J.: Transaction Publishers, 1991.

Further Reading

Remini, Robert V. *Andrew Jackson and the Course of American Empire, 1767–1821.* New York: Harper & Row, 1977.

———. *Andrew Jackson and the Course of American Freedom, 1822–1832.* New York: Harper & Row, 1981.

———. *Andrew Jackson and the Course of American Democracy, 1833–1845.* New York: Harper & Row, 1984.

Watson, Harry L. *Liberty and Power: The Politics of Jacksonian America.* New York: Hill and Wang, 1990.

SELECTED WRITINGS

Jackson, Andrew. *The Correspondence of Andrew Jackson.* Edited by John Spencer Bassett, 7 vols. Washington, D.C.: Carnegie Institution of Washington, 1926–1933.

RELATED ENTRIES

Agrarianism; Class; Democratic Manhood; Dueling; Individualism; Native American Manhood; Patriarchy; Patriotism; Politics; Race; Republicanism; Southern Manhood; Violence; War; Western Frontier; Whiteness; White Supremacism; Working-Class Manhood

—*Caryn E. Neumann*

JAMES, WILLIAM

1842–1910
Philosopher, Educator, and Author

Through his research and his teaching, the philosopher William James sought to mediate between two concepts of middle-class manhood that developed in U.S. culture from the mid-nineteenth to the early twentieth century. The first concept, rooted in antebellum intellectual, religious, and reform movements such as the Second Great Awakening, transcendentalism, and abolitionism, emphasized moral idealism and the authority of individual conscience. The second concept, which emerged after the Civil War, eschewed this antebellum idealism and defined true manliness in terms of duty, obligation, and a "strenuous life"—understood as a struggle toward masculine physical fitness. James sought to combine the ethical principles that informed antebellum reform movements with the new emphasis on the strenuous life to generate a manly, intellectual individualism.

James's vision of manliness had several sources. First, James drew on an Emersonian transcendentalist insistence that truth could never be received secondhand, but had to be discovered, tried, and tested firsthand. Second, James conceptualized manhood in terms of growth and individual autonomy—both of which were part of transcendentalist philosophy and Second Great Awakening theology. Third, James built upon new findings in experimental psychology that challenged the notion that all men possessed distinctive rational and emotive capabilities that could be shaped and reinforced in exact, uniform ways. For example, while James appreciated religious spirituality, he rejected simple solutions such as building moral behavior through physical exercise, as suggested by proponents of "muscular Christianity." Finally, the experiences of Civil War soldiers, such as his brother Wilkinson, confirmed for him both the power of moral idealism and the practical and difficult wartime realities of discipline and perseverance.

Based on these ideas and experiences, James developed a new concept of masculinity. Manhood, he argued, was not a fixed state of being that could be attained and held onto, but an intellectual method and dynamic process by which the self was continually reshaped through ongoing mental struggle. Masculinity, like truth, had to be strenuously fought for—though James defined strenuousness in terms of intellectual rather than physical fitness. James developed this method most fully in *Pragmatism* (1907), where he combined an empirical, rationalistic "tough-minded" stance and an idealist, ethical "tender-minded" stance into a "pragmatic method" by which truth is evaluated and revised based on actual lived experience.

Ultimately, James urged men to believe actively and willfully in a spiritual, transcendent order of the universe and to remain open to continual rethinking, rather than resting passively on old-fashioned, inherited dogmatism. He wished to hold on to moral and ethical values and foundations of society as long as they could be concretely applied in real life; at the same time, he placed a premium on the rigorous use of empirical data, while insisting that their value stood in direct relation to the extent they served larger ethical purposes.

Many others would borrow from James's ideas about manly individualism: He counted among his students President Theodore Roosevelt (whose interpretation of the strenuous life in support of imperialism James publicly opposed); the author Van Wyck Brooks, who advocated the founding of a new, democratic culture that would transcend inherited ideas about manliness; the Harvard philosopher George Santayana; the psychoanalyst Granville Stanley Hall; and the black civil rights activist W. E. B. Du Bois, whose thoughts on race and manhood in *Souls of Black Folk* (1903) reflects James influence.

BIBLIOGRAPHY

Cotkin, George. *William James, Public Philosopher.* Baltimore: Johns Hopkins University Press, 1990.

Fredrickson, George M. *The Inner Civil War: Northern Intellectuals and the Crisis of the Union.* New York: Harper & Row, 1965.

Townsend, Kim. *Manhood at Harvard: William James and Others.* New York: Norton, 1996.

FURTHER READING

Alkana, Joseph. *The Social Self: Hawthorne, Howells, William James, and Nineteenth-Century Psychology.* Lexington: University Press of Kentucky, 1997.

Goodman, Russell B. *American Philosophy and the Romantic Tradition.* Cambridge, England: Cambridge University Press, 1990.

Hansen, Olaf. *Aesthetic Individualism and Practical Intellect: American Allegory in Emerson, Thoreau, Adams, and James.* Princeton, N.J.: Princeton University Press, 1990.

Rose, Anne C. *Victorian America and the Civil War.* New York: Cambridge University Press, 1992.

SELECTED WRITINGS

James, William. *Pragmatism.* 1907. Reprint, edited by Bruce Kuklik. Indianapolis, Ind.: Hackett, 1981.

———. *The Varieties of Religious Experience: A Study in Human Nature.* Edited by Martin E. Marty. New York: Penguin, 1982.

———. *Writings, 1902–1910.* New York: Viking, 1987.

RELATED ENTRIES

Civil War; Education; Emerson, Ralph Waldo; Gilded Age; Hall, Granville Stanley; Imperialism; Militarism; Muscular Christianity; Passionate Manhood; Progressive Era; Religion and Spirituality; Sentimentalism; Strenuous Life; Victorian Era; War

—*Thomas Winter*

JESUS, IMAGES OF

Images of Jesus have articulated changing, and often conflicting, ideas about Christianity and masculinity in the United States. Americans have imagined Jesus as a figure at once human and divine. Yet in depicting him as both a heroic warrior against evil and a compassionate friend, as both conqueror and sinless innocent, they have also imagined him as both masculine and feminine. This has created differing views of Jesus because of the traditional gender division in American society, with traditional masculine traits associated with men and feminine traits with women.

American images of Jesus come primarily from European antecedents. Traditional Catholic images, drawn from a lively tradition of European art, have tended to portray Jesus not as markedly masculine or feminine, but as a sufferer, as the son of Mary, as an innocent child, and, occasionally, as an active adult male. The most common images—those appearing in the fourteen stations of the Way of the Cross, the step-by-step process leading to Jesus' crucifixion and resurrection—portray Jesus' humanity through his pain, tears, and blood, but they do not emphasize masculine qualities over feminine ones. Only occasionally in the past did European and Euro-American Catholic artists portray such masculine images as an angry Jesus (e.g., arguing with Satan or driving merchants from the temple) or a working Jesus.

Most American Protestant groups, on the other hand, have associated iconography with idolatry, and they have therefore been slow to create visual images of Jesus. Leaders of the Protestant Reformation, especially John Calvin, believed churches should refrain from picturing God or Jesus, and most Puritan churches followed suit. But Puritans did depict Jesus in their poetry and sermons, portraying him as decidedly masculine—as the bridegroom of mankind, as a suitor and husband to Christians' souls, and as a stern and righteous savior. Believing that women inherited Eve's sin of disobedience and were more naturally immoral than men, Puritans saw emulation of a masculine Jesus as a key to a Christian social order.

In the nineteenth century a more Romantic version of Christianity produced what some scholars have called a "feminization" of American culture. This coincided with a flowering of apparently feminine physical images of Jesus that depicted him as a great friend to children and a lamb-like innocent with long hair and a flowing robe. Images typically identified Jesus as divine, symbolized by the light surrounding his head, while his direct gaze invited intimacy with Christian believers and characterized him as human. Such images conformed to Victorian ideals of affectionate domestic life, in which parents, especially mothers, offered religious lessons to innocent children. Exemplifying such images of Jesus were deathbed letters during the Civil War, in which soldiers imagined a smiling Jesus welcoming them into a heaven where their families would be reunited.

By the late nineteenth century a growing number of male church leaders—especially evangelical Protestants—began charging that such feminine images of Jesus alienated men from the church. They responded by attempting to masculinize both Jesus and Christian commitment. The Men and Religion Forward movement of 1911–12 wanted an active and vigorous Jesus to help mobilize humanity, both to build strong bodies and to create organizations capable of improving the world. Evangelists such as the former baseball player Billy Sunday offered images of Jesus as an athlete, a carpenter, and a leader of men. During the 1920s, as American notions of manliness became increasingly associated with business success, Bruce Barton's *The Man Nobody Knows* (1924) directly countered the image of Jesus as a self-sacrificing, effeminate kill-joy with images of Jesus as a strong and decisive executive, an outdoorsman, a sociable man, an energetic businessman and, above all, a king.

Physical images of a masculine Jesus proliferated with mass production. The most popular twentieth-century images of Jesus were created by the artist Warner Sallman, whose *Head of Christ* (1940) seems to many American Christians to represent the clearest physical image of Jesus. Encouraged by a faculty member at the Moody Bible Institute in Chicago to "picture a virile, manly Christ," Sallman portrayed Jesus as a stern-jawed man of action, while also drawing on Victorian images that showed Jesus' divinity in the way light from above shone through his hair and eyes. By the 1950s and 1960s some critics called for an even more masculine Jesus who wore shorter hair and looked more at people and less up toward God.

Throughout the twentieth century, images of the manhood of Jesus have varied dramatically. Some groups have sought to de-emphasize femininity and accentuate Jesus' manliness. After World War II, many Catholics worried that their images of Jesus, with long hair, a soft face, and a literally bleeding heart, were too sentimental to deal with contemporary problems. Catholic art of the twentieth century often stressed more abstract visions of Jesus to avoid making his image another consumer product. During the Harlem Renaissance of the 1920s, and again during the black identity movements of the 1960s, African Americans represented Jesus as a black man, purposely rejecting white images of him. African Americans had long identified with Jesus for the way he withstood great pain with dignity, and in the twentieth century they increasingly depicted a courageous Jesus who denounced sin in the face of persecution and emerged as a liberator.

At the same time, several popular films and plays tried to rescue Jesus from notions of masculine excess. In the 1970s, *Jesus Christ Superstar* (1971) and *Godspell* (1971) depicted Jesus as an embodiment of the counterculture, a friend with special powers, whose long hair and androgynous appearance appealed to many young people critical of confining gender roles. The 1988 film *The Last Temptation of Christ,* meanwhile, presented a Jesus characterized by human frailties, including self-doubt and a dream of having sex with Mary Magdalene—a depiction that aroused strong opposition from conservative Christian groups.

The range of images of Jesus also reveals tensions in Christian understandings of the future. For many Christians, particularly those of the Christian Right, Jesus possesses ultimate authority and is ready to return to Earth, punish sinners, and make things right. Some artists, for example, portray Jesus in a variety of conquering images, especially an angry, manly Jesus returning to Earth to overthrow the anti-Christ. For others, often associated with the Christian Left, Jesus is the great friend and mediator, leading humanity, through his lessons and example, to a kinder world that rises above any conventional definitions of masculinity. Answers to the popular question, "What would Jesus do?" continue to reflect conflicting definitions of religion and manhood.

BIBLIOGRAPHY

Barton, Bruce. *The Man Nobody Knows.* Indianapolis, Ind.: Bobbs-Merrill, 1924.

Grubb, Nancy. *The Life of Christ in Art.* New York: Artabras, 1996.

McDannell, Colleen. *Material Christianity: Religion and Popular Culture in America.* New Haven, Conn.: Yale University Press, 1995.

Morgan, David. *Icons of American Protestantism: The Art of Warner Sallman.* New Haven, Conn.: Yale University Press, 1996.

Pelikan, Jaroslav. *The Illustrated Jesus Through the Centuries.* New Haven, Conn.: Yale University Press, 1997.

FURTHER READING

Crown, Carol, ed. *Wonders to Behold: The Visionary Art of Myrtice West.* Memphis, Tenn.: Mustang Publishing, 1999.

Godbeer, Richard. "'Love Raptures': Marital, Romantic, and Erotic Images of Jesus Christ in Puritan New England, 1670–1730." In *A Shared Experience: Men, Women, and the History of Gender,* edited by Laura McCall and Donald Yacovone. New York: New York University Press, 1998.

Maus, Cynthia Pearl. *Christ and the Fine Arts.* Rev. ed. New York: Harper & Row, 1959.

Putney, Clifford. *Muscular Christianity: Manhood and Sports in Protestant America, 1880–1920.* Cambridge, Mass.: Harvard University Press, 2001.

Turner, J. F. *Howard Finster, Man of Visions.* New York: Alfred A. Knopf, 1989.

RELATED ENTRIES

African-American Manhood; Art; Body; Counterculture; Cult of Domesticity, Evangelicalism and Revivalism; Men and Religion Forward Movement; Muscular Christianity; Religion and Spirituality; Sunday, Billy; Victorian Era

—*Ted Ownby*

JEWISH MANHOOD

Jewish manhood in the United States has been marked by two opposing forces. On the one hand, Jewish immigrants and their descendants have perpetuated Jewish traditions that celebrate gentleness, mildness, patience, and scholarship as positive masculine traits and emphasize nonviolent restraint as a desired response to aggression. On the other hand, the image of the tough, violent Jewish man has been an undercurrent throughout Jewish history and has become increasingly salient in the twentieth-century United States as Jews have sought to meet prevailing standards of American manhood.

European Precedents

The image of the gentle Jewish man served as a positive self-identification among Jews—as well as the foundation of anti-Semitic caricatures. In particular, standards of Jewish manhood, both in Europe and the United States, have been historically grounded in the idea of the *mensch*, which means an "admirable person" in Yiddish. In nineteenth-century Europe, a mensch was dependable, patient, modest, and passive—both a kind husband and a devoted scholar. European Christian culture separated such qualities from male sexuality, but Jewish cultures celebrated these characteristics as seductive traits.

Judaism also emphasized a masculine ideal of religious scholarship for boys and men, which contrasted with Euro-Christian martial codes of masculinity. Jewish fathers groomed their sons for religious study and encouraged critical thinking—preconditions for their leadership roles in the synagogue, community, and family. Literacy in Hebrew and knowledge of the bible also were expected of all males. The bar mitzvah, a coming-of-age ritual celebrated on a Jewish male's thirteenth birthday, required initiates to display their intellectual skills and religious responsibility by memorizing and publicly reciting passages of the Torah (the Jewish scripture) in Hebrew.

Because this model of manhood greatly differed from dominant European Christian models, European culture represented Jewish men as either feminine or incompletely masculine at least as far back as the thirteenth century. Circumcision (the removal of the foreskin of the penis for symbolic and hygienic reasons) was a controversial sign of this Jewish manhood. Among Jews, circumcision expresses the covenant between God and Jewish men, and has also been associated with cleanliness. Gentiles (non-Jews) and some assimilated Jews viewed circumcision as a partial castration or feminization of the male body, while some thought that circumcision caused deviant male sexuality (including masturbation) and sexually transmitted diseases such as syphilis. The ambiguity of Jewish men's masculinity was also the basis of Jewish men's close association with hysteria, a nervous disease most often identified with women. In these ways, male Jewish bodies were central to debates about sexuality and health.

The focus in Jewish culture on intellectualism (such as argumentation and the manipulation of language), and the de-emphasis of physical strength, only intensified the Gentiles' identification of Jewish men with traditional feminine traits. Jewish women often worked alongside their husbands to provide for their families, or earned money (frequently as shopkeepers and peddlers) so that their husbands could devote part of the day to religious study. Even working-class Jews who did not engage in sedentary, scholarly lives were perceived as being unmanly by Christian Europeans.

Immigration and Assimilation in Nineteenth- and Twentieth-Century America

Immigration to the United States involved both continuity with and departure from longstanding traditions of Jewish masculinity. The first major migration of Jews to the United States, in the mid-nineteenth century, consisted of German Jews who, having already assimilated to bourgeois European society, accepted a male focus on secular economic success and women's domestication. The second wave of Jewish migration, between 1880 and 1920, was dominated by eastern-European Jews who had not conformed to the middle-class ideology of separate spheres for men and women. The full-time scholar persisted as a masculine ideal (if only rarely a reality) for eastern-European Jews, while women gained some flexibility and autonomy in the public sphere to support men's education.

Although constructions of Jewish manhood shifted on American soil, the Gentile association of Jewish masculinity with effeminacy and deviance persisted. Popular nineteenth-century melodramas, such as John Brougham's *The Lottery of Life* (1868) and Charles Townsend's *The Jailbird* (1893), featured a "sheeny," or Jewish villain, who was effeminate, sexually deviant, greedy, and willing to deceive others to acquire more cash. In addition, his financial duplicity was often tied to unnatural sexual passions. Sheenies expressed effeminacy through language (using affectionate phrases like "my dear"), battles with other men (losing either through cowardice or physical weakness), and nervousness (not concealing their emotions).

Beginning in the mid–nineteenth century, and continuing through the twentieth century, the adaptation to modern American life and the achievement of middle-class status produced a fundamental shift in Jewish manhood. Especially among Reform Jews (those who most thoroughly modified Jewish traditions), but also among Conservative and Orthodox Jews, men sought financial reward and recognition in the public worlds of business and politics, and the traditional link between Jewish manhood and religious study weakened. Although religious education declined among American

Jewish men during this period, the persistence of the traditional scholarly ideal, combined with the new importance of public achievement, led Jews to pursue secular education in the United States with greater commitment than other immigrant groups. In the early twentieth century, second-generation Jews entered universities before other groups that had been part of the wave of immigration after 1880. American Jewish men used their advanced education to pursue prestigious professions, such as medicine and law, while Jewish women sought jobs as teachers and social workers.

The role of Jewish fathers also changed over the course of the twentieth century. Whereas the religious education of sons had rested in the hands of fathers in premodern Jewish culture, fathers in the United States were increasingly absorbed in breadwinning roles and workplace achievement, and they therefore played a smaller part in the development of their children's Jewish identity. In the second half of the twentieth century, Jewish fathers (similar to other American fathers) experienced weakened family authority and were increasingly seen as ineffectual at home as they sought occupational achievement. This development fueled anti-Semitism and anti-immigration sentiment in the United States at the turn of the twentieth century. Stereotypical beliefs about Jewish men's lack of fitness for military service or strenuous labor, and about their propensity for crime, contributed to fears that American stock was being contaminated by inferior and un-American Jewish strains. The passage of the National Origins Act in 1924 sought, in part, to curtail the number of eastern-European Jewish immigrants.

The Tough Jew in Nineteenth- and Twentieth-Century America

Longstanding Jewish ambivalence about the gentle Jewish man is evident in the persistence of an alternative characterization of Jewish manhood—"the tough Jew," a term used by the historian Paul Breines to describe Jews who are violent in the public, political arena. The robust and combative Jew existed in the margins of Jewish culture until the twentieth century, when Zionism, a movement to establish a homeland for a separate Jewish national culture, brought the

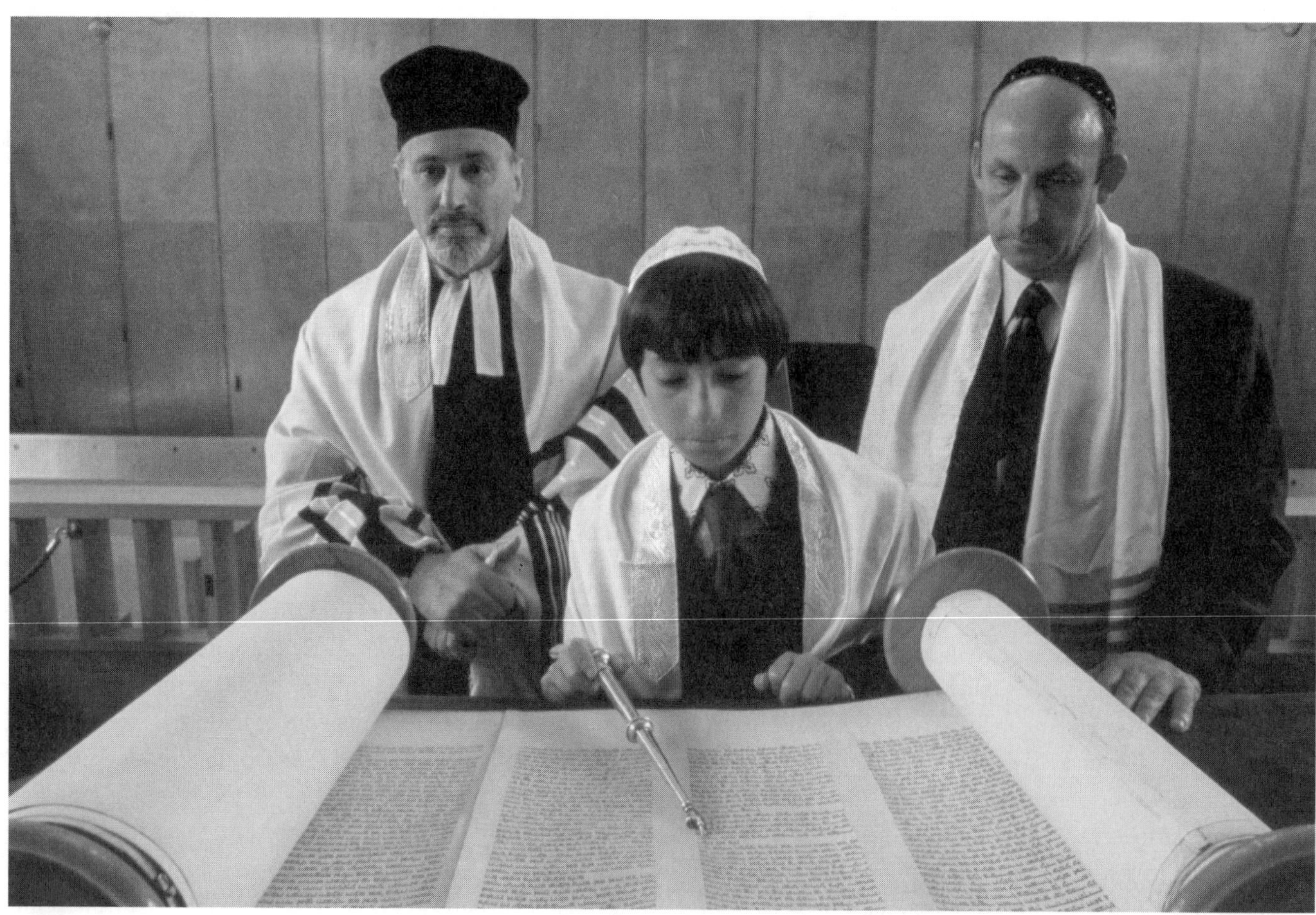

A boy recites from the Torah during his bar mitzvah, a coming-of-age ritual celebrated on a Jewish male's thirteenth birthday. Among many American Jews, the traditional association of manhood with religious study has waned, but the bar mitzvah continues to mark ethnic identity. (© David Reed/Corbis)

tough Jew to the forefront of Jewish culture and politics in America. Prior to the birth of Zionism, the primary images of tough Jews were as martyrs in the Middle Ages, soldiers in various national armies, and gangsters in European and American cities. In the 1890s, however, Austrian physician and Zionist Max Nordau (1849–1923) developed the idea of the *Muskeljudentum*, or "muscle-Jew," as the basis of a strong Jewish state. Zionist groups, such as the Zionist Organization of America, established sports clubs to rejuvenate Jewish bodies and described physically vigorous Jewish men as the ideal citizens of Palestine.

An emphasis on physical toughness in Jewish American culture was evident as early as 1854, when the first Young Men's Hebrew Association (YMHA) was established. Like the Young Men's Christian Association (YMCA), first created in the United States three years earlier, the YMHA sought to develop young men's physical and moral strength through homosocial (male-only) recreation. The YMHA also cultivated strong links with Jewish culture by encouraging Jewish practice and education. The development of the tough Jew accelerated in the United States at the turn of the twentieth century in response not only to growing anti-Semitism, which denigrated Jewish men, but also to the widespread attempts to strengthen manhood in the face of women's rights movements and the emergence of homosexuality as a scientific category and subculture. It coincided with a Protestant Christian movement to promote a "muscular Christianity."

The tough Jew ideal continued to grow in importance over the course of the twentieth century, although images of male Jewish frailty and defenselessness were temporarily reinforced in the 1930s and 1940s by the Nazi genocide. The establishment of Israel in 1948 reinvigorated the tough Jew ideal, however, even though Zionists relied on the image of the disempowered Holocaust victim to provide moral justification for a Jewish state. The victorious defense of Israel against Egypt, Syria, and Jordan in the 1967 Six-Day War was a watershed in the transformation of American Jewish masculinity. According to many scholars, including Paul Breines, images of rugged Israeli soldiers inspired American Jews to reject the tradition of the nonviolent Jew. After 1967, American fiction, including Ken Follett's *Triple* (1979) and Leon Uris's *The Haj* (1984), featured male Jewish spies, detectives, and soldiers. At the same time, historians such as Isaiah Trunk emphasized the strength and heroism of Jewish resistance to the Nazis. American Jewish political organizations, such as the National Jewish Community Relations Council (a coordinating body for community relations in the United States), made Israeli defense a top priority, whereas immigration and the separation of church and state had previously been the main issues. Similarly, the Jewish Defense League, founded in the United States by Meir Kahane in 1968, advocated armed self-defense with its declaration, "For every Jew a .22."

Throughout the nineteenth and twentieth centuries, controversies over Jewish masculinity have been interwoven with questions of American identity. The intellectual and passive mensch has been both an icon of ethnic distinctiveness and a source of embarrassment for Jewish men in modern America. The image of the tough Jew has also sparked concern about the eclipse of nonviolent Jewish traditions and the invisibility of Jewish cultural traditions in the secular world of American abundance. Some critics worry that the tough Jew has become indistinguishable from broader ideals of rugged, violent American masculinity.

BIBLIOGRAPHY

Boyarin, Daniel. *Unheroic Conduct: The Rise of Heterosexuality and the Invention of the Jewish Man.* Berkeley: University of California Press, 1997.

Breines, Paul. *Tough Jews: Political Fantasies and the Moral Dilemma of American Jewry.* New York: Basic Books, 1990.

Erdman, Harley. *Staging the Jew: The Performance of an American Ethnicity, 1860–1920.* New Brunswick, N.J.: Rutgers University Press, 1997.

Gilman, Sander L. *The Jew's Body.* New York: Routledge, 1991.

Gilmore, David G. *Manhood in the Making: Cultural Concepts of Masculinity.* New Haven, Conn.: Yale University Press, 1990

Hyman, Paula. *Gender and Assimilation in Modern Jewish History: The Roles and Representations of Women.* Seattle: University of Washington Press, 1995.

Martel, Elise. "From Mensch to Macho? The Social Construction of a Jewish Masculinity." *Men and Masculinities* 3, no. 4 (2001): 347–369.

Prell, Riv-Ellen. *Fighting to Become Americans: Assimilation and the Trouble between Jewish Women and Jewish Men.* Boston: Beacon Press, 1999.

FURTHER READING

Alexander, Michael. *Jazz Age Jews.* Princeton, N.J.: Princeton University Press, 2001.

Brod, Harry, ed. *A Mensch Among Men: Explorations in Jewish Masculinity.* Freedom, Calif.: Crossing Press, 1988.

Brodkin, Karen. *How the Jews Became White Folks and What That Says about Race in America.* New Brunswick, N.J.: Rutgers University Press, 1998.

Cohen, Rich. *Tough Jews.* New York: Simon & Schuster, 1998.

Follett, Ken. *Triple: A Novel.* New York: Arbor House, 1979.

Trunk, Isaiah. *Jewish Responses to Nazi Persecution: Collective and Individual Behavior in Extremis.* New York: Stein and Day, 1979.
Uris, Leon. *The Haj.* Garden City, N.Y.: Doubleday, 1984.

RELATED ENTRIES
Breadwinner Role; Education; Ethnicity; Fatherhood; Gangsters; Homosexuality; Immigration; Middle-Class Manhood; Muscular Christianity; Nationalism; Sports; Work; Young Men's Christian Association

—*M. Alison Kibler*

JUNGLE, THE

Part muckraking exposé, part naturalist novel, part socialist polemic, Upton Sinclair's *The Jungle* (1906) tells the fictional tale of Jurgis Rudkus, a Lithuanian immigrant who comes to Chicago with his family at the turn of the twentieth century hoping to find a good job and a decent wage. Instead, Jurgis and his family find themselves repeatedly victimized by an exploitative capitalist system. They desperately toil in the dangerous meatpacking industry, struggling to earn enough to survive. All their efforts fail, however, and Jurgis watches his father, wife, and son die in quick succession. In the final chapters of the novel, Jurgis gains a small but promising triumph when he discovers in socialism an incisive critique of the capitalist system and a practical means for affecting social change. This conversion to socialism also transforms Jurgis's gender identity, enabling him to reclaim and reshape the manhood stripped from him in the fiercely competitive working-class "jungle" of urban-industrial America.

When he first arrives in America, Jurgis is a paragon of masculine strength and health, exemplifying an ethic of self-made, independent manhood. Strong and hardworking, he is steadfastly optimistic that he can provide for his family. He responds to all hardships with the defiant refrain "I will work harder," but his faith proves to be tragically naive. Jurgis's manhood is imperiled as poverty and dangerous jobs rob him of both his physical strength and his identity as worker, breadwinner, and family protector. His wife, Ona, and the young children in their family are all eventually forced to work so that they can eke out a meager existence. A greater blow is that Jurgis cannot protect the women of his family from sexual exploitation; Ona submits to the advances of her boss in order to retain her job, and her cousin Marija turns to prostitution to escape poverty. After the death of his son, Jurgis abandons the remaining members of the family and becomes, in turn, an animalistic tramp, a petty thug, a political lackey, and a scab (a nonunion worker who replaces a union worker during a strike). This submission to, and complicity with, the corrupt capitalist system momentarily improves Jurgis's material situation, but only by exacting from him his self-respect.

Sinclair's tale of Jurgis's material and moral demise suggested that individualism and competition—ideals of manliness encouraged by market capitalism—actually emasculate men by depriving them of ways to resist capitalist exploitation. Jurgis ultimately rediscovers and revitalizes his manhood through socialism and working-class political activism, which offer him ways to critique the system and restore his masculine identity. Socialism empowers Jurgis to "no longer be the sport of circumstances" and become "a man, with a will and a purpose." While this radically inflected ethic of manhood was not the norm in America in the early twentieth century, Sinclair's socialist novel drew upon and distilled pervasive anxieties about the demise of an ethos of manhood rooted in hard work, economic independence, and entrepreneurship in what was becoming an increasingly bureaucratic, corporate economy.

BIBLIOGRAPHY
Bederman, Gail. *Manliness and Civilization: A Cultural History of Gender and Race in the United States, 1880–1917.* Chicago: University of Chicago Press, 1995.
Bloodworth, William A. *Upton Sinclair.* Boston: Twayne, 1977.
Montgomery, David. "Workers' Control of Machine Production in the Nineteenth Century." *Labor History* 17 (1976): 485–509.
Sinclair, Upton. *The Jungle.* New York: Doubleday, Page & Co., 1906.

FURTHER READING
Barrett, James R. *Work and Community in the Jungle: Chicago's Packinghouse Workers, 1894–1922.* Urbana: University of Illinois Press, 1987.
Howard, June. *Form and History in American Literary Naturalism.* Chapel Hill: University of North Carolina Press, 1985.
Wilson, Christopher P. *The Labor of Words: Literary Professionalism in the Progressive Era.* Athens: University of Georgia Press, 1985.

RELATED ENTRIES
American Dream; Breadwinner Role; Bureaucratization; Business/Corporate America; Capitalism; Hoboes; Individualism; Labor Movement and Unions; Progressive Era; Self-Made Man; Work; Working-Class Manhood

—*Robert K. Nelson*

Juvenile Delinquency

The term *juvenile delinquency* encompasses much more than a legal definition about violations of law by youthful offenders. Its meaning becomes clear only when one analyzes how society has attempted to define and combat delinquency. Americans first employed the term in the eighteenth century, and since then, although mostly used in a universal way, it has focused on the male delinquent. Authorities have considered the unruly boy and the wayward young man especially dangerous for society. Throughout most of American history, ideas about the roles of young men have been closely connected with notions about the nation's future. The young male delinquent therefore figured as an eminent threat.

One can find examples of delinquent juvenile behavior as early as the colonial period. Both male and female adolescents threatened and violated community norms through vandalism, drinking, theft, and premarital sexual experimentation. While this behavior was often destructive, adults enlarged its meanings and added exaggerated dangers to these acts in order to confirm their authority. Early American communities interpreted such violations in highly gendered ways: While the incriminating behavior of a young female (almost always related to her sexual activity) served as a risk to morality, the aggressiveness and disobedience of male delinquents seemed to threaten the order and stability of the community. At a time when parents and churches were responsible for maintaining discipline, Puritan ministers condemned the unruly conduct of young men and urged them to return to established norms of male adulthood.

In the new nation, the growth of the cities, and the resulting erosion of older community-based mechanisms of maintaining social and moral order, spurred adults' anxieties about male youth. Contemporary commentators strongly associated increasing urban vice and crime with the cities' young male population, and as many chroniclers of urban life observed, gangs were composed largely of boys between the ages of eight and seventeen. Most observers linked the problem of youthful crime and vagrancy to immigration, and many blamed Irish parents for a perceived urban crisis. But as the records of institutions such as the New York House of Refuge reveal, native-born children also contributed to gang membership.

The antebellum denunciation of young urban males stimulated a lively debate on youth as a distinct life stage. Reformers addressed the apparent problem by creating extrafamilial institutions to socialize criminal adolescents, settling, in particular, on the reform school. Unlike the older houses of refuge established and managed by local urban philanthropists, reform schools were usually located in the country (away from the presumed corrupting influences of urban life), were primarily state supported, and were aimed at the reformation of juvenile offenders. Although reformers referred to these institutions with the language of benevolence and environmentalism, most of the reform schools were, in fact, prisons. Before the emergence of the old common-law idea of *parens patriae,* which allowed the state to appoint substitute parents, authorities often committed to these institutions adolescents who were wayward or stubborn, rather than criminal.

Both the discourse on the juvenile delinquent and the institutions built to resocialize them added to and reinforced a certain middle-class perception of working-class masculinity as prone to disorderly behavior—a view which informed a superior notion of Victorian, middle- and upper-class manliness. In the late nineteenth and early twentieth centuries, this distinction weakened, but the creation of the new academic disciplines of adolescent psychology and criminology reconfirmed the established order by lending scientific legitimacy to the idea of the male delinquent as an identifiable and sharply gendered social type.

This logic influenced most initiatives and practices with regard to the young male delinquent in the early twentieth century. Sociologists detected the urban gang as a useful object of investigation, and state legislators drafted numerous bills to integrate scientific explanations into their laws. The most important institutional invention of the Progressive Era with regard to the youthful offender was the Juvenile Court, the first of which was established in Illinois in 1899.

During the twentieth century, moral panics sparked by both real and perceived increases in juvenile delinquency again focused on the male offender. While the debate in the 1920s focused on the dangers of commercialized consumption and a notion of almost universal sexual promiscuity, Depression-era discussions of the "youth problem" again stressed the criminal potential of young men. Although careful criminologists warned about overly simplistic conclusions, juvenile delinquency ranked among the topics most fashionable in the public debate about the nation in crisis. But the line between real offenders and victims of criminalization remained precarious, as the example of the youthful transient, who was very common during the depression, might illustrate. Many of these young hoboes had left their parents in order to fulfill the breadwinner ideal expected from them—or else fled from the pressure that came along with it.

During the 1930s and 1940s, public discussions of juvenile delinquency moved in new directions. The economic perils of the 1930s and wartime conditions of the 1940s prompted a new attention to the unstable family, and the focus of the delinquency issue shifted from such marginalized communities as the working-class, immigrants, and minorities to the center of American society. Furthermore, the absence of many fathers during World War II led a growing number of commentators to address the father's role and responsibility in preventing juvenile delinquency.

During the 1950s, America was especially preoccupied with juvenile delinquency: In black leather on his motorcycle, the young male delinquent represented potentially dangerous sexual and interpersonal power and control over self and environment. Despite rising public anxieties, the market for the teenage consumer boomed, and the "wild one" nevertheless became an American icon, with movie actors like James Dean and Marlon Brando transforming male volatility and rebellion into desirable character traits.

By the early twenty-first century, discourses on juvenile delinquency had undergone important new changes. To be sure, white adolescents remained an important focus of attention—acts of suburban school violence began raising public fear and anxiety during the 1990s. But female offenders, as a group, began invoking greater attention and concern than ever before. Even more importantly, discussions again turned to male members of minority groups. In 2000, the young male African American or Hispanic American figured prominently in public debates about juvenile delinquency.

While teenage crime and antisocial acts still arouse many justified concerns, the history of dealing with juvenile delinquents shows that a scholarly approach to the problem cannot separate the actual behavior from its social perception. Thus, educators, criminologists, and other people in authority often identify young males who act outside societal norms as not properly childlike, and they impose especially strict punishments for people in their early teenage years who commit violent crimes. Such punishments, and the many discussions that they are embedded in, stem from frustration over people not having backgrounds and lives that confirm middle-class standards of proper behavior for young men.

BIBLIOGRAPHY

Alexander, Ruth M. *Adolescence.* Vol. 3 of *Encyclopedia of American Social History,* edited by Mary Kupiec Cayton, Elliott J. Gorn, and Peter W. Williams. New York: Scribner, 1993.

Kett, Joseph F. *Rites of Passage. Adolescence in America, 1790 to the Present.* New York: Basic Books, 1977.

Kimmel, Michael. *Manhood in America. A Cultural History.* New York: Free Press, 1996.

Mennel, Robert M. *Thorns and Thistles; Juvenile Delinquents in the United States, 1825–1940.* Hanover, N.H.: University Press of New England, 1973.

Schneider, Eric C. *In the Web of Class: Delinquents and Reformers in Boston, 1810s–1830s.* New York: New York University Press, 1992.

Sutton, John R. *Stubborn Children: Controlling Delinquency in the United States, 1640–1981.* Berkeley: University of California Press, 1988.

Thompson, Roger. "Adolescent Culture in Colonial Massachusetts." *Journal of Family History* 9, no. 2 (1984): 127–144.

FURTHER READING

Graebner, William. *Coming of Age in Buffalo. Youth and Authority in the Postwar Era.* Philadelphia: Temple University Press, 1990.

Modell, John. *Into One's Own: From Youth to Adulthood in the United States, 1920–1975.* Berkeley: University of California Press 1989.

Schlossman, Steven L. *Love and the American Delinquent: The Theory and Practice of "Progressive" Juvenile Justice, 1825–1920.* Chicago: University of Chicago Press, 1977.

RELATED ENTRIES

Adolescence; African-American Manhood; Alcohol; Brando, Marlon; Breadwinner Role; Character; Citizenship; Class; Dean, James; Education; Fatherhood; Gambling; Gangs; Hoboes; Immigration; Leisure; Nuclear Family; Progressive Era; *Rebel Without a Cause*; Reform Movements; Urbanization; Violence; Youth

—*Olaf Stieglitz*

Kellogg, John Harvey

1852–1943
American Physician and Health Reformer

John Harvey Kellogg, the most popular health reformer of the late nineteenth century, challenged the notion that meat consumption led to good health and increased sexual vigor in men. Sharing Victorian-era concerns about bodily purity, Kellogg argued that the ideal man abstained from participating in violent acts such as hunting, consumed a vegetable diet to avoid illness and increase physical strength, and sustained his energy through sexual continence (abstinence).

Born in Tyrone, Michigan, Kellogg sought not to attack the medical profession, but to convert physicians to his way of thinking. To gain acceptance by the profession, he became a member of it. He received an M.D. in 1875 and joined the American Medical Association that same year. In 1876, Kellogg became the physician-in-chief of Michigan's Battle Creek Sanitarium, a position that he would hold for the next sixty-seven years. Under Kellogg, the sanitarium became a combination health spa and clinic. He prescribed a program of systematic daily exercise, such as gymnastics or machine-aided activity, to be performed vigorously enough to produce fatigue. He advised men to take daily baths, change their undergarments daily, and wear clothing with porous fibers to allow better penetration of light and air.

Of all the factors necessary to maintain health and strength, Kellogg considered a proper diet to be the most important. Through his many writings, including the popular *Home Book of Modern Medicine* (1914), Kellogg elaborated upon his belief that the achievement of ideal physical manhood required obedience to natural laws of health. Along with other proponents of "muscular vegetarianism"—part of a broader late-nineteenth-century concern to strengthen American men against the perceived enervating effects of urban-industrial overcivilization—he argued that digestive disorders were the most common human illnesses, and he attacked the consumption of meat as a drain on physical strength. Challenging conventional beliefs that meat consumption led to superior athletic performance, Kellogg argued that vegetarian men were stronger, faster, and more energetic than those who regularly ate meat.

Like many other nineteenth-century health reformers, Kellogg promoted the theory of "spermatic economy." In *Plain Facts About Sexual Life* (1884), he warned that sexual excitement drew bodily energy and strength from the brain and other vital organs to the penis and testicles, and he recommended a bland dietary regimen as a way to avoid stimulation. Patients who left the sanitarium often had difficulty preparing grains and cereals to Kellogg's standards, and, while most stopped following his dietary advice, some requested that he make his foods available for mail-order purchase. The resulting Kellogg's food company, best known for its cereals, remains in existence today, long after its founder's death.

While Kellogg helped change American eating habits by providing one of the first convenience foods, his theories of manhood have not withstood the test of time. Unable to overcome age-old beliefs about the power of meat, he failed to persuade large numbers of men to become vegetarian or accept vegetarianism as an essential component of masculinity. His sexual theories also faded amid growing twentieth-century challenges to Victorian sexual attitudes. Still, his attempts to change prevailing notions about men's health and his promotion of physical strength contributed to the growing tendency to define manhood in terms of physical aspects, and Kellogg's cereals continue to be marketed to American boys as necessary to the development of manly strength.

Bibliography

Melody, Michael Edward, and Linda Mary Peterson. *Teaching America about Sex: Marriage Guides and Sex Manuals from the Late Victorians to Dr. Ruth.* New York: New York University Press, 1999.

Schwartz, Richard W. *John Harvey Kellogg, M.D.* Berrien Springs, Mich.: Andrews University Press, 1981.

Wharton, James C. "Muscular Vegetarianism: The Debate Over Diet and Athletic Performance in the Progressive Era." *Journal of Sport History* 8 (1981): 58–75.

Further Reading

Butler, Mary, et al. *The Battle Creek Idea: Dr. John Harvey Kellogg and the Battle Creek Sanitarium.* Battle Creek, Mich.: Heritage Publications, 1994.

———. *The Best to You Each Morning: W. K. Kellogg and Kellogg Company.* Battle Creek, Mich.: Heritage Publications, 1995.

Nissenbaum, Stephen. *Sex, Diet, and Debility in Jacksonian America: Sylvester Graham and Health Reform.* Westport, Conn.: Greenwood Press, 1980.

SELECTED WRITINGS

Kellogg, John Harvey. *Plain Facts for Old and Young.* 1881. Reprint, New York: Arno Press, 1974.

———. *The Home Book of Modern Medicine: A Family Guide in Health and Disease.* Battle Creek, Mich.: Good Health Publishing, 1914.

———. *The New Dietetics: A Guide to Scientific Feeding in Health and Disease.* Rev. ed. Battle Creek, Mich.: Modern Medicine, 1923.

———. *Light Therapeutics: A Practical Manual of Phototherapy for the Student and Practitioner.* Battle Creek, Mich.: Modern Medicine, 1927.

RELATED ENTRIES

Advice Literature; Body; Graham, Sylvester; Health; Masturbation; Progressive Era; Reform Movements; Self-Control; Victorian Era

—*Caryn E. Neumann*

KEROUAC, JACK

1922–1969
U.S. Novelist and Poet

Jack Kerouac's life and writing have greatly influenced conceptions of masculinity, gender roles, and sexuality in contemporary American society. Kerouac and other writers of the Beat Generation—which reached its height during the 1950s—rejected what they considered stifling and hypocritical middle-class conventions in favor of intense personal experience, freedom of expression, artistic creation, and spiritual enlightenment. They immersed themselves in alcohol, drugs, jazz culture, and sex. Kerouac's vision of manhood thus diverged radically from the postwar norm of dutiful, impassive figures aspiring to material wealth, security, and nuclear-family life. Rather, like his literary forefather Walt Whitman, Kerouac celebrated an ideal man that lived in the present moment, was emotionally forthright, and sought passionate self-understanding and sensual exhilaration.

The shy, devout son of Catholic French-Canadian immigrants in working-class Lowell, Massachusetts, Kerouac felt like an outsider his entire life. As a youth, the deaths of both his brother and his best friend, and his disillusionment with organized sports and the military, left him seeking intimate male companionship, the recovery of lost innocence, and compassion for all living creatures—themes present in all of his writing. While his sexual partners included men and women, he found intimacy difficult and sexuality became both an obsession and a source of great discomfort for him.

Kerouac chronicled his life in a series of novels he called the "Legend of Duluoz." Its centerpiece is *On the Road* (1957), which follows the adventures of Sal Paradise (modeled on Kerouac himself) and Dean Moriarty (Kerouac's friend Neal Cassady) as they cultivate an intense relationship while traveling across the country in search of "kicks," the American dream, and masculine identity. Dean is an animalistic vessel of raw energy and sexuality, and Sal is his observant, reflective, sensitive sidekick. Sal and Dean attempt to express their deep love for each other, including their vulnerability. This presented a stark contrast to contemporary male figures, for whom visible affection toward a male "buddy" smacked of homosexuality. Women appear in the book largely as sex objects, often left behind when Sal and Dean's adventures resume. Although Sal laments such disrespect for women and sometimes longs for conventional domesticity, the novel lacks a consistent feminist perspective and reflects a long American literary tradition of associating masculinity with travel and freedom from domestic ties.

Upon its publication, *On the Road* was a best-seller, and Kerouac was immediately hailed as the exemplary white, bohemian hipster and the voice of a generation of rebellious youth. He saw himself, however, as a solitary contemplative artist on a spiritual quest for a disappearing American ideal of small-town innocence and simplicity, and later novels show a broadening of his spiritual vision of masculinity. In *The Dharma Bums* (1958), Japhy Ryder introduces Ray Smith (Kerouac) to the wonders of Buddhist meditation and communion with nature, moving him away from the distractions of modern life. *Visions of Cody* (1972) continues Kerouac's spiritual portrait of Neal Cassady, exploring themes including suffering, alienation, detachment, and ultimate redemption.

Kerouac helped pave the way for the counterculture and Sexual Revolution of the 1960s and 1970s. His influence on contemporary notions of masculinity can be seen throughout society, from casual clothing styles and "hip" language to immersion in music and public displays of emotion and affection. Since the 1960s, American men have negotiated masculinity amid an expanding range of options, and Jack Kerouac contributed greatly to this breadth of alternatives.

BIBLIOGRAPHY

Amburn, Ellis. *Subterranean Kerouac: The Hidden Life of Jack Kerouac.* New York: St. Martin's, 1998.

Campbell, James. *This is the Beat Generation: New York, San Francisco, Paris.* Berkeley: University of California Press, 2001.

Kerouac, Jack. *The Portable Jack Kerouac.* Edited by Ann Charters. New York: Penguin, 1996.
Nicosia, Gerald. *Memory Babe: A Critical Biography of Jack Kerouac.* Berkeley: University of California Press, 1994.
Savran, David. *Taking it Like a Man: White Masculinity, Masochism, and Contemporary American Culture.* Princeton, N.J.: Princeton University Press, 1998.

FURTHER READING
Giamo, Benedict. *Kerouac, the Word and the Way: Prose Artist as Spiritual Quester.* Carbondale: Southern Illinois University Press, 2000.
Holmes, John Clellon. *Gone in October.* Hailey, Idaho: Limberlost Press, 1985.
Rolling Stone Book of the Beats: The Beat Generation and American Culture. Edited by Holly George-Warren. New York: Hyperion, 1999.
Theado, Matt. *Understanding Jack Kerouac.* Columbia: University of South Carolina Press, 2000.
Turner, Steve. *Angelheaded Hipster: A Life of Jack Kerouac.* New York: Viking, 1996.

SELECTED WRITINGS
Kerouac, Jack. *On the Road.* 1957. Reprint, New York: Penguin, 1999.
———. *The Dharma Bums.* 1958. Reprint, New York: Penguin, 1986.
———. *Big Sur.* 1962. Reprint, New York: Penguin, 1992.
———. *Visions of Cody.* 1972. Reprint, New York: Penguin, 1993.
———. *Selected Letters, 1940–1956.* Edited by Ann Charters. New York: Viking, 1995.

RELATED ENTRIES

Alcohol; American Dream; Beat Movement; Bisexuality; Counterculture; Crisis of Masculinity; Male Friendship; Religion and Spirituality; Romanticism; Sensitive Male; Sexual Revolution; Travel; Travel Narratives; Whitman, Walt

—*Dominic Ording*

KING, MARTIN LUTHER, JR.

1929–1968
Civil Rights Leader

Martin Luther King, Jr.'s, contributions to African-American constructions of masculinity are often minimized by comparison with his black-nationalist counterparts, whose notions of masculinity were central to their program of liberation. King did, however, offer a vision of black manhood that challenged traditional ideas of black masculinity and affirmed the black man's role as leader.

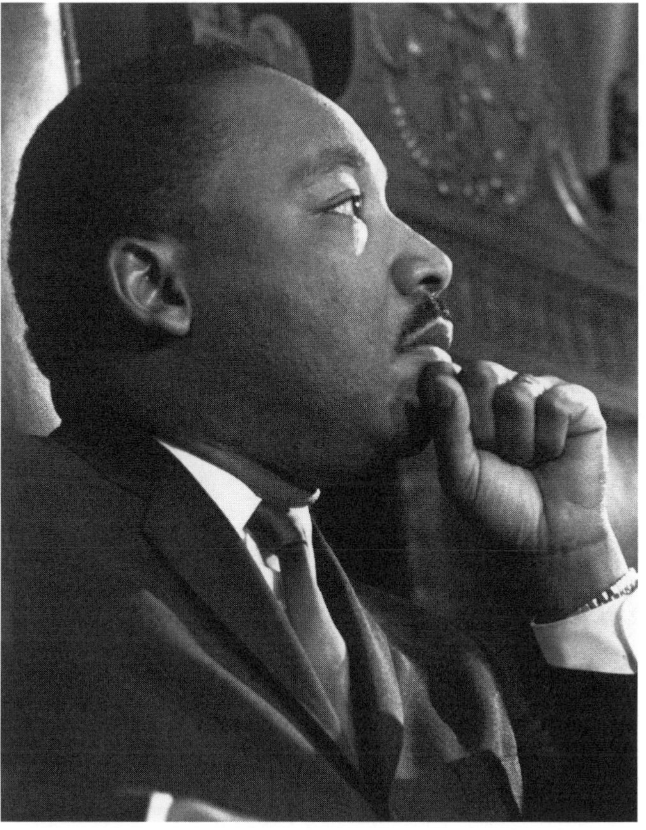

Well-educated and highly articulate, Martin Luther King, Jr., based his leadership of the civil rights movement on an ideal of African-American manhood grounded in passionate spirituality, inward morality, decisive nonviolent action, and commitment to the pursuit of racial and social justice. (© Bettmann/Corbis)

A pastor's son, King developed a passion for religion and social justice that he believed was best exercised from the pulpit. He received a Ph.D. in theology from Boston University in 1953, in the process becoming familiar with the teachings of Mohandas Gandhi, Henry David Thoreau, and other advocates of nonviolence and civil disobedience. In 1954, King accepted his first pastorate in Montgomery, Alabama, where he began a longstanding leadership role in movements for civil and human rights that ended with his assassination in 1968. His experience in these movements, combined with his religious philosophy, formed the basis of his conception of African-American masculinity.

King initially balked at nonviolence, but he soon embraced an approach to social change, and an ideal of African-American masculinity, that was grounded in nonviolent direct action and a spiritually-based struggle for racial and social justice and that implicitly rejected the essentialist idea of men as protectors. He argued in his "Letter from a

Birmingham Jail" (1963) that passive resistance would "help men rise from the dark depths of prejudice" (Carson, 190), and in the Birmingham civil rights campaign of 1963 he pushed for participation by women and children despite concerns that men should not expose them to violent attack. King said that a model of black manhood grounded in struggle for racial justice required not a hypermasculinized emphasis on protection and self-defense, but a willingness to act decisively and to suffer imprisonment and other physical hardships for the cause.

King's masculine ideal emphasized nonviolent action not simply as a tactic to resist white racism but as a fundamental moral principle that would guide men toward true spiritual manhood. Likewise, he defined freedom as an inward state residing in the spirit rather than the body, and not simply outward liberation from societal racism. In *Where Do We Go From Here?* (1967), he urged that an African-American man's response to racial injustice must be to "rise up with an affirmation of his own Olympian manhood" and affirm that "I am a man with dignity and honor" (Carson, 184). By belying stereotypical images of black men as violent, lazy and dangerous, African Americans would demonstrate that society must accept them as equals.

Martin Luther King, Jr., is often contrasted with Malcolm X and other black nationalists who refused to rule out violence, but they shared a belief that men should lead the struggle for racial justice (as was evident both in King's own pronouncements and in female leaders' complaints that he silenced them), and that these movements were an arena for demonstrating a morally grounded African-American spirituality and masculinity.

BIBLIOGRAPHY

Carson, Clayborne, Ralph Luker, and Penny Russell, eds. *The Papers of Martin Luther King, Jr.* Vol. 1, *Called to Serve,* January 1929–June 1951. Berkeley: University of California Press, 1992.

Cone, James. *Martin & Malcolm & America: A Dream or a Nightmare.* New York: Orbis Books, 1992.

Garrow, David. *Bearing the Cross.* New York: Vintage Books, 1988.

King, Coretta Scott. *My Life With Martin Luther King, Jr.* New York: Henry Holt, 1969.

FURTHER READING

Branch, Taylor. *Parting the Waters: America in the King Years, 1954–1963.* New York: Simon & Schuster, 1988.

———. *Pillar of Fire: America in the King Years, 1963–1965.* New York: Simon & Schuster, 1998.

Harper, Phillip Brian. *Are We Not Men? Masculine Anxiety and the Problem of African American Identity.* New York: Oxford University Press, 1996.

Robinson, Jo Ann. *The Montgomery Bus Boycott and the Women Who Started It.* Knoxville: University of Tennessee Press, 1987.

SELECTED WRITINGS

King, Martin Luther, Jr. "Letter from a Birmingham Jail." 1963. In *The Autobiography of Martin Luther King, Jr.* Edited by Clayborne Carson. New York: Warner Books, 2001.

———. *Where Do We Go from Here: Chaos or Community?* New York: Harper & Row, 1967.

———. *The Triumph of Conscience.* New York: Harper & Row, 1968.

———. *A Testament of Hope: The Essential Writings and Speeches of Martin Luther King, Jr.* Edited by James Melvin Washington. San Francisco: Harper & Row, 1986.

RELATED ENTRIES

African-American Manhood; Black Panther Party; Civil Rights Movement; Malcolm X; Nationalism; Nation of Islam; Patriarchy; Race; Religion and Spirituality; Slavery; Thoreau, Henry David; Vietnam War; Violence; White Supremacism

—*David J. Leonard*

KRAMER VS. KRAMER

The film *Kramer vs. Kramer* tells the story of one man's character development—the main character, Ted Kramer, overcomes his traditional masculine identity, defined primarily by career accomplishments, and discovers the simple satisfaction of being a loving father. In this 1979 film, adapted from a 1974 novel by Avery Corman, a father must assume the day-to-day caretaking of his son and his household when his wife decides to leave her unhappy marriage and relinquish her parental responsibility. Set in the late 1970s, the film reflects the rigid attitude prevalent in many social contexts that defined and limited the man's role in the family to that of breadwinner. At the same time, however, *Kramer vs. Kramer* reflects the agenda of an emergent men's movement in its challenge to restricted, gender-defined family roles.

In the beginning of the film, Ted, played by Dustin Hoffman, struggles with having to repair a rather distant relationship with his six-year-old son, Billy, when his wife of eight years, Joanna (played by Meryl Streep), decides to leave the family. The film follows Ted's growing devotion to fathering his son, and then his emotional effort to maintain custody of

Billy when Joanna returns to reclaim their son. The film also dramatizes the discrimination Ted experiences as a single man raising a young child—Ted is fired from his job because his boss feels that Ted's fathering is interfering with his ability to devote his undivided attention to his occupation, and he ultimately loses custody of Billy to Joanna because the judge decides that a young child should reside with the mother.

In the late 1970s the father's role in the family was being re-evaluated due to several social changes prompted by feminism, including the increasing number of women employed outside of the home and the growing divorce rate in the United States. *Kramer vs. Kramer* drew attention to new conceptualizations of fatherhood by presenting a heart-felt story of a man's success in becoming a competent, devoted father. Additionally, the film addressed emerging legal controversies and reform impulses involving single fatherhood in domestic and workplace contexts, and it anticipated several significant legislative initiatives regarding fathers' rights (e.g., paternity establishment, custody laws, parental leave) that were enacted during the last quarter of the twentieth century. Custody decisions favoring fathers' post-divorce involvement with their children became much more common, while legislation such as the Family and Medical Leave Act (1993) awarded both mothers and fathers up to twelve weeks of unpaid leave from work to care for newborn or adopted children.

The film *Kramer vs. Kramer* challenged family roles and conventional notions of fatherhood in the 1970s by recounting one man's personal transformation into a capable and emotionally involved father. As the diversification of the paternal role in the family has also been the focus of later films, such as *Mr. Mom* (1983) and *Mrs. Doubtfire* (1993), motion pictures have aided in portraying a more flexible and inclusive view of the masculine identity.

Bibliography

Corman, Avery. *Kramer versus Kramer: A Novel.* New York: Random House, 1977.

Pleck, E. H., and J. H. Pleck. "Fatherhood Ideals in the United States: Historical Dimensions." In *The Role of the Father in Child Development*, edited by Michael E. Lamb. 3rd ed. New York: Wiley, 1997.

Tamis-LeMonda, S., and N. Cabrera. "Perspectives on Father Involvement: Research and Policy." *Social Policy Report* 2 (1999): 1–26.

Further Reading

Braver, Sanford, and Diane O'Connell. *Divorced Dads: Shattering the Myths.* New York: Tarcher, 1998.

Doherty, W. J., E. F. Kouneski, and M. F. Erickson. "Responsible Fatherhood: A Review and Conceptual Framework." *Journal of Marriage and the Family* 60 (1998): 277–292.

Lamb, M. E., ed. *The Role of the Father in Child Development.* 3rd ed. New York: Wiley, 1997.

Marsiglio, William, Paul Amato, Randal D. Day, and Michael E. Lamb. "Scholarship on Fatherhood in the 1990s and Beyond." *Journal of Marriage and the Family* 62 (2000): 1173–1191.

Palkovitz, R. "Reconstructing 'Involvement': Expanding Conceptualizations of Men's Caring in Contemporary Families." In *Generative Fathering: Beyond Deficit Perspectives*, edited by Alan J. Hawkins and David C. Dollahite. Thousand Oaks, Calif.: Sage, 1997.

Related Entries

Breadwinner Role; Divorce; Fatherhood; Fathers' Rights; Feminism; Hollywood; Marriage; Middle-Class Manhood; *Mr. Mom*; Reverse Sexism; Work; Working-Class Manhood

—Angie M. Schock

Labor Movement and Unions

The organized labor movement in the United States has contributed in important ways to American conceptions of manhood grounded in working-class experience and, usually, in whiteness. While some labor organizations, such as the Knights of Labor, the Industrial Workers of the World (IWW), and sections of the American Federation of Labor, have challenged the association of unions and working-class masculinity solely with white men, most organizations have consistently focused on skilled or semiskilled white male workers and have largely failed to include women, unskilled workers, or nonwhites.

The first labor movement in the United States emerged in the 1820s and 1830s, when industrialization left journeymen (artisans who had completed their apprenticeships) increasingly unable to escape wage work. Journeymen, like other Americans, associated manhood with the political and economic independence made possible by property ownership, and they were fearful that as wage earners they would be forever dependent on others for income. They therefore formed politicized unions to fight the wage system and employers' control of the work process, which they saw as infringements on their liberty and manhood. These nascent unions represented white skilled workers and shunned those Americans they associated with unmanly dependency and wage work, particularly women and African Americans.

Although early unions were often prominent in major urban areas during the antebellum period, it was not until the Civil War that union activity became a widespread and dominant feature of urban, industrial America. Unlike antebellum journeymen, the approximately 200,000 men who joined Civil War–era unions never expected to escape wage work. Instead of seeking property ownership and control of the work process, Civil War–era unionists—applying a definition of masculinity based on their roles as family breadwinners and providers—fought for the job security, wage increases, and shorter workdays they deemed necessary to support and lead a household of dependents.

After the Civil War, as the labor movement grew larger, two main articulations of manhood dominated the movement, the first from the Knights of Labor and the second from the American Federation of Labor. The Knights emerged as a national labor organization in the 1880s, representing 750,000 workers by 1886. The Knights' platform drew heavily on antebellum ideals of manly independence, envisioning a republic without class conflict populated by self-employed men whose economic independence would ensure political virtue. Unlike antebellum journeymen, however, the Knights, at least to a limited degree, challenged older working-class associations of masculinity with whiteness and skilled labor by seeking to organize not only skilled workers, but also women, unskilled workers, and African Americans. In practice, however, the organization remained largely the province of white, skilled, or semiskilled men.

By the late 1880s, as skilled and semiskilled workers increasingly considered independent proprietorship unattainable, and as their interests came to be opposed to those of business owners, they rejected the Knights' reluctance to accept class struggle. Embracing notions of working-class manliness based on economic independence rather than property ownership, they joined the American Federation of Labor (AFL), founded in 1886, in growing numbers. Unlike the Knights, the AFL did not attempt to reassert the power of the male property owner. Instead, the AFL took as its model member the male breadwinner and sought to improve his ability to provide for his family. In the AFL, this model union man was white. Although AFL president Samuel Gompers actively encouraged the inclusion of nonwhites, local unions usually refused. They explicitly saw themselves as protecting the dignity of white breadwinners from employers' attempts to lower wages or dictate work processes, and they excluded women and African American workers, whom they assumed to be naturally subservient.

Not all members of the labor movement shared the AFL's ideal of working-class manhood. The Industrial Workers of the World, founded in 1905, offered a more radical definition of working-class manhood that combined a traditional emphasis on property ownership, a vision of solidarity among all workers (including women and nonwhites), and a call for aggressively militant action. They called for workers to take over factories, seizing control at the point of production. Both the AFL and mainstream America viewed the IWW with some fear, despite its miniscule membership, because its efforts to include nonwhites and women threatened the conventional equation of unions with white men.

General economic prosperity during the 1920s weakened the labor movement (the AFL represented 18.6 percent of the industrial workforce in 1920, but only 12 percent in 1930), leaving it inadequately prepared to respond to the labor crises of the Great Depression. Frustrated by the AFL's lack of success in organizing basic industries during the early years of the depression, a group of union leaders stormed out of the 1935 AFL annual meeting and formed the Congress of Industrial Organizations (CIO). The CIO was devoted to organizing workers by shop—including all the laborers in an auto plant in the same union, for example. Throughout the 1930s the CIO presented itself as the guarantor of American manhood. In one of its advertisement, for example, a tall man standing squarely and facing forward who "work[s] in a union shop" is contrasted with a side profile of a man hunched over who "toils in an open shop." The man in the open shop is said to live with "haunting fear" and a "driving foreman," while the union man reportedly has "humane management" and a "living wage." According to the CIO, union shops created physically strong men who were able to support their families and demand respect (and high wages) from their employers. The CIO's vision of working-class manhood, however, also remained white.

The close association between strong men and unions continued through the 1940s and 1950s. Although large numbers of women entered traditionally male jobs in heavy industry during World War II, they were quickly removed at the end of the war to make way for returning soldiers, thus reinforcing the connection between industrial labor, unions, and male workers. In the postwar era, unions successfully used the assumption that men were their families' sole breadwinners to negotiate high wages for workers.

Still, unions lost both power and prestige throughout the 1950s and 1960s, and membership declined steadily. The 1947 Taft-Hartley Act emasculated unions by severely limiting workers' rights to strike, bargain effectively, or otherwise stand up to management. Employers, especially those in the Sunbelt, renewed their commitment to blocking union organizing. In addition, postwar anticommunism—which identified manliness with patriotism and capitalism—raised suspicions that unions sympathized with, or even promoted, communism, and unions were forced to purge their ranks of suspected communists. As a result, the CIO lost the organizers most committed to expanding membership to nonwhites and women. In popular culture, unions no longer represented strong, proud men, and they were no longer depicted as guarantors of manliness. Instead, unions appeared in films like *On the Waterfront* (1954) as corrupt manipulators of pathetic, defeated workers—in marked contrast to the physically strong, proud worker in CIO posters, in Works Progress Administration public murals, and World War II government propaganda.

By the 1970s, traditional associations of unionism with manliness had further dissolved. As industries such as auto and steel, traditionally union strongholds, declined rapidly and laid off thousands of workers, unions proved unable to defend skilled workers' well-paying jobs. As a result, the connection between union work and the male breadwinner norm was seriously eroded. In the 1970s, working men who had been forced onto welfare or into lower-paying jobs spoke of themselves as emasculated. Corporate and federal union busting, successful throughout the 1970s and 1980s, made male workers appear weak and ineffectual before a greater power. The swift and effective firing of over ten thousand air traffic controllers in 1981 by President Ronald Reagan—whose political appeal lay partly in equating American manliness with business activity and corporate power—not only broke their union but also presented the controllers as powerless in the face of decisive government action.

Although the AFL-CIO (the two organizations merged in 1955) worked hard to revive the labor movement during the late twentieth century, increasing involvement in Democratic Party politics has channeled some of its energy away from industrial action and rhetorical defenses of its members' manhood. In addition, organized labor has continued to find it difficult to organize workers who are not white, male, and highly skilled—often because they work at jobs not traditionally associated with union activity, such as migrant farm work and domestic work. As a result, the image of the union worker has remained white and male.

Throughout most of its history, organized labor in the United States has almost exclusively represented white, male, skilled workers, and the image it portrayed of itself created an ideal constituency of strong men capable of providing for their families and withstanding the assaults of bosses. In the early twenty-first century, however, the labor movement appears confused and weakened, losing both members and power. The model of the skilled male worker no longer serves as a guiding image, but no other model has emerged to take its place.

BIBLIOGRAPHY

Dubofsky, Melvyn. *Industrialism and the American Worker, 1865–1920.* Wheeling, Ill: H. Davidson, 1996.

Green, James. *The World of the Worker: Labor in Twentieth-Century America.* New York: Hill and Wang, 1980.

Johnson, Paul E. *Shopkeepers Millennium: Society and Revivals in Rochester, New York, 1815–1837.* New York: Hill and Wang, 1978.

Laurie, Bruce. *Artisans into Workers: Labor in Nineteenth-Century America.* New York: Hill and Wang, 1989.

Montgomery, David. *The Fall of the House of Labor: The Workplace, the State, and Labor Activism, 1865–1925.* Cambridge, England: Cambridge University Press, 1989.

Painter, Nell Irvin. *Standing at Armageddon: The United States, 1877–1919.* New York: Norton, 1987.

Tomlins, Christopher. *The State and the Unions: Labor Relations, Law, and the Organized Labor Movement in America, 1880–1960.* Cambridge, England: Cambridge University Press, 1985.

Wilentz, Sean. *Chants Democratic: New York City and the Rise of the American Working Class.* New York: Oxford University Press, 1984.

Zeiger, Robert H. *American Workers, American Unions, 1920–1985.* Baltimore: Johns Hopkins University Press, 1986.

FURTHER READING

Babson, Steve. *The Unfinished Struggle: Turning Points in American Labor, 1877–Present.* Lanham, Md.: Rowman & Littlefield, 1999.

Hamper, Ben. *Rivethead: Tales From the Assembly Line.* New York: Warner Books, 1991.

Licht, Walter. *Industrializing America: The Nineteenth Century.* Baltimore: Johns Hopkins University Press, 1995.

Lichtenstein, Nelson. *State of the Union: A Century of American Labor.* Princeton, N.J.: Princeton University Press, 2002.

McCartin, Joseph. *Labor's Great War: The Struggle for Industrial Democracy and the Origins of Modern American Labor Relations, 1912–1921.* Chapel Hill: University of North Carolina Press, 1997.

Moody, Kim. *An Injury to All: The Decline of American Unionism.* London: Verso, 1988.

Roediger, David R. *The Wages of Whiteness: Race and the Making of the American Working Class.* Rev. ed. London: Verso, 1999.

RELATED ENTRIES

Apprenticeship; Artisan; Breadwinner Role; Citizenship; Industrialization; Market Revolution; Property; Race; Reagan, Ronald; Republicanism; Whiteness; Work; Working-Class Manhood

—*Rosanne Currarino*

LATINO MANHOOD

The term *Latino manhood* refers to models of masculinity embraced by men of South American, Central American, or Mexican origin living in the United States. It has historically been complex, dynamic, and in many ways shrouded in stereotype. In the Anglo-American mind, Latino men are often perceived in terms of *machismo*, a generalized set of negatively connoted behaviors ranging from misogyny to belligerence. More specifically, white Americans typically believe Latino men to be heirs to a cultural heritage driven by a veneration of the male and a denigration of the female. The male is supposedly dominant and aggressive, the female subordinate and passive. Within the family, the father is the unquestioned patriarch, provider, lawmaker, and judge. He is obsessed with the need to prove his masculinity, whether by extramarital affairs, excessive drinking, or aggressive behavior toward other men.

Yet while Latino men acknowledge the existence of machismo among them, most regard it as an undesirable cultural trait. Instead, they describe their own masculinity in terms of obligations toward their families, rather than their rights over it. Moreover, historical investigations have demonstrated that, though patriarchal authority did at a specific historical moment become an important component of Hispanic culture, it has been challenged by a variety of factors, including migration in the late nineteenth and twentieth centuries (and its attendant redistribution of authority within the family); the emergence of a Latina feminist consciousness in the 1960s and 1970s; and, at the end of the twentieth century, the conscious rejection by Latino men themselves of behaviors that imperil the survival of their community. Thus, contrary to the stereotype of the Latino man as invariably sexist and violent, Latino masculinity has always been both multifaceted and flexible, sensitive to external socioeconomic pressures and internal reformist urges alike.

Spanish Colonization and the Sources of Machismo

The origins of Latino manhood lay in the cultural interaction and interracial sexual relationships between Amerindians and Spanish colonizers. The indigenous populations that fell subject to the Spanish conquistadors had a variety of gender ideologies that were affected differently by the superimposition of the Spaniards' patriarchal system. On one end of the continuum were the Aztecs in Mexico, whose society was a military patriarchy. Men were raised to be warriors, and women to engage in domestic occupations and subordinate to their spouses. In the case of the Aztecs, therefore, the transition under foreign domination merely reinforced pre-Columbian patriarchal values.

For other groups, however, the conquest involved a revolution in gender relations. When Mexican-born Spanish adventurer Don Juan de Oñate first encountered the Pueblos of New Mexico in 1598, for instance, they were a matrilineal society in which women owned the houses, the fields, and the labor of the men who married into their family. Men spun, wove, hunted, tilled their wives' fields, and protected the community. Under Spanish rule, men were dictated to build, women to weave, and all hunting and warfare to cease. This redistribution of labor was disempowering for women, who lost ownership of their households to the men, and it was often humiliating for men as well. Colonial records indicate that Pueblo men, compelled to do what they perceived as women's work, often abandoned their communities in shame.

These incidents suggest that indigenous men felt emasculated by the Spaniards' imposition of patriarchy, even when it replaced a native matrilineal system. To this day, Mexican men refer to themselves as *hijos de la chingada* (illegitimate children) meaning they are descendants of Amerindian women the Aztec warriors failed to protect from the Spaniards' sexual violence. Furthermore, there is evidence that Franciscan friars in New Mexico at times imposed their authority on recalcitrant Pueblo men by twisting their testicles until their victims collapsed in agony, a gruesome practice that illustrates Spanish men's assertion of power through the emasculation of native men. One common hypothesis for the origin of the cult of machismo among Latinos is that it is a compensatory response for the figural castration suffered by Amerindian men. According to this view, Latino hypermasculinity is designed to mask feelings of impotence and weakness through outward expressions of courage, aggressiveness, and domination.

Latino Masculinity in the United States

The feeling of emasculation that has informed machismo was reinforced by the United States' conquest of the Southwest in the Mexican War (1846–48). Although the Treaty of Guadalupe-Hidalgo, which marked the end of the conflict, promised that Mexican nationals residing in territories ceded to the United States would be granted the constitutional rights of American citizens, including the right to retain their private property, many Mexican landowners were dispossessed. The constitution of Texas, for instance, stipulated that the government could suspend the privileges of anyone who had been disloyal during the rebellion of 1836, when Texas asserted its independence from Mexico and proclaimed itself a republic. Anglos seized the lands of Mexicans who, they claimed, had not sided with the republican government. Similarly, Mexicans in California lost their property when they could not afford the legal fees required to demonstrate the validity of their land claims against Anglo settlers. Unable to provide for their families, Mexican men ousted from their lands experienced a sense of impaired masculinity. As the Californian Pablo de la Guerra put it in a speech to the state legislature in 1856, "old men of fifty and sixty years of age are weeping like children because they have been cast out of their ancestral home" (Kanellos, 112). These words suggest that those who could not discharge the basic requirement of masculinity neither felt nor acted like men.

The industrialization that followed the American conquest of the Southwest further altered the material conditions that had supported the traditional patriarchal family, and thus challenged the domestic authority of Latino men. After 1850 there was an a marked increase in the number of Hispanic female-headed households (including a 27 percent increase in Los Angeles in 1860) due to the temporary absence of fathers who had left their families behind in search of job opportunities. The building of railroads in the newly acquired territories starting in the 1870s, for instance, disrupted the work patterns of thousands of *arrieros*, or teamsters, who went in search of contracts in areas not served by the railways. Similarly, miners in southern Arizona lost their jobs due to the mechanization of labor introduced by American investors, and they opted to extract minerals from placer deposits along the Colorado River to meet their obligation as providers for their families. Paradoxically, these men's efforts to maintain their patriarchal status created a situation that threatened their patriarchal rule, as they were forced to leave mothers as sole decision makers for their families.

Immigration and migration, central aspects of the Latino experience in the United States through the late nineteenth and twentieth centuries, likewise altered the traditional patriarchal order, undermined older notions of masculinity, and prompted shifts in gender roles—especially in the case of "stage migration," in which the father moves before (sometimes years before) the rest of the family. A husband's absence fostered his wife's ability to act independently, while the experience of men in "bachelor communities" of immigrant men forced them to perform basic housekeeping skills. Upon reunification, families were characterized by a higher level of shared decision making and a more equitable division of household labor, especially if a wife had found employment in the United States and made significant financial contributions to the family economy. Even today, researchers have found, Hispanic men spend more time on household labor than white men of the same socioeconomic class. Thus, while the experience of migration has been gendered—that is, initiated and conducted by men with little or no regard for women's desires or objections—it has also eroded traditional patriarchal privileges and created a reorientation of masculinity.

Contrary to the Anglo-American characterization, therefore, gender relations among Latinos have neither been inflexible nor always stratified. When changes have taken place, moreover, they have occurred not because of acculturation to an allegedly more egalitarian American society, as Anglos would like to believe, but rather in response to economic constraints. Indeed, contact with the Anglo world appears to have exacerbated, rather than softened, Latinos' patriarchal stance. According to some analysts of machismo, the emphasis on masculinity among Latinos derives from the historic marginalization and disempowerment of Latino males in the United States. Excluded from positions of authority and denied traditionally valued social roles, they argue, Latino men of the nineteenth and twentieth centuries increasingly and aggressively turned to maleness itself as a basis for asserting their social status and claiming power in their communities. Proponents of this view thus read machismo, and the resulting sexual stratification of Hispanic communities, as a response—indeed, a form of resistance—to racism.

Challenges to Machismo

During the late twentieth century, as Latinos sought to form their own ethnic identities and to overcome the historic effects of Anglo racism, they increasingly challenged the cult of machismo and called for new models of Latino manhood. The earliest challenges to machismo came from women involved in the Chicano, or Mexican American, civil rights movement of the 1960s and 1970s. As they struggled alongside men to unionize farm laborers, end racial ghettoization in the school system, or regain land rights lost to Anglo colonizers, Chicanas, barred from positions of leadership and confined to menial tasks, demanded that the asymmetrical relationship between Latino men and women be altered. When their position was criticized by men in the movement as antifamily and (given the Latino family's historic role in ensuring cultural survival) as antinationalist and anti-Chicano, Chicanas responded that the Hispanic family was founded upon heterosexual and cross-generational bonds of affection rather than on male power and female and filial subjugation. While their calls for a new Latino masculinity grounded in equality rather than dominance were largely ignored, they powerfully reshaped attitudes toward Latino manhood by defining machismo as a social pathology to be eliminated, rather than a cultural value to be preserved.

An equally severe critique of machismo was voiced by the gay community, which had experienced negative physical and psychological consequences due to the complex relation between homosexuality and machismo in Latino culture. Because demonstrating one's manhood through sexual penetration (preferably, though not exclusively, of women) has been a more important marker of masculinity than merely being male, achieving penetration has been particularly important for gay Latino men. In fact, a Latino man who penetrates other men (a *bugarron*) considers himself "straight," and is regarded as such both by his male sexual partners and heterosexual men. Only the sexually passive partner is deemed unmanly, and is thus often disparagingly referred to in feminine terms (e.g., *mariquita*, *loca*) to emphasize his distance from the macho ideal. Internalizing their culture's veneration of sexually aggressive masculinity and its denigrating definition of sexual passivity, Latino homosexuals have been even more concerned than their heterosexual peers to prove their masculinity through sexuality, and they have therefore been reluctant to practice any safe-sex measure that may compromise their capability to penetrate their partners. The elevated frequency of unprotected anal intercourse among Latino gays compared to non-Latinos has, in turn, resulted in a disproportionately high incidence of HIV positivity. In the end, the complex imbrication of the cult of masculinity with homophobia and risky sexual practices has rendered overcoming machismo a matter of emotional and physical survival for Latino gays.

Similarly, in the late twentieth century, and into the twenty-first, concerns for community survival prompted Latino men themselves, regardless of sexual orientation, to call for a reformed Latino masculinity. Growing numbers of Latino men argued that aggressiveness against other men, drunkenness or drug addiction, womanizing, and spousal abuse reflect an antisocial notion of masculinity adverse to the interest of Latinos as a group and must therefore be replaced by a new ideal of manhood based not only on virility, but also on peacefulness, emotional openness, and nurture. The only area where the Latino male should stay aggressive, according to the scholar David T. Abalos, is that of nonviolent militancy for democratic change in American society. There has been increasing agreement among Latinos that masculinity needs to be redefined so that it will support, rather than imperil, the community.

BIBLIOGRAPHY

Abalos, David T. *The Latino Male. A Radical Redefinition.* Boulder, Colo.: Lynne Rienner, 2002.

Díaz, Rafael M. *Latino Gay Men and HIV. Culture, Sexuality, and Risk Behavior.* New York: Routledge, 1998.

González, Ray, ed. *Muy Macho: Latino Men Confront Their Manhood.* New York: Anchor Books, 1996.

Gutiérrez, Ramón A. *When Jesus Came, the Corn Mothers Went Away: Marriage, Sexuality and Power in New Mexico, 1500–1846.* Stanford, Calif.: Stanford University Press, 1991.

Kanellos, Nicolás, ed. *Herencia: An Anthology of Hispanic Literature of the United States.* New York: Oxford University Press, 2002.

Mirandé, Alfredo. *Hombres y Machos: Masculinity and Latino Culture.* Boulder, Colo.: Westview Press, 1997.

Ramírez, Rafael L. *What It Means to Be a Man: Reflections on Puerto Rican Masculinity.* New Brunswick, N.J.: Rutgers University Press, 1999.

FURTHER READING

Baca Zinn, Maxine. "Chicano Men and Masculinity." *Journal of Ethnic Studies* 10 (Spring 1982): 29–44.

Garcia, Alma. "The Development of Chicana Feminist Discourse, 1970–1980." *Gender & Society* 3 (1989): 217–238.

Hondagneu-Sotelo, Pierrette. "Overcoming Patriarchal Constraints: The Reconstruction of Gender Relations among Mexican Immigrant Women and Men." *Gender & Society* 6 (1992): 393–415.

Paz, Octavio. *The Labyrinth of Solitude.* New York: Grove, 1961.

Peña, Manuel. "Class, Gender, and Machismo: The 'Treacherous-Woman' Folklore of Mexican Male Workers." *Gender & Society* 5 (1991): 30–46.

RELATED ENTRIES

Breadwinner Role; Civil Rights Movement; Class; Ethnicity; Feminism; Homosexuality; Immigration; Imperialism; Industrialization; Native American Manhood; Patriarchy; Race; Violence; Working-Class Manhood

—*Paola Gemme*

LAWRENCE, D. H.

1885–1930
British Novelist and Poet

D. H. (David Herbert) Lawrence ranks as one of the great modernist authors and a key influence on the "lost generation" of American writers of the early twentieth century. His provocative novels, questioning Victorian cultural assumptions prevalent on both sides of the Atlantic, heralded the death of the protective and powerful Victorian father figure and the appearance of a more ambiguous post–Victorian picture of masculinity and male sexuality.

Born in Nottinghamshire, England, Lawrence grew up amid the strife of his parents' unhappy marriage, and the tensions between his miner father's working-class sensibilities and his mother's more genteel background dramatically shaped his portrayals of gender. Lawrence depicts this gendered conflict in the autobiographical novel *Sons and Lovers* (1913). Protagonist Paul Morel's father symbolizes sensuality and passion (in opposition to dominant Victorian constructions of middle-class manhood emphasizing self-control and emotional reserve), whereas his controlling mother and obsessively chaste girlfriend Miriam represent social ambition and religious fervor. Paul struggles, and ultimately fails, to develop a masculine identity that balances these competing elements. Lawrence's linked novels, *The Rainbow* (1915) and *Women in Love* (1920), which focus on gender tensions and domestic relationships in the Brangwen family, continue to use battles between strong-willed women and weak men to explore the problem of combining strength and emotional expression into a modernized model of manhood.

Lawrence's representations of demanding women, often portrayed as vampire-like, have spurred psychoanalytic readings of his life and fiction. Drawing on Freudian concepts of the Oedipus complex, these analyses focus on the inability of Lawrence and his fictional characters to separate themselves from strong mother figures and achieve an independent masculinity. His consistent portrayal of men who are unable to achieve healthy relationships with women, some scholars suggest, may also point to latent homosexual or homoerotic tendencies.

Lawrence's treatment of gender was also the product of its historical context. Most of his novels were written during and after World War I, which inaugurated changes in gender roles in both the United States and Britain. As men went off to war, women filled their places in offices and factories on the home front. This shift, occurring alongside agitation for women's suffrage, heralded a change in power structures on both sides of the Atlantic. Thus, Lawrence's work reflects not only personal anxieties, but also broader male concerns about a loss of social, political, and sexual power—and the consequences of this loss on definitions of masculinity. Lawrence's articulation of this social and sexual alienation influenced the work of the lost generation, a group of expatriate writers—including the Americans Ernest Hemingway and F. Scott Fitzgerald—whose novels, like Lawrence's, often involve a protagonist searching for a stable masculine identity in the chaotic modern world.

Only in his later works does Lawrence come close to resolving the conundrum of masculinity, emotion, and power. In *Lady Chatterley's Lover* (1928), Constance Chatterley rejects her invalid husband and finds fulfillment with the groundskeeper, Oliver Mellors. Significantly titled *Tenderness* in its draft form, this controversial novel replaces the overbearing female of Lawrence's earlier works with a strong but nurturing male figure capable of a relationship that is both sexual and emotional.

Stylistically and thematically daring, Lawrence's novels reject the strong patriarchal figure of the nineteenth century and explore the limitations of alternate conceptions of masculine identity, laying the ground for a generation of American male writers and their explorations of American manhood.

Bibliography

Clifford, Stephen P. *Beyond the Heroic "I": Reading Lawrence, Hemingway, and "Masculinity."* Lewisburg, Pa.: Bucknell University Press, 1998.

MacLeod, Sheila. *Lawrence's Men and Women.* London: Heinemann, 1985.

Pilditch, Jan, ed. *The Critical Response to D. H. Lawrence.* Westport, Conn.: Greenwood Press, 2001.

Ruderman, Judith. *D. H. Lawrence and the Devouring Mother: The Search for a Patriarchal Ideal of Leadership.* Durham, N.C.: Duke University Press, 1984.

Further Reading

Balbert, Peter. *D. H. Lawrence and the Phallic Imagination: Essays on Sexual Identity and Feminist Misreading.* New York: St. Martin's, 1989.

"D.H. Lawrence Resources at the University of Nottinghamshire." <http://mss.Nottingam.ac.uk/dhl_home.html> (August 16, 2002).

Hammond, Paul. *Love between Men in English Literature.* New York: St. Martin's, 1996.

Ingersoll, Earl G. *D. H. Lawrence, Desire, and Narrative.* Gainesville: University Press of Florida, 2001.

Storch, Margaret. *Sons and Adversaries: Women in William Blake and D. H. Lawrence.* Knoxville: University of Tennessee Press, 1990.

Selected Writings

Lawrence, D. H. *Sons and Lovers.* 1913. Reprint, edited by Helen and Carl Baron. Harmondsworth, England: Penguin, 2000.

———. *The Rainbow.* 1915. Reprint, edited by Kate Flint. Oxford: Oxford University Press, 1997.

———. *Women in Love.* 1920. Reprint, edited by David Bradshaw. Oxford: Oxford University Press, 1998.

———. *Lady Chatterley's Lover.* 1928. Reprint, Harmondsworth, England: Penguin, 2000.

Related Entries

Body; Emotion; Fitzgerald, F. Scott; Freudian Psychoanalytic Theory; Hemingway, Ernest; Heterosexuality; Homosexuality; Middle-Class Manhood; Mother–Son Relationships; Victorian Era; Working-Class Manhood; World War I

—*Kirsten L. Parkinson*

Leatherstocking Tales

James Fenimore Cooper's Leatherstocking Tales comprise five novels—*The Pioneers* (1823), *The Last of the Mohicans* (1826), *The Prairie* (1827), *The Pathfinder* (1840), and *The Deerslayer* (1841)—chronicling the adventures of the rugged frontiersman, Indian fighter, and British scout, Natty Bumppo. Bumppo, a white man raised among Native Americans, is skilled at survival and hunting on the frontier. He clears the way for western settlers in the eighteenth and nineteenth centuries, though ultimately rejecting settlement for himself. Inspired by English tales of chivalric knights and the mythical exploits of the frontiersman Daniel Boone, and also troubled by the growth of the American republic, Cooper created in the character of Natty Bumppo the archetypal American "Western" male hero, poised between a savage "natural" masculinity (expressed in Bumppo's various nicknames) and "civilized" white Victorian manhood.

The Leatherstocking Tales move back and forth in time, with each story revealing more about Natty Bumppo. In *The Pioneers,* Bumppo is seventy-seven-years old and known as "Leatherstocking." He lives outside the community of Templeton in upstate New York in the 1790s. Although the townspeople see him as a throwback to an earlier time, Leatherstocking and his Indian companion John Mohegan (also known as Chingachgook) instruct Oliver Effingham, the owner of the lands surrounding Templeton, in the ways of the American wilderness. By enhancing his manliness, they make him a more responsible patriarch than the community leader, Judge Marmaduke Templeton.

In *The Last of the Mohicans,* Bumppo is forty-four-year-old "Hawkeye." Fighting with the British during the French and Indian War (1754–63), Hawkeye, Chingachgook, and Chingachgook's son Uncas attempt to rescue Cora and Alice, the daughters of a British colonel, from Mohawk Indians. Here, as in the other Tales, Cooper uses weak, refined heroines to heighten the masculinity of his male characters. In this particular story, he refines his masculine ideal by contrasting Cora and Uncas's interracial sexual attraction with Hawkeye's whiteness and chastity (and uses Cora and Uncas's deaths to prevent the consummation of their relationship).

In *The Prairie,* Bumppo, at age eighty-six, has left Templeton, New York, to live among the nomadic Indians of the American Plains. White civilization intrudes, however, when the squatter Bush clan from Kentucky seeks a new home. Bumppo uses his frontier skills and sacrifices his life to save these white settlers. His death symbolizes the passing of heroic, frontier masculinity and the triumph of genteel, civilized manliness, a transition that troubled Cooper.

The final two novels detail Bumppo's early beginnings. In *The Pathfinder,* forty-two-year-old Bumppo (the "Pathfinder") falls in love with Mabel Dunham, the daughter of a British soldier. Dunham proves too refined for him, however, and marries another, ensuring that Bumppo will remain unredeemed by female domesticity and civilization. *The Deerslayer* describes how the twenty-four-year-old Bumppo (now known as "Deerslayer") befriends the young Delaware chief Chingachcook in upstate New York during the 1740s. In saving Chingachcook's bride from Iroquois marauders, Bumppo allows Chingachcook to reclaim his "natural" masculinity, earns the Indian name "Hawkeye," and acquires a life-long companion in Chingachgook.

Cooper's Natty Bumppo remains an enduring figure in American culture, and his influence can be seen in such figures as the Lone Ranger and Rambo—highly-skilled white men who straddle the line between savagery and civilization. Bumppo's model of manhood appears not only in many portrayals or the western frontier, but also in literary works such as Mark Twain's *Adventures of Huckleberry Finn* (1884), Herman Melville's *Moby Dick* (1851), and Edgar Rice Burroughs's Tarzan series (first introduced in 1912). The Leatherstocking Tales continues to offer an appealing model of "natural" white masculinity that transcends the seemingly artificial realities of modern, industrial America.

BIBLIOGRAPHY

Cooper, James Fenimore. *The Leatherstocking Tales.* New York: Literary Classics of the U.S., 1985.

Slotkin, Richard. *The Fatal Environment: The Myth of the Frontier in the Age of Industrialization, 1800–1890.* Norman: University of Oklahoma Press, 1998.

———. *Regeneration Through Violence: The Mythology of the American Frontier, 1600–1860.* Norman: University of Oklahoma Press, 2000.

Smith, Henry Nash. *Virgin Land: The American West as Symbol and Myth.* Cambridge, Mass.: Harvard University Press, 1978.

Summerlin, Mitchell Eugene. *A Dictionary to the Novels of James Fenimore Cooper.* Greenwood, Fla.: Penkevill, 1987.

FURTHER READING

Fliegelman, Jay. "Familial Politics, Seduction, and the Novel: The Anxious Agenda of an American Literary Culture." In *The American Revolution: Its Character and Limits,* edited by Jack P. Greene. New York: New York University Press, 1987.

Motley, Warren. *The American Abraham: James Fenimore Cooper and the Frontier Patriarch.* Cambridge, England: Cambridge University Press, 1987.

Taylor, Alan. William *Cooper's Town: Power and Persuasion on the Frontier of the Early American Republic.* New York: Knopf, 1995.

RELATED ENTRIES

Adventures of Huckleberry Finn; Agrarianism; Boone, Daniel; Cowboys; Hunting; *Lone Ranger, The*; Male Friendship; Marlboro Man; *Moby Dick*; Native American Manhood; Outdoorsmen; Race; Rambo; Romanticism; Tarzan; Violence; Western Frontier; Westerns; Whiteness

—*Scott Miltenberger*

LEAVE IT TO BEAVER

Leave It to Beaver, a television series that ran from 1957 to 1963, in many ways typifies post–World War II media images of white middle-class family life. The show was set in the suburban town of Mayfield and featured the Cleaver family: father Ward (Hugh Beaumont), mother June (Barbara Billingsley), teenage son Wally (Tony Dow), and younger son Theodore, or "Beaver" (Jerry Mathers). Focusing predominantly on the two boys' relationships—with each other, with their father, and with their friends—the show represented and broadcast postwar American ideals concerning boyhood, adolescence, and manhood to a national audience.

At the time the show first aired, the United States was gripped by the anxieties and aspirations growing out of the Cold War. Conventional definitions of American middle-class manhood, grounded since the late nineteenth century in the ideal of the married suburban breadwinner and family man, were reinforced by concerns that the nation was threatened by a variety of "deviant" male beliefs and behaviors—particularly communism, homosexuality, and juvenile delinquency. Many Americans believed that such threats could be counteracted by socializing boys in a setting of "family togetherness" that would encourage appropriate and conformist male behavior. The firm yet affectionate discipline of fathers—whose absence during World War II had been blamed by many for male deviance—was deemed crucial to this process.

Leave It to Beaver—like *Father Knows Best*, which aired from 1954 to 1963—was devoted to conveying this postwar family ideology. Ward Cleaver, an accountant, is the sole family income earner. His profession suggests the rationality associated with manhood in American culture, and his business suit symbolizes the corporate environment in which he and many middle-class suburban men worked. Yet the show rarely depicts him in his office; instead, the emphasis is on his domestic life. Every episode pivots on the moral problems of boyhood—problems particularly epitomized by Wally's untrustworthy and insincere friend Eddie Haskell (Ken Osmond)—and the gentle yet wise discipline Ward applies when Beaver or Wally encounter trouble. June, meanwhile, is a contented housewife and nurturing mother, though only occasionally a disciplinarian or a source of moral wisdom.

Most of Ward's moral lessons convey the value of those traits that postwar Americans deemed essential to healthy boyhood and manhood: hard work, fairness, self-discipline, business acumen, morality, conformity, getting along with others, and positive relationships with girls. For example, episodes such as "Wally's Test" (1960), and "Beaver's Poster" (1961) teach the importance of doing one's own work; "Wally, the Businessman" (1960), "Eddie Quits School" (1962), and "Stocks and Bonds" (1962) examine the pitfalls of business activity, spending, and investing; "Wally's Haircomb" (1959) involves Wally's troubling experimentation with a faddish hairstyle introduced by Eddie; "The Perfect Father" (1958), "Beaver's Hero" (1959), and "Substitute Father" (1961), offer lessons in ideal fatherhood; "Nobody Loves Me" (1962) explores Beaver's desire to fit in; "The Shave" (1958) and "The Pipe" (1958) show that manhood is achieved gradually; and "Wally's Girl Trouble" (1957) and "Party Invitation" (1958) focus on Beaver's and Wally's awkward relationships with girls.

The ultimate lesson of *Leave It to Beaver* for its insecure national audience was that American life—and American manhood—was firmly grounded in paternal authority, moral principle, corporate business activity, suburban domestic life, and conventional definitions of gender and sexuality. The show went off the air in 1963, as growing numbers of Americans were beginning to question the conformist ideology it represented.

BIBLIOGRAPHY

Kimmel, Michael. *Manhood in America: A Cultural History.* New York: Free Press, 1996.

May, Elaine Tyler. *Homeward Bound: American Families in the Cold War Era.* New York: Basic Books, 1988.

FURTHER READING

Clatterbaugh, Kenneth. *Contemporary Perspectives on Masculinity: Men, Women, and Politics in Modern Society.* 2nd ed. Boulder, Colo.: Westview, 1997.

RELATED ENTRIES

Adolescence; Boyhood; Business/Corporate America; Cold War; Fatherhood; *Father Knows Best;* Marriage; Middle-Class Manhood; Momism; Suburbia; Television

—*Bret E. Carroll*

LEISURE

American men's relationship to leisure is complex, intersected by issues of race, class, religion, and regionalism. An early emphasis on community and public forms of leisure gave way, in the nineteenth century, to a starker differentiation between the domestic and public spheres, a separation that coded labor as masculine and leisure as feminine. The Protestant work ethic espoused by the expanding middle classes further valorized work while associating leisure with femininity and weakness—or with dangerous forms of masculinity. In the twentieth century, however, have alienation from the workplace and the growth of consumerism made leisure more central to American masculinity.

Public Leisure in Early America

In colonial America and the early republic, leisure activities centered on the community. Villages and small towns constituted early American society, and communal gatherings, including church events, dances, court days, and parades, offered ways to develop unity among neighbors and build both a local and a national identity. For example, frolics, or work parties, brought communities together to harvest and preserve food or make other necessary items, but they also provided a space for creating friendships, cementing political alliances, sharing gossip, and matchmaking. For men, these public activities also helped to define their social roles and gender identity. Eighteenth-century definitions of masculine virtue emphasized public interest over self-interest. Through participation in the leisure activities of the community, men could demonstrate their commitment to the larger social good—and thus their masculinity.

In particular, men's involvement in political and religious events solidified their positions as citizens and leaders. Religious observance played an important role in many colonial and early American communities, and participation in church leadership demonstrated one's responsibility and respectability, two traits tied to civic virtue, and therefore to masculinity.

Political activities often revolved around elections, open at this time only to white male property owners. Parades, dinners, and speeches leading up to Election Day offered opportunities for white men to angle for political power and stake a claim to a definition of masculinity closely allied to citizenship. Court days, in which the men of a community resolved property disputes and other legal issues, similarly constituted a space in which to develop one's masculine identity. They reflected an almost fairlike atmosphere in which men would trade news and complete business transactions. Like elections, court days provided an opportunity to learn the rules and responsibilities of governance and economic and political participation in the community, which served to demonstrate one's citizenship and masculinity.

While civic and religious events tied male leisure to concepts of responsibility and citizenship, other forms of male entertainment simultaneously emphasized masculine associations with strength and virility. Taverns, for instance, comprised a largely male space in which men bonded over drinking, cards, and dice. Competition in these games could be fierce, and taverns were also the site of other demonstrations of masculine prowess, including boxing and wrestling matches. Similarly, participation in or attendance at sports such as horse racing, cockfighting, and hunting developed the associations between physicality—especially strength, speed, and virility—and masculinity.

Private Leisure in the Nineteenth Century

As the eighteenth century drew to a close, significant shifts occurred in public life and the constitution of American leisure profoundly impacted masculinity. The rise of evangelicalism, a bourgeois Christian movement, led to widespread disapproval of many earlier forms of leisure, including drinking and dancing. A highly influential group, evangelicals placed a new emphasis on masculine seriousness and sobriety, as well as a steady work ethic. Furthermore, the growth of urban centers and of industrialization, particularly in the North, resulted in a sharper distinction between work and home life. The middle-class ideology of separate spheres defined the work world as masculine and domestic life as feminine. As a result, leisure and domestic consumption became closely tied to the home, and thus to definitions of femininity. Men who did not work, or did not work hard enough, were viewed as lazy, irresponsible, and unmasculine.

Whereas domestic entertainment had once been the province of the male head of household, women now took the lead in organizing balls and dinner parties. Men still took part in such events, but these activities came to be seen as feminine, designed to emphasize courtship and matchmaking. Work and breadwinning, meanwhile, became central components of middle-class masculine identity. A successful man was one whose income allowed leisure for his wife and children, while men whose families had to work to contribute to the budget were considered unmanly. The capitalist ideology of production and consumption left men with a conflicted relationship to leisure, for while domestic life was touted as the ideal, its associations with consumption and femininity simultaneously discouraged men from allying themselves too closely to that more leisured lifestyle. Middle-class male leisure thus frequently focused on business relationships, and much of it moved outside the home to private clubs and fraternal lodges, which offered exclusively masculine spaces not available in the private home. (This gendered structure is still seen occasionally on the golf course and racquetball court). Many cities and towns even included male quarters, which provided goods, services, and entertainment to the men who worked nearby.

In these male-only spaces, men engaged in a variety of rituals, including complex fraternal initiation rites and sporting events. While these activities offered opportunities to cement professional relationships and broker business deals, they also provided a temporary respite from evangelical definitions of masculinity by accentuating such older ideas of masculinity as bravery and strength. This association was particularly crucial for the expanding number of white-collar workers, whose largely sedentary and clerical labor distanced them from this traditional connection between manhood and physical skill. The popularity of sports skyrocketed, with men participating in bodybuilding, running, swimming, baseball, tennis, and golf.

Although working-class men seldom interacted with their middle-class counterparts outside the workplace, the leisure pursuits of both classes paralleled one another in their separation from the feminine domestic world. Like their wealthier counterparts, working men participated in fraternal orders and clubs, where they could join friends for dinners, athletic activities, and conversation. The pall of evangelical morality, however, hung less heavily over working-class men than over the bourgeoisie. Thus, working-class men more openly frequented concert saloons, gambling parlors, variety theaters, and brothels, venues viewed as disreputable by middle-class society but serving in working-class culture as important arenas in which to demonstrate manhood. In these spaces, masculinity was tied to competition, strength, and virility, as men challenged each other to drinking and gambling contests and associated with prostitutes.

Leisure in the South

Whereas the tensions of industrialization and urbanization had a profound effect on male leisure in the North, issues of race and slavery contributed to conceptions of masculinity and leisure in the South. Evangelicalism had a strong hold on the South, as it did on the North, but it competed with even older notions of masculine honor and aristocracy that survived in the South's agricultural society. The sinful and unmasculine connotations of idleness did not have the same power as in the bourgeois-dominated North, and southern male leisure often openly scorned evangelical notions of masculine sobriety and hard work. The plantation lifestyle associated labor with black slaves and thus constructed masculine leisure as a desirable signifier of power and status. Upper-class male activities, including balls, horse racing, and hunting, accentuated this hierarchy by highlighting the wealth and time necessary for participation.

Existing alongside this genteel definition of masculinity, southern white men's conception of honor focused on leisure-time expressions of aggression, competitiveness, and physical courage. Slavery played a crucial role in this definition of masculinity, as the desire to dominate slaves and the fear of a slave revolt led to an emphasis on physical prowess and control. The focus on competition also provided a temporary escape from the strictures of evangelicalism. White men proved their masculinity by participating in a range of physical competitions, including fighting, wrestling, hunting, and marksmanship contests. Whereas fighting and wrestling were frowned upon by the evangelicals, hunting and marksmanship offered a respectable outlet for male aggression and competition. They also constituted crucial rites of passage for boys—the gift of a gun was an important sign of a young man's maturity and masculinity.

Slave leisure might almost seem a contradiction in terms, but the black population of the South regularly carved out time for recreation. Few slave owners required work on Sundays, and they also scattered holidays throughout the year. But the ability of owners to grant freedom or withhold holidays and other leisure time constituted an indirect form of control over their slaves, making it yet another marker of white manhood and paternalism. The culture of slavery constructed black males as unmanly, for subservience and dependence on their owners placed them in a feminine, and even childlike, role. Thus, black men often used their leisure time to resist the demeaning structure of slavery and to reassert their masculinity.

During their free time many black men continued to work, either at paid odd jobs or in their gardens. They did this both to earn money to support their families and to emphasize their dominant role in the household. Slaves also used their leisure time to develop a sense of community by holding barbeques, dances, and parties. Male slaves could regain some measure of control and sense of masculinity by planning and leading these events. They would play instruments and sing songs, as well as tell stories and jokes that satirized the dominant white culture. In this way, music and storytelling both served to challenge the emasculating influences of slavery. Singing in particular, while working and while playing, offered an important form of resistance to white male control; it blurred the lines between work and leisure, providing blacks with the strength to survive the mental and physical degradations of slavery.

Leisure and Masculinity in the Twentieth Century

The advent of the twentieth century brought new challenges to the definitions of manhood and heralded a closer relation between masculinity and leisure. Whereas a steady work ethic and its related duties of responsibility and self-control had been the center of nineteenth-century bourgeois conceptions of masculinity, technological advances and the shifting construction of the workplace left men feeling both divorced from and unsatisfied by their labor. In the new corporate society, few men were self-employed, so the relationship between independence and masculinity prevalent since the colonial period no longer held true for many men. Furthermore, the division of labor that constructed the business world as masculine and the home as feminine came under fire as women fought for more rights and entered the workplace in rising numbers.

As a result, more men turned to leisure as a primary source of masculine identity. The independence lacking in the workplace was now to be found in home ownership and family life. A man's success was measured by the appearance of his home and family, and home and lawn care became important leisure activities for the American male. After World War II, the rise of suburbs, a growing emphasis on family togetherness, and the availability of new consumer products such as televisions, barbeque grills, and swing sets encouraged men to spend time with their families rather than at work. Simultaneously, in male-only leisure activities, men could find the sense of excitement, danger, and aggression that was missing in both their working and home lives. Sports and technology provided outlets for men to test their physical prowess and bravery. Traditional sports such as hunting and fishing maintained their popularity, but men also discovered more physical activities, such as hiking, camping, skiing, bodybuilding, and even skydiving, snowboarding, and bungee jumping, which offered extreme expressions of masculinity. Men also gravitated toward new technology, such as cars, power tools, and, later in the century, video games and computers. Pitting themselves against mechanical and electronic opponents, as well as the elements of nature, men could fight new battles that illustrated their strength and courage.

The emergence of a consumer and corporate economy in the twentieth and early-twenty-first centuries has made leisure, once deemed harmful to masculinity, an increasingly important arena for demonstrating manliness. A culture grounded in consumption has generated a growing array of activities through which men seek to express the independence, physicality, and leadership long fundamental to American constructions of manhood.

Bibliography

Carnes, Mark C. "Middle-Class Men and the Solace of Fraternal Ritual." In *Meanings for Manhood: Constructions of Masculinity in Victorian America*, edited by Mark C. Carnes and Clyde Griffen. Chicago: University of Chicago Press, 1990.

Genovese, Eugene D. *Roll, Jordan, Roll: The World the Slaves Made.* New York: Vintage, 1976.

Isaac, Rhys. *The Transformation of Virginia, 1740–1790.* Chapel Hill: University of North Carolina Press, 1982.

Marsh, Margaret. *Suburban Lives.* New Brunswick, N.J.: Rutgers University Press, 1990.

May, Elaine Tyler. *Homeward Bound: American Families in the Cold War Era.* New York: Basic Books, 1988.

Morgan, Philip D. *Slave Counterpoint: Black Culture in the Eighteenth-Century Chesapeake and Low Country.* Chapel Hill: University of North Carolina Press, 1998.

Ownby, Ted. *Subduing Satan: Religion, Recreation, and Manhood in the Rural South, 1865–1920.* Chapel Hill: University of North Carolina Press, 1990.

Register, Woody. "Everyday Peter Pans: Work, Manhood, and Consumption in Urban America, 1900-1930." In *Boys and Their Toys? Masculinity, Class, and Technology in America*, edited by Roger Horowitz. New York: Routledge, 2001.

Swiencicki, Mark A. "Consuming Brotherhood: Men's Culture, Style, and Recreation as Consumer Culture, 1880–1930." *Journal of Social History* 31, no. 4 (1998): 773–809.

Waldstreicher, David. *In the Midst of Perpetual Fetes: The Making of American Nationalism, 1776–1820.* Chapel Hill: University of North Carolina Press, 1997.

Further Reading

Marsh, Margaret. "Suburban Men and Masculine Domesticity, 1870–1915." In *Meanings for Manhood: Constructions of Masculinity in Victorian America*, edited by Mark C. Carnes and Clyde Griffen. Chicago: University of Chicago Press, 1990.

Meyer, Stephen. "Work, Play, and Power: Masculine Culture on the Automotive Shop Floor, 1930–1960." In *Boys and Their Toys? Masculinity, Class, and Technology in America*, edited by Roger Horowitz. New York: Routledge, 2001.

Peiss, Kathy. *Cheap Amusements: Working Women and Leisure in Turn-of-the-Century* New York. Philadelphia: Temple University Press, 1986.

Rotundo, E. Anthony. *American Manhood: Transformations in Masculinity from the Revolution to the Modern Era.* New York: Basic Books, 1993.

Shackleford, Ben A. "Masculinity, the Auto Racing Fraternity, and the Technological Sublime: The Pit Stop as a Celebration of Social Roles." In *Boys and Their Toys? Masculinity, Class, and Technology in America*, edited by Roger Horowitz. New York: Routledge, 2001.

Veblen, Thorstein. *The Theory of the Leisure Class.* 1899. Reprint, Amherst, N.Y.: Prometheus, 1998.

Related Entries

Baseball; Bodybuilding; Boxing; Class; Consumerism; Evangelicalism and Revivalism; Fishing; Football; Fraternal Organizations; Gambling; Guns; Hunting; Men's Clubs; Middle-Class Manhood; Outdoorsmen; Southern Manhood; Sports; Suburbia; Technology; Working-Class Manhood

—*Kirsten L. Parkinson*

Lincoln, Abraham

1809–1865
Sixteenth President of the United States

Along with fellow presidents George Washington, Andrew Jackson, and Theodore Roosevelt, Abraham Lincoln is widely recognized as an icon of American masculinity. Throughout his political career, Lincoln articulated visions of American identity grounded in contemporary concepts of manhood. After his assassination, he assumed a mythic masculine stature grounded in his rise from humble origins to prominence, his actions as president, and his physical features.

Born in Kentucky, Lincoln grew up in Indiana and received little formal education. As a youth he worked a ferry on the Ohio River and split fence rails. After his family moved to Illinois in 1830, he studied law and entered politics. He developed a reputation for honesty, self-improvement, frontier humor, and physical strength—characteristics that increasingly became associated with manliness in American political culture. He won election to the Illinois legislature as a Whig in 1834, 1836, 1838, and 1840, and to a term in the U.S. Congress

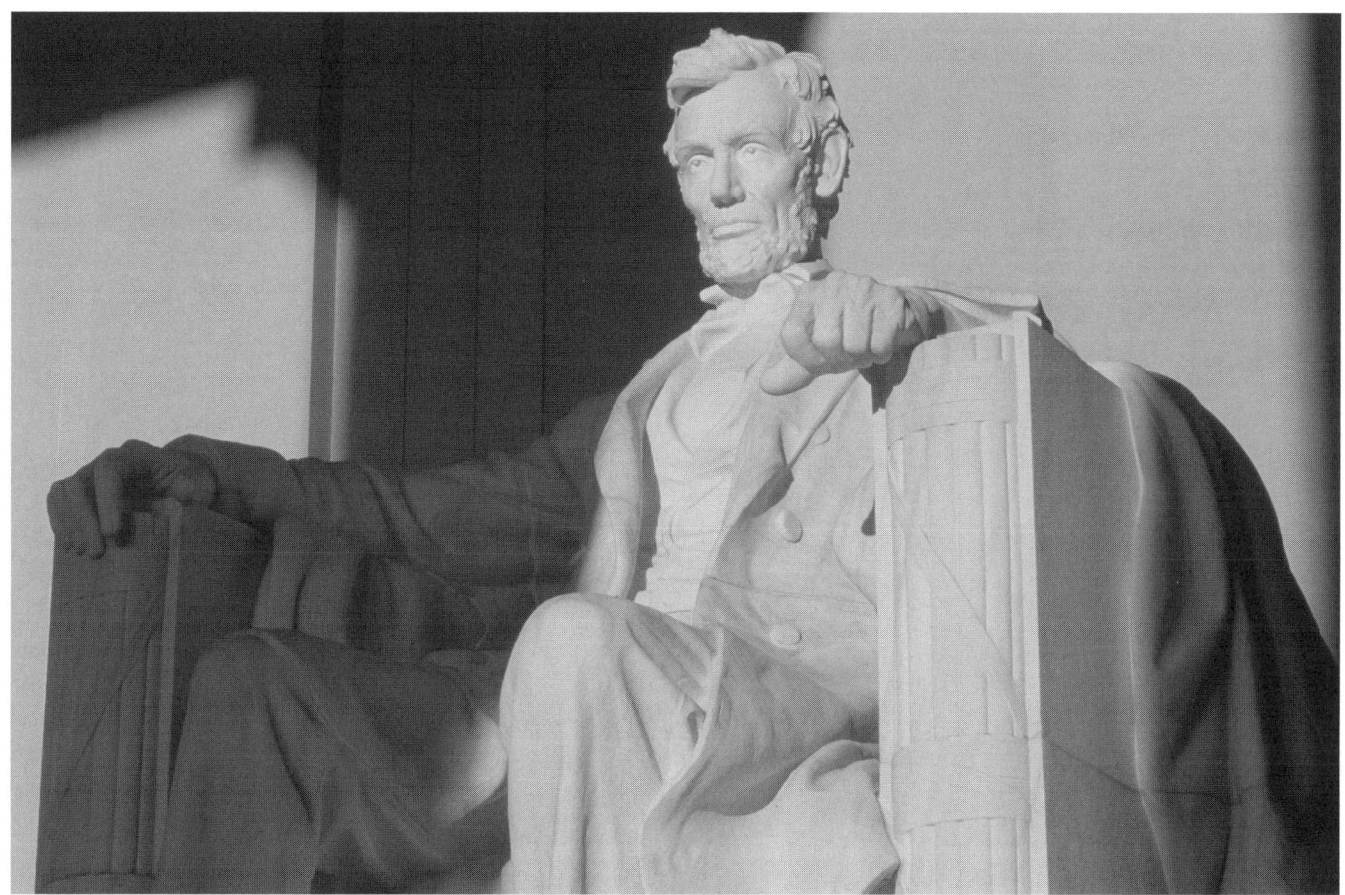

The larger-than-life statue of Abraham Lincoln in the Lincoln Memorial emphasizes the heroic qualities of strength, benevolence, dedication, and idealism widely associated with the sixteenth president. It powerfully conveys Lincoln's mythic stature as a symbol of national identity and an icon of American masculinity. (© James P. Blair/Corbis)

in 1846. He ran for the U.S. Senate in 1858 as a member of the new Republican Party. Although he lost the election, the campaign, highlighted by his debates with the Democratic candidate, Stephen O. Douglas, made him a national figure and led to his successful bid for the presidency in 1860.

Lincoln's rise to national prominence during the 1850s coincided with the rise of the Republican Party, and with his increasingly vocal public opposition to the extension of slavery into new western states and territories. The foundation of this position—and of the Republican Party's growing success in the 1850s—was a vision of America grounded in white manhood. Drawing on Jeffersonian ideals associating national strength and republicanism with economically and politically independent artisans and yeoman farmers, Lincoln's Republican Party adopted the slogan "free soil, free labor, free men," believing that the expansion of African-American slavery limited opportunity for white men. Although Lincoln shared the racist views of most of his white contemporaries, his election to the presidency led Southern states to secede from the Union in 1860 and 1861 and seek independence through civil war.

Between his election and his inauguration, Lincoln grew a beard, a decision that reflected a growing cultural association of facial hair with manliness and established an example followed by several subsequent presidents. As president, Lincoln defended the Union both in rhetoric and through the Civil War, and—particularly in the 1863 address with which he dedicated the national cemetery at Gettysburg—he identified fighting and self-sacrifice for the nation's preservation as the ultimate expression of American heroic manliness. Meanwhile, his political persona generated his growing public image as "Honest Abe."

Lincoln's assassination on April 14, 1865, began his transformation into an American masculine icon. The timing of his assassination—on Good Friday, just days after a Union victory that signaled the return of peace and the impending abolition of slavery—invited comparisons to Jesus and Moses. His successful preservation of the Union made him a symbol of national strength and endurance, while his opposition to slavery and his *Emancipation Proclamation* (1863) made him a heroic defender of American freedom. His path from log cabin to the presidency became a narrative of self-made success. Lincoln's image has also become one of the most highly visible of American national symbols: his tall and lanky frame, brawn, and beard were incorporated into subsequent representations of Uncle Sam, his face has appeared on the penny since 1909, and the larger-than-life statue of him in the Lincoln Memorial endures as a prominent site in the nation's capital.

Bibliography

Oates, Stephen B. "Lincoln: The Man, the Myth." *Civil War Times Illustrated* 22, no. 10 (1984): 10–19.

Peterson, Merrill D. *Lincoln in Modern Memory.* New York: Oxford University Press, 1994.

Purvis, Thomas L. "The Making of a Myth: Abraham Lincoln's Family Background in the Perspective of Jacksonian Politics." *Journal of the Illinois State Historical Society* 75, no. 2 (1982): 148–160.

Schwartz, Barry. "Iconography and Collective Memory: Lincoln's Image in the American Mind." *Sociological Quarterly* 32, no. 3 (1991): 301–319.

Winkle, Kenneth J. "Abraham Lincoln: Self-Made Man." *Journal of the Abraham Lincoln Association* 21, no. 2 (2000): 1–16.

Further Reading

Anderson, Dwight G. *Abraham Lincoln: The Quest for Immortality.* New York: Knopf, 1982.

Braden, Waldo W., ed. *Building the Myth: Selected Speeches Memorializing Abraham Lincoln.* Urbana: University of Illinois Press, 1990.

Foner, Eric, and Olivia Mahoney. *A House Divided: America in the Age of Lincoln.* New York: Norton, 1990.

Holzer, Harold. *Washington and Lincoln Portrayed: National Icons in Popular Prints.* Jefferson, N.C.: McFarland, 1993.

Related Entries

Body; Civil War; Emancipation; Nationalism; Politics; Race; Republicanism; Self-Made Man; Slavery; Uncle Sam; Western Frontier; Whiteness

—*Bret E. Carroll*

London, Jack

1876–1916
Author

Jack London was a highly successful writer of popular fiction. Best known for his novel *The Call of the Wild* (1903), London admired, and promoted in his work, a masculinity that was achieved through physical hardship in inhospitable natural environments. His writings constitute part of a late-nineteenth- and early-twentieth-century discourse concerning masculinity, including a biological definition of manhood, the physical education of the male body, and the promotion of the outdoor life as an antidote to the perceived threat of effeminacy and degeneration posed by the artificial, urban-industrial "overcivilization" of modern American life.

This discourse was inspired by Charles Darwin's theory of natural selection, according to which competition for survival among organisms improves species' adaptation to their natural environments. In *The Call of the Wild, White Fang* (1906), and other writings, London depicts nature as a relentless struggle for survival and supremacy, defining manhood in terms of physical brawn and strength of will. In *The Sea-Wolf* (1904), the impressively muscular and brutally violent ship captain, Wolf Larsen, represents a "natural" predatory masculinity that is achieved at sea. London's stories about realizing manhood in a wild space beyond the frontiers of civilization also reflected contemporary cultural concerns that the future of American masculinity was endangered by the closing of the western frontier at the end of the nineteenth century.

By defining manhood in physical and biological terms, London offered a body-centered masculine ideal. His fiction presents both an unabashed homoerotic appreciation of the beauty of muscular men's bodies—such as that of Wolf Larsen in *The Sea-Wolf* or of Pat Glendon, the boxer hero of *The Abysmal Brute* (1913)—and an emphasis on the redemptive possibilities of physical violence. For London, as for other men of the period who touted the regenerative qualities of war, violence represented a manly and immediate physical experience that seemed increasingly unattainable amid the indirect and genteel relationships of a commercial, bureaucratic society. London sought to inspire men who felt feminized and enervated by civilized gentility to pursue the exciting, as well as muscle- and character-building, experience of physical pain and endurance beyond the frontiers of settled life.

London's understanding of manhood is wrought with contradictions. While he idealized manly yet brutal competition and struggle, he also expressed a socialist sensitivity to inequality and injustice—particularly in *The People of the Abyss* (1903) and *The Iron Heel* (1908). Furthermore, despite London's socialist inclinations and his definition of manliness in opposition to modern American civilization, his valuation of a rugged and competitive individualism resembled and buttressed the ideology of entrepreneurial manhood that underwrote American capitalism.

That London achieved popularity in his lifetime indicates that his promotion of outdoor male adventure and Darwinian view of masculinity powerfully appealed to male readers of the time and reinforced American gender mores. In the twenty-first century, the appeal of leisure activities featuring the pursuit of excitement and danger in natural settings—such as rafting and rock climbing—suggests that London's ideal of masculinity continues to resonate.

BIBLIOGRAPHY

Derrick, Scott. "Making a Heterosexual Man: Gender, Sexuality and Narrative in the Fiction of Jack London." In *Rereading Jack London,* edited by Leonard Cassuto and Jeanne Campbell Reesman. Stanford, Calif.: Stanford University Press, 1996.

Kershaw, Alex. *Jack London: A Life.* New York: St. Martin's, 1998.

Seltzer, Mark. "The Love Master." In *Engendering Men: The Question of Male Feminist Criticism,* edited by Joseph A. Boone and Michael Cadden. New York: Routledge, 1990.

Shor, Francis. "Power, Gender, and Ideological Discourse in The Iron Heel." In *Rereading Jack London,* edited by Leonard Cassuto and Jeanne Campbell Reesman. Stanford, Calif.: Stanford University Press, 1996.

FURTHER READING

Auerbach, Jonathan. *Male Call: Becoming Jack London.* Durham, N.C.: Duke University Press, 1996.

Sinclair, Andrew. *Jack: A Biography of Jack London.* New York: Harper & Row, 1977.

SELECTED WRITINGS

London, Jack. *The Call of the Wild.* 1903. Reprinted in *The Call of the Wild, White Fang, and Other Stories,* edited by Andrew Sinclair. New York: Penguin, 1993.

———. *The People of the Abyss.* 1903. Reprint, London: Pluto Press, 2001.

———. *The Sea-Wolf.* 1904. Reprint, New York: Puffin, 1997.

———. *White Fang.* 1906. Reprinted in *The Call of the Wild, White Fang, and Other Stories,* edited by Andrew Sinclair. New York: Penguin, 1993.

———. *The Iron Heel.* 1908. Reprint, Edinburgh: Rebel, 1999.

———. *The Abysmal Brute.* 1913. Reprint, Lincoln: University of Nebraska Press, 2000.

RELATED ENTRIES

Body; Bodybuilding; Boxing; Bureaucratization; Capitalism; Crisis of Masculinity; Darwinism; Eugenics; Individualism; Outdoorsmen; Self-Made Man; Travel; Travel Narratives; Violence; Western Frontier

—*Michael Kane*

LONE RANGER, THE

One of the most popular dramas of the "Golden Age of Radio," *The Lone Ranger* (1933–54) detailed the adventures of a masked vigilante and his Native American companion, Tonto, in the post–Civil War West. Armed with silver six-guns that never claimed a life, the Lone Ranger helped expand and reinforce the American masculine ideal of physicality tempered by responsibility.

First broadcast on WXYZ in Detroit, *The Lone Ranger* quickly developed into a cultural and commercial phenomenon. Despite, or perhaps because of, the program's unrepentant borrowing from pulp and folkloric sources, the Ranger's comfortingly familiar masculinity elicited a devoted listener response. Audiences not only tuned in three times a week to hear the masked man's signature cry of "Hi-Yo Silver," but they also devoured Lone Ranger comic books, newspaper comic strips, novels, movie serials, and, later, both live-action and cartoon television series. Strong, stoic, and unquestionably patriotic, the masked rider of the plains was part Zorro, part Robin Hood, and wholly American. In rescuing homesteaders from greedy businessmen and burgeoning settlements from outlaw gangs, the Ranger consistently demonstrated that the Wild West could be tamed and the American Dream preserved—though only by a masculinity firmly rooted in the American tradition of protecting the underdog.

Much of the Ranger's appeal lay in his mutability. Whereas other radio heroes were scripted in almost lurid detail, the Ranger's masked face and mysterious origins encouraged listeners to personalize him according to individual taste and desire. Hence, though the Ranger was meant to be an educated white easterner, he was alternately imagined by audiences as Asian, Hispanic, working class, gay, and so forth. Given the challenges to American masculinity posed by woman suffrage, World War I, and the Great Depression, the Ranger's mutability offered men a fluid, and thus potentially more powerful, identity.

The masked man's relationship with Tonto, however, was less dynamic. Although the *kemo sabes* (faithful friends) adventured together in almost all of the 2,956 radio episodes, Tonto was never listed in the program's title. Indeed, he was less a partner than a constant reminder that men of color could never have a starring role. Whereas the Ranger rode Silver, a magnificent white horse, Tonto had only a small but sturdy pinto, or paint pony; in contrast to the masked man's flawless diction, "Old Smoky-Face" spoke in broken English; and when the manly Ranger dealt in six-gun justice, Tonto—in a role many Americans identified with women—succored the sick with "Indian medicines." Not a partnership of equals, their relationship reiterated, rather than challenged, the racism that had long underpinned mainstream American masculinity.

In an era marked by economic depression, the rise of mass popular culture, World War II, and radio's epidemic expansion, *The Lone Ranger* supplied a vision of masculinity that was at once fluid, traditional, and ultimately reassuring. This combination of invention and convention forged a powerful myth that even today defines American notions of heroism. One need only look to masked film and comic book icons such as Batman (with his feminized sidekick Robin) and Spiderman to see the Ranger's continuing influence.

BIBLIOGRAPHY

Basso, Matthew, Laura McCall, and Dee Garceau. *Across the Great Divide: Cultures of Manhood in the American West.* New York: Routledge, 2001.

Calder, Jenni. *There Must Be a Lone Ranger: The American West in Film and in Reality.* New York: McGraw-Hill, 1977.

Harmon, Jim. *Radio Mystery and Adventure: And Its Appearances in Film, Television and Other Media.* Jefferson, N.C.: McFarland, 1992.

Nachman, Gerald. *Raised on Radio: In Quest of The Lone Ranger, Jack Benny, Amos 'n' Andy, The Shadow, Mary Noble, The Great Gildersleeve, Fibber McGee and Molly, Bill Stern, Our Miss Brooks, Henry Aldrich, The Quiz Kids, Mr. First Nighter, Fred Allen, Vic and Sade, The Cisco Kid, Jack Armstrong, Arthur Godfrey, Bob and Ray, The Barbour Family, Henry Morgan, Joe Friday, and Other Lost Heroes from Radio's Heyday.* New York: Pantheon, 1998.

Rothel, David. *Who Was That Masked Man?: The Story of the Lone Ranger.* Rev. ed. San Diego, Calif.: Tantivy Press, 1982.

FURTHER READING

Bickel, Mary E. *Geo. W. Trendle, Creator and Producer of: The Lone Ranger, The Green Hornet, Sgt. Preston of the Yukon, The American Agent, and Other Successes. An Authorized Biography.* New York: Exposition Press, 1971.

Holland, Dave. *From Out of the Past: A Pictorial History of the Lone Ranger.* Granada Hills, Calif.: Holland House, 1988.

MacDonald, J. Fred. *Don't Touch That Dial!: Radio Programming in American Life, 1920–1960.* Chicago: Nelson-Hall, 1979.

Osgood, Dick. *Wyxie Wonderland: An Unauthorized 50-Year Diary of WXYZ Detroit.* Bowling Green, Ohio: Bowling Green University Popular Press, 1981.

Striker, Fran. *The Lone Ranger.* New York: Grosset & Dunlap, 1936.

Striker, Fran, Jr. *His Typewriter Grew Spurs: A Biography of Fran Striker—Writer: Documenting the Lone Ranger's Ride on the Radiowaves of the World.* Landsdale, Pa.: Questco, 1983.

RELATED ENTRIES

Cowboys; Great Depression; Guns; Heroism; Male Friendship; Native American Manhood; Race; Western Frontier; Westerns; World War I

—*Judd Ethan Ruggill*

Malcolm X

1925–1965
African-American Civil Rights Leader

The masculinity of Malcolm X (El Hajj Malik El-Shabazz) is central to his importance within the black community. Malcolm's appeal and continuing legacy stems from his performance and articulation of a vision of black masculinity grounded in black militancy and self-defense.

Malcolm X was born Malcolm Little in Omaha, Nebraska. After white supremacists killed his father and his mother's health deteriorated due to mental illness, Malcolm spent most of his childhood in various foster homes. While in prison for burglary, he joined the Nation of Islam (NOI), a black Muslim group that asserted black pride and embraced Islam as the true religion of nonwhite peoples. When he was released from prison in 1952, Malcolm became a minister, and eventually the national spokesman, for the NOI.

Despite his revolutionary rhetoric, Malcolm accepted and promoted a reactionary and traditional vision of masculinity. To Malcolm, an America dominated by whites required black men to safeguard African-American women and children from whites' hostility and violence. To do this, black men had to function as effective breadwinners and providers in patriarchal families. Citing the brutality faced by female civil rights workers and the history of white rape of black women, Malcolm posited male protection as central to an authentic black masculinity, wondering how black men could "ever expect to be respected as men with black women being beaten and nothing being done about it" (hooks, 186).

Malcolm perceived a historic castration and emasculation of black men as part of their oppressive American experience. He therefore rejected his original surname, which he believed had been given to his ancestors by white slaveholders, and assumed the surname "X" because he believed that black American men had been shorn of meaningful masculine identity when they were involuntarily transported from Africa to America and made subservient to whites. While exposing America's role in the oppression of black men throughout U.S. history, from slavery to police brutality, Malcolm equally blamed black women. Arguing that black liberation and black manhood were impeded by a matriarchal family structure, he often linked black women and whites as joint emasculators of black men and excoriated black women as "the great tool of the devil" (hooks, 187).

Malcolm presented himself and the NOI as the masculine alternative to what he considered a feminized integrationist movement led by Martin Luther King, Jr. He argued that integrationist goals and King's strategy of nonviolence contributed to the brutalization of black women and children at the hands of violent whites and smacked of unmanly passivity, subjugation, and emasculation. He proposed instead self-defense, assertive language, and black autonomy from white America as the bases of black masculinity.

Increasingly frustrated with the NOI's apolitical stances and concerned by accusations that NOI leader Elijah Muhammad had fathered illegitimate children, Malcolm broke from the NOI in 1964. After a pilgrimage to Mecca, an Islamic holy site in Saudi Arabia, Malcolm's views of masculinity and gender changed. He rarely spoke thereafter about liberation being the sole responsibility of men, or of women being complicit in the oppression of black men. Instead, he supported a black masculinity defined less by providing for and protecting black women than by joint sacrifice and struggle in a daily fight against white supremacy. This transformation was halted by his assassination in 1965.

Malcolm X's interpretation of black masculinity serves as the source of both his popularity and shortcomings. Many African-American men continue to revere Malcolm X for his vision of defiant black manhood, but his failure to spark a revolutionary movement that denounced both white supremacy and patriarchy represents the unfulfilled promise of Malcolm's legacy.

Bibliography

Dyson, Michael Eric. *Making Malcolm: The Myth and Meaning of Malcolm X.* New York: Oxford University Press, 1995.

hooks, bell. *Outlaw Culture: Resisting Representations.* New York: Routledge, 1994.

Karim, Benjamin, Peter Skutches, and David Gallen. *Remembering Malcolm.* New York: Carroll & Graf, 1992.

Malcolm X, and Alex Haley. *The Autobiography of Malcolm X.* New York: Ballantine Books, 1964.

Wallace, Michelle. *Black Macho and the Myth of Superwoman.* New York: Dial Press, 1979.

FURTHER READING

Gallen, David, ed. *Malcolm X: As They Knew Him.* New York: Carroll & Graf, 1992.

Goldman, Peter. *The Death and Life of Malcolm X.* New York: Harper & Row, 1973.

Harper, Phillip Brian. *Are We Not Men?: Masculine Anxiety and the Problem of African American Identity.* New York: Oxford University Press, 1996.

Munir, Fareed. "Malcolm X's Religious Pilgrimage: From Black Separatism to a Universal Way." In *Redeeming Men: Religion and Masculinities,* edited by Stephen B. Boyd, W. Merle Longwood, and Mark W. Muesse. Louisville, Ky.: Westminster John Knox Press, 1996.

Perry, Bruce. *Malcolm: The Life of a Man Who Changed Black America.* New York: Station Hill, 1992.

Shabazz, Ilyasha, and Kim McLaurin. *Growing Up X.* New York: Ballantine Books, 2002.

RELATED ENTRIES

African-American Manhood; Black Panther Party; Civil Rights Movement; Cult of Domesticity; Heterosexuality; King, Martin Luther, Jr.; Nationalism; Nation of Islam; Patriarchy; Race; Religion and Spirituality; Self-Control; Slavery; Violence; White Supremacism

—David J. Leonard

MALE FRIENDSHIP

Close relationships between men do not come easily in a society that not only associates masculinity with individualism and competition, but also looks askance at male intimacy as a possible indication of homosexuality. The concept of homosexuality is barely more than a century old, however, and even the emphasis on the self and on competition was not always as strong in American society as it currently is. Additionally, American men and women once occupied much more separate, or homosocial, spaces. Friendships between men are best viewed in this shifting historical context.

Colonial and Nineteenth-Century America

The premodern social conditions of colonial America, in which society consisted of small, homogenous, stable communities, were conducive to the formation of lifelong friendships between men. Defining manhood in terms of one's role in his community and reliability to his neighbors, and considering strong social interdependency essential to community welfare, colonial men typically, and necessarily, formed strong social bonds. Still, while a man might have many friends in this environment, the actual intensity of individual attachments may have been limited by the culture's powerful emphasis on the well-being of the whole community and on one's relationship to God.

During the nineteenth century, several modernizing transformations in American life altered the nature and meaning of male friendships. Urbanization and the market revolution resulted in increased mobility and a new emphasis on competitive individualism, both of which tended to reduce the number of a man's friendships. The increasing primacy of the individual over the community, a growing valuation of emotional expression, and—some historians argue—a diminished role of God-centered devotion prompted the elevation of romantic love between a man and a woman to a new significance in people's lives. These developments may also have made those friendships more psychologically intense, making male friendships an important component of masculine identity.

Indeed, it appears that sometimes there was little division between romance and friendship for men in nineteenth-century America. With men and women frequently living in largely homosocial worlds until—and even in some respects during—their marriages, the object of one's "romantic" attention was often a member of one's own sex. In an era when male expressions of sympathy and sentimentality were prized—and before the concept of homosexuality had been developed and the practice stigmatized—American men were free to speak endearingly to each other and to have what some historians have characterized as "romantic friendships." Daniel Webster, for instance, a U.S. senator from Massachusetts and one of antebellum America's most renowned public figures, usually began letters to one friend with the salutation "Lovely Boy" and closed letters to him with "accept all the tenderness I have." Webster and Abraham Lincoln were among the countless American men of their era to frequently share a bed with a male friend, testimony as much to the extent of unselfconscious intimacy as to the relative shortage of beds.

Some historians have argued that this pervasive intimacy between men in nineteenth-century America was largely confined to young adulthood, before a man would marry (as most eventually did), while others suggest that the intimacy was much more than merely a phase on the way to a man's union with a woman. Additionally, while some scholars have maintained that virtually all of the romantic friendships were nonsexual, others have insisted that the terms of endearment suggest that sexual activity between men of the period was widespread.

Photograph of two American men (c. 1870). Physical intimacy and romance were characteristic of male friendships in Victorian America, but they became less so during the twentieth century as most American men became increasingly aware and fearful of homosexuality. (From John Ibson, Picturing Men: A Century of Male Relationships in Everyday American Photography, *2002)*

Because explicit letters or diary entries are rare, we cannot know for certain how frequently these male friendships were sexual. But abundant photographic evidence suggests that, along with verbal intimacy, a comfort with physical closeness once flourished among American men of various regions, races, and social classes. From the dawn of photography in the 1840s, American men often had their associations commemorated in studio portraits. When snapshots began to have their transforming effect on American lives in the 1890s, there was an initial period, lasting but a few decades, during which men were seemingly quite at ease in appearing close to each other in front of the camera. However, changing attitudes toward male sexuality and emotional expression brought both practices (studio portraits of men together, as well as intimate snapshots) largely to an end by the 1930s.

Two important nineteenth-century institutions, both designed to build or strengthen male character, attest to the importance attached to male friendships and the perceived centrality of such relationships to constructions of manhood. The first was the fraternal organization, which became so widespread during the last third of the nineteenth century—when almost a third of all adult men in the United States belonged to such organizations, which numbered in the hundreds—that the historian Mary Ann Clawson has referred to the period as "American fraternalism's golden age" (Clawson, 111). The second, appealing to new arrivals in America's cities who needed a place to stay or at least get some exercise, was the Young Men's Christian Association (YMCA), branches of which appeared across the country. The contrived quality of the activities in fraternal lodges and YMCAs, including the fervency of efforts to build friendships and construct close relationships among men, suggests a pervasive fear that urban-industrial American life jeopardized such friendships. Yet the fact that American men thought lodges and the "Y" necessary reflected both the strength and the weakness of homosocial friendship.

The Twentieth Century: Male Friendship Transformed

The culture of modern America dramatically altered men's friendships. Increasing mobility and competition surely took their toll, but probably more significant were two fundamental and interrelated changes in the way that Americans thought about sexuality and gender relations. First, psychologists and physicians began examining—and marginalizing—homosexuality. Public fear of male homosexuality, considered by many Americans incompatible with true manhood, became widespread in the United States early in the twentieth century, growing especially intense during the 1950s, when Americans associated homosexuality with communism and viewed both as threatening to American institutions. Second, men and women increasingly emphasized and valued heterosocial interaction. They became more familiar with each other in new urban settings, such as amusement parks and dance halls, and the ideal marriage came to be seen as a union of companions. Together, these developments prompted increasing discomfort with homosocial relationships. Whereas the studio portrait that two nineteenth-century young men might have had taken as a token of their mutual fondness symbolized the quality of men's friendships during that period, the empty seat that two twentieth-century men would sometimes feel compelled to leave between them in a movie theater suggests the very different nature of contemporary male relationships.

As physical intimacy became a less acceptable expression of male friendship in the twentieth century, transformations in American society and culture generated new bases for male association. Beginning late in the nineteenth century, as leisure time increased, outdoor activities and competitive sports received a new emphasis and came to be seen as essential in maintaining vigorous manhood in an urban, industrial society. Further, the development of new corporate philosophies emphasizing teamwork offset, to some degree, the corrosive effects of competitive individualism, encouraging camaraderie in a business culture that most Americans saw as a masculine domain. The growth of suburbia during the twentieth century also created new arenas that fostered male friendships, such as the golf course, the front lawn, and athletic fields where children needed adult coaches.

Nor did many traditional sites of male friendship disappear. Fraternal orders, though much less popular than in their late-nineteenth-century heyday, remained prominent institutions within which men could gather for business advantage, social service, and social interaction. YMCAs became a permanent fixture of American life, remaining predominantly male spaces well into the twentieth century. Military life, especially in wartime, remained an important location for male bonding; indeed, the frequency of American military involvement in distant and unfamiliar environments may have enhanced the importance of war as a basis of male attachment. Male friendship became a central theme in most war dramas, whether literary or cinematic, especially those involving World War II and Vietnam.

The nature of male friendships remained a salient topic of consideration in late-twentieth-century American culture as feminism and the rise of the men's movement sparked a reassessment of traditional constructions of masculinity. Some commentators interpreted men's disinclination to physical contact and verbal expressions of affection as an indication that men lacked the deep friendships enjoyed by women, and they urged men to embrace more emotionally expressive approaches to friendship. Calling for the widespread adoption of a "sensitive male" ideal, they tended to dismiss as superficial or regrettable strong feelings or bonding among soldiers, athletes in violent sports, the socially conservative Promise Keepers, or participants in mythopoetic rituals inspired by Robert Bly's book *Iron John* (1990). Others suggested that the shared recreational activities or expressions of loyalty characteristic of twentieth-century male friendships are more legitimate criteria by which to gauge the depth and intensity of those relationships, and that male friendship required no fundamental reshaping.

The liberalized attitudes toward homosexuality growing out of the 1960s Sexual Revolution produced among some observers a belief that gay men—allegedly free of the constraints that inhibit "straight" men—are able to form close friendships that might serve as models for all men to follow. Others have seen this as a form of gay chauvinism, or at least wishful thinking or selective perception, suggesting that gay and straight men are equally inhibited. Men are men, runs this logic, regardless of the object of their sexual desire.

Conclusion

The structure of everyday life in contemporary America is vastly different from that of the colonial village, and communal manhood and its attendant friendships are matters of a far distant memory. The mobility, self-concern, and homophobia that pervade the contemporary male's existence may not promote friendships that are as openly passionate or emotionally expressive as those of the nineteenth century, but neither has modern life rendered male friendship extinct.

Bibliography

Clawson, Mary Ann. *Constructing Brotherhood: Class, Gender, and Fraternalism.* Princeton, N.J.: Princeton University Press, 1989.

Crain, Caleb. *American Sympathy: Men, Friendship, and Literature in the New Nation.* New Haven, Conn.: Yale University Press, 2001.

Gustav-Wrathall, John Donald. *Take the Young Stranger by the Hand: Same-Sex Relations and the YMCA.* Chicago: University of Chicago Press, 1998.

Ibson, John. *Picturing Men: A Century of Male Relationships in American Everyday Photography.* Washington, D.C.: Smithsonian Institution Press, 2002.

Katz, Jonathan Ned. *Love Stories: Sex between Men before Homosexuality.* Chicago: University of Chicago Press, 2001.

Nardi, Peter M. *Gay Men's Friendships: Invincible Communities.* Chicago: University of Chicago Press, 1999.

Rotundo, E. Anthony. *American Manhood: Transformations in Masculinity from the Revolution to the Modern Era.* New York: Basic Books, 1993.

Rubin, Lillian B. *Just Friends: The Role of Friendship in Our Lives.* New York: Harper & Row, 1985.

Further Reading

Ambrose, Stephen E. *Comrades: Brothers, Fathers, Heroes, Sons, Pals.* New York: Simon & Schuster, 1999.

Kimmel, Michael. *Manhood in America: A Cultural History.* New York: Free Press, 1996.

Lystra, Karen. *Searching the Heart: Women, Men, and Romantic Love in Nineteenth-Century America.* New York: Oxford University Press, 1989.

Mechling, Jay. *On My Honor: Boy Scouts and the Making of American Youth.* Chicago: University of Chicago Press, 2001.

Pollack, William. *Real Boys: Rescuing Our Sons from the Myths of Boyhood.* New York: Random House, 1998.

RELATED ENTRIES

Bachelorhood; Boyhood; Boy Scouts of America; Buddy Films; Counterculture; Dueling; Emotion; Fraternal Organizations; Fraternities; Gangs; Individualism; *Iron John: A Book About Men*; Men's Clubs; Men's Movements; Men's Studies; Military; Nationalism; Nativism; Promise Keepers; Self-Made Man; Sports; War; Whitman, Walt; Young Men's Christian Association

—*John Ibson*

MANIFEST DESTINY

Part romantic sentiment, part bombastic pretense, Manifest Destiny has historically been used to explain and rationalize American territorial expansion. Although derived from the missionary impulses first expressed in Puritan Massachusetts, and later combined with social Darwinian beliefs forged before the Spanish-American War (1898), Manifest Destiny is most closely associated with the Jacksonian era (c. 1815–45), the expansionist agenda of the James K. Polk administration (1845–49), and the territorial goals driving the Mexican War (1846–48). For Americans of that period, Manifest Destiny encapsulated the nation's masculine vigor and purpose and promised the incorporation of new land that would provide the economic independence associated with manhood in republican and agrarian ideology. As both a symptom and a cause of larger historical forces—including gender inequalities, civil turmoil, and sectional strains—Manifest Destiny influenced how Anglo-Saxon men saw themselves, their society, and their nation.

Purportedly coined by New York editor John L. O'Sullivan, the term probably originated with one of O'Sullivan's staff writers, Jane McManus Storm, between 1839 and 1845. According to proponents, Manifest Destiny was a divinely ordained means by which a "superior" and "masculine" America could bring republican institutions to "inferior" and "effeminate" neighbors. American political leaders, military men, and entrepreneurs inspired by the concept hoped that conquering neighboring lands and incorporating them into the United States would provide economic opportunity while counteracting the international ambitions of monarchies like Great Britain (which was perceived by leaders such as Polk to be gaining inordinate influence in modern-day Oregon, the American Southwest, and Latin America).

Recent scholarship, however, has moved beyond associating the rhetoric of Manifest Destiny with a nationalism conceived in terms of masculinity. Historians now view it less as a mystical philosophy of national greatness (often substituting the terms *manifest design* or *manifest dominion*) and more as a rationale for the agency and interests of white men who claimed to act on its basis. As a result, it is seen less as a vehicle of republicanism than as an ideology used by rough-and-tumble fortune hunters to further their economic ambitions and sense of masculine achievement.

During and after the Mexican War, many American men—particularly those prone to violence—grounded their activities in the idea of Manifest Destiny. Inspired by Zachary Taylor, who captured the popular imagination as an archetypal man on horseback during the war, these men hoped for similar adventures in the name of national destiny. Some were led by their ambitions into filibustering (the use of private armies to conquer foreign lands). These men usually found that their actions tarnished them rather than bolstering either their own manhood or the nation's goals. Even William Walker's successful forays into Nicaragua (motivated by his desire to expand U.S. influence and to prove his manhood despite his unprepossessing physical appearance) proved abortive: He governed but briefly (1855–57) before he was executed. Such results dissuaded other men previously inclined toward filibustering.

Other men acting in the name of Manifest Destiny attempted to preserve prevailing notions of manhood and womanhood by acting against the increasingly vocal women's rights movement of the period. As suffragists began to agitate extensively for the vote in 1848, American soldiers defended what they considered traditional American male prerogatives by favorably comparing traditional Mexican women with both the weak, "unmanly" Mexican men who lost the war and the "unsexed females" back home. After they emerged victorious in the Mexican War, U.S. soldiers confirmed their belief in Manifest Destiny, their pride in American manhood, and their sense of national superiority (and some returned home with Mexican wives).

Many American men, however, opposed the bravado of Manifest Destiny, criticizing the actions it spawned and doubting the manhood of its adherents. Opponents of the Mexican War, who generated one of the most vocal antiwar movements in American history, implicitly questioned the bravery and masculinity of those who fought by noting the unevenness of the contest and charging that the war's supporters were subservient to southern slaveholders, whom they viewed as dictating the Polk administration's policies. Urging civil disobedience against the government's expansionist policies, particularly the

Mexican War, the transcendentalist writer Henry David Thoreau argued that a true man followed his conscience rather than the political rhetoric of Manifest Destiny.

Even many men who initially supported Manifest Destiny eventually discerned fundamental problems in the relationship between territorial expansion and nationalism, and they began to doubt that the actions carried out in its name were either manly or right. As the acquisition of new territory from Mexico generated racial fears about the assimilability of its inhabitants, as well as sectional disputes over the expansion of slavery, many of the northern artists, poets, and politicos who had promoted Manifest Destiny (as part of the Young America movement) grew disenchanted with its results between 1848 and 1851. Southerners, meanwhile, fearful that their diminishing status within the Union threatened their manly honor and independence, continued to support desperate filibuster raids in the 1850s in an effort to extend slavery to new territories. Thus, the sectional differences that led to the Civil War grew in part out of differing conceptions over whether, and how, Manifest Destiny fostered manhood. Ironically, Manifest Destiny, intended to enhance national strength, nearly split the nation apart.

During the Civil War the aggressive, adventurous masculinity that had informed Manifest Destiny before the war was challenged by new realities that required increased subordination, regimentation, and technical skill. The term itself has, for all intents and purposes, ceased to be used in modern parlance, yet echoes of Manifest Destiny reverberated in the United States right through the Cold War period. Although its overtly militaristic and imperialistic thrust has been toned down, Manifest Destiny and its associated notion of a masculine United States continue to inform the rhetoric of American foreign policy.

BIBLIOGRAPHY

Greenberg, Amy S. "A Gray-Eyed Man: Character, Appearance, and Filibustering." *Journal of the Early Republic* 20, no. 4 (Winter 2000): 673–699.

Hietala, Thomas R. *Manifest Design: Anxious Aggrandizement in Late Jacksonian America.* Ithaca, N.Y.: Cornell University Press, 1985.

Horsman, Reginald. *Race and Manifest Destiny: The Origins of American Racial Anglo-Saxonism.* Cambridge, Mass.: Harvard University Press, 1981.

Isenberg, Nancy. *Sex and Citizenship in Antebellum America.* Chapel Hill: University of North Carolina Press, 1998.

Johannsen, Robert W. *To the Halls of the Montezumas: The Mexican War in the American Imagination.* New York: Oxford University Press, 1985.

May, Robert E. *Manifest Destiny's Underworld: Filibustering in Antebellum America.* Chapel Hill: University of North Carolina Press, 2002.

FURTHER READING

Hoganson, Kristin L. *Fighting for American Manhood: How Gender Politics Provoked the Spanish-American and Philippine-American Wars.* New Haven, Conn.: Yale University Press, 1998.

Hudson, Linda S. *Mistress of Manifest Destiny: A Biography of Jane McManus Storm Cazneau, 1807–1878.* Austin: Texas State Historical Association, 2001.

Nelson, Dana D. *National Manhood: Capitalist Citizenship and the Imagined Fraternity of White Men.* Durham, N.C.: Duke University Press, 1998.

Stephanson, Anders. *Manifest Destiny: American Expansionism and the Empire of Right.* New York: Hill and Wang, 1996.

Widmer, Edward L. *Young America: The Flowering of Democracy in New York City.* New York: Oxford University Press, 1999.

Wyatt-Brown, Bertram. *Southern Honor: Ethics and Behavior in the Old South.* New York: Oxford University Press, 1982.

RELATED ENTRIES

Civil War; Imperialism; Jackson, Andrew; Militarism; Nationalism; Spanish-American War; Thoreau, Henry David; Western Frontier

—*Robert W. Burg*

MARKET REVOLUTION

The term *market revolution* describes a succession of economic and technological changes that transformed U.S. society between 1825 and 1860. The construction of roads, canals, and railroads; the opening of the West to settlement; the expansion of postal delivery routes; and the introduction of the telegraph drew previously disparate communities closer together and helped to create a national market of commodities, goods, labor, and services. This transformation fundamentally altered American notions of manhood, causing a shift from the eighteenth-century ideal of the community-oriented patriarch and provider to the more modern ideal of the market-oriented breadwinner and "self-made man."

American Manhood before the Market Revolution

Prior to the market revolution, American society was governed more by the natural rhythms of the environment than by the commercial forces of market exchange. Colonial and early national U.S. society consisted of small inland communities and seaboard towns; even such cities as New York, Boston, and

Philadelphia were small by European standards. With the exception of transatlantic commerce, trade remained local and the cost of transport made commercial transactions over longer distances prohibitively expensive. The relative social and economic isolation of colonial and early national American communities affected perceptions of social relations and definitions of gender and manliness.

The fundamental unit of colonial society and the basis for its concepts of manhood was the household, whose male head linked it to social and governmental structures. The responsibilities of the male household head were grounded in notions of duty, obligation, and deference, and his identity was bound up in social relations governed by these principles. Generally, men as well as women accepted their submission to their male superiors in a social order considered as God-given. Although men were regarded as driven by passions such as a desire for power, fame, and wealth, they were expected to govern and control themselves in accordance with social hierarchies and obligations.

During the seventeenth and eighteenth centuries, as American men began to embrace the opportunities offered by transatlantic markets and an expanding commercial capitalism, new notions of male identity emerged that were rooted more in self-assertion, financial risk-taking, and rational individualism than in social duty and obligation. Many men found this to be a difficult transition. For instance, the Puritan businessman Robert Keayne (1595–1656) took great pains to justify business practices that had frequently been criticized and prove that he had fulfilled his obligations to the community through his philanthropic giving. But Benjamin Franklin's *Autobiography* (written between 1771 and 1789), which discussed his rise to wealth and fame in the commercial seaport city of Philadelphia, suggests that Americans had come to embrace an ideal of a gain-oriented, rational masculinity by the late eighteenth century.

The republican and democratic political philosophy that informed the American Revolution and the new nation's government reflected emerging ideas about self-assertion and competition, and thus reinforced these new notions of manhood. In particular, James Madison's "Tenth Federalist," one of eighty-five essays written in support of the Constitution, promoted the idea that individualistic and pluralistic competition in an open marketplace would generate a well-balanced community. Republican ideology also assumed that the ideal male citizen would balance self-interest with concern for the needs of the community and the common good, but its suggestion that the pursuit of self-interest was legitimate when balanced by civic obligation provided crucial momentum and justification for articulations of manliness based on personal gain.

The Rise and Governance of "Marketplace Manhood"

In the period between the 1825 opening of the Erie Canal in upstate New York and the emergence of a railroad network in the Northeast and Midwest by the 1850s, the United States transformed from an agrarian to a commercial economy. These economic changes helped to create a self-conscious middle class that articulated a new entrepreneurial model of masculinity grounded in notions of free competition, acquisitive individualism, and the pursuit of self-interest, limited only by one's talents and abilities and measured by economic performance. This ideal of manliness encouraged men to seek out the possibilities and opportunities of an emerging national market society and to reject many of the communal restraints and duties that had previously anchored manly identity. Middle-class Americans began to celebrate the "self-made man," and male traits considered selfish and dangerous by earlier generations were now considered essential to national economic expansion.

Describing this ideal of marketplace manliness as "self-made" served the needs of middle-class men at the time. It consciously distanced middle-class manliness from aristocratic notions of ascribed status or birthright, while also grounding it in achievements other than landownership or craft, both of which were threatened or made more difficult by urbanization and industrialization. As economic success became increasingly dependent on often anonymous and unpredictable market forces, men of the emerging middle class could ground their manhood in their own agency and focus on developing inner resources of initiative and self-control.

While marketplace manhood substituted independence and autonomy for community-bound duty, it did not condone amoral or unethical behavior. But because it helped remove traditional communal restraints on male behavior and subjected men to temptations on a daily basis, middle-class Americans feared that marketplace manhood could potentially undermine the social and moral order. As they constructed the negative male image of the "confidence man" to reflect these concerns, they developed two major ideological supports to provide marketplace manhood with the necessary moral grounding. The first was the concept of character, defined as the capacity for voluntary self-control. Whereas previous generations had primarily relied on communal restraints to discipline behavior, the marketplace man was to internalize communal mores. Based on this concept, Victorian men found a balance between acquisitive individualism and civilized restraint. Character distinguished the man who had successfully combined communal moral standards, republican civic virtue, and productive, acquisitive habits into a unified self. As the moral cornerstone of marketplace manhood, the character ideal proved especially advantageous to the members of the emerging middle class, justifying their individual pursuit of economic gain while assuring them that this conduct was compatible with notions of self-sacrifice and self-restraint.

The second moral support for marketplace manhood was the ideology of separate spheres, which conceptualized the private sphere of the home (governed by the pious wife and mother) as an essential counterforce to the amoral marketplace. The ideology of separate spheres represented the home as a social space governed by Christian piety and moral purity where men could regain strength in conscience, moral resolve, virtue, and sincerity. Although the ideology of separate spheres implied a critique of market values, it actually coordinated the public conduct of men with the requirements of the marketplace and the rules of commodity capitalism. By offering guidelines of conduct that enabled men to offer themselves up for public scrutiny, examination, and assessment of their trustworthiness by others, the ideology of separate spheres provided ways to legitimize acquisitive impulses that were otherwise looked upon with suspicion and distrust. In short, the ideology of separate spheres enabled a notion of male individualism that followed the rules of capitalist exchange and market relations.

Transforming Marketplace Manhood in the Twentieth Century

By the late nineteenth century, the continuing effects of the market revolution prompted the rise of large corporations and the expansion of bureaucratic structures in both the public and private sectors. These developments, in turn, transformed marketplace manhood. With the corporatization and bureaucratization of the private and public sectors of U.S. society, economic activities previously regulated by market forces became subject to organization and regulation by private corporations and—during the Progressive Era, the New Deal, and both world wars—attempts at government planning. These changes made articulations of manliness less contingent on market forces and more on performance and the mastery of interpersonal skills within corporate and bureaucratic structures. As a result, the man seeking economic success in the twentieth century relied less and less on internally wrought character, and more and more on externally directed personality and salesmanship.

This new style of marketplace manhood became the object of periodic criticism throughout the twentieth century. Amid the economic boom that followed World War II, Arthur Miller's play *Death of a Salesman* (1949) suggested that notions of manhood grounded in personality tragically undermined, rather than bolstered, masculine identity, and William H. Whyte's *The Organization Man* (1956) argued that the pursuit of economic success in a corporate setting destroyed the independence and creativity that constituted true manhood.

During the 1980s and early 1990s, as President Ronald Reagan celebrated entrepreneurial manhood, and as he and his successor George H. W. Bush pursued strongly probusiness policies, such critiques continued. The film *Wall Street* (1987) suggested that success in the stock market rested on a hypermasculine ruthlessness and amorality, while *Regarding Henry* (1991) tells the story of a man who, losing his aggressive masculine identity after suffering a debilitating head injury, finds greater happiness and the respect of others through the formation of a new and more sensitive style of manhood. But the ongoing American celebration of capitalism has kept marketplace manhood at the center of American definitions of masculinity into the early twenty-first century.

BIBLIOGRAPHY

Barker-Benfield, G. J. *The Horrors of the Half-Known Life: Male Attitudes toward Women and Sexuality in Nineteenth-Century America.* 1976. Reprint, New York: Routledge, 2000.

Coontz, Stephanie. *The Social Origins of Private Life: A History of American Families, 1600–1900.* New York: Verso, 1988.

Haltunen, Karen. *Confidence Men and Painted Women: A Study of Middle-Class Culture in America, 1830–1870.* New Haven, Conn.: Yale University Press, 1982.

Keayne, Robert. *The Apologia of Robert Keayne; The Last Will and Testament of Me, Robert Keayne, All of It Written with My Own Hands and Began by Me, Mo: 6:1:1653, Commonly Called August; The Self-Portrait of a Puritan Berchant.* Edited by Bernard Bailyn. Gloucester, Mass.: P. Smith, 1970.

Kimmel, Michael. *Manhood in America: A Cultural History.* New York: Free Press, 1997.

Leverenz, David. *Manhood and the American Renaisssance.* Ithaca, N.Y.: Cornell University Press, 1989.

Sellers, Charles. *The Market Revolution: Jacksonian America, 1815–1846.* New York: Oxford University Press, 1991.

FURTHER READING

Barney, William L. *The Passage of the Republic: An Interdisciplinary History of Nineteenth-Century America.* Lexington, Mass.: D.C. Heath, 1987.

Franklin, Benjamin. *Benjamin Franklin's Autobiography: An Authoritative Text, Backgrounds, Criticism.* Edited by J. A. Leo Lemay and P. M. Zall. New York: Norton, 1986.

Kasson, John F. *Rudeness and Civility: Manners in Nineteenth-Century Urban America.* New York: Hill and Wang, 1990.

Miller, Arthur. *The Death of a Salesman.* 1949. Reprint, New York: Penguin Books, 1999.

Rotundo, E. Anthony. *American Manhood: Transformations in Masculinity from the Revolution to the Modern Era.* New York: Basic Books, 1993.

Ryan, Mary P. *Cradle of the Middle-Class: The Family in Oneida County, New York, 1790–1865.* Cambridge, England: Cambridge University Press, 1981.

Whyte, William H. *The Organization Man.* 1956. Reprint, Philadelphia: University of Pennsylvania Press, 2002.

Related Entries

Advice Literature; Body; Breadwinner Role; Capitalism; Confidence Man; Cult of Domesticity; Individualism; Industrialization; Middle-Class Manhood; Republicanism; Self-Control; Self-Made Man; Sentimentalism; Success Manuals; Urbanization; Victorian Era

—*Thomas Winter*

Marlboro Man

The Marlboro Man is one of the most universally recognized and widely promoted icons of twentieth-century American masculinity. Initiated as part of a cigarette marketing campaign by the Philip Morris company in 1954, the Marlboro Man exemplifies one of the most successful brand promotions in American advertising history. In his most enduring incarnation, he is a strong, independent cowboy with chiseled facial features; his mastery of nature and the western landscape is symbolized by his horse and his ever-present cigarette. The Marlboro Man serves as a visual embodiment of Frederick Jackson Turner's theory that the frontier fostered an American character of rugged manhood and individualism.

The Marlboro brand was originally launched in 1924 as a women's cigarette with the slogan "as mild as May," but Philip Morris repackaged Marlboro in 1954 to counter the prevailing notion that the newly added filters were feminine and tasteless. In doing so, advertiser Leo Burnett drew directly upon the cowboy as "the most generally accepted symbol of masculinity in America" (Burnett, 42). Nevertheless, in a postwar capitalist economy that some Cold War commentators argued made men and the nation soft, early Marlboro advertisements depicted not just wranglers, but also confident males in various professional roles—always with tattoos on the backs of their hands—in order to convey an image of masculine toughness and success. Sales of the brand accelerated after the 1963 "Come to Marlboro Country" campaign, which featured the musical score from the 1960 Western film *The Magnificent Seven.* These ads enshrined the stoic and robust cowboy in his rough western terrain as the company's enduring symbol (replacing a diminutive hotel boy whose "call for Philip Morris" had been heard on the radio since the 1930s). It was this phase of the Marlboro Man campaign that allied the dangerous experience of smoking and the mythic romance of the western wilderness with the figure of the self-sufficient male. After the 1971 prohibition of broadcasting ads for cigarettes, the visual attractions of Marlboro Country

Marlboro Man billboard in San Francisco (c. 1980). The billboard's juxtaposition with its city setting and the men in business suits symbolizes the enduring appeal of the cowboy figure, which was fueled by the processes of urbanization and corporatization in twentieth-century America. (Courtesy of Peter Filene)

in billboards, print media, and promotions helped make Marlboro the best-selling cigarette in the world.

The iconic power of the Marlboro Man led anti-smoking groups to challenge the identification of smoking with male potency. In 1976, the year after Marlboro became the most popular cigarette in the United States, a British documentary called *Death in the West* juxtaposed Marlboro Man advertisements with six real cowboys from the American West who were dying from lung cancer caused by heavy smoking. Philip Morris sued to prevent the film's distribution, and it was not released in the United States until 1981. Such images of the dangers of smoking were magnified when the deaths by lung cancer of former Marlboro Men Wayne McLaren (in 1992) and David McLean (in 1995) were widely reported in the press. Litigation in the late 1990s required the removal of colossal images of the Marlboro Man from billboards across the country, while anti-tobacco billboards have parodied the Marlboro Man by using the phrase "Welcome to Cancer Country" and showing him with a drooping cigarette, with a warning label that reads: "Smoking Causes Impotence."

Despite these challenges, the Marlboro Man endures as a powerful symbol of male independence. Author Larry McMurtry has called him "a last survival of the Western male in the heroic mode" (McMurtry, 17). However, as changes in the public acceptance of smoking affect the romance of smoking, the meaning of this independence will continue to shift.

BIBLIOGRAPHY

Burnett, Leo. "The Marlboro Story: How One of America's Most Popular Filter Cigarettes Got That Way." *New Yorker*, November 15, 1958, 41–43.

Carrier, Jim. "In Search of the Marlboro Man." *Denver Post*, 13–16 January 1991.

———. "Death of a Salesman: Marlboro Man Bows Out." *Denver Post*, 26 August 1996.

Elliot, Stuart. "Uncle Sam Is No Match for the Marlboro Man." *New York Times*, 27 August 1995.

Kluger, Richard. *Ashes to Ashes: America's Hundred-Year Cigarette War, the Public Health, and the Unabashed Triumph of Philip Morris*. New York: Knopf, 1996.

Lohof, Bruce A. "The Higher Meaning of Marlboro Cigarettes." *Journal of Popular Culture* 3 (Winter 1969): 441–450.

McMurtry, Larry. "Death of the Cowboy." *New York Review of Books*, 4 November 1999, 17–18.

FURTHER READING

Twitchell, James B. "The Marlboro Man: The Perfect Campaign." In *20 Ads that Shook the World*. New York: Crown, 2000.

RELATED ENTRIES

Advertising; Cold War; Consumerism; Cowboys; Health; Heroism; Individualism; Self-Control; Self-Made Man; Strenuous Life; Western Frontier; Westerns

—*Timothy Marr*

MARRIAGE

For most of American history, manhood has been closely linked to, and often identified with, marriage. Men's rights and responsibilities as husbands have reflected and reinforced their position in society, and only in the late twentieth century did men in the United States begin to define masculinity apart from marriage.

Colonial America

Marriage was essential to constructions of manhood from the earliest days of European settlement. Colonial Americans regarded the family as a microcosm of society—just as the colonies were under the governance of a monarch, so the family was under the guidance of the male head of the household. It followed, then, that the colonial family was a patriarchy in which men wielded the ultimate authority. The father/husband represented the family's interests in politics, held title to the family's property, and claimed legal guardianship over the children. But men also bore the ultimate responsibility for the family's welfare. Although, in practice, all members of the family contributed to the household economy, the final responsibility for providing for the family fell to the husband, as did the duties of leading the family in worship and providing religious and moral instruction. Marriage, then, was both the source of a man's status in his own community and the arena in which men learned to assert the authority that they possessed in colonial society.

Court records suggest that colonial Americans, recognizing marriage as central to manhood, took marital responsibilities seriously. A man could be fined or jailed for failure to support his family or for his wife's infidelity, which was viewed as a sign that a husband had failed to control his wife. Court records also suggest that, although married men were expected to temper their authority with affection, they occasionally resorted to force to maintain their dominance within marriage. Wives regularly appeared in court to testify to their husbands' verbal and physical abuse.

Revolutionary America

In the late eighteenth century, married men's claims to authority were both challenged and confirmed. Increasingly, married men were encouraged to seek affection rather than exert authority within marriage. At the same time, however, husbands continued to function as the political representatives of the family, and their role as providers increased in importance.

The colonists' political revolution against the monarchy sparked a cultural revolution against patriarchy. The republican ideology that underlay the American Revolution encouraged Americans to view marriage not as a relationship between a stern but kindly patriarch and a loving and submissive wife, but rather as a relationship between equals—one that could prepare the inhabitants of the new nation to take their place in society as citizens rather than as subjects.

New trends in religion, particularly Christianity, also affected ideas about marriage and manhood. The religious awakenings of the eighteenth and early nineteenth centuries legitimated the open expression of emotions and encouraged Americans to invest themselves in their personal relationships. As pastors in evangelical churches emphasized Jesus' love and self-sacrifice, they encouraged married men to follow Christ's example in their interactions with their wives.

Even as married men's traditional bases of authority were eroded by transformations in politics and religion, however, other developments offered them new opportunities for dominance. The rise of industrial capitalism gave men unprecedented opportunities to advance their economic interests, while the concomitant decline in household production increased wives' dependence on their husbands for financial support.

The advent of westward migration made men's role as providers even more pivotal. In the name of advancing the family's fortunes, many men severed their ties with neighbors and kinfolk, isolating their wives and giving themselves a new freedom away from the community oversight that often had functioned to restrict married men's power over their wives.

Men entered the nineteenth century, then, with conflicting expectations for marriage and manhood. The "companionate ideal" urged married men to relinquish their claims to authority and seek happiness in a relationship of mutual love and respect. Yet at the same time, men retained power in politics and in finance—both of which took on new importance in a democratic nation that celebrated the "self-made man."

Antebellum America

For many men in antebellum America, marriage and manhood must have seemed both mutually reinforcing and mutually exclusive. Married men displayed their masculinity by being both affectionate husbands at home and successful wage-earners at work, but companionship and breadwinning often proved to be conflicting rather than complementary roles. Divorce cases, which were increasingly common in the years between the American Revolution and the Civil War, revealed a persistent tension between financial support and companionship in the lives of married men.

The prominent Virginian William Wirt, for instance, found that his success as a lawyer and politician exacted a heavy price in his relationship with his wife, Elizabeth, who resented the time and attention that her husband lavished on his career. Husbandly affection and manly authority vied with each other for dominance in other ways, as well. When Wirt found his attempts to achieve the companionate ideal less than satisfying, he asserted his authority as the head of the household, now buttressed by his centrality as the family's chief support.

If even elite men found it difficult to achieve the Janus-faced ideal of manhood in marriage—being both companion and breadwinner—less fortunate men found it even more so. Denied the ability to provide for their wives (or even to protect them from physical and sexual abuse) male slaves affirmed their manhood by providing their families with material goods (by hunting, fishing, trapping, and woodworking). During the Civil War, many served as soldiers in the Union Army, an activity that afforded them the opportunity both to gain their freedom and to support their families with their earnings.

Working-class men also struggled to exercise masculine authority within marriage. In the uncertain economic atmosphere of the early nineteenth century, few working-class men were able to provide for their families. Some frustrated husbands deserted their wives when confronted by their inability to support them, which they equated with a loss of manhood. For others, patterns of domestic violence revealed both working-class husbands' inability to function as breadwinners and the crude manner in which some asserted their male authority—with their fists.

Victorian America

The period between the Civil War and the beginning of the twentieth century witnessed a reaffirmation of an equation of marriage, work, and citizenship—all of which were deemed necessary to manhood—as well as attempts to extend this definition of masculinity to groups other than white middle-class Protestants.

Emancipation offered African-American men both new possibilities and new pressures to adhere to prevailing ideals of married manhood. Representatives of the Freedmen's Bureau, the government agency responsible for facilitating the transition from slavery to free labor, encouraged African-American

This 1848 marriage certificate identifies marriage with masculine completeness, reflects the companionate standards that shaped Victorian notions of the ideal middle-class husband, and, through its call for male "benevolence" and the bride's downward gaze, suggests the dominance of the male in the marital relationship. (From the collections of the Library of Congress)

men to conform to white middle-class ideals of manhood by adopting both legal marriage and the ideal of the male breadwinner. The link between married manhood and virtuous citizenship was reinforced by the adoption in 1868 of the Fourteenth Amendment (1868), which guaranteed civil rights to all free men by inserting the word *male* into the Constitution as part of the definition of citizenship, thereby ensuring that husbands were the political representatives, as well as the primary providers, of their households.

The U.S. government also promoted an ideal of manhood in which work and marriage were vital components of (male) citizenship in its dealings with Native Americans and Mormons. The Dawes Severalty Act of 1887 encouraged Native Americans to adopt monogamous marriage with a male breadwinner by allotting land to male heads of households, who thereby became both U.S. citizens and the primary providers for their families. The federal government's dogged harassment of the Church of Jesus Christ of Latter-day Saints for its sanction of polygamy likewise reflected the prevalent conviction that monogamous marriage was necessary to both ideal manhood and good citizenship.

Twentieth-Century America

In the early twentieth century, marriage and manhood in the United States were reshaped by sweeping changes in American society, including greater geographical mobility and the rise of a consumer culture that seemed to offer individuals wider opportunities for fun and fulfillment, as well as increased isolation and anomie. The ideal of companionate marriage experienced a wave of renewed popularity as experts advised both men and women to look to marriage for personal (including sexual) gratification. Yet despite these avowedly modern desires for excitement and passion, married men's responsibilities as breadwinners persisted in modern America.

The upheavals of the Great Depression, World War II, and the Cold War challenged men's ability to provide for their families, but they reinforced, rather than eliminated, the ideal of the male breadwinner. New Deal policies supported male authority and female dependence in marriage by increasing penalties for married men's nonsupport of their families, sanctioning discrimination against married women in the workplace, and creating a two-tier welfare state in which men enjoyed entitlements and women and children were cast as needy dependents.

Wartime policies also promoted an ideal of marriage based on a male breadwinner–female homemaker model. World War II propaganda portrayed women's defense work as a temporary aberration—and the war itself was portrayed as a defense of the "traditional" family consisting of a domestic wife and a breadwinning husband. The G.I. Bill of 1944 created additional entitlements for men as husbands and heads of households, including education, job training, and assistance in purchasing homes, and in 1948 the federal income tax pioneered the joint return for married couples, which rewarded marriage but penalized working wives.

In Cold War America, the association between manhood and marriage was strengthened by cultural prescriptions for family togetherness and paternal authority—as exemplified by such popular television programs as *Father Knows Best* (1954–63) and *Leave It to Beaver* (1957–63)—and by a national tendency to look to the home for satisfaction and security in an age of fear and uncertainty. Working-class men's ability to adhere to the standards of married manhood was enhanced by the adoption of a "family wage" by employers such as the Ford Motor Company. In 1965 the now infamous report by Daniel Patrick Moynihan, entitled *The Negro Family: The Case for National Action,* stigmatized allegedly "matriarchal" (female-headed) black families as the source of a "tangle of pathology" in the inner cities, thus reinforcing the links between marriage and manhood and asserting the necessity of both in maintaining (white) middle-class American values.

Contemporary America

But even as the family's centrality in American culture seemed to have reached its ascendancy, marriage began to lose its importance for defining manhood. Beginning in the mid–twentieth century, social critics began to call attention to the costs to men's health and happiness inherent in the breadwinner ethic. The miseries of middle management and the hazards of heart disease ushered in a series of rebellions against this ethic—from pop psychologists' enthusiasm for personal growth to *Playboy* magazine's idealization of bachelorhood—and also corresponded with a rise in the national divorce rate.

At the same time, economic change during the late twentieth century forced increasing numbers of married couples to rely on dual incomes, while the resurgence of feminism prompted criticism of the sole-breadwinner model of married manhood. It had become clear to commentators on both the left and the right of the political spectrum (the former blaming the changing economy, the latter the women's movement) that men were no longer able to base their social status on their incomes. As men lost their authority as breadwinners, they also lost their investment in marriage, and they began to define masculinity apart from, rather than within, matrimony. In a headlong "flight from commitment," men rushed to define themselves in terms of sexual prowess rather than marital responsibilities.

At the dawn of the twenty-first century, the link between marriage and manhood is tenuous at best. While some men have responded to the disappointments of the workplace and the challenges of feminism by devoting themselves to egalitarian marriages, others have rejected matrimony to seek individual fulfillment as carefree bachelors (or, less charitably, as "deadbeat dads"), while still others, such as members of the evangelical Christian organization Promise Keepers, seek to reinvigorate traditional definitions of married manhood. Men in contemporary America find themselves in a society in which definitions of manhood, now severed from marriage, are shifting and contested.

BIBLIOGRAPHY

Cott, Nancy F. *Public Vows: A History of Marriage and the Nation.* Cambridge, Mass.: Harvard University Press, 2000.

Daniels, Christine, and Michael V. Kennedy, eds. *Over the Threshold: Intimate Violence in Early America.* New York: Routledge, 1999.

Ehrenreich, Barbara. *The Hearts of Men: American Dreams and the Flight from Commitment.* Garden City, N.Y.: Anchor Press, 1983.

Gerson, Kathleen. *No Man's Land: Men's Changing Commitments to Family and Work.* New York: Basic Books, 1993.

Gutman, Herbert G. *The Black Family in Slavery and Freedom, 1750–1925.* New York: Random House, 1976.

Jabour, Anya. *Marriage in the Early Republic: Elizabeth and William Wirt and the Companionate Ideal.* Baltimore: Johns Hopkins University Press, 1998.

May, Elaine Tyler. *Homeward Bound: American Families in the Cold War Era.* New York: Basic Books, 1999.

Stansell, Christine. *City of Women: Sex and Class in New York, 1789–1860.* New York: Knopf, 1986.

Wilson, Lisa. *Ye Heart of a Man: The Domestic Life of Men in Colonial New England.* New Haven, Conn.: Yale University Press, 1999.

FURTHER READING

Faludi, Susan. *Stiffed: The Betrayal of the American Man.* New York: William Morrow, 1999.

Fliegelman, Jay. *Prodigals and Pilgrims: The American Revolution against Patriarchal Authority.* Cambridge, England: Cambridge University Press, 1982.

Gordon, Linda. *Heroes of Their Own Lives: The Politics and History of Family Violence.* New York: Viking, 1988.

Griswold, Robert L. *Family and Divorce in California, 1850–1890: Victorian Illusions and Everyday Realities.* Albany: State University of New York Press, 1982.

Lewis, Jan. *The Pursuit of Happiness: Family and Values in Jefferson's Virginia.* Cambridge, England: Cambridge University Press, 1983.

May, Elaine Tyler. *Great Expectations: Marriage and Divorce in Post-Victorian America.* Chicago: University of Chicago Press, 1980.

Mink, Gwendolyn. *The Wages of Motherhood: Inequality in the Early Welfare State, 1917–1942.* Ithaca, N.Y.: Cornell University Press, 1995.

Rotundo, E. Anthony. *American Manhood: Transformations in Masculinity from the Revolution to the Modern Era.* New York: Basic Books, 1993.

Wall, Helena M. *Fierce Communion: Family and Community in Early America.* Cambridge, Mass.: Harvard University Press, 1990.

Weiss, Jessica. *To Have and to Hold: Marriage, the Baby Boom, and Social Change.* Chicago: University of Chicago Press, 2000.

RELATED ENTRIES

African-American Manhood; American Dream; American Revolution; Bachelorhood; Breadwinner Role; Citizenship; Civil War; Cold War; Emancipation; *Father Knows Best;* Great Depression; *Leave It to Beaver;* Men's Movements; Middle-Class Manhood; Native American Manhood; New Deal; Patriarchy; *Playboy* Magazine; Promise Keepers; Republicanism; Self-Made Man; Slavery; Work; Working-Class Manhood; World War II

—*Anya Jabour*

MARTIAL ARTS FILMS

Although martial arts films have received comparatively little critical attention, they reflect widely shared American perceptions of a mysterious, and often stereotyped, Orient, and of Asian masculinity. Distinct from American action films in their focus on physical performance rather than characterization and narrative, martial arts films showcase near-mystical fighting skills that have been gradually separated from their original cultural context and associated with protagonists from different cultures. The martial arts hero's transition from Chinese revolutionary to American action star reflects evolving attitudes in the United States toward Asian manhood—and about masculinity in general.

Although American film and literature have traditionally constructed a feminized Asia that offers exotic delights to Western men, white Americans have been uneasy about Asian masculinity ever since their xenophobic reactions to the late-nineteenth-century influx of Chinese laborers. This reaction featured images of the so-called Yellow Peril, in which allegories of cultural contamination cast Asian males as rapists threatening white women (who embodied Western culture). Mainstream Americans were typically intrigued by Asian men as long as they were feminized, emasculated, and incapable of the cultural "rape" associated with the Yellow Peril. Thus, American films have generally represented Asian males either as demonized villains or as desexualized, amiable, and non-threatening allies.

Although glimpses of the martial arts can be seen in American film since the 1940s, true martial arts movies made their first significant impact in the United States in 1973, when a wave of kung fu movies produced in Hong Kong met with unprecedented box-office success. Most scholars agree that their sudden popularity was a response to U.S. failure during the Vietnam War. The spectacle of a physically small Asian male defeating seemingly insurmountable odds—of an Asian masculinity characterized by quasi-mystical fighting prowess—represented a way of coming to terms with a perceived failure of American masculinity and military might in Vietnam. In an atmosphere increasingly open to Asian religions and philosophies and distrustful of the U.S. government, martial arts films of the 1970s offered disaffected American males a countercultural heroic model.

The early 1970s martial arts hero, embodied by Bruce Lee in films such as *The Chinese Connection* (1973) and *Fists of Fury* (1973), resembled the rebel males who dominated American films of the 1960s and 1970s in that he was hot-headed, impulsive, and resistant to tyranny. Martial arts films were at first marketed primarily to urban minority audiences, playing in inner-city theaters alongside blaxploitation films (a low-budget action genre featuring black protagonists and marketed to African-American audiences). The genre's appeal to minority viewers is understandable: it featured nonwhite protagonists battling imperialist or invading

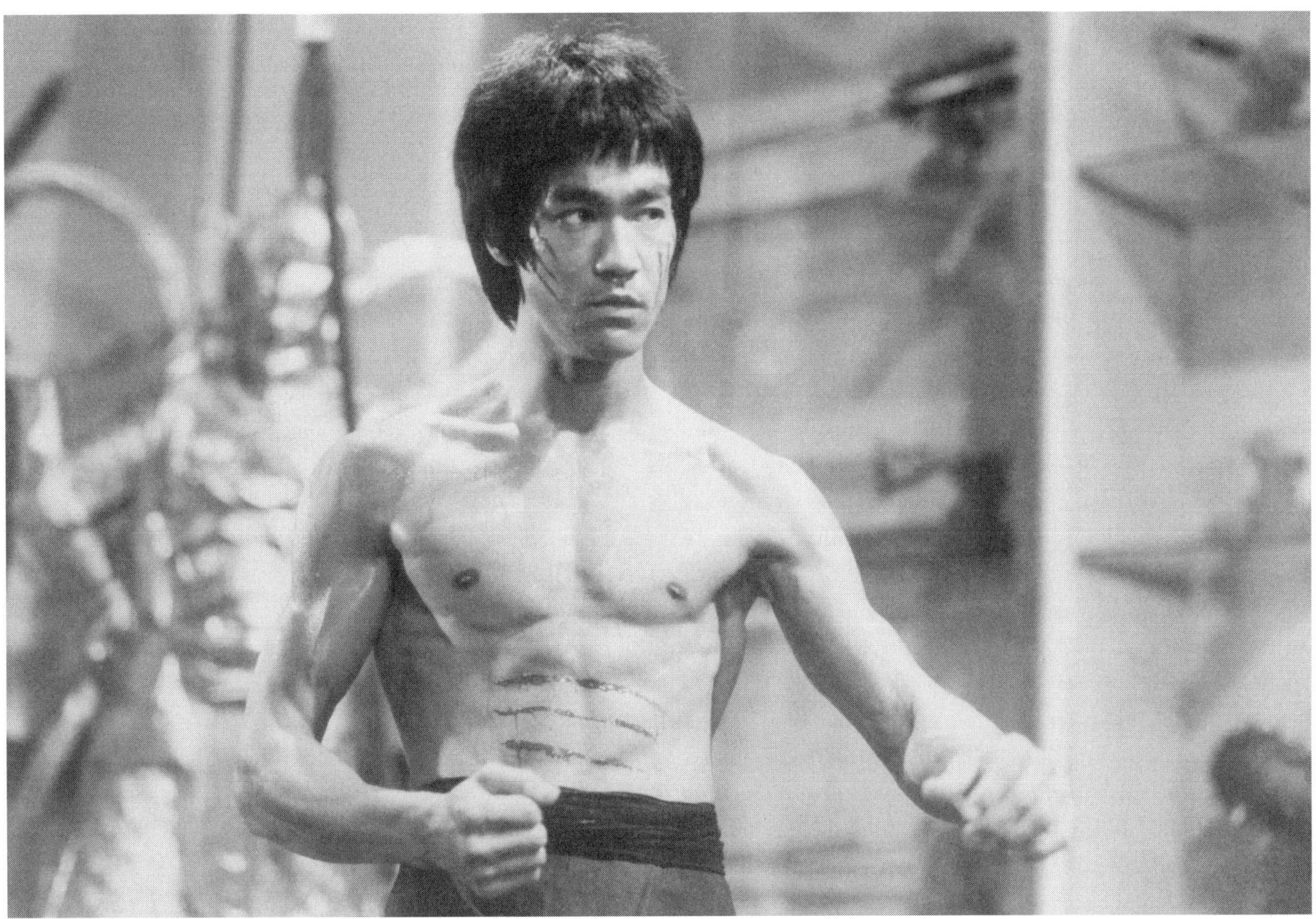

Achieving popularity during the 1970s, martial arts films explained the perceived failure of American masculinity in Vietnam by attributing to Asian men a quasi-mystical fighting prowess. Bruce Lee's triumph over white opponents made marital arts films popular among African-American men, while his stereotypical asexuality contributed to his appeal among whites. (© *Bettmann/Corbis*)

forces, and often defeating white opponents. Soon, blaxploitation films, such as *Black Belt Jones* (1974), began featuring kung fu fights, co-opting the martial arts genre to provide audiences the fantasy of individual martial prowess overcoming cultural oppression.

As martial arts films began seeking and finding white audiences, a profound transformation occurred: The Asian male star became emasculated in order to render the genre palatable to the American public. The transition is clearest in Bruce Lee's *Enter the Dragon* (1973), the first martial arts film made by an American studio with a Hollywood budget, and now generally considered the definitive 1970s martial arts epic. No longer a rebel or revolutionary, Lee plays a British agent who infiltrates a military compound operated by an Asian radical. Lee's character is distinguished by his pacifism—he fights only as a last resort—and by his ascetic asexuality. While his black and Caucasian allies engage in various sexual encounters, Lee is shown meditating and honing his skills. The genre's desexualization of the Asian male increased with its popularity: Even the implicit sexuality of Lee's physical intensity disappeared in the films of Jackie Chan, the unassuming, comic performer who succeeded Lee as the pre-eminent Asian martial arts star.

Although the genre's popularity faded during the late 1970s, it rebounded and was co-opted by whites amid the conservative cultural climate of the 1980s during the administration of President Ronald Reagan. By this time, disillusionment over Vietnam had yielded to a new American nationalism and an increasing emphasis on American military might, especially among the young male demographic targeted by action films. White American karate champion Chuck Norris, who had first appeared as Bruce Lee's opponent in *Return of the Dragon* (1973), is largely responsible for the genre's revival. Norris's films changed the cultural context of the martial arts genre by introducing the white male as hero. The *Missing in Action* (1984, 1985) films, in particular, inverted the stereotypical paradigm of the martial arts film: Norris, schooled in the martial arts as part of his special forces training, returns to Vietnam to rescue prisoners of war, using Asian fighting techniques to defeat the Vietnamese and reasserting white American male dominance over Asia. In these films, Vietnam became a training ground for the white protagonist, rather than a place of subversive Asian power, and the physical feats themselves were presented in a radically different cultural context. Traditional American male action heroes—typically soldiers or policemen—now starred in martial arts films, with Asians confined to roles as villains to be vanquished, or as aging, desexualized masters who impart secrets to their more virile white charges.

The multicultural trend in late-twentieth-century American society generated both a revival of the Asian martial arts film and a revision of the genre's depiction of Asian masculinity and sexuality. Perhaps the most significant example has been Ang Lee's *Crouching Tiger, Hidden Dragon* (2000), which features an all-Asian cast, both male and female protagonists, conspicuous romance and sexuality, and narrative and production values far beyond those of traditional martial arts films. Although Asian female protagonists have long been a mainstay in Hong Kong films, they had largely been excluded from those released in the United States before *Crouching Tiger.* The film significantly revises the traditional martial arts film's desexualization of Asian men, for while the stereotypical chaste warrior who has renounced love in favor of duty is still present (in both male and female incarnations), the film is openly critical of this choice. In addition, the happy ending reunites the rebellious princess with her outlaw lover, thus placing the rebel male hero in a newly sexualized context. The popular and critical success of *Crouching Tiger, Hidden Dragon* may indicate a new openness to depictions of Asian maleness in martial arts films.

BIBLIOGRAPHY

Desser, David. "The Kung Fu Craze: Hong Kong Cinema's First American Reception." In *The Cinema of Hong Kong: History, Arts, Identity,* edited by Poshek Fu and David Desser. Cambridge, England: Cambridge University Press, 2000.

———. "The Martial Arts Film in the 1990s." In *Film Genre 2000: New Critical Essays,* edited by Wheeler Winston Dixon. Albany: State University of New York Press, 2000.

Fore, Steve. "Jackie Chan and the Cultural Dynamics of Global Entertainment." In *Transnational Chinese Cinemas: Identity, Nationhood, Gender,* edited by Sheldon Hsiao-peng Lu. Honolulu: University of Hawaii Press, 1997.

Hsing, Chün (Jun Xing). *Asian America Through the Lens: History, Representations, and Identity.* Walnut Creek, Calif.: AltaMira Press, 1998.

Teo, Stephen. *Hong Kong Cinema: The Extra Dimensions.* London: British Film Institute Publishing, 1997.

FURTHER READING

Meyers, Richard, Amy Harlib, Bill Palmer, and Karen Palmer. *From Bruce Lee to the Ninjas: Martial Arts Movies.* Secaucus, N.J.: Citadel, 1991.

Sarkar, Bhaskar. "Hong Kong Hysteria: Martial Arts Tales from a Mutating World." In *At Full Speed: Hong Kong Cinema in a Borderless World,* edited by Esther C. M. Yau. Minneapolis: University of Minnesota Press, 2001.

Skidmore, Max J. "Oriental Contributions to Western Popular Culture: The Martial Arts." *The Journal of Popular Culture* 25, no. 1 (1991): 129–148.

Tasker, Yvonne. *Spectacular Bodies: Gender, Genre, and the Action Cinema.* London: Routledge, 1993.

RELATED ENTRIES

Antiwar Movement; Asian-American Manhood; Body; Cold War; Ethnicity; Hollywood; Race; Reagan, Ronald; *Shaft*; Vietnam War

—*Anthony Wilson*

MASCULINE DOMESTICITY

Male domesticity emerged as a distinct aspect of male identity, particularly among white middle-class men, when the market revolution of the early nineteenth century began to separate social life into private and public spheres. As income-generating labor was removed from the home, and as the home became redefined as a place of consumption and child-rearing (both associated with women), middle-class articulations of manhood became differentiated into two aspects—domesticity and breadwinning—that were both oppositional and mutually dependent.

The separation of private and public spheres benefited men by creating a "private" domestic space devoid of economic, productive function, which assured men a place seemingly free of financial pressure and yet completely dependent on the support of a male provider. However, men also resisted, and sometimes even resented, this separation, for they perceived domestic life and its affectionate, sentimental characteristics as key components of male identity. After midcentury, middle-class men appear to have largely come to accept this separation, thus putting pressure on themselves to be breadwinners.

But by the early twentieth century, the predictable career paths and increasing leisure time provided by white-collar corporate jobs, combined with the onset of suburbanization, led middle-class men to take a renewed interest in domestic life. Changes in family life and gender roles, such as the rise of an ideal of the "companionate family," and of men as "companionate providers," as well as an emphasis on emotional and sexual fulfillment in marriage, involved men in at least some aspects of domestic life. Alongside these developments, home ownership was increasing and floor plans of houses became more open than previously, leading to a merging of male and female spaces and activities in the home. Publications such as Gustav Stickley's *The Craftsman* (1901–12) urged men to reintegrate domesticity into their definition of masculinity.

While the Great Depression increased pressure on men as wage earners, the New Deal helped ease the demands on men to provide for their families and plan for retirement (particularly through the Social Security Act of 1935), thus enabling them to take a greater interest in parenthood and family life. World War II and its aftermath further encouraged interest in masculine domesticity. During the war, public commentators blamed an increase in juvenile delinquency on the absence of fathers and urged paternal engagement as essential to national social stability. After the war, social scientists lent their support to arguments that the proper psychological and emotional development of children depended upon the domestic presence of men as fathers.

The 1950s witnessed a celebration of masculine domesticity as American men and women, confronted with the possibility of nuclear annihilation, sought security in family life and looked to paternal influence as a source of national strength. *Life* magazine declared 1954 the year of "the domestication of the American Man," and television shows such as *The Adventures of Ozzie and Harriett* (1952–66), *Father Knows Best* (1954–63), and *Leave It to Beaver* (1957–63) showed men as domestic, nurturing beings closely involved in child rearing. At the same time, however, television fathers also spent much less time at home than did the mothers, suggesting the continuing tension between male domesticity and the male breadwinner role. In real life, too, men continued to wrestle with conflicting obligations. For most men domesticity remained difficult to realize. While experts called on fathers to take their place at home, their roles and obligations as providers limited their ability to become active, involved parents.

The most convenient way for a man to be both manly and domestic, if not an involved parent, was to join "the age of do-it-yourself," as *Business Week* called the 1950s in its June 2, 1952 issue. By 1960 there were ten times as many privately owned homes as there had been at the end of the nineteenth century. As a result, Americans increasingly perceived the home as a public manifestation of a man's economic success, and home improvement became both an appropriate extension of men's role as providers and a way to reconcile the conflict between breadwinning and domesticity. Through do-it-yourself tasks, a confluence of suburbanization, growing homeownership, and consumerism, many men began to reintegrate manliness and domesticity.

In the 1960s and 1970s, several developments further encouraged men's attention to domestic tasks and involvement. The counterculture and the gay rights movement helped to destabilize notions of "natural" gender roles, while the feminist movement and the growing number of women in the workforce challenged the idea that public politics or breadwinning were exclusively male purviews. By the 1980s, a new generation of American fathers emerged far more at ease with showing affection and being involved with child rearing. Public acceptance of male domesticity had also crossed racial lines, as indicated by the highly successful *Cosby Show,* starring black actor Bill Cosby in the role of successful surgeon and domestic man. However, the 1980s witnessed both corporate downsizing and a rapid increase in low-income jobs, which, by threatening men's economic security as providers, increased the pressure they felt as breadwinners and complicated their domestic involvement.

Since the emergence of male domesticity as a distinct part of masculinity, men have enjoyed an ambivalent and at times conflicted relation to domesticity. Initially resenting the functional separation of private and public spheres, men came to accept this reorganization of gender roles over the course of the nineteenth century. During the first half of the twentieth century, with the onset of suburbanization and increasing home ownership, men rediscovered the domestic sphere as a masculine realm—a development encouraged and celebrated by the media. Although there was an increasing interest in fatherhood among American men, they also continued to find it problematic to become involved fathers. An expanding twentieth-century consumer culture offered a new outlet for the domestic longings of American men: do-it-yourself. The expansion of home-improvement store chains and the popularity of such television shows as *This Old House* (which premiered in 1979) and the satirical sitcom *Home Improvement* (1991–99) suggest that "Mr. Fix-it"—a man both involved in home life and providing for his family's welfare—seems to have become the most widespread and socially accepted manifestation of the domestic male.

Bibliography

Gelber, Steven M. "Do-It-Yourself: Constructing, Repairing and Maintaining Domestic Masculinity." *American Quarterly* 49, no. 1 (1997): 66–112.

Kimmel, Michael. *Manhood in America: A Cultural History.* New York: Free Press, 1996.

Marsh, Margaret. "Suburban Men and Masculine Domesticity, 1870–1915." In *Meanings for Manhood: Constructions of Masculinity in Victorian America*, edited by Mark C. Carnes and Clyde Griffen. Chicago: University of Chicago Press, 1990.

McCall, Laura. "'Not So Wild A Dream': The Domestic Fantasies of Literary Men and Women, 1820–1860." In *A Shared Experience: Men, Women, and the History of Gender,* edited by Laura McCall and Donald Yacovone. New York: New York University Press, 1998.

Mintz, Steven, and Susan Kellogg. *Domestic Revolutions: A Social History of American Family Life.* New York: Free Press, 1988.

Weiss, Jessica. "Making Room for Fathers: Men, Women, and Parenting in the United States, 1945–1980." In *A Shared Experience: Men, Women, and the History of Gender,* edited by Laura McCall and Donald Yacovone. New York: New York University Press, 1998.

Further Reading

Coontz, Stephanie. *The Social Origins of Private Life: A History of American Families, 1600–1900.* London: Verso, 1988.

Gelber, Steven M. *Hobbies: Leisure and the Culture of Work in America.* New York: Columbia University Press, 1999.

Griswold, Robert L. *Fatherhood in America: A History.* New York: Basic Books, 1993.

LaRossa, Ralph. *The Modernization of Fatherhood: A Social and Political History.* Chicago: University of Chicago Press, 1997.

May, Elaine Tyler. *Homeward Bound: American Families in the Cold War Era.* Rev. ed. New York: Basic Books, 1999.

Palmer, Phyllis. *Domesticity and Dirt: Housewives and Domestic Servants in the United States, 1920–1945.* Philadelphia: Temple University Press, 1989.

Rotundo, E. Anthony. *American Manhood: Transformations in Masculinity from the Revolution to the Modern Era.* New York: Basic Books, 1993.

Related Entries

Advice Literature; African-American Manhood; Arthur, Timothy Shay; Breadwinner Role; Bureaucratization; Cold War; *Common Sense Book of Baby and Child Care, The*; Consumerism; Cult of Domesticity; Divorce; Fatherhood; Father's Day; Fathers' Rights; Great Depression; *Home Improvement*; *Kramer vs. Kramer*; *Leave It to Beaver*; Leisure; Market Revolution; Marriage; Middle-Class Manhood; Momism; *Mr. Mom*; Nuclear Family; *Odd Couple, The*; Promise Keepers; Sentimentalism; Suburbia; Work; World War II

—*Thomas Winter*

Masturbation

From the colonial period to the present day, masturbation—popularly known as *onanism* throughout the nineteenth century—has been particularly associated with male sexual behavior. Over the centuries, the definition of masturbation has changed from a religious and moral framework to a physiological and psychological one. At the same time, attitudes toward masturbation have shifted from anxiety and fear—especially during the nineteenth century—to a more relaxed and accepting approach during the twentieth century.

Colonial Puritan ministers understood masturbation, as they did manhood, within a biblical framework of sin and salvation, and occasionally used the pulpit to condemn the sin of Onan (his wasting of seed, as described in the Old Testament). For clerics like Samuel Danforth, masturbation was a manifestation of deeper human corruption, though it was considered less egregious than sodomy. In his formulation, "self-pollution" was a form of fornication, not unlike adultery. It was less dangerous because it did not cause one to violate the social order, but it was still understood as immoral behavior.

By the early nineteenth century, warnings against masturbation began to stress the physical, as well as the moral, costs of masturbation. In his 1812 text *Medical Inquiries and Observations Upon the Diseases of the Mind,* the physician Benjamin Rush theorized that masturbation caused a stimulus that reverberated through the body and produced ailments by exhausting the nerves and other organs. Similarly, the beliefs of Jacksonian-era sex reformers emphasized the dangers of bodily stimulation in any form. Perhaps most fully articulated in Sylvester Graham's 1834 *A Lecture to Young Men,* the belief of most sex reformers was that stimulating one portion of the body would cause a "sympathetic" response in other organs; agitation of the genitals would thus cause disease throughout the body. While a few authors, such as the Reverend John Todd, retained some elements of European author Samuel A. Tissot's concern with the retention of semen, all of these writers grounded their thought on the physiological principles of bodily "sympathy." Whether framed as a fear of depleting precious semen or, more commonly, as a fear of exhausting the body of its energies through overstimulation, masturbation was believed to drain and weaken the body. Reformers believed that the depletion of mental energies could ultimately produce masturbatory insanity.

The nineteenth century, unlike the colonial period, witnessed a genuine preoccupation with the imagined dangers of masturbation. The transformations associated with the market revolution, such as the consumptive opportunities of an expanding urban economy, caused Jacksonian-era reformers such as Graham, Todd, William Alcott, Samuel B. Woodward, and O. S. Fowler to become strongly concerned about the depletion of bodily energies. Masturbation symbolized all the stimulating possibilities of the city. As new pressures on men to succeed in the marketplace created anxieties about the expenditure of sexual energies and semen, masculinity and sexual self-mastery became highly entwined. If a young man were to prevail in a highly competitive economy—and if a married man were to provide successfully for his wife and children, who themselves drained resources while remaining dependent on him—he would have to exercise great bodily restraint, hoarding his energies and sublimating his sexual urges into the world of work. In some ways, bachelorhood seemed the most desirable state for a man who wanted to succeed in this economy, though it was associated with the greatest temptations to engage in masturbation, and was thus a source of middle-class anxiety.

A new evangelical moral reform impulse also generated growing concern with young men's sexual self-indulgence. Although framed in scientific terms, the flood of texts that appeared in the 1830s and 1840s had a decidedly moral tone, and writers addressing masturbation helped construct a new ideal of sexual chastity and moral purity for young men. Paralleling the writings of temperance advocates, sex reformers stressed the risks of dabbling in sexual indulgence. Stopping men from masturbating, in their view, could also prevent them from engaging in licentious encounters with women. Just as teetotalers saw the first sip of alcohol as the gateway to alcoholism, sex reformers saw masturbation as the first step toward seduction and prostitution. In urging chastity on young men, these sex reformers had to combat increasingly pornographic urban mystery novels and male sporting magazines such as *The Rake, The Flash,* and *The Libertine.* Ironically, these authors may in fact have encouraged masturbation by presenting passages on the ravages of masturbation that bordered on sadomasochism.

By the late nineteenth century, such alarmist descriptions of masturbatory disease worked their way into the world of medicine, psychology, and popular culture. Popular health reformers such as John Harvey Kellogg prescribed complex regimens such as drinking hot water and urinating frequently in order to prevent irritations in the bowels and genitalia that might provoke masturbation. As late-nineteenth-century and early-twentieth-century writers described the sexual dangers attending puberty, they helped construct modern notions of adolescence—particularly male adolescence. The young insane masturbator was an exaggerated but influential image of the stormy adolescent. The psychologist Granville Stanley Hall, who published *Adolescence* in 1904, linked concern about masturbation to his philosophy of eugenics (the theory that human beings could be improved by selective breeding). According to Hall, energy during adolescence had to be preserved—or diverted from sexuality to play—to develop man into his most civilized state. If a young man yielded to sensual desires he would stunt his growth, and, by extension, the growth of his offspring and race.

In the twentieth century, various writers began to challenge Victorian-era fears surrounding masturbation. As Americans became more comfortable with consumption, self-fulfillment, and sexual expression, fears of self-indulgence waned. Writing in the first decade of the twentieth century, the English sexologist Havelock Ellis gained notoriety for his criticisms of Victorian chastity. As part of his wider valorization of sexual expression, Ellis saw masturbation as a healthy and acceptable way to achieve relaxation and sexual self-knowledge. If many early-twentieth-century Americans were not willing to go as far as Ellis in freeing sexual expression, the American embrace of sexuality does seem to have opened the door to autoeroticism as well.

Americans were forced to more fully acknowledge masturbation as a normal male behavior when Alfred Kinsey's 1948 report, *Sexual Behavior in the Human Male,* revealed masturbation to be widespread in the United States and nearly universal in young men. The advent of magazines like *Playboy,* which first appeared in 1953, further liberalized popular attitudes toward male sexual fulfillment (and probably encouraged male masturbation), as did the Sexual Revolution of the 1960s. However, masturbation is still taboo in many circles, and it is still feared as a gateway to dangerous sexual impulses.

BIBLIOGRAPHY

Barker-Benfield, G. J. *The Horrors of the Half-Known Life: Male Attitudes Toward Women and Sexuality in Nineteenth-Century America.* New York: Harper & Row, 1976.

Ellis, Havelock. *Studies in the Psychology of Sex.* New York: Random House, 1936.

Godbeer, Richard. "'The Cry of Sodom': Discourse, Intercourse, and Desire in Colonial New England." *William and Mary Quarterly* 3, no. 52 (1995): 259–286.

Graham, Sylvester. *A Lecture to Young Men.* Providence, R.I.: Weeden and Cory, 1834.

Hall, Granville Stanley. *Adolescence: Its Psychology and Its Relations to Physiology, Anthropology, Sociology, Sex, Crime, Religion, and Education.* 2 vols. New York: D. Appleton, 1904.

Kett, Joseph. *Rites of Passage: Adolescence in America, 1790 to the Present.* New York: Basic Books, 1977.

Kinsey, Alfred, Wardell B. Pomeroy, and Clyde E. Martin. *Sexual Behavior in the Human Male.* Philadelphia: W. B. Saunders, 1948.

Nissenbaum, Stephen. *Sex, Diet, and Debility in Jacksonian America: Sylvester Graham and Health Reform.* Westport, Conn.: Greenwood Press, 1980.

Reynolds, David S. *Beneath the American Renaissance: The Subversive Imagination in the Age of Emerson and Melville.* Cambridge, Mass.: Harvard University Press, 1988.

Rush, Benjamin. *Medical Inquiries and Observations Upon the Diseases of the Mind.* Philadelphia: Kimber and Richardson, 1812.

FURTHER READING

Abzug, Robert H. *Cosmos Crumbling: American Reform and the Religious Imagination.* New York: Oxford University Press, 1994.

Cohen, Patricia Cline. *The Murder of Helen Jewett: The Life and Death of a Prostitute in Nineteenth-Century New York.* New York: Knopf, 1998.

Rosenberg, Charles. *The Cholera Years: The United States in 1832, 1849, and 1866.* Chicago: University of Chicago Press, 1962.

Smith-Rosenberg, Carroll. "Sex as Symbol in Victorian America: An Ethnohistorical Analysis of Jacksonian America." In *Turning Points: Historical and Sociological Essays on the Family,* edited by John Demos and Sarane Spence Boocock. Chicago: University of Chicago Press, 1978.

Walters, Ronald G. *Primers for Prudery: Sexual Advice to Victorian America.* Englewood Cliffs, N.J.: Prentice Hall, 1974.

RELATED ENTRIES

Adolescence; Bachelorhood; Eugenics; Evangelicalism and Revivalism; Graham, Sylvester; Hall, Granville Stanley; Heterosexuality; Insanity; Kellogg, John Harvey; Market Revolution; Marriage; Middle-Class Manhood; *Playboy* Magazine; Pornography; Reform Movements; Seduction Tales; Self-Control; Self-Made Man; Temperance; Youth

—*Rodney Hessinger*

MEDICINE

Throughout much of the history of the United States, medicine has been intimately connected with ideas of masculinity. Physicians, the majority of whom have been men, have often embodied ideas of masculine professionalism. In addition, definitions of health have been intertwined with masculine ideals, and physician advice about disease treatments has reflected and reinforced social, cultural, and political ideas about masculinity. The history of medicine reveals changing ideas about professional identity, masculine character, and the relationship between the two.

Early America

Much analysis of pre-nineteenth-century American medicine has centered on differences between the emerging medical profession in America and the established tradition practiced in Europe. While American medical structures were derived in some ways from their European predecessors, American physicians tended to define themselves in contrast to European doctors and men. This was most clearly articulated by Benjamin Rush, an elite physician and outspoken advocate for American medicine and masculinity. Identifying the vigor of American men with the vigor of the new nation itself, and encouraging American physicians to promote both, Rush advocated ideals of health that connected simple diets and avoidance of overstimulation with healthy American masculinity.

Although Rush was an influential figure, most physicians in early America lacked the social status and cultural authority that would later become central to the physician's masculine professional identity. Education, training, and extent of practice varied widely among American physicians, and the majority of them struggled to make a living. Like American men in other occupations, they derived much of their identity from local circumstances, such as their social and economic position in their families and communities. Beginning in this period, however, and continuing into the twentieth century, male physicians began extending their authority into the process of childbirth, gradually eclipsing the previously accepted authority of midwives.

The Nineteenth Century

In the early nineteenth century, American medicine reflected the antielitism characteristic of Jacksonian democracy, and a variety of physicians and other healers competed in an open marketplace. Both men and women articulated and promoted ideas about health, illness, and treatments for disease, often in explicitly gendered ways. Approaches to health and disease such as homeopathy and the "water cure" were described by their advocates and practitioners (often women) as gentle. In sharp contrast, however, was allopathic medicine, originally promoted by Benjamin Rush and the precursor of today's mainstream medicine. Consisting mainly of bloodletting, purgatives, and other aggressive therapies, it was commonly described as "heroic" and was an exclusively male domain until the mid–nineteenth century (the first woman graduated from an allopathic medical school in 1847).

As allopathic physicians sought to dominate the medical marketplace, they used their authority as men with expertise (as opposed to their later appeal to the cultural authority of science) to gain public authority. A number of them also began to present their opinions publicly, particularly in relation to issues of gender. Some physicians attempted to use biological arguments to support the "cult of domesticity," which defined men as suited to public activity and authority and women as best suited to domestic work. One physician, for example, argued against higher education for girls because of excessive loss of nervous energy during menstruation. (Ironically, the sharp division between male and female worlds in this time period actually helped some women become physicians by allowing them to claim that only women could modestly and appropriately treat other women.) The masculine ideals that permeated allopathic medicine in the late nineteenth century also shaped perceptions of the emergent nursing profession, as nurses (female practitioners) were viewed as helpmates to (male) physicians, reflecting the influence of the cult of domesticity.

Constructions of masculinity and male authority influenced the medical descriptions of diseases and the ways in which physicians prescribed therapeutics for illnesses. For example, although anesthesia was in common use for pain relief during operations by the mid–nineteenth century, soldiers, assumed to be models of masculine toughness, were often considered not to need it. Diagnoses and treatments of neurasthenia—a nervous disease described by physicians during the latter decades of the nineteenth century, and more typically noted among women than among men—were similarly gendered. Doctors attributed male neurasthenia to overwork and overstrain in a changing work environment, while female neurasthenia was seen as evidence that women were straining their nerves by overstepping their social roles. As the feminist Charlotte Perkins Gilman described in *The Yellow Wallpaper* (1899), in which an aspiring woman writer was confined by her husband and her physician to bed rest in an attic, physicians could use neurasthenia to reinforce middle-class Victorian gender norms.

Male physicians embraced medical history to help define and solidify their authority during the late nineteenth century. They used history to illustrate their connection to a chain of great ideas and important male figures, and typically portrayed physicians of the past as models of appropriate medical deportment—models often explicitly described in terms of heroism, reason, and skill. Physicians' practice of employing medical history to celebrate the authority of their own work within the march of medical and scientific progress would continue into the twenty-first century.

The Twentieth Century

By the late nineteenth and early twentieth centuries, physicians began to define medicine as a scientific activity and consolidate their professional identity around a scientific ideal. The invocation of science was based on the assumption that science was a masculine enterprise, characterized by a rational search to penetrate the unknown in nature. A number of American physicians obtained training in Europe and returned to the United States to spread the ideal of the rational scientist-physician. Sinclair Lewis articulated this new ideal in *Arrowsmith* (1925), a novel about a physician who becomes a hero in his search for scientific truth in the face of social and professional obstacles. Not coincidentally, the push toward scientific medicine in the early twentieth century worked to the advantage of the middle- and upper-class men who embraced this ideal, helping to establish medical practice as a marker of middle- and upper-class manhood. Conversely, it resulted in a significant decrease of medical training opportunities for women, minorities, and lower-class men. The changes in early-twentieth-century medicine, including a trend toward specialization, reflected a broader move during the Progressive Era toward an increasing reliance on expertise, growing bureaucratization, and concerns about efficiency.

By the mid–twentieth century, American physicians began to define themselves as not only scientific leaders, but also as experts in expanding medical technologies. Instead of simply providing advice and bedside therapeutics, physicians by the 1950s had a tremendous arsenal of technological interventions in the hospital setting. The expansion of cardiology, which provided diagnostic and therapeutic innovations such as electrocardiograms and cardiac surgery, exemplified the new technological medicine. Along with this incorporation of new technologies, assumptions about men influenced supposedly objective research questions and treatment protocols in the medical field. For example, medical and public discussions about heart disease and its treatment during the 1950s typically assumed that the sufferer would be a man, normally impervious to pain, who suddenly experiences crushing chest pain, usually while he is working hard on his job. When President Dwight Eisenhower suffered a heart attack in office in 1955, the public coverage that followed provided ample exposure of Eisenhower's cardiologist, further reinforcing the masculine identity of both physician and heart patient. This assumption about the link between men and heart disease was so strong that heart disease in women was not fully explored until the 1980s.

The longstanding association between medicine and male authority began to break down during the 1960s and 1970s. While the rational, scientific male technological expert was greatly lauded in popular culture in the 1950s, in the 1960s and 1970s the women's and civil rights movements, as well as the antiauthoritarian and antitechnological impulses accompanying the counterculture and anti–Vietnam War protests, began to challenge this ideal. Growing numbers of Americans looked to Asian and other "alternative" medical therapies, women began to call for more attention to female-specific medical issues, and an increasing number of women entered the field of medicine. As a result of these trends, the conventional public image of the male physician appeared antiquated, and it began to be supplanted by a newer, less patriarchal ideal. In addition, the examination by women physicians of supposedly objective research revealed a number of important gender biases. For example, when women activists protested the exclusion of women from clinical trials in the 1980s, investigators began broadening their horizons and found that heart disease is not just the result of "male" overwork, but is actually quite common in women. Further, the shift away from assumptions about men and heart disease allowed other investigators to see the frequency and consequences of depression (usually seen as a disease of women) in men after heart attack or cardiac surgery.

Future Directions in the Study of Medicine and Masculinity

Medicine, and the scholarly analysis of medicine, has changed in response to many of the social and cultural critiques about patriarchal physicians and inhumane medical practice. By the early twenty-first century, half of the medical school classes at top medical centers were occupied by women. Further, many physicians have sought better communication skills with patients, and humanistic training in fields such as bioethics are being actively taught in medical schools alongside more strictly scientific subjects. Still, there are significant areas (such as surgery) that remain dominated by men, by male assumptions about work patterns, and by traditional approaches to patients.

The changing gender dynamics of medicine and the growth of the history of medicine as an academic field within history have raised an awareness that, with only a few small exceptions, the field of medical history has not yet engaged with the new field of men's studies. Much work is needed to understand the historical and current connections among ideals of masculinity, physician identity, and assumptions about patients, including issues of class, race, and ethnicity. In a new medical era characterized by increased reference to biological differences between people (particularly in genetics), it is vital to understand the ways in which constructions of masculinity have been, and remain, connected to medicine.

Bibliography

Melosh, Barbara. *"The Physician's Hand": Work Culture and Conflict in American Nursing.* Philadelphia: Temple University Press, 1982.

Morantz-Sanchez, Regina Markell. *Sympathy and Science: Women Physicians in American Medicine.* New York: Oxford University Press, 1985.

Numbers, Ronald L., ed. *Medicine in the New World: New Spain, New France, and New England.* Knoxville: University of Tennessee Press, 1987.

Pernick, Martin S. *A Calculus of Suffering: Pain, Professionalism, and Anesthesia in Nineteenth-Century America.* New York: Columbia University Press, 1985.

Rosenberg, Charles E. *No Other Gods: On Science and American Social Thought.* Baltimore: Johns Hopkins University Press, 1976.

Further Reading

Fye, W. Bruce. *American Cardiology: The History of a Specialty and Its College.* Baltimore: Johns Hopkins University Press, 1996.

Numbers, Ronald L., and John Harley Warner. "The Maturation of American Medical Science." In *Sickness and Health in America,* edited by Judith Walzer Leavitt and Ronald L. Numbers. Madison: University of Wisconsin Press, 1997.

Schiebinger, Londa. *Nature's Body: Gender in the Origins of Modern Science.* Boston: Beacon Press, 1993.

Shryock, Richard Harrison. *The Development of Modern Medicine: An Interpretation of the Social and Scientific Factors Involved.* 1936. Reprint, Madison: University of Wisconsin Press, 1979.

Starr, Paul. *The Social Transformation of American Medicine.* New York: Basic Books, 1982.

Related Entries

Body; Cult of Domesticity; Health; Men's Studies; Professionalism; Progressive Era; Reproduction; Technology

—*Laura D. Hirshbein*

MEN AND RELIGION FORWARD MOVEMENT

Cofounded by Fred Smith and Henry Rood in September 1911 as a nationwide campaign, the Men and Religion Forward Movement (MRFM) emerged out of the cooperation between evangelical churches and religious agencies such as the Federal Council of the Churches of Christ, the Young Men's Christian Association, and the Presbyterian Labor Temple. The movement aimed to draw men to Christ and into church membership, as well as to remasculinize Christianity and evangelical churches and to diminish the role that women were increasingly playing in church affairs.

Although the movement never endorsed any political or civic-reform campaign, it adopted an agenda of issues shared by contemporary Social Gospel advocates and Progressive reformers, including social justice, wholesome recreation, better homes, and the elimination of prostitution and saloons. The MRFM was socially more conservative, however, appropriating these issues to promote its goal of remasculinizing evangelical churches. Furthermore, although the movement received support from such prominent women reformers as the settlement-house worker Jane Addams and the Salvation Army national commander Evangeline Booth, it never endorsed women's rights.

The MRFM resembled the "strenuous life" and "muscular Christianity" movements in that it sought to reinvigorate white, middle-class manhood and overturn nineteenth-century Victorian notions of private and public spheres and the "cult of domesticity." White middle-class men had begun to perceive women's longstanding pre-eminent role in church affairs as a problem in the late nineteenth century, when the transition from entrepreneurial to corporate capitalism, the emergence of a mass consumer society, and an intensifying women's rights movement undermined Victorian gender constructs. The movement's organizers hoped to counteract a perceived feminization of American Protestantism and generate a new gender matrix by remodeling evangelical Christianity and its churches through corporate capitalism's sales and advertising techniques, scientific management methods, consumerist appeal, and masculine patterns of control.

The movement ended in April 1912, having attracted more than one million men to meetings in seventy-six cities and more than one thousand towns. Even though it did not realize its goal of bringing three million men to Christ—15,000 fewer men joined a church in 1912 than in 1911—its success in other respects became apparent during the 1920s. In 1923 the Presbyterian Church's all-male general assembly disbanded the women's board. In 1924 the advertising executive Bruce Barton published his bestselling *The Man Nobody Knows*, which depicted the church as a corporate enterprise—and Christ himself as a corporate executive and a virile man. Furthermore, while 39.3 percent of church membership was male in 1906, it had increased to 41.8 percent by 1926.

The MRFM failed to achieve some of its goals, but it appears to have served as a catalyst for the early-twentieth-century shift in the gendered balance of power in U.S. Protestant churches. By attempting to combine masculine and evangelical Christian identities, moreover, it raised issues that remained salient throughout the twentieth century, and it may be considered a forerunner of late-twentieth-century Christian men's movements, such as the Promise Keepers.

BIBLIOGRAPHY

Bederman, Gail. "'The Women Have Had Charge of the Church Work Long Enough': The Men and Religion Forward Movement of 1911–1912 and the Masculinization of Middle-Class Protestantism." *American Quarterly* 41 (September 1989): 432–465.

Curtis, Susan. *A Consuming Faith: The Social Gospel and Modern American Culture.* Baltimore: Johns Hopkins University Press, 1991.

Hopkins, C. Howard. *History of the Y.M.C.A. in North America.* New York: Association Press, 1951.

FURTHER READING

Allen, L. Dean. *Rise Up, O Men of God: The Men and Religion Forward Movement and the Promise Keepers.* Macon, Ga.: Mercer University Press, 2002.

Messages of the Men and Religion Movement. 7 vols. New York: Association Press, 1912.

Smith, Fred B. *Men Wanted.* New York: Association Press, 1911.

———. *A Man's Religion.* New York: Association Press, 1913.

RELATED ENTRIES

Cult of Domesticity; Evangelicalism and Revivalism; Middle-Class Manhood; Muscular Christianity; Progressive Era; Religion and Spirituality; Social Gospel; Victorianism; Young Men's Christian Association

—*Thomas Winter*

MEN'S CLUBS

Since the early 1700s, American men of different classes, ages, races, and ethnicities have established men's clubs to foster conversation and debate, education, business relationships, athletic competition, and social service. Men's clubs have also provided refuge from the pressures of work and family. They are places where like-minded men have gathered to discuss, drink, gamble, and pursue business in private, often sumptuous, surroundings. Despite these varying purposes, all men's clubs achieve status for themselves and their members through exclusive membership practices, and they have been integral to their members' understandings of male identity.

America's earliest men's clubs, grounded in colonial-era and republican conceptions of manhood, promoted intellectual improvement, political awareness, civic spirit, public usefulness, social acumen, and business opportunity. Among these early clubs were the Junto, established by Benjamin Franklin in 1727 for weekly discussions on morals, politics, and natural philosophy, and the "State in Schuylkili," a Philadelphia eating and drinking club founded in 1732. In the late eighteenth and early nineteenth centuries, college students, disappointed by their curriculum and seeking to discuss issues in greater depth, established clubs such as Harvard's Hasty Pudding Club (1770) and Yale's Skull and Bones Society (1832), imagining them as places for the more rigorous pursuit of knowledge. Because of this educational focus, many early men's clubs built impressive private libraries in addition to their sometimes elaborate physical facilities.

For young men not in college, societies such as the Young Men's Christian Association (YMCA), first established in the United States in 1851, could substitute for a formal education by providing access to spirited discussion, debate, and camaraderie. In all such clubs, members were expected to cultivate good manners and begin friendships that would serve them later in life. This focus on cultivating useful relationships gave rise in the early twentieth century to clubs such as Rotary, Lions, and Kiwanis—all oriented toward professional, civic-minded men.

The nineteenth century was the great age for the formation of urban men's clubs, with New York City boasting an estimated five hundred such clubs by the 1920s. Many early clubs, such as New York City's Union, Century, Brook, and University Clubs; Washington, D.C.'s, Metropolitan and Cosmos Clubs; and San Francisco's Bohemian and Olympic Clubs, were established as dinner and discussion clubs. Members could, for an initiation fee and monthly dues, take advantage of such club amenities as large lounges, libraries, bars, theatrical spaces, exercise rooms, baths, billiard parlors, and sleeping accommodations. These amenities encouraged men to engage in the friendly competition, intellectual debate, and social intercourse that club members deemed essential to manliness.

As private spaces, men's clubs also allowed members to pursue behaviors restricted elsewhere, such as drinking, gambling, and bawdy humor, with relative freedom only limited by internal club conventions. Men's clubs thus represented places in which men could engage in behaviors and discuss topics otherwise inappropriate for mixed company. Believing that enacting these dimensions of manhood required a strongly homosocial setting, men's clubs tended to exclude women, inviting them to attend only for limited periods of time or on special occasions. At the same time, in an expression of the domestic longings that many middle-class men of the period associated with complete manhood, men's clubs strove through their furnishings and décor to duplicate a homelike environment. Because of their location in urban centers, close ties to particular professions, and exclusive membership practices, men's clubs mostly served white men and were segregated by economic class. These clubs, catering largely to the middle and upper classes, thus contributed to the process by which their members formed class- and race-based notions of masculinity.

For men of the working classes, local saloons often served the same function as the private men's clubs, becoming quasi-private enclaves where men of similar interests—and, usually, of similar racial and ethnic identities—could gather for drink and discussion. The informal collegiality of saloons represented an American variation of the Working Men's Clubs first established in England in the mid–nineteenth century. For American workingmen, the informal collegiality of the local saloon allowed similar kinds of manly associations to occur along closely aligned class and racial lines. Here again, friendly competition, intellectual exchange, and camaraderie were pursued alongside the vices of drink and gaming in a locale free from women—perhaps with the exception of prostitutes, who occasionally worked out of the saloons and served as another means by which male saloongoers might demonstrate their manliness.

While men's clubs still exist, their popularity has waned. In addition, their traditional emphasis on white homosociality was challenged in the twentieth century. During the Great Depression, fewer men were able to join such clubs, and beginning in the 1950s increasing suburbanization and the availability of entertainment within the home through television and radio removed some of the clubs' traditional social functions. By the late twentieth century, amid the growing impact of feminism and the civil rights and racial identity movements of the 1960s and 1970s, those men's clubs still in existence experienced an intensifying challenge to their status as bastions of privilege for white men. Men's clubs found themselves under increasing pressure to open their memberships to women and nonwhite men. Women were most instrumental in this respect, arguing that the exclusion of women from these clubs limited their ability to make important business contacts. In 1984, New York City passed Local Law 63 (an amendment to the city's Human Rights Law), which redefined private clubs as public accommodations so long as they have more than four hundred members, serve meals, and receive payments from nonmembers for business or trade. Private clubs meeting these criteria found themselves subject to discrimination claims from individuals denied membership on the basis of race or gender. Similar laws followed in many other cities. A 1987 Supreme Court decision allowed women to join Rotary International, where they now make up 11 percent of U.S. membership. Taken together, these developments have made men's clubs a disappearing breed. For working-class men, saloons have largely ceased to exist as exclusively male environments, particularly with the growing acceptance of women as social equals for whom visiting a bar is not seen as inappropriate.

Men's clubs have played a major role in the socialization and professionalization of American men, offering sanctuary from women and social pressures to behave in certain ways. While the variety of men's clubs is impressive, their tendency toward homogeneity and homosociality mark them as remnants of a different era.

Bibliography

Carnes, Mark C. *Secret Ritual and Manhood in Victorian America.* New Haven, Conn.: Yale University Press, 1989.

Hill, Frank Ernest. *Man-Made Culture: The Educational Activities of Men's Clubs.* New York: American Association for Adult Education, 1938.

Kingsdale, Jon M. "The 'Poor Man's Club': Social Functioning of the Urban Working-Class Saloon." In *The American Man,* edited by Elizabeth H. Pleck and Joseph H. Pleck. Englewood Cliffs, N.J.: Prentice Hall, 1980.

Leonard, John. "Breaking the Code." *Ms.* (July 1988): 90.

Rotundo, E. Anthony. *American Manhood: Transformations in Masculinity from the Revolution to the Modern Era.* New York: Basic Books, 1993.

Further Reading

Solly, Henry. *Working Men's Social Clubs and Educational Institutes.* New York: Garland, 1980.

Swiencicki, Mark A. "Consuming Brotherhood: Men's Culture, Style, and Recreation as Consumer Culture, 1880–1930." *Journal of Social History* 31 (1998): 773–808.

Related Entries

Class; Fraternal Organizations; Labor Movement and Unions; Male Friendship; Reform Movements; Republicanism; Working-Class Manhood; Young Men's Christian Association

—*Matthew R. Davis*

Men's Movements

Throughout the twentieth century, men have organized in response to social, cultural, and economic changes affecting conceptions of family, labor, and spirituality. Men's movements however, which are based primarily on issues of masculine identity, have been largely a phenomenon of the late twentieth century. Unlike such early-twentieth-century movements as "muscular Christianity" and the Men and Religion Forward Movement—whose purpose was to assert the virile nature of the Christian faith in response to a perceived feminization of American culture—men's movements of the late twentieth century specifically address themselves to the question of male identity.

The civil rights and liberation movements of the 1960s and 1970s prompted men to begin to organize explicitly on the basis of their identity as men. While some men's movements have been committed to gender equity and to an analysis of the social construction of masculinity, others have sought to renew the traditional claims of white heterosexual men in the public and private spheres. Additionally, while the black power and gay liberation movements raised issues of racial and sexual difference in relation to masculinity and male institutional privilege, the majority of men's movements have universalized their critique of manhood, basing these critiques upon the specific concerns and experiences of white, middle-class, heterosexual men. Although their philosophies and constituencies have differed, these movements have had a significant impact on the understanding of men and masculinity in the changing social and economic climate of the twentieth-century United States.

Feminism and the Men's Liberation Movement

The men's liberation movement emerged in the early 1970s as white, middle-class, college-educated heterosexual men responded to the challenges posed by the women's movement. During the second wave of feminism in the United States in the late 1960s and early 1970s, women launched a widespread critique of male dominance and the social impact of male violence and aggression. In response, some men began to question their own complicity with systems of domination and oppression, and also to explore the limitations that adherence to the male role placed on their own lives and experiences. Although the men's liberation movement acknowledged the negative impact of sexism on women, it was particularly concerned with the emotional and psychological toll traditional conceptions of masculinity exacted from men. Through workshops, newsletters, and "consciousness-raising" groups modeled on those of the women's movement, men questioned the association of masculinity with competitiveness and lack of emotional expressiveness. Books like Warren Farrell's *The Liberated Man* (1974) argued that men (as well as women) were oppressed by a gender system in which men were defined through their public success while restricted in their interpersonal relationships.

By the mid-1970s, the limited usefulness of an approach that focused on the personal costs of masculinity without the framework of a broader analysis of patriarchy was apparent. Responding to the feminist objection that men's liberation posed a false symmetry between men's and women's oppression, a group of men formed an increasingly separate movement, eventually distinguished as the "antisexist" or "profeminist" men's movement. In contrast to the men's liberationists, organizations such as the National Organization for Men Against Sexism (NOMAS) approached male domination and violence as systemic, rather than individual, problems. After the 1970s, the profeminist movement would be largely relegated to the academic community; the American Men's Studies Association (1991) and the *Journal of Men's Studies* (1992) would emerge out of this movement, along with the journal *Men and Masculinities* (1998). Through these institutions, a critical interest in the social and historical construction of masculinity would be encouraged and sustained.

Men's Rights and the Costs of Masculinity

By the late 1970s, the men's liberation movement was largely subsumed under the notion of men's rights. While men's liberationists believed that both men and women suffered under male dominance, men's rights activists considered men to be patriarchy's true victims. Herb Goldberg's *The Hazards of Being Male: Surviving the Myth of Masculine Privilege* (1976) was an early indication of this trend. Goldberg argued that it was men who paid the "costs of masculinity," suffering under social pressures to succeed and emotionally stunted by the imperative to repress their feelings. Dominance itself was constituted as a form of oppression, as the role imposed upon men took a physical and psychological toll evidenced in men's shorter life expectancy and higher rates of heart disease and suicide. As the men's rights discourse became more virulently antifeminist, men were claimed as the victims of traditionally feminist concerns such as domestic violence, pornography, prostitution, and sexist media stereotypes. A major rallying cry was the issue of fathers' rights. Insisting that men were unduly discriminated against in court custody battles, fathers' rights activists lobbied for changes in divorce laws. Organizations such as Men's Rights, Incorporated (1977) and the National Organization for Men (1983) emerged to argue that, while feminist "male-bashing" cast men as the oppressors, women actually wielded the most social power.

The Mythopoetic Men's Movement

Out of the 1970s focus on individual psychological well-being and the increasingly vocal emphasis on the costs (rather than privileges) of masculinity, there emerged the mythopoetic men's movement of the late 1980s and early 1990s. The mythopoets took from Jungian psychoanalysis the notion of essential archetypes conditioning masculine and feminine nature, and combined these with myths from a variety of cultures to produce a philosophy of American male identity and its contemporary ills. The mythopoetic movement eschewed any concrete social or political agenda, focusing instead on a therapeutic program of workshops, conferences, and wilderness retreats through which men who had become soft and unassertive in the face of feminist challenges and the lack of male role models could redress the wounds of masculinity and reconnect with a deep masculine essence. The notion of the "deep masculine" encompassed both traditionally masculine and feminine attributes; rejecting the sensitive male image as well as hypermasculine icons such as John Wayne, the mythopoets understood male aggression as a positive virtue, while also reclaiming nurturance and emotional expressiveness as virile masculine traits.

The most visible text of the mythopoetic movement was poet Robert Bly's best-selling *Iron John* (1990), which lamented that "male energy" was being eroded by industrialization, discredited by the violence of the Vietnam War, and attacked by misguided feminists who disapproved of aggressive behavior in men. According to Bly, industrialized society had deprived men of father figures by separating grown men from boys and consigning the latter to female-dominated homes and schools. In addition, wage labor, market competition, and an emphasis on instrumental rationality had denied them meaningful homosocial bonds and the experience of emotional communion. As an antidote, Bly encouraged men to take to the woods to revitalize their masculinity in the company of other men. These "wild-man weekends," which attracted the often derisive attention of the mass media, combined traditional Native American practices such as drumming circles and sweat lodges with poetry, storytelling, and personal testimonials. In their appropriation of native rituals and association of the outdoor wilderness with the reawakening of the wild man slumbering within the white middle-class professional, such retreats resonated with early-twentieth-century remedies for masculine softness.

Religious Men's Movements of the 1990s

By the mid-1990s, interest in the mythopoetic movement had started to wane, and two religiously informed men's movements took its place in the media spotlight. In October 1995, the Million Man March attracted over 800,000 African-American men to the Mall in Washington, D.C., to pray for "atonement." Co-organized by Louis Farrakhan, the leader of the Nation of Islam, and protesting institutionalized racism and the historical denial of manhood to African-American men, the march called upon those gathered to "stand up" as men and claim moral responsibility for, and leadership of, families and communities.

Two years later, in October 1997, another massive gathering of men descended upon Washington, D.C. These were the Promise Keepers, an overwhelmingly white movement led by former University of Colorado football coach Bill McCartney. Formed in 1990 and tracing its roots to Christian opposition to the feminist and gay liberation movements, the Promise Keepers claimed the participation of hundreds of thousands of men, who gathered together in football stadiums across the country to listen to sermons, sing, and pray. Despite their differences, the Million Man March and the Promise Keepers shared a dominant theme, proclaiming a widespread crisis resolvable only through the restoration of a religiously ordained masculine authority. The Promise Keepers were explicit in their diagnosis of society's ills as stemming directly from men's abdication of their rightful place at the head of the family. Like the muscular Christianity movement of the early twentieth century, which sought to revirilize the image of Jesus, the Promise Keepers sought to recast religious practice as a manly enterprise. The movement decried "sissified" men who would willingly repudiate their God-given authority, and, like the organizers of the Million Man March, issued a call for men to reclaim leadership roles both in public and in private while women returned to their natural care-giving functions as mothers and wives.

Continuity and Change

The notion of men demasculinized by social and economic changes such as industrialization and women's increasing role in the public sphere has enjoyed a long history. Responding specifically to the civil rights and liberation movements of the 1960s and 1970s, men's movements also echo the protests of privileged men across the century who have felt their authority to be under attack. Ultimately, the history of twentieth-century men's movements highlights two related but opposing tendencies: the understanding of masculinity, like femininity, to be a socially constructed rather than an essential identity; and the conviction that the denaturalization of masculinity and male authority is itself the source of contemporary social ills. This latter position (shared by anti-affirmative-action and white-supremacist groups) has resulted in the now frequent charge that white middle-class and upper-middle-class heterosexual men have become the most aggrieved victims of social, cultural, and economic change. Although interest in organized men's movements was waning by the late 1990s, this perception—as well as the ongoing critical interest in the social construction of masculinities—continues to impact the political and cultural landscape of the early twenty-first century.

BIBLIOGRAPHY

Bederman, Gail. *Manliness and Civilization: A Cultural History of Gender and Race in the United States, 1880–1917.* Chicago: University of Chicago Press, 1996.

Clatterbaugh, Kenneth. "Literature of the U.S. Men's Movement." *Signs: Journal of Women in Culture and Society* 25 (Spring 2000): 883–894.

Ehrenreich, Barbara. *The Hearts of Men: American Dreams and the Flight from Commitment.* New York: Anchor, 1984.

Kimmel, Michael, ed. *The Politics of Manhood: Profeminist Men Respond to the Mythopoetic Men's Movement (and the Mythopoetic Leaders Answer).* Philadelphia: Temple University Press, 1995.

Messner, Michael A. *Politics of Masculinities: Men in Movements.* Thousand Oaks, Calif.: Sage, 1997.

Robinson, Sally. *Marked Men: White Masculinity in Crisis.* New York: Columbia University Press, 2000.

Schwalbe, Michael. *Unlocking the Iron Cage: The Men's Movement, Gender Politics, and American Culture.* New York: Oxford University Press, 1996.

FURTHER READING

Bly, Robert. *Iron John: A Book About Men.* Reading, Mass.: Addison-Wesley, 1990.

Clatterbaugh, Kenneth. *Contemporary Perspectives on Masculinity: Men, Women, and Politics in Modern Society.* 2nd ed. Boulder, Colo.: Westview, 1997.

Faludi, Susan. *Stiffed: The Betrayal of the American Man.* New York: William Morrow, 1999.

Farrell, Warren. *The Liberated Man; Beyond Masculinity: Freeing Men and Their Relationship with Women.* New York: Random House, 1974.

Griswold, Robert L. *Fatherhood in America: A History.* New York: Basic Books, 1993.

Hagan, Kay Leigh, ed. *Women Respond to the Men's Movement: A Feminist Collection.* San Francisco: Pandora, 1992.

Jesser, Clinton J. *Fierce and Tender Men: Sociological Aspects of the Men's Movement.* Westport, Conn.: Praeger, 1996.

Kimmel, Michael. *Manhood in America: A Cultural History.* New York: Free Press, 1996.

Pfeil, Fred. "Guerillas in the Mist." In *White Guys: Studies in Postmodern Domination and Difference.* London: Verso, 1995.

RELATED ENTRIES

Antiwar Movement; Breadwinner Role; Counterculture; Crisis of Masculinity; Emotion; Fatherhood; Fathers' Rights; Feminism; Fraternal Organizations; *Home Improvement*; Industrialization; *Iron John: A Book About Men; Kramer vs. Kramer;* Men and Religion Forward Movement; Men's Studies; Middle-Class Manhood; Muscular Christianity; Nation of Islam; Patriarchy; Politics; Promise Keepers; Religion and Spirituality; Reverse Sexism; Sensitive Male; Sexual Revolution; Vietnam War

—*Jonna Eagle*

MEN'S STUDIES

Generally described as the critical analysis of men and masculinities, men's studies emerged as a legitimate field of academic inquiry in the early 1990s. Although men's studies has not yet been widely adopted as a major program at most American colleges and universities, its increasing incorporation and success suggests a growing tendency to rethink the meaning of masculinity in the United States.

Like women's studies, its more widely accepted sister discipline, men's studies is based on the premise that society views all human beings through a gendered lens—a distortion that has traditionally resulted in the general privileging of men over women. While recognizing the inequality of this history, contemporary men's studies also examines aspects of patriarchy not often broached during discussions of gender, particularly the complex, contradictory and at times oppressive cloak of masculinity men are expected to assume. Of highest priority within the discipline is the study of men as unique gendered beings, rather than as the paradigm for generic human existence. As such, men's studies scholars seek to deconstruct terms such as mankind that imply a homogenous worldview and experience shared by men and women of varying age, race, and socioeconomic status.

Men's studies first emerged during the late 1960s and the 1970s as a response, in part, to the second wave of American feminism. Scholarship within the discipline was also influenced by the widespread disillusionment over the Vietnam War, a cynicism that sparked a questioning of patriarchal power structures, traditional male roles, and the male behavioral expectations encouraged by World War II and the Cold War. Courses focusing on men and masculinities began appearing at some of the nation's more liberal institutions in the mid-1970s. The University of California at Berkeley led the way by incorporating the topic into its curriculum in 1976.

Since that time, men's studies scholarship has gone through two discernable waves. The first, running roughly from the mid-1970s to the early 1990s, was concerned primarily with the lived experience of white middle-class men. Much important scholarship resulted from this first wave, most notably Joseph Pleck's *The Myth of Masculinity* (1981) and Peter Filene's *Him/Her/Self: Sex Roles in Modern America* (1986). The establishment and rapid growth of the field were indicated first by the appearance and then by the expansion of Eugene August's 1985 annotated bibliography *Men's Studies.* Originally including about six hundred entries, the book contained over one thousand when it was updated as *The New Men's Studies* less than a decade later. The field's early indebtedness to women's studies and feminist thought was apparent in the theories and observations of Judith Butler, Carol Gilligan, and Barbara Ehrenreich, who produced significant scholarship during this time period.

By the late 1980s, the same rethinking of American masculinity that had produced men's studies had also sparked the emergence of four major men's movements—the profeminist movement, the Promise Keepers, the men's rights movement, and the mythopoetic men's movement. Although the academic examination of men and masculinity is most commonly derived from a profeminist perspective, popular men's studies books tend to focus on the mythopoetic movement and the topics of men's rights, therefore distorting the public's perception of the discipline. For example, mythopoetic men are commonly characterized as New Age fanatics who beat drums and read poetry. Such images have negatively influenced both popular and academic attitudes toward men's studies, although they have had little influence on the academic study of men and masculinities.

Despite these often inaccurate characterizations, men's studies showed signs of evolution and continuing growth during the 1990s. Several new academic journals and organizations were dedicated specifically to the study of men, including the American Men's Studies Association (1991), the *Journal of Men's Studies* (1992) and *Men and Masculinities* (1998). E. Anthony Rotundo's *American Manhood: Transformations in Masculinity from the Revolution to the Modern Era* (1993), the first published history of American masculinities, became a starting point for future scholarship despite criticisms of its narrow focus on white middle-class men.

The 1990s also witnessed calls for a "newer men's studies" as emerging themes surfaced from the scholarship of Harry Brod, Michael Kimmel, and Kenneth Clatterbaugh. Academics leading this second wave of inquiry are primarily concerned with masculinity as a plural and dynamic entity, addressing questions of how men of differing races, sexual orientations, and socioeconomic standing negotiate the boundaries of their gender. This new masculinity scholarship is particularly influenced by gay studies and postcolonialism.

Despite its ostensive focus on disenfranchised groups, contemporary masculinity scholarship also examines the existence and cultural repercussions of the "crisis narrative" of the white, heterosexual, American male. Academics have increasingly recognized that hegemonic masculinity is—and always has been—a dynamic, rather than fixed, construction. Manhood is typically defined in relation to a socioeconomic or cultural "other"—property ownership, nationalism, or paternity, for example. Ideological shifts in any of these spheres—prompted perhaps, by an economic downturn or an elevated consciousness resulting from racial, gender, or sexual liberation movements—necessitates a corresponding shift in cultural definitions of masculinity. As society changes, so do the expectations of men, causing masculine ideals to be perpetually "in crisis."

Uncovering the dynamic nature of manhood has further complicated avenues of inquiry previously considered exhausted by most academics, namely the literary and political canon. This shift has led to revived scholarly interest in the personal lives and work of several prominent "dead white men." This academic trend aroused concern that the current path of men's studies scholarship would reverse the progress that had been made in expanding the academic curriculum to include issues and topics involving women, nonwhites, and homosexuals, and that the interests of these groups would again become subordinated to those of white heterosexual men. The notion that the scholarship of women, men, and homosexuals could best be served under the more general categories of "gender" and "sexuality," rather than in isolated programs such as "women's" or "queer" studies, gained momentum as men's studies assumed the level of academic discipline in its own right in the early 1990s. As a result, some women's studies programs changed their names to conform to the new rubrics.

While the study of American masculinity is indebted to the academic framework of women's studies, which created the vocabulary for discussions of gender-based discrimination and social constructs, the interdependence between men's studies and women's studies does not mean that the two disciplines are inextricably linked. As the scope and breadth of gender studies continues to expand, it becomes increasingly clear that while both men and women are influenced by ever-fluctuating gender dynamics, their experiences are far from uniform. Although barely a decade old, men's studies have succeeded in diversifying our understanding of the American male. Similar breakthroughs are likely to develop as this discipline evolves, ensuring a more balanced perception of manhood and gender in general, as well as a deeper understanding of U.S. history.

Bibliography

Brod, H., and Kaufman, M., eds. *Theorizing Masculinities.* Thousand Oaks, Calif.: Sage, 1994.

Butler, Judith. *Gender Trouble: Feminism and the Subversion of Identity.* New York: Routledge, 1990.

Clatterbaugh, Kenneth. "Literature of the U.S. Men's Movements." *Signs* 25 (Spring 2000): 883–890.

Kimmel, Michael. *Manhood in America: A Cultural History.* New York: Free Press, 1996.

Traister, Bryce. "Academic Viagra: The Rise of American Masculinity Studies." *American Quarterly* 52, no. 2 (2000) 274–304.

Urschel, Joanne K. "Men's Studies and Women's Studies: Commonality, Dependence, and Independence." *Journal of Men's Studies* (Spring 2000): 407–411.

Further Reading

Brod, H., ed. *The Making of Masculinities: The New Men's Studies.* Boston: Allen & Unwin, 1987.

Clatterbaugh, Kenneth. *Contemporary Perspectives on Masculinity: Men, Women, and Politics in Modern Society.* Boulder, Colo.: Westview, 1997.

Pleck, Joseph H. *The Myth of Masculinity.* Cambridge, Mass.: MIT Press, 1981.

Rotundo, E. Anthony. *American Manhood: Transformations in Masculinity from the Revolution to the Modern Era.* New York: Basic Books, 1993.

Related Entries

Education; Fathers' Rights; Feminism; *Iron John: A Book About Men*; Men's Movements; Promise Keepers

—*Kristen M. Kidder*

MIDDLE-CLASS MANHOOD

Middle-class manhood is a paradoxical concept, at once precarious and powerful. It has been marked by fears of failure and inadequacy, while also representing an extraordinarily powerful social position comprising the influence and authority of political and ideological dominance. It represents the experiences, values, and fears of a particular social class, as well as a culturally dominant construction of male gender identity. As a dominant category of social identity, it has been a racially specific one that refers primarily to white men. While men of color may belong to the socioeconomic middle class, their experiences, beliefs, and values have remained outside the historical concept of middle-class manhood.

Self-Made Manhood and the Producer Ethic in the Nineteenth Century

Middle-class manhood first emerged as a distinct social and cultural concept in the early decades of the nineteenth century, a product of industrial capitalism and the emerging middle class. Changes in the scale and mode of production during this period radically altered the economic and demographic landscape, as new technologies and broadening markets created new forms of labor concentrated in rapidly growing urban centers. In the previous century the economic status of the native-born white man had been secured through either land ownership or a skilled trade, and authority was vested in him as the head of a household and an active member in the social and political life of a close-knit community. By the early decades of the nineteenth century, however, small agrarian communities began to splinter under the pressures of industrialization and urbanization. Young men, no longer sure of inheriting their father's land or trade, were increasingly forced into the urban world of business to seek their independent fortunes. Unlike their forefathers, whose identities were tied to relatively stable positions within families and communities, these young men operated in a terrain of social and spatial mobility. Economic success in the marketplace came to define a new conception of manhood, one associated with this class of aspiring urban dwellers.

At the heart of this new model of manhood was the ideology of the "self-made man." According to the principles of self-made manhood, a man's worth was proven and maintained through the economic success he achieved through his own efforts; the inability to succeed economically was understood as a gender, as well as a class, failure. The hallmarks of the self-made man included industry, frugality, hard work, and, above all, self-control. The advice literature of the period called upon men of (or aspiring to) middle-class status to adhere strictly to the principles of restraint, particularly in relation to issues of bodily health.

Rooted in an emergent industrial capitalism, middle-class manhood involved the belief that the male body, like the American capitalist economy itself, had finite resources and required careful management and avoidance of excessive expenditure if it was to be maintained in good health. Men were warned against succumbing to sensual impulses, and sexual activity was of particular concern. Sexual potency was imagined as a force to be conserved rather than recklessly spent, and masturbation was condemned as wasteful, unproductive, and unmanly. Men who indulged their sensual appetites courted both physical and financial ruin, and those who squandered their vital energies were stigmatized as emasculated failures.

Even within marriage, sexual activity was to be infrequent. This not only conserved men's energy for productive labor, but also helped consolidate the middle class by keeping families small and allowing families to invest more of their resources in the education of their sons. Without the assurance of land or a trade to pass on, such education was necessary to ensure the economic and social success of one's sons. In this period, fatherhood itself became a central feature of middle-class masculine identity. Fathers were held responsible for securing the future prosperity of their sons by instilling in them the character traits of the self-made man, for the failure of a father's sons would cast a shadow on his own manhood as well.

Although the middle-class ideology of self-made manhood emphasized autonomy and independence, middle-class men's economic success in the volatile and unstable nineteenth-century marketplace was heavily dependent upon the domestic labor of women. Thus, the definition of middle-class manhood was predicated on a corresponding definition of middle-class womanhood, in which middle-class women managed the home and raised children while middle-class men participated in the public sphere of politics and the marketplace. This doctrine of "separate spheres" infused gender differences with a new moral significance. While aggression, force, and energy were essential to the self-made man's success, middle-class manhood required that such passions be managed and controlled through the moral influence and oversight of middle-class women. In a private domestic sphere, separated from the spaces of productive labor, women were to provide for the hard-working middle-class man a place of warmth, of respite from the ravages of the competitive marketplace, and of the moral and emotional regeneration necessary for effective economic activity.

Overcivilization in the Late Nineteenth Century

As the nineteenth century progressed and the pace of industrialization and urbanization intensified, corporate ownership of the means of production became more common, and opportunities for "self-making" became increasingly rare. By the closing decades of the nineteenth century, more middle-class men found themselves laboring in sedentary white-collar jobs amid vast corporate bureaucracies, within which they had little chance of advancement. Without the dream of autonomy upon which the notion of the self-made man had been founded, ambivalence about the value of restraint and self-denial intensified. In the decades following the Civil War, a new emphasis on the aggressive, forceful, virile nature of manhood emerged, invigorated by the influential theories of social Darwinism that celebrated strength and dominance through the notion of the "survival of the fittest."

This new emphasis on the virtues of the manly passions grew in response to concerns over "overcivilization." It was feared that white, native-born, middle-class men had grown flaccid and soft as a result of their highly civilized—and feminized—state. The fears of feminization were intensified by the increasing presence of women in the public sphere—in reform movements, political organizations, and the labor force itself. A rebellion began to brew against the dictates of self-control and feminine virtues of morality through which the middle class had previously defined itself, and a host of social institutions and leisure activities emerged to encourage "primitive" masculine behavior in middle-class men and boys. The era witnessed a new zeal for competitive sports and military engagements, a boom in fraternal organizations of all kinds, and an increased interest in outdoor adventures such as camping, fishing, and hunting. Such activities, it was hoped, would invigorate the masculinity of young middle-class men whose lives were otherwise directed toward passive and sedentary pursuits. The specter of feminization was warded off through this commitment to the "strenuous life," enacted by seeking revitalization through vigorous physical activities in the company of other men.

The promotion of middle-class vitality, vigor, and strenuous living contributed to a series of late-nineteenth-century developments in middle-class manhood. By reconciling masculine passions with the hierarchical organization that marked the bureaucratic workplace, institutions such as competitive sports and the military encouraged a new model of middle-class masculinity grounded more in teamwork and professionalism than in individual achievement. This model of manhood informed the Progressive social reforms through which the middle class sought a new source of identification and consolidation.

Fears of feminization and the perceived softness of American middle-class life also encouraged a heightened emphasis on the importance of fatherhood in the upbringing of virile middle-class boys. Men such as Theodore Roosevelt—an outspoken advocate of the strenuous life—maintained that active and involved fatherhood was a central responsibility of middle-class men. The doctrine of separate spheres began to break down as men were urged to participate in the running of the home and the raising of children. Finally, the new emphasis on establishing manly prerogatives through leisure pursuits, rather than the marketplace, hinted at the role of consumerism in defining middle-class masculine identity during the twentieth century.

Corporate Capitalism and Consumption in the Twentieth Century

Growing corporatization and consumerism brought about changes in twentieth-century conceptions of middle-class manhood. As corporate white-collar labor increasingly became the norm, the ideology of independent "self-making" could no longer provide the backbone of conceptions of middle-class manhood. Corporate culture encouraged the development of interpersonal skills, and business success increasingly depended upon the abilities of the salesman to charm and influence others. At the same time, a consumer society required a new set of conventions and behaviors, since the value of self-control no longer served the national economy. The growth of a consumer economy and the expansion of mass culture encouraged an emphasis on self-expression through leisure activities and consumer goods. Although individualism and independence remained central concepts in the middle-class conception of manhood, they took on new inflections—rather than economic autonomy, they reflected freedoms associated with commodity consumption. The values of self-restraint gave way to the importance of self-realization.

By the middle of the twentieth century, a new model of middle-class manhood had crystallized in the image of the suburban corporate commuter. The federal government contributed to the development of this model after World War II by expanding educational opportunity, providing housing loans, and constructing the interstate highway system, all of which helped create a new group of white, affluent, suburban-dwelling men. The breadwinner ethic—temporarily shaken by the Great Depression of the 1930s—was reinvigorated by the postwar boom in production and oriented toward a new culture of domestic consumption. Middle-class men were expected to invest their money in household appliances and devote their leisure time to domestic and familial pursuits. In the Cold War era, consumption represented all that was healthy, powerful, and prosperous about capitalist society. Academics and politicians argued that scarcity conditioned men toward deference and submissiveness, while abundance afforded them opportunities for increased independence and self-reliance, albeit as consumers rather than producers.

The increased role of consumption was also apparent in the image of the playboy bachelor, an alternative model of middle-class masculinity increasingly visible at this time. While the bachelor courted the stigma of effeminacy and homosexuality in his hedonistic lifestyle and rejection of marriage and family life, he could also be cast as the beneficiary of the traditional values of independence and autonomy. Buying what he liked, doing what he liked, free from domestic constraints and familial obligations, the bachelor represented another form of male independence, one founded not upon productive labor but upon commodity consumption.

These shifts in middle-class notions of manhood were not without their tensions and ambivalence, however. Corporate labor and the suburban life that it supported—while celebrated as the pinnacle of national and individual prosperity—were simultaneously the targets of criticism. Cultural commentators lamented the loss of the manly self-reliance evident in the era's "organization man," and the image of the "man in the gray flannel suit" expressed the paradox of individualism in an age of conformity, in which men strove to distinguish themselves through the requisite consumption of identical mass commodities. Affluence itself was cause for anxiety, for it eroded self-discipline while intensifying pressures on middle-class men to provide luxury goods for their families. The medical profession raised concerns as well, pointing to the shorter life expectancy and epidemic of coronary heart disease among middle-class men who conformed to the responsible breadwinning ethic of the suburban corporate commuter. Inevitably perhaps, the prescription given to alleviate these corporate pressures was more leisure time and relaxation, and with them the opportunity to enjoy the fruits of a consumer society.

The twentieth century has been host to persistent alarms over the "crisis" of middle-class masculinity, and economic and social changes over the last quarter of the century intensified these fears. The social movements of the 1960s and 1970s challenged middle-class men's prerogatives both at work and in the home. At the same time the counterculture's rejection of traditional middle-class values and lifestyles was taken to represent the failure of middle-class morality and paternal authority: The image of the long-haired anti-establishment hippie embodied the threat of masculine softness resulting from a middle-class culture of affluence and indulgence. The economic recession of the 1970s reinvigorated middle-class fears of downward social mobility and further undercut the viability of middle-class men's role as breadwinner. In the closing decades of the century, the continued shift toward a postindustrial society—characterized by the growth of the service and information sectors and the decline of industrial manufacturing—challenged the traditional foundations of middle-class manhood, while the narcissistic appeals of a mass consumer culture hawking an increasing array of goods and services grew ever more strident.

Conclusion

The notion of middle-class manhood—like all ideological constructs—has encompassed a range of conflicting ideals, representing traditional commitments to manly self-reliance and individualism alongside consumer values of personal freedom and self-expression. The middle class, required to remake itself with each generation, continues to be haunted by fears of both increased and diminished affluence. Such concerns express the inseparability of class and gender, as any alternative to middle-class status has been historically represented as the result of a failure to uphold dominant codes of masculinity.

BIBLIOGRAPHY

Ehrenreich, Barbara. *The Hearts of Men: American Dreams and the Flight from Commitment.* New York: Anchor Press, 1983.

———. *Fear of Falling: The Inner Life of the Middle Class.* New York: HarperCollins, 1989.

Griswold, Robert L. *Fatherhood in America: A History.* New York: Basic Books, 1993.

Halttunen, Karen. *Confidence Men and Painted Women: A Study of Middle-Class Culture in America, 1830–1870.* New Haven, Conn.: Yale University Press, 1982.

Hilkey, J. A. *Character is Capital: Success Manuals and Manhood in Gilded Age America.* Chapel Hill: University of North Carolina Press, 1997.

Leverenz, David. *Manhood and the American Renaissance.* Ithaca, N.Y.: Cornell University Press, 1989.

Nelson, Dana D. *National Manhood: Capitalist Citizenship and the Imagined Fraternity of White Men.* Durham, N.C.: Duke University Press, 1998.

Osgerby, Bill. *Playboys in Paradise: Masculinity, Youth, and Leisure-Style in Modern America.* Oxford: Berg, 2001.

Rotundo, E. Anthony. *American Manhood: Transformations in Masculinity from the Revolution to the Modern Era.* New York: Basic Books, 1993.

Ryan, Mary P. *Cradle of the Middle Class: The Family in Oneida County, New York, 1790–1865.* Cambridge, England: Cambridge University Press, 1981.

FURTHER READING

Bederman, Gail. *Manliness and Civilization: A Cultural History of Gender and Race in the United States, 1880–1917.* Chicago: University of Chicago Press, 1995.

Blumin, Stuart M. *The Emergence of the Middle Class: Social Experience in the American City, 1760–1900.* Cambridge, England: Cambridge University Press, 1989.

Clawson, Mary. *Constructing Brotherhood: Class, Gender, and Fraternalism.* Princeton, N.J.: Princeton University Press, 1989.

Frank, Stephen M. *Life with Father: Parenthood and Masculinity in the Nineteenth-Century American North.* Baltimore: Johns Hopkins University Press, 1998.

Johansen, Shawn. *Family Men: Middle-Class Fatherhood in Early Industrializing America.* New York: Routledge, 2001.

Kimmel, Michael. *Manhood in America: A Cultural History.* New York: Free Press, 1996.

Mangan, J. A., and James Walvin, eds. *Manliness and Morality: Middle-Class Masculinity in Britain and America, 1800–1940.* Manchester, England: Manchester University Press, 1987.

Pendergast, Tom. *Creating the Modern Man: American Magazines and Consumer Culture, 1900–1950.* Columbia: University of Missouri Press, 2000.

Robinson, Sally. *Marked Men: White Masculinity in Crisis.* New York: Columbia University Press, 2000.

Winter, Thomas. *Making Men, Making Class: The YMCA and Workingmen, 1877–1920.* Chicago: University of Chicago Press, 2002.

RELATED ENTRIES

Advice Literature; Alger, Horatio, Jr.; Bachelorhood; Breadwinner Role; Bureaucratization; Business/Corporate America; Capitalism; Class; Consumerism; Crisis of Masculinity; Cult of Domesticity; Darwinism; Individualism; Industrialization; Market Revolution; *Organization Man, The*; *Playboy* Magazine; Professionalism; Progressive Era; Self-Control; Self-Made Man; Strenuous Life; Suburbia; Urbanization; Victorian Era; Work

—*Jonna Eagle*

MILITARISM

The concept of militarism occupies an uncertain place in U.S. history and in the development of American male identity. Militarism exalts the warrior (and masculine) virtues of loyalty, bravery, discipline, and physical strength. It emphasizes war, and preparation for war, as a necessity for national survival and idealizes military service as the highest calling for men. Militarists consider military service to be a rite of passage to manhood, regarding males who have not served in the military as incomplete men. Although military service in wartime has always been part of American male identity, militarism's values clash with the equally masculine virtues of independence and individualism that American culture also idealizes. The result has been an American brand of militarism that extols the citizen soldier while retaining a suspicion of standing armies and aggressive international behavior.

Early American views of militarism and masculinity originated on the colonial frontier, particularly during the American Revolution. Resentment of the large British military presence in the colonies following the French and Indian War (1754–63), combined with the notion that British Army regulars harbored low moral character, produced an image of standing armies as threats to liberty and republican government, and as antithetical to republican manhood. The colonists' victory in the Revolutionary War in 1783 strengthened the ideal of the male citizen-soldier who was a frontiersman, a yeoman farmer, or a shopkeeper. In the early republic, the ambivalent relation between militarism and manhood persisted. The standing national army remained an object of suspicion, constitutionally subject to civilian control, while the male citizen was expected to be willing to serve his family, community, and country in wartime through local and state militias. Women, defined as caregivers and supporters, were to raise and nurture men to be strong enough to serve their country when the United States had to go to war to defend itself, but at the same time they were expected to curtail the glorification of war and large armies that might undermine male republican virtues and foster aggressive international behavior. This view predominated through the Civil War (1861–65).

Several interrelated developments of the late nineteenth and early twentieth centuries led to a change in these attitudes and began to foster a more unambiguously positive relation between militarism and masculinity. First, the presence of large numbers of Civil War veterans generated a mystique that contributed to the rise of American nationalism and glorified military service. Veterans and government officials in both the North and South used the celebration of Memorial Day—the annual commemoration of American soldiers killed in battle—and the dedication of dozens of local Civil War memorials to instill in young men a sense of duty to the state. At about the same time, industrialization and urbanization generated anxiety that modern "overcivilization" had made American men soft; Darwinism identified struggle (sometimes violent) as a norm of existence and a mechanism of evolutionary development; and journalists, intellectuals, and political figures (including Theodore Roosevelt), spurred by these developments, urged the United States toward overseas expansion and increased military strength during and after the 1890s. The crisis that arose with Spain over Cuba and the resulting Spanish-American War in 1898 offered a new generation of males born after the Civil War an opportunity to prove themselves in battle.

The first half of the twentieth century witnessed sharp swings in the debate over the United States' proper role in foreign affairs, the importance of a standing military establishment, and the link between masculinity and military service. In the early years of the century, advocates of a large military saw new threats to American security from Germany and, after its victory in the Russo-Japanese War (1904–05), Japan. Against this backdrop, militarists continued to emphasize the positive impact that military service could have on the development of male character. At the same time, however, opponents of militarism and imperial expansion emphasized the corrosive impact military life could have on individual male creativity and independence, as well as the threat militarism posed to democratic institutions. Women's political and social groups, which surged in the early twentieth century, also frequently expressed antimilitarist sentiments. These swings continued during and after World War I. American intervention in the war in 1917 temporarily strengthened militarist arguments, but postwar disillusionment and isolationism, which grew deeper with the Great Depression, strengthened antiwar sentiment, sparked serious misgivings about American involvement abroad, and undermined militarist arguments regarding the character-building nature of military life.

American participation in World War II, and the onset of the Cold War soon thereafter, prompted a decisive shift in society's views on militarism, military service, and male identity. The onset of World War II, the perceived threat posed by Nazi Germany and Imperial Japan, and American entry into the war once again reinforced the need for enlarged armed forces, but this time, to build support for U.S. involvement, the federal government mounted a strong propaganda campaign. To ease fears that American belligerency might destroy the country's democratic values, government propaganda depicted the armed forces as democratic organizations where servicemen were autonomous beings, while also emphasizing military service as an opportunity for young men to prove their manhood. The cultural reverence for the citizen-soldier as an independent, democratic-minded male ready to defend his home and his freedom was thus vindicated. Associations of national military strength with manliness continued—and were asserted with heightened urgency—during the Cold War, resulting in a large permanent military establishment and a deep imbedding of militarist sentiment in American culture.

During the 1960s the unpopularity of the Vietnam War and the rise of the women's movement revived longstanding mistrust of the association of militarism with manhood, but resurgent conservatism in the late 1970s and 1980s pushed these concerns into the background. Ronald Reagan's election as president in 1980, after a campaign in which he promised to restore an image of American international strength and presented himself as vigorously manly, brought a large military buildup and militarist rhetoric directed against the Soviet Union. The swift and convincing American victory in the Gulf War against Iraq in 1991 strengthened the military mystique, as did the growing military use of computer technology—itself often defined as a "masculine" field. Even the increasing participation of women in the armed forces—and their challenge to patriarchal perceptions of the military—has not diminished the strong use of masculine metaphors in public rhetoric involving military activity. The cultural association between militarism and masculinity, strengthened by developments of the late nineteenth and twentieth centuries, remains powerful.

BIBLIOGRAPHY

Cunliffe, Marcus. *Soldiers and Civilians: The Martial Spirit in America, 1775–1865.* Boston: Little, Brown, 1968.

Elshtain, Jean Bethke. *Women and War.* New York: Basic Books, 1987.

Feinman, Ilene Rose. *Citizenship Rites: Feminist Soldiers and Feminist Antimilitarists.* New York: New York University Press, 2000.

Hoganson, Kristin L. *Fighting for American Manhood: How Gender Politics Provoked the Spanish-American and Philippine-American Wars.* New Haven, Conn.: Yale University Press, 1998.

Pettegrew, John. "'The Soldier's Faith': Turn-of-the-Century Memory of the Civil War and the Emergence of Modern American Nationalism." *Journal of Contemporary History* 31, no. 1 (1996): 49–73.

Vagts, Alfred. *A History of Militarism: Civilian and Military.* Rev. ed. New York: Meridian, 1959.

Van Tuyll, Hubert P. "Militarism, the United States, and the Cold War." *Armed Forces and Society* 20, no. 4 (1994): 519–529.

FURTHER READING

Caulfield, Susan. "Transforming the Criminological Dialogue: A Feminist Perspective on the Impact of Militarism." *Journal of Political and Military Sociology* 27, no. 2 (1999): 291–306.

Conover, Pamela Johnston. "Gender, Feminist Consciousness, and War." *American Journal of Political Science* 37, no. 4. (November 1993): 1079–1099.

Donovan, James A. *Militarism USA.* New York: Scribners, 1970.

Elshtain, Jean Bethke, and Sheila Tobias, eds. *Women, Militarism, and War: Essays in History, Politics, and Social Theory.* Savage, Md.: Rowman & Littlefield, 1990.

Gibson, James William. *Warrior Dreams: Paramilitary Culture in Post-Vietnam America.* New York: Hill and Wang, 1994.

Kaplan, Laura Duhan. "Woman as Caretaker: An Archetype That Supports Patriarchal Militarism." *Hypatia* 9, no. 2 (1994): 123–133.

Regan, Patrick M. "War Toys, War Movies, and the Militarization of the United States, 1900–1985." *Journal of Peace Research* 31, no. 1 (1994): 45–58.

RELATED ENTRIES

American Revolution; Antiwar Movement; Citizenship; Civil War; Cold War; Imperialism; Military; Rambo; Reagan, Ronald; Republicanism; Spanish-American War; Technology; Vietnam War; War; Western Frontier; World War I; World War II

—*Walter F. Bell*

MILITARY

A key element in the construction of gender identity throughout U.S. history has been the almost exclusive male monopoly on the role of warrior and soldier. This role grew from a belief in superior male physical strength, stamina, and courage that has deep roots in Western civilization. The forces that originally defined American culture established a strong tie between masculinity and military service in time of war and conflict.

Throughout American military history, government leaders and the military establishment have used this traditional notion of gender identity and obligations of male citizenship to persuade men to join the armed services and participate in the country's defense in wartime. This process has drawn large numbers of young men into uniform with minimal formal coercion. It has helped to glorify behaviors that encourage a high level of combat effectiveness, such as loyalty to comrades and a willingness to face danger, and it has reinforced accepted gender roles in the wider society that portray men as warriors and protectors and women as supporters and nurturers.

Europeans colonizing North America brought with them the perception, reinforced by medieval concepts of chivalry, that men had the duty of protecting women from outside invasions or internal uprisings. During the Revolutionary War and in the early days of the republic, concepts of male identity that emphasized obligations to fight to guard family and community and to resist tyranny and centralized authority became more pronounced. The republican ideals embodied in the American Revolution stimulated an aversion to large professional armies and a belief in the male citizen soldier who served in local militia forces out of a civic obligation to protect the democratic values of the republic. The values and standards of the predominately small town and rural communities from which these men came shaped their male identities and strengthened the cohesiveness, discipline, and combat effectiveness of the militia units to which they belonged.

The American military experience in nineteenth-century wars, particularly the Civil War, strengthened the notion that military service was the preserve of men. In the conscript armies of World Wars I and II, the Korean War, and the Vietnam War, the military authorities continued to manipulate these gender roles and symbols, placing an added emphasis on the individual soldier's loyalty to his primary unit (squad, platoon, or company). This imbedding of men's identity through linkage to the warrior role has led to the conceptualization of the American military as a male-oriented gendered institution. The masculine culture of the armed forces grew out of this view of military service as a young man's rite of passage, establishing not only citizenship, but also manhood itself.

The twentieth century witnessed increasing challenges to traditional gender roles, including the definition of the warrior/protector role as exclusively male. Forces such as industrialization, urbanization, the mobilization of American society for two world wars, and the growing impact of feminism during the 1960s and 1970s expanded women's occupational opportunities and undermined the traditional notion that certain professions were suitable for men only. Women were allowed into uniform as temporary auxiliaries in clerical roles during World War I. During World War II, women served as

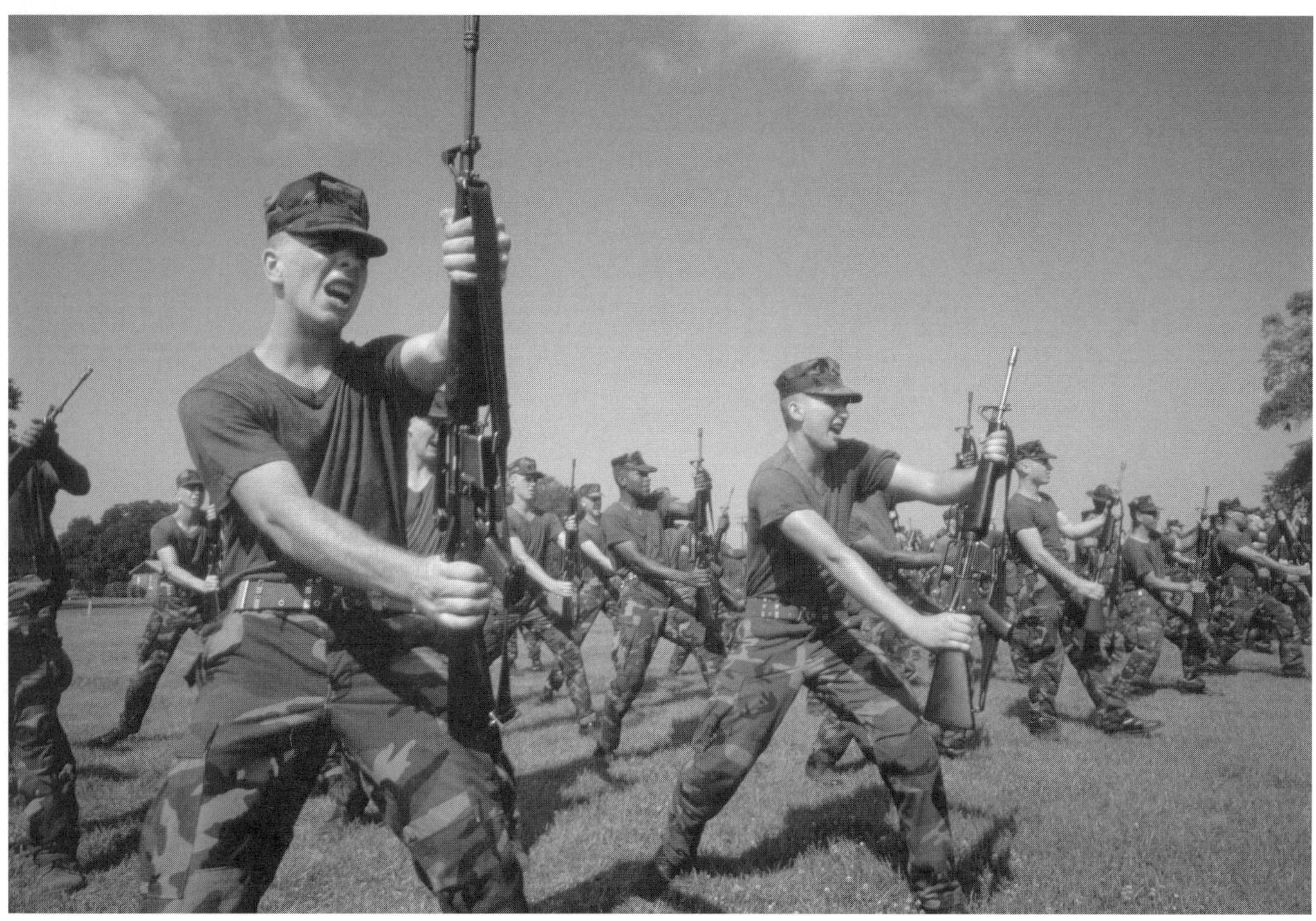

This photograph of U.S. soldiers participating in a training exercise illustrates the traditional elements of American military models of manhood: physical toughness, personal discipline, homosocial bonding, and sometimes violent defense of the nation. (© Bob Krist/Corbis)

members of segregated branches of the armed forces (such as the Women's Army Corps) and performed low-risk support functions. In 1948, Congress passed the Women's Armed Services Integration Act, though there was strong opposition in Congress and in the military. This act established a permanent status for women in both the regular services and the reserves, but it excluded them from combat-related occupations and limited their numbers to no more than 2 percent of authorized strength. Congress abolished these limits when it ended the draft in 1973. Creation of the all-volunteer military brought women into the armed forces in increasing numbers, paving the way for complete gender integration in 1978. In the 1990s, however, Congress relaxed restrictions to allow them to serve on naval combat vessels and to fly jet fighters and helicopters. As of 2002, women were still barred from ground combat units.

This assimilation of women into the military in the 1980s and 1990s intensified the debate, which began during World War II, over their proper role in war. The possibility of women coming under fire conflicts with deeply held beliefs among conservative elements in the military and political leadership about the ability of women in war. Gender integration in the military challenges the notion that men alone are physically and emotionally qualified to participate in governmentally and socially sanctioned violence. This perceived threat to the military's male-centered culture provoked traditionalists to increasingly distinguish between support functions (such as clerical occupations, where most women still serve) and the combat groups, which they define as suitable for men only. Spurred on by heightened concerns over issues of sexual orientation, which further challenges traditional male identity, they resisted attempts by the administration of Bill Clinton during the 1990s to force admission of homosexuals into the nation's armed forces.

Gender integration has forced changes in the traditional training and indoctrination techniques and the customary behavior patterns that, in the all-male military, had affirmed male traits and were thought to foster effective battlefield performance. Efforts to widen women's roles have encountered widespread resistance from traditionalists who argue that gender integration into combat units threatens to undermine qualifying and performance standards, unit morale and cohesion, and general efficiency. This resistance has manifested itself in frequent gender clashes, such as the Tailhook incident, during which male naval aviators abused their female colleagues during a convention in Las Vegas in 1991, and the 1996 allegations of rape and sexual misconduct at the Aberdeen Proving Grounds in Maryland.

While male exclusivity in the military has ended, the assumptions that governed that monopoly still have considerable support. It now appears that the general reappraisal of individual male and female military roles and associated behavioral standards will not occur without intense and prolonged conflict at all levels of the United States' military and political establishments.

BIBLIOGRAPHY

Addis, Elisabetta, et. al., eds. *Women Soldiers: Images and Realities.* New York: St. Martin's, 1994.

Cameron, Craig M. "Gender: Male Identity and the Military." In *The Oxford Companion to American Military History,* edited by John Whiteclay Chambers II. New York: Oxford University Press, 1999.

Field, Kim, and John Nagl. "Combat Roles for Women: A Modest Proposal." *Parameters* 31, no. 2 (Summer 2001): 74–88.

Gutmann, Stephanie. *The Kinder, Gentler Military: Can America's Gender-Neutral Fighting Force Still Win Wars?* New York: Scribner, 2000.

Herbert, Melissa. *Camouflage Isn't Only for Combat: Gender, Sexuality, and Women in the Military.* New York: New York University Press, 1998.

Rotundo, E. Anthony. *American Manhood: Transformations of Masculinity from the Revolution to the Modern Era.* New York: Basic Books, 1993.

Snyder, R. Claire. *Citizen-Soldiers and Manly Warriors: Military Service and Gender in the Civic Republican Tradition.* Lanham, Md.: Rowman & Littlefield, 1999.

Titunik, Regina F. "The First Wave: Gender Integration and Military Culture." *Armed Forces & Society* 26, no. 2 (2000): 229–258.

FURTHER READING

Blacksmith, E. A. *Women in the Military.* New York: Wilson, 1992.

Breuer, William B. *War and American Women: Heroism, Deeds, and Controversy.* Westport, Conn.: Praeger, 1997.

Feinman, Ilene Rose. *Citizenship Rites: Feminist Soldiers and Feminist Antimilitarists.* New York: New York University Press, 2000.

Friedl, Vicki L. *Women in the United States Military, 1901–1995: A Research Guide and Annotated Bibliography.* Westport, Conn.: Greenwood Press, 1996.

Goldstein, Joshua. *War and Gender: How Gender Shapes the War System and Vice Versa.* Cambridge, England: Cambridge University Press, 2001.

Holm, Jeanne. *Women in the Military: An Unfinished Revolution.* Novato, Calif.: Presidio Press, 1982.

Janowitz, Morris, and Roger W. Little. *Sociology and the Military Establishment.* 3rd ed. Beverly Hills, Calif.: Sage, 1974.

Karsten, Peter. "The U.S. Citizen Soldier: Past, Present, and Likely Future." *Parameters* 31, no. 2 (2001): 61–63.

RELATED ENTRIES

American Revolution; Chivalry; Citizenship; Civil War; Gays in the Military; Imperialism; Industrialization; Militarism; Republicanism; Vietnam War; Violence; War; World War I; World War II

—*Walter F. Bell*

MINISTRY

The term *ministry* refers to the work of persons sanctioned by a religious community to administer its sacramental rites and spiritual functions, including preaching, pastoral work, teaching, and community discipline. Although the ministerial office is a part of every major religious tradition, there has been debate over its character and shape particularly in many Christian communities throughout the history of the United States. In the Judeo-Christian tradition, the ministry was defined as a masculine calling in the book of Leviticus, where God commands Moses to consecrate "Aaron and his sons" as priests of the Levite tribe and makes this a "perpetual ordinance." While this concept of the ministry assumed a hierarchical form in most of western European Christendom, a parallel notion of potentially transformative social power—"the priesthood of all believers"—developed as well and became particularly influential during the Protestant Reformation of the sixteenth and seventeenth centuries. As in Europe, many settlements in the New World witnessed an ongoing debate over the meaning and authority of the ministry, and since that time Americans have at times either reasserted or challenged traditional assumptions about the ministerial office as a domicile of divinely ordained masculine authority.

The English Puritans who established the Massachusetts Bay colony in the seventeenth century modeled their society and ecclesiastical life upon their understanding of ancient

Israel, organizing tightly-knit congregations whose members subscribed to a covenant and vested religious authority in properly trained males. Presiding over self-styled covenant communities "in the wilderness," ecclesiastical leaders wielded great power. They justified their authority through a system of biblical interpretation that was intended to protect against theological error, but by requiring an extensive education that was denied to women they also ensured the maintenance of a male oligarchy.

Nevertheless, occasional challenges to Puritan notions of a male-only ministry did arise. In 1635 Anne Hutchinson of Boston's First Church began holding religious meetings in which she publicly questioned the clergy's emphasis on "good works" as proof of one's divine election. That Massachusetts leaders regarded her as a threat to male religious and social authority was evident when, in the 1638 trial that led to her excommunication and banishment, they accused her of acting more like "a Husband than a Wife, and a preacher than a Hearer." Similarly, the Puritans imprisoned New England Quakers, whose rejection of scriptural prohibition against women speaking in church threatened the very foundations of Puritan society.

Between the mid–eighteenth century and the mid–nineteenth century, the Great Awakening, American Revolution, and Second Great Awakening spurred a mistrust of hierarchical structures of religious authority, prompting new notions of ministerial manliness. The disestablishment of state religion, the social and geographic mobility Americans enjoyed, and the impact of emerging republican and democratic notions of manhood created a volatile atmosphere in which the idea of "the priesthood of all believers" took on a new meaning. A new breed of self-made populist preachers held revivals and attracted large audiences. These preachers grounded their authority in their claims to salvation rather than in classical training. Couching their message in an appeal to common sense, individual liberty, and listeners' own ability to interpret the bible, ministers increasingly found that robust, charismatic preaching was more likely to fulfill popular expectations, and thus to assure their social influence than were such earlier markers of ministerial manliness as education and theological sophistication. Significantly, this more democratic notion of ministry did not always challenge the male monopoly on ministerial authority—indeed, it in some ways reinforced that monopoly because of its appeal to contemporary gender assumptions rather than biblical texts that might question such distinctions.

At the same time, however, several cultural currents were working to erode the traditional association between ministry and manhood. Democratization itself, combined with emerging Victorian gender constructs that defined women as naturally more pious than men, encouraged a growing number of women to claim spiritual authority. The abolitionist Sarah Grimké drew analogies between the misuse of biblical texts to justify slavery and their use in the subordination of women. Such liberal denominations as the Unitarians and Universalists began ordaining women in the 1850s and 1860s. The African-American evangelist and missionary Amanda Berry Smith directly challenged established notions of a male ministry by preaching along the east coast and abroad in the 1870s and 1880s. By the close of the century, feminists such as Elizabeth Cady Stanton—author of *The Woman's Bible* (1898)—were increasingly critiquing what they considered a male-dominated church.

The nineteenth century also witnessed what some scholars have called a "feminization" of the ministry. With women outnumbering men two to one in the average congregation, and with Victorian cultural currents emphasizing emotion and compassion in human relationships, ministers increasingly strived to demonstrate in their behavior and emphasize in their sermons certain character traits—such as dignity, humility, piety, and amiableness—that would appeal to feminine tastes. Moreover, evangelicalism's reproach of "worldliness" distanced the ministry from prevailing perceptions of republican manhood that emphasized rationality and competitive impulses.

In response to these trends some Christians attempted to remasculinize the ministry. New expressions of "muscular Christianity" emerged in Protestantism, emphasizing the character and manliness of Jesus, ministers, and the layman's commitment to faith. The preacher Billy Sunday, a former baseball player, became a particularly prominent example of this new model of Christian hypermasculinity. Reflecting the late-nineteenth-century ideal of "passionate manhood," muscular Christianity emphasized action over thought and proclaimed itself "devoid of all the etcetera of creed." Claiming the inerrancy of Scriptures and reconstituting Puritan claims concerning America as a covenant nation, Protestant fundamentalists reasserted biblical archetypes of masculine spiritual leadership and called on men to lead a national crusade of moral reform. Although muscular Christianity waned by the 1920s, it did influence the fundamentalist notions of ministry and masculinity that developed during the Progressive Era and became a powerful cultural force during the late twentieth century.

Nor were fundamentalists alone in their assertion of religious patriarchy. In the South during the twentieth century, male ministers in several black Baptist churches openly opposed the formation of "Bible Bands"—African-American women's groups organized to study Scripture—suggesting these groups ultimately undermined the authority of their office. Opposition to the groups became so pronounced that some Bible Bands were locked out of their home churches and forced to discontinue their study.

Despite such efforts, the twentieth century witnessed a growing erosion of the longstanding definition of ministry as masculine. A small but growing number of Protestant denominations began ordaining women, and the resurgence of feminism in the 1970s generated challenges against those denominations refusing to do so. While some denominations, such as the Episcopal Church, responded to these calls for change, others resisted. Debates over the ordination of women became especially pronounced in the Catholic Church in the United States, prompting the Vatican to reassert the traditional interpretation of the ministry as a male-only calling in its *Declaration on the Question of Admitting Women to the Priesthood* (1976). Still, the debate within the Catholic Church has persisted, and even intensified, as the pool of male divinity candidates has diminished. By the end of the twentieth century, debates about the ordination of homosexuals further expanded the range of contemporary discussion about the relation between ministry and masculinity.

BIBLIOGRAPHY

Bendroth, Margaret Lamberts. *Fundamentalism and Gender, 1875 to the Present.* New Haven, Conn.: Yale University Press, 1993.

Hatch, Nathan O. *The Democratization of American Christianity.* New Haven, Conn.: Yale University Press, 1989.

Higginbotham, Evelyn Brooks. *Righteous Discontent: The Women's Movement in the Black Baptist Church, 1880–1920.* Cambridge, Mass.: Harvard University Press, 1993.

Holifield, E. Brooks. *The Gentleman Theologians: American Theology in Southern Culture, 1795–1860.* Durham, N.C.: Duke University Press, 1978.

Marsden, George M. *Understanding Fundamentalism and Evangelicalism.* Grand Rapids, Mich.: Eerdmans, 1991.

Miller, Perry. *Errand into the Wilderness.* Cambridge, Mass.: Belknap Press, 1956.

Morgan, Edmund S. *The Puritan Family: Religion and Domestic Relations in Seventeenth-Century New England.* New York: Harper & Row, 1966.

Ownby, Ted. *Subduing Satan: Religion, Recreation, and Manhood in the Rural South, 1865–1920.* Chapel Hill: University of North Carolina Press, 1990.

FURTHER READING

Hunter, Jane. *The Gospel of Gentility.* New Haven, Conn.: Yale University Press, 1984.

MacHaffie, Barbara J. *Her Story: Women in Christian Tradition.* Philadelphia: Fortress Press, 1994.

Marty, Martin E. *Modern American Religion.* 2 vols. Chicago: University of Chicago Press, 1986.

Montgomery, William E. *Under Their Own Vine and Fig Tree: The African-American Church in the South, 1865–1900.* Baton Rouge: Louisiana State University Press, 1994.

Pelikan, Jaroslav. *The Christian Tradition: A History and Development of Doctrine.* Vol. 1. Chicago: University of Chicago Press, 1971.

RELATED ENTRIES

Evangelicalism and Revivalism; Jesus, Images of; Muscular Christianity; Passionate Manhood; Promise Keepers; Religion and Spirituality; Republicanism; Sentimentalism; Social Gospel; Sunday, Billy; Victorian Era; Young Men's Christian Association

—*Kent A. McConnell*

MINSTRELSY

Minstrelsy emerged as the premier form of popular theater in the antebellum period, and it remained an important part of American culture through the early twentieth century. Minstrel acts were performed by traveling troops of musicians, dancers, and actors. These were generally white men who impersonated African Americans by blackening their faces. While these shows drew diverse audiences nationwide, they were most popular among young, white, working-class men in the Northeast. As these men assumed an increasingly dependent status within an industrializing economy, the raucous and explicitly sexual characters popular in minstrel shows provided a way for them to examine the meanings of working-class manhood.

The performer Thomas Dartmouth Rice, a white northerner who began his working life as a carpenter's apprentice, was a key popularizer of American minstrelsy. He began his performances as "Jim Crow," a rustic slave, in 1830. Another well-known early minstrel performer was George Washington Dixon, a white Virginian most famous for his portrayal of "Zip Coon," a pretentious urban would-be dandy. Minstrelsy began as a form of theatrical performance consisting of brief musical numbers, dances, and comic monologues and dialogues. By the 1840s, however, minstrel performers had adopted a largely musical program and moved from theaters to more lucrative concert halls, where minstrel troupes with between four and eight members played banjos, fiddles, and the bones. Some of the most noted early minstrel troops were the Christy Minstrels, the Virginia Minstrels, the Virginia Serenaders, and Wood's Minstrels. By the late nineteenth century, minstrelsy had entered the larger tradition of vaudeville performance.

Although minstrels claimed to be presenting their audiences with authentic African-American songs and dances, the actual relationship between black culture and minstrelsy was ambiguous. Many so-called plantation dances and tunes were based on currently popular European dance steps and melodies, and minstrel performances in many ways resembled the "Yankee plays" popular earlier in the nineteenth century, which featured the antics of white rustics, whose manhood audiences deemed inferior. But some scholars have established links between minstrel tunes and dance steps and the music and performance of enslaved and free African Americans, maintaining that minstrelsy was indeed based on African-American cultural forms.

Through minstrel shows, working-class white male audiences expressed a masculine identity based on race and class. This identity was in part an outgrowth of earlier practices whereby white laborers, disempowered by their growing dependence on their employers and landlords, ritually disguised themselves and challenged their social superiors in an effort to assert their own power and social status. In both northern and southern cities in the late eighteenth and early nineteenth centuries, such bands had occasionally blackened their faces in impersonation of African Americans or Native Americans and paraded in a disorderly manner down the streets to celebrate festivities, challenge decisions of local elites, or attack individuals who had violated social norms. Blackface minstrelsy can be seen as a continuation of these often violent but contained cultural practices. The use of blackface to challenge social norms and power structures continued into the Reconstruction period, when groups like the Ku Klux Klan, composed of white males who felt their status threatened by Republican Party dominance in the South, occasionally adopted such disguises in their attacks on freed African-American slaves and white Republicans.

In the nineteenth century, the interest that white workers showed in viewing what they believed to be authentic scenes from plantation life seems to indicate a widespread fascination with African-American culture. Yet blackface actors invariably represented African Americans with such degrading stereotypes and grotesque features that the shows also seem to illustrate a widespread contempt among whites of the period for African Americans and their culture. This attraction and repulsion may be partially explained by white working-class men's ambiguity about their own status within the new industrialized, urbanized economy. Blackface characters bragged about their prowess at sex or fighting—much as white working-class men themselves did—but, in reality, such figures lacked power over their own lives. The comically overt pretensions to manhood of Jim Crow and Zip Coon were amusing to white working-class men largely because achieving the independence constitutive of manhood was absolutely impossible for these African-American characters—and, white male audiences feared, for themselves as well. As the more politicized among the working class complained that white laborers were nothing more than "wage slaves"—a term they used to assert their claims to economic independence as white men—many felt that they were unable to achieve manly autonomy. While they could identify with the failed manhood comically depicted on stage, they despised its implications and struggled to distance themselves from it.

Sexuality was a pervasive theme in minstrelsy. Some of the genre's most popular tunes, such as "Long Tail Blue," were barely veiled references to male sexuality. The stock minstrel characters Jim Crow and Zip Coon presented different versions of manhood, but both boasted about their physical and sexual exploits. It was also common in minstrelsy for male actors to impersonate lustful and manipulative female "wench" characters. Some scholars have argued that white men performing sexuality in blackface were defining white male sexuality in reference to a stereotypically exaggerated African-American sexuality. Others have maintained that blackface performers were not so much attempting to impersonate African-Americans as they were projecting their own sexual tensions and ambiguities onto a black "other." Living in an era that insisted that economic success and moral propriety could be achieved only by restraining one's passions, working-class men had few outlets to express their sexuality. Minstrel shows provided a forum in which they could explore and express sexuality without identifying it as their own.

Minstrelsy survived into the mid–twentieth century, not only in touring minstrel shows but also in such classic films as *Birth of a Nation* (1915) and *The Jazz Singer* (1927). Yet its cultural currency waned as theater competed with movie palaces and dance halls, and as the mass migration of African Americans to northern cities made minstrel shows less exotic to northern audiences. Most significant, however, was the decline of Victorian sexual standards and the rise of a new ideal of masculinity that acknowledged violent and sexual passions as part of white manliness. White men could now embrace their passions rather than projecting them onto African Americans. Minstrelsy's final decline came later in the century as the civil rights movement successfully stigmatized the public stereotyping of African-American men.

BIBLIOGRAPHY

Cockrell, Dale. *Demons of Disorder: Early Blackface Minstrels and their World.* New York: Cambridge University Press, 1997.

Lott, Eric. *Love and Theft: Blackface Minstrelsy and the American Working Class.* New York: Oxford University Press, 1993.

Mahar, William J. *Behind the Burnt Cork Mask: Early Blackface Minstrelsy and Antebellum American Popular Culture.* Urbana: University of Illinois Press, 1999.

FURTHER READING

Nathan, Hans. *Dan Emmet and the Rise of Early Negro Minstrelsy.* 1962. Reprint, Norman: University of Oklahoma Press, 1977.

Roediger, David, R. *The Wages of Whiteness: Race and the Making of the American Working Class.* Rev. ed. New York: Verso, 1999.

Toll, Robert C. *Blacking Up: The Minstrel Show in Nineteenth-Century America.* New York: Oxford University Press, 1974.

RELATED ENTRIES

African-American Manhood; Race; Slavery; Whiteness; Working-Class Manhood

—*Elaine Frantz Parsons*

MOBY DICK

Herman Melville's *Moby Dick; or, The Whale* (1851) describes Captain Ahab of the whaling ship *Pequod* and his quest to kill the white whale that took his leg on an earlier whale hunt. This self-destructive mission ends with the death of Ahab and his crew, with the single exception of Ishmael, the book's narrator. The novel dramatizes the concerns of American middle-class men in the emerging capitalist marketplace of the mid–nineteenth century. The novel negotiates meanings of bourgeois manhood and same-sex relations, as well as man's precarious relationship to nature.

The characters of the novel and their relations with one another represent two models of Victorian manhood: (1) the traditional ideal of "artisanal" manhood, defined through small-producer values, economic autonomy, and self-sufficiency; and (2) an emerging ideal of "entrepreneurial" manhood, defined by competitive individualism, the exploitation of natural resources, and control over other men in the workplace. Artisanal manhood is represented by Ishmael, who goes to sea to escape from urban alienation, and Queequeg, a South Sea islander and harpooner. The two men are joined in a sentimental, homoerotic relationship that enables them to resist Ahab and the entrepreneurial manliness he represents. Ahab's first mate, Starbuck, shares Ishmael and Queequeg's commitment to artisanal manhood, but his attraction to entrepreneurial manhood and desire for economic gain make it impossible for him to resist the madness of the captain's quest.

While Ahab represents the destructive potential of mid-nineteenth-century entrepreneurial capitalism, the white whale represents nature. The purpose of the *Pequod* is to hunt sperm whales for their oil, or "sperm." By means of the whale hunt, capitalist enterprise symbolically converts the masculine erotic energy of nature—represented by the sperm—into cash. Ahab's quest for revenge, however, leads the crew beyond its capitalist purpose of exploiting nature for pecuniary gain and on a path toward the destruction of ship and crew.

In *Moby Dick*, the homoerotic bond between Ishmael and Queequeg serves as the foundation for a radical social critique of capitalist economics and commodity fetishism. The socially and sexually transgressive relation between the two men, who share a bed and undergo a "marriage" ceremony, has liberating potential. Initially drawn to Ahab, Ishmael separates himself from the murderous crusade through his bond with Queequeg. Ishmael and Queequeg's relationship challenges the violently coercive entrepreneurial masculinity and phallic power represented by Captain Ahab, and the noncompetitive union of the two men becomes the foundation for a re-examination of men's relation to one another, and to nature. In the end, only Ishmael survives at sea by using Queequeg's coffin as a flotation device. Queequeg's symbolic reaching out to Ishmael from his own death is suggestive of the maternal love and devotion that Victorian middle-class Americans considered necessary to men's spiritual salvation.

Moby Dick can thus be read as a homoerotic, sentimental critique of bourgeois entrepreneurial manhood, which sustains and perpetuates itself through the exploitation of natural resources and the domination of other men in the workplace. The novel contains a plea for an ideal of artisanal manhood and the need to resist the forces of entrepreneurial capitalism. While the novel suggests that men could prevail over forces of economic change, it also conveys Melville's pessimism about the impact of capitalism on American masculinity.

BIBLIOGRAPHY

Gilmore, Michael T. *American Romanticism and the Marketplace.* Chicago: University of Chicago Press, 1985.

Leverenz, David. *Manhood and the American Renaissance.* Ithaca, N.Y.: Cornell University Press, 1989.

Martin, Robert K. *Hero, Captain, Stranger: Male Friendship, Social Critique, and Literary Form in the Sea Novels of Herman Melville.* Chapel Hill: University of North Carolina Press, 1986.

Melville, Herman. *Moby Dick; or, The Whale.* 1851. Reprint, edited by Hershel Parker and Harrison Hayford. Evanston, Ill.: Northwestern University Press, 2001.

Further Reading

Bellis, Peter J. *No Mysteries Out of Ourselves: Identity and Textual Form in the Novels of Herman Melville.* Philadelphia: University of Pennsylvania Press, 1990.

Cameron, Sharon. *The Corporeal Self: Allegories of the Body in Melville and Hawthorne.* Baltimore: Johns Hopkins University Press, 1981.

Castronovo, Russ. *Fathering the Nation: American Genealogies of Slavery and Freedom.* Berkeley: University of California Press, 1995.

Parker, Hershel. *Herman Melville: A Biography: 1819–1851.* Vol. 1. Baltimore: Johns Hopkins University Press, 1996.

———. *Herman Melville: A Biography: 1851–1891.* Vol. 2. Baltimore: Johns Hopkins University Press, 2002.

Tolchin, Neal L. *Mourning, Gender, and Creativity in the Art of Herman Melville.* New Haven, Conn.: Yale University Press, 1988.

Related Entries

Artisan; Body; Capitalism; Homosexuality; Individualism; Industrialization; Market Revolution; Mother–Son Relationships; Patriarchy; Property; Sentimentalism; Victorian Era; Violence

—*Thomas Winter*

Momism

The "momism" critique, a scathing attack on American mothers during World War II and the early Cold War, asserted that the nation's young men lacked the rugged, independent character possessed by their forefathers and necessary to national strength. Popular writers and psychiatric experts blamed pathological moms who "smother-loved" their children, particularly their boys. They viewed the phenomenon as uniquely American, and largely confined to the middle class.

Momism was rooted in a male reaction to the modernization of gender roles. In the early twentieth century, as women entered the competitive realms of paid labor and politics (achieving national suffrage in 1920), men increasingly questioned the Victorian belief in female moral superiority and challenged the assumption that mother love was a wholly benevolent force. Whereas Victorians had believed that boys became self-governing men by internalizing the moral mother, modern experts began to regard such internalization as an obstacle to healthy masculinity.

Hostility toward maternal influence reached its zenith in the 1940s, and was expressed most memorably by the popular writer Philip Wylie. Wylie coined the term momism after witnessing a Mother's Day spectacle: a division of soldiers spelling, in formation, "MOM." To Wylie, the soldiers' tribute suggested that American men were more skilled at sentimental gestures than heroic acts. In his 1942 bestseller, *Generation of Vipers,* Wylie argued that the decline of manly labor, the saccharine character of radio programming, and the influence of women's clubs all pointed to encroaching momism. During World War II, Wylie's satiric critique resonated with commentators who worried that American men seemed "soft" compared to their fascist enemies.

In the postwar period, psychiatrists and social scientists lent momism a degree of scientific legitimacy by employing it as a kind of diagnosis. In a 1946 bestseller, *Their Mothers' Sons,* the psychiatrist Edward Strecker attributed the high incidence of neuropsychiatric disorders among U.S. draftees and servicemen to widespread maternal pathology. Likewise, in *Childhood and Society* (1950), émigré psychoanalyst Erik Erikson analyzed "Mom" as a distinctive national prototype, the American counterpart to the authoritarian German father. Experts were especially anxious about the role that mothers played in fostering male homosexuality, which became widely associated with communism during the Cold War. To stave off this threat, they urged fathers to forge closer relationships with their sons, portraying engaged fatherhood as the cornerstone of democratic manhood. They also promoted groups like the Boy Scouts that allowed boys to escape the presumably suffocating confines of domesticity.

Historians have tended to view the momism critique as part of an antifeminist movement that sought to re-establish stable gender roles after World War II. Indeed, the critique was decidedly misogynist, and it fueled the rampant homophobia of the postwar era. But its political implications were actually complex. Many liberals, both men and women, supported Wylie's attack on moms, viewing it as an assault on moral hypocrisy, sexual repression, and intolerance. In the 1960s, feminists such as Betty Friedan appropriated the derogatory stereotype of the neurotic suburban mother to argue that women's energies should no longer be confined to the home.

Bibliography

Buhle, Mari Jo. *Feminism and Its Discontents: A Century of Struggle with Psychoanalysis.* Cambridge, Mass.: Harvard University Press, 1998.

Rogin, Michael Paul. "Kiss Me Deadly: Communism, Motherhood, and Cold War Movies." In *Ronald Reagan, the Movie and Other Episodes in Political Demonology.* Berkeley: University of California Press, 1987.

Wylie, Philip. *Generation of Vipers.* 1942. Reprint, Normal, Ill.: Dalkey Archive Press, 1996.

Further Reading

Feldstein, Ruth. *Motherhood in Black and White: Race and Sex in American Liberalism, 1930–1965.* Ithaca, N.Y.: Cornell University Press, 2000.

Terry, Jennifer. "'Momism' and the Making of Treasonous Homosexuals." In *"Bad" Mothers: The Politics of Blame in Twentieth-Century America,* edited by Molly Ladd-Taylor and Lauri Umansky. New York: New York University Press, 1998.

Related Entries

Adolescence, Boyhood, Cold War, Fatherhood, Feminism, Freudian Psychoanalytic Theory, Homosexuality, Mother–Son Relationships, World War II

—*Rebecca Jo Plant*

Mother–Son Relationships

Throughout American history, relationships between mothers and sons have adapted to shifting constructions of masculinity. Mothers' ties to their sons have been both romanticized and criticized, depending on how Americans in various eras viewed the compatibility of this relationship with social and cultural ideals of manhood. The mother–son tie in American culture has thus been alternately a source of celebration and a cause for grave concern.

Mother–Son Relations and Colonial Patriarchy

In the premodern, patriarchal society of colonial America, social order was believed to require both respect for rank and hierarchy and deferential obedience to male domestic, religious, and political authority. Fathers acted as heads of households, and because they were viewed as more rational and more effective disciplinarians, they were considered to be better suited than mothers to raise and educate children. Mothers were to bear, nurse, and care for infants, but were considered too affectionate and lenient to ensure their children's obedience and morality, and therefore ill-suited to raising sons for participation in a stratified and deferential society.

The Nineteenth Century: Mother–Son Relationships Idealized

Beginning in the Revolutionary period, American attitudes regarding mother–son relationships became more favorable, and the responsibility for child rearing increasingly shifted from fathers to mothers. After about the mid–eighteenth century, the advent of republican political theory emphasizing the voluntary bonds between citizens and government generated new theories about child rearing that stressed affection and voluntary obedience over stern discipline. The result was a concept of "republican motherhood," which deemed mothers ideally suited to preparing their sons for citizenship. Because mothers could foster virtue, honesty, and love of liberty in their sons, mother–son relationships became understood as fundamental to the health and stability of the new nation.

Additionally, the impact of Romanticism on American culture in the early to mid-nineteenth century reinforced the emphasis on sentimental affection and nurture over harsh discipline in child rearing. Meanwhile, new gender constructs accompanying the growth of commercial capitalism, which defined men as work-oriented, amoral breadwinners and women as naturally pious, moral, and nurturing, led Americans to view mothers as better suited than fathers to mold the character of their sons. Changing economic patterns, in which economic production and male work increasingly moved outside of the home, meant that mothers were increasingly responsible for day-to-day child care and domestic governance. Beginning around 1830, an explosion of advice literature suggested that mothers would foster in sons the morality, self-restraint, sobriety, and honesty considered essential to well-rounded manhood, successful breadwinning, and the proper functioning of the nation's developing market economy.

At the same time, boys developed an independent culture away from the domestic sphere that encouraged the development of strength, speed, adventure, and courage. This culture assumed that boys required not only the self-restraint and moral virtue taught by mothers at home, but also the individualism, ambition, aggressiveness, and competition they would need as adults participating in the public sphere of their fathers. The idealization of mother–son relations thus coexisted with a continuing mistrust of excessively close mother–son bonding.

The "cult of domesticity" that enshrined the nobility and virtue of white mothers did not extend to slave women.

However, the end of U.S. participation in the international slave trade in 1807 transformed slavery into a system that relied on procreation for its expansion. Although slave families varied in structure, women played a significant role in rearing their sons and earning their love and respect. But several factors disrupted the mother–son tie among slaves, including the forced labor of slave women (and the resulting frequency of slave boys raised collectively); the removal of boys from maternal nurture to a labor regimen at puberty; and the frequent breakup of slave families through sale and "abroad" marriages between men and women living on separate plantations. Still, women were typically more involved in child rearing than were slave men, a circumstance that defined boys' childhoods and often influenced the limited fathering role they would play in their own families.

The Twentieth Century: Critiquing Motherhood

The Victorian idealization of mother–son relationships was increasingly challenged in the late nineteenth century, as cultural critics expressed fears that women's enhanced cultural influence and excessive mothering, combined with the advent of an urban-industrial "overcivilization," had made American men feminized. Critiques of motherhood became the subject of myriad tracts (largely written by men) that redefined child rearing in the language of science—a shift that underscored fears that Victorian maternal sentimentality had ruined America's sons. As organizations like the Boy Scouts emerged to instill more masculine values in young men, and as cultural spokesmen such as Theodore Roosevelt urged young men to pursue a "strenuous life," the primacy of the mother–son relationship was recast as a social problem rather than a cultural pillar. This concern was bolstered in the early decades of the twentieth century by the growing influence of Sigmund Freud and his theories on psychology, which asserted that overattentive mothers could wreak psychosexual damage on their sons.

This same period witnessed a redefinition of African-American manhood—and a concurrent celebration of African-American motherhood. The intellectuals, writers, and artists of the Harlem Renaissance of the 1920s asserted African-American self-reliance and self-respect; rejected prevailing caricatures of black men in favor of a new manhood defined by intelligence, achievement, and strength; and connected this racial progress with virtuous mothers. Extolling the nobility and affection of African-American women, this emphasis on the role of mothers in the rearing of respectful citizens reinforced black men's claims for full cultural and political participation in the United States.

During the 1940s, as American participation in World War II and the subsequent onset of the Cold War raised concerns about American military strength and the toughness of American soldiers, mothers' relationships with their sons became a subject of great interest. The implementation of psychological testing in the military prompted fears that overmothering had made America's young men into sissies and emotional cripples who were ill-equipped to serve and defend the nation. The increased absence of fathers during the war intensified these concerns. At the same time, women's entrance into the workforce during the war provoked fears of expanding female power and accusations that American women were not adequately fulfilling their primary responsibility as mothers. Many of the nation's major concerns during this period—particularly juvenile crime and homosexuality—were attributed to either inadequate or excessive mothering. The belief that American mothers were emasculating their sons, referred to as the "momism" critique, was put forth in such influential works as Philip Wylie's *Generation of Vipers* (1942) and Edward Strecker's *Their Mother's Sons* (1946), as well as in such scientific studies as David Levy's *Maternal Overprotection* (1943).

As the civil rights movement gained momentum, many Americans (both black and white) seeking the causes of blacks' social subordination blamed what they considered excessively strong mother–son relationships and absence of fathers. *The Negro Family: The Case for National Action* (1965), a report issued by the U.S. Department of Labor and authored by sociologist (and future U.S. senator) Daniel Moynihan, argued that the female-headed African-American family inverted dominant cultural norms and wreaked emotional havoc on African-American men. Meanwhile, many black militants looked to strong models of black manhood rather than to black women in their efforts to overcome what they considered African-American men's historic submissiveness.

The second-wave feminism of the 1960s and 1970s prompted a growing number of women to identify excessive mothering as a problem and to rethink their relations with their children. In her seminal book *The Feminine Mystique* (1963), Betty Friedan suggested that women who defined themselves solely as mothers risked smothering their children, thereby making them incompetent adults. Feminists rejected the perceived relegation of women to their reproductive capacities, asserted women's right to have careers, de-emphasized the primacy of motherhood to female identities, and called on fathers to increase their involvement in child rearing.

The various men's movements that developed in feminism's wake in the 1970s, 1980s, and 1990s similarly emphasized the importance of the father–son tie and some of them—such as the mythopoetic movement—echoed earlier anxieties about the effects of mothering on male identity. As domestic responsibilities became less and less the sole purview of women, and as strict gender divisions in child-rearing tactics faded, the importance of the unique mother–son tie diminished. The significance of this relationship has receded in a culture where rigid distinctions between masculinity and femininity have given way to more blurred and fluid gender identities.

Conclusion

Throughout much of American history, Americans have grappled with the question of whether or not men could learn to adopt masculine qualities at their mother's knee. By the end of the eighteenth century, American mothers began to assume control both of the domestic sphere and of raising children. Throughout the Victorian era, mothers and children occupied a sentimental place of primacy within the American imagination. Understood to be men's moral superiors, American mothers were considered the parent best equipped to instill virtues in their children. As the modern age of the twentieth century forced a reconsideration of Victorianism, it consequently prompted a reassessment of the mother–son relationship and the privileged place it had held. While mothers had been seen as conduits of morality and virtue, they were now often seen as transmitters of neuroses and agents of emasculation. The early twenty-first century is seen as a period of reassessment, with the primacy of the mother–son bond that has dominated American familial relations since the Revolutionary era fading away.

Bibliography

Apple, Rima D., and Janet Golden, eds. *Mothers and Motherhood: Readings in American History.* Columbus: Ohio State University Press, 1997.

Buhle, Mari Jo. *Feminism and Its Discontents: A Century of Struggle with Psychoanalysis.* Cambridge, Mass.: Harvard University Press, 1998.

Cable, Mary. *The Little Darlings: A History of Child Rearing in America.* New York: Scribners, 1975.

Degler, Carl N. *At Odds: Women and the Family in America from the Revolution to the Present.* New York: Oxford University Press, 1980.

Douglas, Ann. *Terrible Honesty: Mongrel Manhattan in the 1920s.* New York: Farrar, Straus and Giroux, 1995.

Ehrenreich, Barbara. *The Hearts of Men: American Dreams and the Flight from Commitment.* New York: Anchor Press, 1983.

Franklin, Donna L. *Ensuring Inequality: The Structural Transformation of the African-American Family.* New York: Oxford University Press, 1997.

Friedan, Betty. *The Feminine Mystique.* New York: Norton, 1963.

Genovese, Eugene D. *Roll, Jordan, Roll: The World the Slaves Made.* New York, Pantheon Books, 1974.

Gordon, Linda. "Putting Children First: Women, Maternalism, and Welfare in the Early Twentieth Century." In *U.S. History as Women's History: New Feminist Essays,* edited by Linda K. Kerber, Alice Kessler-Harris, and Kathryn Kish Sklar. Chapel Hill: University of North Carolina Press, 1995.

Kerber, Linda. "The Republican Mother: Women and the Enlightenment—An American Perspective." *American Quarterly* 28 (Summer 1976): 187–205.

Kimmel, Michael. *Manhood in America: A Cultural History.* New York: Free Press, 1996.

Levy, David M. *Maternal Overprotection.* New York: Columbia University Press, 1943.

May, Elaine Tyler. *Homeward Bound: American Families in the Cold War.* New York: Basic Books, 1988.

Pleck, Elizabeth, and Joseph Pleck, eds. *The American Man.* Englewood Cliffs, N.J.: Prentice Hall, 1980.

Rotundo, E. Anthony. "Boy Culture: Middle-Class Boyhood in Nineteenth-Century America." In *Meanings for Manhood: Constructions of Masculinity in Victorian America,* edited by Mark C. Carnes and Clyde Griffen. Chicago: University of Chicago Press, 1990.

———. *American Manhood: Transformations in Masculinity from the Revolution to the Modern Era.* New York: Basic Books, 1993.

Scholten, Catherine. *Childbearing in American Society, 1650–1850.* New York: New York University Press, 1985.

Singleton, Gregory Holmes. "Birth, Rebirth, and the 'New Negro' of the 1920s." *Phylon: A Review of Race and Culture* (March 1982): 29–45.

Stevenson, Brenda. *Life in Black and White: Family and Community in the Slave South.* New York: Oxford University Press, 1996.

Strecker, Edward A. *Their Mothers' Sons: The Psychiatrist Examines an American Problem.* Philadelphia: Lippincott, 1946.

Wylie, Philip. *Generation of Vipers.* New York: Farrar & Rinehart, 1942.

Further Reading

Baker, Paula. "The Domestication of Politics: Women and American Political Society, 1780–1920." *American Historical Review* 89 (June 1984): 620–647.

Bremner, Robert H, ed. *Children and Youth in America: A Documentary History.* Cambridge, Mass.: Harvard University Press, 1974.

Douglas, Ann. *The Feminization of American Culture.* 1977. Reprint, New York: Noonday Press, 1998.

Erikson, Erik H. *Childhood and Society.* 1950. Reprint, New York: Norton, 1993.

Fass, Paula S., and Mary Ann Mason, eds. *Childhood in America.* New York: New York University Press, 2000.

Fliegelman, Jay. *Prodigals and Pilgrims: The American Revolution against Patriarchal Authority, 1975–1800.* Cambridge, England: Cambridge University Press, 1982.

Howard, Sidney. *The Silver Cord.* New York: Samuel French, 1927.

Pollack, William S. *Real Boys: Rescuing Our Sons from the Myths of Boyhood.* New York: Random House, 1998.

Roth, Philip. *Portnoy's Complaint.* 1969. Reprint, New York: Random House, 2002.

RELATED ENTRIES

Adolescence; Advice Literature; Boyhood; Cult of Domesticity; Emotion; Fatherhood; Feminism; Freudian Psychoanalytic Theory; Juvenile Delinquency; Marriage; Masculine Domesticity; Momism; Nuclear Family; Reproduction; Republicanism; Romanticism; Victorian Era; Youth

—*Allison Perlman*

MR. MOM

Mr. Mom (1983), written by John Hughes and directed by Stan Dragoti, is a role-reversal comedy in which the protagonist, Jack Butler (played by Michael Keaton), revises his understanding of masculine identity when he loses his job and, after his wife returns to work, assumes the domestic responsibilities of the household. The film humorously dramatizes Jack's unfamiliarity with household appliances, but the main focus is on his adjustment to his new role as a SAHD (stay-at-home dad) and his gradual acceptance of homemaking as a job to be done with pride rather than as a demotion from his "real" social role as the family's sole breadwinner. As a concept, *Mr. Mom* quickly became a cultural icon, and the term remains a catch-phrase describing fathers with primary domestic responsibility.

Mr. Mom reflects the growing incidence of single and stay-at-home fathers at the time of its release, a trend that resulted from the combined impact of rising divorce rates, economic stagnation, and the growing number of working mothers after the mid-1960s. The film can also be viewed as a response to intensifying feminist critiques of conventional middle-class masculinity and fatherhood. Above all, however, the film expresses a post-1970s examination and rethinking of masculinity, in which defenders of fatherhood lamented the absence of positive representations of fathers in film and television and an emerging men's movement sought to redefine fatherhood as a "growth experience" and liberate men from stereotypical sex roles.

Jack's liberation begins by his becoming "one of the girls"—he socializes with women made single by divorce and develops stereotypical behaviors associated with housewives, such as watching soap operas, gaining weight, and gossiping. However, the film insists that Jack is still very much a man. For example, a male stripper, seeing Jack sitting with his women friends, gives Jack his phone number, but Jack asserts his heterosexuality by passing it along to one of the women. The 1980s was a time of "remasculinization" for white males, and Jack eventually pulls himself together, sharpens his appearance, and becomes a "superdad." He is rewarded by getting his job back without having to compromise his integrity. Thus, although the majority of middle-class American men who take on primary household responsibilities do so because there is no one else to do them, Jack Butler's tenure as a *Mr. Mom* is only temporary. Moreover, because his wife intends to continue working, the family will probably have to hire a nanny.

As a comedy—the typical genre used to represent fatherhood in the 1980s—*Mr. Mom* presents a utopian solution for an issue that had been a disturbing subtext to family relations since the women's liberation movement of the 1970s. While films such as *Kramer vs. Kramer* (1979) and *Ordinary People* (1980) criticized feminist polemics by demonizing women's ambitions and showing fathers as clearly better parents than mothers, who were portrayed as selfish and emotionally inaccessible, *Mr. Mom* rewards both men and women for putting the children first. By depicting what has been called the "new fatherhood" as something other than a reactionary response to feminism, it sought to counteract, and even deny, the divisive gender politics generated by the late-twentieth-century rethinking of gender constructs.

BIBLIOGRAPHY

Case, David. "Mr. Mom's World." *Salon,* May 14, 1999. <http://www.salon.com/mwt/feature/1999/05/14/dads> (May 15, 2003).

Crispell, Diane. "Mr. Mom Goes Mainstream." *American Demographics* 16, no. 3 (1994): 59.

Griswold, Robert L. *Fatherhood in America: A History.* New York: Basic Books, 1993.

Lupton, Deborah, and Lesley Barclay. *Constructing Fatherhood: Discourses and Experiences.* London: Sage, 1997.

Traube, Elizabeth. *Dreaming Identities: Class, Gender, and Generation in 1980s Hollywood Movies.* Boulder, Colo.: Westview Press, 1992.

FURTHER READING

Ehrenreich, Barbara. *The Hearts of Men: American Dreams and the Flight from Commitment.* Garden City, N.Y.: Anchor Press, 1983.

Jeffords, Susan. *The Remasculinization of America: Gender and the Vietnam War.* Bloomington: Indiana University Press, 1989.

Long, Elizabeth. *The American Dream and the Popular Novel.* Boston: Routledge & Kegan Paul, 1985.

Wood, Robin. *Hollywood from Vietnam to Reagan.* New York: Columbia University Press, 1986.

RELATED ENTRIES

American Dream; Breadwinner Role; Crisis of Masculinity; Divorce; Fatherhood; Fathers' Rights; Feminism; Hollywood; Marriage; Masculine Domesticity; Middle-Class Manhood; Sensitive Male; Suburbia

—*Sandy Camargo*

MUSCULAR CHRISTIANITY

"Muscular Christianity" is a philosophy that blends Christian values with men's physical embodiment of masculinity. In the United States, its impact has been especially significant in fusing gender and power relations in two major social institutions: religion and sport.

Muscular Christianity originated in England during the early nineteenth century, and by 1850 it had become a dominant philosophy among Christian reform leaders. It was introduced in the United States during the late nineteenth century in Thomas Hughes' *Tom Brown's Schooldays* (1890), a novel that linked Christian ideology with rugged masculinity through the story of a boy transformed into a man by playing rugby.

Protestant clergy developed muscular Christianity in reaction to several late-nineteenth-century developments in American life: the perceived feminine nature of Victorian religion; the dominance of women parishioners in Protestant churches; a growing feminist movement in the United States; a cultural fear that white, middle-class men were becoming feminized by overcivilization; and a concern that Anglo-Saxon Protestant men were less physically fit than the growing numbers of Catholic immigrants, many of whom worked as manual laborers. Protestant clergy believed that increasing men's church attendance required a masculine religiosity with which men could identify. Proponents of muscular Christianity rejected the feminine Victorian portrait of Jesus as a slight man with a sad face, frail body, and oversized robes in favor of a muscular carpenter with black hair and a stoic heavenward gaze. This image, combining Christian commitment with a brawny physique, represented a new ideal representation of white, middle-class, male spirituality.

This new model of middle-class manhood was spread through several institutions, primarily the Boy Scouts, established in 1910, and the Young Men's Christian Association (YMCA), an English organization first established in the United States in 1851. Both of these organizations encouraged sport in their efforts to promote a model of manliness based on physical fitness and Christian morality. Muscular Christianity was also promoted by such prominent spokesmen as the Congregationalist ministers Josiah Strong and Lyman Abbott, the Unitarian minister Thomas Wentworth Higginson, the YMCA leader Luther Gulick, the psychologist Granville Stanley Hall, and Theodore Roosevelt.

Billy Sunday, a former professional baseball player turned evangelist, became its most famous American advocate. Having grown from a small and sickly child (like Roosevelt) into a strong, successful athlete, Sunday argued that a dedicated Christian man did not have to be feminine, but could, in fact, display great physical strength and toughness. His departure from professional baseball, he said, was not a retreat from manliness but the manly achievement of spiritual fulfillment and a higher moral calling. Sunday preached in an atmosphere that resembled a sporting event, eliciting crowd cheers and responses resembling those at baseball games.

Sunday's successful promotion of muscular Christianity inspired the Men and Religion Forward Movement (1911–12), which was cofounded by Fred Smith and Henry Rood to increase church membership among American men. Emphasizing vigor and steadfast dedication as essential to true Christianity, and urging male leadership both in the home and in church life, it increased men's church attendance in some communities. This movement added a strong element of social concern to its definition of Christian manliness, encouraging participants to oppose local brothels, which the Men and Religion Forward Movement considered potentially detrimental to a muscular Christian style of manliness.

Muscular Christianity was perhaps most powerful during the 1910s, when proponents of American entry into World War I invoked it as a method to remasculinize men on the battlefield, and to provide them an opportunity to demonstrate a moral dedication to the United States through patriotic service. But muscular Christianity declined during the 1920s as a result of a variety of factors: Americans became disillusioned with the war; the Scopes trial publicly embarrassed conservative Christianity by associating it with provincial backwardness; much of the movement's leadership died during the late 1910s and the 1920s; a growing "therapeutic" culture wedded health and fitness less to Christian social transformation and more to personal fulfillment; and middle-class Americans became increasingly absorbed by consumerism. Nonetheless, it remained an influential force in American culture.

The Ku Klux Klan, a secret racist organization that enjoyed a surge of membership in the 1920s, responded to growing urbanization and immigration in the United States by identifying muscular Christianity and a masculine Jesus with what they considered a traditional but beleaguered American national identity. Amid the business prosperity of the 1920s, moreover, the muscular Christian image of Jesus was infused with new entrepreneurial characteristics in support of an expanding business culture. Perhaps the most influential expression of this new type of muscular Christianity was advertising executive Bruce Barton's *The Man Nobody Knows* (1924). Barton's Jesus was "strong" rather than "sissified," a suave, charismatic, organizationally talented, and successful business leader.

Despite the influence of Barton and the Klan, muscular Christianity was further weakened during the 1930s and 1940s as the major economic shifts of the Great Depression and World War II produced the need for a dual-earner income and disrupted the traditional gender order of a male breadwinner and a female homemaker. However, it became revived during and after the 1970s amid the cultural debates sparked by second-wave feminism, the gay and lesbian liberation movement, and the growing influence of conservative Christianity. The theologians Thomas Hearn and Leonard Swidler revived a manly Jesus that addressed feminist concerns, while right-wing Christian organizations resistant to feminism and gay/lesbian awareness responded by espousing the concept of rugged Christian masculinity and domestic patriarchy advanced by the Christian leader Edwin Louis Cole in his book, *Maximized Manhood* (1982).

This latter version of muscular Christianity found its most prominent cultural expression in the early 1990s in the Promise Keepers, a movement founded by the former University of Colorado football coach Bill McCartney to attract men to church membership, unite them through religion, and encourage their return to their "natural" role as family leader. Critics accused McCartney of promoting a backlash against feminist progress in women's equality, but the Promise Keepers insisted that their goals were apolitical. Unsuccessful in their attempt to include men of color, and opposed to homosexuality, which conflicted with their understanding of fatherhood and family, the Promise Keepers' masculine ideal has appealed primarily to a white, conservative, middle- or upper-middle-class, heterosexual male constituency.

As McCartney's leadership of the Promise Keepers suggests, sport remained an important venue for the expression of muscular Christianity during the late twentieth and early twenty-first centuries, and athletes continued to serve as prominent cultural spokespersons for it. Such men as NASCAR driver Jeff Gordan; football players Deion Sanders, Reggie White, Kurt Warner, Cris Carter; basketball player Mark Jackson; and baseball player Oral Hershieser have publicly professed their commitment to Christianity and promoted the muscular Christian image.

Eroded during the twentieth century by high unemployment, shrinking wages, and increasing housing costs that forced middle-class and lower-middle-class families to go from a sole breadwinner income to a dual-earner income, and by feminist and gay-rights challenges to a traditional gender order, muscular Christianity grew weaker at the turn of the twenty-first century. Yet it remains influential in American culture because conservative Christianity, professional sports, and the constructions of masculinity based on these institutions remain potent cultural forces.

Bibliography

Burstyn, Varda. *The Rites of Men: Manhood, Politics, and the Culture of Sport.* Toronto: University of Toronto Press, 1999.

Conrad, Browyn Kara. *Promise Keepers: Gender, Politics, Godly Men, and the Contemporary American Culture Wars.* Ph.D. Diss., Washington State University, 2000.

Crepeau, Richard C. "Playing With God: The History of Athletes Thanking the 'Big Man Upstairs.'" <http://www.poppolitics.com/articles/2001-03-09-sport.shtml> (August 16, 2002).

Kimmel, Michael. *Manhood in America: A Cultural History.* New York: Free Press, 1996.

Lewis, Guy. "The Muscular Christianity Movement." *Journal of Health, Physical Education and Recreation* 37 (May 1966): 27–28, 42.

Messner, Michael A. *Politics of Masculinities: Men in Movements.* Thousand Oaks, Calif.: Sage Publications, 1997.

Niebuhr, Gus. "Men Crowd Stadiums to Fulfill their Souls." *New York Times,* 6 August 1995.

Putney, Clifford. *Muscular Christianity: Manhood and Sports in Protestant America, 1880–1920.* Cambridge, Mass.: Harvard University Press, 2001.

Veenker, Jody. "Muscular Christianity: Sports Stars, Graham Put Grit in the Gospel." *Christianity Today* 43, no. 8 (1999): 19.

FURTHER READING

Hall, Donald E., ed. *Muscular Christianity: Embodying the Victorian Age.* New York: Cambridge University Press, 1994.

Hughes, Tom. *Tom Brown's School Days.* New York: Thomas Y. Crowell, 1890.

Ladd, Tony, and James A. Mathisen. *Muscular Christianity: Evangelical Protestants and the Development of American Sport.* Grand Rapids, Mich.: Baker, 1999.

Messner, Michael A., and Donald F. Sabo. *Sport, Men, and the Gender Order: Critical Feminist Perspectives.* Champaign, Ill.: Human Kinetics, 1990.

Willis, Joe D., and Richard G. Wettan. "Religion and Sport in America—The Case for the Sports Bay in the Cathedral Church or St. John the Divine." *Journal of Sport History* 4, no. 2 (1977) 189–207.

RELATED ENTRIES

Boy Scouts of America; Consumerism; Crisis of Masculinity; Evangelicalism and Revivalism; Fraternal Organizations; Gulick, Luther; Hall, Granville Stanley; Higginson, Thomas Wentworth; Jesus, Images of; Men and Religion Forward Movement; Ministry; Promise Keepers; Religion and Spirituality; Roosevelt, Theodore; Sports; Sunday, Billy; World War I; World War II; Young Men's Christian Association

—Michelle L. Robertson

MUSIC

Although music is, for all intents and purposes, an abstract arrangement of sounds, it can "represent" masculinity. If, as feminist cultural critic Judith Butler claims, gender is performance, a behavior learned and practiced since birth, then the music created and consumed by American men, like other conduits of culture, can reinforce gender norms by embodying "masculine" qualities. Throughout America's history, men (who usually excluded women from public music making) have indeed created music to enforce and reinforce the dominant models of masculinity of their time and culture. At the same time, music has also offered reactions against and alternatives to the mainstream versions of masculinity in music.

Colonial Music

As early as the colonial period, music provided important markers of American manhood. Among white colonists, whose notions of manliness were grounded in concepts of social hierarchy and rank, the ability to make music demonstrated that one could afford the luxuries of a musical education, and was thus a symbol of good breeding and gentlemanly status. Philip Vickers Fithian, a tutor to wealthy children in 1771, observed that "Any young gentleman . . . is presum'd to be acquainted with Dancing, Boxing, playing the Fiddle, & Small-Sword, & Cards" (Hamm, 86). For white gentlemen, music bolstered the cultural authority and colonial power of England—and the masculine privilege that went along with them.

Colonial men's use of music to aspire to English and European styles of aristocratic manhood began to change during the American Revolution, as they sought to define their masculinity in opposition to the perceived decadence and effeteness of Europeans. Anti-English songs such as "Revolutionary Tea" characterized the "mother country" as a greedy old woman not willing to earn her money, while the popular ballad "The Lucky Escape" defined American manhood in terms of hard work and republican virtue. During the Revolutionary era, music—particularly martial music—became an important part of the public political culture and a key means of linking manliness to national identity and support for the Revolution.

The Nineteenth Century

As America grew as a nation, its musical institutions grew in earnest. In the early nineteenth century, music making in the home became more important and songs for piano and voice became very popular, particularly among an emerging middle class. In the private world of the middle-class home, music became a symbol of feminine accomplishment and domestic music making came to be seen as a woman's place. "Masculine" music making took place in public settings and social situations such as clubs, taverns, music halls, and military surroundings.

Communities of men started forming brass bands in large numbers, combining American folk tunes, marches, and dance music. Such bands reinforced a particularly American form of masculinity through their military origins and homosocial surroundings. Military bands had existed in America since before the Revolutionary War—when cavalry used mounted trumpets and kettledrums and foot soldiers marched with fife and drum—but around 1830, amateur groups began forming and becoming popular around the country. Composers such as Stephen Foster and bandleaders such as Patrick S. Gilmore embraced popular music genres like the waltz and quadrille. These leaders paved the way for

John Philip Sousa, the most important composer of military music in America in the last half of the nineteenth century. Brass bands were considered inherently masculine, not only because of their martial origins, but also because, placed in opposition to what many Americans considered a "feminized" European classical music tradition, they seemed to capture a more authentic American folk sensibility. Such music served to link masculinity with patriotism—a function that was strengthened by the nation's rise to global power in the late nineteenth and twentieth centuries.

By the time of the Civil War, brass bands were fully integrated into military units (of both the North and the South), and they served both as the only source of nighttime entertainment for the troops and as performers for soldiers on parade. Popular songs of the Civil War era, meanwhile, can often be viewed not only as inspirations for the military cause, but also as examples of prevailing gender norms. For example, Julia Ward Howe's Union anthem "Battle Hymn of the Republic" was intended to create a clear vision of the male hero, and the traditional tune "Shoot the Buffalo" imagined an idyllic postwar era where women would "knit and sew" and the men would "shoot the buffalo."

During the mid- to late nineteenth century, new forms of music developed and became integral to the newly emerging homosocial spaces in which men forged friendships, often in conscious opposition to what they perceived as the "feminized" spaces of home and church. By the 1840s, as fraternal lodges and college fraternities began forming and achieving wide popularity, sheet-music publishers start printing male-voiced four-part songs for use in these organizations and in other places where men gathered. During the 1860s, when male glee clubs began forming on college campuses, the barbershop quartet—a standardized four-voiced configuration based on a mixture of European hymns with African-American part singing—became popular. A male genre that produced music outside of the home, the barbershop quartet lasted well into the second half of the twentieth century, with both black and white groups achieving success.

For many African-American men, these quartets were vehicles by which to advance the "dignity agenda" promoted by prominent African-American musician James Reese Europe. The main focus of this movement was to present more accurate depictions on stage and in music of African-American masculinity, which was often portrayed in contemporary minstrel music through comic negative stereotypes. African-American men sought to express a more varied and complex range of emotions than these traditional stereotypes would lead a white audience to expect.

The Early Twentieth Century

By the late nineteenth and early twentieth centuries, new cultural contexts generated by industrialization and urbanization began to shape the relation between music and masculinity in American culture. In particular, concern that urban-industrial "overcivilization" and Victorian sentimentalism had weakened and feminized American middle-class men prompted a new emphasis on physical vigor as a criterion of manliness. This imperative, which informed such movements as muscular Christianity and the "strenuous life," was as evident in music as well. Some advocates of muscularity dismissed music as feminizing, but others, such as Charles Ives—generally considered the first important American composer in the classical tradition—sought to create a masculinized music. At the beginning of the twentieth century, Ives's music, which combined loud, clashing brass-band melodies with energetic orchestral dissonance, and which eschewed European musical language, was thought to embody a uniquely American virility. Ives was personally determined to make music that spoke with a masculine voice, as opposed to what he saw as the "feminine" and (applying a concept then being developed by psychiatrists and psychologists in opposition to what they considered normative masculinity) "homosexual" music of other composers. An alternate version of American masculinity in classical music was represented in the music of Virgil Thompson and Aaron Copland. Their depictions in music of both America's heartland and its cities spoke to audiences as examples of the masculine ideas of purity, industry, rationality, and hard work.

African-American men, meanwhile, pioneered new musical genres that conveyed and shaped their experiences. Blues music, with lyrics often featuring unfaithful women and ruthless landlords, emphasized themes of social alienation and emasculation. Jazz, meanwhile, embodied a spontaneity that symbolized a liberating escape from the power of white society. These new forms had a powerful effect on many subsequent forms of American music. Ironically, the evolution of jazz in the 1920s, along with the development of recording and microphone technology, enabled white male singers to challenge "masculine" musical ideals through the popular jazz style of "crooning," a deliberately quiet, delicate form of singing, often in the "feminine" falsetto, that was performed directly into the microphone and emphasized internal feelings.

Popular Music in Postwar America

During the decades after World War II, popular music increasingly overshadowed classical forms and reacted against the perceived feminization in music. The rise of feminism, the growing militancy of gay and lesbian people, and a general challenge by the counterculture to traditional notions of masculinity during the 1960s and 1970s prompted among many male musicians a felt need to "masculinize" their music in overt ways. Bruce Springsteen, for example, produced an energetic form of rock music during the 1970s and 1980s that many American youths perceived—despite Springsteen's avowed commitment to gay rights—as "masculine" and "heterosexual," and therefore as a healthy alternative to the "feminine" or "homosexual" disco music that was popular at the time. The mass burning of disco records in 1979, in a campaign known as "disco sucks," similarly represented an attempt to link rock music to masculinity.

At the same time, however, many rock musicians popular among male Americans during the 1960s and 1970s developed alternative forms of masculinity that challenged existing gender norms. Many of them wore long hair, for example. Some, such as those in the group Kiss, dressed in full make-up and spandex. Others, such as British musician David Bowie, cultivated an intentionally androgynous image or, as in the case of Queen's Freddie Mercury, celebrated homosexuality. Still others revived the image of the nineteenth-century "dandy" and projected images of overt hypersexuality. Robert Plant, the lead singer of the British rock group Led Zeppelin (whose "Whole Lotta Love" featured a musical rendition of sexual intercourse) often performed in crotch-bulging pants, while the group's virtuosic guitarist Jimmy Page wielded his guitar as if it were an extended phallus.

The popular music of the 1960s and 1970s also served as a conduit by which disempowered groups challenged the traditional monopolization of power in American society by white males. During the civil rights movement, for example, music was a focal point for an expression of the power of African-American men to change the world they lived in. The song "We Shall Overcome," which became a virtual anthem for the movement, expressed the nonviolent agitation and Christian manhood preached by Martin Luther King, Jr. The singer James Brown, and others, meanwhile, represented the ideals of the more militant Black Power movement, especially in songs like "I Don't Want Nobody To Give Me Nothing," which combined ideas of independence, strength, and pride. Brown's overt sexuality and masculinity as manifested through his lyrical grunting and in-your-face dancing—both powerful and lascivious—became a confrontational call to arms that challenged a generation of African-American men to stand up for their rights. During this same period, feminists used music to challenge traditional male power, with Helen Reddy's "I Am Woman" as perhaps the best-known example.

Musical challenges to traditional masculinity and patriarchy elicited musical defenses by white male performers. In the 1970s and 1980s, heavy metal, emphasizing technical virtuosity, misogynistic lyrics, and a bad-boy image, was one reaction to this challenge for large segments of white, largely working-class men. Men in country music (who were, and still are, virtually all white) drew upon associations of manliness with stoicism and appealed to more culturally conservative audiences in projecting images of country music as more "manly" and "American" than the extroverted showiness of rock performances. Some country rock and Southern rock bands similarly depicted a masculinity grounded in the personal independence long associated with white southern manhood—in being a "Ramblin' Man" (the Allman Brothers), a "Freebird" (Lynyrd Skynyrd), or a "Long-Haired Country Boy" (Charlie Daniels Band).

During the closing decades of the twentieth century, two new musical genres—rap and hip-hop—emerged as important vehicles for articulating masculinity. Originating in Caribbean DJ culture and European electronic dance music, rap and hip-hop emerged in the late 1970s and early 1980s as vibrant new musical forms. From the beginning, rap has been a largely (if not entirely) male genre, with lyrics ranging from boasting about the artist's skills as a rapper and his abilities in bed to an often complex critique of African-American men's place in contemporary America. Artists such as Ice Cube and Public Enemy (a name that suggests the group's explicit resistance to existing power structures) have continually used rap as a vehicle for social commentary, often criticizing urban black men's abandonment of the traditional role as husband and provider. Whether sung by African-American men or (by the 1990s) white American men, rap and hip-hop lyrics have frequently been characterized by both hypermasculine misogyny and, as the controversies surrounding white rapper Eminem show, homophobia. Nevertheless, many artists and listeners have seen in hip-hop's representation of masculinity an empowering inspiration.

Conclusion

Popular music has been one of the many cultural arenas in which the meaning of American masculinity has been contested, particularly in the late twentieth and early twenty-first centuries. Although alternative representations of masculinity in music have usually been more accepted when they came from outside the United States—the gender-bending musicians that achieved success in the 1980s, including Morrissey, the Pet Shop Boys, DJ Tricky, and cross-dressing singer Boy George, were all from England—some significant male

American musicians, such as Prince and RuPaul, were willing to push the boundaries of traditional masculinity. Beginning in the 1970s, women began contributing in a significant way to mainstream popular music, occasionally in traditionally male genres like rap and heavy metal. In the early twenty-first century, musicians continue to challenge the expectations of listeners, and Americans' conception of "masculinity" in music will inevitably continue to change and adapt to society at large.

BIBLIOGRAPHY

Arnett, Hazel. *I Hear America Singing!: Great Folk Songs from the Revolution to Rock.* New York: Praeger, 1975.

Averill, Gage. *Four Parts, No Waiting: A Social History of American Barbershop Harmony.* New York: Oxford University Press, 2003.

Brett, Philip, Elisabeth Wood, and Gary C. Thomas, eds. *Queering the Pitch: The New Gay and Lesbian Musicology.* New York: Routledge, 1994.

Butler, Judith. *Gender Trouble: Feminism and the Subversion of Identity.* New York: Routledge, 1990.

Fast, Susan. *In the Houses of the Holy: Led Zeppelin and the Power of Rock Music.* New York: Oxford University Press, 2001.

Hamm, Charles. *Music in the New World.* New York: Norton, 1983.

Krims, Adam. *Rap Music and the Poetics of Identity.* New York: Cambridge University Press, 2000.

Ownby, Ted. "Freedom, Manhood, and Male Tradition in 1970's Southern Rock Music." In *Haunted Bodies: Gender and Southern Texts,* edited by Anne Goodwyn Jones and Susan V. Donaldson. Charlottesville: University of Virginia Press, 1997.

Walser, Robert. *Running with the Devil: Power, Gender, and Madness in Heavy Metal Music.* Hanover, N.H.: University Press of New England, 1993.

Whiteley, Sheila, ed. *Sexing the Groove: Popular Music and Gender.* New York: Routledge, 1997.

FURTHER READING

Ammer, Christine. *Unsung: A History of Women in American Music.* Portland, Ore.: Amadeus, 2001.

Austin, William W. *"Susanna," "Jeanie," and "The Old Folks at Home": The Songs of Stephen C. Foster from His Time to Ours.* 2nd ed. Urbana: University of Illinois Press, 1987.

Baraka, Imamu Amiri. *Black Music.* New York: Da Capo Press, 1998.

Crawford, Richard. *America's Musical Life.* New York: Norton, 2001.

Fuller, Sophie, and Lloyd Whitesell. *Queer Episodes in Music and Modern Identity.* Urbana: University of Illinois Press, 2002.

Kramer, Lawrence. *Walt Whitman and Modern Music: War, Desire, and the Trials of Nationhood.* New York: Garland, 2000.

Lomax, John A., and Alan Lomax. *Our Singing Country: Folk Songs and Ballads.* Mineola, N.Y.: Dover, 2000.

Malone, Bill C. *Don't Get Above Your Raisin': Country Music and the Southern Working Class.* Urbana: University of Illinois Press, 2002.

Porter, Eric. *What Is This Thing Called Jazz?: African American Musicians as Artists, Critics, and Activists.* Berkeley: University of California Press, 2002.

RELATED ENTRIES

African-American Manhood, American Revolution; Antiwar Movement; Art; Black Panther Party; Citizenship; Counterculture; Feminism; Heroism; Heterosexuality; Homosexuality; Minstrelsy; Race; *Shaft*; Southern Manhood; Springsteen, Bruce; War, Whiteness, Working-Class Manhood

—*Louis Niebur*

Nationalism

Throughout American history, notions of manliness have been central to concepts of national identity, and devotion to the nation has been deemed fundamental to understandings of American manhood. Yet definitions of manliness in relation to national identity have been multiform, ranging from collectivist ideals emphasizing virtue, sacrifice, and surrender to government and the commonwealth to individualist ideals stressing individualism, pursuit of self-interest, independence, and defiance of authority. Although manhood and nationalism sometimes stand in an ambivalent relation to one another, they have also served as mutually reinforcing codes of cultural and political power in the United States.

Nationalism and Manhood in the Revolutionary Era

Concepts of manhood have been fundamental to American nationalism since the time of the nation's birth. Scholars have described the activities of the Sons of Liberty and the Minute Men (groups that helped to organize resistance against the British) as assertions of a nationalism grounded in notions of republicanism and masculinity, as a revolt against the parental authority of the "mother country," and as an antipatriarchal revolt against the authority of King and Parliament. For patriots, the manliness of their actions involved their heroic defiance of corrupt authority, the defense of liberty (portrayed as feminine), and the establishment of a nation based on republican virtue and male citizenship.

Masculine images and metaphors likewise pervaded debates on the nature of the national government at the Constitutional Convention of 1787, convened to modify the faltering Articles of Confederation. Both Federalist supporters and Anti-Federalist critics of a new and enlarged national government presented their positions as essential to the preservation of American manhood. They agreed that the government should be based on republican virtue (that citizens should cherish their independence while surrendering to legitimate national rule) but disagreed on what sort of national government was most consistent with republican manhood. Anti-Federalists, convinced that the centralized form of government proposed by the Federalists threatened virtue and independence, advocated a more decentralized system that would give freer reign to its male citizens. Federalists James Madison and Alexander Hamilton, on the other hand, favored a strong and vigorous national government and condemned the decentralized Articles government as weak. The Federalists argued that the Constitution would preserve manly virtue and independence, while also promoting national power, growth, and vitality. Fearing civic disorder, the Federalists also proposed the paternal and patriarchal authority of a strong presidency to bolster national stability by embodying national identity and unity.

The framers of the Constitution unanimously agreed that this masculine figure should be the heroic Revolutionary War general George Washington. As president, Washington sought to symbolize national unity and manly dignity by avoiding public statements on divisive national issues, and to symbolize civic order and the strength of the national government by personally leading a group of militia to quell the 1794 Whiskey Rebellion (an armed protest by settlers in western Pennsylvania against a government excise tax on corn whiskey). After his death in 1799, Washington became, in the American imagination, an embodiment of virtue and the patriarchal "father of his country." His birthday remained a major national holiday well into the nineteenth century, and the designers of the Washington Monument, begun in 1848, consciously sought a design that would represent both Washington's heroism and national strength. The monument, the man, and the presidency have remained powerful homogenizing and unifying national symbols.

National Identity and Masculinity in the Early Republic

Through the early nineteenth century, American national identity formed slowly and unevenly, but nationalism was a powerful current that was shaped by notions of masculinity. Conceptions of American national identity pivoted on the political and social ideologies (and the accompanying models of republican manhood) associated specifically with the presidencies of Thomas Jefferson (1801–09) and Andrew Jackson (1829–37). Jeffersonian ideology grounded national character and strength in the figures of the genteel patriarch, the heroic artisan, and the yeoman farmer—the first responsible for benevolent, paternalistic governance, and the latter two representing national productivity and industriousness. These figures ensured the perpetuation of republican virtue and independence. Jacksonianism incorporated the ideals of the artisan and the small farmer, while adding a model of antiauthoritarian egalitarianism appropriate to citizenship in a democratic republic. Literary figures of the early to mid-nineteenth century, such as Ralph Waldo Emerson and Walt Whitman, similarly defined American national identity in terms of self-reliance and a celebration of the everyman. All of these models of American manhood and nationhood found symbolic embodiment in the figure of Uncle Sam, which emerged during the patriotism accompanying the War of 1812 and became a national icon thereafter.

Notions of race and whiteness reinforced this association of masculinity with nation. At a time when political citizenship was confined to white males, articulations and symbols of nationalism tended to remain firmly tied to notions of white manhood. The link between manhood, nationhood, and whiteness was most strongly visible in the idea of Manifest Destiny, which linked America's identity and future to western expansion by industrious white men, and to economic opportunity and political rights for white men. As the nation and national order became defined around the equality of white men, nonwhite males (particularly Native Americans and Mexicans) increasingly became perceived as undisciplined counterpoints to national identity and as violent enemies of the nation. Previous emphases on deference, paternalism, and patriarchy were projected onto African slaves, Native Americans, and Mexicans.

At the same time, heterogeneous local and regional identities persisted. Yet even these were couched in terms of masculine archetypes and became increasingly tied to national identities. The New England "Yankee," for example, a male figure characterized by entrepreneurial drive and ingenuity, became symbolic of American national vigor. The association between localism, nationalism, and manhood was also strong in the case of the republic of Texas (1836–44), whose founders Stephen Austin and Sam Houston couched Texas nationalism in terms of a heroic defense of republican freedom (and of African-American slavery) against Mexican authoritarianism. Perhaps the most obvious association between regional identities, nationalism, and concepts of masculinity involved the growing sectional conflict between the North and South, which defined themselves according to the respective symbolic figures of the entrepreneurial Yankee and the chivalrous "Cavalier."

Civil War, Masculinity, and the Articulation of National Identity

The Civil War (1861–65), though divisive in the short term, ultimately had a homogenizing impact on definitions of manliness and nation. The war valued manly sacrifice in the name of the nation (or region), discredited Southern nationalism as a legitimate form of masculine identification, and ultimately generated an ideal of heroic (white) warrior masculinity and strenuous living, emphasizing usefulness, duty, and commitment to the nation, that both Northern and Southern men could embrace.

Jeffersonian and Jacksonian concepts of republican manhood informed both Confederate and Union definitions of manliness and nation. Confederate nationalism emphasized fierce independence and white paternalism. Union nationalism, grounded in the idea that "free soil" and "free labor" meant "free men" (an idea that became the ideological basis of Abraham Lincoln's Republican Party) —was rooted in the Jeffersonian and Jacksonian idealizations of independent landowning, heroic artisanship, and liberty.

Northern constructions of national identity and masculinity placed a particular emphasis on self-sacrifice. Julia Ward Howe's "Battle Hymn of the Republic" (1862) celebrates Christ-like sacrifice in the name of liberty and freedom, as did President Lincoln's Gettysburg Address and second inaugural address. The Gettysburg cemetery, dedicated in 1863, like other national cemeteries that would follow, starkly symbolized in its orderly arrangement of tombstones the idea that the sacrifice of one's life to the collective national whole is the ultimate expression of manliness.

The Confederate defeat discredited Southern nationalism as a manifestation of American manliness—a point reinforced by Northern claims that Confederate president Jefferson Davis had been apprehended trying to escape dressed in women's clothes. Yet the persistence of Southern nationalism, and its ongoing relationship with Southern manhood, remained apparent in Southern cultural life through the remainder of the nineteenth and twentieth centuries, manifest in the 1867 rise of the Ku Klux Klan, the spectacular success of the 1915 film *Birth of a Nation*, and the continuing visibility of the Confederate flag on state houses and pickup trucks.

Abraham Lincoln, meanwhile, though assassinated in 1865 just after the Civil War, emerged as a new and powerful symbol of manliness and national identity. Having eloquently articulated the meaning of American nationhood in his Gettysburg address and second inaugural address, and having presided over the victorious Union cause, he became an iconic representative of honesty and virtue, national strength and endurance, and the abolition of slavery in the name of freedom. Lincoln's symbolic status was perhaps most apparent in the growing tendency to add Lincolnesque features to renditions of Uncle Sam, and in the design of the Lincoln

Memorial, which was intended to associate his larger-than-life figure with national ideals and strength.

In the aftermath of the Civil War, the ideal of heroic warrior masculinity, with its emphasis on duty, obligation, and the "strenuous life," became the chief model for American nationalism. The emergence of this notion of manliness and its rise to national prominence was apparent as early as 1866 in the first Grand Review of the Grand Army of the Republic. This parade, organized by Union veterans, associated manhood and nationalism with collective identity, defense of union, the Northern cause, and whiteness; it excluded Confederate veterans as well as the women and African Americans who had contributed to Union victory. By defining American national identity as masculine and white, this particular construction of the heroic warrior model helped foreclose the radical potential for social change suggested by the Reconstruction period.

Heroic warrior masculinity and the concept of the strenuous life were also encouraged by renewed western expansion after 1865, and by the growing imperialist impulse of the late nineteenth century. White men, who claimed to be fulfilling their national (as well as gender and racial) destinies, were pitted against nonwhite men along the frontier, as well as in the Caribbean, Latin America, Asia, and the Pacific, further reinforcing the postwar synchronization between manhood and nation. The ongoing definition of the United States in terms of white Anglo-Saxon manhood was further evident in late-nineteenth-century and early-twentieth-century immigration legislation virtually excluding immigration from Asia and from southern and eastern Europe by 1924.

Manhood and National Identity in the Twentieth Century

In the twentieth century, two world wars, the Cold War, and growing anxiety over Middle Eastern terrorism afforded new opportunities to articulate notions of national identity grounded in constructions of masculinity. In World Wars I and II, U.S. propaganda—such as the well-known poster of Uncle Sam calling men to national military service—associated the nation and its male soldiers with a vigorous and aggressive defense against perceived threats to freedom and democracy. American soldiers, in the form of the World War I "doughboy" and the World War II "G.I. Joe," became symbols of nationalism and manliness. During the Cold War, Americans, concerned with asserting and demonstrating the superiority of American institutions to Soviet communism, anxiously defined American life in terms of masculine power, diplomatic and military assertiveness, economic success, sexual and physical prowess, moral righteousness, and patriotism.

Yet traditional articulations of masculinity and nationalism began to shift in the aftermath of World War II. The growing power of the civil rights and racial identity movements after a war in which the defense of American institutions was linked to the defeat of white racism discredited the traditional link between nationalism and whiteness. The new emphasis on a racially inclusive nationalism was dramatically expressed in Martin Luther King, Jr.'s, "I Have a Dream" speech, delivered at the Lincoln Memorial in 1963.

The Vietnam War also challenged traditional associations between manliness and national identity. A widespread antiwar movement questioned the war's moral and democratic aims and associated manhood with a principled resistance to national policy. Furthermore, the loss of that conflict against Asian men deemed inferior and even effeminate undermined the power of the figure of the (male) soldier as a signifier of national strength. This problem was apparent in the debate over the Vietnam Veterans Memorial in Washington, D.C. The memorial committee's decision to use inscriptions on a wall rather than embodied male figures generated a controversy that ended only with the addition of a bronze sculpture of a group of American soldiers symbolizing American warrior masculinity.

A promise to restore the association between nationalism and masculinity in the aftermath of the Vietnam War and the 1979 seizure of American hostages in Iran was a significant element in the successful 1980 presidential campaign of Ronald Reagan. During his presidency (1981–89), Reagan employed the rhetoric of warrior masculinity against the Soviet Union and Middle Eastern terrorism, authorizing military strikes against a leftist government in Grenada and against Libyan leader and suspected terrorist sponsor Muammar al-Qaddafi. His example was followed by his vice president and successor, George H. W. Bush (1989–93), in his approach to Iraqi leader Saddam Hussein during the 1991 Persian Gulf War. President George W. Bush, who took office in 2001, used similar rhetoric against both Hussein and terrorist organizations deemed a threat to American security.

In the aftermath of the attacks on the United States on September 11, 2001, New York mayor Rudolph Giuliani was praised in public discourse for embodying republican traditions of service and civic devotion, while New York City firefighters were upheld as inspiring symbols of manly sacrifice and national loss. These developments made it clear that longstanding associations of masculinity with national identity, sacrifice, and devotion, and the translation of local paragons of manhood into national ones, remain powerful cultural impulses in American life.

BIBLIOGRAPHY

Anderson, Benedict. *Imagined Communities: Reflections on the Origin and Spread of Nationalism.* London: Verso, 1983.

Kann, Mark E. *On the Man Question: Gender and Civic Virtue in America.* Philadelphia: Temple University Press, 1991.

Nagel, Joane. "Masculinity and Nationalism: Gender and Sexuality in the Making of Nations." *Ethnic and Racial Studies* 21 (March 1998): 245–269.

Nelson, Dana D. *National Manhood: Capitalist Citizenship and the Imagined Fraternity of White Men.* Durham, N.C.: Duke University Press, 1998.

O'Leary, Cecilia Elizabeth. *To Die For: The Paradox of American Patriotism.* Princeton, N.J.: Princeton University Press, 1999.

Rogin, Michael Paul. *Fathers and Children: Andrew Jackson and the Subjugation of the American Indian.* New Brunswick, N.J.: Transaction, 1991.

Sharp, Joanne P. "Gendering Nationhood: A Feminist Engagement With National Identity." In *Bodyspace: Destabilizing Geographies of Gender and Sexuality*, edited by Nancy Duncan. London: Routledge, 1996.

Waldstreicher, David. *In The Midst Of Perpetual Fetes: The Making of American Nationalism, 1776–1820.* Chapel Hill: University of North Carolina Press, 1997.

Zelinsky, Wilbur. *Nation Into State: The Shifting Symbolic Foundations of American Nationalism.* Chapel Hill: University of North Carolina Press, 1988.

FURTHER READING

Bederman, Gail. *Manliness and Civilization: A Cultural History of Gender and Race in the United States, 1880–1917.* Chicago: University of Chicago Press, 1996.

Glassberg, David. *American Historical Pageantry: The Uses of Tradition in the Early Twentieth Century.* Chapel Hill: University of North Carolina Press, 1990.

Higham, John. *Strangers in the Land: Patterns of American Nativism, 1860–1925.* 2nd ed. New Brunswick, N.J.: Rutgers University Press, 1994.

Lind, Michael. *The Next American Nation: The New Nationalism and the Fourth American Revolution.* New York: Free Press, 1996.

Rydell, Robert W. *All the World's a Fair: Visions of Empire At American International Expositions, 1876–1916.* Chicago: University of Chicago Press, 1984.

Travers, Len. *Celebrating the Fourth: Independence Day and the Rites of Nationalism in the Early Republic.* Amherst: University of Massachusetts Press, 1997.

RELATED ENTRIES

Agrarianism; American Revolution; Citizenship; Cold War; Democratic Manhood; Emerson, Ralph Waldo; Heroism; Imperialism; Jackson, Andrew; Lincoln, Abraham; Manifest Destiny; Militarism; Nativism; Patriarchy; Patriotism; Politics; Reagan, Ronald; Republicanism; Uncle Sam; Vietnam War; War; Washington, George; Whiteness; Whitman, Walt; World War I; World War II

—*Thomas Winter*

THE NATION OF ISLAM

Arising amidst the segregation, racial violence, and economic disparity of the early twentieth century, the Nation of Islam (NOI) was embraced by black Americans yearning for racial pride. By proposing a model of masculinity founded upon a vigilant defense of African-American society and culture, a quest for financial independence, and a reclaiming of self-mediated identity, the NOI offered a striking alternative to extant white paradigms that devalued black men's intellects and abilities and African-American models that emphasized racial assimilation. Since that time, this movement has continued to promote a style of masculinity and a social agenda welcomed by many African Americans, particularly marginalized ones.

In the 1910s, a surge of black nationalism swept the United States. Groups such as Marcus Garvey's Universal Negro Improvement Association sought self-determination, economic sovereignty, and, often, repatriation to Africa. The NOI surfaced during the Great Depression to address the concerns of large numbers of southern blacks moving to northern cities. Faced with discrimination and an impoverished lifestyle, many of these individuals proved amenable to calls for black separatism and fiscal autonomy. W. D. Fard, a mysterious itinerant peddler, arrived in Detroit in 1930 and began teaching that African Americans were divinely favored by a black God. Far from adhering to strict Islamic law, Fard's eclectic NOI philosophy borrowed from earlier black nationalist movements, the Bible, and his own Afrocentric interpretation of humanity's origins, among other sources. Believed by his followers to be the Messiah who would initiate a racial Armageddon, Fard disappeared under mysterious circumstances in 1934. Elijah Muhammad then assumed leadership of the movement.

Under Muhammad's direction, the NOI accepted Fard as a manifestation of Allah, while also enhancing many of his teachings. Until apocalyptically released from bondage, blacks were counseled to discover their true history, reject their Christian "slave religion" and its implied posture of submissiveness, abide by strict behavioral codes that included bans on tobacco and alcohol, and reinforce patriarchal household relations. Thousands of men embraced Muhammad's message, welcoming the NOI's call for a virile, prideful, and accountable masculinity.

Most active among the lower economic classes, the NOI has historically proselytized to men who are unemployed or unable to provide for their families. By stressing rigid personal morality and self-sufficiency, the movement has sought to reinstate a sense of confident and responsible masculinity. These traits have formed the basis for a disciplined style of manhood deemed capable of furthering the larger causes of black America—a model that paradoxically resembles that of white, middle-class masculinity founded upon work and temperance.

Throughout his forty-year tenure, Elijah Muhammad preached a distinct vision of family life. Claiming that an idealized notion of womanhood was the source of domestic well-being, he encouraged male members to respect and protect their wives and daughters. To restore a sense of female dignity undermined by slavery and oppression, men were prompted to enforce a stringent female code of conduct that emphasized modest behavior and a concentration upon household life. Through such measures, the NOI promoted a masculinity that both reviled liberalizing midcentury gender reforms and embraced a lingering "cult of domesticity" that viewed women as inherently suited to the private world of the home, and men as naturally suited to the public sphere.

Beginning in the 1940s, these proscriptions were inculcated through Muslim Girl's Training and General Civilization Classes and the male-only Fruit of Islam organization. Preaching the value of family responsibility, the Fruit of Islam stressed gender equality while claiming that each sex must fulfill a role for the sake of domestic stability. Additionally, it included a paramilitary component offering instruction on the defense of family and race. By accentuating aggression and violence, the Fruit of Islam gave men the opportunity to embrace a virile mode of manhood often denied to them within the dominant culture, while also acting as vanguards for the pending black revolution. Thus, by defining men as wage earners, family decision makers, and combative guardians, the movement offered a vision of masculinity increasingly at odds with white society's nascent critique of entrenched patriarchy.

By the early 1960s, the NOI began experiencing schisms that would alter its model of masculinity. Under the guidance of Malcolm X, it started to attract middle-class members. Preaching a more socially active message—one that disputed Muhammad's disavowal of the American political system—Malcolm X challenged the movement's leadership. After a pilgrimage to Mecca in 1964, he embraced an orthodox version of Islam and left the NOI to found the Muslim Mosque, Inc. and the Organization of Afro-American Unity. By situating submission to Allah and emulation of his Prophet as primary for the development of masculine identity, he disrupted the NOI's focus on Fard and Muhammad as paradigms of maleness, and in advocating the more egalitarian principles of Sunni Islam and embracing personal independence, he abandoned the NOI's racialized and violent approach to masculinity, as well as its emphasis on obedience to male NOI leaders as primary to idealized manliness. Though assassinated in 1965, Malcolm X's activism and turn to more conventional Muslim beliefs would continue to affect the NOI's ideology for decades.

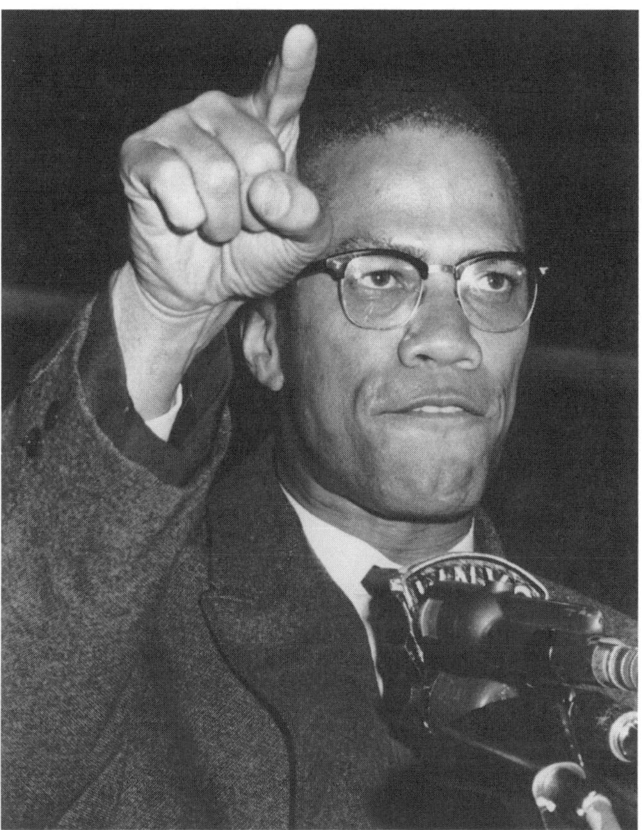

Nation of Islam leader Malcolm X preached an ideal of African-American manhood emphasizing racial pride, militancy, social activism, self-discipline, and responsibility to family and community. After converting to orthodox Islam, he abandoned the Nation of Islam's racialized and violent approach to masculinity. (From the collections of the Library of Congress)

At the death of Elijah Muhammad in 1974, his son, Wallace, assumed control of the organization and created the more traditional World Community of Al-Islam in the West (later known as the American Muslim Mission). Embracing the teachings of Sunni Islam, he eliminated gender-segregated training classes and placed greater focus upon women's intellectual capacities. But, inspired by the Koran, he continued to emphasize the centrality of the family and of the man's responsibility for familial welfare. He also maintained the traditional NOI emphasis on men's "natural" prowess in the marketplace and the public sphere.

Although the vast majority of contemporary African-American Muslims adhere to Wallace Muhammad's stances, in 1978 Louis Farrakhan restored the Nation of Islam's original goals by reorganizing the movement, reinstating classes to teach proper male and female conduct, and re-emphasizing a gendered public/private divide. As the principal organizer of the 1995 Million Man March, he brought together hundreds of thousands of black men to affirm virtues of sobriety, commitment, and racial pride. Calling for men to take responsibility for their families and to dedicate themselves to fighting drugs, violence, and unemployment, Farrakhan and his movement reiterated a time-honored NOI model of maleness.

By offering an ideology founded upon racial purity, domestic leadership and defense, economic independence, and the cultivation of self-esteem, the NOI has granted black men the opportunity to rework their identities amid oppression and bigotry. Although the nature of black Muslim belief and practice in the United States has changed since the death of Elijah Muhammad, events such as the Million Man March and the continued controversial notoriety of Louis Farrakhan demonstrate that the NOI's masculine paradigm persists as a viable option for many.

BIBLIOGRAPHY

Akbar, Na'im. "Family Stability Among African-American Muslims." In *Muslim Families in North America,* edited by Earle H. Waugh, Sharon McIrvin Abu-Laban, and Regula Burckhardt Qureshi. Edmonton: University of Alberta Press, 1991.

Gardell, Mattias. *In the Name of Elijah Muhammad: Louis Farrakhan and the Nation of Islam.* Durham, N.C.: Duke University Press, 1996.

Lincoln, C. Eric. *The Black Muslims in America.* 3rd ed. Grand Rapids, Mich.: Eerdmans, 1993.

Marsh, Clifton E. *From Black Muslims to Muslims: The Transition from Separatism to Islam, 1930–1980.* Metuchen, N.J.: Scarecrow Press, 1994.

Miller, Timothy. "Black Jews and Black Muslims." In *America's Alternative Religions,* edited by Timothy Miller. Albany: State University of New York Press, 1995.

Munir, Fareed. "Malcolm X's Religious Pilgrimage: From Black Separatism to a Universal Way." In *Redeeming Men: Religion and Masculinities,* edited by Stephen B. Boyd, W. Merle Longwood, and Mark W. Muesse. Louisville, Ky.: Westminster John Knox Press, 1996.

FURTHER READING

Clegg, Claude Andrew. *An Original Man: The Life and Times of Elijah Muhammad.* New York: St. Martin's, 1997.

Essien-Udom, E. U. *Black Nationalism: A Search for an Identity in America.* Chicago: University of Chicago Press, 1971.

Lee, Martha F. *The Nation of Islam: An American Millenarian Movement.* Syracuse, N.Y.: Syracuse University Press, 1996.

RELATED ENTRIES

African-American Manhood; Civil Rights Movement; Class; Cult of Domesticity; Emancipation; Great Depression; Malcolm X; Militarism; Nationalism; Nuclear Family; Patriarchy; Race; Religion and Spirituality; Self-Control; Slavery; Temperance; Urbanization; Violence; Working-Class Manhood

—*Aaron K. Ketchell*

NATIVE AMERICAN MANHOOD

Of all the historical images of the Native American man, perhaps none has endured as well as that of the lone warrior. Whether recalling the Sioux war-chief Sitting Bull or the horse-mounted militants of 1950s Westerns, Americans tend to imagine Indian men either fighting valiantly on the frontier or stoically accepting inevitable military defeat. This one-dimensional representation masks the complexity of both historical and contemporary Indian manhood. For more than four hundred years, Native American men have played a host of other roles that have shaped American history in concrete ways and that offer important insights into the construction of masculine identities and the social structures that support them.

Contact and Colonization in Early America

Some of the most telling episodes in the first century of Indians' interactions with European newcomers center on clashing understandings of masculinity. Almost all Indian societies of the fifteenth and sixteenth centuries trained boys by example, ritual, and shame that becoming a man meant developing skills as a successful hunter and potent warrior. In many cases, this meant participating in a vision quest, a rite of passage undertaken at puberty during which adolescent boys would seek inspiration and power through altered states of consciousness. After this or a similar rite of passage, a young man would participate in his first hunting or raiding expedition. Thereafter, social custom demanded that he avoid all domestic and agricultural duties, which were deemed emasculating and demeaning for men. Among the many Indian societies that relied heavily on agriculture for subsistence, such as the Iroquois or Pueblo, this customary prohibition checked men's power by excluding a village's most important material resources from their control. In these cases, however, men governed many of the spiritual resources believed to be necessary for healing, successful harvests and hunts, and community safety.

Many Europeans brought to North America concepts of manhood that accorded poorly with Indian gender roles. The French explorer Jacques Cartier, for example, wrote in 1535 that the Iroquoian men of the St. Lawrence River Valley were lazy and exploitative because "the women . . . work beyond comparison more than the men, both at fishing, which is much followed, as well as at tilling the ground and other tasks" (Biggar, 70). To the English of Virginia in the early seventeenth century, Indian men were "idle" not because they were inactive, but because they neglected to take responsibility for agriculture, as European men were trained to do. Thus, early English colonists justified their seizure of Indian lands by pointing to the failure of Indian men to subdue the earth with the plow.

Indians also scorned European men. To begin with, European men did not physically measure up to the standards of Indian masculinity. Not only were European men generally shorter and in poorer physical condition than Indian men, but Indians also detested the facial hair worn by Europeans to signify their transition to adult manhood. In 1632, for example, a Jesuit missionary wrote that the natives believed that facial hair "makes people more ugly and weakens their intelligence" (Jaenen, 24). When European men used the hoe, the plow, or the scythe, Indians judged them to be effeminate and thus easily defeated.

Yet many Indian men did not conform to the ideal types prescribed by their social customs, and the ambivalence with which Indian societies dealt with these cases reveals a great deal about their concepts of masculinity. Europeans observed among many Indian peoples men who have come to be known as *berdache* (meaning "slave" or "prostitute"), biological males who assumed the clothing, demeanor, and sexual role of women. Historians have long debated the status of these men within seventeenth- and eighteenth-century Indian societies. According to one interpretation, the berdache symbolized harmony between the sexes and the potential for fluidity in gender roles. In this view, these men were "two-spirit peoples" who possessed metaphysical powers of both sexes in one body, and therefore occupied a position of special importance. Others have adhered more closely to the term *berdache*, suggesting that these men were marginalized and victimized for their deviation from gender norms.

Although surviving evidence may never permit a conclusive answer to this question, the documents yield two important insights. First, the particular attention paid to these men by both Native American and European cultures, whether positive or negative, reveals the importance of masculinity in Native social organization. The social status of these men depended, for better or worse, on the basic integrity of gender divisions, for they were defined by their position outside the norm. Second, the actual status of the berdache seems to have varied among Indian societies, depending on the relative power exercised by men and women within a given village, tribe, or nation. The greater the authority exercised by women, the less disempowering it was for these men to assume a female role. For example, among the Pueblo of New Mexico, where women controlled property and grain, Spanish observers reported less abuse and derision of the berdache than they witnessed among the Nahua (Aztec), a much more male-dominant culture.

However, it would be misleading to suggest that only conflict and difference characterized Indian–European understandings of masculinity. Throughout the colonial period, Native Americans and Europeans also forged economic and military alliances that relied heavily on some shared assumptions about men and masculinity. Particularly when it came to war, Indian and European gender norms reinforced each other. Indian men appealed to a common language of manhood to goad others into fighting or to demean conquered enemies. When the Delaware Indians refused to join the Iroquois as allies in war, the Iroquois taunted: "You delaware Indians doe nothing but stay att home & boill yor potts, and are like women, while wee Onondages & Senekaes goe abroad & fight" (Shoemaker, 242). The Iroquois used the same tactic to convince reluctant English colonists to "fight like Men."

The Nineteenth Century

With the removal of the French from North America in 1763 and the defeat of the British in the American Revolution, Indians faced new pressures that continued to reveal and influence Native American masculinity. During the nineteenth century, Americans moved with unprecedented rapidity into Indian country, provoking Indian resistance in areas previously allowed to remain under their control. Following a long tradition of captivity narratives, American publishers thrived on tales of rapacious Indian men skulking at the woods' edge for vulnerable white women. These images of Indian men provided the justification many sought for forcibly removing Indian peoples from the lands desired by white settlers and speculators. During the 1820s and 1830s especially, state and national governments adopted a policy of forced relocation, symbolized by the tragic march of the Cherokee on the Trail of Tears in 1838.

Ironically, during the same period, other segments of American society began to embrace a more romantic vision of Indian men as the vanishing remnants of an epic past. In James Fenimore Cooper's collection of five novels known as the Leatherstocking Tales (1823–41), for instance, a few caricatured Indian men served as emblems of a disappearing race doomed either to death or removal to the West. Others, such as the transcendentalist and romantic movements, appealed to an idealistic image of the Indian male to critique what they saw as the emasculating effects of urbanization and industrialization.

As white Americans consumed these contrasting, yet mutually reinforcing, images of Native American men, hundreds of thousands of real Indian men struggled to adapt to new social and demographic pressures. Within those groups most resistant to American encroachments, male revival leaders such as the Shawnee prophet Tenskwatawa or the Seneca visionary Handsome Lake struggled to lead their communities against increasing odds. Within historically matriarchal Indian cultures, male revival leaders faced stern resistance from women accustomed to playing a greater role in village politics, family relations, and religion. Because the United States increasingly associated Indian politics with violent removal, however, it became harder for Indian groups to separate the masculine function of warrior from the more gender-neutral realm of village politics.

By midcentury, most Indian nations east of the Mississippi faced either sharp population declines or dangerous relocation onto unfamiliar lands. Given the close relationship between Indian gender divisions and the range of subsistence activities within a community, ecological and demographic pressures had a powerful influence on Indian masculinity. At the turn of the nineteenth century, for example, the eastern Sioux were shifting from a more gender-balanced hunting and gathering economy to one centered almost entirely on male bison hunting. Conversely, many Indian women expanded their economic role as male hunting activities became much more difficult to sustain in their new western homeland.

During the second half of the nineteenth century, the U.S. government worked to coerce Indians to adopt farming as their primary means of subsistence. Indian men therefore faced a dual threat to their sense of masculinity. Government agents, and even sympathetic reformers, questioned the manhood of Indian males who refused to farm and "provide" for their families. However, in many cases, peers within Indian communities persisted in shaming those men who agreed to do the "women's work" of caring for crops. Access to government and community resources often depended on a man's willingness to choose one masculine ideal over another.

Between 1854 and 1890, more than fifty major battles and massacres reinvigorated Indian men's role as warrior, among Indians and non-Indians alike. Especially during and after the Civil War, American armies invaded Indian country, killing thousands and destabilizing Indian communities all across the

Lakota Sioux war-chief Sitting Bull (Tatanka Iyotake), photographed in about 1884. His spiritual leadership and his 1876 defeat of George Custer at Little Bighorn made him heroically symbolic of traditional ideals of Native American manhood, which were being reinvigorated amid the antiwhite resistance movements of the late nineteenth century. (From the collections of the Library of Congress)

West. When a coalition of Indian men defeated the army of General George Armstrong Custer at the Battle of Little Bighorn (in the Montana Territory) in 1876, they gained prestige among their own people and reinforced prescribed masculine roles in warfare. To non-Indian Americans, however, this manifestation of Indian masculinity only confirmed the importance of changing Indian men from fighters into passive farmers or industrial workers.

Following the American defeat of the Sioux at Wounded Knee in South Dakota, in 1890, Indian men again faced a crisis of masculinity that the warfare of the past generation had only temporarily masked. In fundamental ways, Indian communities at the end of the nineteenth century had to re-envision the role of men within Indian cultures. Disruptions in subsistence activities, demographic and geographic change, and new legal and political realities all encouraged the redefinition of masculine roles. White Americans, however, continued to consume images of masculinity that encouraged them to pursue a "primitive" virility—as long as it did not get in the way of white progress. In this era, popular culture perfected the image of the vanishing Indian warrior, even as it encouraged white men to reclaim some of the "savage" masculinity of a fading past.

The Twentieth Century and Beyond

In the twentieth century, Native American men found diverse answers to the problem of defining masculinity in a changing world. For some, survival meant finding ways to fit historical definitions of manliness, including bravery and fearlessness, into viable means of subsisting. Thus, during the 1920s, a large number of Mohawk men found work doing the dangerous, high-altitude welding required to build New York City's high-rise buildings. These Mohawk "sky walkers," as they came to be known, gained renown for their brave handling of these dangerous tasks, earning the respect of more traditional men and women at home and the praise of employers who struggled to fill these treacherous positions. Given the increasing concentrations of Indian peoples in cities across the country, such innovative adaptations of historical mores to new circumstances proved highly valuable as models for other Indian men.

In other cases, definitions of masculinity simply changed. Among the Navajo, for instance, farming became an increasingly legitimate occupation for men, no longer associated with women as it once had been. Although livestock herding accounted for much of the Navajos' wealth, farming provided most of their subsistence. By the twentieth century, men played the dominant role in both.

These and similar changes in gender roles forced Indian communities of the twentieth century to formulate a sense of identity and continuity with their past that could reconcile shifting definitions of masculinity with efforts to reinvigorate past traditions. Living in a world where fixed gender norms and exclusive spheres of authority no longer met social and legal standards of propriety, Indian men struggled to reclaim those portions of their past that allowed for such fluidity.

In November 2001, the all-female Sweetgrass Road Drum Group traveled to St. Paul, Minnesota, to perform at a powwow organized by the University of St. Thomas. The Indian men who organized the festival sent them away, claiming that drumming was a traditionally male activity and that the women's participation would thus render the powwow inauthentic. Incensed, the female drummers promptly filed suit for sexual discrimination. The case touched off a firestorm of debate in Indian communities about the history of Indian gender divisions and the propriety of maintaining historical divisions in traditional activities. This case, and the controversies it has inspired, indicate the ongoing importance of male gender definitions among American Indians and suggest that issues involving masculinity will continue to shape Indian life.

Bibliography

Biggar, H. P., ed. *The Voyages of Jacques Cartier.* Toronto: University of Toronto Press, 1993.

Brown, Kathleen M. "The Anglo-Algonquian Gender Frontier." In *American Indians,* edited by Nancy Shoemaker. Malden, Mass.: Blackwell, 2001.

Jaenen, Cornelius J. *Friend and Foe: Aspects of French-Amerindian Cultural Contact in the Sixteenth and Seventeenth Centuries.* Toronto: McClelland and Stewart, 1976.

"Powwow Dispute Highlights Male–Female Divide in Indian Country." *Associated Press State and Local Wire,* December 18, 2001.

Shoemaker, Nancy. "An Alliance between Men: Gender Metaphors in Eighteenth-Century American Indian Diplomacy East of the Mississippi." *Ethnohistory* 46 (Spring 1999): 239–263.

Thomas, David, et al. *The Native Americans: An Illustrated History.* Atlanta: Turner Publishing, 1993.

White, Richard, "The Winning of the West: The Expansion of the Western Sioux in the Eighteenth and Nineteenth Centuries." *Journal of American History* 45 (September 1978): 319–343.

Further Reading

Crow Dog, Leonard Erdos, and Richard Erdoes. *Crow Dog: Four Generations of Sioux Medicine Men.* New York: HarperCollins, 1995.

Deloria, Philip J. *Playing Indian.* New Haven, Conn.: Yale University Press, 1998.

Gutierrez, Ramon. *When Jesus Came, the Corn Mothers Went Away: Marriage, Sexuality, and Power in New Mexico, 1500–1846.* Stanford, Calif.: Stanford University Press, 1991.

White, Richard. *The Middle Ground: Indians, Empires, and Republics in the Great Lakes Region, 1650–1815.* Cambridge, England: Cambridge University Press, 1995.

Related Entries

Agrarianism; Breadwinner Role; Crisis of Masculinity; Family; Homosexuality; Industrialization; Leatherstocking Tales; Military; Property; Race; Religion and Spirituality; Transvestism; Urbanization; War; Western Frontier; Westerns

—*Brett Rushforth*

Nativism

Historians of the United States apply the term *nativism* to political and cultural ideologies developed and embraced primarily by white men. Although these men share the racial, ethnic, and religious background of the most powerful groups in the culture, they feel economically and politically disadvantaged in relation to those they deem alien to the society. Nativism has been both a component and reflection of the masculinity of these disaffected white males.

Nativist ideology in the United States has typically defined new immigrants (and often nonimmigrant racial and religious minorities) as unable or unwilling to become "true Americans" or "real men," and also as threats to the rightful dominance of white, Protestant, heterosexual males. Most nativist groups have believed that legal—and sometimes illegal—actions are imperative to "preserve" the United States from the pernicious influence of the groups they have identified as un-American and unmanly, and thus unsuited for the rights and privileges of citizenship. At different points in American history, U.S. nativists have identified as "inferior" members of nondominant races (any nonwhite group), nondominant ethnicities (e.g., Irish and Asian immigrants), nondominant religions (e.g., Catholicism, Judaism, and Mormonism), and even members of unpopular groups (e.g., members of the Masonic Brotherhood).

Periods of large-scale immigration and difficult economic situations have often coincided with and helped to produce nativist activity, particularly among working-class men seeking to preserve the perceived link between Americanness, manhood, and economic self-sufficiency. In the mid–nineteenth century an influx of Irish-Catholic immigrants, combined with the rapidly fluctuating economic conditions generated by industrialization, prompted the rise of a number of nativist groups. The Know-Nothings (a semi-secret political party originally named the Order of the Star Spangled Banner and later called the American Party) was the most prominent and most successful, significantly affecting a number of elections in both the northern and southern states during the 1850s. The Know-Nothings defined the "true American" man as a white heterosexual who had been born—and whose parents had been born—in the United States. Know-Nothing publications provided idealized images of American nativists: young, beardless, and blandly handsome men with curling blond or brown hair and dark eyes. One description of the representative Know-Nothing (called "Sam") portrayed him as "a tall American whose forefathers fought in the battles of the Republic," with a "sound head and a pure heart" that was "as tender as his nerves are strong" (Overdyke, 181–83). Other nineteenth-century nativists conceived the ideal American man similarly: He was an industrious, frugal Protestant who made a living doing "honest" (usually physical) labor.

Nativist ideology has generally defined "alien" males as either excessively or insufficiently masculine. During the mid–nineteenth century, for example, nativists portrayed the Irish laborers they saw threatening their livelihood as lazy, immoral, stupid, and lacking the qualities nativists associated with manliness. Nativist literature of the period was typified by the novel *Stanhope Burleigh: The Jesuits in Our Home* (1855), which titillated readers with a plot contrasting the pure manly love of Know-Nothing patriots with lascivious, violent attacks on American women by hypersexualized Irish priests. Later nativist writings similarly attributed sexual violence against women and "white slavery" to immigrants and other target groups. In the early twentieth century, fiction, popular theatre, and films incorporated nativist images that reinforced stereotypes of Irish Catholic priests, Asian males, and African-American men as sexual threats against whom the "true American" man served as a defender of female virtue.

After the Civil War, groups like the Ku Klux Klan (founded in 1865), The American Protective Association (founded in 1887), and the Immigration Restriction League (founded in 1894) arose in response to the political and economic impact of newly emancipated African Americans, immigration from southern and eastern Europe, and Asian immigration to the western United States. Like the Know-Nothings, these later nativists defined their masculinity in contrast to the groups they feared and distrusted. Nativists described Asians, Jewish immigrants, and other target groups with imagery similar to that found in Sax Rohmer's novels (originally published during the 1910s) about the arch-villain

Dr. Fu Manchu, whom Rohmer described (using terms his audiences associated with femininity and moral depravity) as "lean and feline, high-shouldered, with a brow like Shakespeare and a face like Satan, a close-shaven skull, and long, magnetic eyes . . . with all the cruel cunning of an entire Eastern race . . . " (Rohmer, 94).

The close association between American nativism and masculinity has been equally apparent in nativists' stance on gender roles. Women have been welcome to participate in nativist activities, provided they accept male leadership and a construction of gender that identifies men with public leadership and women with dependence and submission. Nativists have consistently understood gender (like race and ethnicity) in terms of hierarchy and essentialism. To nativists, men's dominance over, and difference from, women is as natural as the "true American" man's dominance over, and difference, from other males. They ardently defend a patriarchal model of gender relations and promote a model of the nuclear family in which women and children benefit from their dependence and inequality. They have considered any attempt by women to achieve equality and independence—whether as members of a convent, as suffragists in the nineteenth century, or as advocates of economic and sexual autonomy in the twentieth century—as threatening to their masculinity.

The twentieth century saw the emergence of new nativist movements, such as the "English Only" and "Christian Identity" movements, which incorporated nativist definitions of masculinity in their ideologies. Like earlier groups, twentieth-century nativists have used both legal and illegal activities in an attempt to influence politics and social conditions and defend their notions of manhood against perceived alien threats. Although Irish Catholics are no longer the targets of late-twentieth-century nativists—indeed, some Irish Americans have embraced nativist ideologies—immigrants from Mexico and other Latin American countries have taken their place. At the end of the twentieth century, conservative political groups—along a continuum that stretches from the conservative pundit Patrick J. Buchanan to secret and semi-secret militia groups—again used traditional nativist imagery in resisting the perceived negative social effects of multiculturalism, feminism, and acceptance of homosexuality. On numerous Web sites, television programs, radio talk shows, and other outlets, spokespersons for cultural conservatism portray hardworking, white, native-born males as heroic upholders of American values, contrasting them with the "welfare bums," illegal aliens, "feminazis," and supporters of a "homosexual agenda" that they believe threaten traditional American manhood.

The persistence of nativism in the United States reflects the persistence of economic, political, and social conflict in American life, as well as the continuing appeal of the nativist ideology of masculinity—particularly to white men. Echoes of aspects of nativist masculinity are present in film, fiction (including romance and spy fiction), and television. At the same time, the increasing multiculturalism of the United States, and its acceptance and celebration in public discourse, provides both an implicit and explicit challenge to nativist beliefs and ideology. Television programs such as *All in the Family* (1971–79) and films such as *American History X* (1998), for example, have broadcast sharp critiques of nativist versions of American masculinity. Thus, although nativist ideas may continue to attract significant sympathy from groups of disadvantaged white males, it is unlikely to become a dominant force in American culture.

BIBLIOGRAPHY

Anbinder, Tyler. *Nativism and Slavery: The Northern Know-Nothings and the Politics of the 1850s.* New York: Oxford University Press, 1992.

Bennett, David. *The Party of Fear: From Nativist Movements to the New Right in American History.* Chapel Hill: University of North Carolina Press, 1988.

Berlet, Chip, and Matthew N. Lyons. *Right-Wing Populism in America: Too Close for Comfort.* New York: Guilford Press, 2000.

Billington, Ray Allen. *The Protestant Crusade, 1800–1860: A Study of the Origins of American Nativism.* New York: Macmillan, 1938.

Higham, John. *Strangers in the Land: Patterns of American Nativism, 1860–1925.* 2nd ed. New Brunswick, N.J.: Rutgers University Press, 1988.

Kimmel, Michael, and Abby L. Ferber. "'White Men Are This Nation': Right-Wing Militias and the Restoration of Rural American Masculinity." *Rural Sociology* 65, no. 4 (2000): 582–604.

Lee, Robert G. *Orientals: Asian Americans in Popular Culture.* Philadelphia: Temple University Press, 1999.

Lester, Ellen (Brown). *Stanhope Burleigh: The Jesuits in our Homes.* New York: Stringer and Townsend, 1855.

Levine, Bruce. "Conservatism, Nativism, and Slavery: Thomas R. Whitney and the Origins of the Know-Nothing Party." *Journal of American History* 88, no. 2 (September 2001): 455–488.

Overdyke, W. D. *The Know-Nothing Party in the South.* New Orleans: Louisiana State University Press, 1950.

Rohmer, Sax. *Fu Manchu: Four Classic Novels.* Secaucus, N.J.: Citadel Press, 1983.

Wu, William F. *The Yellow Peril: Chinese Americans in American Fiction, 1850–1940.* Hamden, Conn.: Archon, 1982.

FURTHER READING

Blee, Kathleen. *Women of the Klan: Racism and Gender in the 1920s.* Berkeley: University of California Press, 1991.

Chalmers, David M. *Hooded Americanism: The History of the Ku Klux Klan.* 1965. Reprint, Durham, N.C.: Duke University Press, 1987.

Cose, Ellis. *A Nation of Strangers: Prejudice, Politics, and the Populating of America.* New York: William Morrow, 1992.

Kasson, John F. *Houdini, Tarzan, and the Perfect Man: the White Male Body and the Challenge of Modernity in America.* New York: Hill and Wang, 2001.

Kimmel, Michael. *Manhood in America: A Cultural History.* New York: Free Press, 1996.

RELATED ENTRIES

Citizenship; Democratic Manhood; Ethnicity; Immigration; Politics; Race; Republicanism; Whiteness; White Supremacism; Working-Class Manhood

—*JoAnn E. Castagna*

NEW DEAL

The New Deal era (1933–39) witnessed a major shift in government control of labor and social policies, with the federal government taking over many responsibilities that were formerly controlled by the individual states. A similar change occurred in the definition of citizenship rights and government responsibilities for providing individual economic security. Growing from conventional notions of men as productive workers and women as providers of child care, New Deal policies protected traditional work- and family-based ideals of masculinity. They reinforced prevailing gender norms despite President Franklin D. Roosevelt's appointment of the first woman to the Cabinet (Frances Perkins as secretary of labor), the presence an unprecedented number of women in administrative posts, and First Lady Eleanor Roosevelt's social activism.

Prior to the 1930s, government and societal attitudes about work and provision for the needy centered on traditional ideas of masculinity and the family. Nineteenth-century working-class men measured their worth by their jobs and their success as family providers; thus, men who failed to hold a job fell short of true manhood. Unemployment relief was the province of the states and private charities, and males who had to rely on such services were held in contempt. State and local welfare policies were limited to the provision of pensions for indigent single mothers and their children. Federal unemployment insurance and old-age assistance programs for breadwinners did not exist.

The Great Depression, beginning in 1929, caused massive unemployment. By 1932 nearly 25 percent of workers were jobless. Americans responded by rearticulating their assumptions concerning the relationship of government to wage work and family life. While most Americans believed that men, as providers, deserved priority in the competition for scarce jobs, public opinion moved from staunch opposition to federal intervention in the economy to a willingness to sanction experiments in government mediation between the marketplace and the work lives of men (but not women). This shift manifested itself in Franklin D. Roosevelt's election as president in 1932, and in the resulting government relief and social programs of the New Deal. The Roosevelt administration's policies addressed the depression's economic dislocations on two levels: They provided short-run work and financial relief for the unemployed and, through long-term national social and labor legislation, created a permanent safety net for American workers.

In implementing these programs, New Deal policymakers based their decisions on gender-based views concerning work and the traditional role of men as family breadwinners. Relief programs were administered through numerous government agencies, such as the Federal Emergency Relief Administration and the Works Progress Administration. The majority of these work-relief jobs, and the highest paying, involved construction and employed only men. Women, who were restricted to one-sixth of enrollees in federal work relief, held positions that mirrored household chores, such as growing and canning food, or traditionally female occupations, such as secretarial work.

Conventional notions of American manhood were also apparent in federal cultural programs. Administrators of New Deal arts programs cultivated an image of labor that depicted American wageworkers as heroic masculine figures who embodied the work ethic and manifested the manly virtues of strength, individuality, and determination. The post office murals of Leo Raiken depicted the utility of blue-collar drillers, stonecutters, and professional-class engineers and architects, but included few representations of women's work. Such portraits counteracted depression-era worries about the impact of unemployment on the ideal of male breadwinning.

The gendered assumptions of the New Deal era had a lasting impact on social insurance and labor policy. The most significant social legislation of the 1930s—which involved old-age assistance, unemployment insurance, and aid to dependent children—favored the male provider. The Social

Two Civilian Conservation Corps (CCC) workers construct a farm building in 1937. The CCC and other New Deal public-works programs reinforced conventional gender norms by bolstering the traditional association between masculinity, work, and the provider role—and in most cases by employing only men. (From the collections of the Library of Congress)

Security Act of 1935 provides an instructive example. The act linked social citizenship to independence (as defined by wage earning), unless the earners were in an excluded and devalued occupation such as domestic service or agricultural field work. White males constituted a large majority of workers who had worked long enough and had earned enough to gain national standing and the right to old-age benefits. Other citizens were left as subjects of the states, forced to depend on a paternalistic system of public assistance and private benevolence to sustain them in impoverished old age. The act was subsequently amended to include the widows of breadwinners, which granted middle-class women who outlived their husbands higher benefits than women working in the service sector and low-wage industries. These measures institutionalized and rewarded the patriarchal family model, fragmenting social insurance along gender lines.

The Social Security Act supported the same traditional assumptions in its shaping of unemployment insurance and welfare policies. In providing unemployment benefits in the manufacturing and heavy-industry sectors, the act's framers again emphasized the importance of the male breadwinner. Unemployment insurance for workers in these predominately male industries, although decentralized and administered by the states, incorporated a federal tax and provided for federal control over the distribution of funds. Welfare policy, centering on the Aid to Families with Dependent Children program and reflecting prevailing norms about the appropriate roles of mothers in raising children, was left to the states. State and local governments frequently acted as a "father figure" in child care, regulating the behavior of their clients at the lowest cost possible. Child care thus had a lower value in the structure of economic rewards than male occupations.

Similarly, labor legislation and the upsurge in union activity in the Roosevelt years mainly benefited white male workers. Both the National Labor Relations Act of 1935 and the Fair Labor Standards Act of 1938, which guaranteed the right of workers to their own labor unions and established a minimum wage, affected male-dominated industries. The Congress of Industrial Organizations (CIO) also sought to organize unskilled workers in mainly female occupations, such as clothing and textiles, but the presence of women in CIO unions remained low. Clerical, domestic, and agricultural occupations employing mainly African Americans and single women did not benefit from New Deal labor laws.

The effect of New Deal social policies was to institutionalize a conventional set of ideas about manhood and to implement a limited concept of social rights that granted full benefits to white men. The structuring of these obligations guaranteed higher priority on the federal level to the white male provider, but left aid to lower categories of workers to the states—thus relegating blacks, working women, and poor mothers to whatever benefits the states granted them. The gendered assumptions underlying this division, which reinforced white male dominance, were not widely questioned until the civil rights revolution and the rise of feminism in the 1960s and 1970s.

Bibliography

Doss, Erika. "Toward an Iconography of American Labor: Work, Workers, and the Work Ethic in American Art, 1930–1945." *Design Issues* 13, no. 1 (1997): 53–66.

Gordon, Linda. *Pitied But Not Entitled: Single Mothers and the History of Welfare, 1890–1935.* New York: Free Press, 1994.

Kessler-Harris, Alice. *In Pursuit of Equity: Women, Men, and the Quest for Economic Citizenship in Twentieth-Century America.* New York: Oxford University Press, 2001.

Mettler, Suzanne. *Dividing Citizens: Gender and Federalism in New Deal Public Policy.* Ithaca, N.Y.: Cornell University Press, 1998.

Mink, Gwendolyn. *The Wages of Motherhood: Inequality in the Welfare State, 1917–1942.* Ithaca, N.Y.: Cornell University Press, 1995.

Nelson, Barbara J. "The Origins of the Two-Channel Welfare State: Workmen's Compensation and Mothers' Aid." In *Women, the State, and Welfare,* edited by Linda Gordon. Madison: University of Wisconsin Press, 1990.

Rose, Nancy E. "Discrimination Against Women in New Deal Work Programs." *Affilia: Journal of Women and Social Work* 5, no. 2 (1990): 23–45.

Further Reading

Brock, William Ranuff. *Welfare, Democracy, and the New Deal.* New York: Cambridge University Press, 1988.

Long, Jennifer. "Government Job Creating Programs: Lessons from the 1930s and 1940s." *Journal of Economic Issues* 33, no. 4 (1999): 903–918.

Mink, Gwendolyn. *Welfare's End.* Ithaca, N.Y.: Cornell University Press, 2000.

Park, Marlene, and Gerald E. Markowitz. *Democratic Vistas: Post Offices and Public Art in the New Deal.* Philadelphia: Temple University Press, 1984.

Patterson, James T. *America's Struggle Against Poverty in the Twentieth Century.* Cambridge, Mass.: Harvard University Press, 2000.

Rose, Nancy E. "Gender, Race, and the Welfare State: Government Work Programs from the 1930s to the Present." *Feminist Studies* 19, no. 2 (1993): 318–343.

Skocpol, Theda. *Protecting Soldiers and Mothers: The Political Origins of Social Policy in the United States.* Cambridge, Mass.: Harvard University Press, 1992.

Swain, Martha H. *Ellen S. Woodward: New Deal Advocate for Women.* Jackson: University Press of Mississippi, 1995.

Ware, Susan. *Partner and I: Molly Dewson, Feminism, and New Deal Politics.* New Haven, Conn.: Yale University Press, 1987.

Related Entries

Breadwinner Role; Capitalism; Citizenship; Class; Great Depression; Industrialization; Labor Movement and Unions; Old Age; Progressive Era; Urbanization; Work; Working-Class Manhood; World War II

—*Walter F. Bell*

Noyes, John Humphrey

1811–1886
U.S. Religious Leader

John Humphrey Noyes, the founder and leader of the utopian Oneida Community (established in 1848), developed a radical conception of masculinity and sexuality. His spiritual and religious convictions led him to criticize the dominant heterosexual family structure in the United States, as well as the changes wrought on U.S. work culture by nineteenth-century industrialization.

In 1831, after a year of studying law, Noyes was converted during a religious revival of the Second Great Awakening, after which he entered the Andover Theological Seminary in Massachusetts. Finding Andover's theological approach too restrictive, he left and entered the Yale Divinity School, where he was influenced by Nathaniel Taylor's doctrine of Perfectionism. According to this doctrine, which assumed major importance in American religious thinking during the Awakening, Christ's redemption freed human beings from sin and allowed them to attain perfection.

Noyes's conceptualization of masculinity and of gender and sexual relationships rests on his own controversial interpretation of Perfectionism. He posited a fully redeemed world in which men and women may escape sin through their spiritual and intellectual understanding. He used his prolific writings and the example of the Oneida Community to try to convert the world to his beliefs.

Noyes advocated "male continence," a method for controlling ejaculation during sexual activity, and "complex marriage," a heterosexual, polygamous arrangement in which all male and female members of the community considered themselves married. These ideas grew out of the basic component of Noyes' Perfectionist ideology, which he called "ascending association." Noyes believed that interaction with those more advanced in spiritual development could increase one's own spiritual gifts, and that any such relationship should be controlled by the person of higher spiritual rank. At Oneida, however, while older women might have higher spiritual rank than the youngest men, male community members were seen as ultimately having a higher spiritual rank. As Noyes noted, "in the fellowship between men and women . . . man is naturally superior" (Noyes 1975, 205). Noyes therefore put men firmly in charge of sexual virtue. Challenging the contemporary Victorian idea that men needed women's help to control their unruly sexual impulses, the practice of male continence assumed men's willingness and ability to control their most intimate sexual activities.

Noyes, reflecting prevalent societal values, believed men were more active than women—and more able to lead and inspire. He considered women more passive and receptive than men. However, Noyes encouraged men to cultivate and develop what he considered feminine qualities: the ability to listen as well as talk, to learn as well as teach. In the Oneida Community, Noyes returned men to the center of the family as spiritual leaders, and he returned wage-earning labor to the home. His beliefs displaced women who, in the dominant U.S. culture, were identified as leaders in the home environment. At Oneida, men did not leave home to go to a separate workplace; manufacturing and most (but not all) domestic duties were shared by men and women, generally under the leadership of men.

It is difficult to assess the precise influence that Noyes and the Oneida experiment have had on U.S. culture. Only a few hundred people ever joined the Oneida Community, but nineteenth-century "sex radicals" and twentieth-century sexual ethicists were influenced by the experiences of those who lived there. The Oneidans exemplified sexual intimacy within a loving community without jealousy or exclusivity, they emphasized the value of sexuality separate from reproduction, and they recognized the importance of male attention to female sexual pleasure.

Bibliography

DeMaria, Richard. *Communal Love at Oneida: A Perfectionist Vision of Authority, Property, and Sexual Order.* New York: Mellen, 1978.

Fogarty, Robert S., ed. *Desire and Duty at Oneida: Tirzah Miller's Intimate Memoir.* Bloomington: Indiana University Press, 2000.

Foster, Lawrence. *Religion and Sexuality: Three American Communal Experiments of the Nineteenth Century.* New York: Oxford University Press, 1981.

Kern, Louis J. *An Ordered Love: Sex Roles and Sexuality in Victorian Utopias: the Shakers, the Mormons, and the Oneida Community.* Chapel Hill: University of North Carolina Press, 1981.

Klaw, Spencer. *Without Sin: The Life and Death of the Oneida Community.* New York: Allen Lane, 1993.

Thomas, Robert David. *The Man Who Would Be Perfect: John Humphrey Noyes and the Utopian Impulse.* Philadelphia: University of Pennsylvania Press, 1977.

Further Reading

Carden, Maren Lockwood. *Oneida: Utopian Community to Modern Corporation.* 1969. Reprint, Syracuse, N.Y.: Syracuse University Press, 1998.

Noyes, George Wallingford. *Free Love in Utopia: John Humphrey Noyes and the Origin of the Oneida Community.* Edited and with an introduction by Lawrence Foster. Urbana: University of Illinois Press, 2001.

Robertson, Constance Noyes. *Oneida Community Profiles.* Syracuse, N.Y.: Syracuse University Press, 1977.

Robertson, Constance Noyes, ed. *Oneida Community: An Autobiography, 1851–1876.* Syracuse: Syracuse University Press, 1970.

Selected Writings

Noyes, John Humphrey. *Male Continence, Together with Essay on Scientific Propagation, Dixon and his Copyists, [and] Salvation from Sin.* 1872–1876. Reprint, New York: AMS Press, 1974.

———. *Home-talks.* Edited by Alfred Barron and George Noyes Miller. 1875. Reprint, New York: AMS Press, 1975.

RELATED ENTRIES

Capitalism; Cult of Domesticity; Heterosexuality; Industrialization; Market Revolution; Marriage; Masculine Domesticity; Nuclear Family; Reform Movements; Religion and Spirituality; Self-Control; Victorian Era; Work

—*JoAnn E. Castagna*

NUCLEAR FAMILY

The nuclear family is traditionally defined as a unit composed of a husband and wife and their biological children, all working together to perform changing economic and emotional functions. The nuclear family has historically been tied to American masculinity by serving as a measure of an adult man's social achievements, by potentially offering emotional support to men, and by serving as the setting in which young boys are nurtured and first learn gender roles. As expectations for the family have changed, the role of men within the family has evolved, impacting the construction and health of American masculinity. Across these varying definitions of family, a man's position as the head of the household continues to be one marker of successful manhood and a stable society.

The Nuclear Family in Early America

Scholars' opinions differ as to when the nuclear family became the dominant familial structure in America. Although most scholars see this shift from the extended to the nuclear family as occurring in the nineteenth century, other historians date the nuclear family's prominence to colonial times. During the first centuries of American settlement, the family was the primary producing unit. Unlike the European family, which functioned as a "little monarchy," the family on American soil operated more democratically, as a kind of "little commonwealth," with the family working together. In this setting, the male head of the household functioned as the embodiment of all family members, serving as the link to the community and as the family's voting representative. A man's status was thus linked to the happy and orderly functioning of his family. This order was valued by the community for preserving political stability, sustaining piety, and ensuring the community's productivity. While parenting was a shared duty, fathers were particularly involved in preparing their sons for their future responsibilities as household heads.

Every person had to find a place within a family, and a man's male identity was based on his position within a household. Unmarried adults or adults with children whose nuclear families had been disrupted by death or temporary separation generally joined the household of another nuclear family, making a male head of household responsible for more than his own wife and children. As late as the nineteenth century, a third or more households included a secondary family, or subfamily, in addition to the primary nuclear family. However, the one constant was that the head of the household tended to be male. The father was responsible for the education, religious instruction, and future of all members of his household, including his nuclear family and any residing subfamily, apprentices, or servants.

By the late eighteenth and early nineteenth centuries, several developments began to redefine men's relationships to their nuclear families. The ideologies of republicanism and Romanticism discouraged authoritarianism and encouraged affection as a basis for family bonding, resulting in a growing respect for women and mothers as uplifting and moral influences on their families. At the same time, families were becoming smaller and husbands were spending more of the day away from home, separating them from their families.

The Nuclear Family in Industrial America

With the rise of industrialization and the move toward a market economy, many significant changes occurred in the relation between manhood and the nuclear family. As the family ceased to be the primary site of economic production, its emotional importance for men increased. The nineteenth-century French writer Alexis de Tocqueville described the American home, specializing primarily in child rearing, as a source of emotional retreat from the impersonal marketplace in which men worked. With the family's declining economic importance came a new focus on the comfort and welfare of every family member, as well as a growing tendency to limit the family to a smaller nuclear unit. This new view of the nuclear family was codified in the ideology of separate spheres, which associated women with the domestic sphere of the home and men with the public sphere of economics and politics. But the notion of separate spheres may have exaggerated the father's emotional distance from the family, for although fathers may have had less energy and time to spend in the nuclear-family setting, they still considered domestic engagement central to their masculine identities. Furthermore, by providing education and mortal guidance for their sons and models of ideal middle-class manhood for their daughters, they sought to bolster their identities by perpetuating their families' middle-class status.

The decline of the family's economic functions, the decline in family size, and the ideology of domesticity were more prevalent among white, Protestant, and middle- and upper-class families than among African-American or other ethnic working-class families. Among working-class families, traditions of patriarchy and related notions of masculine identity survived well into the nineteenth century. In slave families, the labor regimen and the plantation owner's role as provider weakened the influence of African-American fathers, although many slave fathers continued to provide food by hunting small game and fishing. Although most slave families did manage to provide paternal and maternal care for their children, fathers were separated from their children more often than were mothers. This pattern continued after emancipation in the nineteenth century due to problems of racial violence, agricultural poverty, the necessity of frequent movement in search of income, and urban underemployment, all of which led to a pronounced incidence of multigenerational, mother-headed households. Nonetheless, African-American families tended, by a margin of about two to one, to be nuclear and father-headed.

Toward the Modern Family

The responsibilities and influence of the male head of household narrowed as the nuclear family moved into the twentieth century. Households became smaller and, with more available housing, less likely to include servants or extended family members. At the same time, the government played a larger role in functions that were formerly the responsibility of the family patriarch, including education and the care of disadvantaged or older relatives. However, in delegating these duties, families lost some of their power to shape behavior previously considered private. The government also attempted to shape the family in accordance with current ideals through various government programs. For example, New Deal and G.I. Bill programs of the 1930s and 1940s worked specifically to support the position of the male breadwinner, while providing disincentives for married women to work.

The advent of modern psychology and social science in the early twentieth century produced new approaches to examining the nuclear family. Experts portrayed nuclear-family life as normative and urged domestically involved fatherhood in nuclear families as essential both to the well-being of fathers and the raising of boys to become emotionally healthy adults. The growing power of scientific experts drew some child rearing authority away from men, further reducing their influence, but also provided new foundations for paternal identity and pride among those men who heeded the experts' advice.

The relation between male identity and the nuclear family was also dramatically affected by large-scale economic changes in American life. As a result of industrialization, the family unit became, by the early twentieth century, far less a place of production than it had once been, and primarily a site of consumption. In this new setting, male household heads increasingly assessed their masculine identities, and determined their success or failure as men, in terms of the amount of leisure time they spent with their families and their ability to provide their wives and children with specific consumer items.

During the 1940s and 1950s, as World War II and the ensuing Cold War made American military strength and fears of perceived threats to social and political order into national concerns, the nuclear family loomed increasingly large as a source of anxious hope and concern. American political and cultural leaders, fearful of what they labeled "deviance" (especially communism, homosexuality, and juvenile delinquency) looked to father-headed nuclear-family life as a source of healthy manhood and the chief bastion of social and political stability. Such popular television programs as *The Adventures of Ozzie and Harriet* (1952–66), *Father Knows Best* (1954–63), and *Leave It to Beaver* (1957–63) broadcast to millions of Americans the idea that (white) nuclear-family life, male breadwinning, heterosexual masculinity, and Americanism were inextricably intertwined.

Of course, this family model was not equally available to all American families. But many Americans understood it as a norm, any deviation from which could generate social ills. Thus Daniel Patrick Moynihan's 1965 report *The Negro Family: The Case for National Action,* prompted by the civil rights movement, attributed the problems facing African-American families to a perceived high incidence of father absence and female heads of households. Calling on black families to establish patriarchal nuclear-family structures as the best means of achieving stability, Moynihan's report both reflected and reinforced stereotypical notions about African-American family life and African-American men, reflecting the powerful cultural association between the nuclear-family ideal and dominant constructions of masculinity.

Challenges to the Nuclear-Family Ideal

Yet this association began to erode during the 1960s and 1970s. Under the impact of feminism, increasing opportunities for women's economic independence, the gay rights movement, and a growing incidence of divorce, more and more Americans lived outside of conventional nuclear-family structures and began to perceive the standard nuclear family as only one of many options, including single-parent (mother or father) families, blended families, joint-custody households, and families headed by same-sex parents. These variations provided a greater range of familial roles for men, and several of them operate entirely without adult men. As single women and gay couples struggled for recognition as parents capable of raising male children with secure masculine identities, heterosexual men became less likely to be seen as essential to the nuclear family, and the nuclear family was less likely to be considered essential to an individual's achievement of mature American manhood.

These changes aroused opposition from (usually religious) conservative groups that—defending what they termed "family values"—sought to defend the earlier nuclear-family ideal as best suited to moral stability. The Republican Party, in particular, sought to politicize this issue during the 1990s, and Vice President Dan Quayle, campaigning for re-election in 1992, criticized the single motherhood of television comedy character Murphy Brown and urged the importance of fathers and fatherhood. The incident received widespread media attention, demonstrating how hotly contested the issue of the relation between masculinity and the nuclear family had become by the late twentieth century.

BIBLIOGRAPHY

Connell, R. W. *Masculinities.* Berkeley: University of California Press, 1995.

Faludi, Susan. *Stiffed: The Betrayal of the American Man.* New York: William Morrow, 1999.

Frank, Stephen. *Life with Father: Parenthood and Masculinity in the Nineteenth Century American North.* Baltimore: Johns Hopkins University Press, 1998.

Habermas, Jurgen. *The Structural Transformation of the Public Sphere: An Inquiry into a Category of Bourgeois Society.* Translated by Thomas Burger. Boston: MIT Press, 1989.

Kimmel, Michael. *Manhood in America: A Cultural History.* New York: Free Press, 1996.

———. *The Gendered Society.* New York: Oxford University Press, 2000.

May, Elaine Tyler. *Homeward Bound: American Families in the Cold War Era.* New York: Basic Books, 1988.

Rotundo, E. Anthony. *American Manhood: Transformations in Masculinity from the Revolution to the Modern Era.* New York: Basic Books, 1993.

Seward, Rudy Ray. *The American Family: A Demographic History.* London: Sage, 1978.

FURTHER READING

Casper, Lynne M., and Suzanne M. Bianchi. *Continuity and Change in the American Family.* Thousand Oaks, Calif.: Sage, 2002.

Coontz, Stephanie, Maya Parson, and Gabrielle Raley. *American Families: A Multicultural Reader.* New York: Routledge, 1999.

Hunter, Jean E., and Paul T. Mason, eds. *The American Family: Historical Perspectives.* Pittsburgh: Duquesne University Press, 1991.

Johansen, Shawn. *Family Men: Middle-Class Fatherhood in Early Industrializing America.* New York: Routledge, 2001.

LaRossa, Ralph. *The Modernization of Fatherhood: A Social and Political History.* Chicago: University of Chicago Press, 1997.

Lehr, Valerie. *Queer Family Values: Debunking the Myth of the Nuclear Family.* Philadelphia: Temple University Press, 1999.

Levitan, Sar A., Richard S. Belous, and Frank Gallo. *What's Happening to the American Family?: Tensions, Hopes and Realities.* Baltimore: Johns Hopkins University Press, 1988.

Mintz, Steven, and Susan Kellogg. *Domestic Revolutions: A Social History of American Family Life.* New York: Free Press, 1988.

The New American Family: Significant and Diversified Lifestyles. New York: Simmons Market Research Bureau, 1992.

Skolnick, Arlene S. *Embattled Paradise: The American Family in an Age of Uncertainty.* New York: Basic Books, 1991.

South, Scott J., and Stewart E. Tolnay, eds. *The Changing American Family: Sociological and Demographic Perspectives.* Boulder, Colo.: Westview Press, 1992.

Wallace, Michele. *Black Macho and the Myth of Superwoman.* New York: New Left Books, 1999.

RELATED ENTRIES

African-American Manhood; Bachelorhood; Boyhood; Breadwinner Role; Divorce; Fatherhood; *Father Knows Best*; *Iron John: A Book About Men*; *Leave It to Beaver*; Marriage; Men's Movements; Middle-Class Manhood; Mother–Son Relationships; Old Age; Patriarchy; Suburbia; Working-Class Manhood

—*Elizabeth Abele*

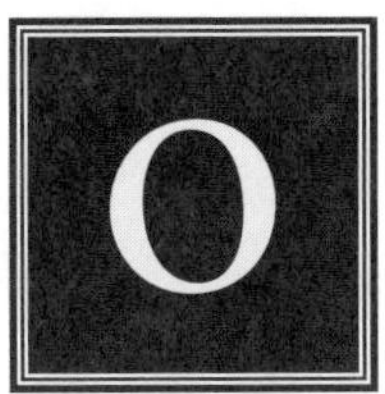

Odd Couple, The

Playwright Neil Simon's *The Odd Couple* premiered on Broadway in 1965 as racial unrest, a resurgence of feminism, the youth counterculture, and a sharp rise in the divorce rate challenged conventional images of the dependable white middle-class husband/provider. At the same time, the success of *Playboy* magazine (established in 1953) heralded a new male ideal of bachelorhood, leisure, and conspicuous consumption. Simon's play addressed these shifting understandings of manhood.

A humorous story of two single white middle-class men thrust together through desperation and divorce, the play featured Walter Matthau as the chronic slob Oscar Madison and Art Carney as the emotional neatnik Felix Unger. Simon's story would eventually appear in both film and television versions, as well as a revamped stage version, providing an ongoing vehicle for the investigation of gender roles, male bonding, bachelorhood, and homosocial living in America.

The Odd Couple questioned *Playboy*'s glamorized notion of the carefree playboy: Felix is completely unable to function outside of wedlock, and Oscar's repugnant apartment suggests his inability to realize *Playboy*'s hip bachelor pad. Instead, the play's opening poker game—rife with smoke, warm beer, and rotten sandwiches—establishes an unappealing male world of divorcés, bachelors, and absentee husbands. As the various characters struggle to forge stable homosocial (and sometimes heterosocial) bonds (and to comfort the suicidal Felix), they reveal both the vulnerability and the emotional sensitivity generated in men by the experience of divorce.

By focusing mainly on the homosocial world of men, and by juxtaposing the traditionally pejorative male characteristics of Oscar (lascivious, loud, irresponsible, and sloppy) with the classically feminine characteristics of Felix (emotional, domestic, priggish, and henpecking—the very traits that led to his divorce), the play ultimately suggests that masculinity is a fluid and changeable identity, rather than a natural and fixed group of characteristics. As Oscar and Felix battle for control, they compromise, each unknowingly absorbing a bit of the other's traits. As a result, they find a new masculine identity—one that resembled the emerging sensitive male ideal of the 1970s—and emerge independent at the end of the play.

In 1968, *The Odd Couple* re-emerged as a film starring Jack Lemmon as Felix and Matthau reprising his stage role. The film remained textually loyal to the original, but differed in that the action extended from the apartment to include restaurants, strip clubs, and bowling alleys. This spatial diversity facilitated the inclusion of women who symbolize the desired but mysterious and elusive female sex. By highlighting the uncertainty of the world outside the apartment, these figures underscore both the men's homosocial bonding and their vulnerability.

Recycling the script further, Jack Klugman and Tony Randall reprised Oscar and Felix in television's *The Odd Couple* (1970–75), as did the African-American actors Demond Wilson and Ron Glass in *The New Odd Couple* (1982–83). The latter served as one of the few prime-time shows of the period that featured African Americans in leading roles. A female version of the play opened on Broadway in 1985, with Rita Moreno as Olive (Oscar) and Sally Struthers as Florence (Felix). This incarnation fared poorly, however, perhaps because a looser cultural rein on images of femininity rendered the juxtaposition less effective. Throughout its multiple incarnations, Simon's script has reflected an ongoing cultural exploration of the ties that bind popular notions of American gender roles.

Bibliography

Gross, Edward. *Still Odd After All These Years: The 25th Anniversary Odd Couple Companion.* Las Vegas, Nev.: Pioneer Books, 1989.

Kitman, Marvin. "Odd Couples." *New Leader,* 10 January 1983, 21–22.

Nadel, Norman. "Carney, Matthau Hilarious in 'Odd Couple.'" *New York World Telegram,* 11 Mar 1965.

Rich, Frank. "Theatre: 'Odd Couple,' A Remix and Rematch." *New York Times,* 12 Jun 1985.

Taubman, Howard. "Theatre: Neil Simon's 'Odd Couple.'" *New York Times,* 11 Mar 1965.

Further Reading

Johnson, Robert K. *Neil Simon.* Boston: Twayne, 1983.

Koprince, Susan. *Understanding Neil Simon.* Columbia: University of South Carolina Press, 2002.

Marc, David, and Robert J. Thompson. *Prime Time, Prime Movers: From I Love Lucy to L. A. Law–America's Greatest TV Shows and the People Who Created Them.* Boston: Little, Brown, 1992.

McGovern, Edythe M. *Not-So-Simple Neil Simon: A Critical Study.* Van Nuys, Calif.: Perivale Press, 1978.

Newcomb, Horace, and Robert S. Alley. *The Producer's Medium: Conversations with Creators of American TV.* Oxford: Oxford University Press, 1983.

Related Entries

Bachelorhood; Breadwinner Role; Consumerism; Cult of Domesticity; Divorce; Emotion; Fatherhood; Gambling; Hollywood; Marriage; Masculine Domesticity; Middle-Class Manhood; Passionate Manhood; *Playboy* Magazine; Sensitive Male; Sports; Television; Whiteness

—*Kelly Kessler*

Old Age

Throughout U.S. history, American attitudes to aging among males have changed from veneration to condescension to an emerging understanding of the potential rewards of a long life. These shifts, along with changing expectations about reaching old age, have transformed the social and cultural relations between old age and masculinity. The relative rarity of old age among men in early America both enhanced and detracted from the status it carried. Only about 2 percent of the first European colonists could expect to reach the age of sixty-five, and until the mid–twentieth century only a minority of American men lived to old age. More recently, an increasing expectation of a longer and fuller life span—brought about by advances in science and social agency—has prompted both the troubling prospect of lengthened dependency and more positive attitudes toward old age. Retirement, for example, is now seen as offering an opportunity to fulfill lives once entirely dominated by work.

Colonial and Revolutionary America

In colonial America, the association of masculine identity with patriarchal household leadership, as well as the rarity of old age, created an environment in which old age among men was venerated as an enhancement of their masculine status. Euro-American colonists typically associated aging manhood with heightened wisdom and spirituality and upheld an image of God as an old man with a white beard. The oldest members of a church congregation held a higher position within the community, and therefore sat nearest the pulpit during services. As a consequence, social mores dictated that appearing older than one's years was of definite advantage to the aspiring male. Many men that sought or achieved high social or political status purposefully accentuated their age by powdering their hair, wearing white wigs, dressing dourly, and cultivating a serious public manner. Yet at the same time, colonial associations of manhood with public usefulness meant that the declining faculties caused by aging left men feeling less certain of their manliness.

Between 1770 and 1820, the American Revolution, the establishment of the new republic, and the global impact of the French Revolution caused a social revolution and redefined the position of both younger and aged males. Challenges to established structures of political and social authority and innovative approaches to social and political institutions prompted a drastic shift in attitudes toward judges, law enforcers, educators, and churchmen, all once valued for their seniority. The elderly were beginning to be seen as feebleminded and corruptible compared to the more astute and vigorous youth of the emerging nation. Looking older became less of a personal or political advantage, and fashions items such as wigs and powder were replaced by knee breeches and well-tailored coats, along with toupees and hair dye to disguise advancing years. Nationalistic identifications of America with newness required more vibrant visions and versions of masculinity.

The Nineteenth Century

In the early republic, the relation between old age and masculinity remained problematic. The republican association of manhood with independence, a product of the Revolutionary era, exerted a powerful cultural influence and caused aging men to fear the dependency that came with a decline in physical vigor. The onset of the market revolution, which linked manliness to work, aggressive competitiveness, and financial success further encouraged a stigmatization of old age. As work came to define a man's standing in society, gerontophobia (the fear of the aged and of aging) increased, resulting in the introduction of a mandatory retirement age and growing rates of discrimination against older retired men. This created a class of impoverished retirees, who were housed in old-age homes, or "poor houses." Physically and symbolically removed from the public world of masculine endeavor to insulated institutions, aging males—like criminals and the insane, similarly institutionalized for failing to maintain masculine behavioral ideals—were hidden from social view and ignored by society at large. With the rise and spread of the factory system during the mid- to late nineteenth century, more and more men were forced into retirement, which increased poverty among a growing number of older men.

During the late nineteenth century, as the impact of Darwinian biology and concerns about the effect of urban-industrial overcivilization on male vigor generated increasingly body-centered definitions of masculinity that emphasized physical strength, old age became even further separated from prevailing notions of masculinity. The increasing association of aging with emasculating physical decline was evident in new developments in the linguistic meaning of words used to describe older men. For example, *gaffer*, a corruption of grandfather, became a term of contempt, as did *fogy*, once a term to describe a wounded military veteran or a war hero.

The Twentieth Century

Because of advances in medicine, a decrease in the arduousness of many Americans' work, and growing leisure time, old age became increasingly common in the twentieth century. By 1900 about 50 percent of Americans were surviving to age sixty, up from about 30 percent in 1830. The average life expectancy of American men jumped from forty-seven in 1900 to the unprecedented figure of seventy-four by 2000. In that year, 25 million American men were over fifty-five years of age. The problem of dependency, and the accompanying feeling of weakness and emasculation, was compounded by the emergence of the welfare state during the 1930s. Aging males, already dependent on their families or on institutionalized care, now became public wards as well.

The association of youthfulness with manliness, and of aging with loss of manly virility, intensified as well. Beginning in the 1920s and accelerating with the post–World War II baby boom, American culture became increasingly characterized by a "cult of youth" that associated youth with activity and—in contrast to earlier attitudes—with wisdom. As manufacturers in a growing consumer economy targeted youthful markets, advertisers increasingly saturated American popular culture with images equating youth with perfection. Particularly during the latter half of the century, the growing number of older Americans became the target of advertisers hawking the cult of youth. New vanity and medical products—such as dietary supplements, health foods, herbal and natural remedies, cosmetic surgery, hair-coloring products, hair-replacement procedures, and sex-enhancing drugs—encouraged older American men to equate manliness with youthfulness and activity and to resist the physical effects of aging.

The presidential campaigns of 1960 and 1980, in particular, highlighted the cultural association of masculinity with youth and of old age with enfeeblement. In 1960, forty-three-year-old John F. Kennedy presented himself to voters as a youthful alternative to outgoing president Dwight Eisenhower, who had suffered a heart attack in office and turned seventy during the campaign. In 1980, sixty-nine-year-old Ronald Reagan worked to convince voters that he was not too old for the presidency, both through the use of hair dye and television commercials featuring him engaged in vigorous activities.

Associations of aging with a decline in manly virility were further reinforced by emerging social and medical issues that accompanied the growth of the senior population during the late twentieth century. One set of issues, involving health care and insurance, the social security program, and nursing-home facilities, highlighted the problems involved in providing adequate care for older Americans, and thus reinforced gerontophobic associations of aging with unmanly dependency. Concerns also emerged relating to medical problems associated with aging, such as Alzheimer's disease, which gradually destroys mental functioning. Ronald Reagan's announcement in 1994 that he had Alzheimer's disease, followed by his withdrawal from public life and a growing media interest in his deteriorating condition, contributed to public identifications of aging with a decline in masculinity.

At the same time, countervailing developments suggested that aging and masculine stamina were compatible. Increased mechanization and the advent of computer technology allowed men to prolong their working lives and reduce their dotage and dependency. At the turn of the twenty-first century, 19 percent of American men over sixty-five still classified themselves as workers. While advances in medical technology encouraged associations of manliness with youth, they also allowed men to lead more active lives further into old age. For growing numbers of American men, retirement meant greater possibilities for the kinds of outdoor activities long identified with masculinity in American culture. According to a *Los Angeles Times* survey, by 1999 only 25 percent of men over age seventy would acknowledge that they looked and felt their age, suggesting not only that they identified youthfulness with manliness, but that they felt a genuine sense of continuing vitality.

At the end of the twentieth century, many public male figures offered American men inspiring examples of masculine potency: from 1981 to 1989, Ronald Reagan served as president in his seventies; in October 1998 Senator John Glenn became an astronaut for the second time at the age of seventy-seven; and at the 1992 Academy Awards ceremony, the seventy-two-year-old actor Jack Palance displayed one-armed push-ups, a feat intended as a critical reference to older actors having to prove themselves to directors. Along with these developments came more positive depictions of older men in such films as *On Golden Pond* (1981), *The Straight Story* (1999), and *About Schmidt* (2002), all of which depicted aging American males as honest, decent, dependable, fair-minded men with a capacity to take the most from life. By the early twenty-first century, the new pride of older American men was apparent in their references to the concept of a "Super Second Life" and their willingness to present themselves as "chronologically gifted."

BIBLIOGRAPHY

Barrow, G. M., and P. A. Smith. *Aging: The Individual and Society.* St. Paul, Minn.: West Publishing, 1983.

Browne, W. P., and L. Katz Olson. *Aging and Public Policy: The Politics of Growing Old in America.* Westport, Conn.: Greenwood Press, 1983.

Carlsen, M. B. *Creative Aging: A Meaning-Making Perspective.* New York: Norton, 1991.

Demos, J. *Past, Present, and Personal: The Family and the Life Course in American History.* New York: Oxford University Press, 1986.

Erikson, Erik H., Johan M. Erikson, and Helen Q. Kivnick. *Vital Involvement in Old Age.* New York: Norton, 1986.

Fischer, D. H. *Growing Old in America.* New York: Oxford University Press, 1978.

Timiras, P. S., ed. *Physiological Basis of Aging and Geriatrics.* Boca Raton, Fla.: CRC Press, 1994.

FURTHER READING

Belt, B. D. *The 21st Century Retirement Security Plan.* Washington, D.C.: Center for Strategic and International Studies, 1999.

Butler, A. *Aging: Recent Advances and Creative Responses.* London: Croom, 1985.

Dychtwald, K. *Age Power: How the 21st Century Will Be Ruled by the New Old.* New York: Jeremy P. Tarcher, 1999.

Lowenthal, Marjorie Fiske, and David A. Chiriboga. *Change and Continuity in Adult Life.* San Francisco: Jossey–Bass, 1990.

Skinner, B. F., and M. E. Vaughan. *Enjoy Old Age: A Practical Guide.* New York: Norton, 1997.

RELATED ENTRIES

Body; Consumerism; Health; Medicine; Middle-Class Manhood; Patriarchy; Reagan, Ronald; Religion and Spirituality; Work; Youth

—*Michael John Pinfold*

ORGANIZATION MAN, THE

Published in 1956 by William H. Whyte, editor of the upmarket business magazine *Fortune, The Organization Man* offered a portrait of American manhood suffocating under a blanket of dull conformity fostered by American corporate culture. After World War II an economic boom had brought prosperity, but for many commentators of the time the ensuing rise of faceless business corporations and the inexorable expansion of suburbia had pushed American masculinity into the paralyzing doldrums of uniformity. *The Organization Man* exemplified these perceptions through its portrayal of a white-collar bureaucracy that rewarded conformity rather than initiative, crushing individual identity and autonomy beneath the collective will of the organization.

Drawing on evidence from a study of a new middle-class housing development in Illinois called Park Forest, *The Organization Man* depicted a rising generation of junior executives whose embrace of a new social ethic threatened to undermine national vigor. Whyte argued that, in place of the traditional masculine ideals of hard work, thrift, self-reliance, and competitive struggle, the middle-class male was heavily pressured by economic prosperity to meet his breadwinning obligations, and therefore he adopted a value system that privileged group interests over those of the individual. The developing business culture of conformity, conventionality, and consensus, he feared, threatened to overwhelm the traditional manly virtues of individuality, autonomy, and entrepreneurship by demanding personality traits in which ambition, imagination, and creativity were suppressed in favor of genial group-mindedness, consistency, and affable compliance. Similarly, Whyte believed that suburbia fostered the "organization" mentality of docile orthodoxy and conformism through voluntary associations and informal neighborhood groups that provided for community cohesion and mutual support, but at the price of an oppressive social homogeneity.

The Organization Man was part of a body of literature that, during the 1950s, portrayed middle-class American manhood as being in a state of decline. David Riesman's *The Lonely Crowd* (1950) lamented the rise of the "other-directed man" who, instead of being self-reliant and "inner-directed," blindly followed the lead of those around him in a desperate search to "belong." C. Wright Mills, in *White Collar* (1951), presented American business corporations as monolithic bureaucracies in which employees were dehumanized by monotonous work routines. The very title of Sloan Wilson's novel, *The Man in the Gray Flannel Suit* (1955), provided an enduring emblem for the debilitating malaise and loss of selfhood that plagued American middle-class men. Within such studies, the erosion of individuality was invariably configured in gendered terms: "Masculine" dynamism, autonomy, and self-control were presented as drowning in a sea of feminine passivity, and American manhood was seen as being emasculated by enervating white-collar jobs and soft suburban living.

One of the most widely read and influential social critiques of the 1950s, *The Organization Man* is noteworthy not simply for its damning appraisal of American business practices. Whyte's book also gave currency to contemporary perceptions of a crisis in masculine identity—a premise that became a recurring theme in American cultural debate throughout the late twentieth century.

BIBLIOGRAPHY

Breines, Wini. "The 1950s: Gender and Some Social Science." *Sociological Inquiry* 56 (1986): 69–92.

Jezer, Marty. *The Dark Ages: Life in the United States, 1945–1960.* Boston: South End Press, 1982.

Whyte, William H. *The Organization Man.* New York: Simon & Schuster, 1956.

FURTHER READING

Ehrenreich, Barbara. *Fear of Falling: The Inner Life of the Middle Class.* New York: HarperPerennial, 1990.

Leinberger, Paul, and Bruce Tucker. *The New Individualists: The Generation After the Organization Man.* New York: HarperCollins, 1991.

Mills, C. Wright. *White Collar: The American Middle Classes.* New York: Oxford University Press, 1951.

Reisman, David. *The Lonely Crowd.* New Haven, Conn.: Yale University Press, 1950.

Wilson, Sloan. *The Man in the Gray Flannel Suit.* New York: Simon & Schuster, 1955.

RELATED ENTRIES

Breadwinner Role; Bureaucratization; Business/Corporate America; Crisis of Masculinity; Individualism; Masculine Domesticity; Middle-Class Manhood; Professionalism; Self-Control; Suburbia; Work

—*Bill Osgerby*

OUTDOORSMEN

The outdoorsman has long been an American cultural ideal, combining physical skills and closeness to nature with such manly qualities as individualism and courage. The antecedents of modern-day outdoorsmen were the pioneers of the eighteenth and nineteenth century who opened up the West, lived off the land, and established a history synonymous with the advancement of American values. Early trackers such as Davy Crockett came to represent a "natural" frontier masculinity that resisted social conformity, reform, and the niceties of genteel civilization and, as such, has entered American mythology. Fur traders explored and settled the Northeast, while the transcontinental railway pushed westward in the 1860s, allowing men to explore and settle western lands more easily. These early outdoorsmen cultivated a rigorous, energetic version of masculinity that was associated with the ownership, settlement, and exploitation of land.

As industrialization and urbanization brought a greater number of men to America's cities to work in factory jobs in the nineteenth century, a growing number of men, fearing that these developments undermined masculine vigor, looked to the values associated with outdoorsmen and sought to revitalize American manhood through recreational activities in natural settings. Such concerns informed the establishment of the Boy Scouts of America (1910), the preservation movements at the turn of the twentieth century, and the establishment of national parks, beginning with Yellowstone in 1872. Theodore Roosevelt, who was a conservation leader, outdoor enthusiast, and avid hunter, urged American men to pursue a "strenuous life" by engaging in activities that forged a link with the natural world.

While industrialization was perceived by many American men as a threat to masculine vigor, its fostering of consumerism and leisure also encouraged the spreading and embedding of the outdoor ideal in American culture during the twentieth century. As men increasingly sought fulfillment and self-definition through activities other than their work, they turned to such outdoor sports and activities as cycling, skiing, camping, canoeing, hiking, tracking, sledding, archery, and, more recently, mountain biking and snowboarding. Such activities have opened up a consumer market that offers all American men the chance to buy reassurance of their manhood despite being surrounded by modern amenities—and to escape both a corporate existence and the domestication of married life. The film *City Slickers* (1991)—released as the media declared that late-twentieth-century life had generated a "crisis" in American masculinity—exemplifies these developments: It depicts a group of urbanized male friends who spend a vacation driving cattle in the West in an attempt to reclaim their masculinity through outdoor pursuits.

The symbol of the outdoorsman continues to exert a powerful influence on American culture. Some—such as the journalist Elizabeth Gilbert, who titled her profile of outdoorsman Eustace Conway *The Last American Man* (2002)—have suggested that modern American life has left few American men capable of living up to the ideal of the outdoorsman. Yet it has played a part in recent political developments. For instance, some members of the gun lobby argue that every American possesses the right to own a gun—a vestigial symbol of life on the frontier where guns were necessary for protection and hunting game for survival. More recently, in response to the terrorist attacks on September 11, 2001, outdoorsmen communities fervently answered President George W. Bush's call for "standby volunteers." Since the settling of America, the mythic notion of the heroic outdoorsman has remained a persistent theme in defining American masculinity.

Bibliography

Davis, William C. *The American Frontier: Pioneers, Settlers, and Cowboys.* Norman: University of Oklahoma Press, 1999.

Roosevelt, Theodore. *The Strenuous Life: Essays and Addresses.* New York: The Century Company, 1900.

Townsend, Tom. *Davy Crockett: An American Hero.* Burnet, Tex.: Eakin Publications, 1987.

Further Reading

Gilbert, Elizabeth. *The Last American Man.* New York: Viking, 2002.

Young, Margaret Blair, and Darius Aidan Gray. *One More River to Cross.* Salt Lake City, Utah: Bookcraft, 2000.

Related Entries

Boy Scouts of America; Cowboys; Crockett, Davy; Fishing; Guns; Hunting; Leatherstocking Tales; Leisure; London, Jack; Men's Movements; Patriotism; Roosevelt, Theodore; Strenuous Life; Western Frontier; Westerns

—*Michael John Pinfold*

Passionate Manhood

Introduced into historical analyses of American men and masculinities by E. Anthony Rotundo in 1993, the concept of "passionate manhood" refers to four connected articulations of middle-class manliness: (1) the body, (2) forms of "primitive" masculinity, (3) martial and military virtues, and (4) competition in sports and business. These articulations of manliness emerged after 1850 and became increasingly influential in the 1880s and 1890s.

This shift toward a passionate manhood represented a decisive departure from earlier ideals of manliness. During the late eighteenth century, the American Revolution had generated an ideal of manhood emphasizing moral, social, and political qualities, such as independence, autonomy, virtue, and distrust of hierarchies and inherited status, that were considered conducive to responsible democratic citizenship and public order. After 1850, urbanization, industrialization, the development of a competitive market economy, and, later, the impact of Darwinian biology created a new ideal of manliness emphasizing bodily strength and more passionate, aggressive, and less self-restrained forms of expression—traits that an earlier generation had considered dangerous to the social fabric and the body politic. Whereas antebellum middle-class Americans valued sentimental self-expression, emotional candor, and rational thought as essential qualities of a man, by the late nineteenth century true manhood was increasingly associated with the absence of sentiment and complex feelings, as well as with an aversion to deep, rational thought and reflection. Instead, masculinity became defined in terms of decisive and assertive action unencumbered by grand moral or ethical considerations.

As a part of this shift, men of the latter half of the nineteenth century increasingly expressed their manhood through attention to their physique and physical strength. Even before the Civil War, the body—particularly one's dress, diet, posture, and gestures—was considered a reflection of one's character. By the 1880s, however, the emphasis on the body, especially a man's physical strength, became even more pronounced in gauging manly character. A man who lacked physical stamina or strength was perceived as lacking character and the ability to enforce his decisions. Not coincidentally, it was during the late nineteenth and early twentieth centuries that such bodybuilders as Eugen Sandow and Charles Atlas achieved national prominence. Advocates of "muscular Christianity," a late nineteenth-century Protestant movement closely akin to passionate manhood, went so far to argue that physical strength and moral conduct were inseparable.

Critical to this new emphasis was the discovery and positive valuation of the "primitive" in men. After about 1850, American middle-class men became increasingly concerned with the allegedly effeminizing effects of urban, industrial civilization. They therefore sought to revitalize masculinity by attempting to recover a rugged masculine self through boxing and other athletics, outdoor activities (especially in the West, considered a landscape unsullied by eastern "overcivilization"), and strenuous activity in general. Advice to recover a primitive masculine passion and savage energy was directed particularly at men in routine white-collar occupations.

In the aftermath of the Civil War, middle-class American men also began to value military discipline and martial valor. In the 1880s and 1890s, influenced by social Darwinist ideas of "survival of the fittest," men saw life as a combat-like struggle in which success required self-control and physical strength. Whereas some, such as the philosopher William James, hoped to harness military discipline and valor toward peaceful purposes, others, such as Theodore Roosevelt, felt that war, as a release of passion through violence, would most effectively reinvigorate masculinity. Men who shared Roosevelt's attitude linked passionate manhood to imperialism, nationalism, whiteness, and a racial theory of Anglo-Saxon superiority and capacity for self-government and discipline. They also strongly supported U.S. involvement in the Spanish-American War of 1898.

Evidenced in the 1880s by mushrooming membership in male fraternal organizations, which were characterized by hierarchical organization and primitive rituals, the embrace of military discipline led men to abandon older republican ideals of manliness that questioned inherited or ascribed status and resisted concentrations of power in the hands of the few. Instead, promoters of military discipline valorized an unquestioning submission to authority and touted the virtues of hierarchical bonds between men. This development involved an incorporation of the individualistic competitive impulses of entrepreneurial manhood into a "team spirit" approach that was considered necessary among men in an increasingly corporatized and bureaucratic society.

Similarly, organized sports were increasingly promoted as an outlet for men's competitive impulses. To be sure, economic competition had been an accepted, even an expected and encouraged, aspect of manly behavior since the late eighteenth century—one sanctioned by the economic theories of Adam Smith and the political writings of James Madison. However, after midcentury, competition for its own sake became a pervasive principle directing all aspects of men's lives in U.S. society, generating among men an obsession with competitive sports. Team sports enabled men, whether participants or spectators, to balance new demands for disciplined conduct and submission of the individual to the collective will with a culturally inscribed mandate of personal competitiveness. Games such as baseball, football, basketball, and volleyball promised to build character, develop military virtues, and foster self-control, while also enabling men to act passionately through aggressive competition.

Passionate manhood meshed well with such fundamental changes in the late nineteenth-century United States as urbanization, the growth of modern bureaucratic and administrative apparatuses, and the shift from entrepreneurial to corporate capitalism (with its emphasis on professional hierarchies, routinized career paths, and a division of labor). These developments destabilized older foundations of manliness and required new articulations of masculinity that would socialize men into a changing social and political matrix. The emphasis on bodily strength and male passions encouraged forms of behavior that earlier men might have considered antisocial, but passionate manhood adapted men and masculinity to a new world of depersonalized and dispersed authority.

Passionate manhood continues to influence cultural definitions of masculinity in contemporary U.S. society. Although no longer limited to men, this influence is evident in such body-centered leisure activities as mountain climbing and bicycling, as well as in the ongoing appeal of aggressive athletic competition. It is further reflected in Americans' consistent admiration of assertiveness and resolute action, particularly in their presidents. Finally, passionate manhood has been exemplified most recently in the mythopoetic men's movement and, more generally, in the persistent appeal of achieving contact with a more true and pure inner self.

Bibliography

Bederman, Gail. *Manliness and Civilization: A Cultural History of Gender and Race in the United States, 1880–1917.* Chicago: University of Chicago Press, 1996.

Budd, Michael Anton. *The Sculpture Machine: Physical Culture and Body Politics in the Age of Empire.* New York: New York University Press, 1997.

Kasson, John F. *Houdini, Tarzan, and the Perfect Man: The White Male Body and the Challenge of Modernity in America.* New York: Hill and Wang, 2001.

Kwolek-Folland, Angel. *Engendering Business: Men and Women in the Corporate Office, 1870–1930.* Baltimore: Johns Hopkins University Press, 1994.

Rotundo, E. Anthony. *American Manhood: Transformations in Masculinity from the Revolution to the Modern Era.* New York: Basic Books, 1993.

White, Kevin. *The First Sexual Revolution: The Emergence of Male Heterosexuality in Modern America.* New York: New York University Press, 1993.

Further Reading

Armstrong, Tim. *Modernism, Technology, and the Body: A Cultural Study.* Cambridge, England: Cambridge University Press, 1998.

Carnes, Mark C. *Secret Ritual and Manhood in Victorian America.* New Haven, Conn.: Yale University Press, 1989.

Gorn, Elliott J. *The Manly Art: Bare-Knuckle Prize Fighting in America.* Ithaca, N.Y.: Cornell University Press, 1986.

Kimmel, Michael. *Manhood in America: A Cultural History.* New York: Free Press, 1996.

Putney, Clifford. *Muscular Christianity: Manhood and Sports in Protestant America, 1880–1920.* Cambridge, Mass.: Harvard University Press, 2001.

Seltzer, Mark. *Bodies and Machines.* New York: Routledge, 1992.

Stearns, Peter N. *Battleground of Desire: The Struggle for Self-Control in Modern America.* New York: New York University Press, 1999.

Related Entries

Atlas, Charles; Baseball; Body; Bodybuilding; Boxing; Boy Scouts of America; Bureaucratization; Character; Crisis of Masculinity; Darwinism; Football; Fraternal Organizations; Gilded Age; Gulick, Luther; Hall, Granville Stanley; Imperialism; Individualism; James, William; Middle-Class Manhood; Militarism; Muscular Christianity; Nationalism; Outdoorsmen; Progressive Era; Republicanism; Spanish-American War; Sports; Strenuous Life; Violence; War; Western Frontier

—*Thomas Winter*

Patriarchy

Patriarchy—the governance of the household and its members by the male *paterfamilias* (father of the family), and the social relations this arrangement entails—has empowered men in both private and public life and defined male gender identity throughout U.S. history. A male-governed household has often been perceived as a model of good public order. Patriarchy, while supporting social hierarchies and power relationships based on gender, has also served as a foundation for power systems based on race, ethnicity, and class, and thus created the impression that social hierarchies based on these categories are part of the natural order. Women, nonwhites, and other disempowered groups, however, have challenged patriarchal power.

Patriarchy in Early America

European colonists brought to America social systems in which the male-headed household was the fundamental unit, male household heads represented their families politically, and men exercised power over their families (especially their sons) through the promise of the inheritance of land and other real estate. Colonists also adhered to the belief that these patriarchal social and political patterns were divinely instituted and necessary for a well-ordered society. These assumptions informed such early visions of American society as the Mayflower Compact (1620) and Massachusetts governor John Winthrop's Model of Christian Charity (1630)—both of which were, effectively, contracts among men about social order and the purpose of their colonial undertaking.

Colonial societies in New England, the Chesapeake Bay region, and elsewhere sought to maintain a strict patriarchal order. The Puritan leadership of the Massachusetts Bay colony perceived the gathering of both male and female religious dissenters at the house of Anne Hutchinson as a threat to their patriarchal power, and they expelled her and a group of her followers in 1638. Scholars have argued that the witchcraft accusations in Salem in 1692 (with a large majority of the accused being women) suggests an attempt to counteract challenges to pervasive patriarchal power. Seventeenth-century Chesapeake laws about the status of black servants grounded slavery in a legally constructed system of race-based patriarchy. Colonists in both regions defined Native American societies as uncivilized because their gender relations did not conform to European patriarchal patterns.

The era of the American Revolution witnessed both an ideological challenge to patriarchy and its affirmation in the drafting of the Constitution. Boycotts of English goods drew women into political activism and encouraged such women as Abigail Adams and Judith Sargent Murray—supported by such male patriot leaders as Thomas Paine and Benjamin Rush—to seek political equality with men in the emerging republic. Furthermore, the republican ideology that justified resistance to England's King George III also called for a softening of patriarchal governance in families and households. Despite these challenges to patriarchal leadership, citizenship and political power in the new nation were confined to white male property owners, and national identity formed around a notion of white male patriarchy embodied in the figure of wartime leader George Washington.

Patriarchy in the New Nation

During the first six decades of the nineteenth century, economic developments such as the market revolution and industrialization tended to undermine earlier forms of patriarchy and forced its regrounding, particularly in the northern states. The market and industrial revolutions forced a reconfiguration of male patriarchy by causing a decline in the significance of land ownership as a foundation of male economic and political power. Instead, male power became increasingly grounded in the forces of market exchange and men's ability to respond to them, and a new rationale for middle-class male authority promoted free competition, acquisitive individualism, and the pursuit of economic self-interest. A concomitant ideology of "separate spheres" defined men as alone suited to administer and participate in public political and economic life. Patriarchal power—at least for the middle class—depended increasingly on fathers' abilities as breadwinners and their capacity to provide education and guidance, especially to their sons. Linking manhood to income-generating activities gave men a greater share of economic power than they had held in the traditional patriarchal household.

In addition, an emerging emphasis on the equality of white men (grounded in republican notions of equality) and the practice of universal white-male suffrage that became widespread in the 1820s challenged earlier patriarchal notions that had assigned public political power to a propertied male elite. Yet this emerging notion of equality, which did not include women or nonwhite men, perpetuated patriarchy by preserving the male monopolization of political power.

Western expansion and frontier migration had ambivalent consequences for definitions of male patriarchy. On one hand, state and federal policy relied on notions of male patriarchy, with the white, male U.S. government serving as the paterfamilias, in defining Native Americans as child-like wardens of the government and relocating them further and further west. Similarly, the ideology of Manifest Destiny cast white males as divinely ordained instruments by which republican institutions would be spread across North America. On the other hand, the conditions accompanying westward migration forced a rethinking of the patriarchal relations that had developed in the industrializing, urbanizing East. The physically and emotionally demanding trip forced men and women to work more closely together on a basis of greater equality than they had previously. This process created new settler societies based on social experiences in which patriarchy proved to be less useful in guaranteeing survival than more equitable forms of social organization. As a result, the new western states of the late nineteenth century were among the first to jettison a key element of political patriarchy by granting women's suffrage.

Feminist challenges to patriarchal power arrangements gained momentum during this period. Beginning in the 1830s, abolitionist women and men made comparisons between the authority men held over women and the power male slaveholders wielded over their slaves, formulating a wide-ranging critique of masculine patriarchal power and control. Radical Quakers, spiritualists, and transcendentalists developed notions of gender equality based on spiritual grounds. In 1848 women's rights activists congregated at Seneca Falls, New York, drawing on the model of the Declaration of Independence and its case against tyranny to critique male patriarchal power and demand political equality.

In the agrarian economy and slave society of the South, however, patriarchy in its more traditional form thrived and gained significance as the foundation of public order and social relations. Southern plantation owners perceived their family members and their slaves (some of whom were their own offspring) as an extended household under their patriarchal control—and non-slave-holding yeoman farmers supported their patriarchal power and governance. Defenders of slavery, such as George Fitzhugh, the author of *Cannibals All!* (1857), argued that the patriarchal social relations of the slave system provided more humane working conditions for its laborers than did the impersonal, market-driven economy of industrial capitalism. The defeat of the Confederacy in the Civil War began to undermine race-based patriarchy in the South as the Fourteenth and Fifteenth Amendments (1868 and 1870, respectively) extended suffrage and other rights of citizenship to black males—although white Southern males responded by resisting these changes and seeking to salvage prewar patriarchal relations.

Men and Patriarchy: The Late Nineteenth and Early Twentieth Centuries

Social and economic developments of the late nineteenth and early twentieth centuries generated new challenges to patriarchal structures. Urbanization and the accompanying expansion of white-collar managerial work created a sense of uncertainty among men who now carried neither the power of property ownership nor entrepreneurial authority. Middle-class men, feeling a loss of patriarchal power, felt what historians have called a "crisis in masculinity."

In addition, a resurgent women's rights movement demanded suffrage and challenged male patriarchal authority in the realm of public politics. Many women began proposing maternalist models of city politics based on the notions of "municipal housekeeping." The feminist Charlotte Perkins Gilman proposed such a maternal state in her utopian novel *Herland* (1915). In 1920 woman suffragists succeeded in erasing one key element of patriarchy—the male monopolization of political power—with the ratification of the Nineteenth Amendment granting women the vote. Male social and political reformers, such as educator John Dewey, social scientists Lester Frank Ward and Thorstein Veblen, socialist writer Upton Sinclair, and African-American civil rights activist W. E. B. Du Bois, joined women reformers in arguing that patriarchy was unsuitable for a democratic society.

Challenges to patriarchy did not affect only white, native-born men. The immigrants that came to the United States between 1880 and 1914 from southern and eastern Europe frequently brought with them social relations grounded in traditional notions of patriarchal power. Yet the social and economic environment they entered offered opportunities that allowed individual family members to challenge and escape patriarchal power, leaving many immigrant fathers feeling that their masculine identities had been compromised.

U.S. foreign relations served as an ideological stage for affirming and renegotiating male patriarchy. Politicians such as Theodore Roosevelt promoted U.S. imperialism in the late nineteenth century on the grounds that colonial governance by white men would protect weaker, nonwhite people against the irresponsibility of their governments—as well as making American men more assertive rulers abroad and uncontested patriarchs at home. During both world wars, U.S. propaganda called on men to exercise their duties as patriarchal defenders of women's virtue and to gain women's allegiance to their patriarchal rule by enlisting to fight. During the Cold War years, and beyond, American presidents and policymakers would continue to use patriarchal arguments (protecting weaker people) to justify military intervention.

Patriarchy Crumbling: Recent America

The decades after World War II witnessed intensifying and increasingly successful challenges to gender- and race-based patriarchy by civil rights and feminist activists. The 1964 Civil Rights Act eroded patriarchal prerogatives by prohibiting discrimination along lines of both race and gender, and the 1965 Voting Rights Act guaranteed suffrage rights to African Americans. Resisting a system of race-based patriarchy gave African Americans of both sexes a sense of empowerment. But it also made women of both races even more keenly aware of the nature and strength of patriarchy in U.S. society. Likewise, the resurgence of feminism in the 1960s mounted a formidable challenge to male patriarchy, although the fate of the resulting Equal Rights Amendment (ERA) suggests that their success in uprooting it was only partial: Passed by Congress in 1972, the ERA failed to achieve ratification by the requisite number of states by 1982, due in large part to strong resistance from conservatives, who feared a breakdown of the traditional patriarchal family.

Many males participated in the challenge to gender patriarchy. Profeminist men—including gay author Gore Vidal, African-American civil rights activists Martin Luther King, Jr., and Jesse Jackson, rock musician John Lennon (who released "Woman is the Nigger of the World" in 1972), and actors Ed Asner and Alan Alda—spoke out against patriarchy and sought to articulate new models of manhood that separated male identity from gender hierarchy and claims to power over women.

The challenge to patriarchy was evident in academia as feminist studies, women's studies, and men's studies emerged as important new scholarly fields. Scholars in these areas produced systematic historical, sociological, anthropological, and literary analyses of patriarchal structures in American life. Historians, in particular, argued that standard narratives of the American past had often implicitly posited a white male "center," thereby serving to justify and legitimate patriarchal political, social, and economic structures. Using postmodernist approaches, gender scholars contributed to the ongoing rejection of patriarchy by producing new, decentered narratives of American life.

In the 1970s, deindustrialization began to erode the economic foundations of male patriarchy. With the decline of key industries, economic power and the ability to provide for a family became increasingly problematic, and American families increasingly required a second income (a female as well as a male breadwinner) to get by or to afford a certain standard of living. In addition, the national divorce rate and the number of single-parent, female-headed families rose, especially, but not exclusively, among racial and ethnic minority groups. As a result, Americans became increasingly aware of alternatives to the conventional male-headed, patriarchal household.

The late-twentieth-century erosion of patriarchal power prompted a renewed sense among many American men that masculinity was in crisis. It also sparked the emergence of social movements intended to reground and bolster male power. During the 1980s and 1990s, religious conservatives increasingly urged the importance of preserving the male-headed family and relocating women from the workforce back to the home. Similarly, the Promise Keepers, an evangelical Christian group founded in 1991, sought to reground male household authority in men's emotional and spiritual commitment to their families.

Conclusion

Throughout U.S. history, male patriarchy has served as an important reference point for the formation of male identity, the distribution of power, the organization of private and public relations, and the shaping of domestic and foreign politics. Economic change, feminism, and American democracy itself have consistently forced reconfigurations and erosions of patriarchal power. However, while profound challenges to patriarchy have occurred in the decades since World War II, bastions of male privilege remain, ranging from the U.S. Senate (where men are represented far out of proportion to their percentage of the population) to Georgia's Augusta National Golf Club, the target in 2003 of feminist protests over the club's all-male membership policy. Patriarchy thus remains a powerful, if contested, reality of American life.

Bibliography

Braude, Ann. *Radical Spirits: Spiritualism and Women's Rights in Nineteenth-Century America.* Boston, Mass.: Beacon Press, 1989.

Brown, Elaine. *A Taste of Power: A Black Woman's Story.* New York: Random House, 1994.

Coontz, Stephanie. *The Social Origins of Private Life: A History of American Families, 1600–1900.* New York: Verso, 1988.

Demos, John. *A Little Commonwealth: Family Life in Plymouth Colony.* New York: Oxford University Press, 1970.

Ehrenreich, Barbara. *The Hearts of Men: American Dreams and The Flight from Commitment.* New York: Doubleday, 1983.

Enloe, Cynthia. *The Morning After: Sexual Politics at The End of the Cold War.* Berkeley: University of California Press, 1993.

Faludi, Susan. *Stiffed: The Betrayal of Modern Man.* New York: Vintage, 1999.

Fliegelman, Jay. *Prodigals and Pilgrims: The American Revolution Against Patriarchal Authority, 1750–1800.* New York: Cambridge University Press, 1982.

Kann, Mark. *A Republic of Men: The American Founders, Gendered Language, and Patriarchal Politics.* New York: New York University Press, 1998.

Karlsen, Carol. *The Devil in the Shape of a Woman: Witchcraft in Colonial New England.* New York: Norton, 1987.

Kimmel, Michael. *Manhood in America: A Cultural History.* New York: Free Press, 1996.

Kimmel, Michael, and Thomas E. Mosmiller, eds. *Against the Tide: Pro-Feminist Men in the United States, 1776–1990.* Boston: Beacon Press, 1992.

McCurry, Stephanie. *Masters of Small Worlds: Yeoman Households, Gender Relations, and the Political Culture of the Antebellum South Carolina Low Country.* New York: Oxford University Press, 1995.

Norton, Mary Beth. *Founding Mothers and Fathers: Gendered Power and the Forming of American Society.* New York: Vintage, 1997.

Stearns, Peter N. *Be A Man! Males in Modern Society.* 2nd ed. New York: Holmes & Meier, 1990.

FURTHER READING

Brown, Kathleen M. *Good Wives, Nasty Wenches, and Anxious Patriarchs: Gender, Race, and Power in Colonial Virginia.* Chapel Hill: University of North Carolina Press, 1996.

Lerner, Gerda. *The Creation of Patriarchy.* New York: Oxford University Press, 1986.

Murray, Mary. *The Law of the Father?: Patriarchy in the Transition from Feudalism to Capitalism.* London: Routledge, 1995.

Pateman, Carole. *The Sexual Contract.* Stanford, Calif.: Stanford University Press, 1988.

Radway, Janice A. *Reading the Romance: Women, Patriarchy, and Popular Literature.* 1984. Reprint, Chapel Hill: University of North Carolina Press, 1991.

Rotundo, E. Anthony. *American Manhood: Transformations in Masculinity from the Revolution to the Modern Era.* New York: Basic Books, 1993.

Stoltenberg, John. *Refusing to Be a Man: Essays on Sex and Justice.* New York: Penguin, 1990.

Walby, Sylvia. *Theorizing Patriarchy.* Oxford: Basil Blackwell, 1990.

RELATED ENTRIES

American Revolution; Citizenship; Class; Crisis of Masculinity; Cult of Domesticity; Democratic Manhood; Feminism; Immigration; Imperialism; Industrialization; Labor Movement and Unions; Manifest Destiny; Market Revolution; Marriage; Masculine Domesticity; Men's Movements; Men's Studies; Military; Nationalism; Patriotism; Politics; Postmodernism; Promise Keepers; Race; Religion and Spirituality; Republicanism; Sexual Harassment; Sexual Revolution; Slavery; Suffragism; Television; Violence; War; Washington, George; Western Frontier; Whiteness; White Supremacism; Work; Working-Class Manhood

—Thomas Winter

PATRIOTISM

Patriotism and definitions of manliness have a shared history in the United States. While the pressure to be "patriotic" has been especially strong in times of national crisis or war, patriotism in general has been perceived as a significant component of manliness. Although women have been called upon to be patriotic as well, women's patriotism has been linked to the private realms of home, family, and motherhood, whereas men's has been connected to public politics and the military.

Revolutionary and Early National America

American patriotism first appeared with intensifying resistance to British colonial policies in the 1760s and 1770s. American opponents of British laws identified themselves as "Patriots" and, defining their cause as a heroic defense of liberty, formed organizations such as the Sons of Liberty. An association between manliness and patriotism thus underlay the formation of national identity in the United States.

Still, patriotic devotion to an abstract concept of American nationhood took form only gradually and unevenly. During the debates surrounding the writing of the Constitution, devotion to the nation was identified with the civic virtue that early Americans considered essential to liberty under a republican form of government. Yet there were differences over the implications of manly patriotism: Both Federalist supporters of the Constitution and a strong national government and their Anti-Federalist critics associated their positions with republican manhood and the true fulfillment of Revolutionary patriotism. In light of such divisions, the figure of General George Washington (soon to be President Washington) served as both a powerful masculine symbol for national integration and a focus for patriotic sentiment. His birthday remained an important occasion for public celebrations of manly patriotism through much of the nineteenth century.

The Antebellum Period

Patriotic devotion to the American nation intensified during and after the War of 1812—sometimes considered a second war for independence—and again during the 1830s and 1840s as white Americans linked westward expansion to Manifest Destiny, patriotic duty, and masculinity. In this context, the independence of Texas and the unsuccessful 1836 defense of the Alamo by so-called freedom fighters such as Davy Crockett served as symbols for masculine patriotic perseverance. Many white Americans regarded geographic expansion in the Pacific during the 1840s and the nation's expansionist war against Mexico as a fulfillment of a patriotic continental vision of the United States as a nation. At the same time, opponents of the Mexican War, such as transcendentalist Henry David Thoreau, regarded resistance to the war as an expression of American ideals and a mark of manly patriotism.

Race, ethnicity, and religion figured implicitly, yet prominently, in antebellum definitions of patriotism and manliness. Western expansion carried a promise of free land and economic opportunities for white men. The removal of nonwhite, non-Protestant men (Native Americans and Mexicans) from western lands was justified by a race-coded, patriotic manliness. Similarly, nativists defined their opposition to Irish immigration in terms of a race-coded manly patriotism: They portrayed the Roman Catholic Irish as nonwhite, devoted to an authority outside the United States (the pope in Rome), and therefore incapable of undivided patriotism.

Antebellum patriotism ultimately fractured along sectional lines and became entwined with conflicting concepts of American manhood. Northerners associated their patriotic devotion to the nation with a vision of manliness grounded in independent farming, "free soil," and free labor; many of them regarded John Brown's violent resistance to slavery and his 1859 execution as an act of patriotic and heroic martyrdom. Southern notions of patriotic manliness relied on commitment to a patriarchal social order, racial hierarchy, slavery, and regional identity. These conflicting definitions of patriotism, manliness, and nation contributed to secession and Civil War (1861–65) and became bases on which both sides rallied their populations and armies.

The Late Nineteenth and Early Twentieth Centuries

In the aftermath of the Civil War, Americans, from both North and South, redefined notions of patriotism and manliness as they tried to reconstruct the nation. Northern men were inclined to view Abraham Lincoln (assassinated in 1865 after the end of the Civil War) as a patriotic martyr to freedom and national unity. White Southerners, meanwhile, retained a regionally based patriotic manhood expressed in celebrations of the "Lost Cause." African Americans associated the cause of emancipation with a manly, patriotic commitment to national ideals of liberty. Black Union-army veterans celebrated Emancipation Day and articulated a vision of patriotic manliness based on racial equality. However, in the name of national reconciliation, white Americans eventually elevated Southern soldiers from traitors to loyal sons of the nation. Notions of patriotic manliness thus acquired a racial dimension, for the military valor of white men eclipsed loyalty to the nation as a mark of manly patriotism. The Civil War came to be perceived as a heroic cause that had strengthened national bonds and joined Northern and Southern men in shared patriotic resolve.

Race and class became increasingly significant dimensions of U.S. patriotism and masculinity in the late nineteenth century. The Spanish-American War (1898), the Philippine-American War (1902), and the founding of the Boy Scouts of America (1910) reinforced notions of martial valor and Anglo-Saxonism as appropriate expressions of manly patriotism and fused them to a commitment and devotion to the nation. After 1880, meanwhile, an influx of immigrants from southern and southeastern Europe and from Asia—perceived as nonwhite and alien to U.S. society and culture—further reinforced white Americans' belief that patriotism belonged properly to white men. Emerging national trade unions such as the Knights of Labor and the American Federation of Labor associated working-class pride, equality, and economic justice with manly patriotism. Yet these same ideals also led trade unions to advocate the exclusion of Asian workers, who were perceived as unmanly. Working-class definitions of manliness and patriotism thus became linked to notions of race.

The World Wars

The two world wars of the twentieth century sparked strong expressions of patriotic masculinity in American culture. In both wars, patriotic devotion to the United States was portrayed as the highest expression of manliness, whereas war resisters were depicted as unmanly, effeminate, and unpatriotic. During this period the figure of Uncle Sam became one of the most visible and powerful symbols of manly patriotism.

These years also witnessed the creation of several other icons embodying patriotic manhood. The Lincoln Memorial, dedicated in 1922 in Washington, D.C., and featuring a larger-than-life statue of President Lincoln as the "Great Emancipator," stands as a tribute to patriotic sacrifice and unity of the nation. Likewise, the presidential monument at Mount Rushmore, South Dakota (dedicated in 1927 and completed in 1939) features the busts of Presidents George Washington, Thomas Jefferson, Theodore Roosevelt, and Abraham Lincoln, a grouping that, to some, associates patriotism and nation with white patriarchy.

Cold War America

The onset of the Cold War between the United States and the Soviet Union created a new framework for patriotic manliness. Politically, the anticommunist position exemplified by Republican senator Joseph R. McCarthy of Wisconsin was perceived by many as an expression of patriotic manhood—a perception that McCarthy himself articulated explicitly and, sometimes, bombastically. Conversely, dissent from U.S. Cold War policies was construed as unpatriotic and unmanly—and was often associated with homosexuality. A true man, according to Cold War American ideology, showed his patriotism through his dedication to the capitalist system in his work, and by giving proof of his heterosexuality by fathering offspring within the confines of marriage. Another outlet for patriotic manliness in the 1950s included "preparedness" for possible

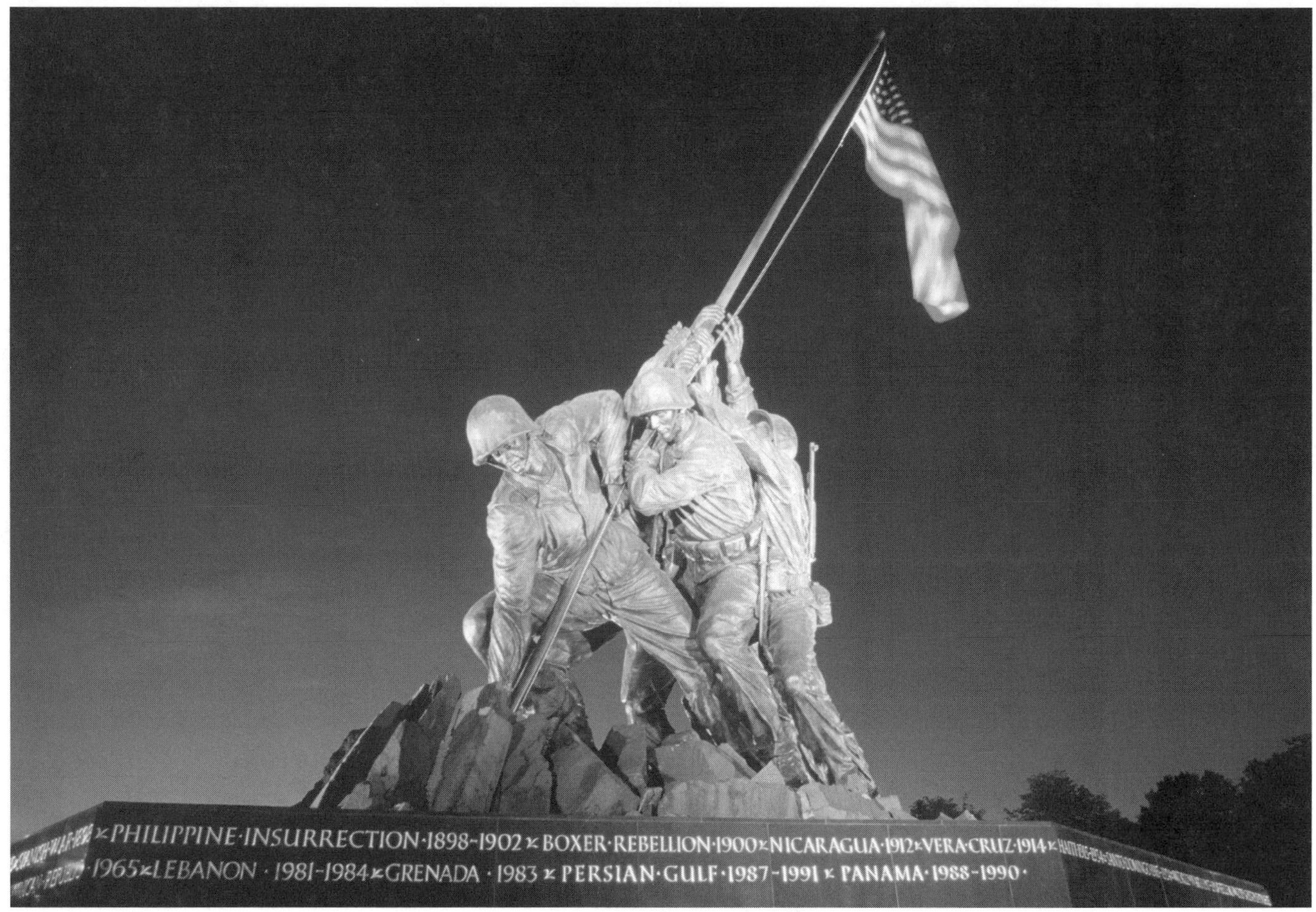

The U.S. Marine Corps memorial statue Iwo Jima *symbolizes the close association in American culture between masculinity, patriotism, military service, and national identity. (© William Manning/Corbis)*

nuclear conflict, such as the installation of a bomb shelter for the protection of one's family in one's backyard.

By the 1960s, ideas of what constituted manly patriotism became contested both at home and abroad. Movements for social justice, such as the civil rights, Chicano, and American Indian movements (with nonwhites and sometimes women in positions of leadership), successfully challenged the idea that patriotic dedication to liberty and equality is the sole purview of white men. Support of U.S. involvement in the Vietnam War was initially portrayed as patriotic, yet as resistance to the war mounted, antiwar activists argued that manly patriotism required a commitment to social justice rather than unquestioning support of government policy.

Post–Cold War America

The end of the Cold War problematized previous definitions of patriotism and manliness. But Americans applied the rhetoric of bellicose patriotism and masculinity to newly identified enemies, such as Japan, perceived during the 1990s as an economic competitor to American commercial prowess, and Iraqi dictator Saddam Hussein, a target of American military attacks in 1991 and 2003. In the absence of a rival superpower, even the American government itself became the target of domestic militia groups such as the Montana Freemen, who identified themselves as manly patriots defending liberty against overreaching federal power. Timothy McVeigh, who led the bomb attack on the Murrah Federal Building in Oklahoma City in 1995, certainly saw himself as an exponent of a patriotic masculinity—and he viewed his 2001 execution as a form of martyrdom. In the aftermath of the terrorist attacks of September 11, 2001, definitions of, and reverence for, manly patriotism gained new currency, as exemplified in widespread accolades for New York City police officers and firefighters.

Conclusion

Associations between patriotism and manliness as key components of citizenship have played a significant role in American culture, both contributing to definitions of national identity and serving at times as powerful foci of national reconciliation. Yet definitions of patriotism and manliness have not been the sole cultural property of people or groups in power. Black Civil War veterans, participants in the labor movement, Vietnam veterans, proponents of social justice, and others have availed themselves of the vocabulary of patriotic masculinity as well. A strong connection between patriotism and manliness remains fundamental to American civic culture.

Bibliography

Bodnar, John. *Remaking America: Public Memory, Commemoration, and Patriotism in the Twentieth Century.* Princeton, N.J.: Princeton University Press, 1992.

Bodnar, John, ed. *Bonds of Affection: Americans Define Their Patriotism.* Princeton, N.J.: Princeton University Press, 1996.

Boime, Albert. *The Unveiling of the National Icons: A Plea for Patriotic Iconoclasm in a Nationalistic Era.* Cambridge, England: Cambridge University Press, 1998

Fried, Richard M. *The Russians Are Coming! The Russians Are Coming! Pageantry and Patriotism in Cold-War America.* New York: Oxford University Press, 1998.

O'Leary, Cecilia Elizabeth. *To Die For: The Paradox of American Patriotism.* Princeton, N.J.: Princeton University Press, 1999.

Further Reading

Frank, Dana. *Buy American: The Untold Story of Economic Nationalism.* Boston, Mass.: Beacon Press, 1999.

Gerstle, Gary. *Working-Class Americanism: The Politics of Labor in a Textile City, 1914–1960.* Princeton, N.J.: Princeton University Press, 2002.

Glassberg, David. *American Historical Pageantry: The Uses of Tradition in the Early Twentieth Century.* Chapel Hill: University of North Carolina Press, 1990.

Hoganson, Kristin L. *Fighting for American Manhood: How Gender Politics Provoked the Spanish-American and Philippine-American Wars.* New Haven, Conn.: Yale University Press, 1998.

Kammen, Michael. *Mystic Chords of Memory: The Transformation of Tradition in American Culture.* New York: Knopf, 1991.

Lembcke, Jerry. *The Spitting Image: Myth, Memory, and the Legacy of Vietnam.* New York: New York University Press, 1998.

Zelinsky, Wilbur. *Nation into State: The Shifting Symbolic Foundations Of American Nationalism.* Chapel Hill: University of North Carolina Press, 1988.

Related Entries

African-American Manhood; *Birth of a Nation*; Boy Scouts of America; Citizenship; Civil War; Cold War; Crockett, Davy; Emancipation; Gilded Age; Imperialism; Irish-American Manhood; Militarism; Nationalism; Nativism; Race; Southern Manhood; Spanish-American War; Strenuous Life; Vietnam War; Violence; War; Washington, George; Whiteness; World War I; World War II

—*Thomas Winter*

Playboy Magazine

Launched by publisher Hugh Hefner in 1953, *Playboy* magazine became a huge commercial success by combining softcore pornography and up-market lifestyle features for men in one magazine. Between the 1950s and the 1970s, its soaring circulation became the basis for an international business empire embracing publishing, movie production, and a chain of nightclubs, casinos, and hotels. *Playboy*'s success marked not only a transformation in American sexual morals and a greater legitimacy of pornography within mainstream culture, but also the ascendance in U.S. society of masculine identities that eschewed moderation and the work ethic in favor of hedonistic consumption, recreation, and personal gratification. Its mascot, a white rabbit sporting a bowtie, symbolized this model of masculinity by connoting affluence, sophistication, lighthearted leisure, and sexual license.

Playboy was highly controversial throughout the 1950s and 1960s, facing opposition from moral crusaders, who viewed its nude pictorials as lewd and indecent, and from the growing feminist movement, which objected to what it considered to be sexual exploitation of women. *Playboy* was nonetheless a publishing triumph. Monthly sales climbed to nearly 1 million by 1959 and to more than 4.5 million by 1969 as *Playboy* became a totem of the Sexual Revolution. Primarily appealing to urban, white, middle-class men, its circulation was highest in the East, California, and metropolitan enclaves in between. *Playboy* also successfully pitched itself to a young market, with college students comprising over a quarter of its readership. Although *Playboy* posed as a champion of footloose bachelorhood, during the 1950s married men made up slightly more than half its readership, perhaps because they were attracted by the magazine's vicarious fantasies of independent hedonism.

In 1960 the first Playboy Club was opened in Chicago, and by 1967 Hefner owned seventeen nightclubs and hotels. Based in cosmopolitan cities such as New York, Miami, and San Francisco, and staffed by scantily costumed female "Bunnies," the Playboy Clubs boasted a membership of half a million during the late 1960s and turned an annual profit of nearly $25 million. Merchandising items of stylish male consumption—including ties, cigarette lighters, golf clubs, and polo

A 1962 photo of Playboy *magazine publisher and editor Hugh Hefner, surrounded by "bunnies" who staffed his Playboy clubs. Hefner's model of masculinity, characterized by bachelorhood, affluence, sophistication, leisure, consumerism, and freewheeling heterosexuality, challenged the post–World War II model of the married suburban father and heralded the 1960s Sexual Revolution. (From the collections of the Library of Congress)*

shirts, all emblazoned with *Playboy*'s Bunny insignia—was another lucrative sideline.

Much of *Playboy*'s success lay in its appeal to a new generation of upwardly-mobile men whose gender identities were pre-eminently constructed around leisure and personal consumption. *Playboy*'s inclusion of semi-pornographic content established it as an avowedly masculine and heterosexual magazine; its features and advertisements dealing with fashion, entertainment, foreign travel, and interior décor grounded masculine identity in the universe of modern consumerism; and its literary features, political commentary, investigative journalism, and interviews with major public figures were intended to infuse this new model of American manhood with cultural sophistication.

In September 1972, *Playboy*'s circulation exceeded 7 million—its highest total ever. During the mid-1970s, however, its image began to look anachronistic as competing titles such as *Penthouse* (a British magazine launched in America in 1969) and *Hustler* (launched in 1974) offered more sexually explicit material. *Playboy*'s dipping sales prompted marketing reappraisals and cost-cutting measures that ultimately led to the closing of the Playboy Clubs in the 1980s. During the late 1990s, however, *Playboy*'s international circulation still totaled 4.5 million, while steady expansion into video sales, cable TV, and Internet services maintained the financial success of its parent company, Playboy Enterprises.

The rise of *Playboy* magazine both contributed to and reflected profound shifts in American masculine identities during the second half of the twentieth century. *Playboy's* image of free-wheeling sexuality and hedonistic consumption appealed to men who were increasingly eschewing the traditional male role of responsible, family-focused breadwinner in favor of material pleasure and personal indulgence.

Bibliography

Brady, Frank. *Hefner.* London: Weidenfeld & Nicolson, 1975.

Ehrenreich, Barbara. *The Hearts of Men: American Dreams and the Flight From Commitment.* New York: Anchor Press, 1984.

Miller, Russell. *Bunny: The Real Story of Playboy.* London: Michael Joseph, 1984.

Further Reading

Dines, Gail. "'I Buy It For the Articles': Playboy Magazine and the Sexualization of Consumerism." In *Gender, Race and Class in Media: A Text-Reader,* edited by Gail Dines and Jean M. Humez. Thousand Oaks, Calif.: Sage, 1995.

Weyr, Thomas. *Reaching for Paradise: The Playboy Vision of America.* New York: NYT Times Books, 1978.

Related Entries

Advertising; Bachelorhood; Consumerism; Fashion; Feminism; Heterosexuality; Leisure; Middle-Class Manhood; Pornography; Sexual Revolution

—Bill Osgerby

Politics

In the United States politics has traditionally been the province of men. The public sphere of politics has historically been conceived in opposition to the private (and feminine) sphere of the home, and it is one of the central arenas in which American masculinity has been experienced and enacted. From the early colonial settlers to the most recent immigrants of the late twentieth century, engaging in political activity has been a way of becoming a man. However, the gradual emancipation and enfranchisement of women, alongside the inexorable democratization of access to political office, has transformed American politics over the centuries from a privileged bastion of wealthy white men to a far more complex arena in which many models of manhood—and womanhood—compete.

The Colonial Era

In the early colonies of New England, the sphere of politics was entirely subordinated to religious authority. The rulers of the Puritan colonies were deeply religious men who based their authority on Old Testament models of patriarchy. Thus, the Puritan pastor and religious scholar Cotton Mather, in his *Magnalia Christi Americana: or, The Ecclesiastical History of New-England* (1702), compared his chronicles to the books of Moses, which recorded the lives of the "Ante-Diluvian Patriarchs." Political manhood in the Puritan colonial tradition derived from the prophetic and evangelical tradition of Protestant Christianity—political power and the manhood it defined were understood in terms of maintaining and expanding the community of Christians in the "wilderness" of the New World.

Although this political system was based on the idea of the religious covenant, it was not democratic in the modern electoral sense. Leaders did not campaign, nor were they popularly elected, as such a process was understood to appeal to selfish interests, not to the spiritual health and political integrity of the community. But their selection for office signified community acknowledgment of their spiritual strength and soundness of judgment—in short, of their manhood.

In the southern colonies, economic gain and the extension of European royal authority were more important than prophetic mission, and the gradual expansion of slavery into the plantation system resulted in an aristocratic paternalism that contrasted considerably with the developing political tradition in the New England colonies. Over the course of the eighteenth century, the South bred an entire generation of gentlemen farmers, including George Washington, Thomas Jefferson, James Madison, and many others, whose combination of political and paternalistic authority would dominate the early decades of the post-Revolutionary government. In many ways, this model of masculine political authority was based on European models of aristocratic privilege, in which manhood and power derived from land ownership and good "breeding." Although these leaders were elected, the franchise (vote) was still restricted to propertied males (who affirmed a candidate's manliness through their votes). Campaigning, in the modern sense, had not yet emerged. Rather, wealthy candidates would organize social events for party members at which alcohol was generously distributed as a mechanism of forging political community among likeminded men.

The Eighteenth Century

In the rapidly growing cities and towns of eighteenth-century America, another model of political manhood emerged that would contribute much of the energy and manpower behind the Revolution. The independent artisan, whose masculinity derived from economic autonomy and a communal identification based in independent crafts and trades, was a powerful political force in the colonies. While the founding fathers deliberated over the Declaration of Independence in the Philadelphia State House, these men demonstrated in the streets and argued in the local taverns, enacting a more boisterous and rowdy model of American democracy.

Indeed, it was as an independent craftsman (a printer) that Benjamin Franklin forged the model of manhood that eventually came to dominate the rhetoric, if not the reality, of the American political scene. This was the "self-made man," the solitary male who was able to gain political and economic power without relying on religious institutions or family background. His astonishing rise from poverty and obscurity to worldwide renown and influence became a model for manhood in post-Revolutionary America, vying against the more genteel and traditional aristocratic masculinity embodied by the early presidencies of Washington, Jefferson, Madison, and James Monroe.

The genteel aristocrat, the laborer/artisan, and the self-made man (all of which, by the Revolutionary era, were defined in relation to political republicanism) were the political models of masculinity that made up the Sons of Liberty, a patriotic organization that rebelled against the mother country. Their principal victim in the new nation, however, would be the Puritan father, whose authority was permanently undermined by the constitutional separation of church and state. After the Revolution, religious authority was, in essence, feminized, for ministers without political power now preached to congregations of mostly women, while political leaders, appealing to "manly" republican citizens, attempted to organize and educate a rapidly expanding male electorate. At this point in time the term democracy was associated with chaos and mob rule, and politicians achieved political power and influence through pamphleteering and, increasingly, the party system that was organized around boisterous rallies and a highly partisan press.

The Nineteenth Century

When Thomas Jefferson assumed the presidency in 1800, he instituted a model of political manhood that would have a profound influence during the nineteenth century. Jefferson was the model of the yeoman farmer, a sort of combination of the genteel aristocrat and the urban artisan. He thought that republican government could only work if citizens achieved economic autonomy through the ownership of land. Deeply distrustful of industrialization and city life, he envisioned a republic of independent and enfranchised farmers, with small cities and no industrialization.

With the election of Andrew Jackson to the presidency in 1828, Jefferson's genteel aristocracy was supplanted by a rugged, frontier individualism that appealed to the poorer, landless whites who had recently been granted voting rights through universal male suffrage. Such men became the principal constituents of what became known as Jacksonian democracy. Jackson's promoters emphasized his crude, backwoods style and heroic performance as a general during the War of 1812 to suggest the effeminacy and ineffectuality of southern and the northeastern elites. The male persona of the Indian-killing pioneer became the central expression of the frontier, and military prowess became one of the most promising avenues to political office. Furthermore, Jackson's election marked the beginning of the modern campaign system. His opponent, John Quincy Adams, considered public appearances and solicitation of votes vulgar and common, while Jackson was able to win by parading his soldierly authority and liberally casting slurs on Adams' manhood. Declaring one's masculinity to a male electorate became a perennial feature of American electioneering.

The South's defeat in the Civil War further severed the connection between aristocratic privilege and political power. By the end of the nineteenth century, the principal model for political manhood was Franklin's self-made man, now embodied, and indeed consecrated, in the figure of Abraham Lincoln. However, with the rise of industrial and corporate capitalism after the war, the self-made man was increasingly associated with big business, particularly as tycoons such as Andrew Carnegie and John D. Rockefeller became prominent public figures. Politicians of this era tended to be businessmen, or at least to have strong connections to the business world, and they typically associated manhood with business success. Opponents of such figures charged them with dependence on (and subservience to) big business; cronyism; undermining the manly integrity of political office; and an unmasculine softness borne of excessive wealth and overcivilization.

Furthermore, the increasing presence of women, freedmen, and immigrant ethnic populations in the workforce and the public world demanded considerations that most white male politicians were reluctant to offer. The woman suffrage movement was increasingly visible and vocal during this era, but most men continued to believe that women were biologically unfit for politics. Likewise, when Reconstruction presented the vision of African-American male voters and politicians, white society responded, for the most part, with ridicule, asserting that the freedmen were unmanly, infantile, lazy, and incapable of self-rule. Nevertheless, the increasing presence in politics of women and minorities generated an anxiety among white men—called by some scholars a "crisis" in white masculinity—that would come to characterize twentieth-century political manhood.

The Twentieth Century

The passage of the Nineteenth Amendment in 1920, giving women the right to vote, was a clear turning point in American politics. The ideals of the suffrage movement—that the enfranchisement of women would cleanse politics of corruption and infuse it with a higher morality—failed to be realized, but the exclusive relation between masculinity and politics was irreversibly severed. As a result, most models of political manhood in the twentieth century became almost archaic throwbacks to earlier versions. In the opening decade of the twentieth century, President Theodore Roosevelt tried desperately to resuscitate the frontier spirit; in the following decade, Woodrow Wilson attempted to embody what was left of the southern gentleman; and Franklin D. Roosevelt, whose presidency lasted from 1933 to 1945 (the longest in American politics), represented the persistence of the old New England patrician aristocracy. All three men struggled against accusations of effeminacy.

In the early 1960s, John F. Kennedy briefly seemed to offer a new model of heroic manhood for the modern age. During his campaign for the presidency, his youth, dashing good looks, and his rhetoric of action and a "New Frontier" were all contrasted with a kindly but elderly and enfeebled Dwight Eisenhower. The novelist Norman Mailer summarized the change when he proclaimed that America no longer needed a father; it needed a leading man. But Kennedy's presidency was brief, and his assassination in 1963 was followed by the devastating entanglement in Vietnam, the rise of second-wave feminism, and an extended economic downturn that would permanently damage job security, all of which were experienced as further assaults on American masculinity. Once again, the political world responded with throwbacks, all of which further undercut conventional models of political manhood. Lyndon B. Johnson, who took over from Kennedy, exposed the crude macho bravado behind the southern gentleman; Richard M. Nixon, in the 1970s, revealed the amoral vindictiveness behind the self-made man; and Ronald Reagan, in the 1980s, became the senile caricature of frontier individualism.

Bill Clinton's election in 1992 marked the emergence of a new model of political manhood in the United States. The first baby-boomer president, Clinton grew up with the challenges posed to conventional masculine political leadership by feminism. Consequently, his administration included many women, including his wife Hillary Rodham, in positions of power, and was more receptive to women's issues than any prior administration. In Clinton's Cabinet, politics was no longer a homosocial affair. Consequently, Clinton was highly popular with female voters, who had put such issues as abortion and gender equality permanently on the American political agenda.

Furthermore, Clinton himself had a public image as an empathic and emotionally sensitive man, signaling that it has become more acceptable for political men to exhibit conventionally feminine characteristics. Clinton's accommodation of feminism and femininity was further illustrated by his willingness to subordinate himself to Hillary's Senate career, and his implicit support for her possible presidential bid. Overall, the Clinton marriage represents the disintegration of male dominance and prerogative in American politics, and the emergence of a model of political manhood more attuned to the issues and qualities conventionally associated with American women.

BIBLIOGRAPHY

Cawelti, John G. *Apostles of the Self-Made Man.* Chicago: University of Chicago Press, 1965.

Douglas, Ann. *The Feminization of American Culture.* New York: Noonday Press, 1998.

Genovese, Michael A. *The Power of the American Presidency, 1789–2000.* New York: Oxford University Press, 2001.

Hofstadter, Richard. *The American Political Tradition and the Men Who Made It.* New York: Vintage, 1989.

Kimmel, Michael. *Manhood in America: A Cultural History.* New York: Free Press, 1996.

Mailer, Norman. *The Presidential Papers.* New York: Berkeley, 1970.

Rogin, Michael. *Ronald Reagan, The Movie and Other Episodes in Political Demonology.* Berkeley: University of California Press, 1987.

Wills, Gary. *Nixon Agonistes: The Crisis of the Self-Made Man.* Atlanta, Ga.: Cherokee, 1990.

FURTHER READING

Faludi, Susan. *Stiffed: The Betrayal of the American Man.* New York: William Morrow, 1999.

Hodgson, Godfrey. *All Things to All Men: The False Promise of the Modern American Presidency.* New York: Simon & Schuster, 1980.

Miroff, Bruce. *Icons of Democracy: American Leaders as Heroes, Aristocrats, Dissenters, and Democrats.* Lawrence: University of Kansas Press, 2000.

Posner, Richard A. *An Affair of State: The Investigation, Impeachment, and Trial of President Clinton.* Cambridge, Mass.: Harvard University Press, 1999.

Rogin, Michael Paul. *Fathers and Children: Andrew Jackson and the Subjugation of the American Indian.* New Brunswick, N.J.: Transaction Publishers, 1991.

Warner, Michael. *The Letters of the Republic: Publication and the Public Sphere in Eighteenth-Century America.* Cambridge, Mass.: Harvard University Press, 1990.

Wills, Gary. *Inventing America: Jefferson's Declaration of Independence.* New York: Vintage, 1979.

———. *The Kennedy Imprisonment: A Meditation on Power.* New York: Pocket Books, 1983.

———. *Lincoln at Gettysburg: The Words That Remade America.* New York: Simon & Schuster, 1992.

RELATED ENTRIES

Alcohol; American Dream; American Revolution; Civil War; Democratic Manhood; Franklin, Benjamin; Individualism; Jackson, Andrew; Lincoln, Abraham; Patriarchy; Patriotism; Property; Reagan, Ronald; Republicanism; Roosevelt, Theodore; Self-Made Man; Sons of Liberty; Southern Manhood; Vietnam War; Washington, George

—Loren Glass

POPULISM

American populism is an enduring and prominent intellectual and political tradition, as well as a specific political movement of the late nineteenth century. Populism lionizes the middle-class "producer" as a model of ideal manhood while blaming both the rich and the poor for the perceived decline of the white patriarchal family. This ideal, seen by its adherents as the foundation of the American republic, is based on a concept of masculinity grounded in breadwinning, protection of family, and citizenship.

Often infused with moral and evangelical fervor, populism has sought to restore an idealized past era of small-scale capitalism in which white male producers had the economic power to support their families, acted as independent citizens, and succeeded or failed on their own merits. Its promise to restore this lost status to a deserving "natural" elite of white working- and middle-class males has tended to attract men from these groups who feel dispossessed of economic privilege or political power, particularly during times of economic or social upheaval.

A populist ideology that advocated male superiority emerged in colonial America as an abundance of land and periodic shortages of labor fostered a perception that all enterprising white men could succeed by their own efforts. During the Revolutionary era, republicanism connected this economic ideology to a political narrative pitting a "producer" class (those who actually made things) against beneficiaries of inherited wealth and centralized power. According to the tenets of republican manhood (an important foundation of populism) only the male producer could maintain the vigilance, moral uprightness, and economic independence needed to sustain a democratic republic.

Populist masculinity took on added dimensions between the 1820s and 1850s, as industrialization and westward expansion began transforming the American economy. Jacksonian political ideology and an emerging working class emphasized an antielitist agenda that set "the people" (i.e., small-town businessmen, small western and southern farmers, and skilled urban workers) against both the rising power of northern industrialists and what they perceived as hypersexualized and degenerate immigrants, Catholics, blacks, and Native Americans competing with them for jobs and land. (Later in the nineteenth century, populism categorized Asian and Jewish immigrants similarly.) Building on real economic grievances, populist rhetoric featured images of the besieged patriarchal family man protecting his wife and children. Also emphasized were the importance of white-male suffrage, affordable land, and a family wage to the male provider. Populism thus asserted an inextricable connection between manhood, independence, and whiteness.

During the late nineteenth century, the Knights of Labor, a labor organization, and the populist movement attempted to combine populism's established antielitist political and economic agenda with a new and more progressive attitude toward women, racial minorities, and the poor. Hoping to unite various disempowered groups by loosening populism's moorings in masculinity and whiteness, the Knights hired women organizers, supported woman suffrage, and sought to establish "mixed" local organizations that would include blacks, the poor, the working class, and the middle class. But the Knights also drew on the ideology of manly producerism and envisioned a perfect society where a man would be able to earn enough to be the sole breadwinner of his family. The Knights' disintegration by the late 1890s ended this more broadly egalitarian populism.

The populist movement, which gained much of its strength from the agrarian National Farmers' Alliance and Industrial Union, likewise challenged certain aspects of populist masculinity while embracing others. Strongest in the South and the Great Plains, the National Farmers' Alliance and Industrial Union accepted women as equal members, allowed them to be officers (although rarely beyond the local level), stressed family-based events, and used a moral political rhetoric akin to the women's political movements of the time. Their challenge to conventional notions of political masculinity provoked Democrats and Republicans alike to mock male Alliance members as unmanly business failures who had strayed from the masculine arena of the two-party system. Women Alliance leaders were portrayed as unfeminine harpies invading the male political sphere.

When the National Farmers' Alliance and Industrial Union established the national Populist Party in 1892, however, it fell back on traditional populist masculinism, emphasizing men's responsibilities as voters and breadwinners, casting women and children as passive victims requiring protection, and dropping such traditional women's issues as suffrage and prohibition. Similarly, the Southern Farmers' Alliance, though somewhat less progressive on women's issues, attempted to transcend the earlier racist assumptions and actions of southern populists. Identifying the old associations of whiteness and manhood as the means of their oppression, white southern populists organized blacks as well as whites and eschewed racist demagoguery. But race-baiting and intimidation eventually destroyed the nascent biracial movement and replaced it with a virulently racist populism that reinforced the association of masculinity, whiteness, and citizenship.

The patterns that emerged in the mid-1890s have largely repeated themselves in populist movements during the twentieth century. Political, social, and cultural agendas based on ideological associations among masculinity, whiteness, Protestant Christianity, and citizenship (and in hostility to African Americans, Jews, and nonwhite immigrants) defined the Ku Klux Klan in the 1920s (a movement strongest in the Midwest and far West), the John Birch Society (founded in 1958), George Wallace's presidential campaigns in 1968 and 1972, and the militia movements that arose in the 1990s. Many of these movements admitted women to supporting roles, but all sought as their central goal to preserve white male breadwinning and dominance amid economic uncertainty and the growing power of movements for racial and gender equality.

During the Great Depression of the 1930s, Louisiana politician Huey Long's "Share the Wealth" movement revived the attempt at broad inclusiveness, employing the rhetoric of the besieged patriarchal family while eschewing most of populism's other prejudices. But after Long's 1936 assassination, his supporters were drawn into parallel movements that used traditional populist rhetoric of white solidarity, patriarchal responsibility, and the supposed conspiracies of the rich to support fascist, racist, and anti-Semitic ideologies.

Masculine-oriented populist movements have thrived by tapping into the frustrations caused by the failure of democratic capitalist masculinity to fulfill its promise to make, in the words of Long's campaign, "every man a king." Their traditionalist idealization of a more egalitarian capitalism and less egalitarian family structure does not easily fit the progressive, modernizing thrust of corporate capitalism and socially liberal politics. But its continuing presence demonstrates the unresolved tensions among masculinity, whiteness, democracy, and capitalism in a changing society.

Bibliography

Berlet, Chip, and Matthew N. Lyons. *Right-Wing Populism in America: Too Close for Comfort.* New York: Gilford Press, 2000.

Goldberg, Michael. *An Army of Women: Gender and Politics in Gilded Age Kansas.* Baltimore: Johns Hopkins University Press, 1997.

Kazin, Michael. *The Populist Persuasion: An American History.* New York: Basic Books, 1995.

Further Reading

Brinkley, Alan. *Voices of Protest: Huey Long, Father Coughlin, and the Great Depression.* New York: Knopf, 1982.

Carter, Dan T. *The Politics of Rage: George Wallace, the Origins of the New Conservatism, and the Transformation of American Politics.* New York: Simon & Schuster, 1995.

Goodwyn, Laurence. *The Populist Moment: A Short History of the Agrarian Revolt in America.* New York: Oxford University Press, 1978.

MacLean, Nancy. *Behind the Mask of Chivalry: The Making of the Second Ku Klux Klan.* New York: Oxford University Press, 1994.

McMath, Robert C. *American Populism: A Social History, 1877–1898.* New York: Hill and Wang, 1993.

Saxton, Alexander. *The Rise and Fall of the White Republic: Class Politics and Mass Culture in Nineteenth-Century America.* New York: Verso, 1990.

Related Entries

Agrarianism; American Dream; Class; Democratic Manhood; Gilded Age; Great Depression; Jackson, Andrew; Labor Movement and Unions; Patriarchy; Politics; Race; Republicanism; Whiteness; White Supremacism; Working-Class Manhood

—Michael Lewis Goldberg

Pornography

Pornography is sexually explicit material designed specifically for sexual arousal. Since at least the early nineteenth century, pornography and public discussions of it have been intertwined with debates about the definition of masculinity and the role of male sexuality in the United States.

Intense concern with pornography developed in the United States during the nineteenth century, when the market revolution created a middle class that defined itself and social stability in terms of self-control and self-restraint, and when urbanization and the growth of commercial capitalism raised fears about the erosion of traditional restraints on male morality. Many middle-class Americans considered pornography—usually depicting female sexuality, produced by men, and aimed at male consumers—to be a threat to moral and social order. In the 1840s, local obscenity laws made it possible for officials to arrest publishers and distributors of "sporting" magazines that depicted the lifestyle of sophisticated urban young men, especially in New York City, who frequented brothels, dance halls, and other places associated with urban nightlife. These magazines seemed to target young men who recently had arrived in the city from the rural countryside. Evaluations and descriptions of brothels read like insiders' accounts but were more likely guides for the greenhorn. During the Civil War, federal officials were concerned about activities that could undermine soldiers' resolve, and they feared the effects of imported French postcards and pictures of nude and semi-nude women that were being sold and traded among the soldiers. In 1865 the U.S. postmaster general was given limited rights to confiscate obscene materials in the mail.

After the Civil War, reformers focused on young males' access to cheap crime-story newspapers such as the *Police Gazette.* These papers, with their tales of urban crime, sexuality, divorce, and other morally questionable activities, were easily accessible to young boys in railroad stations and barber shops. Reformers feared that crime-story papers and dime novels would lead boys and young men into corruption, and thus create moral and social chaos in the nation's cities.

In 1873 the Young Men's Christian Association (YMCA) hired the reformer Anthony Comstock to lobby the U.S. Congress to pass a federal obscenity law. The resulting

Comstock Act of 1873 allowed for the regulation and suppression of obscene materials that were sent through the mail. It also indicated the federal government's willingness to enforce middle-class standards of appropriate masculine behavior. Voluntary reform organizations, fearing a loss of control over young men's behavior and moral development, also actively monitored and resisted pornography. Supported by a psychiatric profession equally concerned about defining sexual norms and promoting moral order, reformers argued that immoral popular culture produced imitative behavior in young men and threatened to lead them to criminality, masturbation, and premarital sex—all of which they considered ruinous to a young man's manhood and future prospects.

Thus, male vice societies such as the New York Society for the Suppression of Vice (NYSSV) focused attention on the young male viewer of obscenity, and women's reform groups like the Woman's Christian Temperance Union (WCTU) opposed obscene materials on the grounds that young men should be held to the same Victorian standards of sexual purity to which young women were held. To combat immorality in books and movies, and to limit its effects on young men, the WCTU founded a Department for the Suppression of Impure Literature in 1881 and a Department of Motion Pictures in 1925.

During the 1920s a growing challenge to Victorian sexual mores allowed for a more expressive female sexuality, a coeducational youth culture in many of the nation's universities, a car-oriented dating culture, and an acceptance of illegal drinking in speakeasies. This sexual revolution allowed young men and women to express their sexuality more openly and increased toleration for (veiled) sexuality in literature and movies. The new attitude toward sexually suggestive imagery was apparent in the national fame achieved by actresses such as Clara Bow (the "It" girl) and Mae West.

Pornography itself entered the cultural mainstream in the second half of the twentieth century. Beginning in the late 1940s, there was an increasing tendency to consider pornography as an important and acceptable part of men's sexual-identity formation. Liberalized attitudes toward male sexuality were evident in, and accelerated by: (1) the publication of Alfred Kinsey's report, *Sexual Behavior in the Human Male* (1948); (2) the popularity of psychologist Herbert Marcuse's *Eros and Civilization* (1955), which identified the sublimation of sexuality to work as the chief fault of Western (especially American) civilization; and (3) the growing popularity of *Playboy* magazine (established in 1953). The advertisements and stories in *Playboy* critiqued the family-centered culture of the 1950s by ridiculing domesticity and offering men an alternative image of masculinity grounded in leisure, consumption, and liberated sexuality. By 1956, *Playboy* was reaching half a million readers each year. During the 1960s Sexual Revolution, pornography continued to enjoy an increasing social acceptability—and a growing audience.

The emergence of the Christian Right and the feminist movement as significant political forces during the 1970s led to rising concerns about the effects of widespread pornography. Christian conservatives condemned pornography as a dangerous medium that threatened Christian manhood, the traditional gender hierarchy, and the stable patriarchal family by tempting men to adultery and depicting women in positions of sexual dominance. In contrast, antipornography feminists, urging new definitions of masculinity based on gender equality, argued that pornography encouraged such undesirable male behaviors as the sexual objectification of women and sexual violence against women. Antipornography feminists argued that male sexual behavior is based on a desire for male supremacy, and that women would not be truly liberated until they were free from sexual subordination to men.

Debates about pornography and masculinity continued through the late twentieth century. The Supreme Court's refusal during the 1980s (on First Amendment grounds) to accept feminist-proposed antipornography civil-rights ordinances encouraged free-speech activists to reject the charge that pornography incites male sexual violence. Instead, some suggested that it actually promoted healthy masculine behavior by serving as an outlet for anger (or a type of safety valve for sexual fantasies), or by being used by male viewers (especially young males) for practical sex education.

By the early twenty-first century, discussions of pornography, while remaining focused on the male viewer, increasingly dealt with electronic forms and the creation and use of "virtual" (contrived) images. Courts addressing the issue raised concerns by suggesting that child pornography using virtual images would be considered legal for adults (while pornography using actual images would not). Other discussions concerned the impact that electronic sources of pornography, which are less easily monitored than printed forms, would have on the healthy sexual development of young males. In the ongoing debate over men and pornography, electronic pornography has complicated matters by introducing new kinds of censorship issues, new possibilities for male sexual predation, and renewed anxiety over male sexuality.

BIBLIOGRAPHY

Butler, Judith. *Excitable Speech: A Politics of the Performative.* New York: Routledge, 1997.

Cornell, Drucilla, ed. *Feminism and Pornography.* Oxford: Oxford University Press, 2000.

Dworkin, Andrea. *Pornography: Men Possessing Women.* New York: Putnam, 1981.

Kimmel, Michael, ed. *Men Confront Pornography.* New York: Meridian, 1991.

MacKinnon, Catharine, and Andrea Dworkin, eds. *In Harm's Way: The Pornography Civil Rights Hearings.* Cambridge, Mass.: Harvard University Press, 1997.

McLaren, Angus. *The Trials of Masculinity: Policing Sexual Boundaries, 1870–1930.* Chicago: University of Chicago Press, 1997.

Parker, Alison M. *Purifying America: Women, Cultural Reform, and Pro-Censorship Activism, 1873–1933.* Urbana: University of Illinois Press, 1997.

Segal, Lynn, and Mary McIntosh, eds. *Sex Exposed: Sexuality and the Pornography Debate.* New Brunswick, N.J.: Rutgers University Press, 1993.

Stoltenberg, John. *Refusing to Be a Man: Essays on Sex and Justice.* Portland, Oreg.: Breitenbush Books, 1989.

Strossen, Nadine. *Defending Pornography: Free Speech, Sex, and the Fight for Women's Rights.* New York: Scribner, 1995.

FURTHER READING

Barry, Kathleen. *Female Sexual Slavery.* New York: New York University Press, 1984.

Harrison, Maureen, and Steve Gilbert, eds. *Obscenity and Pornography Decisions of the United States Supreme Court.* Carlsbad, Calif.: Excellent Books, 2000.

MacKinnon, Catharine. *Only Words.* Cambridge, Mass.: Harvard University Press, 1993.

Russell, Diana. *Against Pornography: The Evidence of Harm.* Berkeley, Calif.: Russell, 1993.

Snodgrass, Jon, ed. *For Men Against Sexism: A Book of Readings.* Albion, Calif.: Times Change Press, 1977.

RELATED ENTRIES

Bachelorhood; Cult of Domesticity; Masturbation; *Playboy* Magazine; Sexual Revolution; Victorian Era

—*Alison M. Parker*

POSTMODERNISM

The term *postmodernism* originally stemmed from the field of architecture in the 1960s and referred to the conservative efforts of designers to incorporate styles from periods prior to the Modern movement into contemporary buildings. By the late 1960s the term had been adopted by the humanities (particularly philosophy, literary criticism, and history), where it became intertwined with the Yale University and French schools of poststructuralism and deconstructionism. Postmodernism marked a critical challenge to concepts and approaches to knowledge that had become widely accepted as objective truth in the "modern" Western world of the late nineteenth and twentieth centuries.

Among the concepts challenged by postmodernism was an understanding of heterosexual masculinity (including a power structure based on the hegemony of the heterosexual white male) that had so far remained relatively intact in the Western world. Postmodernists argued that traditional perceptions of masculinity, far from being universally valid, were social and cultural constructions that had been imposed and supported by the heterosexual white males traditionally in power. They claimed that these constructs shifted in relation to experiences of "gender," "self," and "identity." Likewise, they argued that the ideologies, or "master narratives," of the past were usually developed by men and intended to bolster the existing social and cultural structures that privileged male authority. Postmodernists therefore called for a plurality of thinking that allowed for multiple new definitions of masculinity and gender, fostering the idea that gender is a fluid construct. This perspective has had a profound impact on American historical and cultural studies, since it has generated among scholars an awareness that traditionally dominant narratives about American life—which imply the centrality of white males and typically excluded women, nonwhites, and homosexuals—represent only one of many possible narratives.

In American culture, the impact of postmodernism coincided with the rise of second-wave feminism and the racial and sexual identity movements of the 1960s and 1970s. The resulting advent of women's studies, gender studies, and queer theory in American academia has challenged the established notion of a natural or absolute "maleness." These developments also sparked the development of men's studies, an interdisciplinary field that assumes the social and cultural variability of experiences and definitions of masculinity and seeks to connect such variations to power dynamics.

Outside academia during this period, the idea that gender and masculinity are fluid and changeable challenged the traditional notion of the dominant male breadwinner and subordinate female homemaker. Growing numbers of Americans sought to redefine gender roles and distinctions, producing role reversals in which men embraced domestic engagement as an essential element of their identities. This blurring of gender distinctions was apparent in American popular culture in such films as *Mr. Mom* (1983), in which a male executive becomes a homemaker; *Tootsie* (1982), in which a male actor advances his career by pretending to be a woman; and *Mrs. Doubtfire* (1993), in which a divorcé dresses as a woman and poses as a housekeeper, thus highlighting his "femininity," in order to spend time with the children he considers necessary to his sense of self.

Postmodernism has also influenced such central features of American culture as television, as well as the new "virtual reality" created by the World Wide Web. Because postmodernist theory asserts that reality does not exist in any objective sense and instead refers to a "hyperreality" (a simulation of reality), postmodernists claim that representations seen on television or the Internet sometimes seem more "real" than everyday life because of their immediacy and technical standard. Postmodernists also believe that Americans have constructed their definitions of manhood and their masculine identities on the basis of written and visual images—ranging from Natty Bumppo to Theodore Roosevelt to John Wayne to Rambo to Homer Simpson—rather than through personal experience. Postmodern theorists have also argued that urban experiences, in which individuals view and are viewed by others, expose the subjective viewer to a multitude of male lifestyles, and thus highlight and reinforce the variability, fluidity, and image-based nature of masculine identity.

The consequences of postmodern perspectives were evident in other areas of American life in the late twentieth century. Growing critiques of what were often called "good-old-boy networks," including local men's clubs, corporate management, and the nation's political institutions, resulted in the labeling of these networks as instruments of hegemonic white heterosexual masculinity. The postmodern challenge to these traditional structures of masculinity and male power prompted a sense of displacement among white heterosexual men and growing public discussions of a "crisis of masculinity." It also motivated the growth of conservative movements critical of academia and devoted to defending both traditional understandings of American manhood and the belief in an objectively real and universally experienced maleness. This crisis has become most evident in language, where the traditional focus on the meaning of a word has given way to a growing sense of a free-floating meaning of various words. Therefore, to attempt even a semantic definition of *masculinity* would—according to postmodernists—result in a whole range of different and, most likely, contradictory results. In short, American culture has been fundamentally transformed by a debate over whether there is any clear, universally agreed-upon notion of masculinity.

The ongoing debate about the impact of postmodernism has shaped the cultural landscape and historical memory of the United States in various ways. The combination of new currents in academia; the increasingly vocal assertiveness of such groups as nonwhites, nonheterosexuals, and nonmales; and the impact of technology has generated in American life a fundamental reassessment of what constitutes a man. The incorporation of postmodernism into academic curricula and the currents of everyday life suggest that it will have long-term impact, but it is still too early to judge the precise impact of postmodern thinking in general. Whether it will survive or prove evanescent remains to be seen.

Bibliography

Baudrillard, Jean. *Simulations.* Translated by Paul Foss, Paul Patton, and Philip Beitchman. New York: Semiotext(e), 1983.

Lyotard, Jean-François. *The Postmodern Condition: A Report on Knowledge.* Translated by Geoff Bennington and Brian Massumi. Foreword by Fredric Jameson. Manchester, England: Manchester University Press, 1984.

McLuhan, Marshall, and Quentin Fiore. *War and Peace in the Global Village.* New York: McGraw-Hill, 1968.

Further Reading

Berman, Marshall. *All That is Solid Melts into Air: The Experience of Modernity.* London: Verso, 1995.

Bertens, Hans. *The Idea of the Postmodern: A History.* London: Routledge, 1995.

Brooker, Peter, ed. *Modernism, Postmodernism.* London: Longman, 1999.

Cahoone, Lawrence E., ed. *From Modernism to Postmodernism: An Anthology.* Cambridge, Mass.: Blackwell, 1997.

Derrida, Jacques. *Of Grammatology.* Translated by Gayatri Chakravorty Spivak. Baltimore: John Hopkins University Press, 1990.

Eagleton, Terry. *The Illusions of Postmodernism.* Oxford: Blackwell, 1997.

Foster, Hal, ed. *The Anti-Aesthetic: Essays on Postmodern Culture.* New York: New Press, 1998.

Habermas, Jürgen. *The Philosophical Discourse of Modernity: Twelve Lectures.* Translated by Frederick Lawrence. Cambridge, Mass.: MIT Press, 1987.

Harvey, David. *The Condition of Postmodernity: An Enquiry into the Origins of Cultural Change.* Oxford: Blackwell, 1990.

Jencks, Charles. *What is Post-Modernism?* Lanham, Md.: National Book Network, Inc., 1996.

Sarup, Madan. *An Introductory Guide to Post-Structuralism and Postmodernism.* New York: Harvester Wheatsheaf, 1993.

Wellmer, Albrecht. *The Persistence of Modernity: Essays on Aesthetics, Ethics, and Postmodernism.* Translated by David Midgley. Cambridge, Mass.: MIT Press, 1991.

RELATED ENTRIES

Feminism; Individualism; Men's Studies; Romanticism; Television; Urbanization

—*Markus Oliver Spitz*

PROFESSIONALISM

Ideals of professionalism, like those of work more generally, have often been articulated in conjunction with notions of manliness, at least since what are commonly called "the professions" (law, medicine, and the ministry) emerged in the mid–eighteenth century. Large numbers of American men have often rooted their masculine identities in specialized training, technical expertise, and professional credentials. While the impersonal and bureaucratic codes that govern conduct and advancement in the professions constitute a departure from earlier definitions of masculinity grounded in autonomy and manual labor, the characteristics associated with professional endeavors—social indifference; intellectual power; adherence to abstract, impersonal rules; mastery of expert knowledge; an emphasis on rational behavior and thought; and a premium on advancement and achievement—have been gendered as masculine in American culture. In this way, professionalism has been central to the formation of modern constructions of manhood.

Manhood and the Professions: 1750–1880

While the term profession dates back to Roman times, it acquired a particular meaning in the mid–eighteenth century, when a professional occupation came to be associated with status as an educated upper-class gentleman and conveyed on the practitioner a sense of honor and dignity. Men in these professions derived a sense of authority and masculinity from the intellectual labor of their work—which did not require productive effort, entrepreneurial drive, or physical labor or prowess—and from the superior position that came from their mastery of specialized knowledge and employment in highly structured and hierarchical settings. Through these professions, the authority and aristocratic honor of the gentleman became transferred to bourgeois constructions of manhood during the eighteenth and early nineteenth centuries.

The professions played a critical role in shaping the male-gendered concept of American national identity that emerged in the late eighteenth and early nineteenth centuries. Whereas some leading revolutionaries, such as George Washington and Thomas Jefferson, were farmers, many others, such as Alexander Hamilton and James Madison, both lawyers, and Benjamin Rush, a physician, came from the professions. Alexander Hamilton (in Federalist Paper No. 35, one of eighty-five essays written in support of the Constitution) and James Madison (in Federalist Paper No. 54) accorded professionals a special status as neutral arbiters and mediators, hoping that they would stabilize the new republic by mediating between different interest groups while remaining bound by duty, occupational responsibility, and dispassionate professional conduct. Yet at least one of the professions, the clergy, experienced a setback in terms of its occupational authority and status, since the disestablishment clause in the First Amendment to the Constitution explicitly withheld official authority from the churches. In contrast, the special licensing laws by which the states regulated access to medicine and the law perpetuated the particular authority and codes of manhood associated with these professions.

Between the 1830s and 1880, several social and political developments challenged older ideals of professional manhood. Political democratization, the market revolution, industrialization, and urbanization generated entrepreneurial ideals of "marketplace manhood" and "self-made manhood" and created an egalitarian notion of "democratic manhood" that undermined older professional codes of manliness grounded in aristocratic notions of rank and hierarchy. The term gentleman, previously a preserve of professionals, began to refer to all white men who conducted themselves in a proper, orderly fashion. The egalitarian and sometimes antiauthoritarian impulses produced by the religious revivals of the Second Great Awakening further undermined those claims to special authority upon which the professions had relied. Finally, intensifying political partisanship undermined the ideal of the professional as neutral arbiter. In a social setting that tended to be hostile to prescribed social order and hierarchies, all the states took their special licensing laws off the books in the 1830s, opening up access to a wide variety of fields to men without special training and blurring boundaries between rightful and wrongful practitioners. Amid these transformations, the professional codes of manliness that had formed since the mid–eighteenth century lost their social force and momentum.

The Culture of Professionalism: 1880–1945

Developments of the mid- to late nineteenth century laid the foundations of new ideals of manly professionalism. A growing concern with distinguishing legitimate from illegitimate practitioners in a variety of fields prompted increasing efforts to define proper credentialing, usually in terms of scientific methodology and technical expertise (both gendered male in contemporary culture). The emergence and expansion of universities provided the advanced education and specialized training by which would-be professionals (not only physicians and lawyers, but also scientists, engineers, and academics) could establish their credentials and articulate masculine identities grounded in professional achievement and conduct. At the same time, growing bureaucratization in many areas of American life found expression in the establishment of national organizations, such as the American Bar Association (founded in 1878), which codified standards of conduct in their respective professions and provided grounding for emerging notions of professional identity. Previously established societies, such as the American Medical Association (established in 1847), assumed similar functions and benefited from the increasing power and influence of the professions in U.S. society. Two key Supreme Court decisions—*Bradley* v. *Illinois* (1872), in which the Supreme Court affirmed the rights of the states to exclude women from the professions, and *Dent* v. *West Virginia* (1888), in which the Supreme Court ruled that no individual had the right to practice a profession without necessary qualification, as determined by competent authorities—solidified the ideal of the true professional as a credentialed, highly trained male.

During the late nineteenth and early twentieth centuries, middle-class professionals—who were overwhelmingly male—rose to social and cultural prominence as they sought to address social issues through scientific scrutiny, the application of dispassionate expertise, and organization. The new cultural authority and status of the male professional was well illustrated in Edward Bellamy's utopian novel *Looking Backward, 2000–1887* (1888). Bellamy's ideal society, organized on the foundation of professional, technocratic expertise, was also a thoroughly masculine society based on gender segregation. Women do have voice and power in the novel, yet only in regard to expressly female concerns. In Bellamy's utopia, and in reality, the professions helped to create an integrated national culture predicated on a masculine matrix of professional values. His vision resonated powerfully at a time when many men felt that urbanization, industrialization, and bureaucratization had undermined traditional bases of masculine power and destabilized the meaning of manhood.

The first half of the twentieth century was a golden age for the professions and for professionals. Progressive Era reforms, which aimed to cure social ills through technocratic efficiency, emphasized the necessity of professional expertise and planning. By the 1910s and 1920s, public intellectuals such as Walter Lippmann and Herbert Croly argued that the problems of modern society were best addressed not through democratic processes, but through the leadership of professional male experts who would apply their dispassionate, technocratic knowledge to a wide array of social issues. Similarly, African-American activist W. E. B. Du Bois looked to a cadre of black professionals he called the "talented tenth" to resolve the particular issues confronting African Americans.

While visions of a technocratic elite failed to materialize, the New Deal and World War II gave a renewed boost to the role, power, and masculine authority of professionals. Under the New Deal, President Franklin D. Roosevelt and his "brain trust" of mostly male academics, intellectuals, and other professional experts expanded the administrative and regulatory capacities of the U.S. government, extending its reach into new realms. Wartime planning as a result of the U.S. entry into World War II in 1941 further increased the needs for professionals and their specialized expertise, and the association of their efforts with national power and eventual victory greatly enhanced the public image of professionals as paragons of manliness.

Gender and Professionalism since World War II

During the post–World War II period, professionalism and its association with manhood have been reinforced in some ways and challenged in others. During the 1950s, some critics questioned the desirability of a society led by a middle-class professional elite, worrying that the impersonal nature of American bureaucratic structures threatened masculinity by reducing male professionals to bland conformists. These concerns were exemplified by C. Wright Mills in *White Collar* (1951) and *The Power Elite* (1956), and by William H. Whyte in *The Organization Man* (1956). At the same time, however, the postwar period witnessed a widening reach of professional codes in American occupational and social life, and the authority of the professional expert continued to significantly empower men.

Challenges to the ideal and authority of the male professional intensified during the 1960s. Both the critiques of professional elites and the continuing expansion of male professionals' power prompted a broad challenge to the ideal of the male expert by the counterculture, the New Left (heavily inspired by C. Wright Mills), and a resurging feminist movement. These new forces charged that the dispassionate professional male exacerbated rather than resolved the problems American society was facing. At the same time, legislation against sex discrimination—and the growing preference by women for female obstetricians and gynecologists as issues of women's health assumed new public prominence—opened the professions to women at an unprecedented level.

Yet the power of the professional male persisted through the late twentieth century. Despite a growing presence of women in a wide variety of professions, some, such as engineering and science, remained so thoroughly dominated by men that many critics began to suggest that the educational process discouraged women from success in these fields beginning at an early age. Technological advances of the late twentieth century, such as the computer and information revolution, undermined any direct association between gender and professionalism, and the presence of personal computers in more and more households made society less dependent on professional experts by democratizing access to technology. Yet the growing cultural prominence of the "computer geek" (a figure typically imagined as male, and as possessing greater technological knowledge than most people) has enhanced the power of the male professional. In the early twenty-first century, it appears that the traditional association between masculinity and the power of professional expertise has endured.

Bibliography

Bellamy, Edward. *Looking Backward, 2000–1887.* 1888. Reprint, New York: Penguin, 1982.

Bledstein, Burton J. *The Culture of Professionalism: The Middle Class and the Development of Higher Education in America.* New York: Norton, 1976.

Chandler, Alfred D., Jr. *The Visible Hand: The Managerial Revolution in American Business.* Cambridge, Mass.: Belknap Press, 1977.

Ehrenreich, Barbara, and John Ehrenreich. "The Professional-Managerial Class." In *Between Labor and Capital,* edited by Pat Walker. Boston: South End Press, 1979.

Haber, Samuel. *The Quest for Authority and Honor in the American Professions, 1750–1900.* Chicago: University of Chicago Press, 1991.

Haskell, Thomas L., ed. *The Authority of Experts: Studies in History and Theory.* Bloomington: Indiana University Press, 1984.

Kimmel, Michael. *Manhood in America: A Cultural History.* New York: Free Press, 1996.

Lubove, Roy. *The Professional Altruist: The Emergence of Social Work As a Career, 1880–1930.* Cambridge, Mass.: Harvard University Press, 1965.

Mills, C. Wright. *White Collar: The American Middle Classes.* New York: Oxford University Press, 1951.

Riesman, David, with Nathan Glaser, and Reuel Denney. *The Lonely Crowd: A Study of the Changing American Character.* New Haven, Conn.: Yale University Press, 1950.

Whyte, William H. *The Organization Man.* New York: Simon & Schuster, 1956.

Wiebe, Robert H. *The Search For Order, 1877–1920.* New York: Hill and Wang, 1967.

Further Reading

Abbott, Andrew Delano. *The System of Professions: An Essay on The Division of Expert Labor.* Chicago: University of Chicago Press, 1988.

Beniger, James R. *The Control Revolution: Technological and Economic Origins of the Information Society.* Cambridge, Mass.: Harvard University Press, 1986.

Blumin, Stuart M. *The Emergence of the Middle-Class: Social Experience in the American City, 1760–1900.* New York: Cambridge University Press, 1989.

Braverman, Harry. *Labor and Monopoly Capital: The Degradation of Work in the Twentieth Century.* New York: Monthly Review Press, 1998.

Davis, Clark. *Company Men: White-Collar Life and Corporate Cultures in Los Angeles, 1892–1941.* Baltimore: Johns Hopkins University Press, 2001.

Galbraith, John Kenneth. *The New Industrial State.* 1967. Reprint, Boston: Houghton Mifflin, 1985.

Geison, Gerald L., ed. *Professions and Professional Ideologies in America.* Chapel Hill: University of North Carolina Press, 1983.

Giddens, Anthony. *The Class Structure of the Advanced Societies.* New York: Harper & Row, 1975.

Gouldner, Alvin. *The Future of the Intellectuals and the Rise of the New Class.* New York: Seabury Press, 1979.

Hall, Peter Dobkin. *The Organization of American Culture, 1700–1900: Private Institutions, Elites, and the Origins of American Nationality.* New York: New York University Press, 1982.

Mills, C. Wright. *The Power Elite.* 1956. Reprint, New York: Oxford University Press, 1999.

Trachtenberg, Alan. *The Incorporation of America: Culture and Society in the Gilded Age.* New York: Hill and Wang, 1982.

Wilson, Christopher. *The Labor of Words: Literary Professionalism in the Progressive Era.* Athens: University of Georgia Press, 1985.

Wilson, Sloan. *The Man in the Gray Flannel Suit.* 1955. Reprint, New York: Four Walls Eight Windows, 2002.

Related Entries

Breadwinner Role; Bureaucratization; Business/Corporate America; Capitalism; Class; Consumerism; Crisis of Masculinity; Education; Gilded Age; Individualism; Industrialization; Medicine; Middle-Class Manhood; Ministry; Nationalism; Nuclear Family; Patriotism; Progressive Era; Self-Made Man; Sentimental Manhood; Sports; Suburbia; Technology; Urbanization; Work

—*Thomas Winter*

Progressive Era

Definitions of manliness during the Progressive Era (1890–1915) were often ambiguous and contradictory. While a more assertive and aggressive masculinity (with origins in the Gilded Age of the late nineteenth century) spilled over into the twentieth century and continued in the Progressive Era, new articulations of manliness were emerging that emphasized a greater foundation in social networks and political associations and a scientific approach to examining and understanding society and politics. These new definitions, which sought to balance notions of liberal individualism and social justice with notions of social bonds, social order, the common good, and social efficiency, began to reign in and temper the more aggressive concepts of masculinity common in the Gilded Age.

Since the Civil War, U.S. society had seen the emergence of new administrative capacities that expanded the reach and powers of the nation, while corporate capitalism had transformed the economic model of U.S. society by concentrating production (and political power) in the hands of large industrial conglomerates. These developments challenged prevailing ideals of manhood, bringing about what contemporaries referred to as a "crisis of masculinity" and prompting, particularly among middle-class men, the ideal of a "strenuous life" and hedonistic articulations of a "passionate manhood." By the early twentieth century a reform-oriented state, geared toward correcting the worst abuses of the system, sought to assure men of their status, rights, and opportunities as autonomous individuals in a liberal, capitalist society and offered new outlets for masculine activity. This resulted in new loyalties between the federal government and the voting (male) citizenry.

During the Progressive Era, men continued to speak a language of masculine individualism, which was manifested in a strong opposition to corporate monopolies and an insistence on an open, liberal marketplace. Yet the stress on male individual autonomy was balanced by stresses on the commonwealth and social efficiency. Definitions of manhood stood in opposition to arbitrary and unregulated sources of power, and men accepted a critical break with nineteenth-century notions of the autonomous individual. Instead, they acknowledged the necessity to intervene in people's lives and to regulate social and economic processes to improve social conditions and to restore economic opportunity. To realize this goal, Progressives not only accepted, but also demanded, an enlarged government role in their lives.

Theodore Roosevelt serves as one outstanding example of the simultaneous commitment to individual autonomy, social obligation, and the acceptance of an enlarged role of the state. During the Spanish-American War (1898), Roosevelt led the 1st U.S. Volunteer Cavalry, known as the "Rough Riders," in Cuba in a specially tailored uniform. As spokesmen for the "strenuous life," he journeyed to the West to recapture a more pure and true masculinity. As president (1901–09), he announced a "square deal" for Americans and sought to use the power of the state to break up trusts and ameliorate social abuses, thus helping to create the twentieth-century notion of the interventionist state.

Concerns with men's commitment to social justice and the common good did not remain limited to presidential politics. Authors such as Randolph Bourne, Van Wyck Brooks, Waldo Frank, and Lewis Mumford felt that the nineteenth-century ideal of the autonomous self-made man had proven to be a failure. The "Young Americans," as they were called, set out to reconcile notions of community and society in a new, inclusive, and participatory democratic society by formulating a masculine ideal grounded in a notion of the common good.

Some men took such commitments a step further and embraced women's suffrage. Randolph Bourne, Max Eastman, Floyd Dell, Hutchins Hapgood, William Sanger (husband of birth control advocate Margaret Sanger), and John Dewey organized the Men's League for Women's Suffrage in 1910. Such men embraced women's social and legal equality as a statement about their own confidence in their masculinity and sense of security in their position as men.

Yet this new emphasis on a socially embedded manhood also subjected men to the judgment and scrutiny of informed, scientifically inclined, professional communities of experts, such as lawyers, doctors, politicians, advertisers, and efficiency experts, such as Frank and Lillian Gilbreth and Frederick Winslow Taylor. While the Gilbreths sought to apply principles of scientific management to such places as their own home and household, Taylor, through his time-motion studies, gave employers new tools to subvert male craft-workers' control over the shop floor and extract greater productivity from them.

Progressives also defined socially embedded notions of manliness in terms of religion. Around the turn of the twentieth century, the Social Gospel movement, with its commitment to social reform and social justice, emerged in U.S. Protestant churches. No longer certain of the meanings of manhood, but convinced that masculine spirituality involved a concern with social salvation as much as with individual salvation, Social Gospelers defined an ideal of manliness that promised to reconcile an urban-industrial society with spiritual needs and interests. This ideal of a Christian manhood espoused service, self-sacrifice, and teamwork, and it rejected an ideal of an entrepreneurial, self-made manhood.

The emphasis on the socially rooted individual and the concern with social justice raised vexing issues and questions that exposed uncertainty and contention over the meaning of American manhood and its relation to citizenship. Working-class men sought to defend their leisure practices and its spaces—such as the saloon, which they saw as fundamental to their masculine identities—against attacks from middle-class Progressive reformers, who felt that such practices were antisocial and antithetical to true manhood. At the same time, however, working-class men, their unions, and middle-class politicians agreed that "American" masculinity did not include Asian immigrant men, whom they believed lacked the type of manliness necessary for citizenship. African-American reformers inspired by Progressive ideals, such as W. E. B. Du Bois, organized the National Association for the Advancement of Colored People (NAACP). They insisted that black men possessed the kind of manhood that could be expected of men as citizens, arguing that social justice demanded that black men be treated equally with white men and urging Progressive reformers to devote greater attention to issues of race. Meanwhile, the very connection between masculinity and citizenship increasingly came under assault as suffragists, organized in the National American Woman Suffrage Association (NAWSA), argued that social justice and the common good ultimately required that women be given the right to vote and that manliness was no longer a valid criterion for access to the rights and privileges of citizenship.

Progressive Era articulations of masculinity consisted of overlapping, and at times contradictory, notions and images. Progressive Era articulations of manliness, by emphasizing social obligation, civic commitment, and social change, questioned static and exclusive notions of masculine identity and pointed the way toward the increasingly complex understandings of manhood characteristic of American society in the twenty-first century.

Bibliography

Banta, Martha. *Taylored Lives: Narrative Productions in the Age of Taylor, Veblen, and Ford.* Chicago: University of Chicago Press, 1993.

Blake, Casey Nelson. *Beloved Community: The Cultural Criticism of Randolph Bourne, Van Wyck Brooks, Waldo Frank, and Lewis Mumford.* Chapel Hill: University of North Carolina Press, 1990.

Buenker, John D. "Sovereign Individuals and Organic Networks: Political Cultures in Conflict during the Progressive Era." *American Quarterly* 40 (June 1988): 187–204.

Diner, Steven J. *A Very Different Age: Americans of the Progressive Era.* New York: Hill and Wang, 1998.

Kimmel, Michael. *Manhood in America: A Cultural History.* New York: Free Press, 1996.

Rodgers, Daniel T. "In Search of Progressivism." In *Reviews in American History.* Vol. 10, *The Promise of American History: Progress and Prospects,* edited by Stanley I. Kutler and Stanley N. Katz. Baltimore: Johns Hopkins University Press, 1982.

Further Reading

Crunden, Robert M. *Ministers of Reform: The Progressives' Achievement in American Civilization, 1889–1920.* Urbana: University of Illinois Press, 1984.

Fink, Leon. *Progressive Intellectuals and the Dilemmas of Democratic Commitment* Cambridge, Mass.: Harvard University Press, 1997.

Link, Arthur, and Richard McCormick. *Progressivism.* Arlington Heights, Ill.: Harlan Davidson, 1983.

Quandt, Jean. *From the Small Town to the Great Community: The Social Thought of Progressive Individuals.* New Brunswick, N.J.: Rutgers University Press, 1970.

Rotundo, E. Anthony. *American Manhood: Transformations in Masculinity from the Revolution to the Modern Era.* New York: Basic Books, 1993.

Related Entries

African-American Manhood; Body; Bureaucratization; Business/Corporate America; Citizenship; Consumerism; Feminism; Gilded Age; Individualism; Industrialization; Leisure; Reform Movements; Roosevelt, Theodore; Social Gospel; Strenuous Life; Suffragism; Urbanization; Working-Class Manhood

—Thomas Winter

Promise Keepers

Founded in 1991 by Bill McCartney, a former football coach at the University of Colorado, Promise Keepers is an international evangelical Christian organization designed specifically to appeal to men and promote a masculinity centered upon "traditional" definitions of home, family, marriage, and Christianity.

Promise Keepers began as a late-twentieth century manifestation of "muscular Christianity," a movement that emerged in Great Britain and the United States in the mid–nineteenth century to make Christianity more appealing to men by encouraging masculine expressions of religious devotion and using athletic metaphors to describe Christian commitment. Promise Keepers asks its members to maintain an ideal of Christian manhood that focuses on being faithful, devoted husbands and fathers and adhering to what they consider "good Christian morals." Promise Keepers are particularly concerned with abstaining from what they have labeled "sexual sins," such as lust, pornography, adultery, fornication, and homosexuality, which they believe threaten proper male behavior and family devotion.

To help members maintain their commitment, Promise Keepers advocates "shepherding," in which small groups of men submit to the authority of spiritual leaders who form a network extending to organizational headquarters in Colorado. Through shepherding, McCartney argues, the Promise Keepers can make a difference in society as men, implying that their identity as Christian men is critical not only to their construction of masculinity, but also to the success of their movement. Members of Promise Keepers form groups of no more than five men, typically operating within a church, and are expected to submit all aspects of their lives to review. Each member answers questions concerning such key aspects of masculine identity as marriage, family, finances, sexuality, and business activity. These groups are led by a "Point Man" who answers to an "Ambassador," who reports directly to headquarters in Boulder.

The Promise Keepers movement grew rapidly in the mid-1990s. McCartney attracted only 4,200 attendees to the Promise Keepers' first meeting, held in 1991 in a University of Colorado basketball arena, but between 1995 and 1996 Promise Keepers held twenty-two events, attracting 1.1 million men, with many rallies being held in sports stadiums. The movement's popularity peaked in 1997, when more than 600,000 men attended the "Stand in the Gap" rally in Washington D.C., and 638,297 men attended eighteen regional stadium conferences.

Critics of Promise Keepers argue that it reflects a conservative backlash against gains made by racial minorities, women, and homosexuals during the civil rights movement. They point to a conspicuous lack of racial minorities among its members, and to its profoundly conservative views of women and homosexuals, to support their claim that Promise Keepers is nothing more than an attempt by middle-class white males to reassert their authority in mainstream American society. Other scholars contend that, while this may be true, Promise Keepers does provide a "safe" place for white men to come together and reaffirm their faith and values.

Although the source of Promise Keepers' appeal remains open for debate, it became clear in the late-1990s that its success would be short-lived. Promise Keepers experienced a drastic decline in popularity after 1997 due to a changing political climate and its insistence on maintaining a strict system of shepherding. It cancelled or scaled down many of its rallies and relied on volunteer staff. Yet its emergence reflects an ongoing concern in American life to define Christian commitment as a marker of manhood.

Bibliography

Bellant, Russ. "Promise Keepers: Christian Soldiers for Theocracy." In *Eyes Right! Challenging the Right Wing Backlash,* edited by Chip Berlet. Boston: South End Press, 1995.

Boston, Rob. *Close Encounters with the Religious Right: Journeys into the Twilight Zone of Religion and Politics.* Amherst, N.Y.: Prometheus, 2000.

Claussen, Dane S., ed. *Standing on the Promises: The Promise Keepers and the Revival of Manhood.* Cleveland, Ohio: Pilgrim Press, 1999.

Further Reading

Allen, L. Dean. *Rise Up, O Men of God: The Men and Religion Forward Movement and the Promise Keepers.* Macon, Ga.: Mercer University Press, 2002.

Brickner, Bryan W. *The Promise Keepers: Politics and Promises.* Lanham, Md.: Lexington Books, 1999.

Clatterbaugh, Kenneth C. *Contemporary Perspectives on Masculinity: Men, Women, and Politics in Modern Society.* Boulder, Colo.: Westview Press, 1997.

Claussen, Dane S., ed. *The Promise Keepers: Essays on Masculinity and Christianity.* Jefferson, N.C.: McFarland, 2000.

Messner, Michael A. *Politics of Masculinities: Men in Movements.* Thousand Oaks, Calif.: Sage, 1997.

Related Entries

Breadwinner Role; Civil Rights Movement; Class; Crisis of Masculinity; Cult of Domesticity; Divorce; Emotion; Evangelicalism and Revivalism; Fatherhood; Feminism; Fraternal Organizations; Heterosexuality; Homosexuality; Male Friendship; Marriage; Men and Religion Forward Movement; Men's Movements; Middle-Class Manhood; Muscular Christianity; Nuclear Family; Patriarchy; Religion and Spirituality; Self-Control; Sensitive Male

—*Michael A. Rembis*

Property

The term property generally refers to the physical possessions an individual owns. Legally, there are two types of property: real and personal. In the United States, concepts of real property focused primarily on land ownership. However, the transition from an agricultural society to an industrial society changed concepts of property, moving the focus to personal property, both tangible and intangible. Physical labor exemplifies intangible personal property, while tangible personal property exists in the form of home ownership. Because manhood and freedom have historically been tied to property, ownership of property has taken on specific importance for American males.

From the time of the Greek philosopher Aristotle, Western thought identified property ownership as a necessary condition for citizenship, political virtue, and liberty—all of which have historically been understood as central to male social identity. From the colonial period through the early nineteenth century, Americans accepted this association, which became central to Jeffersonian republicanism and agrarianism. It was believed that men with land had the means to support their families, and thus were independent. Ownership of land took on further importance in American history because white men tended to be the main property owners, using it to dominate economic, political, and social institutions.

Private property gave men, even of differing classes, common interests that they believed government was obligated to protect. Thus, with the exception of colonial New England, ownership of property, particularly land, determined who voted and held elected office. Men also used gender to determine access to property, especially property that produced wealth. Fathers passed property such as land, buildings, and livestock on to sons, while daughters inherited moveable personal property like furniture. However, patriarchal laws granted control of women's real property to husbands or heads of households, thereby negating the rights that property entitled women to exercise and maintaining the connection between manhood, property, and citizenship. In addition, the fact that only large property holders served as elected officials beyond the local level corresponded with the belief that government's primary objective was protecting the right to own property.

In the years before the American Revolution, American men interpreted duties and acts passed by the English Parliament as infringing on their personal liberty, and thus on their very manhood, because they taxed property. The new government resulting from the Revolution reflected these principles, and the Constitution protected personal property from a democratic majority by limiting suffrage to those with property over a specified monetary value. By the third decade of the nineteenth century, however, the traditional relationship between citizenship and property ownership had begun to erode, for political democratization led the states to adopt universal white-male suffrage and eliminate property qualifications for voting. Yet property itself remained fundamental to American conceptions of manhood—especially white manhood—throughout the antebellum period. In the northern states, homestead legislation facilitating white men's access to western land gained momentum–with strong support from landless men, while southern men measured their manhood in terms of ownership of land and slaves.

The Union victory in the Civil War freed millions of African-American slaves, who hoped to achieve manly independence through land ownership. Yet they remained without easy access to property other than their own physical labor. The same was true for growing numbers of white laborers. The abolition of slavery, the Fourteenth Amendment's extension of suffrage to all adult males in 1868, and rapid industrialization all combined to lessen the importance of agricultural property in guaranteeing manly independence. Furthermore, the liberalization of laws governing women's control of property—and African Americans' continuing push for equal economic opportunity—challenged the earlier association between real property ownership and white manhood. As a result, men increasingly identified labor itself—their personal property—as a valuable commodity, an intangible property they could use not only to attain physical possessions, but also to determine self-worth and manhood. Men also identified specific types of labor in factories, mills, and coal mines as male domains.

In the twentieth century, sexual integration of the workplace, growing mechanization in factories, and the growth of bureaucratized white-collar work compromised many men's sense that they owned and controlled their own labor, particularly after World War I. Therefore, men looked for other ways and places to articulate property-based notions of masculinity. Single-home ownership, which increased exponentially from under 3 million in 1890 to over 30 million by 1950, enabled men to apply their productive labor to create valuable personal property and reasserted male control over property. The transition to suburban life in the 1950s—and the increasing currency of the saying "a man's home is his castle"—illustrated the new expression of masculinity through the ownership of domestic property. Men now displayed their maleness through yards groomed with heavy tools and equipment such as lawn tractors and power trimmers. While some advocates of the 1960s counterculture attempted to develop new notions of manhood divorced from property ownership, the continuing association of home ownership with manhood into the twenty-first century suggests that property-based concepts of manhood remain strong in American society.

BIBLIOGRAPHY

Paul, Ellen Frankel, Fred D. Miller, and Jeffrey Paul, eds. *Property Rights.* Cambridge, England: Cambridge University Press, 1994.

Ryan, Alan. *Property.* Minneapolis: University of Minnesota Press, 1987.

Tully, James. *A Discourse on Property: John Locke and His Adversaries.* Cambridge, England: Cambridge University Press, 1980.

FURTHER READING

Ditz, Toby L. *Property and Kinship: Inheritance in Early Connecticut, 1750–1820.* Princeton, N.J.: Princeton University Press, 1986.

Sydnor, Charles S. *American Revolutionaries in the Making: Political Practices in Washington's Virginia.* New York: Free Press, 1965.

RELATED ENTRIES

Agrarianism; Citizenship; Class; Democratic Manhood; Patriarchy; Politics; Republicanism; Self-Made Man; Slavery; Southern Manhood; Suburbia

—*Eugene VanSickle*

PROSTITUTION

Prostitution is the exchange of sexual services for payment. Although it has been practiced by both sexes, the term generally refers to men seeking the sexual services of women. Throughout American history, therefore, attitudes toward prostitution have reflected and contributed to cultural constructions of masculinity and male sexuality.

In colonial America, little attention was paid to "deviant" sexuality. But in a patriarchal society in which men were expected to produce large families for agricultural labor and legitimate heirs to family property, men who sought the sexual services of prostitutes were perceived as failing to meet the responsibilities of manhood. Because most colonial Euro-Americans assumed that men's sexual aberrations resulted from weakness of the flesh, while women's stemmed from innate spiritual depravity, prostitutes bore the brunt of public sanctions, which included whippings and hard labor.

By the middle of the eighteenth century, "bawdy houses" became more widespread, especially in seaport cities where men engaged in the growing maritime trade. In the misogynistic subcultures that flourished among urban male laborers, prostitution, along with sodomy, interracial sex, and adultery, existed within such homosocial male spaces as taverns and billiard halls. To colonial authorities mistrustful of these subcultures, prostitution signified a declining moral sensibility, and citizen groups and politicians frequently raided brothels.

Throughout the nineteenth century, prostitution flourished wherever men gathered. The market revolution and urbanization eroded the traditional moral constraints imposed by familial control in rural and village settings, and growing numbers of young unmarried men began to congregate in the nation's burgeoning cities. As prostitution moved into the urban marketplace, cities developed "red light" districts in which brothels were concentrated. In many cities, male visitors could purchase "gentlemen's guides" to locate the best brothels in the area.

Prostitution became intertwined with the new class-based definitions of manhood taking form in this new social setting. Although men of all social classes frequented the commercial sexual establishments of the nineteenth-century city, brothels were typically located in the working-class sections of cities, where older laborer subcultures endured and working-class men resisted the bourgeois morality of their employers. Meanwhile, an emerging middle class began associating manhood with self-control, marriage, domesticity, and economic success—and sexual activity for purposes other than reproduction came to be regarded as a wasteful expenditure of bodily fluids and energy. Middle-class social reformers targeted working-class men and—fueled by cultural assumptions that likened working-class sexuality with the behavior of animals—were particularly concerned about what they considered an excessive number of workingmen who solicited prostitutes.

Still, there was a general tolerance for prostitution among the Victorian middle class, which applied a double standard that held middle-class women to strict guidelines for purity while defining men as naturally inclined to moral weakness—and therefore allowing them considerable freedom to indulge their sexual appetites. Since middle-class men defined prostitutes as working women to whom middle-class standards of purity did not apply, prostitution supported middle-class gender constructs by providing an avenue for men's sexual release while protecting the virtue of Victorian women. It also allowed men a sexual license while they conformed to genteel moral standards in their marriages and their public lives. Prostitution was also important for bachelors, for late marriages and prolonged bachelorhood became more common during the nineteenth century, and celibate bachelorhood was considered unnatural and unhealthy.

By 1880 certain cultural developments—particularly the growing impact of Darwin's theory of natural selection and a massive influx of non-Protestant immigrants from southern and eastern Europe—prompted new attitudes about the relation between masculinity and prostitution. As fertility rates among the white middle class declined, there was concern that African-American and immigrant laboring men, who were deemed inferior, were surpassing the white middle class in the Darwinian competition for survival. This trend was partly blamed on sexually transmitted diseases (STDs) spread by prostitution, which caused infertility and raised fears of a "race suicide" among the white middle class. By the turn of the century these concerns prompted middle-class reformers to target prostitution, birth control, abortion, and women's growing participation in the labor force for their perceived negative effect on family structure. Doctors and medical experts involved in this reform effort began defining dalliance with prostitutes as a form of sexual deviance and urged men to confine their sexuality to marriage and procreation.

This xenophobically driven antiprostitution sentiment culminated with the 1910 passage of the Mann Act, which prohibited the interstate and international trafficking of women for "immoral" purposes. The legislative effort was fueled in part by a 1909 article in *McClure's* magazine that attributed the trafficking of women, and thus the decline of white middle-class fertility, to immigrant men—especially Italians, as well as Austrians, Russians, and Hungarian Jews. Immigrant lodging homes, perceived as a haven for prostitutes, came under frequent attack.

The twentieth-century rise of U.S. global power and the accompanying concern to maintain American military strength intensified antiprostitution activity, particularly in the armed forces. Although prostitution was usually tolerated by the military as an outlet for men's natural sexual urges, an alarming rise in the incidence of sexually transmitted diseases among soldiers prompted the 1941 passage of the May Act, which made it a federal offense to practice prostitution near military bases. Still, the growing number of military men infected with venereal diseases suggested the prevalence of prostitution. Despite official military policy, persisting toleration of prostitution was evident during the postwar American occupation of Europe. Some officers argued it was more prudent to regulate brothels, since military personnel would still visit them. After the 1944 landing of Allied forces in Normandy, U.S. soldiers in France could visit houses of prostitution run specifically for them and guarded by military police. These brothels were racially segregated, reflecting the importance of race in shaping American military officials' notions of masculinity and gender.

New perspectives on male sexuality in the 1960s and 1970s complicated public attitudes toward masculinity and prostitution. On the one hand, liberalized attitudes about sexuality, evident in the growing popularity of *Playboy* magazine (established in 1953) and other pornographic publications, encouraged an association of masculinity with freewheeling sexuality. On the other hand, the growing impact of feminism prompted a growing critique of traditional understandings of masculinity and appropriate male behavior, especially the sexual double standard. While Nevada gradually legalized prostitution during the 1970s and 1980s, most states accepted feminist claims that prostitution victimizes women and depends on male consumers and expanded their anti-prostitution laws, including efforts to punish male customers, known as "johns." Some cities began experimenting with two-day programs known as "Johns Schools," which educated men arrested for soliciting prostitutes about the potential dangers associated with commercial sex, such as STDs, criminal activity, and marital discord. Public awareness of AIDS in the 1980s added a new caution in men's attitudes toward prostitution. But while some cities, such as San Francisco and Buffalo, New York, reported a decline in repeat offenders, the persistence of prostitution was apparent: The overall number of solicitation arrests remained unaffected.

Approaches to prostitution have reflected changing constructions of male sexuality and a persistent ambivalence about its relation to masculinity. Associations of manhood with sexual purity and physical health and strength have generated campaigns motivated at least in part by a belief that prostitution threatened to disrupt prevailing concepts of masculinity. Yet the belief that a strong sex drive and the need for sexual release are inherent to male behavior has produced an enduring double standard that has tolerated, and even encouraged, the solicitation of prostitutes as a natural male activity.

Bibliography

Burnham, John C. "The Progressive Era Revolution in American Attitudes Toward Sex." *The Journal of American History* 59, no. 4 (1973): 885–908.

D'Emilio, John, and Estelle B. Freedman. *Intimate Matters: A History of Sexuality in America.* New York: Harper & Row, 1988.

Feldman, Egal. "Prostitution, the Alien Woman, and the Progressive Imagination, 1910–1915." *American Quarterly* 19, no. 2 (1967): 192–206.

Griswold, Robert L. "Law, Sex, Cruelty, and Divorce in Victorian America, 1840–1900." *American Quarterly* 38, no. 5 (1986): 721–745.

Ota, Nancy K. "Flying Buttresses." *DePaul Law Review* 49 (Spring 2000): 1–21.

Rosenberg, Charles E. "Sexuality, Class and Role in 19th-Century America." *American Quarterly* 25, no. 2 (1973): 131–153.

Stansell, Christine. *City of Women: Sex and Class in New York, 1789–1860.* New York: Knopf, 1986.

Vitzthum, Virginia. "Reform School: A Program for First-Time Johns Lets Offenders off the Hook in Exchange for Their Attendance at a Daylong Session Taught by Ex-Hookers." Salon.com. October 17, 2000. <www.salon.com/sex/col/vitz/2000/10/17/johns> (May 8, 2003).

Walkowitz, Judith R. *Prostitution and Victorian Society: Women, Class, and the State.* Cambridge, England: Cambridge University Press, 1980.

Willoughby, John. "The Sexual Behavior of American GIs During the Early Years of the Occupation of Germany." *Journal of Military History* 62, no. 1 (1998): 155–174.

Further Reading

Browne, Jan, and Victor Minichiello. "The Social Meanings behind Male Sex Work: Implications for Sexual Interactions." *British Journal of Sociology* 46, no. 4 (1995): 598–622.

Cordasco, Francesco. *The White Slave Trade and the Immigrant.* Detroit, Mich.: Blaine Ethridge, 1981.

Holzman, Harold R., and Sharon Pines. "Buying Sex: The Phenomenology of Being a John." *Deviant Behavior* 4 (1982): 89–116.

Kempadoo, Kamala, and Jo Doezema. *Global Sex Workers: Rights, Resistance, and Redefinition.* New York: Routledge, 1998.

Smith-Rosenberg, Carroll. *Disorderly Conduct: Visions of Gender in Victorian America.* New York: Knopf, 1985.

Weitzer, Ronald. *Sex for Sale: Prostitution, Pornography, and the Sex Industry.* New York: Routledge, 2000.

Related Entries

Bachelorhood; Crisis of Masculinity; Feminism; Heterosexuality; Middle-Class Manhood; Military; *Playboy* Magazine; Pornography; Progressive Era; Victorian Era; Working-Class Manhood

—*Sharon A. Abbott*

Race

Race is a factor that has had, and will for the foreseeable future continue to have, a profound effect on masculinities within the United States. Throughout American history, racial designations have been crucial in organizing, and often limiting, men's ambitions, expectations, and opportunities. This has been true of all the arenas in which masculinity has traditionally been constructed or proved, including the workplace, the family, sexual relationships, and the body.

Race, Class, and Ethnicity

Most biologists and anthropologists now agree that there are no biological characteristics or genetic patterns capable of classifying a person as belonging to a certain race. Yet while race lacks scientific grounding, belief in its reality determines many aspects of social conduct. Race is therefore best understood as a social and cultural construction, the result of a historically conditioned process of racialization by which individuals automatically attempt to differentiate people according to what a culture constitutes as different races. It also involves the association of certain cultural and social traits with certain races. Frequently, racialization accompanies a sense of culturally belonging to a certain race; that is, participation in a group history, a set of cultural practices, and shared experiences.

The process of racialization often interacts with the process—equally social, cultural, and historical in nature—of constructing gendered identities. Crucial to the establishment of both racial and gendered identities are encounters with those who are perceived as "other"—those individuals or groups who come to embody characteristics seen as alien to one's own racialized and gendered identity. When this process exists alongside imbalances of power between such groups, as it usually does, the dominant group (white men, through much of American history) often ascribes the less powerful group a set of undesirable characteristics that define it as inferior and unsuitable for positions of public authority, responsibility, or power. For example, women and racial minorities have been labeled childish, irresponsible, excitable, irrational, "natural," and corporeal since the foundation of the colonial territories, and they have, thereby, been restricted in their opportunities and access to jobs and services. By contrast, whiteness and maleness have often been associated with adulthood, responsibility, calmness, rationality, culture, and intelligence, all characteristics that have generally been highly valued. It is important to recognize, therefore, that just as masculinity cannot be understood without reference to femininity, racial identities defined as "nonwhite" cannot be understood without reference to whiteness.

Throughout U.S. history, therefore, white masculinity has often been defined in opposition to characteristics identified with racial minorities, especially African Americans. Indeed, it has been argued that the black/white binary has been the crucial organizing structure for racialization in the United States, and that the racialization of Asian Americans, Native Americans, Latino Americans, and masculinities of other racial groups, although exhibiting their own specificities, cannot be understood without reference to this binary.

Racialized male identities have also been intertwined with the formation of class identities. White middle-class men have often applied to working-class men the same negative descriptors that they applied to women and nonwhite men, and they have excluded nonwhite men from the economic mechanisms of achieving middle-class status. Furthermore, the early-twentieth-century African-American sociologist W. E. B. Du Bois (as well as some recent historians) has argued that white racial identity was a fundamental element of working-class manhood and provided an additional "wage" for male workers consisting of the benefits (e.g., services, rights, access to positions of authority, and general psychological well-being) accrued from simply being white. The resulting affirmation of racial difference often prevented the white working class from affiliating with the nonwhite working classes.

Concepts of racial male identity in the United States have been complicated by attempts to distinguish between race and ethnicity. Broadly speaking, ethnic male identities have commonly been grounded in a sense of cultural, religious, or national heritage (Italian American or Jewish American, for example) rather than the more physiological characteristics often associated with racial categorization. Yet some scholars consider racial identity the most significant factor in ethnic identity, while others contend that racial identity is a special case that needs to be treated separately.

While the formation of racialized male identities has been a constant throughout U.S. history, it is also important to understand the historical fluidity of the process. For example, native-born white men refused at times during the nineteenth century to recognize Irish and Jewish men as white or fully masculine, though both of these groups eventually—to quote the historian Noel Ignatiev—"became white." In addition, the 1960 alteration to the census policy that allowed for the self-determination of race has greatly increased the number of American men who identify themselves as Native American.

Masculinity, Americanness, and Exclusion

Along with the concentration of political, economic, and social power in the hands of white men through much of U.S. history has been an identification of the practices and aesthetics of white manhood as "normal" and "American." This identification of Americanness with whiteness and masculinity led Du Bois to describe his identity as a black American as a condition of "double consciousness." Such racialized definitions of nationhood and manhood have been used to define nonwhite men as un-American, and thus to justify their exclusion from the rights of U.S. citizenship and from economic opportunity. White men have often used racialized understandings of their masculinity to construct concepts of equality and citizenship grounded specifically in white manhood.

The effects of this identification of white masculinity with American identity pervade the American past. Nativist and white supremacist sentiment have recurred through U.S. history, as has discrimination against nonwhite men in the workplace, in access to the right to vote, in establishing segregated residential areas and public facilities often inferior to those enjoyed by whites, and in limiting the cultural representation of nonwhite people. Native American peoples and cultures were displaced from their ancestral American lands; African Americans were enslaved and long excluded from the rights of citizenship; and, in the late nineteenth century, notions of white American racial superiority infused with Darwinian notions of natural competition and struggle for survival stimulated U.S. imperialism in Asia and Latin America.

Racialized Masculinity, Sexuality, and the Primitive

Constructions of racialized male identity in the United States have been inseparable from images of sexuality and the primitive. White men have constructed their masculinity not only by infantilizing and patronizing nonwhite men but also by representing them (especially black men) as primitive, emotionally uncontrollable, prone to criminality, and hypersexual. Such representations have been common since the time of the initial contact of English traders with sub-Saharan African peoples in the 1550s, and they still exist in the twenty-first century. Thus, for example, the archetypes of black men in the white imagination have included not only the childlike and servile slave Uncle Tom of Harriet Beecher Stowe's *Uncle Tom's Cabin* (1852), but also Bigger Thomas, the antihero, murderer, and rapist of Richard Wright's *Native Son* (1940), and the hyperphysical, hypersexual athlete represented by the boxer Jack Johnson. These images of nonwhite masculinity—and attempts by African American and other nonwhite men to contend with them—remain apparent in media coverage of figures like the boxer Mike Tyson.

The displacement of physicality, sexuality, and criminality onto "blackness" as a way of constructing white masculinity means that the relationship of white masculinity to black masculinity was not always marked purely by contempt and fear, but also by desire. The association of black masculinity with the transgressive and the sexual has appealed to white men questioning conventional constructions of white middle-class manhood and seeking to construct new alternative masculine identities. This can be seen in many of the bohemian communities of the Jazz Age and Beat era, as well as in various other youth cultures of the twentieth century. This cross-racial male desire and fantasy has been evident in attempts by white rock-and-roll musicians of the 1950s to adopt African-American styles, in the contemporary popularity of rap and hip-hop among young white American men, and in the imitation of Native American rituals by recent men's groups hoping to reconnect to a more primal side of their identity.

Interracial desire and fear have been most emotive for American masculinity, particularly in the twentieth century, in matters involving interracial sex, especially between black men and white women. Interracial marriage between black and white, perceived as a threat to racialized (especially white) male identities, was prohibited as early as the seventeenth century in the English colonies. For much of the history of the United States black men were punished for having sex with white women, often by corporal or capital means (which at various times included castration and lynching). This prohibition on black-male/white-female sexual intercourse continued for much of the twentieth century, especially in the southern states. Enforcing it became a central way of asserting and protecting white men's supremacy—and was a central part of white supremacist rhetoric in organizations such as the Ku Klux Klan. For many black men, challenging this prohibition offered a way to defy this system.

Masculinity and Resistance to Racialization

Feelings of having suffered a history of emasculation at the hands of white oppression have led nonwhite men to form and articulate their own racialized constructions of manhood. These male identities have pervaded the rhetoric and strategies of resistance enacted by men of American racial minorities. For example, the word *man* became a common term of address between African-American men partly in response to whites' demeaning use of *boy* to address grown African-American men. There were also angry reactions to Daniel Patrick Moynihan's controversial 1965 report *The Negro Family: The Case for National Action,* which suggested that many problems in African-American communities stemmed from the inability of black men to participate effectively in family life. The civil rights movements of the 1960s and 1970s, and especially the militant Black Power movement, used heavily gendered and even hypermasculine rhetoric to reclaim and assert a distinctly African-American manhood that participants thought had been long inhibited by America's history of racism. Much of this rhetoric was misogynistic and homophobic, but it presented an empowering vision of black masculinity that many young black men found appealing. Similarly, leaders of Chicano militant political groups in the 1960s and 1970s drew upon *machismo* to form Chicano male identities and to emphasize the manliness and affirmative value of their resistance politics.

Conclusion

Race has been of crucial importance to American masculinity, a situation heavily conditioned by the nation's history of slavery, and by its territorial expansion at the expense of indigenous peoples. For white men, it has often provided a bulwark to a hierarchical view of masculinity that draws much of its currency from competition and exclusion. It has secured them privilege in the workplace, in public life, and in cultural representation. The formation of nonwhite masculinities has been profoundly affected by engagement with this oppression, both in the emasculating feelings it has produced and in the feelings of cultural and historical cohesion it has generated. Whether American concepts of masculinity remain tightly anchored in the categories of black and white, in light of the fact that Latinos now represent the nation's largest ethnic minority, is an important question about the future of race and gender in the United States. Questions about the efficacy of affirmative action as a means of promoting the manhood of nonwhite men, and about the value of an identity politics that grounds nonwhite masculinities in the self-conscious use of racial, cultural, and political affiliation, will continue to be raised for the foreseeable future. It is clear in any case that constructions of masculinity in the United States cannot be fully understood apart from the factor of race.

Bibliography

Baldwin, James. *Nobody Knows My Name: More Notes of Native Son.* New York: New York: Vintage, 1993.

Bernasconi, Robert, ed. *Race.* Malden, Mass.: Blackwell, 2001.

Carroll, Peter N., and David W. Noble. *The Free and the Unfree: A New History of the United States.* 2nd ed. New York: Penguin, 1988.

Cleaver, Eldridge. *Soul on Ice. New York:* Delta Trade Paperbacks, 1999.

Delgado, Richard, and Jean Stefancic, eds. *Critical White Studies: Looking Behind the Mirror.* Philadelphia: Temple University Press, 1997.

Dyer, Richard. *White.* London: Routledge, 1997.

Gutman, Herbert G. *The Black Family in Slavery and Freedom, 1750–1925.* New York: Vintage, 1977.

Hammerback, John C., Richard J. Jensen, and Jose Angel Gutierrez. *A War of Words: Chicano Protest in the 1960s and 1970s.* Westport, Conn.: Greenwood Press, 1985.

Ignatiev, Noel. *How the Irish Became White.* New York: Routledge, 1995.

Jordan, Winthrop D. *White Over Black: American Attitudes Towards the Negro, 1550–1812.* Chapel Hill: University of North Carolina Press, 1968.

Kimmel, Michael. *Manhood in America: A Cultural History.* New York: Free Press, 1996.

Roediger, David R. *The Wages of Whiteness: Race and the Making of the American Working Class.* London: Verso, 1999.

Sollors, Werner. *Beyond Ethnicity: Consent and Descent in American Culture.* New York: Oxford University Press, 1986.

Trigger, Bruce G., and Wilcomb E. Washburn. *The Cambridge History of the Native Peoples of the Americas.* Vol. 1, Part 2. Cambridge, England: Cambridge University Press, 1996.

West, Cornel. *Race Matters.* Boston: Beacon Press, 2001.

Further Reading

Bederman, Gail. *Manliness and Civilization: A Cultural History of Gender and Race in the United States, 1880–1917.* Chicago: University of Chicago Press, 1996.

Carby, Hazel V. *Race Men.* Cambridge, Mass.: Harvard University Press, 1998.

Eng, David L. *Racial Castration: Managing Masculinity in Asian America.* Durham, N.C.: Duke University Press, 2001.

Fanon, Frantz. *Black Skin, White Masks.* 1952. Reprint, translated by Charles Lam Markmann, New York: Grove Press, 1991.

Franklin, John Hope, and Alfred A. Moss, Jr. *From Slavery to Freedom: A History of Negro Americans.* 6th ed. New York: Knopf, 1988.

Harper, Phillip Brian. *Are We Not Men? Masculine Anxiety and the Problem of African American Identity.* New York: Oxford University Press, 1996.

hooks, bell. *Outlaw Culture: Resisting Representations.* New York: Routledge, 1994.

Lipsitz, George. *The Possessive Investment in Whiteness: How White People Profit from Identity Politics.* Philadelphia: Temple University Press, 1998.

Saxton, Alexander. *The Rise and Fall of the White Republic: Class Politics and Mass Culture in Nineteenth-Century America.* London: Verso, 1996.

Somerville, Siobhan B. *Queering the Color Line: Race and the Invention of Homosexuality in American Culture.* Durham, N.C.: Duke University Press, 2000.

RELATED ENTRIES

African-American Manhood; American Dream; Asian-American Manhood; Black Panther Party; Body; Capitalism; Citizenship; Civil Rights Movement; Civil War; Counterculture; Darwinism; Emancipation; Ethnicity; Eugenics; Immigration; Imperialism; Irish-American Manhood; Italian-American Manhood; Jewish Manhood; Latino Manhood; Minstrelsy; Nationalism; Nation of Islam; Native American Manhood; Slave Narratives; Slavery; Whiteness; White Supremacism; Work

—*Mark Whalan*

RAMBO

The film character John Rambo, played by Sylvester Stallone, became an icon in the United States during the 1980s. A former Green Beret, Rambo's manly assertiveness represented the conservatism and aggressive global interventionism of the Reagan era, as well as a widespread rejection of the liberal policies of the 1960s and 1970s.

Rambo first appeared in 1972 as the main character in *First Blood,* a novel by the Canadian-American writer David Morrell. The film version of the novel, directed by Ted Kotcheff, was released in 1982 and was followed by two sequels: *Rambo: First Blood II* (1985), directed by George Pan Cosmatos; and *Rambo III* (1988), directed by Peter MacDonald. Rambo successfully fights bland politicians and smug bureaucrats in the United States (*First Blood*) and the proxy governments of the Soviet Union in Southeast Asia (*Rambo: First Blood II*) and Afghanistan (*Rambo III.*) Critics praised the first film, and, despite the critical rejection of the sequels, the public embraced Rambo. The character embodied a masculine, patriotic, and national toughness well suited to the conservative political and cultural climate of the period. Rambo and Stallone, who also co-wrote the screenplays, became symbols of a conservative, nationalistic America.

The John Rambo character draws on several archetypes associated in American popular culture with masculine and national strength. His combined white European (German) and Native American ancestry gives him superior physical endurance and helps him survive in hostile environments. He also plays the role of rescuer common in captivity narratives (much like James Fenimore Cooper's character "Hawkeye" Natty Bumppo in his Leatherstocking Tales). These traits make Rambo a modern hero of the mythic American frontier. The Rambo films present a white, muscular male American hero who patronizes and protects non-whites abroad, strengthening the myth of benevolent imperialism that had come to define U.S. foreign policy during the twentieth century. Rambo's paramilitary prowess and the success of his missions mirrored President Ronald Reagan's promises to strengthen the U.S. military and restore the international respect that the United States had lost due to the Vietnam War and the embarrassing Middle East foreign policy crises of the 1970s (all of which Reagan blamed on liberals).

In the three films, as well as in the novel, Rambo reflects Reagan's defense of manly individual initiative against big government, as well as his emphasis on militarism and warlike masculinity. Rambo resents Americans who refuse to accord the same honor to Vietnam War veterans that was given to veterans of the nation's prior wars. In *First Blood,* a wailing Rambo complains that "somebody"—by which he means the civilian bureaucrats that had conducted the war in Vietnam—"wouldn't let us win." Supported emotionally by Colonel Tautman, a fatherly military figure modeled on John Wayne's character in the film *The Green Berets* (1968), Rambo believes that the pusillanimous but pervasive political establishment should be replaced by a more aggressive one. Reagan's rhetoric of conventional gender hierarchy, military strength, and conservative triumph over liberalism were embodied in Rambo's transformation from enraged outcast in *First Blood* into a brawny warrior in its sequels.

Rambo has become an important cultural window on postliberal America. Representing masculine strength and aggressive nationalism, he articulates a mythology traditionally shaped by white males in America, many of whom emerged in the 1980s as a key conservative constituency.

BIBLIOGRAPHY

Bates, Milton J. *The Wars We Took To Vietnam: Cultural Conflict and Storytelling.* Berkeley: University of California Press, 1996.

Jeffords, Susan. *The Remasculinization of America: Gender and the Vietnam War.* Bloomington: Indiana University Press, 1989.

Further Reading

Gibson, James William. *Warrior Dreams: Violence and Manhood in Post-Vietnam America.* New York: Hill and Wang, 1994.

Johnson, Haynes. *Sleepwalking through History: America in the Reagan Years.* New York: Anchor Books, 1992.

Mintz, Steven, and Randy Roberts, eds. *Hollywood's America: United States History through Its Films.* St. James, N.Y.: Brandywine Press, 1993.

Shafer, D. Michael, ed. *The Legacy: The Vietnam War in the American Imagination.* Boston: Beacon Press, 1990.

Slotkin, Richard. *Gunfighter Nation: The Myth of the Frontier in Twentieth-Century America.* Norman: University of Oklahoma Press, 1998.

Related Entries

Body; Boone, Daniel; Bureaucratization; Cold War; Heroism; Imperialism; Leatherstocking Tales; Male Friendship; Militarism; Military; Nationalism; Patriotism; Populism; Race; Reagan, Ronald; Vietnam War; Wayne, John; Western Frontier; World War I; World War II

—*Juan José Cruz*

Reagan, Ronald

1911–
American Actor, Politician, and President

Ronald Reagan enjoyed careers in radio, film, and politics, and he served as the fortieth president of the United States (1981–89). Partly through his acting career, but primarily through his highly popular presidency and his conservative political policies, he became an icon of American masculinity.

Reagan graduated in 1932 from Eureka College, where he played football, and became a radio sports announcer. In 1937 he turned to acting. Appearing in fifty-three films over the following two decades—most notably *Knute Rockne: All American* (1940) and *King's Row* (1941)—he played roles that identified manliness with patriotism, football, military heroism, and the West.

After making army training and morale films during World War II, Reagan became president of the Screen Actors' Guild (1947–52). While he initially held liberal and Democratic views, growing Cold War fears of communism made him increasingly conservative, anticommunist, and militaristic in his outlook. Amid controversy involving his co-operation with the House Un-American Activities Committee's investigation of communism in the film industry in the 1950s, Reagan left the acting business. He then became a national spokesman for

Ronald Reagan, elected president in 1980, embodied a conservative and nostalgic vision of American masculinity emphasizing physical vigor, patriotism, military strength, morality, and capitalism. His success heralded a Republican ascendancy in American politics that lasted into the early twenty-first century. (© Hulton/Archive)

General Electric, giving speeches that associated masculinity and patriotism with business, capitalism, and conservatism.

In the 1960s, supported by business leaders who admired his inspirational speaking style, Reagan sought political office as a Republican. After two terms as governor of California (1967–75), he won the Republican presidential nomination in 1980. In his successful campaign, which tapped concerns that the nation had been weakened during the 1970s by economic stagnation, defeat in Vietnam, and Middle Eastern terrorists, Reagan promised to reinvigorate the nation militarily and economically, identifying his masculinity with national strength. By contrast, he portrayed his Democratic opponent, the incumbent president Jimmy Carter, as a weak president who had been ineffective at addressing economic malaise and confronting terrorists holding Americans hostage at the U.S. embassy in Iran. Reagan's campaign image of manly vigor, typified by television commercials depicting him wearing a cowboy hat or splitting wood, also addressed concerns raised by the fact that, at age sixty-nine, he was seeking to become the oldest president in American history.

As president, Reagan continued to associate patriotism, military strength, capitalism, and moral righteousness with masculinity. He used tough rhetoric in his dealings with the Soviet Union, ordered an invasion of the Caribbean island nation of Grenada to topple a Communist-backed government in 1983, and, responding to a series of terrorist acts during the early 1980s, launched a military strike aimed at Libyan leader Muammar al-Qaddafi in 1986. Identifying manliness with entrepreneurship and economic expansion, he supported a probusiness agenda that reduced both corporate taxes and federal regulation on corporate activity. His conservative positions on issues of family, gender, and sexuality won him the support of the Christian Right, whose leaders believed that the 1960s counterculture and feminist challenges to traditional patriarchal domestic relations had undermined moral values and the stability of the family. But Reagan's masculine image was eroded during the Iran-Contra affair, when his claim that he was unaware of secret government sales of weapons to Iran to raise money for anticommunist guerillas in Nicaragua renewed concerns that advancing age had left him too weak to function effectively as president. His critics claimed confirmation of these suspicions following Reagan's 1994 announcement that he had Alzheimer's disease.

The growing appeal of the Republican Party and its conservative ideology during and after his presidency—particularly to white males—suggests that Reagan's association of masculinity, patriotism, business, military prowess, and moral conservatism powerfully impacted American political and cultural life into the twenty-first century.

Bibliography

Combs, James. *The Reagan Range: The Nostalgic Myth in American Politics*. Bowling Green, Ohio: Bowling Green State University Popular Press, 1993.

Dallek, Robert. *Ronald Reagan: The Politics of Symbolism*. Cambridge, Mass.: Harvard University Press, 1984.

Wills, Gary. *Reagan's America: Innocents at Home*. Garden City, N.Y.: Doubleday, 1987.

Further Reading

Cannon, Lou. *President Reagan: The Role of a Lifetime*. New York: Public Affairs, 2000.

Greenstein, Fred I., ed. *The Reagan Presidency: An Early Assessment*. Baltimore: Johns Hopkins University Press, 1983.

McManus, Doyle, and Jane Mayer. *Landslide: The Unmaking of the President, 1984–88*. Boston: Houghton Mifflin, 1988.

Related Entries

Business/Corporate America; Capitalism; Cold War; Football; Heroism; Hollywood; Militarism; Patriotism; Politics; Vietnam War; Western Frontier; Westerns

—*Bret E. Carroll*

Rebel Without a Cause

Directed by Nicholas Ray and starring James Dean, Sal Mineo, and Natalie Wood, *Rebel Without a Cause* (1955) portrays white middle-class American teenagers alienated from—and in a political rebellion against—the materially comfortable but emotionally empty world of their parents. The film contemplates what it means to be a young male in midcentury America, and it made James Dean a lasting icon of restless American manhood.

Both the traditional family and the prevailing model of post–World War II white middle-class fatherhood, which were exalted in such popular 1950s television series as *Father Knows Best*, function poorly in *Rebel Without a Cause*, victims of a failed adult manhood and a disorienting reversal of traditional gender and generational roles. "You're tearing me apart!" Dean's character Jim Stark screams resentfully to his befuddled parents. Hungering for a manhood more admirable than that of his inept, apron-wearing, wife-fearing father (played by Jim Backus), Jim Stark even wonders if things would be better if his father "had the guts to knock mom cold once." Jim moves beyond verbal assaults, attacking his father physically at one point, prompting his mother to plead, "Stop it! You'll kill him, Jim! Do you want to kill your father?" The question stays unanswered.

Despite his anger, Jim is able to express his own vulnerability, as well as tender feelings for others his own age, male and female alike. Natalie Wood's Judy appreciates this unconventional approach to maleness in Jim, "a man who can be gentle and sweet." She thinks Jim's distinctive way of "being strong" makes him the sort of man "a girl wants."

Males are drawn to Jim as well. Even Buzz, the tough male accidentally killed in a "chickie run" contest with Jim (in which the two drive stolen cars at full speed toward a cliff, the one who jumps out first being the loser), had admitted, "I like you, you know." Feeling trapped by the cultural emphasis on male competition, Jim was moved to ask in reply, "Buzz? What are we doing this for?" Much more powerfully attracted to Jim is Plato, played by Sal Mineo. Abandoned by his father, Plato wishes Jim "could have been my dad," and Jim reciprocates with warm affection. Interestingly, some critics see homoeroticism in Plato's attraction to Jim; but the fact that they care deeply for each other does not necessarily suggest sexual yearning on either's part. Significantly, however, both male objects of Jim's affection, Buzz and Plato, are dead by the end of the movie, suggesting the era's widespread discomfort with any sort of passionate attachment between males.

Before Plato is killed by police gunfire, he retreats to an abandoned mansion with Jim and Judy, briefly establishing an alternative sense of family vastly more fulfilling than anything the three had experienced with their own families. Jim and Judy eventually surrender to the police, however, and, in an ambiguous ending, Jim is reunited with his parents.

Ultimately, *Rebel Without a Cause* is as at odds with itself as Jim Stark is conflicted. Jim's ambivalent embrace of both rage and tenderness mirrors the film's inconsistent explanations of male adolescent alienation. The film suggests that a new cultural definition of manhood is in order, yet its ending implies that a return to traditional male authority is the better solution. What is clear is the considerable questioning that lay beneath the apparently solid acceptance of prevailing constructions of manhood during the 1950s.

Bibliography

Alexander, Paul. *Boulevard of Broken Dreams: The Life, Times, and Legend of James Dean.* New York: Viking, 1994.

Kreidl, John Francis. *Nicholas Ray.* Boston: Twayne, 1977.

Further Reading

Dalton, David. *James Dean, The Mutant King: A Biography.* Chicago: A Cappella, 2001.

DeAngelis, Michael. *Gay Fandom and Crossover Stardom: James Dean, Mel Gibson, and Keanu Reeves.* Durham, N.C.: Duke University Press, 2001.

Related Entries

Adolescence; American Dream; Dean, James; Emotion; Hollywood; Juvenile Delinquency; Sensitive Male

—*John Ibson*

Reform Movements

Issues of men and masculinity have often been central to American reform movements. By definition, such movements have sought to change some aspect of culture, politics, or the economy, and they have attempted to reconfigure, sometimes in limited and sometimes in grandiose ways, power relationships in American society. Given the centrality of gendered language and concepts to the ways power relationships are understood and articulated, defining and promoting a particular vision of masculinity (and, for that matter, femininity) has often been a central strategy of different reformers attempting to accomplish social and cultural change. This relationship between reform and masculinity characterizes the three most important reform impulses in U.S. history: that of the antebellum period (1820–60), the Progressive Era (1890–1915), and the various reform movements of the 1960s and 1970s.

Antebellum Reform

The four decades preceding the Civil War witnessed an explosion of reform efforts in the United States. Fueled by the utopian spirit of both the American Revolution and the religious revivals of the Second Great Awakening, tens of thousands of men and women during this period tried to improve their society in ways as diverse as ending slavery in the South, reforming Americans' dietary habits, and encouraging their countrymen not to drink. Yet, however diverse, most of these movements were preoccupied with defining an ideal relationship between the individual and society, and very often that ideal was conceptualized and promoted in terms of some perceived standard of "manly" behavior.

A new concept of masculinity that emphasized the liberty and rights of the individual emerged in the nineteenth century. With the trend toward extending voting rights to all white men and the ascendancy of a more profit-oriented economy (what historians call the "market revolution"), a cultural ideal of manhood emerged that defined men as self-interested participants in both the political arena and the economic marketplace. While this individualistic concept of manhood often created a sense of empowerment for some, for the society as a whole it was also a source of considerable social anxiety. Many feared that the social and economic changes of the period were eroding the bonds that held American society together. They worried that new understandings of manhood were not indicative of increased individual liberty, but instead promoted self-interested acquisitiveness and civic irresponsibility.

Many of the reform movements of the period were therefore directed at creating a sense of social stability. These movements usually did not seek to reverse the social and cultural changes of the market revolution; instead, they worked to mitigate anxieties about those changes. Addressing fears about the erosion of older mechanisms of social control, several movements offered a vision of masculine identity based upon self-control. For example, by building organizations where men pledged to give up alcohol and eat only healthy foods, temperance societies and dietary reform movements such as Grahamism (influenced by the health reformer and minister Sylvester Graham) provided reassuring evidence that American men—particularly entrepreneurial, middle-class men—balanced their pursuit of self-interest with voluntary self-restraint.

Abolitionist activists also celebrated self-control. While many sincerely considered slavery a momentous injustice, the abolitionist critique of slavery also functioned as a symbolic repository of all the perceived problems of America's increasingly fragmented society. In this view, slavery—not American society as a whole or its entrepreneurial middle-class men—was economically exploitative, driven by greed and aggressiveness. In contrast, the ideal man in abolitionist ideology was not driven by self-interest, but was restrained by his moral sense and religious beliefs. Although attitudes toward market capitalism varied widely between different reform movements, the vision of self-restrained manhood promoted by antebellum reformers helped ease concerns about the effects of social atomization during the period.

Progressivism

If many antebellum Americans feared that their society's ideals of manhood might promote a dangerous individualism, by the turn of the twentieth century Americans felt compelled to defend an individualistic manly identity that they thought was imperiled by an increasingly bureaucratic society and corporate economy. The final decades of the nineteenth century witnessed what the historian Richard Hofstadter labeled a "status revolution" in American cultural politics: Middle-class white men increasingly felt that they were losing power and prestige in their local communities, and in the nation as a whole. With the emergence of enormous, powerful corporations; the accumulation of large personal fortunes by industrialists such as Andrew Carnegie and John D. Rockefeller; and the growth of large unions like the Knights of Labor and the American Federation of Labor, an individualistic ideal of manhood rooted in entrepreneurship no longer seemed tenable. Instead of aspiring to ownership of a small business, for example, middle-class men at the turn of the century faced the reality of spending their careers filling modest positions in enormous bureaucratic hierarchies—of being small cogs in large corporate machines.

While some men of the period tried to revitalize a failing sense of manhood by engaging in such hypermasculine activities as prizefighting and bodybuilding, or by joining fiercely patriarchal fundamentalist sects, others sought to regain social power and status through organized reform movements. From the 1890s to World War I, a pervasive reform sensibility, often labeled Progressivism by historians, found expression in diverse, even conflicting, reform efforts. Celebrated Progressives included such different figures as the social reformer and Hull House founder Jane Addams and "trust buster" Theodore Roosevelt, who served as U.S. president from 1901 to 1909. Although no specific political strategy or objective unified Progressives, they did share a commitment to mitigating the perceived excesses of large-scale corporate capitalism and administering a dose of morality and justice to civic and economic life. For some men, Progressive reform reaffirmed their manhood; accomplishing reform meant individual men still possessed manly authority in the political life of the nation.

The corporate trust was the embodiment of the problems Progressives saw in politics and the economy. Many Progressives thought that the trusts, through such corporate strategies as price fixing and vertical integration, destroyed or absorbed smaller-scale businesses, and thus threatened the link between hard work and economic independence central to traditional American notions of manhood. Breaking up corporate trusts through legislative and executive actions provided reassuring evidence of the continued power of manly citizens and offered the promise that small-scale businesses built by independent men might yet remain viable. Other Progressive reforms—such as wresting city governments from the control of corrupt political machines and granting the electorate more power through initiatives and referendums—also aimed to restore power to the virtuous, independent male citizen.

The 1960s and 1970s

Antebellum reformers' and Progressives' ideals of manhood generally reflected the perspectives of the dominant social group of those periods—in both cases, white middle-class males. Throughout the nineteenth century and into the twentieth, prevailing ideals of American manhood were defined against the perceived "unmanliness" of African Americans, nonheterosexuals, and, of course, women. In the post–World War II era, particularly during the 1960s and 1970s, those groups began to challenge the hegemony of white middle-class males in the United States through organized reform movements such as the civil rights movement, the second-wave of feminism, and the gay liberation movement. In the process of seeking to restructure power relationships, they contested the dominant ideal of manliness in American culture and proposed new ideals of their own.

The civil rights movement produced competing ideals of manhood. Martin Luther King, Jr., grounded both his understanding of African-American manhood and his strategy for social change in nonviolent civil disobedience and the dignity of African-American men. Malcolm X and the Black Panthers offered very different models of manhood based upon more militant challenges to white power. Yet whatever their differences, leaders of all civil rights and African-American identity movements insisted that black men be considered "men."

Feminism presented the most direct critique of traditional manhood. Feminist critics, particularly the National Organization of Women (NOW; founded in 1966), challenged the notion that public life was the exclusive domain of men and the domestic home that of women. They insisted, with some success, that women should be granted opportunities in the workplace, and that men should assume more responsibilities in the home and develop new models of manhood divorced from traditional patriarchal assumptions and notions of gender hierarchy.

The gay liberation movement of the 1970s questioned the equation of manhood with heterosexuality and sought to empower gay men by proposing new models of masculinity grounded in homosexual identity. Some gay men, for example, adopted hypermasculine personas, sporting mustaches and muscular bodies. The politicization of same-sex eroticism in the gay liberation movement functioned as a self-conscious critique of the patriarchal ideology institutionalized in heterosexual marriage.

For African-American and gay men, staking a claim to manhood in the larger culture has been perceived as a means of asserting authority and social dignity. For women, critiquing and reshaping traditional gender roles has been, and continues to be, considered a central and essential step toward achieving true equality. Like their antebellum and Progressive predecessors, the civil rights, feminist, and gay liberation movements highlight the longstanding, problematic equation between the manhood and power in American culture.

BIBLIOGRAPHY

Dorsey, Bruce. *Reforming Men and Women: Gender in the Antebellum City.* Ithaca, N.Y.: Cornell University Press, 2002.

Hofstadter, Richard. *The Age of Reform: From Bryan to F.D.R.* New York: Knopf, 1955.

Kimmel, Michael. *Manhood in America: A Cultural History.* New York: Free Press, 1997.

Muncy, Robyn. "Trustbusting and White Manhood in America, 1898–1914." *American Studies* 38 (Fall 1997): 21–42.

Stewart, James Brewer. *Holy Warriors: The Abolitionists and American Slavery.* New York: Hill and Wang, 1976.

FURTHER READING

Abzug, Robert H. *Cosmos Crumbling: American Reform and the Religious Imagination.* New York: Oxford University Press, 1994.

Bederman, Gail. *Manliness and Civilization: A Cultural History of Gender and Race in the United States, 1880–1917.* Chicago: University of Chicago Press, 1995.

Evans, Sara. *Personal Politics: The Roots of Women's Liberation in the Civil Rights Movement and the New Left.* New York: Vintage, 1980.

Sitkoff, Harvard. *The Struggle for Black Equality, 1954–1992.* Rev. ed. New York: Hill and Wang, 1993.

Stauffer, John. *The Black Hearts of Men: Radical Abolitionists and the Transformation of Race.* Cambridge, Mass.: Harvard University Press, 2002.

RELATED ENTRIES

Abolitionism; African-American Manhood; Alcohol; Antiwar Movement; Black Panther Party; Bureaucratization; Business/Corporate America; Capitalism; Citizenship; Civil Rights Movement; Counterculture; Douglass, Frederick; Feminism; Graham, Sylvester; Heterosexuality; Homosexuality; Individualism; *Jungle, The*; Malcolm X; Market Revolution; Middle-Class Manhood; Politics; Populism; Progressive Era; Race; Republicanism; Roosevelt, Theodore; Self-Control; Suffragism; Temperance; Work

—*Robert K. Nelson*

RELIGION AND SPIRITUALITY

In the United States, spiritual and religious expression has historically been highly diverse, and devotion has taken a multiplicity of forms contingent upon individual and group identity, social and cultural milieu, geographic location, and other variables. American men's attempts to locate themselves in relation to the divine have historically constituted a complex set of beliefs and practices determined by these and other factors. Some ideological strains and influential constructs have at times contributed to an overarching, frequently hegemonic notion of masculine spirituality, but the spiritual identities of American men have both conditioned, and been conditioned by, the ever increasing pluralism of American religiosity. Racial and ethnic identities have also been interwoven with religious affiliations, enhancing the broad range of masculine spiritual and religious manifestations in the United States.

Religion and Spirituality among Native American Men

The vast array of Native American social, cultural, and religious stances have produced myriad notions of masculine spirituality. It is feasible, however, to identify a number of prevalent models. For instance, archetypes such as the aggressive hunter/warrior or the authoritative ritual leader have possessed much vitality within many Native American groups, especially during the pre-Columbian period. For Plains Indians, communal livelihood depended upon successful buffalo hunts, thus making the ability to secure prey a pivotal marker of manliness. In the Southwest, Hopi women were barred from participation in kiva ritual ceremonies, while men directed a variety of rituals meant to link an agricultural people with a deified terrain. Many groups inculcated masculine spirituality through rite-of-passage vision quests or all-male sweat-lodge ceremonies, rituals valorizing manly virtues such as personal fortitude or solitary introspection. At the same time, however, indigenous American religiosity has frequently rejected exclusionary gender dualisms, recognizing a nurturing Mother Earth and wise female healers. Among the Cheyenne, Lakota, and others, for example, this ambivalence about gender dualism has been exemplified by the *berdache*, a ritual leader and shaman whose transvestism crosses the boundaries of conceptual categories to unleash creative power and mediate between natural and supernatural realms.

Beginning in the sixteenth century, new modes of male spirituality emerged as indigenous societies were altered by the encroachments of white settlement. Occasionally, conquest prompted vigorous and defensive religious responses among Native Americans, such as the late-nineteenth-century Ghost Dance, which represented a combination of native apocalypticism and renewed vigilance toward white aggressors. Conversely, the Native American Church, a movement begun among the Kiowa in about 1890 and formally incorporated in 1918, has integrated Christian visions of male spirituality into its beliefs and practices, emphasizing industriousness and restraint while resisting absolute assimilation through the maintenance of pan-native moral principles and the sacramental consumption of peyote.

Religion and Spirituality among Protestant Men

The Puritans of seventeenth-century New England emphasized male governance of the political, familial, and religious realms, and they conceptualized male spirituality in relation to these leadership roles. At the same time, however, their vision of faith as an erotic union of a masculine God and a feminized, submissive believer led them to portray both sexes as "brides of Christ" and to equate male and female piety alike with humility and subordination. By 1700, the communal nature of colonial America began to give way to a market economy, and religious language underwent a process of masculinization. Positing passion as injurious to proper economic functioning, Puritan clergymen created a masculine form of sanctity grounded in rationality and restraint.

Rapid modernization and industrialization during the nineteenth century increasingly separated men from the domestic sphere, furthered a view of masculinity based upon competitiveness, and created a split between the "profane" world of work and the increasingly sanctified world of home. Many American men—especially those of the urban middle-class—grew concerned that Protestant spiritual and domestic life had become excessively feminized, a concern underscored by changes in Protestant Christology: Jesus was portrayed as an exemplar of love and passivity, visual images gave him distinctly feminine features, and wives and mothers served as a spiritually empowered contrast to the amoral male world of marketplace competition. Many commentators have marked this split as the origin of a crisis in male spirituality that persists in various contemporary forms.

By the mid–nineteenth century, countless men had retreated from what they perceived as the feminizing influences of the church, the sentimental domestic sphere, and urban overcivilization in order to pursue a distinctly robust form of spirituality at the Young Men's Christian Association (YMCA) or within fraternal orders. Seeking out male fellowship through an integration of faith and sport, or by partaking in Calvinist-derived initiation rites at a lodge, these men fashioned a form of religiosity more amenable to the masculine public sphere and sought to tap a primitive and natural inner self that they considered fundamental to male spirituality. Later in the century, Social Gospel advocates similarly promoted a "muscular Christianity," urging the cultivation of a hardy physique and the combating of social evils with manly ferocity. In the early twentieth century, the Men and Religion Forward Movement of 1911–12, the first evangelistic campaign to target a specific gender, stressed a masculine spirituality allied with church leadership, social service, and domestic responsibility. Purveyors of religious art, meanwhile, attempted to divest representations of Jesus of feminine attributes and emphasize Christ's manliness. Although direct calls for a more vigorous Christianity decreased by the 1920s, throughout the twentieth century fundamentalist Protestants reasserted a biblically based spiritual and familial patriarchy in the face of liberal, antiliteralist readings of scripture and, especially during the last third of the century, feminist theology.

Beginning in the late 1980s, advocates of the mythopoetic perspective reiterated historical themes by claiming that men were overwhelmed by feminism and oppressed by the conditions of modern labor. Urging readers to realize the "wild man" within, authors such as Robert Bly recommended male spiritual empowerment through archetype-rich homosocial rituals. Finally, the Promise Keepers, an evangelical Christian men's movement begun in 1990, has attempted to combat "moral collapse" by accentuating God-given male leadership ability and Christ-like family governance. Thus, for many, a perceived crisis in male spirituality continues to highlight the relationship between gender and piety.

Religion and Spirituality among Catholic Men

Catholic men in nineteenth-century America also identified a tension between manhood and piety, positing virtues such as industriousness and temperance as vital for a cultivated masculine spirituality. Faced with a sociocultural context different from that in their European homelands, first-generation immigrants were nonetheless familiar with models that portrayed women as naturally religious. Drawing upon a Catholic tradition that described this paradigm as designed by God, exemplified by the Virgin Mary, and revealed through natural law, such men promoted a notion of separate spheres more vehemently than many other Christians. Despite similarities between Catholic and Protestant men, most Catholic men's working-class status, ethnic identification, and more hostile relationships with male religious authorities contributed to the construction of masculinities that often differed from those of Protestant men.

Unable to locate a set of labor-driven virtues in the frequently chaotic and threatening industrial realm, Catholic men placed an even greater emphasis on the sanctity and orderliness of the home. While expecting wives and daughters to function as the familial representatives of the sacred, they often developed an antagonistic stance toward piety. Resenting close relationships between priests and female family members, they feminized the priesthood while opposing such friendships. This cautious approach to institutional Catholicism has been most evident among southern Italian and Mexican men, who have often restricted their spiritual expressions to the public space of the streets, thus devaluing the necessity of parish life.

After World War II, with the onset of a suburban lifestyle that threatened men's ability to oversee the home, Catholic devotional manuals sought to construct a non-ethnic male religiosity and emphasize the father's role in domestic religion. But piety remained largely a female undertaking. At the end of the twentieth century, Catholic men continued to seek out modes of masculine spirituality, rather than the traditional spirituality of the celibate priest. Modernizing tendencies promoted by the Second Vatican Council, theological attempts to realign gendered discussions of godliness by female Catholic theologians, and fervent debates over the viability of a female priesthood continue to contribute to modifications of Catholic male spiritualities.

Religion and Spirituality among Jewish Men

Whereas mainstream Christianity has historically identified women as the bearers of piety, the culture of nineteenth-century eastern-European Jewish immigrants defined spirituality as a male responsibility. Stationing men at the forefront of familial religiosity and emphasizing sacred learning as an exclusively male undertaking, Orthodox Jews initially inverted standard American conceptions by bestowing the burden of a child's religious education upon the father and advocating contemplative male pursuits. Separate synagogue seating for men and women functioned as a material reminder of these separate roles. Although this practice has been maintained among Orthodox Jews, the Reform and Conservative traditions, influenced by modernization and American values of domestic unity and sexual equality, have worked since the mid–nineteenth century to promote less male-exclusive forms of piety.

If many Protestant men have historically defined their spiritualities through a lens of social and economic privilege, Jewish-American men have alternately situated their religious experiences within a cultural climate of oppression and marginalization. Hebrew Scripture often associates closeness to God with male delicateness and domesticity, and the stories of Isaac, Joseph, and others emphasize the merits of intimate mother–son relationships and the value of intellectualism—traits that have been deemed less than heroic within the gender ideologies of American Christianity.

With these traditions of strong mothering and an emphasis upon literacy, American Jewish men have often been viewed by the dominant culture as emotional and fragile—therefore lacking the vigor essential to most American models of masculinity and male spirituality. Experiences of anti-Semitism and a concomitant Jewish male air of restraint in the face of persecution have served to compound this dissonant relationship between Jewish masculinities and prevailing American views. Thus, Jewish men have often been asked to construct a mode of spirituality mired in contrasts. Faced with a traditional understanding of family that heralded the piety of husbands and sons, they have been subject to American ideologies that deemed their intellectualism and familial intimacy as contrary to a male religiosity founded upon success in the public sphere and disassociation from domesticity.

Religion and Spirituality among African-American Men

Like Jewish men, African-American males have often defined their spirituality through a vantage of marginality. The experience and legacy of slavery, the development of distinct black churches, the varying personalities of their leaders, and the influence of white racism have contributed to the construction of numerous models of male spirituality capable of negotiating a context of domination. Forced to abandon indigenous traditions, African slaves nevertheless maintained emotive and confident aspects of tribal religiosity that would be integrated into expressions of both black Christianity and black masculinity. As an advocate of liberation, the antebellum male slave preacher demonstrated self-assertive masculinity and functioned as a model of integrity for his audiences, drawing upon heroic exemplars such as Moses for scriptural precedent, as well as on American republican ideals of manly independence. The male leaders of the separate black churches that developed during the Revolutionary era continued this tradition of independence by forming congregations that could offer a forceful voice of dissent in the face of bigotry and oppression.

During the late nineteenth century, African-American men began to cultivate more thorough associations with Africa, with many claiming that an authentic black male spirituality could only arise when individuals were loosed from the geographical confines and the cultural grip of white America. Marcus Garvey's Universal Negro Improvement Association—and its support of the African Orthodox Church, a new Christian denomination established in 1921—continued this initiative of separation during the 1910s and 1920s. Beginning in the 1930s, Black Muslims (later known as the Nation of Islam), advanced an often militant theology of racial superiority that reviled what they considered to be the polluting effects of white culture and religion upon black spirituality. At the same time, these groups sought to restore the spirituality of black men through such traditional elements of white masculinity as thrift and patriarchal family leadership.

Other African-American men sought to reconcile black manhood with Christianity by identifying the latter with a vigorous pursuit of liberation and social justice. During the civil rights movement of the 1950s and 1960s, men such as Martin Luther King, Jr., a Baptist minister, drew upon transcendentalism, the Gandhian concept of *ahimsa* (belief in the sacredness of all living creatures and the necessary avoidance of violence), and the peace-seeking Gospel tradition to encourage male spiritualities couched in forceful yet nonviolent modes of resistance.

A continuing sense of crisis of identity among young black men and a perceived lack of male leadership within the black family prompted Nation of Islam leader Louis Farrakhan to organize the Million Man March in 1995. Attracting over one million individuals to Washington, D.C., participants in the march sought personal atonement alongside spiritual and social transformation, reiterating the themes of self-responsibility and freedom that have permeated constructions of black male spirituality throughout American history.

Religion and Spirituality among Muslim Men

Islam is often stereotyped as heavily patriarchal, but the gender codes in its sacred text, the Koran, are in fact more ambivalent. The Koran does include passages codifying divinely sanctioned male superiority but, unlike Judeo-Christian texts, it does not describe Eve (woman) as inherently subservient to Adam (man), it does not assign Eve responsibility for humanity's downfall, and it claims that women and men have the same spiritual nature. Apparent manifestations of male dominance in Muslim practice, such as polygamy for men and requirements of modest dress and behavior for women, are the product less of Koranic injunction than of sociocultural context and adherence to Shariah (Islamic law based upon specific interpretations of the Koran). Muslim men's spiritual expressions are similarly grounded in specific sociocultural contexts, and are therefore diverse.

Like Judaism, Islam situates the family as the fundamental organizational unit of the faith. Recognizing a gendered public/private divide that casts men as the representatives of the familial unit outside of the home and in the mosque, Islamic men have historically cited the prophet Muhammad as an exemplar of idealized masculinity. As a paradigm, Muhammad represents qualities of civic assertiveness, evangelical fervor, spiritual mastery, and family governance that continue to guide contemporary masculine models. Although Muslim mothers are expected to make substantial contributions to the religiosity of their children, fathers have traditionally resisted notions that divest them of their sacred authority, and they thus have continued to position familial religious leadership as integral to definitions of maleness.

Entering a sociocultural climate more amenable to ideas of female liberation and participation in the public sphere than their countries of origin, American Muslim men have often been urged to modify their stances regarding male and female piety. For instance, Muslim women in America are more likely to attend mosques than women in Islamic countries, with several mosques even allowing for mixed worship. In regard to the traditional Islamic dress code, some women practice full veiling while others opt for this attire only for religious occasions. However, despite these changes, Muslim men in the United States continue to express their spiritual prowess and their desire to guide public familial behavior by disallowing female *imams* (traditional leaders of worship), outnumbering women at Friday mosque services, and exercising their domestic authority by demanding modest dress and behavior among wives and daughters. Therefore, the religious and spiritual stances of Muslim men continue to be reshaped through the balancing of traditional elements and Americanizing influences.

Conclusion

Since the early 1970s, a formalized men's movement has sought to complicate the notion of hegemonic or entrenched masculinities. This initiative addresses numerous social and cultural agendas, but attempts to reconceptualize male spirituality have been central to it. Profeminist men, in an attempt to isolate and combat traditional American notions of male spirituality, have called for the integration of traditionally "feminine" emotions and religious perspectives into male identity in order to promote ideas of mutuality and to assuage the stereotyping of masculinity as a bastion of self-reliance. But men's piety has never been monolithic—it has always been conditioned by class, race, ethnicity, and geographic context. Men's spiritual expressions have historically reflected the vast pluralism of both American religion and American masculinity.

Bibliography

Becker, William H. "The Black Church: Manhood and Mission." *Journal of the American Academy of Religion* 40, no. 3 (1972): 316–333.

Brod, Harry, ed. *A Mensch Among Men: Explorations in Jewish Masculinity.* Freedom, Calif.: Crossing Press, 1988.

Carnes, Mark C., and Clyde Griffen. *Meanings for Manhood: Constructions of Masculinity in Victorian America.* Chicago: University of Chicago Press, 1990.

Carroll, Bret E. "Masculine Spirituality." In *Contemporary American Religion,* edited by Wade Clark Roof. New York: Macmillan, 2000.

Clatterbaugh, Kenneth. *Contemporary Perspectives on Masculinity: Men, Women, and Politics in Modern Society.* Boulder, Colo.: Westview, 1997.

Juster, Susan. "The Spirit and the Flesh: Gender, Language, and Sexuality in American Protestantism." In *New Directions in American Religious History,* edited by Harry S. Stout and D. G. Hart. New York: Oxford University Press, 1997.

McDannell, Colleen. "Catholic Domesticity, 1860–1960." In *Religion and American Culture: A Reader,* edited by David G. Hackett. New York: Routledge, 1995.

Mernissi, Fatima. *Beyond the Veil: Male-Female Dynamics in Modern Muslim Society.* Bloomington: Indiana University Press, 1987.

Putney, Clifford. *Muscular Christianity: Manhood and Sports in Protestant America, 1880–1920.* Cambridge, Mass.: Harvard University Press, 2001.

Taves, Ann. "Sexuality in American Religious History." In *Retelling U.S. Religious History,* edited by Thomas A. Tweed. Berkeley: University of California Press, 1997.

Further Reading

Boyd, Stephen B., Merle W. Longwood, and Mark W. Muesse. *Redeeming Men: Religion and Masculinities.* Louisville, Ky.: Westminster John Knox Press, 1996.

Carnes, Mark C. *Secret Ritual and Manhood in Victorian America.* New Haven, Conn.: Yale University Press, 1989.

Ownby, Ted. *Subduing Satan: Religion, Recreation, & Manhood in the Rural South, 1865–1920.* Chapel Hill: University of North Carolina Press, 1990.

Welter, Barbara. "The Feminization of American Religion: 1800–1860." In *Religion in American History: A Reader,* edited by Jon Butler and Harry S. Stout. New York: Oxford University Press, 1998.

Related Entries

African-American Manhood; Beecher, Henry Ward; Civil Rights Movement; Crisis of Masculinity; Cult of Domesticity; Emancipation; Evangelicalism and Revivalism; Fraternal Organizations; Immigration; Industrialization; Jesus, Images of; Jewish Manhood; King, Martin Luther, Jr.; Malcolm X; Market Revolution; Men and Religion Forward Movement; Men's Movements; Ministry; Muscular Christianity; Nation of Islam; Native American Manhood; Noyes, John Humphrey; Progressive Era; Promise Keepers; Social Gospel; Sunday, Billy; Temperance; Urbanization; Young Men's Christian Association

—*Aaron K. Ketchell*

Reproduction

Reproduction, as both a biological and social function, has been a salient element in defining masculinity and the lives of men in the United States. For men, reproduction has represented the continuation of a genealogical line, the establishment of social position as a household head, the demonstration of virility through fertility, and the assumption of the role and responsibilities of fatherhood. Historically, American men have more consistently defined their identities apart from their reproductive capacities and accomplishments than women have. But with the rise, spread, and then decline of the traditional two-parent nuclear family in industrial and postindustrial America, both biological and social reproduction have come to play more central roles in defining masculinity.

Reproduction in the Colonies: 1640–1800

Reproduction in the colonial and early post-Revolutionary periods directly reflected the economic necessities of agricultural production and an expansionist attitude aimed at strengthening the colonies and, later, the nation through population growth. This attitude toward nation building, reflected in high fertility rates and large families, persevered in the frontier areas of the United States into the mid–nineteenth century. American men expected to sire large families, not only to reap the economic potential of children in a household-based economy, but also to secure positions within communities as patriarchal heads of households. In Puritan New England, this patriarchal line of authority extended from God to government officials to the family father. Because they rarely passed down their inheritance to the firstborn son alone, most white men would head their own households. Following the high mortality rates in the early colonies, comparatively low mortality rates and phenomenal fertility rates drove rapid population growth in the eighteenth century.

Slavery directly affected the reproduction of thousands of men. Grounding their understanding of manhood and its social functions in whiteness, slave owners viewed male slaves in terms of their reproductive capacities, but separated slaves' reproduction from considerations of family and fatherhood. During slavery, slave owners "bred" black men to increase their labor force. While white men saw black slaves as a sexual threat to white women, they viewed their own reproductive engagement with slave women as a prerogative of racial patriarchy, overlooking, and even condoning, the rearing of children resulting from relations between white male slave owners and female slaves.

The U.S. Demographic Transition: 1800–1900

Changing masculine roles coincided with a demographic shift and the resulting fertility decline that occurred in the United States in the nineteenth century prior to the Industrial Revolution. During this period, life expectancy increased and mortality levels at all ages dropped, followed by a decline in the average family size. Thus, while the U.S. population continued to double every twenty years until 1860, the total fertility rate decreased almost in half, from 7.1 children per woman among white Americans in 1800 to 3.6 in 1900. From 1850 to 1900, total fertility among black women also declined, from 7.9 to 5.6. The later age at which couples first married and their increased participation in marital contraception (particularly by means of withdrawal) precipitated this decline. As the United States moved from a household-based and largely agricultural economy into an urban, industrial one, the economic cost of individual children increased. Children thus became less of an economic asset and more of a social and personal investment, and couples responded by delaying marriage and having fewer children.

With this economic and demographic transition came a change in the relation between masculinity and reproduction. Women and children became less involved in economic activities, and the separation for men of home and workplace reinforced the notion of men as the primary providers for families and women as domestic guardians. This increasing gender disparity in economic roles occurred in the context of men's lack of involvement in child rearing, which enhanced men's growing monopoly of work outside the home. Men's reproductive role became increasingly connected to financial provision for their children.

The Victorian Era to World War II: 1850–1945

The nineteenth-century demographic transition, along with social theories of human reproduction, would shape Victorian-era male norms of sex and sexuality. Prior to the dramatic changes in fertility rates and family structure, the male desire for sex was acceptable within marriage because it led to reproduction. Laws dating to colonial times condemned such acts as masturbation and oral and anal sex as crimes against nature because they involved sexual organs in nonprocreative ways. Victorian-era medical experts continued to marginalize nonreproductive male sexuality, but they increasingly identified sexual deviance as distinct individual pathologies, decrying the ill physical effects of immoral sexual activities such as masturbation, premarital sex, and prostitution. The criminalization of prostitution, in particular, reflected gendered attitudes toward sex, with laws inflicting harsher penalties on female prostitutes than on their male clients.

Racist stereotypes about sexuality, spurred by reproductive fears, persisted even after the abolition of slavery. Whites, especially in southern states, portrayed free black men as hypersexual and animalistic. These attitudes fueled fears among white southerners of the rape of white women by black men and of the birth of mixed-race children, leading to both unfair prosecution of, and violence toward, black men premised on sexual crimes.

In the late nineteenth and early twentieth centuries, Darwinian thought greatly influenced attitudes toward men's reproductive roles. In the works *On the Origin of Species* (1854) and *The Descent of Man* (1876), Charles Darwin argued that the male sex in most species faced much lower reproductive costs than females, given that males do not gestate or lactate. Many Americans interpreted Darwinism to suggest that it is men's "nature" to compete with other men to produce as many offspring with as many women as possible. Darwinists justified an aggressive male sexuality that disconnected men's sexual acts from the bearing and rearing of children, thus reinforcing existing norms of male sexual desire and promiscuity. The theory also placed new value on men's reproductive capacity, and many Americans came to associate procreation with "maleness." At the same time, some moral reformers associated reckless male sex with a less evolved state, encouraging social development through managed reproduction. Using Darwinian theory to define reproduction by "less fit" men as a social problem, eugenicists in the beginning of the twentieth century supported miscegenation and sterilization laws that predominantly targeted immigrants, the poor, the mentally handicapped, and criminals. Eugenics laws and programs also particularly targeted men, who were assumed to be the active, determinant element of reproduction.

World Wars I and II—and the growth of American global power and accompanying concerns about national military strength that these wars fostered—profoundly affected ideas about reproduction in the United States. During both wars, soldiers received sexual education and condoms in order to prevent the transmission of venereal disease. Before World War I, the U.S. government had been reluctant to legalize the manufacturing of condoms or other contraceptives. But this attitude changed as soldiers in World War I became seriously debilitated by sexually transmitted diseases contracted overseas. While the interwar period in the United States did not witness specific state-directed reproduction programs, as seen in countries such as Germany, eugenicists nonetheless associated the management of reproduction with the possibility of physically defeating an enemy in war.

New Reproductive Technologies: 1900–Present

New reproductive technologies have greatly influenced the relation among reproduction, men, and masculinity in the twentieth and twenty-first centuries. Generally, women have used these technologies, while men have designed and implemented them. During the late nineteenth and early twentieth centuries, professional male doctors medicalized and assumed control of pregnancy and delivery, leading campaigns to displace, and eventually outlaw, lay female midwives who had previously controlled childbirth. Men's domination of the field of obstetrics led to valuable medical practices—including hospitalized birth, anesthesia, cesarean sections, episiotomies, and restrained birth positions—that eased the labors of childbearing and reduced infant and maternal mortality. But these practices may also have alienated women from the childbearing process.

Masculine norms also influenced—and continue to influence—developing scientific understandings of the role of male and female sex cells (sperm and eggs) during conception and gestation. Physiological understandings of reproduction into the late nineteenth century had assigned men a determinate role, with semen characterized as carrying the full potential for a human child (a *homunculus*, or wholly-formed human, was once thought to exist in sperm). While advances in genetics and embryology in the twentieth century elucidated the role of sperm and ova, gender norms continued to influence physiological depictions and understandings of reproduction. Medical texts described sperm production as a physiological marvel (in contrast to wasteful menstruation), while sperm were incorrectly assigned a more active role in fertilization than ova. Sperm are, in fact, swept to ova in a relatively passive manner, while ova actively attract sperm.

Beginning in the 1960s and 1970s, the availability of reliable, user-controlled hormonal contraceptives and safer, legalized abortion procedures changed the meanings of reproduction for both men and women. Hormonal contraceptives and abortion, both considered to be the responsibility of women, meant that men became less involved in decisions about conception and pregnancy. These trends may also have caused men to feel less accountable both for contraception decisions and parenting after childbirth. With the rise of HIV/AIDS in the late twentieth century, men became increasingly involved in decisions about barrier contraceptives, such as condoms, as sexual activity is associated with risk of infection.

The development of paternity tests created more direct legal links between men and their offspring, leading to an increasingly genetic basis of paternity. Genetic matching allowed for the enforcement of laws that hold men socially and economically responsible for their genetic children, and also gave fathers more legal rights during pregnancy and infancy.

Men's role in reproduction also changed in the late twentieth century through technologies such as sperm donation and infertility treatment. Men can now separate reproduction from heterosexual activity, genetically reproducing through sperm donation without any contact with a partner. At the same time, popular and medical attention has increasingly been focused on male-related infertility, which is believed to account for more than half of all cases of couple infertility. The traditional association of fulfilled manhood with reproduction has generated an emotional burden for infertile men, many of whom have turned to in vitro fertilization to bolster their sense of masculine identity.

Continuing Shifts in the Role of Men in the American Family

Americans in early-twenty-first-century, postindustrial society have witnessed the escalating instability of the traditional nuclear family. Men are more likely to cohabit, less likely to marry or remarry, and more likely to divorce than their fathers and grandfathers. Men's declining commitment to the nuclear family has both been a factor in and a result of women's increased participation in labor and economic independence. Increasingly, more children in the United States are born outside of marriage, and men's level of social and economic support of their offspring has declined. Men are also more likely to have biological children with whom they do not live, and to live with children not biologically theirs. These new roles for men in the family have led some conservatives to push for a return to traditional "family values" and more strongly gendered household roles, while some liberal feminists have pushed for increased female autonomy and lessened male involvement in reproductive decision making. These positions point to tension between traditional structures of male authority in the household and shifting rationales for male involvement in reproduction for both men and women.

BIBLIOGRAPHY

D'Emilio, John, and Estelle B. Freedman. *Intimate Matters: A History of Sexuality in America.* New York: Harper & Row, 1988.

Ehrenreich, Barbara, and Deirdre English. *For Her Own Good: 150 Years of the Experts' Advice to Women.* Garden City, N.Y.: Anchor Press, 1978.

Goldscheider, Frances K., and Gayle Kaufman. "Fertility and Commitment: Bringing Men Back In." *Population and Development Review* 22S (1996): 87–99.

Hawkins, Mike. *Social Darwinism in European and American Thought, 1860–1945: Nature as Model and Nature as Threat.* Cambridge, England: Cambridge University Press, 1997.

Kimmel, Michael. *The Gendered Society.* New York: Oxford University Press, 2000.

Martin, Emily. *The Woman in the Body: A Cultural Analysis of Reproduction.* Boston: Beacon Press, 2001.

Shorter, Edward. *The Making of the Modern Family.* New York: Basic Books, 1975.

Tone, Andrea. *Devices and Desires: A History of Contraceptives in America.* New York: Hill and Wang, 2001.

FURTHER READING

Gordon, Linda. *Woman's Body, Woman's Right: A Social History of Birth Control in America.* New York: Grossman, 1976.

Hobson, Barbara, ed. *Making Men into Fathers: Men, Masculinities, and the Social Politics of Fatherhood.* New York: Penguin, 1990.

Kline, Wendy. *Building a Better Race: Gender, Sexuality, and Eugenics from the Turn of the Century to the Baby Boom.* Berkeley: University of California Press, 2001.

RELATED ENTRIES

Darwinism; Heterosexuality; Homosexuality; Eugenics; Fatherhood; Fathers' Rights; Marriage; Medicine; Technology

—*Matthew R. Dudgeon and Jenny Higgins*

REPUBLICANISM

The term *republicanism* refers to an ideology that outlined principles of social and political order and the privileges and obligations of citizenship in the Anglo-American world from the seventeenth century through the early nineteenth century. Because it developed in a setting in which masculinity was a prerequisite of citizenship, republicanism necessarily constituted a prescription for ideal manhood as well. Frequently ambivalent and contradictory, republicanism embraced a range of ideas about political society, including notions of hierarchical and organic social order that emphasized mutual obligation over the pursuit of self-interest; a liberal, possessive individualism that stressed the individual's right to seek, accumulate, and dispose of property; and a civic humanism that called for devotion to the public good as the primary responsibility of citizenship. It also required both resistance to tyranny and subordination to legitimate rule and authority.

As a prescriptive code of manliness, republicanism aimed to inspire men to exercise their rights and obligations as citizens in an orderly society. Its critical task was to constrain self-interest and redirect it into socially and politically desirable channels. The central quality of ideal citizenship and ideal republican manhood was virtue, defined as the capacity to control, and sometimes sacrifice, one's selfish interests for the common good. Only in the 1820s did states begin to introduce universal adult white-male suffrage, so, prior to this, the full privileges of republican citizenship and the status of republican manhood were confined to a white, propertied, patriarchal elite.

In republican ideology, the duties and privileges of citizenship and the foundations of male identity lay in a man's status as an owner of land and the head of a household, both of which integrated him into the bonds of political society. The true republican man was a patriarch who governed his household like a well-ordered commonwealth in harmony with the mandates of public order. He was also married, since marriage would provide the basis for his establishment of a household, and he would sublimate his passions in work to support that household, channel his sexuality into the production of offspring, and provide a framework for raising his offspring according to the political dictates of republican society. By siring offspring who would inherit his land holdings, a republican man demonstrated that he respected his birthright and the privileges of citizenship it conferred upon him. His doing so also ensured the perpetuation of the economic and political independence necessary to republican order.

If republican ideology understood the married household head as the ideal man, and as the basis of society, it portrayed single men as a grave danger to republican order. The bachelor, free to express his sexuality and passions outside the bonds of household, marriage, and civic fraternal society, was perceived as a source of moral licentiousness and democratic excess. During this period, male-male sexual relations were redefined from a mortal sin to a crime against republican political order. Single men were expected to give up the freedom of bachelorhood for the social contract implied in the responsibilities of marriage and household.

The property interests of the republican man, who was bound to rule over, protect, and provide for others, would encourage him and his sons to support political stability and the rule of law. A republican man's devotion to political stability allowed him to enter fraternal society and caused him to accept the leadership and protection of the government. Men of exceptional worth, meanwhile, who through self-restraint

This painting of the signing of the Declaration of Independence in 1776 conveys the grounding of early American republican manhood in ideals of disinterested civic devotion and white patriarchy, and suggests George Washington's stature as a model of heroic republican manliness. (From the collections of the Library of Congress)

and virtue were able to exercise power without corruption or aristocratic ambition, constituted a propertied patriarchal male elite that contributed to social order and the longevity of the republic by providing leadership and guidance.

By associating liberty and citizenship with masculinity, republicanism, by definition, excluded all women from such privileges, except when mediated through fathers or husbands. Yet republican theory accorded women functions crucial to the formation and maintenance of republican manhood. Isolated from public politics and denied the right to vote, women remained confined to the household and economically dependant on fathers and husbands—thus highlighting men's patriarchal status. Yet republicanism also understood mothers as critical to the reproduction of republican society, not only sexually, but also socially, since it defined women as exemplars of moral virtue who would raise their sons to become responsible republican citizens. Furthermore, because wives tied their husbands to their households and counteracted the corrupting effects of political power, women were deemed essential to grounding men in republican civil society.

During the early nineteenth century the concept of republican manhood became increasingly problematic and contested as the new nation was transformed by industrialization, urbanization, the market revolution, political democratization, and western expansion. These developments stimulated the development of newer concepts of manhood—such as the Yankee entrepreneur, the "self-made man," and an egalitarian ideal of democratic manhood—that undermined the notions of hierarchy and organic social order that had previously framed republican manhood. These trends presented a challenge to the traditional monopolization of political power by propertied male elites. Furthermore, while republicanism was intended by men to relegate women to subordinate social and political roles, it also opened the way to women's empowerment by stimulating a women's rights movement that resisted the male monopoly on political power, while the ideal of republican motherhood also encouraged the education of women. Similarly, African-American abolitionists interpreted republican manhood in ways that challenged its traditional association with whiteness.

Slavery and antebellum sectional conflict raised other issues that complicated notions of republican manhood. Diverging northern and southern versions of republican manhood developed in the 1840s and 1850s. The northern version, articulated in the ideologies of the Free-Soil and Republican parties, emphasized ideas of political and economic independence grounded in Jeffersonian agrarianism, Jacksonian democracy, and an emerging capitalist market. The southern version, meanwhile, prioritized notions of patriarchy, hierarchy, and an organic social order, casting southern men as patriarchal rulers over extended households and as landowners who provided for their families (including slaves). Southerners portrayed the northern free-labor system as antithetical to paternal benevolence and social harmony; northerners viewed southern slaveholders as an aristocratic element detrimental to republican notions of manly liberty; and abolitionists charged that slaveholders, through their sexual access to female slaves, separated sexual desire from marital obligation and practiced the sins associated with disorderly bachelors. These diverging interpretations of republican theory and republican manhood made reconciliation difficult and helped to exacerbate the sectional divisions that culminated in the Civil War.

Republicanism and republican manhood would give way to different ideals of manliness and political order over the course of the nineteenth century. However, it also created an enduring cultural legacy in U.S. culture by suggesting that: (1) manhood is not innate, but must be earned and acquired; (2) manliness requires self-discipline and a devotion to the responsibilities of citizenship; and (3) men must procreate as a rite of passage to full manliness. In their broad outlines, republican notions of responsible citizenship have endured into the twenty-first century, although they are no longer confined to white males.

Bibliography

Bloch, Ruth H. "The Gendered Meanings of Virtue in Revolutionary America." *Signs: Journal of Women in Culture and Society* 13 (1987): 37–58.

Boydston, Jeanne. *Home and Work: Housework, Wages, and the Ideology of Labor in the Early Republic.* New York: Oxford University Press, 1994.

Kann, Mark E. *On The Man Question: Gender and Civic Virtue in America.* Philadelphia: Temple University Press, 1991.

———. *A Republic of Men: The American Founders, Gendered Language, and Patriarchal Politics.* New York: New York University Press, 1998.

Kimmel, Michael. *Manhood in America: A Cultural History.* New York: Free Press, 1996.

Norton, Mary Beth. *Founding Mothers and Fathers: Gendered Power and the Forming of American Society.* New York: Knopf, 1996.

Shalhope, Robert E. *The Roots of Democracy: American Thought and Culture, 1760–1800.* Boston: Twayne, 1990.

Further Reading

Fliegelman, Jay. *Prodigals and Pilgrims: The American Revolution Against Patriarchal Authority, 1750–1800.* Cambridge, England: Cambridge University Press, 1982.

Greven, Philip. *The Protestant Temperament: Patterns of Child-Rearing, Religious Experience, and Self in Early America.* New York: Knopf, 1977.

Gross, Robert. *The Minutemen and Their World.* New York: Hill and Wang, 1976.

Lockridge, Kenneth. *On the Sources of Patriarchal Rage: The Commonplace Books of William Byrd and Thomas Jefferson and the Gendering of Power in the Eighteenth Century.* New York: New York University Press, 1992.

Nelson, Dana. *National Manhood: Capitalist Citizenship and the Imagined Fraternity of White Men.* Durham, N.C.: Duke University Press, 1998.

Rotundo, E. Anthony. *American Manhood: Transformations in Masculinity from the Revolution to the Modern Era.* New York: Basic Books, 1993.

Wilentz, Sean. *Chants Democratic: New York City and the Rise of the American Working Class, 1788–1850.* New York: Oxford University Press, 1984.

Zagarri, Rosemarie. "Morals, Manners, and the Republican Mother." *American Quarterly* 44 (June 1992): 192–215.

Related Entries

Agrarianism; American Revolution; Bachelorhood; Citizenship; *Contrast, The*; Crèvecoeur, J. Hector St. John; Democratic Manhood; Franklin, Benjamin; Individualism; Market Revolution; Marriage; Mother–Son Relationships; Nationalism; Patriarchy; Patriotism; Politics; Property; Self-Made Man; Slavery; Southern Manhood; Washington, George; Western Frontier; Whiteness; Work

—*Thomas Winter*

Reverse Sexism

The concept of reverse sexism, an idea developed in the late twentieth century and most frequently articulated by men, asserts that feminism has generated discourses and practices that disadvantage men. Because these discourses and practices have been grounded in a belief that traditional notions of masculinity are to blame for a range of legal, social, political, cultural, and sexual inequities in the United States, public debates about reverse sexism have focused on the position of men and the meaning of manhood in American life.

In the late 1960s the advent of second-wave feminism in the United States generated an often strident critique of patriarchy and the development of a strongly antipatriarchal body of theory and discourse. In its most extreme forms this discourse suggested that men were, by their very nature, aggressive oppressors, and that ideals of masculinity were to blame for the oppression of women. The more moderate theories underlying reverse sexism argued that masculinity was a social and cultural construction that had been developed by men to justify their power over women, and that conventional power structures and notions of manhood should be revised in order to create a more equitable political, social, economic, and legal system in the United States.

The 1970s saw feminism-driven legal reforms involving pay levels, housework, divorce, and custody, and many men began arguing that women were actually being given unfair preference. Some of these men sought legal acknowledgement that they were discriminated against. As a variety of men's movements and organizations began publicizing the issue and seeking legal remedies during the 1970s and 1980s, the idea of reverse sexism—like that of reverse discrimination more broadly—gained increasing currency.

Legal actions involving claims and incidents of reverse sexism increased during the late twentieth century. During the 1990s more than two hundred men in the United States filed sexual harassment charges with the Equal Employment Opportunity Commission, and 14 percent of the federal workers in the U.S. Merit Systems Protection Board reported such harassment. The legal issues associated with reverse sexism also became visible in the mass media. The film *Kramer vs. Kramer* (1979), for example, highlighted apparent discrimination against men as parents, and the film *Disclosure* (1994) demonstrated that men were subject to sexist advances in the workplace—and that they could seek legal redress.

Reverse sexist rhetoric and imagery often took the form of what its critics called "male-bashing." It defined masculinity in terms of the negative characteristics often associated with it—violence, hypersexuality, excessive absorption in work, insensitivity to women's needs, and alienation from domestic life—though its proponents differed over whether these characteristics were the result of socialization or were inherent to maleness. In popular culture, this trend fueled reverse-sexist humor from sources ranging from Hallmark cards ("Men are scum. Excuse me. For a second there I was feeling generous.") to comedian Joan Rivers ("Want to know why women don't blink during foreplay? Not enough time."). A popular 1980s television advertisement for Folger's coffee depicted a husband unable to prepare breakfast for his wife until a package of coffee fell out of a pantry, literally at his feet. A flyer published in 1994 by the Women's Issues Advocate of the Office for Women's Issues at the University of Southern California, stating that "There are no good men," caused a considerable furor.

Reverse-sexist discourse took other forms as well. In some cases it advocated an overturning of traditional power relations between men and women. Actor Sharon Stone, for example, appearing on the *David Letterman Show* in 1990, stated: "The more famous and powerful I get, the more power I have to hurt men." In other cases, particularly common in advertising, it involved the use of the sexually objectified male body to sell products. For instance, a television commercial for Diet Coke, featuring a group of women gazing at a construction worker removing his shirt, became the subject of public discussion.

Reverse sexism affected the development of American masculinity in complex ways. For one, it made men conscious that they are being assessed, often negatively, by the women around them. It also made them feel increasingly threatened, both legally and physically. In 1993, male anxieties about severe forms of reverse sexist abuse were heightened following an incident in which John Wayne Bobbitt's penis was severed by his wife after a marital dispute. Surgery replaced the penis, and Bobbitt himself was interviewed in various media outlets (as was his wife) and went on to appear on *The Oprah Winfrey Show* (and in the 1994 pornographic movie *John Wayne Bobbitt . . . Uncut*). The incident left men aware of their physical vulnerability in their sexual relationships—and in fear of the possibility that their manhood was open to attack.

On the other hand, reverse sexism has prompted many men to examine their own position within patriarchal power structures and to pursue reforms to eliminate inequities and abuses. It has also encouraged the development of revised masculine identities and behaviors that acknowledge oppressive structures, accept the politicized discourse of the feminist agenda, and seek to eliminate those aspects of conventional masculinity deemed offensive to its critics. Reverse-sexist practice has likewise initiated a concern to promote more positive images of men and masculinity.

In particular, the men's movement, which emerged in the 1970s in response to the impact of feminism, has tried to offer a version of masculinity that is tolerant of others, both in gendered and sexual terms, and to defy reverse sexism. It has argued that reverse sexism is a very real social and cultural problem, and it posits that a cultural version of reverse sexism suppresses male emotions, restricts male sensitivity, and conditions the parameters of male-to-male and male-to-female relationships. Such organizations as the Men's Defense Association, founded in 1971, emerged to assist individuals facing reverse-sexist discrimination in divorce and custody cases, and to protect the rights of fathers.

Reverse sexism has generated new ways of thinking about the behavior of men and the meaning of masculinity in the United States. This has allowed a form of masculinity to emerge that values the contributions of maleness to the culture at large, and that acknowledges that men—as a monolithic group—cannot be accused of abusive behavior. A more positive approach by men to their own maleness affords a more tempered view of the position of men in the twenty-first century.

BIBLIOGRAPHY

Brownmiller, Susan. *Against Our Will: Men, Women and Rape.* New York: Simon & Schuster, 1975.

Dworkin, Andrea. *Our Blood: Prophecies and Discourses on Sexual Politics.* New York: Harper & Row, 1976.

French, Marilyn. *The Women's Room.* New York: Jove, 1977.

Greer, Germaine. *The Female Eunuch.* 1970. Reprint, New York: Farrar, Straus and Giroux, 2002.

Griffin, Susan. *Rape: The Politics of Consciousness.* New York: Harper & Row, 1979.

Morgan, Robin. *The Demon Lover.* New York: Norton, 1989.

FURTHER READING

Badinter, Elisabeth. *XY: On Masculine Identity.* New York: Columbia University Press, 1995.

Boone, J., and M. Cadden. *Engendering Men: The Question of Male Feminist Criticism.* London: Routledge, 1990.

Chapman, R., and J. Rutherford, eds. *Male Order: Unwrapping Masculinity.* London: Lawrence and Wishart, 1988.

Dworkin, Andrea. *Woman Hating.* New York: Dutton, 1974.

Horrocks, Roger. *Masculinity in Crisis.* New York: St. Martin's, 1994.

Messner, M. *The Politics of Masculinities: Men in Movements.* Thousand Oaks, Calif.: Sage, 1997.

RELATED ENTRIES

Advertising; Crisis of Masculinity; Divorce; Fatherhood; Fathers' Rights; Feminism; *Kramer vs. Kramer;* Men's Movements; Men's Studies; Sensitive Male; Sexual Revolution

—Michael John Pinfold

ROMANTICISM

Romanticism was a cultural and artistic movement rooted in eighteenth- and nineteenth-century Europe and highly influential among American writers and intellectuals of the nineteenth century. Its emphasis on the experiences and the autonomy of the self as the primary basis of knowledge and truth greatly influenced cultural constructions of American masculinity and its key concepts of emotion and nature shaped perceptions and definitions of the American male.

Individualism

Perhaps the central element of Romanticism's definition of manhood is individualism. In particular, American writers influenced by Romanticism—including Ralph Waldo Emerson, Henry David Thoreau, Nathaniel Hawthorne, Herman Melville, and Walt Whitman—emphasized the idea that the individual was, by nature, divine. The intuitive, emotional self, thoroughly grounded in nature and divinity, was therefore the most reliable source of truth. This idea meant that individual expression was all-important in the artistic process and fundamental to true manliness. Emerson declared, for example, that "Whoso would be a man, must be a nonconformist," that "Society everywhere is in conspiracy against the manhood of every one of its members," and that the "great man" maintains "the independence of solitude" (Emerson 1965, 242–244).

Romantic masculinity also required a continual introspective striving for greater knowledge of self, nature, and divinity. This understanding of manhood meshed well with, and may well have played a role in inspiring, American ideals of republican manhood, which similarly emphasized independence and resistance to tyranny. It also reflected a broader American emphasis on self-improvement and the cultivation of inner character, both important components of nineteenth-century constructions of manhood. Finally, Romantic masculinity served the needs of the Romantic writers themselves, who were attempting to establish careers as authors in a society that was disinclined to view writing or other forms of intellectual work as true labor, and therefore regarded male writers as unmanly and effeminate.

Romantic Heroes and Antiheroes

Another important motif in Romantic thought and literature is that of the male protagonist as hero or conqueror. While in European Romanticism this figure operated in fantastic settings and was characterized by a high degree of emotional courtship, the American version was rooted in a much more realistic stance and in a harsh natural setting. Conquering and expanding the western frontier, for instance, inspired a more conservative view on gender, in which the male explorer became the counterpart of the effeminate poet, while the female was to a large extent desexualized, rather than romantically idealized, because she was expected to play her part in overcoming the hardships of life on the trail. The works of nineteenth-century historian Francis Parkman, which emphasize white Americans' conquest of the spectacular natural environment into which they are nonetheless thoroughly integrated, typify this approach to American manhood.

Not only white American men served as heroes in Romantic tales, however. Drawing on French philosopher Jean-Jacques Rousseau's idea that civilization was responsible for social inequality—and that there was no inequality in nature—American Romantic authors portrayed some non-white men as "noble savages" characterized by a natural masculinity that placed them in harmonious balance with their natural environment and with each other. Yet as the term itself suggests, this perception of a natural masculinity was wrought with ambivalence. On the one hand, the "savage" individual was presented as a positive counterpoint to the aggressive, colonizing white representatives of so-called civilized society—in accordance with the view held by Romantics that the imaginative powers of the human mind should rule over its rational dimension. Yet Romantic writers often produced overly romantic and condescending images of indigenous American peoples, as is evident in such male fictional characters as Queequeg in *Moby Dick* (1852), Geronimo, and Tarzan. These images had a strong impact on the shaping and perception of male identity in nineteenth- and twentieth-century America.

Romanticism also produced a marked antiheroic type: The literary subcategory of "Gothic" or "Dark" Romanticism portrayed the horror that resulted from masculine individualism run amok. Featuring oversensitive and idiosyncratic types whose nervousness, excessive rejection of reason, and overindulgence in emotion and introspection produce a total distortion of the mind, these works suggest that extreme versions of Romantic masculinity actually undermine true manhood by casting men into forms of savagery. *Moby Dick*'s Captain Ahab, for example, absorbed in a quixotic and obsessive quest to capture and destroy a whale, ultimately destroys his own navigational instruments and becomes a frightening figure far more savage than Queequeg. Such self-destructive and emotionally tortured masculine characters are also common in the works of Nathaniel Hawthorne and Edgar Allen Poe.

Impact of Romanticism

The legacy and continuing impact of Romanticism remained visible in American culture throughout the twentieth century. Romanticism and its notions of ideal masculinity were particularly strong influences on the works of the Beat writers of the 1950s, who sought to develop their masculine identities in rejection of what they perceived to be the excessively conformist and suburban society around them. Nonconformist approaches to maleness and the ideal of a harmonious relation between man and nature also characterized the countercultural and environmental movements of the 1960s.

More broadly, American men continued to oppose any form of restraint, stressing the desire to live their lives according to their own projections. The heroic conqueror living in close proximity to nature and in an ambivalent relation to Euro-American civilization became a standard masculine ideal that has persisted in film productions of the Western genre. The introspective, nonconformist, emotionally sensitive, yet tortured young male soul searching for truth became an iconic film type beginning with James Dean's performance in *Rebel Without a Cause* (1955). Romanticism thus remains a powerful influence on American ideals of manhood.

Bibliography

Emerson, Ralph Waldo. *The Journals and Miscellaneous Notebooks.* Edited by William H. Gilman and J. E. Parsons. Cambridge, Mass.: Belknap Press, 1960.

———. *Selected Essays, Lectures, and Poems.* Edited by Robert E. Spiller. New York: Washington Square Press, 1965.

Hawthorne, Nathaniel. *The Scarlet Letter. Centenary Edition of the Works of Nathaniel Hawthorne.* Vol. I. Columbus: Ohio State University Press, 1963.

Leverenz, David. *Manhood and the American Renaissance.* Ithaca, N.Y.: Cornell University Press, 1989.

Melville, Herman. *Moby Dick, or the Whale. The Writings of Herman Melville.* Northwestern-Newberry Edition. Edited by Harrison Hayford, Hershel Parker, and G. Thomas Tanselle. Vol. VI. Evanston, Ill.: Northwestern University Press, 1988.

Rousseau, Jean-Jacques. *The Discourses and Other Early Political Writings.* Edited by Victor Gourevitch. Cambridge, England: Cambridge University Press, 1997.

Whitman, Walt. *Leaves of Grass.* Edited by Sculley Bradley and Harold W. Blodgett. New York: Norton, 1973.

Further Reading

Andrews, William L., ed. *Literary Romanticism in America.* Baton Rouge: Louisiana State University Press, 1981.

Bell, Michael Davitt. *The Development of American Romance: The Sacrifice of Relation.* Chicago: University of Chicago Press, 1980.

Bradfield, Scott. *Dreaming Revolution: Transgression in the Development of American Romance.* Iowa City: University of Iowa Press, 1993.

Carton, Evan. *The Rhetoric of American Romance.* Baltimore: Johns Hopkins University Press, 1985.

DeMott, Robert J., and Sanford E. Marovitz, eds. *Artful Thunder: Versions of the Romantic Tradition in American Literature.* Kent, Ohio: Kent State University Press, 1975.

Fulford, Tim. *Romanticism and Masculinity: Gender, Politics, and Poetics in the Writings of Burke, Coleridge, Cobbett, Wordsworth, DeQuincey, and Hazlitt.* New York: St. Martin's, 1999.

Goodman, Russel B. *American Philosophy and the Romantic Tradition.* Cambridge, England: Cambridge University Press, 1990.

Morse, David. *American Romanticism.* 2 vols. New York: Barnes and Noble, 1987.

Taylor, Beverly, and Robert Bain, eds. *The Cast of Consciousness: Concepts of the Mind in British and American Romanticism.* New York: Greenwood Press, 1987.

Wu, Duncan, ed. *A Companion to Romanticism.* Oxford: Blackwell, 1998.

Related Entries

Art; Beat Movement; Character; Counterculture; Emerson, Ralph Waldo; Heroism; Individualism; Kerouac, Jack; *Moby Dick*; Native American Manhood; Postmodernism; Republicanism; Tarzan; Thoreau, Henry David; Western Frontier; Whitman, Walt

—*Bret E. Carroll and Markus Oliver Spitz*

Roosevelt, Theodore

1858–1919
U.S. President

At the beginning of the twentieth century, many white middle-class Americans feared that a shift in lifestyles—from manual labor and frontier expansionism to professional careers and urban living—would make men weak. Theodore Roosevelt, who came of age at a time when these changes caused considerable anxiety about the future of American manhood, created a new image of masculinity that combined education, physical strength, and rugged individualism. As president of the United States (1901–09), Roosevelt extended these ideals from the individual to the national level.

As a boy, Theodore Roosevelt was often ill. His health improved during his teens when he forced himself to increase his physical strength. In 1881, at the age of twenty-three, he won a seat in the state assembly of New York, where, despite his healthy physique, the local press ridiculed him as effeminate. While this may have been due to class differences between Roosevelt and other local politicians, Roosevelt responded by purchasing a ranch in the Dakota Territories where he could prove his manhood. There, he immersed himself in ranch life and wrote *Hunting Trips of a Ranchman* (1885), in which he stressed the importance of vigor and courage in hunting wild animals, as well as qualities such as thrift and restraint. Through hunting and writing, Roosevelt contributed to an emerging image of western white men as rugged individuals. By 1886, when he ran for mayor of New York City, he had reconstructed himself into a robust cowboy; nonetheless, he was defeated.

Throughout his life, Roosevelt remained an active politician. In 1889, President Benjamin Harrison appointed him to the Civil Service Commission, and he was reappointed to a second term in 1893. In 1898, Roosevelt resigned his position as Assistant Secretary of the Navy to participate in the Spanish-American War. He received a commission as colonel and formed a cavalry regiment. The men in the regiment were from Ivy League colleges and western ranches, thus demonstrating Roosevelt's belief that both education and outdoorsmanship were important to masculine living. Roosevelt invited members of the press to travel with his men. Consequently the press provided the public with extensive coverage of the regiment's activities and, because of their colorful antics, dubbed them the "Rough Riders." As a result of the regiment's success, Roosevelt returned to the United States as a war hero and was elected governor of New York. The following year he was running mate to victorious presidential candidate William McKinley. When McKinley was assassinated in 1901, Roosevelt became president of the United States.

Theodore Roosevelt, pictured (center) with members of the Rough Riders in 1898, advocated a model of masculinity combining education, physical strength, outdoorsmanship, and military prowess. His successful command of the Rough Riders during the Spanish-American War made Roosevelt a national war hero and helped propel him to the presidency. (AP/Wide World Photos)

As president, Roosevelt used his office to extend his masculine ideologies to national politics. He gave speeches and wrote public letters that called on white men to be active in politics and strong patriarchs at home. He also argued that it was their public responsibility to procreate. In 1903 he published his now infamous letter on "race suicide," promoting his belief in the superiority of the white race in America and abroad. In addition, he advocated a strong military, increased the size of the U.S. navel force (his stated policy was to "speak softly and carry a big stick"), and began the building of the Panama Canal.

After leaving office in 1909, Roosevelt went to Africa on a hunting expedition; his published account of this adventure recorded his hunting of rhinos, elephants, and lions. In 1912, Roosevelt again ran for president under the banner of the Progressive Party, which had split from the Republican Party and was called the "Bull Moose" Party because Roosevelt claimed to feel as strong as a bull moose. This was Roosevelt's last campaign for public office, and he won 27.4 percent of the popular vote.

In his lifetime, Theodore Roosevelt came to symbolize white masculinity. He valued western frontiersmen as exemplary American men and encouraged the men of his generation to embrace rigorous living through sports and outdoor recreation. A highly visible public figure, he produced and spread a new image of white masculinity that combined rugged frontier values with qualities such as education, public service, and self-restraint.

BIBLIOGRAPHY

Bederman, Gail. *Manliness and Civilization: A Cultural History of Gender and Race in the United States, 1880-1917.* Chicago: University of Chicago Press, 1996.

Friedenberg, Robert V. *Theodore Roosevelt and the Rhetoric of Militant Decency.* New York: Greenwood Press, 1990.

Keller, Morton. *Theodore Roosevelt: A Profile.* New York: Hill and Wang, 1967.

Kerr, Joan Paterson, ed. *A Bully Father: Theodore Roosevelt's Letters to His Children.* New York: Random House, 1995.

Testi, Arnaldo. "The Gender of Reform Politics: Theodore Roosevelt and the Culture of Masculinity" *Journal of American History* 81, no. 4 (1995): 1509–1533.

FURTHER READING

Alfonso, Oscar M. *Theodore Roosevelt and the Philippines, 1897–1909.* Quezon City: University of the Philippines Press, 1970.

Morris, Edmund. *The Rise of Theodore Roosevelt.* New York: Coward, McCann & Geoghegan, 1979.

———. *Theodore Rex.* New York: Random House, 2001.

SELECTED WRITINGS

Roosevelt, Theodore. *Hunting Trips of a Ranchman: Sketches of Sport on the Northern Cattle Plains.* New York: Putman, 1885.

———. *The Strenuous Life.* New York: The Century Co., 1900.

———. *African Game Trails: An Account of an American Hunter-Naturalist.* New York: Scribner's, 1910.

RELATED ENTRIES

Body; Cowboys; Crisis of Masculinity; Education; Hunting; Imperialism; Individualism; Industrialization; Militarism; Nationalism; Progressive Era; Reproduction; Self-Control; Spanish-American War; Strenuous Life; Urbanization; War; Western Frontier; Whiteness

—*Linda Heidenreich*

Sandow, Eugen

1867–1925
Bodybuilder

Eugen Sandow, born in East Prussia as Friederich Wilhelm Muller, rose from a sideshow muscleman in the 1880s to international fame as a premier bodybuilder and, in the United States and Europe, a representative of an ideal physical masculine type. His image shaped the aesthetic and erotic sensibilities of millions of nineteenth- and twentieth-century fans, and the phrase "as strong as Sandow" became a byword for a strong man.

Sandow began bodybuilding in the midst of the *Turnvereine*, the German gymnastic movement of the 1880s. His professional career began with a circus in 1885 but changed significantly in Brussels when he met the German impresario Louis Attila, who trained Sandow as a weightlifter and music hall entertainer. Attila was soon encouraging Sandow to pose for sculptors, painters, and photographers, who documented his remarkable physique and self-control. Sandow then moved to London, where he became an international celebrity, performing on stage in a leopard skin, tights, and sandals. Lifting a piano or a small horse on stage, he thrilled audiences by displaying his physique and strength, as well as his wit, intelligence, and agility. In 1893 the Broadway producer Florenz Ziegfeld expanded Sandow's show business career by bringing his act to New York City. Together they made bodybuilding glamorous and popular in the United States.

Sandow's fame reflected and reinforced a fundamental transformation in American concepts of masculinity in the late nineteenth century. Amid the growing influence of Darwinian biology (such as the theories of natural selection and "survival of the fittest") and increasing anxiety that modern urban life had sapped the physical vigor of white middle-class American men, Sandow represented a new emphasis on bodily strength as a basic marker of manhood. He therefore appealed to a culture that was developing new ideas of "muscular Christianity" and the "strenuous life." Sandow's emphasis on proper diet, exercise, and a positive mental attitude coincided with the Victorian-era concern for self-discipline and physical purity. That Sandow was white and German inspired Anglo-Saxon Americans, who were concerned about the influx of immigrants from eastern and southern Europe and Asia.

Touted as the perfect man, Sandow became an entrepreneur for bodybuilding. He wrote articles connecting strength with health in *Cosmopolitan* magazine, published inspirational books, and sold his own dumbbells and exercise lessons. His performance at the World's Columbian Exposition in Chicago in 1893 inspired the young Bernarr Macfadden (who became another prominent exponent of muscular masculinity) and introduced physical training to millions of Americans.

Perhaps Sandow's greatest impact occurred when he organized the first nationwide bodybuilding competition in England in 1901, thus stimulating other national contests elsewhere. French contests also judged the most handsome athlete, and German contests rewarded the strongest weightlifter, but Americans combined these competitions in the 1930s to find "Mr. America," the man with the finest physique. All of these exhibitions and performances, like modern sports in general, linked a strong manly body with a strong manly character.

By the time of his death in 1925, Sandow had become such a popular figure that his wife, Blanche, buried him in an unmarked grave at the Putney Vale Cemetery in London. But Sandow's influence extended far beyond his death; the emphasis on physique and health that he helped establish as gauges of manhood has persisted into the twenty-first century.

Bibliography

Adam, G. Mercer, and Eugen Sandow. *Sandow on Physical Training: A Study in the Perfect Type of the Human Form.* New York: J. S. Tait & Sons, 1894.

Chapman, David L. *Adonis: The Male Physique Pin-Up, 1870–1940.* Boston: Alyson Publications, 1989.

———. *Sandow the Magnificent: Eugen Sandow and the Beginnings of Bodybuidling.* Urbana: University of Illinois Press, 1994.

Kasson, John F. *Houdini, Tarzan, and the Perfect Man: The White Male Body and the Challenge of Modernity in America.* New York: Hill and Wang, 2001.

Kimmel, Michael. *Manhood in America: A Cultural History.* New York: Free Press, 1996.

Mainardi, Robert, ed. *Strong Man: Vintage Photos of a Masculine Icon.* San Francisco: Council Oak Books, 2001.

Rotundo, E. Anthony. *American Manhood: Transformations in Masculinity from the Revolution to the Modern Era.* New York: Basic Books, 1993.

FURTHER READING

Bederman, Gail. *Manliness and Civilization: A Cultural History of Gender and Race in the United States, 1880–1917*. Chicago: University of Chicago Press, 1995.

Green, Harvey. *Fit for America: Health, Fitness, Sport and American Society*. New York: Pantheon, 1986.

SELECTED WRITINGS

Sandow, Eugen. *Strength, and How to Obtain It*. London: Gale and Polden, 1901.

RELATED ENTRIES

Body; Bodybuilding; Darwinism; Health; Middle-Class Manhood; Muscular Christianity; Self-Control; Sports; Strenuous Life; Victorian Era

—*Peter C. Holloran*

SAWYER, TOM

Tom Sawyer and his best friend, Huckleberry Finn, are featured in four novels by Mark Twain: *Adventures of Tom Sawyer* (1876), *Adventures of Huckleberry Finn* (1884), *Tom Sawyer Abroad* (1894), and *Tom Sawyer, Detective* (1896). Although Huck Finn is the older boy and the narrator of the last three novels, Tom Sawyer is the undisputed leader and inventor of their adventures. Huck may be a rough boy of nature, but Tom Sawyer is the ultimate "bad" good boy, a trickster who also serves as an emblem of American boyhood.

Mark Twain's intention with *Adventures of Tom Sawyer* was less to create a classic boy's book than to write a gentle parody of the moralistic children's literature written by authors such as Horatio Alger, Jr., and Louisa May Alcott. Written for adults, this novel is a more honest and complex portrait of childhood than contemporary novels, which featured ideal (good) boys and girls.

The Tom Sawyer novels, which include slave playmates and storytellers, were influenced by Twain's integrated childhood, which explains Tom and Huck's appeal across racial boundaries. The literary figure that Tom most resembles is his contemporary Brer Rabbit, of Joel Chandler Harris' Uncle Remus stories. The way Tom Sawyer cons his friends into paying for the privilege of doing his chores by proclaiming the joys of whitewashing a fence is similar to Brer Rabbit's famous ploy of begging "whatever you do, don't throw me into the briar patch" when that is exactly where he wants to go. Tom only appears in the last section of *Adventures of Huckleberry Finn*, yet he completely drives the narrative after his arrival. For instance, Tom insists on orchestrating a fittingly dramatic escape for the slave Jim, rather than reveal to Huck that Jim was legally freed months earlier.

Although Huck longs to "light out for the territories"—in keeping with nineteenth-century models of manhood requiring an escape from a stifling urban life—Tom's mischief requires a community setting. Tom, more like the urban street urchin than the frontier loner, rebels against nothing except adult control. He uses games, pranks, and superstitions to balance the feminine-controlled middle-class community. Tom understands the rules of society, and he beats society at its own game. As an orphan raised by his Aunt Polly, Tom has all the comforts of a small-town, middle-class home life—but without the expectations of parents. His male identity is thus grounded equally in domesticity and a "natural" boyishness. While Alger's urban good boys demonstrated the value of paternalistic nurture, Tom actively resists any attempts at paternal or maternal control, possibly to the point of usurping paternal authority himself and exercising it over Huck and his other friends. Fishing appears as a common scene in the novels, serving as a refuge from adult influence. While family may be tangential to Tom, friendship with other boys is Tom's highest priority—at least when it does not interfere with his self-centered need for adventure.

Tom Sawyer has remained a major figure in popular American images of boyhood through the continued popularity of Twain's novels and their adaptations into plays, film, and television. He serves as the exemplar for twentieth-century boy tricksters like Dennis the Menace, Calvin of *Calvin and Hobbes*, Bart Simpson, and many other young male characters who rebel against the expectations of adult society and the ideals of middle-class domesticity by demanding more adventure from life.

BIBLIOGRAPHY

Fishkin, Shelley Fisher. *Was Huck Black? Mark Twain and African-American Voices*. New York: Oxford University Press, 1993.

Norton, Charles A. *Writing Tom Sawyer: The Adventures of a Classic*. Jefferson, N.C.: McFarland, 1983.

Railton, Stephen. "Adventures of Tom Sawyer." In *Mark Twain in His Times*. Electronic Text Center, University of Virginia. <http://etext.lib.Virginia.edu/railton> (January 20, 2003).

Scharnhorst, Gary, ed. *Critical Essays on the Adventures of Tom Sawyer*. New York: G. K. Hall, 1993.

FURTHER READING

de Koster, Katie, ed. *Readings on the Adventures of Huckleberry Finn*. San Diego, Calif.: Greenhaven Press, 1998.

Griswold, Jerome. *Audacious Kids: Coming of Age in America's Classic Children's Books.* New York: Oxford University Press, 1992.
Hutchinson, Stephen, ed. *Mark Twain, Tom Sawyer and Huckleberry Finn.* New York: Columbia University Press, 1999.

RELATED ENTRIES
Adventures of Huckleberry Finn; Alger, Horatio, Jr.; Boyhood; Fishing; Male Friendship; Middle-Class Manhood; Slavery; Southern Manhood; Urbanization; Youth

—*Elizabeth Abele*

SCHWARZENEGGER, ARNOLD

1947–
Film Star and Bodybuilder

During the 1980s, Arnold Schwarzenegger visibly symbolized an ideal of muscularized masculinity that gained currency as Republican president Ronald Reagan, promising to restore national strength after the economic and foreign policy woes of the 1970s, presented himself and his policies as tough and aggressive. As the 1990s approached, Schwarzenegger, continuing to reflect a conservative cultural agenda, successfully reinvented himself as a signifier of men's attempt to reclaim a domestic authority that had been challenged since the 1970s.

Schwarzenegger, who won the Mr. World, Mr. Universe, and Mr. Olympia titles before his retirement from professional bodybuilding in 1975, first became a widely known symbol of hypermuscular masculinity in the United States when he was featured in the documentary film *Pumping Iron* (1977), which chronicled the behind-the-scenes action at the Mr. Olympia competition. Previously considered a narcissistic and, thereby, feminized preoccupation, bodybuilding found a new appreciation among American men in the 1970s amid a growing cultural emphasis on self-realization and self-fulfillment. It allowed American men to embrace the softer, more self-centered brand of masculinity that the culture required, while they also maintained such requisite traits of traditional masculinity as strength, health, and heroism.

Schwarzenegger achieved even greater national fame through his films of the 1980s and 1990s, in which he offered models of ideal masculinity that changed with the times. During the 1980s, as Reagan sought to appeal to white middle-class men by promoting corporate growth, reducing the size of the federal government, and pursuing an aggressive foreign policy, Schwarzenegger starred in action films as an extraordinary-everyman figure. These films fed masculine fantasies of escape from the pressures of corporate work

Arnold Schwarzenegger on the beach at the 1977 Cannes Film Festival in France, where his documentary film Pumping Iron *was presented. Schwarzenegger fueled a new cultural appreciation of bodybuilding and, during the 1980s, symbolized an ideal of muscular masculinity that reflected an anxious concern with national military strength. (AP/Wide World Photos)*

and suburban life, supported Reagan's militaristic policies by seeking justice through violence, and indirectly praised Reagan's approach to government by featuring heroic military figures who defied inefficient institutional bureaucracies that stood in the way of social improvement. Such films as *Commando* (1985), *Predator* (1987), and *The Running Man* (1987) addressed the concerns of white middle-class men who feared marginalization within a society in which minorities and women were competing for their jobs and challenging their authority.

In the 1990s a growing men's movement advised men to embrace their emotional and nurturing sides and spawned a fathers' rights movement. At the same time, cultural conservatives urged the importance of fatherhood, criticized feminism and single motherhood, and stirred national political debates about "family values." In response, Schwarzenegger's films shifted toward a softer form of masculinity. In films like *Kindergarten Cop* (1990) and *Terminator 2: Judgment Day* (1991), Schwarzenegger's characters begin as cold-hearted killing machines but gradually learn to use their skills in defense of traditional family values. Fathering becomes the vehicle for portraying masculine emotions, ethics, and commitments; for reasserting patriarchal authority; and for counteracting deficient parenting by career women and single mothers. In *Terminator 2,* for example, Sarah Connor's obsessive efforts to prevent the end of the world have landed her in a mental institution and her son in foster care.

Since the early 1990s, Schwarzenegger's allure seems to have faded amid new cultural developments. As contemporary American masculinity has begun to look inward in order to assign blame for the supposed erosion of its authority, cultural representations of masculinity have become more concerned with exploring male anxieties and neuroses than in constructing fantasies of male heroism.

BIBLIOGRAPHY

Flynn, John L. *The Films of Arnold Schwarzenegger.* Secaucus, N.J.: Carol Publishing Group, 1993.

Jeffords, Susan. *Hard Bodies: Hollywood Masculinity in the Reagan Era.* New Brunswick, N.J.: Rutgers University Press, 1994.

Tasker, Yvonne. *Spectacular Bodies: Gender, Genre, and the Action Cinema.* London: Routledge, 1993.

FURTHER READING

Andrew, Nigel. *True Myths: The Life and Times of Arnold Schwarzenegger.* New York: Birch Lane Press, 1996.

Dyer, Richard. "The White Man's Muscles." In *The Masculinity Studies Reader,* edited by Rachel Adams and David Savran. Malden, Mass.: Blackwell, 2002.

RELATED ENTRIES

Body; Bodybuilding; Business/Corporate America; Emotion; Fatherhood; Feminism; Health; Heroism; Hollywood; Men's Movements; Militarism; Patriarchy; Reagan, Ronald; Sensitive Male; Suburbia; Violence

—*Avi Santo*

SEDUCTION TALES

In the late eighteenth century, American presses began to produce a stream of seduction tales for young female readers. These narratives, detailing the seduction and abandonment of young women by male predators, were inspired by the mid-eighteenth-century writings of British author Samuel Richardson. Growing anxieties in America surrounding courtships, which were no longer under the strict surveillance of parents and the community, ensured the popularity of these stories. Initially displaying considerable imagination and flexibility regarding masculinity, seduction tales ultimately propagated a vision of men as aggressive and lustful.

This model of virile manhood marked a significant departure from colonial thinking. Colonists believed that women, as descendants of Eve, were more lustful than men, while men were thought more capable of rational control over their animal appetites. But by the nineteenth century most Americans assumed that men were more sexually driven than women. Seduction tales were critical to this reformulation. The image of the male seducer, paired with the image of the chaste female victim, helped establish an emerging sexual double standard in which male sexual aggression was accepted as natural and a strong female sexuality was considered abnormal.

Social Context for Early Seduction Tales

Among the most popular of the early American seduction tales were Susanna Rowson's *Charlotte Temple* (1794), which was the most widely published novel in America until the publication of *Uncle Tom's Cabin* in 1852, and Hannah Foster's *The Coquette* (1797). In the 1780s and 1790s, American periodicals were also producing a broad range of short stories about sexual betrayal. Such fiction resonated with the American public, for by the late eighteenth century American youth were exercising considerably greater sexual freedom than had their parents—as evidenced by rising premarital pregnancy and bastardy rates. By the Revolutionary era, nearly a third of first-born children were being conceived out of wedlock. As the supply of inheritable land declined, particularly in the urban Northeast, parents lost influence over the courtship of their children. Ideological attacks on patriarchy in the Revolutionary era also contributed to growing freedom for the young; parents who interfered with matters of the heart were deemed to be tyrants similar to the British king.

Sexual independence had obvious benefits for the young, but it also entailed risks. Most obviously, a growing geographic mobility meant that men were more liable to leave a pregnant woman behind. Mobile young men represented a threat not only to family but to political order, for a rise in seduction jeopardized the republican emphasis on a virtuous citizenry. For republican thinkers, marriage, as a consensual and honorable union, imitated the relationship among citizens in a republic. As trust in men eroded, wives were expected to act as a positive influence on husbands. A republic of young men cut loose from such influence was feared as a place rife with contention.

A Frustrated Message of Reform

Seduction tales not only expressed social and political anxieties but also offered strategies to resolve them. A handful of tales that drew on eighteenth-century Enlightenment theories, such as the moral-sense philosophies of David Hume and Adam Smith, suggested that male sensibility might prevent the seduction of women. These ideas represent a path mostly not taken in American masculinity. According to prevailing definitions of sensibility, men and women alike had the ability to feel sympathy for others in pain. This idea had the potential to blur distinctions between men and women, since sensibility challenged prevailing expectations that men assume a stoic demeanor when confronting distress. Following this logic, authors such as Hannah Foster tried to instruct young men about the consequences of seduction. Foster's seducer character, Major Sanford, felt guilty and regretful when he realized that his actions had led to the death of heroine Eliza Wharton. Presumably, men who read seduction tales might learn to avoid Sanford's mistakes. Thus, some seduction tales explored a model of masculinity aimed at engendering male responsibility for premarital chastity. Yet even authors who explored male sensibility undermined the influence of this masculine ideal by spending much more time in their stories depicting the dangerous qualities of men.

Crafting a Double Standard

Seduction tales, which ultimately depicted men as deceptive and immoral, implicitly endorsed predatory behavior in men. By suggesting that men were naturally more lustful than women, and thus beyond hope for reform, authors placed the burden on women to work to avoid being ensnared by deceptive men. The most extremely dangerous seducers, the young male dandies, can be seen as symbolic of the lure of British luxuries. However, these tales transcended republican discourse. Most men were painted with a broad brush that put them all within the pale of suspicion.

The central villain figure in these tales, the young male seducer, became a stereotype that was used to scare young women into seeking parental guidance in marriage. At the very least, women were to exercise chastity before wedlock. The male seducers used stratagems such as false promises of marriage to gain sexual access to women. Authors hurled a range of epithets at young men in these tales, such as "designing villain," "cruel robber," "base dissembler," and "betraying enemy," all of which reflected the men's less than virtuous intentions.

While the primary lesson of the tales was targeted at women, men could hardly avoid making meaning of them. Seduction tales opened the door for a legitimation, and even valorization, of male libertinism. By the mid–nineteenth century a variety of periodicals appeared in urban America—including *The Rake, The Whip, The Flash,* and *The Libertine*—that deliberately catered to and endorsed a virile, sexually aggressive masculinity. Such publications cultivated a male sporting culture in which aggression against women was celebrated. Across American culture, images of male immorality and female chastity reinforced one another as opposites. Their mutual articulation laid essential groundwork for the "cult of domesticity," an ideology that rationalized female homemaking and male economic and political power by suggesting the need to shelter female purity and compassion from the dangerous and aggressively competitive world of men.

Seduction Narrative Unravels

Although seduction tales created enduring constructions of masculinity and femininity in American culture, they began to lose credibility as the nineteenth century proceeded, for they failed to capture the complexity of American sexual life. The concept of seduction retained resonance, but writers increasingly imagined that men as well as women could fall prey to sexual ploys. The stereotypes of female victim and male predator were especially strained when moral reformers in the nineteenth century began working with prostitutes. Early-nineteenth-century moral reformers assumed prostitutes were the victims of male villainy, but reformers in the urban North became frustrated with women who were willing to play their assigned roles as wronged and repentant women for only so long before returning to the streets again. By midcentury, male reformers began to develop a darker picture of prostitutes and more sympathy for young men. According to their formulation, if courtesans had once been victims of seduction, they had become seducers in turn, luring young men into illicit commerce and augmenting the dangers awaiting naive country boys in the city. Although reformers still worried about the dangers posed by young men, they increasingly saw them as corruptible and sought to protect them in their innocence. The fact that men had a stronger libido than women merely meant that they were all the more vulnerable to the ploys of courtesans. New seduction narratives—such as Joseph Holt Ingraham's *Frank Rivers* (1843), in which women wielded sex as a weapon against men—mirrored the trajectory of popular reform thought.

These challenges to the standard seduction narrative, however, did not fundamentally undermine notions of female purity and male virility, for reformers and writers increasingly observed a class boundary between chaste middle-class women and lecherous working class women. From this perspective, only women from the dangerous immigrant and working classes were liable to violate purity; middle-class women continued to be understood as morally and sexually pure. Images of masculinity were transformed even less. Although some female reformers, such as those joining female moral reform societies of the 1830s and 1840s, armed themselves with a more strident version of the seduction narrative and called on men to adopt chastity and accept responsibility for their sexual misdeeds, most Americans assumed that men were, by nature, more lustful than women. Even sex reformers who warned young men against the dangers of masturbation believed that men had stronger natural urges for sex. While they believed that women could exist without any desire, men were urged to sublimate their sexual energy into economic endeavors. In a growing market economy, male sexuality was important and even necessary, and men were considered to be at a competitive advantage with their reservoir of sexual energy.

As a coherent and consistent stock narrative, the seduction tale disappeared by the middle of the nineteenth century. Undermined by sexually promiscuous women and fears for innocent men, it could not fully comprehend the American sexual landscape, but many of the themes and ideas it developed persist to the present, however. In the twenty-first century, the stigma attached to women who violate chastity persists, and while women who do so are called "sluts," American culture lacks a similarly familiar term for a sexually aggressive male. The seduction tale's notions about manhood also endure. Fantasies of male virility, first stoked in seduction tales, continue to inform popular portrayals of men. The sexually charged, dark, and handsome man of romance novels and soap operas continues to allure and frighten.

Bibliography

Cohen, Patricia Cline. *The Murder of Helen Jewett: The Life and Death of a Prostitute in Nineteenth-Century New York.* New York: Knopf, 1998.

Cott, Nancy F. "Passionlessness: An Interpretation of Victorian Sexual Ideology, 1790–1850." *Signs* 4, no. 2 (1978): 219–236.

Davidson, Cathy N. *Revolution and the Word: The Rise of the Novel in America.* New York: Oxford University Press, 1986.

Fliegelman, Jay. *Prodigals and Pilgrims: The American Revolution Against Patriarchal Authority, 1750–1800.* New York: Cambridge University Press, 1982.

Hessinger, Rodney. "Insidious Murderers of Female Innocence": Representations of Masculinity in the Seduction Tales of the Late Eighteenth Century." In *Sex and Sexuality in Early America,* edited by Merril D. Smith. New York: New York University Press, 1998.

———. "Victim of Seduction or Vicious Woman? Conceptions of the Prostitute at the Philadelphia Magdalen Society, 1800–1850." *Explorations in Early America Culture: Supplemental Issue on Pennsylvania History* 66 (1999): 201–222.

Further Reading

Gross, Robert A. *The Minutemen and Their World.* New York: Hill and Wang, 1976.

Lewis, Jan. "The Republican Wife: Virtue and Seduction in the Early Republic." *William and Mary Quarterly* 3, no. 44 (1987): 689–721.

Reynolds, David S. *Beneath the American Renaissance: The Subversive Imagination in the Age of Emerson and Melville.* Cambridge, Mass.: Harvard University Press, 1989.

Smith-Rosenberg, Carroll. "Domesticating 'Virtue': Coquettes and Revolutionaries in Young America." In *Literature and the Body: Essays on Population and Persons,* edited by Elaine Scarry. Baltimore: Johns Hopkins University Press, 1988.

Related Entries

Advice Literature; American Revolution; *Contrast, The*; Cult of Domesticity; Heterosexuality; Masturbation; Patriarchy; Prostitution; Reform Movements; Republicanism; Sentimentalism; Youth

—*Rodney Hessinger*

Self-Control

"Control yourself!" is a common message that Americans of both sexes begin hearing at a young age, though it is an admonition that often carries greater intensity and has wider implications when addressed to males. Over the course of American history, different aspects of restraint—sometimes emotional, at other times sexual or economic—have been stressed. The call for self-control has roots in the Puritans' scrutiny of their thoughts and actions, but it began to have a particular significance for men, both politically and personally, after the American Revolution, an event that was essentially about self-governance. Subsequently—whether resisting women's desire for a wider role in society or justifying discrimination against blacks and other minorities—white Protestant males often claimed a greater capacity for self-control and labeled it an essential requirement for full participation in a political democracy. Even after women and ethnic minorities became full political participants, self-control remained a matter of greater importance for men in private life. Sometimes celebrated and sometimes criticized, an emphasis on self-control has been at the heart of dominant cultural requirements for manhood.

In sixteenth-century Europe, the Protestant Reformation introduced the proposition that the most legitimate earthly authority governing human actions was the individual. New England Puritans saw themselves as the most faithful upholders of this belief. The Puritans did not overtly link control of self to their sense of manhood, but they did consider men's activities of more consequence than those of women. The American Revolution put into much wider practice the notion that the best authority was not external to the person governed. The republican ideology informing the revolution linked self-control more tightly to manhood by confining political activity to men and making control of the self—the subordination of self-interest to civic spirit—an important political value. In the new nation, a woman's most important role was to train her sons for republican citizenship by instilling in them self-reliance and self-control.

The generation of the American Revolution believed that the success of their experiment in republican government required male self-control. John Adams worried liberty might lead to wealth, which in turn might produce unseemly self-indulgence. Thomas Jefferson, too, frequently expressed concern about unchecked indulgence of physical urges. Benjamin Rush, a political thinker, physician, and the founder of American psychiatry, wrote extensively about the need to cultivate a new type of personality that suited a republican society's need for self-controlled men. Drawing on Enlightenment notions linking manhood, political order, self-control, and a mechanistic cosmology, Rush urged that American males must become no less than "republican machines" who shunned unproductive play and idleness.

The onset of industrialization, urbanization, and the market revolution in the nineteenth century further reinforced the premium on male self-control. The rapidly industrializing society prized orderliness, time-consciousness, industriousness, and restraint, and the unprecedented situations that many men encountered in their new urban environments—as well as the new market economy itself—lent a fresh urgency to self-control and prompted the appearance of a growing body of advice literature. Men were increasingly urged to avoid drinking and shun excessive selfishness in their pursuit of wealth. Masturbation became a particularly worrisome example of a man's loss of self-control, a concern addressed by Rush and apparently widely shared by nineteenth-century Americans. So serious was the worry that a man might overspend himself sexually, sapping vital energy needed for work, that the historian G. J. Barker-Benfield has written of the era's "economy of sperm." Men of an emerging middle class linked manhood, whiteness, and self-control, justifying their social position and economic success through the notion that they controlled themselves better than did black or working-class males.

As economic growth generated a gradual shift from production to consumption in the late nineteenth and early twentieth centuries, however, the culture's emphasis on restraint became increasingly problematic. If Americans were too restrained in a society of expanding production, the manufacturers' nightmare of warehouses overflowing with products might be realized. While self-control hardly disappeared as a cultural priority, mixed messages began to emerge as Americans were urged to spend as never before in what historian William Leach has called "the land of desire." Initially, consumption was seen as a womanly activity, especially in the new palaces of consumption, department stores. But economic necessity required a loosening of the association of consumption with femininity, and males were increasingly urged to indulge themselves as consumers as the twentieth century progressed. Similarly, American society grew more at ease with sexual pleasure for men and women alike, and earlier taboos on masturbation faded. For instance, the 1953 appearance of *Playboy* magazine heralded a new ethic of male consumerism and free sexuality.

However, as much as men might be urged to "let go" economically in a consumer culture, the emphasis on male emotional restraint has remained. Further, not only has the control of the self remained a gendered issue, but so has the control of others. Although men and women might share control of more everyday situations than ever before, many Americans of both sexes still view being in control—of a corporation or of one's self—as something more natural to men. As such, shopping is still widely perceived as a feminine activity, while male shopping is often seen as most appropriate on items culturally defined as essentially masculine, such as automobiles, sporting goods, or power tools.

At the same time, however, cultural associations of masculinity with self-control have faced a range of new challenges. There was growing concern during the late twentieth century over the physical and psychological price of excessive self-control, believed to be more common among men. Psychologists identified the "Type A" personality of those who put too much emphasis on self-discipline and control with proneness to heart disease and other disorders. The Harvard psychologist William Pollack, meanwhile, reflecting and promoting increasing concern over the troubled states of young American men, argued in his best-selling book *Real Boys* (1998) that

American boys had become excessively self-disciplined and trapped in emotional cages of their own construction. Unlike the nation's founders, many Americans began to worry that men exercise too much, not too little, self-control.

Bibliography

Farrell, Warren. *Why Men Are the Way They Are.* New York: McGraw-Hill, 1986.

Pugh, David G. *Sons of Liberty: The Masculine Mind in Nineteenth-Century America.* Westport, Conn.: Greenwood Press, 1983.

Rotundo, E. Anthony. *American Manhood: Transformations in Masculinity from the Revolution to the Modern Era.* New York: Basic Books, 1993.

Takaki, Ronald T. *Iron Cages: Race and Culture in Nineteenth-Century America.* New York: Oxford University Press, 1990.

Further Reading

D'Emilio, John, and Estelle B. Freedman. *Intimate Matters: A History of Sexuality in America.* 2nd ed. Chicago: University of Chicago Press, 1997.

Kasson, John F. *Houdini, Tarzan, and the Perfect Man: The White Male Body and the Challenge of Modernity in America.* New York: Hill and Wang, 2001.

Kimmel, Michael. *Manhood in America: A Cultural History.* New York: Free Press, 1996.

Leach, William. *Land of Desire: Merchants, Power, and the Rise of a New American Culture.* New York: Pantheon, 1993.

Pollack, William. *Real Boys: Rescuing Our Sons from the Myths of Boyhood.* New York: Random House, 1998.

Related Entries

Adolescence; Advertising; Advice Literature; Alcohol; Bachelorhood; Boyhood; Breadwinner Role; Character; Citizenship; Consumerism; Democratic Manhood; Emotion; Gambling; Health; Individualism; Industrialization; Leisure; Masturbation; Medicine; Middle-Class Manhood; Passionate Manhood; Republicanism; Self-Made Man; Sensitive Male; Sexual Revolution; Temperance

—John Ibson

Self-Made Man

The concept of the "self-made man"—the idea that a man can achieve success and fulfill the expectations of manhood through his own merit and hard work—has been central to American constructions of masculinity since the early nineteenth century. First articulated by the politician Henry Clay in 1832, the idea flourished during the Jacksonian era and became a nostalgic hope in the industrial and postindustrial eras.

Puritans grounded their concepts of manhood in family, church, and community, distrusting the man severed from these institutions as sinful and potentially barbaric. Most young men in colonial America achieved their social and economic stations with the help of established patriarchs who bestowed their sons and apprentices with land or training in a skilled trade. In his calling, a man was to serve God and community, not strive to advance his station. In keeping with this vision, all members of colonial society imagined themselves as part of a hierarchically arranged chain of being in which authority rested in patriarchs, kings, and God and relationships of patronage bound superiors and inferiors. Men were not understood to stand or succeed on their own merits in colonial society.

In the late eighteenth and early nineteenth centuries, however, the American Revolution and the market revolution eroded older notions of economic hierarchy and generated new emphases on self-governance and self-mastery. American men, particularly those of the emergent middle class, increasingly tied masculinity to their own ability to succeed in a competitive economic arena. This development was apparent in the writings of Benjamin Franklin. He presented in his *Autobiography*, written between 1771 and 1789, a model of success achieved through ingenuity and hard work. Franklin came to be seen as a heroic embodiment of self-made manhood during the Jacksonian period, when—despite an uneven distribution of wealth and the confinement of economic opportunity largely to white men—most men were self-employed and believed that they were in charge of their own destinies. Regarding self-control as necessary to success, advice writers instructed young men they were only truly "manly" when they had learned to check all indulgent impulses.

The ideal of self-made manhood was apparent not only in economic matters, but also in religion, as Americans increasingly rejected teachings about predestination in favor of the view that each man possessed free will and could achieve his own salvation. Similarly, the essayist Ralph Waldo Emerson urged self-reliance (dependence on the self alone for reaching truth) as the basis of American manhood. The idea of self-made manhood assumed its most exaggerated form in literary images of western frontiersman, self-sufficient men who lived wholly outside the constraints of women and cities.

During the late nineteenth and twentieth centuries, the idea of self-made manhood became increasingly problematic as the growth of industries and corporations left men increasingly in positions of economic dependency. No longer did self-employed master artisans ply their trade; instead, blue-collar workers labored in large factories with little hope of achieving economic independence. Middle-class men answered to bosses and became embedded in complex bureaucracies. Nonwhite men had yet another layer of limits put on their aspirations when architects of scientific racism sought to strengthen the tie between self-made manhood and whiteness by insisting that only white men could achieve upward mobility. Most men continued to define masculinity in relation to earnings, but they increasingly turned to other markers of male identity as well. Suburban lawns—where men still might shape their surroundings through home improvement and yardwork—became a compensatory frontier for office-bound men. For most American men, self-made manhood became an elusive, and therefore heroic, achievement—a symbol of a bygone era rather than a living reality.

Bibliography

Cawelti, John G. *Apostles of the Self-Made Man.* Chicago: University of Chicago Press, 1965.

Franklin, Benjamin. *Benjamin Franklin: The Autobiography and Other Writings.* Edited by L. Jesse Lemisch. New York: Signet Classics, 2001.

Horlick, Allan Stanley. *Country Boys and Merchant Princes: The Social Control of Young Men in New York.* Lewisburg, Penn.: Bucknell University Press, 1975.

Kimmel, Michael. *Manhood in America: A Cultural History.* New York: Free Press, 1996.

Further Reading

Halttunen, Karen. *Confidence Men and Painted Women: A Study of Middle-Class Culture in America, 1830–1870.* New Haven, Conn.: Yale University Press, 1982.

Smith-Rosenberg, Carroll. "Davy Crockett as Trickster: Pornography, Liminality, and Symbolic Inversion in Victorian America." In *Disorderly Conduct: Visions of Gender in Victorian America.* New York: Knopf, 1985.

Wall, Helena M. *Fierce Communion: Family and Community in Early America.* Cambridge, Mass.: Harvard University Press, 1990.

Related Entries

Advice Literature; American Dream; American Revolution; Apprenticeship; Bureaucratization; Capitalism; Character; Crockett, Davy; Darwinism; Emerson, Ralph Waldo; Evangelicalism and Revivalism; Franklin, Benjamin; Individualism; Industrialization; Jackson, Andrew; Market Revolution; Masturbation; Middle-Class Manhood; Patriarchy; Self-Control; Suburbia; Success Manuals; Western Frontier

—Rodney Hessinger

Sensitive Male

American culture commonly discourages males from expressing emotions associated with tenderness and vulnerability. The "sensitive male" is often thought a weakling, a sissy, or perhaps gay. Yet this stigmatizing of men's sensitivity developed only in the late nineteenth century, when middle-class men's fear of overcivilized softness and homosexuality prompted a new cultural emphasis on male toughness. A half century or so later, fuelled by feminism's questioning of traditional gender roles, there emerged a fresh appreciation of male sensitivity, though emphasis on emotional restraint remained widespread.

Before the late nineteenth century, men were free to express tender feelings—to women and to each other—with politicians as uninhibited as poets. "Accept all the tenderness I have," wrote Massachusetts senator Daniel Webster in a letter to college friend James Hervey Bingham, while the salutations "Lovely Boy" and "Dearly Beloved" opened their letters to each other. Early photographs often show men holding hands, one sitting on the other's lap, or casually reclining against each other. Pictured alone, men often struck poses of gentle reflection. The mainstream masculine ideal was apparently one that would later seem an androgynous combination of male and female qualities.

Facing new demands from women entering politics and the workplace, as well as work's altered nature due to urban living and machine production, many men of the late nineteenth century anxiously sought to redefine their manhood. Sports became more popular as well as more violent, and much more directly linked to definitions of masculinity. As physical power became increasingly unnecessary in everyday life, many men overcompensated, prizing strength as never before. *Homosexual* and *heterosexual*, two newly coined words, came to describe not just activities but distinct identities, with homosexuals stereotyped as weaklings. Sensitivity became the province of women or effeminate men.

The allegedly uniform sensitivity of women was used to justify their exclusion from certain domains of public life. A revived feminism in the 1960s and 1970s, therefore, commonly criticized the designation of sensitivity as an exclusively feminine trait. Many women and men gradually came to recognize the emotional (and physical) price that males of all ages paid for their fervent efforts not to appear sensitive. Bookstore shelves bulged with examinations of men's troubled emotional lives, and a loosely structured men's movement brought many men together, sometimes simply to talk about their feelings. The "sensitive guy" increasingly became a cultural ideal during the late twentieth century, and the term became a buzzword. Even the Promise Keepers, a conservative group devoted to maintaining traditional male authority in the family, encouraged men's emotional expression.

New sorts of men were portrayed heroically in films, as when Billy Dee Williams and James Caan played professional football players Gales Sayers and Brian Piccolo in the 1971 film *Brian's Song*. Depiction of the depth of their friendship and of Sayers's grief when Piccolo died made *Brian's Song* a new kind of sports movie—one that grounded manhood equally in physical toughness and emotional vulnerability. However, some critics' designation of such films as "male weepies" suggested continuing discomfort with men's sensitivity. Efforts to develop a model of American manhood that embraced emotional honesty continued through the end of the twentieth century, as William Pollack's best-selling *Real Boys* (1998) suggested. Yet the cultural tension between old habits and the renewed appreciation of sensitive men (by men as well as women) persists.

BIBLIOGRAPHY

Ibson, John. *Picturing Men: A Century of Male Relationships in Everyday American Photography.* Washington, D.C.: Smithsonian Institution Press, 2002.

Kimmel, Michael. *Manhood in America: A Cultural History.* New York: Free Press, 1996.

Pollack, William. *Real Boys: Rescuing Our Sons from the Myths of Boyhood.* New York: Random House, 1998.

Rotundo, E. Anthony. *American Manhood: Transformations in Masculinity from the Revolution to the Modern Era.* New York: Basic Books, 1993.

FURTHER READING

Pleck, Joseph H., and Jack Sawyer, eds. *Men and Masculinity.* Englewood Cliffs, N.J.: Prentice Hall, 1974.

Real, Terrence. *I Don't Want to Talk about It: Overcoming the Secret Legacy of Male Depression.* New York: Fireside, 1998.

RELATED ENTRIES

Crisis of Masculinity; Fathers' Rights; Feminism; Freudian Psychoanalytic Theory; Homosexuality; *Iron John: A Book About Men; Kramer vs. Kramer;* Male Friendship; Masculine Domesticity; Men's Movements; Mother–Son Relationships; *Mr. Mom*; Passionate Manhood; Promise Keepers; Self-Control; Sentimentalism

—*John Ibson*

SENTIMENTALISM

A central part of Victorian middle-class culture from about 1830 to the 1870s, sentimentalism shaped cultural constructions of gender by prescribing types of bodily conduct, including speech, posture, gestures, dress, and proper etiquette among both men and women. The goal of these prescriptions was the same for men and women: to foster perfect sincerity, truthfulness, and candor in social relations. But Victorian sentimentalism had different practical implications for men and women because middle-class Americans assumed women to be naturally expressive of their feelings, and therefore naturally sincere, while men were assumed to be naturally more rational, better able to control their emotions, and therefore less sincere. Sentimentalism therefore required of men a strict standard of proper conduct—a conscious performance of behavior appropriate to given situations—that became basic to Victorian constructions of middle-class manhood.

The Victorian concern with interpersonal sincerity, particularly among men, was a response to the new types of social relations and gender definitions being fostered by the market revolution and urbanization. As American economic life grew increasingly competitive and urban life increasingly impersonal, middle-class Americans feared that men, who were being encouraged to pursue entrepreneurial success in this anonymous urban capitalist marketplace, would be tempted to prey on and deceive others to gain advantage. While the middle class was created by, and benefited economically from, the new market economy, its members worried that the new kinds of economic relationships that supported their status, and which did not require the familiar moral obligations of face-to-face small-town exchange, threatened men's ethical grounding. The cultural archetype of the confidence man—who used false sincerity to gain the confidence of others for the purpose of ruining them—became perhaps the most powerful symbol of the morally unconstrained male entrepreneur.

Sentimental prescriptions for middle-class men were formulated in large part as a counterpoint to this negative model. Fearful of the impersonal competitive marketplace, the middle class rooted their ideals of male conduct in the home or domestic sphere—a social space characterized by a companionate family ideal built around emotive, affectionate, and caring relations. They hoped that men might carry the warm, personal character of domestic relationships into their interactions outside the home as well. Men would thus develop a genuine sincerity, honesty, and trustworthiness that could withstand public scrutiny—a solid "character" both inwardly wrought and socially enforced. Sentimental codes of conduct, then, assumed that the intimacy of domestic interactions provided the most promising basis for a model of manhood that guaranteed social trust in a society comprised of strangers.

The sentimental insistence on sincerity was based on the notion that reason, while a fundamental aspect of masculinity, could be deceptive, but that "feminine" emotion was always a genuine expression of the inner self. Thus, sentimental requirements of manhood were based on gender concepts that called into question men's capacity for emotional honesty. This problem was further complicated by the fact that while middle-class Victorians condemned any artificial cultivation of mere public image, they valued outward social reputation and deemed it essential to the business success expected of men. They therefore urged the display of proper manners and appearances in public, but also insisted that such surface expressions reflect one's inner moral principles and true feelings. Middle-class Victorians sought to combine outward conduct and inward sentiment by developing—and pressing with particular urgency upon men—a code of social etiquette called "genteel performance" by the historian Karen Halttunen. Victorians believed that for the truly sincere, adherence to these rules would come naturally.

Victorians devised such strategies of sentiment for a variety of settings and situations. Broadly speaking, sentimentalism provided for three sets of rules that regulated social interaction: (1) rules of politeness and courtesy in public settings, (2) rules of tact, and (3) rules of acquaintanceship. These rules provided a social framework intended to assure that one was not falsely acting sincere, and they also served to mark and reinforce middle-class status. For example, sentimental rules of conduct prescribed that men wear a three-piece suit, a top hat, and, even in summer, a thin overcoat in public. Because the required clothing consisted of luxury items, conformity to the sentimental code indicated that one enjoyed the financial means associated with middle-class status.

Indeed, sentimental conduct was closely tied to the emerging commodity culture being created by the market revolution. Middle-class Victorians perceived sentimentalism as an antidote to the impersonal social and economic relations of market capitalism, and also as a counterforce to the possibility that men might cynically promote false public images in the economic marketplace. But sentimentalism actually reinforced the rules of commodity capitalism and enabled men's participation in public politics and economic exchange. Because the behavioral techniques men used to signify trustworthiness became a cultural capital that required reciprocation by others, sentimentalism followed the logic of capitalist exchange and extended behavioral patterns suitable to market capitalism into the make-up of the male self.

Sentimentalism further shaped Victorian middle-class manhood by bridging a cultural gap between two important facets of male public life in nineteenth-century America: involvement in the market economy and participation in a political republic. On the one hand, economic competition was grounded in the pursuit of self-interest; on the other, civic responsibility was supposed to require subordinating self-interest to the collective good. Sentimental manhood provided a way to resolve that contradiction. Men's activities in the public sphere were motivated not by economic self-interest or political partisanship, but by responsibility to their households and those who depended on them. Men who could display candor and sincerity in their public conduct could outwardly disassociate themselves from their identity as market-oriented beings and present themselves as domestic beings and selfless "family men." Thus, by claiming the mantle of public virtue and seeming to elevate themselves above their selfish interests, sentimental men could appear well suited to participate in the public sphere.

Sentimentalism profoundly influenced new constructions of manhood that emerged in the late nineteenth and twentieth centuries. By the late nineteenth century, the insistence on the primacy of feelings had prompted the emergence of a "passionate manhood" that emphasized the healthy display of an inner masculine savage as a counter to the constraints of urban-industrial life. By the early twentieth century, the superficial display of sincerity (regarded by nineteenth-century Victorians as the art of the confidence man) had become an accepted part of a middle-class ideology of manhood. This development involved not so much a departure from the ideal of sincerity as a redefinition of its gendered core. Managing the body and one's feelings—once subordinated to the cultivation of genuine inner character—now stood independently as features of true manliness. In an increasingly urbanized and corporatized consumer society, the need to purposefully manufacture appearances to compete with others for the attention and support of superiors in social and occupational settings became increasingly important for achieving personal and professional success.

By the beginning of the twenty-first century, Americans had long since come to accept and negotiate what nineteenth-century middle-class men (and women) would have considered hypocrisy—the ability to change behavior according to the demands of the situation. Still, emotional sincerity remains important to American cultural constructions of "real" manhood and, indeed, formed the core of the ideal of the "sensitive male" that emerged during the late twentieth century. In 1994, for example, *Time* magazine carried an extensive story about former president George H. W. Bush's frequent weeping in public. In that same year, the film adaptation of Winston

Groom's 1986 novel *Forrest Gump* became a box office hit, in part because the title character was both a war hero and a quintessentially sentimental man.

BIBLIOGRAPHY

Brown, Gillian. *Domestic Individualism: Imagining the Self in Nineteenth-Century America.* Berkeley: University of California Press, 1990.

Burgett, Bruce. *Sentimental Bodies: Sex, Gender, and Citizenship in the Early Republic.* Princeton, N.J.: Princeton University Press, 1998.

Chapman, Mary, and Glenn Hendler, eds. *Sentimental Men: Masculinity and the Politics of Affect in American Culture.* Berkeley: University of California Press, 1999.

Douglas, Ann. *The Feminization of American Culture.* New York: Knopf, 1977.

Halttunen, Karen. *Confidence Men and Painted Women: A Study of Middle-Class Culture in America, 1830–1870.* New Haven, Conn.: Yale University Press, 1982.

Kasson, John F. *Rudeness and Civility: Manners in Nineteenth-Century Urban America.* New York: Hill and Wang, 1990.

Lystra, Karen. *Searching The Heart: Women, Men, and Romantic Love in Nineteenth-Century America.* New York: Oxford University Press, 1989.

FURTHER READING

Baym, Nina. "Melodramas of Beset Manhood: How Theories of American Fiction Exclude Women Authors." In *Feminism and American Literary History: Essays,* edited by Nina Baym. New Brunswick, N.J.: Rutgers University Press, 1992.

Kelley, Mary. *Private Woman, Public Stage: Literary Domesticity in Nineteenth-Century America.* New York: Oxford University Press, 1984.

Kete, Mary Louise. *Sentimental Collaborations: Mourning and Middle-Class Identity in Nineteenth-Century America.* Durham, N.C.: Duke University Press, 2000.

Noble, Marianne. *The Masochistic Pleasures of Sentimental Literature.* Princeton, N.J.: Princeton University Press, 2000.

Samuels, Shirley, ed. *The Culture of Sentiment: Race, Gender, and Sentimentality in Nineteenth-Century America.* New York: Oxford University Press, 1992.

Sánchez-Eppler, Karen. *Touching Liberty: Abolition, Feminism, and the Politics of the Body.* Berkeley: University of California Press, 1993.

Sedgwick, Eve Kosofsky. *Epistemology of the Closet.* Berkeley: University of California Press, 1990.

Tompkins, Jane. *Sensational Designs: The Cultural Work of American Fiction, 1790–1860.* New York: Oxford University Press, 1985.

RELATED ENTRIES

Advice Literature; Art; Body; Capitalism; Confidence Man; Cult of Domesticity; Emotion; Market Revolution; Masculine Domesticity; Middle-Class Manhood; Passionate Manhood; Republicanism; Self-Control; Sensitive Male; Urbanization; Victorian Era

—*Thomas Winter*

SEXUAL HARASSMENT

Sexual harassment, which includes sexual advances, requests for sexual favors, and other verbal or physical conduct of a sexual nature, was part of the wider realm of American power relations and gender dynamics long before it came to be legally defined in the 1970s. Because prevailing gender roles defined the world of economic production and exchange as the domain of men well into the twentieth century, the workplace was a traditionally homosocial male space. Thus, women who challenged their prescribed domestic roles faced the possibility of harassment. Although women have engaged in acts of sexual harassment, such actions have primarily been used by men in public arenas as a mechanism designed to keep women "in their place." Legal controversies involving sexual harassment thus became closely intertwined with larger cultural issues over sex discrimination, women's rights, and appropriate male conduct.

American women's challenges to the notion of the all-male workplace developed along with organized women's rights activism itself. As early as the Seneca Falls convention of 1848, Lucretia Mott urged the necessity of "securing to woman an equal participation with men in the various trades, professions, and commerce" (Kerber and DeHart, 209). Women's growing presence in the workforce during the late nineteenth and twentieth centuries, particularly as a result of the expansion of the service sector, raised concerns over workplace equality and conduct.

At the same time, feminists of the early twentieth century began emphasizing women's right to control their own bodies. But into the mid–twentieth century, women in the United States were frequently blamed for enticing men to rape them, and they were expected to tolerate sexual taunts as natural male behavior. President John F. Kennedy began to address the issue of women's workplace rights in 1961 by appointing a commission on the status of women, led by the former First Lady Eleanor Roosevelt. This commission was instrumental in the passage of the Equal Pay Act of 1963, the inclusion of sexual discrimination in the Civil Rights Act of 1964, and the attention to sex discrimination in the activities of the Equal Employment Opportunity Commission, established in 1965.

But while these measures established what became the legal basis for sexual-harassment litigation, they did not make sexual harassment specifically a matter of public concern.

Sexual harassment began to emerge as a public issue beginning in the late 1960s, when the resurgent feminist movement encouraged broad public discussion not only of traditional workplace issues such as equal opportunity and equal pay, but also of sexual issues such as rape and the objectification of women, such as in pornography. Activists also criticized what they considered the conventional and sometimes boorish male behavior that underlay men's power, urging men to embrace models of male behavior more sensitive to women's concerns, needs, and aspirations. Better educated than the working women of earlier generations, women of the late-twentieth-century workplace brought with them a sharpened awareness of the relation between male sexuality and male power, a heightened sensitivity to the routine sexual harassment to which they were subjected, and a growing desire to reform conventional patterns of male workplace conduct.

This new social awareness led U.S. federal courts to make a growing number of rulings on sex discrimination in education and the workplace during the 1970s, and in 1986, in *Meritor Savings Bank* v. *Vinson*, the U.S. Supreme Court decided (under Title VII of the Civil Rights Act of 1964) that sexual harassment is a form of sex discrimination. American law similarly sought to curb sexual harassment in education: Title IX of the federal Education Amendments of 1972 banned sex discrimination, including sexual harassment, from any federally funded educational program. Public discussion and legal litigation increasingly identified instances of sexual harassment by men (and sometimes women) in their roles as boss, client, or coworker; as teacher, fellow student, or counselor; and as military superior or military peer.

American law distinguishes between two types of employment-related sexual harassment: *quid pro quo,* in which a superior demands sexual favors from an employee in exchange for a job related favor; and *hostile environment,* in which a supervisor or fellow employee is guilty of behavior that makes one's job unpleasant enough to adversely affect one's work (e.g., making sexual comments, telling sexual jokes, displaying pornographic pictures). The Supreme Court offered its most precise definition of a hostile working environment and of ideal male workplace deportment in the *Meritor* case, ruling that Title VII is violated when a work space is affected by "discriminatory intimidation, ridicule, and insult" that is "sufficiently severe or pervasive to alter the conditions of the victim's employment and create an abusive working environment." The Supreme Court also ruled that sexual harassment required sustained patterns, rather than isolated incidents, of inappropriate male conduct.

While legal proceedings easily identified and outlawed the most obvious and crude forms of sexual harassment, subtler forms proved more persistent and more difficult to pinpoint legally. Many gray areas therefore remained, generating continuing efforts to refine both cultural definitions of appropriate male workplace behavior and legal definitions of sexual harassment. The intertwining of the legal controversy surrounding sexual harassment with ongoing disagreement over the cultural definition of appropriate male workplace behavior was particularly apparent in the Supreme Court's ruling in *Harris* v. *Forklift Systems, Inc.* (1993), which states: "If the victim does not subjectively perceive the environment to be abusive, the conduct has not actually altered the conditions of the victim's employment, and there is no Title VII violation."

The many forms of sexual harassment identified by American courts during the late twentieth century, including various kinds of speech and other types of inappropriate conduct, indicate the extent to which women have actively explored and publicized the ways in which men have used workplace behaviors to bolster traditional patriarchal power and subjugate those at a power disadvantage. Public discussions and legal controversies about the issue have gauged the nature and intensity of late-twentieth-century attempts to redefine masculinity in American culture.

BIBLIOGRAPHY

Cahill, Mia L. *The Social Construction of Sexual Harassment Law: The Role of the National, Organization, and Individual Context.* Burlington, Vt.: Ashgate, 2001.

de Beauvoir, Simone. *The Second Sex.* New York: Knopf, 1953.

Dobrich, Wanda. *The Manager's Guide to Preventing a Hostile Work Environment.* New York: McGraw-Hill, 2002.

Friedan, Betty. *The Feminine Mystique.* New York: Norton, 1963.

Griffith, Benjamin E., ed. *Sexual Harassment in the Public Workplace.* Chicago: American Bar Association, 2001.

Gulledge, Jo, ed. *Avoiding Sexual Harassment Claims: Guide for the Educator.* Gaithersburg, Md.: Aspen, 2002.

Hajdin, Mane. *The Law of Sexual Harassment: A Critique.* London: Associated University Presses, 2002.

Kerber, Linda, and Jane Sherron DeHart, eds. *Women's America: Refocusing the Past.* New York: Oxford University Press, 2000.

Kulick, Don, and Margaret Wilson, Eds. *Taboo: Sex, Identity, and Erotic Subjectivity in Anthropological Fieldwork.* London: Routledge, 1995.

Sanday, Peggy Reeves. *A Woman Scorned: Acquaintance Rape on Trial.* New York: Doubleday, 1996.

Stan, Adele M., ed. *Debating Sexual Correctness: Pornography, Sexual Harassment, Date Rape, and the Politics of Sexual Equality.* New York: Delta, 1995.

Zimmer, Michael J. *Cases and Materials on Employment Discrimination.* New York: Aspen Law & Business, 2000.

FURTHER READING

Laqueur, Thomas. *Making Sex: Body and Gender from the Greeks to Freud.* Cambridge, Mass.: Harvard University Press, 1990.

Ortner, Sherry B., and Harriet Whitehead. "Introduction: Accounting for Sexual Meanings." In *Sexual Meanings: The Cultural Construction of Gender and Sexuality.* Cambridge, England: Cambridge University Press, 1981.

Peach, Lucinda Joy. *Women in Culture: A Women's Studies Anthology.* Malden, Mass.: Blackwell, 1998.

Sanday, Peggy Reeves, and Ruth G. Goodenough. *Beyond the Second Sex: New Directions in the Anthropology of Gender.* Philadelphia: University of Pennsylvania Press, 1990.

RELATED ENTRIES

Business/Corporate America; Feminism; Patriarchy; Sensitive Male; Work

—*Frank A. Salamone*

SEXUAL REVOLUTION

The Sexual Revolution of the 1960s and 1970s significantly affected the development of masculinity in the United States. During this period, relationships between men and women shifted, and established expectations concerning sexual expression began to alter. There was an increasing liberation of attitudes toward premarital sex, homosexuality, pornography, divorce, abortion, birth control, and sex therapy; and sex itself took on a form of political expression with the increasing power of the feminist and gay rights movements. As a result, versions of masculinity began to emerge that required that men behave in ways that were less authoritative and controlling; they had to recognize the rights of women and sexual minorities and allow voices other than those of the dominant male to be heard. In one way this challenged a status quo that continued to privilege a masculine social ethos, but in another way it offered men the possibility of adopting a different social and cultural position. This revolution encouraged male expressiveness and a loosening of restrictions, and thus privileged male sexuality in an unprecedented way.

The Sexual Revolution had its roots in social, cultural, scientific, and intellectual areas. Socially and culturally, the peace demonstrations and draft-dodging of the 1960s allowed men to avoid or denigrate the machismo that had characterized American masculinity since World War II, while countercultural movements embracing a drug and sex culture pushed permissiveness to the fore and politicized the expression of masculine sexuality. "Make love, not war" was a popular slogan of the 1960s. This atmosphere encouraged the publication of more sexually explicit material for men (pornography became more available after the initial publication of *Playboy* magazine in 1953) and a growing awareness through school and college courses that masculinity and human sexuality can be carefree (contraceptives such as the birth-control pill, approved by the U.S. government in 1960, prevented pregnancy), promiscuous (awareness of sexually transmitted diseases sharply increased), and experimental (gay and bisexual lifestyles became valid).

In scientific terms, debates about sexuality had become popularized through the distribution of the work of Sigmund Freud (The Hogarth Press's *Standard Edition* of his complete works appeared between 1953 and 1974), and these became increasingly significant to understanding masculinity after the publication of Alfred Kinsey, Wardell Pomeroy, and Clyde Martin's book *Sexual Behavior in the Human Male* (1948). Enormous media interest in this book furthered public debate about male sexuality, affecting perceptions of masculinity as a subject of study. William Masters and Virginia E. Johnson furthered the empirical study of sexuality, and in 1966 they published *Human Sexual Response*, which detailed five stages of sexual encounter: desire, excitement, plateau, orgasm, resolution. They advocated the idea of a healthy and multiform human sexuality, furthering a developing masculine consciousness. Their 1970 book *Human Sexual Inadequacy* prefigured male anxieties such as premature ejaculation and impotency, which came to be spoken about more openly.

Scientific research was mirrored by intellectual inquiry. Herbert Marcuse, in *Eros and Civilisation: A Philosophical Inquiry into Freud* (1955), argued that sexuality is varied and should be freed from social restriction, an argument that influenced his students at the University of California, Berkeley. At about the same time, Wilhelm Reich developed a theory of orgonamy, which offered liberation in purely genital terms and argued for a primeval and elemental sexual force of which human sexuality was only a part. Reich's book, *The Sexual Revolution: Towards a Self-Regulating Character Structure* appeared posthumously in 1974. Marcuse and Reich fused the theories of Marxism and psychoanalysis into a revolutionary sexual radicalism that shaped understandings of masculinity and sexuality for the remainder of the twentieth century. Their work created a new awareness of male sexuality, which previously had been taken for granted.

Debates about male sexuality were further repositioned in the light of increased feminist consciousness during the 1960s and 1970s. Simone de Beauvoir's *The Second Sex* (1953), Betty Friedan's *The Feminine Mystique* (1963), and Kate Millett's *Sexual Politics* (1970) challenged men to recognize and reconsider those mechanisms of female expression that had kept them in power and to rethink their core suppositions about themselves. In their intimate relationships, men were re-educated about women's and men's bodies. In the workplace, sexual harassment legislation reset the parameters of relationships men could have with female coworkers and, in particular, sought to curb the use of sexuality as an instrument of male domination.

At the same time, an alternative and increasingly public discourse on male homosexuality offered another option to men. In 1950, Harry Hay founded the Mattachine Society in Los Angeles, promoting what came to be known as gay rights, and by 1961 Illinois had become the first state to decriminalize homosexual acts. Throughout the decade, gay rights demonstrations allowed men to consider homosexuality as a life choice and to become politically active in demanding equal rights. On June 27, 1970, the first Gay Pride march took place in New York City, and homosexuality became an increasingly viable option for American men. As such, it impacted considerably upon perceptions of masculinity as a whole, encouraging a process whereby both straight (heterosexual) men and gay men were expected to adopt and live openly a particularized lifestyle. Sexuality entered the arena of public expression, and on very personal terms. Significant debates also emerged around transsexuality, as science offered the opportunity for male-to-female transgendering (acquisition of female genitalia and secondary female sexual characteristics), and as social mores recognized this possibility. The well-publicized case of Renee Richards, who transgendered in 1975 at the age of forty and went on to have a significant tennis career, exemplified for the masses that masculinity was not as stable as it had been assumed.

During the Sexual Revolution of the 1960s and 1970s, these changes significantly altered societal understanding of masculinity, encouraging and forcing men to reconsider their attitudes about, and enactments of, their own developing sexual expression. The Sexual Revolution and its reconfiguration of male sexuality in the United States continued to unfold in the early twenty-first century under the impact of an emergent cyberculture, the anonymity and technological sophistication of which greatly expanded the possible scope and range of men's sexual encounters and expressions.

BIBLIOGRAPHY

de Beauvoir, Simone. *The Second Sex.* Edited and translated by H. M. Parshley. New York: Knopf, 1953.

D'Emilio, John, and Estelle B. Freedman. *Intimate Matters: A History of Sexuality in America.* Chicago: University of Chicago Press, 1997.

Friedan, Betty. *The Feminine Mystique.* London: Gollancz, 1963.

Kinsey, Alfred, Wardell P. Pomeroy, and Clyde E. Martin. *Sexual Behavior in the Human Male.* 1948. Reprint, Bloomington: Indiana University Press, 1998.

Masters, William, and Virginia E. Johnson. *Human Sexual Response.* Boston: Little, Brown, 1966.

———. *Human Sexual Inadequacy.* Boston: Little, Brown, 1970.

Millett, Kate. *Sexual Politics.* 1970. Reprint, Urbana: University of Illinois Press, 2000.

Reich, Wilhelm. *The Sexual Revolution: Towards a Self-Regulating Character Structure.* New York: Farrar, Strauss and Giroux, 1974.

FURTHER READING

Badinter, Elizabeth. *XY: On Masculine Identity.* New York: Columbia University Press, 1995.

Bailey, Beth. *Sex in the Heartland.* Cambridge, Mass.: Harvard University Press, 1999.

Connell, R. W. *Masculinities.* Berkeley: University of California Press, 1995.

D'Emilio, John. *Sexual Politics/Sexual Communities: The Making of a Homosexual Minority in the United States, 1940–70.* 2nd ed. Chicago: University of Chicago Press, 1998.

Duberman, Martin. *Stonewall.* New York: Plume, 1994.

Odzer, Cleo. *Virtual Spaces: Sex and the Cyber Citizen.* New York: Berkley, 1997.

RELATED ENTRIES

Bisexuality; Counterculture; Divorce; Feminism; Freudian Psychoanalytic Theory; Heterosexuality; Homosexuality; Marriage; *Playboy* Magazine; Pornography; Sexual Harassment; Transsexuality

—*Michael John Pinfold*

SHAFT

Directed by Gordon Parks, *Shaft* was released by MGM in 1971. Based on a novel by white writer Ernest Tidyman, the film focuses on black private detective John Shaft (played by Richard Roundtree), who has been hired by a Harlem crime boss to rescue his kidnapped daughter from the Mafia. But Shaft's significance lays less in its plot than in its handsome, intelligent, and dynamic black hero, who captivated audiences and was a landmark in the history of representations of African-American masculinity in mainstream cinema.

At least since *Birth of a Nation* (1915), film representations of African-American men had been dominated by the dual racist stereotypes of the animalistic, sexually threatening primitive and the subservient, asexual jester. Shaft, which was released in the aftermath of 1960s civil rights activism and the rise of the Black Power movement (with its confrontational political stance and hostility to white liberalism) articulated a new African-American masculinity characterized by self-assurance and strength. The sharp-witted, tough, and stylish detective heralded the arrival of a new brand of enigmatic African-American action hero. Shaft's confident poise seemed to personify the defiant spirit of Black Power radicalism, while his black turtleneck sweaters and trademark leather trenchcoat offered a slick and glamorous image of black masculinity that was widely imitated in popular fashion. Isaac Hayes's pulsating score, a musical representation of Shaft's sexual charisma and street-smart edge, also influenced subsequent soul and hip-hop artists such as Barry White and Snoop Doggy Dogg.

Shaft's box-office success prompted two sequels, *Shaft's Big Score* (1972) and *Shaft in Africa* (1973), and a short-lived TV series. It also laid the way for films such as *Superfly* (1972), *Black Belt Jones* (1974), and other action movies featuring maverick black heroes. Low-budget, and often lurid in their depiction of sex and violence in a stylized ghetto setting, these films became known as blaxploitation due to their use of African-American stereotypes and brash commercial hype.

While some critics have praised Shaft for its representation of strong, self-assured African-American masculinity, others consider it to be a stock action film repackaged to appeal to black audiences, rather than a meaningful exploration of racial politics. The film's representation of Shaft's numerous sexual relationships with women has also been criticized for reproducing earlier racist stereotypes of an African-American masculinity distinguished by physical prowess and sexual potency. More widely, the blaxploitation genre that followed the release of Shaft has been attacked for sexually objectifying women, encouraging homophobia and misogyny, and reproducing racist stereotypes through the celebration of virulent masculine heterosexuality and violence.

Despite these criticisms, *Shaft* represented an important moment in the development of representations of black masculinity in American popular culture. At a time when many African Americans were socially and economically disenfranchised, *Shaft* offered an image of strength and empowerment, and many young African-American men drew inspiration from the central character's attitude and style. The film's legacy remained detectable decades later in popular fashion, music, and numerous film releases—including a new film version of *Shaft* in 2000.

Bibliography

Bogle, Donald. *Toms, Coons, Mulattoes, Mammies, and Bucks: An Interpretive History of Blacks in American Films.* New York: Continuum, 2001.

Reid, Mark A. *Redefining Black Film.* Berkeley: University of California Press, 1993.

Further Reading

Diawara, Manthia, ed. *Black American Cinema.* New York: Routledge, 1993.

James, Darius. *That's Blaxploitation! Roots of the Baadasssss 'Tude (Rated X By an All-Whyte Jury).* New York: St. Martin's Griffin, 1995.

Koren, Mikel J. *Blaxploitation Cinema.* North Pomfret, England: Trafalgar Square, 2001.

Related Entries

African-American Manhood; *Birth of a Nation*; Black Panther Party; Civil Rights Movement; Cop Action Films; Detectives; Fashion; Gangsters; Heterosexuality; Hollywood; Martial Arts Films; Race; Violence

—*Bill Osgerby*

Slave Narratives

A genre of American writing popular between 1830 and 1860, the slave narrative was one of the earliest forms of African-American self-expression. Typically written by escaped slaves, these gripping accounts of American slave life were read in the northern United States by abolitionists—an audience made up mostly of white women working to end the practice of African slavery. Slave narrators thus wrote with a sense of moral purpose, and also for the more practical reason of making an income from their writing.

In order to elicit sympathy from a northern audience unfamiliar with the wretched conditions of slave life, slave narratives often dwelled on graphic scenes of inhuman cruelty. Some readers did not want to confront the fact that the United States condoned the atrocities of chattel slavery, and these narratives were sometimes read with skepticism. Not only did the slave narrative seek to expose the barbaric treatment of black slaves by their southern white owners, they also made a case for recognizing the shared humanity of black and white

Americans. In their eloquent indictments of the nation's failure to extend the rights of Americans to all of its inhabitants, slave narratives provided the foundation for later attempts by African Americans to participate fully in the life and promise of their country. They also illuminate the ways in which their narrators constructed concepts of masculinity grounded in the experiences both of slavery and of writing about slavery.

Fatherhood and Masculinity in Slave Narratives

The American slave narrative typically displays a number of characteristics that reveal the narrator's understanding of masculinity. First, the male slave narrator often invokes a sense of lost origins, usually depicted in terms of the destruction of his family through separation and death. Slavery's destruction of the black family—its "traffic in humans" torn from parent, child, and sibling—came to function as one of the genre's central indictments of slavery. As a system of human ownership, slavery denied the patriarchal rights of fathers to make decisions about their children, which is to say that black fatherhood under slavery was invisible or ineffectual. When a female slave conceived a child through rape by her owner, the child she bore faced the dilemma of being "owned" by the biological father. Slave narratives thus suggested that being a slave presented enormous challenges to achieving a model of manhood that valued the rights and obligations of fatherhood. Despite a slave's desire to create traditional family structures, opportunities to attain personal autonomy or fulfill family obligations often conflicted with one another. In *The Narrative of William W. Brown, A Fugitive Slave* (1847), for instance, the author attempts to escape slavery with his mother, only to leave her in slavery in order to ensure his own release. Thus, Brown's achievement of the freedom of manhood comes only through his failure to protect his mother.

Violence and Masculinity in Slave Narratives

Slave narratives also focus on scenes of physical brutality as a way of bearing witness to the cruelty slavery inflicts on its victims. To some extent, the culture of slavery dominated both male and female slaves through intimidation and acts of physical violence; thus, the threat of the whip and chain were often highlighted in the slave narrative. Slave narratives also suggest a tension between the heroic masculinity represented by resistance to slavery and the white codes of genteel or refined masculinity that deplored physical violence. On the one hand, slave narrators such as Frederick Douglass and Solomon Northrup identified a slave's combat with a white slaveholder or overseer as a mark of acquired manhood. "You have seen how a man was made a slave," Douglass remarks on the threshold of his famous fight with Edward Covey, a slavebreaker, "you will now see how a slave was made a man" (Douglass 1960, 97).

On the other hand, slave narratives emphasized the narrators' desire for literacy—for verbal rather than physical prowess—as a way of demonstrating that African-American slaves were capable of learning to reason and acquiring the marks of civilization. Thus, violent physical resistance, which some white readers expected to read in slave narratives, potentially undermined the slave's and the narrator's claims to genteel manhood.

In his *Narrative* (1845), Frederick Douglass recognized this tension between physical and verbal manhood, particularly in his depiction of the fight with Covey. In this scene, Douglass presents himself as a reluctant combatant, reduced to fighting with an irrational slaveholder not because he desires confrontation, but because Covey is incapable of acting with honor or reason. In this way, Douglass does not so much out-fight Covey as prove himself a better man.

Literacy and Self-Made Manhood in Slave Narratives

A third feature of the slave narrative is the narrator's depiction of his acquisition of literacy and subsequent elevation from lowly origins. This reflects the mythology of self-reliance and self-made manhood so important to antebellum American constructions of masculinity—and so clearly denied to men who were regarded as owned objects and deprived of access to education. The importance of written literacy emerges intriguingly in the often recounted episode of the forged "pass," in which slaves capable of writing attempted to escape from slavery by forging a pass that would permit them to travel freely. When narrators like Douglass, Northrup, William Wells Brown, and Henry Bibb, speak of "writing oneself into freedom," the forged pass thus takes on literal meaning.

Slave narratives also presented the narrative of escape as a written signal of the writer's acquisition of freedom and autonomy, for the ability to write and publish a slave narrative depended first on the slave's successful escape from slavery, and, second, on his ability to use his literacy as a means of that escape. Yet, on several levels, the ability to achieve autonomy through writing was limited. Forged passes usually proved ineffective, and they also recalled the issue of the written manumission, the legally binding and written emancipation of a slave by his or her owner. Both the pass and the manumission signaled the fact that white men might dispose of their slaves through acts of writing; in other words, the freedom of a slave was a manmade, rather than a "God-given" or "natural" right.

Additionally, in some cases a man would be born into freedom, only to be enslaved later in his life; such is the case of Northrup, who was born free and kidnapped into a twelve-year enslavement that was rendered "legal" through the superior legal authority of southern whites. Such examples suggest that a status so easily "written" might also be, and often was, "unwritten."

Sentimentalism, Manhood, and the Female Audience

A similarly paradoxical situation emerges in the slave narrative's characteristic appeal to a white audience for financial and moral support. Male slave narrators may have claimed manhood through their writing, but in doing so they found themselves curiously dependent on their primary audience of northern, white, middle-class women. To appeal to this readership, narrators used one of their most effective rhetorical strategies: the sentimental invocation of the destroyed black family. Although the emotional appeal to the domestic values of women successfully outraged white female readers, it required male narrators to adopt "unmanly" sentimental displays. Male slave narrators employed strategies for managing this conflict and preserving their manhood. One tendency—exemplified by Frederick Douglass's famous depiction of the brutal beating of his Aunt Hester—was to describe the physical abuse of a female slave and minimize accounts of physical beatings endured by the narrator himself. By this means, male narrators deflected readers' sentimental responses away from themselves. A second strategy was to depict moments of male physical resistance to brutality.

The Narrators' Manhood and the White Audience

The slave narrative nearly always includes letters and statements written by white men attesting to the moral integrity of the narrator. This highlighted the male slave's dependence on a white community of readers to validate the claims they make about slavery. Bibb, Northrup, Douglass, and Brown all presented their testimonies against slavery with such prefatory letters, nearly all written by white men. These letters attested either to the truthfulness of the narrative, or to the good moral character of its author.

For example, the radical abolitionist William Lloyd Garrison wrote one such introduction to Douglass's *Narrative*, while Brown included letters from prominent white abolitionists in his *Narrative of William W. Brown*. Such authenticating documents helped market the texts to the intended audience of northern abolitionists, but also called the narrators' manhood into question. For instance, these letters reinforced many whites' stereotypical assumptions that black men lacked moral character. Additionally, they challenged the slave narrators' truthfulness by suggesting that these writers depended on the words of white men to corroborate their indictments of slavery.

Conclusion

Having written themselves into freedom, escaped male slave narrators still found themselves chasing the elusive ideals of American masculinity. For example, even in the comparatively free conditions of the nonslaveholding northern states, escaped slaves like Douglass and Brown still lacked many of the privileges that defined white American masculinity during the nineteenth century, most notably the rights to vote, to congregate freely, and, in some states at least, to be heard in court and sit on juries. African-American men continued to fight for these rights after the Civil War (when discriminatory Jim Crow laws replaced the slave codes in the south), and well into the twentieth century with the rise of the civil rights movement.

BIBLIOGRAPHY

Andrews, William L. *To Tell a Free Story: the First Century of Afro-American Autobiography.* Urbana: University of Illinois Press, 1986.

Baker, Houston A. *Blues, Ideology, and Afro-American Literature: A Vernacular Theory.* Chicago: University of Chicago Press, 1987.

Leverenz, David. *Manhood and the American Renaissance.* Ithaca, N.Y.: Cornell University Press, 1989.

Nelson, Dana D. *The Word in Black and White: Reading "Race" in American Literature, 1838–1867.* New York: Oxford University Press, 1992.

Sundquist, Eric J., ed. *Frederick Douglass: New Literary and Historical Essays.* New York: Cambridge University Press, 1990.

FURTHER READING

Blassingame, John W. *The Slave Community: Plantation Life in the Antebellum South.* Rev. ed. New York: Oxford University Press, 1979.

Carby, Hazel V. *Race Men.* Cambridge, Mass.: Harvard University Press, 1998.

Gates, Henry Louis. *The Signifying Monkey: A Theory of Afro-American Literary Criticism.* New York: Oxford University Press, 1988.

Jacobs, Harriet A. *Incidents in the Life of a Slave Girl.* 1859. Reprint, New York: Penguin, 2000.

Stowe, Harriet Beecher. *Uncle Tom's Cabin.* 1852. Reprint, Oxford: Oxford University Press, 2002.

SELECTED WRITINGS

Bibb, Henry. *The Life and Adventures of Henry Bibb: An American Slave.* Madison: University of Wisconsin Press, 2001.

Brown, William Wells. *Narrative of William W. Brown: A Fugitive Slave.* 1847. Reprint, New York: Johnson Reprint Corp., 1970.

Douglass, Frederick. *Narrative of the Life of Frederick Douglass, an American Slave.* 1845. Reprint, Cambridge, Mass.: Belknap Press, 1960.

———. *My Bondage and My Freedom.* 1855. Reprint, Amherst, N.Y.: Humanity Books, 2002.

———. *The Life and Times of Frederick Douglass.* 1881. Reprint, New York: Gramercy Books, 1993.

Northrup, Solomon. *Twelve Years a Slave.* 1853. Reprint, New York: Dover, 1970.

RELATED ENTRIES

Abolitionism; African-American Manhood; Douglass, Frederick; Emancipation; Emotion; Fatherhood; Race; Self-Control; Self-Made Man; Sentimentalism; Slavery; Violence; Work

—*Bryce Traister*

SLAVERY

Between 1619 and 1865, as many as eight million slaves lived within the current boundaries of the United States, making slavery one of the nation's most profoundly influential institutions. For millions of male slaves, fashioning a masculine identity became an important means of coping with slavery's oppressive and degrading conditions. The ideals and experiences generated within the crucible of slavery set enslaved men apart from their white counterparts, even as they strove to find a place for themselves within white-dominated southern society.

Family

During the colonial period, slaves' concept of masculinity often came from Africa, where husbands and fathers normally exercised patriarchal authority (contrary to common misconceptions that African societies were predominantly matriarchal) and aspired to be great men as warriors, village politicians, or spiritual leaders, although women often joined men in the latter role. Enslaved men in the Americas strove, within the constraints of slavery, to approximate these roles as they protected their families, negotiated with other slave households, and provided spiritual leadership as conjurers, healers, or teachers. The masculine ideals forged in the colonial period remained vital into the nineteenth century, with slave men aspiring both to demonstrate physical prowess and to become culturally powerful teachers and negotiators.

The importance of fatherhood and family life to male slaves' identity was reinforced when a decline in transatlantic slave importation (beginning in the 1750s) and its legal termination in 1807 made natural increase the primary means of augmenting the slave population. Slaveholders encouraged marriage and family among their slaves, realizing that enslaved men with families were less likely to run away. "It is necessary that the Negroes have wives," one of them wrote, "and you ought to know that nothing attaches them so much to a plantation as children" (Genovese, 452). Masters usually allowed male slaves some leeway in conducting their family relations, especially on large plantations, as long as they avoided violence and continued to work.

Yet slaveholders defined their own manhood through notions of racial hierarchy and patriarchal control of their farms and plantations, and they intervened in many ways to disrupt slave families and challenge the authority of men in the slave quarters. Nothing was more destructive to male slaves' participation in the family than the domestic slave trade. Slaveholders frequently divided families, and children rarely accompanied their fathers to a new location. In addition, many plantation owners threatened to sell disobedient male slaves away from their families. These men faced a horrific choice between two alternatives—submitting to their master's cruel authority or losing their families—either of which threatened their masculine identities. When allowed the choice, most stayed with their families, seeking new ways to assert their independence and manhood that would draw less attention from the master.

Violence and Submission

Slaveholders likewise challenged enslaved men's role as protectors of their families. Very rarely could slave husbands shield their wives from the whip, for example, although on some occasions a master would allow a man to stand in and be beaten for his wife. Enslaved men were usually powerless to prevent the cruelest of slavery's abuses: rape. On one occasion, an overseer attempted to rape a slave woman and her husband beat him nearly to death. The next day, when the overseer told the master, the slave received one hundred lashes with the whip, and then had his ear nailed to a post and cut off. Such punishments circumscribed, but did not obliterate, notions of slave manhood. Slave men were not expected, either by their families or by other men, to risk being maimed for something they were powerless to prevent.

When the tables were turned, with black men threatening white women, southern society, perceiving in such actions a threat to white patriarchy and racial hierarchy, responded violently and swiftly. Although there is no evidence that slave men posed a disproportionate threat as rapists of white women,

An 1860 depiction of a slave being sold away from his family. While many male slaves grounded their identities in fatherhood, the division of their families through sale—often because of their resistance to slaveholders' authority—emphasized their limited access to ideals of masculinity within a system of white patriarchy. (From the collections of the Library of Congress)

many white men, associating black masculinity with hypersexuality, believed that they did. Male slaves therefore had to exercise caution in their relationships with white women to avoid the appearance of impropriety, which would inevitably result in severe punishment.

In fact, much of what enslaved men did in the presence of their masters, mistresses, and overseers was calculated to appeal to white demands and stereotypes. Enslaved men often put on "masks of obedience" (Wyatt-Brown), pretending to be the docile, submissive, and happy slaves that their masters idealized. Slaveholders interpreted this submission as a sign of black men's inferior manhood, while the slaves themselves recognized that their public performance of childlike compliance did not define who they really were. This divide between slaves' apparent emasculation and their real assertion of choice has divided historians. Some have suggested that the institution of slavery was so oppressive and destructive to human psychology that enslaved men lost their sense of self and developed a childlike dependence on their masters. Since the late 1960s, however, most historians have rejected this position, suggesting that this so-called Sambo personality was an invention of hopeful slaveowners who wanted to believe that black men were less capable of exercising freedom than themselves.

Assertions of Manhood

One way that enslaved men asserted their independent identity and masculinity was to commit acts of violence, both within the slave quarters and against their masters. Some slave men, unable to assert manly authority outside the slave community, overcompensated within their families by abusing their wives and children. Others fashioned a masculine identity around their bold and often violent resistance against oppression. Slaves such as Nat Turner planned or led violent armed rebellions, seeing them as heroic expressions of manliness. But acts of violent resistance were rare; more common acts of defiance could include standing up to an abusive overseer or fighting against the whip. The former slave Frederick Douglass summarized his feelings after wrestling down a cruel slave breaker: "I was nothing before; I was a man now" (Douglass, 143).

More often, however, enslaved men affirmed their masculinity in ways less costly to them and their families. One of the more important ideals that developed within the slave quarters was the responsibility of male slaves to provide extra food and clothing for their families. Most enslaved men with families routinely hunted for small game to enrich their families' diets with meat and provide furs and skins for childrens' clothing and blankets. Single male slaves used hunting as a badge of honor, comparing their skills with other slave men on the plantation.

Men also claimed positions of cultural prominence in slave communities as spiritual leaders in both African and Christian traditions. Especially in the colonial period, when African influences were stronger, enslaved men gained prestige as healers and conjurers, demonstrating in these otherworldly pursuits a much-admired skill. As Christianity became increasingly common among slaves, men sought to lead their fellow slaves as preachers, often encouraged by self-congratulating masters who viewed slavery as a Christianizing institution. These Christian preachers, frequently practicing and teaching elements of African religion at the same time, symbolized the independence and public influence denied to most slaves. Slaveholders' patriarchal ideals encouraged male religious leadership among slaves, which eclipsed women's roles in traditional African religions and strengthened the social power of male slave preachers.

Towering over all other aspects of a male slave's life was his daily work. Although a majority of slaves worked as agricultural laborers, many worked in skilled or semiskilled positions such as carpentry or blacksmithing. Because white gender norms attributed these tasks to men, slaveholders assigned skilled labor far more to male than to female slaves. Thus, slave men had greater access to the benefits of skilled labor, including more frequent travel, wider social circles, and, occasionally, the ability to earn their own money. Some, like Gabriel Prosser, incorporated into their male identities the republican emphasis on economic independence common among the white artisans with whom they sometimes intermingled.

From Slavery to Freedom

In many ways, slaves' sense of manhood paralleled the ideals of nineteenth-century white men, who also defined themselves as protectors, providers, and successful workers. In one of the most important matters, however, there could be no parity. As the nineteenth century and the market revolution progressed, white men increasingly viewed themselves as "self-made men," asserting their independent abilities to produce in the marketplace and govern in the public sphere. Slaveholders vigorously denied their slaves the means of claiming such pride, dictating their daily work as well as stealing the fruits of their labors. Many antislavery activists, judging slavery against the marketplace model of manhood, considered this the system's greatest injustice, as it deprived male slaves of becoming "true men."

This "free labor" ideology, based on white conceptions associating manhood with whiteness and economic independence, became the rallying point of northern politicians, helping Abraham Lincoln win the presidential election in 1860 and inspiring the South to secede from the Union in 1860–61. The Civil War not only ended with the abolition of slavery, but it also began to transform slaves' ideals of masculinity. Nearly 200,000 black men, many of them former slaves, fought as soldiers in the war, exclaiming, as one South Carolinian slave did, "I's a man now!" (Hine and Jenkins, 489). Many male slaves hoped to become independent landowners after the war, and thus achieve the economic autonomy they considered fundamental to full manhood. Most, however, ultimately became sharecroppers and found that their aspirations to manhood in American society would be difficult to realize. Much of the civil rights agenda that followed was grounded in this realization.

Conclusion

The cruelties inherent to slavery demanded a unique set of masculine ideals appropriate to the social and cultural setting within which male slaves lived. Although some men despaired, like the former slave Lewis Clarke, who concluded that "a slave can't be a man" (Hine and Jenkins, 384), many slaves asserted their manhood as husbands, fathers, laborers, craftsmen, hunters, musicians, and spiritual leaders. Others expressed their masculinity through violent acts of resistance, or by fleeing slavery altogether. Slaves thus constructed ideals of masculinity that fit their circumstances, adjusting those ideals as the conditions of slavery changed over time, and laying the foundations for post-emancipation conceptions of black manhood.

Bibliography

Bardaglio, Peter W. *Reconstructing the Household: Families, Sex, and Law in the Nineteenth-Century South.* Chapel Hill: University of North Carolina Press, 1995.

Blassingame, John W. *The Slave Community: Plantation Life in the Antebellum South.* New York: Oxford University Press, 1972.

Douglass, Frederick. *Narrative of the Life of Frederick Douglass, an American Slave.* 1845. Reprint, New York: Collier, 1892.

Egerton, Douglas. *Gabriel's Rebellion: The Virginia Slave Conspiracies of 1800 and 1802.* Chapel Hill: University of North Carolina Press, 1993.

Elkins, Stanley. *Slavery: A Problem in American Institutional and Intellectual Life.* Chicago: University of Chicago Press, 1959.

Genovese, Eugene D. *Roll, Jordan, Roll: The World the Slaves Made.* New York: Vintage, 1974.

Hine, Darlene Clark, and Ernestine Jenkins, eds. *A Question of Manhood: A Reader in U.S. Black Men's History and Masculinity.* Vol. 1, *"Manhood Rights": The Construction of Black Male History and Manhood, 1750–1870.* Bloomington: Indiana University Press, 1999.

Morgan, Philip D. *Slave Counterpoint: Black Culture in the Eighteenth-Century Chesapeake and Lowcountry.* Chapel Hill: University of North Carolina Press, 1998.

Stevenson, Brenda E. *Life in Black and White: Family and Community in the Slave South.* New York: Oxford University Press, 1996.

Wyatt-Brown, Bertram. "The Mask of Obedience: Male Slave Psychology in the Old South." *American Historical Review* 93 (1988): 1228–1252.

Further Reading

Berlin, Ira. *Many Thousands Gone: The First Two Centuries of Slavery in North America.* Cambridge, Mass.: Harvard University Press, 1998.

Greenberg, Kenneth S. *Honor and Slavery: Lies, Duels, Noses, Masks, Dressing as a Woman, Gifts, Strangers, Humanitarianism, Death, Slave Rebellions, The Proslavery Argument, Baseball, Hunting, and Gambling in the Old South.* Princeton, N.J.: Princeton University Press, 1996.

Kolchin, Peter. *American Slavery: 1619–1877.* New York: Hill and Wang, 1993.

White, Deborah Gray. *Ar'n't I a Woman?: Female Slaves in the Plantation South.* New York: Norton, 1999.

Wyatt-Brown, Bertram. *Southern Honor: Ethics and Behavior in the Old South.* Chapel Hill: University of North Carolina Press, 2001.

RELATED ENTRIES
Abolitionism; African-American Manhood; Artisan; Breadwinner Role; Civil War; Douglass, Frederick; Emancipation; Fatherhood; Lincoln, Abraham; Patriarchy; Race; Religion and Spirituality; Republicanism; Slave Narratives; Southern Manhood; Violence; War; Work; Working-Class Manhood

—*Brett Rushforth*

SOCIAL GOSPEL

The Social Gospel movement, led largely by male ministers, emerged in American Protestant churches in the 1880s. The movement sought to redefine the spiritual and socioeconomic dimensions of manhood and the gospel of Christ in a secularizing, urbanizing, and industrializing culture. Believing that these developments generated social problems that prevented individual and social salvation, and threatened Christian manliness and the role of Protestant Christianity in society, Social Gospelers articulated an ideal of manhood that confronted these challenges while remaining grounded in morality and spiritual commitment. They rejected older ideals of entrepreneurial, self-made manhood in favor of a model of Christian manhood that emphasized service, self-sacrifice, and teamwork.

The men at the core of the Social Gospel movement sought new meanings for manhood and Christianity on the basis of their own upbringing, religious experience, and social environment. Often influenced by their parents' examples, Social Gospelers attempted to integrate their fathers' discipline and work ethic with their mothers' model of sentimentality and self-sacrifice into a new male identity. The Massachusetts minister Charles McFarland, for example, grounded his identity in the memory of his father's rigorous biblical instruction, in his reverence for his father's physical labor and loss of life in erecting a monument to the Plymouth Pilgrims, in his experience of working to support his mother and himself after his father's death, and in his strong bond with his mother (whose wedding band he wore into his thirties).

In addition to their upbringing, Social Gospelers such as Washington Gladden, a minister in Columbus, Ohio, and Walter Rauschenbusch, whose first ministerial assignment was in New York's Hell's Kitchen neighborhood, were heavily influenced by the labor unrest of the 1870s and 1880s and by the misery caused by urbanization and industrialization. Such experiences convinced them that a progressive, manly, social Christianity must be committed to social justice. This conviction was apparent in the titles of Gladden's *Applied Christianity* (1886), Rauschenbusch's *Christianity and the Social Crisis* (1907) and *Christianizing the Social Order* (1912), and the best-selling author and minister Charles M. Sheldon's *In His Steps* (1896), which by 1933 had sold twenty-three million copies (more than any other Social Gospel work).

Despite their parents' influence, Social Gospelers were led by their own experiences to reject their parents' stern, individualistic faith, which linked poverty and misfortune to sinfulness. The social ethos of individual responsibility and self-control their parents had (often literally) preached no longer seemed adequate to secure economic success, spiritual fulfillment, or manhood. They instead articulated an ideal of Christian manhood grounded in social usefulness and communal spiritual experience.

By the 1880s an institutional infrastructure committed to social salvation and the promotion of a social ideal of Christian manliness began to emerge. In 1877 the Young Men's Christian Association (YMCA) formed a railroad department, followed by an industrial department in 1903, which sought to minister to working men in urban industries. In 1893, the Congregationalist minister Josiah Strong and the labor economist Richard T. Ely founded the American Institute of Christian Sociology. In 1905, thirty-three religious organizations and churches formed the Federal Council of Churches of Christ to promote the application of Christianity to social issues.

Social Gospelers' commitment to manly effort and maternal sacrifice led them to engage in and masculinize—as a form of paternal nurture—several activities traditionally associated with women. They opposed alcohol, prostitution, and gambling as detrimental to men's moral integrity and familial responsibility; they operated soup kitchens, settlement houses, bathing facilities, gymnasiums, and social clubs; they distributed used clothing in an attempt to nurture and uplift the urban poor; they provided industrial training to help impoverished men become breadwinners; and they evangelized working men through lunchtime meetings that portrayed Christianity as a manly commitment.

Similarly, Social Gospelers redefined the figure of Jesus Christ. During the mid–nineteenth century, Jesus had been represented as feminine, sentimental, tender, and nurturing. Social Gospelers, by contrast, combined his caring and nurturing qualities with a new emphasis on his manliness and assertiveness. A carpenter by training, Jesus became a noble craftsman, a reformer, and a "man's man" in such books as Thomas DeWit Tallmadge's *From Manger to Throne* (1890), Gladden's *Tools and the Man* (1893), Bouck White's *The Call of the Carpenter* (1913), and Harry Emerson Fosdick's *The Manhood of the Master* (1913). Social Gospelers remade Jesus in the image of the masculine ideal toward which they themselves aspired.

The Social Gospel movement stood in a complex relation to such related contemporary phenomena as muscular Christianity and the Men and Religion Forward Movement (MRFM), both of which shared Social Gospelers' interest in masculinizing Christianity. But whereas muscular Christians prioritized individual salvation and the achievement of spiritual manliness through physical exercise, Social Gospelers prioritized social salvation. Similarly, some Social Gospelers, such as the politician, settlement-house worker, and women's rights advocate Raymond Robins; the labor reformer Charles Stelzle, and the settlement-house worker Graham Taylor, sought to take advantage of the MRFM's momentum to promote their own vision of a Progressive social and masculine Christianity, while rejecting the movement's sometimes antifemale slant.

During the early twentieth century, the message of the Social Gospel movement changed as notions of Christian manliness adapted to an increasingly materialistic and business-minded ethos in American culture. In particular, the Social Gospel's emphasis on community, teamwork, and service as bases of a manly social Christianity began to incorporate notions of efficiency and businesslike promotion. Whereas Social Gospelers of the 1910s identified Jesus' manliness with the artisansal ruggedness of the craftsman, by the 1920s they defined it in terms of Jesus' personality—his ability to win over, convince, organize, and lead people in the manner of a corporate executive. Rufus Jones presented Christ in this way in his *Life of Christ* (1926), much as the advertising executive Bruce Barton had in his highly popular *The Man Nobody Knows* (1924). This new emphasis on personality over morality in the Social Gospel message represented a significant change through which the movement contributed to new ideas about Christian manliness; yet it also remained consistent with the movement's original goal of redefining Christian manhood to handle the challenges of an urban, industrial, and secularizing society.

During the 1920s the new cultural emphasis on business and personality overshadowed the Social Gospel message of social justice, and the movement's influence declined. By the 1930s, moreover, the movement was eclipsed as the federal government was prompted by the onset of the Great Depression to turn to policies of paternalistic social nurture.

The "cult of personality" to which the Social Gospel movement contributed grew in strength through the mid–twentieth century, peaking in strength with the Reverend Norman Vincent Peale's *The Power of Positive Thinking for Young People* (1952). Ironically, the Social Gospelers' emphasis on communal experience, service, and teamwork, which was intended to preserve Christian manhood against the increasing secularization and commercialization of U.S. culture, implicitly helped to further a shift toward a manliness that increasingly reflected secular trends rather than following spiritual dictates.

Bibliography

Curtis, Susan. *A Consuming Faith: The Social Gospel and Modern American Culture.* Baltimore: Johns Hopkins University Press, 1991.

Fishburn, Janet Forsythe. *The Fatherhood of God and the Victorian Family: The Social Gospel in America.* Philadelphia: Fortress Press, 1981.

Kimmel, Michael. *Manhood in America: A Cultural History.* New York: Free Press, 1996.

May, Henry F. *Protestant Churches and Industrial America.* New York: Harper & Row, 1949.

Further Reading

Bederman, Gail. "'The Women Have Had Charge of the Church Work Long Enough': The Men and Religion Forward Movement of 1911–1912 and the Masculinization of Middle-Class Protestantism." *American Quarterly* 41 (September 1989): 432–465.

Carter, Paul. *The Spiritual Crisis of the Gilded Age.* DeKalb: Northern Illinois University Press, 1971.

Crunden, Robert M. *Ministers of Reform: The Progressives Achievement in American Civilization, 1889–1920.* New York: Basic Books, 1982.

Fones-Wolf, Ken. *Trade Union Gospel: Christianity and Labor in Industrial Philadelphia, 1865–1915.* Philadelphia: Temple University Press, 1989.

Related Entries

Character; Cult of Domesticity; Evangelicalism and Revivalism; Industrialization; Men and Religion Forward Movement; Middle-Class Manhood; Muscular Christianity; Progressive Era; Religion and Spirituality; Sentimentalism; Urbanization; Victorian Era; Young Men's Christian Association

—Thomas Winter

Sons of Liberty

The Sons of Liberty was organized in 1765 to protest Britain's passage of the Stamp Act, which was enacted to raise revenue through colonial taxation. A secret intercolonial organization of men that cut across class lines, the Sons of Liberty expanded definitions of male citizenship and republican manhood by mobilizing thousands for political action. Previously, traditional notions of social and political deference had effectively confined legitimate political activity to elite men, despite the high proportion of men eligible to vote by virtue of property ownership. The Sons of Liberty offered much wider access to public politics, thus expanding the social reach of the responsibilities and privileges of citizenship.

The organization's very name was rooted in the gendered nature of English republican political ideology and practice. Like the radical politicians in eighteenth-century England who challenged the growing power of the monarchy, American patriot leaders tended to portray liberty and political virtue as feminine and to cast themselves as liberty's masculine defenders.

The Sons of Liberty included men with previously limited access to democratic participation. Local leaders were men from middling backgrounds—including small merchants, seamen, and artisans—who assumed positions of political importance by organizing public demonstrations and acting as middlemen between political elites and laboring men. On August 14, 1765, the Boston chapter of the Sons of Liberty organized a mob protest in response to the Stamp Act. The demonstration, the first known organized action by the group, was led by shoemaker Ebenezer McIntosh, probably in concert with wealthy and powerful politicians such as Samuel Adams and James Otis. After hanging effigies of Stamp Distributor Andrew Oliver and the Earl of Bute, McIntosh led two thousand of Boston's laboring men to Oliver's genteel house, where they demolished his elegant furniture and destroyed his wines. This crowd action resulted in Oliver's resignation as stamp distributor. The anti–Stamp Act demonstration exemplifies the Sons of Liberty's broadening of republican manhood and its challenge to older notions of deference and elite rule.

Despite its potentially radical widening of republican citizenship and encouragement of political protest, the Sons of Liberty attempted to discourage social upheaval and ultimately offered a conservative definition of manhood rooted in property ownership. Their experiences during the August 14 demonstration convinced them that recruiting lower-class crowds for political purposes involved risks to the security of propertied men, since they could not ensure control over these crowds. Subsequent street protests in 1765, which involved pillaging symbols of wealth and power, made apparent the risks of radicalizing the lower classes through empowering notions of republican manhood. Boston crowds attacked Lieutenant Governor Thomas Hutchinson's mansion, destroying his furniture, wine, and other objects of value, while New York crowds dragged Governor Cadwallader Colden's coach, and his effigy, through the streets before burning both in front of the royal fort.

In denouncing these later attacks while continuing to celebrate what they considered the legitimate activities of August 14, the Sons of Liberty revealed class differences and tensions over the meaning of republican manhood during the Revolutionary period. Patriot leaders established formal delegations for intercolonial committees, held town meetings, and published public notices and political pamphlets. They were interested in pursuing radical political agendas and targeting symbols of royal authority, but theirs was a socially conservative version of republican manhood that remained grounded in traditional notions of social hierarchy, and was therefore suspicious of the unchecked power of mobs. However, the laboring men who participated in antigovernment crowd actions embraced a socially and politically radical version of republican manhood; their belief in property-based citizenship, infused with class resentment, led them to target symbols of wealth and to conclude that existing property arrangements should be overthrown. The middling artisans and small merchants who were the early members of the Sons of Liberty used their position between elite patriot leaders and the laboring poor to give themselves political legitimacy and enter the fold of republican manhood. Through their ability to influence and control extralegal crowd action, these men gained access to legitimate channels of political control.

Occupying the middle ranks of Revolutionary American society, the Sons of Liberty both maintained and challenged the traditional stance of social deference toward authority, and paradoxically extended and delimited the social scope of republican manhood. Keeping the definition of republican manhood firmly rooted in male property ownership, they contributed to the conservatism of the American Revolution and, in the longer term, opened a door to the more radically inclusive notions of republican manhood and citizenship that shaped American life in the nineteenth and twentieth centuries.

BIBLIOGRAPHY

Countryman, Edward. *A People in Revolution: The American Revolution and Political Society in New York, 1760–1790.* New York: Norton, 1989.

Hoerder, Dirk. "Boston Leaders and Boston Crowds, 1765–1776." In *The American Revolution: Explorations in the History of American*

Radicalism, edited by Alfred Young. DeKalb: Northern Illinois University Press, 1976.

Morgan, Edmund Sears, and Helen Morgan. *The Stamp Act Crisis: Prologue to Revolution.* Chapel Hill: University of North Carolina Press, 1953.

Nash, Gary B. *The Urban Crucible: The Northern Seaports and the Origins of the American Revolution.* Cambridge, Mass.: Harvard University Press, 1979.

Further Reading

Bushman, Richard L. *King and People in Provincial Massachusetts.* Chapel Hill: University of North Carolina Press, 1985.

Fliegleman, Jay. *Prodigals and Pilgrims: The American Revolution against Patriarchal Authority, 1750–1800.* New York: Cambridge University Press, 1982.

Lemisch, Jesse. *Jack Tar vs. John Bull: The Role of New York's Seamen in Precipitating the Revolution.* New York: Garland, 1997.

Maier, Pauline. *From Resistance to Revolution: Colonial Radicals and the Development of American Opposition to Britain, 1765–1776.* New York: Knopf, 1972.

Wood, Gordon S. *The Creation of the American Republic, 1776–1787.* Chapel Hill: University of North Carolina Press, 1969.

Young, Alfred Fabian. *The Shoemaker and the Tea Party: Memory and the American Revolution.* Boston: Beacon Press, 1999.

Related Entries

American Revolution; Citizenship; Democratic Manhood; Patriotism; Politics; Property; Republicanism

—*Jeffrey Trask*

Southern Manhood

Definitions of manhood in the American South have developed out of diverse relationships—particularly those between white and black, free and slave, farmers and the land, and men and women. Many of these definitions emerged either to justify domination or to resist it. Self-consciously southern definitions have generally involved white men resisting interference from outside the region. African-American men in the South, meanwhile, have often had to construct understandings of manhood within or against the boundaries created by slavery, segregation, and poverty.

White Manhood in the Old South

By the eighteenth century, white southern men applied at least five definitions of manhood. One, the ideal of paternalism, called for benevolent men to rule as fathers over extended families and ultimately over society. A second, the notion of independence, suggested that white men should work for themselves and associated taking orders with women, slaves, and children. Another definition involved honor, which focused on the need to prove one's character and protect one's reputation among equals. A fourth, imbued with racist meanings, suggested that white men should assert mastery over black men and could claim sexual authority over black women. Finally, there was the image of the "helluvafella," a term the historian W. J. Cash used to describe the man whose focus was "to toss down a pint of raw whiskey in a gulp, to fiddle and dance all night, to bite off the nose or gouge out the eye of a favorite enemy, to fight harder and love harder than the next man" (Cash, 52).

These dimensions of white southern manhood grew out of the conditions and experiences of early southern life. The large majority of males in the first generations of English settlers in Virginia struggled against each other, against Native Americans, and against the environment in their attempts to become independent and, increasingly during the seventeenth and eighteenth centuries, slaveholding landholders. By the early nineteenth century, white southern men measured their manhood by the degree to which they had achieved freedom from dependent labor and credit. Among slaveholding whites, ownership of land and slaves (and paternalistic control over the latter) were also markers of manhood.

Notions of honor and paternalism worked together to suggest that powerful men deserved their authority. Beginning in the mid–eighteenth century, slave owners imagined themselves as patriarchs who treated their dependents kindly and received respect and affection in return. The abolitionist movement prompted slave owners to argue that rule by benevolent father figures protected a harmonious, hierarchically arranged, organic society against excessive individualism, crime, vice, and disorder. Notions of honor suggested that elite men should protect their reputations and family names from any criticism.

Meanwhile, among white indentured servants, the rough and often temporary nature of early colonial life in the South often encouraged frontier rashness, a characteristic apparent in the floating saloons catering to that group. By the late colonial period, southerners and nonsoutherners writing about the southern frontier began producing helluvafella images of lower-class southern whites as fun-loving rustics fond of boastful talk, ready to fight, and expert at hunting and other physical skills. In the mid–nineteenth century, southwestern humor writers built on these descriptions to create long-lasting images of rural white southerners as uncouth men of nature who lived beyond the rules of polite society.

This 1844 lithograph depicts an antebellum ideal of southern manhood based on benevolent patriarchy, racial and gender hierarchy, family honor, and chivalry. (Harry T. Peters, "America on Stone" Lithography Collection, National Museum of American History, Behring Center, Smithsonian Institution)

African-American Manhood in the Old South

African-American men in the South, meanwhile, often constructed understandings of manhood shaped by slavery, segregation, poverty, and racism. Early in southern history, white men depicted African-American men either as childlike figures requiring and benefiting from kindly paternalism, or as hypersexual brutes with a sexual potency they both feared and envied. Living in a society where people with power often compared them to children, and sometimes denied their very humanity, African-American males often emphasized their manhood either through great dignity and self-control or through aggressive retaliation. Other definitions of African-American manhood stressed the ability to support and maintain a household in the face of great obstacles.

African men came from societies based on hierarchy and honor, but as slaves they faced severe challenges to their honor and their family roles. Slave owners had the authority to break up slaves' families. Large numbers of slave husbands and wives—perhaps more than half—did not live together. Also, slave laws identified slave children's status with the status of their mothers. This relative powerlessness, combined with the real possibility of physical punishment for acts of disobedience, meant that men faced great challenges in understanding or asserting their manhood. For many men, the tensions of slave life could lead to violence against other slaves, both male and female.

Survival sometimes meant suffering in silence. Some scholars see cool resolve in the face of suffering as a West African trait. For many, however, finding ways to resist authority became central to their definition of manhood. Frederick Douglass, for example, recalled that he had almost accepted his slave status before he fought back against an abusive overseer and found a way to escape. Douglass helped establish a literary tradition in which individual men asserted their manhood by showing how they escaped oppression through flight.

White Manhood during the Civil War and Reconstruction

The Civil War and the Confederate military experience brought white southerners' definitions of manhood together, although not without conflict, and merged them with ideas of Confederate government and nationhood. White men claimed to be fighting against forces and distant authorities that threatened their honor by insulting the nature of their society and challenged their independence by questioning their right to own slaves, resisting efforts to take these slaves west, and invading their land. To lead their military regiments, Confederates elected prominent local men who generally claimed to offer paternal care over their forces. Men in the army increasingly feared the freedoms asserted by black men, both on the home front and in the Union army.

The outcome of the war, and the Reconstruction process that followed, further cemented traditional definitions of southern manhood. White men responded to military defeat, growing financial problems, and loss of control over both African-American slaves and (briefly) the political system by asserting their manhood even more strongly through an emphasis on violence and domination. Whites' representations of black men became even more exaggerated, ranging from overdressed drunken stooges incapable of caring for themselves to brutish killers or rapists loose on the highways. In the late 1860s the Ku Klux Klan emerged, claiming the right and responsibility of southern white men to defend their honor and traditional independence by using violence in their local communities to overturn the illegitimate power of black men and northern Republicans. From the late 1880s through the 1910s, groups of white men often lynched black men who had been accused, but not convicted, of crimes, defending such actions by stressing the need to assert white manhood and protect white women in a new and uncertain South.

Rethinking African-American Manhood after Emancipation

For African Americans of the Civil War and Reconstruction periods, manhood represented a range of possibilities. It meant fighting for freedom in the Civil War and then memorializing that fight with Memorial Day celebrations. Many defined manhood as working to unite families, claiming and using political rights, and pursuing economic independence outside the control of white landlords and the federal government.

As always, African-American manhood in the South included the rejection of racist images. Minstrel images of black men as fun-loving comic musicians who accepted inferior roles and had limited ambitions became central to southern justifications for blacks' disempowerment. African Americans rejected such images with two responses. One, represented by Booker T. Washington and numerous church leaders, was to embrace a demeanor of self-control, dignity, hard work, and racial uplift—images that were at first extremely Victorian and intended to appeal to whites.

The other strategy seized a form of power by emphasizing qualities white men already feared. Some African-American men, in both northern and southern cities developed a street corner culture that stressed the ability to live outside conventional rules and identities. African-American folklore upheld "bad man" characters such as Stagolee, who gained respect by being fearless. Leaving the farm for the road offered the possibility of new identities, especially for the young men who were usually the first in a family and community to migrate. The lyrics of blues songs, originating in the Deep South, combined the freedom to ramble from place to place with a pride in surviving through wits and physical skill. Mississippi native Richard Wright wrote about young black men for whom manhood meant the ability to move and, sometimes, to fight back. His short story "Almos' a Man" (1940) dramatizes the frustrations of a southern teenager who, unable to prove his manhood to his parents or employer, tries to prove it by getting a gun and heading out of town.

White Manhood in the New South

Increasing African-American assertiveness was only one of several challenges to white southerners' traditional meanings of manhood. Industrial growth also challenged white men's sense of themselves as independent farmers and masters of households. Railroad construction, mining, and timber and levee work took men away from their families, while the textile and garment mills that emerged around 1900 challenged patriarchy by employing men, women, and children at similar jobs. Particularly troubling for southern white men was the fact that the low wages of factory work offered no escape from dependent labor.

Tensions among white southerners' definitions of manhood became especially prominent during the Southern Renaissance, an intellectual movement in the 1920s and 1930s that attempted to portray Confederate men as heroes while also embracing a more modern world. Conservative writers such as William Alexander Percy and the Vanderbilt Agrarians—who, led by John Crowe Ransom, published *I'll Take My Stand* (1929)—bemoaned the economic and cultural forces that undercut the independence of farmers and the paternalism of traditional elites. On the other hand, William Faulkner and other Renaissance authors like W. J. Cash, author of *The Mind of the South* (1941), were troubled by flaws of character (e.g., sexual excess, dishonesty, unprovoked violence) that undercut the status and leadership of apparently heroic father figures.

The Civil Rights Movement

The civil rights movement, gaining force in the late 1950s, dramatized earlier differences among conflicting images of black manhood. The solemn and dignified image found its champion in Martin Luther King, Jr., for whom commitment to nonviolent protest was not merely a strategy but a dedication to conducting a dignified and disciplined struggle. The second male image in the civil rights movement was far more militant, combining pride in blackness, an emphasis on individual achievement, readiness for self-defense, and an unwillingness to compromise. This image was embraced by such diverse people as Kentucky-born boxer Cassius Clay (Mohammad Ali), who rejected the name of the white abolitionist for whom he was named; South Carolina singer James Brown, who, in 1968, created the anthem "Say It Loud—I'm Black and I'm Proud"; Robert Williams, author of *Negroes with Guns* (1962); and Black Power spokesman Stokely Carmichael. Like King and many other preachers, these men offered images of self-control in the face of great pressure, but their pride also included forms of bravado. Ali proclaimed, for example, "I am the greatest."

White-supremacist thinking and action during the civil rights years drew on traditional meanings of manhood. Many southern opponents of civil rights portrayed the movement as the work of meddlers from outside the region, and as intending to integrate black males and white females in public schools. Citizens' Councils, which formed in the Mississippi Delta in 1954, claimed to be the white supremacist organizations of the traditional elite and argued that their traditional paternalistic leadership made them the best forces to restore order. Many businessmen claimed the mantle of paternalism, arguing that investors would not come to a South where people repeatedly broke the laws, turned fire hoses on children, bombed churches, and threatened to close the schools.

Manhood in the Recent and Contemporary South

Changes in southern life have challenged most traditions of southern white manhood and prompted great interest in symbolism and cultural politics. Agricultural independence, upper-class paternalism, face-to-face communities based on honor, and clear claims to racial domination have faded as living realities. Perhaps as a response, many white southerners have grasped the helluvafella image in music and sports. It is no coincidence that Southern Rock music—exemplified by Charlie Daniels' plea for white male southerners to "Get loud and be proud," and by his plea as a white southern man to "leave this long-haired country boy alone"—developed among young white southerners in the years following the civil rights movement. In this music, independence, once tied to mastery of place and household, now meant the freedom to keep moving without domestic ties or permanent connections—to be, in Lynyrd Skynyrd's phrase, "free as a bird." The helluvafella male image lives on among NASCAR drivers and fans, though corporate domination of the sport has eclipsed the Appalachian tradition of fleeing revenue agents that helped give birth to the sport.

Many political disputes in the South draw on traditional concerns about manhood. Southern men often take pride in gun ownership and oppose gun-control laws, usually in the name of protecting their households and being free to hunt. Southern conservatives' opposition to welfare programs often taps traditional notions of black men's moral failings. In recent debates about displaying the Confederate flag in South Carolina and Mississippi, white men interpreted opposition to the flag as a dishonoring of their male ancestors, while many African Americans identified the flag with inequality and indignity. Such controversies suggest that issues of masculinity, historically fundamental to southern consciousness, remain central to the region's society and culture.

Bibliography

Ayers, Edward L. *Vengeance and Justice: Crime and Punishment in the 19th Century American South.* New York: Oxford University Press, 1984.

Brown, Kathleen M. *Good Wives, Nasty Wenches, and Anxious Patriarchs: Gender, Race, and Power in Colonial Virginia.* Chapel Hill: University of North Carolina Press, 1996.

Cash, W. J. *The Mind of the South.* New York: Alfred A. Knopf, 1941.

Dailey, Jane, Glenda Elizabeth Gilmore, and Bryant Simon, eds. *Jumpin' Jim Crow: Southern Politics from Civil War to Civil Rights.* Princeton, N.J.: Princeton University Press, 2000.

Hale, Grace Elizabeth. *Making Whiteness: The Culture of Segregation in the South, 1890–1940.* New York: Vintage, 1999.

Jordan, Winthrop D. *White Over Black: American Attitudes toward the Negro, 1550–1812.* New York: Norton, 1977.

McCurry, Stephanie. *Masters of Small Worlds: Yeoman Households, Gender Relations, and the Political Culture of the Antebellum South Carolina Low Country.* New York: Oxford University Press, 1995.

Oliver, Paul. *The Meaning of the Blues.* New York: Collier, 1972.

Ownby, Ted. "Freedom, Manhood, and Male Tradition in 1970's Southern Rock Music." In *Haunted Bodies: Gender and Southern Texts,* edited by Anne Goodwyn Jones and Susan V. Donaldson. Charlottesville: University of Virginia Press, 1997.

Stevenson, Brenda E. *Life in Black and White: Family and Community in the Slave South.* New York: Oxford University Press, 1997.

Williamson, Joel. *The Crucible of Race: Black/White Relations in the American South Since Emancipation.* New York: Oxford University Press, 1984.

Wyatt-Brown, Bertram. *Southern Honor: Ethics and Behavior in the Old South.* New York: Oxford University Press, 1982.

———. *The Shaping of Southern Culture: Honor, Grace, and War, 1760s–1890s.* Chapel Hill: University of North Carolina Press, 2001.

Further Reading

Bardaglio, Peter W. *Reconstructing the Household: Families, Sex, and the Law in the Nineteenth-Century South.* Chapel Hill: University of North Carolina Press, 1995.

Bercaw, Nancy, ed. *Gender and the Southern Body Politic: Essays and Comments.* Jackson: University Press of Mississippi, 2000.

Dudley, David L. *My Father's Shadow: Intergenerational Conflict in African American Men's Autobiography.* Philadelphia: University of Pennsylvania Press, 1991.

Gilmore, Glenda Elizabeth. *Gender and Jim Crow: Women and the Politics of White Supremacy in North Carolina, 1896–1920.* Chapel Hill: University of North Carolina Press, 1996.

Hall, Jacquelyn Dowd, James Leloudis, Robert Korstad, Mary Murphy, Lu Ann Jones, and Christopher B. Daly. *Like a Family: The Making of a Southern Cotton Mill World.* Chapel Hill: University of North Carolina Press, 2000.

Kantrowitz, Stephen. *Ben Tillman and the Reconstruction of White Supremacy.* Chapel Hill: University of North Carolina Press, 2000.

Levine, Lawrence W. *Black Culture and Black Consciousness: Afro-American Folk Thought from Slavery to Freedom.* Oxford: Oxford University Press, 1978.

Littlefield, Daniel C. "Blacks, John Brown, and a Theory of Manhood." In *His Soul Goes Marching On: Responses to John Brown and the Harpers Ferry Raid,* edited by Paul Finkelman. Charlottesville: University Press of Virginia, 1995.

Ownby, Ted. *Subduing Satan: Religion, Recreation, and Manhood in the Rural South, 1865–1920.* Chapel Hill: University of North Carolina Press, 1990.

Proctor, Nicholas W. *Bathed in Blood: Hunting and Mastery in the Old South.* Charlottesville: University Press of Virginia, 2002.

RELATED ENTRIES

African-American Manhood; Agrarianism; Character; Chivalry; Civil Rights Movement; Civil War; Dueling; Guns; Hunting; Minstrelsy; Patriarchy; Property; Race; Slavery; Victorian Era; Violence; Whiteness; White Supremacism; Wright, Richard

—*Ted Ownby*

SPANISH-AMERICAN WAR

The Spanish-American War, fought in 1898 between the United States and Spain over interests in Cuba, was triggered by an alleged Spanish attack on the U.S. battleship *Maine.* The war occurred during the Gilded Age (1873–1900), a period of changing definitions of middle-class masculinity. Since the mid–nineteenth century, American middle-class men had been articulating new definitions of masculinity (associated with the notion of a "strenuous life" by contemporaries and described as a "passionate manhood" by historians) that emphasized the body, martial virtues, and military discipline. At the same time, the United States began to emerge as a world power that sought to emulate European colonial powers. The Spanish-American War, referred to at the time as a "splendid little war," lasted a mere four months, yet it reflected an important convergence of new articulations of masculinity and U.S. foreign policy.

Prior to the outbreak of the war, American men had begun to voice increasing concerns over both their manliness and the status of the United States as an emerging world power. The emergence of the "new woman" in the late nineteenth century appeared to challenge men's position of power in public life, while urbanization and industrialization seemed to undermine middle-class American manhood by separating men from nature and removing physical exertion from their working lives. Meanwhile, the scramble for colonies among European nations after 1889 and the publication of Alfred Thayer Mahan's *The Influence of Sea-Power Upon History* (1890), which linked national greatness to control over trade, military strength, and colonial possessions, awakened fears among some American men that the United States was too weak to compete with the European nations that were carving out large territorial empires in Africa and Asia. For American men afraid of having become "soft" at home and abroad, the Spanish-American War presented an opportunity to assert national strength and reinvigorate white, middle-class masculinity.

American support for the Cuban resistance against Spain served as a defense of an ideal of male chivalry and well-ordered gender relations at home. By idealizing Cuban men as "gallant revolutionaries" and Cuban women as models of chaste femininity, American supporters of a war with Spain depicted Cuba as a society that still defined masculinity and gender relations in terms of an early-nineteenth-century notion of republican manhood and a nineteenth-century, middle-class "cult of domesticity." The events surrounding the arrest and liberation of Cuban activist Evangelina Cisneros in 1897 reflected the convergence of U.S. concerns regarding masculinity, gender relations, and foreign policy. The daughter of a prominent Cuban family, Cisneros had been arrested by Spanish authorities on the suspicion that she had aided the resistance. *The New York Journal* and its publisher, William Randolph Hearst, arranged Cisneros's subsequent rescue and transport to the United States. The Cisneros affair allowed prointerventionists in the United States to cast Cuba in the role of the damsel in distress. By aiding Cuba, American men upheld their own revolutionary republican traditions, which suggested that manhood must be earned and supported male patriarchical control over both the household and the nation.

Not all Americans, however, were eager for war. Initially, President William McKinley tried to remain neutral and resolve the conflict through arbitration. As a result, McKinley and his policies became embroiled in American debates over the nature of manhood, war, and political leadership. McKinley's critics, such as Assistant Secretary of the Navy Theodore Roosevelt, called him "Wobbly Willy" and accused him of lacking the physical ability to enforce his demands—a severe accusation at a time when American men increasingly saw the body as the core of male gender identity. McKinley's supporters, however, saw the president's arbitrationist stance as a sign of his moral stamina, sound character, and manly resolve and courage. After the *Maine* incident, however,

McKinley found that his arbitrationist position became impossible to uphold and he declared war on Spain. As a result of the United States' victorious intervention, McKinley was praised for his manly leadership during the conflict.

In the aftermath of the Spanish-American War, American men felt reinvigorated as forceful rulers abroad and at home. Validating a masculinity grounded in military discipline and martial valor, the war abetted a larger process of reconciliation in the nation, which was still divided by memories of the Civil War, bringing northern and southern men closer together under a banner of a shared manly citizenship.

Wartime events contributed to a shift in middle-class understandings of manliness. Whereas nineteenth-century American men had understood male identity in terms of a stable and static inner self, the Spanish-American War fostered the emergence of new notions of middle-class masculinity as an identity constructed and enacted by men themselves. The career of Theodore Roosevelt, who created himself as the archetype of the vigorous and aggressive, yet civilized and chivalric, white man, is an example. Educated at Harvard, Roosevelt resigned at the outset of the war from his post as assistant secretary of the navy and led the 1st U.S. Volunteer Cavalry—known as the "Rough Riders"—to Cuba and up San Juan Hill in a uniform designed and tailored to his specifications. Recognizing the political value of Roosevelt's military service and the virile masculinity the public had come to associate with him, New York senator Thomas Collier Platt offered him the Republican Party nomination in the 1898 New York gubernatorial election. In 1900, McKinley (whose initial reluctance about going to war Roosevelt had publicly attacked) chose him as his vice-presidential candidate.

Just like the prointerventionists, anti-interventionists such as Senator George Frisbie Hoar of Massachusetts made important contributions to ongoing debates over the nature of masculinity and its place in American society and politics. They promoted values such as manly honor and self-restraint, arguing that Spain was an inferior adversary, unworthy of being engaged in combat by the United States. Additionally, anti-interventionists introduced new ideas about manhood based on a dispassionate application of professional expertise and a faith in institutional forms and arrangements, such as treaties—a definition of masculinity that would gain currency during the Progressive Era (1890–1915) and the 1920s.

The Spanish-American War served as a catalyst for new definitions of manhood that emerged after the Civil War. Perceived as an opportunity to reinvigorate American manhood, the war gave rise to an ideal of manliness grounded in physical vigor, combative qualities, and physical aggressiveness, while its opponents argued for a manliness based on professionalism and middle-class respectability. After 1900, new emphases associated with Progressive Era reforms—such as professionalism, efficiency, and a renewed emphasis on middle-class respectability—tempered the aggressive masculine impulses fostered by the war.

Bibliography

Bederman, Gail. *Manliness & Civilization: A Cultural History of Gender and Race in the United States, 1880–1917.* Chicago: University of Chicago Press, 1996.

Boose, Linda. "Techno-Muscularity and the 'Boy Eternal.'" In *Cultures of United States Imperialism*, edited by Amy Kaplan and Donald E. Pease. Durham, N.C.: Duke University Press, 1993.

Edwards, Rebecca. *Angels in the Machinery: Gender in American Party Politics from the Civil War to the Progressive Era.* New York: Oxford University Press, 1997.

Hoganson, Kristin L. *Fighting for American Manhood: How Gender Politics Provoked the Spanish-American and Philippine-American Wars.* New Haven, Conn.: Yale University Press, 1998.

Linderman, Gerald F. *The Mirror of War: American Society and the Spanish-American War.* Ann Arbor: University of Michigan Press, 1974.

Further Reading

Budd, Michael Anton. *The Sculpture Machine: Physical Culture and Body Politics in the Age of Empire.* New York: New York University Press, 1997.

Hooper, Charlotte. *Manly States: Masculinities, International Relations, and Gender Politics.* New York: Columbia University Press, 2001.

Jacobson, Matthew Frye. *Barbarian Virtues: The United States Encounters Foreign Peoples at Home and Abroad, 1876–1917.* New York: Hill and Wang, 2000.

Rowe, John Carlos. *Literary Culture and U.S. Imperialism: From the Revolution to World War II.* New York: Oxford University Press, 2000.

Wexler, Laura. *Tender Violence: Domestic Visions in an Age of U.S. Imperialism.* Chapel Hill: University of North Carolina Press, 2000.

Related Entries

Chivalry; Citizenship; Cult of Domesticity; Gilded Age; Heroism; Imperialism; Industrialization; Middle-Class Manhood; Militarism; Military; Nationalism; Passionate Manhood; Politics; Professionalism; Progressive Era; Roosevelt, Theodore; Strenuous Life; Violence; War; Whiteness

—*Thomas Winter*

SPORTS

Sports have been intertwined with American ideals of (and fears about) masculinity since achieving cultural prominence in the late nineteenth century. For much of the twentieth century, a "rough" model of sports masculinity prevailed, largely defined by forceful physical contact or *mano a mano* (hand-to-hand) competition. Although this model remained powerful in the late twentieth and the early twenty-first centuries, it was challenged by critics because of its perceived hypermasculine excess. Such challenges both illustrated and influenced broadening concepts of American sports masculinity.

Masculinity and Organized Sports

Before the mid–nineteenth century, most white Americans defined manhood through work and spirituality, rather than through leisure activity and physical prowess, and mainstream American society generally considered game-playing incompatible with true manhood. Sports existed in recognizable forms, but they were not highly organized.

During the late nineteenth century, however, organized sports grew in America amid an increasing cultural emphasis on the physical aspects of manhood. As Darwinian theory encouraged Americans to equate life with physical struggle, and as industrialization and urbanization prompted concerns that the work of American men (particularly middle-class men) had become insufficiently vigorous, cultural spokespersons began emphasizing the importance of athletics to the moral and physical dimensions of healthy manhood. Advocates of "muscular Christianity" urged organized sports programs for American males, and proponents of a "strenuous life" ideal likewise encouraged men to pursue challenging outdoor activity. These impulses prompted the incorporation of sports into the activities and facilities of the Young Men's Christian Association (YMCA); the formation of sports programs for men in the nation's colleges and elite high schools; the promotion of sports and outdoor activity by such boys' organizations as the Boy Scouts of America (established in 1910); and, especially in cities, a national proliferation of professional sports teams.

Although many Americans hoped that sports would foster the physical vigor and moral virtue they considered essential to ideal middle-class manhood, many professional athletes themselves demonstrated a model of sports-related masculinity more akin to urban working-class models grounded in boisterousness. John L. Sullivan, for instance, a descendant of Irish immigrants and the most famous bare-knuckle boxing champion of the late nineteenth century, was renowned as much for his prodigious drinking as for his exploits in the ring. To the delight of middle-class sport advocates, Sullivan began advocating temperance after his boxing career, warning boys that alcohol undermined, rather than demonstrated, manliness.

Early-twentieth-century developments encouraged growing numbers of American men to participate in sports. Reduced working hours, a growing alienation from factory and office work, and a burgeoning consumer culture encouraged them to define their masculinity through leisure activities and consumption rather than through work, while corporate culture increasingly touted the virtues of team spirit and loyalty as markers of manhood. Many American men expressed their manhood through direct engagement in sports, while many others, particularly in and near the nation's cities, also participated as spectators. This consumer activity promoted male camaraderie and friendships grounded in admiration of athletes' physical prowess, in shared loyalty to a local team, and often in the consumption of alcohol. The connections among masculinity, organized sports, consumerism, and corporate culture became increasingly strong during the twentieth century, as demonstrated by the promotion of "masculine" products (e.g., sports equipment, automobiles, beer) in sports stadiums and during televised sports events (which excluded women's athletics for most of the century), as well as by the naming of sports stadiums for large corporations.

Corporatism and consumerism encouraged the perpetuation of the rough model of sports masculinity during the early twentieth century—a point illustrated by the career of professional baseball player George Herman "Babe" Ruth, a charismatic and successful athlete also known for his drinking and sexual indulgence. Ruth set the Major League single-season home-run record in 1927, helped lead the New York Yankees to four World Series titles, and presented himself as a model of American masculine bravado. In a corporatized and bureaucratized society, he became a national masculine icon because of his remarkable individual productivity and physical achievement. At the same time, his enthusiasm for gambling and spending money reflected and reinforced the consumeristic attitudes of the Roaring Twenties, while his immoderate behavior symbolized rebellion against an increasingly mechanized culture.

The differing models of masculinity in sports represented by muscular Christianity, the strenuous life, and athletes such as Ruth—and by the cultural tensions between them—persisted through the twentieth century, but the waning of the muscular Christianity movement after World War I greatly reduced the relative visibility of the Christian athlete.

Sports, Race, and Ethnicity

Participation in sports, whether professionally or in youth organizations, was at first largely confined to white males, and thus reinforced a broader association that most white Americans drew between manhood and whiteness. During the twentieth century, however, sports increasingly became an arena in which nonwhite men sought to combat racial prejudice and assert their claims to equal manhood. African Americans, in particular, formed separate sports leagues and institutions beginning in the late nineteenth century but they also pushed for admission to white leagues so that they might demonstrate their masculinity in direct competition with white men.

Several black athletes became heroes, particularly to African Americans, by becoming models of black manhood and outperforming whites: Track star Jesse Owens publicly disproved Adolph Hitler's white supremacist beliefs by winning four gold medals at the 1936 Berlin Olympics; Brooklyn Dodgers' star Jackie Robinson became the first African American to play in the major leagues in 1947; heavyweight boxing champion Cassius Clay publicized the growing African-American embrace of Islam when he changed his name to Muhammad Ali and then refused induction into the U.S. Army in 1967 because of his Muslim faith; sprinters Tommie Smith and John Carlos attracted national attention to racial justice issues by raising black-gloved fists as a political gesture after being presented with medals during the 1968 Olympics; and baseball player Henry "Hank" Aaron achieved fame by breaking Babe Ruth's career home run record in 1974.

Blacks' efforts to demonstrate their masculinity in sports had a dual impact on the interaction between race relations and constructions of masculinity in the United States. On the one hand, they reinforced white stereotypes that defined African-American masculinity in terms of physical prowess. Furthermore, African Americans continued to be largely excluded from such elite sports as golf (until Tiger Woods achieved fame during the late 1990s). In some cases, nonwhite men in sport—Muhammad Ali, for example—often emphasized their differences from, and even superiority to, white men. In these ways, sport reinforced racial tensions and notions of cultural difference.

Sports also allowed participants from several racial and ethnic groups to counteract prejudice and challenge racial and ethnic boundaries through a cross-racial and cross-ethnic form of masculinity emphasizing teamwork and friendship. Major League baseball, in particular, exposed American fans to players from increasingly diverse backgrounds. In the 1950s, for example, the fame of Joe DiMaggio counteracted many Americans' previously negative perceptions of Italian-American men. Latino baseball players, whose increasing visibility beginning in the early 1970s coincided with the rise of Hispanic identity movements, sought recognition and parity in the major leagues as part of a broader effort to achieve equality in the United States (while also conveying loyalty to their respective countries of origin). Likewise, Asians' increasing prominence in professional baseball beginning in the 1990s began counteracting white Americans' tendency to stereotype Asian and Asian-American men as unmasculine. Furthermore, in recent years sports have encouraged identification and hero worship across color lines, as exemplified by white suburban youths during the 1990s who idolized professional basketball player Michael Jordan (and purchased the Air Jordan athletic shoes that he promoted)—as well as Tiger Woods, Texas Rangers' shortstop Alex Rodriguez, and, more recently, Seattle Mariners' outfielder Ichiro Suzuki.

Challenges to Traditional Sports-Related Manhood

Cultural developments of the late twentieth and early twenty-first centuries both reinforced and challenged traditional models of sports masculinity, particularly in professional sports. In one important development, the growing impact of feminism and the men's movement after about 1970 sparked increasing concern that the rough model of manhood in sport promotes potentially dangerous hypermasculinity. This challenge was especially apparent in growing media attention to instances of violence (particularly against women) by professional athletes. Critics charged that such antisocial behavior represented an undesirable model of manhood for young male sports fans.

A related critique claimed that the premium on physical performance encouraged behaviors that either threatened or called into question athletes' manhood. The traditional expectation that athletes would endure physical pain and bodily injury—an outgrowth of the late-nineteenth-century belief that strenuous living and physical struggle bolstered one's masculinity—was challenged as it became clear that repeated injury sometimes produced serious health problems. The broken-down former athlete became an increasingly distinct masculine type. Similarly, the association of masculinity with performance led growing numbers of athletes to use performance-enhancing drugs, though the belief that such drugs delegitimized athletic accomplishments caused many sports to ban their use.

At the same time, the renewed cultural prominence of evangelical Christianity during and after the 1970s prompted the resurgence of the Christian athlete ideal. The new intertwining of sports and evangelical Christianity, apparent in the ritual gestures of many athletes during sporting events, was also evident in the growth of Promise Keepers, an evangelical men's organization that was founded in 1991 by former University of Colorado football coach Bill McCartney and held several public gatherings in sports stadiums.

While some by-products of the traditional emphasis on strenuousness have been criticized, opportunities for young males to demonstrate masculinity through personal physical adventurousness rather than hand-to-hand competition have proliferated, raising new issues about the meanings of both sports and masculinity. The growing popularity of such "extreme sports" as skateboarding, freestyle bicycling or motocross riding, freestyle skiing, and street luge—activities once associated with boyish irresponsibility rather than manliness—eventually prompted their coverage on cable television, thus gaining these sports a measure of legitimacy. As these sports began to move within the range of socially approved American male activities, the range of respectable masculinities broadened to include extreme sport practitioners, who began to be considered manly—a trend apparent in motorcycle stuntman Evel Knievel's achievement of iconic status in the 1970s and, more recently, the fame of professional skateboarder Tony Hawk. Sport thus continues to contribute to evolving American understandings of manhood.

BIBLIOGRAPHY

Baker, Aaron, and Todd Boyd, eds. *Out of Bounds: Sports, Media, and the Politics of Identity.* Bloomington: Indiana University Press, 1997.

Kimmel, Michael, and Michael A. Messner. *Men's Lives.* New York: Allyn & Bacon, 2000.

Messner, Michael A., and Donald F. Sabo. *Sex, Violence, and Power in Sports: Rethinking Masculinity.* Freedom, Calif.: Crossing Press, 1994.

Putney, Clifford. *Muscular Christianity: Manhood and Sports in Protestant America, 1880–1920.* Cambridge, Mass.: Harvard University Press, 2001.

Rail, Genevieve, ed. *Sport and Postmodern Times.* Albany: State University of New York Press, 1998.

Regalado, Samuel O. *Viva Baseball!: Latin Major Leaguers and Their Special Hunger.* Urbana: University of Illinois Press, 1998.

Susman, Warren. *Culture As History: The Transformation of American Society in the Twentieth Century.* New York: Pantheon, 1984.

FURTHER READING

Gorn, Elliott. *The Manly Art: Bare-Knuckle Prize Fighting in America.* Ithaca, N.Y.: Cornell University Press, 1986.

Lehman, Peter. *Masculinity: Bodies, Movies, Culture.* New York: Routledge, 2001.

McKay, Jim, Michael A. Messner, and Don Sabo, eds. *Masculinities, Gender Relations, and Sport.* Thousand Oaks, Calif.: Sage, 2000.

Messner, Michael A. *Power at Play: Sports and the Problem of Masculinity.* Boston: Beacon Press, 1992.

Nixon, Sean. *Hard Looks: Masculinities, Spectatorship, and Contemporary Consumption.* New York: St. Martin's, 1996.

RELATED ENTRIES

Advertising; Baseball; Body; Boyhood; Consumerism; Crisis of Masculinity; Football; Heroism; Leisure; Male Friendship; Muscular Christianity; Professionalism; Promise Keepers; Race; Strenuous Life; Sunday, Billy; Urbanization; Young Men's Christian Association

—Sean Heuston

SPRINGSTEEN, BRUCE

1949–
American Rock Singer and Songwriter

Bruce Springsteen's work reflects the impact of social and cultural change on masculinity in America during the late twentieth century. His upbringing in the manufacturing town of Freehold, New Jersey, exposed him to the conservative, patriarchal ethos of a white working-class ethnic community, but his early fondness for rock and roll in the 1950s and the "British Invasion" of the 1960s eventually transformed his view of social and gender relations.

Early in his career, Springsteen relied on the constructions of masculinity prevalent in working-class environments. His early songs feature men resolved to flee small towns "full of losers" (as in "Thunder Road" [*Born to Run*, 1975]), as well as the more passive attitude of the "little girls" who may or may not go along with them. Paradoxically, it was Springsteen who remained tied to his working-class neighborhood after his family left New Jersey for California in the late 1960s. While moving back and forth between his native Freehold and the declining beach resort of Asbury Park, he met the musicians that would make up the E-Street Band, with whom he has performed with continually since 1971 (with some early personnel changes).

In the 1980s, Springsteen began to question prescribed gender constructions and to address the personal circumstances of both men and women. His music became less tied to his New Jersey roots, and a changing social environment demanded more complex characters in his songs. During this period, well-paid blue-collar jobs vanished, while a new service economy provided mostly dead-end jobs at lower wages. Downward social mobility would consequently undermine the role of men as the sole breadwinner of the family, especially when women, driven by economic necessity and the impact of feminism, entered the job market. This symbolic emasculation of American men can be found in releases from *The River* (1980), *Nebraska* (1982), and *Born in the U.S.A.* (1984).

Springsteen's most characteristic themes are working-class populism, male bonding, and the will to overcome difficulties. These themes overlapped with, and sometimes reinforced, the resurgent conservatism of the 1980s. His antiwar song "Born in the U.S.A.," for example, was reinterpreted (or misinterpreted) by the public as a nationalist anthem, and President Ronald Reagan hailed him as an example of the self-made individual that Reagan's administration supported. Springsteen's masculine image in his performances also coincided with the conservative religious belief that gender differences are "divinely ordered." Yet Springsteen himself resisted such conservative constructions, and instead expressed an emergent "sensitive male" ideal that embraced pacifism and accepted homosexuality. For example, he kissed E-Street band saxophone player Clarence Clemmons onstage and added an antimilitaristic introduction to Edwin Starr's "War" on his recording *Live 1975–1985* (1986)—but these actions received much less public notice.

After the mid-1980s, Springsteen's liberal attitudes on race, ethnicity, and sexuality became increasingly central to his work. Nonwhite and non-English-speaking workers ("American Skin," on *New York City Live*, 2001), gay men ("My Lover Man," on *Tracks*, 1998), and poor working women ("Spare Parts," on *Tunnel of Love*, 1987) became his protagonists, replacing the unemployed or class-resentful males who had once been his focus of attention.

Masculinity is thus an important marker of social relations in all of Bruce Springsteen's music, though in a far more subdued form in his work in the 1980s and 1990s. The changing archetypes of men featured in his songs reflect changing perceptions of gender in America throughout the last quarter of the twentieth century.

Bibliography

Garman, Bryan K. *A Race of Singers: Whitman's Working-Class Hero from Guthrie to Springsteen.* Chapel Hill: North Carolina University Press, 2000.

Further Reading

Alterman, Eric. *It Ain't No Sin to Be Glad You're Alive: The Promise of Bruce Springsteen.* Boston: Little, Brown, 1999.

Cullen, Jim. *Born in the USA: Bruce Springsteen and the American Tradition.* New York: Harper Collins, 1997.

Lipsitz, George. *Time Passages: Collective Memory and American Popular Culture.* Minneapolis: University of Minnesota Press, 1990.

Mackey-Kallis, Susan, and Ian McDermott. "Bruce Springsteen, Ronald Reagan, and the American Dream." *Popular Music and Society* 16, no. 4 (1992).

Scheurer, Timothy E. *Born in the U.S.A.: The Myth of America in Popular Music from Colonial Times to the Present.* Jackson: University Press of Mississippi, 1991.

Shelvin, David, Janet Zandy, and Larry Smith, eds. *Writing Work: Writers on Working-Class Writing.* Huron, Ohio: Bottom Dog Press, 1999.

Related Entries

American Dream; Antiwar Movement; *Grapes of Wrath, The;* Heroism; Heterosexuality; Homosexuality; Individualism; Labor Movement and Unions; Male Friendship; Nationalism; Patriotism; Race; Rambo; Reagan, Ronald; Self-Made Man; Sensitive Male; Vietnam War; Working-Class Manhood

—Juan José Cruz

Strenuous Life

Emerging out of the historical context of western expansion in the 1840s, the ideal of a "strenuous life" was initially articulated in opposition to the humanitarian idealism of antebellum reform movements. In the aftermath of the Civil War, this ideal—emphasizing duty, military valor, and perseverance in overcoming obstacles—came to shape middle-class masculinity in U.S. society. By the late nineteenth century, contemporaries agreed on key masculine virtues, though they tended to disagree on the exact form and outlets that the strenuous life should take.

The concept had its origin in the social thought of the historian and naturalist Francis Parkman. A scion of Boston's upper class, Parkman and others of his class resented what seemed an erosion of status barriers and an increase in social and political egalitarianism in Jacksonian America. Parkman particularly scorned the political softness and sentimentalism of antebellum reform movements that, heavily influenced by women, advocated gender and racial equality and the admission of lower-class white men to the political process. Parkman felt that upper-class white men could retain their power and influence in U.S. society only by adopting a new ideal of manliness. Traveling to the Oregon territory in 1846—a journey he subsequently chronicled in *The Oregon Trail* (1847)—Parkman believed he found this model of manliness in the example of the frontiersman, who possessed endurance, physical courage, and social usefulness in blazing trails for civilization to follow.

Parkman's ideals failed to spark interest until the Civil War united men around a national crisis. The realities of combat convinced many Northern men who volunteered for military service that war had less to do with moral ideals and humanitarian commitments than with duty and perseverance. Even the transcendentalist philosopher Ralph Waldo Emerson (1803–82) began to perceive war as a manifestation of men's vigor and the nation's vitality, extending his concept of self-reliance from its original meaning of manly intellectual independence to include duty and service in a larger cause.

After the war, the ideal of the strenuous life—temporarily shorn of Parkman's emphasis on physical endurance—became a middle-class social ideal, defining manhood in terms of an active and socially useful life. For a post–Civil War generation of middle- and upper-class men, public service in peacetime required self-discipline and the ability to overcome obstacles, just as military service in wartime did. By the 1880s, however, as growing numbers of Americans embraced imperialist foreign policy goals and perceived the world in terms of a Darwinian struggle for racial and national survival, this ideal regained its earlier focus on physical strife, as well as a heightened emphasis on military valor among men. On April 10, 1899, Theodore Roosevelt exhorted his all-male audience at Chicago's elite Hamilton Club to embrace a strenuous life conceived in these terms. What had been a prescription for the restoration of upper-class male hegemony in the days of Parkman became a doctrine of masculine, national, and Anglo-Saxon racial superiority.

Not all contemporaries agreed with this interpretation of the strenuous life. The Harvard philosopher and anti-imperialist William James was a particularly prominent spokesman for an alternative understanding of strenuous living. James agreed that American men—especially young men—required discipline and a higher cause to direct their energies toward, but his reading of the strenuous life involved moral and intellectual, rather than physical and military, exertion. In "The Moral Equivalent of War" (1910), James suggested that the strenuous discipline and martial valor used to fight wars could be pragmatically applied to the solving of social and ethical problems.

For several reasons, the ideal of a strenuous life faded in the aftermath of World War I. First, the war, and particularly its results, was somewhat unpopular among the American public, and therefore was unable to serve to unite Americans behind a cause, suggesting that victory and defeat on the battlefield were viewed as being decided more by mutual attrition than by individual military valor and discipline. Second, the isolationist mood of the 1920s and early 1930s proved inhospitable to an ideal of masculinity grounded in valorization of war and notions of imperialist exploit. Lastly, the burgeoning consumer culture of the 1920s provided new outlets and opportunities for men to establish their manliness. James's version of the strenuous life, however, which stressed a moral dimension, persisted in the New Deal's Civilian Conservation Corps, which put unemployed youth to work in conserving natural resources. This ideal was also revived in John F. Kennedy's Peace Corps in the 1960s, and in increasing calls toward the close of the twentieth century for men to participate in national service.

Bibliography

Bederman, Gail. *Manliness and Civilization: A Cultural History of Gender and Race in the United States, 1880–1917.* Chicago: University of Chicago Press, 1995.

Fredrickson, George M. *The Inner Civil War: Northern Intellectuals and the Crisis of the Union.* New York: Harper & Row, 1965.

Gorn, Elliott J. *The Manly Art: Bare-Knuckle Prize Fighting in America.* Ithaca, N.Y.: Cornell University Press, 1986.

Townsend, Kim. *Manhood at Harvard: William James and Others.* New York: Norton, 1996.

Further Reading

Budd, Michael Anton. *The Sculpture Machine: Physical Culture and Body Politics in the Age of Empire.* New York: New York University Press, 1997.

Hoganson, Kristin. *Fighting for American Manhood: How Gender Politics Provoked the Spanish-American War.* New Haven, Conn.: Yale University Press, 1998.

Kasson, John F. *Houdini, Tarzan, and the Perfect Man: The White Male Body and the Challenge of Modernity in America.* New York: Hill and Wang, 2001.

Kimmel, Michael. *Manhood in America: A Cultural History.* New York: Free Press, 1996.

Putney, Clifford Wallace. *Muscular Christianity: Sports in Protestant America, 1880–1930.* Cambridge, Mass.: Harvard University Press, 2001.

Roberts, Gerald Franklin. "The Strenuous Life: The Cult of Manliness in the Era of Theodore Roosevelt." Ph.D. diss., Michigan State University, 1970.

Rotundo, E. Anthony. *American Manhood: Transformations in Masculinity from the Revolution to the Modern Era.* New York: Basic Books, 1993.

Related Entries

Body; Capitalism; Civil War; Crisis of Masculinity; Darwinism; Democratic Manhood; Gilded Age; Imperialism; James, William; London, Jack; Middle-Class Manhood; Muscular Christianity; Nationalism; Passionate Manhood; Progressive Era; Roosevelt, Theodore; Spanish-American War; Sports; Tarzan; Victorian Era; War; Western Frontier; Whiteness

—*Thomas Winter*

SUBURBIA

The American suburb—a social and geographic space typically consisting of single-family homes and economically connected to nearby cities in which suburban homeowners (usually male) work—emerged in the mid–nineteenth century. Suburbia expanded rapidly around the turn of the twentieth century due to the growth of white-collar work and the impact of new transportation systems such as the railroad and street cars, and again during the 1950s due to the increased popularity of the automobile. The experience of suburban living combined several existing concepts of masculinity with new social experiences to form a new kind of male identity. Both conceptually and in reality, suburban manhood was contradictory: Men sought to reconcile the autonomy of independent property ownership with the loss of control entailed in white-collar office work, and their roles as provider and protector with the physical reality of increasing geographic distance and time away from their families.

The Emergence of Suburban Manhood in the Nineteenth Century

Suburban manhood drew on several major sources. The first was the Jeffersonian agrarian ideal of the early nineteenth century, according to which owning and working land as a yeoman farmer in close physical proximity to one's family made a man complete. The social reality behind this ideal faded during the late nineteenth and early twentieth centuries, as increasingly fewer American men (particularly those living in suburbia) farmed for a living or worked near their homes. But the ideal itself persisted, and many urban men alienated by their corporate work experiences sought to counteract their sense of distance from nature, family, and an idealized rural American past by owning a small plot of land, a home, and often a garden.

A second source of suburban male identity, which developed during the early to mid–nineteenth century, was a growing separation of work from the home (and the division of labor by gender that accompanied it), called by historians the "cult of domesticity." According to this social construct, men were solely responsible for providing economic support for their families through paid labor—and for representing the family's interests in the public sphere. This role gave the male breadwinner a feeling of empowerment and autonomy, even as the corporate work that underwrote it allowed most men little control over the nature of their work and often afforded them little personal satisfaction. The cult of domesticity was not unique to the suburban experience, but it was magnified by the physical separation of suburbia from the male workplace.

During the late nineteenth century, in particular, suburban manhood (and the move to suburbia generally) was informed by the husband/father's belief that leaving urban areas protected his family, or at least protected white, middle-class family ideals. Concerns over the social unrest and urban violence produced by growing immigration, nativism, class and racial conflict, and escalating crime rates resulted in an important ideological underpinning of suburban masculinity: the perceived duty of protecting women and children in a new and safe haven.

Suburban Manhood in the Twentieth Century

Between the 1880s and 1920s, the growth of suburban living generated a suburban model of manhood, sometimes called by scholars "masculine domesticity." This emergent male identity emphasized an interest in the physical aspects of the house and property, an engagement in family life, a reaction against the female-centered domesticity characteristic of Victorian culture in the United States, and a desire to counteract consequent feminization of the home and children. Feeling separated from domestic life by the increasing distances between the home and the workplace, men who aspired to this style of maleness sought to replace the mid-nineteenth-century image of the dispassionate and often emotionally and physically absent patriarch. Suburban design—from the layout of streets, parks, and social clubs to the architecture of suburban homes—emphasized the family as a complete unit and reflected the suburban man's role as participant and caregiver.

Suburban growth was briefly slowed, and suburban manhood temporarily challenged, by the Great Depression of the 1930s; but both rebounded after World War II. The accessibility of new suburban developments was greatly enhanced by a booming economy, home development programs begun during the New Deal, Veterans Administration's guaranteed mortgages, and the Interstate Highway Act of 1956. Economic prosperity fueled an enormous growth in consumer purchasing, reinforcing the importance of the suburban father/husband as breadwinner. Most suburban families remained dependent on his single income, and his full-time employment made possible the purchase of domestic items, such as television sets, automobiles, and electric washers and dryers, that came to be perceived as necessities and badges of successful suburban manhood. But suburban living and suburban manhood remained sharply circumscribed by race; the suburbs of the 1950s remained as predominantly white and middle-class, as they had been a half-century before.

Yet the postwar experience of suburban manhood entailed new sources of psychological discomfort. In addition to the already existing tension between the autonomy of the independent breadwinner role and the alienation of white-collar work, expanding consumerism intensified pressures on suburban men to provide for their families and adorn their homes with luxury items (meaning harder work and longer hours), and also to participate actively in domestic life. Furthermore, Cold War fears about nuclear annihilation and perceived challenges to the American way of life generated considerable insecurity and uncertainty among many Americans. As a result, suburban men looked increasingly to suburban life and the family as a psychological refuge. Suburban manhood meant, more than ever, seeking satisfaction, fulfillment, recreation, and fun in domesticity—and seeking autonomy and security in the suburban home.

Postwar ideals of suburban manhood were not only shaped by the social and economic realities of the period, but they were broadcast on the televisions that were increasingly part of suburban homes. Families watching such weekly programs as *The Adventures of Ozzie and Harriet* (1952–66), *Father Knows Best* (1954–63), and *Leave It to Beaver* (1957–63) saw idealized images of—and templates for—suburban living,

The growth of suburbia, particularly during the 1950s, generated a model of masculinity grounded in the suburban experience and emphasized independent property ownership, domestic engagement and leadership, breadwinning, and home maintenance and improvement. Barbecuing was a common suburban experience that symbolized a man's provider role and attachment to the outdoors. (© Josef Scaylea/Corbis)

male breadwinning, and father-centered domesticity. Although the social dynamics on screen did not always represent actual daily life, they presented powerful ideologies to which many men (and women) attempted to conform. Other forms of suburban recreation also suggested the dual identity of suburban men as distant providers and family leaders: golfing and bowling removed them from family life into the company of similarly situated men; barbecuing symbolized their role as family leaders and providers; and going to social clubs, picnics, and neighborhood (couples) card games required family participation. Hence, in both work and leisure, suburban manhood required both independence from and dependence on the family.

By the 1950s, suburbia and suburban manhood had become sufficiently prominent features of American life to generate critical concern. Such critiques as William H. Whyte's *The Organization Man* (1956) lamented the conformity, banality, and emptiness of suburban masculinity. Yet such stereotyped caricatures of suburban men failed to capture the complex realities of their lives and identities, for suburban manhood was not reducible to either absentee fatherhood or bland conformity. Rather, it combined providing for and participating in the family, autonomy from and dependence on family life, and economic power over and dependent interaction with family members.

Contemporary Issues and Representations of Suburban Manhood

During the late twentieth century, suburbia changed in important ways, including growth in size; increasing racial, ethnic, and economic diversity; and the development of corporate parks, shopping malls, townhouse subdivisions, and intersuburban highways. The trends that have perhaps had the greatest impact on gender roles and suburban manhood, however, have been an accelerated divorce rate (beginning in the 1960s), the emergence of second-wave feminism in the late 1960s, and the increasing necessity, since the 1970s, of dual incomes (the paid employment of both husbands and wives) for suburban household maintenance. As a result, suburban men have been increasingly unlikely to enjoy the authority and mystique that accompany sole-breadwinner status, and they are more likely to be targets of criticism. Still, these changes have not erased the 1950s archetype of the suburban father/husband from the American imagination.

Television and film images of the late twentieth century reflect both the persistence of and the challenges to suburban masculinity. The nostalgic but comical television program *The Wonder Years* (1988–93), for example, features a family plagued by internal discord and a father who, while balancing absence and involvement in the manner of the classic suburban father, is characterized by frequent angry outbursts rather than the calm paternalism of his 1950s television forebears. Sitcoms such as *Married with Children* (1987–97), *The Simpsons* (premiered in 1989), and *Home Improvement* (1991–99) carry the critique of suburban manhood even further by featuring bumbling, incompetent, fiscally irresponsible, and even violent fathers. Still, these programs all stopped short of challenging the suburban father's role as absentee provider, authority figure, and, at least figuratively, head of the family. Similarly, in the film *She's Having a Baby* (1988), Kevin Bacon plays a suburban husband whose loss of freedom is made apparent through scenes of lawn mowing in unison with his neighbors and laborious but unfulfilling urban work. But while Bacon's character at first seeks to escape suburbia and the responsibilities of impending fatherhood, the birth of his child prompts his full embrace of suburban manhood. In all of these media images, the basis of suburban manhood remains intact: The suburban father/husband seeks to balance providing and participating, and also to find validation as a man through his home and family.

The reality of suburban masculinity has no doubt changed in the modern era, impacted by larger changes in the social, political, and economic landscape. Yet the archetype of suburban masculinity—including notions of male patriarchy, masculine domesticity, and male prerogative—has persisted, remaining largely static, perhaps in an attempt by middle-class Americans to retain familiar social and cultural patterns amid fundamental transformations in American life.

BIBLIOGRAPHY

Carnes, Mark C., and Clyde Griffen, eds. *Meanings for Manhood: Constructions of Masculinity in Victorian America.* Chicago: University of Chicago Press, 1990.

Douglass, Harlan Paul. *The Suburban Trend.* 1925. Reprint, New York: Johnson Reprint Corp., 1970.

Kelly, Barbara M., ed. *Suburbia Re-examined.* New York: Greenwood Press, 1989.

Marsh, Margaret. "Suburban Men and Masculine Domesticity, 1870–1915." *American Quarterly* 40 (1988): 165–186.

———. *Suburban Lives.* New Brunswick, N.J.: Rutgers University Press, 1990.

May, Elaine Tyler. *Homeward Bound: American Families in the Cold War Era.* New York: Basic Books, 1999.

Muller, Peter O. "Everyday Life in Suburbia: A Review of Changing Social and Economic Forces that Shape Daily Rhythms Within the Outer City." *American Quarterly* 34 (1982): 262–277.

O'Connor, Carol. "Sorting Out the Suburbs: Patterns of Land Use, Class, and Culture." *American Quarterly* 37 (1985): 382–394.

Sharpe, William, and Leonard Wallock. "Bold New City or Built-Up 'Burb?' Redefining Contemporary Suburbia." *American Quarterly* 46 (March 1994): 1–30.

FURTHER READING

Baumgartner, M. P. *The Moral Order of a Suburb.* New York: Oxford University Press, 1999.

Bennett, Thomas L. *Suburbia: The American Dream and Dilemma.* Garden City, N.Y.: Anchor Press, 1976.

Cowan, Ruth Schwartz. *More Work for Mother: The Ironies of Household Technology from the Open Hearth to the Microwave.* New York: Basic Books, 1983.

Halberstam, David. *The Fifties.* New York: Villard, 1993.

Muller, Peter O. *Contemporary Suburban America.* Englewood Cliffs, N.J.: Prentice Hall, 1981.

RELATED ENTRIES

Agrarianism; American Dream; Automobile; Breadwinner Role; Business/Corporate America; Cold War; Cult of Domesticity; Crisis of Masculinity; Fatherhood; *Father Knows Best*; Hollywood; *Home Improvement*; Industrialization; *Leave It to Beaver*; Masculine Domesticity; Middle-Class Manhood; Nuclear Family; *Organization Man, The*; Television; Urbanization; Victorian Era; Work; Working-Class Manhood; World War II

—*Elizabeth Myers*

SUCCESS MANUALS

The ideal of success has been a pervasive theme in American life, and prescriptions for achieving success have assumed a wide range of cultural forms. One of these has been the success manual, which experienced its greatest proliferation and impact on U.S. culture during the Gilded Age (1873–1900) and Progressive Era (1890–1915). Tailored toward male, middle-class audiences, success manuals equated success with manliness and gave detailed advice not only on choosing an occupation and developing a career, but on all forms of public and private behavior.

Advice literature, which has had a long history in American society, gained in significance with the onset of industrialization and economic expansion from the 1830s through 1850s. Books such as Sylvester Graham's *A Lecture to Young Men* (1834), John Todd's *The Student's Manual* (1835), William Alcott's *The Young Man's Guide* (1846), and Timothy Shay Arthur's *Advice to Young Men* (1848) counseled young men on dietary habits, urged temperance, and exhorted them against masturbation. These advice manuals promoted self-control as a mark of manliness in all walks of life.

By the 1870s, the success manual emerged as a distinct literary form, and the wide circulation of these manuals suggests their strong influence on ideas about manliness. Between 1870 and 1910, 144 new success manuals appeared on the market. Written by ministers, educators, and professional authors, they ranged from 300 to 800 pages in length. Sold by traveling agents on subscription plans, success manuals sold anywhere from 10,000 to 100,000 copies per title. Each title cost between two and four dollars—about one-quarter to one-half of an average weekly salary—with the most expensive manuals costing five dollars. Their content was culled from popular biographies, histories, and encyclopedias, and was heavily adorned with evocative illustrations. Two of the six national nonfiction bestsellers between 1870 and 1910—Thomas L. Haines and Levi W. Yaggy's *The Royal Path of Life, or Aims and Aids to Success and Happiness* (1879) and Frank Channing Haddock's *The Power of Will: A Practical Companion Book for Unfoldment of the Powers of Mind* (1907)—belonged to the success manual genre.

The authors of these success manuals experienced the transformations of the market revolution and were uniquely positioned to articulate changing currents of masculinity. More educated than most Americans, yet often of rural background, they belonged to a distinct generation that came of age between 1835 and 1880. Perhaps the most famous success manual author was Orison Swett Marden (1848–1924). Orphaned as a child, Marden grew up in five different foster families but went on to become an accomplished man. By 1882, he had acquired several degrees, including a medical degree from Harvard University and a law degree from Boston University. In 1894, he published *Pushing to the Front,* the first and most popular of his thirty success manuals. It went through 12 editions in 1894, and by 1925 had gone through 250 editions and been translated into 25 languages; one million copies were sold in Japan alone. In addition to his prolific efforts as an author and compiler of such success manuals, Marden also became the founder and editor of *Success Magazine* (1897–1911). Marden and other success-manual authors offered readers the simple message that hard work and good habits—called character by nineteenth-century Americans—contributed to manhood and success.

The achievements of writers like Marden appeared to validate their prescriptions for success and their character-based definitions of manhood. Amid late-nineteenth-century economic insecurity, social upheaval, and labor unrest, contemporary audiences needed such reassurances. Success manuals provided encouragement and comfort to their lower middle-class readers by offering a familiar antebellum ideal of success and manly achievement that emphasized independent entrepreneurship and a work ethos of virtue, sobriety, frugality, self-discipline, and self-sacrifice. Their advice on choosing a "calling" invoked traditional notions of work associated with self-employment, continuity of social mobility across generational lines, and small-scale production in a preindustrial setting. Writers praised a simple life and exhorted their audiences to avoid ostentatious, extravagant living in favor of moderation and respectability. Defining success in preindustrial terms, success-manual authors assured their audiences that economic ills could still be overcome by individual effort, and that true success and manliness remained tied to one's moral qualities rather than to economic achievement alone.

Despite their appeal to traditional notions of manliness and work, success manuals facilitated a shift from a producer-oriented ideal of manhood grounded in character to a consumer-oriented ideal of manhood grounded in a personality geared toward influencing and convincing others. Some of Marden's works, such as *The Power of Personality* (1906) and *Masterful Personality* (1921), reflected this shift. By the 1920s, prescriptions for manhood and success through the cultivation of one's personality increasingly became the norm as a modern business culture emphasizing notions of salesmanship took form. Examples would include Dale Carnegie's *How to Win Friends and Influence People* (1936) and the Reverend Norman Vincent Peale's *The Power of Positive Thinking* (1952).

By the 1970s, as a severe economic recession led to diminishing expectations of financial success and as feminist advances prompted a feeling that masculinity was in crisis, the tone of success books changed. New works such as Robert J. Ringer's *Winning through Intimidation* (1974) and Michael Korda's *Power: How to Get It and How to Use It* (1975) exemplified a new emphasis on the use of power and aggression. Since the 1980s, books like Charles J. Givens's *Wealth Without Risk* (1988) and *More Wealth Without Risk* (1991) sought to reassure audiences that everybody could be successful without imperiling their economic well-being. These books signaled a greater desire for security and a decreased readiness among men to take risks needlessly. The idea of being successful and of finding the best way to achieve affluence continues to retain a great fascination for many Americans, most especially for American men, for success has often been equated with manliness.

Bibliography

Burns, Rex. *Success in America: The Yeoman Dream and the Industrial Revolution.* Amherst: University of Massachusetts Press, 1976.

Cawelti, John G. *Apostles of the Self-Made Man.* Chicago: University of Chicago Press, 1965.

Hilkey, Judy. *Character Is Capital: Success Manuals and Manhood in Gilded Age America.* Chapel Hill: University of North Carolina Press, 1997.

Weiss, Richard. *The American Myth of Success: From Horatio Alger to Norman Vincent Peale.* 1969. Reprint, Urbana: University of Illinois Press, 1988.

Wyllie, Irvin G. *The Self-Made Man in America: The Myth of Rags to Riches.* New York: Free Press, 1966.

Further Reading

Huber, Richard M. *The American Idea of Success.* New York: McGraw-Hill, 1971.

Kilmer, Paulette D. *The Fear of Sinking: The American Success Formula in the Gilded Age.* Knoxville: University of Tennessee Press, 1996.

Kimmel, Michael. *Manhood in America: A Cultural History.* New York: Free Press, 1996.

Rodgers, Daniel T. *The Work Ethic in Industrial America, 1850–1920.* Chicago: University of Chicago Press, 1978.

Shi, David E. *The Simple Life: Plain Living And High Thinking in American Culture.* Athens: University of Georgia Press, 2001.

Related Entries

Alger, Horatio, Jr., American Dream; Arthur, Timothy Shay; Breadwinner Role; Bureaucratization; Business/Corporate America; Capitalism; Character; Class; Crisis of Masculinity; Franklin, Benjamin; Gilded Age; Graham, Sylvester; Individualism; Industrialization; Market Revolution; Middle-Class Manhood; Progressive Era; Property; Self-Control; Self-Made Man; Temperance; Work

—*Thomas Winter*

Suffragism

In 1776 the Declaration of Independence proclaimed that "all men are created equal," but for the next two centuries American suffrage laws implicitly limited who counted as a "man." Voting regulations reflecting beliefs about class, race, gender, and age restricted participation in the American political process. These beliefs were tied to ideas of virtue central to definitions of masculinity, particularly that independent men had a right and a responsibility to participate in public life and community governance through voting. During the twentieth century, however, concepts of masculinity were gradually divorced from definitions of citizenship and suffrage.

During the colonial and Revolutionary periods, suffrage rights were restricted to male landowners on the basis of the eighteenth-century belief that manhood and civic virtue (the ability and willingness to act in the public interest rather than out of self-interest) were grounded in property ownership and the economic and political independence it bestowed. The virtuous man of independent means embodied self-sufficiency, respectability, and stability; while those without property—particularly women, children, and slaves—were seen as dependents not adequately invested in the affairs of the state to have a voice in them.

The upheaval of the American Revolution forced a reexamination of these assumptions, since many men who were not qualified to vote fought for American independence. These soldiers argued that if they were man enough to die for their country, then they were entitled to a stake in the fledgling nation. In response, several of the new states eliminated the property requirement for voting, replacing it with a less restrictive tax-paying requirement. The notion of "republican manhood" maintained the earlier associations between manhood, public virtue, and suffrage, but it now expanded to include those without property.

During the early nineteenth century the concept of masculine political virtue became completely separated from property ownership, for property restrictions on voting disappeared entirely and industrialization produced a class of nonpropertied wage earners. As a result, the belief spread that the right to vote should be connected to the man and not to property, and virtuous manhood became grounded in racial and gender identity rather than class status. White men asserted this modified idea of masculine political virtue ever more strongly as abolitionism, slave riots, and, beginning in 1848, the push for woman suffrage challenged their power. They characterized African Americans, women, and Native Americans as weak, dependent, and, therefore, unsuited to the rights of citizenship.

The Civil War (1861–65) again made the question of the vote—and its relation to manhood and to whiteness—a major national issue. Like nonpropertied men during the American Revolution, freed blacks who fought for the Union believed that their military service demonstrated their manhood and entitled them to suffrage rights. Furthermore, with the abolition of slavery many black males sought full citizenship, including the right to vote. The Fourteenth (1868) and Fifteenth (1870) Amendments offered them citizenship and suffrage respectively. These measures also represented the federal government's first attempt to define citizenship and voting rights—a decision that previously had been the province of the states. The North did little to enforce the new amendments, however, and southern white men excluded blacks from the public realm of politics and voting by reinstating property requirements and implementing poll taxes, literacy tests, complex registration requirements, and white-only primaries that successfully excluded the black voting population. Seeking to preserve the association between whiteness, manhood, and citizenship, southern white men denied full voting rights to African-American men and initiated racial segregation, or "Jim Crow" laws, to return black men to their positions of dependence. Significantly, women's attempts to gain the vote at this time also failed, further emphasizing the continued association of suffrage and citizenship with masculinity.

The passage of the Nineteenth Amendment in 1920, which gave women the right to vote, marked the first real disruption in the traditional linkage among manhood, citizenship, and suffrage. Furthermore, while the continued exclusion of poor and minority males from the voting booth—through pauper laws, revitalized property requirements and other voting loopholes—suggested the persistence of the old associations of masculinity and suffrage, the economic suffering of the Great Depression led the government to revise laws that kept the poor from voting. As millions of men lost their jobs, government officials recognized that self-sufficiency was not essential to masculinity, and could therefore no longer be feasibly connected to voting rights.

Similarly, World War II represented a watershed event in the separation of suffrage rights from race and class identities. Like previous wars, it raised the problem of mobilized men who could not vote. Even more importantly, the racial bigotry of the Nazis required Americans to examine their own longstanding prejudices about who counted as a "man." Many Americans believed that the United States, which had fought for democracy around the world, could not continue to exclude a significant portion of its own population from suffrage. The Soldier Voting Act of 1942 eliminated the poll tax for black soldiers, and in 1944 the Supreme Court, in *Smith* v. *Allwright*, declared white-only primaries unconstitutional, thus removing two obstacles to black suffrage. Minorities, meanwhile, began to actively resist the practices that excluded them.

The erosion of the traditional association between suffrage rights and white masculinity became complete during the 1960s, when the federal government definitively took control of the regulation of voting rights away from the states. The Voting Rights Act of 1965, in particular, eliminated many of the

This 1885 lithograph honoring female suffragist leaders suggests the continuing grounding of American concepts of suffrage in white patriarchy during the late nineteenth century. (From the collections of the Library of Congress)

remaining restrictions on voting by legislating federal oversight of southern voting practices and suspending a number of exclusionary practices. In its wake, most other voting limitations, including pauper laws, literacy tests, poll taxes, and lengthy residency requirements, were outlawed. As a result, approximately a million black voters were registered and finally given the full citizenship they had been granted a century before.

One of the final changes made to voting rights, and to the definition of manhood on which those rights rested, came again in response to war. Since the founding of the colonies, legal citizenship—and by implication, full manhood—had begun at the age of twenty-one. Yet during the Vietnam conflict men younger than that were regularly dying overseas in the service of their country, and students at home protesting the war could not formally vote for or against the politicians and policies involved. The Twenty-Sixth Amendment (1971) expanded suffrage to include all Americans over the age of eighteen.

Through two hundred years of voting regulations, it is possible to trace a shifting relationship among suffrage, citizenship, and masculinity. While concepts of virtue were initially central to definitions of manhood and suffrage, changing ideas of human sovereignty have expanded definitions of manhood—and consequently of citizenship, making it the province of all Americans.

Bibliography

Bloch, Ruth H. "The Gendered Meanings of Virtue in Revolutionary America." *Signs: Journal of Women in Culture and Society* 13, no. 1 (1987): 37–58.

Keyssar, Alexander. *The Right to Vote: The Contested History of Democracy in the United States.* New York: Basic Books, 2000.

Pocock, J. G. A. "Virtue and Commerce in the Eighteenth Century." *Journal of Interdisciplinary History* 3, no. 1 (1972): 119–134.

Scholastic, Inc. "Research Starters: Suffrage." <http://teacher.scholastic.com/researchtools/rsearchstarters/women/> (March 11, 2003).

Williamson, Chilton. *American Suffrage from Property to Democracy 1760–1860.* Princeton, N.J.: Princeton University Press, 1960.

Further Reading

Nelson, Dana D. *National Manhood: Capitalist Citizenship and the Imagined Fraternity of White Men.* Durham, N.C.: Duke University Press, 1998.

Rogers, Donald W., ed. *Voting and the Spirit of American Democracy: Essays on the History of Voting and Voting Rights in America.* Urbana: University of Illinois Press, 1992.

Scriabine, Christine Brendel, ed. *Black Voting Rights: The Fight for Equality.* Amawalk, N.Y.: Golden Owl, 1993.

U.S. Department of Justice. "The Right to Vote: How Federal Law Protects You." Washington, D.C.: USDOJ, 2000.

Zelden, Charles L. *Voting Rights on Trial: A Handbook with Cases, Laws, and Documents.* Santa Barbara, Calif.: ABC–CLIO, 2002.

Related Entries

African-American Manhood; American Revolution; Antiwar Movement; Citizenship; Civil Rights Movement; Civil War; Class; Democratic Manhood; Emancipation; Native American Manhood; Politics; Race; Republicanism; Southern Manhood; Vietnam War; War; Whiteness; World War I; World War II

—Kirsten L. Parkinson

Sunday, Billy

1862–1935
American Christian Evangelist

The most widely known revivalist of the early twentieth century, and a participant in the "muscular Christianity" movement, William Ashley "Billy" Sunday sought to bring men into Protestantism by emphasizing the strength needed to be a Christian. His ministry both reflected and addressed concerns about perceived perils to the state of American manhood and the feminization of American Christianity in the late nineteenth and early twentieth centuries.

Born in Story County, Iowa, Sunday spent years struggling in poverty before being sent to the Soldiers' Orphans Home in 1872. At the orphanage, Billy discovered his ability to outrun other boys, and he parlayed his speed into a position with the Chicago White Stockings baseball team. His baseball career made Sunday a household name, and his embrace of Christianity in 1886 garnered publicity in newspapers across the country. As a devoutly religious, nondrinking, nonswearing baseball player, Sunday rejected a common urban model of male behavior and became a popular attraction at churches. No organization courted him more than the Young Men's Christian Association (YMCA), an organization that espoused the muscular Christian belief that strength of body, mind, and spirit were inextricably linked. Sunday began touring small towns and cities across the United States for the YMCA, using his athletic fame to show groups of boys and men that one could be both a Christian and a "real man."

In 1891, increasingly uncomfortable with the amorality of baseball, Sunday quit to become a full-time evangelist and Bible instructor for the Chicago YMCA. After working as an assistant to a traveling preacher, Sunday began holding his own evangelical meetings around the nation in 1896. A captivating speaker with a combative, energetic style, Sunday cultivated a tough streetwise image. Using slang, with his coat off and sleeves rolled up, Sunday described faith in martial terms and emphasized his own willingness to fight for Jesus. To be a Christian required toughness, he said, and American Protestantism had been weakened by women's leadership in the nation's churches. He regularly criticized what he considered the insidious influence of "flabby-cheeked, brittle-boned, weak-kneed, thin-skinned, pliable, plastic, spineless, effeminate, ossified three-karat Christianity" (Bruns, 85).

Challenging the notion that devoutness left a man too weak to battle successfully in the world of business, Sunday argued that men needed to be strong to accept religion and repent for the sins that threatened their masculinity. He lamented that too many men had become libertines responsible for the deterioration of the American home and the decadence of modern American society. He espoused a rural, nineteenth-century vision of manhood emphasizing sobriety, hard work, piety, perseverance, courtesy, and family responsibility. He sought to ban dancing, opposed profanity, scorned the theater, and labeled birth control a device of the devil. Sunday's popularity waned in the 1920s as muscular Christianity and evangelical Christianity lost their cultural force, but his supporters estimated that he had converted over a million men and women by the time he succumbed to a heart attack in 1935.

Millions of Americans saw Sunday as the embodiment of masculinity, a Christian soldier who made the evils of the world seem uncomplicated and feared nothing except God. Through his virile persona, dramatic flair, and affirmation of manliness, Sunday persuaded enormous numbers of men to embrace a Christianity that made religious commitment a badge of manhood.

Bibliography

Bruns, Roger A. *Preacher: Billy Sunday and Big-Time American Evangelism.* New York: Norton, 1992.

Dorsett, Lyle W. *Billy Sunday and the Redemption of Urban America.* Grand Rapids, Mich.: Eerdmans, 1991.

Martin, Robert F. "Billy Sunday and Christian Manliness." *The Historian* 58, no. 4 (1996).

Putney, Clifford. *Muscular Christianity: Manhood and Sports in Protestant America 1880–1920.* Cambridge, Mass.: Harvard University Press, 2001.

Further Reading

Brown, Elijah P. *The Real Billy Sunday: The Life and Work of Rev. William Ashley Sunday, D. D. the Baseball Evangelist.* New York: Fleming H. Revell, 1914.

Ellis, William T. *"Billy" Sunday: The Man and His Message, With His Own Words Which Have Won Thousands for Christ.* Philadelphia: John C. Winston, 1914.

Ladd, Tony. *Muscular Christianity: Evangelical Protestants and the Development of American Sport.* Grand Rapids, Mich.: Baker, 1999.

McLaughlin, William G., Jr. *Billy Sunday Was His Real Name.* Chicago: University of Chicago Press, 1955.

Rodeheaver, Homer. *Twenty Years with Billy Sunday.* Nashville, Tenn.: Cokesbury Press, 1936.

Thomas, Lee. *The Billy Sunday Story: The Life and Times of William Ashley Sunday, an Authorized Biography.* Grand Rapids, Mich.: Zondervan, 1961.

Selected Writings

Sunday, William A. *Billy Sunday Speaks.* 1937. Reprint, New York: Chelsea House, 1970.

Related Entries

Alcohol; Baseball; Crisis of Masculinity; Evangelicalism and Revivalism; Gilded Age; Jesus, Images of; Men and Religion Forward Movement; Middle-Class Manhood; Ministry; Muscular Christianity; Progressive Era; Religion and Spirituality; Young Men's Christian Association

—*Caryn E. Neumann*

Superman

Debuting in *Action Comics* #1 in 1938, Superman became an icon of American masculine heroism and has been featured in comics, radio, television, movies, a musical, and various product tie-ins. Throughout most of his career, Superman embodied a normative white heterosexual masculinity that adapted to broader currents in the cultural construction of American manhood.

Created by writer Jerry Siegel and cartoonist Joe Schuster, Superman was rocketed as an infant from the dying planet Krypton and its red Sun to Earth, where the yellow Sun and weaker gravity gave him incredible powers. Through the "Man of Steel" and his alter-ego Clark Kent, Siegel and Schuster, both Jewish, expressed their ambivalent relationship to American masculinity. Kent, a mild-mannered, bespectacled, newspaper reporter in the fictional city of Metropolis, reflected stereotypical notions of Jewish men as urban, timid, overly intellectual, sexually inept, and feminized. Yet Kent was also thoroughly grounded in the rural midwestern values of his foster parents, the presumably gentile Kents of Smallville. Superman, meanwhile, was an immigrant shorn of Jewish characteristics and possessed of a heroic muscularity that drew on dominant cultural images of ideal manhood.

Superman's strength and foes changed over time, reflecting broader American fears and anxieties. Prior to World War II, Superman's powers were enormous but limited, and, in the context of the Great Depression of the 1930s, he displayed a social conscience that led him to target rapacious businessmen rather than menacing aliens. After the United States entered World War II, however, Superman put aside criticism of the economic order to urge the defeat of what Superman's creators called the "Japanazis." Because Clark Kent accidentally failed his eye examination, Superman had to battle homefront saboteurs and urge Americans to buy bonds.

During World War II and the Cold War, Superman represented American manhood at its most conservative: clean-cut and muscular, politically neutral, respectful of authority, and a faithful worker. In the face of hostile military powers and such rival ideologies as fascism and communism, he asserted that "truth, justice and the American way" (as the 1950s television series put it) were essentially the same things (and were backed up by tremendous physical strength). In the late 1950s and the 1960s, Superman's physical powers escalated to nearly infinite levels. To humanize the character and retain plot tension, Superman's writers created Kryptonite, irradiated fragments of the hero's home planet, which weakened him when he was exposed to it.

In keeping with broader notions of middle-class manhood during the 1950s and 1960s emphasizing fatherhood and family togetherness, Superman gained new domestic responsibilities, and his family expanded to include Superboy, Supergirl, and various superpets. Writers also gave Superman's love life more attention, with Lois Lane and Lana Lang vying for his affections. Superman even considered marriage; but even in this era of the valorization of home and family he seemed unable to reconcile himself to suburban fatherhood, perhaps because marriage implied emotional dependence, and thus weakness.

By the late 1960s, Superman was again reassessed amid growing resistance to the Vietnam War, increasing doubts about the moral rightness of American military actions, and the rise of feminism and identity movements among nonwhite and gay men. His near omnipotence lost favor with readers aware that normative American manhood faced challenges in a politically and economically complex world. In the late 1970s and the 1980s, however, a series of four Superman movies starring Christopher Reeve revived the character's popularity.

The 1980s and 1990s brought two signal events in the history of Superman: marriage and death. In 1990 Lois Lane accepted Clark Kent's proposal, ending the bachelorhood that differentiated him from most American men. Before the wedding, however, he died and was reborn. The reborn Superman (actually four Supermen, including a cyborg, a teenage clone, and an African American) suggests that American manhood itself had grown too diverse and problematic for one "Man of Steel" to contain.

Bibliography

Brod, Harry. "Of Mice and Superman: Images of Jewish Masculinity." In *Redeeming Men: Religion and Masculinities,* edited by Stephen B. Boyd, W. Merle Longwood, and Mark W. Muesse. Louisville, Ky.: Westminster John Knox Press, 1996.

Daniels, Les. *Superman: The Complete History.* San Francisco, Calif.: Chronicle, 1998.

Land, Jeffrey S., and Patrick Trimble. "Whatever Happened to the Man of Tomorrow? An Examination of the American Monomyth and the Comic Book Superhero." *Journal of Popular Culture* 22, no. 3 (1988): 157–173.

Stern, Roger. *The Death and Life of Superman: A Novel.* New York: Bantam, 1993.

Further Reading

Eco, Umberto. "The Myth of Superman." Translated by Natalie Chilton. *Diacritics* 2, no. 1 (1977): 14–22.

Siegel, Jerry, and Joe Schuster. *Superman: The Action Comics Archive.* Vol. 1. New York: DC Comics, 1998.

———. *Superman: The Sunday Classics, Strips 1–183, 1939–1943.* Timonium, Md.: Diamond Comic, 2000.

Related Entries

Body; Cold War; Heroism; Heterosexuality; Jewish Manhood; Patriotism; Television

—Trent Watts

Tarzan

Created by the author Edgar Rice Burroughs the fictional character Tarzan was born Lord Greystoke, a member of an aristocratic British family. Stranded in the African jungle as a small child, Tarzan is found and raised by a group of primates. The character was first introduced to the public in 1912 in *Tarzan of the Apes,* which appeared in the magazine *All-Story.* The twenty-five novels that followed between 1912 and 1947 were a huge commercial success, with over 100 million copies sold, and Tarzan has become symbolic of a primal form of masculinity untouched by Western industrial civilization, as well as an escapist fantasy for generations of boys and men.

The Tarzan novels share certain plot features: The peace and order of the African jungle, maintained by Tarzan, is disturbed by the arrival of a group of Europeans in search of treasure, usually associated with a lost civilization; the expedition often includes a white woman, typically of middle-class background, who is abducted and subsequently rescued; and Tarzan restores order in the jungle through a mixture of animal instinct, cunning, and sheer physical prowess.

Burroughs' novels negotiate meanings of masculinity by using the figure of Tarzan to address Victorian notions of race and civilized self-restraint, Gilded Age fears of overcivilization, and early-twentieth-century demands for a "strenuous life" and a "passionate manhood." Tarzan owes his masculine power to a combination of his Anglo-Saxon racial heritage, which endowed him with "civilized" behavioral traits, and a childhood in the wilds of Africa that steels his masculinity by forcing on him a Darwinistic struggle for survival. This model of masculinity suggests an ambivalent relation between manhood and civilization: only men of allegedly civilized races are endowed with true manliness, but this civilization stifles masculinity by removing men from invigorating contact with nature. Only in the African jungle can an otherwise effeminate English aristocratic boy achieve his full masculine potential. In the end, Tarzan represents an imperialistic fantasy: While it is the more primitive masculinity that enables Tarzan to prevail over his enemies, it is his Anglo-Saxon heritage that enables him to create order out of chaos in the jungle.

Tarzan's appeal was not limited to the readers of mass-market pulp magazines, but influenced scientific thinking about masculinity as well. Granville Stanley Hall, the father of American psychology, enjoyed Tarzan so much that he taught *Tarzan of the Apes* in his course on human development at Clark University. For Hall, who encouraged parents to nurture evolutionary remnants of savagery in boys as an antidote to the effeminizing effects of modern industrial civilization, Tarzan represented an example of the synthesis he hoped for young American men to achieve.

Tarzan represents the fantasy of a natural masculine identity that exists outside of civilization but is not incompatible with it. This fantasy has had more recent manifestations, particularly in the mythopoetic men's movement and such writings as Douglas Gillette's *King, Warrior, Magician, Lover: Rediscovering the Archetypes of the Mature Masculine* (1991) and Robert Bly's *Iron John: A Book About Men* (1990). The escapist fantasy that such texts represent signifies the desire of many men for an unchanging blueprint for manhood that is preordained by nature.

Bibliography

Bederman, Gail. *Manliness and Civilization: A Cultural History of Gender and Race in the United States, 1880–1917.* Chicago: University of Chicago Press, 1996.

Holtsmark, Erling B. *Edgar Rice Burroughs.* Boston: Twayne, 1986.

Kasson, John F. *Houdini, Tarzan, and the Perfect Man: The White Male Body and the Challenge of Modernity in America.* New York: Hill and Wang 2001.

Further Reading

Budd, Michael Anton. *The Sculpture Machine: Physical Culture and Body Politics in the Age of Empire.* New York: New York University Press, 1997.

Burroughs, Edgar Rice. *Tarzan of the Apes.* 1912. Reprint, with an introduction by Gore Vidal. New York: New American Library, 1990.

———. *The Return of Tarzan.* 1913. Reprint, New York: Ballantine Books, 1990.

———. *The Son of Tarzan.* 1916. Reprint, Sandy, Utah: Quiet Vision, 2000.

———. *The Jungle Tales of Tarzan.* 1919. Reprint, Sandy, Utah: Quiet Vision, 2000.

Holtsmark, Erling B. *Tarzan and Tradition: Classical Myth in Popular Literature.* Westport, Conn.: Greenwood Press, 1981.

Porges, Irvin. *Edgar Rice Burroughs: The Man Who Created Tarzan.* Provo, Utah: Brigham Young University Press, 1975.

RELATED ENTRIES

Darwinism; Hall, Granville Stanley; Heroism; Imperialism; Industrialization; *Iron John: A Book About Men*; Men's Movements; Middle-Class Manhood; Passionate Manhood; Progressive Era; Race; Roosevelt, Theodore; Whiteness

—*Thomas Winter*

TECHNOLOGY

American masculinity has long been linked to mastering technology. From the first axe to the spinning jenny to the McCormick reaper, inventions designed by and for men have shaped United States settlement and industry. Yet, more than a masculine tool for cultivation and industry, technology has also been a force for masculine identity. Three technological movements illustrate the ways in which American masculinities are interwoven with technologies. They make it clear that while American men have long been concerned with making machines, machines have long been at work making men.

"Tinkering" Technology: From the Eighteenth to the Twentieth Century

In the eighteenth-century, technology was essential for claiming masculinity; a man owned his own tools and could not claim status as an independent man until he possessed the right equipment for the job, be it farming or blacksmithing. The association between tools, crafts, and masculinity went unchallenged until the late nineteenth century, when mechanized innovations and industrialization changed the meaning of technology in men's lives —those with the proper "tools" became scientists, "tinkerers," and factory owners. This transformation turned craftsmen into workers and dramatically altered definitions of masculinity.

The new relation between technology and masculinity was evident by the early twentieth century, when many American men considered such technological innovators as Thomas Edison and Henry Ford the great heroes of the day. Edison, creator of hundreds of inventions, including electric lighting and motion pictures, and Ford, originator of the assembly line and the Model T automobile, represented the best of an era of unbridled male inventiveness. Together, they signaled for many that a new age had arrived in which self-taught "tinkerers" could master technology to revolutionize the world's products, processes, and systems.

Ford and Edison became heroic figures not merely on the strength of their inventions. Rather, it was their hands-on approach to invention that defined their manliness and fascinated the American public. Edison, often called the Wizard of Menlo Park, was well known for the relentless energy and strict work ethic that he and his "insomnia squad" of assistants celebrated. At a time when many American men associated intellectualism with effeminacy, Edison and Ford eschewed university-educated engineers in favor of experienced tinkerers, surrounding themselves with carpenters and machinists who favored craftsmanship and experimentation over theories and book learning.

Ford and Edison dominated an era in which men's bodies seemed capable of creating, harnessing, and directing technological power. If American men could neither be in charge of the industries nor shape the work processes that technology created, they could nonetheless take pride in their ability to control their machines. Popular representations of Ford's River Rouge Factory in Detroit, Michigan, reveal an assumption that these powerful new inventions would make powerful new men. For instance, Diego Rivera's murals depict muscular workers directing the flow of technological energy, while Charles Sheeler's photographs and paintings place the factory and its workers in a celebratory, spiritual light. Although technology had its critics, including Henry Adams, who wrote about the fearful implications of machine power for men, its celebrants were more numerous. When men worshiped the prowess of an Edison or a Ford, they anticipated a new era governed by those who mastered technological systems rather than those who labored with their own tools.

Post–World War II: "Do-it-Yourself" Technology

During and after World War II, as factories grew increasingly systematized and management became professionalized, the educated engineer began to assume the status of male American hero and to challenge the primacy of the workplace tinkerer. But although hands-on technological wizards like Ford and Edison were increasingly replaced by distant bureaucrats, the tinkerer (and the model of masculinity he represented) found refuge in the home. Between 1920 and 1950, American men transformed the home's gendered spaces as they embraced a new ethic of do-it-yourself technology.

Do-it-yourself movements did not appear until the early twentieth century. Previously, after the nineteenth-century rise of separate spheres in which men sought employment in the world outside the home and women remained "employed" within the home, wives, daughters, and hired male laborers were expected to care for the home. According to Andrew Jackson Downing, a popular nineteenth-century architect and writer of "country house" plan books, the only proper way to have one's lawn maintained was to hire someone to do it. This

This sketch panel of Diego M. Rivera's Detroit Industry, North Wall *(1932–33) illustrates the twentieth-century association of masculine identity and labor with the harnessing and directing of technological power. (Gift of Edsel B. Ford, Photograph © 2001 The Detroit Institute of Arts)*

perspective began to change in the 1920s, when the first wave of suburbanization made single-family homes affordable to the middle class and encouraged a new model of manhood grounded in home maintenance and improvement. New magazines aimed primarily at men, such as *Popular Mechanics,* included plans for designing labor-saving devices such as battery-powered hedge trimmers, bicycle-powered lawn mowers, and chicken-operated hen-house doors. Such technological gadgets, designed to appeal to men with tinkering skills, allowed men to complete laborious tasks in short periods of time, but they also served a psychological function. Captions in plan guides frequently suggested that these "work hobbies" could be easily made by even "amateur mechanics." Their popularity suggests that many men had begun to regard their lawns and garages as miniature Menlo Parks, sites where they could take pride in their technological mastery.

After World War II, as technologies were converted from foreign to domestic use, it became easier for increasing numbers of men to embrace do-it-yourself technology. No longer would one have to be even an amateur mechanic to use technologies at home. The arrival of new power tools, such as drills, saws, and lawn mowers, inspired consumers (primarily male) to spend roughly $5 billion on tools and materials in the 1950s. Advertising campaigns, particularly for power lawn mowers, portrayed postwar families in which mom gardened, children played, and dad mowed the lawn. The new vision of the suburban male became one of domestic technological mastery, with a power tool in one hand and grill mitt in the other.

In the 1970s and 1980s, the dad as "weekend warrior" became a part of popular culture. Warehouse stores like Home Depot became family destinations, and comedian Tim Allen's television series *Home Improvement* emerged as a highly rated sitcom. The popularity of television shows like PBS's *This Old House* and cable channels dedicated to home improvement, such as HGTV, attest to home repair's continued importance to American men.

The Late Twentieth Century: High-Tech Masculinity

The era of the industrial and home tinkerer, however, faced a serious challenge in the 1990s, due to the proliferation of computer and other electronic technologies and the rise of a hi-tech culture in the 1990s. Articles and editorials increasingly suggested that even home technologies were becoming too complex for the average American handyman. Oft-told jokes about children being enlisted to program the family VCR reflect an increasing anxiety about a technologically complex society that may be outpacing the capacities of men (and women) raised without DVDs, MP3s, and the Internet.

At the beginning of the twenty-first century, hands-on performers and expert engineers co-exist, if uneasily. Skilled trades and construction, where physical strength and technological gadgetry are combined, continue to be male domains where experience and strength are prized. Yet it is "expert" engineers, also predominantly male, who increasingly command the knowledge necessary to maintain complex technological systems and structures. Further strengthening the hold of the experts are a new generation of hi-tech mavens, led by Steve Jobs and Bill Gates. While men still dominate these new technological fields, they are increasingly valued more for brains than brawn and for their knowledge of the immaterial instead of the physical. The new vogue of the hi-tech "geek" was strengthened by reports on the "dot-com lifestyle" of the late 1990s, in which young men—and increasing numbers of women—traded their hi-tech knowledge for long hours, sugar-stocked refrigerators, impromptu ping pong, and a chance at early retirement via stock options. In spite of the downturn in dot-com fortunes, their emphasis on computer expertise and relatively equal gender representation already marked the late-twentieth-century relationship between masculinity and technology as different from that of the past.

Current pharmaceutical technologies, meanwhile, continue to bolster older ideals of manhood by enhancing masculine physical power, even as it is increasingly usurped in the workplace. Substances like Viagra and creatine allow men to use technologies to build sexual and physical strength. Because of such substances, many men are finding that while the new hi-tech world may appear to threaten manly physical vigor by demanding less from them physically, it may also offer them much in return.

BIBLIOGRAPHY

Banta, Martha. *Taylored Lives: Narrative Productions in the Age of Taylor, Veblen, and Ford.* Chicago: University of Chicago Press, 1993.

Gelber, Steven. "Do-It-Yourself: Constructing, Repairing, and Maintaining Domestic Masculinity." In *The Gender and Consumer Culture Reader,* edited by Jennifer Scanlon. New York: New York University Press, 2000.

Hitt, Jack. "The Second Sexual Revolution." *New York Times Magazine,* 20 February 2000.

Hughes, Thomas. *American Genesis: A Century of Invention and Technological Enthusiasm, 1870–1970.* New York: Penguin, 1990.

Nye, David E. *Electrifying America: Social Meanings of a New Technology, 1880–1940.* Cambridge, Mass.: MIT Press, 1997.

Pursell, Carroll. *The Machine in America: A Social History of Technology.* Baltimore: Johns Hopkins University Press, 1995.

FURTHER READING

Faludi, Susan. *Stiffed: The Betrayal of the American Man.* New York: William Morrow, 1999.

Gideon, Siegfried. *Mechanization Takes Command: A Contribution to Anonymous History.* 1948. Reprint, New York: Norton, 1969.

Israel, Paul. *Edison: A Life of Invention.* New York: John Wiley, 1998.

Marvin, Carolyn. *When Old Technologies Were New: Thinking About Electric Communication in the Late Nineteenth Century.* New York: Oxford University Press, 1988.

Nye, David E. *American Technological Sublime.* Cambridge, Mass.: MIT Press, 1994.

Rabinbach, Anson. *The Human Motor: Energy, Fatigue, and the Origins of Modernity.* Berkeley: University of California, 1992.

Tichi, Cecelia. *Shifting Gears: Technology, Literature and Culture in Modernist America.* Chapel Hill: University of North Carolina Press, 1987.

RELATED ENTRIES

Artisan; Automobile; Body; Business/Corporate America; Fatherhood; *Home Improvement*; Industrialization; Working-Class Manhood

—*Carolyn Thomas de la Peña*

TELEVISION

Television, perhaps the most popular medium in the United States since the 1950s, has been central to the cultural history of American masculinity. Its stylized masculine images have reflected historically changing notions of normative male identity and, by giving high visibility to certain masculine types, helped shape those notions.

In programs ranging from sports events to commercials to game shows to children's cartoons, television has reinforced men's cultural dominance and authority by representing them as trim, handsome, and heterosexual, by promoting the sexual appeal of such images, and, in the case of sports, by marketing visions of male physical power and prowess to the near total exclusion of women's sporting events. But while this pattern remained more or less unchanged into the twenty-first century, such popular genres as family comedies and crime dramas have offered historically shifting images of American manhood.

The 1950s

Television became increasingly widespread in American middle-class homes during the late 1940s and the 1950s. At the time, many Americans feared that communism threatened American institutions and that American men and boys, softened by middle-class suburban lifestyles and endangered by homosexuality and juvenile delinquency, were not strong enough to meet these dangers. Television programming responded with an anxious effort to broadcast the superiority of American life and the strength and authority of white middle-class men through idealized images. Family comedies such as *The Adventures of Ozzie and Harriet* (1952–66), *Father Knows Best* (1954–63), and *Leave It to Beaver* (1957–63) portrayed white middle-class men both as effective breadwinning professionals and as suburban husbands and fathers who exercised unquestioned domestic authority and taught their sons lessons on the morality and economics of heterosexual middle-class manhood. Westerns such as *Gunsmoke* (1955–75) featured male archetypes long considered icons of American manhood, while crime dramas such as *Perry Mason* (1957–66) similarly depicted strong and emotionally reserved masculine paragons of law, order, and moral rectitude who protected submissive female characters.

The occasional exceptions effectively proved the rule. *The Honeymooners* (1952–57) featured a childless working-class family living in a sparsely furnished urban apartment. But Ralph Kramden, a loudmouthed bus driver who lacked his wife's maturity and wisdom, represented an ineffectual working-class manhood that reflected a broader decline in the cultural status of working-class manhood during the 1950s and 1960s. Kramden continually aspired to achieve middle-class status through abortive or ill-conceived schemes. *I Love Lucy* (1951–57) featured an urban apartment-dwelling childless couple and a Cuban household head. But the show underscored the normativeness of Anglo-Saxon masculinity and middle-class suburban fatherhood by giving the boyishly named Ricky Ricardo such stereotypical Latino characteristics as authoritarianism and hotheadedness, making Ricky a father by writing a child into the show, and eventually relocating the family to a suburban home. *Amos 'n Andy* (1928–53), which began on radio and moved to television in 1951, celebrated white manhood through its stereotyping of African-American males.

The 1960s and 1970s

Television images of American manhood began to change dramatically during the 1960s and 1970s as feminism, rising divorce rates, the youth counterculture, and racial, ethnic, and sexual identity movements challenged the cultural dominance of white middle-class masculinity. As alternative models of American manhood received public acceptance, television images became increasingly diverse and complex.

Family programs continued to feature white males and emphasize the normativeness of middle-class family life, but they now included remarried fathers, as on *The Brady Bunch* (1969–74); single fathers, as in *My Three Sons* (1960–72) and *The Courtship of Eddie's Father* (1969–72); and divorcés, as on *The Odd Couple* (1970–75). Several of these male types remained authoritative and effective fathers; Mike Brady, for example, whose job as an architect paralleled his leadership role in constructing a new family, experienced no difficulty in establishing his authority over his stepchildren. But *The Odd Couple*'s Felix Unger and Oscar Madison—an emotionally depressed neatnik and an irresponsible and emotionally distant slob, respectively—represented a masculinity undermined by divorce. Their unhappy lifestyle, highlighted by Felix's longings for reunion with his wife, refuted the model of glamorous male bachelorhood made popular by *Playboy* magazine and suggested the necessity of marriage and domesticity for masculine completeness. Meanwhile, *All in the Family* (1971–83) upheld the middle-class father by highlighting a negative working-class example: Archie Bunker, a narrow-minded would-be patriarch whose paternal authority was frequently questioned.

Television's models of masculinity during the 1960s and 1970s did not always serve such culturally conservative purposes. Whereas the characters in 1950s westerns, crime dramas, and family comedies invariably upheld law, order, nuclear-family life, and the moral rightness of American values, television now presented new male types whose actions associated manliness with an irreverent questioning of conventional American patriotism and institutions. *M*A*S*H* (1972–83), which centered around an army hospital staff in the Korean War, premiered toward the end of the increasingly unpopular Vietnam War. The sitcom pitted the antiwar, antimilitary, antiauthoritarian, highly sexualized, perpetually unmarried, swill-drinking, yet heroic doctor "Hawkeye" Pierce (significantly nicknamed for the fictional freedom-loving frontier hero of James Fenimore Cooper's nineteenth-century Leatherstocking Tales) against the rulebound, immature, and foolish wimp Frank Burns. Similarly, *All in the Family* featured the tense relationship between the bigoted and anti-intellectual Archie Bunker and his long-haired, anti-establishment, politically liberal, college-educated, and sexually charged stepson Mike Stivic.

Likewise, the impact of feminism and the growing call for a new model of "sensitive manhood" was apparent in 1970s images of men who questioned masculine ideals based on physical power and brawn. *The Incredible Hulk* (1977–82) depicted a man who had become thoroughly alienated from his own body. Periodically transforming into a hypermasculine, hypermuscular green monster, its main character, Dr. David Banner, sought to control the violent impulses within. *The Six Million Dollar Man* (1974–78) similarly featured a man whose superhuman strength (the result of bionic parts received after an aeronautic accident) left him seeking to understand and control his hypermasculinized body.

Television images of American manhood diversified racially and ethnically as well, though they offered only limited challenges to stereotypical images of nonwhite men. *Chico and the Man* (1974–78) featured a Latino main character, but Latino activists criticized the show for portraying

Chico Rodriguez as lazy and irresponsible. Portrayals of African-American manhood became numerous during the 1970s, when shows such as *Sanford and Son* (1972–77), *Good Times* (1974–79), and *The Jeffersons* (1975–85) premiered. But these programs offered ambiguous images of African-American masculinity. *Good Times* featured a conscientious father and *The Jeffersons* featured a successful businessman who had entered the middle class, but *Sanford and Son* and *Good Times* were derided for depicting African-American men as ghetto-bound; *Sanford and Son* and *The Jeffersons* were charged with identifying black men as hypermasculine and verbally abusive, particularly of women; and George Jefferson's self-consciousness about his middle-class status suggested a fundamental incongruity between his racial and class identities. Only later did *The Cosby Show* (1984–92), in which father and physician Cliff Huxtable exercised a strong and father-knows-best style of paternal authority, present an image of middle-class African-American manhood relatively devoid of such stereotypes. The impact of feminism on television fatherhood was also apparent in the fact that Cliff fully shared domestic authority with his lawyer wife Clair.

The 1980s to the Twenty-First Century

Television images during the 1980s and 1990s indicated an increasing introspectiveness and uncertainty about the meaning of manhood in American life. Contributing to this new attitude were the ongoing questioning of traditional patriarchal authority, the growing visibility of gay masculinities, the emergence of the men's movement, and a developing public perception of a "crisis of masculinity" in American life.

The dysfunctional white father became a standard and familiar male type. In the highly successful *The Simpsons,* which premiered in 1989, Homer Simpson's lack of both intelligence and paternal authority provides much of the show's humor and appeal. Al Bundy of *Married with Children* (1987–97) offered a similar portrait of ineffectual suburban fatherhood. The decline of traditional fatherhood on television prompted considerable public commentary, particularly after television's masculine-named woman journalist *Murphy Brown* (1988–98) decided to become a single mother, provoking a sharp complaint from the conservative U.S. vice president Dan Quayle in 1992 about the cultural invisibility of fathers—and about the perceived role of television and feminism in contributing to this development.

The uncertainties of white suburban masculinity were addressed perhaps most explicitly on *Home Improvement* (1991–99), a program influenced by the suggestion of the contemporary men's movement that men reject conventional notions of manliness and seek spiritual grounding, emotional self-awareness, and identities grounded in family life. The main character, Tim "The Toolman" Taylor, was portrayed as stereotypically hypermasculine and egocentric, but also as bumbling in matters of home repair, marriage, and fatherhood. With the help of his neighbor Wilson, an abundant source of spiritual wisdom, and his bearded but sensitive cohort Al Borland, Tim continually sought to become more responsive to the needs of his wife, Jill.

The crime drama *Magnum, P.I.* (1980–88) offered a very different perspective on the new, more introspective American masculinity. The feature character, Thomas Magnum, a strong, handsome private investigator, was much like the hard-boiled detective that for decades had been an iconic masculine type in American culture. His freewheeling bachelor lifestyle also reflected a popular model of manliness. But unlike the emotionally reserved detective or the carefree bachelor, Magnum, a Vietnam War veteran, demonstrated an emotional vulnerability resulting from the psychological wounds brought on by the war, and he maintained strong ties to war buddies T. C. and Rick. The show regularly reminded viewers of these tender friends' decided heterosexuality.

The late-twentieth-century rethinking of masculinity was evident as well in the increasing appearance of gay male television images. The earliest example served largely to underscore the normativeness of heterosexual masculinity: Jack Tripper of *Three's Company* (1977–84) feigned homosexuality to a homophobic landlord in order to share an apartment with two women, and he did so through exaggerated stereotypical behaviors. In the landlord's absence, however, he constantly flaunted his heterosexuality. But by the 1990s, homosexuality in gay male characters was either celebrated or accepted as a given. Furthermore, such programs as *Will & Grace* (premiered 1999) represented a range of gay masculinities by juxtaposing the "straight-acting" and symbolically named Will Truman and the more flamboyantly gay Jack McFarland. By the early twenty-first century, televised images suggested that American masculinity had become racially and sexually diverse, inclined to self-exploration, and distanced from its traditional monopoly on power.

BIBLIOGRAPHY

Butsch, Richard. "Class and Gender in Four Decades of Television Situation Comedy." *Critical Studies in Mass Communication* 9 (1992): 387–399.

Cantor, M.G. "Prime-Time Fathers: A Study in Continuity and Change." *Critical Studies in Mass Communication* 7 (1990): 275–285.

Craig, Steve, ed. *Men, Masculinity, and the Media.* Newbury Park, Calif.: Sage, 1992.

Jones, Gerard. *Honey, I'm Home!: Sitcoms, Selling the American Dream.* New York: Grove Weidenfeld, 1992.

Leibman, Nina. *Living Room Lectures: The Fifties Family in Film and Television.* Austin: University of Texas Press, 1995.

FURTHER READING

Hamamoto, Darrell Y. *Nervous Laughter: Television Situation Comedy and Liberal Democratic Ideology.* New York: Praeger, 1989.

Javna, John. *The Critics' Choice: The Best of TV Sitcoms: Burns and Allen to the Cosby Show, The Munsters to Mary Tyler Moore.* New York: Harmony, 1988.

Schwalbe, Michael. *Unlocking the Iron Cage: The Men's Movement, Gender Politics, and American Culture.* New York: Oxford University Press, 1996.

RELATED ENTRIES

Advertising; African-American Manhood; Bachelorhood; Cold War; Counterculture; Crisis of Masculinity; Divorce; Fatherhood; *Father Knows Best;* Hollywood; *Home Improvement*; Homosexuality; Latino Manhood; *Leave It to Beaver*; Marriage; Men's Movements; Middle-Class Manhood; *Odd Couple, The*; *Playboy* Magazine; Sensitive Male; Suburbia; Westerns; Working-Class Manhood

—*Bret E. Carroll*

TEMPERANCE

The temperance movement, which flourished from the early nineteenth century through the early twentieth century, attempted to limit or eliminate alcohol consumption. Although both men and women drank alcoholic beverages, temperance reformers generally focused on male drinking because they considered intoxication harmful to dominant middle-class constructions of manhood. Drinking, they believed, profoundly threatened social order by preventing men from being responsible citizens and patriarchs.

Many Americans of the colonial and Revolutionary periods objected to excessive drinking on the grounds that it challenged two traits thought basic to manhood: moderation and moral autonomy. But a substantial social movement against alcohol began only during the 1810s and 1820s (particularly in industrializing New England), sparked by the development of a market economy, the increasing mechanization of production, the emergence of identifiable middle and working classes, and the development of a middle-class "cult of domesticity" and the "breadwinner" model of manhood. Such early organizations as the Massachusetts Society for the Suppression of Intemperance (1813) and the American Temperance Society (1826), led by elites and the middle class, advocated moderate alcohol use and were most concerned about public drinking among working-class men. They branded drinking men as unreliable workers and inadequate breadwinners who lacked in self-control and were liable to depend on charity in times of crisis. Middle-class reformers claimed that sobriety, self-control, and hard work—values they considered central to male responsibility and to their own social and economic status—would allow men to support their families and improve their station in life. Thus, they attributed such troubling social problems as poverty and labor unrest to working men's use of alcohol, rather than to inequities in the new industrial economy.

In the 1840s a new type of temperance society emerged, exemplified by the Washingtonians and the Sons of Temperance. Inspired by the impulse toward religious perfectionism emerging from the revivals of the Second Great Awakening, these new societies called for total abstention from alcoholic beverages. By describing immoral behavior as "enslavement to vice," and therefore as a failure of the will, they emphasized moral purity and self-control as constitutive of manhood. While these societies, like their predecessors, understood masculinity in terms of hard work and breadwinning, they were also fraternal organizations that fostered strong homosocial bonds among their members and associated manliness with mutual support and social activism. Their initiation rituals, like those of other fraternal organizations, enacted a rebirth of the new member into a family of men, and they frequently represented their temperance work in martial terms, parading in uniform and describing themselves as armies of reform. In this way, they claimed that sobriety and participation in the reform of others (sometimes associated with female benevolence) were essentially masculine behaviors. Much less exclusive than older groups, they drew large working- and middle-class memberships and spread throughout the nation.

While antebellum temperance activity was usually intended to support the power and status of middle-class men, after the Civil War it became an important means for women to challenge male political and social dominance. Founded in 1874, the Women's Christian Temperance Union (WCTU) quickly became the largest nondenominational women's organization of the nineteenth century. It soon expanded its purpose from battling the saloon to confronting other social problems, particularly women's lack of political and social rights. Advocates for women's rights often successfully used

This certificate of membership for a nineteenth-century temperance society, in which a man prepares to pledge temperance with the encouragement of his family, suggests the middle-class Victorian association of sobriety with domestically responsible manhood. (From the collections of the Library of Congress)

male drinking as an argument for decreasing male power. Two of the most important legal rights won by married women in the nineteenth century—the right to own property in their own name and the right to bring lawsuits on their own behalf—were won largely by evoking the image of the inebriate husband and his oppressed wife.

Even as the WCTU challenged male prerogatives, however, its leaders insisted that their goal was to rescue men from the alcohol that sapped their manhood and restore them to their proper position within the family and community. In the organization's view, men could achieve true manhood only by yielding to the moral influence of female family members and reformers. Since men, who were thrown into the chaotic, impersonal, and amoral world of public commerce, were much more vulnerable to vicious influences than women, who were protected and morally fortified in private domestic spaces, women had the ability and responsibility to protect them.

The end of the nineteenth century saw the emergence of a new, male-led, organization—the Anti-Saloon League (founded in 1895)—which set out to prove that only men were organized and powerful enough to eliminate drinking. The Anti-Saloon League touted itself as more practical and businesslike than the WCTU. Like the WCTU, it perceived a crisis in male roles and behaviors, but while the WCTU aimed chiefly to make men better household heads, the Anti-Saloon League focused more heavily on politicizing its members and encouraging men to exercise leadership in civic affairs. As ideals of manly behavior came to emphasize aggression, passion, and power, and as many women moved from temperance into more focused woman suffrage groups, the Anti-Saloon League surpassed the WCTU as the vanguard of the temperance movement. In 1919 the WCTU's groundwork and the Anti-Saloon League's organizational and political strategies brought about the Eighteenth Amendment to the U.S. Constitution, which prohibited the manufacture, sale, or transportation of intoxicating liquors, and the Volstead Act, which was enacted to enforce the Eighteenth Amendment.

During the twentieth century, temperance messages became increasingly grounded in the newly emerging cultural authority of the medical and psychological professions. Now emphasized were alcohol's deleterious effects on men's physical, sexual, and mental health. Although temperance as an organized nationwide movement barely survived national prohibition, the WCTU and other temperance groups exist to this day, concentrating on alcohol education in the schools and antidrug campaigns. Additionally, newer groups like Alcoholics Anonymous and Mothers Against Drunk Driving (MADD) have emerged. While MADD continues the tradition of woman-led temperance reform, and while popular cultural images of problem drinkers sometimes focus on gendered issues such as wife abuse, gender has become substantially less central in discussions of the problem of excessive drink. Like their predecessors, postprohibition temperance groups emphasize that excessive alcohol use causes both social and familial problems. At the same time, however, they acknowledge that both men and women become alcoholics, and that women's drinking can be just as devastating (and in much the same ways) as men's. This change of focus reflects both the rise of widespread female public drinking and the diminishing difference between women's and men's roles in political, economic, and domestic life over the course of the twentieth century.

BIBLIOGRAPHY

Blocker, Jack S. *"Give To the Winds Thy Fears": The Women's Temperance Crusade, 1873–1874.* Westport, Conn.: Greenwood Press, 1985.

Bordin, Ruth Birgitta Anderson. *Woman and Temperance: The Quest for Power and Liberty, 1873–1900.* New Brunswick, N.J.: Rutgers University Press, 1990.

Murdock, Catherine Gilbert. *Domesticating Drink: Women, Men, and Alcohol in America, 1870–1940.* Baltimore: Johns Hopkins University Press, 1998.

Tyrrell, Ian R. *Sobering Up: From Temperance to Prohibition in Antebellum America, 1800–1860.* Westport, Conn.: Greenwood Press, 1979.

FURTHER READING

Epstein, Barbara Leslie. *The Politics of Domesticity: Women, Evangelism, and Temperance in Nineteenth-Century America.* Middletown, Conn.: Wesleyan University Press, 1981.

Gusfield, Joseph R. *Symbolic Crusade: Status Politics and the American Temperance Movement.* Urbana: University of Illinois Press, 1986.

Pegram, Thomas R. *Battling Demon Rum: The Struggle for a Dry America, 1800–1933.* Chicago: Ivan R. Dee, 1998.

RELATED ENTRIES

Alcohol; Arthur, Timothy Shay; Breadwinner Role; Cult of Domesticity; Fraternal Organizations; Industrialization; Middle-Class Manhood; Patriarchy; Progressive Era; Reform Movements; Self-Control; Suffragism; Victorian Era; Work; Working-Class Manhood

—*Elaine Frantz Parsons*

THOREAU, HENRY DAVID

1817–1862
Philosopher and Author

Henry David Thoreau shared with Ralph Waldo Emerson and other transcendentalists an ideal of manhood grounded in scholarly activity, self-awareness, and self-reliance. More radical in his advocacy of dissent, Thoreau espoused an environmentally conscious definition of manhood that encompassed, at least in part, the tenets of capitalism. Whereas Emerson initially eschewed market capitalism, only to embrace it wholeheartedly after 1860, Thoreau accepted market exchange, but rejected the exploitation of both labor and nature.

Thoreau graduated from Harvard in 1837, and then returned to his native Concord, Massachusetts, to take a position as a teacher in the town's public school. During the 1840s, he observed that the market revolution was undermining Concord's identity as a small fishing village. The town experienced firsthand the selective forces of capitalism when, in 1843, the opening of the Boston & Fitchburg Railroad reduced traffic along the Middlesex Canal (which served the town) and forced the filling in of a section of nearby Walden Pond.

Thoreau responded to these changes in 1854 by moving to Walden Pond, where he tried to realize an agrarian ideal of manliness that valued productive labor as the true basis of wealth. While he accepted market exchange and economic gain, he also saw nature as an aesthetic, sensual, and invigorating antidote to industrial civilization. He sought, not seclusion, but a critical juncture between nature and industrial change where he could live a life embedded in social patterns of obligation, exchange, and communal reciprocity. For instance, Thoreau partially built his cabin himself, while part of it was contracted out, and he worked in a variety of jobs to make ends meet, as well as planting vegetables for sale and consumption. Thoreau did not resist market capitalism, but he sought to explore the conditions of subsistence during a time of rapid change.

In *Walden* (1854), the literary product of this sojourn, Thoreau added a spiritual dimension to this masculine ideal, conceiving of manhood as a transcendental awareness of the inner self as discovered through nature. His naturalist and travel writings, such as *A Week on the Concord and Merrimack Rivers* (1849), *Cape Cod* (1855) and "Walking" (1862), reflect his belief that an excursion into nature is a journey into the self.

Thoreau's understanding of manliness also emphasized an unwavering commitment to the principles discovered in the inner self—both as the root of moral action and civic consciousness and as the only acceptable foundation for political society. This understanding of individual autonomy led him, in 1848, to oppose the Mexican-American War by refusing to pay his poll tax (for which he spent a night in jail) and to write "Resistance to Civil Government" (1849; now known by the title "Civil Disobedience"), in which he elevated the authority of the conscience over that of the state.

Like other transcendentalists, Thoreau supported the abolitionist movement. In 1859, he spoke out in support of what he considered the moral heroism of John Brown, who had been sentenced to death for leading an attack on the Harpers Ferry Armory and attempting to incite a slave rebellion.

Thoreau's commitment to individual integrity, the environment, abolitionism, and women's political equality helped to lay the foundations for a democratic, tolerant, and nonsexist concept of manhood that remains influential. Environmentalists, leaders of the 1960s counterculture, Beat poets such as Allen Ginsberg, and African-American leaders such as Martin Luther King, Jr., have cited Thoreau as an influence and as a model of firm moral commitment.

BIBLIOGRAPHY

Buell, Lawrence. *The Environmental Imagination: Thoreau, Nature Writing, and the Formation of American Culture.* Cambridge, Mass.: Belknap Press, 1995.

Gilmore, Michael T. *American Romanticism and the Marketplace.* Chicago: University of Chicago Press, 1985.

Porte, Joel. *In Respect to Egotism: Studies in American Romantic Writing.* Cambridge, England: Cambridge University Press, 1991.

Richardson, Robert D., Jr. *Henry David Thoreau: A Life of the Mind.* Berkeley: University of California Press, 1986.

Teichgraeber, Richard, III. "'A Yankee Diogenes': Thoreau and the Market." In *The Culture of the Market: Historical Essays,* edited by Thomas L. Haskell and Richard F. Teichgraeber, III. Cambridge, England: Cambridge University Press, 1996.

FURTHER READING

Cavell, Stanley. *The Senses of Walden.* Chicago: University of Chicago Press, 1992.

Fink, Steven. *Prophet in the Marketplace: Thoreau's Development as a Professional Writer.* Columbus: Ohio State University Press, 1999.

Milder, Robert. *Reimagining Thoreau.* Cambridge, England: Cambridge University Press, 1995.

Smith, David Clyde. *The Transcendental Saunterer: Thoreau and the Search for the Self.* Savannah, Ga.: Frederick C. Beil, 1997.

Warner, Michael. "Walden's Erotic Economy." In *Comparative American Identities: Race, Sex, and Nationality in the Modern Text,* edited by Hortense J. Spillers. New York: Routledge, 1991.

SELECTED WRITINGS

Thoreau, Henry David. *A Week on the Concord and Merrimack Rivers; Walden, Or, Life in the Woods; The Maine Woods; Cape Cod.* Edited by Robert F. Sayre. New York: Viking, 1985.

———. *Collected Essays and Poems.* Edited by Elizabeth Hall Witherell. New York: Library of America, 2001.

RELATED ENTRIES

Agrarianism; Beat Movement; Capitalism; Counterculture; Emerson, Ralph Waldo; Individualism; Kerouac, Jack; Market Revolution; Middle-Class Manhood; Reform Movements; Religion and Spirituality; Self-Control; Self-Made Man; Travel Narratives; Victorian Era

—*Thomas Winter*

TRANSSEXUALITY

Transsexuality, in which members of one biological sex assume the identity of the other, existed before there was a word for the phenomenon. Transsexuality emerged as a separate identity during the mid–twentieth century when practitioners of medicine and psychology, who had sought to define gender and sexual identities since the late nineteenth century, began to distinguish it from homosexuality (sexual attraction to the same sex) and transvestism (wearing the clothing of the opposite sex). Typically, doctors and psychologists, seeking to maintain gender norms they considered necessary to social order, defined these identities negatively, contrasting with what they considered a normative heterosexual masculinity. The history of transsexuality has therefore been closely intertwined with that of masculinity in American culture.

Transsexuality in Western society has been defined with reference to a sharp gender dichotomy: An individual is understood as either male or female, and a transsexual is one who moves from one to the other of these identities. Yet the earliest Americans, like many other non-Western societies, recognized more than two sexes. In many indigenous American cultures, for example, transsexuality as such does not exist, and individuals regarded as neither "masculine" nor "feminine" are not considered aberrant. At one time, many Native American cultures acknowledged not simply two genders, but also an additional, third gender that anthropologists often refer to as *berdache.* Such persons, far from being considered abnormal, enjoyed enhanced status. Among the Cheyenne, berdaches served as medicine people. Navajo berdaches were holy people who acted as mediators in community disputes, and among the Crow they were tribal historians. Among Euro-Americans, however, the same bigendered social system that created gender inequalities privileging men and masculinity over women and femininity has also led to a stigmatization of those who, like transsexuals, challenge that system, and are thus perceived as a threat to masculinity and male power.

The growth of medical technology in the twentieth century allowed individuals in the United States to express their identities through a change of anatomical structure. The earliest cases of sex reassignment surgery (SRS) occurred in Scandinavia, and the first known transsexual in the United States, Christine Jorgenson, had to travel there for SRS in 1952. The combination of media attention and the conservative cultural climate of Cold War America—where fear of communism often intertwined with fears of perceived sexual deviance and a self-conscious defense of patriarchal nuclear-family structures—prevented Jorgensen from successfully reintegrating into society. But Jorgensen's high profile did increase Americans' awareness of the difference between transsexuality and transvestism, prompting hospitals in the United States to begin offering SRS, at least to men. Women

In 1952, George W. Jorgensen, Jr., became Christine Jorgenson, the nation's first known transsexual. Publicity surrounding Jorgenson's operation increased Americans' awareness of transsexuality, but also stigmatized it because most Americans considered transsexuality a threat to "normative" masculinity and to the bigendered system underlying male power. (© Bettmann/Corbis)

seeking SRS continued to face strong discouragement, a difference due in part not only to the difficulties of constructing an artificial phallus, but also to cultural resistance to allowing women to claim masculinity and its associated status.

American perceptions of transsexuality and masculinity changed considerably during the 1960s and 1970s as feminism, the gay rights movement, and postmodernist notions of the fluidity of gender challenged both heterosexual male patriarchy and conventional understandings of gender and sexuality. A cultural climate more hospitable to men wishing to change their gender identities encouraged growing numbers of American men (and women) to seek SRS. Such cases as that of Jan Morris, who had SRS in 1972 after having climbed Mount Everest as James Morris in 1953, and Renée Richards, who played tennis in the U.S. Open in 1977 after relinquishing her earlier identity as physician Richard Raskin, attracted national attention. Several high-profile transsexuals published autobiographies that critiqued conventional models of American masculinity, especially the ways in which men are taught to view women as sexual objects, and urged new approaches to gender and masculinity that broke free of traditional views. Their authors addressed the complex relation between biological and psychological gender identity, arguing that male genitalia were not necessarily accompanied by self-identification as a man. By the late twentieth century, several states began offering legal recognition of this new reality about sex and gender, allowing biological men who undergo SRS to change their gender status, amend their birth certificates, and live as women. The ratio of female-to-male and male-to-female transsexuals also began to level out.

Transexuality remained a controversial issue at the beginning of the twenty-first century, and transsexuals continued to face considerable discrimination. In addition to discrimination in employment and housing, opponents of transsexuality, continuing to judge transsexuals against conservative definitions of masculinity and gender, questioned whether transsexuals should be able to teach school, marry, and adopt children. As a result, transsexuals established dozens of support and advocacy organizations during the late twentieth century, including the American Educational Gender Information Service (1990), the International Conference of Transgender Law and Employment Policy (1991), and, for female-to-male transsexuals, FTM International (1994). While such organizations continue to struggle for legal protections, by the end of 2003, only Minnesota, New Mexico, and Rhode Island had adopted laws prohibiting discrimination against transgender people. Yet as the procedure becomes more common, support resources for transsexuals strengthen and multiply, and Americans grow increasingly disinclined to perceive transsexuality as a threat to masculinity, the phenomenon is attracting less public attention.

BIBLIOGRAPHY

Benjamin, Harry. *The Transsexual Phenomenon.* New York: Julian Press, 1966.

Bullough, Bonnie, Vern L. Bullough, and James Elias, eds. *Gender Blending.* Amherst, N.Y.: Prometheus, 1997.

Conn, Canary. *Canary: The Courageous and Moving Story of a Transsexual.* 1974. Reprint, New York: Bantam, 1977.

Feinberg, Leslie. *Transgender Warriors: Making History from Joan of Arc to RuPaul.* Boston: Beacon Press, 1996.

Hausman, Bernice L. *Changing Sex: Transsexualism, Technology, and The Idea of Gender.* Durham, N.C.: Duke University Press, 1995.

Jorgensen, Christine. *Christine Jorgensen: A Personal Autobiography.* New York: Bantam, 1967.

Savitsch, Eugene de. *Homosexuality, Transvestism, and Change of Sex.* Springfield, Ill.: Charles C. Thomas, 1958.

Transgender Law and Policy Institute. <http://www.transgenderlaw.org> (May 7, 2003).

FURTHER READING

Bolin, Anne. *In Search of Eve: Transsexual Rites of Passage.* New York: Bergin and Garvey, 1988.

Brevard, Aleshia. *The Woman I Was Not Born to Be: A Transsexual Journey.* Philadelphia: Temple University Press, 2001.

D'Emilio, John, and Estelle B. Freedman. *Intimate Matters: A History of Sexuality in America.* New York: Harper & Row, 1988.

Hodgkinson, Liz. *Michael, Née Laura: The Story of the World's First Female-to-Male Transsexual.* London: Columbus, 1989.

Richards, Renée. *Second Serve: The Renée Richards Story.* New York: Random House, 1983.

Williams, Walter L. *The Spirit and the Flesh: Sexual Diversity in American Indian Cultures.* 1986. Reprint, Boston: Beacon Press, 1992.

RELATED ENTRIES

Body; Feminism; Homosexuality; Transvestism

—Bret E. Carroll and Linda Heidenreich

TRANSVESTISM

Transvestism emerged as a term for cross-dressing when, in 1910, the physician and pioneering sexologist Magnus Hirschfeld published his work *Transvestites.* Like later works, Hirschfeld's study focused on male, rather than female, cross-dressing, in part because male cross-dressers received a disproportionate amount of attention from the general population. In Western cultures, where masculine gender roles are valued over feminine ones and masculinity is typically associated with authority, male cross-dressing has been condemned by the church, the state, and medical professions. Yet cross-dressing, specifically male cross-dressing, has persisted from the beginnings of written history.

Records dating as early as the fifth century B.C.E. tell of instances of male cross-dressing. The Greek historian Herodotus, for example, wrote of Scythians who dressed as women. From the indigenous American *berdache* (a male who adopted the clothing and work of women) to the *hijra* community of India (a group of eunuchs, transsexuals, and cross-dressers), many traditional cultures have invested cross-dressers with spiritual power. These cross-dressing men differed from transvestites in the modern United States in that they also rejected masculine gender roles, embracing both feminine dress and lifestyles. This suggests that the insistence on two rigidly defined gender roles and the stigmatization of cross-dressing that characterize Western and American culture are not universal, but culturally rooted in Judeo-Christian religious traditions.

The stigma attached to cross-dressing has erased much of the early history of transvestism in the United States. Some stories claim that Edward Hyde, Lord Cornbury, the governor of the provinces of New York and New Jersey (1702–08) was a transvestite. Rumors have him opening the colonial assemblies while dressed as a woman, and a portrait from his time shows the Lord dressed as Queen Anne. Early university dress codes provide more substantial evidence of colonial cross-dressing. In 1734, for example, the laws of Harvard College were revised to explicitly forbid women's clothing. Students found cross-dressing could be "publicly denigrated" or expelled.

Transvestism entered the medical canon in the late nineteenth century, just as middle-class men in the United States and northern Europe began to suffer from a growing anxiety about the meaning of masculinity. As they increasingly entered the professions, living in city environments away from the rugged life of the frontier and feeling a loss of autonomy in their work environments, growing numbers of them sought new ways to construct masculinity and bolster their masculine identities. The result was the rise of a new ideal of manliness that sharply distinguished men from women and valued physical exertion, aggression, and martial discipline.

In this cultural environment, transvestism—like homosexuality, with which many Americans associated it—seemed to many Americans incompatible with true manhood. Thus, American physicians and psychologists accepted the idea, presented in works by the German sexologist Richard von Krafft-Ebing, that cross-dressing was a sexual "perversion." Later works by Magnus Hirschfeld (1868–1935) and Havelock Ellis (1859–1939) took a more positive view toward male cross-dressing, yet most medical texts classified transvestism as a sickness. By 1952 the American Psychiatric Association listed male, but not female, transvestism, as an illness in its *Diagnostic and Statistical Manual* (DSM). In 1996, transvestism remained listed as an illness in the fourth edition of the DSM.

Only in the late twentieth century—as the Sexual Revolution, the counterculture, second-wave feminism, and a growing men's movement prompted new attention to the male sensitivity—did transvestites, as a minority community, organize in the United States. In the 1960s, Virginia Prince, also known as Charles Prince, began organizing transvestites who wanted to articulate a new kind of masculine identity by expressing their "woman within." Prince was a biochemist whose wife left him in 1950 when he disclosed his transvestism to her. Following his divorce, he founded the magazine *Transvestia.* Originally printed on a low budget and mimeographed, the publication soon failed, but it was revived in 1960 as a full-scale magazine "by, for, and about Transvestites."

In 1961, Prince founded Hose and Heels, the first known cross-dressing support group in the United States. In 1962, Hose and Heels was incorporated into Full Personality Expression (FPE), the first national transvestite support organization. In 1976, FPE and Mamselle (another support group) merged to form the Society for the Second Self, the largest heterosexual transvestite organization to date. In 1987, heterosexual and homosexual transvestites founded the Renaissance Education Association, an advocacy and support group.

New definitions of masculinity that incorporate transvestism still struggle for broad cultural acceptance. While the vast majority of transvestites, including the members of organizations such as the Society for the Second Self, are heterosexual, popular images of transvestism have focused on homosexual female impersonators and the media has continued to portray transvestites as homosexual. Recent studies of male transvestites have revealed that many dress in men's clothing by day and wear women's clothing for the purpose of sexual arousal. Modern transvestism, then, is a complex phenomenon that illuminates the fluidity and variability of masculine identities.

Bibliography

Allen, J. J. *The Man in the Red Velvet Dress: Inside the World of Cross-Dressing.* New York: Carol Publishing, 1996.

Bullough, Bonnie, Vern L. Bullough, and James Elias, eds. *Gender Blending.* Amherst, N.Y.: Prometheus, 1997.

Bullough, Vern L., and Bonnie Bullough. *Cross Dressing, Sex, and Gender.* Philadelphia: University of Pennsylvania Press, 1993.

Feinberg, Leslie. *Transgender Warriors: Making History from Joan of Arc to RuPaul.* Boston: Beacon Press, 1996.

Garber, Marjorie. *Vested Interests: Cross-Dressing and Cultural Anxiety.* New York: HarperPerennial, 1993.

Further Reading

Epstein, Julia, and Kristina Straub, eds. *Body Guards: The Cultural Politics of Gender Ambiguity.* New York: Routledge, 1991.

Feinbloom, Deborah Heller. *Transvestites and Transsexuals: Mixed Views.* New York: Dell, 1977.

Hirschfeld, Magnus. *Transvestites: The Erotic Drive to Cross-Dress.* 1910. Reprint, translated by Michael A. Lombardi-Nash. Amherst, N.Y.: Prometheus Books, 1991.

Woodhouse, Annie. *Fantastic Women: Sex, Gender and Transvestism.* New Brunswick, N.J.: Rutgers University Press, 1989.

Related Entries

Crisis of Masculinity; Heterosexuality; Homosexuality; Religion and Spirituality; Transsexuality

—Linda Heidenreich

Travel

Travel has offered American men unique opportunities to establish, reinforce, and test the boundaries of masculinity. Travel in the United States and abroad has allowed Americans to compare their customs and beliefs with those of foreigners, and has thus been a significant means through which Americans have developed a sense of national identity. It has also allowed men to rehearse a variety of masculine roles in unfamiliar settings. The history of travel in the United States highlights male travelers' displacement from conventional social relations, even as class and gender assumptions have traveled with them as cultural "baggage." More than just a test of prevailing masculinities, however, travel has also given men the opportunity to transform meanings of manhood in America.

The Nineteenth Century

Although a limited number of colonial Americans traveled regularly in the eighteenth century, it was not until the early nineteenth century that recreational travel became a well-organized activity in the United States. New means of transportation, such as steamships and railroads, made it possible for Americans to travel in relative comfort throughout the continent or across the ocean. Recreational travel also required destinations that people wished to visit, and entrepreneurs first turned New England spas, Appalachian resorts, and tourist attractions such as Niagara Falls into preferred places for travelers to meet, socialize, and sightsee. Later in the century, commercial tour companies guided customers to western states and through the nations of Europe. Most significantly, travel required money—only the affluent could afford to travel far and regularly before 1900.

Because wealthy men were the first to travel frequently, a specific form of upper-class masculinity was the first to be exhibited through American travel. Spas and mountain resorts that attracted the elite traveler in the early nineteenth century were home to fashionable displays of gentility and privilege based upon a man's economic standing and his public interaction with women. Both bachelors and men who traveled with their wives were expected to act as sophisticated gentlemen at resort balls and dinners. A man's dancing skills, knowledge of etiquette, and power of conversation became barometers of his manhood and social status. Travel to exclusive resorts before the Civil War thus demonstrated an interweaving of class and gender dynamics.

Expensive tours of Europe relied upon the same mixture of sophistication and manliness. Men who traveled through such European cities as Paris and Rome followed prescribed routes made fashionable in earlier centuries and promoted themselves as schooled in the finer arts of high society. Trips to art museums and palatial estates allowed wealthy American men to associate themselves with the discerning taste and formal social rules of the European gentry. Above all, genteel travel reinforced the privileges of upper-class Americans by emphasizing their freedom from the demands of daily work.

For middle-class men who could not afford European excursions, travel in the nineteenth century often provided an opportunity to expand their sense of masculinity beyond the workplace. The rise of white-collar occupations and business culture led many men to question their usefulness and independence in an increasingly industrial society—a society that still valued the traditional work ethic of physical toil and autonomy. Leisure travel allowed middle-class men to escape the constraints of their working lives, if only temporarily. Travel offered a sense of manly independence that few white-collar jobs could provide, allowing men to set challenging itineraries and assert themselves without supervision. Henry David Thoreau provided a model for the journey of self-discovery with *A Week on the Concord and Merrimack Rivers* (1849), in which he wrote of travel's "buoyancy and freedom" as an integral part of his experience. Whereas the late-nineteenth-century popular press classified resort vacations as decidedly feminine excursions, middle-class camping vacations and long-distance sightseeing tours reproduced a sense of labor for men who lamented the lack of physical work in their professional lives. Significantly, American mills and factories became popular destinations in the last quarter of the century, as tourists combined their pursuit of leisure travel with their romanticized view of working-class manhood.

Closely connected to men's search for purpose was a desire for adventure and danger. Due to pervasive concerns that urbanization, industrialization, and bureaucratization had weakened men, travel to rough locales became a means for men to prove that they could cope and even thrive in primitive environments. The American West, in particular, became popularly associated with the revitalization of manhood during this period. Traveling shows such as Buffalo Bill's Wild West, which made stops in cities from Chicago to Richmond, transformed the American West into a mythic region to which men of the East might travel in order to strengthen their bodies and renew their manly vigor. Theodore Roosevelt supported conservation of the nation's western landscape during his presidency (1901–09) in order to maintain the region's wild areas. Africa and South America were similarly seen as destinations for men looking for adventure—in *African Game Trails* (1910), Roosevelt described his 1909 African safari as a strenuous exercise that tested a man's character and improved his physique through dangerous encounters. Dangerous travel gave discontented "modern" men a chance to create a new model of manliness that armed them for battle in the public sphere of politics and business. As the daily life of many middle-class men became managerial, travel and the world beyond the workplace became increasingly associated with a rugged masculinity more akin to the frontiersman than the businessman.

The Twentieth Century

The democratization of travel in the early twentieth century gave people of limited means the chance to travel farther than ever before. In the 1920s, labor researchers and social scientists promoted the benefits of vacation time for workers, arguing that time spent in leisurely travel produced better performance in the workplace. By the 1930s, most industrial employers began offering their workers paid summer vacations.

Mass production of the automobile also brought leisure travel within reach for many Americans; the number of car owners grew from under 500,000 in 1910 to 19.2 million in 1926. The car also generated a culture of its own: thrill-seeking men who were willing to face the hardships of transcontinental driving for the glory of setting new speed records. The dangers of early automobiles made each trip a well-publicized effort to conquer nature through manly ingenuity and skill. As automobile travel became more routine in the 1920s, manufacturers and social critics alike touted the car as a social leveler, a device that made the wealthy and the poor traveling peers. In the 1950s, car advertisements still offered men of all classes a sense of power based on their ability to command this marvelous yet accessible machine.

Automobile travel in twentieth-century America also featured a most domestic institution, the family vacation. With the advent of the interstate highway system in the 1950s, the annual summer journey became a widespread phenomenon, one that placed the nuclear family on a voyage of education and relaxation. As fathers and husbands, men were often imagined as the captains of vacations, guiding their families on new adventures, while also recuperating from the rat race of work and business. The family vacation gave men license to explore a more domestic form of masculinity, even as they reasserted their authority within the family unit.

A central theme of travel for men in the twentieth century continued to be the promise of escape from the monotony of stationary life. From the rambling ethic embraced by folksinger Woody Guthrie in the 1930s and 1940s to Jack Kerouac's celebration of constant movement in *On the Road* (1957), travel became a way of life for men who took to the road to find freedom of expression and to reject an increasingly commercial and corporate American culture. The manly culture of the road produced thousands of truck stops, gas stations, and travelers' motels noted for their rough atmosphere. The manliness of the road journey was commodified in the 1960s and 1970s, turning the economic desperation of Depression-era hoboes into another form of touristic adventure. By the late twentieth century, the high school or college "road trip" had become an established rite of passage for many American men, a journey in which they were permitted to abandon social responsibility one last time as a segueway into manhood.

In the twenty-first century, travel remains a central leisure activity in American culture. With adventure travel and ecotourism emerging as the fastest-growing types of tourism, some men will continue to find in travel the sensations of freedom and risk that they associate with masculinity. Of course, these ventures into the wild will compete with the increasingly commercialized and conventional forms of travel marketed to families by entertainment conglomerates and heritage organizations. Moreover, the ongoing growth of business travel will mean that a trip between American cities or around the world will perhaps become less an adventure than just another form of commuting. Whether in the guise of the fearless adventurer, the average tourist, or the corporate globetrotter, however, American men will continue to develop their identity through travel, finding both an escape from gender conventions and an arena in which to address them directly.

Bibliography

Belasco, Warren James. *Americans on the Road: From Autocamp to Motel, 1910–1945.* Baltimore: Johns Hopkins University Press, 1997.

Sherrill, Rowland A. *Road-Book America: Contemporary Culture and the New Picaresque.* Urbana: University of Illinois Press, 2000.

Stowe, William W. *Going Abroad: European Travel in Nineteenth-Century American Culture.* Princeton, N.J.: Princeton University Press, 1994.

Thoreau, Henry David. *A Week on the Concord and Merrimack Rivers.* 1849. Reprint, New York: Penguin, 1998.

Further Reading

Aron, Cindy S. *Working at Play: A History of Vacations in the United States.* New York: Oxford University Press, 1999.

Dulles, Foster Rhea. *Americans Abroad: Two Centuries of European Travel.* Ann Arbor: University of Michigan Press, 1964.

Dunlop, M. H. *Sixty Miles from Contentment: Traveling the Nineteenth-Century American Interior.* Boulder, Colo.: Westview Press, 1998.

Jakle, John A. *The Tourist: Travel in Twentieth-Century America.* Lincoln: University of Nebraska Press, 1985.

McConnell, Curt. *Coast to Coast by Automobile: The Pioneering Trips, 1899–1908.* Stanford, Calif.: Stanford University Press, 2000.

Sears, John F. *Sacred Places: American Tourist Attractions in the Nineteenth Century.* Amherst: University of Massachusetts Press, 1998.

Shaffer, Marguerite S. *See America First: Tourism and National Identity, 1880–1940.* Washington, D.C.: Smithsonian Institution Press, 2001.

Sutton, Horace. *Travelers: The American Tourist from Stagecoach to Space Shuttle.* New York: Morrow, 1980.

Related Entries

Automobile; Bachelorhood; Class; Consumerism; Cowboys; Crisis of Masculinity; Hoboes; Leisure; Middle-Class Manhood; Outdoorsmen; Roosevelt, Theodore; Technology; Thoreau, Henry David; Western Frontier; Work; Youth

—*Edward Slavishak*

Travel Narratives

Since the colonial period, American travel narratives have explored competing ideas of what it means to be a man. Whether taking the form of brief sketches published in newspapers or full-length books, travel narratives have dealt both explicitly and implicitly with issues of manhood. The act of writing about travel has given authors the opportunity to present the varying qualities of masculinity that emerge on personal journeys. Moreover, assumptions about the purpose of travel have been informed by notions of masculinity, underscoring the central importance of gender in the literature of travel.

The travel narrative first emerged in the late eighteenth century as a result of a man's presumed duty to produce knowledge. Men's travel narratives were considered to be both accurate descriptions of the world and evidence of authority in matters of science, geography, politics, and economics. J. Hector St. John de Crèvecoeur's *Letters from an American Farmer* (1782) and William Bartram's *Travels* (1791) are two early examples of American travel narratives that attempted to record, classify, and measure the new nation for European audiences. Through their accounts, Crèvecoeur and Bartram conveyed knowledge of New England and the Southeast, respectively—information considered useful and significant, at least in part, because the traveling writers were men. While women's writings were often devalued as frivolous, men's travel narratives became accepted accounts of America's social and natural features.

The early nineteenth century also saw the rise of travel literature meant to entertain as well as inform. Humorous or dramatic accounts of trips to Europe or throughout the United States may seem to have little to do with notions of masculinity, yet the act of writing such an account was itself an expression of concern about men's social and cultural obligations. Writing about their travels became a primary way for men of privilege in the nineteenth century to make their leisure activities productive. The middle-class work ethic that determined a man's worth also exerted its influence on those who had the means to avoid a life of toil. Upper-class men transformed trips that seemed idle and unmanly into literary output, creating evidence of work by producing something tangible out of their travel experience. In a culture that respected hard work, a man's travel writing gave him license to pursue a life of leisure.

In the nineteenth century, as tourists flooded the new commercial attractions erected in the United States, many domestic travelers sought authenticity and risk beyond the artifice of such crowded sites as New York's Niagara Falls and Mammoth Cave in Kentucky. By mid-century, tales of adventurous travel became the most popular type of general reading, partly due to contributions from such established writers as Washington Irving and Mark Twain. Irving's *A Tour on the Prairies* (1835) chronicled an excursion to the Oklahoma territories, replete with tales of hunting trips and the ruggedly virile life of Native Americans. Similarly, Twain's *Roughing It* (1872) presented the American West as a lawless land of violence and coarse manners. By journeys' end, both Irving and Twain had adopted a new narrative persona, that of the experienced male traveler, ravaged by the road but stronger for the adventure.

The West was the ultimate site of domestic adventure, yet the settled regions of the East also offered literary vistas. Henry David Thoreau's introspective travel account, *A Week on the Concord and Merrimack Rivers* (1849), claimed that because a traveler was "born again on the road," even journeys through the woods and rivers of New England allowed men to reinvent themselves spiritually (Thoreau, 247). The cultural anxiety about masculinity that emerged later in the nineteenth century, fueled by pervasive concerns about the softening effects of white-collar occupations, consumer culture, and modern conveniences, prompted many American men to seek a sense of challenge beyond the bounds of home and work. Narratives of rugged masculinity on trails and rivers suggested that there were still places to find vivid examples of hardy and capable men, even in the heart of the industrialized East.

In the late nineteenth and early twentieth centuries, reports of travel to parts of the world that Americans viewed as exotic became central texts in which white male writers juxtaposed their masculinity with that of native, nonwhite men. Travelers to South America, Africa, and Asia admired indigenous men for their ability to survive in harsh conditions, yet ridiculed their seemingly feminine qualities. American writers championed the values of Western civilization, and they typically criticized the indigenous men they encountered for their lack of self-control, undeveloped rules of social etiquette, and ignorance of modern science. The birth of *National Geographic* magazine in 1888 provided a regular forum for exotic travel narratives in which foreign peoples around the world were classified in terms of crudeness and compared to American writers' supposedly advanced masculinities.

Twentieth-century travel narratives emphasized much of the same manly adventures and exotic interactions that characterized nineteenth-century narratives. One theme that became more apparent, however, was the connection between travel and the traveler's sense of individual freedom. Many "road books" of the twentieth century described a trip through the United States as an expression of manly independence. Jack Kerouac's *On the Road* (1957) and John Steinbeck's *Travels with Charley* (1962) both narrated tales of continuous movement through Cold-War America in which the freedom to keep traveling gave a man his sense of self. The belief that spatial freedom is connected to a man's autonomy continued to be expressed in such late-twentieth-century narratives as Peter Jenkins' *A Walk Across America* (1979) and William Least Heat Moon's *Blue Highways* (1982), in which male narrators discovered themselves while on the road as they experienced the pleasures and pains of travel.

As a literary genre that has spanned three centuries of American history, the travel narrative has served as a text on both journeys and gender. Accounts of trips have allowed men to define their masculinity as a product of the analytical, adventurous, disorienting, or liberating experience of travel. The narrative of a trip, addressing both discoveries and misfortunes, has been particularly conducive to explorations of masculinity. In 1782, Crèvecoeur asked: "What then is the American, this new man?" (Crèvecoeur, 43) Ever since, male travel writers from the United States have sought answers to this enduring question.

Bibliography

Crèvecoeur, J. Hector St. John de. *Letters from an American Farmer.* 1782. Reprint, Oxford: Oxford University Press, 1997.

Dulles, Foster Rhea. *Americans Abroad: Two Centuries of European Travel.* Ann Arbor: University of Michigan Press, 1964.

Edwards, Justin D. *Exotic Journeys: Exploring the Erotics of U.S. Travel Literature, 1840–1930.* Hanover, N.H.: University Press of New England, 2001.

Regis, Pamela. *Describing Early America: Bartram, Jefferson, Crèvecoeur, and the Rhetoric of Natural History.* DeKalb: Northern Illinois University Press, 1992.

Stowe, William W. *Going Abroad: European Travel in Nineteenth-Century American Culture.* Princeton, N.J.: Princeton University Press, 1994.

Thoreau, Henry David. *A Week on the Concord and Merrimack Rivers.* 1849. Reprint, New York: Penguin, 1998.

Further Reading

Brown, Sharon Rogers. *American Travel Narratives as a Literary Genre from 1542–1832: The Art of a Perpetual Journey.* Lewiston, N.Y.: E. Mellen Press, 1993.

Caesar, Terry. *Forgiving the Boundaries: Home as Abroad in American Travel Writing.* Athens: University of Georgia Press, 1995.

Day, Laura Anne. "The History of Every One of Us: A Gender Study of America's Antebellum Travel Writers." Ph.D. diss., Purdue University, 1988.

Kerouac, Jack. *On the Road.* New York: Viking Press, 1957.

Lueck, Beth. *American Writers and the Picturesque Tour: The Search for National Identity, 1790–1860.* New York: Garland Publishing, 1997.

Sherrill, Rowland A. *Road-Book America: Contemporary Culture and the New Picaresque.* Urbana: University of Illinois Press, 2000.

Theroux, Paul, ed. *The Best American Travel Writing, 2001.* New York: Houghton Mifflin, 2001.

Ziff, Larzer. *Return Passages: Great American Travel Writing, 1780–1910.* New Haven, Conn.: Yale University Press, 2000.

Related Entries

Beat Movement; Crèvecoeur, J. Hector St. John; Crisis of Masculinity; *Easy Rider*; Individualism; Kerouac, Jack; Leisure; Middle-Class Manhood; Thoreau, Henry David; Travel; Twain, Mark; Western Frontier; Whiteness; Work

—Edward Slavishak

Twain, Mark

1835–1910
American Novelist, Journalist, and Humorist

Commonly viewed as the quintessential American writer, Mark Twain defined a brand of rugged masculinity through works such as *Roughing It* (1872) and *Life on the Mississippi* (1883) while his best-known works, *Adventures of Huckleberry Finn* (1884) and *Adventures of Tom Sawyer* (1876), drew affectionate portraits of nineteenth-century American boyhood. Twain's use of humor and colloquial language and his valorization of a new type of frontier male hero, which was a renunciation of the feminizing influences associated with the urban, industrial East, helped to shape the genre of Western American literature.

Born Samuel Langhorne Clemens, Twain grew up in the frontier town of Hannibal, Missouri. His youthful adventures as a riverboat pilot and prospector supplied material for his autobiographical works and comic stories, which frequently involve a rough, overtly masculine frontiersman triumphing over a more dignified and feminized easterner. Seen in such stories as "The Notorious Jumping Frog of Calaveras County" (1865), this approach champions a new kind of male hero: uneducated but clever, uncouth but charming, and socially unconnected but physically powerful. *Roughing It* tells of Twain's own transformation from greenhorn to savvy western man during his time in Nevada and California in the early 1860s. These early writings glorified the still evolving West as a primitive, dusty, masculine place refreshingly free of the emasculating influences that middle-class Victorians associated with nineteenth-century civilization and industrialization in the eastern United States.

Twain's later work, however, paints a more ambiguous picture of the conflict between roughness and civilization, a shift occasioned perhaps by Twain's marriage into a prominent eastern family. The mischievous hero of the often comic *Adventures of Tom Sawyer* seeks to escape the feminine, domestic world of his Aunt Polly and the town of St. Petersburg, Missouri, and to discover a masculine world of adventure—a world repeatedly associated with nature. But Tom comes to recognize the dangers of an unbridled, untamed, "natural" masculinity through his contact with the murderous Injun Joe, a social and racial outsider. While Joe is punished with death at the end of the novel, the rebellious Tom achieves manhood by becoming tamed and reintegrated into the community.

Twain's masterpiece, *Adventures of Huckleberry Finn,* offers a still more biting commentary on the challenges of American manhood amid the nineteenth-century tensions of social class, slavery, and greed. Huck and the slave Jim are outcasts from Tom's world of white, middle-class masculinity—Huck by virtue of his poverty and Jim because of his race. Their adventures as runaways teach them the value of male friendship as they encounter a variety of crooks and confidence men who seek to cheat them and women who aim to control them. Huck and Jim are eventually redeemed and masculinized—Jim gains his freedom and Huck learns that his good-for-nothing father has died and has left him a small fortune. The novel closes more equivocally than its predecessor, however, for Huck ends where he began, preparing to run away, forever resistant to the rules of feminine domestic life.

Twain's combination of humor, colorful description, colloquial language, and social insights have made him one of the most beloved American writers. His heroes, whether boys or men, have intertwined concepts of masculinity with images of physicality, bravado, freedom, and nature in the American consciousness.

Bibliography

Bloom, Harold, ed. *Mark Twain.* New York: Chelsea House, 1986.

Cardwell, Guy. *The Man Who Was Mark Twain: Images and Ideologies.* New Haven, Conn.: Yale University Press, 1991.

Hutchinson, Stuart, ed. *Mark Twain: Critical Assessments.* 3 vols. Mountfield, East Sussex, England: Helm Information, 1993.

Stoneley, Peter. *Mark Twain and the Feminist Aesthetic.* Cambridge, England: Cambridge University Press, 1992.

Further Reading

Messent, Peter. *Mark Twain.* New York: St. Martin's, 1997.

Robinson, Forrest G., ed. *The Cambridge Companion to Mark Twain.* New York: Cambridge University Press, 1995.

Skandera-Trombley, Laura. *Mark Twain in the Company of Women.* Philadelphia: University of Pennsylvania Press, 1994.

Stahl, J. D. *Mark Twain, Culture, and Gender: Envisioning America through Europe.* Athens: University of Georgia Press, 1994.

Stone, Albert. *The Innocent Eye: Childhood in Mark Twain's Imagination.* Hamden, Conn.: Archon Books, 1970.

Selected Writings

Twain, Mark. *Roughing It.* 1872. Reprint, edited by Hamlin Hill. Harmondsworth, England: Penguin, 1982.

———. *Life on the Mississippi.* 1883. Reprint, edited by James M. Cox. Harmondsworth, England: Penguin, 1985.

———. *Adventures of Huckleberry Finn.* 1884. Reprint, New York: Bantam, 1989.

———. *Adventures of Tom Sawyer.* 1876. Reprint, edited by Lee Clark Mitchell. New York: Oxford University Press, 1998.

———. "The Notorious Jumping Frog of Calaveras County." *The Norton Anthology of American Literature.* 3rd ed. Vol. 2. New York: Norton, 1989.

Related Entries

Abolitionism; Adolescence; *Adventures of Huckleberry Finn*; African-American Manhood; Boyhood; California Gold Rush; Confidence Man; Race; Sawyer, Tom; Slavery; Travel Narratives; Western Frontier

—*Kirsten L. Parkinson*

Uncle Sam

A national patriotic symbol created by a series of cartoonists, Uncle Sam became a highly popular representation of masculinity—defined in terms of republican independence, patriotic commitment, whiteness, national vigor, and morality. First appearing in 1832, Uncle Sam was designed to serve as a more serious and manly representation of America than the then common images of the callow youth Brother Jonathan (also known as Yankee Doodle) and the Native American woman Columbia.

Uncle Sam's origin is usually traced to Samuel Wilson, a meatpacker from Troy, New York. The barrels of meat that he supplied to the army during the War of 1812 were stamped "U.S." to indicate that they were the property of the United States. This identification is said to have led to widespread use of Uncle Sam to refer to the federal government. The first recorded use of the term appeared in 1813 in Wilson's hometown newspaper, the *Troy Post*, which referred to war losses that weighed "upon Uncle Sam's shoulders." A 1961 Congressional resolution recognized Wilson as Uncle Sam's namesake.

The first drawing of Uncle Sam, an unsigned 1832 lithograph entitled Uncle Sam in Danger conveys bitterness over Andrew Jackson's effort to destroy the Second Bank of the United States. This Uncle Sam reflects the contemporary artisan archetype of manhood—young, white, muscular, honest, and hard working—to which Jackson's enemies sought to appeal. By the mid-nineteenth century, as the nation expanded westward, the market economy grew, and an emergent middle class rose to cultural prominence, artists' depictions of Uncle Sam shifted to reflect these societal changes. His body became less muscular to reflect a new ideal thin physique, his frame grew taller to suggest national strength and heroism, and his hair turned white to suggest national maturity. These versions remained frozen in 1830s dress: top hat, vest, striped trousers, and swallow-tailed coat.

During and after the Civil War, Uncle Sam increasingly began to resemble President Abraham Lincoln, perceived in the North as a defender of national unity. To northerners, Uncle Sam, like Lincoln, came to represent manly resolve, courage, power, and a lack of cultivated refinement, (Confederate cartoonists never drew Uncle Sam). During the 1870s, the best-known cartoonist of the day, Thomas Nast of *Harper's Weekly*, widely popularized Sam as a lanky Lincoln look-alike. Another

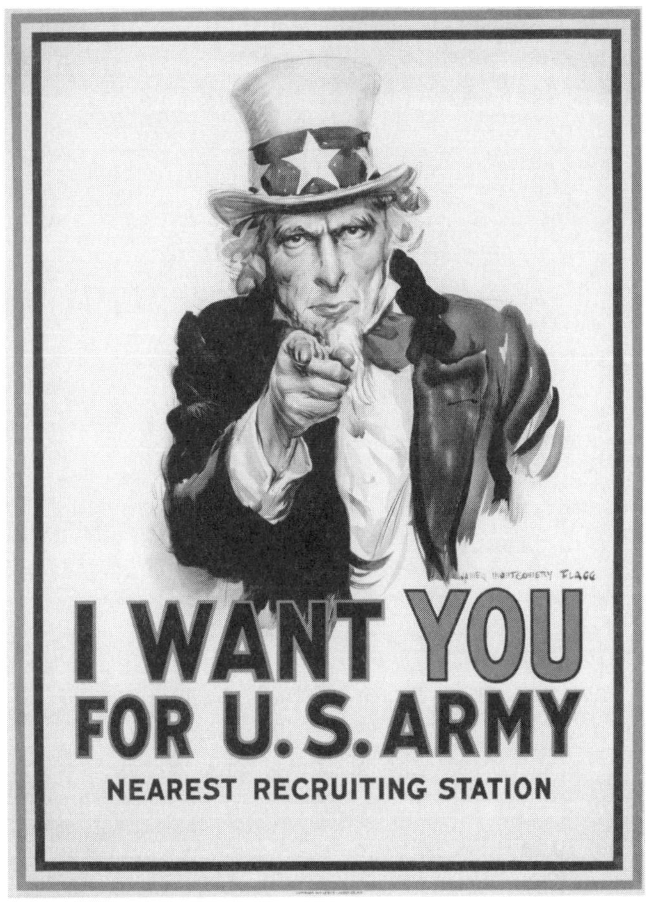

James Montgomery Flagg's well-known 1917 U.S. Army recruiting poster featuring Uncle Sam powerfully illustrates the American cultural association between masculinity, nationalism, patriotic service, and—into the early twentieth century—whiteness. (© Swim Ink/Corbis)

physical change in Uncle Sam, the sporting of a beard, reflected a broader trend in the decades following the Civil War, during which middle-class American men resisted the perceived feminizing influences of urban, industrial civilization by accentuating their physical distinctiveness from women.

During World War I, Uncle Sam's reputation as an American symbol of national unity, citizenship, and courage received another boost. In 1917, James Montgomery Flagg created the best-known version of the icon for a U.S. Army recruitment poster, which depicts Uncle Sam pointing out at the public while stating "I Want You." By urging patriotic self-sacrifice and encouraging heroism among men, this poster became a classic that was used again for recruitment purposes during World War II.

During the 1960s, the Vietnam conflict challenged ideas of American military power while political and social movements, such as the civil rights and feminist movements, questioned white men's dominance in American life and undermined confidence in American national unity. As traditional associations of national identity with masculinity, whiteness, and military strength became increasingly archaic, the image of Uncle Sam faded from prominence.

Bibliography

Bivins, Thomas H. "The Body Politic: The Changing Shape of Uncle Sam." *Journalism Quarterly* 64, no.1 (1987): 13–20.

Ketchum, Alton. *Uncle Sam: The Man and the Legend.* New York: Hill and Wang, 1959.

Kimmel, Michael. "Consuming Manhood: The Feminization of American Culture and the Recreation of the Male Body, 1832–1920." *Michigan Quarterly Review* 33 (1994): 7–36.

Matthews, Albert. *Uncle Sam.* Worcester, Mass.: Davis Press, 1908.

Meagher, Cecile Ann. *America's Favorite Uncle: Cartoonists Draw a Legacy.* Milton, Fla.: CALM Productions, 1998.

Further Reading

Horwitz, Elinor Lander. *The Bird, the Banner, and Uncle Sam: Images of America in Folk and Popular Art.* Philadelphia: Lippincott, 1976.

Steward, Nicholas, and Gail Manchur, eds. *James Montgomery Flagg: Uncle Sam and Beyond.* Portland, Oreg.: Collectors Press, 1997.

Related Entries

Artisan; Body; Citizenship; Civil War; Crisis of Masculinity; Heroism; Lincoln, Abraham; Middle-Class Manhood; Militarism; Nationalism; Patriotism; Politics; Republicanism; Vietnam War; War; Whiteness; World War I

—*Caryn E. Neumann*

Urbanization

Urbanization has changed constructions of manliness in U.S. society since the 1830s, when the nation experienced its first surge of urban expansion. Urbanization (the growth of cities and the built environment) has affected codes of manliness in a variety of ways. Coinciding with processes of economic expansion, such as the market revolution, industrialization, and the emergence of a mass consumer society, as well as a relaxation of traditional communal mores, urbanization has expanded opportunities for articulating and enacting manliness and male sexuality. In addition, the replacement of open space with a built environment can be seen as an expression of male domination of nature. In short, urbanization and articulations of manliness have significantly influenced one another over the course of U.S. history.

Manhood in Pre-Urban America

In the small, rural, farm-based communities of colonial America, face-to-face relations, patterns of deference, strict communal controls, and sanctions on individual conduct regulated social life. Seaport cities, such as Boston, New York, and Philadelphia, were only a fraction of the size of their European counterparts. In this social and demographic context, manliness was defined largely within an agrarian frame of reference. Commentators and politicians such as J. Hector St. John de Crèvecoeur and Thomas Jefferson praised the ideal of the yeoman farmer—the independent, self-sufficient farmer and domestic patriarch—as the basis of civic society and the highest ideal to which a man could aspire. Mistrusting the city as a threat to manly virtue, they hoped America would remain an agrarian society of independent producers.

Still, urban-bound definitions of manliness began to appear in the late eighteenth century. Jefferson himself praised the artisan as the farmer's urban counterpart, and Benjamin Franklin's *Autobiography*, written between 1771 and 1789, presented the reader with an urban, rational ideal of manhood propelled by disciplines of time, capitalist accumulation, and credit. Urban-centered articulations of manliness became much more salient in the nineteenth century.

Urban Masculinity in Antebellum America

After 1815, urbanization drew increasing numbers of young men from the countryside into the nation's burgeoning cities. This migration, abetted by surging immigration after 1840, eroded previous forms of social control through family, community, and church. This process had an ambivalent impact on the men inhabiting these new urban environments. Among the emerging middle class, growing cities, as sites of commerce and manufacture, promoted codes of manliness rooted in individual autonomy, self-control, entrepreneurial activity, and economic performance.

At the same time, urbanization encouraged the emergence of less genteel, more hedonistic, and sometimes violent definitions and practices of manliness by offering an expanding range of leisure activities, fostering the growth of an industrial working class, and providing spaces for self-expression. Urban entrepreneurship itself produced the frighteningly hedonistic masculine type of the confidence man. The confidence man took advantage of other, often transient, young men, gaining their trust and luring them into the emerging urban subculture of theaters, brothels, and gambling dens. Meanwhile, urban working-class men seeking to compensate for economic marginalization and other alienating aspects of industrial work formed subcultures consisting largely of single white men working in urban factories or as clerks in expanding merchant businesses. These men were fiercely egalitarian in their politics, belligerent in defending the equality of white men, and openly scornful of urban middle-class gentility. They also asserted their masculinity by claiming the right to control and coerce women, invading African-American neighborhoods, and reveling in their assaults on prostitutes and blacks. Many young white men articulated such codes of manliness by forming and joining youth gangs, such as New York's Bowery B'hoys. These codes of masculinity have remained an intricate part of urbanization and city life into the early twenty-first century.

The working-class and hedonistic models of masculinity generated by urbanization prompted anxious concern among many middle-class Americans, who feared that the absence of traditional moral restraints on male conduct in cities threatened to produce social chaos. They responded through various efforts to control and discipline such models of manliness. First, cities increasingly formed organized police forces—voluntary at first, then paid—to monitor and curtail male behaviors deemed dangerous to society. The police patrolman, mediating between rough male urban groups and legal standards of normative manhood, in turn became another new urban masculine type. Moral reform represented another attempt to define and enforce standards of manly conduct. Spearheaded by an evangelically inclined emergent middle class and usually aimed at the working class, moral reformers included temperance organizations, bible and tract societies, and antiprostitution groups, all of which began organizing in the 1820s.

Urban Masculinities in the Late Nineteenth and Early Twentieth Centuries

Male urban subcultures further proliferated after 1880 as migration from rural areas intensified. At the same time, a new wave of immigration brought millions of men from southern and eastern Europe to the nation's cities, a "great migration" brought millions of African-American men from the South to northern urban centers, and improvements in transportation enhanced cities' significance as places of work and commerce. These men—arriving from other settings, settling in already crowded cities that lacked infrastructure appropriate for integrating them, and acculturating to varying degrees to urban industrial life—formed masculinities grounded in their work and business habits and in the holidays, festivals, and honor- and community-bound codes of manliness they brought from their previous cultural environments. Thus, urbanization produced a growing diversity of ethnically and racially defined American masculinities.

In addition to fostering racially and ethnically defined male subcultures, urbanization encouraged new patterns of male sexuality. Relatively free from strictures of community, family, and church, migrants and immigrants experimented with their own sexuality. By the 1880s, cities witnessed the rise of male homosexual communities, which offered gay men support, a means to express their sexuality and their preference for male partners, and a space in which to develop models of masculinity grounded in homosexuality. Heterosexual men, too, found the city, with its entertainments, brothels, and theater district, to be a place of experimentation with sexuality and sexual promiscuity free from communal surveillance. Late-nineteenth-century urbanization was the golden age of the bachelor, who could, if he had the discretionary income, choose from a wide range of activities and negotiate definitions of manhood through them.

Accompanying late-nineteenth-century urbanization was the large-scale organization of such sports as baseball and football. Organized sports served an important function in the urban setting by providing controlled settings in which men both expressed and channeled such potentially dangerous behaviors as competitiveness, aggressiveness, and hedonism. Most participants were spectators who found in the shared experience of spectatorship new sources of urban masculine identity grounded in friendship, camaraderie, pride in one's city or neighborhood, and a sense of ethnic, racial, or class solidarity. As commercial displays of male competition, organized sports constituted a form of consumption that served to appropriate unruly masculine impulses.

Attempts to control proliferating urban male subcultures produced new, distinct, and powerful masculine types. One was the political "boss," who assumed patriarchal control over large numbers of urban men by providing services, assistance, and jobs in exchange for loyalty, support, and votes. Another was the urban philanthropist, described by the historian Kathleen McCarthy as a "masculine civic steward" (McCarthy, 53). While there were important women who contributed to a variety of philanthropic causes, most philanthropists were men who established their manliness by influencing a sprawling urban society and culture through their support of such institutions as theaters, museums, and moral-reform societies. A third urban male type was the city planner, who, believing that the chaos and artificiality of the city could have a negative influence on human behavior, sought to master the urban environment, order the conduct of those living in it, and express his professional expertise through rational arrangement and the addition of "natural" features. Frederick Law Olmstead, for example, designed for the city of Boston a system of lakes and parks surrounding the core city in the late nineteenth century.

There were also more broadly based institutional efforts to mold urban society by offering male migrants and immigrants prescriptions of manliness conducive to middle-class perceptions of good public morale and civic order. One such urban institution, aimed specifically at men, was the Young Men's Christian Association (YMCA). First established in the United States in 1851, and initially targeting native-born middle-class men, the YMCA began in the 1870s to approach railroad workers (especially in urban areas) as well as urban industrial workers (both native- and foreign-born) and African-American migrants. The YMCA sought to regenerate urban society and shape urban manhood by offering programs and activities of moral uplift and an ideal of manliness grounded in service, piety, cleanliness, temperance, and middle-class respectability.

Another such institution was the settlement house. Established by middle-class reformers in several American cities during the late nineteenth century, settlement houses sought to replace ethnic- and working-class-based codes of masculinity (often grounded in loyalty to a group) with codes grounded in individual autonomy and self-restraint. By the early twentieth century, Progressive reformers targeted urban bosses and the political machines through which they controlled city politics, seeking to replace their arbitrary power with forms of masculine civic administration grounded in bureaucratic rationality and professional expertise. Other Progressive reform efforts aimed to improve public health, targeting, in particular, bachelors who patronized prostitutes—and thus threatened to spread sexually transmitted diseases.

Both new opportunities for leisure and consumption and the attempt to shape to urban society generated what may be the most urban of male archetypes: the male flaneur, who asserted his masculine authority by scrutinizing and assessing public life. With urbanization came boulevards, parks, cafes, beer gardens, and department stores, all spaces for the flaneur's masculine gaze and his consumption of urban life. This figure could be a reformer who investigated urban vice districts and published his reports for an expanding urban readership, a journalist uncovering crime and corruption in municipal governments, or merely the man-about-town who enjoyed urban scenes and sights.

Urban Masculinities in the United States since 1945

Most American cities and urban masculinities were strongly affected after World War II by suburbanization, which separated where men lived from where they worked and made leisure activities, entertainment, and retail stores increasingly available to them outside of urban settings. The many middle-class and working-class men who relocated from urban residences to suburbia developed new ideals of manliness apart from city life, while continuing to view cities as places of concentrated entertainment and leisure activity.

Those poorer urban men unable to join the flight to suburbia continued to participate in male urban subcultures and street gangs, whose rough qualities were intensified by the abandonment and collapse of the inner city. The aftermath of 1960s urban race riots, mostly associated with African-American males between eighteen and twenty-four years of age, combined with deindustrialization in the 1970s and 1980s and the continuing relocation of businesses to the suburban fringe, produced an image of socially scarred inner cities. Yet the inner city with its central business district remains a powerful site for the enactment of bureaucratic and corporate articulations of masculinity in government and business. Urban nonwhite men, however, having experienced a paucity of meaningful work and career opportunities, have cultivated a countercultural masculine style that has often been expressed through gang activity and various forms of popular music, such as rap and hip-hop. These subcultures reflect anger, social and economic problems, and the specific issues of inner city life, while also celebrating libidinal and consumer excess.

Conclusion

Throughout U.S. history, urbanization has enabled men to live and choose from a widening range of definitions of manliness. Yet the proliferation of urban masculinities has raised concerns about moral order in American life almost from the time urbanization began. The recent growth of gang activity and intensifying middle-class anxieties about the perceived dangers of urban male behavior suggest that the historical tension between the proliferation of urban masculine identities and the maintenance of social order persists.

Bibliography

Boyer, Paul. *Urban Masses and Moral Order in America, 1820–1920.* Cambridge, Mass.: Harvard University Press, 1978.

Chauncey, George. *Gay New York: Gender, Urban Culture, and the Making of the Gay Male World, 1890–1940.* New York: Basic Books, 1994.

Chudacoff, Howard. *The Age of the Bachelor: Creating an American Culture.* Princeton, N.J.: Princeton University Press, 1999.

McCarthy, Kathleen. *Noblesse Oblige: Charity and Cultural Philanthropy in Chicago, 1849–1929.* Chicago: University of Chicago Press, 1982.

Mjagkij, Nina. *Light in the Darkness: African Americans and the YMCA, 1852–1946.* Lexington: University of Kentucky Press, 1994.

Mohl, Raymond A. *The New City: Urban America in the Industrial Age, 1860–1920.* Wheeling, Ill.: Harlan Davidson, 1985.

Riess Steven A. *Sport in Industrial America, 1850–1920.* Wheeling, Ill.: Harlan Davidson, 1995.

White, Kevin. *The First Sexual Revolution: The Emergence of Male Heterosexuality in Modern America.* New York: New York University Press, 1993.

Winter, Thomas. *Making Men, Making Class: The YMCA and Workingmen, 1877–1920.* Chicago: University of Chicago Press, 2002.

Further Reading

D'Emilio, John, and Estelle B. Freedman. *Intimate Matters: A History of Sexuality in America.* 2nd ed. Chicago: University of Chicago Press, 1997.

Franklin, Benjamin. *Benjamin Franklin's Autobiography: An Authoritative Text, Backgrounds, Criticism.* Edited by J.A. Leo Lemay and P.M. Zall. New York: Norton, 1986.

Kimmel, Michael. *Manhood in America: A Cultural History.* New York: Free Press, 1996.

Machor, James L. *Pastoral Cities: Urban Ideals and the Symbolic Landscape of America.* Madison: University of Wisconsin Press, 1987.

Teaford, Jon C. *The Twentieth-Century City.* Baltimore: Johns Hopkins University Press, 1993.

Wilentz, Sean. *Chants Democratic: New York City and the Rise of the American Working Class, 1788–1850.* Oxford: Oxford University Press, 1986.

Related Entries

African-American Manhood; Confidence Man; Democratic Manhood; Gangs; Heterosexuality; Homosexuality; Immigration; Individualism; Industrialization; Middle-Class Manhood; Prostitution; Sexual Revolution; Suburbia; Temperance; Working-Class Manhood; Young Men's Christian Association

—Thomas Winter

Victorian Era

The Victorian Era (1837–1901) is the period in history during which Queen Victoria reigned over Great Britain. This includes both British and American cultural history from the 1830s to the end of the nineteenth century, though Victorian mores and practices had begun to fade during the 1880s. As a set of cultural conventions of male gender identity, Victorianism was generated by the fundamental social and economic changes of the nineteenth century, particularly industrialization, urbanization, and the market revolution. The term usually refers to prescriptions of middle-class manliness and emphasizes self-control in public conduct, companionship and emotional expressiveness in private life, and competitiveness and success in men's occupational lives.

Social and Economic Sources of Victorian Manhood

With the onset of the market revolution after 1820, the cultural foundation of manliness shifted from patriarchal control over the household and communal obligations to an emphasis on an acquisitive individualism that found affirmation through economic performance in an expanding, open marketplace. The market revolution led to a functional differentiation between private life and public life by disrupting the spatial link between men's homes and their workplaces. In the United States, this new notion of manliness, primarily grounded in individual entrepreneurial ability and economic performance, created an idealized man, variously labeled as the "masculine achiever," the male breadwinner, the "self-made man," and the "Yankee." While this new definition of manhood, grounded in capitalist market economics and profit-oriented performance, offered new opportunities for monetary gain and social experimentation, it also made male self-worth contingent upon economic structural forces increasingly beyond individual control. As such, it bore not only new possibilities, but new anxieties. The transcendentalist philosopher Henry David Thoreau captured this in *Walden* (1854) when he referred to the market as a "'place of humiliation'" (Kimmel, 43). To prepare themselves for the vagaries of the market and the public sphere, men articulated new modes of self-control and self-representation, including prescriptions for genteel manners, etiquette, conduct, fashion, and sexuality, that defined Victorian middle-class manhood.

Victorian Gentility

Eighteenth-century American society and social relations were characterized by small communities and face-to-face interactions, but social relations changed as American society urbanized and a market revolution began to generate interregional, and eventually national, markets. A society consisting of fairly insular neighborly communities became a society of strangers lacking communally enforced standards of conduct. Social relationships became more impersonal and anonymous, and therefore increasingly uncertain and unpredictable. In an attempt to restore predictability to social relations, Victorians conceived a variety of rules of personal conduct and social interaction that, while applicable to both men and women, carried a particular urgency in male behavior, since men's lives were more firmly grounded in the new public world of market exchange. Genteel male deportment in this new amoral world required, above all, self-control, moral discipline, and sincerity. These imperatives shaped Victorian male manners, etiquette, and fashion.

Such nineteenth-century advice and etiquette book authors as Timothy Shay Arthur and Samuel Goodrich promoted genteel manhood and its association with elegance, gracefulness, and politeness. These etiquette books offered a blueprint for public male behavior in a society that had drifted from its traditional communal bases for polite and moral conduct. The application of their advice promised to produce a trustworthy style of manhood that would stand up to public scrutiny and examination.

Fashion became one of the major areas for expressing and signaling gentility. Whereas eighteenth-century middle-class and (especially) upper-class men tended to wear clothes in an array of flamboyant colors and materials ranging from satin to silk to velvet as an expression of their status and wealth, by the 1830s men's fashion had become increasingly somber, with black as the predominant color. A man who chose to dress differently was considered a dandy who was incapable of discipline and self-control, thus inviting the ridicule of his peers. Tall dark hats, double-breasted suits, and a thin overcoat (even in summer) signified the fashionable sobriety of Victorian middle-class manliness.

Another way to indicate one's standing as a genteel man was through polite deportment and manners. A man was respectful toward other men, always courteous to women, and in command of himself in any given situation—both in his emotional and his physical conduct. Moreover, a genteel man comfortably handled a vast array of rules regulating conduct at the dinner table, including what forks or spoons to use, what glass to use for what beverage, and how to choose topics for conversation.

This rigor and self-control in public life transferred into men's private, reproductive lives as well. Advice writers such as Sylvester Graham, William Alcott, and John Harvey Kellogg promoted a male ethos of bodily purity, applying it to male nutrition, digestive functions, and reproduction. Contemporary advice books urged sexual restraint both before and within marriage. Insistence on bodily purity and sexual moderation was intended, in part, as a cultural defense against the rapid social and economic changes resulting from urbanization, industrialization, and the market revolution, yet it also reinforced a capitalist ethos of delayed gratification.

Victorian gentility and Victorian manhood had implications for both race and class. These codes were accessible and were appropriated by nonwhite men, such as the abolitionist Frederick Douglass, whose indictment of slavery relied heavily on appealing to Victorian sensibilities. His autobiographical *Narrative of the Life of Frederick Douglass* (1845) derived much of its appeal from demonstrating that slavery in all its forms—its subversion of autonomy, its reliance on physical force and use of physical cruelty, the labor demands it placed on women—violated Victorian cultural beliefs about gender. In turn, white middle-class Americans, perceiving African Americans as childlike, tended to respond to these abolitionist appeals with paternalistic pity. With regard to social class and class difference, Victorian emphases on self-restraint, physical and emotional composure, and admonitions against excess served to distinguish white, middle-class men from the alleged excesses of working-class and immigrant men, such as the Irish, whom they perceived as racially different, brutish, and lacking in self-control. Victorian manhood was constructed in conscious opposition to urban working-class manhood, and to the leisure practices and street politics of Jacksonian America.

Male Emotion and Companionship

Victorian men compensated for this extreme rigor in public life and private sexuality through a new emphasis on emotional expressiveness and companionship in their personal relationships. While they used a language of civilized morality and cultural sobriety when speaking of their business lives and careers, they used a highly romantic and sentimental language when discussing their marriages and friendships. Bemoaning the spatial separation between business and household, they described the home as a place where they could be more truly themselves, and they perceived affectionate domestic relationships as a key aspect of male gender identity. Indeed, both men and women cherished emotional self-expression, which no longer seemed possible in the superficial public sphere, as a way of sharing their sacred, innermost selves within the sanctity of the home.

Victorian men practiced this private, emotive style in homosocial as well as heterosocial settings, and they understood sentimental, even romantic, relationships with other men as central to their identities as men. Before the twentieth century, men routinely formed emotionally and physically intimate (though usually nonsexual) friendships with other men, and they attached deep spiritual significance to these friendships. While men perceived sexuality and their physical relations with their wives as a part of their mutually expected and cherished self-expression, intense, long-lasting friendships among men were valued because they lacked an association with sex or physical consummation. Such friendships not only represented a way to facilitate the transition from youth to adulthood, but they also expressed men's ability to love. These friendships lasted even after the men got married, and men's wives not only knew of these friendships, but appreciated them as a sign of their chosen partners' capacity for love and affection.

Challenges to Victorian Manhood

Victorian definitions of manhood were often ambiguous and ambivalent. While they affirmed an emerging capitalist market and the resulting commodification of social relations, they also suggested resistance to these developments by offering compensatory behavior. Victorian ideas about masculinity were increasingly challenged during the early twentieth century by the emergence of a consumer society, by new ideas about sexuality and the body, and by the formation and expansion of corporate and bureaucratic sectors in society. The expanding array of leisure activities offered by consumer culture and urban areas undermined a Victorian insistence on sexual self-restraint and sobriety. Furthermore, Americans interpreted the ideas of Sigmund Freud, which gained in popularity in the United States, as supportive of heterosexual self-expression as a source and an indication of psychological well-being.

At the same time, psychologists' invention and stigmatization of homosexuality rendered suspect intensely emotional male-male friendships. In addition, while emerging corporate and bureaucratic cultures incorporated the Victorian emphasis on sobriety into new professional codes of manliness, they also encouraged a style of manhood (one viewed with suspicion by Victorians) that emphasized external impressions over inner character. Victorian definitions of manliness focusing on the outward representation of a true and unchanging inner self lost influence with the twentieth-century shift to the notion of a self that was grounded in interpersonal relations and that emphasized role playing.

Bibliography

Halttunen, Karen. *Confidence Men and Painted Women: A Study of Middle-Class Culture in America, 1830–1870.* New Haven, Conn.: Yale University Press, 1982.

Kasson, John F. *Rudeness and Civility: Manners in Nineteenth-Century Urban America.* New York: Hill and Wang, 1990.

Kimmel, Michael. *Manhood in America: A Cultural History.* New York: Free Press, 1996.

Lystra, Karen. *Searching The Heart: Women, Men, and Romantic Love in Nineteenth-Century America.* New York: Oxford University Press, 1989.

Rosenberg, Charles E. "Sexuality, Class, and Role in 19th-Century America." *American Quarterly* 25 (May 1973): 131–153.

Yacovone, Donald. "'Surpassing the Love of Women': Victorian Manhood and the Language of Fraternal Love." In *A Shared Experience: Men, Women, and The History of Gender,* edited by Laura McCall and Donald Yacovone. New York: New York University Press, 1998.

Further Reading

Coontz, Stephanie. *The Social Origins of Private Life: A History of American Families, 1600–1900.* New York: Verso, 1988.

Freedman, Estelle B., and John D'Emilio. *Intimate Matters: A History of Sexuality in America.* New York: Harper & Row, 1988.

Haller, John S., and Robin M. Haller. *The Physician and Sexuality in Victorian America.* New York: Norton, 1974.

Rotundo, E. Anthony. *American Manhood: Transformations in Masculinity from the Revolution to the Modern Era.* New York: Basic Books, 1993.

Related Entries

Advice Literature; Body; Breadwinner Role; Capitalism; Class; Confidence Man; Douglass, Frederick; Fashion; Heterosexuality; Individualism; Industrialization; Male Friendship; Market Revolution; Marriage; Middle-Class Manhood; Race; Romanticism; Self-Control; Self-Made Man; Sentimentalism; Temperance; Urbanization; Working-Class Manhood

—*Thomas Winter*

Vietnam War

U.S. involvement in the Vietnam War (1965–73) reflected and shaped American articulations of masculinity. Because the figure of the male soldier has long been an icon of both national and masculine identity in America, the United States' intervention in Vietnam offered two opportunities. First, within a larger context of Cold War rivalry, it could establish the superiority of U.S. military power and American masculinity over an Asian people and the Communist powers (the Soviet Union and the People's Republic of China) that backed them. Second, it could reinvigorate masculinity at home at a time when such social forces as a resurgent women's rights movement, an emerging gay rights movement, the counterculture, and the economic downturn of the late 1960s and early 1970s undercut notions of a stable definition of manliness. Although only a small number of American men eligible for the draft actually served in Vietnam, masculinity was at stake at many levels during and after U.S. involvement in the war. Since connecting manhood to the war made masculinity contingent upon a decisive victory in the conflict, U.S. failure to achieve that victory complicated cultural constructions of masculinity.

The application of masculine metaphors to the conflict by top-level policymakers suggested a broad cultural equation of U.S. military involvement and support for the war with a tough, virile masculinity. In National Security Council meetings, President Lyndon B. Johnson appeared to be greatly concerned to take a sufficiently masculine approach on U.S. policy in South Vietnam. On one occasion, Johnson expressed concern that he might compare less than favorably to his predecessor John F. Kennedy, who cultivated a youthful, virile image. Reflecting such concerns with a sufficiently masculine stance in Southeast Asia, President Johnson stated after the 1966 Christmas bombings of North Vietnam that he "did not just screw Ho Chi Minh" but "cut his pecker off" (Fasteau, 396). Johnson thus compared U.S. military action in Southeast Asia to domineering sexual penetration, culminating in the castration of allegedly inferior Asian males. Johnson's rhetoric, in particular, indicated the importance of masculine imagery in both domestic political life and in Cold War foreign policy.

Not all American men accepted the identification of intervention in Vietnam with American strength and masculinity. Conscientious objectors and participants in the antiwar movement, such as the Vietnam Veterans Against the War, formed in 1967, tended to identify their conscience-based resistance to what they perceived as an unjust and needless war as a marker of a more genuine manhood grounded in a commitment to responsible citizenship and social justice. Tensions between the war's supporters and opponents revolved around differing conceptions of manhood and would remain powerful long after the war had ended.

Following America's defeat in Vietnam, returning veterans confronted new problems relating to definitions of masculinity. Disabilities sustained in combat forced many veterans to rethink the meaning of their manhood in light of their physical injuries and emotional suffering. In particular, veterans experiencing medical problems caused by Agent Orange, a defoliating substance used during the war, suffered physically and psychologically, particularly since the Veterans Administration and U.S. government denied for many years that the substance had any harmful effects on humans.

Wartime setbacks and the final U.S. defeat sparked attempts to reinvent (white) masculinity and to reassert America's "manly" national strength. In the aftermath of the war, American men and U.S. mass culture generated new articulations of male identity that integrated into male toughness new elements of sensitivity, male friendship, and—as was especially apparent in the POW/MIA (prisoners of war/missing in action) controversy—the white male victim. This definition of masculinity became fundamental to a cultural "remasculinization" of U.S. society in the 1970s and 1980s.

This remasculinization process was evident in several U.S. television programs and movies. The *Rambo* film series, for example, features Sylvester Stallone as a Vietnam veteran and hypermasculine American hero often adorned with heavy weaponry. Such 1980s television shows as *The A Team, Magnum P.I.,* and *Miami Vice* pivot on the homosocial male bonds carried from Vietnam into civilian life. In the films *Uncommon Valor* (1983) and *Garden of Stone* (1987), a group of Vietnam veterans form family-like bonds that transfer back and forth between battlefield and civilian life.

More recent films have carried the remasculinization process further, turning the Vietnam veteran from a victim to a heroic leader of others. In *Air Force One* (1997) the president, a Medal of Honor winner and Vietnam veteran, single-handedly protects his family and demonstrates American toughness by defeating a group of terrorists seeking to capture him and his plane. Meanwhile, Cabinet members on the ground, pushing the female vice president to assume presidential power, represent the specter of an effeminate government ready to abandon its soldiers (in this case, the president himself) on the front line. The president's triumph rescues American masculinity from the stigma of Vietnam and signifies that it remains capable of prevailing over international threats.

This remasculinization process has implications for racial definitions of manhood. In American popular cultural representations, the Vietnam veteran is usually white, but in reality disproportionate numbers of African-American draftees served in frontline units.

At a time when the African-American population hovered around 11 percent, black soldiers made up close to 30 percent of frontline units. Black men shared the burden and costs of the war, but cultural narratives excluding them from combat have in effect suggested that remasculinization—and thus manhood itself—is a white men's prerogative. While African Americans figure as soldiers in many Vietnam films, only *Dead Presidents* (1995) featured African-American men as its main characters.

The Vietnam War and the Vietnam veteran remain critical signifiers in ongoing discussions of men and manhood in the United States. Public controversy during the 1980s over the construction of a war memorial revolved around the issue of whether the memorial should commemorate heroic manliness or recognize the war's emotional costs. Similarly, a mushrooming of fabricated stories about military exploits by men who did not see combat in Southeast Asia, and attempts to make former president Bill Clinton's draft-dodging an issue during his election campaigns, suggest that many Americans continue to regard Vietnam service, or any military service as an important badge of national pride and masculinity. As recently as 2002, the film *We Were Soldiers*, which hints at the U.S. defeat in Vietnam but also celebrates the masculine bonds between soldiers forged in battle, indicated that Americans continue to view the Vietnam War through the lens of masculinity.

BIBLIOGRAPHY

Faludi, Susan. *Stiffed: The Betrayal of the American Man.* New York: William Morrow, 1999.

Fasteau, Marc Feigen. "Vietnam and the Cult of Toughness in Foreign Policy." In *The American Man*, edited by Elizabeth H. Pleck and Joseph H. Pleck. Englewood Cliffs, N.J.: Prentice-Hall, 1980.

Hass, Kristin Ann. *Carried to the Wall: American Memory and the Vietnam Veterans Memorial.* Berkeley: University of California Press, 1998.

Jeffords, Susan. *The Remasculinization of America: Gender and the Vietnam War.* Bloomington: Indiana University Press, 1989.

Kimmel, Michael. *Manhood in America: A Cultural History.* New York: Free Press, 1996.

Lembcke, Jerry. *The Spitting Image: Myth, Memory, and the Legacy of Vietnam.* New York: New York University Press, 1998.

Savran, David. *Taking it Like a Man: White Masculinity, Masochism, and Contemporary American Culture.* Princeton, N.J.: Princeton University Press, 1998.

FURTHER READING

Appy, Christian G. *Working-Class War: American Combat Soldiers and Vietnam.* Chapel Hill: University of North Carolina Press, 1993.

Bates, Milton. *The Wars We Took to Vietnam: Cultural Conflict and Storytelling.* Berkeley: University of California Press, 1996.

Franklin, H. Bruce. *Vietnam and Other American Fantasies.* Amherst: University of Massachusetts Press, 2000.

Gibson, James William. *Warrior Dreams: Paramilitary Culture in Post-Vietnam America.* New York: Hill and Wang, 1994.

Hooper, Charlotte. *Manly States: Masculinities, International Relations, and Gender Politics.* New York: Columbia University Press, 2001.

Sturken, Marita. *Tangled Memories: The Vietnam War, the AIDS Epidemic, and the Politics of Remembering.* Berkeley: University of California Press, 1997.

Suran, Justin David. "Coming Out Against the War: Antimilitarism and the Politicization of Homosexuality in the Era of Vietnam." *American Quarterly* 53, no. 3 (2001): 452–488.

Westheider, James E. *Fighting on Two Fronts: African Americans and the Vietnam War.* New York: New York University Press, 1997.

Young, Marilyn B. *The Vietnam Wars, 1945–1990.* New York: HarperCollins, 1991.

RELATED ENTRIES

Antiwar Movement; Cold War; Conscientious Objection; Crisis of Masculinity; Guns; Heterosexuality; Homosexuality; Militarism; Military; Nationalism; Patriarchy; Patriotism; Rambo; Sexual Revolution; Technology; Violence; War; World War I; World War II

—*Thomas Winter*

VIOLENCE

Violence—defined as intentional, aggressive, direct physical harm inflicted by one person on another—has long been associated with masculinity. While women can be violent, men have been the main perpetrators and victims of violence across history and cultures. While biologists have increasingly sought the biological and evolutionary roots of male violence, historians and social scientists—presupposing an evolutionary, biological basis for male proclivities toward violence—have addressed the role of society and culture in encouraging or restraining male violence. The damage caused by male violence has lent special urgency to the search for its patterns, its causes, and its historical, social, and cultural contexts.

Historical and Cultural Contexts

Historians have revealed distinctive patterns of male violence in the history of the European settlement of North America and, later, in the history of the United States. The historian David Courtwright has suggested that demographics play a primary role in these patterns. Most violence in the world is committed by young, unmarried men (from twelve to twenty-eight years old). Through much of American history, even into the twentieth century, population movement and settlement patterns meant that an unusually large proportion of the population, particularly in places such as the western frontier, consisted of young, unmarried men. The specific periods and regions that experienced this population pattern have seen higher rates of violence and disorder.

Historians and other social scientists have also grounded associations between masculinity and violence in specific social and cultural contexts. Historians specializing in southern and western history note that men who belong to cultures emphasizing honor as a component of manliness often tend to resort to violence to protect or restore their reputation. In the multiracial, multiethnic society of the United States, conditions of racism and other sorts of ethnocentrism or xenophobia (fear of the outsider) have produced instances of violence—sometimes by the men in power, who often view "alien" men as either unmanly or hypermasculine threats to social order, and sometimes by the men being oppressed or excluded, who consider protection of their communities and assertions of pride necessary duties of manhood. Alcohol and other drug consumption contribute to an inclination to commit violence, so male subcultures in which these practices are common have also historically witnessed an elevated incidence of violence. Religious-studies scholars have shown that religious beliefs sometimes help restrain violence, such as when a religion identifies peacefulness as a requirement of male spirituality. At other times, however, such as when male spirituality is associated with acts of "righteous anger," religious beliefs can be used to legitimate violence.

Public Violence

The traditional association of manhood with the maintenance of public order (brought to colonial America by European colonizers) has led to the sorts of sanctioned, structural, institutional violence evident in slavery, the penal system, and state reactions to street demonstrations or striking workers. At the same time, longstanding associations in the United States between manhood and resistance to authority, and between masculine duty and public leadership, have prompted many men to organize sometimes violent public actions in pursuit of or defense of group interests against perceived concentrations of corrupt official power.

American history has witnessed many riots, mob actions (e.g., lynchings), and other large-scale public disorders driven by particular social, political, or economic causes. During the years preceding the American Revolution, street protests against British policy were carried out in the name of manly defense of liberty against tyrannical power, organized by such patriotic groups as the Sons of Liberty. Many working-class white men participated in violent draft riots during the Civil War out of fear that the emancipation of African-American slaves would undermine their status as workers. During the decades following emancipation, southern white men often lynched black men, ostensibly for sexual predation against white women, but more fundamentally for their perceived threat to a traditional social system that privileged white males.

These same decades witnessed bloody clashes pitting striking workers, seeking to assert working-class pride and become more effective breadwinners, against private or public police forces hired by industrial leaders seeking to fortify their power. The civil rights demonstrations, anti-war demonstrations, and urban riots of the 1960s featured young men who identified their manhood with their commitment to activism and social justice. Each of these public actions has raised the important question of whether economic, social, or political injustice sometimes warrants violent action in the name of justice.

At the same time, other men, often inspired by religious beliefs, have equated manliness with nonviolent social, economic, and political protest. The traditional peace churches (Moravian, Amish, and Quakers) provide a small but notable example, but there have been nonviolent traditions within larger religious and political organizations. Martin Luther King, Jr., and others in the 1960s formulated nonviolent strategies for protesting civil rights violations and the war in Vietnam. Yet even King built violence into his strategy, counseling followers to expect physical suffering for their cause and expecting media images of violent reactions by southern white men to arouse controversy and sympathy among Americans.

The association of manliness with violence in the name of justice has raised vexing questions about the legitimacy of violence in protest and the legitimacy of the use of violence by the government to restore order. The African-American activist Malcolm X and the militant Black Panther Party, for example, defended violence in the name of social justice, citing the American Revolution and Civil War as examples of justifiable violence. They aroused fears, however, among white Americans and public officials uncertain that their own positions were legitimate. The federal government urged male (and, more recently, female) citizens to violent military action in several bloody wars in the twentieth century, thus legitimating violence as a manly expression of patriotic duty and as an instrument of both national and foreign policy. Yet many government actions have provoked strong opposition from those unconvinced that their goals were just. Furthermore, the long-term effects of military training on male psychology aroused growing public concern during the late twentieth century, since many soldiers were found to retain a propensity for violence long after their service ended. Violent actions by right-wing "patriot" organizations during the 1990s—such as the 1995 bombing of the Murrah Federal Building in Oklahoma City—were deemed illegitimate acts of cowardice by most Americans, even though their perpetrators defended them in the familiar rhetoric of manly duty and republican liberty.

During the twentieth century, two world wars and the urban race riots of the 1960s prompted the U.S. government to sponsor interdisciplinary inquiries into the roots of violence and war. Analyses of the authoritarian personality, mob psychology, and the causes of civil disorder (including racism, poverty, and social alienation), did not overlook the clear gender pattern in the search for solutions to problems of public violence. The rise of second-wave feminism, a series of profeminist men's movements, and academic fields in gender studies during the 1960s and 1970s added new force, sophistication, and scope to studies of male violence and its historical, social, and cultural contexts.

Juvenile Violence

Beginning in the nineteenth century, as urbanization drew increasing numbers of young unmarried males into cities, adults worried about violence committed by adolescents. By the late nineteenth century the growth of immigrant populations and an industrial labor force in the nation's urban areas led experts in the emerging social sciences to identify and examine juvenile delinquency, focusing mainly (though not entirely) on the male delinquent. Their studies drew heavily on Darwinian biology (which defined violence as a natural behavior, particularly in male animals) and often proposed the channeling of violent impulses through competitive sports.

By the latter half of the twentieth century, a growing youth subculture and counterculture and intensifying racial unrest fueled increasing attention to youthful male violence. By the 1990s public concern reached new heights as a series of highly publicized violent crimes by boys as young as six lent new urgency to the issue of socialization and male violence and prompted fears of a "crisis" among boys. At first the media attention focused on cases of very young African-American and Latino gang members enlisted to commit murder—thus linking male violence to social issues of race and ethnicity—but in the 1990s a series of school shootings in white, suburban communities (and the occasional case of a white boy killing a sibling or playmate) called greater attention to maleness itself as a problem. At the same time, the mass media's biographical reconstructions of the boyhoods of notorious mass murderers (predominantly male) purported to uncover disturbing patterns of sociopathy originating in childhood. By the end of the decade, a series of books, news stories, and magazine articles—such as William Pollack's best-selling *Real Boys* (1998)—were outlining the problem of preadolescent and adolescent male violence and proposing new ways of socializing boys into masculinity that would reduce inclinations to violent behavior.

Domestic and Sexual Violence

Historians and sociologists have suggested that close and affectionate domestic ties have often been identified as a key marker of manhood, and that marriage and family generally seem to constrain male violence. But they have also paid growing attention to domestic violence (primarily committed by men against women, children, and other men) as a significant social and historical problem.

Domestic violence in the United States traces its roots in part to the patriarchal social systems brought by the earliest English and European colonists. Many colonial Americans understood fathers as the primary domestic disciplinarians, accepting stern assertions of patriarchal authority (and occasional corporal punishment) against both wives and children as male prerogatives necessary to household order. Beginning in the late eighteenth century, however, new approaches to family governance based on the Enlightenment emphasis on human reason and the republican ideology of resistance to tyrannical authority called the use of corporal punishment into question.

The nineteenth century also saw a new emphasis on romantic love within marriage, further discrediting domestic violence. Child-rearing literature showed a general shift away from the unquestioned use of corporal punishment, and models of ideal fatherhood, particularly those articulated by the middle class, increasingly emphasized paternal nurture and affection. By the late nineteenth century, specialists in the emerging field of psychology began offering new, "scientific" child-rearing advice that emphasized the use of psychological punishments and rewards in motivating children's behavior. Such approaches proliferated with the further development of psychology during the twentieth century, and by the late twentieth century an increasingly visible and powerful feminist movement added new voices to the growing public resistance to domestic violence.

Corporal punishment and other forms of male domestic violence remained more pronounced outside the northern middle class. In the South, nineteenth-century courts tended to sanction domestic violence as a legitimate means of addressing marital conflict. Likewise, older patriarchal assumptions and prerogatives persisted among working-class and immigrant fathers into the twentieth century, including a greater inclination than middle-class parents to spank their children as a routine form of discipline. Corporal punishment remains uneasily at the edge of sanctioned and unsanctioned violence, but its growing stigmatization was apparent by the late twentieth century in parents' increasing reluctance to spank their children in public places.

During the latter decades of the twentieth century, feminist women and men called increasing public attention to sexual violence by men against girls and women. Feminists and profeminist men became interested in understanding why men rape, arguing that rape is a complex act of violent aggression grounded in the desire for power and the deep anger toward women long important to many men's male identities. Extreme feminists even concluded that all men are potential rapists. Few Americans accepted this view, but most were inclined to agree that males were socialized to view women as sexual objects and to see violence as acceptable male behavior—and that this tendency contributed to an environment that fostered, and perhaps even encouraged, male acts of rape. Several highly publicized events of "wilding" in the 1990s, many of them by white, middle-class fraternity members, shocked the white, middle-class public by revealing how easily homosocial settings and peer influence could transform their sons into rapists.

Violence in Popular Culture

Around the turn of the twentieth century, urban theater in working-class and immigrant neighborhoods and the rise of popular fiction for boys of all classes prompted public discussions about the influence of popular culture images on what boys perceived as normative male behavior. Because theater and fiction (dime novels in the nineteenth century, and adventure, spy, and mystery series in the twentieth) often purveyed images of men engaging in acts of violence, many adults worried that exposure to these entertainments was harmful for boys. This controversy persisted through the twentieth century as emerging media raised new concerns. Beginning in the 1930s, and continuing through the 1950s, adults attributed the heightened visibility of the juvenile delinquent to the influence of popular culture, and comic books became a source of public alarm.

During the latter half of the century, many Americans worried that popular music—from rock and roll in the 1950s and 1960s to gangsta rap and grunge in the 1990s—encouraged violence among young males. During the 1980s and

1990s, violent video games, films, and television programs, most of them aimed at males in their teens and early twenties, became topics of controversy. Professional sports such as football and wrestling, targeting similar audiences, also aroused concerns. By the 1990s, as ever younger boys engaged in violent crimes, growing numbers of Americans favored some form of censorship of popular culture materials.

Conclusion

Male violence has been a perennial American social problem and cultural concern. Much of the public debate over male violence has addressed the social and cultural factors fueling it, as well as the nature, effects, and legitimacy of systematic, institutionalized male violence. The "nature versus nurture" issue pervades this debate, as people try to understand the respective roles of biology and culture in prompting men to violence. The variability of male violence across time and cultures suggests the strong influence of sociocultural factors. One must conclude that American boys and men are socialized in a culture that expresses much ambivalence about curbing male violence.

Bibliography

Beneke, Timothy. *Men on Rape.* New York: St. Martin's, 1982.

Blum, Deborah. *Sex on the Brain: The Biological Differences Between Men and Women.* New York: Viking, 1997.

Blumenthal, Monica, et al., eds. *Justifying Violence: Attitudes of American Men.* Ann Arbor: Institute for Social Research, University of Michigan, 1972.

Cassell, Justine, and Henry Jenkins, eds. *From Barbie to Mortal Kombat: Gender and Computer Games.* Cambridge, Mass.: MIT Press, 1998.

Courtwright, David T. *Violent Land: Single Men and Social Disorder from the Frontier to the Inner City.* Cambridge, Mass.: Harvard University Press, 1996.

Ehrenreich, Barbara. *Blood Rites: Origins and History of the Passions of War.* New York: Metropolitan Books, 1997.

Friedman, David M. *A Mind of Its Own: A Cultural History of the Penis.* New York: Free Press, 2001.

Gibson, James William. *Warrior Dreams: Violence and Manhood in Post-Vietnam America.* New York: Hill and Wang, 1994.

Gilbert, James. *A Cycle of Outrage: America's Reaction to the Juvenile Delinquent in the 1950s.* New York: Oxford University Press, 1986.

Greven, Philip. *Spare the Child: The Religious Roots of Punishment and the Psychological Impact of Physical Abuse.* New York: Vintage, 1992.

Jewett, Robert, and John Shelton Lawrence. *The American Monomyth.* Garden City, N.Y.: Anchor Press, 1977.

O'Toole, Laura L., and Jessica R. Schiffman, eds. *Gender Violence: Interdisciplinary Perspectives.* New York: New York University Press, 1997.

Slotkin, Richard. *Regeneration through Violence: The Mythology of the American Frontier, 1600–1860.* Middleton, Conn.: Wesleyan University Press, 1973.

Further Reading

Lefkowitz, Bernard. *Our Guys: The Glen Ridge Rape and the Secret Life of the Perfect Suburb.* New York: Vintage, 1998.

Levine, Sylvia, and Joseph Koenig, eds. *Why Men Rape: Interviews with Convicted Rapists.* London: W. H. Allen, 1982.

Miedzian, Myriam. *Boys Will Be Boys: Breaking the Link Between Masculinity and Violence.* New York: Anchor Press, 1992.

Pollack, William. *Real Boys: Rescuing Our Sons from the Myths of Boyhood.* New York: Random House, 1998.

Sanday, Peggy Reeves. *Fraternity and Gang Rape: Sex, Brotherhood, and Privilege on Campus.* New York: New York University Press, 1990.

Sapolsky, Robert M. *The Trouble with Testosterone.* New York: Scribner, 1997.

Slotkin, Richard. *Gunfighter Nation: The Myth of the Frontier in Twentieth-Century America.* Norman: University of Oklahoma Press, 1998.

Related Entries

Adolescence; Alcohol; Boyhood; Civil Rights Movement; Cop Action Films; Darwinism; Dueling; Fatherhood; Feminism; Gangs; Guns; Heroism; Juvenile Delinquency; King, Martin Luther, Jr.; Malcolm X; Martial Arts Films; Men's Movements; Middle-Class Manhood; Militarism; Military; Patriarchy; Sexual Harassment; Slavery; Southern Manhood; Sports; Vietnam War; War; Western Frontier; Westerns; Working-Class Manhood; World War I; World War II; Youth

—Jay Mechling

War

Throughout U.S. history, war has carried a special meaning for the status of men in American society. Wartime military service has long been regarded both as an obligation of male citizenship and as a rite of passage to manhood. Wartime emergencies have also created opportunities for social and cultural change, and have frequently threatened basic assumptions concerning gender, race, and class, but cultural myths defining war as a white masculine undertaking have historically served to limit opportunities for minorities and to preserve gender distinctions by prescribing different wartime duties for men and women. Historically, men have been expected to protect their women, homes, and families through military service, while women have had indirect roles, such as maintaining homes and raising and supporting strong men. Instances of female heroism in war have been played down in propaganda and subsequent historical accounts, thus allowing some wartime flexibility without actually overturning traditional gender roles.

Colonial and Revolutionary America

Gender roles during wartime have been contested since the early colonial wars and the American Revolution. During these conflicts, women frequently served in combat and supporting roles with only minimal recognition. During the American Revolution, in particular, women's political engagement and their management of family farms and businesses in men's absence encouraged them to challenge patriarchal power structures. Yet the war ultimately upheld existing gender norms, and therefore served to reinforce these ideals. The definition of masculine and feminine citizenship that evolved during the Revolutionary and the early national eras grew out of men's wartime service in the state militias and the Continental Army, as well as in the predominance of men (such as George Washington) among the war's heroes. Males controlled political institutions, political discourse, and the development of gender identities and cultural norms, which were products of the new nation's experience. Whereas the founding fathers linked men's citizenship to wartime military service, female citizenship required supporting men's participation in war and raising sons who were strong enough to fulfill their masculine military roles.

Nineteenth-Century America

The definition of citizenship and its relation to wartime gender roles that developed during the Revolutionary era prevailed throughout the early republic and the nineteenth century. At the outbreak of the Civil War, military and political leaders in both the North and South couched their rhetoric in gendered terms. Northern soldiers saw themselves as solid family men and household protectors fighting for their families and communities, and as heroic patriots seeking to return their childlike Southern brothers to the Union. Southerners also saw themselves as fighting to protect their families—by seeking to prevent marauding Union intruders from destroying their homes and degrading their women.

Yet the war also strained these accepted norms. In both the North and the South, women gained acceptance as nurses and in some other support functions. In the South, where wartime strains on resources and manpower were more severe, women's roles widened. Plantation mistresses and women on smaller farms frequently assumed management responsibilities when their husbands departed for war. Moreover, as the war went on, the increasing inability of Confederate armies to protect much of the South from Union forces frequently left Southern women in occupied territory at the mercy of the Federal authorities, forcing them to devise survival strategies independent of male guidance. The result was a weakening of the Southern gender system. Many women lost confidence in the Confederacy's ability to protect them from Yankee attacks, which seriously undermined Southern morale and the fighting ability of its armies, and this contributed to the South's defeat.

During the late nineteenth century, major social and economic changes generated gender-based anxieties that manifested themselves in militarism and war. Industrialization, the resultant materialism, and intensifying women's activism inspired a pervasive feeling that the "masculine" virtues of independence, honor, chivalry, and stamina were under attack. Younger generations saw these virtues in Civil War veterans from both the North and South, while the romantic mystique that grew around the collective public memory of the war fueled a desire for new martial challenges. This yearning manifested itself in the Spanish-American War of 1898 and the subsequent American war against Philippine insurrectionists from 1899 to 1902, both of which were portrayed by jingoists as opportunities for strong men to assert themselves. Pro-war groups successfully employed gender-based arguments to mobilize support for both wars and to intimidate dissenters. Reports of atrocities committed by American forces in the Philippines angered antiwar and anti-imperialist Americans, who argued that prolonged wars against peoples in underdeveloped areas actually threatened the character of young men sent to fight them. Nevertheless, American success in the Philippines and in limited military actions in China and Latin America seemed to reinforce arguments concerning the uses of war to build male character.

Twentieth-Century America and Beyond

In the twentieth century, World Wars I and II differed radically from the smaller wars in which the United States had participated during the late nineteenth and early twentieth centuries. These world wars required the mobilization of all elements of the civilian population to support the war effort, the building of large armies through conscription, and the massive organization of industry for war production. Mobilization strategies—exemplified by James Montgomery Flagg's well-known poster of Uncle Sam declaring "I Want You"—typically involved the use of masculine rhetoric. At the same time, the increasing number of women entering the workforce—and the ensuing social and economic dislocations—stimulated concerns that mobilizing women might undermine traditional gender and sexual roles. During and after World War I, women's contributions to the war effort in war industries, nursing, and service work in organizations such as the Young Men's Christian Association (YMCA) strengthened support for woman suffrage and contributed to the ratification, in 1920, of the Nineteenth Amendment, which gave all women the vote and ended the longstanding exclusive association of citizenship rights with manhood.

World War II required an even higher degree of female participation, and therefore posed a far greater threat to the male role of warrior, protector, and provider. In reaction, government and media propaganda emphasized the ways in which women could contribute to the war effort through their traditional roles, such as planting "victory gardens" and canning perishable foods. For the unprecedented numbers of women moving into the workforce, "Rosie the Riveter" propaganda (which encouraged the hiring of women in war-related industries) created the image of women working for strictly patriotic reasons, and that they would return to the home when the war ended. At the same time, the female domination of the home caused by men's wartime absence raised fears that American boys were being overmothered to the detriment of national strength. Female service in the armed forces was restricted to nursing or support functions and was justified as freeing men to fight.

Both world wars were fought away from the continental United States, thus maintaining the distinction between the home front and battle front—and reinforcing the male role as protector. Propaganda during World War II boosted men's protector image by emphasizing the potential danger an Axis victory would pose to American women. Posters portrayed enemy soldiers (particularly the Japanese) as hypersexualized beasts terrorizing white women. At the same time, pinups of female movie stars, models, and girlfriends, which appeared everywhere from footlockers to the fuselages of warplanes, served as reminders of the citizenship obligations men were fighting to fulfill. The women in these images served as objects of desire, symbolizing the sexual rewards servicemen might reap if they succeeded in protecting their homes and families. The *Iwo Jima* memorial outside Washington, D.C., dedicated in 1954 to commemorate the famous World War II battle, powerfully symbolized the war's role in reinforcing traditional associations between masculinity and wartime heroism.

In the Cold War era of the late 1940s and 1950s, both political rhetoric and media advertising emphasized the importance of the traditional patriarchal nuclear family—and the role of women as wives and mothers—in the maintenance of social stability and national survival in the struggle with the Soviet Union. However, these sentiments could not conceal the extent to which social and economic changes initiated by the world wars created new chances for women to challenge the traditional gender system. These changes in women's consciousness helped prompt the modern feminist movement of the 1960s and 1970s, which in turn opened up opportunities for women in the armed forces and in American society.

In the 1960s, events surrounding the Vietnam War further challenged the traditional gender paradigm. Thousands of young men questioned the obligation to serve in the military and fight a war they viewed as morally wrong. Debates over the war exposed conflicting notions of masculinity: Traditionalists accused antiwar males of cowardice, while antiwar activists promoted a notion of manhood based on social justice and responsible citizenship. The first war lost by the United States, the Vietnam conflict left a confused cultural legacy in several respects: (1) a significant number of young men had refused and challenged the rite of passage that wartime military service had always provided; (2) for the first time, large segments of American society, including both antiwar individuals and veterans of previous wars, questioned the actions of returning veterans; and (3) military defeat raised doubts about the effectiveness of American military men.

The controversial legacy of Vietnam helped prompt the emergence of a conservative political and cultural environment in the 1980s and 1990s in which U.S. leaders sought to reassert American military might. Military successes, beginning with Grenada (1983) and Panama (1989) and culminating in the U.S. victories in the Gulf Wars of 1991 and 2003, suppressed memories of rebellious males and of the wider antiwar discourse of the Vietnam era. These conflicts also bolstered traditional notions of male wartime heroism. Significantly, perhaps the most famous woman combatant, Jessica Lynch, achieved fame by being rescued (by men) from captivity during the 2003 Iraq war. Yet questions about gender roles remained. The large female presence in the volunteer military and women's service in the Gulf War proved to many Americans that war and military service should no longer be a male preserve and that men and women should share equal citizenship. Supporters of gender equality, pointing to changes in military technology that put less of a premium on physical strength and endurance, consider the notion of war as a rite of passage affirming male identity to be obsolete. However, the current emotional debate over women in the military is proof that traditionalists still value that rite and the gender system that it supports.

BIBLIOGRAPHY

Campbell, D'Ann. "The Regimented Women of World War II." In *Women, Militarism, and War: Essays in History, Politics, and Social Theory,* edited by Jean Bethke Elshtain and Sheila Tobias. Savage, Md.: Rowman & Littlefield, 1990.

Clinton, Catherine, and Nina Silber, eds. *Divided Houses: Gender and the Civil War.* New York: Oxford University Press, 1992.

Hoganson, Kristin L. *Fighting for American Manhood: How Gender Politics Provoked the Spanish-American and Philippine-American Wars.* New Haven, Conn.: Yale University Press, 1998.

Jeffords, Susan. *The Remasculinization of America: Gender and the Vietnam War.* Bloomington: Indiana University Press, 1989.

Kennedy, David M. *Over Here: The First World War and American Society.* New York: Oxford University Press, 1980.

Kerber, Linda K. "'May All Our Soldiers be Citizens and All Our Citizens Soldiers': The Ambiguities of Female Citizenship in the New Nation." In *Women, Militarism, and War: Essays in History, Politics, and Social Theory,* edited by Jean Bethke Elshtain and Sheila Tobias. Savage, Md.: Rowman & Littlefield, 1990.

Meyer, Leisa D. "Gender and War." In *The Oxford Companion to American Military History,* edited by John Whiteclay Chambers II. New York: Oxford University Press, 1999.

Mitchell, Reid. *The Vacant Chair: The Northern Soldier Leaves Home.* New York: Oxford University Press, 1993.

Westbrook, Robert R. "'I Want a Girl, Just Like the Girl That Married Harry James': American Women and the Problem of Political Obligation in World War II." *American Quarterly* 42, no. 4 (1990): 587–616.

FURTHER READING

Bourke, Joanna. *An Intimate History of Killing: Face to Face Killing in the 20th Century.* New York: Basic Books, 1999.

Burk, James. "The Military Obligation of Citizens Since Vietnam." *Parameters* 31, no. 2 (2001): 48–60.

Cooke, Miriam, and Angela Woollacott, eds. *Gendering War Talk.* Princeton, N.J.: Princeton University Press, 1993.

Elshtain, Jean Bethke. *Women and War.* 1987. Reprint, Chicago: University of Chicago Press, 1995.

Goldstein, Joshua. *War and Gender: How Gender Shapes the War System and Vice Versa.* Cambridge, England: Cambridge University Press, 2001.

Kaplan, Laura Duban. "Woman as Caretaker: An Archetype That Supports Patriarchal Militarism." *Hypatia* 9, no. 2 (1994): 123–133.

Treadwell, Mattie E. *The Women's Army Corps.* Washington, D.C.: Office of the Chief of Military History, Department of the Army, 1954.

Whites, LeeAnn. *The Civil War as a Crisis in Gender.* Athens: University of Georgia Press, 1995.

RELATED ENTRIES

American Revolution; Antiwar Movement; Civil War; Cold War; Heroism; Imperialism; Industrialization; Militarism; Military; Momism; Nationalism; Patriotism; Spanish-American War, Suffragism; Uncle Sam; Vietnam War; World War I; World War II

—*Walter F. Bell*

WASHINGTON, GEORGE

1732–1799
Commander of Revolutionary Army and First U.S. President

Commander of the Continental Army during the American Revolution and the first president of the United States (1789–97), George Washington was arguably the most crucial figure in the achievement of American independence and the establishment of American nationhood. In that capacity he became, and remains today, an iconic representation of American manhood and political virtue.

Born into colonial Virginia's gentry, Washington cultivated an aristocratic style of manhood that emphasized civility and honor. He established his class credentials by becoming the surveyor of Culpeper County at the age of twenty, and by then accumulating land. During the 1750s he became a military hero and the commander of the Virginia regiment during the French and Indian War (1754–63).

Washington was appointed commander of the Continental Army in 1775, but he was both a symbolic and a military leader of the patriot cause. Americans infused him with traits of masculine heroism, including piety, rationality, benevolence, civic virtue, devotion to liberty, and self-sacrifice. By 1777 he was being called the "father of his country," which reflected contemporary notions of patriarchal governance. He was admired not for military brilliance—which he lacked (and which many Americans associated with a potential dictatorship)—but for possessing "the righteous willfulness of the republican soldier" (Schwartz 1983, 23). His voluntary resignation of his commission in 1783, following his military victory, cemented his stature as an embodiment of ideal republican manhood. He represented the self-sacrificing citizen-soldier who devoted himself to defending liberty, eschewed political power, and embraced agrarian and domestic pursuits.

Symbolizing the close cultural association between republicanism, patriotism, national identity, and manliness, Washington became the fledgling nation's most crucial political figure. Because of his prestige and his reputation for public virtue, he was asked to preside over the 1787 Constitutional Convention, and his support was crucial to the Constitution's ratification. Aware that much of the populace feared a monarchy but trusted Washington, the framers of the Constitution saw him alone as suited to be the nation's first president.

In office, Washington maintained the conservative style of presidential manhood he deemed crucial to national stability and the success of the young republic. He projected an image of dignified aloofness, emphasized political order, led the military force that quelled the 1794 Whiskey Rebellion, and refused a third term. By emphasizing moral character as an essential presidential trait, he set a standard by which subsequent presidents were measured.

Washington remained a paragon of heroic republican manliness after his death. Americans constructed his masculinity to suit varying political and social—and often class-based—purposes. Antebellum biographers, usually genteel conservatives mistrustful of democratization, emphasized his aristocratic bearing. After the Civil War, Washington's masculine image became more multiform. Americans disdainful of the new industrial order continued to see in Washington an aristocratic gentleman; those who felt displaced by it saw in him a simple farmer or artisan; and those who benefited from industrialism made Washington a symbol of their bourgeois wealth. The disappearance of the frontier prompted romantic portrayals of Washington as representative of frontier manhood, while Progressive reformers determined to curtail political corruption and the power of industrial capitalists regarded Washington as a symbol of public virtue. Amid the Victorian valuation of domesticity, Washington became an affectionate father and husband, yet middle-class men fearful that urban-industrial overcivilization threatened their masculine virility saw in Washington the man of impulse demanded by their ideal of "passionate manhood." By the 1920s, advocates of the nation's business culture interpreted Washington as a model corporate businessman. During the 1960s, a growing mistrust of the nation's political leaders and criticism of white patriarchy prompted disparaging caricatures of Washington, but such images underscored his persistence as a central cultural icon.

Scholars disagree about whether Washington's character was genuine or performed, but Washington remains a powerful cultural and political symbol of American masculinity. His visage remains omnipresent, and in Washington, D.C., no building is permitted to ascend higher than the Washington Monument. During the 1989 bicentennial of Washington's inauguration, former president George H. W. Bush praised Washington for his "integrity" and for being the "master builder" of the government (Lindgren, 705), suggesting that Washington continues to serve as a cultural nexus of republicanism and American manhood, and that the nation's political culture remains strongly grounded in ideals of masculinity.

BIBLIOGRAPHY

Lindgren, James M. "Pater Patriae: George Washington as Symbol and Artifact." *American Quarterly* 41 (1989): 705–713.

McDonald, Forrest. "Presidential Character: The Example of George Washington." *Perspectives on Political Science* 26 (1997): 134–139.

Miller, Eugene F., and Barry Schwartz. "The Icon of the American Republic: A Study in Political Symbolism." *Review of Politics* 47 (1985): 516–543.

Sayen, William Guthrie. "George Washington's 'Unmannerly' Behavior: The Clash Between Civility and Honor." *Virginia Magazine of History and Biography* 107 (1999): 5–36.

Schwartz, Barry. "George Washington and the Whig Conception of Heroic Leadership." *American Sociological Review* 48 (1983): 18–33.

———. "The Character of Washington: A Study in Republican Culture." *American Quarterly* 38 (1986): 202–222.

———. *George Washington: The Making of an American Symbol.* New York: Free Press, 1987.

Wood, Gordon S. "The Greatness of George Washington." *Virginia Quarterly Review* 68 (1992): 189–207.

FURTHER READING

Albanese, Catherine L. *Sons of the Fathers: The Civil Religion of the American Revolution.* Philadelphia: Temple University Press, 1976.

Hay, Robert P. "George Washington: American Moses." *American Quarterly* 21 (1969): 780–791.

Holzer, Harold. "'Columbia's Noblest Sons': Washington and Lincoln in Popular Prints." *Journal of the Abraham Lincoln Association* 15 (1994): 23–69.

Morgan, Edmund S. *The Genius of George Washington.* New York: Norton, 1980.

Rabinowitz, Howard N. "George Washington as Icon." In *Icons of America,* edited by Ray B. Browne and Marshall Fishwick. Bowling Green, Ohio: Popular Press, 1978.

Reaves, Wendy Wick. *George Washington: An American Icon.* Charlottesville: University of Virginia Press, 1982.

Rhodehamel, John. *The Great Experiment: George Washington and the American Republic.* New Haven. Conn.: Yale University Press, 1998.

Royster, Charles. *A Revolutionary People at War: The Continental Army and American Character, 1775–1783.* 1979. Reprint, Chapel Hill: Published for the Institute of Early American History and Culture, 1986.

Wills, Garry. *Cincinnatus: George Washington and the Enlightenment.* Garden City, N.Y.: Doubleday, 1984.

RELATED ENTRIES

American Revolution; Heroism; Nationalism; Patriotism; Politics; Republicanism; Southern Manhood; War

—*Bret E. Carroll*

WAYNE, JOHN

1907–1979
American Actor, Director, and Producer

As a movie actor, director, producer, and right-wing political activist, John Wayne (nicknamed "The Duke") became an iconic symbol of an idealized model of American masculinity that reflected American cultural and political concerns during the mid–twentieth century.

Wayne began his career in 1928 as a prop man on movie sets, after an injury prevented him from completing his football scholarship at the University of Southern California. He began acting in films in 1930 and appeared in approximately seventy films before achieving stardom as Ringo Kid in John Ford's *Stagecoach* (1939). The film became a model for subsequent film Westerns, and Wayne became a model for portrayals of masculinity in the Western film genre: the lone, tough, confident, emotionally reserved, yet humane cowboy-warrior, unwaveringly committed to justice and the protection of the weak.

Wayne went on to play similar roles in nearly 150 more Western and war films from the 1940s to the 1970s, achieving superstar status through his role as isolated cattleman Tom Dunson in *Red River* (1949) and his Oscar-nominated performance as Sergeant Stryker of the Marine Corps in *The Sands of Iwo Jima* (1949). Consciously seeking to cultivate an on-screen image of manliness, Wayne rarely acknowledged his birth name of Marion Morrison and was trained by stunt performer Yakima Canutt to develop what became his trademark speech pattern and swagger. Such later films as *True Grit* (1969), for which he won an Academy Award for Best Actor, and *The Shootist* (1976), his final film, added elements of patriarchy and paternalism to his masculine persona.

Wayne's performances offered American audiences an ideal of masculinity that served their need for assurance of American toughness and moral righteousness amid the tribulations of World War II and the subsequent Cold War. For Americans wanting to discourage boys and adolescent males from behaviors considered deviant—such as homosexuality, delinquency, and communism—Wayne's films provided a model worthy of emulation.

Off-screen, Wayne sought to associate his masculine persona with his right-wing political posture and a particular brand of patriotism. This commitment led him to support Republican presidential candidate Barry Goldwater in 1964 and Republican president Richard M. Nixon, who served from 1969 to 1974. It also motivated his financing, directing, and producing of *The Alamo* (1960), which associated the United States, and particularly the American West, with masculine heroism and the defense of freedom. Wayne responded to opponents of the Vietnam War by denouncing them as effeminate and cowardly, and by producing, directing, and starring in *The Green Berets* (1968), a war film that advocated U.S. intervention in Vietnam. In the 1970s he recorded the record album *America: Why I Love Her* (1973) and filmed television commercials for the Marine Corps.

Wayne's status as an icon of American masculinity was clearly evident when the Veterans of Foreign Wars awarded him its National Americanism Gold Medal in 1973, when Congress awarded him the Congressional Gold Medal in 1979, and, most recently, when the U.S. Army named a RAH-66 helicopter "The Duke" in 1998. The continuing familiarity of Wayne's film persona testifies to its continuing power to shape American understandings of masculinity.

BIBLIOGRAPHY

Davis, Ronald L. *Duke: The Life and Image of John Wayne.* Norman: University of Oklahoma Press, 1998.

Mellen, Joan. *Big Bad Wolves: Masculinity in the American Film.* New York: Pantheon Books, 1977.

Roberts, Randy, and James S. Olson. *John Wayne: American.* Lincoln: University of Nebraska Press, 1995.

Trice, Ashton D., and Samuel A. Holland, eds. *Heroes, Antiheroes, and Dolts: Portrayals of Masculinity in American Popular Films, 1921–1999.* Jefferson, N.C.: McFarland, 2001.

Wills, Gary. *John Wayne's America: The Politics of Celebrity.* New York: Simon & Schuster, 1997.

FURTHER READING

Cohan, Steven, and Ina Rae Hark, eds. *Screening the Male: Exploring Masculinities in Hollywood Cinema.* New York: Routledge, 1993.

Wayne, Pilar. *John Wayne: My Life with the Duke.* New York: McGraw-Hill, 1987.

Zolotow, Maurice. *Shooting Star: A Biography of John Wayne.* New York: Simon & Schuster, 1974.

RELATED ENTRIES

Cold War; Emotion; Heroism; Hollywood; Patriarchy; Patriotism; Vietnam War; Western Frontier; Westerns; World War II

—*Bret E. Carroll and Annette Richardson*

WESTERN FRONTIER

In 1893, historian Frederick Jackson Turner introduced his "frontier thesis," which advanced the concept of the West as an untamed region of free land stretching out endlessly and breeding masculine individualism, heroic action, democratic citizenship, and national progress through adventurous exploration and the arduous work of settlement. This idea has held great sway over the American imagination. Popular culture has long romanticized prosaic elements of western history, transforming cattle drives into man-making odysseys and labor disputes into epic wars, while the cowboy himself has metamorphosed from underpaid laborer to archetype of American heroism. The imaginary West persists as a place free of culture, appearing in American literature and film as an escape from a feminized civilization—a natural setting that could free men from the genteel social constraints of European tradition and the dehumanizing effects of industrialization.

Since the first European encounters with the New World, the idea of the frontier has exercised a powerful influence on American cultural self-conception, particularly in constituting and defining ideals of masculinity. The movement westward, motivated by a pervasive drive to master the wilderness and build a new nation, has always been evoked through metaphors of male sexuality—whether in the form of exploration of and union with a virgin wilderness, or in the more troubling form of invasion, subjugation, and "rape" of the land and its natural resources. The construction of westward expansion as masculine domination of feminized, virgin terrain implicitly excluded women from meaningful participation in the endeavor. This masculine rhetorical conception of frontier exploration, along with the division of labor dictated by accustomed gender roles, kept women largely on the periphery of contact with the unsettled frontier. Women were understood as the embodiment and keepers of civilization. While men expanded its borders, frontier women cultivated domestic havens on civilization's advancing edge. Imagined as a space free of cultural constraint, and considered to be a region suited solely for male experience, the metaphor of the frontier provides a unique index to shifting cultural understandings of masculinity throughout American history.

Early Encounters

To the first European explorers, all of America was a frontier. The earliest European accounts of America came from all-male expeditions led by explorers like Cabeza de Vaca, Christopher Columbus, and Giovanni da Verazanno, who described an untamed land characterized by the savagery of its indigenous and non-Christian inhabitants. Native Americans, identified with the wildness of the new land, were represented in European accounts in much the same way as the land itself: with a combination of fear and fascination. European travelers sent back reports that told tales of horrific savagery or painted romanticized pictures of noble savages among the inexhaustible American bounty. Native Americans' impressions of early European settlers were equally influenced by conflicting cultural attitudes and notions of masculinity. For instance, Native Americans regarded the white settlers as effeminate due to their smaller physical size and their performance of agricultural tasks that were typically relegated to women in Native American tribes. The settlers, in turn, found Indian men unmanly due to their neglect of the same duties. These initial reactions would develop into an evolving relationship between Native American and European masculine traditions that would determine the nature of frontier masculinity.

In the early seventeenth century, Puritan settlers in New England, informed by those early accounts and inspired by their profound religious convictions, conceptualized America's wilderness (synonymous with the frontier) as a new

Eden that not only promised religious freedom, but also offered a virgin paradise when properly settled. According to the Puritan settlers' deeply religious outlook, the wilderness was a place where God's chosen must enter to be tried and redeemed, as the Israelites were in the desert during biblical times. The Puritans conceived of their enclave as a kind of holy "City on a Hill," as John Winthrop, the first governor of Boston, described it—a new Jerusalem, outside of which all was demonically charged chaos. The mission of the Puritans was to encounter and subdue the wilds—and to claim them in God's name. The active agents in this divinely ordained plan would always be male; women, in Puritan narratives, remained within the borders of civilization, entering the wilderness only if captured by Native Americans. It remained the responsibility of the men to encounter, battle, and subdue the wilderness that would become their civilization.

In the eighteenth century, with the dawn of the Age of Enlightenment, the Puritan's strictly religious interpretation of the western frontier faded before a new, practical nationalism. A new conception of the West emerged that reflected the potential for commercial and national expansion rather than divine mandates for exploration. Thomas Jefferson, among others, advanced the idea that the settlement of the West would lead to a utopian American society, and he promised agricultural prosperity and moral and cultural regeneration with the settlement of the West. In the American mind, the West became a land of limitless potential that promised financial prosperity and offered the possibility of self-determination. This new practical understanding of the frontier gave rise to another American masculine ideal, the "self-made man" who created his own wealth and social position on the basis of land ownership and usage, independent of the familial and class structures that governed advancement in Europe. The discovery and exploitation of frontier wealth was strictly a male province: as men expanded the boundaries of America, women typically remained within settled civilization.

The Ideal of the Frontiersman

The Victorian era's ideal of masculinity emphasized self-restraint, emotional sensibility, and gentlemanly conduct. But as early as the 1830s, this ideal was challenged by a notion of the western frontiersman as a tough and physically capable being who, unconstrained by, and sometimes disdainful of, bourgeois gentility, would use a passionate strength to assert his will over both wilderness and savagery. This masculine ideal found early expressions in the 1828 election of President Andrew Jackson; in the career of frontier politician and storyteller Davy Crockett (particularly as conveyed in the *Crockett Almanacs* [1835–56]); and in the Whig party's "log cabin and hard cider" presidential campaign for William Henry Harrison in 1840.

This concept became increasingly powerful over the course of the nineteenth century as industrialization and urbanization progressed and independence from societal constraints became a prerequisite for male heroism. An archetype of American manhood tied to the allure and promise of the Western frontier held particular appeal for middle- and upper-class men. These men rebelled against the overly civilized society brought about by industrial expansion and moneyed leisure—and against a real or perceived feminization of American culture brought about by the "cult of domesticity," the advent of the woman suffrage movement, and the intensification of such women-led political causes as the temperance movement.

By the late nineteenth century, the cowboy had become the chief embodiment of frontier masculinity. Theodore Roosevelt, for instance, was elected president in 1904 after transforming his public image from that of the genteel and effete aristocrat into that of the tough, heroic two-fisted "Cowboy of the Dakotas." The image of the rugged, individualistic cowboy mastering a romanticized western landscape became a widely recognized icon of gender ideology, one that persisted through the twentieth century as a uniquely American masculine ideal. The cinematic and literary Western remains one of a few genres of indisputably American origin, and many of the most influential icons of American masculinity, such as John Wayne, Gary Cooper, and Clint Eastwood, established their screen personae in Westerns.

Native American Cultural Influence

Ever since the Europeans' early explorations of the New World in the sixteenth century, the frontier had always been a site of persistent white colonial encounters with racial "others"—most often Native Americans. The Indian, indelibly associated in the popular imagination with the western frontier, exercised a strong influence on American male identity. Usually portrayed or imagined as either a bloodthirsty savage or a noble son of nature, the Native American man was alternately depicted as one to be destroyed in pursuit of western expansion and resources or as one to be emulated as an example of pure and natural manhood. In many ways, the West was a place for the white male to emulate, or to fantasize about emulating, a romanticized vision of the Native American male as a socially unencumbered warrior untouched by urban and industrial overcivilization and intuitively bonded to the landscape.

This notion of Native American manhood influenced nineteenth-century depictions of American masculinity in popular accounts and literary works. Heroic masculine archetypes from the wilderness emerged as uniquely American heroes—ranging from fictional ones such as Natty Bumppo, who appeared in James Fenimore Cooper's Leatherstocking Tales, to legendary historical frontiersmen such as Davy Crockett and Daniel Boone. The mythic construction of the woodland hero portrayed a solitary male connecting and engaging with the wilderness, adopting characteristics associated with Native American males, such as hunting prowess and stealth, and yet remaining separate from the natives' perceived savagery by virtue of their whiteness.

Although the white male may have emulated those Native American traits he admired, the cultural exchange was dominated primarily by American imperialism, an institutionalized form of the male drive to conquer and master the continent. White response to Native American culture was always mediated by the prevailing idea that the European settlers were destined to control not only the land, but also whatever people might inhabit it. More often than not, cultural interaction took the form of violent conflict and conquest. To support this imperialist ideology, white Americans developed an attitude of self-serving paternalism toward Native Americans. During the Jacksonian era, the idea of Manifest Destiny required the displacement of indigenous tribes, leading to a series of Indian wars and a great deal of bloodshed and slaughter, particularly in the last half of the nineteenth century. White Americans depicted the Indians who opposed Jackson's removal policies not as men, but as culturally immature children who would benefit from Americans' control of their people and land.

Rethinking Masculinity and the Frontier

Beginning in the last decades of the twentieth century, historians have increasingly questioned both Turner's frontier thesis and American frontier mythology, which focus primarily on the deeds of white male heroes and see other cultures as either peripheral to the central narrative of progress or as an opposition to be overcome. These historians—notably Richard Slotkin and Michael Rogin—have sought to replace the simple concept of white civilization versus wild frontier with a more complex image of cultural intersections between the expanding European-American culture and other civilizations whose cultures predated it, primarily Native American and Latin American. In so doing, they have replaced the glorified idea of Americans settlement of the West with an acknowledgment of the violent conquest and cultural displacement that accompanied this westward expansion.

Other scholars, such as Annette Kolodny and Susan J. Rosdowski, have also replaced the monotonal notion of the male frontier hero with a more complex exploration of the frontier as a site of interacting gender systems and models of manliness. Alongside these reconceptions have been efforts to demythologize the frontier experience, emphasizing the market forces driving westward expansion, rather than the traditional notion of frontier conquest as a spiritual or nationalistic quest, as well as broadening the previously male-dominated understanding of the pioneer experience to include women's roles. The frontier was a borderland, a place on the fringe of civilization, society, and established nationhood, and scholars and historians are only beginning to explore the complexities of race and gender interaction that accompanied westward expansion. As they do so, the prevailing image of the frontier as a space reserved for the rugged, solitary, self-determined white male (one of the central foundational myths of American masculinity) must inevitably be revised.

Despite the clearer understanding of American history offered by these necessary, if belated, reconceptions, the prevailing myth of the western frontier remains powerful. The idea of the frontier as a place of escape from social constraints and of endless potential for masculine self-actualization still exercises a powerful hold on the American imagination, however disconnected it may be from historical fact. Film and television still celebrate the frontiersman and the cowboy, usually with only a tacit recognition of the distance between the fantasy they portray and reality. The individualistic, self-determining hero persists as an American masculine archetype. It remains to be seen if and how a newly emerging, revised history of the West and the long-standing and pervasive American frontier myth can coexist.

BIBLIOGRAPHY

Basso, Matthew, Laura McCall, and Dee Garceau, eds. *Across the Great Divide: Cultures of Manhood in the American West.* New York: Routledge, 2001.

Rogin, Michael Paul. *Fathers and Children: Andrew Jackson and the Subjugation of the American Indian.* New Brunswick, N.J.: Transaction Publishers, 1991.

Slotkin, Richard. *The Fatal Environment: The Myth of the Frontier in the Age of Industrialization.* Norman: University of Oklahoma Press, 1998.

———. *Gunfighter Nation: The Myth of the Frontier in Twentieth Century America.* Norman: University of Oklahoma Press, 1998.

———. *Regeneration Through Violence: The Mythology of the American Frontier, 1600–1860.* Norman: University of Oklahoma Press, 2000.

Smith, Henry Nash. *Virgin Land: The American West as Symbol and Myth.* 1950. Reprint, Cambridge, Mass.: Harvard University Press, 1978.

Further Reading

Fiedler, Leslie. *Love and Death in the American Novel.* 1960. Reprint, Normal, Ill.: Dalkey Archive Press, 1997.

Kolodny, Annette. *The Land Before Her: Fantasy and Experience of the American Frontiers, 1630–1860.* Chapel Hill: University of North Carolina Press, 1984.

Mitchell, Lee Clark. *Westerns: Making the Man in Fiction and Film.* Chicago: University of Chicago Press, 1996.

Rosowski, Susan J. *Birthing a Nation: Gender, Creativity, and the West in American Literature.* Lincoln: University of Nebraska Press, 1999.

Related Entries

Boone, Daniel; California Gold Rush; Cooper, Gary; Cowboys; Crockett, Davy; Eastwood, Clint; Heroism; Imperialism; Individualism; Industrialization; Jackson, Andrew; Leatherstocking Tales; Manifest Destiny; Marlboro Man; Native American Manhood; Outdoorsman; Passionate Manhood; Roosevelt, Theodore; Self-Made Man; Suffragism; Temperance; Travel; Travel Narratives; Urbanization; Victorian Era; Violence; Wayne, John; Whiteness

—*Anthony Wilson*

Westerns

The Western, in both literature and film, has been a key genre through which authors, scholars, artists, and filmmakers have established standards of American masculinity and male identity. The many issues that the Western has addressed—nationalism, honor, family, politics, the environment, capitalism—all intersect with masculinity. A variety of Westerns have appeared since the late nineteenth century, the most common being the "Indian" Western and the "gunfighter" Western. In all of the variations of this genre, however, the theme of manliness remains central.

Westerns in Literature

Westerns, and the concepts of masculinity they promote, trace their origins to the myth of the American frontier. This myth originated in New England in the 1680s in the aftermath of King Phillips War, which saw the appearance of captive narratives (mostly centered on females) and tales lionizing the frontiersman/Indian fighter. In his frontier romances, published between 1823 and 1850, James Fenimore Cooper created the masculine western archetype upon which subsequent authors and filmmakers built. His hero "Hawkeye" from the Leatherstocking Tales, modeled on the historical figure of Daniel Boone, embodies the masculine virtues of courage, loyalty, and endurance, which could only be fully realized, it was believed, by a white man, and only after abandoning a corrupt eastern "civilization" for a more natural western environment. Balancing an untamed and wild masculinity with a civilized genteel manhood, this was the masculine ideal of the warrior/protector willing to stand against "savage" Indians or ignorant and greedy whites.

Authors of dime novels wrote Westerns between 1870 and 1900 and, in a variation on Cooper's model embodying the balance between wildness and gentility, framed their protagonists as heroic badmen. Such was the case with Edward Wheeler's "Deadwood Dick" novels, which appeared in the late 1870s. Set in the Black Hills of South Dakota during the Great Sioux War, these tales juxtapose menacing Indians and corrupt easterners against a Hawkeye-type character who knows the wilderness and its natives, embodies the masculine virtues of physical bravery and resourcefulness, and is willing to take risks to save the female protagonist from Indian captivity. Reflecting the social unease created by urbanization, industrialization, and the rise of large corporations, however, Wheeler's protagonist achieves masculine heroism less by fighting Indians than by robbing stagecoaches and trains to take revenge against the eastern capitalists who wronged him.

Other dime novelists, such as Ned Buntline and Frank Tousey, used a similar format. Western fiction of the 1870s and 1880s romanticized historical outlaws such as Jesse James and Billy the Kid, attributing to them the same masculine characteristics demonstrated by Hawkeye and other fictional frontier heroes. Likewise, more serious Western novelists such as Owen Wister (author of *The Virginian* [1902], the first full-length Western novel) and Zane Grey featured heroes who embodied courage and stood by their principals regardless of the strength of the opposition. In their writings, Grey, Wister, and other early dime novelists reflected gender tensions and discontent with what they perceived as the soft, materialistic culture of the industrialized East where they were born and educated.

While the featured characters of the early Western novels were male, women played important, but secondary and stereotyped, roles, serving either as objects of contention or as redeemers who helped excessively savage outlaw males achieve the necessary moral grounding. As with Cora Munro in Cooper's *Last of the Mohicans* (1826), Molly in *The Virginian*, or Alice Terry in the Deadwood Dick novels, the featured women provided the male hero with an opportunity to serve as warrior, protector, and rescuer. On the other hand, women in the stories who challenged gender conventions and male power, such as female suffragists and reformers, were portrayed as old maids or harridans.

Westerns in Film

The male models established in nineteenth-century Western literature were transferred to the screen early in the twentieth century. The silent film *The Great Train Robbery* (1903) ran only ten minutes, but its model of heroic western manhood proved highly popular and set the tone for subsequent Western movies. The hero, a telegraph operator who symbolizes civilized manhood, organizes a posse to pursue bandits who have just robbed a train; his daring outlaw antagonist, who represents "savage" masculinity, is ultimately cornered and killed. Both men display the male virtues of courage, daring, and skill by which later heroes of the Western genre will be measured.

In the early twentieth century, constructions of masculinity in Western films—whether through their heroes or villains—mirrored racial, gender, and social conflicts of the period. These trends first manifested themselves in the productions of William S. Hart, who both produced and starred in several motion pictures between 1905 and 1920. Hart's formulaic productions feature a male hero characterized by courage, endurance, skill with a gun and knife, and strong political and social convictions for which he is willing to fight. His enemies are urban saloonkeepers, tinhorn gamblers, and outlaws who appear as dark-skinned "halfbreeds" or Hispanics. Hart's images of the male Western hero reflect the social and racial tensions of the Progressive Era. In these films, "Progressive" white male heroes resist the alien forces of unreformed capitalism and unrestrained ethnic and racial minorities concentrated in the nation's cities.

The appearance of the "epic" Western in the 1920s signaled the next step in the development of the Western film and its male hero. Combining history with visual effects, these movies involved location shooting, which highlighted the physical environment and allowed filmmakers to define masculinity in vivid relation to nature. In films such as James Cruze's *The Covered Wagon* (1923), John Ford's *The Iron Horse* (1924), and Wesley Ruggles's *Cimarron* (1931), the white male lead establishes his masculinity by showing his ability to master and understand the western landscape and its nonwhite inhabitants. Since the 1920s, the forging of male toughness and heroism in a natural western setting has remained central to the genre. The western environment itself has consistently defined the essential traits of manhood: John Ford's character Ethan Edwards emerges from the flatlands of west Texas as tough and unyielding, and Sergio Leone's "man with no name" is chiseled from the barren desert in which he roams.

Although the basic characteristics of the male hero in Westerns persisted through the twentieth century, continuing to appeal to an increasingly industrialized and urbanized society, "outlaw" and "gunfighter" protagonists varied in their responses to changes in America's social and political setting. During the 1950s, post–World War II social pressures and anxieties and the onset of the Cold War prompted the cultural elevation of the male loner as a heroic symbol. the best-known Western movies of this period—particularly *Red River* (1949), *High Noon* (1952), *Shane* (1953), and *The Searchers* (1956)—feature male "outsiders" who feel alienated from their communities and try to cope with social and economic change. The characters portrayed by John Wayne (in *Red River* and *The Searchers*) Gary Cooper (*High Noon*), and Alan Ladd (*Shane*) all represent male symbols of the Old West who do not fit in with changing attitudes associated with civilization and are compelled by their own values to fight against evils that threaten their communities. These male characters represent updated versions of Progressive Era heroes: They defend the forces of capitalism and modernization even though they are alienated from these very forces. This formula also applied to the several Western series that appeared on network television in the 1950s and early 1960s and featured heroic "loner" male leads—most prominently *Gunsmoke* (1955–75).

Whereas the "outsider" Westerns of the 1950s affirmed the ideas of capitalism and progress, Westerns of the 1960s and early 1970s, increasingly influenced by domestic, social, and racial conflicts and the Vietnam War, used a countercultural and anticapitalist variation of the outsider formula. This trend can be seen in *Butch Cassidy and the Sundance Kid* (1969) and, more violently, *The Wild Bunch* (1969). In both of these films, the male protagonists are outlaw heroes who are opposed to a corrupt and pitiless social system, but whose courage and skills are irrelevant in twentieth-century industrial America.

During the 1970s, as defeat in Vietnam, the Watergate scandal, and economic stagflation undermined traditional American notions of masculine heroism and achievement, Western motion pictures declined in popularity, and virtually no new Westerns appeared. But during the late 1980s and the 1990s, population shifts to the west of the Mississippi River and a willingness to re-examine the frontier myth in the cultural openness of the post–Cold War period prompted a revival of the Western film. These films, such as *Dances with Wolves* (1990), Clint Eastwood's *Unforgiven* (1992), and *Tombstone* (1993) keep the basic male norms of the genre in place: They all feature leading men willing to kill to avenge wrongdoing, be it the disfiguring of a young prostitute, the murder of a brother, or—in a reversal of one of the genre's traditional themes—the injustice done to Native Americans. Yet these films also display a willingness to explore the roles of women and ethnic minorities. They are also far more inclined toward moral ambiguity, suggesting—in keeping with the emergent "sensitive male" ideal of the late twentieth century—that there is little redemption in violence, and that a new standard for the definition of manhood and masculinity is needed in a postindustrial society trying to redefine gender relations.

BIBLIOGRAPHY

Cawelti, John G. *The Six-Gun Mystique.* Bowling Green, Ohio: Bowling Green State University Popular Press, 1999.

Coyne, Michael. *The Crowded Prairie: American National Identity in the Hollywood Western.* New York: I. B. Taurus, 1997.

Hardy, Phil. *The Overlook Film Encyclopedia: The Western.* Woodstock, N.Y.: Overlook Press, 1994.

Luhr, William. "The Scarred Woman Behind the Gun: Gender, Race, and History in Recent Westerns." *Bilingual Review* 20, no. 1 (1995): 37–42.

Mitchell, Lee Clark. *Westerns: Making the Man in Fiction and Film.* Chicago: University of Chicago Press, 1996.

Slotkin, Richard. *Gunfighter Nation: The Myth of the Frontier in Twentieth-Century America.* New York: Macmillan, 1992.

Tompkins, Jane. *West of Everything: The Inner Life of Westerns.* New York: Oxford University Press, 1992.

FURTHER READING

Aquila, Richard. *Wanted Dead or Alive: The American West in Popular Culture.* Urbana: University of Illinois Press, 1996.

Buscombe, Edward, and Roberta E. Pearson, eds. *Back in the Saddle Again: New Essays on the Western.* London: British Film Institute, 1998.

MacReynolds, Douglas J. "Alive and Well: Western Myth in Western Movies." *Literature Film Quarterly* 26, no. 1 (1998): 46–52.

Studlar, Gaylyn, and Matthew Bernstein. *John Ford Made Westerns: Filming the Legend in the Sound Era.* Bloomington: Indiana University Press, 2001.

Wellmann, Jeffrey. *The Western: Parables of the American Dream.* Lubbock: Texas Tech University Press, 1999.

RELATED ENTRIES

Boone, Daniel; Cold War; Cooper, Gary; Cowboys; Crockett, Davy; Eastwood, Clint; Gilded Age; Heroism; Hollywood; Industrialization; Leatherstocking Tales; Nativism; Populism; Progressive Era; Television; Urbanization; Victorian Era; Vietnam War; Violence; Wayne, John; Western Frontier

—*Walter F. Bell*

WHITENESS

Throughout U.S. history, whiteness as a marker of racial identity, like masculinity as a gender identity, has often been associated with power, dominance, and the marginalization (and sometimes oppression) of others. Both whiteness and maleness have often derived their cultural force and power from being represented as universal categories, rather than expressly acknowledged as simply signifiers of race or gender. Whiteness and manhood have reinforced one another in U.S. society, usually through attempts by white males in power to deny that nonwhite males are true "men," and thereby to exclude them from the privileges, rights, and opportunities associated with manhood in American culture.

Whiteness and Masculinity: 1619–1840

During the seventeenth century, as white indentured servants and African slaves coexisted in colonial America, and as colonial societies were still in a state of social flux, definitions of masculinity were not explicitly tied to whiteness. During the late seventeenth and early eighteenth centuries, however, the decline of indentured servitude and the racialization of unfree labor were accompanied by an increasingly close link between freedom and manhood on the one hand and whiteness on the other.

By the 1780s commentators consciously tied manhood to whiteness. The independent producer and property owner celebrated by J. Hector St. John Crèvecoeur in his *Letters From An American Farmer* (1782) was both male and white. When Thomas Jefferson wrote in 1776 that all men are created equal, he was referring to white men. In *Notes on the State of Virginia* (1784), Jefferson declared nonwhites unfit for republican citizenship and participation in a form of government based on political equality. The U.S. Constitution, written in 1787, enacted the notion of the ideal citizen as a white male subject who is protected in his right to acquire property—including the right to own blacks as slaves. The Naturalization Act of 1790 limited the privilege of naturalization, and therefore the rights of political manhood, to those who were white.

Political change further reinforced the ideological link between whiteness and male citizenship and showed that white masculinity, despite its exclusionary functions, had powerful assimilative consequences along class lines. By 1820 all the U.S. states had adopted universal white-male suffrage. States such as Connecticut (1818) and New York (1821), for example, further limited the rights of free blacks as they expanded the rights of free white men. Connecticut excluded blacks from suffrage, and New York imposed property qualifications and prohibitive residence requirements on black suffrage. In effectively making class insignificant as a determinant of who counted as a citizen, universal white-male suffrage—and the concept of democratic manhood it generated—magnified the importance of, and the association between, whiteness and masculinity.

Competition in the capitalist marketplace—from which women and nonwhite men were largely excluded—served as another arena for affirming the identification of manliness with whiteness. Among middle-class Americans, the market revolution generated a model of masculinity that emphasized breadwinning, economic advancement, and domesticity, and which was closely associated with whiteness. White middle-class men generally denied that women and nonwhites possessed the "masculine" characteristics—rationality, industry, sobriety, and thrift—necessary for success in the emerging market economy. But because free rivalry among men in the marketplace meant that some would gain while others would lose, the market revolution set in motion processes of social differentiation and class formation that assigned some white men positions of masculine, entrepreneurial power over other white men in the workplace. Working-class men complained that they were being reduced to the status of "wage slaves," a choice of words that implied that their whiteness entitled them to the economic independence they deemed necessary to full manhood.

Whiteness Challenged and Affirmed: 1840–1924

Antebellum immigration, ushering in nearly eighty years of high rates of immigration, further fueled attempts to affirm the association between masculinity and whiteness. Scientists of the 1840s and 1850s argued that Americans were a mixed white race of Anglo-Germanic, or Teutonic, origin. Irish immigrants, arriving in large numbers during the 1840s and 1850s, were depicted in American public discourse—particularly in the rhetoric of the nativist movements that emerged during the period—not as white Anglo-Saxons, but as uncivilized "Celts" lacking the qualities of true manhood and unfit for citizenship. Indeed, they were often called the "black Irish," building on European associations between blackness and evil, and grouped with African Americans. Mexicans incorporated into the United States after the Mexican War (1846–48) were similarly perceived as insufficiently white and masculine to merit the privileges and opportunities accorded men in American society. Indeed, the ideology of Manifest Destiny by which Americans justified the conquest of Mexican territory assumed that only white men were capable of guiding the political and economic development of North America. Under the U.S. government, many Mexicans lost title to their land, considered by many Americans to be a key signifier of manhood.

The extension of suffrage rights to black males under the Fifteenth Amendment in 1870 prompted new affirmations that only white males were true men. Especially in the South, white men responded with new ways of denying black men the privileges and rights of manhood on the basis of race. The Ku Klux Klan, founded in 1866 in Tennessee, espoused an ideology of white male supremacy and sought to intimidate, socially discipline, and murder African Americans, and black men in particular. In addition, southern states began to implement a system of social segregation through so-called Jim Crow laws, which were sanctioned by their respective constitutions after 1890. While the limitations of these laws applied to both black men and black women, the penal system, including convict leasing, chain gangs, and peonage, specifically sought to curtail the privileges and immunities of black men as citizens.

Outside the South, other groups of males defined as nonwhite were treated similarly. In part, such treatment grew out of the concern that urbanization and industrialization had sapped the physical vigor of white middle-class males and undermined their ability to compete with nonwhite men (who were arriving as immigrants in growing numbers) in the struggle for existence and social supremacy. White males responded by seeking in several ways to reinforce the link between whiteness and masculinity. Many cultural spokesmen advocated an ideal of the "strenuous life," which they felt would reinvigorate masculinity and promote the survival of the white Anglo-Saxon race. Similarly, many American men looked to competitive sport, particularly boxing, for demonstrations of white men's physical superiority.

Another response was to limit immigration by peoples defined as nonwhite. In 1882, Congress passed its first Asian exclusion law, eliminating further immigration from China and Japan and denying Asian men the access to American economic opportunity that white men enjoyed. At the same time, the Spanish-American War (1898), the Philippine-American War (1899–1902), the rise of the United States to the status of a world power, and the often imperialistic foreign policy of the U.S. government during the early twentieth century provided new outlets to apply the belief that only white males were capable of global leadership. The "Great White Fleet" sent around the globe by President Theodore Roosevelt in 1908 to demonstrate U.S. naval and military power was clearly intended to assert a specific militaristic brand of white manliness.

Whiteness Expanded and Weakened: 1924–1965

During the middle decades of the twentieth century, the traditional association between masculinity and whiteness in American society was both strengthened and challenged. The

Johnson-Reed Act (or Native Origins Act) of 1924, which excluded further immigration from southern and eastern Europe and privileged immigrants from northern and western Europe, was grounded in longstanding notions of which immigrants counted as white, and therefore as men. Yet at the same time, this legislation prompted a demographic settling of the population and reduced native-born Americans' previous tendency to regard Jews, Italians, and Irish as nonwhite. Instead, whiteness became a broader category affirming the national belonging and the manliness of ethnic populations. Al Jolson's character in *The Jazz Singer* (1927), Jakie Rabinowitz, illustrates this process when he becomes the blackface actor Jack Robin—a transformation that conceals his Jewish identity, accentuates his whiteness, and facilitates his assimilation. Meanwhile, the Nineteenth Amendment (1920), which granted women the right to vote, de-emphasized masculinity as the basis for the rights of citizenship, and the National Association for the Advancement of Colored People (NAACP), established in 1909, increasingly pressed for extending the privileges of manhood to African-American men.

However, as white masculinity became more ethnically inclusive, the lines of racial difference persisted. Important labor and welfare legislation of the New Deal, such as the 1934 Federal Housing Act, the 1935 Social Security Act, and the 1936 National Labor Relations (or Wagner) Act, all intended to bolster the male role of breadwinner and provider, privileged whites. Many other New Deal programs, especially in the South, were segregated by race. This exclusive association of whiteness with masculinity did not go unchallenged. In the 1930s the Communist Party of the United States of America (CPUSA) called on white male workers to join blacks in defending a vision of manhood grounded in class rather than race. But the CPUSA's limited appeal underscored the power of white identity among American workers.

The identification of masculinity with whiteness began to erode substantially during World War II. As Nazi Germany and its allies promoted a racist and patriarchal ideology, U.S. wartime propaganda de-emphasized whiteness and sought to highlight the racial inclusiveness of American society. The growing significance of civil rights groups, such as the NAACP and the Congress of Racial Equality (CORE), and federal measures such as the creation of the Fair Employment Practices Commission in 1961, reflected a growing effort in the United States to extend rights once associated with whiteness to nonwhites as well. Books such as Ashley Montagu's *Race: Man's Most Dangerous Myth* (1942), Gunnar Myrdal's *An American Dilemma* (1944), and Franz Boas' *Race and Democratic Society* (1945) argued that whiteness should not be made the basis for special treatment in a democratic society. Yet whiteness remained a basis for privilege. The wartime relocation imposed on Japanese Americans in the West, for instance, was never imposed on German Americans.

During the postwar period, amid Cold War emphases on political conformity and conventional male domestic roles, cultural critics grew increasingly concerned that white masculinity was narrow, bland, and self-repressed. In response, a growing number of white men embraced the image of the nonconformist white man, represented most effectively by James Dean, Marlon Brando, and Elvis Presley. The centrality of whiteness to this new masculine image was particularly apparent in Jack Kerouac's *On the Road* (1957), in which main characters Sal Paradise and Dean Moriarty reject middle-class conformity and find masculine fulfillment only through cultural contact with African Americans and Mexicans. Equally telling was white Americans' concern to appropriate rock and roll, a controversial new musical form pioneered by blacks, through the crowning of Elvis Presley as its "king."

The civil rights and black nationalist movements of the 1950s and 1960s delivered a powerful blow to traditional associations of manhood with whiteness. In ways ranging from the nonviolent, moralistic, and Christian approach of civil rights leader Martin Luther King, Jr., to the militancy of Nation of Islam spokesman Malcolm X to the aggressive, arms-bearing posture of the Black Panther Party, African Americans asserted their claims to equal status with whites in American society. The passage of the Civil Rights Act of 1964 and Voting Rights Act of 1965 signified that whiteness would no longer entail privileged legal and political status.

Whiteness on the Defensive: 1965–Present

The 1965 Immigration and Nationality Act amendments, overturning the restrictive quota system of the 1924 National Origins Act, inaugurated a new period in the history of whiteness and masculinity in American history. Ethnic differences became increasingly less important for reinforcing masculinity, yet race remained a significant parameter for manliness.

In American culture, white masculinity was increasingly depicted as being on the defensive in the face of growing civil rights and multiculturalism. White men in U.S. culture began to cast themselves as victims of circumstances beyond their control, thus inhabiting a stereotypically nonmasculine, nonwhite position. This tendency is evident in a number of popular culture images of the late twentieth century, including the character Archie Bunker of the television series *All in the Family* (1971–79); the boxer Rocky Balboa in the *Rocky* film series, who rises from urban obscurity to success only through intense and physically brutal struggle; and the white rap musician Eminem, who rose to fame during the 1990s by celebrating his cultural victimization. Likewise, in social reality, white supremacist groups enjoyed growing success in appealing to young white men who felt victimized by nonwhites and sought the empowerment to which they feel entitled by American tradition.

Conclusion

Complicated by streams of immigration and the subsequent incorporations of ethnic populations into U.S. society, as well as by tendencies to celebrate a more multicultural society, white masculinity has become a progressively more problematic, and somewhat less influential, identity marker over the course of the twentieth century. Powerful, yet somehow victimized, the white male finds it increasingly difficult to stabilize his identity around male (hetero)sexuality, race, and class. What has been portrayed as a late-twentieth-century "crisis of masculinity" may be the uneasy emergence of a fragmented, postmodern self that transcends signifiers such as gender, race, and sexuality and shatters the longstanding association between whiteness and masculinity in American life.

BIBLIOGRAPHY

Bederman, Gail. *Manliness and Civilization: A Cultural History of Gender and Race in the United States, 1880–1917.* Chicago: University of Chicago Press, 1995.

Brodkin, Karen. *How Jews Became White Folks and What That Says About Race in America.* New Brunswick, N.J.: Rutgers University Press, 1998.

Gossett, Thomas F. *Race: The History of an Idea in America.* 1963. Reprint, New York: Schocken, 1965.

Ignatiev, Noel. *How the Irish Became White.* New York: Routledge, 1995.

Jacobson, Matthew Frye. *Whiteness of a Different Color: European Immigrants and the Alchemy of Race.* Cambridge, Mass.: Harvard University Press, 1998.

Lipsitz, George. *The Possessive Investment in Whiteness: How White People Benefit from Identity Politics.* Philadelphia: Temple University Press, 1995.

Roediger, David R. *The Wages of Whiteness: Race and the Making of the American Working Class.* New York: Verso, 1991.

Savran, David. *Taking It Like a Man: White Masculinity, Masochism, and Contemporary American Culture.* Princeton, N.J.: Princeton University Press, 1998.

Saxton, Alexander. *The Rise and Fall of the White Republic: Class Politics and Mass Culture in Nineteenth-Century America.* New York: Verso, 1990.

FURTHER READING

Delgado, Richard, and Jean Stefanic, eds. *Critical White Studies: Looking Behind the Mirror.* Philadelphia: Temple University Press, 1997.

Kasson, John F. *Houdini, Tarzan, and the Perfect Man: The White Male Body and the Challenge of Modernity in America.* New York: Hill and Wang, 2001.

Nelson, Dana D. *National Manhood: Capitalist Citizenship and the Imagined Fraternity of White Men.* Durham, N.C.: Duke University Press, 1998.

Takaki, Ronald T. *Iron Cages: Race and Culture in Nineteenth-Century America.* 1979. Reprint, New York: Oxford University Press, 2000.

Wray, Matt, and Annalee Newitz, eds. *White Trash: Race and Class in America.* New York: Routledge, 1997.

RELATED ENTRIES

African-American Manhood; Beat Movement; Brando, Marlon; Capitalism; Citizenship; Dean, James; Democratic Manhood; *Easy Rider*; Immigration; Imperialism; Individualism; Industrialization; Manifest Destiny; Nationalism; Nativism; Patriarchy; Politics; Postmodernism; Race; *Rebel Without a Cause*; Republican Manhood; Roosevelt, Theodore; Vietnam War; Western Frontier; White Supremacism

—*Thomas Winter*

WHITE SUPREMACISM

The belief in white supremacy forms an integral part of U.S. history. It is inherent in the country's founding, and gave shape to its social, political, and economic institutions in both subtle and explicit ways. The assertion of white supremacy is based on a belief in the innate superiority of white manhood, and the dominance of white manhood has historically served as both the proof and guarantee of white racial supremacy. Given the centrality of manhood to the constitution of white supremacy, challenges to white male power and authority have been viewed as threats to white supremacy itself. White supremacist movements have thus been primarily concerned with the maintenance of white male authority in both public and private spheres, insisting upon the essential nature of this authority while voicing anxieties over its instability or demise.

Ideologies and Institutions of White Supremacy

For much of its history, the United States has defined citizenship through the notion of white male independence and authority, and it conferred political and economic rights accordingly. In a country whose founding doctrines assert the inalienable rights of the individual, the institution of slavery and the expropriation of land from Native Americans required an ideology of racial supremacy that cast nonwhites as savage, heathen, libidinous, and animalistic others. Historians debate whether systematic antiblack racial discrimination preceded slavery or resulted from it. Some believe that long-held beliefs in the inferiority of Africans provided the basis for slavery in the United States, while others argue that it was the institutionalization of slavery itself, motivated and perpetuated by economic incentives, that established the foundations for white supremacist views that denied African Americans basic human rights, along with any claim to civil rights and political equality.

Patriarchy and white supremacy have historically reinforced one another, as white men's authority in the home (where they held dominion over women, children, and slaves) qualified them as participants in the government of the nation. Potential divisions among men along class, ethnic, and sectional lines (e.g., among the ruling elite and laboring men in the north, or plantation owners and small farmers in the south) have been smoothed over by a common investment in white manhood, and the possibilities of interracial class coalitions have been foreclosed through the shared assumption of white male superiority.

During the nineteenth century, white supremacist policies underwrote the extension of the nation's geographic reach and political power through westward expansion and imperialistic exploits. Manifest Destiny asserted the divinely ordained fate of the Anglo-Saxon race to conquer nonwhite peoples and civilizations, and the idea of the "white man's burden" similarly encouraged the United States' budding imperialism at the turn of the twentieth century by asserting that it was white men's duty to annex and control nonwhite populations deemed unfit to govern themselves. Advocates of imperialism, such as Theodore Roosevelt, argued that neglecting this duty would contribute to a decay of white manhood. Anti-imperialists defended their position in similar terms, insisting that such exploits would lead to racial intermixing and the contamination of Anglo-American stock.

Turn-of-the-century notions of white supremacy, white masculinity, and racial decay were grounded primarily in biological and social Darwinism. Many white American men believed that their superiority resided in the essential manliness and virility of the white race, but they worried that Anglo-Saxon evolution from savage to civilized states was producing a state of overcivilization, which in turn resulted in racial atrophy and degeneration. Belief in a competitive struggle among races also prompted concern among white men that the declining birthrate among Anglo-American women, the increasing social and political autonomy of these women, the "softening" of Anglo-American men, and the growing immigration of non-Anglo Saxon peoples from southern and eastern Europe would lead to "race suicide."

White men of the late nineteenth century sought to bolster the virility and supremacy of Anglo-American manhood through a variety of means. Growing calls for a "strenuous life" emphasized the importance of sports, outdoor activity, physical exertion, and martial discipline to maintaining the health and dominance of white men. Similarly, many men looked to military service and the opportunities afforded by battle—particularly in the Spanish-American War (1898). Wars in Cuba and the Philippines further strengthened white supremacism in the United States by helping to restore the national unity that had been weakened by the Civil War, as northern and southern men came together to fight for a common cause under the shared banner of white manhood.

White Supremacist Movements

Organized white supremacist groups first developed in the post–Civil War South, as emancipation and Reconstruction in the 1860s and 1870s terminated white men's monopoly on the so-called manhood rights of citizenship. The end of slavery and the devastation of the South made the economic future of many southern white men insecure. The Ku Klux Klan emerged during this period, waging a campaign of intimidation, violence, and terror in a brutal effort to restore antebellum racial hierarchies. The Klan saw its mission in explicitly gendered terms: the redemption of chivalric southern manhood and the protection of pure white southern womanhood. Through the "myth of the black rapist," African-American men were cast as sexual aggressors seeking not simply political rights, but also the ultimate prerogative of white manhood: sexual access to white women. The myth was used as justification for an epidemic of lynchings against black men in the South. (It also functioned as a perverse disavowal of the long history of the sexual abuse of African-American women that white men considered their privilege.) However, in less than one-third of these lynchings was rape even alleged; instead, African-American men were attacked for exerting their rights to property ownership, political organization, and the defense of themselves and their families. In addition to the policing of African-American communities and the enforcement of the prohibition on interracial relationships, the myth facilitated the intense surveillance of white women, upon whose purity the honor of white manhood depended. White womanhood has played a central and conflicted role in the ideology of white supremacism ever since. As potential mothers, white women represent the reproductive possibility of the white racial future, and are thus revered. At the same time, they can betray this future, and thus their sexuality must be assiduously patrolled.

In 1915, as nonwhite and non-Protestant immigration swelled and nativist sentiment intensified, the Klan reemerged under the leadership of William J. Simmons. Contemporaneous with and contributing to this reemergence was the release of D. W. Griffith's notorious account of the Civil War and Reconstruction, *The Birth of a Nation* (1915). Based upon the novel *The Clansman* by Thomas Dixon, Griffith's film was a powerful example of the rewriting of southern history, with white southern men cast as the true victims of Reconstruction and the Klan celebrated as the salvation of white manhood and white womanhood alike. By the mid-1920s, the Klan had become an economically and politically powerful institution, with millions of white, native-born Protestant men pledging their loyalty.

Like the first Klan, the second Klan was explicit in its concerns about white manhood. The Klan pledged itself to the restoration of traditional values, as manifested in men's authority in the home and public sphere and women's primary commitment to childbearing and child rearing. They positioned themselves against all individuals and groups, including Jews, Catholics, labor activists, feminists, and others deemed a threat to white male authority. They sought recruits by waging "purity campaigns" dedicated to wiping out any immorality threatening the home and the traditional gender roles upon which it was founded. Concerned to preserve the moral purity of white manhood itself, the Klan disciplined and sometimes terrorized white men who were accused of drinking, domestic abuse, or inappropriate sexual liaisons.

The civil rights and liberation movements of the 1960s and 1970s significantly influenced white supremacism in the United States. Subsequent white supremacist organizations, such as the Aryan Nations, White Aryan Resistance, and the National Association for the Advancement of White People (founded by politician David Duke), echo many of the attitudes and anxieties of their predecessors but they also target new enemies such as multiculturalism and globalism, which blur cultural and national boundaries and undercut the white supremacist fantasy of a pure race or nation. White supremacists blame feminism for what they see as the contemporary emasculation and softening of men (echoing the complaints of other contemporary men's movements). They also represent white men as the victims of feminist attacks on male privilege, institutional commitments to affirmative action, and calls for multiculturalism, all of which they hold responsible for the deterioration of white men's authority and the undue privileging of women and minorities at white men's expense.

Gender, race, and sexuality continue to be closely entwined in white supremacist discourse, and there is an intense focus on white women's sexuality, the issue of homosexuality, the sexuality of nonwhite men, and the prospect of interracial coupling. Since the 1960s, however, the view of the federal government has shifted radically. Unlike the avowedly patriotic Ku Klux Klan of the 1920s, contemporary movements see the federal government as an enemy. Entrusted with the legislative and judicial enforcement of civil rights and affirmative action, the government is cast alongside feminism as a primary agent in the emasculation of white men.

Conclusion

The power of white supremacist discourse lies in the social and institutional entrenchment of white male supremacy in the United States, and the history of white supremacism reveals the difficulty of creating a conception of white American manhood not based in the presumption of domination over others. While overt racist expression became less acceptable in the latter half of the twentieth century, white supremacist discourse continues to resonate with mainstream cultural critiques of race and gender, and white supremacist commentators and politicians continue to impact social policy.

BIBLIOGRAPHY

Bederman, Gail. *Manliness and Civilization: A Cultural History of Gender and Race in the United States, 1880–1917.* Chicago: University of Chicago Press, 1996.

Bonilla-Silva, Eduardo. *White Supremacy and Racism in the Post-Civil Rights Era.* Boulder, Colo.: Lynne Rienner, 2001.

Daniels, Jessie. *White Lies: Race, Class, Gender, and Sexuality in White Supremacist Discourse.* New York: Routledge, 1997.

Ferber, Abby L. *White Man Falling: Race, Gender, and White Supremacy.* Lanham, Md.: Rowman and Littlefield, 1998.

Hofstadter, Richard. *Social Darwinism in American Thought.* 1945. Reprint, Boston: Beacon Press, 1992.

Horsman, Reginald. *Race and Manifest DestiN.Y.: The Origins of American Racial Anglo-Saxonism.* Cambridge, Mass.: Harvard University Press, 1981.

Kantrowitz, Stephen. *Ben Tillman and the Reconstruction of White Supremacy.* Chapel Hill: University of North Carolina Press, 2000.

MacLean, Nancy. *Behind the Mask of Chivalry: The Making of the Second Ku Klux Klan.* New York: Oxford University Press, 1994.

Roediger, David R. *The Wages of Whiteness: Race and the Making of the American Working Class.* Rev. ed. London: Verso, 1999.

Further Reading

Burlein, Ann. *Lift High the Cross: Where White Supremacy and the Christian Right Converge.* Durham, N.C.: Duke University Press, 2002.

Chalmers, David M. *Hooded Americanism: The History of the Ku Klux Klan.* 3rd ed. Durham, N.C.: Duke University Press, 1987.

Dobratz, Betty A., and Stephanie L. Shanks-Meile. *White Power, White Pride! The White Separatist Movement in the United States.* New York: Twayne, 1997.

Dyer, Thomas G. *Theodore Roosevelt and the Idea of Race.* Baton Rouge: Louisiana State University Press, 1980.

Ezekiel, Raphael S. *The Racist Mind: Portraits of American Neo-Nazis and Klansmen.* New York: Viking, 1995.

Feagin, Joe R., and Hernán Vera. *White Racism: The Basics.* 2nd ed. New York: Routledge, 2001.

Hale, Grace Elizabeth. *Making Whiteness: The Culture of Segregation in the South, 1890–1940.* New York: Vintage, 1999.

Lipsitz, George. *The Possessive Investment in Whiteness: How White People Profit From Identity Politics.* Philadelphia: Temple University Press, 1998.

Ridgeway, James. *Blood in the Face: The Ku Klux Klan, Aryan Nations, Nazi Skinheads, and the Rise of a New White Culture.* 2nd ed. New York: Thunder's Mouth Press, 1995.

Related Entries

Agrarianism; *Birth of a Nation*; Chivalry; Citizenship; Civil Rights Movement; Crisis of Masculinity; Darwinism; Eugenics; Fraternal Organizations; Imperialism; Manifest Destiny; Men's Movements; Minstrelsy; Nativism; Patriarchy; Politics; Populism; Race; Romanticism; Roosevelt, Theodore; Slavery; Southern Manhood; Strenuous Life; Violence; Whiteness

—*Jonna Eagle*

Whitman, Walt

1819–1892
American Poet

Walt Whitman devoted his work and his persona to constructing an American model of manhood in a changing cultural context. His *Leaves of Grass* (1855) is perhaps the most influential work of nineteenth-century American romantic poetry. Whitman revised *Leaves* continually, but retained a passage asking, "What is a man anyhow?" His written and lived answer was always complex and contradictory.

The dress and posture of Walt Whitman in this image, the frontispiece of the 1855 edition of Leaves of Grass, *conveys Whitman's idealized American masculine persona: a rugged working-class everyman. (From the collections of the Library of Congress)*

The son of a downwardly mobile house-builder, Whitman abandoned his father's trade to pursue journalism and poetry. From 1838 to 1855 he edited newspapers in New York City, Brooklyn, and New Orleans, wrote short stories, and drafted poems that he would later assemble into *Leaves.* During the Civil War, Whitman volunteered as a nurse in Washington, D.C., then moved to Camden, New Jersey, where he spent the remainder of his life in semiretirement, revising and expanding *Leaves* and nurturing his reputation as a poet.

Influenced by the transcendentalist Ralph Waldo Emerson, who defined American manhood in terms of inner spirituality and self-reliance, Whitman presented himself as an idealized American man, a rugged individualist softened by a vision of transcendental oneness. The frontispiece to the first edition of *Leaves* portrayed Whitman as "one of the roughs," a working-class New Yorker who venerated the everyman and spurned florid language for plain English. Associating American manhood with nationalism and liberty and casting himself as the nation's "bard," Whitman wrote poetry celebrating the United States as an empire of freedom. Yet his self-assertive rhetoric was intended to promote a spiritual and contemplative vision of manliness. Whitman sought liberation from capitalist individualism and the violence of empire-building, stating in "Song of Myself" that "every atom belonging to me as good belongs to you," and summoning his readers to "loafe" with him on the grass. His service as a nurse during the Civil War involved an explicit and principled rejection of regular military duty. Moreover, Whitman rejected the gender and racial hierarchies by which Victorian men defined masculinity, proposing instead a radical equality for women, slaves, and Native Americans. In his final years, he led a life of genteel poverty, rejecting the materialism of the Gilded Age.

Whitman's challenge to Victorian mores was especially apparent in matters of sexuality, which he viewed as the primary means by which a culture maintains its solidarity. Accepting both opposite-sex and same-sex relationships, he explored the range of sexuality from the platonic to the erotic with a frankness remarkable for the Victorian era, particularly in "The Children of Adam" (1860) and "Calamus" (1860). Whitman's homoerotic passages were initially seen by most readers as expressions of a romanticized "male friendship" that was not unusual in Victorian culture, but as sexual behavior became increasingly categorized and policed by medical and legal discourse in the late nineteenth century, critics increasingly interpreted his work (and Whitman himself) as advocating homosexuality. In an 1882 article, the "muscular Christianity" advocate Thomas Wentworth Higginson charged that Whitman represented an "unmanly manhood."

During the twentieth century, many of Whitman's admirers defended him against charges of unmanliness and homosexuality. But Whitman's ideal of spiritual liberation and sexual freedom made his model of manhood attractive to the 1950s Beat Generation and the 1960s counterculture. With the advent of gender and sexuality studies during the 1980s and 1990s, scholars achieved new and complex understandings of Whitman's masculinity by rejecting simplistic homo- and heterosexual binaries that Whitman himself did not recognize.

Bibliography

Emerson, Ralph Waldo. *Essays and Lectures.* Edited by Joel Porte. New York: Library of America, 1983.

Fone, Byrne R. S. *Masculine Landscapes: Walt Whitman and the Homoerotic Text.* Carbondale: Southern Illinois University Press, 1992.

Higginson, Thomas Wentworth. "Unmanly Manhood." *Woman's Journal* 13 (April 1882): 1.

Leverenz, David. *Manhood and the American Renaissance.* Ithaca, N.Y.: Cornell University Press, 1989.

Further Reading

Killingsworth, M. Jimmie. *Whitman's Poetry of the Body: Sexuality, Politics, and the Text.* Chapel Hill: University of North Carolina Press, 1989.

Moon, Michael. *Disseminating Whitman: Revision and Corporeality in Leaves of Grass.* Cambridge, Mass.: Harvard University Press, 1991.

Pollak, Vivian R. *The Erotic Whitman.* Berkeley: University of California Press, 2000.

Rivers, W. C. *Walt Whitman's Anomaly.* London: George Allen, 1913.

Selected Writings

Whitman, Walt. *The Correspondence of Walt Whitman.* Edited by Edwin Haviland Miller. 6 vols. New York: New York University Press, 1961–77.

———. *The Early Poems and the Fiction.* Edited by Thomas L. Brasher. New York: New York University Press, 1963.

———. *Prose Works, 1892.* Edited by Floyd Stovall. 2 vols. New York: New York University Press, 1963.

———. *Leaves of Grass: Comprehensive Reader's Edition.* Edited by Sculley Bradley and Harold W. Blodgett. New York: New York University Press, 1965.

Related Entries

Beat Movement; Emerson, Ralph Waldo; Higginson, Thomas Wentworth; Homosexuality; Male Friendship; Nationalism; Populism; Religion and Spirituality; Romanticism; Victorian Era; Working-Class Manhood

—*William Pannapacker*

WORK

Work has been central to constructions of American masculinity since the colonial period, though this relationship has shifted greatly over time. In the eighteenth and nineteenth centuries, productive work was believed to ensure manly independence and virtue, as well as upward social mobility. The harsh economic and social realities of industrial America, however, demonstrated that hard work was rarely sufficient to secure social mobility or independence. In the twentieth and twenty-first centuries, work has remained integral to masculine identity, even while increasingly failing to ensure it. A cultural emphasis on the importance of consumption rather than production, the rising number of women in the permanent workforce, and the growing automation of work processes have all contributed to the disassociation of work and manliness.

Productive Labor in Colonial America

Since the founding of Plymouth Plantations in 1620, work has been central to American conceptions of masculinity. Sixteenth-century Protestant colonists asserted that consistent, hard work was both the condition and the reward of life on Earth. Idleness, which suggested a rejection of God's plan, was to be avoided at all costs. For them, a man's hard work represented an outward display of faith and virtue and marked him as an upright citizen, whereas idle men invited ridicule and censure.

By the eighteenth century, popular understandings of the role of work had changed. Work was still the foundation of a moral life, but now it was linked to civic life. The work ethic of the eighteenth and nineteenth centuries centered around the image of *homo faber*, "the man who makes," a concept inherited from European political economists such as Adam Smith and John Locke. In the United States, *homo faber* was linked specifically to the health and success of the republic. Only the unstinting and productive labor of men could propel the economy of the United States forward through the creation of useful commodities for exchange and profit—a kind of work that was almost exclusively male.

Productive work was embodied in the public imagination by the yeoman farmer and the urban artisan, both of whom combined great physical strength with the masculine virtues of self-reliance and property ownership. In addition, the work of yeoman farmers and urban artisans provided food, shelter, and comfort for dependent wives and children. Not only would hard work and consistent production ensure national success, but hard work was also the avenue to true personal success—to becoming a "self-made man." Failure to achieve economic stability or provide for a family indicated that a man lacked moral fiber and determination.

However, contempt for unproductive men remained the same: Idle men were perceived as leeches on society who depended on the hard work of other men for their survival. Similarly, women were dependent on their husbands, fathers, or brothers for food, shelter, clothing, and any luxuries. Their own hard work within the home was considered distinct from manly work precisely because it did not support the family. In cases where a woman did become the primary breadwinner, popular commentary emphasized that this situation was far from normal. Often, it was ascribed to a husband's unmanliness, emasculation (whether through excessive drinking or gambling), or to the tragedy of a husband's death. Thus, examples of female breadwinners were often used to reinforce the assumed connection between masculinity and work—and between idleness and unmanliness.

Male and female labor were further distinguished during the early nineteenth century by the growing division between public and private areas of life. Increasingly, middle-class men went out in public to work as merchants, manufacturers, salesmen, clerks, and accountants while women stayed within the home. The cult of true womanhood, which defined the ideal woman in terms of the domestic functions she should perform within the home, also created an ideal of middle-class manhood defined by nonmanual, well-remunerated labor outside the home. Even artisans who worked in the ground-floor workshops of their houses labored in a public setting. Although many artisans' wives helped in their husbands' shops, either keeping books or aiding customers, their primary responsibilities were within the home. "Real" masculine work—work that would support a family—thus became something done outside the home.

Wage Work in the Nineteenth Century

Beginning in the 1830s, the rise of factories and the growing dominance of wage work challenged the association of hard work with financial success. In the 1830s and 1840s, northern white workers, fearing permanent wage-earner status and its impact on their manhood, began constructing a definition of masculinity grounded in whiteness rather than in control of the means of production or property ownership. In particular, they compared themselves to African-American slaves, calling themselves white slaves or wage slaves. White workers used such terms to suggest that wage work had degraded their status to the level of black slave labor; but, far from expressing solidarity with slaves, such rhetoric insisted that slavery, whether wage or chattel, was inappropriate for them as white working men and implied, by contrast, that slavery was appropriate for African Americans. For antebellum white semi-skilled and skilled workers, then, blackness became equated with dependency and whiteness with independence, regardless of whether white workers labored for themselves or for a wage. Workers in the north rallied around such rhetoric, creating an activist working class that was, in fact and image, white. Furthermore, this white working class considered the interests of semiskilled and skilled workers to be more legitimate than those of female laborers, unskilled factory laborers, farm laborers, slaves, and free African Americans.

Demographic, economic, and technological changes, however, further eroded the connections between masculinity and productive work in the nineteenth century. American men viewed rampant unemployment, compounded by the severe cyclical depressions (such as those of the 1870s, 1880s, and 1890s), as a threat to male independence. Since the 1820s, women had begun to seriously challenge men in the workforce, taking jobs that had previously been reserved for males, particularly in the textile industry. Employers, like the owners of the textile mills in Lowell, Massachusetts, sought to maximize profits by turning away from skilled men and toward unskilled workers (usually women) whose labor was less expensive. Increasingly employed as wageworkers, working men found themselves dependent on employers, rather than on themselves, for an income. Instead of determining their own work paces, schedules, and breaks, they were bound to work underneath a foreman and to adhere to established hours and schedules.

In the second half of the nineteenth century, labor unions attempted to reverse the perceived emasculation of wage-earning men by shifting the focus of working-class masculinity from production and manual labor to consumption and leisure, and by reasserting the traditional association between manhood, whiteness, work, and breadwinning. For example, Samuel Gompers, the president of the American Federation of Labor (AFL), made his the largest and most successful union of the late nineteenth century by pushing for a program of "pure and simple" unionism that emphasized shorter hours and higher wages for wageworkers. Better pay and more leisure time, he insisted, would allow working men to participate more fully in the rapidly growing consumer economy, enhance their status as family breadwinners, and provide more time for family involvement. The continued importance of breadwinning and whiteness to working-class manhood was apparent in the labor movement's reluctance to organize women or nonwhite male workers.

Wage Work in the Twentieth Century

As the association between manual labor and masculinity became more tenuous in the late nineteenth and early twentieth centuries, it persisted and became romanticized in popular culture. At the turn of the twentieth century, artists and photographers such as Lewis Hine increasingly glorified the physical strength required for industrial labor. Images of steelworkers and construction workers, for example, focused on the burly bodies of the male subjects, emphasizing the physical aspects of the work while downplaying or eliminating the mental aspects. However, manual labor, though picturesque, became increasingly associated with uneducated, uncouth, and socially immobile men trapped in urban working-class neighborhoods. As these images proliferated, blue-collar workers continued to see themselves as emasculated.

Despite the reassertion of the male breadwinner norm after both World War I and World War II, when returning soldiers quickly replaced women in high-paying industrial jobs, industrial labor no longer created a secure and stable image of masculinity. A 1964 sociological study of factory workers, *Alienation and Freedom*, by Robert Blauner, found men frustrated by the lack of control they had over the production process, the increasing specialization of tasks, and their isolation from management. Economic declines in heavy industry in the 1970s and 1980s and the quest for cheaper labor outside of the United States have led to unemployment for many American men, effectively eliminating their positions as breadwinners.

White-collar work has had an even more troubled association with masculinity in the twentieth century. In part, the tenuousness of white-collar work's relationship to masculinity resulted from its nonmanual nature. During the Progressive Era at the beginning of the century, as men of an emerging middle class entered sedentary managerial or clerical jobs, masculinity became more closely associated with a "strenuous life." Men such as Theodore Roosevelt rejected the relatively inactive kinds of work spawned by urbanization and industrialization as being specifically feminine and sought to reinvigorate the manliness of middle-class men through physical activities.

However, not all white-collar workers were labeled unmanly. Successful businessmen remained masculine through their association with power. For instance, Cyrus McCormick, the head of International Harvester during the mid- to late nineteenth century, typified nineteenth- and twentieth-century industrialists' understanding of manliness by presenting himself as the embodiment of successful, powerful manhood—his will determined the fate of the company and he controlled large numbers of wageworkers. Professional men, such as doctors and lawyers, appeared to be their own bosses, secure in their retention of specialized knowledge. But middle managers, office workers, and salesmen retained a more fragile grip on masculinity. Not only was their work not physical or strenuous, but they appeared to conform to corporate authority at the expense of their individual autonomy. In contrast to vigorous blue-collar workers, white-collar workers appeared as physically and mentally weak "pencil pushers."

The valorization of manual work over nonmanual work, however, obscured the economic and class distinctions between white-collar and blue-collar workers. Blue-collar men's physical labor may have made them more "manly" in the abstract, but their lower economic and social capital assured that they remained in the working class, whereas white-collar workers' higher incomes and access to more elite cultural activities kept them in the middle or upper class. Furthermore, throughout the twentieth century, white-collar workers increasingly moved out of urban neighborhoods into suburbs strictly segregated by class and race.

By the mid–twentieth century, the problematic relation between manhood and white-collar work began to attract considerable literary comment. Arthur Miller's play *Death of a Salesman* (1949) depicts the appropriately named Willie Loman as a pathetic and ineffectual member of society who is unable to sufficiently provide for his family. In the 1950s, sociological studies like C. Wright Mills' *White Collar* (1951) and William H. Whyte's *The Organization Man* (1956) condemned male corporate workers as emasculated conformists unable to control their lives at work. Such images of white-collar men pervaded popular culture as well. Calvin Baxter, the much-abused renter in Billy Wilder's 1960 film *The Apartment,* is constantly ousted from his own home by his bosses' demands to use his apartment to conduct extramarital affairs. Ultimately, his promotion depends not on his hard work or ability but on his willingness to submit to his bosses and hand over his keys. Accounts of socially impotent white-collar male workers like these reflected an increasing anxiety about the emasculating effects of professional work. Increasingly, such men sought to reassert their masculinity outside of work in recreational activities, such as male-only sports.

Conclusion

Work remains an integral part of masculinity in America. Idle men, or men who rely on their wives' incomes, continue to be viewed as irresponsible, weak, or childlike. The very act of work, as well as one's earnings for it, is considered to be a sign of adulthood. However, in the twenty-first century, a single income can no longer provide the standard of living that was possible previously. Furthermore, rising numbers of women in the workforce means that work is increasingly less of a masculine domain. Greater use of computers and computerized equipment, both in manual and nonmanual jobs, has further separated the act of work from individual autonomy. While work remains a necessary component of American masculinity, work is no longer a sufficient guarantor of it.

Bibliography

Blauner, Robert. *Alienation and Freedom: The Factory Worker and His Industry.* Chicago: University of Chicago Press, 1967.

Blumin, Stuart M. *The Emergence of the Middle Class: Social Experience in the American City, 1760–1900.* New York: Cambridge University Press, 1989.

Daniels, Roger. *Asian America: Chinese and Japanese in the United States Since 1850.* Seattle: University of Washington Press, 1988.

Fabian, Ann. *Card Sharps, Dream Books, and Bucket Shops: Gambling in Nineteenth-Century America.* Ithaca, N.Y.: Cornell University Press, 1990.

Kimmel, Michael. *Manhood in America: A Cultural History.* New York: Free Press, 1996.

Laurie, Bruce. *Artisans into Workers: Labor in Nineteenth-Century America.* Urbana: University of Illinois Press, 1997.

Rodgers, Daniel T. *The Work Ethic in Industrial America, 1850–1920.* Chicago: University of Chicago Press, 1978.

Roediger, David R. *The Wages of Whiteness: Race and the Making of the American Working Class.* New York: Verso, 1999.

Further Reading

Dabakis, Melissa. *Visualizing Labor in American Sculpture: Monuments, Manliness, and the Work Ethic, 1880–1935.* New York: Cambridge University Press, 1999.

Davis, Clark. *Company Men: White Collar Life and Corporate Cultures in Los Angeles, 1892–1941.* Baltimore: Johns Hopkins University Press, 2000.

Halle, David. *America's Working Man.* Chicago: University of Chicago Press, 1984.

Halttunen, Karen. *Confidence Men and Painted Women: A Study of Middle-Class Culture in America, 1830–1870.* New Haven, Conn.: Yale University Press, 1982.

Hamper, Ben. *Rivethead: Tales from the Assembly Line.* New York: Warner Books, 1991.

Horowitz, Roger, ed. *Boys and Their Toys?: Masculinity, Class, and Technology in America.* New York: Routledge, 2001.

Johnson, Paul E. *Shopkeepers Millennium: Society and Revivals in Rochester, New York, 1815–1837.* New York: Hill and Wang, 1978.

Joyce, Patrick, ed. *The Historical Meanings of Work.* New York: Cambridge University Press, 1987.

Mills, C. Wright. *White Collar: The American Middle Classes.* New York: Oxford University Press, 1951.

Montgomery, David. *The Fall of the House of Labor: The Workplace, the State, and American Labor Activism, 1865–1925.* New York: Cambridge University Press, 1989.

Way, Peter. *Common Labour: Workers and the Digging of North American Canals, 1780–1860.* New York: Cambridge University Press, 1993.

Wilentz, Sean. *Chants Democratic: New York City and the Rise of the American Working Class.* New York: Oxford University Press, 1986.

Related Entries

Agrarianism; Alcohol; Alger, Horatio, Jr.; Apprenticeship; Artisan; Body; Breadwinner Role; Bureaucratization; Citizenship; *Death of a Salesman*; Industrialization; Labor Movement and Unions; Market Revolution; *Organization Man, The*; Property; Reagan, Ronald; Republicanism; Self-Made Man; Slavery; Success Manuals; Technology; Temperance; Whiteness; Working-Class Manhood

—*Rosanne Currarino*

WORKING-CLASS MANHOOD

Since the late eighteenth century, conceptions of working-class manhood have emphasized workers' independence, but the meanings of *independence* have changed greatly over time. Early definitions of independent working-class manhood focused on property ownership and craft skills. By the latter part of the nineteenth century, working-class manhood stressed the ability to provide comfortably for a family while skill level remained important. In the twentieth century, working-class manhood became more firmly associated with the male breadwinner norm, and less with highly skilled work. Changes in the workforce, however, as well as the decline of the organized labor movement after the post–World War II era, have complicated popular conceptions of working-class manhood, depicting it as physically weak and dependent—as well as strong and independent.

Artisanal Manhood

In the late eighteenth and early nineteenth centuries, the artisan provided the model of working-class masculinity. A highly skilled craftsman, the artisan owned his own shop, hired journeymen and apprentices to work for him, provided for his family, and was a solid member of the political community. He exemplified independent republican manhood, assuring his personal independence from the influence of other men through property ownership—and demonstrating the power of that independence though prudent political participation and his ability to care for, and command the work of, dependent family members and employees. In contrast to the independent manhood of the white artisan, women, children, wage earners (who relied on other men for their livelihood), and African-American slaves were without these advantages.

By the early nineteenth century, however, fewer skilled white men were likely to achieve the independence of the property-owning artisan. Economic downturns prevented journeymen from acquiring sufficient capital to buy their own shops; job competition, which increased with immigration and urbanization, lowered journeymen's wages; and employers hired larger numbers of journeymen to produce more, and cheaper, goods. In northeastern cities like New York, Philadelphia, and Boston, journeymen formed political parties and unions to protest what they saw as their disfranchisement. They staged elaborate parades emphasizing their craft skills and asserting that knowledge and skill assured their political and social independence.

Such demonstrations, however, subtly altered the sources and meaning of independence and manhood. Manly independence, these unions and parades suggested, could now be assured through the skilled production of useful commodities. Journeymen continued to assert both their manhood and their whiteness by contrasting themselves to women and slaves, whose perceived inability to produce commodities without supervision and guidance continued to ensure their dependent status. But journeymen also contrasted themselves to nonproductive men, such as stockbrokers, gamblers, lawyers, and speculators, who profited off others' labor without actually making anything themselves.

Industrial Manhood

One dominant labor organization of the postbellum period, the Knights of Labor, continued to assert the close connections among manhood, producing, and independence. The Knights' platform demanded "the abolition of wage slavery" and emphasized the desirability of cooperatively owned factories. They envisioned a nation of independent producers, who themselves owned and controlled the means of production. The Knights' understanding of *producer* was quite broad: Anyone who made things, whether male or female, working-class or middle-class, white or black, qualified as a producer. The Knights sought an alliance of all producers, and called for the inclusion of the middle class, women, African Americans, and unskilled workers in the organization. Yet in practice the union represented mostly skilled white men.

The Knights' equation of independent working-class manhood with property ownership was not the only version of working-class manhood in the Gilded Age. Working-class leisure activities reasserted connections between masculinity and independence, though independence here relied on a man's ability to "treat" his fellows rather than his control of the work process. Saloons, for example, played a central role in the lives of most working men. Although temperance advocates (including the Knights) depicted saloons as dens of inebriation, most saloons functioned more as meeting places for male workers from a particular neighborhood or factory. Union business was frequently contracted in saloons, making them centers of organized labor information and activity. More importantly, perhaps, saloons acted as male spaces in which men created a working-class male community based on mutuality (treating comrades to drinks) and shared concerns. There were limits to the community, however. Most saloons catered to only one ethnic group, neighborhood, or factory. While saloons fostered a working-class male camaraderie, they also re-emphasized divisions within the urban working class along lines of race, ethnicity, and gender.

By the late 1880s and the 1890s, the popularity of the Knights and its version of working-class manhood had faded in favor of the American Federation of Labor (AFL), founded in 1886 by Samuel Gompers. Its definition of manly independence was grounded not in one's identity as a producer, but in high wages and the ability of a working man to provide a high standard of living for his dependent family. The male breadwinner began to embody the most significant aspect of working-class manhood. Also unlike the Knights, the AFL held that class conflict—a struggle for power in the workplace between opposing groups of men—was an inevitable part of industrial capitalism. Since employers, they argued, would seek to emasculate and control workers, workers had to assert their manhood and resist emasculation by demanding higher wages, bolstering male workers' positions as breadwinners, and—since older work-based notions of manliness persisted—preserving whatever control workers still retained on the job.

Changes in factory organization and production, however, made the association of manhood with control of one's work increasingly tenuous. Individual workers no longer made whole products, but repetitively performed a single task that was part of the larger productive process. Workers had increasingly little control over their work; managers and machinery colluded to set the pace and determine the methods of production. By the late nineteenth century, middle-class experts like Frederick Winslow Taylor had appeared to tell men how to "best" and most efficiently perform their work. Workers greatly resented Taylor's efforts, arguing that he made them into unthinking and emasculated machines that worked faster but more sloppily.

The emergence of Fordism in the early twentieth century furthered the decline of workers' control of production. Based on the idea of Henry Ford, Fordism removed workers from all decision-making processes, replacing them with moving assembly lines, repetitive tasks, and higher wages. Despite the higher wages, workers saw the system as a direct threat to their independence and manhood. A worker's wife wrote to Ford accusing him of being a "slave driver," while Charlie Chaplin satirized Ford's system in the movie *Modern Times* (1936). Chaplin's character, a pointedly unnamed operative, fails repeatedly at his high-speed, repetitive tasks. Chaplin's film highlights the inhumane qualities of assembly-line production while also portraying Chaplin's character as pathetic, downtrodden, and emasculated. He realizes independent property ownership only in a daydream.

As the workplace and the work process became more tenuous sources of male identity, working-class manhood was increasingly created and affirmed through leisure activities. Saloons and alcohol consumption continued as important sites of male leisure, while formally and informally organized sports like football, baseball, and boxing began to play important roles in constructing working-class masculinity. Contact sports like football and boxing, in particular, equated masculinity with brute force, strength, endurance, and the ability to withstand pain. These same qualities were celebrated by middle-class observers of football matches and prize fights, but these observers correlated such attributes with a rough working-class masculinity inclined to violence and drinking.

Some labor organizations, like the Industrial Workers of the World (IWW; also known as the Wobblies), founded in 1905, attempted to reverse the loss of male workers' control of production and halt what they saw as the continued emasculation of American men. The IWW urged workers to seize control of their workplaces at the point of production, thus reclaiming both their masculinity and the fruits of their labor. Like the Knights, the IWW called for the inclusion of African Americans, women, and unskilled workers in their "One Big Union," but, also like the Knights, the union represented mostly skilled white men.

The CIO and Working-Class Manhood

The weak labor movement in the 1920s did little to substantially alter existing understandings of white working-class manhood and independence. White men retained their hold on higher-paying productive and industrial jobs; women who entered the work force were relegated to jobs that emphasized service or routine tasks; and in the African-American communities that grew in northern cities after the Great Migration during World War I, African-American women overwhelmingly labored only in domestic service, while men worked in low-paying industrial jobs. Employers' preference for white workers could be seen in their policies of hiring black workers last and firing them first. For workers on the margins of American society, though, the gender divisions of labor broke down. In agricultural labor in California, for example, entire families worked together; the low wages and atrocious living conditions effectively made the male breadwinner an untenable model of manhood.

During the Great Depression of the 1930s, however, the newly formed Congress of Industrial Organizations (CIO), founded in 1935, suggested new ways of representing and describing working-class manhood. As the CIO aggressively organized the previously nonunionized auto and steel industries, they depicted unionization, defined as organized action and collective class identity, as the root of working-class manhood. Publicity campaigns connected images of strong, virile working men with union membership. The CIO, which organized by shop and not by craft, also encouraged men to identify with the community of men they worked with each day. The much publicized images of the CIO's first great successful action, the 1936–37 strike at General Motor's Flint Plant in Michigan, showed groups of men reading and relaxing together. The workers' breadwinner role was also enforced by newsreel pictures of wives helping their striking husbands by bringing them casseroles and sandwiches.

The CIO's equation of unionism, worker identity, manly strength, and breadwinning was mirrored in contemporary beliefs about who should hold jobs during the Great Depression. Most Americans believed that working women should relinquish their jobs to men, who needed them to support their families. Many also believed that white men deserved to work more than nonwhites or eastern or southern Europeans. Employers quickly fired African Americans, while they retained white workers. Additionally, the federal government forcibly deported nearly 500,000 Mexicans and Mexican Americans to Mexico, despite the fact that many of the deportees were American citizens. Workplace segregation was mirrored in the racial segregation of working-class leisure activities such as baseball, football, and movie-going.

Although women and nonwhites did enter industrial jobs previously held by white men during World War II, their removal from the workforce after the war reasserted the male (and white) breadwinner norm and reaffirmed the connection between working-class masculinity and providing for one's family. The AFL and the CIO (unified as the AFL-CIO in 1955) both actively promoted this correlation among working-class manhood, the male breadwinner norm, and high-paying, unionized jobs. Although this image remained strong in the popular imagination of the 1950s, 1960s, and 1970s, the association of unionism with manhood also began to erode, particularly in the public's perception.

While unions and working men continued to stress their skill at industrial labor and their ability to provide for their families, antiunion campaigns argued that workers and unions demanded too many luxuries. Images of corpulent and corrupt union officials countered images of physically strong, hardworking men. Such images were reinforced by union leaders like Teamsters' president Jimmy Hoffa, who used workers' pensions funds for personal investment and speculation and closely associated themselves with members of organized crime.

In popular culture, particularly television, however, working-class men have appeared as stereotypically loud and crass but essentially good-hearted. The self-consciously white character of Archie Bunker from *All in the Family* (1971–79), for instance, heckled his family from the depths of his famous recliner and, beer in hand, consistently made disparaging remarks about different ethnic groups and races as well as women and homosexuals. But the show's writers made sure that, in the end, he almost always "did the right thing," however grudgingly. The figure of Homer Simpson in the cartoon series *The Simpsons*, which premiered in 1990, has built upon the image of working-class manhood presented in *All in the Family* and earlier characters like Ralph Kramden in *The Honeymooners* (1955–56). Homer, who works at an unfulfilling job in a nuclear power plant, appears as an overweight slob, usually dressed in an undershirt and guzzling a beer. Homer's masculinity is defined through his understanding of his role as head of a family and his position in a group of male friends who meet regularly to drink at Moe's Tavern. Socially and financially inept, he continually leads his family and friends into embarrassment or ruin. In the end, however, his decency, which is well hidden throughout each episode, saves the day, though often through his bumblings rather than his premeditated intentions.

In the early twenty-first century, working-class manhood continues to be defined as "independent," but what constitutes that independence remains unclear. Workers have less control over the work process as companies increasingly turn to automated assembly lines in an effort to cut labor costs, thus making the association of working-class manhood and independence with control over the work process ever more tenuous. As corporations threaten to move production facilities out of the United States in search of cheaper labor, they directly threaten the male worker's role as a family breadwinner. Although workers have fought to keep jobs in the United States, it seems likely that increasing numbers of corporations will locate production in other countries. As working-class manhood can no longer rely on work and earnings to define itself, it has become increasingly centered around sex-segregated leisure activities.

Bibliography

Dubofsky, Melvyn. *Industrialism and the American Worker, 1865–1920.* 3rd ed. Wheeling, W. Va.: Harlan Davidson, 1996.

Glickman, Lawrence B. *A Living Wage: American Workers and the Making of Consumer Society.* Ithaca, N.Y.: Cornell University Press, 1997.

Green, James R. *The World of the Worker: Labor in Twentieth-Century America.* Urbana: University of Illinois Press, 1998.

Halle, David. *America's Working Man: Work, Home, and Politics Among Blue-Collar Property Owners.* Chicago: University of Chicago Press, 1984.

Johnson, Paul E. *Shopkeepers Millennium: Society and Revivals in Rochester, New York, 1815–1837.* New York: Hill and Wang, 1978.

Laurie, Bruce. *Artisans into Workers: Labor in Nineteenth-Century America.* Urbana: University of Illinois Press, 1997.

Nelson, Daniel. *Managers and Workers: Origins of the New Factory System in the United States, 1880–1920.* Madison: University of Wisconsin Press, 1975.

Powers, Madelon. *Faces Along the Bar: Lore and Order in the Workingman's Saloon, 1870–1920.* Chicago: University of Chicago Press, 1998.

Wilentz, Sean. *Chants Democratic: New York City and the Rise of the American Working Class, 1788–1850.* New York: Oxford University Press, 1986.

Zeiger, Robert H. *American Workers, American Unions.* 2nd ed. Baltimore: Johns Hopkins University Press, 1994.

FURTHER READING

Dubofsky, Melvyn. *We Shall Be All: A History of the Industrial Workers of the World.* 2nd ed. Urbana: University of Illinois Press, 1988.

Fink, Leon. *Workingmen's Democracy: The Knights of Labor and American Politics.* Urbana: University of Illinois Press, 1985.

Hamper, Ben. *Rivethead: Tales From the Assembly Line.* New York: Warner Books, 1991.

Lichtenstein, Nelson. *State of the Union: A Century of American Labor.* Princeton, N.J.: Princeton University Press, 2002.

Nelson, Bruce. *Divided We Stand: American Workers and the Struggle for Black Equality.* Princeton, N.J.: Princeton University Press, 2001.

Phillips, Kimberley L. *Alabama North: African-American Migrants, Community, and Working-Class Activism in Cleveland, 1915–1945.* Urbana: University of Illinois Press, 1999.

Roediger, David R. *The Wages of Whiteness: Race and the Making of the American Working Class.* Rev. ed. London: Verso, 1999.

Vaught, David. *Cultivating California: Growers, Specialty Crops, and Labor, 1875–1920.* Baltimore: Johns Hopkins University Press, 1999.

RELATED ENTRIES

Alcohol; Apprenticeship; Artisan; Breadwinner Role; Business/Corporate America; Citizenship; Consumerism; Fatherhood; Industrialization; Labor Movement and Unions; Leisure; Market Revolution; Middle-Class Manhood; Property; Race; Reagan, Ronald; Republicanism; Television; Whiteness; Work

—*Rosanne Currarino*

WORLD WAR I

When the United States joined its European allies and declared war against Germany in 1917, the nation was experiencing profound social and economic transformations that challenged traditional understandings of manhood and generated new concepts of masculinity. In particular, urbanization and the growth of industrial capitalism had created a middle class that emphasized moral purity and self-control, while also prompting concerns that white-collar managerial and bureaucratic work had demasculinized men by removing them from physical labor. Growing immigration and the influence of Darwinism, meanwhile, had left many middle-class men harboring racialized anxieties that white Anglo-Saxon manhood in the United States was being endangered by alien men perceived as physically and sexually hypermasculine. These changes led to the emergence of the ideals of Progressive manhood, with many Anglo-Saxon men embracing calls for a "strenuous life," a "muscular Christianity," and a "passionate manhood." These ideals offered new constructions of American manhood based on physical labor and struggle, moral and spiritual toughness, aggressive competitiveness, and the superiority of white middle-class Americanism. For men embracing these ideals of Progressive manhood, World War I represented an opportunity to demonstrate and revitalize American masculinity.

War department officials and President Woodrow Wilson—supported by Progressive reformers, many church leaders, and other cultural spokespersons—used these ideals of Progressive manhood in their efforts to recruit soldiers and create broad-based support for military service. Whereas Americans had traditionally considered soldiers to be immoral and potentially dangerous, leaders made a concerted effort to bring the popular image of soldiers more in line with the emerging definitions of masculinity, presenting military service as honorable, patriotic, and manly. They suggested that service in the military in defense of democracy, as well as the strenuous physical demands of soldiering, would be both physically and spiritually invigorating. These ideals of masculinity were used not only to encourage support, but also to ridicule of any opposition to the war, which was portrayed as unmasculine cowardice and lack of patriotism. Mobilization likewise became a public ritual of masculinity. Recruitment posters depicting Uncle Sam declaring "I Want You" and a young woman stating "Gee I Wish I were a Man—I'd Join the Navy" suggested that soldiering was not only a patriotic duty, but a privilege reserved for real men. These efforts were apparently successful, as men from all walks of life volunteered to serve in the war. Those ineligible for service sought to demonstrate their manliness through participation in other aspects of war mobilization, such as serving on a draft board or being a member of a Liberty Bond committee.

The federal government also appealed to notions of patriotic manliness in its efforts to popularize the first conscription since the Civil War. Wilson declared that men registering for the draft would become enrolled on "lists of honor," while government officials labeled draft-dodgers and those slow to enlist as "slackers." The Justice Department conducted "slacker raids," as did private citizens, such as those of the American Protective League, which enforced the wartime definition of manhood by spying and reporting on Americans they deemed disloyal. Twenty-four million men registered for the draft, and by war's end four million men were in the military. In contrast, before April 1917 the entire U.S. Army stood at about 120,000 men. By May 1918 over 500,000 soldiers were in France as part of the American Expeditionary Force commanded by General John J. Pershing. Eventually, over two million American troops were deployed in Europe.

While recruiters appealed to notions of physical manhood and patriotism in an effort to redefine the public image of soldiering, Progressive reformers promoted their ideals of masculinity grounded in mental and moral purity, which also influenced the actual experience of military service. Drawing upon white middle-class notions of manhood, military officials emphasized the need for soldiers to maintain sexual self-control in order to be "fit to fight." In contrast to traditional images of immoral and dangerous soldiers, the army would help create a moral manhood and a new sexual identity for men. Training camps urged upon new recruits a model of manhood combining muscularity and virility with morality and self-discipline.

For Progressive reformers and military leaders, the physical and moral manhood achieved through soldiering was a mechanism by which immigrant men could be molded to American middle-class ideals of masculinity. A national unity was forged around soldiers' common experiences as men. But while no one doubted the benefits of men of different classes and ethnicities serving together, racialized definitions of American manhood continued to constrain the experiences of African-American soldiers. The issue of recruitment of African Americans created heated debate, as many southern political leaders adamantly opposed the idea, while many draft boards defined African-American men as insufficiently manly for military service and combat. However, black leaders viewed wartime service as an opportunity to assert African-American masculinity and, as a result of their pressure, the first camp for training and commissioning black infantry officers was opened in 1917. Still, most army officials continued to deem blacks unfit for combat, and only 42,000 of the 200,000 African-American army troops in Europe served in combat (most served instead in labor battalions). Thus, while military service during the war helped to consolidate the emerging ideals of Progressive manhood and celebrate national unity, it did so within a highly racialized context that emphasized the whiteness of masculinity.

While American soldiers never experienced the horrifying trench-warfare stalemates of the early years of the war, many nonetheless were profoundly changed by their wartime experience. Given an opportunity to see more of the world than they had before, many young men—especially those from small towns and rural areas—became more inclined to associate manliness with cosmopolitanism and urban sophistication. As one of the popular songs of the era asked, "how you gonna keep 'em down on the farm after they've seen gay Paree?" Many farm boys, like the future U.S. president Harry S. Truman, never returned to their rural communities after the war.

Many war veterans saw their military service as having defined their manhood, prompting them to join such veterans' organizations as the newly formed American Legion. These groups served to reinforce the strong association that veterans had formed between their military service and their manliness. Yet other men, such as the author Ernest Hemingway, became disillusioned after the Versailles Peace Conference in 1919 rejected most of Wilson's idealistic war aims and the U.S. Senate rejected membership in a proposed League of Nations. Hemingway's *The Sun Also Rises* (1926), which examines the postwar experiences of a veteran rendered sexually impotent by a combat injury, suggests that many American men viewed the war as having sapped, rather than bolstered, their masculinity by failing to achieve the idealistic goals of world peace for which it had supposedly been fought.

Bibliography

Bristow, Nancy K. *Making Men Moral: Social Engineering during the Great War.* New York: New York University Press, 1996.

Coffman, Edward M. *The War to End All Wars: The American Military Experience in World War I.* New York: Oxford University Press, 1968.

Farwell, Byron. *Over There: The United States in the Great War, 1917–1918.* New York: Norton, 1999.

Ford, Nancy Gentile. *Americans All! Foreign-Born Soldiers in World War I.* College Station: Texas A&M University Press, 2001.

Kennedy, David M. *Over Here: The First World War and American Society.* New York: Oxford University Press, 1980.

Putney, Clifford. *Muscular Christianity: Manhood and Sports in Protestant America, 1880–1920.* Cambridge, Mass.: Harvard University Press, 2001.

Shenk, Gerald E. "Race, Manhood, and Manpower: Mobilizing Rural Georgia for World War I." *Georgia Historical Quarterly* 81, no. 3 (1997): 622–662.

Veterans History Project. "The Doughboy Center." <http://www.worldwar1.com/dbc> (March 29, 2003).

Further Reading

Bederman, Gail. *Manliness and Civilization: A Cultural History of Gender and Race in the United States, 1880–1917.* Chicago: University of Chicago Press, 1995.

Brandt, Allan M. *No Magic Bullet: A Social History of Venereal Disease in the United States Since 1880.* New York: Oxford University Press, 1985.

Carnes, Mark C., and Clyde Griffen, eds. *Meanings for Manhood: Constructions of Masculinity in Victorian America.* Chicago: University of Chicago Press, 1990.

Dubbert, Joe L. "Progressivism and the Masculinity Crisis." In *The American Man,* edited by Elizabeth H. Pleck and Joseph H. Pleck. Englewood Cliffs, N.J.: Prentice Hall, 1970.

Keene, Jennifer D. *Doughboys, the Great War and the Remaking of America.* Baltimore: Johns Hopkins University Press, 2001.

Related Entries

Crisis of Masculinity; Ethnicity; Hemingway, Ernest; Immigration; Industrialization; Military; Muscular Christianity; Nativism; Patriotism; Progressive Era; Race; Self-Control; Social Reform; Strenuous Life; Urbanization; War

—*Rebecca Hartman*

World War II

United States participation in World War II entailed an unprecedented level of social, economic, and military mobilization and affected gender roles in ways that both reinforced and undermined traditional concepts of maleness and masculinity. Newfound economic and social mobility for both men and women challenged traditional male and female roles, while at the same time these shifts triggered anxieties relating to changing gender standards. The World War II era was a time of gender confusion, and the resulting tensions have had lasting consequences.

Traditional images of men and women pervaded popular wartime culture, and the male role of warrior and protector received powerful reinforcement. American cultural norms had portrayed military service both as a rite of passage from boyhood to manhood and as a fulfillment of a man's obligations to his family, community, and country. Thus, during the war, government and media propaganda presented the war as an opportunity for boys to prove their manhood. Marketing experts used recruiting posters and advertisements to appeal to the male's self-image as protector. Men classified as physically unfit for military service were pitied and often despised. Conscientious objectors and others avoiding the draft were deemed unmanly and unpatriotic, and these individuals faced scorn, social ostracism, and, frequently, imprisonment. Likewise, wartime propaganda, such as movies, radio programs, and advertising, emphasized the domestic measures that women could take to aid the war effort.

Images of Americans in combat projected the manly warrior ideal. Movies and news reports profiled American soldiers as homespun heroes with characteristics associated with the traditional male virtues of physical toughness, resourcefulness, individuality, courage, and loyalty. They embodied the strengths of small-town middle- and working-class America. The link between wartime service and masculinity was also forged in men's actual wartime experience, for the shared ordeal of combat and prolonged separation from home and family generated strong male bonds and a sense of masculine identity grounded in patriotic service and sacrifice.

Although popular culture, media images, and the war experience strengthened traditional constructions of masculinity, other social and economic developments challenged them. As men entered the armed forces and labor shortages spread, traditionally male occupations, such as those in the basic manufacturing sectors and the skilled trades, began to be filled by women. Between 1940 and 1944, over three million women took jobs in war-related industries. Male-dominated unions and corporations grew increasingly concerned about job competition from women and the possible loss of both wages and economic status. Labor and business leaders reacted to this threat through frequent job and wage discrimination often keeping women segregated in low-skill (and lower-paying) clerical and service positions. "Rosie the Riveter" propaganda (which encouraged the hiring of women in war-related industries) notwithstanding, the male economic establishment resisted the challenge that the increasing number of women in the workforce posed to one of the cornerstones of masculinity—the role of breadwinner and provider.

Furthermore, wartime needs did not eliminate social and psychological concerns regarding the sexualization and masculinization of wartime females, particularly married women from middle-class homes, as they left their traditional duties and entered public spaces. Employment gave women an unparalleled degree of personal freedom and economic autonomy that, to many conservatives, threatened traditional sexual morality, family values, and social stability. Barriers between male preserves (e.g., the workplace, the neighborhood bar, union meeting halls) and the female place in the home virtually disappeared under wartime pressures, further threatening masculine culture and identity. Women who frequented bars and dance halls unaccompanied by men, and who otherwise challenged accepted gender norms, undermined the existing social order. Gender tensions surrounding these developments found expression in campaigns against venereal disease, prostitution, female promiscuity, and homosexuality.

Traditionalists also worried about the transformation of the family. The wartime absence of fathers from their homes and the increase in female-headed households caused concerns about the impact of such developments on male children. Many observers feared what became known as "momism," the notion that young boys without a male role model present would be subject to cross-gender identification that would undermine their male identity.

Possibly the greatest perceived threat to traditional masculinity arose in 1942 when the War Department established the Women's Army Auxiliary Corps (WAAC; later the Women's Army Corps, or WAC), which was followed by similar organizations for the U.S. Navy, Air Force, and Marines. Even though women's branches were strictly segregated and women were to be recruited only for support roles (thus freeing more men for male-exclusive combat functions), recruitment of women encountered widespread resistance. Many men feared that female recruits would abdicate their traditional responsibilities, usurp the male warrior/protector role, lose their femininity, or sexually tempt male recruits. In response, government officials took steps to minimize women's exposure to combat, and to monitor their sexual behavior. Training facilities in the United States were segregated by sex, and those few women who were sent overseas often found themselves housed in heavily guarded compounds surrounded by barbed wire. These measures notwithstanding, gender tensions in the wartime military remained, finding expression in frequent witch-hunts for promiscuous women, lesbians, and gay men.

Postwar homecomings often exacerbated tensions resulting from wartime changes. Husbands and fathers returned from overseas, often from conditions entailing severe hardship and danger, to female-dominated households where wives and children had managed without them. As returning men sought to reassert their traditional domestic authority, marital clashes often occurred over domestic issues such as child discipline, household budgets, and whether or not the wife should work. Disabled veterans faced even greater difficulties, for they had to readjust both to an altered physical self-image and to changed family conditions in a social setting where a disability was tantamount to male disempowerment. Divorce rates soared in the immediate postwar years, and by 1950 more than one million veterans had been divorced.

The mixed signals that characterized gender relations during the war years were complicated by the return of demobilized servicemen to the workforce—and of millions of women to the home. Challenges to traditional gender roles, and the resulting tensions, remained unresolved, and women in the burgeoning middle-class suburbs of the 1950s grew increasingly restless with their limited roles as housewives and mothers. Their discontent would manifest themselves in the 1960s and 1970s with the rise of the women's movement and growing controversies surrounding sex discrimination in the workplace and social issues such as birth control and abortion rights.

Bibliography

Blum, John Morton. *V was for Victory: Politics and American Culture during World War II.* New York: Harcourt Brace Jovanovich, 1976.

Hegarty, Marilyn. "Patriot or Prostitute: Sexual Discourses, Print Media, and American Women during World War II." *Journal of Women's History* 10, no. 2 (1998): 112–136.

Lipman-Blumen, Jean. "A Crisis Framework Applied to Microsociological Family Changes: Marriage, Divorce, and Occupational Changes Associated with World War II." *Journal of Marriage and the Family* 37, no. 4 (1975): 889–902.

Meyer, Leisa D. "Creating G.I. Jane: The Regulation of Sexual Behavior in the Women's Army Corps during World War II." *Feminist Studies* 18, no. 3 (1992): 581–601.

Milkman, Ruth. *Gender at Work: The Dynamics of Job Segregation by Sex during World War II.* Urbana: University of Illinois Press, 1987.

O'Brien, Kenneth Paul, and Lynn Hudson Parsons, eds. *The Home-Front War: World War II and American Society.* Westport, Conn.: Greenwood Press, 1995.

Treadwell, Mattie E. *The Women's Army Corps.* Washington, D.C.: Center of Military History, United States Army, 1954.

Tuttle, William M., Jr. *"Daddy's Gone to War": The Second World War in the Lives of America's Children.* New York: Oxford University Press, 1993.

Further Reading

Aldrich, Mark. "The Gender Gap in Earnings during World War II." *Industrial and Labor Relations Review* 42, no. 3 (1989): 415–429.

Cooper, Patricia, and Ruth Oldenziel. "Cherished Classifications: Bathrooms and the Construction of Gender/Race on the Pennsylvania Railroad during World War II." *Feminist Studies* 25, no. 1 (1999): 7–41.

Fussell, Paul. *Wartime: Understanding and Behavior in the Second World War.* New York: Oxford University Press, 1989.

Goodman, Jack, ed. *While You Were Gone: A Report on Wartime Life in the United States.* New York: Simon & Schuster, 1946.

Goossen, Rachel Waltner. *Women Against the Good War: Conscientious Objection and Gender on the American Home Front, 1941–1947.* Chapel Hill: University of North Carolina Press, 1997.

Honey, Maureen. *Creating Rosie the Riveter: Class, Gender, and Propaganda during World War II.* Amherst: University of Massachusets Press, 1984.

Polenberg, Richard. *War and Society: The United States, 1941–1945.* Westport, Conn.: Greenwood Press, 1980.

Westbrook, Robert B. "I Want a Girl, Just Like the Girl that Married Harry James: American Women and the Problem of Obligation in World War II." *American Quarterly* 42, no. 4 (1990): 587–614.

RELATED ENTRIES

Advertising; Boyhood; Citizenship; Conscientious Objection; Divorce; Fatherhood; Gays in the Military; Heroism; Hollywood; Labor Movement and Unions; Militarism; Military; Momism; Mother–Son Relationships; Patriotism; Urbanization; Violence; War; Working-Class Manhood; World War I

—*Walter F. Bell*

WRIGHT, RICHARD

1908–1960
African-American Writer

Richard Wright explored the experiences of black men in America, focusing on their despair under, and resistance to, the racism of the early to mid-twentieth century. Several of Wright's novels problematize African-American masculinity by questioning the possibility that black men can achieve true manhood while also confronting a code of capitalism and white supremacy that defines all black males as "boys."

Born in Mississippi, Wright was deserted by his sharecropper father at the age of ten. After a youth spent sporadically working and going to school, he moved to Chicago during the Great Depression and became involved in politics. He joined the Communist Party in the early 1930s and began writing novels celebrating communism as a guarantor of equality and justice—and as a vehicle for realizing black manhood. He continued to advocate communism and class struggle throughout his career, arguing in *Lawd Today* (published posthumously in 1963) that the black nationalism embraced by such groups as the Nation of Islam offered only psychological solace and failed to rectify the emasculating realities of capitalism.

Wright typically employed Marxist and psychoanalytical concepts to examine black masculinity. Considering a reasonable wage, economic independence, and the ability to support one's family crucial to a fulfilled black masculinity, he believed that black men were prevented from fulfilling their prescribed manly roles, that they were emasculated and infantilized, both by whites' racism and by their own responses to it. Wright maintained that black men—relegated to "boy" status and forced to depend on their wives, mothers, and daughters for financial support—responded through regressive actions that only underscored and reinforced their boyishness, whether it be by killing their white father (literally or symbolically), embracing black nationalism, or remaining submissive. To Wright, standard black responses to American racism highlighted the elusiveness of an African-American manhood.

These themes of infantilization and impotence recur in Wright's works. In *Native Son* (1940), for instance, the large, tough, and brutish protagonist Bigger Thomas responds to the harshness of postemancipation Chicago—with its pernicious landlords, brutal police, and unscrupulous politicians—by bullying his family, carrying a gun, and robbing stores. Larger and more violent (but no more effectual a man) than a stereotypical "Uncle Tom," Bigger Thomas tragically internalizes and becomes trapped by the "boy" stereotype. Bigger's sexuality further demonstrates his inability to achieve manhood. From masturbating in a movie theater to forming abortive sexual relationships with his girlfriend Bessie and his boss's daughter Mary Dalton (ending in the murder of both), he yearns for sensation without regard for consequences. Similarly, in *Lawd Today,* the main character, Jake, deals with his feelings of confinement and alienation through infantilized fantasies of quick fixes, immediate (sexual) gratification, and a yearning for maternal love. Wright's autobiographical *Black Boy* (1945) concludes that the black man's inability to transcend boyhood leads to an absolute despair that reinforces submission.

Wright addressed many themes and issues, but his career (and the power of his work) was grounded in his frank exploration of futility and unfulfilled black manhood—themes that continue to resonate in contemporary black America.

BIBLIOGRAPHY

Baker, Houston. "On Knowing Our Place." In *Richard Wright: Critical Perspectives Past and Present,* edited by Henry Louis Gates, Jr., and K. A. Appiah. New York: Amistad, 1993.

Beacham, Walton, ed. "Richard Wright: 1908–1960." In *Beacham's Popular Fiction, 1950–Present.* Washington, D.C.: Beacham Publishing, 1987.

Dawahare, Anthony. "From No Man's Land to Mother-Land: Emasculation and Nationalism in Richard Wright's Depression Era Urban Novels." *African American Review* 33, no. 3 (1999), 451–466.

Rowley, Hazel. *Richard Wright: The Life and Times.* New York: Henry Holt, 2001.

Further Reading

Black, Daniel. *Dismantling Black Manhood: A Historical and Literary Analysis of the Legacy of Slavery.* New York: Garland, 1997.

Boyd, Herb, and Robert Allen, eds. *Brotherman: The Odyssey of Black Men in America.* New York: Fawcett, 1996.

Carbado, Devon W. *Black Men on Race, Gender, and Sexuality: A Critical Reader.* New York: New York University Press, 1999.

Clark, Keith. *Black Manhood in James Baldwin, Ernest J. Gaines, and August Wilson.* Urbana: University of Illinois Press, 2002.

Selected Writings

Wright, Richard. *Native Son.* 1940. Reprint, New York: HarperPerennial, 1993.

———. *Black Boy.* 1945. Reprint, New York: HarperPerennial, 1993.

———. *Lawd Today!* 1963. Reprint, Boston: Northeastern University Press, 1993.

Related Entries

African-American Manhood; Freudian Psychoanalytic Theory; *Invisible Man*; Nationalism; Nation of Islam; Patriarchy; Race; Violence; White Supremacism

—David J. Leonard

Young Men's Christian Association

Emerging out of an early-nineteenth-century wave of evangelical reform, the Young Men's Christian Association (YMCA) offered a wholesome environment to young unmarried men coming to large cities in search of work. In response to rapid industrialization and urbanization, the YMCA sought to propagate a model of masculinity that emphasized the merits of Christian propriety and physical proficiency, while condemning the urban vice that its leaders feared would overtake susceptible youths. This paradigm was frequently embraced by white, middle-class men, though it was often being remade or challenged by working-class, African-American, and gay males. Although the YMCA has instituted significant ideological and structural changes in the twentieth century, its emphasis upon the unity of mind, body, and spirit—symbolized by an inverted red triangle—continues to underscore both its overarching mission and its promotion of a distinct masculinity.

The original YMCA was founded in London in 1844. The organization was brought to the United States by Thomas Sullivan, who formed a Boston branch in 1851. By establishing a physical presence in American cities, the YMCA addressed a mid-nineteenth-century population shift that brought huge numbers of rural white migrants to urban areas in search of industrial labor. In addition, by 1880 half of the young men in American cities were foreign-born by birth or parentage, a group that YMCA authorities marked as especially vulnerable to metropolitan temptations because of their lack of the traditional socialization mechanisms of home and church. YMCA leaders feared that these male newcomers would both become subject to vices such as drinking, gambling, and prostitution and disrupt the social and commercial culture of cities if not subjected to a moralizing influence. Promoting Protestant virtues such as thrift, temperance, and industriousness, the YMCA sought to fill a void within an impersonal, urban-industrial life by creating facilities (known as YMCAs) for the production of a mode of manhood that reviled the indiscretions of modern urban existence.

YMCAs were originally designed to proffer an environment conducive to the pursuit of religiosity. However, by the 1870s religious efforts were augmented with social, educational, and athletic interests as leaders sought to minister to the "wholeness" of life. Catering primarily to white, middle-class Protestants during this era, YMCAs encouraged a conservative style of masculinity by sponsoring programs that promoted the preservation of separate gender spheres and endorsing physical regimes necessary to combat the perceived feminizing influences of domestic sentimentality. Lamenting a decline in vigorous outdoor labor and the ascendance of sedentary white-collar work, the YMCA became one of the chief promoters of "muscular Christianity," an ideology that viewed maintenance of the body as essential for both worldly success and otherworldly salvation.

During the late nineteenth century, the YMCA's attempt to build male character was also welcomed on college campuses by both undergraduates and administrators. It was believed that students, once free from the virtuous confines of home, were privy to the same unethical influences as their urban counterparts. Therefore, university men were viewed as equally in need of a homosocial institution to help them construct an appropriate masculinity.

While many middle-class and college men were willing to adopt this paradigm, members of the late-nineteenth-century working class often challenged efforts to mold them into morally driven laborers. Sent to YMCAs by their companies, workers frequently shunned Bible study and disputed notions of middle-class decency by spitting on floors, playing banned games such as billiards, and resorting to violence when association leaders collaborated with strikebreakers during labor disputes. Through such measures, workers challenged an initiative to manufacture both genteel men and complacent employees.

The late nineteenth century also witnessed the emergence of independent African-American YMCAs. Linked to the larger movement on a "separate but equal" basis, these associations advanced a vision of idealized masculinity similar to that of their white counterparts, but they pursued this model for different reasons. Whereas white YMCAs sought to reduce anxieties over immigration, industrialization, and feminization, black association leaders hoped to combat the stereotyping of African-American males as lazy or shiftless by placing members within the dominant construct of Victorian manhood. Aspiring toward a refined Christian gentility supplemented with physical prowess, black YMCA leaders expected such exhibitions to lead to the transcendence of racial barriers. Although African-American YMCAs were guided by this assimilationist impulse, they also functioned as sanctuaries for black men confronting

This undated photo of a locker room at a Young Men's Christian Association (YMCA) in Chicago highlights the emphasis on masculine athleticism that, while originally linked to the promotion of Christian morality and resistance to urban vice, gradually became an end in itself during the twentieth century. (Courtesy of the Chicago Historical Society)

the emasculations of lynching, race riots, and disfranchisement. Born out of racism, black YMCAs nevertheless offered a safe, public space for the cultivation of African-American communal sentiment prior to the YMCA's desegregation in 1946.

The YMCA has often been a site for the development of gay masculinities. As viable arenas for homoerotic encounters due to their same-sex environment, associations have inadvertently facilitated urban gay subcultures since the 1890s. While gay cruising at YMCAs seems paradoxical due to a historical promotion of chastity, by providing accessible spaces prefaced upon overt physicality the movement allowed for much sexual experimentation. The ability to share a room with another man without suspicion or to participate in nude bathing presented multiple opportunities to subvert the YMCA's promotion of unsullied heterosexuality. Ironically, the emergence of a militant gay rights movement in the late 1960s brought much attention to these dissident uses. By advocating open expressions of homosexual identity, gay rights activists also increased public awareness of cruising, making this activity at YMCAs more scrutinized and dangerous.

During the twentieth century, the YMCA gradually integrated international and familial concerns into its mission. Spread worldwide under the leadership of John R. Mott, general-secretary of the International Committee of the YMCA from 1915 to 1928 and president of the organization's World Committee from 1926 to 1937, the movement served 30 million people in 120 countries in 2002. Reacting to a climate of post–World War II suburbanization that placed greater emphasis upon the nuclear family, YMCAs also saw an increased membership among married men. In addition, although it is believed that the first female member of a YMCA joined in Brooklyn, New York, in the late 1850s, the 1950s witnessed the initial growth of a sizeable female membership. Finally, during the 1900s, physical fitness came to be viewed by the organization as an end in itself, rather than a mere contributor to Christian character. Globalization, demographic shifts, and a more secular approach have created a contemporary YMCA that is much different than its nineteenth-century predecessor. However, the YMCA still formally advocates programs that employ Christian principles to build healthy spirits, minds, and bodies. Within this new manifestation, the emphasis upon constructing a distinct mode of masculinity remains integral to the organization's goals.

Bibliography

Gustav-Wrathall, John Donald. *Take the Young Stranger by the Hand: Same-Sex Relations and the YMCA*. Chicago: University of Chicago Press, 1998.

Ladd, Tony, and James A. Mathisen. *Muscular Christianity: Evangelical Protestants and the Development of American Sport.* Grand Rapids, Mich.: Baker Books, 1999.

Macleod, David I. *Building Character in the American Boy: The Boy Scouts, YMCA, and Their Forerunners, 1870–1920.* Madison: University of Wisconsin Press, 1983.

Mjagkij, Nina. *Light in the Darkness: African Americans and the YMCA, 1852–1946.* Lexington: University Press of Kentucky, 1994.

Mjagkij, Nina, and Margaret Spratt, eds. *Men and Women Adrift: The YMCA and the YWCA in the City.* New York: New York University Press, 1997.

FURTHER READING

Davidann, Jon Thares. *A World of Crisis and Progress: The American YMCA in Japan, 1890–1930.* Bethlehem, Pa.: Lehigh University Press, 1998.

Hopkins, Charles Howard. *History of the YMCA in North America.* New York: Association Press, 1951.

Putney, Clifford. *Muscular Christianity: Manhood and Sports in Protestant America, 1880–1920.* Cambridge, Mass.: Harvard University Press, 2001.

RELATED ENTRIES

African-American Manhood; Body; Bodybuilding; Boy Scouts of America; Business/Corporate America; Character; Crisis of Masculinity; Heterosexuality; Homosexuality; Immigration; Industrialization; Leisure; Middle-Class Manhood; Muscular Christianity; Religion and Spirituality; Sports; Suburbia; Temperance; Urbanization; Victorian Era; Violence; Work; Working-Class Manhood; Youth

—*Aaron K. Ketchell*

YOUTH

Youth, a life stage situated between childhood and adulthood, was an important social category in America through the late nineteenth century. Eventually replaced by the concept of *adolescence*—a more truncated life stage ending by the end of one's teens—youth in early American society had less to do with one's age than with whether one had taken on manly responsibilities such as marriage and an occupation. Americans understood male youth as preparatory to manhood, and the full assumption of independence marked the end of one's youth. However, the degree of dependency experienced in youth—and, therefore, the precise relation between youth and manhood—was historically and regionally variable.

For males in the American colonies, youth was generally a period of exaggerated and prolonged dependency. In colonial subsistence farm communities, young men's claims to manhood were problematic. Masculinity was predicated upon independent mastery of a household, but parents relied heavily on their sons' labor and were slow to let them establish their own families. With a highly restricted land market and few opportunities for wages, sons had to wait for an inheritance before they could become self-sufficient. Furthermore, parents controlled, and often delayed, their sons' independence by having a significant say over prospective partners. Puritan fathers negotiated patrimonies and dowries before agreeing to any proposed match, while Quaker men and women investigated young couples through committees of their Monthly Meetings before allowing a couple to wed. Where patriarchy was strong, adults closely controlled young men's entry into adulthood.

Yet the nature of patriarchy and the extent of patriarchal restrictions on male youths varied. Some young men in the colonies, especially those living in regions where agriculture was an avenue for profit rather than subsistence, could escape patriarchal rule more easily. Young men from Europe who crossed the Atlantic to become indentured servants, for example, no longer had to answer to their parents, though they were expected to obey the quasi-paternal household authority of their masters. On southern plantations, the presence of slave labor allowed household patriarchs to be more indulgent with their youthful sons, who themselves had control over slaves—and thus exercised a fundamental prerogative of southern manhood—long before reaching adulthood.

Traditional barriers between youth and manhood were lowered by challenges to fathers' patriarchal rule during the era of the American Revolution. In the decades approaching and following the war, Americans consumed English novels that decried fathers' interference in marriage. Overthrowing a patriarchal king further delegitimized patriarchy in the young country. In addition, fathers lost much of their economic leverage over their sons as land supplies were depleted by successive partible (divisible) patrimonies in older village communities. Declining patriarchy is apparent in the booming rates of premarital pregnancy in these years. Some young men forced their fathers to assent to a proposed match, and thus verify their arrival at manhood, by impregnating a young woman.

Adults fought back, however, using seduction tales to express growing concerns about the ability of young people to negotiate marriage on their own. Bemoaning the wiles of young male seducers, authors urged chastity to stem the tide of sex and pregnancy among the young. Although parents never reassumed control of courtship, they did succeed in curtailing premarital pregnancy. Thus, young males' control over this route from youth to full manhood had been substantially reduced by the early nineteenth century.

The market revolution of the early nineteenth century provided new opportunities for youthful males to stake claims to manhood, for their power as consumers led purveyors of culture to seek their attention by appealing to their desire to achieve masculine adulthood. Moralist authors and advice writers such as William Alcott and Daniel Eddy, for example, sold books and built careers by offering young males guidance on how to become self-made men. Revivalists seeking larger audiences encouraged the young to seek God and spiritual maturation on their own, telling them to forsake the wisdom of parents and reject the mediation of traditional ministers. More conservative ministers, fearing the depletion of their churches, offered young men positions as teachers in Sunday schools. Colleges were likewise forced to make manhood more easily accessible, as male youths, influenced by notions of democracy, challenged professors' stern rule and resisted perceived threats to their manhood. Students demanded that degrees, and the resulting independence, come more quickly. At Dickinson College in Pennsylvania, for example, students managed to force professors to agree to a program that could be finished in a single year.

At the same time, however, many Americans were concerned that democratization and the manifold temptations presented by an emerging market economy threatened the social and moral order by pushing young males into the responsibilities of manhood before they were able to demonstrate self-control. Thus, while moralist authors pandered to young men's desire for success, they also resisted their claims on independence and devised strategies to control them. By exaggerating how precarious it was to cross the threshold from the home into the world, antebellum moralists made the passage from youth to manhood seem like a dangerous journey that demanded paternal guidance. With confidence men hawking sex, alcohol, and dangerous books on every city corner, and masturbation a constant temptation, young men were liable to lose their self-mastery to flights of fancy and passion. Authors such as Sylvester Graham and Samuel B. Woodward went so far as to depict young men as weak and effeminate. As writers and moralists increasingly depicted youth as a dangerous stage of life, they were laying the groundwork for the late-nineteenth-century concept of *adolescence.*

During the mid- to late nineteenth century, self-styled protectors of youth began building institutions that helped turn the period of youth into that of adolescence. As high schools and urban rescue institutions like the Young Men's Christian Association (YMCA) segregated young people from the world of adults, the image of the immature, awkward adolescent replaced the manly youth of the antebellum era. Granville Stanley Hall's tome *Adolescence* (1904), an extended meditation on the volatility and immaturity of young men, would crystallize a trend well under way in the late nineteenth century.

By the twentieth century, *youth* had disappeared as a meaningful category in American culture. While certainly the word still carried shades of meaning, it no longer referred to a discrete period in the life cycle. Gone too were its opportunities for cultivating manliness. During the early nineteenth century this life stage had been a ladder upon which one accrued responsibilities leading to manhood, but young men now approached adulthood as if coming to the edge of a dangerous precipice. Adolescence became an extended dependency, an extension of childhood that offered few opportunities for independent action.

Bibliography

Fliegelman, Jay. *Prodigals and Pilgrims: The American Revolution Against Patriarchal Authority, 1750–1800.* Cambridge, England: Cambridge University Press, 1982.

Greven, Philip. *Four Generations: Population, Land and Family in Colonial Andover, Massachusetts.* Ithaca, N.Y.: Cornell University Press, 1970.

Hemphill, C. Dallett. *Bowing to Necessities: The History of Manners in America, 1620–1860.* New York: Oxford University Press, 1999.

Kett, Joseph. *Rites of Passage: Adolescence in America, 1790 to the Present.* New York: Basic Books, 1977.

Further Reading

Gross, Robert A. *The Minutemen and Their World.* New York: Hill and Wang, 1976.

Halttunen, Karen. *Confidence Men and Painted Women: A Study of Middle-Class Culture in America, 1830–1870.* New Haven, Conn.: Yale University Press, 1982.

Hessinger, Rodney. "'The Most Powerful Instrument of College Discipline': Student Disorder and the Growth of Meritocracy in the Colleges of the Early Republic." *History of Education Quarterly* 39 (Fall 1999): 237–262.

Ryan, Mary P. *Cradle of the Middle Class: The Family in Oneida County, New York, 1790–1865.* Cambridge, England: Cambridge University Press, 1981.

Related Entries

Adolescence; Advice Literature; American Revolution; Apprenticeship; Arthur, Timothy Shay; Boyhood; Confidence Man; Evangelicalism and Revivalism; Graham, Sylvester; Hall, Granville Stanley; Market Revolution; Marriage; Masturbation; Patriarchy; Reform Movements; Seduction Tales; Self-Control; Self-Made Man; Southern Manhood; Young Men's Christian Association

—*Rodney Hessinger*

Bibliography

Art and Literature 516

Body, Emotion, and Health 517

Business, Technology, and Work 518

Class Identities 519

Consumption and Leisure 519

Ethnic and Racial Identities 519

Family, Fatherhood, and Marriage 521

General Anthologies, Histories, and Reference 522

Icons and Symbols 523

Media and Popular Culture 524

Military and War 525

Movements and Organizations 525

Nationalism and Politics 526

People 527

Political and Social Issues 528

Regional Identities 528

Religion and Spirituality 529

Sexual Identities and Sexuality 530

Sports 532

Theoretical Works 532

ART AND LITERATURE

Auerbach, Jonathan. *Male Call: Becoming Jack London.* Durham N.C.: Duke University Press, 1996.

August, Eugene R. "Death of a Salesman: A Men's Studies Approach." *Western Ohio Journal* 7 (Spring 1986): 53–71.

Balbert, Peter. *D. H. Lawrence and the Phallic Imagination.* New York: St. Martin's, 1989.

Baym, Nina. "Melodramas of Beset Manhood: How Theories of American Fiction Exclude Women Authors." In *Feminism and American Literary History: Essays,* edited by N. Baym. New Brunswick, N.J.: Rutgers University Press, 1992.

Bertolini, Vincent J. "Fireside Chastity: The Erotics of Sentimental Bachelorhood in the 1850s." *American Literature* 68, no. 4 (1996): 707–737.

Callow, Heather Cook. "Masculine and Feminine in Death of a Salesman." In '*The Salesman Has a Birthday': Essays Celebrating the Fiftieth Anniversary of Arthur Miller's Death of a Salesman,* edited by Stephen A. Marino. Lanham, Md.: University Press of America, 2000.

Carew-Miller, Anna. "The Language of Domesticity in Crèvecoeur's *Letters from an American Farmer.*" *Early American Literature* 28 (1993): 242–254.

Chapman, Mary, and Glenn Hendler, eds. *Sentimental Men: Masculinity and Politics of Affect in American Culture.* Berkeley: University of California Press, 1999.

Cheyfitz, Eric. *Trans-Parent: Sexual Politics in the Language of Emerson.* Baltimore: Johns Hopkins University Press, 1981.

Clark, Keith. *Black Manhood in James Baldwin, Ernest J. Gaines, and August Wilson.* Urbana: University of Illinois Press, 2002.

Clifford, Stephen P. *Beyond the Heroic "I": Reading Lawrence, Hemingway, and "Masculinity."* Lewisburg, Pa.: Bucknell University Press, 1998.

Crain, Caleb. *American Sympathy: Men, Friendship, and Literature in the New Nation.* New Haven, Conn.: Yale University Press, 2001.

Dabakis, Melissa. *Visualizing Labor in American Sculpture: Monuments, Manliness, and the Work Ethic, 1880–1935.* New York: Cambridge University Press, 1999.

Dawahare, Anthony. "From No Man's Land to Mother-Land: Emasculation and Nationalism in Richard Wright's Depression Era Urban Novels." *African American Review* 33, no. 3 (1999): 451–466.

Derrick, Scott. "Making a Heterosexual Man: Gender, Sexuality, and Narrative in the Fiction of Jack London." In *Rereading Jack London,* edited by Leonard Cassuto and Jeanne Campbell Reesman. Stanford, Calif.: Stanford University Press, 1996.

Dudley, David L. *My Father's Shadow: Intergenerational Conflict in African American Men's Autobiography.* Philadelphia: University of Pennsylvania Press, 1991.

Edwards, Justin D. *Exotic Journeys: Exploring the Erotics of U.S. Travel Literature, 1840–1930.* Hanover: University of New Hampshire, 2001.

Ellison, Julie. "The Gender of Transparency: Masculinity and the Conduct of Life." *American Literary History* 4, no. 4 (1992): 584–606.

Fliegelman, Jay. "Familial Politics, Seduction, and the Novel: The Anxious Agenda of an American Literary Culture." In *The American Revolution: Its Character and Limits,* edited by Jack P. Greene. New York: New York University Press, 1987.

Fone, Byrne R. S. *Masculine Landscapes: Walt Whitman and the Homoerotic Text.* Carbondale: Southern Illinois University Press, 1992.

Golden, Thelma. *Black Male: Representations of Masculinity in Contemporary American Art.* New York: Whitney Museum of American Art, 1994.

Griswold, Jerome. *Audacious Kids: Coming of Age in America's Classic Children's Books.* New York: Oxford University Press, 1992.

Hendershot, Cyndy. *The Animal Within: Masculinity and the Gothic.* Ann Arbor: University of Michigan Press, 1998.

Horner, Carl S. *The Boy inside the American Businessman: Corporate Darwinism in Twentieth-Century American Literature.* Lanham, Md.: University Press of America, 1992.

Jacobson, Marcia. *Being a Boy Again: Autobiography and the American Boy Book.* Tuscaloosa: University of Alabama Press, 1994.

Kelley, Mary. *Private Woman, Public Stage: Literary Domesticity in Nineteenth-Century America.* New York: Oxford University Press, 1984.

Killingsworth, M. Jimmie. *Whitman's Poetry of the Body: Sexuality, Politics, and the Text.* Chapel Hill: University of North Carolina Press, 1989.

Leverenz, David. *Manhood and the American Renaissance.* Ithaca, N.Y.: Cornell University Press, 1989.

Martin, Robert K. *Hero, Captain, Stranger: Male Friendship, Social Critique, and Literary Form in the Sea Novels of Herman Melville.* Chapel Hill: University of North Carolina Press, 1986.

Martin, Stoddard. *California Writers: Jack London, John Steinbeck, the Tough Guys.* New York: St. Martin's, 1984.

Melosh, Barabara. *Engendering Culture: Manhood and Womanhood in New Deal Public Art and Theater.* Washington, D.C.: Smithsonian Institution Press, 1991.

Motley, Warren. *The American Abraham: James Fenimore Cooper and the Frontier Patriarch.* New York: Cambridge University Press, 1987.

Nelson, Robert K., and Kenneth M. Price. "Debating Manliness: Thomas Wentworth Higginson, William Sloane Kennedy, and the Question of Whitman." *American Literature* 73 (2001): 497–524.

Pollak, Vivian R. *The Erotic Whitman.* Berkeley: University of California Press, 2000.

Radway, Janice A. *Reading the Romance: Women, Patriarchy, and Popular Literature.* Chapel Hill: University of North Carolina Press, 1984.

Roskowski, Susan J. *Birthing a Nation: Gender, Creativity, and the West in American Literature.* Lincoln: University of Nebraska Press, 1999.

Samuels, Shirley, ed. *The Culture of Sentiment: Race, Gender and Sentimentality in Nineteenth-Century America.* New York: Oxford University Press, 1992.

Sattelmeyer, Robert, and J. Donald Crowley, eds. *One Hundred Years of Huckleberry Finn: The Boy, His Book, and American Culture.* Columbia: University of Missouri Press, 1985.

Savran, David. *Communists, Cowboys, and Queers: The Politics of Masculinity in the Work of Arthur Miller and Tennessee Williams.* Minneapolis: University of Minnesota Press, 1992.

Shamir, Milette, and Jennifer Travis, eds. *Boys Don't Cry?: Rethinking Narratives of Masculinity and Emotion in the U.S.* New York: Columbia University Press, 2002.

Shor, Francis. "Power, Gender and Ideological Discourse in The Iron Heel." In *Rereading Jack London,* edited by Leonard Cassuto and Jeanne Campbell Reesman. Stanford, Calif. Stanford University Press, 1996.

Smith, Terry. *In Visible Touch: Modernism and Masculinity.* Chicago: University of Chicago Press, 1997.

Snyder, Katherine. *Bachelors, Manhood, and the Novel, 1850–1925.* New York: Cambridge University Press, 1999.

Stevenson, Warren. *Romanticism and the Androgynous Sublime.* Rutherford, N.J.: Fairleigh Dickinson University Press, 1996.

Sweeney, J. Gray. *The Columbus of the Woods: Daniel Boone and the Typology of Manifest Destiny.* St. Louis, Mo.: Washington University Gallery of Art, 1992.

Tolchin, Neal L. *Mourning, Gender, and Creativity in the Art of Herman Melville.* New Haven, Conn.: Yale University Press, 1988.

Vance, Norman. *The Sinews of the Spirit: The Ideal of Christian Manliness in Victorian Literature and Religious Thought.* Cambridge, England: Cambridge University Press, 1985.

Wadlington, Warwick. *The Confidence Man in American Literature.* Princeton, N.J.: Princeton University Press, 1975.

Wallace, Maurice O. *Constructing the Black Masculine: Identity and Ideality in African American Men's Literature and Culture, 1775–1995.* Durham, N.C.: Duke University Press, 2002.

White, G. Edward. *The Eastern Establishment and the Western Experience: The West of Frederic Remington, Theodore Roosevelt, and Owen Wister.* New Haven, Conn.: Yale University Press, 1968.

BODY, EMOTION, AND HEALTH

Balsamo, Anne. *Technologies of the Gendered Body.* Durham, N.C.: Duke University Press, 1996.

Berrett, Jesse. "Feeding the Organization Man: Diet and Masculinity in Postwar America." *Journal of Social History* 30, no. 4 (Summer 1997): 805–826.

Bordo, Susan. *The Male Body: A New Look at Men in Public and Private.* New York: Farrar, Straus and Giroux, 1999.

Borish, Linda J. "The Robust Woman and the Muscular Christian: Catharine Beecher, Thomas Higginson, and Their Vision of American Society, Health, and Physical Activities." *International Journal of the History of Sport* 4 (1987): 139–154.

Budd, Michael Anton. *The Sculpture Machine: Physical Culture and Body Politics in the Age of Empire.* New York: New York University Press, 1997.

Burgett, Bruce. *Sentimental Bodies: Sex, Gender, and Citizenship in the Early Republic.* Princeton, N.J.: Princeton University Press, 1998.

Chapman, David L. *Adonis: The Male Physique Pin-Up, 1870–1940.* Boston: Alyson Publications, 1989.

———. *Sandow the Magnificent: Eugen Sandow and the Beginnings of Bodybuilding.* Urbana: University of Illinois Press, 1994.

Corrigan, John. *Business of the Heart: Religion and Emotion in the Nineteenth Century.* Berkeley: University of California Press, 2002.

Daniels, Christine, and Michael V. Kennedy, eds. *Over the Threshold: Intimate Violence in Early America.* New York: Routledge, 1999.

Dutton, Kenneth R. *The Perfectible Body: The Western Ideal of Physical Development.* New York: Continuum, 1995.

Dyer, Richard. "The White Man's Muscles." In *The Masculinity Studies Reader,* edited by Rachel Adams and David Savran. Oxford: Blackwell, 2002.

Engelhardt, H. Tristram. "The Disease of Masturbation: Values and Concepts of Disease." In *Sickness and Health in America.* Madison: University of Wisconsin Press, 1978.

Epstein, Julia, and Kristine Straub, eds. *Body Guards: The Cultural Politics of Gender Ambiguity.* London: Routledge, 1991.

Fair, John D. *Muscletown USA: Bob Hoffman and the Manly Culture of York Barbell.* University Park: Pennsylvania State University Press, 1999.

Friedman, David M. *A Mind of Its Own: A Cultural History of the Penis.* New York: Free Press, 2001.

Hall, Donald E., ed. *Muscular Christianity: Embodying the Victorian Age.* New York: Cambridge University Press, 1994.

Haller, John S., and Robin M. Haller. *The Physician and Sexuality in Victorian America.* Urbana: University of Illinois Press, 1974.

Kasson, John. *Houdini, Tarzan, and the Perfect Man: The White Male Body and the Challenge of Modernity in America.* New York: Hill and Wang, 2001.

Kimmel, Michael. "Consuming Manhood: The Feminization of American Culture and the Recreation of the Male Body, 1832–1920." *Michigan Quarterly Review* 33 (1994): 7–36.

Klein, Alan M. *Little Big Men: Bodybuilding Subculture and Gender Construction.* Albany: State University of New York Press, 1993.

Krondorfer, Björn. *Men's Bodies, Men's Gods: Male Identities in a Post-Christian Culture.* New York: New York University Press, 1996.

Laqueur, Thomas. *Making Sex: Body and Gender from the Greeks to Freud.* Cambridge, Mass.: Harvard University Press, 1990.

Lehman, Peter. *Running Scared: Masculinity and the Representation of the Male Body.* Philadelphia: Temple University Press, 1993.

Lehman, Peter, ed. *Masculinity: Bodies, Movies, Culture.* New York: Routledge, 2001.

Lord, Alexandra M. "Models of Masculinity: Sex Education, the United States Public Health Service, and the YMCA, 1919–1924." *Journal of the History of Medicine and Allied Sciences* 58, no. 2 (2003): 123–152.

Lucas, John A. "Thomas Wentworth Higginson: Early Apostle of Health and Fitness." *Journal of Health, Physical Education, and Recreation* 42 (February 1971): 30–33.

Luciano, Lynne. *Looking Good: Male Body Image in Modern America.* New York: Hill and Wang, 2001.

Money, John. *The Destroying Angel: Sex, Fitness and Food in the Legacy of Degeneracy Theory: Graham Crackers, Kellogg's Corn Flakes, and American Health History.* Amherst, N.Y.: Prometheus Books, 1985.

Pope, Harrison G., Katharine A. Phillips, and Roberto Olivardia. *The Adonis Complex: The Secret Crisis of Male Body Obsession.* New York: Free Press, 2000.

Putney, Clifford. *Muscular Christianity: Manhood and Sports in Protestant America, 1880–1920.* Cambridge, Mass.: Harvard University Press, 2001.

Shamir, Milette, and Jennifer Travis, eds. *Boys Don't Cry?: Rethinking Narratives of Masculinity and Emotion in the U.S.* New York: Columbia University Press, 2002.

Smith, Geoffrey. "National Security and Personal Isolation: Sex, Gender, and Disease in the Cold-War United States." *International History Review* 14 (May 1992): 307–337.

Sokolow, Jayme. *Eros and Modernization: Sylvester Graham, Health Reform, and the Origins of Victorian Sexuality in America.* Rutherford, N.J.: Fairleigh Dickinson University Press, 1983.

Stearns, Carol Zisowitz, and Peter N. Stearns. *Anger: The Struggle for Emotional Control in America's History.* Chicago: University of Chicago Press, 1986.

Stearns, Peter N. "Girls, Boys, and Emotions: Redefinitions and Historical Change." *Journal of American History* 80 (1993): 36–68.

———. *Battle Ground of Desire: The Struggle for Self-Control in Modern America.* New York: New York University Press, 1999.

Tasker, Yvonne. *Spectacular Bodies: Gender, Genre and the Action Cinema.* London: Routledge, 1993.

Toon, Elizabeth, and Janet Golden. "'Live Clean, Think Clean, and Don't Go to Burlesque Shows': Charles Atlas as Health Advisor." *Journal of the History of Medicine* 57 (January 2002): 39–60.

Wharton, James C. "Muscular Vegetarianism: The Debate Over Diet and Athletic Performance in the Progressive Era." *Journal of Sport History* 8 (Spring 1981): 58–75.

Business, Technology, and Work

Allmendinger, Blake. *The Cowboy: Representations of Labor in American Work Culture.* New York: Oxford University Press, 1995.

Aron, Cindy Sondik. *Ladies and Gentlemen of the Civil Service: Middle-Class Workers in Victorian America.* New York: Oxford University Press, 1987.

Baron, Ava, ed. *Work Engendered: Toward a New History of American Labor.* Ithaca, N.Y.: Cornell University Press, 1991.

Blewett, Mary H. *Men, Women, and Work: Class, Gender, and Protest in the New England Shoe Industry, 1780–1910.* Urbana: University of Illinois Press, 1988.

Catano, James V. "The Rhetoric of Masculinity: Origins, Institutions, and the Myth of the Self-Made Man." *College English* 52, no. 4 (1990): 421–436.

Cawelti, John. *Apostles of the Self-Made Man: Changing Concepts of Success in America.* Chicago: University of Chicago Press, 1965.

Cooper, Patricia A. *Once a Cigar Maker: Men, Women, and Work Culture in American Cigar Factories, 1900–1919.* Urbana: University of Illinois Press, 1987.

Dabakis, Melissa. *Visualizing Labor in American Sculpture: Monuments, Manliness, and the Work Ethic, 1880–1935.* New York: Cambridge University Press, 1999.

Daniels, Christine. "From Father to Son: Economic Roots of Craft Dynasties in Eighteenth-Century Maryland." In *American Artisans: Crafting Social Identity, 1750–1850,* edited by Howard B. Rock, et al. Baltimore: Johns Hopkins University Press, 1995.

Davis, Clark. *Company Men: White-Collar Life and Corporate Cultures in Los Angeles, 1892–1941.* Baltimore: Johns Hopkins University Press, 2000.

———. "The Corporate Reconstruction of Middle-Class Manhood." In *The Middling Sorts: Explorations in the History of the American Middle Class,* edited by Burton Bledstein and Robert Johnson. New York: Routledge, 2001.

DeVault, Ileen A. "To Sit among Men: Skill, Gender, and Craft Unionism in the Early American Federation of Labor." In *Labor Histories: Class, Politics, and the Working-Class Experience,* edited by Eric Arnesen, et al. Urbana: University of Illinois Press, 1998.

Ditz, Toby L. "Shipwrecked; or Masculinity Imperiled: Mercantile Representations of Failure and the Gendered Self in Eighteenth-Century Philadelphia." *Journal of American History* 81 (1994): 51–80.

Halle, David. *America's Working Man: Work, Home, and Politics among Blue-Collar Property Owners.* Chicago: University of Chicago Press, 1984.

Hilkey, Judy. *Character Is Capital: Success Manuals and Manhood in Gilded Age America.* Chapel Hill: University of North Carolina Press, 1997.

Horner, Carl S. *The Boy inside the American Businessman: Corporate Darwinism in Twentieth-Century American Literature.* Lanham, Md.: University Press of America, 1992.

Horowitz, Roger, ed. *Boys and Their Toys: Masculinity, Class, and Technology in America.* New York: Routledge, 2001.

Kessler-Harris, Alice. *In Pursuit of Equity: Women, Men, and the Quest for Economic Citizenship in Twentieth-Century America.* New York: Oxford University Press, 2001.

Kilmer, Paulette D. *The Fear of Sinking: The American Success Formula in the Gilded Age.* Knoxville: University of Tennessee Press, 1996.

Kwolek-Folland, Angel. *Engendering Business: Men and Women in the Corporate Office, 1870–1930.* Baltimore: Johns Hopkins University Press, 1994.

Lewchuk, Wayne A. "Men and Monotony: Fraternalism as a Managerial Strategy at the Ford Motor Company." *Journal of Economic History* 5, no. 4 (1993): 824–856.

Milkman, Ruth. *Gender at Work: The Dynamics of Job Segregation By Sex During World War II.* Urbana: University of Illinois Press, 1987.

Oldenziel, Ruth. *Making Technology Masculine: Men, Women, and Modern Machines in America, 1870–1945.* Amsterdam: Amsterdam University Press, 1999.

Peter, Gregory, Michael Mayerfield Bell, Susan Jarnagin, and Donna Bauer. "Coming Back across the Fence: Masculinity and the Transition to Sustainable Agriculture." *Rural Sociology* 65, no. 2 (2000): 215–233.

Sandage, Scott A. "Gender and the Economics of the Sentimental Market in Nineteenth-Century America." *Social Politics* 6, no. 2 (1999): 105–130.

Class Identities

Appy, Christian. *Working-Class War: American Combat Soldiers and Vietnam.* Chapel Hill: University of North Carolina Press, 1993.

Aron, Cindy Sondik. *Ladies and Gentlemen of the Civil Service: Middle-Class Workers in Victorian America.* New York: Oxford University Press, 1987.

Blewett, Mary H. *Men, Women, and Work: Class, Gender, and Protest in the New England Shoe Industry, 1780–1910.* Urbana: University of Illinois Press, 1988.

Butsch, Richard. "Class and Gender in Four Decades of Television Situation Comedy: Plus ca Change . . ." *Critical Studies in Mass Communication* 9 (1992): 387–399.

Carman, Bryan K. *A Race of Singers: Whitman's Working-Class Hero from Guthrie to Springsteen.* Chapel Hill: University of North Carolina Press, 2000.

Clawson, Mary Ann. *Constructing Brotherhood: Class, Gender, and Fraternalism.* Princeton, N.J.: Princeton University Press, 1989.

Daniels, Jessie. *White Lies: Race, Class, Gender, and Sexuality in White Supremacist Discourse.* New York: Routledge, 1997.

Davis, Clark. "The Corporate Reconstruction of Middle-Class Manhood." In *The Middling Sorts: Explorations in the History of the American Middle Class,* edited by Burton Bledstein and Robert Johnson. New York: Routledge, 2001.

Halttunen, Karen. *Confidence Men and Painted Women: A Study of Middle-Class Culture in America, 1830–1870.* New Haven, Conn.: Yale University Press, 1982.

Herman, Daniel J. "The Other Daniel Boone: The Nascence of a Middle-Class Hunter Hero, 1784–1860." *Journal of the Early Republic* 18, no. 3 (1998): 429–457.

Horowitz, Roger, ed. *Boys and Their Toys: Masculinity, Technology, and Class in America.* New York: Routledge, 2001.

Kasson, John F. *Rudeness and Civility: Manners in Nineteenth-Century Urban America.* New York: Hill and Wang, 1990.

Lott, Eric. *Love and Theft: Blackface Minstrelsy and the American Working Class.* New York: Oxford University Press, 1993.

Peña, Manuel. "Class, Gender, and Machismo: The 'Treacherous-Woman' Folklore of Mexican Male Workers." *Gender & Society* 5 (1991): 30–46.

Powers, Madelon. *Faces along the Bar: Lore and Order in the Workingman's Saloon, 1870–1920.* Chicago: University of Chicago Press, 1998.

Roediger, David. *Wages of Whiteness: Race and the Making of the American Working Class.* London: Verso, 1991.

Rosenberg, Charles E. "Sexuality, Class and Role in 19th-Century America." *American Quarterly* 25, no. 2 (1973): 131–153.

Ryan, Mary. *Cradle of the Middle Class: The Family in Oneida County, New York, 1790–1835.* New York: Cambridge University Press, 1981.

Saxton, Alexander. *The Rise and Fall of the White Republic: Class Politics and Mass Culture in Nineteenth-Century America.* New York: Verso, 1990.

Sutton, William R. *Journeymen for Jesus: Evangelical Artisans Confront Capitalism in Jacksonian Baltimore.* New York: Garland, 1998.

Traube, Elizabeth. *Dreaming Identities: Class, Gender, and Generation in 1980s American Movies.* Boulder, Colo.: Westview Press, 1992.

Winter, Thomas. *Making Men, Making Class: The YMCA and Workingmen, 1877–1920.* Chicago: University of Chicago Press, 2002.

Consumption and Leisure

Breazeale, Keanon. "In Spite of Women: *Esquire* Magazine and the Construction of the Male Consumer." *Signs: Journal of Women in Culture and Society* 20, no. 1 (1994): 1–22.

Edwards, Tim. *Men in the Mirror: Men's Fashions and Consumer Society.* London: Cassell, 1997.

Herman, Daniel Justin. *Hunting and the American Imagination.* Washington, D.C.: Smithsonian Institution Press, 2001.

Osgersby, Bill. *Playboys in Paradise: Masculinity, Youth, and Leisure-Style in Modern America.* Oxford: Berg, 2001.

Ownby, Ted. *Subduing Satan: Religion, Recreation, and Manhood in the Rural South, 1865–1920.* Chapel Hill: University of North Carolina Press, 1990.

Paoletti, Jo B. "Ridicule and Role Models as Factors in American Men's Fashion Change, 1880–1910." *Costume* 19 (1985): 121–134.

———. "Clothing and Gender in America: Children's Fashions, 1890–1920." *Signs* 13, no. 1 (1987): 136–143.

Parsons, Elaine Franz. "Risky Business: The Uncertain Boundaries of Manhood in the Midwestern Saloon." *Journal of Social History* 34, no. 2 (Winter 2000): 283–307.

Proctor, Nicolas W. *Bathed in Blood: Hunting and Mastery in the Old South.* Charlottesville: University Press of Virginia, 2002.

Powers, Madelon. *Faces along the Bar: Lore and Order in the Workingman's Saloon, 1870–1920.* Chicago: University of Chicago Press, 1998.

Swiencicki, Mark A. "Consuming Brotherhood: Men's Culture, Style, and Recreation as Consumer Culture, 1880–1930." *Journal of Social History* 31, no. 4 (1998): 773–809.

Ethnic and Racial Identities

Ames, Christopher. "Restoring the Black Man's Lethal Weapon: Race and Sexuality in Contemporary Cop Films." *Journal of Popular Film and Television* 20, no. 3 (1992): 52–60.

Anderson, Warwick. "The Trespass Speaks: White Masculinity and Colonial Breakdown." *American Historical Review* 102, no. 5 (1997): 1343–1370.

Baca Zinn, Maxine. "Chicano Men and Masculinity." *Journal of Ethnic Studies* 10 (Spring 1982): 29–44.

Becker, William H. "The Black Church: Manhood and Mission." *Journal of the American Academy of Religion* 40, no. 3 (1972): 316–333.

Bederman, Gail. *Manliness and Civilization: A Cultural History of Gender and Race in the United States, 1880–1917.* Chicago: University of Chicago Press, 1995.

Black, Daniel P. *Dismantling Black Manhood: An Historical and Literary Analysis of the Legacy of Slavery.* New York: Garland, 1997.

Bogle, Donald. *Toms, Coons, Mulattoes, Mammies, and Bucks: An Interpretive History of Blacks in American Films.* 3rd ed. Oxford: Roundhouse, 1994.

Booker, Christopher B. *"I Will Wear No Chain": A Social History of African American Males.* Westport, Conn.: Praeger, 2000.

Boyarin, Daniel. *Unheroic Conduct: The Rise of Heterosexuality and the Invention of the Jewish Man.* Berkeley: University of California Press, 1997.

Boyd, Herb, and Robert Allen, eds. *Brotherman: The Odyssey of Black Men in America.* New York: Fawcett, 1996.

Breines, Paul. *Tough Jews: Political Fantasies and the Moral Dilemma of American Jewry.* New York: HarperCollins, 1990.

Brod, Harry, ed. *A Mensch among Men: Explorations in Jewish Masculinity.* Freedom, Calif.: Crossing Press, 1988.

Brown, Kathleen M. "The Anglo-Algonquian Gender Frontier." In *American Indians,* edited by Nancy Shoemaker. Malden, Mass.: Blackwell, 2001.

Carbado, Devon. *Black Men on Race, Gender, and Sexuality: A Critical Reader.* New York: New York University Press, 1999.

Clark, Keith. *Black Manhood in James Baldwin, Ernest J. Gaines, and August Wilson.* Urbana: University of Illinois Press, 2002.

Cohen, Rich. *Tough Jews: Fathers, Sons, and Gangster Dreams.* New York: Simon & Schuster, 1998.

Daniels, Jessie. *White Lies: Race, Class, Gender, and Sexuality in White Supremacist Discourse.* New York: Routledge, 1997.

Dawahare, Anthony. "From No Man's Land to Mother-Land: Emasculation and Nationalism in Richard Wright's Depression Era Urban Novels." *African American Review* 33, no. 3 (Fall 1999): 451–466.

Devens, Carol. "Separate Confrontations: Gender as a Factor in Indian Adaptation to European Colonization." *American Quarterly* 38 (1986): 461–480.

Díaz, Rafael M. *Latino Gay Men and HIV: Culture, Sexuality, and Risk Behavior.* New York: Routledge, 1998.

Doss, Erika. "Imaging the Panthers: Representing Black Power and Masculinity, 1960s–1990s." *Prospects* 23 (1998): 483–516.

Dudley, David L. *My Father's Shadow: Intergenerational Conflict in African American Men's Autobiography.* Philadelphia: University of Pennsylvania Press, 1991.

Dyer, Richard. "The White Man's Muscles." In *The Masculinity Studies Reader,* edited by Rachel Adams and David Savran. Oxford: Blackwell, 2002.

Dyer, Thomas G. *Theodore Roosevelt and the Idea of Race.* Baton Rouge: Louisiana State University Press, 1980.

Eng, David L. *Racial Castration: Managing Masculinity in Asian America.* Durham, N.C.: Duke University Press, 2001.

Ferber, Abby L. *White Man Falling: Race, Gender, and White Supremacy.* Lanham, Md.: Rowman and Littlefield, 1998.

Ferguson, Ann Arnett. *Bad Boys: Public Schools in the Making of Black Masculinity.* Ann Arbor: University of Michigan Press, 2000.

Gayfield, Donnie. "On the Periphery of Manhood: The African American Community's Marginalization of Black Male Homosexuality." *The 2000 Berkeley McNair Research Journal* (Winter 2000). <http://www-mcnair.berkeley.edu/2000journal/Gayfield/Gayfield.html> (April 9, 2003).

Golden, Thelma. *Black Male: Representations of Masculinity in Contemporary American Art.* New York: Whitney Museum of American Art, 1994.

González, Ray, ed. *Muy Macho: Latino Men Confront Their Manhood.* New York: Anchor Books, 1996.

Guerrero, Ed. "The Black Image in Protective Custody: Hollywood's Biracial Buddy Films of the Eighties." In *Black American Cinema,* edited by Manthia Diawara. New York: Routledge, 1993.

Harper, Phillip Brian. *Are We Not Men? Masculine Anxiety and the Problem of African American Identity.* New York: Oxford University Press, 1996.

Hawkeswood, William G., and Alex W. Costley, eds. *One of the Children: Gay Black Men in Harlem.* Berkeley: University of California Press, 1996.

Hine, Darlene Clark, Earnestine Jenkins, and Bill Strickland. *A Question of Manhood: A Reader in U.S. Black Men's History.* Bloomington: Indiana University Press, 2001.

Hondagneu-Sotelo, Pierrette. "Overcoming Patriarchal Constraints: The Reconstruction of Gender Relations among Mexican Immigrant Women and Men." *Gender & Society* 6 (1992): 393–415.

Horton, James Oliver, "The Manhood of the Race: Gender and the Language of Black Protest in the Antebellum North." <http://www.law.yale.edu/outside/pdf/centers/sc/Horton-Manhood.pdf> (July 7, 2003).

Kimmel, Michael, and Abby L. Ferber. "White Men Are This Nation: Right-Wing Militias and the Restoration of Rural American Masculinity." *Rural Sociology* 65, no. 4 (2000): 582–604.

Ling, Peter J., and Sharon Monteith, eds. *Gender in the Civil Rights Movement.* New York: Garland, 1999.

Littlefield, Daniel C. "Blacks, John Brown, and a Theory of Manhood." In *His Soul Goes Marching On: Responses to John Brown and the Harpers Ferry Raid,* edited by Paul Finkelman. Charlottesville: University Press of Virginia, 1995.

Martel, Elise. "From Mensch to Macho? The Social Construction of a Jewish Masculinity." *Men and Masculinities* 3, no. 4 (2001): 347–369.

Matthews, Tracye. "'No One Ever Asks, What a Man's Role in the Revolution is': Gender and the Politics of The Black Panther Party, 1966–1971." In *The Black Panther Party Reconsidered,* edited by Charles E. Jones. Baltimore: Black Classic Press, 1998.

McDannell, Colleen. "Catholic Domesticity, 1860–1960." In *Religion and American Culture: A Reader,* edited by David G. Hackett. New York: Routledge, 1995.

Mirandé, Alfredo. *Hombres y Machos: Masculinity and Latino Culture.* Boulder, Colo.: Westview Press, 1997.

Mjagkij, Nina. *Light In The Darkness: African Americans and the YMCA, 1852–1946.* Lexington: University of Kentucky Press, 1994.

Muncy, Robyn. "Trustbusting and White Manhood in America, 1898–1914." *American Studies* 38 (Fall 1997): 21–42.

Peña, Manuel. "Class, Gender, and Machismo: The 'Treacherous-Woman' Folklore of Mexican Male Workers." *Gender & Society* 5 (1991): 30–46.

Pfeil, Fred. *White Guys: Studies in Postmodern Domination and Difference.* London: Verso, 1995.

Prell, Riv-Ellen. *Fighting to Become American: Assimilation and the Trouble between Jewish Women and Jewish Men.* Boston: Beacon, 1999.

Ramírez, Rafael L. *What It Means to Be a Man: Reflections on Puerto Rican Masculinity.* New Brunswick, N.J.: Rutgers University Press, 1999.

Robinson, Sally. *Marked Men: White Masculinity in Crisis.* New York: Columbia University Press, 2000.

Roediger, David. *Wages of Whiteness: Race and the Making of the American Working Class.* London: Verso, 1991.

Rogin, Michael Paul. *Fathers and Children: Andrew Jackson and the Subjugation of the American Indian.* New York: Knopf, 1974.

Savran, David. *Taking It Like a Man: White Masculinity, Masochism, and Contemporary American Culture.* Princeton, N.J.: Princeton University Press, 1998.

Saxton, Alexander. *The Rise and Fall of the White Republic: Class Politics and Mass Culture in Nineteenth-Century America.* New York: Verso, 1990.

Shenk, Gerald E. "Race, Manhood, and Manpower: Mobilizing Rural Georgia for World War I." *Georgia Historical Quarterly* 81, no. 3 (1997): 622–662.

Shoemaker, Nancy. "An Alliance between Men: Gender Metaphors in Eighteenth-Century American Indian Diplomacy East of the Mississippi." *Ethnohistory* 46 (Spring 1999): 239–263.

Somerville, Siobhan B. *Queering the Color Line: Race and the Invention of Homosexuality in American Culture.* Durham, N.C.: Duke University Press, 2000.

Spraggins, Johnnie David, Jr. "African American Masculinity: Power and Expression." *Journal of African American Men* 4 (Winter 1999): 45–72.

Stecopoulos, Harry, and Michael Uebel. *Race and the Subject of Masculinities.* Durham, N.C.: Duke University Press, 1997.

Thomas, Kendall. "'Ain't Nothing' Like the Real Thing': Black Masculinity, Gay Sexuality, and the Jargon of Authenticity." In *The House That Race Built*, edited by Wahneema Lubiana. New York: Vintage, 1998.

Tillner, George. "Masculinity and Xenophobia: The Identity of Dominance." Paper presented at UNESCO conference. *Masculinity and Male Roles in the Perspective of a Culture of Peace*, September 1997. <http://mailbox.univie.ac.at/~tillneg8/xenomale/OSLO.html> (March 28, 2003).

Wallace, Maurice O. *Constructing the Black Masculine: Identity and Ideality in African American Men's Literature and Culture, 1775–1995.* Durham, N.C.: Duke University Press, 2002.

Wyatt-Brown, Bertram. "The Mask of Obedience: Male Slave Psychology in the Old South." *American Historical Review* 93 (1988): 1228–1252.

FAMILY, FATHERHOOD, AND MARRIAGE

Bardaglio, Peter W. *Reconstructing the Household: Families, Sex, and Law in the Nineteenth-Century South.* Chapel Hill: University of North Carolina Press, 1995.

Bertolini, Vincent J. "Fireside Chastity: The Erotics of Sentimental Bachelorhood in the 1850s." *American Literature* 68, no. 4 (1996): 707–737.

Cantor, M. G. "Prime-Time Fathers: A Study in Continuity and Change." *Critical Studies in Mass Communication* 7 (1990): 275–285.

Carew-Miller, Anna. "The Language of Domesticity in Crèvecoeur's *Letters from an American Farmer.*" *Early American Literature* 28 (1993): 242–254.

Carroll, Bret E. "'I Must Have My House in Order': The Victorian Fatherhood of John Shoebridge Williams." *Journal of Family History* 24, no. 3 (1999): 275–304.

Chudacoff, Howard. *The Age of the Bachelor: Creating an American Subculture.* Princeton, N.J.: Princeton University Press, 1999.

Coontz, Stephanie. *The Social Origins of Private Life: A History of American Families, 1600–1900.* New York: Verso, 1988.

———. *The Way We Never Were: American Families and the Nostalgia Trap.* New York: Basic Books, 1992.

Daniels, Christine, and Michael V. Kennedy, eds. *Over the Threshold: Intimate Violence in Early America.* New York: Routledge, 1999.

Demos, John. "The Changing Faces of Fatherhood." In *Past, Present, and Personal: The Family and the Life Course in American History*, edited by John Demos. New York: Oxford University Press, 1986.

Dixon, Chris. *Perfecting the Family: Antislavery Marriages in Nineteenth-Century America.* Amherst: University of Massachusetts Press, 1997.

Edwards, Laura F. "The Politics of Marriage and Households in North Carolina during Reconstruction." In *Jumpin' Jim Crow: Southern Politics from Civil War to Civil Rights*, edited by Jane Dailey, Glenda Elizabeth Gilmore, and Bryant Simon. Princeton, N.J.: Princeton University Press, 2000.

Fishburne, Janet Forsythe. *The Fatherhood of God and the Victorian Family: The Social Gospel in America.* Philadelphia: Fortress Press, 1981.

Fliegelman, Jay. *Prodigals and Pilgrims: The American Revolution against Patriarchal Authority, 1750–1800.* New York: Cambridge University Press, 1982.

———. "Familial Politics, Seduction, and the Novel: The Anxious Agenda of an American Literary Culture." In *The American Revolution: Its Character and Limits*, edited by Jack P. Greene. New York: New York University Press, 1987.

Foster, Thomas A. "Deficient Husbands: Manhood, Sexual Incapacity, and Male Marital Sexuality in Seventeenth-Century New England." *William and Mary Quarterly* 56 (October 1999): 723–744.

Frank, Stephen M. *Life with Father: Parenthood and Masculinity in the Nineteenth-Century American North.* Baltimore: Johns Hopkins University Press, 1998.

Gelber, Steven M. "Do-It-Yourself: Constructing, Repairing, and Maintaining Domestic Masculinity." *American Quarterly* 49, no. 1 (1997): 66–113.

Griswold, Robert L. "Law, Sex, Cruelty, and Divorce in Victorian America, 1840–1900." *American Quarterly* 38, no. 5 (1986): 721–745.

———. *Fatherhood in America: A History.* New York: Basic Books, 1993.

Gutiérrez, Ramón A. *When Jesus Came, the Corn Mothers Went Away: Marriage, Sexuality, and Power in New Mexico, 1500–1846.* Stanford, Calif.: Stanford University Press, 1991.

Hobson, Barbara, ed. *Making Men into Fathers: Men, Masculinities, and the Social Politics of Fatherhood.* New York: Cambridge University Press, 2002.

Jabour, Anya. *Marriage in the Early Republic: Elizabeth and William Wirt and the Companionate Ideal.* Baltimore: Johns Hopkins University Press, 1998.

Johansen, Shawn. *Family Men: Middle-Class Fatherhood in Early Industrializing America.* New York: Routledge, 2001.

LaRossa, Ralph. *The Modernization of Fatherhood: A Social and Political History.* Chicago: University of Chicago Press, 1997.

Leibman, Nina C. *Living Room Lectures: The Fifties Family in Film and Television.* Austin: University of Texas Press, 1995.

Lupton, Deborah, and Lesley Barclay. *Constructing Fatherhood: Discourses and Experiences.* London: Sage, 1997.

Lystra, Karen. *Searching the Heart: Women, Men, and Romantic Love in Nineteenth-Century America.* New York: Oxford University Press, 1989.

Marsh, Margaret. "Suburban Men and Masculine Domesticity, 1870–1915." *American Quarterly* 40 (June 1988): 165–186.

May, Elaine Tyler. *Great Expectations: Marriage and Divorce in Post-Victorian America.* Chicago: University of Chicago Press, 1980.

———. *Homeward Bound: American Families in the Cold War Era.* New York: Basic Books, 1988.

McDannell, Colleen. *The Christian Home in Victorian America, 1840–1900.* Bloomington: Indiana University Press, 1986.

Mintz, Steven. *A Prison of Expectations: The Family in Victorian Culture.* New York: New York University Press, 1985.

———. "Mothers and Fathers in America: Looking Backward, Looking Forward." Gilder Lehrman Institute of American History, 2001. <http://www.gliah.uh.edu/historyonline/mothersfathers.cfm> (July 7, 2003).

Mintz, Steven, and Susan Kellogg. *Domestic Revolutions: A Social History of American Family Life.* New York: Free Press, 1988.

Murray, Mary. *The Law of the Father: Patriarchy in the Transition from Feudalism to Capitalism.* London: Routledge, 1995.

Nelson, Claudia. *Invisible Men: Fatherhood in Victorian Periodicals, 1850–1910.* Athens: University of Georgia Press, 1995.

Parke, Ross D., and Peter N. Stearns. "Fathers and Child Rearing." In *Children in Time and Place: Developmental and Historical Insights,* edited by Glen H. Elder, Jr., John Modell, and Ross D. Parke. Cambridge, England: Cambridge University Press, 1993.

Pleck, Elizabeth H., and Joseph H. Pleck. "Fatherhood Ideals in the United States: Historical Dimensions." In *The Role of the Father in Child Development,* edited by Michael E. Lamb. 3rd ed. New York: Wiley, 1997.

Robson, David W. "The Republican Father: The Family Letters of Charles Nisbet." In *The American Family: Historical Perspectives,* edited by Jean E. Hunter and Paul T. Mason. Pittsburgh, Pa.: Duquesne University Press, 1991.

Rogin, Michael Paul. "Kiss Me Deadly: Communism, Motherhood, and Cold War Movies." In *Ronald Reagan, the Movie, and Other Episodes in Political Demonology.* Berkeley: University of California Press, 1987.

Rotundo, E. Anthony. "American Fatherhood: A Historical Perspective." *American Behavioral Scientist* 29 (1985): 7–23.

Ruppel, Tim. "Gender Training: Male Ambition, Domestic Duties, and Failure in the Magazine Fiction of T. S. Arthur." *Prospects* 24 (1999): 311–337.

Ryan, Mary. *Cradle of the Middle Class: The Family in Oneida County, New York, 1790–1835.* New York: Cambridge University Press, 1981.

Snyder, Katherine. *Bachelors, Manhood, and the Novel, 1850–1925.* New York: Cambridge University Press, 1999.

Terry, Jennifer. "'Momism' and the Making of Treasonous Homosexuals." In *"Bad" Mothers: The Politics of Blame in Twentieth-Century America,* edited by Molly Ladd-Taylor and Lauri Umansky. New York: New York University Press, 1998.

Wallach, Glenn. *Obedient Sons: The Discourse of Youth and Generations in American Culture, 1630–1860.* Amherst: University of Massachusetts Press, 1997.

Wexler, Laura. *Tender Violence: Domestic Visions in an Age of U.S. Imperialism.* Chapel Hill: University of North Carolina Press, 2001.

Wilson, Lisa. *Ye Heart of a Man: The Domestic Life of Men in Colonial New England.* New Haven, Conn.: Yale University Press, 1999.

Zagarri, Rosemarie. "Morals, Manners, and the Republican Mother." *American Quarterly* 44 (June 1992): 192–215.

General Anthologies, Histories, and Reference

Adams, Rachel, and David Savran, eds. *The Masculinity Studies Reader.* Malden, Mass.: Blackwell, 2002.

August, Eugene. *The New Men's Studies: A Selected and Annotated Interdisciplinary Bibliography.* Englewood, Colo.: Libraries Unlimited, 1994.

Bederman, Gail. *Manliness and Civilization: A Cultural History of Gender and Race in the United States, 1880–1917.* Chicago: University of Chicago Press, 1995.

Booker, Christopher B. *"I Will Wear No Chain": A Social History of African American Males.* Westport, Conn.: Praeger, 2000.

Brod, Harry, ed. *The Making of Masculinities: The New Men's Studies.* Boston: Allen & Unwin, 1987.

Carnes, Mark C., and Clyde Griffen, eds. *Meanings for Manhood: Constructions of Masculinity in Victorian America.* Chicago: University of Chicago Press, 1990.

Ehrenreich, Barbara. *The Hearts of Men: American Dreams and the Flight from Commitment.* New York: Anchor-Doubleday, 1983.

Faludi, Susan. *Stiffed: The Betrayal of the American Man.* New York: William Morrow, 1999.

Filene, Peter Gabriel. *Him/Her/Self: Sex Roles in Modern America.* Baltimore: Johns Hopkins University Press, 1986.

Gilmore, David D. *Manhood in the Making: Cultural Concepts of Masculinity.* New Haven, Conn.: Yale University Press, 1990.

Kimmel, Michael. *Changing Men: New Directions in Research on Men and Masculinity.* Newbury Park, Calif.: Sage, 1987.

———. *Manhood in America: A Cultural History.* New York: Free Press, 1996.

Kimmel, Michael, and Michael A. Messner. *Men's Lives.* New York: Allyn & Bacon, 2000.

Mangan, J. A., and J. Walvin, eds. *Manliness and Morality: Middle-Class Masculinity in Britain and America, 1800–1940.* Manchester, England: Manchester University Press, 1987.

McCall, Laura, and Donald Yacovone, eds. *A Shared Experience: Men, Women, and the History of Gender.* New York: New York University Press, 1998.

Morgan, David. "Masculinity, Autobiography, and History." *Gender & History* 2, no. 1 (1990): 34–39.

Mosse, George L. *The Image of Man: The Creation of Modern Masculinity.* New York: Oxford University Press, 1996.

Pleck, Elizabeth H., and Joseph H. Pleck, eds. *The American Man.* Englewood Cliffs, N.J.: Prentice Hall, 1980.

Pleck, Joseph H., and Jack Sawyer, eds. *Men and Masculinity.* Englewood Cliffs, N.J.: Prentice Hall, 1974.

Pugh, David G. *Sons of Liberty: The Masculine Mind in Nineteenth-Century America.* Westport, Conn.: Greenwood Press, 1983.

Rotundo, E. Anthony. "Body and Soul: Changing Ideals of American Middle-Class Manhood, 1770–1920." *Journal of Social History* 16 (1983): 23–38.

———. *American Manhood: Transformations in Masculinity from the Revolution to the Modern Era.* New York: Basic Books, 1993.

Smith-Rosenberg, Carroll. *Disorderly Conduct: Visions of Gender in Victorian America.* New York: Knopf, 1985.

Stearns, Peter N. *BE A MAN!: Males in Modern Society.* New York: Holmes and Meier, 1979.

Traister, Bryce. "Academic Viagra: The Rise of American Masculinity Studies." *American Quarterly* 52 (June 2000): 274–304.

Urschel, Joanne K. "Men's Studies and Women's Studies: Commonality, Dependence, and Independence." *Journal of Men's Studies* (Spring 2000): 407–411.

Icons and Symbols

Allmendinger, Blake. *The Cowboy: Representations of Labor in American Work Culture.* New York: Oxford University Press, 1995.

Bivins, Thomas H. "The Body Politic: The Changing Shape of Uncle Sam." *Journalism Quarterly* 64, no. 1 (1987): 13–20.

Carman, Bryan K. *A Race of Singers: Whitman's Working-Class Hero from Guthrie to Springsteen.* Chapel Hill: University of North Carolina Press, 2000.

Davis, Ronald L. *Duke: The Life and Image of John Wayne.* Norman: University of Oklahoma Press, 1998.

Hay, Robert P. "George Washington: American Moses." *American Quarterly* 21 (1969): 780–791.

Holzer, Harold. "'Columbia's Noblest Sons': Washington and Lincoln in Popular Prints." *Journal of the Abraham Lincoln Association* 15 (1994): 23–69.

Lindgren, James M. "*Pater Patriae*: George Washington as Symbol and Artifact." *American Quarterly* 41 (1989): 705–713.

McCann, Graham. *Rebel Males: Clift, Brando and Dean.* New Brunswick, N.J.: Rutgers University Press, 1993.

McDonald, Forrest. "Presidential Character: The Example of George Washington." *Perspectives on Political Science* 26 (1997): 134–139.

Miroff, Bruce. *Icons of Democracy: American Leaders as Heroes, Aristocrats, Dissenters, and Democrats.* New York: Basic Books, 1993.

Oates, Stephen B. "Lincoln: The Man, the Myth." *Civil War Times Illustrated* 22, no. 10 (1984): 10–19.

Rabinowitz, Howard N. "George Washington as Icon." In *Icons in America,* edited by Ray B. Browne and Marshall Fishwick. Bowling Green, Ohio: Popular Press, 1978.

Roberts, Randy, and James S. Olson. *John Wayne: American.* Lincoln: University of Nebraska Press, 1995.

Ruth, David E. *Inventing the Public Enemy: The Gangster in American Culture, 1918–1934.* Chicago: University of Chicago Press, 1996.

Savage, William W. *The Cowboy Hero: His Image in American History and Culture.* Norman: University of Oklahoma Press, 1979.

Schwartz, Barry. "George Washington and the Whig Conception of Heroic Leadership." *American Sociological Review* 48 (1983): 18–33.

———. "The Character of Washington: A Study in Republican Culture." *American Quarterly* 38 (1986): 202–222.

———. *George Washington: The Making of an American Symbol.* New York: Free Press, 1987.

———. "Iconography and Collective Memory: Lincoln's Image in the American Mind." *Sociological Quarterly* 32, no. 3 (1991): 301–319.

Sklar, Robert. *City Boys: Cagney, Bogart, Garfield.* Princeton, N.J.: Princeton University Press, 1992.

Susman, Warren I. "Culture Heroes: Ford, Barton, Ruth." In *Culture as History: The Transformation of Society in the Twentieth Century,* edited by Warren I. Sussman. New York: Pantheon, 1984.

Sweeney, J. Gray. *The Columbus of the Woods: Daniel Boone and the Typology of Manifest Destiny.* St. Louis, Mo.: Washington University Gallery of Art, 1992.

Wadlington, Warwick. *The Confidence Man in American Literature.* Princeton, N.J.: Princeton University Press, 1975.

Wick, Wendy C. *George Washington: An American Icon.* Charlottesville: University of Virginia Press, 1982.

Winkle, Kenneth J. "Abraham Lincoln: Self-Made Man." *Journal of the Abraham Lincoln Association* 21, no. 2 (2000): 1–16.

Wyllie, Irvin G. *The Self-Made Man in America: The Myth of Rags to Riches.* New York: Free Press, 1966.

Media and Popular Culture

Ames, Christopher. "Restoring the Black Man's Lethal Weapon: Race and Sexuality in Contemporary Cop Films." *Journal of Popular Film and Television* 20, no. 3 (1992): 52–60.

Bingham, Dennis. *Acting Male: Masculinities in the Films of James Stewart, Jack Nicholson, and Clint Eastwood.* New Brunswick, N.J.: Rutgers University Press, 1994.

Bogle, Donald. *Toms, Coons, Mulattoes, Mammies, and Bucks: An Interpretive History of Blacks in American Films.* 3rd ed. Oxford: Roundhouse, 1994.

Browne, Ray B., Marshall Fishwick, and Michael T. Marsden, eds. *Heroes of Popular Culture.* Bowling Green, Ohio: Bowling Green University Popular Press, 1972.

Butsch, Richard. "Class and Gender in Four Decades of Television Situation Comedy: Plus ca Change . . ." *Critical Studies in Mass Communication* 9 (1992): 387–399.

Cantor, M. G. "Prime-Time Fathers: A Study in Continuity and Change." *Critical Studies in Mass Communication* 7 (1990): 275–285.

Carman, Bryan K. *A Race of Singers: Whitman's Working-Class Hero from Guthrie to Springsteen.* Chapel Hill: University of North Carolina Press, 2000.

Cassell, Justine, and Henry Jenkins, eds. *From Barbie to Mortal Kombat: Gender and Computer Games.* Cambridge, Mass.: MIT Press, 1998.

Cohan, Steven. *Masked Men: Masculinity and the Movies in the Fifties.* Bloomington: Indiana University Press, 1997.

Cohan, Steven, and Ina Rae Hark, eds. *Screening the Male: Exploring Masculinities in Hollywood Cinema.* London: Routledge, 1993.

Craig, Steve. *Men, Masculinity, and the Media.* Newbury Park, Calif.: Sage, 1992.

———. "More (Male) Power: Humor and Gender in *Home Improvement.*" *The Mid-Atlantic Almanack,* 5 (1996): 61–84.

Davies, Jude, and Carol R. Smith. *Gender, Ethnicity, and Sexuality in Contemporary American Film.* Edinburgh: Keele University Press, 1997.

Davis, Robert Murray. *Playing Cowboys: Low Culture and High Art in the Western.* Norman: University of Oklahoma Press, 1991.

DeAngelis, Michael. *Gay Fandom and Crossover Stardom: James Dean, Mel Gibson, and Keanu Reeves.* Durham, N.C.: Duke University Press, 2001.

Delamater, Jerome, and Ruth Prigozy, eds. *The Detective in American Fiction, Film, and Television.* Westport, Conn.: Greenwood Press, 1988.

Dines, Gail, and Jean M. Humez, eds. *Gender, Race, and Class in the Media: A Text Reader.* Thousand Oaks, Calif.: Sage, 1995.

Ehrenstein, David. *Open Secret: Gay Hollywood, 1928–1998.* New York: William Morrow, 1998.

Greene, Theodore. *America's Heroes: The Changing Models of Success in American Magazines.* New York: Oxford University Press, 1970.

Gross, Larry. *Up from Invisibility: Lesbians, Gay Men, and the Media in America.* New York: Columbia University Press, 2001.

Guerrero, Ed. "The Black Image in Protective Custody: Hollywood's Biracial Buddy Films of the Eighties." In *Black American Cinema,* edited by Manthia Diawara. New York: Routledge, 1993.

Holzer, Harold. "'Columbia's Noblest Sons': Washington and Lincoln in Popular Prints." *Journal of the Abraham Lincoln Association* 15 (1994): 23–69.

Ibson, John. *Picturing Men: A Century of Male Relationships in American Everyday Photography.* Washington, D.C.: Smithsonian Institution Press, 2002.

Jeffords, Susan. *Hard Bodies: Hollywood Masculinity in the Reagan Era.* New Brunswick, N.J.: Rutgers University Press, 1994.

King, Neal. *Heroes in Hard Times: Cop Action Movies in the U.S.* Philadelphia: Temple University Press, 1999.

Kirkham, Pat, and Janet Thumim, eds. *You Tarzan: Masculinity, Movies, and Men.* New York: St. Martin's, 1993.

———. *Me Jane: Masculinity, Movies, and Women.* New York: St. Martin's, 1995.

Krutnik, Frank. *In a Lonely Street: Film Noir, Genre, Masculinity.* London: Routledge, 1991.

Lehman, Peter, ed. *Masculinity: Bodies, Movies, Culture.* New York: Routledge, 2001.

Leibman, Nina C. *Living Room Lectures: The Fifties Family in Film and Television.* Austin: University of Texas Press, 1995.

Lott, Eric. *Love and Theft: Blackface Minstrelsy and the American Working Class.* New York: Oxford University Press, 1993.

Luhr, William. "The Scarred Woman behind the Gun: Gender, Race, and History in Recent Westerns." *Bilingual Review* 20, no. 1 (1995): 37–42.

MacKinnon, Kenneth. *Love, Tears, and the Male Spectator.* Madison, N.J.: Fairleigh Dickinson University Press, 2002.

McCann, Graham. *Rebel Males: Clift, Brando, and Dean.* New Brunswick, N.J.: Rutgers University Press, 1993.

McDonald, Archie P., ed. *Shooting Stars: Heroes and Heroines of Western Film.* Bloomington: Indiana University Press, 1987.

McEachern, Charmaine. "Bringing the Wildman Back Home: Television and the Politics of Masculinity." *Australian Journal of Media & Culture* (1994): 1–15.

Mellen, Patricia. *Big Bad Wolves: Masculinity in the American Film.* New York: Pantheon, 1977.

Mitchell, Lee Clark. *Westerns: Making the Man in Fiction and Film.* Chicago: University of Chicago Press, 1996.

Munby, Jonathan. *Public Enemies, Public Heroes: Screening the Gangster from Little Caesar to Touch of Evil.* Chicago: University of Chicago Press, 1999.

Ownby, Ted. "Freedom, Manhood, and Male Tradition in 1970's Southern Rock Music." In *Haunted Bodies: Gender and Southern Texts,* edited by Anne Goodwyn Jones and Susan V. Donaldson. Charlottesville: University of Virginia Press, 1997.

Pendergast, Tom. *Creating the Modern Man: American Magazines and Consumer Culture, 1900–1950.* Columbia University Press, 2000.

Rogin, Michael Paul. "Kiss Me Deadly: Communism, Motherhood, and Cold War Movies." In *"Ronald Reagan," the Movie, and Other*

Episodes in Political Demonology. Berkeley: University of California Press, 1987.

Ruppel, Tim. "Gender Training: Male Ambition, Domestic Duties, and Failure in the Magazine Fiction of T. S. Arthur." *Prospects* 24 (1999): 311–337.

Russo, Vito. *The Celluloid Closet: Homosexuality in the Movies.* Rev. ed. New York: HarperCollins, 1987.

Sklar, Robert. *City Boys: Cagney, Bogart, Garfield.* Princeton, N.J.: Princeton University Press, 1992.

Spoto, Donald. *Camerado: Hollywood and the American Man.* New York: New American Library, 1978.

Studlar, Gaylyn. *This Mad Masquerade: Stardom and Masculinity in the Jazz Age.* New York: Columbia University Press, 1996.

Tasker, Yvonne. *Spectacular Bodies: Gender, Genre, and the Action Cinema.* London: Routledge, 1993.

Traube, Elizabeth. *Dreaming Identities: Class, Gender, and Generation in 1980s American Movies.* Boulder, Colo.: Westview Press, 1992.

Trice, Ashton D., and Samuel A. Holland, eds. *Heroes, Antiheroes, and Dolts: Portrayals of Masculinity in American Popular Films, 1921–1999.* Jefferson, N.C.: McFarland, 2001.

Trujillo, N. "Hegemonic Masculinity on the Mound: Media Representations of Nolan Ryan and American Sports Culture." *Critical Studies in Mass Communication* 8 (1991): 290–308.

Yaquinto, Marilyn. *Pump 'Em Full of Lead: A Look at Gangsters on Film.* New York: Twayne, 1998.

MILITARY AND WAR

Appy, Christian. *Working-Class War: American Combat Soldiers and Vietnam.* Chapel Hill: University of North Carolina Press, 1993.

Bristow, Nancy K. *Making Men Moral: Social Engineering during the Great War.* New York: New York University Press, 1996.

Clinton, Catherine, and Nina Silber, eds. *Divided Houses: Gender and the Civil War.* New York: Oxford University Press, 1992.

Cooper, Patricia, and Ruth Oldenziel. "Cherished Classifications: Bathrooms and the Construction of Gender/Race on the Pennsylvania Railroad during World War II." *Feminist Studies* 25, no. 1 (1999): 7–41.

Gibson, James William. *Warrior Dreams: Violence and Manhood in Post-Vietnam America.* New York: Hill & Wang, 1994.

Goldstein, Joshua. *War and Gender: How Gender Shapes the War System and Vice Versa.* New York: Cambridge University Press, 2001.

Higginbotham, Don. *George Washington and the American Military Tradition.* Athens: University of Georgia Press, 1985.

Hoganson, Kristin. *Fighting for American Manhood: How Gender Politics Provoked the Spanish-American War.* New Haven, Conn.: Yale University Press, 1998.

Humphrey, Mary Ann. *My Country, My Right to Serve: Experiences of Gay Men and Women in the Military, World War II to the Present.* New York: HarperCollins, 1988.

Jeffords, Susan. *The Remasculinization of America: Gender and the Vietnam War.* Bloomington: Indiana University Press, 1989.

Kaplan, Laura Duban. "Woman as Caretaker: An Archetype That Supports Patriarchal Militarism." *Hypatia* 9, no. 2 (1994): 123–133.

Milkman, Ruth. *Gender at Work: The Dynamics of Job Segregation By Sex During World War II.* Urbana: University of Illinois Press, 1987.

Shenk, Gerald E. "Race, Manhood, and Manpower: Mobilizing Rural Georgia for World War I." *Georgia Historical Quarterly* 81, no. 3 (1997): 622–662.

Shilts, Randy. *Conduct Unbecoming: Lesbians and Gays in the U.S. Military, Vietnam to the Persian Gulf.* New York: St. Martin's, 1993.

Whites, LeeAnn. *The Civil War as a Crisis in Gender: Augusta, Georgia, 1860–1890.* Athens: University of Georgia Press, 1995.

Willoughby, John. "The Sexual Behavior of American GIs During the Early Years of the Occupation of Germany." *The Journal of Military History* 62, no. 1 (1998): 155–174.

MOVEMENTS AND ORGANIZATIONS

Clatterbaugh, Kenneth. "Literature of the U.S. Men's Movement." *Signs: Journal of Women in Culture and Society* 25 (Spring 2000): 883–894.

Clawson, Mary Ann. *Constructing Brotherhood: Class, Gender, and Fraternalism.* Princeton, N.J.: Princeton University Press, 1989.

Dorsey, Bruce. *Reforming Men and Women: Gender in the Antebellum City.* Ithaca, N.Y.: Cornell University Press, 2002.

Gustav-Wrathall, John Donald. *Take the Young Stranger by the Hand: Same-Sex Relations and the YMCA.* Chicago: University of Chicago Press, 1998.

Harding, Christopher, ed. *Wingspan: Inside the Men's Movement.* New York: St. Martin's, 1992.

Hoganson, Kristin. "Garrisonian Abolitionists and the Rhetoric of Gender, 1850–1860." *American Quarterly* 45 (December 1993): 558–595.

Jesser, Clinton J. *Fierce and Tender Men: Sociological Aspects of the Men's Movement.* Westport, Conn.: Praeger, 1996.

Kimmel, Michael. *The Politics of Manhood: Profeminist Men Respond to the Mythopoetic Men's Movement (and the Mythopoetic Leaders Answer).* Philadelphia: Temple University Press, 1995.

Ling, Peter J., and Sharon Monteith, eds. *Gender in the Civil Rights Movement.* New York: Garland, 1999.

Lord, Alexandra M. "Models of Masculinity: Sex Education, the United States Public Health Service, and the YMCA, 1919–1924." *Journal of the History of Medicine and Allied Sciences* 58, no. 2 (2003): 123–152.

MacLean, Nancy. *Behind the Mask of Chivalry: The Making of the Second Ku Klux Klan.* New York: Oxford University Press, 1994.

Macleod, David I. "Act Your Age: Boyhood, Adolescence, and the Rise of the Boy Scouts of America." *Journal of Social History* 16, no. 2 (1983): 3–20.

———. *Building Character in the American Boy: The Boy Scouts, YMCA, and Their Forerunners, 1870–1920.* Madison: University of Wisconsin Press, 1983.

Mechling, Jay. *On My Honor: Boy Scouts and the Making of American Youth.* Chicago: University of Chicago Press, 2001.

Messner, Michael A. *Politics of Masculinities: Men in Movements.* Thousand Oaks, Calif.: Sage, 1997.

Mjagkij, Nina. *Light in the Darkness: African Americans and the YMCA, 1852–1946.* Lexington: University of Kentucky Press, 1994.

Mjagkij, Nina, and Margaret Spratt. *Men and Women Adrift: The YMCA and the YWCA in the City.* New York: New York University Press, 1997.

Schwalbe, Michael L. *Unlocking the Iron Cage: The Men's Movement, Gender Politics, and American Culture.* New York: Oxford University Press, 1996.

Winter, Thomas. *Making Men, Making Class: The YMCA and Workingmen, 1877–1920.* Chicago: University of Chicago Press, 2002.

Nationalism and Politics

Anderson, Warwick. "The Trespass Speaks: White Masculinity and Colonial Breakdown." *American Historical Review* 102, no. 5 (1997): 1343–1370.

Bercaw, Nancy, ed. *Gender and the Southern Body Politic: Essays and Comments.* Jackson: University Press of Mississippi, 2000.

Bloch, Ruth H. "The Gendered Meanings of Virtue in Revolutionary America." *Signs: Journal of Women in Culture and Society* 13, no. 1 (1987): 37–58.

Boose, Linda. "Techno-Muscularity and the 'Boy Eternal.'" In *Cultures of United States Imperialism,* edited by Amy Kaplan and Donald E. Pease. Durham, N.C.: Duke University Press, 1993.

Brown, Kathleen M. *Good Wives, Nasty Wenches, and Anxious Patriarchs: Gender, Race, and Power in Colonial Virginia.* Chapel Hill: University of North Carolina Press, 1996.

Burgett, Bruce. *Sentimental Bodies: Sex, Gender, and Citizenship in the Early Republic.* Princeton, N.J.: Princeton University Press, 1998.

Burstyn, Varda. *The Rites of Men: Manhood, Politics, and the Culture of Sport.* Toronto: University of Toronto Press, 1999.

Cuordileone, Kyle A. "'Politics in an Age of Anxiety': Cold War Political Culture and the Crisis in American Masculinity, 1949–1960." *Journal of American History* 87 (September 2000): 515–545.

Dean, Robert D. *Imperial Brotherhood: Gender and the Making of Cold War Foreign Policy.* Amherst: University of Massachusetts Press, 2001.

Edwards, Laura F. *Gendered Strife and Confusion: The Political Culture of Reconstruction.* Urbana: University of Illinois Press, 1997.

Edwards, Rebecca. *Angels in the Machinery: Gender in American Party Politics from the Civil War to the Progressive Era.* New York: Oxford University Press, 1997.

Epstein, Barbara. "Anti-Communism, Homophobia, and the Construction of Masculinity in the Postwar U.S." *Critical Sociology* 20 (1994): 21–44.

Greenberg, Amy S. "A Gray-Eyed Man: Character, Appearance, and Filibustering." *Journal of the Early Republic* 20 (Winter 2000): 673–699.

Hooper, Charlotte. *Manly States: Masculinities, International Relations, and Gender Politics.* New York: Columbia University Press, 2001.

Isenberg, Nancy. *Sex and Citizenship in Antebellum America.* Chapel Hill: University of North Carolina Press, 1998.

Kann, Mark E. *On the Man Question: Gender and Civic Virtue in America.* Philadelphia: Temple University Press, 1992.

———. *A Republic of Men: The American Founders, Gendered Language, and Patriarchal Politics.* New York: New York University Press, 1998.

———. *The Gendering of American Politics: Founding Mothers, Founding Fathers, and Political Patriarchy.* Westport, Conn.: Praeger, 1999.

Lewis, Jan. "The Republican Wife: Virtue and Seduction in the Early Republic." *William and Mary Quarterly* 3, no. 44 (1987): 689–721.

Lockridge, Kenneth. *On the Sources of Patriarchal Rage: The Commonplace Books of William Byrd and Thomas Jefferson and the Gendering of Power in the Eighteenth Century.* New York: New York University Press, 1992.

McCurry, Stephanie. *Masters of Small Worlds: Yeoman Households, Gender Relations, and the Political Culture of the Antebellum South Carolina Low Country.* New York: Oxford University Press, 1995.

Mettler, Suzanne. *Dividing Citizens: Gender and Federalism in New Deal Public Policy.* Ithaca, N.Y.: Cornell University Press, 1998.

Milkman, Ruth. "Gender, Race, and the Welfare State: Government Work Programs from the 1930s to the Present." *Feminist Studies* 19, no. 2 (1993): 318–343.

Miroff, Bruce. *Icons of Democracy: American Leaders as Heroes, Aristocrats, Dissenters, and Democrats.* New York: Basic Books, 1993.

Nagel, Joane. "Masculinity and Nationalism: Gender and Sexuality in the Making of Nations." *Ethnic and Racial Studies* 21 (March 1998): 245–269.

Nelson, Dana A. *National Manhood: Capitalist Citizenship and the Imagined Fraternity of White Men.* Durham, N.C.: Duke University Press, 1998.

Norton, Mary Beth. *Founding Mothers and Fathers: Gendered Power and the Forming of American Society.* New York: Knopf, 1996.

Rogin, Michael Paul. "Kiss Me Deadly: Communism, Motherhood, and Cold War Movies." In *"Ronald Reagan," the Movie, and Other Episodes in Political Demonology.* Berkeley: University of California Press, 1987.

Rose, Nancy E. "Discrimination against Women in New Deal Work Programs." *Affilia: Journal of Women and Social Work.* 5, no. 2 (1990): 23–45.

Sharp, Joanne P. "Gendering Nationhood: A Feminist Engagement With National Identity." In *Bodyspace: Destabilizing Geographies of Gender and Sexuality,* edited by Nancy Duncan. London: Routledge, 1996.

Smith, Geoffrey. "National Security and Personal Isolation: Sex, Gender, and Disease in the Cold-War United States." *International History Review* 14 (May 1992): 307–337.

Smith, Rogers. *Civic Ideals: Conflicting Visions of Citizenship in U.S. History.* New Haven, Conn.: Yale University Press, 1997.

Smith-Rosenberg, Carroll. "Domesticating 'Virtue': Coquettes and Revolutionaries in Young America." In *Literature and the Body,* edited by Elaine Scarry. Baltimore: Johns Hopkins University Press, 1988.

Testi, Arnaldo. "The Gender of Reform Politics: Theodore Roosevelt and the Culture of Masculinity." *Journal of American History* 81, no. 4 (1995): 1509–1533.

Wexler, Laura. *Tender Violence: Domestic Visions in an Age of U.S. Imperialism.* Chapel Hill: University of North Carolina Press, 2001.

Zagarri, Rosemarie. "Morals, Manners, and the Republican Mother." *American Quarterly* 44 (June 1992): 192–215.

Zalewski, Marysia, and Jane Parpart, eds. *The "Man" Question in International Relations.* Boulder, Colo.: Westview Press, 1998.

PEOPLE

Auerbach, Jonathan. *Male Call: Becoming Jack London.* Durham N.C.: Duke University Press, 1996.

Bingham, Dennis. *Acting Male: Masculinities in the Films of James Stewart, Jack Nicholson, and Clint Eastwood.* New Brunswick, N.J.: Rutgers University Press, 1994.

Butters, Ronald R. "Cary Grant and the Emergence of Gay 'Homosexual.'" *Dictionaries: Journal of the Dictionary Society of North America* 19 (1998): 188–204.

Chapman, David L. *Sandow the Magnificent: Eugen Sandow and the Beginnings of Bodybuilding.* Urbana: University of Illinois Press, 1994.

Cheyfitz, Eric. *Trans-Parent: Sexual Politics in the Language of Emerson.* Baltimore: Johns Hopkins University Press, 1981.

Clark, Keith. *Black Manhood in James Baldwin, Ernest J. Gaines, and August Wilson.* Urbana: University of Illinois Press, 2002.

Clifford, Stephen P. *Beyond the Heroic "I": Reading Lawrence, Hemingway, and "Masculinity."* Lewisburg, Pa.: Bucknell University Press, 1998.

Cullen, Jim. *Born in the USA: Bruce Springsteen and the American Tradition.* Westview, Colo.: Harper-Perennial, 1997.

Davis, Ronald L. *Duke: The Life and Image of John Wayne.* Norman: University of Oklahoma Press, 1998.

Dawahare, Anthony. "From No Man's Land to Mother-Land: Emasculation and Nationalism in Richard Wright's Depression Era Urban Novels." *African American Review* 33, no. 3 (1999): 451–466.

DeAngelis, Michael. *Gay Fandom and Crossover Stardom: James Dean, Mel Gibson, and Keanu Reeves.* Durham, N.C.: Duke University Press, 2001.

Derrick, Scott. "Making a Heterosexual Man: Gender, Sexuality, and Narrative in the Fiction of Jack London." In *Rereading Jack London,* edited by Leonard Cassuto and Jeanne Campbell Reesman. Stanford, Calif.: Stanford University Press, 1996.

Dyer, Thomas G. *Theodore Roosevelt and the Idea of Race.* Baton Rouge: Louisiana State University Press, 1980.

Fone, Byrne R. S. *Masculine Landscapes: Walt Whitman and the Homoerotic Text.* Carbondale: Southern Illinois University Press, 1992.

Hay, Robert P. "George Washington: American Moses." *American Quarterly* 21 (1969): 780–791.

Herman, Daniel J. "The Other Daniel Boone: The Nascence of a Middle-Class Hunter Hero, 1784–1860." *Journal of the Early Republic* 18, no. 3 (1998): 429–457.

Higginbotham, Don. *George Washington and the American Military Tradition.* Athens: University of Georgia Press, 1985.

Killingsworth, M. Jimmie. *Whitman's Poetry of the Body: Sexuality, Politics, and the Text.* Chapel Hill: University of North Carolina Press, 1989.

Lindgren, James M. "*Pater Patriae*: George Washington as Symbol and Artifact." *American Quarterly* 41 (1989): 705–713.

Lucas, John A. "Thomas Wentworth Higginson: Early Apostle of Health and Fitness." *Journal of Health, Physical Education, and Recreation* 42 (February 1971): 30–33.

Martin, Robert F. "Billy Sunday and Christian Manliness." *The Historian* 58, no. 4 (1996): 811–812.

McCann, Graham. *Rebel Males: Clift, Brando, and Dean.* New Brunswick, N.J.: Rutgers University Press, 1993.

McDonald, Forrest. "Presidential Character: The Example of George Washington." *Perspectives on Political Science* 26 (1997): 134–139.

Motley, Warren. *The American Abraham: James Fenimore Cooper and the Frontier Patriarch.* New York: Cambridge University Press, 1987.

Oates, Stephen B. "Lincoln: The Man, the Myth." *Civil War Times Illustrated* 22, no. 10 (1984): 10–19.

Pollak, Vivian R. *The Erotic Whitman.* Berkeley: University of California Press, 2000.

Rabinowitz, Howard N. "George Washington as Icon." In *Icons in America,* edited by Ray B. Browne and Marshall Fishwick. Bowling Green, Ohio: Popular Press, 1978.

Roberts, Randy, and James S. Olson. *John Wayne: American.* Lincoln: University of Nebraska Press, 1995.

Rogin, Michael Paul. *Fathers and Children: Andrew Jackson and the Subjugation of the American Indian.* New York: Knopf, 1974.

Ruppel, Tim. "Gender Training: Male Ambition, Domestic Duties, and Failure in the Magazine Fiction of T. S. Arthur." *Prospects* 24 (1999): 311–337.

Sayen, William Guthrie. "George Washington's 'Unmannerly' Behavior: The Clash Between Civility and Honor." *Virginia Magazine of History and Biography* 107 (1999): 5–36.

Schwartz, Barry. "George Washington and the Whig Conception of Heroic Leadership." *American Sociological Review* 48 (1983): 18–33.

———. "The Character of Washington: A Study in Republican Culture." *American Quarterly* 38 (1986): 202–222.

———. *George Washington: The Making of an American Symbol.* New York: Free Press, 1987.

———. "Iconography and Collective Memory: Lincoln's Image in the American Mind." *Sociological Quarterly* 32, no. 3 (1991): 301–319.

Skandera-Trombley, Laura. *Mark Twain in the Company of Women.* Philadelphia: University of Pennsylvania Press, 1994.

Sklar, Robert. *City Boys: Cagney, Bogart, Garfield.* Princeton, N.J.: Princeton University Press, 1992.

Stahl, J. D. *Mark Twain, Culture, and Gender: Envisioning America through Europe.* Athens: University of Georgia, 1994.

Stoneley, Peter. *Mark Twain and the Feminist Aesthetic.* Cambridge, England: Cambridge University Press, 1992.

Sweeney, J. Gray. *The Columbus of the Woods: Daniel Boone and the Typology of Manifest Destiny.* St. Louis, Mo.: Washington University Gallery of Art, 1992.

Testi, Arnaldo. "The Gender of Reform Politics: Theodore Roosevelt and the Culture of Masculinity." *Journal of American History* 81, no. 4 (1995): 1509–1533.

Townsend, Kim. *Manhood at Harvard: William James and Others.* New York: Norton, 1996.

Wick, Wendy C. *George Washington: An American Icon.* Charlottesville: University of Virginia Press, 1982.

Wills, Garry. *Cincinnatus: George Washington and the Enlightenment.* New York: Doubleday, 1984.

Winkle, Kenneth J. "Abraham Lincoln: Self-Made Man." *Journal of the Abraham Lincoln Association* 21, no. 2 (2000): 1–16.

Wood, Gordon S. "The Greatness of George Washington." *Virginia Quarterly Review* 68 (1992): 189–207.

Political and Social Issues

Blumenthal, Monica, et al., eds. *Justifying Violence: Attitudes of American Men.* Ann Arbor: Institute for Social Research, University of Michigan, 1972.

Boone, J., and M. Cadden. *Engendering Men: The Question of Male Feminist Criticism.* London: Routledge, 1990.

Clatterbaugh, Kenneth. *Contemporary Perspectives on Masculinity: Men, Women, and Politics in Modern Society.* Boulder, Colo.: Westview, 1997.

Courtwright, David. *Violent Land: Single Men and Social Disorder from the Frontier to the Inner City.* Cambridge, Mass.: Harvard University Press, 1996.

Digby, Tom, ed. *Men Doing Feminism.* New York: Routledge, 1998.

Dubbert, Joe. "Progressivism and the Masculinity Crisis." *Psychoanalytic Review* 61 (Fall 1974): 433–455.

Faludi, Susan. *Backlash: The Undeclared War against American Women.* New York: Crown, 1991.

Ferguson, Ann Arnett. *Bad Boys: Public Schools in the Making of Black Masculinity.* Ann Arbor: University of Michigan Press, 2000.

Fraser, John. *America and the Patterns of Chivalry.* Cambridge, England: Cambridge University Press, 1982.

Gilbert, James. *A Cycle of Outrage: America's Reaction to the Juvenile Delinquent in the 1950s.* New York: Oxford University Press, 1996.

Gordon, Lynn D. *Gender and Higher Education in the Progressive Era.* New Haven, Conn.: Yale University Press, 1990.

Horrocks, Roger. *Masculinity in Crisis.* London: Macmillan, 1994.

Kimmel, Michael. *The Politics of Manhood: Profeminist Men Respond to the Mythopoetic Men's Movement (and the Mythopoetic Leaders Answer).* Philadelphia: Temple University Press, 1995.

Kimmel, Michael, ed. *Men Confront Pornography.* New York: Meridian, 1990.

Kimmel, Michael, and Thomas E. Mosmiller, eds. *Against the Tide: Pro-Feminist Men in the United States, 1776–1990, A Documentary History.* Boston: Beacon Press, 1992.

Lesko, Nancy, ed. *Masculinities at School.* Thousand Oaks, Calif.: Sage, 2000.

Lewis, Robert A., ed. *Men in Difficult Times: Masculinity Today and Tomorrow.* Englewood Cliffs, N.J.: Prentice Hall, 1981.

Lingard, Bob, and Peter Douglas. *Men Engaging Feminism: Pro-Feminism, Backlashes, and Schooling.* Buckingham, England: Open University Press, 1999.

May, Larry. *Masculinity and Morality.* Ithaca, N.Y.: Cornell University Press, 1998.

Messner, Michael A. *Politics of Masculinities: Men in Movements.* Thousand Oaks, Calif.: Sage Publications, 1997.

Miedzian, Myriam. *Boys Will Be Boys: Breaking the Link Between Masculinity and Violence.* New York: Doubleday, 1991.

Murdock, Catherine Gilbert. *Domesticating Drink: Women, Men, and Alcohol, 1870–1940.* Baltimore: Johns Hopkins University Press, 1998.

O'Toole, Laura L., and Jessica R. Schiffman, eds. *Gender Violence: Interdisciplinary Perspectives.* New York: New York University Press, 1997.

Pleck, Joseph. *The Myth of Masculinity.* Boston: M.I.T. Press, 1981.

Real, Terrence. *I Don't Want to Talk about It: Overcoming the Secret Legacy of Male Depression.* New York: Fireside, 1998.

Sanday, Peggy Reeves. *Fraternity and Gang Rape: Sex, Brotherhood, and Privilege on Campus.* New York: New York University Press, 1990.

Segal, Lynne, and Mary McIntosh, eds. *Sex Exposed: Sexuality and the Pornography Debate.* New Brunswick, N.J.: Rutgers University Press, 1992.

Seidler, Victor. "Masculinity, Violence, and Emotional Life." In *Emotions in Social Life: Critical Themes and Contemporary Issues,* edited by Gillian Bendelow and Simon J. Williams. New York: Routledge, 1998.

Smith, Paul, ed. *Boys: Masculinities in Contemporary Culture.* Boulder, Colo.: Westview Press, 1996.

Regional Identities

Bardaglio, Peter W. *Reconstructing the Household: Families, Sex, and Law in the Nineteenth-Century South.* Chapel Hill: University of North Carolina Press, 1995.

Basso, Matthew, Laura McCall, and Dee Garceau, eds. *Across the Great Divide: Cultures of Manhood in the American West.* New York: Routledge, 2001.

Bercaw, Nancy, ed. *Gender and the Southern Body Politic: Essays and Comments.* Jackson: University Press of Mississippi, 2000.

Bruce, Dickson. *Violence and Culture in the American South.* Austin: University of Texas Press, 1979.

Edwards, Laura F. *Gendered Strife and Confusion: The Political Culture of Reconstruction.* Urbana: University of Illinois Press, 1997.

———. "The Politics of Marriage and Households in North Carolina During Reconstruction." In *Jumpin' Jim Crow: Southern Politics from Civil War to Civil Rights,* edited by Jane Dailey, Glenda Elizabeth Gilmore, and Bryant Simon. Princeton, N.J.: Princeton University Press, 2000.

Faragher, John Mack. *Women and Men on the Overland Trail.* New Haven, Conn.: Yale University Press, 1979.

Greenberg, Kenneth S. *Honor and Slavery; Lies, Duels, Noses, Masks, Dressing as a Woman, Gifts, Strangers, Humanitarianism, Death, Slave Rebellions, The Proslavery Argument, Baseball, Hunting, and*

Gambling in the Old South. Princeton, N.J.: Princeton University Press, 1996.

Horlick, Allan Stanley. *Country Boys and Merchant Princes: The Social Control of Young Men in New York.* Lewisburg, Pa.: Bucknell University Press, 1975.

Johnson, Susan Lee. *Roaring Camp: The Social World of the California Gold Rush.* New York: Norton, 2000.

Kamensky, Jane. "Talk Like a Man: Speech, Power, and Masculinity in Early New England." *Gender and History* 8 (1996): 22–47.

McCurry, Stephanie. *Masters of Small Worlds: Yeoman Households, Gender Relations, and the Political Culture of the Antebellum South Carolina Low Country.* New York: Oxford University Press, 1995.

Norton, Mary Beth. "Gender and Defamation in Seventeenth-Century Maryland." *William and Mary Quarterly* 44 (1987): 3–39.

Ownby, Ted. *Subduing Satan: Religion, Recreation, and Manhood in the Rural South, 1865–1920.* Chapel Hill: University of North Carolina Press, 1990.

———. "Freedom, Manhood, and Male Tradition in 1970's Southern Rock Music." In *Haunted Bodies: Gender and Southern Texts,* edited by Anne Goodwyn Jones and Susan V. Donaldson. Charlottesville: University of Virginia Press, 1997.

Proctor, Nicolas W. *Bathed in Blood: Hunting and Mastery in the Old South.* Charlottesville: University Press of Virginia, 2002.

Rosa, Joseph G. *Age of the Gunfighter: Men and Weapons on the Frontier, 1840–1900.* Norman: University of Oklahoma Press, 1999.

Shenk, Gerald E. "Race, Manhood, and Manpower: Mobilizing Rural Georgia for World War I." *Georgia Historical Quarterly* 81, no. 3 (1997): 622–662.

Slotkin, Richard. *The Fatal Environment: The Myth of the Frontier in the Age of Industrialization, 1800–1890.* New York: Atheneum, 1985.

———. *Gunfighter Nation: The Myth of the Frontier in Twentieth-Century America.* New York: HarperPerennial, 1993.

———. *Regeneration through Violence: The Mythology of the American Frontier.* Norman: University of Oklahoma Press, 2000.

Stowe, Steven M. *Intimacy and Power in the Old South: Ritual in the Lives of the Planters.* Baltimore: Johns Hopkins University Press, 1987.

White, G. Edward. *The Eastern Establishment and the Western Experience: The West of Frederic Remington, Theodore Roosevelt, and Owen Wister.* New Haven, Conn.: Yale University Press, 1968.

Whites, LeeAnn. *The Civil War as a Crisis in Gender: Augusta, Georgia, 1860–1890.* Athens: University of Georgia Press, 1995.

Wyatt-Brown, Bertram. *Southern Honor: Ethics and Behavior in the Old South.* New York: Oxford University Press, 1982.

———. "The Mask of Obedience: Male Slave Psychology in the Old South." *American Historical Review* 93 (1988): 1228–1252.

Religion and Spirituality

Abraham, Ken. *Who Are the Promise Keepers?: Understanding the Christian Men's Movement.* New York: Doubleday, 1997.

Allen, L. Dean. *Rise Up, O Men of God: The "Men and Religion Forward Movement" and the "Promise Keepers."* Macon, Ga.: Mercer University Press, 2002.

Becker, William H. "The Black Church: Manhood and Mission." *Journal of the American Academy of Religion* 40, no. 3 (1972): 316–333.

Bederman, Gail. "'The Women Have Had Charge of the Church Work Long Enough': The Men and Religion Forward Movement of 1911–1912 and the Masculinization of Middle-Class Protestantism." *American Quarterly* 41 (September 1989): 432–65.

Bendroth, Margaret Lamberts. *Fundamentalism and Gender: 1875 to the Present.* New Haven, Conn.: Yale University Press, 1993.

Bilhartz, Terry D. "Sex and the Second Great Awakening: The Feminization of American Religion Reconsidered." In *Belief and Behavior: Essays in the New Religious History,* edited by Philip R. VanderMeer and Robert P. Swierenga. New Brunswick, N.J.: Rutgers University Press, 1991.

Boyd, Stephen B., W. Merle Longwood, and Mark W. Muesse, eds. *Redeeming Men: Religion and Masculinities.* Louisville, Ky.: Westminster John Knox Press, 1996.

Brickner, Bryan. *The Promise Keepers: Politics and Promises.* Lanham, Md.: Lexington Books, 1999.

Brod, Harry, ed. *A Mensch among Men: Explorations in Jewish Masculinity.* Freedom, Calif.: Crossing Press, 1988.

Carnes, Mark. *Secret Ritual and Manhood in Victorian America.* New Haven, Conn.: Yale University Press, 1989.

Carroll, Bret E. "The Religious Construction of Masculinity in Victorian America: The Male Mediumship of John Shoebridge Williams." *Religion and American Culture: A Journal of Interpretation* 7, no. 1 (1997): 27–60.

———. "'A Higher Power to Feel': Spiritualism, Grief, and Victorian Manhood." *Men and Masculinities* 3, no. 1 (2000): 3–29.

Claussen, Dane, ed. *Standing on the Promises: The Promise Keepers and the Revival of Manhood.* Cleveland, Ohio: Pilgrim Press, 1999.

———. *The Promise Keepers: Essays on Masculinity and Christianity.* Jefferson, N.C.: McFarland, 2000.

Corrigan, John. *Business of the Heart: Religion and Emotion in the Nineteenth Century.* Berkeley: University of California Press, 2002.

Fishburne, Janet Forsythe. *The Fatherhood of God and the Victorian Family: The Social Gospel in America.* Philadelphia: Fortress Press, 1981.

Hackett, David G. "Gender and Religion in American Culture, 1870–1930." *Religion and American Culture: A Journal of Interpretation* 5, no. 2 (1995): 127–157.

Hall, Donald E., ed. *Muscular Christianity: Embodying the Victorian Age.* New York: Cambridge University Press, 1994.

Higgs, Robert J. "'In a Different Voice': Male and Female Narratives of Religious Conversion in Post-Revolutionary America." *American Quarterly* 41 (1989): 34–62.

———. *God in the Stadium: Sports and Religion in America.* Lexington: University Press of Kentucky, 1995.

Juster, Susan. "The Spirit and the Flesh: Gender, Language, and Sexuality in American Protestantism." In *New Directions in American Religious History,* edited by Harry S. Stout and D. G. Hart. New York: Oxford University Press, 1997.

Juster, Susan, and Lisa MacFarlane, eds. *A Mighty Baptism: Race, Gender, and the Creation of American Protestantism.* Ithaca: N.Y.: Cornell University Press, 1996.

Kirkley, Evelyn A. *Rational Mothers and Infidel Gentlemen: Gender and American Atheism, 1865–1915.* Syracuse, N.Y.: Syracuse University Press, 2000.

Krondorfer, Björn. *Men's Bodies, Men's Gods: Male Identities in a Post-Christian Culture.* New York: New York University Press, 1996.

Ladd, Tony. *Muscular Christianity: Evangelical Protestants and the Development of American Sport.* Grand Rapids, Mich.: Baker, 1999.

Lippy, Charles H. "Miles to Go: Promise Keepers in Historical and Cultural Context." *Soundings* 80, no. 2–3 (1997): 289–304.

Martin, Robert F. "Billy Sunday and Christian Manliness." *The Historian* 58, no. 4 (1996): 811–812.

McDannell, Colleen. "Catholic Domesticity, 1860–1960." In *Religion and American Culture: A Reader,* edited by David G. Hackett. New York: Routledge, 1995.

Mernissi, Fatima. *Beyond the Veil: Male-Female Dynamics in Modern Muslim Society.* Bloomington: Indiana University Press, 1987.

Ownby, Ted. *Subduing Satan: Religion, Recreation, and Manhood in the Rural South, 1865–1920.* Chapel Hill: University of North Carolina Press, 1990.

Putney, Clifford. *Muscular Christianity: Manhood and Sports in Protestant America, 1880–1920.* Cambridge, Mass.: Harvard University Press, 2001.

Reynolds, David S. "The Feminization Controversy: Sexual Stereotypes and the Paradoxes of Piety in Nineteenth-Century America." *New England Quarterly* 53 (1980): 96–106.

Sutton, William R. *Journeymen for Jesus: Evangelical Artisans Confront Capitalism in Jacksonian Baltimore.* New York: Garland, 1998.

Vance, Norman. *The Sinews of the Spirit: The Ideal of Christian Manliness in Victorian Literature and Religious Thought.* Cambridge, England: Cambridge University Press, 1985.

Sexual Identities and Sexuality

Barker-Benfield, G. J. *The Horrors of the Half-Known Life: Male Attitudes toward Women and Sexuality in Nineteenth-Century America.* New York: Routledge, 2000.

Beemyn, Brett, and Erich Steinman, eds. *Bisexual Men in Culture and Society.* New York: Haworth Press, 2002.

Bertolini, Vincent J. "Fireside Chastity: The Erotics of Sentimental Bachelorhood in the 1850s." *American Literature* 68, no. 4 (1996): 707–737.

Bérubé, Allan. *Coming Out under Fire: The History of Gay Men and Women in World War Two.* New York: Free Press, 1990.

Boyarin, Daniel. *Unheroic Conduct: The Rise of Heterosexuality and the Invention of the Jewish Man.* Berkeley: University of California Press, 1997.

Bullough, Bonnie, Vern L. Bullough, and James Elias, eds. *Gender Blending.* Amherst, N.Y.: Prometheus, 1997.

Bullough, Vern L., and Bonnie Bullough. *Cross Dressing, Sex, and Gender.* Philadelphia: University of Pennsylvania Press, 1993.

Burgett, Bruce. *Sentimental Bodies: Sex, Gender, and Citizenship in the Early Republic.* Princeton, N.J.: Princeton University Press, 1998.

Butters, Ronald R. "Cary Grant and the Emergence of Gay 'Homosexual.'" *Dictionaries: Journal of the Dictionary Society of North America* 19 (1998): 188–204.

Carbado, Devon. *Black Men on Race, Gender, and Sexuality: A Critical Reader.* New York: New York University Press, 1999.

Chauncey, George. *Gay New York: Gender, Urban Culture, and the Making of the Gay Male World, 1890–1940.* New York: Basic Books, 1994.

Cheyfitz, Eric. *Trans-Parent: Sexual Politics in the Language of Emerson.* Baltimore: Johns Hopkins University Press, 1981.

Corber, Robert J. *Homosexuality in Cold War America: Resistance and the Crisis of Masculinity.* Durham, N.C.: Duke University Press, 1997.

Cott, Nancy F. "Passionlessness: An Interpretation of Victorian Sexual Ideology, 1790–1850." *Signs: Journal of Women in Culture and Society* 4 (Winter 1978): 219–236.

Daniels, Jessie. *White Lies: Race, Class, Gender, and Sexuality in White Supremacist Discourse.* New York: Routledge, 1997.

DeAngelis, Michael. *Gay Fandom and Crossover Stardom: James Dean, Mel Gibson, and Keanu Reeves.* Durham, N.C.: Duke University Press, 2001.

D'Emilio, John. *Sexual Politics, Sexual Communities: The Making of a Homosexual Minority in the United States, 1940–1970.* Chicago: University of Chicago Press, 1983.

D'Emilio, John, and Estelle Freedman. *Intimate Matters: A History of Sexuality in America.* 2nd ed. Chicago: University of Chicago Press, 1997.

Derrick, Scott. "Making a Heterosexual Man: Gender, Sexuality, and Narrative in the Fiction of Jack London." In *Rereading Jack London,* edited by Leonard Cassuto and Jeanne Campbell Reesman. Stanford, Calif.: Stanford University Press, 1996.

Díaz, Rafael M. *Latino Gay Men and HIV: Culture, Sexuality, and Risk Behavior.* New York: Routledge, 1998.

Duberman, Martin. *About Time: Exploring the Gay Past.* New York: Penguin, 1991.

Duberman, Martin, Martha Vicinus, and George Chauncey, Jr. *Hidden From History: Reclaiming the Gay and Lesbian Past.* New York: Penguin, 1989.

Edwards, Justin D. *Exotic Journeys: Exploring the Erotics of U.S. Travel Literature, 1840–1930.* Hanover: University Press of New England, 2001.

Ehrenstein, David. *Open Secret: Gay Hollywood, 1928–1998.* New York: William Morrow, 1998.

Engelhardt, H. Tristram. "The Disease of Masturbation: Values and Concepts of Disease." In *Sickness and Health in America.* Madison: University of Wisconsin Press, 1978.

Enloe, Cynthia. *The Morning After: Sexual Politics at the End of the Cold War.* Berkeley: University of California Press, 1993.

Epstein, Barbara. "Anti-Communism, Homophobia, and the Construction of Masculinity in the Postwar U.S." *Critical Sociology* 20 (1994): 21–44.

Epstein, Julia, and Kristine Straub, eds. *Body Guards: The Cultural Politics of Gender Ambiguity.* London: Routledge, 1991.

Feinberg, Leslie. *Transgender Warriors: Making History from Joan of Arc to Dennis Rodman.* Boston: Beacon Press, 1996.

Foster, Thomas A. "Deficient Husbands: Manhood, Sexual Incapacity, and Male Marital Sexuality in Seventeenth-Century New England." *William and Mary Quarterly* 56 (October 1999): 723–44.

Friedman, David M. *A Mind of Its Own: A Cultural History of the Penis.* New York: Free Press, 2001.

Garber, Marjorie. *Vested Interests: Cross-Dressing and Cultural Anxiety.* New York: HarperCollins, 1993.

Gayfield, Donnie. "On the Periphery of Manhood: The African American Community's Marginalization of Black Male Homosexuality." *The 2000 Berkeley McNair Research Journal* (Winter 2000). <http://www-mcnair.berkeley.edu/2000journal/Gayfield/Gayfield.html> (April 9, 2003).

Godbeer, Richard. *Sexual Revolution in Early America.* Baltimore: Johns Hopkins University Press, 2002.

Greenberg, David F. *The Construction of Homosexuality.* Chicago: University of Chicago Press, 1990.

Gross, Larry. *Up from Invisibility: Lesbians, Gay Men, and the Media in America.* New York: Columbia University Press, 2001.

Gustav-Wrathall, John Donald. *Take the Young Stranger by the Hand: Same-Sex Relations and the YMCA.* Chicago: University of Chicago Press, 1998.

Gutiérrez, Ramón A. *When Jesus Came, the Corn Mothers Went Away: Marriage, Sexuality, and Power in New Mexico, 1500–1846.* Stanford, Calif.: Stanford University Press, 1991.

Haller, John S., and Robin M. Haller. *The Physician and Sexuality in Victorian America.* Urbana: University of Illinois Press, 1974.

Hausman, Bernice L. *Changing Sex: Transsexualism, Technology, and The Idea of Gender.* Durham, N.C.: Duke University Press, 1995.

Hawkeswood, William G., and Alex W. Costley, eds. *One of the Children: Gay Black Men in Harlem.* Berkeley: University of California Press, 1996.

Humphrey, Mary Ann. *My Country, My Right to Serve: Experiences of Gay Men and Women in the Military, World War II to the Present.* New York: HarperCollins, 1988.

Juster, Susan. "The Spirit and the Flesh: Gender, Language, and Sexuality in American Protestantism." In *New Directions in American Religious History,* edited by Harry S. Stout and D. G. Hart, eds. New York: Oxford University Press, 1997.

Katz, Jonathan Ned. *Gay American History: Lesbians and Gay Men in the U. S. A.* Rev. ed. New York: Meridian, 1992.

———. *The Invention of Heterosexuality.* New York: Dutton, 1995.

———. *Love Stories: Sex between Men before Homosexuality.* Chicago: University of Chicago Press, 2001.

Kern, Louis J. *An Ordered Love: Sex Roles and Sexuality in Victorian Utopias: The Shakers, the Mormons, and the Oneida Community.* Chapel Hill: University of North Carolina Press, 1981.

Killingsworth, M. Jimmie. *Whitman's Poetry of the Body: Sexuality, Politics, and the Text.* Chapel Hill: University of North Carolina Press, 1989.

Kline, Wendy. *Building a Better Race: Gender, Sexuality, and Eugenics from the Turn of the Century to the Baby Boom.* Berkeley: University of California Press, 2001.

Lewis, Jan. "The Republican Wife: Virtue and Seduction in the Early Republic." *William and Mary Quarterly* 3, no. 44 (1987): 689–721.

Lord, Alexandra M. "Models of Masculinity: Sex Education, the United States Public Health Service, and the YMCA, 1919–1924." *Journal of the History of Medicine and Allied Sciences* 58, no. 2 (2003): 123–152.

McLaren, Angus. *The Trials of Masculinity: Policing Sexual Boundaries, 1870–1930.* Chicago: University of Chicago Press, 1997.

Messner, Michael A., and Donald F. Sabo. *Sex, Violence, and Power in Sports: Rethinking Masculinity.* Freedom, Calif.: Crossing Press, 1994.

Nardi, Peter M. *Gay Men's Friendships: Invincible Communities.* Chicago: University of Chicago Press, 1999.

Plummer, David. *One of the Boys: Masculinity, Homophobia, and Modern Manhood.* Binghamton, N.Y.: Harrington Park Press, 1999.

Pollak, Vivian R. *The Erotic Whitman.* Berkeley: University of California Press, 2000.

Richardson, Diane, ed. *Theorizing Heterosexuality: Telling It Straight.* Buckingham, England: Open University Press, 1996.

Rosenberg, Charles E. "Sexuality, Class and Role in 19th-Century America." *American Quarterly* 25, no. 2 (1973): 131–153.

Rupp, Leila J. *A Desired Past: A Short History of Same-Sex Love in America.* Chicago: University of Chicago Press, 1999.

Russo, Vito. *The Celluloid Closet: Homosexuality in the Movies.* Rev. ed. New York: HarperCollins, 1987.

Segal, Lynne. *Straight Sex: Rethinking the Politics of Pleasure.* Berkeley: University of California Press, 1994.

Segal, Lynne, and Mary McIntosh, eds. *Sex Exposed: Sexuality and the Pornography Debate.* New Brunswick, N.J.: Rutgers University Press, 1992.

Shilts, Randy. *Conduct Unbecoming: Lesbians and Gays in the U.S. Military, Vietnam to the Persian Gulf.* New York: St. Martin's, 1993.

Smith, Geoffrey. "National Security and Personal Isolation: Sex, Gender, and Disease in the Cold-War United States." *International History Review* 14 (May 1992): 307–337.

Smith, Merril D., ed. *Sex and Sexuality in Early America.* New York: New York University Press, 1998.

Smith-Rosenberg, Carroll. "Sex as Symbol in Victorian America: An Ethnohistorical Analysis of Jacksonian America." In *Turning Points: Historical and Sociological Essays on the Family,* edited by John Demos and Sarane Spence Boocock. Chicago: University of Chicago Press, 1978.

———. "Domesticating 'Virtue': Coquettes and Revolutionaries in Young America." In *Literature and the Body,* edited by Elaine Scarry. Baltimore: Johns Hopkins University Press, 1988.

Sokolow, Jayme. *Eros and Modernization: Sylvester Graham, Health Reform, and the Origins of Victorian Sexuality in America.* Rutherford, N.J.: Fairleigh Dickinson University Press, 1983.

Somerville, Siobhan B. *Queering the Color Line: Race and the Invention of Homosexuality in American Culture.* Durham, N.C.: Duke University Press, 2000.

Suran, Justin David. "Going Out against the War: Antimilitarism and the Politicization of Homosexuality in the Era of Vietnam." *American Quarterly* 53 (September 2001): 452–488.

Terry, Jennifer. "'Momism' and the Making of Treasonous Homosexuals." In *"Bad" Mothers: The Politics of Blame in Twentieth-Century America,* edited by Molly Ladd-Taylor and Lauri Umansky. New York: New York University Press, 1998.

Thomas, Kendall. "'Ain't Nothing' Like the Real Thing': Black Masculinity, Gay Sexuality, and the Jargon of Authenticity." In *The House That Race Built: Black Americans, U.S. Terrain,* edited by Wahneema Lubiana. New York: Vintage, 1998.

Walters, Ronald G., ed. *Primers for Prudery: Sexual Advice to Victorian America.* Baltimore: Johns Hopkins University Press, 2000.

White, Kevin. *The First Sexual Revolution: The Emergence of Male Heterosexuality in Modern America.* New York: New York University Press, 1993.

Williams, Walter L. *The Spirit and the Flesh: Sexual Diversity in American Indian Cultures.* Boston: Beacon Press, 1992.

Sports

Burstyn, Varda. *The Rites of Men: Manhood, Politics, and the Culture of Sport.* Toronto: University of Toronto Press, 1999.

Cavallo, Dominick. *Muscles and Morals: Organized Play and Urban Reform, 1880–1920.* Philadelphia: University of Pennsylvania Press, 1981.

Gorn, Elliot J. *The Manly Art: Bare-Knuckle Prize Fighting in America.* Ithaca, N.Y.: Cornell University Press, 1986.

Gustav-Wrathall, John Donald. *Take the Young Stranger by the Hand: Same-Sex Relations and the YMCA.* Chicago: University of Chicago Press, 1998.

Higgs, Robert J. *God in the Stadium: Sports and Religion in America.* Lexington: University Press of Kentucky, 1995.

Ladd, Tony. *Muscular Christianity: Evangelical Protestants and the Development of American Sport.* Grand Rapids, Mich.: Baker, 1999.

McKay, Jim, Michael A. Messner, and Don Sabo, eds. *Masculinities, Gender Relations, and Sport.* Thousand Oaks, Calif.: Sage, 2000.

Messner, Michael A. *Power at Play: Sports and the Problem of Masculinity.* Boston: Beacon Press, 1992.

Messner, Michael A., and Donald F. Sabo. *Sport, Men, and the Gender Order: Critical Feminist Perspectives.* Champaign, Ill.: Human Kinetics Books, 1990.

———. *Sex, Violence, and Power in Sports: Rethinking Masculinity.* Freedom, Calif.: Crossing Press, 1994.

Putney, Clifford. *Muscular Christianity: Manhood and Sports in Protestant America, 1880–1920.* Cambridge, Mass.: Harvard University Press, 2001.

Riess, Steven A. *Sport in Industrial America, 1850–1920.* Wheeling, Ill.: Harlan Davidson, 1995.

Trujillo, N. "Hegemonic Masculinity on the Mound: Media Representations of Nolan Ryan and American Sports Culture." *Critical Studies in Mass Communication* 8 (1991): 290–308.

Theoretical Works

Badinter, Elizabeth. *XY: On Masculine Identity.* New York: Columbia University Press, 1995.

Baumli, Francis, ed. *Men Freeing Men: Exploding the Myth of the Traditional Male.* Jersey City, N.J.: New Atlantis Press, 1985.

Berger, Maurice, Brian Wallis, and Simon Watson. *Constructing Masculinity.* New York: Routledge, 1995.

Beynon, John. *Masculinities and Culture.* Buckingham, England: Open University Press, 2001.

Boone, Joseph A., and Michael Cadden, eds. *Engendering Men: The Question of Male Feminist Criticism.* New York: Routledge, 1990.

Brenkman, John. *Straight Male Modern: A Cultural Critique of Psychoanalysis.* New York: Routledge, 1993.

Brod, Harry, and Michael Kaufman, eds. *Theorizing Masculinities.* Thousand Oaks, Calif.: Sage, 1994.

Chapman, Rowena, and Jonathan Rutherford, eds. *Male Order: Unwrapping Masculinity.* London: Lawrence & Wishart, 1988.

Connell, R. W. *Masculinities.* Berkeley: University of California Press, 1995.

David, Deborah Sarah, and Robert Brannon, eds. *The Forty-Nine Percent Majority: The Male Sex Role.* Reading, Mass: Addison-Wesley, 1976.

Dubbert, Joe. *A Man's Place: Masculinity in Transition.* Englewood Cliffs, N.J.: Prentice Hall, 1983.

Farrell, Warren. *Why Men Are the Way They Are.* New York: McGraw-Hill, 1986.

Frosh, Stephen. *Sexual Difference: Masculinity and Psychoanalysis.* London: Routledge, 1994.

Gilmore, David G. *Manhood in the Making: Cultural Concepts of Masculinity.* New Haven, Conn.: Yale University Press, 1990.

Kimmel, Michael. *The Gendered Society.* New York: Oxford University Press, 2000.

Lerner, Gerda. *The Creation of Patriarchy.* New York: Oxford University Press, 1986.

Lunbeck, Elizabeth. *The Psychiatric Persuasion: Knowledge, Gender, and Power in Modern America.* Princeton, N.J.: Princeton University Press, 1994.

Middleton, Peter. *The Inward Gaze: Masculinity and Subjectivity in Modern Culture.* London: Routledge Press, 1992.

Pleck, Joseph. *The Myth of Masculinity.* Boston: M.I.T. Press, 1981.

Richardson, Diane, ed. *Theorizing Heterosexuality: Telling It Straight.* Buckingham, England: Open University Press, 1996.

Segal, Lynne. *Slow Motion: Changing Masculinities, Changing Men.* New Brunswick, N.J.: Rutgers University Press, 1990.

Walby, Sylvia. *Theorizing Patriarchy.* Oxford: Basil Blackwell, 1990.

Contributors

Abbott, Sharon A.
Assistant Professor, Department of Sociology and Anthropology
Fairfield University, Fairfield, Connecticut

Abele, Elizabeth
Instructor, English Department
Nassau Community College
State University of New York, Garden City, New York

Adrian, Lynne M.
Associate Professor, Department of American Studies
University of Alabama, Tuscaloosa, Alabama

Allen, Holly
Assistant Professor, American Literature and Civilization Department
Middlebury College, Middlebury, Vermont

Andrews, Matthew
Doctoral Candidate, Department of History
University of North Carolina, Chapel Hill, North Carolina

Arthur, Erica
Doctoral Candidate, American Studies
School of American and Canadian Studies
University of Nottingham, Nottingham, United Kingdom

Barnard, Timothy
Visiting Assistant Professor, Department of English
James Madison University, Harrisonburg, Virginia

Beatty, Greg
Instructor
University of Phoenix, Phoenix, Arizona

Bell, Walter F.
Reference Librarian
Lamar University, Beaumont, Texas

Borg, Kevin L.
Assistant Professor, Department of History
James Madison University, Harrisonburg, Virginia

Burg, Robert W.
Doctoral Candidate, Department of History
Purdue University, West Lafayette, Indiana

Camargo, Sandy
Resident Instruction Assistant Professor, Department of English
University of Missouri–Columbia, Columbia, Missouri

Castagna, JoAnn E.
Independent Scholar
Iowa City, Iowa

Combest, Eric
Instructor, History Department
University of North Carolina, Chapel Hill, North Carolina

Cruz, Juan José
Associate Professor, Department of English
Universidad de La Laguna, Canary Islands, Spain

Currarino, Rosanne
Assistant Professor, Department of History
Queen's University, Kingston, Ontario, Canada

Davis, Matthew R.
Visiting Assistant Professor, Department of English
University of Puget Sound, Tacoma, Washington

Dudgeon, Matthew R.
Doctoral Candidate, Department of Anthropology
Emory University, Atlanta, Georgia

Eagle, Jonna
Doctoral Candidate, Department of American Civilization
Brown University, Providence, Rhode Island

Eaklor, Vicki L.
Professor of History
Chair, Division of Human Studies
Alfred University, Alfred, New York

Estes, Steve
Assistant Professor, Department of History
Sonoma State University, Rohnert Park, California

Ezra, Michael
Assistant Professor, American Multicultural Studies Department
Sonoma State University, Rohnert Park, California

Flood, Karen P.
Lecturer, History and Literature Program
Harvard University, Cambridge, Massachusetts

Gardaphe, Fred
Professor, Department of European Languages, Literatures, and Cultures and Department of English
State University of New York, Stony Brook, New York

Gates, Philippa
Assistant Professor, Department of English and Film Studies
Wilfrid Laurier University, Waterloo, Ontario, Canada

Gemme, Paola
Assistant Professor, Department of English
Arkansas Tech University, Russellville, Arkansas

Glass, Loren
Assistant Professor, Department of English
Towson University, Towson, Maryland

Goldberg, Michael Lewis
Associate Professor, Interdisciplinary Arts and Sciences/ American Studies Concentration
University of Washington, Bothell, Washington

Griswold, Robert L.
Professor, Department of History
University of Oklahoma, Norman, Oklahoma

Hartman, Rebecca
Doctoral Candidate, Department of History
Rutgers University, New Brunswick, New Jersey

Heidenreich, Linda
Assistant Professor, Department of Women's Studies
Washington State University, Pullman, Washington

Hessinger, Rodney
Assistant Professor, Department of History
Hiram College, Hiram, Ohio

Heuston, Sean
Assistant Professor, Department of English
The Citadel, Charleston, South Carolina

Higgins, Jenny
Doctoral Candidate, Women's Studies
MPH Candidate, International Health
Emory University, Atlanta, Georgia

Hirshbein, Laura D.
Clinical Instructor, Department of Psychiatry
University of Michigan, Ann Arbor, Michigan

Hodgdon, Tim
Doctoral Candidate, Department of History
Arizona State University, Tempe, Arizona

Holloran, Peter C.
Assistant Professor, Department of History
Worcester State College, Worcester, Massachusetts

Ibson, John
Professor, Department of American Studies
California State University, Fullerton, California

Jabour, Anya
Associate Professor, Department of History
University of Montana, Missoula, Montana

James, Anthony W.
Instructor, Department of History
Coastal Carolina Community College, Jacksonville, North Carolina

Kane, Michael
Lecturer in German
Blanchardstown Institute of Technology, Dublin, Ireland

Kessler, Kelly
Doctoral Candidate, Department of Radio-Television-Film
University of Texas, Austin, Texas

Ketchell, Aaron K.
Doctoral Candidate, American Studies Program
University of Kansas, Lawrence, Kansas

Kibler, M. Alison
Assistant Professor, American Studies
Franklin and Marshall College, Lancaster, Pennsylvania

Kidder, Kristen M.
Lecturer, Department of Communication Studies
Northeastern University, Boston, Massachusetts

Kuhlman, Erika
Assistant Professor, Department of History
Idaho State University, Pocatello, Idaho

Laipson, Peter
Head, Department of History
Concord Academy, Concord, Massachusetts

Lee, Calinda N.
Assistant Professor, Department of History
University of Maryland University College, College Park, Maryland

Leonard, David J.
Assistant Professor, Comparative Ethnic Studies
Washington State University, Pullman, Washington

MacKinnon, Kenneth
Professor, Department of Humanities, Arts, and Languages
London Metropolitan University, London, United Kingdom

Marr, Timothy
Assistant Professor, Curriculum in American Studies
University of North Carolina, Chapel Hill, North Carolina

Maybrey, Catherine
Doctoral Candidate and Teaching Fellow, Department of History
Loyola University, Chicago, Illinois

McConnell, Kent A.
Visiting Professor, Department of Religion
Dartmouth College, Hanover, New Hampshire

Meadows, Michael R.
Assistant Professor, Department of Communication Arts
Ashland University, Ashland, Ohio

Mechling, Jay
Professor, American Studies Program
University of California, Davis, California

Miller, Elisa
Doctoral Candidate, Department of History
University of Illinois at Urbana–Champaign, Urbana, Illinois

Miltenberger, Scott
Doctoral Candidate, Department of History
University of California, Davis, California

Myers, Elizabeth
Doctoral Candidate, Department of History
Loyola University, Chicago, Illinois

NELSON, ANGELA M. S.
Associate Professor, Department of Popular Culture
Bowling Green State University, Bowling Green, Ohio

NELSON, ROBERT K.
Doctoral Candidate, American Studies Program
College of William and Mary, Williamsburg, Virginia

NEUMANN, CARYN E.
Doctoral Candidate and Instructor, Department of History
Ohio State University, Columbus, Ohio

NIEBUR, LOUIS
Doctoral Candidate, Department of Musicology
University of California, Los Angeles, California

ORDING, DOMINIC
Doctoral Candidate, Department of American Studies
Michigan State University, East Lansing, Michigan

OSGERBY, BILL
Senior Lecturer, Department of Cultural Studies
University of North London, London, United Kingdom

OWNBY, TED
Professor, Department of History and Department of Southern Culture
University of Mississippi, University, Mississippi

PANNAPACKER, WILLIAM
Assistant Professor, Department of English
Hope College, Holland, Michigan

PARKER, ALISON M.
Associate Professor, Department of History
State University of New York, Brockport, New York

PARKINSON, KIRSTEN L.
Assistant Professor, Department of English
Hiram College, Hiram, Ohio

PARSONS, ELAINE FRANTZ
Assistant Professor, Department of History
University of Wisconsin, Oshkosh, Wisconsin

PATELL, CYRUS R. K.
Associate Professor, Department of English
Director of Undergraduate Studies
New York University, New York, New York

DE LA PEÑA, CAROLYN THOMAS
Assistant Professor, American Studies Program
University of California, Davis, California

PERLMAN, ALLISON
Doctoral Candidate, Department of American Studies
University of Texas, Austin, Texas

PINFOLD, MICHAEL JOHN
Field Chair, Department of Film Studies
University of Gloucestershire, Cheltenham, United Kingdom

PLANT, REBECCA JO
Assistant Professor, Department of History
University of California, San Diego, California

REGENHARDT, CHRISTY ERIN
Doctoral Candidate, Department of History
University of Maryland, College Park, Maryland

REMBIS, MICHAEL A.
Visiting Assistant Professor, Department of History
University of Arizona, Tucson, Arizona

RICHARDSON, ANNETTE
Adjunct Associate Professor, Department of Educational Policy Studies, Faculty of Education
University of Alberta, Edmonton, Alberta, Canada

ROBERTSON, MICHELLE L.
Doctoral Candidate, Department of Sociology
Washington State University, Pullman, Washington

ROBINSON, ANGELO RICH
Assistant Professor, Department of English
Goucher College, Baltimore, Maryland

RODRÍGUEZ, CARLOS
Assistant Professor, Department of Literature and Language
Dominican University of California, San Rafael, California

RUGGILL, JUDD ETHAN
Doctoral Candidate, Comparative Cultural and Literary Studies
University of Arizona, Tucson, Arizona

RUSHFORTH, BRETT
Assistant Professor, Department of History
College of William and Mary, Williamsburg, Virginia

SALAMONE, FRANK A.
Professor of Anthropology, Department of Sociology
Iona College, New Rochelle, New York

SANTO, AVI
Doctoral Candidate, Department of Radio-Television-Film
University of Texas, Austin, Texas

SCHOCK, ANGIE M.
Assistant Professor, Department of Family and Consumer Sciences
California State University, Northridge, California

SCHWARTZ, DANIELLE K.
Doctoral Candidate, Department of Art History and Communications Studies
McGill University, Montreal, Québec, Canada

SLAVISHAK, EDWARD
Visiting Assistant Professor, Department of History
Susquehanna University, Selinsgrove, Pennsylvania

SPITZ, MARKUS OLIVER
Doctoral Candidate, Department of German
School of Modern Languages
University of Exeter, Exeter, United Kingdom

Stieglitz, Olaf
Assistant Professor, Department of History
Institute for British and North American History
Cologne University (Universität Köln), Cologne, Germany

Stott, Richard
Associate Professor, Department of History
George Washington University, Washington, D.C.

Sussman, Herbert
Professor Emeritus, Department of English
Northeastern University, Boston, Massachusetts

Thompson, Jenny
Independent Scholar
Evanston, Illinois

Tolley-Stokes, Rebecca
Assistant Professor, Cataloger/Reference Librarian
East Tennessee State University, Johnson City, Tennessee

Traister, Bryce
Associate Professor, Department of English
University of Western Ontario, London, Ontario, Canada

Trask, Jeffrey
Doctoral Candidate, Department of American History
Columbia University, New York, New York

VanSickle, Eugene
Doctoral Candidate, Department of History
West Virginia University, Morgantown, West Virginia

Watts, Trent
Assistant Professor, Department of History
James Madison University, Harrisonburg, Virginia

Whalan, Mark
Lecturer, American Literature and Culture
University of Exeter, Exeter, United Kingdom

Wilson, Anthony
Instructor, Department of English
Vanderbilt University, Nashville, Tennessee

Winter, Thomas
Assistant Professor and Acting Chair, Department of American Culture and Literature
Bilkent University, Bilkent, Ankara, Turkey

Index

Note: Page numbers in **boldface** refer to main entries; page numbers in *italic* refer to illustrations and photographs.

A

Aaron, Henry "Hank," 436
Abalos, David T., 265
Abbott, Lyman, 323
abolitionism, **5–7**
  African-American manhood and, 5, 16
  Douglass and, 134
  feminism and, 5–6, 168–69
  self-control and, 388
  slave narratives and, 420
  Thoreau and, 457
  Victorian Era and, 474
About Schmidt (2002), 349
Abysmal Brute, The (London), 274
acculturation, 151
Adams, Abigail, 28, 168
Adams, Henry, 450
Adams, John, 20, 411
Adams, John Quincy, 364
Addams, Jane, 299, 388
Address to Slaves (Garnett), 16
adolescence, **7–9**
  advice literature and, 13, 14, 15
  Beat movement and, 50
  Catcher in the Rye and, 84–85
  Dean's films and, 125–26
  Dr. Spock and, 102
  emotional expression and, 148
  Father Knows Best and, 164–65
  fraternities and, 178–80
  gangs and, 184–86
  guns and, 199
  Hall's theories and, 7–8, 201
  heterosexuality and, 208
  Iron John and, 241
  juvenile delinquency, 66, 102, 253–54, 320, 478–79
  Leave It to Beaver and, 268–69
  masturbation and, 295
  momism and, 318
  Native American manhood and, 334–35
  organic memory concept and, 197
  Rebel Without a Cause and, 386–87
  self-control and, 411–12
  Tom Sawyer and Huckleberry Finn and, 9–10, 406, 465–66
  violence and, 8, 478–79
  See also boyhood; youth
Adolescence (Hall), 7–8, 201, 295, 514
adonis complex, 58
Adventures of Huckleberry Finn (Twain), **9–10,** 66, 211, 406, 465
Adventures of Ozzie and Harriet, The (1952–66), 67, 293, 345, 441, 452–53
Adventures of Tom Sawyer (Twain), 9, 10, 66, 406, 465
adventure travel, 462, 463, 464
advertising, **10–13**
  Atlas and bodybuilding, 41
  body image and, 57
  fashion and, 159, 160
  Father's Day and, 166
  Marlboro Man and, 285–86
  old age and, 349
  Playboy magazine, 11, 361
  reverse sexism and, 400
  World War I and, 505
advice literature, **13–15**
  alcohol and, 23
  Arthur and, 36
  Boone and, 62
  character and, 86
  confidence man skills and, 103
  fatherhood and, 163, 164
  industrialization and, 234
  Irish-American manhood and, 240
  Kellogg and, 255
  mother–son relationships and, 319
  self-control and, 411
  success manuals, 442–44
  Victorian Era, 473
  youth and, 13, 14, 513
Advice to Young Men (Arthur), 36
AFL-CIO, 262, 504
African-American manhood, **15–20,** 493
  abolitionism and, 5, 16
  adolescence and, 7, 8
  advertising and, 12
  agrarianism and, 21
  American Dream and, 26, 27
  American Revolution and, 28
  antiwar movement and, 29
  art and, 34
  automobiles and, 42, 43
  Black Panther Party and, 17, **54–56,** 88, 160, 185, 389, 478
  Black Power movement, 327, 383, 420, 431
  boyhood and, 66–67
  breadwinner role and, 16, 72–73
  chivalry and, 88
  citizenship and, 90
  civil rights movement and, 17, 92, 93, 383
  Civil War and, 95
  Douglass and, 134–35
  education and, 66–67, 141, 142–43
  eugenics and, 154
  fashion and, 160
  fatherhood and, 18
  fraternal organizations and, 177
  fraternities and, 179
  gambling and, 183
  gangs and, 185
  gangsters and, 187
  guns and, 198, 199
  heroism and, 206
  Hollywood and, 52–53, 74, 111, 212, 213, 214, 290–91, 419–20
  immigration and, 225
  individualism and, 230
  Invisible Man and, 237
  Jesus, images of, 248
  juvenile delinquency and, 254
  King and, 257–58
  labor movement and unions and, 261
  Malcolm X and, 277
  marriage and, 287–88, 289
  middle-class manhood and, 306
  military service and, 92, 95, 105, 143–44, 476
  Million Man March and, 18, *18,* 118, 303, 334
  minstrelsy and, 315–17
  mother–son relationships and, 320
  music and, 50, 187, 326, 327
  myth of the black rapist, 88, 93, 495–96
  Nation of Islam and, 17, 277, **332–34,** 392
  nativism and, 338
  nuclear family and, 345
  patriarchy and, 356–57
  patriotism and, 359
  politics and, 364
  professionalism and, 372
  Progressive Era and, 375
  property and, 377
  racialization and, 381, 382, 383
  reform movements and, 389
  religion and spirituality and, 392
  reproduction and, 394–95
  republicanism and, 398
  in the South, 430, 431, 432
  sports and, 48, 63, 64, 436
  suffrage and, 92, 93, 144, *144,* 145, 444–45
  television and, 453, 454
  urbanization and, 470
  urban migration and, 469
  violence and, 478
  working-class manhood and, 503
  World War I and, 506
  Wright and, 509
  See also slavery
African-American YMCA, 511–12
African Game Trails (Roosevelt), 462
African Orthodox Church, 392
Agent Orange, 476
aging. *See* old age
agrarianism, **20–22**
  Crèvecoeur and, 20, 25, 115–16, 223, 468
  Emerson and, 146
  fatherhood and, 161
  Grapes of Wrath and, 194–95

agrarianism (*continued*)
Jefferson and, 20, 89, 194, 329, 365, 468
Native American manhood and, 335, 336, 337
patriarchy and, 356
populism and, 366
Southern manhood and, 429, 431
suburbia and, 440
Thoreau and, 457
urbanization *vs.*, 468
work, role of, 499
See also land ownership
AIDS (acquired immunodeficiency syndrome), 54, 210, 218, 219, 379, 395
Aid to Families with Dependent Children, 341–42
Air Force One (1997), 476
Alamo, The (1960), 485
alcohol, **22–24**
advertising and, 12
California Gold Rush and, 81, 82
election day consumption, 89, 363
fraternities and, 179
gangsters and, 186
immigrants and, 22, 224
Irish-American manhood and, 238, 240
leisure and, 270
men's clubs and, 300
Social Gospel movement and, 426
sports and, 435
temperance movement, 23, 35, 192, 388, 455–56
violence and, 477
working-class manhood and, 233, 502, 503
Alcoholics Anonymous, 456
Alcott, William, 13, 192, 234, 295, 474, 514
Alexander, John L., 68
Alger, Horatio, Jr., 10, **24–25,** 206
Ali, Muhammad, 17, 64, 105, 431, 436
Alice's Restaurant (1969), 140
Alienation and Freedom (Blauner), 500
Allen, Tim, 215–16
Allen, Woody, 214
All in the Family (1971–79), 339, 453, 493, 504
Allman Brothers, 327
allopathic medicine, 296–97
"Almos' a Man" (Wright), 431
alternative medicine, 298
America: Why I Love Her (1973), 485
American and Foreign Anti-Slavery Society, 6
American Anti-Slavery Society, 6
American Bar Association, 372
American Dilemma, An (Myrdal), 493
American Dream, **25–27,** 126, 173, 252, 275
American Educational Gender Information Service, 459
American Fathers' Coalition, 167
American Federation of Labor (AFL), 97, 191, 233, 239, 261, 262, 388, 500, 503
American History X (1998), 339
American Institute of Christian Sociology, 426
American Manhood: Transformations in Masculinity from the Revolution to the Modern Day (Rotundo), 305
American Medical Association, 372
American Men's Studies Association, 302, 305
American Party (Know-Nothing Party), 90, 338
American Physiological Society, 192
American Protective League, 506
American Psychiatric Association, 218, 460
American Revolution (1775–83) and Revolutionary period, 2–3, **27–29**
abolitionism and, 6
apprenticeship and, 32
chivalry and, 88
conscientious objection and, 104
Crèvecoeur and, 116
divorce and, 132
feminism and, 168
Franklin and, 175
gays in the military, 188
gender roles in, 481
guns and, 198
health and, 202
heroism and, 205
immigration and, 223–24
individualism and, 229
marriage and, 286–87
militarism and, 309
military and, 311
mother–son relationships and, 319
music, 325
nationalism and, 329
old age and, 348
patriarchy and, 355
patriotism and, 358
politics, 363
premarital pregnancy, 408
property and, 377
self-control and, 410, 411
self-made man and, 412
Sons of Liberty, 28, 329, 358, 363, **427–29,** 478
suffragism and, 444
violence and, 478
Washington and, 28, 33, 104, 329, 358, 363, **483–85**
youth and, 513
American Temperance Society, 455
Amos 'n Andy (1928–53), 18, 453
"Analysis of a Phobia in a Five-Year-Old Boy" (Freud), 181
anarchism, 112–13
Andover Academy, 142
Andover Theological Seminary, 343
anesthesia, 297
Anglo-Saxonism. *See* whiteness
Animal House (1978), 180
anorexia, reverse, 58
Anti-Federalists, 329, 358
antifeminism movement, 318
antiheroes
art and, 34–35
Bogart's films and, 60–61
Eastwood's films and, 139
Hollywood and, 212, 214
Romanticism and, 401
Westerns and, 490
anti-immigrant sentiment. *See* nativism
anti-imperialist movement, 226, 227, 482, 495
anti-intellectualism, 109
anti-militarism, 310
Anti-Saloon League, 456
anti-Semitism, 249, 250, 251
antiwar movements, **29–31,** 281–82, 438, 475–76, 482, 507
Apartment, The (1960), 501
Applied Christianity (Gladden), 426
apprenticeship, 7, 22, **31–33,** 37, 65, 141
Arbus, Diane, 35
Aristotle, 147
Arm and Hammer, *37*
Arrowsmith (Lewis), 297
art, **33–35**
African-American manhood and, 17
American Revolution and, 28
Beat movement, **49–51**
Jesus, images of, 191, 247–48, 299, 323, 324, 390, 426–27
New Deal and, 340
Uncle Sam, 274, 330, 467, 505
Arthur, Timothy Shay, **35–36,** 473
artisans, **36–38,** 502
alcohol and, 22
apprenticeship and, 31–32
class and, 96, 97
Gilded Age and, 191
industrialization and, 37–38, 232, 233
Lincoln and, 273
Moby Dick and, 317
nationalism and, **36–38,** 329–30
politics and, 363
Uncle Sam and, 467
urbanization and, 468
work, role of, 499
Aryan Nations, 496
Asian-American manhood, **38–41**
citizenship and, 91
eugenics and, 154
gangsters and, 187
Hollywood and, 213, 214
immigration and, 39–40, 151, 152, 225
martial arts films and, 40–41, 214, 290–92
nativism and, 338–39
racialization and, 381
sports and, 436
assembly-line production, 503
assimilation, 151
A Team, The (1980s), 476
Atlantic Monthly, 209
Atlas, Charles, **41–42,** 56, 59, 203, 353
Attila, Louis, 405

August, Eugene, 304
Austin, Stephen, 330
Autobiography. See Benjamin Franklin's Autobiography
Autobiography of an Ex-Colored Man (Johnson), 17
automobiles, **42–43**
business/corporate America and, 78, 79
consumerism and, 42, 107
do-it-yourself technology and, 450
travel and, 42, 462

B

Bachelor, The (2002), 47
bachelorhood, **45–47**
advertising and, 11
boxing and, 63
consumerism and, 106, 107
heterosexuality and, 208
hoboes and, 211
Magnum, P.I., 454
masturbation and, 295
middle-class manhood and, 308
Odd Couple and, 347
Playboy magazine and, 46–47, 361
prostitution and, 378
republicanism and, 397
television and, 47, 453
Bacon, Kevin, 442
Baden-Powell, Robert S. S., 68
Bakker, Jim, 156
baldness, 58
Baldwin, James, 17
Ball, Thomas, 34
barbershop quartets, 326
Barker-Benfield, G. J., 411
bar mitzvah, 249, *250*
Barnett, Ross, 93
Barton, Bruce, 247, 299, 324, 427
Bartram, William, 463
baseball, **47–49,** 323, 435, 436, 446
basketball, 436
Battle Creek Sanitarium, 255
"Battle Hymn of the Republic" (Howe), 326, 330
"Bear, The" (Faulkner), 221
Beard, Charles A., 117
Beard, Daniel Carter, 68
Beard, George M., 190, 201, 203, 235
beards (facial hair), 273, 274, 335
Beat movement, **49–51**
American Dream and, 26
Brando films and, 70
business/corporate America and, 79
fashion and, 160
Kerouac and, 256
Romanticism and, 401
Beautiful and Damned, The (Fitzgerald), 173
Beecher, Catharine, 86
Beecher, Henry Ward, **51–52**
Bell, Daniel, 98
bella figura, 243
Bellamy, Edward, 77, 372
Benevolent and Protective Order of Elks (BPOE), 176
Benjamin Franklin's Autobiography, 25, 86, 134, 175, 283, 412
berdache, 335, 390, 458, 460
Berg, Vernon, III, 188
Best Years of Our Lives, The (1946), 213
Beverly Hills Cop (1984), 111
Bibb, Henry, 421, 422
Bible Bands, 315
biggerexia, 58
"Big Two-Heated River" (Hemingway), 172
biker gangs, 185
BiNet, 54
birth control, 395, 418
Birth of a Nation (1915), 18, **52–53,** 88, 95, 212, 316, 496
Bisexual Center, 54
bisexuality, **53–54,** 218
Bisexuality: A Reader and Sourcebook (Geller), 54
BiWays, 54
Black Belt Jones (1974), 291
Black Boy (Wright), 66–67, 509
Black Caesar (1973), 187
blackface. *See* minstrelsy
black manhood. *See* African-American manhood
Black Panther Party, 17, **54–56,** 88, 160, 185, 389, 478
Black Power movement, 327, 383, 420, 431
blarney, 239
Blauner, Robert, 500
blaxploitation, 290, 291, 420
blue-collar workers. *See* working-class manhood
blues music, 326
Bly, Robert, 77, 118, 149, 170, 209, 215, 216, 241, 302, 449
Blythe, David Gilmour, 34
Boas, Franz, 493
Bobbitt, John Wayne, 400
body and body image, **56–59**
advertising and, 12, 57
advice literature and, 13–14
art and, 33
cop action films and, 111
crisis of masculinity, 117
fashion and, 159, 160
football and, 174
Gulick and, 197–98
Hollywood Silent Era and, 212
Hudson and, 219–10
Jewish manhood and, 251
London and, 274
old age and, 349
passionate manhood and, 353, 354
Rambo and, 384
self-control and, 234
Superman and, 447–48
technology and, 450
transsexuality and, 458–59
Uncle Sam, 467
Victorian Era and, 56, 474
war and, 95
YMCA and, 511
See also bodybuilding; health and fitness
bodybuilding, **59–60**
Atlas and, 41–42
body image and, 56, 57, 58
health and, 203, 204
passionate manhood and, 353
Sandow and, 56, 59, 203, 353, **405–6**
Schwarzenegger and, 57, 407
Bogart, Humphrey, **60–61,** *213*
Bohemian Club, 300
Bond, James, 12
Bonnie and Clyde (1967), 140
Book of the Courtier, The (Castiglione), 242
Boone, Daniel, **61–62,** 128, 205–6
Boone and Crockett Club, 221
Booth, Evangeline, 299
Born in the U.S.A. (Springsteen), 438
Born to Run (Springsteen), 437
Boston University, 443
Boucicault, Dion, 239
Bourne, Randolph, 374
Bowery B'hoys, 106, 129, 184, 469
Bowie, David, 327
boxing, **62–65,** 129, 237, 435, 436
Boy and His Gang, The (Puffer), 185
Boy George, 327
boyhood, **65–68**
advice literature and, 13, 14, 15
Alger and, 24
apprenticeship, 31–33, 65
Boy Scouts and, 66, 69
Dr. Spock and, 102
education and, 66–67, 141–42
emotional expression and, 147, 148
Father Knows Best and, 164–65
gangs and, 184–86
guns and, 199
hunting and, 221
Iron John and, 241
Jewish manhood and, 249
Leave It to Beaver and, 67, 268–69
momism and, 318
Native American manhood and, 334–35
pornography and, 367
self-control and, 411–12
Tom Sawyer and Huckleberry Finn and, 9–10, 66, 406, 465–66
Wright and, 509
See also adolescence; youth
Boy Problem, The (Forbush), 14
Boy Scouts of America, 14, 66, **68–70,** 148
guns and, 199
momism and, 318
mother–son relationships and, 320
muscular Christianity and, 323
as outdoorsmen, 351
sports and, 435
boy *vs.* man, use of terms, 383, 509
Boyz 'n the Hood (1991), 19, 185
Bradley v. *Illinois*, 372
Brady Bunch (1969–74), 453
Brando, Marlon, 8, 50, **70–71,** 254
breadwinner role (provider role), **71–73**
advertising and, 11
advice literature and, 14
African-American manhood and, 16
alcohol and, 455
Black Panther Party and, 55
class and, 71, 72, 97, 98
consumerism *vs.*, 106, 107
Crèvecoeur and, 116

breadwinner role (*continued*)
crisis of masculinity and, 118
Death of a Salesman and, 126, 127
divorce and, 132, 133
domesticity *vs.*, 120
fashion and, 159
fatherhood and, 161, 162, 163
feminism and, 169–70
Great Depression and, 72, 195–96
heterosexuality and, 208
industrialization and, 232, 233
The Jungle (Sinclair) and, 252
Kramer vs. Kramer and, 258–59
labor movement and unions and, 71, 261, 262
Malcolm X and, 277
marriage and, 286, 287, 288, 289
masculine domesticity *vs.*, 292, 293
middle-class manhood and, 71, 72, 306, 307–8
New Deal and, 340
nuclear family and, 345
Organization Man and, 350
patriarchy and, 355, 357
populism and, 365–66
postmodernism and, 369
Springsteen's music and, 437–38
suburbia and, 440, 441
Victorian Era and, 473
work and, 499, 500, 501
working-class manhood and, 71–72, 503
World War II and, 72, 507
Breines, Paul, 250, 251
Brian's Song (1971), 414
Bringing Up Baby (1938), 193
brinkmanship, 100
Brod, Harry, 305
Brooks, Van Wyck, 246, 374
Brougham, John, 249
Brown, James, 327, 431
Brown, John, 6, 359, 457
Brown, William W., 421, 422
Brown v. *Board of Education of Topeka* (1954), 67, 92
Buchanan, Patrick J., 339
buddy films, **73–75**, 111, 127–28
Buffalo Bill, 62, 206
Bumppo, Natty. *See* Leatherstocking Tales
Buntline, Ned, 489
bureaucratization, **75–78**
character *vs.* personality, 76, 86, 195
crisis of masculinity and, 117
market revolution and, 284
Organization Man and, 76, 350
passionate manhood and, 353
professionalism and, 371, 372
reform movements and, 388
travel and, 462
Burlingame Treaty (1881), 39
Burnett, Leo, 285
Burr, Aaron, *136*, 137
Burroughs, Edgar Rice, 79, 124, 449
Burroughs, William S., 49, 50
Bush, George H. W., 31, 101, 284, 331, 415, 484
Bush, George W., 31, 331
Bushnell, Horace, 86, 155
business/corporate America, 3–4, **78–80**
advertising and, 10–12
Arthur and, 35, 36
bureaucratization of, 76
character *vs.* personality, 86, 195, 443
class and, 97–98
emotional expression and, 148
fashion in, 159, 160
fraternities and, 179
individualism and, 230, 231
Jewish manhood and, 249–50
labor movement and unions and, 262
Leave It to Beaver and, 269
leisure and, 271
male friendship and, 280
market revolution and, 283–84
men's clubs and, 300, 301
middle-class manhood and, 307, 308
Organization Man and, 79, 350–51
Reagan and, 79, 284, 385, 386
reform movements and, 388
self-made man and, 412–13
sexual harassment and, 416–17
Social Gospel movement and, 427
sports and, 49, 174, 435
technology and, 450
Washington portrayals and, 484
work and, 500–501
World War II and, 507
Butch Cassidy and the Sundance Kid (1969), 74, 490
Butler, Judith, 304, 325

C

Cagney, James, 239, 240
Cahan, Abraham, 206
California, University of, at Berkeley, 304
California Gold Rush, **81–82**
Call of the Carpenter, The (White), 426
Call of the Wild (London), 274
Cameron, James, 215
Cammermeyer, Greta, 189
Camp, Walter, 173–74
Campbell, Joseph, 241
Cannibals All! (Fitzhugh), 356
Canutt, Yakima, 485
Cape Cod (Thoreau), 457
capitalism, 3, **82–84**
agrarianism and, 21
Alger and, 24
American Dream and, 25, 26
Arthur and, 36
Beecher and, 51
boyhood and, 66
class and, 97–98
communism *vs.*, 83–84, 99–100
crisis of masculinity and, 117
Darwinism and, 123
democratic manhood and, 129–30
Douglass and, 134, 135
dueling and, 137
emotional expression and, 147
fishing and, 172
gambling and, 183, 184
gangsters and, 186
Graham and, 192
homosexuality and, 217
individualism and, 230
The Jungle and, 252
leisure and, 270
London and, 274
market revolution and, 284
marriage and, 287
Men and Religion Forward Movement and, 299
middle-class manhood and, 306, 307–8
Moby Dick and, 317
mother–son relationships and, 319
passionate manhood and, 354
patriotism and, 359
populism and, 365, 366
Progressive Era and, 374
Reagan and, 385, 386
sentimentalism and, 415
Thoreau and, 457
Victorian Era and, 473
Westerns and, 490
Wright and, 509
Capone, Al, 186, *187*, 243
captains of industry, 97, 230
cardiology, 297
Carlos, John, 436
Carmichael, Stokely, 17, 431
Carnegie, Andrew, 206, 388
Carnegie, Dale, 76, 86, 103, 195, 443
Carroll, James, 30
Carroll, Joseph, 30
Carson, Kit, 62, 206
Carter, Chris, 324
Carter, Jimmy, 385–86
Cartier, Jacques, 335
Casablanca (1942), *213*
Cash, W. J., 429
Castiglione, Baldassare, 242
Castro, Fidel, 101
Catcher in the Rye, The (Salinger), **84–85**
Catholicism, 90, 392
Jesus, images of, 247, 248
Irish-American manhood and, 238
ministry and, 315
nativism and, 338
patriotism and, 359
Century Club, 300
Chan, Jackie, 74
Chandler, Raymond, 130–31
Chaplin, Charlie, 211, 212, 503
character, **85–89**
advice literature and, 13
Boone and, 62
Boy Scouts and, 69
football and, 174
market revolution and, 283–84
muscular Christianity and, 209
passionate manhood and, 353
personality *vs.*, 86–87, 195, 284, 427, 443
sentimentalism and, 414
success manuals and, 443
Charlie Daniels Band, 327
Charlotte Temple (Rowson), 408
Chavez, César, 206
Cherokee, 336
Cheyenne, 390, 458

Chico and the Man (1974–78), 453–54
Childhood and Society (Erikson), 318
Chin, Frank, 40
Chinese-American manhood. *See* Asian-American manhood
Chinese Connection, The (1973), 290
Chinese Exclusion Act (1882), 39, 91
Chinese immigrants, 39, 91
chivalry (protector role), **87–89**
  Father Knows Best and, 164
  guns and, 198, 199
  heroism and, 205
  imperialism and, 226, 227, 228
  Italian-American manhood and, 242
  The Jungle and, 252
  King and, 257–58
  Latino manhood and, 264
  military and, 311–12
  patriarchy and, 356
  populism and, 365, 366
  slavery and, 423, 425
  Spanish-American War and, 433
  suburbia and, 440, 441
  war and, 481, 482
  white supremacism and, 495–96
  World War II and, 507, 508
Christian Identity movement, 339
Christianity
  Catholicism (*See* Catholicism)
  Darwinism and, 124
  evangelicalism (*See* evangelicalism and revivalism)
  Jesus, images of, 247–48
  marriage and, 287
  ministerial authority and, 313–15
  muscular (*See* muscular Christianity)
  politics and, 363
  pornography and, 368
  Protestantism (*See* Protestantism)
  slavery and, 424
  sports and, 436–37
  See also religion and spirituality
Christianity and the Social Crisis (Rauschenbusch), 426
Christianizing the Social Order (Rauschenbusch), 426
Christian Right, 156
Church of Jesus Christ of Latter-day Saints, 288
Cicero, 242
cigarettes, 12, 285–86
Cilley, Jonathan, 137
Cimarron (1931), 490
circumcision, 249
Cisneros, Evangelina, 433
Citizen's Council, 92, 431
citizenship, **89–92**
  African American, 90, 144, 145
  agrarianism and, 20
  American Revolution and, 28, 89
  apprenticeship and, 31, 32
  Asian Americans, 38–39, 91
  Boy Scouts and, 69
  democratic manhood and, 128, 130
  health and, 202
  heroism and, 205
  marriage and, 288
  military service and, 311
  mother–son relationships and, 319, 320
  New Deal and, 340
  patriarchy and, 355
  patriotism and, 360–61
  populism and, 365–66
  Progressive Era and, 90–91, 375
  property and, 377
  race and, 89–91, 382
  republicanism and, 89, 396–98
  Sons of Liberty and, 428
  Spanish-American War and, 434
  suffragism and, 444–46
  war and, 481, 482
  whiteness and, 89, 90, 491
citizen soldiers, 309, 310, 311, 484
city planners, 469–70
City Slickers (1991), 351
civil disobedience, 257–58
"Civil Disobedience" (Thoreau), 457
Civilian Conservation Corps (CCC), *341*, 439
Civilization and Its Discontents (Freud), 124
Civil Rights Act (1964), 93, 416, 417, 493
civil rights movement, 4, **92–94**, 388, 389, 493
  advertising and, 11–12
  African-American manhood and, 17, 92, 93, 383
  Ali and, 64
  Black Panther Party and, 54
  conscientious objection and, 105
  Du Bois and, 16, 17, 142, 246, 356, 372, 375, 381, 382
  King and, 17, 93, 257–58, 389
  Malcolm X and, 277
  men's clubs and, 300
  Mexican-American (Chicano), 265
  music and, 327
  Southern manhood and, 431–32
Civil Service Commission, 75, 403
Civil War (1861-65), **94–96**
  African-Americans soldiers, 95, 143–44, 425
  conscientious objection and, 104
  dueling and, 137
  fraternal organizations and, 176–77
  fraternities and, 178
  gender roles, 481
  imperialism and, 226
  labor movement and unions and, 261
  Lincoln and, 273–74
  Manifest Destiny and, 282
  militarism and, 309–10
  military service and, 95, 143–44, 188, 311
  music and, 326
  nationalism and, 330–31
  patriotism and, 359
  politics and, 364
  pornography and, 367
  republicanism and, 398
  Southern manhood and, 94–95, 430
  strenuous life and, 438–39
Clansman, The (Dixon), 496
Clarke, Lewis, 425
Clark University, 201, 449
class, **96–99**
  alcohol and, 22
  bachelorhood and, 45, 46
  boxing and, 63, 64
  boyhood and, 65, 66
  character and, 86
  chivalry and, 88
  cop action films and, 111
  dueling and, 135
  education and, 141, 142
  fishing and, 172
  fraternities and, 179
  gambling and, 183
  Grapes of Wrath and, 194
  Great Depression and, 195
  hunting and, 220, 221
  industrialization and, 96–97, 232–33, 234
  Jackson and, 245
  men's clubs and, 300
  minstrelsy and, 316
  neurasthenia and, 236
  patriotism and, 359
  prostitution and, 378
  race and, 381–82
  seduction tales and, 410
  Sons of Liberty and, 428
  strenuous life and, 438, 439
  suffragism and, 444, 445
  Tom Sawyer and Huckleberry Finn and, 465
  Victorian cultural beliefs and, 474
  See also middle-class manhood; upper-class manhood; working-class manhood
Clatterbaugh, Kenneth, 305
Clawson, Mary Ann, 279
Clay, Cassius. *See* Ali, Muhammad
Clay, Henry, 412
Claytor, Graham, 188
Cleburne, Patrick Ronayne, 188
Clemmons, Clarence, 438
Clinton, Bill, 31, 87, 189, 365
Clinton, Hillary Rodham, 365
clothing. *See* fashion
Coalition of American Divorce Reform Elements (CADRE), 167
Code of Honor or Rules for the Government of Principles and Seconds in Duelling (Wilson), 136
Cody, William (Buffalo Bill), 62, 206
coeducation, 141–42
Cohan, George M., 240
Colden, Cadwallader, 428
Cold War, **99–101**
  adolescence and, 8
  body image and, 57
  boyhood during, 67
  Boy Scouts and, 69
  Brando's films and, 70

Cold War (*continued*)
capitalism *vs.* communism, 83–84, 99–100
Cooper's films and, 110
cop action films and, 111
crisis of masculinity and, 118
detectives and, 131
domesticity and, 99–100, 121
Father Knows Best and, 164–65
feminism and, 169
Freudian psychoanalytic theory and, 182
gender roles, 482
homosexuality and, 218
immigration and, 225
militarism and, 99, 100, 310
momism and, 318
nationalism and, 331
nuclear family and, 345
patriotism and, 359–60
suburbia and, 441
Superman and, 448
Vietnam War and, 475
Cole, Edwin Louis, 324
colleges. *See* universities and colleges
colonial America
American Dream and, 25
boyhood and, 65–66
breadwinner role and, 71
citizenship and, 89
divorce and, 132
emotion and, 147
fashion and, 159
fatherhood and, 161
gambling and, 183
hunting and, 220
immigration and, 223
individualism and, 229
insanity treatment, 235
juvenile delinquency and, 253
leisure, 269–70
male friendship and, 279
market revolution and, 282–83
marriage and, 286
medicine and, 296
men's clubs, 300
music, 325
Native American manhood and, 334–35
nuclear family and, 344
old age and, 348
patriarchy and, 355, 412
politics and, 363
prostitution and, 378
reproduction and, 394
slavery and, 423
Southern manhood and, 429
suffragism and, 444
wartime gender roles, 481
whiteness and, 491
work, role of, 499
Colored Farmers' National Alliance, 21
Colt, Samuel, 198
Columbine High School, 12
Columbus, Christopher, 486
Common Sense Book of Baby and Child Care, The (Spock), 67, **102,** 148
Common Sense (Paine), 28
communes, 113, 343
communism
capitalism *vs.,* 83–84, 99–100
homosexuality and, 218
individualism *vs.,* 230
labor movement and unions and, 262
patriotism and, 359–60
Reagan and, 385
Superman and, 448
whiteness and, 493
Wright and, 509
Communist Manifesto, The (Marx, Engels), 83
Communist Party of the United States of America (CPUSA), 493
Compleat Angler, or the Contemplative Man's Recreation, The (Walton), 171
computer geeks, 373, 452
computers, 451–52
Comstock, Anthony, 367–68
Comstock Act (1873), 368
"Concord Hymn" (Emerson), 198
Conduct of Life, The (Emerson), 146
Confederate flag, 432
confidence man, 83, **103–4,** 109, 230, 283, 414, 468–69
Confidence-Man: His Masquerade (Melville), 103
Congressional Gold Medal, 485
Congress of Industrial Organizations (CIO), 98, 225, 262, 342, 503–4
Congress of Racial Equality (CORE), 93, 493
conscientious objection, **104–6,** 475–76, 507
consumerism, **106–8**
advertising and, 11
American Dream and, 26
automobiles and, 42, 43, 107
bachelorhood and, 46–47
Beat movement and, 50
boyhood and, 67
Death of a Salesman and, 126, 127
divorce and, 132–33
fashion and, 159
Father's Day and, 165–66
gangsters and, 186
Gilded Age and, 190, 191
health and, 203
leisure and, 270, 271
middle-class manhood and, 107, 307, 308
nuclear family and, 345
Playboy magazine and, 107, 361, 362
self-control and, 411
sports and, 435
suburbia and, 107, 440, 441
Victorian cultural beliefs and, 474
working-class and, 106, 500
contraceptives (birth control), 395, 418
Contrast, The (Tyler), 28, **108–9**
Control of the Tropics, The (Kidd), 123
Conway, Eustace, 351
Coolidge, Calvin, 78
Cooper, Gary, **109–10**
Cooper, James Fenimore, 88, 121, 267–68, 336, 488, 489
cop action films, 74, **110–12**
See also detectives
Copland, Aaron, 326
Coppola, Francis Ford, 187
Coquette, The (Foster), 408
corporate America. *See* business/corporate America
corporate trusts, 388
Cosby Show, The (1984–92), 19, 293, 454
Cosmatos, George Pan, 384
Cosmos Club, 300
Costello, Frank, 243
counterculture, **112–14**
advertising and, 11–12
American Dream and, 26
antiwar movement and, 29
body image and, 57
consumerism and, 107–8
corporate condemnation, 79
Easy Rider and, 140
fashion and, 160
heterosexuality and, 208
individualism and, 231
Jesus, images of, 248
Kerouac and, 256
middle-class manhood and, 308
professionalism and, 372–73
property and, 377
Sexual Revolution and, 418
country music, 327
Court days, 270
courtesy, 415, 474
Courtship of Eddie's Father, The (1969–72), 453
Courtwright, David, 477
Covered Wagon, The (1923), 490
Covey, Edward, 134, 143, 421
cowboys, **114–15**
City Slickers, 351
Gilded Age and, 191
Lone Ranger, 275–76
Marlboro Man, 285–86
Roosevelt and, 403
Wayne and, 485
Western frontier and, 486, 487, 488
creatine, 452
Crèvecoeur, J. Hector St. John, 20, 25, **115–17,** 223, 463, 468, 491
crisis of masculinity, **117–19**
advice literature and, 13, 14–15
body-image anxiety, 57–58
buddy films and, 74
Catcher in the Rye and, 85
counterculture and, 112
Death of a Salesman and, 126–27
Deliverance and, 127–28
football and, 174
fraternities and, 178–79
Freudian psychoanalytic theory and, 182
hunting and, 221
men's movements and, 303
men's studies and, 305
middle-class manhood and, 308
Organization Man and, 350
outdoorsmen and, 351
patriarchy and, 356
postmodernism and, 370
Progressive Era and, 374
Crittenden Report, 188

Crockett, Davy, 62, 67, **119–20,** 130, 351, 358, 487
Crockett Almanacks, The (1835–56), 119, 487
Croly, Herbert, 372
crooning, 325–26
cross-dressing. *See* transvestism
Crouching Tiger, Hidden Dragon (2000), 292
Crow, 458
Cruze, James, 490
Cuba, 101, 227, 433–34
Cuban Missile Crisis (1961), 101
Cukor, George, 212–13
cult of domesticity, **120–22**
breadwinner role and, 71, 120
Cold War and, 99–100
Darwinism and, 123
divorce and, 132
Father Knows Best and, 164
feminism and, 169
fraternal organizations and, 176–77
Jewish manhood and, 249
middle-class manhood and, 120–21
mother–son relationships and, 319
Nation of Islam and, 333
Odd Couple and, 347
physician support of, 297
seduction tales and, 409
suburbia and, 440
cult of personality, 86–87, 195, 284, 427, 443
cult of sensibility, 147
cult of true womanhood, 499
cultural pluralism, 151
Curtis, Tony, 107
Custer, George Armstrong, 336, 337

D

Daley, Richard J., 239, 240
Dances with Wolves (1990), 490–91
dandies, 128
Danforth, Samuel, 294
Daniels, Charlie, 432
Darwin, Charles, 123, 153
Darwinism, **123–25**
advice literature and, 14
Beecher and, 51
capitalism and, 83
emotional expression and, 148
ethnic superiority and, 151
eugenics and, 153
evangelicalism and, 156
Gilded Age and, 190
heterosexuality and, 207
imperialism and, 226
individualism and, 230
London and, 274, 275
prostitution and, 378, 379
reproduction and, 395
strenuous life and, 439
Tarzan and, 449
violence and, 478
white supremacism and, 123, 124, 495
Das Kapital (Marx, Engels), 83
Davis, Jefferson, 94, 330
Dawes Severalty Act (1887), 288
Deadbeat dads, 164
Dead Presidents (1995), 476
Deadwood Dick novels, 489
Dean, James, 8, 50, **125–26,** 254, 386–87
Death in the West, 286
Death of a Salesman (Miller), 79, **126–27,** 284, 501
Death of Jane McCrea, The (Vanderlyn), 34
Declaration on the Question of Admitting Women to the Priesthood, 315
Deer Hunter, The (1978), 221
Deerslayer, The (Cooper), 268
deindustrialization, 308, 357
Deliverance (1972), **127–28,** 221
Dell, Floyd, 374
democratic manhood, 20, 28, 90, **128–30,** 314, 371
Democratic Party, 90
Dempsey, Jack, 64
Denny, Dallas, 54
Dent v. *West Virginia,* 372
DePalma, Brian, 187
depression, 236, 298
Descent of Man, The (Darwin), 123, 395
detectives, **130–31,** 212
cop action films, 111
Magnum, P.I., 131, 454
Shaft, 419–20
Dewey, John, 117, 356, 374
Dharma Bums, The (Kerouac), 256
Diagnosis and Statistical Manual (American Psychiatric Association), 460
Diagnosis Murder, 131
Die Hard films, 111, 131
Diggers, 113
dignity agenda, 326
DiMaggio, Joe, 243, 436
Dimensional Man (Marcuse), 148
Dirty Harry films, 131, 139, 214
Disclosure (1994), 399
disco music, 327
divorce, **131–34**
fatherhood and, 133, 164
fathers' rights and, 133, 166–67
Kramer vs. Kramer and, 259
nuclear family and, 345–46
Odd Couple and, 347
reverse sexism and, 399, 400
suburbia and, 441
television and, 453
World War II and, 508
Divorce and Custody for Men (Metz), 167
Divorce Racket Busters, 167
Dixon, George Washington, 315
Dixon, Thomas, 496
DJ Tricky, 327
Dodd, Sonora Smart, 165
Dog Day Afternoon (1975), 74
do-it-yourself, 293, 450–51
Dole, Bob, 189
domesticity. *See* cult of domesticity; masculine domesticity
dominant masculinity, 150, 151, 152
Dooner, P. W., 39
Do the Right Thing (1989), 19
double consciousness, 382
double standard, 408, 409
Douglas, Ann, 117
Douglass, Frederick, **134–35**
African-American manhood and, 16, 134–35
feminism and, 169
individualism and, 230
slave narratives and, 134, 421, 422, 424, 430
Victorian beliefs and, 474
Downing, Jackson, 450
Doyle, Arthur Conan, 130
Doyle, Richard, 167
Dr. Jekyll and Mr. Hyde (Stevenson), 124
Dr. Strangelove, Or, How I Stopped Worrying and Learned to Love the Bomb (1963), 100
Dragnet, 131
Dress for Success (Molloy), 160
Du Bois, W. E. B., 16, 17, 142, 356, 372, 375, 381, 382
dueling, 87, **135–37,** 245
Dunne, John Gregory, 240
Durand, Asher B., 34
Durant, Henry, 117
Dwight, Timothy, 86
Dynamic of Manhood, The (Gulick), 197

E

Eakins, Thomas, 33
Eastman, Max, 117, 374
East of Eden (1955), 125
Eastwood, Clint, 131, **139,** 213–14
Easy Rider (1969), 74, **140–41**
economy of sperm theory, 255, 411
Eddy, Daniel, 86, 514
Edison, Thomas, 450
education and schools, **141–43**
African-American boyhood and, 66–67
American Dream and, 26
character development and, 86
desegregation, 67, 92
football and, 174
Jewish manhood and, 249, 250
middle-class manhood and, 306
ministerial authority and, 314
professionalism and, 371, 372, 373
See also universities and colleges
Edwards, Jonathan, 155
efficiency experts, 374, 503
Ehrenreich, Barbara, 304
Eighteenth Amendment (1919), 456
Eisenhower, Dwight D., 100, 297–98, 364
electronic pornography, 368
Ellis, Havelock, 53, 295, 460
Ellison, Ralph, 17, 237
Ely, Edward, 81
Ely, Richard T., 426
emancipation, 16–17, 34, 95, 134, **143–45,** 273–74
Emancipation (Ball), 34
Emancipation Proclamation (1863), 95, 143
Emerson, Ralph Waldo, **146–47**
Beat movement and, 49–50
emancipation and, 134
emotion and, 148
guns and, 198
individualism and, 146, 401
nationalism and, 330
self-reliance and, 412

Emerson, Ralph Waldo (*continued*)
strenuous life and, 439
Eminem, 152, 327, 494
emotion, **147–50**
advice literature and, 14, 15
boyhood and, 67
dueling and, 136–37
evangelicalism and revivalism and, 155, 156
Gulick and, 197
Kerouac and, 256
Lawrence and, 266–67
male friendship and, 278, 279, 280
mythopoetic men's movement and, 302
Odd Couple and, 347
Romanticism and, 400, 401
Schwarzenegger's films, 407
self-control and, 147, 410, 411
sensitive male and, 149, 413, 414
sincerity of, 414–15
television and *(Magnum, P.I.)*, 454
Victorian Era and, 414–15, 474
Endangered Black Family, The (Hare and Hare), 18
engineers, 450
English Only movement, 339
Enlightenment
corporal punishment and, 479
cult of sensibility, 147
feminism and, 168
Franklin and, 175
individualism and, 161
insanity treatment and, 235
rationality and, 83
Rush and, 411
seduction tales and, 409
Enter the Dragon (1973), 291
Episcopal Church, 315
Equal Pay Act (1963), 416
Equal Rights Amendment (ERA), 357
Erikson, Erik, 318
Eros and Civilization (Marcuse), 148, 368, 418–19
Esquire (magazine), 50, 107, 159
ethnicity, **150–53**
boxing and, 62, 63, 64
gangs and, 185
gangsters and, 187
Great Depression and, 196
heroism and, 206
immigration and, 223–25
nativism and, 338
race and, 150, 381–82
sports and, 436
Springsteen's music and, 438
television and, 453–54
urbanization and, 469
violence and, 477
whiteness and, 493
See also specific ethnicities
etiquette, 473, 474
eugenics, **153–55**
Eureka College, 385
Europe, James Reese, 326
evangelicalism and revivalism, **155–57**
general, 390
Great Awakening, 155
Jesus, images of, 247
leisure and, 270, 271
marriage and, 287, 289
masturbation and, 295
Men and Religion Forward Movement, 156, 247, **299,** 323, 390, 427
ministerial authority and, 314
Promise Keepers (*See* Promise Keepers)
Second Great Awakening, 81, 155, 192, 202, 343
Social Gospel movement, 426–27
sports and, 436–37
Sunday, Billy, 156, 247, 314, 323, **446–47**
youth and, 514
evolution. *See* Darwinism
extreme sports, 437

F

facial hair, 273, 274, 335
Fairbanks, Douglas, 212
Fair Labor Standards Act (1938), 342
family. *See* nuclear family
Family and Medical Leave Act (1993), 259
Fard, W. D., 332
Farewell to Arms, A (Hemingway), 204
Farm, The, 113
farmers. *See* agrarianism; yeoman farmers
Farnham, Eliza W., 81
Farrakhan, Louis, 18, *18,* 303, 334, 392
Farrell, Warren, 14, 149, 302
fashion, **159–61**
advertising and, 12
consumerism and, 106
Playboy magazine and, 361
Victorian Era and, 473
fatherhood, **161–64**
advice literature and, 14, 15, 163, 164
boyhood and, 66, 67
breadwinner role and, 161, 162, 163
corporal punishment and, 479
Crèvecoeur and, 115–16
Death of a Salesman and, 126, 127
divorce and, 133, 164
Dr. Spock and, 102
emotional expression and, 147–48, 149
Father Knows Best and, 164–65
Father's Day and, 165–66
fathers' rights movement and, 166–67
fishing and, 171
immigrants and, 224
industrialization and, 233
Irish-American manhood and, 240
Iron John and, 241
Jewish manhood and, 249, 250, 251
juvenile delinquency and, 254
Kramer vs. Kramer, 133, **258–59,** 322, 399
Leave It to Beaver and, 268–69
masculine domesticity and, 293
middle-class manhood and, 162, 163, 306, 307
Mr. Mom and, 322
mythopoetic men's movement and, 241, 302
nuclear family and, 344, 345, 346
patriarchy and, 161
Rebel Without a Cause and, 386–87
reproduction, 394, 395, 396
Schwarzenegger's films, 408
slavery and, 421, 423
suburbia and, 440, 441, 442
Superman and, 448
television and, 452–53, 454
Father Knows Best (1954–63), 102, 121, **164–65,** 289, 293, 441, 452–53
Father's Day, **165–66**
fathers' rights, **166–68**
divorce and, 133
genetic matching and, 167, 395
Kramer vs. Kramer and, 259
men's rights movement and, 302
reverse sexism and, 399, 400
Faubus, Orval, 93
Faulkner, William, 221
Federal Bureau of Investigation, 188
Federal Council of the Churches of Christ, 299
Federal Emergency Relief Administration, 340
Federalists, 329, 358
Federal Reserve Board, 76
Feminine Mystique, The (Friedan), 320, 419
femininity/feminization
African-American men and, 16
Asian men and, 39, 40
boyhood and, 66
circumcision and, 249, 250
communism and, 99–100
consumerism and, 106, 411
cult of domesticity and, 120
education and, 141, 142
emotion and, 147, 148, 415
evangelicalism and, 155–56
fashion and, 159
football and, 174
fraternal organizations and, 176
gangs and, 185
homosexuality and, 217–18
hunting and, 221
Jesus, images of, 247
imperialism and, 227, 228
Jewish manhood and, 249
leisure and, 269, 270
London's novels and, 274
middle-class fears of, 307
ministry and, 314
music and, 326
sensitive male and, 413
feminism, **168–71**
abolitionism and, 5–6, 168–69
advertising and, 12
advice literature and, 14
Black Panther Party and, 55
breadwinner role and, 289
chivalry and, 88
civil rights movement and, 93
counterculture and, 113
crisis of masculinity and, 117
Douglass and, 135, 169

Dr. Spock and, 102
eugenics and, 154
fatherhood and, 163
fathers' rights movement and, 166–67
Freudian psychoanalytic theory and, 182
heterosexuality and, 208
Hollywood and, 214
Kramer vs. Kramer and, 259
men's clubs and, 300
men's movements and, 301–2
men's studies and, 304
military service and, 311–13
momism and, 318
mother–son relationships and, 320
Mr. Mom and, 322
muscular Christianity and, 323, 324
nativism and, 339
nuclear family and, 345–46
patriarchy and, 356, 357
politics and, 364, 365
pornography and, 368
postmodernism and, 369
professionalism and, 372–73
prostitution and, 379
reform movements and, 389
reverse sexism and, 399
sexual harassment and, 416, 417
Sexual Revolution and, 418, 419
sexual violence and, 479
sports and, 436
suburbia and, 441
white supremacism and, 496
Ferlinghetti, Lawrence, 50
FHM (magazine), 108
Fifteenth Amendment (1870), 90, 144, 444
54th Massachusetts Infantry, 95
Filene, Peter, 304
Film. *See* Hollywood
Filmer, Robert, 45
Finn, Huckleberry, **9–10,** 66, 211, 406, 465
Fire in the Belly (Keen), 77
First Blood (1972), 384
Fisher King, The (1991), 74
fishing, **171–72,** 205, 406
Fistful of Dollars, A (1964), 139
Fists of Fury (1973), 290
Fithian, Philip Vickers, 325
fitness. *See* body and body image; bodybuilding; health
Fitzgerald, F. Scott, 107, **172–73**
Fitzhugh, George, 16, 356
Flagg, James Montgomery, 467
flaneur, 470
Fliegelman, Jay, 28
fogy, 349
Follett, Ken, 251
Fonda, Peter, 140
football, **173–75**
For a Few Dollars More (1965), 139
Forbush, William B., 14
Ford, Henry, 42, 78, 79, 450, 503
Ford, John, 485, 490
Fordism, 503
Forrest, Edwin, 129
Forrest Gump (1986), 415–16
48 Hours (1982), 74, 111
For Whom the Bell Tolls (Hemingway), 204
Fosdick, Harry Emerson, 426
Foster, Hannah, 408, 409
Foster, Stephen, 325
Foster, William Z., 230
Fountainhead (Rand), 77
Fourteenth Amendment (1868), 90, 144, 288, 444
Fowler, O. S., 13, 295
Fox, William, 213
Foyt, A. J., 43
franchise. *See* suffragism
Frank, Waldo, 374
Franklin, Benjamin, **175–76**
agrarianism and, 20
character and, 86
Junto men's club and, 300
market revolution and, 283
self-made man and, 25, 175, 363, 412
Steuben and, 188
urbanization and, 468
Frank Rivers (Ingraham), 409
Fraternal Order of Eagles (FOE), 176
fraternal organizations, **176–78**
adolescence and, 7
alcohol and, 23
chivalry and, 88
Gilded Age and, 191
Ku Klux Klan (*See* Ku Klux Klan)
leisure and, 270
male friendship and, 176–77, 279, 280
music and, 326
passionate manhood and, 353
religion and spirituality and, 390
temperance movement and, 455
See also men's clubs
fraternities, 142, **178–71,** 326
Frazier, Joe, 64
Fredrickson, George M., 117
"Freebird" (Lynyrd Skynyrd), 327
Freedmen's Bureau, 75
Free-Soil Party, 6, 21
Freudian psychoanalytic theory, **181–82**
Darwinism and, 124
Dr. Spock and, 102
insanity and, 182, 236
Lawrence and, 266
mother–son relationships and, 181, 182, 320
sexuality and, 181, 207, 418
Friedan, Betty, 318, 320, 419
friendship. *See* male friendship
From Manger to Throne (Tallmadge), 426
Fruit of Islam, 333
Full Personality Expression (FPE), 461
Fu Manchu, 339

G

gaffer, 349
gambling, 81, 82, 109, **183–84,** 300, 426
gangs, 14, **184–86,** 253, 469, 470, 478
gangsta rap, 187
gangsters, 107, **186–87,** 212, 243, 244, 251
Garden of Stone (1987), 476
Gardiner, Augustus Kingsley, 234
Garlits, Don, 43
Garnett, Henry Highland, 16
Garrison, William Lloyd, 5, 6, 169, 422
Garvey, Marcus, 17, 332, 392
Gaskin, Stephen, 113
Gates, Bill, 451
Gates, Henry Louis, 143
Gay Liberation Front (GLF), 53
Gay Pride, 419
gay rights movement, 218, 388, 389
advertising and, 12
heterosexuality and, 208
nuclear family and, 345–46
Sexual Revolution and, 418, 419
gays in the military, 31, **188–89,** 312
Geller, Thomas, 54
Generation of Vipers (Wylie), 182, 318, 320
genetic matching, 167, 395
genteel performance, 415
gentility, 473–74
Gentlemen's Quarterly (magazine), 107, 159
George Balcombe (Tucker), 121
George III, King of England, 28
Gerber, Henry, 218
German-Americans, 152
German immigrants, 223, 224
Germany, 310
Gettysburg Address, 273, 330
Ghost and the Darkness (1996), 221
Ghost Dance, 390
G.I. Bill (1944), 26, 289
G.I. Joe, 67
Giant (1955), 125
Gibson, Mel, 74, 111
Gilbert, Elizabeth, 351
Gilbreth, Frank and Lillian, 374
Gilded Age (1873–1900), **189–92**
Alger and, 24
Darwinism and, 123, 190
heroism and, 206
Spanish-American War, 433–34
success manuals and, 442
Tarzan and, 449
Gillette, Douglas, 77, 449
Gilligan, Carol, 304
Gilman, Charlotte Perkins, 297, 356
Gilmore, Patrick S., 325
Ginsberg, Allen, 49, 50
Gitlin, Todd, 30
Giuliani, Rudoph, 331
Givens, Charles J., 443
Gladden, Washington, 426
glee clubs, 326
Glenn, John, 349
globalism, 228
Glover, Danny, 74
Godfather, The (1972), 70, 152, 244
Godspell (1971), 248
Goldberg, Herb, 149, 302
Gold Rush. *See* California Gold Rush
Goldwyn, Samuel, 213
Gompers, Samuel, 71, 261, 500, 503

Gone With The Wind (1939), 212–13
Good, the Bad, and the Ugly, The (1967), 139
good-old-boy networks, 370
Goodrich, Samuel, 473
Good Times (1974–79), 19, 454
Gordan, Jeff, 324
government, bureaucratization of, 75–77
Graham, Sylvester, 13, 56, **192–93,** 202, 234, 294, 295, 388, 474, 514
Graham Journal of Health and Longevity, 192
Grand Review of the Grand Army of the Republic, 331
Grand United Order of Odd Fellows in America, 177
Grange, The, 176
Grant, Cary, **193–94**
Grapes of Wrath, The (Steinbeck), 21, **194–95**
Graves, William, 137
Great Awakening, 155
Great Depression, **195–96**
  adolescence and, 8
  advertising during, 11
  agrarianism and, 21
  American Dream and, 26
  Bogart films and, 60
  breadwinner role and, 72, 195
  class and, 97–98, 195, 196
  consumerism and, 107
  domesticity and, 121
  fatherhood and, 163
  Father's Day and, 166
  feminism and, 169
  gangsters and, 186
  Grapes of Wrath and, 194–95
  heroism and, 206
  individualism and, 230
  labor movement and unions and, 196, 262
  militarism and, 310
  muscular Christianity and, 324
  Nation of Islam and, 332
  New Deal (*See* New Deal)
  populism and, 367
  suffragism and, 445
  Superman and, 448
  working-class manhood and, 195, 196, 503
Great Gatsby, The (Fitzgerald), 107, 172, 173
Great Train Robbery, The (1903), 490
Great White Fleet, 492
Green Berets, The (1968), 485
Grenada, 483
Grey, Zane, 489
Griffith, D. W., 52, 95, 212, 496
Grimké, Angelina, 5
Grimké, Sarah, 5, 314
Grinnell, George Bird, 220–21
Groom, Winston, 415–16
Gross Clinic, The (Eakins), 33
Guadalupe-Hidalgo, Treaty of (1848), 264
Gulf War (1991), 310, 483
Gulf War (2003), 483
Gulick, Luther Halsey, **197–98,** 323
guns, 55, **198–99,** 351–52, 432
Gunsmoke (1955–75), 453, 490
Guthrie, Woody, 206, 462

H

Haddock, Frank Channing, 443
Haines, Thomas L., 443
hair, 58, 273, 274, 335, 348
Haj, The (Uris), 251
Hall, Granville Stanley, **201–2**
  adolescence and, 7–8, 14, 66, 148, 514
  masturbation and, 295
  muscular Christianity and, 323
  Tarzan and, 449
Hamilton, Alexander, *136,* 137, 329, 371
Hamlet (Shakespeare), 147
Hammett, Dashiell, 131
Hampton University (Hampton Normal and Agricultural Institute), 142
Handsome Lake (Seneca), 336
Hare, Nathan and Julia, 18
Harlem Renaissance, 17, 248, 320
Harrigan, Edward, 239
Harris, David, 30
Harrison, William Henry, 90, *129,* 130, 487
Harris v. *Forklift Systems, Inc.* (1993), 417
Hart, William S., 114, 115, 490
Harvard Divinity School, 209
Harvard University (Harvard College), 142, 300, 443, 457, 460
Hasty Pudding Club, 300
Hawaii, annexation of, 227
Hawk, Tony, 437
Hawthorne, Nathaniel, 148, 401
Hay, Harry, 419
Hayden, Tom, 30
Hazards of Being Male: Surviving the Myth of Masculine Privilege (Goldberg), 302
Head of Christ (Sallman), 248
healing ritual, 241
health and fitness, **202–4**
  alcohol and, 456
  Atlas and, 41–42
  breadwinner role and, 289
  circumcision and, 249
  emotional expression and, 149
  fashion and, 160
  Graham and, 192–93, 202
  heart disease, 308
  insanity and, 235–36
  Kellogg and, 255
  masturbation and, 294–95
  medicine and, 296–98
  muscular Christianity and, 209–10, 323–24
  old age and, 349
  Sandow and, 405
  self-control and, 306
  smoking and, 286
  sports and, 436
  Vietnam War and, 476
  YMCA and, 511, 512
  See also body; bodybuilding
Hearn, Thomas, 324
Hearst, William Randolph, 433
heart disease, 297–98, 308
Heat Moon, William Least, 464
Hefner, Hugh, 361
Hell's Angels, 185
helluvafella image, 429, 432
Hemingway, Ernest, 88, **204–5**
  Cooper and, 110
  fishing and, 171–72, 205
  Fitzgerald and, 173
  hunting and, 204, 221
  war and, 204, 506
Herland (Gilman), 356
heroism, **205–7**
  art and, 33–34
  Bogart's films and, 60–61
  Cooper's films and, 109–10
  cop action films and, 74, 110–12
  Crockett and, **119–20**
  detectives and, 130–31
  Eastwood's films and, 139
  gangsters and, 186–87
  Grant's films and, 193–94
  Grapes of Wrath and, 194–95
  guns and, 198
  Hemingway and, 204–5
  Hollywood and, 212, 213, 214
  imperialism and, 226, 227
  inventors and, 450
  Jackson and, 245
  Jewish manhood and, 251
  Leatherstocking Tales and, 267–68
  Lone Ranger, 275–76
  martial arts films and, 290–92
  nationalism and, 329, 330, 331
  physicians and, 297
  Rambo and, 384
  Romanticism and, 401
  Roosevelt and, 403
  Schwarzenegger's films and, 407
  self-made man and, 412, 413
  Shaft and, 419–20
  slavery and, 424
  sports and, 436
  Superman and, 447–48
  Tarzan and, 449
  Twain and, 465–66
  Vietnam and, 476
  war and, 205, 481, 482, 483
  Washington and, 484
  Wayne and, 485
  Western frontier and, 486, 487, 488
  Westerns and, 275–76, 489, 490
Hershieser, Oral, 324
heterosexuality, **207–9**
  advice literature and, 14, 15
  bachelorhood and, 46–47
  bisexuality *vs.,* 53
  Boy Scouts and, 69
  Catcher in the Rye and, 85
  Freudian psychoanalytic theory and, 181–82
  Grant's films and, 193–94
  Hollywood and, 212
  homosexuality *vs.,* concepts of, 207–8, 217, 218–19
  Kellogg's theories, 255
  men's movements and, 301, 303
  Noyes and, 342–43
  Playboy magazine and, 361–62
  postmodernism and, 369, 370
  prostitution and, 378–79
  seduction tales and, 408–10
  sensitive male and, 413
  Sexual Revolution and, 418–19
  television and, 452

transvestism and, 461
HGTV, 451
Higginson, Thomas Wentworth, **209–10,** 323, 497
Higham, John, 117
High Noon (1952), 110, 490
high-tech masculinity, 451–52
hijra, 460
Him/Her/Self: Sex Roles in Modern America (Filene), 304
Hine, Lewis, 34, 500
hip-hop, 327
hippies, 112–14
Hirschfeld, Magnus, 460
Hispanic Americans, 225. *See also* Latino manhood
HIV, 265, 395
Hoar, George Frisbie, 434
hoboes, 34–35, 196, **210–11,** 253, 463
Hoffa, Jimmy, 504
Hoffman, Bob, 59
Hoffman, Dustin, 258–59
Hofstadter, Richard, 388
Hollywood, **212–15**
African-American manhood and, 19, 52–53, 212, 213, 214, 420
Asian-American manhood and, 40–41, 214, 290–92
Birth of a Nation, 18, **52–53,** 88, 95, 212, 316, 496
body image and, 57
Bogart's films, 60–61
Brando's films, 8, 50, **70–71,** 254
breadwinner role and, 72
buddy films, **73–75,** 111, 127–28
Cold War and, 100
consumerism and, 107
Cooper's films, 109–10
cop action films, 74, **110–12**
cowboys (*See* cowboys)
Davy Crockett films, 119
Dean's films, 8, 50, **125–26,** 254, 386–87
Deliverance, **127–28,** 221
detectives, 111, 131, 212
Eastwood's films, 139, 213–14
Easy Rider, 74, **140–41**
fatherhood and, 133, 258–59, 322, 386–87, 399, 408
feminism and, 170
Freudian psychoanalytic theory and, 182
gangsters and, 186, 187, 212
Grant's films, 193–94
homosexuality and, 212–13, 219
hunting and, 221
Irish-American manhood and, 239, 240
Italian-American manhood and, 243, 244
Jesus, images of, 248
Kramer vs. Kramer, 133, **258–59,** 322, 399
market revolution and, 284
martial arts films, 40–41, 214, 290–92
masculine domesticity and, 133, 293, 322
Mr. Mom, 170, **322–23,** 370
old age and, 349
Reagan and, 385
Rebel Without a Cause, 8, 50, 125, *125,* 126, **386–87**
reverse sexism and, 399
Romanticism and, 401
Schwarzenegger's films, 57, 59, 111–12, 214, 407, **407–8**
sensitive male and, 414
suburbia and, 442
Superman, 448
Vietnam veterans and, 476
violence and, 479, 480
Wayne's films, 114, 115, 206, **485–86**
Westerns (*See* Westerns)
Holmes, Sherlock, 130
Home Book of Modern Medicine (Kellogg), 255
Home Depot, 451
home improvement, 293, 450–51
Home Improvement (1991–99), 170, **215–16,** 293, 442, 451
home ownership, 293, 377, 440, 441
homo faber, 499
homosexuality, **216–19**
Alger and, 24
antiwar movement and, 31
art and, 35
bachelorhood and, 46
Beat movement and, 50
bisexuality and, 53, 54
body image and, 57
Boy Scouts and, 69
Brando's films and, 70
Catcher in the Rye and, 85
Cold War and, 99
communism and, 218
Darwinism and, 123
Dean and, 126
Deliverance and, 127–28
fatherhood and, 164
fraternities and, 180
Freudian psychoanalytic theory and, 181, 182
gay rights movement, 12, 218, 388, 389
gays in the military, 31, **188–89,** 312
Gilded Age and, 190
Great Depression and, 195, 196
heterosexuality *vs.,* concepts of, 207–8, 217, 218–19
hoboes and, 211
Hollywood and, 70, 126, 127–28, 212–13, 387
Hudson and, 219–10
Invisible Man and, 237
Italian-American manhood and, 243
Latino manhood and, 265
male friendship and, 278, 279, 280
men's studies and, 305
ministry and, 315
Moby Dick and, 317
momism and, 318
mother–son relationships and, 320
music and, 326, 327
Native American manhood and, 335
nativism and, 339
Promise Keepers and, 376
Rebel Without a Cause and, 387
reform movements and, 388, 389
republicanism and, 397
sensitive male and, 413
Sexual Revolution and, 419
Springsteen and, 438
television and, 219, 454
transsexuality and, 458
transvestism and, 460, 461
urbanization and, 469
Victorian Era and, 474
Whitman and, 497
YMCA and, 512
Honeymooners, The (1955–56), 504
honor, 136, 137, 477
Hoover, Herbert, 230
Hoover, J. Edgar, 188
Hopper, Dennis, 140
Hose and Heels, 461
hostile environment, 417
Houdini, Harry, 56
Houston, Sam, 330
Howe, Julia Ward, 326, 330
Howl (Ginsberg), 49, 50
How to Win Friends and Influence People (Carnegie), 76, 86, 103, 195, 443
Huckleberry Finn, **9–10,** 66, 211, 406, 465
Hudson, Rock, 107, **219–10**
Hudson River School, 33–34
Hughes, John, 322
Hughes, Langston, 17
Hughes, Thomas, 209, 323
Human Sexual Response (Masters and Johnson), 418
Hume, David, 409
hunting, **220–22**
Boone and, 61, 62
Crockett and, 119
guns and, 198, 199
Hemingway and, 204
heroism and, 206
Leatherstocking Tales and, 267
leisure and, 271
Native American manhood and, 65, 334, 335
Roosevelt and, 402, 403
slaves and, 424
Hunting Trips of a Ranchman (Roosevelt), 402
Hussein, Saddam, 360
Hutchins, Hapgood, 374
Hutchinson, Anne, 314
Hutchinson, Thomas, 428
Hyde, Edward, Lord Cornbury, 460
hysteria, 249

I

"I Am Woman" (Reddy), 327
Ice Cube, 327
Ignatiev, Noel, 239
I'll Take My Stand (Ransom), 431
I Love Lucy (1951–57), 453
Immigration Act (1924), 91
Immigration and Nationality Act (1952), 39
Immigration and Nationality Act amendments (1965), 40, 225, 493
immigration/immigrants, 4, **223–26**

immigration/immigrants (*continued*)
alcohol and, 22, 224
anti-immigration, 90, 91, 123, 184, 250, **338–40**
Asian, 38, 39–40
bachelorhood and, 46
bodybuilding and, 59
boxing and, 64
boyhood and, 66, 67
citizenship and, 90–91
Crèvecoeur and, 116, 223
ethnic masculinity and, 150–52
eugenics and, 153, 154
gangs and, 184–85
Great Depression and, 196
Irish, 223, 224, 225, 237–38
Jewish, 249
juvenile delinquency and, 253
Latino manhood and, 264–65
nationalism and, 331
nativism, 90, 91, 123, 184, 250, 338–39
patriarchy and, 223, 224, 356
prostitution and, 378–79
reproduction and, 395
urbanization and, 468, 469
whiteness and, 492, 493
working-class manhood and, 502
Immigration Restriction League, 338
imperialism, **226–29**
chivalry (protector role) and, 88, 226, 227, 228
Darwinism and, 123
emotional expression and, 148
Latino manhood and, 263–64
militarism and, 310
nationalism and, 331
passionate manhood and, 353
patriarchy and, 226–28, 356
Philippines, 226, 227, 228, 481–82
Rambo and, 384
Spanish-American War, 226, 227, 310, 353, 374, 403, **433–34,** 481–82
strenuous life and, 439
Tarzan and, 449
Western frontier and, 488
whiteness and, 226–28, 492
white supremacism and, 226–27, 495
Improved Benevolent and Protective Order of Elks of the World, 177
Incredible Hulk, The (1977–82), 453
Independent Order of Good Samaritans and Daughters of Samaria, 177
Independent Order of Odd Fellows (IOOF), 176
individualism, **229–31**
art and, 34–35
Asian-American manhood and, 40
baseball and, 48, 49
body image and, 56
Bogart's films and, 61
Boone and, 61–62
boxing and, 63, 64
bureaucratization and, 76–77
Dean's films and, 125–26
Douglass and, 134, 135
Easy Rider and, 140
Emerson and, 146
Hemingway and, 204
heroism and, 205
James and, 246
The Jungle and, 252
London and, 274
male friendship and, 278
market revolution and, 283, 284
Marlboro Man and, 286
middle-class manhood and, 307, 308
militarism and, 309
ministry and, 314
Moby Dick and, 317
Organization Man and, 350
postmodernism and, 370
Progressive Era and, 374
Rambo and, 384
reform movements and, 387
republicanism and, 396
Romanticism and, 401
Roosevelt and, 402, 403
self-control and, 411
Social Gospel movement and, 426
sports and, 435
success manuals and, 443
Thoreau and, 457
travel narratives and, 464
urbanization and, 469
Victorian Era and, 473
Western frontier and, 486, 487
Whitman and, 497
industrialization, **231–35**
alcohol and, 22, 233
American Dream and, 25
apprenticeship and, 32
artisans and, 36, 37–38
automobiles and, 42
bodybuilding and, 41
boyhood and, 66
breadwinner role and, 232, 233
Civil War and, 94
class and, 96–97, 98, 232–33, 234
cowboys and, 114
democratic manhood and, 128–30
emotional expression and, 147, 148
fashion and, 159
football and, 174
Gilded Age and, 190, 191
Graham and, 192
health and, 202, 203
hoboes and, 210–11
hunting and, 220
immigrants and, 223–24
Iron John and, 241
labor movement and unions and, 261–62
Latino manhood and, 264–65
leisure and, 270
Native American manhood and, 336
nuclear family and, 344, 345
outdoorsmen and, 351
passionate manhood and, 353
patriarchy and, 231, 232, 233–34, 355
self-control and, 411
sexuality and, 234
Social Gospel movement and, 426
tinkering technology and, 450
travel and, 462
Western frontier and, 486, 487
working-class manhood and, 232–33, 234, 502–3
YMCA and, 511
Industrial Workers of the World (IWW), 261–62, 503
infertility, 396
Influence of Sea-Power Upon History, The (Mahan), 226, 433
Ingraham, Joseph Holt, 409
In His Steps (Sheldon), 426
insanity, **235–36**
Irish-American manhood and, 240
masturbation and, 295
momism and, 318
neurasthenia, 190, 201, 203, 235–36, 297
insurance industry, 164, 176–77
International Committee of the YMCA, 512
International Conference of Transgender Law and Employment Policy, 459
Internet, 15, 167, 451
Interpretation of Dreams, The (Freud), 181
Interstate Highway Act (1956), 440
interventionist state, 374
Invisible Man (Ellison), **237**
Iran-Contra affair, 386
Irish-American manhood, 152, **237–41**
boxing and, 63, 64
gangsters and, 187
immigration and, 151, 223, 224, 225, 237–38, 492
patriotism and, 239–40, 359
Iron Horse, The (1924), 490
Iron John: A Book About Men (Bly), 77, 118, 149, 170, 209, 215, 216, **241–42,** 302, 449
Iroquois, 335
Irving, Washington, 171, 464
Islam, 392–93. *See also* Nation of Islam
Israel, 251
Italian-American manhood, 152, **242–44**
Catholicism and, 392
gangs and, 185
gangsters and, 187
Hollywood and, 214
immigration and, 151, 224, 225, 242–43
sports and, 436
Ives, Charles, 326
Iwo Jima memorial, *360,* 482

J

Jackson, Andrew, **245–46**
agrarianism and, 20–21
bureaucratization and, 75
common man and, 90
Crockett and, 119
democratic manhood and, 128, 129
dueling and, 135–36

Manifest Destiny and, 281
nationalism and, 329, 330
politics and, 364
populism and, 366
Western frontier and, 487, 488
Jackson, Jesse, 357
Jackson, Mark, 324
Jailbird, The (Townsend), 249
James, Henry, 243
James, William, **246–47,** 353, 439
Japan, 310, 360
Japanese immigrants, 39–40, 91
Jay-Z, 19
jazz, 50, 326
Jazz Age, 172
Jazz Singer, The (1927), 316, 493
Jefferson, Thomas, 364, 468
agrarianism and, 20, 89, 194, 329, 365, 468
Declaration of Independence and, 28
nationalism and, 329–30
Western frontier and, 487
whiteness and, 491
Jeffersons, The (1975–85), 19, 454
Jenkins, Peter, 464
Jesus, images of, **247–48**
Gilded Age and, 191
Men and Religion Forward Movement and, 299
muscular Christianity and, 323, 324
Protestantism and, 390
Social Gospel movement and, 426–27
Jesus Christ Superstar (1971), 248
Jewish Defense League, 251
Jewish manhood, **248–52**
gangsters and, 187
Hollywood and, 213
immigration and, 224, 248, 249–50, 338
religion and spirituality and, 391–92
Superman and, 447–48
whiteness and, 493
Jim Crow laws, 145, 492
Jim Crow (minstrelsy character), 315, 316
Jobs, Steve, 451
John, Dale, 86
John Birch Society, 366
Johnson, Jack, 64, 382
Johnson, James Weldon, 17
Johnson, Lyndon B., 76, 93, 101, 365, 475
Johnson, Virginia E., 418
Johnson-Reed Act (1924), 225, 493
John Wayne Bobbitt . . . Uncut (1994), 400
Jolson, Al, 493
Jones, Rufus, 427
Jordan, Michael, 436
Jorgenson, Christine, 458, *459*
Journal of Men's Studies, 302, 305
journeymen, 31, 33, 37, 38, 97, 502
Jung, Carl, 241, 302
Jungle, The (Sinclair), **252**
Junior (1994), 112
Junto, 300
Juvenile Court, 253
juvenile delinquency, 66, 102, **253–54,** 320, 478–79

K

Kahane, Meir, 251
Kant, Immanuel, 147
Keaton, Buster, 212
Keaton, Michael, 322
Keayne, Robert, 283
Keen, Sam, 77
Keitel, Harvey, 214
Kellert, Stephen, 221
Kellogg, John Harvey, 56, 203, **255–56,** 474
Kennedy, John F., 100–101, 203, 349, 364, 416, 439
Kennedy, William, 187
Keppel, Francis, 179
Kerouac, Jack, 49, 50, **256–57,** 462–63, 464, 493
Kidd, Benjamin, 123
Kilrain, Jake, *63*
Kimmel, Michael, 170, 305
Kindergarten Cop (1990), 112, 407
Kindred Spirits (Durand), 34
King, Martin Luther, Jr., **257–58**
African-American manhood and, 431
American Dream and, 27
civil rights movement and, 17, 93, 257–58, 389
Malcolm X and, 258, 277
nonviolence and, 257, 258, 478
patriarchy and, 357
religion and spirituality and, 257, 392
King, Warrior, Magician, Lover (Moore, Gillette), 77, 449
Kingsley, Charles, 209
King's Row (1941), 385, 386
Kinsey, Alfred, 53, 99, 208, 295, 368, 418
Kiowa, 390
Kiss, 327
Kiss Me Deadly (Spillane), 99
kitchen debate, 100
Kiwanis, 300
Knievel, Evel, 437
Knights of Columbus, 176
Knights of Labor, 38, 97, 233, 239, 261, 366, 388, 502–3
Knights of Pythias (KOP), 176
Knights of Pythias of North America, 177
Know-Nothings, 90, 338
Knute Rockne: All American (1940), 385
Kolodny, Annette, 488
Komarovsky, Mira, 195
Korda, Michael, 443
Korean War, 29, 92, 311
Kotcheff, Ted, 384
Kraditor, Aileen, 120
Krafft-Ebing, Richard von, 207, 460
Kramer vs. Kramer (1979), 133, **258–59,** 322, 399
Ku Klux Klan, 492, 495–96
Birth of a Nation and, 52–53, 88
civil rights and, 90, 92–93, 145, 177
eugenics and, 154
interracial marriage and, 382
minstrelsy and, 316
muscular Christianity and, 324
nationalism and, 330
nativism and, 338
populism and, 366
Southern manhood and, 95, 177, 430–31

L

labor movement and unions, **261–63**
American Dream and, 26
American Federation of Labor (AFL), 97, 191, 233, 239, 261, 262, 388, 500, 503
apprenticeship and, 32
artisans and, 38
breadwinner role and, 71, 261–62
class and, 97
Congress of Industrial Organizations (CIO), 98, 225, 262, 342, 503–4
consumption and leisure and, 500
Gilded Age and, 191
Great Depression and, 196
immigrants and, 224–25
individualism *vs.*, 230
industrialization and, 233
Industrial Workers of the World (IWW), 261–62, 503
Irish-American manhood and, 239
Knights of Labor, 38, 97, 233, 239, 261, 366, 388, 502–3
New Deal and, 342
populism and, 366
Progressivism and, 388
violence and, 478
working-class manhood and, 502–4
World War II and, 507
Lady Chatterley's Lover (Lawrence), 266–67
Laemmle, Carl, 213
la Guerra, Pablo de, 264
Lakota, 390
LaLanne, Jack, 57, 203
Lamarck, Jean-Baptiste-Pierre-Antoine de Monet Chevalier de, 201
land ownership, 20–21, 376–77
African-American manhood and, 16, 144
American Dream and, 25
class and, 96, 97
Grapes of Wrath and, 194
Latino manhood and, 264
outdoorsmen and, 351
patriarchy and, 355
politics and, 363, 364
Southern manhood and, 429, 430, 431
suffragism and, 444
Western frontier and, 487
youth and, 513
Last American Man, The (Gilbert), 351
Last Days of the Republic (Dooner), 39
Last of the Mohicans, The (Cooper), 267, 489
Last Tango in Paris (1972), 70
Last Temptation of Christ (1988), 248
Latino manhood, **263–66**
gangs and, 185
heroism and, 206

Latino manhood (*continued*)
juvenile delinquency and, 254
racialization and, 381, 383
sports and, 48, 64, 436
television and, 453–54
Lawd Today (Wright), 509
Lawrence, D. H., 115, 148, **266–67**
Leach, William, 411
Leatherstocking Tales, 62, 205–6, **267–68,** 336, 488, 489
Leave It to Beaver (1957–63), 67, 121, **268–69,** 289, 293, 441, 452–53
Leaves of Grass (Whitman), 497–98
Lectures to Young Men (Beecher), 51
Lecture to Young Men, A (Graham), 192, 294
Led Zeppelin, 327
Lee, Bruce, 214, 290, 291, *291*
Lee, Joseph, 197
Lee, Spike, 19, 214
leisure, **269–72**
bachelorhood and, 46, 47
consumerism and, 106, 107
crisis of masculinity and, 118
divorce and, 132–33
fashion and, 159, 160
fatherhood and, 162–63
Father's Day and, 166
fishing, 171–72
gambling and, 183–84
Gilded Age and, 190
insanity and, 235
middle-class manhood and, 307, 308
outdoorsmen and, 351
Playboy magazine and, 361, 362
travel and, 461–63, 464
urbanization and, 468
working-class manhood and, 500, 503
Lemmon, Jack, 74
Lennon, John, 357
Leone, Sergio, 139
Lethal Weapon films, 74, 111
"Letter from a Birmingham Jail" (King), 257–58
Letters from an American Farmer (Crèvecoeur), 20, 25, 115, 116, 463, 491
Levine, Jack, 35
Levy, David, 320
Lewis, Sinclair, 297
Liberated Man, The (Farrell), 14, 302
Liberator (newspaper), 5
Life of Christ (Jones), 427
Life on the Mississippi (Twain), 465
Life Outside: The Signorile Report on Gay Men (Signorile), 57
Life with Father (1953), 72
Lincoln, Abraham, 34, **272–74,** 330, 364, 467
Lincoln Memorial, *273,* 274, 330–31, 359
Lions Club, 300
Lippmann, Walter, 372
literacy, 421–22
Little Bighorn, Battle of, 336, 337
Little Caesar (1930), 187, 243
Live 1975–1985 (Springsteen), 438
Locke, Alain, 17
Locke, John, 499
Lodge, Henry Cabot, 226
lodges. *See* fraternal organizations
London, Jack, 124, **274–75**
Lonely Crowd, The (Riesman), 77, 79, 350
Lone Ranger, The (1933–54), 115, 268, **275–76**
Long, Huey, 367
"Long-Haired Country Boy" (Charlie Daniels Band), 327
Long Way from Home, A (McKay), 17
Looking Backward, 2000–1887 (Bellamy), 77, 372
Looking Good (Luciano), 57
Lottery of Life, The (Brougham), 249
Louis, Joe, 64
Lowenstein, Allard, 30, 31
Lucas, George, 214
Luciano, Lucky, 243
Luciano, Lynne, 57
Lynch, Jessica, 483
Lynd, Robert S. and Helen M., 195

M

Macbeth (Shakespeare), 147
MacDonald, Peter, 384
Macfadden, Bernarr, 59, 86
Machiavelli, Niccolò, 242
machismo, 263–65, 383
Maclean, Norman, 171
Macready, William Charles, 129
Madden, John, 174
Madison, James, 283, 329, 354, 371
Magnalia Christi Americana: or, The Ecclesiastical History of New-England (Mather), 363
Magnum, P.I. (1980–88), 131, 454, 476
Mahan, Alfred Thayer, 226, 433
Mailer, Norman, 77, 221, 364
Maine, USS, 433
Malcolm X, 17, **247–78,** 258, 333, *333,* 389, 478
male-bashing, 399
male bonding. *See* male friendship
male continence, 343
male friendship, **279–81**
alcohol and, 22, 23
bachelorhood and, 45, 46, 47
Beat movement and, 50
buddy films and, **73–75**
California Gold Rush and, 81
Deliverance and, 127–28
dueling and, 136, 137
education and, 142
fraternal organizations and, 176–77
fraternities and, 178–80
homosexuality and, 217
hunting and, 221
Kerouac and, 256
Lone Ranger and Tonto, 275–76
Odd Couple and, 347
Rebel Without a Cause and, 387
sensitive male and, 413
sports and, 435, 469
Springsteen's music and, 438
television and *(Magnum, P.I.),* 454, 476
Tom Sawyer and Huckleberry Finn and, 406, 465
Victorian Era and, 474
Vietnam veterans and, 476
Whitman and, 497
Maltese Falcon, The (1941), 131
Manchurian Candidate, The (1962), 100
Manhood of the Master, The (Fosdick), 426
Manifest Destiny, **281–82**
Boone and, 62
chivalry and, 88
nationalism and, 281, 330
Native Americans and, 488
patriarchy and, 355
patriotism and, 358
white supremacism and, 495
Man in the Grey Flannel Suit, The (Wilson), 98, 159, 350
Mann Act (1910), 379
Man Nobody Knows, The (Barton), 247–48, 299, 324, 427
mano a mano competition, 435
manumission, 421
man *vs.* boy, use of terms, 383, 509
Mapplethorpe, Robert, 35
Marcuse, Herbert, 77, 148, 368, 418–19
Marden, Orison Swett, 443
market revolution, 5, **282–85**
American Dream and, 25
class and, 96–97
confidence man and, 103, 283
Emerson and, 146
gambling and, 183
individualism and, 229–30, 283, 284
masculine domesticity and, 292
masturbation and, 295
passionate manhood and, 353
patriarchy and, 355
professionalism and, 371
prostitution and, 378
reform movements and, 387–88
self-control and, 411
self-made man and, 412
sentimentalism and, 415
sincerity and, 414, 415
success manuals and, 443
Thoreau and, 457
Victorian Era and, 473
whiteness and, 492
youth and, 514
Marlboro Man, 114, **285–86**
marriage, **286–90**
bachelorhood and, 45
emancipation and, 145
Father Knows Best and, 164
feminism and, 169
Great Depression and, 195, 196
heterosexuality and, 208
interracial, 382
Noyes and, 343
Promise Keepers and, 375, 376
reproduction and, 394
republicanism and, 397
seduction tales and, 409
slavery and, 423
Superman and, 448
television and, 452, 453, 454
violence and, 479
World War II and, 508
youth and, 513
Married with Children (1987–97), 442, 454

martial arts films, 40–41, 214, **290–92**
Marx, Karl, 83
masculine domesticity, **292–94**
Crèvecoeur and, 116
cult of domesticity and, 121
Easy Rider and, 140
emancipation and, 145
evangelicalism and revivalism, 155
Father's Day and, 166
feminism and, 169
hoboes and, 210
Home Improvement and, 215–16
Latino manhood and, 264–65
Odd Couple and, 347
postmodernism and, 369–70
sentimentalism and, 414
suburbia and, 440, 441
masculine mystique, 118
masculinists, 167
*M*A*S*H* (1972–83), 453
Masonic Order, 176
Massachusetts Society for the Suppression of Intemperance, 455
massive retaliation, 100
mass murderers, 479
Masterful Personality (Marden), 443
Masters, William, 418
masturbation, 14–15, 192, 234, 235, 249, **294–96,** 306, 411
Maternal Overprotection (Levy), 320
Mather, Cotton, 363
Matlovich, Leonard, 188
Mattachine Society, 218, 419
Matthau, Walter, 74
Maximized Manhood (Cole), 324
Maxim (magazine), 107
May Act (1941), 379
Mayer, Louis B., 213
Mayflower Compact (1620), 355
McCarthy, Joseph R., 100, 110, 240, 359
McCarthy, Kathleen, 469
McCartney, Bill, 303, 324, 375–76, 437
McClure's (magazine), 107
McCormick, Cyrus, 500
McCracken, Henry Noble, 117
McFadden, Bernarr, 203
McFarland, Charles, 426
McGovern, James R., 117
McGuire, Mark, 49
McIntosh, Ebenezer, 428
McIntyre, James Francis, 239, 240
McKay, Claude, 17
McKinley, William, 433–34
McLaren, Wayne, 286
McLean, David, 286
McLuhan, Marshall, 148
McMurtry, Larry, 286
McNamara, Craig, 30
McNamara, Robert S., 30
McVeigh, Timothy, 360
Meany, George, 239
Mechanical Bride, The (McLuhan), 148
Medical Inquiries and Observations Upon the Diseases of the Mind (Rush), 294
medicine, **296–98**
insanity and, 235–36
old age and, 349
pharmaceutical technologies, 452
professionalism and, 371, 372
reproduction and, 395, 396
sex reassignment surgery (SRS), 458–59
Meek, Harry C., 165
melancholia, 240
melting pot *vs.* mixed salad, 151
Melville, Herman, 103, 148, 172, 401
Memorial Day, 310
Men, The (1950), 70
Menace II Society (1993), 19
Men and Masculinities, 302, 305
Men and Religion Forward Movement, 156, 247, **299,** 323, 390, 427
mensch, 249, 250, 251
men's clubs, 23, 176–81, **299–301**
Men's Defense Association, 400
Men's Fitness (magazine), 57
Men's Health (magazine), 57, 107
Men's League for Women's Suffrage, 374
men's liberation movement, 301–2
men's movements, **301–4**
advice literature and, 14
crisis of masculinity and, 118
emotional expression and, 149
health issues and, 203–4
hunting and, 221
men's liberation, 301–2
men's rights, 167, 302, 304
men's studies and, 304
mother–son relationships and, 320–21
Mr. Mom and, 322
mythopoetic movement, 149, 170, 221, 241, 302–3, 304, 354, 391, 449
profeminism, 168, 170, 302, 357
religious, 303 (*See also* Million Man March; Promise Keepers)
reverse sexism and, 399, 400
sensitive male and, 413
sports and, 436
Men's Rights, Incorporated, 302
Men's Rights Association (MRA), 167
men's rights movement, 167, 302, 304
men's studies, **304–5**
crisis of masculinity and, 118
feminism and, 170, 304
medicine and, 298
Middletown in Transition and, 195
patriarchy and, 357
postmodernism and, 369
profeminist movement and, 302, 304
Men's Studies (August), 304
mental illness. *See* insanity
Mercury, Freddie, 327
Mercury Rising (1998), 111
Meritor Savings Bank v. *Vinson,* 417
Metropolitan Club, 300
Metropolitan Life Insurance, 78, 79
Metz, Charles V., 167
Mexican-American (Chicano) manhood, 265, 383, 391, 492, 504. *See also* Latino manhood
Mexicans, 263–64, 330
Mexican War (1846–47), 104, 264, 281, 358
Miami Vice (1980s), 476
middle-class manhood, 2, 3, 96, 97, 98, **306–9**
abolitionism and, 5–6
adolescence and, 7, 8
advertising and, 11
alcohol and, 23
Arthur and, 35–36
bachelorhood and, 45, 46, 308
Beat movement and, 50
Beecher and, 51
bodybuilding and, 59
body image and, 57
Boone and, 62
boyhood, 66
Boy Scouts and, 69
breadwinner role and, 71, 72, 307–8
Civil War and, 94
concept of character, 85, 86
confidence man and, 103
consumerism and, 106, 107
cop action films and, 111
crisis of masculinity and, 117, 308
cult of domesticity and, 120–21
Death of a Salesman and, 126
divorce and, 132
Douglass and, 134, 135
education and, 141, 142
fashion and, 159
fatherhood and, 162, 163, 306, 307
Father Knows Best and, 164–65
fraternal organizations and, 176–77
gambling and, 183
gangs and, 185–86
Gilded Age and, 190–91, 191
Graham and, 192
Great Depression and, 195, 196
Gulick and, 197–98
health and, 203
hoboes and, 210–11
Home Improvement and, 216
hunting and, 220–21
industrialization and, 232, 233, 234
Irish-American manhood and, 238, 240
James and, 246
Leave It to Beaver and, 268–69
leisure and, 270
market revolution and, 283
medical profession and, 297
Men and Religion Forward Movement, 299
men's movements and, 301, 303
men's studies and, 304–5
Moby Dick and, 317
momism and, 318
Mr. Mom and, 322
muscular Christianity and, 209, 210, 323, 324
neurasthenia and, 190, 201, 203, 235–36, 297
nuclear family and, 344

middle-class manhood (*continued*)
- *Odd Couple* and, 347
- *Organization Man* and, 350
- passionate manhood and, 353–54
- patriarchy and, 356
- populism and, 365
- pornography and, 367
- producers, 365–66
- professionalism and, 372
- Progressive Era and, 374
- prostitution and, 378, 379
- race and, 381
- *Rebel Without a Cause* and, 386
- reform movements and, 388
- Roosevelt and, 402, 403
- self-control and, 306, 411
- self-made man and, 306, 412, 413
- sentimentalism and, 414–15
- Spanish-American War and, 433, 434
- sports and, 48, 174, 435
- strenuous life and, 439
- suburbia and, 440
- success manuals and, 442–43, 443
- Superman and, 448
- television and, 452
- temperance and, 455
- travel and, 462
- urbanization and, 468, 469, 470
- Victorian Era and, 306–7, 473, 474
- Vietnam War and, 29–30
- Washington portrayals and, 484
- Western frontier and, 487
- whiteness and, 492
- work, role of, 500
- World War I and, 505
- World War II and, 507
- YMCA and, 511

Middletown in Transition (Lynd and Lynd), 195
Midnight Cowboy (1969), 74
midwives, 395
migration, 264–65, 355, 468, 469
militarism, **309–11**
- advertising and, 12
- Cold War and, 99, 101
- Manifest destiny and, 281–82
- passionate manhood and, 353–54
- Reagan and, 12, 57, 101, 310, 385, 386
- Roosevelt and, 403

military, **311–13**
- conscientious objection, **104–6,** 475–76, 507
- gays and, 188, 312
- Irish-American manhood and, 239–40
- Italian-American manhood and, 243
- male friendship and, 280
- militarism and, 309
- music and, 325–26
- prostitution and, 379
- Vietnam War, 476
- women in, 311–13, 508
- World War I and, 505, 506
- World War II and, 507, 508

military bands, 325–26
military discipline, 353
military education, 141
militia groups, 339, 360, 366
militias, local and state, 309, 311, 481
Mill, John Stuart, 147
Miller, Arthur, 79, 126–27, 284, 501
Miller, Stuart, 167
Millett, Kate, 208, 419
Million Man March, 18, *18,* 118, 303, 334, 392
Mills, C. Wright, 26, 77, 79, 99, 127, 159, 350, 372, 501
Mineo, Sal, 386, 387
ministry, 51–52, **313–15,** 363
minstrelsy, **315–17,** 431
Minute Men, 329
Missing in Action (1984), 291–92
Mitchell, John, 71
Moby Dick (Melville), 172, **317–18,** 401
model minority, 40
Model of Christian Charity, 355
Modern Times (1936), 503
Mohawk sky walkers, 337
Molloy, John, 160
momism, 182, 241, **318–19,** 320, 508
Monroe Doctrine, 88
Montagu, Ashley, 493
Montana Freemen, 360
Moore, Michael, 98
Moore, Robert, 77
"Moral Equivalent of War, The" (James), 439
Morgan, Winona, 195
Morrell, David, 384
Morris, Jan, 459
Morrissey, 327
Mothers Against Drunk Driving (MADD), 456
mother–son relationships, **319–22**
- adolescence and, 7
- Freudian psychoanalytic theory and, 181, 182
- Italian-American manhood and, 242
- Jewish manhood and, 391
- Lawrence and, 266
- momism, 182, 241, 318, **318–19,** 320, 508
- mythopoetic movement and, 241
- republicanism and, 319, 398
- Social Gospel and, 426

motorcycles, 185, 254
Mott, John R., 512
Mott, Lucretia, 169, 416
Mount Rushmore, 359
Moynihan, Daniel Patrick, 18, 72, 93, 185, 289, 320, 345, 383
Mr. America, 405
Mr. Mom (1983), 170, **322–23,** 370
Mr. Olympia, 407
Mrs. Doubtfire (1993), 133, 370
Muhammad, Elijah, 105, 277, 332–33
Muhammad, Wallace, 333–34
multiculturalism, 292, 339, 493, 496
multi-ethnic masculinity, 152
Mumford, Lewis, 374
Murphy, Eddie, 74
Murphy Brown (1988–98), 346, 454
Murrah Federal Building (Oklahoma), 360, 478
Murray, Judith Sargent, 168
muscle dysmorphia, 58
muscle-Jew, 251
muscular Christianity, **323–25**
- advice literature and, 14
- Beecher and, 51
- body and body image and, 56
- Boy Scouts and, 68
- evangelicalism and, 156
- general, 390
- Gilded Age and, 191
- Gulick and, 197
- Hall and, 201
- health and, 203
- ministry and, 314
- music and, 326
- passionate manhood and, 353
- Social Gospel *vs.,* 427
- sports and, 435
- Sunday and, 446–47
- YMCA and, 511

muscular vegetarianism, 255
music, **325–28**
- adolescence and, 8
- American Revolution and, 325
- "Battle Hymn of the Republic" (Howe), 326, 330
- Colonial, 325
- country, 327
- Guthrie and, 206, 462
- hip-hop, 327
- jazz, 50, 326
- military, 325–26
- rap, 187, 327
- Springsteen's, 206, 327, 437–38
- violence in, 479, 480

Muskeljudentum, 251
Muslim Girl's Training and General Civilization Classes, 333
Muslims, 392–93. *See also* Nation of Islam
Myrdal, Gunnar, 493
mysticism (mystical hippies), 113
Myth of Masculinity, The (Pleck), 304
myth of the black rapist, 88, 93, 495–96
mythopoetic movement, 149, 170, 221, 241, 302–3, 304, 354, 391, 449
My Three Sons (1960–72), 453

N

Naked City, The (1948), 131
Naked Lunch (Burroughs), 49
Narrative (Douglass), 421
Narrative of the Life of David Crockett, A (Crockett), 119
Narrative of the Life of Frederick Douglass (Douglass), 134, 143, 474
Narrative of William W. Brown, A Fugitive Slave (Brown), 421, 422
Nast, Thomas, 467
National American Woman Suffrage Association (NAWSA), 375
National Association for the Advancement of Colored People (NAACP), 16, 52, 53, 375, 493

National Association for the Advancement of White People, 496
National Bisexual Liberation Group, 53
National Congress for Fathers and Children, 167
National Congress of Men (NCM), 167
National Farmer's Alliance and Industrial Union, 366
National Geographic (magazine), 464
nationalism, **329–32**
  capitalism and, 82
  homosexuality and, 217
  hunting and, 220
  Jewish manhood and, 250–51
  Manifest Destiny and, 281, 282
  nativism and, 338
  passionate manhood and, 353
  patriotism and, 358
  race and, 382
  Rambo and, 384
  strenuous life and, 439
  Uncle Sam and, 467
  Western frontier and, 486
  Whitman and, 497
Nationality Act (1870), 38–39
National Jewish Community Relations Council, 251
National Labor Relations Act (1935), 342
National Organization for Men, 302
National Organization for Men Against Sexism (NOMAS), 302
National Organization of Women (NOW), 167, 389
National Origins Act (1924), 225, 493
National Rifle Association (NRA), 198–99
Nation of Islam, 17, 277, **332–34,** 392
Native American Church, 390
Native American manhood, **334–38**
  alcohol and, 22
  American Dream and, 26
  art and, 34
  berdache, 335, 390, 458, 460
  boyhood and, 65, 334–35
  homosexuality and, 217
  hunting and, 206, 220, 334, 335
  Jackson and, 245
  Leatherstocking Tales and, 267–68
  marriage and, 288
  nationalism and, 330
  patriarchy and, 355
  racialization and, 381, 382
  Rambo and, 384
  religion and spirituality and, 390
  Romanticism and, 401
  Tonto and, 275–76
  Western frontier and, 486, 487–88
  Westerns and, 489, 490, 491
Native Son (Wright), 382, 509
nativism, 90, 91, 123, 184, 250, **338–40**
Naturalization Act (1870), 91
natural selection, 123
nature, 171, 317, 400, 401, 457, 468, 490. *See also* outdoorsmen; Western frontier
Nature (Emerson), 146
Navajo, 458
Nazism, 153
Nebraska (Springsteen), 438
necessary roughness, 74
"Negro Artist and the Racial Mountain, The" (Hughes), 17
Negroes with Guns (Williams), 431
Negro Family, The: The Case for National Action (Moynihan), 18, 72, 93, 185, 289, 320, 345, 383
neurasthenia, 190, 201, 203, 235–36, 297
New Deal, 195, 196, **340–42**
  art and, 34, 340
  bureaucratization and, 76
  individualism and, 230
  professionalism and, 372
  strenuous life and, 439
  whiteness and, 342, 493
New England Courant, 175
New Men's Studies, The (August), 304
Newton, Huey, 54–55
New York Draft Riots, 184
New York Herald, 103
New York Society for the Suppression of Vice (NYSSV), 368
Nicaragua, 281, 386
Nineteenth Amendment (1920), 445
Nixon, Richard, 76, 100, 365
noble savages, 401
Nolte, Nick, 74
nonviolence, 93, 257, 258
Nordau, Max, 251
Norris, Chuck, 291–92
Northrup, Solomon, 421, 422
Notes on the State of Virginia (Jefferson), 20, 491
Noyes, John Humphrey, **342–44**
nuclear family, **344–46**
  bisexuality and, 54
  character and, 86
  Death of a Salesman and, 126–27
  emotional expression and, 148
  fatherhood and, 162–64, 344, 345, 346
  hoboes and, 210–11
  industrialization and, 232
  Nation of Islam and, 333
  nativism and, 339
  Promise Keepers and, 375–76
  Rebel Without a Cause and, 386–87
  religion and spirituality and, 391, 392, 393
  slavery and, 287, 319–20, 420, 421, 422, 423, 430
  television and, 164–65, 215–16, 268–69, 452–53
  travel and, 462
  World War II and, 508
  YMCA and, 512
nursing profession, 297, 481, 482

O

O'Brien, Pat, 239, 240
Odd Couple, The (play, Simon), **347–48**
Odd Couple, The (television series, 1970–75), 74, 347, 453
Oedipus complex, 181, 266
Okies, 21
old age, 46, **348–50**
Old Man and the Sea (Hemingway), 172
Olivardia, Roberto, 57–58
Oliver, Andrew, 428
Olmsted, Frederick Law, 470
Olympic Club, 300
onanism, 294
Oñate, Don Juan de, 264
One-Dimensional Man (Marcuse), 77
Oneida Community, 342–43
One Lonely Night (Spillane), 99
On Golden Pond (1981), 349
On the Origin of Species (Darwin), 123, 395
On the Road (Kerouac), 49, 50, 256, 462–63, 464, 493
On the Waterfront (1954), 70, 262
Order of Patrons of Husbandry, 176
Ordinary People (1980), 322
Oregon Trail, The (Parkman), 438
organic memory, 197
Organization Man, The (Whyte), 76, 79, 98, 99, 148, 230, 284, **350–51,** 372, 441, 501
orgonamy, theory of, 418
Oriard, Michael, 174
"Our Countrymen in Chains" (Whittier), 5
outdoorsmen, **351–52**
  fishing and, 171–72
  football and, 174
  Hemingway, 204
  hunting and, 220–21
  London's novels and, 274–75
  mythopoetic men's movement and, 302–3
  Natty Bumppo (Leatherstocking Tales), 267–68
  passionate manhood and, 353
  retirees, 349
  Roosevelt and, 351, 403
Outlaw Josey Wales, The (1976), 139
outlaws, 74, 113, 140
overcivilization
  cowboys and, 115
  feminism and, 169
  gangs and, 185
  Hall and, 201
  health and, 203
  imperialism and, 226, 310
  London and, 274
  middle class and, 307
  mother–son relationships and, 320
  muscular Christianity and, 323
  passionate manhood and, 353
  Tarzan and, 449
Owens, Jesse, 436

P

pacifism, 29, 85, 104–6, 249
Packard, Vance, 26
padrone system, 224
Page, Jimmy, 327
Paine, Thomas, 28
Palance, Jack, 349
Panama, 483
parens patriae, 253
Parents' Day, 166
Park Forest (Illinois), 350
Parkman, Francis, 401, 438
Parsons, Talcott, 72
party man, 103
passionate manhood, **353–54**
  chivalry and, 88
  Civil War and, 95
  domesticity and, 121
  emotional expression and, 148
  ministry and, 314
  Progressive Era and, 374
  Tarzan and, 449
paterfamilias, 354
paternity tests, 395
Pathfinder, The (Cooper), 268
patriarchy, **354–58**
  American Revolution and, 27, 28, 355
  apprenticeship and, 32
  Asian-American manhood and, 38, 39
  divorce and, 132
  education and, 143
  emotional expression and, 147
  fatherhood and, 161
  Father Knows Best and, 164
  fathers' rights and, 167
  feminism and, 168, 169
  Franklin and, 175
  gangsters and, 186
  immigration and, 223, 224
  imperialism and, 226–28, 356
  industrialization and, 231, 232, 233, 234
  Islam and, 392
  Italian-American manhood and, 242
  Latino manhood and, 263, 264, 265
  Malcolm X and, 277
  marriage and, 286
  medical profession and, 298
  men's movements and, 302
  mother–son relationships and, 319
  Nation of Islam and, 333
  nativism and, 339
  nuclear family and, 344, 345
  old age and, 348
  populism and, 365–66, 366, 367
  property and, 377
  reproduction and, 394
  republicanism and, 397, 398
  Schwarzenegger's films, 408
  self-made man *vs.,* 412
  sexual harassment and, 417
  slavery and, 423, 424
  Southern manhood and, 429
  Spanish-American War and, 433
  violence and, 479
  white supremacism and, 495
  youth and, 513
patriotism, **358–61**
  Boy Scouts and, 69
  chivalry and, 88
  Cold War and, 359–60
  conscientious objection and, 104, 105
  democratic manhood and, 128, 129
  heroism and, 205
  Irish-American manhood and, 239–40
  Lone Ranger and, 275
  Reagan and, 385
  terrorism and, 360
  Uncle Sam and, 467
  Washington and, 484
  Wayne and, 485
  World War I and, 359, 505–6
  World War II and, 359
Peace Corps, 439
Peacock Revolution, 107
Peale, Norman Vincent, 427, 443
Pendergast machine, 239
Pendleton Act (1883), 75
penis-enlargement surgery, 58
Penn, Sean, 239
Pennsylvania Hospital, 235
Pennsylvania State University study, 73
People's Party, 21
Percy, William Alexander, 431
Perfectionism, 343
Perry Mason (1957–66), 453
Pershing, John J., 506
personality, cult of, 86–87, 195, 284, 427, 443
Petrified Forest, The (1936), 60
Pet Shop Boys, 327
Petty, Richard, 43
Phi Beta Kappa, 178
Philadelphia Story, The (1940), 193
philanthropists, 469
Philippines, 226, 227, 228, 481–82
Phillips, David Graham, 117
Phillips, Katharine, 57–58
Phillips Exeter, 142
phrenology, 147
Physical Culture (magazine), 59, 86
physical fitness. *See* health and fitness
physicians. *See* medicine
Piano, The (1993), 214
Pioneers, The (Cooper), 267
Plain Facts About Sexual Life (Kellogg), 255
Plant, Robert, 327
Playboy magazine and culture, **361–62**
  advertising and, 11, 361
  as advice literature, 14
  bachelorhood and, 46–47, 133, 361
  Beat movement and, 50
  consumerism and, 107
  fashion and, 160, 361
  masturbation and, 295
  Odd Couple and, 347
  pornography and, 361–62, 368
  sexuality and, 179, 208
Play Misty for Me (1971), 213–14
Pleck, Joseph, 149, 304
Poe, Edgar Allen, 130
Poitier, Sidney, 214
police forces, 469, 478
Police Gazette, 367
police procedurals, 111
political bosses (political machines), 129, 239, 388, 469, 470
politics, **362–65**
  colonial America and, 269–70
  Crockett and, 119
  democratic manhood and, 129
  evangelicalism and, 155
  feminism and, 169
  Franklin and, 363
  gangs and, 184
  Irish-American manhood and, 239
  Jewish manhood and, 251
  The Jungle and, 252
  labor movement and unions and, 262
  men's clubs and, 300
  patriarchy and, 355
  populism and, 365–67
  postmodernism and, 370
  republicanism, 396–98
  Southern manhood and, 432
  suffragism, 444–46
  See also specific presidents
Polk, James K., 281
Pollack, William, 67, 149, 411–12, 414, 479
Pope, Harrison, 57–58
Popular Mechanics (magazine), 451
populism, 21, 179, **365–67**
Populist Party, 366
pornography, 169, 295, 361–62, **367–69,** 418
Port Huron Statement, 230
postmodernism, 35, 219, **369–71**
post-traumatic stress disorder (shell shock), 182, 236
poverty, 426, 455
Powderly, Terence, 239
Powell, Colin, 189
Power: How to Get It and How to Use It (Korda), 443
power dressing, 160
Power Elite, The (Mills), 372
Power of Personality, The (Marden), 443
Power of Positive Thinking (Peale), 427, 443
Power of Will: A Practical Companion Book for Unfoldment of the Powers of Mind (Haddock), 443
Pragmatism (James), 246
Prairie, The (Cooper), 268
Presbyterian Church, 299
Presbyterian Labor Temple, 299
Presley, Elvis, 152
priesthood of all believers, 314
Prince, 328
Prince, Charles, 460–61
Prince, The (Machiavelli), 242
Prince, Virginia, 460–61
Prince Hall Freemasonry, 177
Princeton, 142
profeminism, 117, 168, 170, 302, 304, 357, 393
professionalism, **371–73**
  capitalism and, 83, 84
  education and, 141, 142
  emotional expression and, 148
  industrialization and, 233
  men's clubs and, 300, 301

neurasthenia and, 236
physicians, 296, 297
work, role of, 500
Progressive Era (1890–1915), **374–75,** 388
bureaucratization and, 76
citizenship and, 90–91
Darwinism and, 123
ethnicity and, 151
eugenics and, 153
feminism and, 169
Gulick and, 197
health and, 203
hunting and, 221
medical profession and, 297
middle-class manhood and, 307
professionalism and, 372
Social Gospel movement and, 374–75, 427
success manuals and, 442
urbanization and, 470
Washington portrayals and, 484
Westerns and, 490
World War I and, 505
Prohibition, 23, 186, 456
Promise Keepers, 156, 303, **375–76,** 391
crisis of masculinity and, 118
emotion and, 149
fatherhood and, 167
feminism and, 170
marriage and, 289
muscular Christianity and, 324
patriarchy and, 357
sensitive male and, 413–14
sports and, 437
property, **376–78**
abolitionism and, 6
agrarianism and, 20
American Revolution and, 28, 377
apprenticeship and, 31, 32
artisans and, 37
capitalism and, 83, 84
citizenship and, 89, 90
class and, 96–97
labor movement and unions and, 261, 262
Latino manhood and, 264
patriarchy and, 355, 377
politics and, 363
republicanism and, 397
Sons of Liberty and, 428
suburbia and, 440, 441
suffrage and, 377, 444
working-class manhood and, 502
See also land ownership
Prosser, Gabriel, 424–25
prostitution, 169, 211, 299, 377, **378–79,** 409, 426
protector role. *See* chivalry (protector role)
Protestant Ethic and the Spirit of Capitalism (Weber), 25
Protestantism, 390–91
Darwinism and, 124
emotional expression and, 147
ethnicity and, 151
evangelicalism (*See* evangelicalism and revivalism)
fraternities and, 179
Jesus, images of, 247
Men and Religion Forward Movement, 156, 247, **299,** 323, 390, 427
ministerial authority and, 313–14, 315
muscular Christianity (*See* muscular Christianity)
nativism and, 338
Promise Keepers (*See* Promise Keepers)
self-control and, 410–11
Social Gospel movement, 191, 374–75, 390, **426–27**
work, role of, 499
YMCA and, 511
provider role. *See* breadwinner role
Psychological Care of Infant and Child (Watson), 66
Psychopathia Sexualis (Krafft-Ebing), 207
Public Enemy, 327
Pueblos, 335
Puff Daddy, 19
Puffer, J. Adam, 185
Pugh, David, 117
Pumping Iron (1977), 407
Puritans, 390
alcohol and, 22
American Dream and, 25
boxing and, 62
boyhood and, 65
fatherhood and, 161
gambling and, 183
masturbation and, 294
ministerial authority and, 313–14
patriarchy and, 355
politics and, 363
reproduction and, 394
self-control and, 411
Western frontier and, 486–87
Pushing to the Front (Marden), 443

Q

Quaker Committee of Friends on Bisexuality, 53
Quayle, Dan, 346, 454
queer theory, 182, 208, 219, 369
Quidor, John, 34

R

Rabbit series (Updike), 124
race, **381–84**
American Dream and, 26, 27
antiheroes and, 34
automobiles and, 42, 43
buddy/cop films and, 74, 111
California Gold Rush and, 81
class and, 381–82
corporate workplace and, 79
Darwinism and, 123
education and, 141, 142
ethnicity and, 150, 381–82
fatherhood and, 162
fraternal organizations and, 177
fraternities and, 179
gangs and, 184–85
Gilded Age and, 190–91
Great Depression and, 195, 196
Hall's theories and, 201
heroism and, 206
Hollywood and, 212, 213, 214
immigration and, 225
imperialism and, 226–27, 228
Irish-American manhood and, 239
martial arts films and, 290–92
men's clubs and, 300, 301
men's studies and, 305
minstrelsy and, 315–17
nationalism and, 330
organic memory concept and, 197, 201
passionate manhood and, 353
patriarchy and, 355, 356
patriotism and, 359
populism and, 366
Progressive Era and, 375
reproduction and, 394–95
Roosevelt and, 403
Shaft and, 420
sports and, 48, 62, 63–64, 436
Springsteen's music and, 438
strenuous life and, 439
suburbia and, 440
suffragism and, 444–46
television and, 453–54
Tom Sawyer and Huckleberry Finn and, 406, 465
travel narratives and, 464
urbanization and, 469, 470
Victorian beliefs, 474
Vietnam War and, 476
violence and, 478
war and, 481
World War I and, 506
YMCA and, 511–12
See also specific races
Race: Man's Most Dangerous Myth (Montagu), 493
Race and Democratic Society (Boas), 493
race riots, 470
racial justice, 257–58
radio, 275–76, 447
Raiken, Leo, 340
railroads, 283
Rainbow, The (Lawrence), 266
"Ramblin' Man" (Allman Brothers), 327
Rambo, 12, 57, **384–85,** 476
Rand, Ayn, 77
Ransom, John Crowe, 431
rape, 167, 169, 416, 423–24, 479
rap music, 187, 327
Rauschenbusch, Walter, 426
Reagan, Ronald, **385–486**
business and, 79, 284, 385, 386
Cold War and, 101
consumerism and, 107
Dirty Harry catch-phrase and, 139
heroism and, 205
individualism and, 231
militarism and, 12, 310
nationalism and, 331
old age and, 349
Rambo and, 384
unions and, 262
welfare and, 91
Real Boys: Rescuing Our Sons from the Myths of Boyhood (Pollack), 67, 149, 411–12, 414, 479
Rebel Without a Cause (1955), 8, 50, 125, *125,* 126, **386–87**
recapitulation theory of play, 197
Reconstruction, 144, 145

Reddy, Helen, 327
Redford, Robert, 214–15
Red River (1949), 485, 490
Reflections in a Golden Eye (1967), 70
reform movements, **387–89**
abolitionism (*See* abolitionism)
antebellum, 387–88
antiwar movement, 29–31
Beecher and, 51
civil rights (*See* civil rights movement)
evangelicalism and, 155
feminism (*See* feminism)
gay rights (*See* gay rights movement)
James and, 246
Kellogg and, 255
masturbation and, 294–95
Noyes and Perfectionism, 343
pornography and, 368
Progressivism (*See* Progressive Era)
seduction tales and, 409
temperance, 455–56
reform schools, 253
Regarding Henry (1991), 284
Reich, Wilhelm, 418–19
religion and spirituality, **389–93**
African-American men and, 392
Beat movement and, 49–50
body image and, 57
Boy Scouts and, 69
California Gold Rush and, 81, 82
character and, 86
colonial leisure and, 269–70
conscientious objection and, 104–5
Darwinism and, 123, 124
dueling and, 137
Emerson and, 146
ethnic masculinity and, 151
fatherhood and, 161, 164
Father's Day and, 165, 166
fathers' rights and, 167
feminism and, 168, 170
fishing and, 171
fraternal organizations and, 176
Gulick and, 197
Higginson and, 209–10
homosexuality and, 217
immigration and, 223, 224
individualism and, 229
James and, 246
marriage and, 286, 287, 288
masturbation and, 294, 295
men's movements and, 303
ministry and, 313–15, 363
mystical hippies and, 113
Native American men and, 390
nativism and, 338
Noyes and Perfectionism, 343
old age and, 348
politics and, 363
professionalism and, 371
Progressive Era and, 374–75
Reagan and, 386
self-made man and, 412
slaves and, 424
Springsteen's music and, 438
transvestism and, 460
violence and, 477, 478
Western frontier and, 487
work, role of, 499
YMCA and, 511
See also specific religions and denominations
remasculinization, 476
Remington, Frederic, 114, 115
Renaissance Education Association, 461
reproduction, 123, 124, 234, **393–96,** 398
republicanism, **396–99**
adolescence and, 7
agrarianism and, 20
Alger and, 24
American Revolution and, 27, 28
apprenticeship and, 31, 32
Arthur and, 36
artisans and, 36, 37
Boone and, 61
citizenship and, 89, 396, 397, 398
Contrast and, 108–9
Franklin and, 175
gambling and, 183
guns and, 198
health and, 202
individualism and, 229, 396
Lincoln and, 273
ministry and, 314
mother–son relationships and, 319, 398
nationalism and, 329, 330, 331
patriarchy and, 355, 397, 398
patriotism and, 358
politics and, 363, 364
populism and, 366
Romanticism and, 401
self-control and, 411
sentimentalism and, 415
Sons of Liberty and, 428
suffragism and, 444, 445
Uncle Sam and, 467
Washington and, 484
work and, 499
working-class manhood and, 502
republican motherhood, 319, 398
Republican Party, 94, 273, 346
"Resistance to Civil Government" (Thoreau), 457
retirement, 348, 349
"Retiring from Business" (Arthur), 36
Return of the Dragon (1973), 291
reverse anorexia, 58
reverse sexism, 259, **399–400**
revivalism. *See* evangelicalism and revivalism
Revolutionary War. *See* American Revolution
Rice, Thomas Dartmouth, 315
Richards, Renée, 419, 459
Richardson, Samuel, 408
Riesman, David, 26, 77, 79, 350
Ringer, Robert J., 443
River, The (Springsteen), 438
Rivera, Diego, mural, 450, *451*
River Rouge Factory (Detroit), 78, 79, 450
A River Runs Through It (Maclean), 171
Rivers, Joan, 399
Roberts, Gerald Franklin, 117
Robins, Raymond, 427
Robinson, Edgar M., 68
Robinson, Jackie, 436
Rockefeller, John D., 388
Rocky film series, 244, 493
Rodgers, Tara, 49
Rodriguez, Alex, 436
Rodriguez, Richard, 206
Roger and Me (1988), 98
Rohmer, Sax, 338–39
rollback, 100
romantic friendships, 278
Romanticism, **400–402**
advice literature and, 14
boyhood and, 65–66
heroes and antiheroes, 401
individualism and, 401
mother–son relationships and, 319
Native American manhood and, 336
Whitman and, 497–98
Rood, Henry, 323
Roosevelt, Eleanor, 416
Roosevelt, Franklin D., 340, 364, 372
Roosevelt, Theodore, **402–4**
bodybuilding and, 59
chivalry and, 88
fatherhood and, 307
football and, 174
hunting and, 220, 402, 403
imperialism and, 226, 227, 356
militarism and whiteness, 492
muscular Christianity and, 323
outdoorsman, 351, 403
politics and, 364
Progressive Era and, 374, 388
Spanish-American War and, 433, 434
strenuous life and, 64, 115, 190, 203, 246, 320, 439
travel and, 462
Western frontier and, 403, 487
Roots (1977), 19
Rosdowski, Susan J., 488
Roseanne (1988–97), 122
Rotary Club, 300, 301
Rotundo, E. Anthony, 305, 353
Roughing It (Twain), 464, 465
Rough Riders, 374, 403, *403,* 434
Rousseau, Jean-Jacques, 147, 401
Rowson, Susanna, 408
Royal Path of Life, or Aims and Aids to Success and Happiness (Haines and Yaggy), 443
RuPaul, 328
Rush, Benjamin, 202, 235, 294, 296, 371, 411
Rush Hour films, 74
Rustin, Bayard, 105
Ruth, George Herman "Babe," 435

S

Sacco, Nicola, 243
SAHD (stay-at-home-dad), 322
Salinger, J. D., 84–85
Sallman, Warner, 248
saloons and taverns, 22–23, 270, 502, 503
Salvation Army, 156
Samoa, 227
Sandage, Scott, 96
Sanders, Deion, 324

Sandow, Eugen, 56, 59, 203, 353, **405–6**
Sands of Iwo Jima, The (1949), 485
Sanford and Son (1972–77), 19, 454
Sanger, William, 117, 374
Saturday Night Fever (1977), 244
Sawyer, Tom, 9, 10, 66, **406–7,** 465
Scarface (1932), 187
schizophrenia, 240
Schmeling, Max, 64
schools. *See* education and schools
Schuster, Joe, 447
Schwarzenegger, Arnold, 57, 59, 111–12, 214, **407–8**
Scopes trial, 124, 324
Scorsese, Martin, 187
Scott, Randolph, 193
Scythians, 460
Seale, Bobby, 54–55
Searchers, The (1956), 490
Sea-Wolf, The (London), 274
Second Bank of the United States, 129, 245
Second Great Awakening, 81, 155, 192, 202, 343
seduction tales, **408–10,** 513
self-control, **410–12**
  advice literature and, 13
  alcohol and, 22, 23, 455
  Boone and, 62
  emotional, 147, 148, 411–12
  Franklin and, 175
  Graham and, 192–93
  health and, 202
  insanity and, 235, 236
  Italian-American manhood and, 242
  middle-class manhood and, 306, 307
  passionate manhood and, 353
  reform movements and, 388
  republicanism and, 396–97
  self-made man and, 306
  Victorian Era and, 473, 474
  Washington (Booker T.), and, 142
  World War I and, 505
  youth and, 514
self-knowledge, 146
self-made man, **412–13**
  agrarianism and, 21
  Alger and, 24
  American Dream and, 25
  Beecher and, 51
  confidence man and, 103
  Crèvecoeur and, 116
  Emerson and, 146
  Fitzgerald and, 172–73
  Franklin and, 175, 363
  gangsters as, 186
  heroism and, 206
  individualism and, 229
  Lincoln as, 272–74
  market revolution and, 283
  middle-class manhood and, 306
  politics and, 363, 364
  professionalism and, 371
  slavery and, 425
  success manuals and, 443
  Victorian Era and, 473
  Western frontier and, 487
  youth and, 514
self-reliance, 134, 146, 412, 439, 457
"Self-Reliance" (Emerson), 134, 146
Selleck, Tom, 131
Seneca Falls convention, 169, 356, 416
sensitive male, **413–14**
  boyhood experience and, 67
  buddy films and, 74
  cop action films and, 111–12
  detectives, 131
  emotional expression and, 149, 413–14
  feminism and, 170
  Hollywood and, 212, 213, 214
  Home Improvement and, 216
  Kerouac and, 256
  male friendship and, 280, 413, 414
  Odd Couple and, 347
  politics and, 365
  Springsteen as, 438
  television and, 453
  Victorian sentimentalism and, 415
sentimentalism, **414–16**
  bachelorhood and, 45, 46
  Crèvecoeur and, 115–16
  emotional expression and, 148
  male friendship and, 278
  slave narratives and, 422
separate spheres, 120, 121, 284, 292, 306, 355
September 11, 2001, terrorist attacks, 331, 352, 360
Seton, Ernest Thompson, 68
settlement houses, 470
sexism, reverse, 259, **399–400**
sex reassignment surgery (SRS), 458–59
Sexual Behavior in the Human Male (Kinsey), 53, 99, 295, 368, 418
sexual-enhancement drugs, 58
sexual harassment, 399, **416–18**
sexuality
  feminism and, 169
  Freudian psychoanalytic theory and, 181–82, 207, 418
  Hall's theories on, 201
  industrialization and, 234
  Victorian Era and, 394
  Whitman and, 497
  World War I and, 506
  See also bisexuality; heterosexuality; homosexuality; Sexual Revolution; transsexuality
sexually transmitted diseases (STDs), 379, 395
Sexual Politics (Millett), 208, 419
Sexual Revolution, **418–19**
  Kerouac and, 256
  male friendship and, 280
  masturbation and, 295
  Playboy magazine and, 361
  pornography and, 368
  transvestitism and, 460
Sexual Revolution, The: Towards a Self-Regulation Character Structure, 418–19
Shaft (1971), 19, 187, 419
Shakespeare, William, 147
Shane (1953), 490
Share the Wealth movement, 367
Shariah, 392
Shawnee, 336
Shawshank Redemption, The (1994), 74
Sheeler, Charles, 450
Sheen, Martin, 239
sheenies, 249
Sheldon, Charles M., 426
shell shock, 182, 236
shepherding, 376
She's Having a Baby (1988), 442
Shootist, The (1976), 485
Siegel, Jerry, 447
Signorile, Michelangelo, 57
Simmons, William J., 496
Simpsons, The (1989–), 122, 442, 454, 504
Sinatra, Frank, 243
sincerity, 414–15, 473
Sinclair, Upton, 117, 356
Sioux, 336, 337
Sitting Bull, 334, *336*
Six Million Dollar Man, The (1974–78), 453
Sixties, The: Years of Hope, Days of Rage (Gitlin), 30
Skull and Bones Society, 300
Slater, Samuel, 232
slave narratives, **420–23**
slavery, *5,* **423–26**
  adolescence and, 7
  African-American manhood and, 16
  boyhood, 65
  Civil War and, 95
  Douglass and, 134
  emancipation, 143
  family and, 287, 319–20, 420, 421, 423, 430
  leisure and, 271
  literacy and, 421–22
  Manifest Destiny and, 282
  marriage and, 287
  narratives of, **420–23**
  patriarchy and, 355, 423, 424
  religion and spirituality and, 392
  reproduction and, 394
  republicanism and, 398
  Southern manhood and, 429–30
  submission to, 424
  Tom Sawyer and Huckleberry Finn and, 10, 406, 465
  violence and, 421, 423–24
  white supremacism and, 495
  See also abolitionism
Slavic immigration, 224–25
Smith, Adam, 82–83, 354, 409, 499
Smith, Angelina Berry, 314
Smith, Betty, 240
Smith, Fred, 323
Smith, Tommie, 436
Smith v. *Allwright* (1944), 445
social citizenship, 91
social Darwinism. *See* Darwinism
Social Gospel movement, 191, 374–75, 390, **426–27**
socialism, 230, 252, 274
social justice, 374–75
Social Security Act (1935), 340, 349
Social Security Administration (1935), 76
Society for Human Rights, 218

Society for the Second Self, 461
Soldier Voting Act (1942), 445
"Song of Myself" (Whitman), 134
Sons and Lovers (Lawrence), 266
Sons of Liberty, 28, 329, 358, 363, **427–29,** 478
Sons of Temperance, 455
Sopranos, The (1999–), 244
Souls of Black Folk, The (Du Bois), 16, 246
Sousa, John Philip, 326
Southern Christian Leadership Conference (SCLC), 93
Southern Farmers' Alliance, 366
Southern manhood, **429–33**
  adolescence and, 7
  African-American, 430, 431–32
  boxing and, 62
  chivalry and, 87, 88
  civil rights movement and, 92–93
  Civil War and, 94–95, 430, 481
  Darwinism and, 124
  domestic violence and, 479
  dueling and, 135–37, 198
  emancipation and, 144
  gambling and, 183
  Huckleberry Finn and, 9–10
  Jackson and, 245
  leisure and, 271
  Manifest Destiny and, 282
  ministry and, 314–15
  music and, 327
  nationalism and, 330
  politics and, 363
  populism and, 366
  republicanism and, 398
  white supremacism and, 431–32, 495–96 (*See also* Ku Klux Klan)
Southern Renaissance, 431
Southern Rock music, 432
Soviet Union, 99–100
Soyer, Raphael, 34–35
Spalding, Albert, 48
Spanish-American War (1898), **433–34,** 481–82
  imperialism and, 226, 227
  militarism and, 310
  passionate manhood and, 353
  Roosevelt and, 374, 403, 433, 434
Spanish colonization, 263–64
Spencer, Herbert, 123
spermatic economy (economy of sperm), 255, 411
Spielberg, Steven, 214
Spillane, Mickey, 99
spirituality. *See* religion and spirituality
Spock, Benjamin, 67, 102, 148
sporting men, 128
sports, **435–37**
  auto racing, 42–43
  baseball, **47–49,** 323, 435, 436, 446
  basketball, 436
  bodybuilding, 59–60, 405, 407
  boxing, **62–65,** 129, 237, 435, 436
  education and, 142
  ethnicity and, 436
  football, **173–75**
  gambling and, 183–84
  heroism and, 206
  Irish-American manhood and, 239
  leisure and, 270, 271
  male friendship and, 280
  middle-class manhood and, 307
  muscular Christianity and, 323, 324
  outdoorsmen and, 351
  passionate manhood and, 353, 354
  race and, 436
  sensitive male and, 413, 414
  urbanization and, 469
  violence and, 480
  working-class manhood and, 503
  wrestling, 57
sprezzatura, 242
Springsteen, Bruce, 206, **437–38**
Stagecoach (1939), 485
Stagolee, 431
Stallone, Sylvester, 57, 214, 384, 476
Stamp Act (1765), 28, 427, 428
Stanhope Burleigh: The Jesuits in Our Home, 338
Stanton, Elizabeth Cady, 169, 314
State in Schuylkili, 300
Steelworker (Hine), 34
Steinbeck, John, 21, 194–95, 464
Stelzle, Charles, 427
sterilization laws, 154, 395
Steuben, Baron Von, 188–89
Stevenson, Robert Louis, 124
Stone, Sharon, 400
Storm, Jane McManus, 281
Stowe, Harriet Beecher, 159, 382
Straight Story, The (1999), 349
Strauss, Levi, 160
Strecker, Edward, 182, 318, 320
Streetcar Named Desire, A (1951), 70
strenuous life, **438–39**
  bodybuilding and, 59
  Boone and, 62
  boxing and, 64
  Civil War and, 94, 95, 438–39
  cowboys and, 115
  democratic manhood and, 130
  domesticity and, 121
  football and, 174
  Gilded Age and, 190
  Gulick and, 197
  health, 203
  Hemingway and, 204–5
  hoboes and, 211
  James and, 246
  middle-class manhood and, 307
  mother–son relationships and, 320
  music and, 326
  nationalism and, 331
  Progressive Era and, 374
  Roosevelt and, 64, 115, 190, 203, 246, 320, 439
  sports and, 435, 436, 437
  Tarzan and, 449
  white supremacism and, 495
Strong, Josiah, 323, 426
Student Nonviolent Coordinating Committee (SNCC), 17, 93
Students for a Democratic Society (SDS), 30, 230
Studies in Classic American Literature (Lawrence), 148
suburbia, **440–42,** 470
  automobiles and, 42–43
  Beat movement and, 50
  class and, 98
  consumerism and, 106–7
  Easy Rider and, 140
  Father Knows Best and, 164
  gangs and, 185–86
  Home Improvement and, 216, 441, 454
  Italian-American manhood and, 243
  Leave It to Beaver and, 269
  leisure and, 271, 441
  male friendship and, 280
  masculine domesticity and, 293
  men's clubs and, 300
  middle-class manhood and, 307, 308
  Organization Man and, 350
  property and, 377
  technology and, 451
success manuals, 62, 103, **442–44**
Sudden Impact (1983), 139
suffragism (voting rights, franchise), **444–46**
  African-American, 16, 92, 93, 144, *144,* 145, 444–46
  American Revolution and, 28, 444
  citizenship and, 89–91
  civil rights movement and, 92, 93
  feminism and, 169
  patriarchy and, 355, 356
  politics and, 364
  populism and, 366
  Progressive Era and, 374, 375
  property and, 363, 377
  whiteness and, 491–92, 492
Sullivan, John L., *63,* 64, 239, 435
Sullivan, Thomas, 511
Sun Also Rises, The (Hemingway), 172, 204, 506
Sundance Film Festival, 214–15
Sunday, Billy, 156, 247, 314, 323, **446–47**
Superfly (1972), 19
Superman, **447–48**
Suzuki, Ichiro, 436
Swaggart, Jimmy, 156
Sweetgrass Road Drum Group, 337
Swidler, Leonard, 324
Sylvia Scarlett (1935), 193
System (magazine), 79

T

Tacitus, 242
Taft-Hartley Act (1947), 262
Tailhook incident, 313
Talese, Gay, 187
Tallmadge, Thomas DeWit, 426–27
Tammany Hall, 129, 239
Tango and Cash (1989), 111
Tappan, Arthur and Lewis, 6
Tarzan, 56, 79, **449–50**
Taylor, Frederick Winslow, 374, 503
Taylor, Graham, 427
Taylor, Nathaniel, 343
Taylor, Zachary, 281

team player/team spirit, 75, 76, 117, 174, 353
technology, **450–52**
automobiles and, 42, 450
do-it-yourself, 450–51
leisure and, 271–72
medicine and, 297, 452
old age and, 349
pornography and, 368
professionalism and, 373
reproduction and, 395–96
television, **452–55**
advertising, 11, 12
African-American manhood and, 18–19
bachelorhood and, 47
body image and, 57
boxing and, 64
boyhood and, 67
breadwinner role and, 72
cowboys, 114, 115
Daniel Boone, 62
detectives, 131, 454
domesticity and, 121, 122
fatherhood and, 268–69
Father Knows Best, 102, 121, **164–65,** 289, 293, 441, 452–53
feminism and, 170
Home Improvement, 170, **215–16,** 293, 442, 451
homosexuality and, 219, 454
Italian-American manhood and, 244
Leave It to Beaver, 67, 121, **268–69,** 289, 293, 441, 452–53
nativism and, 339
nuclear family, 164–65, 215–16, 268–69, 345, 453
postmodernism and, 370
suburbia and, 441–42, 454
Superman, 447
Vietnam veterans and, 476
violence and, 480
Westerns and, 490
working-class manhood and, 504
temperance, 23, 35, 192, 388, **455–57**
Tender Comrade (1943), 72–73
Ten Nights in a Bar-Room and What I Saw There (Arthur), 35
Tenskwatawa (Shawnee prophet), 336
Terminator films, 12, 57, 407–8
Texas independence, 264, 330, 358
Their Mothers' Sons (Strecker), 182, 318, 320
This Old House (1979–), 293, 451
This Side of Paradise (Fitzgerald), 172, 173
Thomas, Norman, 230
Thompson, Samuel (William), 103
Thompson, Virgil, 326
Thoreau, Henry David, **457–58**
capitalism and, 457, 473
conscientious objection and, 104, 358, 457
fishing and, 171
Manifest Destiny and, 282
Romanticism and, 401
travel and, 462, 464
Three's Company (1977–84), 454
Thunderbolt and Lightfoot (1974), 74
Thurmond, Strom, 189
Tidyman, Ernest, 419
Till, Emmett, 92
Tilton, Theodore, 16, 51
tinkering technology, 450, 451
Tissot, Samuel A., 294
Tocqueville, Alexis de, 344
Todd, John, 234, 294, 295
Tom Brown's Schooldays (Hughes), 323
Tombstone (1993), 490–91
Tom Sawyer, 9, 10, 66, **406–7,** 465
Tonto, 275–76
tools, 450, 451
Tools and the Man (Gladden), 426
Tootsie (1982), 170, 370
Touch of Evil (1958), 131
Tour on the Prairies, A (Irving), 464
Tousey, Frank, 489
Townsend, Charles, 249
Tracy, Spencer, 239
Tramp Acts (1870s), 211
transactional manhood, 96, 97
transcendentalism, 146, 246, 457–58, 497
Transients (Soyer), 34–35
transsexuality, **458–60**
art and, 35
berdache and, 335, 390, 458, 460
Sexual Revolution and, 419
Transvestia magazine, 460
transvestism, 390, **460–61**
Transvestites (Hirschfeld), 460
travel, 9–10, 42, 194, 256, **461–63**
travel narratives, 9–10, 140, 194, 256, 457, **463–65**
Travels (Bartram), 463
Travels with Charlie (Steinbeck), 464
Travolta, John, 152
Tree Grows in Brooklyn, A (Smith), 240
Triple (Follett), 251
True Grit (1969), 485
Trumbull, John, 28, 33
Tucker, Chris, 74
Tucker, Nathaniel Beverly, 121
Turner, Frederick Jackson, 25, 226, 285, 486
Turner, Henry McNeal, 95
Turner, Nat, 424
Turnvereine, 405
Tuskegee Institute, 16, 142
Twain, Mark, 9–10, 88, 189–90, 464, **465–66**
Twenty-Sixth Amendment (1971), 446
Tyler, Royall, 28, 108–9
Type A personality, 411
Tyson, Mike, 19, 64, 382

U

Uncle Sam, 274, 330, **467–68,** 505
Uncle Tom's Cabin (Stowe), 382
Uncommon Valor (1983), 476
unemployment, 72, 195, 340, 341, 499
Unforgiven (1992), 139, 490–91
Union Club, 300
unions. *See* labor movement and unions
United States Divorce Reform, 167
United States v. *Seeger* (1965), 105
Universal Negro Improvement Association (UNIA), 17, 332, 392
universities and colleges, 141, 142, 143
football and, 174
fraternities, 178–80
men's clubs and, 300
men's studies and, 304–5
postmodernism and, 369, 370
YMCA and, 511
youth and, 514
University Club, 300
Updike, John, 124
Up From Slavery (Washington), 16
upper-class manhood, 2, 96–97
dueling and, 135
education and, 141, 142
football and, 174
hunting and, 220–21, 221
leisure and, 271
market revolution and, 283
medical profession and, 297
men's movements and, 303
music and, 325
professionalism and, 371
strenuous life and, 438, 439
travel and, 461–62, 464
Washington and, 483–84
Western frontier and, 487
urbanization, **468–71**
alcohol and, 22
American Dream and, 25
bachelorhood and, 45–46
Boone and, 61–62
confidence men and, 103, 468–69
cowboys and, 114
crisis of masculinity and, 117
Darwinism and, 123–24
Deliverance and, 127
democratic manhood and, 128–30
emotional expression and, 148
fashion and, 159
Gilded Age and, 190
health and, 202, 203
hunting and, 220, 221
immigrants and, 223–24
juvenile delinquency and, 253
leisure and, 270
Moby Dick and, 317
Native American manhood and, 336, 337
passionate manhood and, 353, 354
patriarchy and, 356
pornography and, 367
postmodernism and, 370
prostitution and, 378
sincerity and, 414, 415
Social Gospel movement and, 426
Tom Sawyer and, 406
travel and, 462
Western frontier and, 486, 487
YMCA and, 470, 511
Uris, Leon, 251
U.S. Army, *467*, 506. *See also* military

V

Vaca, Cabeza de, 486
Valentino, Rudolph, 212, 243
Vanderbilt Agrarians, 431
Vanderlyn, John, 34
van Dyke, Dick, 131
Vanity Fair (magazine), 107
Van Winkle, Rip, 171
Vanzetti, Bartolomeo, 243
Veblen, Thorstein, 356
vegetarianism, 202, 203, 255
venereal diseases, 379, 395
Verazanno, Giovanni da, 486
Veterans Administration, 440
Viagra, 58, 452
Victorian Era (1837-1901), **473–75**
  adolescence and, 7
  Adventures of Huckleberry Finn and, 9–10, 465
  alcohol and, 23
  Beecher and, 51
  boxing, 63
  boyhood in, 66
  breadwinner role and, 71
  chivalry, 88
  confidence man and, 103
  cowboys, 115
  Darwinism and, 123, 124
  detectives, 130
  divorce and, 132
  domesticity and, 120–21
  Freudian psychoanalytic theory and, 181
  gangs and, 184–85
  gentility, 473–74
  Graham and, 192–93
  Gulick and, 197–98
  Hall and, 201
  health and, 202, 203
  heterosexuality and, 207
  Higginson and, 209–10
  imperialism and, 226–27
  Jesus, images of, 247
  juvenile delinquency in, 253
  Lawrence and, 266
  market revolution and, 283–84
  marriage and, 287–88
  masturbation and, 295
  medicine, 297
  middle-class manhood and, 306–7, 473, 474
  ministry and, 314
  Moby Dick and, 317
  mother–son relationships and, 319, 320, 321
  muscular Christianity and, 323
  pornography in, 367–68
  prostitution in, 378
  reproduction and, 394–95
  Sandow and bodybuilding, 405
  sentimentalism and, 414–16
  strenuous life and, 438–39
  Tarzan and, 449
  Washington portrayals and, 484
  Western frontier and, 487
  Whitman and, 497
  YMCA and, 511–12
Vietnam Veterans Against the War, 475–76
Vietnam Veterans Memorial, 331, 476
Vietnam War (1965–73), **475–77,** 482–83
  adolescence and, 8
  antiwar movement and, 29–31, 101, 102, 475
  conscientious objection and, 105, 475
  martial arts films and, 290, 292
  men's studies and, 304
  militarism and, 310
  military service and, 311
  nationalism and, 331
  patriotism and, 360
  post-traumatic stress disorder and, 236
  Rambo and, 384
  suffragism and, 446
  Wayne and, 485
vigilante cop films, 111, 131, 139
violence, **477–80**
  adolescence and, 8, 67, 184, 185–86, 478–79
  Adventures of Huckleberry Finn and, 9, 10
  advertising and, 12
  African-American manhood and, 19
  Black Panther Party and, 54, 55
  civil rights movement and, 92–93
  cop action films and, 111
  Deliverance and, 127–28
  domestic, 479
  dueling, 135–37
  Eastwood's films and, 139
  Easy Rider and, 140
  emotional expression and, 147
  gangs and, 184, 185–86
  gangsters and, 187
  guns and, 199
  Hollywood and, 127–28, 139, 140, 214, 407, 480
  Irish-American manhood and, 239, 240
  Italian-American manhood and, 243–44
  Jackson and, 245
  Jewish manhood and, 250–51
  King and, 257, 258
  Latino manhood and, 263, 264, 265
  London's novels and, 274
  Nation of Islam and, 333
  passionate manhood and, 353
  popular culture and, 479
  Schwarzenegger's films and, 407
  sexual, 479
  slavery and, 6, 143, 421, 423–24, 430
  sports and, 64, 129, 174, 436
  Western frontier and, 488
Virginia Military Institute, 141, 142
Virginian, The (Wister), 114, 191, 489
virtual pornography, 368
Visions of Cody (Kerouac), 256
vocational education, 142
voting rights. *See* suffragism
Voting Rights Act (1965), 93, 445–46, 493

W

wage slaves, 38, 499
Wagner Act (1935), 98
Walden (Thoreau), 457, 473
Walk Across America, A (Jenkins), 464
Walker, David, 16
Walker, William, 281
"Walking" (Thoreau), 457
Wallace, George, 93
Wall Street (1987), 284
Walton, Isaak, 171
war, **481–83**
  antiwar movements, **29–31,** 281–82, 438, 475–76, 482, 507
  conscientious objection and, **104–6,** 475–76, 507
  gender roles and, 481–83
  Hemingway and, 204–5
  heroism and, 205, 481, 482, 483
  Hollywood and, 212
  insanity and, 236
  Jackson and, 245
  Korean War, 29, 92, 311
  London's novels and, 274
  male friendship and, 280
  militarism and, 309
  nationalism and, 329, 330, 331
  Native American manhood and, 334, 335, 336–37
  passionate manhood and, 353
  patriotism and, 358, 359, 360
  regenerating manhood, 95
  strenuous life and, 438–39
  violence and, 478
  See also militarism; *specific wars*
Ward, Lester Frank, 356
Warhol, Andy, 35
Warner, Charles Dudley, 189–90
Warner, Jack, 213
Warner, Kurt, 324
War of 1812, 245
Washington, Booker T., 16, 17, 142, 145, 431
Washington, George, 28, 33, 104, 329, 358, 363, **483–85**
Washingtonians, 455
Watson, John B., 66, 67
Wayne, John, 114, 115, 206, **485–86**
Way to Win, The (John), 86
Wealth of Nations, The (Smith), 82–83
Wealth Without Risk (Givens), 443
Weber, Max, 25
Webster, Daniel, 278, 413
weekend warriors, 451
Week on the Concord and Merrimack Rivers, A (Thoreau), 457, 462, 464
Welcome Home (Levine), 35
welfare state, 91
Welsh v. United States (1970), 105
Welter, Barbara, 120
"We Shall Overcome," 327
Wesley, John, 155
West, James E., 68
Western frontier, **486–89**
  agrarianism and, 20–21
  American Dream and, 25
  Boone and, 61, 62
  cowboys and, 114–15, 486, 487, 488
  crisis of masculinity and, 117
  Crockett and, 119
  Death of a Salesman and, 126

democratic manhood and, 129, 130
Easy Rider and, 140
gambling and, 183
guns and, 198, 199
hunting and, 220
imperialism and, 226
individualism and, 229, 230
Jackson and, 245, 488
Leatherstocking Tales and, 267–68
London and, 274
Marlboro Man and, 285
Native American manhood and, 336, 486, 487–88
outdoorsmen and, 351
patriarchy and, 355
Reagan and, 385, 386
Romanticism and, 401
Roosevelt and, 403, 487
self-made man and, 412, 487
strenuous life and, 438
travel and, 462, 464
Twain and, 465
Washington portrayals and, 484
Westerns, 212, 453, 487, **489–91**
boyhood and, 67
Cooper's films, 109–10
cowboys and, 114, 115
Eastwood's films, 139
Easy Rider and, 140
Lone Ranger, The, 275–76
Wayne and, 485
West Point, 141, 142
We Were Soldiers (2002), 476
Wheeler, Edward, 489
Where Do We Go From Here? (King), 258
Whig Party, 27, 90, 119, 129–30
Whiskey Rebellion (1794), 329
White, Bouck, 426
White, Reggie, 324
White Aryan Resistance, 496
White Collar (Mills), 77, 79, 99, 159, 350, 372, 501
white-collar workers
business/corporate America and, 78–79
class and, 98
consumerism and, 106–7
fashion and, 159
fatherhood and, 163
Gilded Age and, 190
leisure and, 270
Organization Man and, 350
suburbia and, 440
work, role of, 500, 501
White Fang (London), 274
Whitefield, George, 155
white male victim, 476
"White Negro, The" (Mailer), 77
whiteness, 2–4, **491–94**
Adventures of Huckleberry Finn and, 9–10
advertising and, 12
agrarianism and, 21
American Dream and, 26–27
American Revolution and, 28
art and, 33, 34–35
artisans, 37, 38
baseball and, 48
Boone and, 62
California Gold Rush and, 81
chivalry and, 88
citizenship and, 89, 90, 91
democratic manhood and, 128, 129, 130
Douglass and, 134
education and, 141, 142
fashion and, 159
Father Knows Best and, 164, 165
football and, 174
fraternal organizations and, 176, 177
fraternities and, 179
gangs and, 184, 185–86
Gilded Age and, 190–91
heroism and, 205–6
Hollywood and, 212, 213
hunting and, 220, 221
imperialism and, 226–28
individualism and, 231
Invisible Man and, 237
Irish-American manhood and, 239
juvenile delinquency and, 254
Kerouac and, 256
labor movement and unions and, 261, 262
Leatherstocking Tales and, 267–68
Leave It to Beaver and, 268–69
leisure and, 271
Lincoln and, 273
Men and Religion Forward Movement, 299
men's clubs and, 300
men's movements and, 301, 303
men's studies and, 304–5
middle-class manhood and, 306
minstrelsy and, 315–17
music and, 325, 327
nationalism and, 330, 331
nativism and, 338, 339
New Deal and, 342
organic memory concept and, 197
passionate manhood and, 353
patriarchy and, 355
patriotism and, 358–59
politics and, 363
populism and, 365–66
postmodernism and, 369
Promise Keepers and, 376
property and, 377
racialization and, 381
Rambo and, 384
reform movements and, 388
republicanism and, 397, 398
Romanticism and, 401
Roosevelt and, 402, 403
Sandow and, 405
self-control and, 410–11
self-made man and, 412, 413
Southern manhood and, 429, 430, 431–32
strenuous life and, 438, 439
suburbia and, 440
suffragism and, 444, 445, 492
Tarzan and, 449
television and, 164, 165, 268–69, 452, 454
travel narratives and, 464
Uncle Sam and, 467
urbanization and, 469
Victorian Era and, 474
war and, 476, 481, 505, 506
Western frontier and, 488
Westerns and, 489, 490
working class and, 499
YMCA and, 511
white supremacism, **494–97**
Birth of a Nation and, 18, **52–53,** 88, 95, 212, 316, 496
Black Panther Party and, 55
boxing and, 64
civil rights movement and, 92–93
Civil War and, 95
Darwinism and, 123
eugenics and, 154
imperialism and, 226–28
Ku Klux Klan and (*See* Ku Klux Klan)
Malcolm X and, 277
nativism and, 338, 339
populism and, 366
Roosevelt and, 403
Southern manhood and, 429, 430, 431–32
sports and, 436
Wright and, 509
Whitman, Walt, 49–50, 134, 188, 210, 330, 401, **497–98**
Whittier, John Greenleaf, 5
Why are We in Vietnam? (Mailer), 221
Whyte, William, 26, 76, 79, 98, 99, 127, 148, 230, 284, 350–51, 372, 441
wigs, 348
Wild Bunch, The (1969), 490
Wilder, Billy, 501
wilding, 479
wild-man weekends, 302–3
Wild One, The (1953), 8, 50, 70, 185
Wilentz, Sean, 184
Will & Grace (1999–), 454
Williams, Robert, 93, 431
Willis, Bruce, 111, 131
Wilson, John Lyde, 136
Wilson, Samuel, 467
Wilson, Sloan, 98, 159, 350
Wilson, Woodrow, 364, 505, 506
Winning through Intimidation (Ringer), 443
Winthrop, John, 30, 355, 487
Wirt, William, 121, 287
Wister, Owen, 114, 115, 191, 489
Wolfe, Tom, 231
Woman's Bible, The (Stanton), 314
Women in Love (Lawrence), 266
Women's Armed Services Integration Act (1948), 312
Women's Army Corps (WAC), 508
Women's Christian Temperance Union (WCTU), 23, 368, 455, 456
women's studies, 304, 305, 369
Wonder Years, The (1988–93), 441–42
Wood, Natalie, 386
Woods, Tiger, 436
Woodward, Samuel B., 295, 514
work, **498–501**
alcohol and, 22
apprenticeship, 31–33
artisans (*See* artisans)
Asian-American manhood and, 39, 40
class status and, 96–98
corporate, 78–79
Death of a Salesman and, 126–27

work (*continued*)
fatherhood and, 161–62
fishing and, 172
Gilded Age and, 190, 191
Great Depression and, 195–96
hoboes and, 210–11
immigration and, 223, 224
Kramer vs. Kramer, 258–59
New Deal and, 340
old age and, 348, 349
Organization Man and, 350–51
professionalism, 371–72
property and, 377
sexual harassment and, 416–17
slavery and, 424–25
suburbia and, 440, 441
success manuals and, 443
travel narratives and, 464
working-class manhood, 97, 98, **502–5**
alcohol and, 22, 455, 502, 503
American Dream and, 26
antiwar movement and, 29
apprenticeship and, 31–32
artisans (*See* artisans)
baseball and, 48
boxing and, 63, 64
boyhood and, 66
breadwinner role and, 71–72
capitalism and, 83
Catholicism and, 392
Civil War and, 94
consumerism and, 106
cop action films and, 111
corporate work, 78
democratic manhood and, 128–30
domesticity and, 121
education and, 142
gambling and, 183
gangs and, 184–85, 186
Gilded Age and, 191
Great Depression and, 195, 196
heroism and, 206
hoboes and, 211
industrialization and, 232–33, 234
Irish-American manhood and, 238, 239
Italian-American manhood and, 242–43
Jackson and, 245
The Jungle and, 252
labor movement and unions and (*See* labor movement and unions)
leisure and, 270, 503
marriage and, 287, 289
men's clubs and, 300, 301
minstrelsy and, 316
neurasthenia and, 236
New Deal and, 340
nuclear family and, 345
patriotism and, 359
populism and, 366
Progressive Era and, 375
prostitution and, 378
race and, 381
self-control and, 411
sports and, 435, 503
Springsteen's music and, 437–38
technology and, 450
television and, 453, 504
travel and, 462
urbanization and, 468, 469
work, role of, 499–501
World War II and, 507
YMCA and, 511
Working Men's Clubs, 300
Works Progress Administration, 340
World War I, **505–7**
conscientious objection and, 105
gender roles, 482
insanity and, 236
Lawrence and, 266
militarism and, 310
military service and, 188, 311–12, 505, 506
muscular Christianity and, 323
nationalism and, 331
patriotism and, 359, 505, 506
reproduction and, 395
strenuous life and, 439
World War II, **507–9**
antiwar movement and, 29
Bogart's films and, 61
breadwinner role and, 72
conscientious objection and, 104, 105
Freudian psychoanalytic theory and, 182
gays in the military, 188
gender roles, 482
Italian-American manhood and, 243
Japanese-American soldiers in, 40
masculine domesticity and, 293
militarism and, 310
military service and, 40, 188, 243, 311–12
mother–son relationships and, 318, 320, 508
muscular Christianity and, 324
nationalism and, 331
patriotism and, 359
professionalism and, 372
reproduction and, 395
suffragism and, 445
Superman and, 448
whiteness and, 493
working-class manhood and, 504
wrestling, 57
Wright, Richard, 17, 66–67, 382, 431, **509–10**
Wyandotte (Cooper), 121
Wylie, Philip, 182, 318, 320

Y

Yaggy, Levi W., 443
Yale Divinity School, 343
Yale University, 142, 300, 369
Yankee Doodle Dandy (1942), 240
Yankee plays, 316
Yankees, 330, 473
Yellow Peril, 39, 290
Yellow Wallpaper, The (Gilman), 297
yeoman farmers, 96, 329–30, 364, 468, 499
yin and *yang*, 113
YMCA. *See* Young Men's Christian Association
Young Americans, 374
Young Man in Curlers at Home on West Twentieth Street (Arbus), 35
Young Man's Friend (Eddy), 86
Young Men's Christian Association (YMCA), 300, **511–13**
African Americans and, 511–12
Beecher and, 51
Gulick and, 197
health and, 203
homosexuality and, 512
male friendship and, 279, 280
pornography and, 367
regeneration of urban society, 470
religion and spirituality and, 156, 299, 323, 390, 426, 511
sports and, 63, 435
Sunday and, 446
Young Men's Hebrew Association (YMHA), 251
youth, **513–14**
Adventures of Huckleberry Finn and, 9–10
apprenticeship and, 31–32
California Gold Rush, 81–82
Catcher in the Rye and, 84–85
Easy Rider and, 140
Fitzgerald and, 172–73
fraternities and, 178–80
gangs and, 184–86
juvenile delinquency, 253–54
masturbation and, 295
Playboy magazine and, 361
pornography and, 367, 368
prostitution and, 378
seduction tales and, 408, 409
suffragism and, 446
urbanization and, 468–69
violence and, 477, 478–79
See also adolescence; boyhood
Yuppies, 107

Z

Ziegfeld, Florenz, 405
Zionism, 250–51
Zip Coon, 315, 316
Zukor, Adolph, 213